Encyclopedia of
Educational
Research

Encyclopedia of Educational Research

FIFTH EDITION

Sponsored by the American Educational Research Association

Editor in Chief

Harold E. Mitzel

Associate Editors

John Hardin Best and William Rabinowitz

Volume 1

THE FREE PRESS, *A Division of Macmillan Publishing Co., Inc.*, NEW YORK

Collier Macmillan Publishers, LONDON

THE FREE PRESS
A Division of Macmillan Publishing Co., Inc.
866 Third Avenue, New York, NY 10022

Collier Macmillan Canada, Inc.

Library of Congress Catalog Card Number: 82–2332

Printed in the United States of America

printing number
1 2 3 4 5 6 7 8 9 10

Library of Congress Cataloging in Publication Data
Main entry under title:

Encyclopedia of educational research.

  Includes bibliographies and index.
    1. Educational research—United States—Directories.
2. Education—Bibliography. 3. Universities and colleges
—United States—Directories. 4. Education—Dictionaries.
I. Mitzel, Harold E. II. Best, John Hardin. III. Rabino-
witz, William. IV. American Educational Research Associa-
tion.
L901.E57 1982   370′.7′8073   82–2332
ISBN 0–02–900450–0 (set)   AACR2

Contributors' acknowledgments, some of which are relevant
to the copyright status of certain articles, appear in a
special section at the back of volume 4.

Consulting Editors

Contents

Preface

AN ENCYCLOPEDIA IS A WORK that instructs the reader on a variety of subjects. One of the roots of the word is the Greek *enkuklios*, meaning "circular" or perhaps "well-rounded." This is a quality that the editors have attempted to incorporate into the fifth edition of the *Encyclopedia of Educational Research*. A comprehensive compendium of educational research cannot, of course, go into great depth about one or even a few topics; neither can it treat its subject matter superficially. Between these extremes, this edition is offered for the use of students, scholars, critics, and advocates for education.

Since its inception in 1941, successive editions of this work, each sponsored by the American Educational Research Association (AERA), have presented "a critical synthesis and interpretation of reported educational research." As a general reference work, it has a number of audiences. First, there are the graduate and undergraduate students who have a serious commitment to education and who seek a thorough reference to the field. These are the young people who will become part of the more than three million employed professional educators in the nation. A second audience is composed of professionals in education (e.g., teachers, supervisors, coordinators, specialists, and administrators) who need information about topics in which they are not currently active scholars. (It should be observed here that this encyclopedia is not meant to be a handbook for active researchers in their own areas of scholarship.) A third major audience is composed of thoughtful inquirers who are not professionals in education. Some examples include a journalist preparing a feature article about a curricular controversy, a legislator who must decide how to vote on an important bill dealing with education, and anyone who decides to stand for election as a member of a local school board. These interested "nonprofessionals" need relatively short briefings to help them interpret various aspects of education.

The first edition of the *Encyclopedia of Educational Research* was published in 1941. Edited by Professor Walter S. Monroe of the University of Illinois, it had 188 contributors and contained 1,344 double-column pages. A revised edition, by the same editor, was published in 1950. Dramatic growth in the U.S. educational enterprise during the 1950s soon made it imperative that another edition be available quickly. Professor Chester W. Harris, then at the University of Wis-

TABLE 1. *Comparison of fourth and fifth editions of the*
Encyclopedia of Educational Research

Characteristic	Fourth ed.	Fifth ed.
Number of signed entries	164	256
Number of words of text	780,000	1,700,000
Number of contributors	185	317
Number of entries in index	3,000	12,000

consin, was invited by AERA to develop a third edition, which appeared in 1960. Increased federal support for education and particularly for educational research during the 1960s again presaged the need for a revision. Professor Robert L. Ebel at Michigan State University responded to the invitation of the AERA Publications Committee to prepare the fourth edition, which was published in 1969. The thirteen-year interval between the fourth and fifth editions has seen tumultuous changes in education generally and research in particular.

Table 1 details for comparative purposes some of the ways in which this edition differs from the fourth edition and reflects the expansion of educational research during the 1970s. Although the number of entries has increased by 57 percent, the amount of text provided by authors has increased by nearly 118 percent. We believe these data reflect the appearance of new ideas and concepts as well as an increase in the amount of new information about familiar topics.

Because membership in AERA includes a sizable portion of the men and women who produce research in the field, it is instructive to compare the status of the organization in 1968, the year before the fourth edition appeared, with data from 1981, the year just prior to publication of the present edition. In July 1968, AERA had 8,350 members; by November 1981, there were 14,006. At the 1968 annual meeting held in Chicago there were 160 sessions on professional topics. At the Los Angeles meeting in 1981 there were 803 sessions in the same category. We do not hold that the quality of research in education has increased as much as the quantity during this period, but we believe that the fifth edition does faithfully reflect changes in the broad sweep of educational research in more than a decade.

For example, the fourth edition contains a single entry called "Curriculum." The present edition has five entries related to curriculum, as follows: "Curriculum and Instruction in Higher Education," "Curriculum Development and Organization," "Curriculum History," "Curriculum Research," "Qualitative Curriculum Evaluation." The expansion in educational research between the late 1960s and the early 1980s can also be seen in the change in entries on methodology. The 1969 edition carried a single entry called "Statistical Methods." In the present volumes there are seven entries reporting on methodology research under the following titles: "Analysis of Variance and Covariance," "Causal Modeling," "Factor Analysis," "Log-Linear Analysis," "Multivariate Analysis," "Path Analysis," "Regression Analysis."

In spite of change and a flood of new knowledge some topics covered in the previous edition retain a timeless quality. Here are some titles that are the same for 1969 and 1982 with about the same amount of space devoted to their reviews: "Discipline," "Elementary Education," "Handwriting," "Individual Differences," "Learning," "Spelling."

The phenomenon of "old wine in new bottles" is also part of the picture needed to compare the fourth edition with the new fifth edition. "Outdoor Education" has been dropped in favor of "Environmental Education." Similarly, "Data Processing" no longer seems as relevant as "New Technologies in Education." In like fashion "Correspondence Study" has been replaced by "Distance Education" and "Independent Study." We have attempted to develop entry titles that reflect state-of-the-art usage in educational research and have not been hesitant to adapt old ideas to current practice.

Examples of new concepts and topics that do not appear in previous editions are as follows: "Computer-Based Education," "Drug Abuse Education," "Equity Issues in Education," "Ethnography," "Neurosciences."

These changes reflect recent events and developments in American society to which education must attend.

The editor and two associate editors for the fifth edition were authorized in October 1979 by the AERA president, Ellis Page, to begin development of the work. An editorial board of nine distinguished educational researchers was invited to meet with the editors, the chairman of the AERA Publications Committee, the AERA executive officer, and the AERA director of publications at AERA central offices in the City of Washington, December 13–14, 1979. The board reviewed and endorsed the preliminary work of the editors in devising an organizing scheme of entries. The final version of our scheme, which immediately follows this preface, shows the eighteen broad headings that provided the basic structure of the fifth edition. Under each heading there are two levels of entry titles, one somewhat more generic than the other. We tried a number of different classification schemes but could not find a symmetrical rubric that would lead to a unique slot for every entry title. Our final scheme is a compromise that reflects our best collective judgment about the appropriate interrelationships among the 256 entries.

In addition to making suggestions regarding topical coverage of the field, the editorial advisory board nominated authors and alternates to be invited to prepare entries. In its collective wisdom, the board also suggested appropriate word allotments for each entry. Because of the scope of the venture, the editorial board recommended that we seek the services of a group of eighteen consulting editors, one for each major subdivision of our organizing scheme of entries.

The consulting editors agreed to contribute their time and talent to the development of the work and were invited to meet with the editors individually during the 1980 annual meeting of AERA held in Boston. Consulting editors were asked to do two tasks for each of 5 to 35 projected entries: (a) prepare a brief statement of the scope of the entry and (b) nominate potential authors.

In August of 1980, we, the editors, began the process of commissioning authors for specific entries. Authors for entries were given the edited scope statements prepared by consulting editors. Our instructions to authors emphasized, however, that the scope statements contained only suggestions for content and organization. Authors were given maximum freedom in choice of research to be reviewed and summarized.

Early in 1981, manuscripts began to arrive, and we began our editorial review. Most manuscripts were overlong, and we found that our chief task was judicious trimming, to avoid redundancy and to achieve overall balance of coverage. We tended to accept author construction and organization, making revisions only where they seemed necessary for clarity and consistency of style. By the first week of September, our substantive editing was completed and 256 manuscripts had been forwarded to the publisher.

In communicating the original task to the authors who had agreed to prepare entries, we requested them to discuss the policy implications of the research reviewed. It seems to us that research findings in every field are subject to the pertinent question "So what?" Because the *Encyclopedia of Educational Research* seeks to reach an audience of nonspecialists, we believed that this edition would be substantially strengthened by conscious attention of the authors to the policy implications of the findings of recent research. Our suggestion was carefully implemented by some of the authors and given somewhat less attention by others. The reader will have to judge whether the question of "So what?" has been answered by the authors.

A publication effort of this scope and duration touches many lives and demands contributions of skill, resources, service, and good will from a wide circle of colleagues, coworkers, and well-wishers. We can never appropriately acknowledge all of the people and organizations who have contributed to this work. There are, however, a number of people whose contributions must be acknowledged.

We and the AERA are grateful to Dean Henry J. Hermanowicz of the College of Education at The Pennsylvania State University for support of this project from its inception. During a time when his budget was being assaulted by the twin demons of inflation and retrenchment, he gave our project his highest priority. He has continued a tradition begun by the University of Illinois and continued by the University of Wisconsin and Michigan State University of providing editorial services, space, and personnel support for the development of successive editions of this encyclopedia.

Our thanks go to Claude Conyers, senior project editor, and to the editorial and production staff at the Macmillan Publishing Company. Our respect for their skill and experience in transforming a pile of manuscripts into a sophisticated reference work has grown by leaps and bounds during these past months.

We have been blessed with a clerical and secretarial staff that demonstrated as much interest in the publications as we had ourselves. Correspondence with authors was well done by Beverly Hosband, Rose Marie Ferguson, and Marsha Castiglione. Judy Fox developed and debugged an invaluable manuscript control program for an APPLE microcomputer. A master file for the word processor containing data on entries, authors, and editors was ably developed and maintained by Suzanne Harpster over a period of eighteen months.

Central office personnel of AERA in Washington who provided outstanding support on contract development and manuscript handling resources included William Russell, executive officer, and Anita King, director of publications.

The National Institute of Education, through the good offices of Robert Chesley and Spencer Ward of the ERIC system, contributed to the development of entry references for this edition by funding searches of the ERIC data base for those authors who requested the service. Many authors located additional references as the result of this service. In addition, ERIC clearinghouses provided document numbers for all references available through the ERIC system. We are certain that the value of the volume as a scholarly source has been enhanced by the participation of the ERIC team at the National Institute of Education and the field clearinghouses. In connection with the provision of document numbers, we gratefully acknowledge the individual work of Lynn Smart of the Clearinghouse on Handicapped and Gifted Children, and Cheryl Chase, project monitor for ERIC.

We acknowledge, with deep appreciation, the work of Ann Lamiel Landy who served as editorial assistant for this edition. She carefully reviewed every manuscript and frequently communicated with authors about editorial matters. Her red pencil gave some authors pause, but her steady insistence on crisp prose and clear meaning has made this a better work than it might otherwise be.

Finally, we acknowledge the prodigious efforts of the authors. Many were unable to obtain badly needed secretarial and reference services from their institutions. They cheerfully funded travel and typing services from their own resources. When manuscripts were returned to authors or telephone inquiries were made for clarification, we were unfailingly treated with respect, with concern for the urgency of the situation, and with good humor. The importance of the project had obviously also been communicated by the authors to their secretaries and their assistants with whom we spoke. It is perhaps the mark of a very mature group of scholars that they can voluntarily contribute to the development of a major reference work for the benefit of a profession without seeking personal gain or recompense.

The Pennsylvania State University   Harold E. Mitzel
University Park, Pennsylvania   John Hardin Best
November 25, 1981   William Rabinowitz

Organizing Scheme

THE PLANNED ENTRIES FOR THE FIFTH EDITION of the *Encyclopedia of Educational Research* are here classified under eighteen broad headings, shown below in alphabetical order in boldface type. Under each heading, entry titles are listed at either one or two levels of specificity. One heading, for example, is "Organization and Administration." There is no entry in the body of work with this title, but there are several general articles that cover various aspects of the topic. The first, alphabetically, of these is "Administration of Educational Institutions." Related to this article, but more specifically focused, are "Business Administration," "Collective Negotiations," and "School Personnel Policies," which are listed at the second level of specificity. Entry titles enclosed by parentheses were commissioned by the editors, but for a variety of reasons manuscripts were not obtained from authors after reasonable extensions of deadlines. In most instances, the resulting gaps in our planned contents were filled by expanding sections of closely related entries.

Curriculum Areas (continued)

Social Studies Education
Citizenship Education
Economic Education
Geography
History as Subject Matter

Development of Human Characteristics

Cognitive Development
Emotional Development
Language Development
Moral Development
Motor Skills Development
Physical Development
Social Development

Developmental Levels

Adolescent Development
Adult Development
Aging
Early Childhood Development
Infant Development
Life-Span Development
Middle Years Development
Preadolescent Development

Disciplinary Studies

Anthropology
Economics and Education
History of Education
Curriculum History
(Linguistics)
Neurosciences
Philosophy of Education
Aesthetic Education
Philosophy of Science in Education
Political Science
Psychology
Cognition and Memory
Creativity
Individual Differences
Intelligence
Learning
Mathematical Behavior of Children
Motivation
Perception
Personality Theory
Readiness
Sex Differences
Transfer of Learning
Sociology of Education
Culture and Education Policy
Family Studies
Group Processes

Education in National and International Development

(Assessment of Schooling)
Change Processes
(Demographic Trends)
Comparative Education
Comparative Education Administration
Comparative School Achievement
(Future Studies and Education)
International Education
National Development and Education

Education of Exceptional Persons

Behavior Problems
Truants and Dropouts
Behavioral Treatment Methods
Deinstitutionalization of the Handicapped
Gifted Persons
Handicapped Individuals
Attitudes toward the Handicapped
Hearing Impairment
Learning Disabilities
Mental Retardation
Speech-Language Services
Visual Impairment
(Mainstreaming)
Preschool Education for the Handicapped
Special Education

Education Related to Identifiable Groups

Correctional Education
Equity Issues in Education
Labor and Education
Multicultural and Minority Education
American Indian Education
Asian-American Education
Black Education
Hispanic-American Education
Parent Education
(Racial Integration)
Religion and Education
Catholic Schools
Jewish Education
Protestant Education
Rural Education
Urban Education
Women's Education

Influences on Education Policy

Federal Influence on Education
U.S. Department of Education
Governance of Schools
Judicial Decisions
Legislation
Local Influences on Education
School Boards

List of Articles

Encyclopedia of
Educational
Research

ACADEMIC FREEDOM AND TENURE

The relationship between academic freedom and tenure can be examined best by discussing each concept separately.

Academic Freedom. A general definition of academic freedom will always need some explanation and clarification, but the following definition is a useful point of departure:

Academic freedom consists in the absence of, or protection from, such restraints or pressures—chiefly in the form of sanctions threatened by state or church authorities or by the authorities, faculties, or students of colleges and universities, but occasionally also by other power groups in society—as are designed to create in the minds of academic scholars (teachers, research workers, and students in colleges and universities) fears and anxieties that may inhibit them from freely studying and investigating whatever they are interested in, and from freely discussing, teaching, or publishing whatever opinions they have reached. (Machlup, 1955, p. 753)

This definition, as well as most other definitions and discussions of academic freedom, refers to colleges and universities, suggesting that academic freedom applies only to these institutions. But although the issue may have centered on higher education historically, and although the best-known controversies have arisen there, the concept of academic freedom is no longer so restricted. In recent years it has been applied to elementary and secondary schools, as well as to such nonschool educational institutions as museums, the media, and expositions and displays that may be considered to serve the public interest (Beale, 1936; Fischer, Schimmel, & Kelly, 1981).

No modern society can reasonably make the claim to be open and democratic without prizing intellectual freedom above other freedoms. The freedom of those involved in academic life is at the very center of the intellectual life of a culture and indispensable for the achievement and dissemination of new knowledge. The intellectual de-velopment of a culture and the equal accessibility of new knowledge for all the population thus depend on it (Dewey, 1919; Hutchins, 1953).

The ideal of academic freedom is more of a moral precept than a legal principle. It antedates general freedom of speech by hundreds of years, and its development was quite separate (Machlup, 1955). In its most widely accepted sense, it includes freedom for researchers to pursue lines of inquiry within their specialties, wherever such inquiry may lead, and to publish their findings; as well as for teachers to disseminate their ideas in classrooms and on campus as they see fit. There is less agreement on the extent to which this ideal applies to students, though freedom to teach and to learn are related. Logically, in schools freedom to learn presupposes the freedom to teach, but the converse is not necessarily true. However, in an open, democratic society, the two reinforce each other and strengthen a comprehensive view of academic freedom. Such a comprehensive view would also apply to academic administrators in any responsibilities and activities that relate to the intellectual life of the campus.

Academicians have insisted on the principle that scholars and researchers be judged by their professional peers when the legitimacy of scholarly pronouncements is at issue (Hook, 1971). At the same time, when speaking off-campus as private citizens, academicians should make clear to their audiences that they do not represent their institutions and are not speaking in their official, academic capacities. Because of the special position of faculty members in the community, there is an obligation in extramural contexts to be accurate, to exercise restraint, and to show respect for the opinions of others (American Association of University Professors, 1941).

It is clear that academic freedom covers at least the activities of teaching, research, and publishing. On college and university campuses it is even more broadly defined. It includes library acquisitions and use, art displays, musical and dramatic performances, and lectures by members of the campus and by guests. The extent to which the ideal encompasses faculty governance and student organizations and activities is controversial. There are those who support a narrow concept of the ideal, whereas others spread a generous umbrella to protect a wide variety of faculty, administration, and student interests.

Justification. There are three lines of reasoning offered in justification of academic freedom: first, that it is a high moral value, ultimately derived from a religious conception of the nature of human beings (Kirk, 1955); second, that it is a value in itself and an intrinsic part of an open, democratic society; and third, that it has an instrumental value in the improvement of the quality of life in our society (Hutchins, 1953; Hook, 1953; Reisman, 1956).

The intrinsic value of academic freedom is derived by logic from a basic conception of the nature of man, a conception that holds consistent with Aristotle, that the development of intellectual virtues is man's highest and thus most godlike achievement. Others urge that inherent in the meaning of "democracy" or of "open society" is a commitment to freedom of inquiry and thus, of necessity, to academic freedom (Dewey, 1916, 1919).

The instrumental value of academic freedom is the easiest to establish in our culture, where change and novelty are highly valued and where institutions of higher education are expected to generate new solutions to life's unending problems. Once we expect universities to expand our area of knowledge and to produce new and better solutions to the practical problems of life, we must accept them as centers of free thought and inquiry—places where "the winds of freedom blow." Society's problems, whether social, technological, moral, aesthetic, or other, are more likely to be ameliorated when inquiry is fostered and protected by academic freedom. The best of human critical abilities are most likely to flourish in an atmosphere that encourages free intellectual exploration and discussion and mutual scholarly scrutiny. Such an atmosphere is not always a peaceful one; in fact it may bristle with disagreement and tension. Truth more often emerges from a campus where vigorous criticism abounds than from its placid counterpart. If we believe that knowledge is never complete, that there are always new and perhaps better solutions to human problems, there is no alternative to academic freedom. Our search for the good life requires it, and the leading of an adventurous, creative life, full of intellectual and artistic achievement, demands it (McMurrin, 1969).

History. The roots of academic freedom go back to classical antiquity. Western accounts of its origin typically begin at the Academy of Plato and the Lyceum of Aristotle, although some writers trace the idea's beginning to the rise of the European universities in the twelfth century (Hofstadter & Metzger, 1955; Jaeger, 1943). Clearly, the idea of intellectual freedom was central in the work and life of Socrates in ancient Athens, but since organized universities did not come into being until the Middle Ages,

it also makes sense to consider that period as the beginning of the struggle for academic freedom.

From the very beginning of institutionalized schooling, educators and institutions came under powerful pressures from political and church authorities to conform to prevailing orthodoxy. The resistance to such pressures by Plato and Aristotle formed the early basis for Western intellectual freedom and influenced the efforts to achieve autonomous institutions in Europe during the Middle Ages. Particularly at the great universities of Bologna, Paris, and Oxford, a genuine spirit of free inquiry prevailed, and these institutions became quite autonomous centers of thought and learning and achieved powerful influence over contemporary life (Hofstadter & Metzger, 1955). These and other medieval universities, which typically began as self-constituted communities of scholars, came under the sponsorship and authority of a church, with clerics constituting most of the faculty. Whether the church was Catholic or Protestant, faculties often found it necessary to struggle against attempts to control scholarly activities. Such struggles within universities paralleled a more general human effort to escape various forms of restrictions imposed by both political and church authorities. Attempts at control and censorship persisted through the ages, and vestiges are still with us today. At such great universities as Cambridge and Oxford, for example, religious tests and restrictions for students persisted into the second half of the nineteenth century (Hofstadter & Metzger, 1955).

The earliest colleges in the United States were church-related, with the preparation of ministers and the propagation of religious dogma serving as their central missions. Concern for academic freedom was not on their agenda and did not become an issue there until after the Civil War. In the antebellum period, colleges had not developed broad and varied purposes; thus wide-ranging inquiry and the expansion of knowledge in multiple directions had not developed. Furthermore, faculty had very little interest in governance, an activity fraught with controversy in later years. During this period, most conflicts involved college presidents rather than professors (Hofstadter & Metzger, 1955).

After the Civil War various developments influenced an increased concern for academic freedom in American higher education. Among them were the rise of public institutions, the controversies related to the spread of Darwinian thought, the growth of secularism, with a concomitant decline of religion, and a general trend toward liberalism. The influence of Darwinism was particularly important, not only on the biological sciences but also on the social sciences, philosophy, and religion. Its open-ended world view encouraged critical examination of matters that many believed settled and closed. With the decline of religious control and influence in our colleges and with a newfound interest in higher education in Germany, where a large number of our students went for advanced schooling, the German ideal of academic freedom made a powerful impact on American thought.

In Germany the teacher's freedom, *Lehrfreiheit,* was complemented by the students' *Lernfreiheit.* Students were free to study where they wished, to visit various institutions, and to govern their own conduct. They were held accountable through comprehensive final examinations at the conclusion of their studies. Although the German ideal of academic freedom was not imported to America *in toto,* partly because of the different pattern of institutional development, it did push thinking in the direction of freedom. American institutions became corporate entities, whether public or private, and accepted the position of *in loco parentis* with reference to students. In short, this meant that the college had parietal responsibilities over the students and corresponding power to regulate their lives and academic activities. The doctrine of *in loco parentis* controlled college relationships with students until the latter half of the twentieth century, when it was supplanted by a growing recognition that the rights guaranteed by the Constitution apply to students in public colleges and universities. *In loco parentis* still may apply to private institutions, although even there it has been substantially eroded by student activism and militancy during the 1960s and 1970s.

With the weakening of religious influence over American higher education and with the increasing importance of the research function, new conflicts arose as a result of professional inquiry challenging accepted conservative doctrines, particularly in economics and politics. Simultaneously, the professoriate was becoming more organized, articulate, and even militant (Hofstadter & Metzger, 1955).

Academic freedom, like freedom in general, remains an unfinished business, and the twentieth century has witnessed a variety of controversies surrounding this idea. Most of these derived from political, social, and economic issues, though efforts to control, based on religion, were not completely absent. The two world wars, the great Depression, the rise and spread of communism, and the involvement of the United States in the Vietnam War generated a variety of reactions that often bordered on hysteria and led to various efforts threatening academic freedom by government, political bodies, trustees, administrators, and even professors and students.

Wars tend to create internal pressures for expressions of loyalty and suppression of dissent. In the United States the climate of opinion generated by wars has brought professors under suspicion for their criticism of government policy. As a reaction to the spread of communism and the fear of subversion, special loyalty oaths were enacted by legislatures, including disclaimer oaths for teachers whereby they swore not to be members of certain organizations labeled subversive. The most intensive use of such oaths occurred after World War II during the McCarthy era, when investigative activities approximated witchhunting. During this period, there was also widespread scrutiny of campus speakers and censorship of texts, teaching materials, and libraries, and suspicion hung over the teaching profession (MacIver, 1955; Fidler, 1965). The po-

litically generated suppression of dissent spread throughout the country, and schools were particularly vulnerable to it. Professors were dismissed for refusing to sign loyalty oaths. A dramatic example of such dismissals occurred at the highly respected University of California, where thirty-six professors, some of world renown, were discharged. Ultimately, the California courts struck down the disclaimer oaths as unconstitutional and reinstated the professors, none of whose competence had been questioned (Gardner, 1967).

The Vietnam era and its aftermath were reflected in various threats to academic freedom, the most serious among them being student efforts to close down campuses and silence some professors and guest speakers (Hook, 1971; Woodward, 1975). Speakers or professors who took unpopular stands on racial issues, on women's liberation, or on affirmative action also had the speaker's podium denied to them on many campuses. Recent discussions have concerned the application of academic freedom to campus governance activities. The question was placed in the limelight when a federal district judge ordered that a University of Georgia professor be held in contempt of court for refusing to disclose, in a judicial proceeding, how he had voted while serving on a personnel committee.

Subcollegiate schooling. Historically academic freedom was an issue in higher education and was not considered applicable to elementary and secondary schools. This position makes sense if the exclusive purpose of such freedom is the encouragement of inquiry in order to generate new knowledge, that is, the research function. If, however, the methods and materials teachers use are also protected by academic freedom, then good reason exists for its extension to subcollegiate schooling. The fact that elementary and secondary school students are less mature and are in school under compulsory attendance laws is not sufficient ground for denying academic freedom, although its applications might well be limited to those appropriate to the maturity and experience of the students. Academic freedom is not absolute at any level. The principle can only remain the same for all levels of schooling, whereas its application must be governed by the situation, as judged by mature and knowledgeable educators, ultimately answerable to the public through the political process or in the courts (Fischer, Schimmel, & Kelly, 1981).

Whether one supports the extension of academic freedom to subcollegiate schooling also depends on one's conception of the purposes of education at those levels. There are those who claim that the mission of these schools is to socialize children in ways determined by local political forces. This view holds such mission inconsistent with free inquiry and dissemination (Nordin, 1978). A different view—one that emphasizes the development of attitudes and skills favorable to reflection, inquiry, and publication—would extend academic freedom to all levels of schooling (Dewey, 1916; Schaefer, 1967). The controversy between these two conceptions persists, but most schools today subscribe, at least at the rhetorical level, to the importance of both goals; cultural transmission and socialization as well as the development of reflective, critical aptitudes. Thus, arguments favoring some degree of academic freedom are increasingly looked upon with favor even during the years of compulsory schooling and have, on occasions, been supported by the courts.

Constitutional protection. Academic freedom, although not mentioned specifically in the Constitution, is being increasingly recognized as a special application of the First Amendment right to free speech. Although there is no authoritative Supreme Court ruling specifically establishing the right of professors and teachers to academic freedom, various statements in its support can be found in concurring opinions, in dissents, and in the scholarly speeches and out-of-court writing of the justices of the Court. Furthermore, federal courts of appeal, district courts, and state courts have recognized such a right in various cases.

The best known of these cases arose during the communist scare and loyalty oath eras of the 1950s and 1960s (*Weiman* v. *Updegraff*, 1952; *Sweezy* v. *New Hampshire*, 1957; *Keyishian* v. *Board of Regents*, 1967). These cases included some impressive statements from justices Frankfurter and Douglas, in which they referred to teachers as the "priests of our democracy," whose special status fosters enlightened public opinion and responsible citizenship. Douglas's oft-quoted statement on behalf of academic freedom appears in *Keyishian:* "Our nation is deeply committed to safeguarding academic freedom, which is a transcendent value to all of us and not merely to the teachers concerned. That freedom is therefore a special concern of the First Amendment which does not tolerate laws that cast a pall of orthodoxy over the classroom" (p. 603).

The Supreme Court has declared unconstitutional the disclaimer oaths enacted by various states but has upheld simple oaths affirming loyalty to the Constitution. Such oaths do not violate academic freedom or any other constitutional right. The questions of whether or not they serve any purpose and whether it is wise to have them are not for courts to decide.

Historically college professors have had latitude in the selection of teaching materials and methods. During recent times some elementary and secondary school teachers have claimed similar professional freedom, based in part on the maturing of the professions and in part on progressive education theories and research results. Many legal disputes have arisen from such exercises in freedom, and courts are by no means uniform in either recognizing academic freedom or applying such a right to the use of controversial methods and materials by teachers. The general trend of decisions is in the direction of recognizing the teacher's right to select the methods and materials of instruction provided that they (1) are relevant to agreed-upon objectives, (2) are appropriate to the age, maturity, and experience of the students, and (3) do not cause substantial or material disruption of the processes of schooling. The claim of academic freedom may not be used to protect incompetence or irrelevance; it does not protect indoctrination, religious, ideological, or political; nor is it an excuse to discard required texts or established curricula.

With these criteria, courts have protected the rights of teachers who brought into the classroom controversial reprints from magazines, objectionable language, guest speakers, and others supplementing the specified curricula. The basic authority, however, to decide what shall be taught in the public schools, at what levels, and with what materials rests with school officials and school boards. They, of course, must function within the boundaries specified for them by state law and the U.S. Constitution. Since the Constitution is the basic law of the land, and since its First Amendment has been interpreted to embody protection for academic freedom, public school officials must not violate such freedom.

It is also clear that private institutions do not come under the same legal principles, for the First and Fourteenth amendments apply only when "state" actions are involved, and whereas officials of public schools have been characterized as "state" officials for purposes of constitutional law, private school officials have not. Thus, private schools may determine for themselves whether or not they will accept the principle of academic freedom. Independently of legal requirements, high-quality private schools have respected this freedom perhaps even more than public institutions, for they have recognized its significance for both teachers and students.

Student academic freedom. Students were free to move about and to select their studies, their teachers, and their places of residence in the early universities of Europe; this tradition never developed in America. In fact, the idea that academic freedom also applies to students has gained adherents only recently. During the Vietnam era, there were widespread efforts to establish "free universities" or "minicolleges," in which students selected teachers, specified areas to be studied, and removed all restrictions found in more conventional institutions of learning. These efforts were short-lived, and perhaps their only lasting impact was the challenging of the rigidities of traditional schools. In general, aside from some elective courses, students still must follow curricula defined by the faculties and learn materials prescribed by teachers. On their own, of course, they are free to use school libraries and other facilities as well as work through the formal and informal organizations on campuses to bring about changes they deem desirable.

During their years of compulsory schooling, students do not have the right to determine course content or methods or to select their textbooks. Courts differ, however, on the question of student access to controversial library materials. There are no Supreme Court cases on this issue, and federal circuit courts have reached different conclusions, some respecting students' "right to know" as an aspect of the First Amendment and others upholding school boards' prerogatives in selecting books for libraries and removing objectionable books from their shelves (Fischer,

1981). However, officials may remove books for reasons of obsolescence, irrelevance, obscenity, or space limitations and not because they might contain controversial social or political ideas.

Students do not lose their right to free expression when they enter a school. The landmark *Tinker* case announced this principle, and the case has been used subsequently to recognize a variety of constitutional rights that must be respected by public school officials (*Tinker* v. *Des Moines*, 1969). Thus, if academic freedom for students encompasses freedom of speech in schools and outside of classes and freedom to publish in school newspapers, such freedom is now well established under the authoritative ruling of the U.S. Supreme Court. Restrictions are upheld only if substantial and material disruption of schooling has occurred, if there is objective evidence that it is very likely to occur, or if the content of the expression is obscene or defamatory. Within these restrictions, students are free to criticize public officials and policy, including school officials and school policies.

Extramural pronouncements. It is interesting to note that in medieval Germany, whose principles of *Lehrfreiheit* and *Lernfreiheit* so influenced American conceptions of academic freedom, professors had little freedom outside their institutions of learning. Within an authoritarian larger environment, the universities functioned as islands of free inquiry and exposition. In the United States, the constitutional protection of free speech applies to everyone and should apply, on the face on it, to teachers and professors in their roles as general citizens. Despite the logic of this position, educators have often found themselves in trouble for so-called extramural pronouncements, their oral or written statements away from their institutions of teaching and learning.

At the college and university levels of education, it was long believed that the public attributed professors' off-campus pronouncements to the institution and treated them as the official voice of the college or university. Furthermore, university officials feared that controversial statements by professors would offend donors, alumni, or government officials, bringing disfavor upon the institution. Thus, time and again, professors were reprimanded, disciplined, and even dismissed for controversial statements made off-campus. Acceptance of some restrictions on freedom of expression is implicit even in "Academic Freedom and Tenure: 1940 Statement of Principles" of the American Association of University Professors (1941), where it is stated that a professor's "special position in the community imposes special obligations." Professors must be accurate at all times, respect others' opinions, and make every effort to indicate that they are not speaking for an institution. No such restrictions on free expression are accepted by other occupational groups. In fact, according to constitutional scholars, this self-restraint is more stringent than any restriction the government could impose on professors' freedom of speech (Van Alstyne, 1975). The claim has been made that the organized profes-

soriate has exchanged some of its civil rights for procedural safeguards of personnel policies and actions and particularly of tenure rights (Slaughter, 1980).

Extramural pronouncements of public school teachers have always come under close public scrutiny and have been subject to severe restrictions. Until fairly recently, these teachers could not make a claim to a private life and were expected to be model citizens twenty-four hours a day. Local communities could dismiss them alsmost at will, and controversial speech in public by teachers was seldom tolerated (Beale, 1936). Major changes during the latter half of the twentieth century have substantially eliminated these restrictions, to the point where courts today will accord the same right of free expression to teachers, in their role as general citizens, as to the rest of the population. Teachers retain this right even when they speak critically on social issues, the government, and school policies (Morris, 1980). Although controversies still remain, and although teachers and professors in private institutions may not fall under the protection of the Constitution, the courts protect teachers' and professors' extramural remarks as they protect those of other citizens under the First Amendment.

Tenure. Although in the popular mind tenure is associated with teachers' interest in security, the strongest justification for it and the historical reasons for its development are to be found in its protection of academic freedom. "Tenure" is the term used to describe the right to a continuous contract granted to a teacher or professor upon the successful completion of probationary years of employment. It is similar to the tenure granted by the Constitution to federal judges, whose tenure is for life and who may be removed only by impeachment. Teachers' tenure is not for life, but until retirement—the only reasons for its termination being proven incompetence, gross personal misconduct, financial exigency, or program retrenchment.

Just as we grant judges tenure to protect them from political pressures and thus enhance their fairness and objectivity, we grant tenure to protect academic freedom. It is clear from the historical record that teachers have been all too vulnerable to political and ideological pressures as well as to undue influence by organized religion, school administrators, boards of trustees, and others. Although by no means foolproof or without its shortcomings, in difficult times and situations tenure has proved to be a fairly effective and worthwhile means to protect teachers' right to free inquiry and teaching (Machlup, 1964).

Tenure is not universally granted in our schools and colleges, nor is it a constitutional right. Where it is, it is generally granted either by law or by contract, although in some situations it is the result of a "moral commitment under a widely accepted academic code" and at times it derives from "courtesy, kindness, timidity, or inertia" (Machlup, 1964, p. 114). In many states tenure is granted in public institutions pursuant to state law; when it is the law must be specifically followed both for the conferral of tenure and for its denial. Such laws also specify the grounds for breaking tenure and the process to be followed in order to dismiss a tenured teacher. Courts have held that a legislature that has created tenure through law also has the power to abrogate such laws as a matter of new social policy. Depending upon the wording of the state law, tenure might become a contractual right, in which case even legislation that wipes out tenure applies only prospectively and not to those already tenured.

Private institutions that grant tenure do so by contract, since state tenure laws do not apply to them. Similarly, in states without statewide tenure laws, individual school districts or colleges may, by contract, grant tenure. And while tenure through courtesy, timidity, kindness, inertia, or moral commitment does not carry a legal obligation, the Supreme Court has recognized that *de facto* tenure might accrue to teachers when there is no formal tenure but when the circumstances are such that the teachers could reasonably consider themselves permanently employed (Fischer, Schimmel, & Kelly, 1981). Once tenure is acquired by any of the means noted above, the teacher gains a "property" right in continuous employment, a right that can be taken away only by following due process of law. In short, although tenure is not a constitutional right, the Constitution protects tenure, once acquired, as it protects other property rights.

There are disadvantages to the operation of tenure, some of which accrue to institutions and some to individual scholars. The most often-noted disadvantages for institutions are the claims that (1) tenure generates "deadwood," which prevents the institution from upgrading its faculty within a reasonable time period, (2) the probationary period is often too short for bright but slowly developing young faculty, (3) the system makes it difficult to staff high-enrollment lower-division courses with good teachers, for these are usually taught by junior faculty, among whom the turnover is the greatest, and (4) in a time of enrollment decline, minority and women faculty, who tend to be untenured, are among the first to lose their teaching positions.

Although there is something to each of these arguments, there is no substantial empirical support for the first two. What little evidence exists does not support the contention that somehow the security of tenure makes teachers lazy or dull. Clearly, some mediocrity is shielded by tenure, but it can be avoided from the start if the screening processes are adequate. Subcollegiate institutions grant or deny tenure after a three-year probationary period, whereas this period tends to be six years in higher education. For many young scholars this is too short a period to reach the mature productivity that merits tenure. Thus, they often must move on before their scholarly contributions become evident. This turnover is a loss to the first institution but a gain to the subsequent one. Furthermore, it is argued that even if scholars leave academia for industry or government, society has not lost them.

It is generally admitted that in large institutions, where lower-division instruction is usually relegated to the junior faculty, the high rate of turnover in those ranks hurts the quality of such instruction. Some colleges and universities attempt to cope with this problem by requiring top-ranked tenured faculty to share in lower-division instruction, and many schools factor affirmative action considerations into tenure decisions.

The tenure system also works to the disadvantages of individual teachers who would rather opt for higher income than security, whose entrepreneurial spirit is thwarted by tenure rules, particularly those who work in noncontroversial academic areas. Young professors often prefer a longer probationary period in order to develop in the twin areas of teaching and scholarly productivity. However, individuals may not opt out of the tenure system, for ultimately it is not created and maintained for their benefit or for the benefit of the schools. The ultimate beneficiary of tenure is society at large. The main benefit and final justification for tenure lie in its protection of academic freedom, from which society gains in various ways. Clearly, one by-product of tenure is security for the individual, but that is a by-product and not the central purpose. In an excellent treatment of the subject, the following claim is made: "Academic freedom and tenure do not exist because of a peculiar solicitude for the human beings who staff our academic institutions. They exist, instead, in order that society may have the benefit of honest judgment and independent criticism which otherwise might be withheld because of fear of offending a dominant social group or transient social attitude" (Byse & Joughin, 1959, p. 4).

Some criticism of the tenure system has been heard throughout its existence. During recent years, as academic enrollments have reached a no-growth state and even gone into decline, more and more voices have criticized tenure. Demographic analyses reveal an aging professoriate, with relatively few young professors entering the ranks during the next ten years. As more and more departments become saturated with tenured professors and with little opportunities for academic mobility resulting from enrollment decline, there is fear of stagnation and talk of alternatives to tenure.

The major alternatives so far identified are no tenure or multiple-year contracts. The first alternative has been considered and rejected by schools that initially opted for the tenure system. The second is increasingly discussed, but it is clearly fraught with difficulties. Limited experience with it—for example, at Hampshire College in Amherst, Massachusetts—indicates that many problems of the tenure system also surface in the use of multiple-year contracts. Furthermore, there is reason to argue that the faculty anxiety and the time-consuming work necessary to reach a tenure decision must also go into each contract decision at each contract-renewal time throughout the faculty member's career at the institution. Thus, an inordinate amount of professorial time is spent on preparing files of evidence relevant to contract renewal and in serving on committees to make recommendations on the contracts of colleagues. The alternative of turning all such decisions over to administrators is unacceptable to mature faculties or to better institutions, since personnel decisions go to the heart of academic quality. Giving up participation in self-governance, as it relates to personnel matters, also constitutes a serious threat to the academic freedom that took many years for the professoriate to achieve.

In spite of these considerations, there are professors who would abandon tenure and opt for a free marketplace ideology for schools and colleges (O'Toole, 1979). And there are even those who would borrow a model used in professional sports, with rules to govern free agents, reservations of individuals, first refusal, trading, and salary arbitration. Whether or not an "academic czar" would be needed was not decided by the proponents of this position (Dworkin & Johnson, 1979).

In sum, despite the problems associated with tenure, particularly in times of declining enrollment, no one has yet found an adequate and workable substitute for it that would protect academic freedom in the same way.

Collective Bargaining. Recent years have seen the advent of collective bargaining at all levels of schooling. Although earlier experience with industrial models of employer-employee negotiations influenced this development, there are many aspects of education that are unique and do not fit models borrowed from other fields. Among these unique features are academic freedom, tenure, and at the college level, the processes whereby personnel decisions are made. They are not merely "management" prerogatives, for the faculties have primary responsibility over the quality of programs and personnel. Therefore, untried provisions must be introduced into collectively negotiated contracts.

Although some of these contracts are silent on the subject of academic freedom, many specifically endorse it and incorporate past principles and policies. There has been at least one court ruling, however, that held that in their contract, public school teachers negotiated away the right to select teaching materials for their classes. This is a curious and dangerous ruling by a federal district court, for academic freedom is primarily for the benefit of the public, not the teachers—and if it is a constitutional right, it cannot be abrogated by a contract (*Cary* v. *Board of Education*, 1977).

Organizational Protection. Academic freedom is protected mainly by certain professional societies, although the American Civil Liberties Union has also championed its cause and has often gone to court in its behalf. In higher education, the American Association of University Professors (AAUP) has been the central force, since its birth in 1915, for the protection of academic freedom and tenure and for developing adequate procedures for their maintenance. Below the college level, the National Education Association (NEA) and the American Federation of Teachers (AFT) have both been active on behalf of developing and protecting teachers' rights.

In 1915 the AAUP's Committee A produced a "Declara-tion of Principles," setting forth the reciprocal rights and responsibilities between the professoriate and the rest of society. Although its task was primarily that of formulating principles and procedures related to academic freedom, Committee A quickly became involved in investigations of alleged violations and in making recommendations. Institutions found guilty of violating accepted principles can be censured by the AAUP, and such censures are published, as are the removals of the sanctions ("Report of Committee A," 1980). The AAUP collaborated with other scholarly organizations, such as the American Economic Association, the American Political Science Association, and the American Sociology Society, in a shared effort to further the cause of academic freedom, and the 1915 "Declaration of Principles" was the result of this cooperation. This document became the basis for the "1925 Conference Statement of Academic Freedom and Tenure" of the American Council on Education and of several other national organizations. The principles embodied in the 1925 statement were further refined and evaluated in the currently accepted "1940 Statement of Principles" (AAUP, 1941). This statement has since been endorsed by the major educational and scholarly associations and by the faculties and administrations of large numbers of colleges and universities in America.

The AAUP's "Statement on Procedural Standards in Faculty Dismissal Proceedings" in 1958 (AAUP, 1964) was intended as a procedural guide to implement the norms announced in the 1940 statement. The latest major AAUP document in effect reissued the 1940 statements with 1970 interpretative comments (AAUP, 1977), following lawsuits arising out of the campus turmoils of the 1960s. Concerning students, the AAUP approved a statement related to their freedom in the classroom and on campus, the privacy and disclosure of their records, freedom from discrimination, disciplinary procedures, and off-campus activities (AAUP, 1965). Although such declarations are important, most conflicts related to students' freedom in public institutions are controlled by law, which today extends significant protection to students (Millington, 1979).

Summary Academic freedom is a moral ideal that is necessary for the flourishing of an open democratic society and its institutions of learning. It encompasses the freedom to teach, to learn, and to do research and publish research results, as well as the freedom of libraries, art displays, performances, and lectures on campuses and in schools. Such freedom is justified as a moral precept by some, as an intrinsic part of democracy by others, and as an instrumental value to society by still others. Although the roots of this freedom go back to classical antiquity, it is traceable primarily to the great medieval universities in Europe. In America it was adapted from its European forms and shaped through the unique history of our schools and the cultural conflicts resulting from wars, religious diversity, and ideological and economic currents of thought.

In a departure from the traditions of Europe, America has, to some extent, extended the principle of academic freedom to subcollegiate institutions, though with modifications to account for differences in age and experience. The legal bases of academic freedom are still somewhat shaky. Although impressive statements on its behalf have been made by justices of the Supreme Court, these were always in the form of *obiter dicta* or in private writing. Important cases protecting professors' freedoms were decided on grounds other than that of academic freedom—for example, the right to association or to due process. Lower courts, however, have recognized academic freedom as part of the freedom of expression guaranteed by the First Amendment, and if a case should arise squarely on that point, the Supreme Court will probably also recognize it. These principles apply only to public schools, because as a general rule, the Constitution does not apply to private schools.

Students in American schools do not have academic freedom in the sense of determining course content or selecting texts. However, they do have the right to freedom of expression as long as they do not disrupt ordinary teaching-learning processes. Similarly, they have a right to freedom of the press as long as their written expression is not obscene or defamatory and does not cause disruption.

It is generally held that in their off-campus statements, professors should be careful and respectful of others and should indicate that their statements are not official pronouncements. This cautious stance, a self-restraint by professors, seems to be more restrictive than what courts would impose.

Historically, tenure was developed as a means to protect academic freedom, society being the chief beneficiary of such protection. Although not universal, tenure is usually provided for by state law for public institutions and by contract in private ones. Laws or contracts that grant tenure also specify the grounds for breaking it and the procedures to follow in such cases. During recent years tenure has come under some criticism, and some alternatives to tenure have been proposed. Collective bargaining in educational institutions is another recent development that may have an impact on both academic freedom and tenure in the years ahead.

Historically, the AAUP has been the most important organization protecting academic freedom and tenure. In recent years the American Civil Liberties Union, the National Education Association, and the American Federation of Teachers have also made significant contributions to the protection of the rights of teachers.

Louis Fischer

See also Evaluation of Teachers; Faculty Development; Higher Education; History and Philosophy of Higher Education; Judicial Decisions; School Personnel Policies.

REFERENCES

American Association of University Professors. Academic freedom and tenure: 1940 statement of principles. *Bulletin of American Association of University Professors*, 1941, *27*, 40–43.

American Association of University Professors. Statement on procedural standards in faculty dismissal proceedings. *Bulletin of American Association of University Professors*, 1964, *50*, 69–71.

American Association of University Professors. Statement on the academic freedom of students. *Bulletin of American Association of University Professors*, 1965, *51*, 447–449.

American Association of University Professors. Academic freedom and tenure: 1940 statement of principles and (1970) interpretive comments. *American Association of University Professors Policy Documents and Reports*. Washington, D.C.: AAUP, 1977.

Beale, H. K. *Are American Teachers Free?* New York: Scribner, 1936.

Byse, C., & Joughin, L. *Tenure in American Higher Education*. Ithaca, N.Y.: Cornell University Press, 1959.

Cary v. *Board of Education of Adams-Arapahoe*, 427 F. Supp. 945 (D. Colo., 1977).

Dewey, J. *Democracy and Education*. New York: Macmillan, 1916.

Dewey, J. Academic freedom. In P. Monroe (Ed.), *Cyclopedia of Education*. New York: Macmillan, 1919, pp. 700–705.

Dworkin, J. B., & Johnson, R. W. A sporting alternative to tenure. *Bulletin of American Association of University Professors*, February 1979, pp. 41–45.

Fidler, W. P. Academic freedom in the South today. *Bulletin of American Association of University Professors*, 1965, *51*, 413–421.

Fischer, L.; Schimmel, D.; & Kelly, C. *Teachers and the Law*. New York: Longmans, 1981.

Gardner, D. P. *The California Oath Controversy*. Berkeley: University of California Press, 1967.

Hofstadter, R., & Metzger, W. P. *The Development of Academic Freedom in the United States*. New York: Columbia University Press, 1955.

Hook, S. *Heresy, Yes—Conspiracy, No*. New York: John Day, 1953.

Hook, S. *In Defense of Academic Freedom*. New York: Pegasus, 1971.

Hutchins, R. M. *The University of Utopia*. Chicago: University of Chicago Press, 1953.

Jaeger, W. *Paideia: The Ideals of Greek Culture* (Vol. 3), (G. Highet, Trans.). New York: Oxford University Press, 1943.

Keyishian v. *Board of Regents*, 385 U.S. 589 (1967).

Kirk, R. *Academic Freedom: An Essay in Definition*. Chicago: Regnery, 1955.

Machlup, F. G. On some misconceptions concerning academic freedom. *Bulletin of American Association of University Professors*, 1955, *41*, 753–784.

Machlup, F. G. In defense of academic tenure. *Bulletin of American Association of University Professors*, 112–124.

MacIver, R. M. *Academic Freedom in Our Time*. New York: Columbia University Press, 1955.

McMurrin, S. M. Academic freedom. In R. L. Ebel (Ed.), *Encyclopedia of Educational Research* (4th ed.). New York: Macmillan, 1969.

Millington, W. G. *The Law and the College Student*. St. Paul: West Publishing Co., 1979.

Morris, A. A. *The Constitution and American Education*. St. Paul: West Publishing Co., 1980.

Nordin, V. D. The legal protection of academic freedom. In C. P. Hooker (Ed.), *The Courts and Education: The Seventy-seventh Yearbook of the National Society for the Study of Education* (Part I). Chicago: University of Chicago Press, 1978.

O'Toole, J. *Tenure: Three Views*. New Rochelle, N.Y.: Change Magazine Press, 1979.

Reisman, D. *Constraint and Variety in American Education.* Lincoln: University of Nebraska Press, 1956.

Report of Committee A, 1979–1980. *Academe: Bulletin of American Association of University Professors,* September 1980, *66*(5).

Schaefer, R. J. *The School as a Center of Inquiry.* New York: Harper & Row, 1967.

Slaughter, S. The danger zone: Academic freedom and civil liberties. *Annals of the American Academy of Political and Social Science,* March 1980, *448.*

Sweezy v. *New Hampshire,* 354 U.S. 234 (1957).

Tinker v. *Des Moines Independent School District,* 393 U.S. 503 (1969).

Van Alstyne, W. The specific theory of academic freedom and the general issue of civil liberty. In E. L. Pincoff (Ed.), *The Concept of Academic Freedom.* Austin: University of Texas Press, 1975.

Weiman v. *Updegraff,* 344 U.S. 183 (1952).

Woodward, C. V. (Chairman). *Report to the Committee of Freedom of Expression at Yale.* New Haven, Conn.: Yale University, 1975.

ACCELERATED PROGRESS

See Gifted Persons; Promotion Policy.

ACCREDITATION

The function of self-regulation through accreditation is one of the unique characteristics of American higher education. Its emergence and evolution are attributable in part to the fact that state and federal education agencies were primarily concerned with precollegiate education until relatively recent years. Accreditation has its origins in late-nineteenth-century efforts to define a college and to determine requirements for admission. In the twentieth century, the concept evolved into a concern for the quality and integrity of educational institutions and some of their specialized and professional programs. This account of accreditation in higher education presents a brief history of its development; describes its basic premises, organizational structure, and procedures; and notes the changing environment of higher education in which accrediting bodies have become increasingly interrelated with federal and state governments.

Purpose and Types. Institutional accreditation today is closely linked to an institution's continuing efforts to assess its effectiveness and to ensure the fullest possible realization of its mission and goals. It does not require similarity of aims, uniformity of process, or comparability among institutions. Rather, it indicates that, in the judgment of responsible members of the academic community, an institution's goals are soundly conceived and appropriate, that its educational programs have been intelligently planned and are competently conducted, and that the institution is accomplishing the majority of its goals substan-

tially and has the resources to continue doing so for the foreseeable future.

"Institutional accreditation" embraces all educational endeavors conducted by a single institution regardless of its complexity. "Specialized" or "programmatic accreditation" deals with schools, programs, or other segments of institutions, except those professional schools (medical, dental, law, theological, etc.) that are independent or free-standing entities. Specialized accreditation tends to be specific and prescriptive, in part to ensure that the purposes and attainments of specialized programs meet the needs of society and the professions. Because of differing emphases and approaches, institutional accreditation is not equivalent to the specialized accreditation of each of the several programs in an institution. This is an important distinction, because graduation from an accredited program is a prerequisite for many state-licensure examinations in the health fields, accountancy, law, and several other professions.

Development of Accrediting Agencies. Institutional accreditation developed along regional lines as a result of the formation of several associations of schools and colleges. The New England Association led the way (1885), followed by the Middle States Association (1887), the North Central and the Southern associations (1895), the Northwest Association (1917), and the Western College Association (1924). Originally, these organizations focused principally on school-college articulation, especially in relation to college admission standards. A by-product of these activities was the creation, in 1900, of the College Entrance Examination Board.

The regional associations are institutional-membership organizations supported by annual dues from the institutions they accredit. All have separate, elected commissions for the various educational levels: postsecondary, secondary, middle, and, in some cases, elementary schools. Expenses for accrediting activities are borne by the institutions on a cost basis that is kept low by the extensive use of volunteers on evaluation visits. The regional commissions share a common philosophy, and many of their policies and procedures are similar, but there are also differences in emphasis and approach stemming from idiosyncratic characteristics of the geographic areas served.

In contrast, the specialized accrediting agencies vary greatly: some are part of professional associations supported by individual members; others are composed of specialized schools or departments, usually part of a college or university, such as social work, home economics, or architecture. Most are national in scope, with distinctive definitions of eligibility, accrediting criteria, and operating procedures. In general, specialized accrediting bodies are more specific than the institutional accreditors in their requirements for accreditation and more prescriptive in their recommendations for change or improvement. This fact leads at times to charges that they are protectionist and place professional self-interest above that of the public or of the educational institutions with which they are involved. The steady proliferation of specialized accrediting agencies has become one of the most serious and controversial issues in higher education.

Specialized accreditation was introduced by the American Medical Assoication in 1906, when it published a list of acceptable medical schools. Law school accreditation followed in the early 1920s, and before that decade ended, teacher, nursing, collegiate business, library science, optometry, music, and landscape architecture education joined the parade. In the 1930s, dentistry, engineering, social work, and theology were among the fields engaged in specialized or programmatic accreditation.

The idea of institutional accreditation evolved slowly and against the resistance of many reputable institutions and educators. The North Central Association was the first regional association to publish a list of accredited institutions in 1913, followed by the Southern Association in 1919 and by the Middle States Association in 1921. The Northwest Association also assumed accrediting responsibility in 1921, but the Western Association did not follow until 1948, and the New England Association held out until 1952.

The initial lists of accredited institutions were compiled arbitrarily and included chiefly the prestigious liberal arts colleges and major universities. Teachers colleges, engineering schools, and two-year institutions were excluded, and the black colleges of the South did not gain full membership in the Southern Association until the mid-1950s. Gradually, the regional associations expanded their eligibility criteria, until by the early 1970s, they accredited virtually the entire spectrum of postsecondary educational institutions, including proprietary schools.

National coordination. Until 1949, there was neither a public agency nor a private organization in a position to coordinate or oversee the accrediting agencies. Institutions had controlling votes in the regional associations, but they had little influence in the specialized accrediting bodies controlled by the professions. This situation led, in 1949, to the formation of the National Commission on Accrediting (NCA), supported by most of the nation's leading universities and colleges in the hope that accrediting bodies could be brought under some sort of orderly control.

In that same year, the first meeting of the National Committee of Regional Accrediting Agencies marked the beginning of continuing efforts to achieve commonality and consistency in policies and procedures among the regions. The committee was reorganized, in 1964, as the Federation of Regional Accrediting Commissions of Higher Education (FRACHE), a more formal and purposeful step toward greater cooperation. Eight years later, in 1972, further steps were taken to consolidate the influence of FRACHE by establishing a national office in Washington and appointing a full-time executive director.

While the NCA and FRACHE were still in their formative years, Congress, in 1952, passed Public Law 82-250, designed to eliminate abuses of sections of the World War II GI Bill providing educational benefits to veterans. Sec-

tion 253 of the law required the U.S. Commissioner of Education to publish a list of nationally recognized accrediting agencies, a requirement satisfied for the next sixteen years chiefly by the commissioner's duplicating the list of agencies recognized by the NCA and by adding the names of the regional accrediting commissions. However, profound changes in the relationship of the federal government to higher education occurred during those same years and eventually brought about a major shift in posture toward accreditation. The U.S. Commissioner of Education's role remained passive until 1968, when the Accreditation and Institutional Eligibility Staff (AIES) was established in the U.S. Office of Education to oversee accrediting agencies. An advisory committee was established, a set of criteria for recognition was published, and the federal government was quickly and actively engaged in reviewing all agencies whose recognition could be utilized as a basis for determining eligibility to participate in federal funding programs for higher education. Some of the recognition criteria were strongly opposed, and some were modified, but most of the institutional and specialized accrediting agencies satisfied the criteria sufficiently to have their recognition continued on a four-year cycle.

Nevertheless, the specter of federal control of higher education, through the regulation of accrediting, loomed steadily larger in the early 1970s, thus raising new pressures on the accrediting bodies to get their houses in order. The result was a merger, in 1975, of the NCA and FRACHE to form the Council on Postsecondary Accreditation (COPA). After years of obscurity and deliberately low-profile activity, accreditation had entered the goldfish bowl of public attention. In its first few years, COPA could claim modest success in the improvement and coordination of accrediting agencies through its own policies. Improvement in the practices of some agencies must also be credited to the recognition function of AIES, which, in 1975, became the Division of Eligibility and Agency Evaluation (DEAE). Sponsored and supported by the leading national educational organizations, as well as by the regional and specialized accrediting agencies, COPA was in a strategic position to serve as a countervailing balance against the intrusion of federal control in higher education. A prime example was its successful struggle, in 1979–1980, to have the federal government continue using accreditation as a basis of eligibility for federal funding and, at the same time, to resist the expansion of regulatory government controls. As the 1980s began, the federal relationship to accreditation was obscured by the uncertain future of the Department of Education.

State involvement. At the state level, however, there was a steadily rising interest and growing involvement in accreditation in higher education. Until the 1950s, state involvement, with few exceptions, was limited to funding state universities and teachers colleges. In the 1950s and 1960s, states, counties, and even municipalities established hundreds of new institutions, transformed normal schools and teacher-training institutions into general-purpose colleges, and made state colleges into universities. Much of this change occurred without plan or design, but it soon became apparent that central planning and structure were needed to organize the elements into a coherent whole. Gradually, state systems, boards of higher education, coordinating councils, and other variations of centralized supervision began to emerge. At first the state agencies affected only public institutions, but as private colleges and universities began to receive subsidies, those institutions also became subject to state scrutiny. The spreading necessity for statewide master planning, the rising demands for consumer protection in education, and the expansionist tendency of bureaucracies resulted in the growing impact of state government in higher education affairs.

The pattern of this involvement has been as varied as the fifty states, ranging from nearly absolute control in New York, where the Board of Regents has had virtually total authority over all levels of education in the state since 1784, to virtually no control in states that tolerate almost anything, including the mail-order sale of pseudo-degrees. Authority to license or charter educational institutions rests historically and constitutionally with the states, but this power has been exercised erratically. Under the aegis of the Education Commission of the States, model legislation for licensing educational institutions was developed in 1973, but its adoption has progressed slowly.

State interest in some form of surveillance over existing institutions rose rapidly in the 1970s, although there were sharp conflicts in many states about the extent of state jurisdiction over private institutions, including those receiving state subsidies. The issues were further confused by failure to distinguish between licensure and accreditation, and, in several states, conflict occurred between government agencies and accrediting bodies. Institutions were unfortunately caught in the middle. One answer to the problem is the triad concept, a triangular relationship involving the states, the accrediting commissions, and the federal government. States would be responsible for licensing educational institutions, accrediting bodies would attest to the quality and integrity of the institutions, and the federal government would keep all of them honest. That obviously oversimplifies a complex problem, but nonetheless it represents the essence of what many believe to be a desirable division of labor and responsibility. Whether or how well the triad concept can work is a prominent question for the 1980s.

Process of Accreditation. There were other issues of debate, as accreditation continued to evolve: minimum standards versus standards of excellence, objective criteria versus subjective criteria, and process versus outcomes in measuring quality or effectiveness. When accrediting was inaugurated, the criteria used by the regional commissions were entirely quantitative: number of faculty, square footage per student, volumes in the library, size of endowment, hours of instruction, and so on. No reliable basis was established for selecting these particular measures.

Once an institution was accredited under the old criteria, it remained on the accreditation roster indefinitely. By the mid-1930s, however, disenchantment with the quantitative approach set in, and a shift toward qualitative considerations became evident. Slowly the sophistication of the accrediting process was elevated. Questions like "What is this institution's educational purpose?" and "How well is it fulfilling that purpose?" became the focus of institutional accreditation in the 1940s. The indefinite duration of accreditation also became an issue that was resolved by instituting the periodic reevaluation of accredited institutions in the 1950s.

To prepare for such evaluations, the process of institutional self-study was introduced. Its guiding principles include broad constituent involvement, candor, and a willingness to take an honestly critical look at all aspects of the institution. A twelve-month to twenty-four-month period of self-study precipitates a report that serves to inform a visiting team of professional peers and the accrediting commission of the nature and purpose of the institution and to convey the institution's own assessment of its effectiveness. With continual refinement and adaptation, self-study and periodic evaluation are now essential features of all institutional and most specialized accrediting.

Standards and effects. Through the years, the debate over the issue of standards has waxed and waned: "Should there be minimum standards so that any institution meeting them can be accredited?" or "Should there be absolute standards of excellence allowing only the "best" institutions to be accredited and who shall determine these standards?" There has never been any widely accepted agreement on the answers, nor is there likely to be, but a new emphasis has emerged recently in the continuing effort to assess educational effectiveness. For most of its history, accreditation relied on a series of assumptions related to the process of education: if a carefully selected student spent enough hours in class with a properly credentialed professor and had ready access to a well-stocked library, if the curricula were clearly defined and the requirements sufficiently rigorous, and if the grading patterns followed a respectable curve and attrition was not too high, then *ipso facto*, good education was being provided, and the institution deserved accreditation. The evidence of cause-and-effect relationships was limited at best, and legislators, consumer-protection groups, and the general public have become more insistent that educators find better ways of demonstrating the tangible results of the educational experiences of students.

In response, outcomes assessment is being studied more carefully than ever before in American higher education. In essence, outcomes assessment seeks to determine the extent to which an institution is fulfilling its educational goals and objectives as reflected in the attainments of its students. It is being stressed by a number of accrediting commissions as a means of strengthening accreditation and enhancing its credibility. At the same time, accreditors are concerned that subjective considerations not be subordinated entirely, the more so, because the development of sound and discriminating judgment is a paramount goal of all education.

Specialized accreditation has also begun to look more searchingly at outcomes data, although in some of the professional fields success in licensing examinations is a ready measure of success. However, the specialized agencies have traditionally been more quantitatively oriented in their requirements and procedures. Until the 1970s, when COPA and DEAE pressured them, few of the specialized agencies required self-study as part of their accrediting procedures. Check sheets and extensive questionnaires were completed by the institution or program under scrutiny, and the outside visitor's role was primarily to verify data that required little or no judgment. That pattern is changing, and the pace will accelerate as the pressure for greater coordination between institutional and specialized accrediting continues to build. This will be a major thrust of COPA through the 1980s, and the results will certainly affect the future of nongovernmental accreditation.

In the final analysis, however, the future of nongovernmental accreditation hinges more directly on the integrity of educational institutions and on the responsibility of their leaders. Accreditation is not well understood within higher education, let alone by the general public. Few are aware of its achievements (1) in fostering excellence in education through development of criteria and guidelines for assessing institutional effectiveness; (2) in encouraging institutional improvement through continual self-study and evaluation; (3) in assuring the academic community, the general public, the professions, and other agencies that an institution or program has clearly defined and appropriate educational objectives, has established conditions to facilitate their achievement, appears in fact to be achieving them substantially, and is so organized, staffed, and supported that it can be expected to continue doing so; (4) in providing counsel and assistance to established and developing institutions; and (5) in protecting institutions from encroachments that might jeopardize their educational effectiveness or academic freedom.

Impressive as it is, not even that record will protect or perpetuate independent accreditation without institutional involvement and commitment. All the standards in the world will make no difference if educational leaders compromise their own or their institution's integrity merely to survive. That will be the challenge and the test for higher education and accreditation in the 1980s.

The literature about accreditation increased rapidly during the 1970s, a reflection of both the growing interest and the importance of the subject. In 1979, the *Journal of Higher Education* devoted its entire March-April issue to the discussion of key topics pertaining to accreditation. These topics included the relationship of accreditation to quality assurance in higher education, credentialing, nontraditional education, federal and state governments, and analyses of the accrediting process. The articles and references in that issue, along with the entries in the bibliography prepared by Kells and Robertson (1980), clearly demonstrate that accreditation has emerged from a long history of low-profile activity and relative obscurity to become one of the central issues of higher education in the 1980s.

Robert Kirkwood

See also Higher Education; Licensing and Certification; Professional Organizations; Professions Education; State Influences on Education; Teacher Certification.

REFERENCES

Journal of Higher Education, 1979, *50*, 115–232.
Kells, H. R., & Robertson, M. P. Postsecondary accreditation: A current bibliography. *North Central Association Quarterly*, 1980, *54*, 411–426.

ACHIEVEMENT TESTING

"Achievement testing" as defined here refers to the assessment of the outcomes of formal instruction in cognitive domains, with "instruction" defined as subject matter that is explicitly taught. This instruction carries with it the expectation that it will produce observable changes in the behavior of those who are being instructed. "Achievement" as discussed in this article does not cover such domains as creativity, motivation, or ethical sense.

Achievement testing is often thought of as a sample of indicators of a student's knowledge taken at a particular point in time (Ebel, 1979). In practice, however, the use of such indicators, or the interpretation of test results, implies a comparison of the sample behavior either with another sample of behavior taken at a different point in time or with a sample of behavior taken from another student or group of students. This type of comparison is most characteristic of norm-referenced test uses. One can also think of an achievement test as a sample of behavior that provides an opportunity for comparison with a performance standard, as in criterion-referenced testing (Gronlund, 1973; Hambleton et al., 1978; Popham, 1978). One of the factors contributing to the development of criterion-referenced testing has been the perceived closeness of the norm-referenced orientation to aptitude constructs. Proponents of criterion-referenced testing point out that normative comparisons of achievement are often misinterpreted as comparisons of aptitude and may further be wrongly construed as indicating fixed rather than malleable abilities. The criterion-referenced testing orientation, in its focus on clearly defined behavioral samples, is less susceptible to this type of misinterpretation.

Achievement is often defined in relation to the concept of aptitude by a simple contrast: measuring the learning that takes place during a definable course of instruction is achievement testing; measuring the outcomes of a very lengthy and diffuse set of learning experiences is aptitude testing. Aptitude has, in fact, been characterized as "curriculum-free" (Angoff, 1980). If one accepts this contrast, achievement may be thought of simply as being more closely related in time to instruction than is aptitude. Although this orientation in itself implies a continuum rather than a dichotomy, in practice it represents a distinction that is useful, if not intellectually rigorous.

It seems useful to distinguish between aptitude and achievement tests in two additional ways: the directionality of the inferences made on the basis of such tests and the expected improvement as a function of instruction. Achievement tests are typically used to assess the outcomes of previous schooling, whereas aptitude tests are usually intended to aid in prediction of success in schooling or later employment. In addition, performance on tests labeled achievement tests will be expected to improve relatively rapidly as a function of instruction, whereas performance on tests labeled aptitude tests may be expected to improve more slowly, even with additional specific instruction. But it should be remembered that these distinctions, although of considerable practical significance for some problems, are not clear-cut in many ordinary situations.

Reading comprehension provides an example of the difficulty of attempting to maintain a distinction between aptitude and achievement based on instructional constructs alone. Reading comprehension is a skill that is widely taught at the elementary level and that forms the basis for later achievement at every level of instruction. It is a skill that diverges from explicit instruction at a very early stage, around third grade for most learners. Reading practitioners endorse this early separation from specific instruction, and the separation is reflected in achievement testing as well as in curriculum materials and course structure. Students are expected, at a very early stage, to generalize the reading skills that they have been specifically taught to other reading tasks. Thus reading comprehension, although prototypical of an achievement skill, is also thought of and widely used as an aptitude measure. Is it useful to say that a test of reading is an achievement test for a student in second grade and an aptitude test for a student in ninth grade? In contrast, mathematics continues to be taught as a series of new skills to be acquired throughout the elementary and secondary school years and into college.

The distinction between the retrospective and prospective orientations of aptitude and achievement tests is also not so fixed as it may seem at first glance. This distinction may explain the intent of the testing; it is interesting, if not instructive or comforting, to note that in validity studies based on predicting success in the next level of schooling, achievement tests often outperform aptitude tests in terms of relative predictive efficiency (Wilson, 1974, 1979).

It should also be noted that the philosophical orientation of aptitude testing for postsecondary admissions is currently changing. Admissions tests have often been mistakenly regarded as tests of pure aptitude or even of innate ability. Publishers now emphasize that these tests assess "developed abilities," thus maintaining the distinction between aptitude and achievement tests on the basis of the length of time required to develop the specific abilities on which the test content is based.

Thus, it is not possible to maintain rigorous theoretical distinctions between aptitude and achievement tests. One can measure only crystalized achievements (in larger or smaller units), not innate abilities. Any presumed indicator of ability must rely heavily on an individual's previous learning experiences.

Types of Achievement Tests. A fundamental distinction in achievement testing, and the basic issue in the selection of test format, is the relative desirability of recall versus recognition item types. "Recall" item types require the test taker to recall or supply information from memory (this is also called the "free-response" type and includes the essay item); "recognition" item types require the test taker to recognize the correct answer among a number of alternatives supplied.

Although the archetype of the recall question is the essay and that of the recognition item type is the multiple-choice question, there are many forms of both the free-response and the objective test question. The free-response question ranges from a lengthy and complex essay that requires the interaction of content and highly developed cognitive skills to the short-answer completion that simply requires inserting a single word or phrase in an incomplete statement. Likewise, the objective test question may range from the multiple-choice question requiring difficult inferences and evaluation to be chosen from among highly similar but subtly different distractors, through matching sets, to the simple true/false statement.

The range of objective item types suggested in recent years is truly awesome. Test constructors have argued the merits of two-, three-, four-, and five-choice multiple-choice questions, discrete items or interdependent sets, the matching set or related series of facts, and such semiobjective item types as cloze paragraphs (words systematically deleted from reading comprehension paragraphs) using either free-response or supplied choices to fill in the blanks. Wesman (1971) provided a helpful summary of the strengths and limitations of major item types. Table 1 summarizes some of the major advantages and disadvantages of five widely used item types.

Cronbach (1970), in characterizing the contrast between recall and recognition as a major issue in educational testing, emphasized the relationship of item type to test use; for example, essay and other free-response item types are especially useful where the purpose of teaching is to produce the ability to recall information from memory or invent new solutions. The range of available item types, however, in both the objective and the free-response mode is so great that it is not possible to make categorical statements about their appropriate uses; further qualifiers are

TABLE 1. *Advantages and disadvantages of common item types*

Type	Advantages	Disadvantages
Essay	Measures complex skills directly Easy to write questions Difficult to obtain high scores by chance or guessing	Time-consuming to administer and score Difficult to score reliably Limited sample of knowledge can be assessed
Multiple-choice	Can be used to assess wide range of skills Large sample of knowledge can be assessed in a brief period Efficient to score, even for large numbers of takers Can be made highly reliable	Time-consuming to write Measures complex skills indirectly Possible to answer correctly by guessing
True/false	Many can be administered in a short time Efficient to assess factual knowledge Efficient to score Moderately easy to write	Largely restricted to factual material High probability of guessing correctly Many depend heavily on extraneous clues
Short-answer	Many can be administered in a short time Relatively efficient to score for small numbers of students Moderately easy to write	Time-consuming to construct defensible criteria for correct answers Limited to questions that can be answered or completed in very few words
Performance	Provides a direct sample of relevant complex behaviors	Developing reliable and valid scoring systems is difficult Must be individually administered and scored

needed. As mentioned earlier, essay or free-response questions may tap only the simplest and most minimal skills whereas objective test questions may tap the most complex cognitive skills. On the other hand, the reverse is demonstrably true as well.

Although it is appropriate to focus on the intended use of a test in recommending recall or recognition item types, the debate has been informed by considerable research as well. Historically, the recall item type has predominated in achievement testing. The free-response or essay format has been the most widely used in teacher-made classroom examinations everywhere and in external examinations, currently in Western Europe but formerly in the United States as well. Early in the twentieth century, the emerging specialty of educational measurement adopted a critical stance toward the essay examination. Starch and Elliott (1912, 1913a, 1913b) conducted some classic studies of the reliability of teacher grading of essays in English, mathematics, and social studies. In these studies, Starch and Elliott asked a number of teachers to grade the same examination papers and found extremely wide variation in the grades assigned to the same essays. (Later studies confirmed these same findings in a variety of contexts.)

Even then, it was apparent that the unreliability of essay grades stems from two sources: the small number of questions that can be asked in a given time and differences in graders' standards for scores. Because essays are time-consuming for the student to write relative to answering multiple-choice questions, fewer of them can be required of students in any given time period. Ebel (1979) put this quite simply: "Students spend most of their time in thinking and writing when taking an essay test. They spend most of their time reading and thinking when taking an objective test" (p. 100). Thus, the student's score is highly dependent upon "the luck of the draw": A fortunate student may benefit greatly from being asked about the few things he or she knows, and an unfortunate student may suffer from being asked about only those few things she or he does not know.

Arguments in favor of the essay or free-response testing mode are somewhat diffuse and rely extensively on tradition, but the core of the pro-essay position is that such questions provide a direct measure of desirable complex behaviors. As in performance testing, a student provides an actual sample of the relevant behaviors. Examples include such testing tasks as foreign language pronunciation tests as well as the more familiar English composition. In addition to measuring complex behavior, another advantage noted by proponents of essay testing is that guessing does not materially affect scores on an essay test, as it does on tests in which the student is to choose among given responses. An additional advantage of the essay type is that even a high-quality essay question requires a much smaller investment of preparation time for the test developer than does preparation of multiple-choice material of comparable quality requiring the same testing time.

Proponents of essay testing have also argued that the increasing use of objective item types, particularly on standardized tests, has caused educational institutions of all levels to forsake, wholly or partially, instruction in writing in favor of skills measured more prominently by multiple-choice tests. They further argue that such an emphasis on objective testing creates a situation in which students do not learn to write because they are not tested directly on their writing skills.

The arguments in favor of the multiple-choice test can be summarized succinctly. This format provides highly efficient and flexible measurement, particularly for large groups of students. Multiple-choice test questions of high quality can be quite time-consuming to construct, but they are very simple and reliable to score either by hand or with electronic equipment. By hand, a punched-out stencil or simple tally will, with the proper quality control procedures, enable even untutored scorers to arrive at the same score for a given paper. With the assistance of modern electronic scanning equipment, literally millions of responses per hour can be graded. Multiple-choice test questions are also able to provide reliable measurement because a very large sample of questions may be asked of the students within the allotted testing time. As mentioned previously, careful construction techniques can produce test questions assessing a very wide range of cognitive skills and subject matter content.

It has become commonplace in tests-and-measurement courses to say that objective tests are difficult to prepare and easy to score, whereas essay or free-response tests are easy to prepare and difficult to score. One of the central issues in assessing the appropriateness of free-response item types is the reliability of scoring. Essay questions are typically graded in one of two ways, which are not completely distinct: analytic scoring and holistic scoring. "Analytic scoring" closely resembles the teacher's traditional method of scoring classroom tests. The scorer specifies points to be allocated for various aspects of the essay, such as the number of points given for handwriting, the number subtracted for capitalization and punctuation errors, the number given for content, the number given for creativity, and so forth. The student's score is simply the sum of the points awarded. In "holistic scoring," the scorer disregards specific points of strength or weakness in the piece of writing and reacts to the piece as a whole.

Each of these methods has its own advantages and limitations as well as appropriate and inappropriate uses. The analytic method is certainly a quite reliable method of scoring essays, if sufficiently detailed criteria are provided to the scorer and if reasonably adequate quality control measures are taken. Much of the benefit of the essay question is lost, however, when analytic scoring procedures can be specified rigorously enough to enable a clerical

assistant to grade essays. In this instance, the judgment of the student's complexity of thought and marshaling of facts in support of a thesis is lost. On the other hand, essays scored holistically require the scorer to be well versed in the subtleties of the subject matter. The scoring of essays in this fashion, when reliability of scoring is considered to be of prime importance, depends heavily on agreement among scorers as to what constitute acceptable standards or grades. Indeed, to achieve even minimal reliability of scoring, each essay must certainly be read by more than one qualified individual.

A tradition of research on this topic dating to the early 1930s suggests that a well-constructed essay examination can be graded reliably through either the analytic or the holistic scoring method, provided the questions themselves are well constructed and more than one reader is available to read and score each essay (Coffman, 1971). Maximum reliability also requires that each test taker is, in fact, attempting the same task. This means that the time-honored tradition of allowing a student to choose, for example, three out of five questions to attempt in an essay test must be forsaken in the interest of increased reliability. Reliability of scoring is also increased by grading each group of essays on the same topic separately, rather than grading on a total student-by-student basis.

A scattered body of research has indicated that, despite problems with reliability of free-response tests, moderate correlations can be obtained between material tested through essay questions and comparable material tested with multiple-choice questions. Coffman (1971) provided a good summary of these data and a helpful interpretation of the relationship. There is some evidence, however, that item types may interact with personal characteristics of the test taker. Murphy (1977) noted a small but consistent sex difference associated with item format. Murphy studied performance on a wide range of subject areas assessed for Great Britain's General Certificate of Education examinations as the examiners experimented with moving from their traditional all-essay format to inclusion of a multiple-choice component. He found that, overall, assessing the same content with multiple-choice rather than essay questions gave a small but distinct advantage to male students.

Given that, in general, a strong and consistent relationship exists between free-response and objective test question formats of various types, it must also be the case that selection of a test format and associated item types should be determined primarily by the specific test use and the resources available to those charged with the testing. Factors to be considered include the testing time available, the number of individuals to be tested, the importance of the reliability of judgments about individuals, the amount of staff time available for multiple grading of essays, and access to equipment such as electronic scoring machines.

Uses. Coffman (1971) outlined five major uses of achievement tests: student motivation, teacher feedback, certification and selection, credit for courses or advanced standing, and historical record-keeping and policy-making aids. Brown (1980), following Cronbach (1970), differentiated between two major types of test use: decision-making uses and descriptive uses. Decision-making uses include situations in which applicants are being selected for particular employment or academic opportunities, assignment to instructional groups, occupational certification, or the use of test scores as a dependent or criterion measure (for example, when evaluating educational programs). In descriptive uses, on the other hand, the main goal of testing is to provide information that can help the test user understand or assist an individual test taker. Brown noted that descriptive uses generally are most appropriate when there is a continuing relationship between the test taker and the test user, and the information obtained from the assessment can be modified in light of further information. Because descriptive uses of tests are more individualized than decision-making uses, the applicability of standards for test use differs between these two broad categories of test use.

Grades. Achievement tests have long been used to motivate students to study by forming a partial basis (or the major basis) for course grades. Many teachers also use achievement tests to signal important material or key concepts within a course. An emphasis on achievement tests as an aid to teacher feedback has been important in the development of criterion-referenced testing. In a typical theoretical model of criterion-referenced assessment, the teacher feedback cycle is approximately as follows: The teacher sets a series of skill or knowledge objectives; the concepts underlying these objectives are taught to the students; the teacher tests the students on these particular concepts; the teacher reviews the results of this testing; the teacher reteaches the material, usually in a different way (or the teacher goes on to the next objective).

Selection. The use of achievement tests for certification and selection is widespread throughout the world, particularly in Western Europe, to assess student progress at the end of secondary school and for admission to higher education. In the United States, achievement-type examinations are also widely used as supplementary information for postsecondary admissions. The use of achievement tests is becoming very widespread in occupational and professional licensing situations as well.

Credit by examination. The last fifteen years have seen a great increase in the practice of awarding credit by examination or advanced standing in college documented by examinations. Perhaps the best-known examples are the College Entrance Examination Board's Advanced Placement Examinations and College-Level Examination Program. The Advanced Placement program is based on a common syllabus to be taught in subject matter areas, followed by a common examination on this material. Student examinations, typically a combination of essay and multiple-choice questions, are then scored at a single reading by groups of subject matter experts.

Colleges set their own rules concerning acceptance of scores for advanced standing in their institution. In the College-Level Examination Program, students take subject matter examinations to demonstrate competence in areas where they may not have had formal instruction, but where they have acquired knowledge and skills through experience or independent study.

Policy making. Achievement tests or groups of achievement test items have also been used recently as a historical record and as an aid to policy making at all levels of government. Many state programs assess student skills in such basic areas as reading and mathematics at selected grade levels, with the primary purpose of assessing student progress across school districts or across time. In recent years, controversy has arisen over the issue of withholding student diplomas on the basis of such testing and the related problem of possible adverse impact of such practices on minority-group students.

The National Assessment of Educational Progress (NAEP) takes a somewhat different approach to achievement testing for the historical record on a national level. NAEP differs from other achievement testing situations in that scores are reported only on the item level. Interpretation is then made at the item level by inspection of the data on the percentage of students in each selected age-group who have answered the question correctly. An obvious disadvantage of NAEP's unique approach, however, is that direct comparisons with other types of achievement test data are not possible.

Norm-referenced versus criterion-referenced tests. As mentioned earlier, a major distinction in test use that has been recognized largely within the past decade is between norm-referenced and criterion-referenced testing. This distinction can best be conceptualized as a matter of score interpretation, with "norm-referenced" testing aimed at comparisons with a group of test takers designated as a norm group (typically national norms or other appropriate comparison groups) and "criterion-referenced" testing aimed at comparison with a specified standard of performance or behavior. Few meaningful distinctions can be made between norm-referenced tests and criterion-referenced tests at the item level, although Ebel (1979) pointed to a tendency for items on criterion-referenced tests to be highly specific and to cluster around a limited number of specific objectives. This is in contrast to norm-referenced tests in which one item may attempt to assess several points simultaneously. Larger distinctions can be made, however, in the manner in which criterion-referenced and norm-referenced test items are assembled and administered to students. "Pure" exemplars of criterion-referenced tests are typically assembled in shorter blocks of items (five and ten are not uncommon numbers), to be administered to students at any time the teacher considers the student ready to take that test. Norm-referenced tests are more likely to be administered in larger numbers at a single testing session, reflecting the interdependent, survey nature of these tests.

Standards. An important issue that has been highlighted by the development of criterion-referenced testing is the setting of appropriate cutting scores (passing scores or standards). Test users have only recently recognized that a cutting score is not inherent in an achievement test itself, but is a product of judgment, and have taken steps to incorporate this insight into their testing practice. It is intuitively obvious, for example, that a traditional passing grade of 65 percent has very different meaning on a difficult test than on an easy test and that there are situations in which 50 or 90 may be more appropriate passing scores. Several helpful surveys of methods to set appropriate passing scores are available (Hambleton & Eignor, 1980; Meskauskas, 1976; Zieky & Livingston, 1977).

Confidentiality. Confidentiality of scores is also a major issue related to test use. Federal legislation, such as the Buckley amendment, gives students and their parents the right to all educational information concerning those students, including their test scores. In addition, this legislation prohibits disclosure of these records, except with the prior written consent of the students or their parents, to other than certain school officials or other authorized users (Brown, 1980). Thus, legislation and current test standards require that achievement test score information be kept confidential, but be available to students and their parents.

Current controversies. Attention is currently being focused on the use of achievement tests as measures of effectiveness of schooling. A problem arises in attempting to assess achievement with a single outcome measure when the educational input (students) is not controlled or is known to vary in systematic ways. This is an important point to consider in evaluating such complex phenomena as the observed decline in college admission test scores. A common oversimplification of this issue overlooks both any aptitude-achievement distinction as well as the problem of noncomparable input. Insofar as scholastic aptitude test scores are designed to be independent of specific curricula and to draw on students' out-of-school learning experiences as well as formal instruction, they are inappropriate as measures of school effectiveness or the quality of secondary instruction. Such outcomes are better measured with tests closely related to instructional objectives, administered in an appropriate evaluation design.

Test disclosure. Legislation enacted in the late 1970s and early 1980s requires disclosure of the content of standardized tests (as well as the students' answer sheets and the intended keys) to those taking them. This legislation resulted from a larger controversy concerning the advantages of tests' content being new to all test takers, on the one hand, and the advantages to the test takers of being able to review and evaluate tests that are influential in their lives, on the other. In particular, proponents of test disclosure have largely focused their attention on postsecondary admissions tests, but the issues are germane to achievement tests as well. Developers of standardized tests typically reuse test forms or test items, arguing that to develop new items for each test administration would be wasteful. Further, many standardized testing programs use test-equating methods that require readministration of previously used items. This would not be possible if the items were to be disclosed. Those in favor of test disclosure characterize these considerations as obstacles that can be overcome, arguing for the precedence of a test-taker's right to review and comment on the test questions he or she has actually taken and the importance of the right of the test taker, as a consumer, to inspect the questions and answers for errors, ambiguity, or bias. As of 1981, most developers of standardized tests have complied with test disclosure requirements and are seeking ways to overcome the financial and technical problems associated with these actions.

Test Construction Issues. A major task of the group or individual charged with developing an achievement test, that of writing test materials, may still be characterized as an art to which some scientific procedures and experientially derived judgments make only modest contributions (Wesman, 1971). Even such widely respected works as Ebel's *Essentials of Educational Measurement* (1979) deal with the consensus of professional judgment regarding item-writing issues, rather than with reports and conclusions drawn from a body of research. Not surprisingly, this orientation has troubled many researchers. Recent works, such as that of Roid and Haladyna (1981), have attempted to conceptualize various approaches to a technology of item writing. These approaches, however, remain useful largely at the theoretical level. Some techniques proposed include objective-based item writing, amplified objectives, item forms, facet design, domain-referenced testing, and computerized applications. Currently, applications of these theoretical orientations are largely restricted to lower-level cognitive skills, and each of these theoretical orientations lacks generalizability, remaining restricted to a limited subject matter domain (most often science or mathematics). Nonetheless, these attempts at investigating the bases and mechanics of item writing do serve the valuable function of focusing attention on the necessity for a close match between test items and the material they are intended to assess, a central element in evaluating an assessment cycle. This relationship between the material that has been taught and the items themselves is of particular significance at this time because of recent court decisions (such as those in Florida's case *Debra P. v. Turlington*) that have declared invalid, in minimum-competency testing, any individual use of test questions on material that cannot be demonstrated to have been explicitly taught to each student.

Specifications. Test specifications are of crucial significance in achievement testing. Professional standards for achievement tests require the presence of test specifications, while leaving unspecified the level of detail at which specifications must be given. The result is that achievement test specifications, even for standardized achievement tests, are extremely variable in type and level of specificity. They may range from a simple statement and description of the general area to be covered (e.g., "reading comprehension") to extremely detailed item forms, such as those proposed by Hively, Patterson, and Page (1968). Specifications for individually or locally made achievement tests may also be drawn from a particular course or content area syllabus or may be adapted or used "as is" from commercial banks of objectives. The areas typically covered in detailed achievement test specifications include item content, item context, presence of sex- or ethnic-relevant material, test length, testing time, target reliability, and target difficulty.

In establishment of content specifications for large-scale assessment or standardized achievement testing programs, the basis of decision rests largely on established authority (in the form of consensus of judgments) in delineating the skills or knowledge to be tested. Content specifications are typically established by a committee of subject matter or other relevant experts. Empirical validation of many of their judgments is subsequently possible through pretesting and item analysis, but does not usually form the basis for content specifications.

Context specifications, descriptions of the external context in which substantive questions are set, are applicable primarily to verbal areas, such as reading comprehension, but are also used in certain other applications, such as applied mathematics problems. Context specifications may, for example, call for an even distribution of reading comprehension passages dealing with technical or scientific topics on the one hand and with humanities-oriented topics on the other. The relationship of test item context to such personal characteristics as race and sex has been widely assumed but only sporadically investigated (Dwyer, 1976; Graff & Riddel, 1972; Milton, 1957, 1959; Strassberg-Rosenberg & Donlon, 1975). Test specifications also generally include guidelines for inclusion of sex- and ethnically relevant materials where appropriate, but this is a relatively recent development and is not typical of tests more than a few years old.

Several authors have addressed the question of the appropriate number of choices to be included in a multiple-choice item. Proponents of large numbers of choices point to the diminished advantage of guessing when the student has a relatively large number of distractors from which to choose. Proponents of smaller numbers of choices point to the decreased amount of reading associated with two- or three-choice questions and suggest that more questions can be given in an alloted testing time, thus leading to increased reliability and content coverage. Smith (1958) investigated the use of two-choice items and found them satisfactory for some purposes. Ebel and Williams (1957) examined the effect of varying the number of item alternatives from two to four and found all of them satisfactory for some purposes as well. In a later work, however, Ebel (1979) concluded that "there is no magic in four alternatives and no reason why all items in a test should have the same number of alternatives. It is quite possible to

write a good multiple-choice test item with only two distractors (three responses), and occasionally one distractor" (1979, p. 150). Ebel also advised classroom teachers that three options are sufficient for classroom tests. Standardized test makers seem to favor three options in tests for students up to grade 3, four options for students from grades 4 through high school, and five options for college entrance through higher education and occupational assessment.

Statistical or psychometric specifications affect item writing in a number of ways. Setting a target level of difficulty that is based on such needs as test appropriateness for a particular population or the establishment of cut scores can be achieved through a combination of professional judgments as to the probable difficulty of individual items and review of item analysis information obtained from pretesting where this is feasible. Common examples are designing a test with many difficult items to aid in selecting applicants for a graduate fellowship (scores will cluster at the low end of the scale), or designing a test with many relatively easy items to determine minimum competency for occupational certification (scores will cluster at the high end of the scale). Reliability is also largely a function of item appropriateness for the population and the integrity of individual items.

In setting specifications for test length and testing time, most large-scale or published achievement tests now try to eliminate speededness. Current psychometric thinking generally considers speed not to be intrinsic to most academic tasks; there is also the possibility of interaction of test speededness with personal and background characteristics of the test taker, such as willingness to take risks or sex and ethnicity. In any event, the speededness of achievement tests is assessed largely through somewhat arbitrary criteria, such as the commonly used rule of thumb that 80 percent of the test takers should reach the last question, and virtually all reach the question that marks the completion of 75 percent of the test items (Swineford, 1974).

Item writing. Many specific test construction practices used by large-scale test makers have evolved from attempts to eliminate factors extraneous to the material being tested that might distract test takers or irrelevantly influence their scores. Extraneous factors that are commonly controlled by item writers and and test editors include such points as the avoidance of any words or phrases that may serve as specific determiners of the correct answer. Test makers attempt to ensure that all the options are of approximately the same length, all options are grammatically parallel, words such as "none" or "all" (which the intelligent but uninformed student may simply recognize as seldom being true) are avoided, and each option follows grammatically from the stem. Test writers also avoid the use of offensive or stereotypical language that may be upsetting or distracting to the test taker and material dealing with highly controversial topics (where understanding of these topics themselves is not being measured).

Test assembly. In the context of an entire test, test assemblers and editors also consider the number and distribution of correct keys. Long runs of correct answers with the same designation (for example, all "A"'s or "B"'s) are avoided. Throughout the test, each key position should be approximately equally represented. It is commonly thought by test developers that key placement can also affect item difficulty. An item may be made slightly easier by moving the correct answer to an earlier key position ("A" or "B") and slightly more difficult by moving the correct key to a later key position ("D" or "E"). Test developers also typically attempt to order items by difficulty distribution and content. Conventional test development wisdom decrees that each test should start with a few easy items to "warm up" the student. In fact, moving any item to the first position in a test will make that item slightly more difficult than it would be if placed anywhere else in the test. It is for this reason that the first item in a test is avoided as part of an equating set. (An "equating set" is a set of items repeated in subsequent forms of a test that enables score comparisons to be made between parallel forms of a test. Items in equating sets must remain completely unchanged.) In achievement tests, items are typically arranged roughly in order of difficulty from the easiest to the hardest. Within this difficulty distribution, small subgroupings of items of similar content are also arranged.

Bias. Construction of achievement tests currently faces a number of unanswered questions. Chief among these is the question of test bias and how this may be detected and avoided in test construction. Bias remains a problem for achievement tests as well as for aptitude tests, despite the former's clear link to the instructional process. Most test publishers now adhere to sets of guidelines aimed at eliminating sex and ethnic bias in tests of all types. Many publishers have developed their own sets of principles, whereas others rely on published guidelines such as those of the American Psychological Association (1975) and others (Macmillan, 1975; McGraw Hill, 1974; Weston & Stein, 1978). Such guidelines address themselves primarily to the elimination of offensive or stereotypic language and concepts. The interaction of such offensive material with an individual's test score remains largely obscure at this point, but test makers assume that, regardless of the potential impact of offensive test materials on scores, such material should be excluded for the sake of basic fairness. Empirical studies of test bias by a number of methods have also been carried out, but it is often difficult, once items have been identified as biased by some criterion, to determine what aspect of the item has caused it to perform differentially for the groups being studied (Rudner, Getson, & Knight, 1980; Scheuneman, 1980).

Parallel forms. Another largely unresolved issue in test development relates to parallelism of alternate test forms. Parallel forms are necessary or desirable in a number of educational assessment situations, but there is no commonly agreed-upon definition of parallelism. Some writers consider two tests to be parallel when they have the same mean and standard deviation for a given sample, whereas others would require identical content specifications, with or without equivalence of statistical specifications. Tests may also be considered nonparallel at the item level, when different item types have been used to cover the same specifications at different educational or age levels. This is a problem particularly when vertical parallelism (across age or ability levels) is required. In some instances, scores on alternate forms of an achievement test need to be completely interchangeable. In these instances, simply covering the same specifications in the same proportion as the base form is insufficient; score equating must be carried out to ensure interchangeability of individual scores from one form of the test to another. In general, this requires a separate equating study, such as administering two forms of a test that have been judged to be parallel in content to a single group of students.

Norms. Gathering normative data for standardized achievement tests is yet another problematic area. Many test publishers supply only user norms, and this practice makes it difficult to generalize from the user population to a more broadly representative group. Given the heterogeneity of American society, there is also difficulty conceptualizing the meaning of, for example, a national average. Beyond these conceptual problems, however, there is the practical problem of gathering a representative national sample. Although many highly defensible sampling methodologies exist, these are all ultimately dependent on securing the cooperation of institutions and test takers once they have been selected. It is not uncommon for major standardized testing programs to be refused by 80 percent of the schools they ask to participate in a norming study. This situation quite obviously exposes such studies to criticism on the grounds of nonrepresentativeness of the norming sample, which can in no sense be considered random at these levels of participant refusal (Baglin, 1981).

Yet the fact remains that raw scores are not intuitively meaningful, and a basis of comparison, even though flawed, may serve as a helpful general guideline for test users, such as school districts, who may wish to compare their students with an external group.

Evaluation of Test Quality. Questions concerning the evaluation of test quality apply to both published standardized tests and teacher-made classroom tests. The concerns implicit in the evaluation of test quality rest upon the issues described in the previous sections. Conclusions regarding quality of a particular test must ultimately rest on the correspondence of that test to one's particular measurement needs. Of necessity, specific judgments about a test are based largely on the quality, accuracy, and appropriateness of the information provided by the test's developer or publisher. Although much of the information that is needed to evaluate an achievement test's technical quality will be found in a test manual or technical report, the evaluator must not fail to inspect the actual test questions and the directions to the test takers.

Some crucial areas in an evaluative description of an achievement test are specifications, test development and refinement procedures, the quality and appropriateness of test questions, and availability and appropriateness of experimental data. Above all, the person who wishes to evaluate an achievement test must seek evidence that sound procedures were followed in the conceptualization and development of the test. First, one must investigate the test specifications. As mentioned previously, these may be present in various levels of detail or may take such forms as sets of behavioral objectives. All too often, specifications information is completely lacking or is restricted to a few general phrases. Sufficient information on specifications should be provided to enable an evaluator to judge the appropriateness of the match between them and both the immediate measurement needs and the test questions that are intended to measure them. In general, the minimum amount of detail necessary for good specifications is that which would allow another test developer to replicate the test in its essential aspects.

In inspecting the test items themselves, the first question is "Are these test questions relevant to the specifications?" It is highly desirable that a publisher of a standardized test indicate what section of the specifications each question is intended to assess. The person evaluating the achievement test will then look at the appropriateness of the test questions for measuring the particular specifications to which they are linked and check the correctness of the intended answer. In addition, as already described, the items should be free of obvious flaws and ambiguities that would distort interpretation of the test scores obtained.

One must also examine the available materials for information concerning the appropriateness of the development procedures and the individuals associated with the development of a particular achievement test. In the case of standardized tests, one should consider the qualifications of the author or authors of the test. In general, more than one individual should have contributed materials to or reviewed the test. No single individual, no matter how qualified, is capable of producing the highest level of achievement test single-handedly. The experiences and qualifications of the test's authors should also provide assurance that these individuals are, in fact, knowledgeable about the subject matter area being tested.

In addition, one should look for evidence of procedures used to refine the test in its preliminary or draft stages. Descriptions of pretesting activities for preliminary item analyses should be provided. Data gathered from relevant experiments should also be provided for the inspection of the potential test user. Relevant data include indications of the level of difficulty of the material, item analysis information, and evidence of reliability. Information concerning level of difficulty will indicate the likely appropriateness of this material for the particular group of test takers at hand. Item analysis information should be supplied as a check on the professional judgment of appropriateness of the test materials to the test takers for whom it was

developed and appropriateness of the subject matter coverage.

Evidence of test reliability should be provided in detail. Simply presenting a chart of correlation coefficients is insufficient. The test publisher should explain why a particular reliability index was chosen. Wesman (1952) provided a useful summary of how to interpret reliability coefficients provided by test publishers. Some important points to consider include the following: Is subtest reliability information provided along with total test reliability information, when you wish to use subtest scores? Has the use of internal consistency indices of reliability been avoided when there is an indication of speededness in the test? In recent years, questions concerning the appropriateness of reliability indices for criterion-referenced tests have been raised by several authors (e.g., Livingston, 1980). The basic distinction to be made between reliability indices for norm-referenced and for criterion-referenced tests relates to the amount of score variance expected in the two kinds of tests. In theory, criterion-referenced tests will often show little variability since students may be expected to be either masters or nonmasters of the material that is being tested. In this case, score variance would be greatly diminished and some widely used reliability statistics would be inappropriate. In practice, however, there is ordinarily not so great a disparity in score variance between norm-referenced and criterion-referenced measures as to make this point a crucial one.

When dealing with a test that is used to classify test takers into groups on the basis of their scores, the reliability of classification should also be taken into account. It should be noted that this is not the same statistic as those used to determine the reliability of test scores. It refers to the consistency with which an individual's score would be classified as, for example, passing or failing. The reliability of classification depends in part upon the reliability of the scores themselves, but also on the nearness of the test scores to the cut point or standard that has been identified. The reliability of classification may be low even when the scores themselves are quite reliable, and vice versa.

In general, when considering the technical qualities of a particular achievement test, one must expect full and detailed descriptions of every aspect of the development procedures as well as access to a sample test or the test questions themselves.

The issue of evaluating the validity of achievement tests is a highly controversial one. The controversy centers on the role played by content validity in achievement testing. Opinion is polarized at these extremes: writers such as Ebel (1979) assert that content validity is the only relevant aspect of validity for achievement testing; writers such as Messick (1980) assert that content validity is "not validity at all" (p. 48). It is agreed, however, that "content validity" refers both to the relevance of the test content to the specifications and the skill that is intended to be tested; and to content coverage, that is, the representativeness of the content of this particular test in covering the domain of interests. It is also widely accepted that content validity refers only to test materials themselves and not to the test scores produced on the basis of this material. Proponents of construct validation consider content validity to be one of the components of a construct validation process. But the constuct validity orientation places strong emphasis on underlying processes or characteristics of the test taker rather than on the accomplishment of objectively specified tasks. This distinction seems most central to the argument concerning content validity. The construct validation position outlined by Messick (1980) clearly points to a way to measure achievement more certainly, but with less ability to demonstrate clearly how that measurement has been effected. The position outlined by Ebel (1979), on the other hand, results in less scientific or logical certainty that the construct of interest has been measured, but it does yield a practical demonstration of what measurement has occurred.

Messick made the point that content validity is limited by its nature as a unidirectional concept: "Although it may undergird certain straightforward interpretations for high scorers (such as "they possess suitable skills to perform the tasks correctly, because they did so repeatedly"), it provides no basis for interpreting low scores in terms of incompetence or lack of skill. To do that requires the discounting of plausible counter-hypotheses about such irrelevancies in the testing as anxiety, defensiveness, inattention, or low motivation" (1980, p. 1018). He then went on to remind us that empirical discounting of plausible rival hypotheses is the hallmark of construct validation. The same question of unidirectional validity is a relevant issue in assessing effectiveness of criterion-referenced tests, where a similar problem exists in accounting for the failure of students who do not meet the standard.

Another problem in evaluating the quality of achievement tests is the appropriateness of norms when they are provided. As mentioned previously, there is considerable question about the representativeness of many national norming samples for standardized tests and the possible distorting effects of having a group of volunteer subjects rather than a true random sample. Users of tests should be particularly wary of reports of norming studies in which emphasis is on the large numbers of students participating, with little detail provided as to how those students or their schools were chosen. Such norming studies are likely to be based on test users alone rather than on any systematic sampling plan. Users should also consider what type of norms are most appropriate for their test use. In many cases, local norms collected over a number of years or state or regional norms give more pertinent information than national norms. Some test publishers also provide national or user norms separately by race, sex, or socioeconomic status. These should be used only when there is a clear-cut need on the part of the user to do so and when there is a substantial rationale for differential actions to be taken or interpretations of data to be made for the various subgroups.

In certain circumstances it is also appropriate for the potential test user to evaluate the parallelism of test forms.

It may be appropriate to investigate the parallel structure of alternate forms of the same level of this same test as well as the parallel continuity of content and other relevant factors from one level of the test to the next. As mentioned earlier, "parallel" is an elusive concept in test construction. The potential test user should determine which aspects of parallelism are most appropriate to one's current measurement problem and evaluate the pairs of tests under consideration from that specific point of view.

A number of excellent resources are available to those seeking general information about the quality of published tests for typical uses. Especially recommended are the Buros *Mental Measurements Yearbooks.* Readers are also referred to the latest issue of the *Standards for Educational and Psychological Tests* (1974) of the Joint Committee of the American Psychological Association, American Educational Research Association, and National Council on Measurement in Education. These standards are updated periodically, and a new edition is expected in the near future. An invaluable source of information on achievement testing is R. L. Thorndike's *Educational Measurement* (1971).

Carol A. Dwyer

See also Aptitude Measurement; Competency Testing; Individual Differences; Intelligence Measurement; Instructional Time and Learning; Marking Systems; Measurement in Education; Norms and Scales.

REFERENCES

American Psychological Association Task Force on Issues of Sexual Bias in Graduate Education. Guidelines for nonsexist use of language. *American Psychologist,* 1975, *30,* 682–684.

Angoff, W. H. Distinctions between aptitude and achievement tests. In Educational Testing Service (Ed.), *Issues in Testing.* Princeton, N.J.: Educational Testing Service, 1980.

Baglin, R. F. Does "nationally" normed really mean nationally? *Journal of Educational Measurement,* 1981, *18,* 97–107.

Brown, F. G. *Guidelines for Test Use: A Commentary on the Standards for Educational and Psychological Tests.* Washington, D.C.: National Council on Measurement in Education, 1980. (ERIC Document Reproduction Service No. ED 193 247)

Buros, O. K. (Ed.). *Eighth Mental Measurements Yearbook.* Highland Park, N.J.: Gryphon Press, 1978.

Coffman, W. E. Essay examinations. In R. L. Thorndike (Ed.), *Educational Measurement* (2nd ed.). Washington, D.C.: American Council on Education, 1971.

Cronbach, L. J. *Essentials of Psychological Testing* (3rd ed.). New York: Harper & Row, 1970.

Donlon, T. F. Content factors in sex differences on test questions. In *Research Memorandum 73-28.* Princeton, N.J.: Educational Testing Service, 1973.

Dwyer, C. A. Test content and sex differences in reading. *Reading Teacher,* 1976, *29,* 753–757.

Ebel, R. L. *Essentials of Educational Measurement* (3rd ed.). Englewood Cliffs, N.J.: Prentice-Hall, 1979.

Ebel, R. L., & Williams, B. J. The effect of varying the number of alternatives per item on multiple-choice vocabulary test items. In *The Fourteenth Yearbook of the National Council on Measurements Used in Education.* East Lansing: Michigan State University, 1957.

Graff, R. G., & Riddel, J. C. Sex differences in problem-solving as a function of problem context. *Journal of Educational Research*, 1972, *65*, 451–452.

Gronlund, N. E. *Preparing Criterion-referenced Tests for the Classroom*. New York: Macmillan, 1973.

Hambleton, R. K., & Eignor, D. R. Competency test development, validation, and standard setting. In R. M. Jaeger & C. K. Tittle (Eds.), *Minimum Competency Achievement Testing: Motives, Models, Measures, and Consequences*. Berkeley, Calif.: McCutchan, 1980.

Hambleton, R. K.; Swaminathan, H.; Algina, J.; & Coulson, D. B. Criterion-referenced testing and measurement: A review of technical issues and developments. *Review of Educational Research*, 1978, *48*, 1–47.

Hively, W.; Patterson, H. L.; & Page, S. A. A "universe-defined" system of arithmetic achievement tests. *Journal of Educational Measurement*, 1968, *5*, 275–290.

Katz, M. *Selecting an Achievement Test: Principles and Procedures* (2nd ed.). Princeton, N.J.: Educational Testing Service, 1961.

Livingston, S. A. Test reliability and "error of measurement." In Educational Testing Service (Ed.), *Issues in Testing*. Princeton, N.J.: Educational Testing Service, 1980.

Macmillan Publishing Co., Inc. *Guidelines for Creating Positive Sexual and Racial Images in Educational Materials*. New York: Macmillan, 1975. (ERIC Document Reproduction Service No. ED 117 687)

McGraw-Hill Book Company. *Guidelines for Equal Treatment of the Sexes in McGraw-Hill Book Company Publications*. New York: McGraw-Hill, 1974. (ERIC Document Reproduction Service No. ED 098 574)

Meskauskas, J. A. Evaluation models for criterion-referenced testing: Views regarding mastery and standard-setting. *Review of Educational Research*, 1976, *46*, 133–158.

Messick, S. Test validity and the ethics of assessment. *American Psychologist*, 1980, *35*, 1012–1027.

Milton, G. A. The effects of sex-role identification upon problem-solving skill. *Journal of Abnormal and Social Psychology*, 1957, *55*, 208–213.

Milton, G. A. Sex differences on problem-solving as a function of role appropriateness of problem content. *Psychological Reports*, 1959, *5*, 705–708.

Murphy, R. J. L. *Sex Differences in Examination Performance: Do These Reflect Differences in Ability or Sex-role Stereotypes?* Paper presented at the International Conference on Sex-role Stereotyping, Cardiff, Wales, July 1977. (ERIC Document Reproduction Service No. ED 154 265)

Popham, W. J. *Criterion-referenced Measurement*. Englewood Cliffs, N.J.: Prentice-Hall, 1978.

Roid, G. H., & Haladyna, T. M. The emergence of an item-writing technology. *Review of Educational Research*, 1980, *50*, 293–314.

Rudner, L. M.; Getson, P. R.; & Knight, D. L. Biased-item detection techniques. *Journal of Educational Statistics*, 1980, *5*, 213–233.

Scheuneman, J. D. Latent-trait theory and item bias. In L. J. Th. van der Kamp, W. S. Langarac, & D. N. M. de Gruijter (Eds.), *Psychometrics for Educational Debates*. New York: Wiley, 1980.

Schmeiser, C. B., & Ferguson, R. L. Performance of black and white students on test materials containing content based on black and white cultures. *Journal of Educational Measurement*, 1978, *15*, 193–200.

Smith, K. An investigation into the use of "double-choice" items in testing achievement. *Journal of Educational Research*, 1958, *51*, 387–389.

Standards for Educational and Psychological Tests. Washington, D.C.: American Psychological Association, 1974.

Starch, D., & Elliott, E. C. Reliability of grading high school work in English. *School Review*, 1912, *20*, 442–457.

Starch, D., & Elliott, E. C. Reliability of grading high school work in History. *School Review*, 1913, *21*, 676–681. (a)

Starch, D., & Elliott, E. C. Reliability of grading high school work in Mathematics. *School Review*, 1913, *21*, 254–259. (b)

Strassberg-Rosenberg, B., & Donlon, T. F. *Content Influences on Sex Differences in Performance on Aptitude Tests*. Paper presented at the annual meeting of the National Council on Measurement in Education, Washington, D.C., March 1975. (ERIC Document Reproduction Service No. ED 110 493)

Swineford, F. *The Test Analysis Manual* (ETS SR 74-06). Princeton, N.J.: Educational Testing Service, 1974.

Thorndike, R. L. (Ed.). *Educational Measurement* (3rd ed.). Washington, D.C.: American Council on Education, 1971.

Wesman, A. G. Reliability and confidence. In Psychological Corporations, *Test Service Bulletin*, 1952, *44*.

Wesman, A. G. Writing the test item. In R. L. Thorndike (Ed.), *Educational Measurement* (2nd ed.). Washington, D.C.: American Council on Education, 1971.

Weston, L. C., & Stein, S. L. A content analysis of publications guidelines for the elimination of sex-role stereotyping. *Educational Researcher*, 1978, *7*, 13–14.

Wilson, K. M. *The Validity of a Measure of "Academic Motivation" for Forecasting Freshman Achievement at Seven Liberal Arts Colleges* (RB 74-29). Princeton, N.J.: Educational Testing Service, 1974. (ERIC Document Reproduction Service No. ED 163 016)

Wilson, K. M. *The Validation of GRE Scores as Predictors of First-year Performance in Graduate Study: Report of the GRE Cooperative Validity Studies Project*. Princeton, N.J.: Educational Testing Service, 1979. (ERIC Document Reproduction Service No. ED 183 569)

Zieky, M. J., & Livingston, S. A. *Manual for Setting Standards on the Basic Skills Assessment Tests*. Princeton, N.J.: Educational Testing Service, 1977.

ADMINISTRATION OF EDUCATIONAL INSTITUTIONS

This article is focused on the internal administration of educational organizations and thus implicates concepts of organizations and organizational behavior. Locating administration in an organizational setting requires us to consider the relationship between the institution and its environment, as well as the relationships across various levels of the organization (see Parsons, 1958; Thompson, 1967). Both normative discourse about, and descriptive treatment of, administrators and of administration receive attention.

After an introductory note on the literatures of educational administration, the article presents (1) a portrayal of the setting within which educational administration has recently taken place; (2) a description of the "traditional paradigm," which has influenced the majority of disciplined inquiry; (3) an identification of emergent challengers to the traditional paradigm; and (4) a review of recent studies of administrator work and effects.

Literatures

Three major forms and contents comprise the literature on educational administration: (1) the professional-normative, (2) the scholarly-normative, and (3) the scholarly-descriptive. In the first category, professional-normative, fall primarily exchanges of practitioners with each other. The producers of this body of literature are educational administrators at various levels, and often executives of associations of administrators, who take the time and effort to share "war stories" (mostly successful) or strongly held convictions with audiences of colleagues. The bulk of this class of literature consists of anecdotes and prescriptive recommendations for courses of action to improve administrative practice and schooling. Only rarely do the authors locate either their anecdotes or prescriptions in a matrix of previous research findings, or even the reported or recorded experiences of fellow practitioners. Primary outlets for such articles are the journals and house organs of the various associations of school administrators and supervisors. On occasion these professional-normative sources present a scholarly-normative, or even a scholarly-descriptive, piece on a currently lively topic. But the primary contributions of professional-normative literature reside in its vigorous portrayal of the concerns and problems that practitioners experience and in its restive exploration of actual or potential solutions. Reliance on a substantial research foundation hardly constitutes a hallmark of the professional-normative literature.

Producers of the second class of literature, scholarly-normative, come primarily from two subsets of professors of educational administration. The first cadre numbers those professors who remain fundamentally practitioner-oriented, in that they devote their professional careers to preparing practitioners and to working as consultants. The second subset of professors of educational administration devotes a substantial proportion of its time to original research or scholarship, but its members also involve themselves voluntarily (or by invitation) in finding and attempting to solve current problems in the administration of educational institutions. (For a more detailed description of the characteristics of the two sets of professors of educational administration and of their publication activity, see Campbell & Newell, 1973; Immegart, 1977.)

The modal character of the scholarly-normative literature derives from conscientious efforts by its authors to distill the output of scholarship and research for use by practitioners. Often, ideation or informed opinion, rather than research *per se*, serves as the author's platform. Much of the scholarly-normative output is not published in journals but appears in the form of special purpose reports prepared for the various professional associations and in collections of essays that represent the joint efforts of professors alone or of professors and practitioners joining hands. By far the most voluminous and readily available of the scholarly normative literature appears in textbooks. Sometimes authors attempt to link descriptions of management models drawn from noneducational sources to the management of schools. In general, texts reflect the tendency of the literature in educational administration to lag behind developments in public and private sector administration (see March, 1974; Boyan, 1981b). Virtually all the texts exhibit consistent agreement on the primary task areas of educational administration: program or curriculum; personnel (pupils, faculty, and staff); finance; business management and facilities; school-community relations; and increasingly, assessment and evaluation as an administrative function (Glasman, 1979). Few texts, however, systematically develop or treat connections across task areas, administrative processes, theoretical developments, research findings, and patterns of work. In recent years, texts have systematically stressed the distinction between normative and descriptive treatments of administration, but they still tend to leave undeveloped and undefined the connections between what "is" and what "ought to be."

Another source of scholarly-normative literature is the set of publications from the Educational Resources Information Center (ERIC) Clearinghouse on Educational Management at the University of Oregon. Clearinghouse publications include (1) *The Best of ERIC;* (2) *The Best of the Best of ERIC;* (3) reviews; (4) research analysis papers; and (5) state-of-the-knowledge monographs (general, school law, administrator preparation). The monographs themselves merit classification as scholarly-descriptive rather than scholarly-normative (e.g., Iannaccone & Cistone, 1974; Piele & Hall, 1973; Tucker & Zeigler, 1980).

Volume in the scholarly descriptive class of literature, even after more than twenty-five years of notable expansion in the size of the professoriate and presumed focus on research, remains small as compared with professional-normative and scholarly-normative output. Consistently, studies of the scholarly productivity of professors of educational administration have revealed that only a small proportion thereof devote themselves continuously and systematically to disciplined inquiry and associated scholarly publication (Campbell & Newell, 1973). Professors as a group contribute materially to a form of scholarship by way of directing a total of 1,000–1,200 dissertations per year, most of which reach publication only in *Dissertation Abstracts*. The doctoral candidate remains the producer of volume in inquiry in educational administration (see Boyan, 1981b; Immegart, 1977).

Primary outlets for scholarly-descriptive literature include several well-regarded journals, monographs, edited collections, and commissioned papers. Journals which consistently seek to publish the scholarly descriptive literature of educational administration number the *Administrator's*

Notebook, the *Educational Administration Quarterly,* and the *Journal of Educational Administration* (an Australian publication). Of more recent vintage are *Educational Administration* (a United Kingdom publication) and the *Executive Review* (like the *Administrator's Notebook,* a single-topic, four-page publication). Another journal which provides a useful outlet for scholarly-descriptive productivity is the *Journal of Educational Administration and History.* Other journals of mostly scholarly-descriptive tilt but not identified exclusively with educational administration often publish quite pertinent manuscripts, notably *Education and Urban Society, Educational Evaluation and Policy Analysis, Journal of Collective Negotiations in the Public Sector, Journal of Law and Education, School Law Journal, Sociology of Education,* and *Urban Education.* Only occasionally do reports of research in educational administration appear in the *Administrative Science Quarterly,* a journal that many scholars in educational administration consider it imperative to consult regularly. One of the characteristics of the scholarly descriptive literature which leaps at the reviewer is the increasing specialization and fragmentation which has come to mark research in educational administration (see Boyan, 1981b; Immegart, 1977; Immegart & Boyd, 1979). This article on the internal administration of public elementary and secondary schools will draw primarily on the scholarly-descriptive literature.

A Note on Setting

Four major sources of uncertainty have pervaded the environment of educational institutions over the past decade and have materially conditioned their administration. Demographic conditions precipitously converted education from a growing to a declining industry, creating attendant problems of reductions in force, of school closings, and of managing decline instead of growth. Political and economic conditions, including pressure by the federal establishment for equity and school reform under varying and uneven arrangements (which generally involved increased regulations), contributed to a sense of uncertainty, exacerbated by evidence of a loss of confidence in education. Other contributors to reduced support for education included (1) a shift in policy priorities to issues of income maintenance, welfare, and social security; (2) evidence of decreased productivity in the schools; (3) evidence, or at least belief, that crime and violence were rampant; (4) teacher militancy and organized collective action; (5) rapidly escalating inflation coupled with declining enrollments, creating a sense of education for fewer students, costing more than was reasonable; (6) pressure for school finance reform in behalf, primarily, of equity; (7) tax resistance and revolt; (8) contradictory pulls for affirmative action desiderata and seniority provisions in accommodating layoffs; (9) pressure for broader and deeper public participation in school affairs and for greater professional responsiveness; (10) professional and public interests in promoting school site management at authentically meaningful levels; (11) pressure for more accountability and more evaluation, and for the adoption of more rational and efficient planning and management tools; (12) pressure for competency-based education and associated assessment systems, including raising hurdles to pupil progress and making more obviously public the performance of teachers, administrators, schools, and school systems.

Against this backdrop of turbulence and uncertainty, we shall explore the research productivity generated by the "traditional paradigm," which has guided research in educational administration; the emergence of challenges to the older paradigm; and new ways of looking at administrator work, as well as conflicting views about the effects of administrator activity.

The Traditional Paradigm

Almost all the best known textbooks in educational administration take their readers over much the same ground in treating the historical development of views of the worker-in-organization and of organizational management (Campbell, Bridges, & Nystrand, 1977; Hanson, 1979; Hoy & Miskel, 1978; Kimbrough & Nunnery, 1976; Knezevich, 1975; Lipham & Hoeh, 1974; Morphet, Johns, & Reller, 1974; Owens, 1981; Saxe, 1980; Sergiovanni & Carver, 1980; Sergiovanni et al., 1980). The classical, scientific management school, with its emphasis on the worker as a machine and on rationality in designing organizational structure and process, receives its due. The contributions of Fayol (1949) and Taylor (1911) to the development and spread of scientific management attract comment, usually with concomitant citation of Callahan's critical observations (1962) about the undue influence of concern for efficiency on public discourse in educational administration.

Gulick and Urwick (1937) appear, typically, as the synthesizers of the classical scientific management school, but some time after Follet (1924) had introduced views about persons in organizations that laid a useful foundation for the human relations movement. The place of the Western Electric studies at the Hawthorne plant, and the central roles played by Mayo (1946) and by Roethlisberger and Dixon (1939), regularly receive mention in representation of the antithesis to scientific management. Human relations as a way of looking at the life and work of people in organizations spread rapidly and continues to show influence in training programs for executives and supervisors, in organizational research agendas, and in organizational interventions such as training groups and organizational development programs. Other scholars whose names have typically appeared in the human relations lineup include Argyris (1957), Likert (1961, 1967), and McGregor (1960). According to Owens (1981) the human relations school tended to attract considerably more attention in first-line supervisor circles than at the superintendency level.

Just as the human relations movement introduced a

conception of worker-in-organization that departed materially from the classical, scientific management view, it also gave ground to the "modern" or "behavioral" orientation (Etzioni, 1964; Perrow, 1972). The "behavioral" viewpoint encompasses a wide variety of ways of looking at, studying, describing, and explaining organizational behavior. The several points of view and approaches that scholars of educational administration have borrowed or derived from the behavioral orientation have collectively come to constitute the "traditional paradigm," which has, until very recently, dominated inquiry and discourse about educational administration.

Component theoretical constructs within the traditional paradigm that warrant commentary include (1) social system and role, (2) bureaucracy and bureaucratization, (3) decision making, (4) leadership and leader behavior, and (5) motivation and satisfaction.

Social System and Role Perspectives. For some students of educational administration, the view of the school as a social system begins and ends with the pioneering formulation by Getzels and Guba (Getzels, 1952; Getzels & Guba, 1957), their empirical work, and the many investigations for which the Getzel–Guba model has served as the heuristic foundation. (See Getzels, Lipham, & Campbell, 1968, for a summary of the conceptual statement and a full report of investigations through the mid-1960s.) For others, including Willower (1979a, 1979b, 1980), the social system perspective covers a much wider range, antedates the Getzels–Guba model, and encompasses empirical work well into the 1970s, receiving stimulation and guidance from other sources. Willower traces social system inquiry to Waller's description of schools as miniature societies (Waller, 1932). (See Bidwell, 1965, for a compact summary of Waller's classic, and also of studies in the same genre by Coleman, 1961, and Gordon, 1957.) Other early works of a social systems orientation, according to Willower, include (1) Becker's analyses of authority structure and relationships (Becker, 1952, 1953); (2) Iannaccone's description of informal organization and its connection to formal organization (Iannaccone, 1962, 1964; for earlier investigations in this vein, see Boyan, 1951; Congreve, 1957); (3) Carlson's analysis of the importance for schools of the characteristics of their clients and sources of support (Carlson, 1964; see Bidwell, 1965, 1970, for additional insights on the influence and meaning of client characteristics); (4) Miles's examination of social systems properties (Miles, 1967); and (5) Jackson's report on life in classrooms (Jackson, 1968).

Without question, the social system perspective materially shaped conceptual thinking and empirical inquiry in the internal administration of education during the 1960s and continued its sway during much of the 1970s. For useful summaries of the components of the perspective, which build and expand on the earlier presentation by Getzels et al. (1968), see Hoy and Miskel (1978), and Lipham and Hoeh (1974). Examples of work following the social system theme during the 1970s include (1) Gross,

Giaquinta, and Bernstein (1971) on description and analysis of specific instances of innovation; (2) the detailed post mortem by Smith and Keith (1971) of the rise and fall of change in an elementary school; (3) the in-depth portrayal of student culture by Cusick (1973); and (4) Lortie (1975), on detailed analysis of the life of the teacher and teacher socialization. In addition to individual inquiries and reports of the variety cited, three substantial lines of inquiry following the social system perspective deserve special mention. The first set includes the work contributed by Willower, his colleagues, and his students on teacher subcultures and the salience of adult concern for pupil control (see Willower, Eidell, & Hoy, 1967, 1973; Willower, 1975, 1977; Smyth, 1977). The second theme includes the investigations on work structure and governance structure within purported and documented conditions of change, offered by the University of Oregon group (some of the studies involving crucial participation by colleagues at the University of Wisconsin–Madison; see Pellegrin, 1976; Packard et al., 1978). The third set incorporates several lines of inquiry located within the Environment for Teaching Program of the Center for Research on Teaching at Stanford University (see Meyer & Cohen, 1971; Packard et al., 1978).

Collectively, the pupil control studies, the two sets of Oregon studies, the Stanford studies, and the several individual investigations cited demonstrate the versatility of the social system perspective for generating useful and enlightening information about schools and their operation. Willower (1980) identifies the two common features of the social system literature that cut across variation in specifics. (1) The school shows itself as vulnerable to external environmental forces; and at the same time vulnerable to internal strains related to the particular composition of client groups and their sentiments about the services and activities that the school provides. (2) Schools exhibit various protective structures for adult members of the organization, and other structures to foster student adjustment and control (such as norms and traditions as well as more formal rules, regulations, and routines), mostly designed to reduce uncertainty and to enhance predictability by containing variety and threat.

As for role theory's contributions in the 1970s, Corwin (1974) confirms Griffiths's earlier observation that use of role models experienced a noticeable decline in guiding investigations of social organizations in general and of school organizations in particular (Griffiths, 1969a). Corwin based his assessment on a count of papers inspired by role theory that had appeared in the *American Sociological Review* and the *American Journal of Sociology* over twenty years. Despite evidence of some revived interest in role studies in Israel (Inbar, 1977, 1980; Gaziel, 1979), Willower (1980) reports that his own examination of trends in recent issues of *Dissertation Abstracts, Educational Administration Quarterly,* and the *Journal of Educational Administration* confirms the estimates of both Griffiths and Corwin.

Bureaucracy and Bureaucratization. Argument and discourse about the appropriateness and utility of viewing schools as bureaucracies has ebbed and flowed for some time (see Abbott, 1965; J. Anderson, 1966, 1967a, 1967b, 1967c, 1968; Bidwell, 1965; Bridges, 1965; Clear & Seager, 1971; Corwin, 1974; Gracey, 1972; Hill, 1969; Hills, 1966; Hoy & Miskel, 1978, chap. 4; Isherwood & Hoy, 1972, 1973; Moeller, 1962; Moeller & Charters, 1966; Rogers, 1968; Solomon, 1967; Willower, 1980). Hills (1966) sensibly urged participants to focus on extent of bureaucratization, a position that has yet to drive out a preference for arguing over whether schools are indeed bureaucracies. Because of the salience of issues of control in education, two features regularly identified with the bureaucratic phenomenon have continuously engaged the attention of students of educational administration: (1) hierarchy of authority; and (2) the life of professionals in organizations.

Among the characteristics of ideal-type bureaucracy stipulated by Weber (see Bendix, 1962), hierarchy of authority has regularly commanded the interest of students of organizations as a salient structural property or descriptor. A useful way of tracing the hierarchy of authority is to plot the distribution of rights to exercise control (Boyan, 1981a). One of the more systematic series of analyses of schools along this line appears in the work of "the Canadian group" (B. Anderson, 1971, 1973; Kolesar, 1967; MacKay, 1964, 1969; Punch, 1969, 1970). MacKay and Punch made major conceptual and methodological contributions, whereas Anderson and Kolesar concentrated on assessing the association of variability in client alienation and sense of powerlessness with variability in extent of bureaucratization.

Of particular interest is the regularity with which several investigators unearthed evidence of two hierarchies rather than one hierarchy of authority: the first associated with the managerial life of schools; the second with their instructional life. This empirically identified differentiation recalls the findings of Becker's case study and supports the views of organizational analysts who had previously reported conflict between professional and bureaucratic orientations (Becker, 1953; see Corwin, 1965, 1970; Kuhlman & Hoy, 1974; Thornton, 1971).

Bishop and George (1973), from a vantage point related to but separate from bureaucratization, reported two distinct hierarchies of authority of the same persuasion as the Canadian group: the one arranged around managerial matters; the other associated with expertise in curriculum and instruction. The consistency in the findings of the Canadian group, and of Bishop and George about two hierarchies of authority rather than one, strongly suggest that considerable care must be applied when plotting the distribution of authority rights in schools, when designing modifications of the distribution of those rights, when tracing the effects of variability in the exercise of the rights, and when assessing zones of indifference and acceptance (see Barnard, 1938; Simon, 1957) among professionals in organizations. The empirical data also provide support for a task-specific view of authority rights (see Brunetti, 1970).

The flip side of authority as a control mechanism is autonomy, a characteristic of schools and teaching that has received considerable attention (see Bidwell, 1965; Lortie, 1969, 1973, 1975; Goodlad & Klein, 1970; Packard et al., 1978). Three particular inquiries into the association of extent of bureaucratization with autonomy or its surrogate, sense of power, merit mention. The first, reported by Moeller and Charters (1966), yielded unexpected results. The investigators had hypothesized that teachers in a larger school district displaying characteristics of more bureaucratization would report a lower sense of power than teachers in a smaller, less bureaucratized district. Their data yielded almost directly contradictory results. Isherwood and Hoy (1973) took the unexpected results reported by Moeller and Charters under advisement in a later study in which they added the mediating variable of teacher position on organizational or professional orientation (following Corwin, 1965, 1970). Isherwood and Hoy found that although teachers generally reported higher levels of powerlessness in authoritarian as compared to professional structures, professionally oriented teachers expressed more acute sense of powerlessness than organizationally oriented teachers. Still later, Marjoribanks (1977) reported that autonomy displayed curvilinear rather than unilinear relationships with organizational characteristics regularly assumed to be indicators of bureaucratization.

Inquiry and exposition in and around bureaucracy and bureaucratization permit at least the conclusion that any effort to construct a useful theory of legitimate social control for the school must somehow make provision for (1) the empirically verified presence of multiple hierarchies of authority that attend to different purposes (i.e., management and instruction) and that appear to rest on different foundations; and (2) the reality of substantial amounts of autonomy related in complex ways to any particular distribution of authority rights. Otherwise, the application of bureaucratic theory to schools looks problematic at best. Corwin (1974) concluded his own review with the trenchant observation that use of the bureaucratic model tended to oversimplify the realities of educational organizations, which exhibit more variety and complexity than the model can likely accommodate. Willower (1979b) reached essentially the same conclusion, for basically the same reasons.

Decision Making. Theorizing about, and investigation into, decision making in educational institutions reach back to the 1950s, with two main streams of activity discernible then and now. The first has focused attention on the centrality of decision making in the administrative process, with two primary tributaries, one derived from organizational analysis, the other from political analysis. The second main stream has flowed almost exclusively through the territory of the participation hypothesis, touching on the meaning to organizational members of participating in various decision domains and types under different structural and affective conditions.

Decision-making process. Stimulation for much of the work on the decision-making process came from statements by Gregg (1957) and Griffiths (1958, 1959). Gregg argued vigorously along lines earlier drawn by McCamy (1947), a scholar in public administration, in favor of viewing decision making as the central activity of the administrative process. On his part, Griffiths urged primary attention to control of the decision-making process versus the making of decisions *per se* as the *sine qua non* of administrative activity. Griffiths drew heavily on earlier expositions by Barnard (1938) and Simon (1945). Simon himself collaborated later with March (March & Simon, 1958) in identifying control of decision-making premises as the single most important organizational process for managers and other participants to comprehend and accommodate. Both Gregg and Griffiths accepted the assumptions associated with a rational model of organizational behavior. March and Simon had already showed signs of uneasiness about rationality, a concern that was to raise serious questions for the traditional paradigm at a later date.

Gregg's work, along with students and colleagues, helped to establish the University of Wisconsin–Madison as a center for substantial activity addressed to decision making in education. Lipham has summarized many of the Wisconsin studies via textbook publication (Lipham & Hoeh, 1974) and has projected some of its learnings via essays aimed at practicing school administrators (e.g., Lipham, 1974). As late as 1978, an Australian investigator reported use of the Decision Point Analysis Instrument developed at Wisconsin to assess congruence of expectations about organizational decisions (see Telfer, 1978a, 1978b).

Griffiths participated in major empirical and conceptual work from the late 1950s through the close of the 1960s (see Griffiths, 1969b; Hemphill, Griffiths, & Frederiksen, 1962). Following publication of the decision-making section of a major taxonomic project, which he directed (Griffiths, 1969b), Griffiths's firsthand involvement in attempting to advance inquiry on decision making declined noticeably.

Although the lines and paths of inquiry on organizational decision making viewed internally have continued, another major topic has appeared: the process and product of decision making viewed as an integral component of educational planning and policy making. The new source raises questions and issues of (1) resource acquisition and allocation (Smith, 1971; Bumbarger & Thiemann, 1972; Thiemann & Bumbarger, 1972; Elboim-Dror, 1973; Dufty, 1976; Thomas, Kemmerer, & Monk, 1978; Monk, 1979); (2) public and professional insertion and processing of educational desiderata (Gaynor, 1971; McGivney & Haught, 1972; Mann, 1974, 1975, 1976a, 1976b; Wiles, 1974; Schwille, Porter, & Gant, 1980; Hentschke, 1980); and (3) values and precedent in establishing and implementing policies (Skilbeck, 1972; Glasman & Sell, 1972; Fletcher, 1974; Weatherley & Lipsky, 1977). Politics of education, rather than organizational analysis considered more narrowly, represent the linkages across this particular set of statements and reports on decision making.

Parallel to and intermingled with the planning and policy perspective on decision making have appeared position papers and reports on the technology available to planners, policy makers, and decision makers. (1) On management information systems, see Nias (1973), Hayman (1974), Mellor (1977), Clemson (1978). (2) On Program Planning and Budgeting Systems, see van Geel (1973). On the use of computers and computer simulation, see Mellor (1976), Pogrow (1978), and Clemson (1980). On management by objectives, see Hacker (1971) and Shetty and Carlisle (1974). On issues pertaining to accountability, see Hencley (1971), Hills (1973, 1974), and Crowson (1974). On mathematical modeling, see McNamara (1976). On planning in general, see Thomas (1971 and 1974).

A vigorous exchange of opinion between Sharples (1975, 1977) and Johnson (1976) over the use of economic analysis and models in educational planning well illustrates the restiveness about extent of and limits to rationality in planning and decision making that made its presence felt increasingly during the 1970s. Crowson (1975) speaks to this point, as does Marks (1978) in his contrastive treatment of analytic versus anthrocentric management. Coleman (1974) offered to a Canadian audience a model of organizational decision making that placed political processes and conflict as central, a view close to that developed by Baldridge (1971; see Griffiths, 1979a, for a criticism of the Baldridge interpretation). Mann's trenchant analysis of non–decision making, which drew on a combination of conventional social system perspectives and emerging political perspectives to document and explain the absence of conscious choice making among secondary school principals in New York City, provides another demurrer to the place of rationality in decision making (Mann, 1976b).

Withal, the most severe contradictions to conceptions of decision making as primarily rational came from two widely disparate sources. The first was Allison's dramatic treatment of the Cuban missile crisis, in which he parades for inspection the influence of organizational processes and routines and of bureaucratic-political considerations as competitors to the rational model of organizational behavior (Allison, 1971). The second was the line of work promulgated by March and his associates which has popularized views of educational institutions as organized anarchies in which a "garbage can" model of decision making prevails (Cohen, March, & Olsen, 1972; Cohen & March, 1974; March & Olsen, 1976; Sproull, Weiner, & Wolf, 1978).

Participation hypotheses. For the second main line of work on decision making, Bridges had set the benchmark by the early 1970s with his think pieces and related inquiries: on teacher participation in general (1964); on a model for shared decision making (1967); on the effects of hierarchical differentiation on group decisions (see Bridges, Doyle, & Mahan, 1968; see Doyle, 1969; Doyle & Ahlbrand, 1973, for additional reports in this vein); on subjective and objective aspects of demands for involvement (1969). In addition, Bridges (1970) opened the door for looking at the administrator as a recipient as well as an originator of action (see Campbell, Bridges, & Nystrand, 1977, chapter 10). A later report by Erickson (1972) extended this line of thought by addressing the powerlessness as well as the powerfulness of educational administrators.

During the 1970s, Alutto and Belasco (Belasco & Alutto, 1972; Alutto & Belasco, 1973) initiated a set of investigations of their own and stimulated others, adding further insight to the relationship between participation in organizational decision making and the affective state of participants. Alutto and Belasco developed a scale of decisional participation that permitted locating teachers along a continuum, according to the divergence between the level of participation in twelve areas of activity that they desired and that they reported actually experiencing. They found that (1) the desire for increased participation varied among teachers; (2) there is no simple association between expressed desire for increased participation and organizational outcomes; (3) commitment and integration into school organization may be independent of any particular pattern of decisional participation; and (4) shared decision making may simply not constitute a viable administrative strategy for all segments of the school population. The Alutto–Belasco studies add useful dimension to views expressed earlier by Bridges (1970) on the need to recognize variability in zones of acceptance among teachers when considering how, where, and how much to seek their involvement in decision making.

Conway (1976) extended the Alutto–Belasco treatment of decision states by testing the linearity of teachers' participation in decision making and their perception of schools as organizations. He found (1) a curvilinear relationship between perceived versus desired levels of participation on one side and perception of organizational operation on the other, with the peak occurring at roughly a state of decisional equilibrium (desired state equals actual state). In his 1978 study, Conway contributed a comparative perspective to the discourse on decision making through reporting on the relationship of school heads and the participation of teachers in school affairs in eight schools in northwest England. He found that school heads have retained control in areas where tangible rewards and sanctions clearly count even while supporting teacher participation in less central or less vital areas. Conway used an adapted form of the original Alutto–Belasco decisional state scale in England with satisfactory results. Inkpen, Ponder, and Crocker (1975) questioned a group of Canadian elementary school teachers about desired versus actual level of participation in decision making in several areas. They found, like others, that desire for more participation varies considerably by area or type of decision involved.

Mohrman, Cooke, and Mohrman (1978) introduced an imaginative variation into the Alutto–Belasco instrument by applying Parsons's view of three salient levels in organizations: institutional, managerial, and technical (Parsons, 1958). They predicted that teachers would care much more about level of participation in the technical than in the managerial domain. Teachers did report higher levels of both actual and desired participation in the technical activity set than in the managerial set. Levels of satisfaction and role ambiguity among teachers showed a consistent association only with decisional state in the technical domain. Participation level in the managerial area revealed no statistically significant relationship with level of satisfaction.

More enlightenment on extent of teacher desire to participate comes from investigations reported by Duke, Showers, and Imber (1979, 1980). Duke and his associates explored teachers' perceptions of potential costs and benefits for involvement in school as compared to classroom decision making. On the potential cost side, the investigators found that most of the teachers considered only loss of time as particularly burdensome and saw none of the other alternatives presented to them (loss of autonomy, risk of collegial disfavor, subversion of collective bargaining, and threats to career advancement) as important reasons for avoiding shared decision making. Clearly, some costs weighed more heavily with some teachers than others, illustrating again the complexity of zones of acceptance. On the benefits side, the majority of teachers expressed the opinion that shared decision making offered some potential utilities. The teachers also identified several possible benefits that the investigators had not included in their set. Despite apparent evidence of sentiment that potential costs would be low and that potential benefits could be high, the investigators found that the teacher groups were not particularly anxious to take part in shared decision making at the schoolwide level. Not only did most feel less than anxious to participate, but those who had participated expressed relatively little satisfaction about their experiences and considerable skepticism over whether their involvement had made any difference in the scheme of things. Duke and his associates concluded that experience had taught a significant proportion of teachers in the study that shared decision making does not equal shared influence.

Altogether, the studies by Alutto and Belasco, Conway, Mohrman and associates, and Duke and associates have raised knowledge about participative decision making above the level that prevailed a decade ago. Teacher sentiments about participation in decision making vary widely. Teachers have become increasingly sophisticated about weighing the costs and benefits of shared decision making; they readily distinguish between their proximal and distal concerns; and they also distinguish between sharing and effective influencing. In these respects the findings of the decision-making inquiries square nicely with the findings of the Oregon and Stanford studies. (For a useful, brief summary of several reports on participative decision making, see the *Research Action Brief,* published by the ERIC Clearinghouse on Educational Management, July 1977).

Of comparative interest, Brown (1970) found that business administrators exhibited more risk propensity and achievement motivation in decision-making activities than school administrators, whereas Hy and Mathews (1978) concluded that both public and educational administrators employed about the same repertoire in working on everyday problems, with neither group using much in the way of systematic decision-making procedures.

Study of Leadership. The 1970s opened with a serious effort to take stock of leadership study in education, the Twelfth Annual Phi Delta Kappa Symposium on Educational Research, held in March 1971 (Cunningham & Gephart, 1973). Substantively, the several essays, responses thereto, and general discussions thereon serve more usefully to document the status of leadership study at the close of the 1960s than to identify major departures for the future. A major point of consensus was that scholars should pay much more attention to the behavior of followers than they had in previous decades, particularly to how leading behavior elicited following behavior. A second point of consensus was that Lipham's distinction between administration as maintenance-oriented and leadership as change-oriented required adjustment (Lipham, 1964). Otherwise, as Gephart's summary of the proceedings demonstrates, the group hardly laid a strong foundation for future leadership study (Gephart, 1973). Illustrative of a dissension that characterized much of the symposium stand the presentation by Immegart (1973) on a desired agenda for research on leadership in education and the response by Guba (1973). Where Immegart advocated experimental designs in the interest of supporting stronger inferences, Guba countered with argument for more direct observation in natural settings in the interest of reaching clearer understanding of the salient variables implicated in leading behavior as contrasted to leader behavior. The give-and-take involving all presenters and discussants that followed Guba's reaction to Immegart's presentation vividly documents the spread in views on both concepts and methodology that characterized the study of leadership in education at the time of the symposium and that still remains.

Application of Fiedler's contingency theory. Hanson (1979) observes that the Contingency Theory of leadership, in which Fiedler's contributions stand most central and cogent (Fiedler 1967; Fiedler & Chemers, 1974), displaced during the 1970s the domination that research employing the Leader Behavior Description Questionnaire (LBDQ) had enjoyed during the 1960s (see Hemphill & Coons, 1950; Halpin 1956). The respite from broadside use of the LBDQ in research on educational institutions occasioned little regret (see Griffiths, 1969a).

McKague (1970) presented a compact discussion of Fiedler's theory, comparing it to other approaches in the study of leadership with special emphasis on its value for viewing the leader in the situation; and he summarized four Canadian studies covering the years 1967–1969. He clearly identified the relevant pieces of the Fiedler concept: (1) leadership style—measured by the leader's score on the Least Preferred Coworker instrument, completed by the leader, with a high score indicating a relations-oriented style and a low score suggesting a task-oriented style; (2) situational favorableness—measured by a combination of three interacting conditions, which run in descending order of importance from leader-member relations through task structure to power position. The score for leader-member relations derives from the Group Atmosphere Scale, which again the leader completes. High-low or good-poor dichotomies on each of the three dimensions permit the creation of eight octants, along a continuum of situations from favorable through moderate to unfavorable. Data from hundreds of studies led Fiedler to conclude that task-oriented leaders secure more effective performance from groups when the situation is highly favorable or highly unfavorable; relations-oriented leaders secure best group performance when the situation is moderately favorable. The other two conditions that contribute to situational favorableness, task structure and positive power, derive from the core technology of the group and the (primarily) formal authority location of the group leader. One of the crucial features of Fiedler's theory is availability of a relatively unequivocal measure of group effectiveness, a requirement that introduces problems for applying the theory to educational organizations.

Additional empirical work on the application of Fiedler's theory to educational sites includes (1) an exploration of principal-staff relations as a mediator in explaining leader effectiveness (Williams & Hoy, 1971); (2) an examination of the leader behavior of principals vis-à-vis other members of teacher probation committees (Martin, Isherwood, & Lavery, 1976); (3) an investigation of the valence of leader-member interaction on organizational effectiveness (Garland & O'Reilly, 1976); (4) a study of leadership style with risk-taking inclination also considered (Holloway & Niazi, 1978); (5) an inquiry into the combinations of leadership styles exhibited by principals and their deputies in a set of Australian high schools (Badcock, 1980). Dufty and Williams (1979) tested a slightly different version of the contingency model in an Australian institution of higher education. Counting the four studies of the late 1960s reported by McKague, the box score includes four applications in U.S. schools, four in Canadian schools, one in an Australian high school, and one in an Australian postsecondary institution. The studies display a variety of measures of effectiveness, which collectively demonstrate that unequivocal indications of productivity are elusive, a thorny problem for investigators who desire to apply the Fiedler theory to schools and postsecondary units. Nevertheless, Fiedler has contributed meaningfully to viewing and analyzing leadership in education by way of focusing attention operationally on the interaction of personal, group, and situational variables; and especially by postulating a variability in favorableness-of-situation, which interacts in a complicated, rather than a simplistic, way with leader style.

Loyalty to superior.   Hoy continued his inquiries into subordinate-superior loyalty relationships. With Williams (Hoy & Williams, 1971), he was unable to find support for the thesis that teachers would show less loyalty to principals who exhibited high loyalty to superordinates than to principals who exhibited less loyalty. The investigators did find that principals who displayed higher levels of emotional detachment commanded more loyalty than principals with lower levels of detachment. When correlating a combination of dependence and emotional detachment with loyalty, they found that as they held emotional detachment constant, hierarchical dependence did reveal a positive association with loyalty. (See also Hoy & Rees, 1974.) In a second study, Hoy, Newland and Blazovsky (1977) examined the relationship between subordinate loyalty and *esprit* in connection with the structural characteristics of centralization and formalization. The investigators found, as hypothesized, that *esprit* and loyalty varied inversely with degree of centralization. They report that hierarchy of authority showed the strongest independent influence on both *esprit* and loyalty. However, Hoy and associates also report, in surprise, that schools appear to be skewed toward centralization in contrast to social welfare agencies. As for the relationships between centralization with *esprit* and loyalty, the investigators report that rule observance varied inversely with job codification only when they statistically controlled the influence of job codification; that job codification varied inversely with *esprit* when they statistically controlled the influence of rule observance and enforcement. The investigators infer that teachers appear generally to desire a relatively structured job environment but react negatively to vigorous enforcement of rules and regulations. They find this interpretation consistent with that offered by Moeller and Charters (1966) on explaining the unexpected finding of a higher sense of power in more bureaucratized settings, but inconsistent with the findings reported by Isherwood and Hoy (1973). In a third study, Hoy, Tarter, and Forsyth (1978) looked at loyalty against (1) the LBDQ components of consideration and initiation of structure; (2) the thrust subscale of the Organizational Climate Description Questionnaire (OCDQ); (3) authoritarianism, as construed by Blau and Scott (strict to lenient); and (4) emotional detachment, also as construed by Blau and Scott (1962). Across a set of forty public elementary and secondary schools, Hoy's group found that the four independent variables ordered themselves in the degree of association with loyalty as follows: thrust, consideration, initiation of structure, and nonauthoritarianism. Thrust stands out as most influential across all schools, but consideration and initiation of structure reverse their relative influence from elementary to secondary schools. The investigators suggest that possibly, in

elementary schools, emphasis on group maintenance elicits more loyalty, whereas in secondary schools, emphasis on group achievement does so. The studies of subordinate loyalty to superiors provide useful information on one dimension of leader behavior.

Leader rule administration behavior.   A completely different line of inquiry on leader behavior comes to light in a piece by Caldwell and Lutz (1978), tying more recent work to an earlier field study by Lutz and Evans (1968) on principal rule-administration behavior within the context of union contracts. Gouldner's tripartite classification of administrator rule behavior in bureaucratic organizations (mock-centered, representative-centered, and punishment-centered) provided the conceptual foundation, first for Lutz and Evans, and then for Caldwell and Lutz. The investigators employed a newly developed Rule Administration Scale to score principals' behavior as the independent variable, and the Gross-Herriott Educational Professional Leadership Scale (1965) to score the dependent variable. Caldwell and Lutz summarize findings across the several investigations as follows. (1) Elementary school principals who were high on representative-centered behavior, or high on a combination of representative-centered and punishment-centered rule administration behavior, received high leadership scores. (2) Elementary school principals who were high on mock-centered rule behavior (exemplified by nonenforcement of existing rules) received low scores. (3) Secondary school principals who were high on representative-centered behavior received high scores. (4) Secondary school principals who were high on punishment-centered behavior received low scores. (5) Secondary school principals who were high on mock-centered behavior received the lowest scores of all. (6) Initiation of grievances revealed an association with a combination of principal rule behavior and superintendents' management behavior. (7) Open superintendent management behavior and principal representative-centered rule behavior showed the lowest association with the initiation of grievances by teachers.

Caldwell and Lutz have systematically and helpfully documented the contribution of principal rule-administration behavior to teachers' estimates of executive performance. Introduction of perceptions of superintendent management behavior in combination with perceptions of rule administration behavior to account for variability in teacher militancy, as inferred from the objective measure of initiation grievances, comprises a distinct advance over typical single-variable inquiries.

Use of the LBDQ.   Tronc (1970) assessed the level of promotional aspirations of approximately 1,000 Canadian teachers, some 65 vice-principals, and a like number of principals. The more ambitious vice-principals and principals, as distinguished from the less aspirant via Seeman's Mobility Achievement Scale, perceived significantly higher superordinate frequency on the initiating structure and significantly lower frequency on the consideration dimensions of the LBDQ. Teacher responses were similar.

Tronc concludes that conflict between teachers and administrators could occur as teachers increase their level of professional aspiration.

Kunz and Hoy (1976) report a study involving use of LBDQ investigating the relationship between (1) location of principals in one of the standard four quadrants formed by combination of high and low scores on the consideration and initiation of structure dimensions; and (2) the zone of acceptance reported by teachers to directives issued by principals on professional matters. The widest zone of acceptance appeared in instances where principals scored high on both consideration and initiation. But for principals high on initiating structure and low on consideration, teachers reported almost as large an acceptance score as in the high-high cases. Analysis of partial correlations revealed that, with the effect of initiating structure held constant, the value for consideration fell below statistical significance.

Miscellaneous contributions. Punch and Ducharme (1972) found no support for the effect of the Life Cycle Leadership Theory for school situations. (For a later, more positive exposition, see Gates, Blanchard, & Hersey, 1977.) Miskel investigated the relationship with principals' perceived effectiveness of (1) innovation effort, (2) level of technology (modern administrative practices) exhibited in the school district, and (3) interpersonal climate. Innovation efforts at the individual school level are related to the level of technology maintained across the school district; perceptions reported by teachers and superordinates of principals' effectiveness are positively correlated; where teachers report favorable interpersonal climate, they also rate the principal high on effectiveness (Miskel, 1974b, 1977a, 1977b). Moyle (1979) concluded that the leadership exhibited by the principal was related to the performance of instructional improvement committees. Martin, Isherwood, and Rapagna (1978) confirmed the utility of goal-oriented supervision. Brennan (1973) found that twenty New South Wales high school principals responded in nonbureaucratic manner to a set of in-basket items, leading him to conclude that they performed as leaders rather than bureaucrats. Maddock and Hyams (1979) learned that teachers in four South Australian high schools rated the influence of senior subject teachers on professional matters over the influence of both principals and deputy principals. Swan (1980), in a revival of interest in the relative effects of authoritarian, democratic, and laissez faire styles, found lowest absentee rates among teachers during the term of a democratic faculty head; that the head exhibiting the democratic style was most in tune with faculty priorities; and that faculty reactions to the democratic head were much more favorable than to the two other heads.

Motivation and Satisfaction. Two conceptual frameworks, Herzberg's two-factor theory of motivators and dissatisfiers and Maslow's hierarchy of needs, have contributed significantly to thought and inquiry in educational administration. Useful summaries of the development of both frameworks and their application in various organizational settings, including education, appear in Hoy and Miskel (1978) and in a set of textbooks involving Sergiovanni as author (see Sergiovanni & Carver, 1980; Sergiovanni & Elliott, 1975; Sergiovanni & Starratt, 1979).

Sergiovanni employed Herzberg's two-factor theory as far back as the late 1960s in a report on factors that affect teacher satisfaction and dissatisfaction (Sergiovanni, 1967). He found strong support for Herzberg's contention that satisfiers (called motivators) and dissatisfiers (called hygienes) tend to operate separately; the former contributing distinctively to satisfaction, the latter contributing uniquely to dissatisfaction.

Miskel also tested the Herzberg two-factor theory in educational situations. He and Fuller (Fuller & Miskel, 1972) reported difficulty in classifying the responses of some 500 educators into a simple two-way break of motivators or hygienes; but they did find that teacher-student relationships count for a great deal with teachers. Both reports square with the conceptual and empirical foundations for the work of Willower and colleagues on pupil control ideology and behavior (see Willower, 1977). In 1973, Miskel and Heller reported the development of an instrument to study educational work components, which enabled merger of Herzberg's two-factor theory with the notion of risk orientation and also prompted adaptation of the two-factor set into three parts: motivators, ambients (which can cut both ways), and hygienes. Miskel (1973) applied the new Educational Work Components Study (EWCS) instrument in a study of 550 educators in three school districts. He found that (1) principals display more tolerance for work pressure than elementary school teachers; (2) central office administrators exhibit less need for security than elementary school teachers; and (3) the higher the reported level of aspiration of subjects, the greater the desire for risk taking and for motivator rewards. Later he extended his reach by incorporating business managers into a comparative study (Miskel, 1974a). Business managers at one end exhibit high risk inclination and less concern for hygienes; educational administrators in the middle show high concern for hygienes and security but look more like business managers than teachers when risk combines with motivators. Teachers at the other end display low-risk propensity and a high concern for hygiene factors.

Spuck (1974) examined via Herzberg-type instrumentation reward structures in a group of high schools. The motivator-type rewards showed high levels of association with teacher absenteeism, recruitment (disposition to enter the system), and retention (disposition to remain in the system). Levels of association with recruitment may be spurious because so few of the participants were teachers new to their districts. For another, different perspective on organizational incentives, see Stephens's (1974) account of how school districts' reward systems influence extent of innovative teaching practices, including reference to the salient position of the principal in dispensing or withholding rewards. Schmidt (1976) conducted a straight-out Herzberg type investigation among secondary school administrators with results which paralleled those of Sergiovanni's 1967 report and which provided further support for the application of the two-factor theory in educational institutions.

Fewer pieces which apply Maslow's formulation of need hierarchy appear in the scholarly educational administration outlets than reports involving Herzberg's two-factor theory. Trusty and Sergiovanni (1966) presented an initial study in the mid 1960s. Carver joined Sergiovanni in a second report in the early 1970s (Carver and Sergiovanni, 1971). The several available pieces permit Sergiovanni and Carver (1980) to essay comparative analyses, across geography and over time. They report that while, relatively speaking, teachers appear generally satisfied with the fulfillment of the two lower-order needs (security and affiliation), they signal considerably less satisfaction with the three higher-order needs (esteem, autonomy, and self-actualization). In both time periods, concern over the three higher-order needs exceeds concern for the two lower-order needs.

Miskel and Gerhardt (1974) found that (1) hierarchy of authority and rules and regulations served as significant predictors of conflict; (2) experience, sex, and teaching level added more information about variability in conflict; (3) level of conflict varied inversely with satisfaction; and (4) voluntarism and central life interests varied directly with job satisfaction. Earlier, Miskel and two associates completed a report for the U.S. Office of Education which detected, by way of employing an indirect measure of satisfaction, a discernibly lower proportion of satisfied and highly satisfied teachers. (Miskel, Glasnapp, & Hatley, 1972).

The same authors (1975) also elaborated an inequity hypothesis to guide subsequent investigations. The inequity hypothesis treats job satisfaction as a reflection of the divergence between a worker's view of ideal conditions and his or her perception of actual conditions. Study findings provided support for the pertinence of the inequity hypothesis in educational settings. Somewhat later, with a different set of associates, Miskel undertook an investigation that looked at satisfaction against a pattern of perceived school effectiveness, extent of participation in organizational decision making, extent of formalization of general rules, and the level of complexity of professional activity (Miskel, Fevurly, & Stewart, 1979). The findings support the expectation that teachers consider schools that provide less centralized decision-making structures and more participative organizational processes, and those schools that support higher order and more complex professional activity, to be more effective. An unexpected finding was that teachers also view more formalized general rules as a characteristic of effective schools (see Hoy, Newland, & Blazovsky, 1977, for similar report). High formalization on general rules, low centralization on decision making, participative principal leadership, and level of principal's experience covary with job satisfaction. Miskel et al. (1979) found that structural and process variables are more complex and varied than traditional paradigms propose.

Grassie and Carss (1973) found that the satisfaction of teachers who valued theory was more strongly related to ratings of structural conditions and to principals' leadership than was the satisfaction of teachers who placed lower value on theory. An inquiry of somewhat similar stripe by Fraser (1980), on the relationship between supervisory behavior and teacher satisfaction, documented that (1) many of the Montana teachers from whom responses came would prefer to experience more exposure to the 31 exemplary supervisory practices the investigator presented for their reaction; (2) satisfaction levels covaried directly with the difference between scores revealing extent of actual experience versus level of desired experience with the practices; (3) responses to several of the items depended on sex, years of teaching experiences, or teaching level.

Hollon and Gemmill (1976) also found sex differences in the responses among 321 community college faculty members. Women reported experiencing a sense of low participation in decision making, less job involvement, more job-related tension, and less overall job satisfaction. Holdaway (1978) explored the relationship between facet (specific job factor) and overall satisfaction. He affirmed earlier findings that teachers report themselves as generally satisfied, with distinctions across teaching levels (elementary school teachers more satisfied than secondary school teachers), between sexes (women more satisfied than men), and across age groups (older more satisfied than younger). Bridges (1980) inferred from his multivariate analysis of the relationship between job satisfaction and teacher absenteeism that there was at best only a tenuous association between the two variables among the elementary school teachers who participated in his study, but that the association might be affected by the level of work interdependence. Conway and Ables (1973) noted that congruence of belief systems across team members and between team members and leader showed a positive relationship with a measure of morale within teaching teams. Shetty and Carlisle (1974) observed differential responses across a university faculty to introduction of a program of management-by-objectives (MBO): lower-rank, nontenured members reported more success for the program than higher-rank, tenured members.

Overall, research has yet to establish a definitive relationship between satisfaction and performance. Until inquiry addresses that vital relationship, educators will continue to find themselves basing their views on extrapolations from business and industry, which consistently reveal only a low, positive level of association between satisfaction and performance.

Challenges to the Traditional Paradigm

Discontent with predominant concepts and constructs has prompted a quest to identify more useful ways of describing and explaining organizational life. In some instances philosophical bent or ideological tilt stimulated both the initiation and the development of the challenge to organizational analysis in general as well as in educational institutions.

Classifying Organizational Perspectives. Bidwell and Abernathy (1979) and Scott (1981a, 1981b) have produced excellent comparative analyses of organizational models. According to Scott, 1960 marks the dividing line between earlier emphasis on closed systems models in organizational theory and later emergence of open systems models. Within each of the two time periods, Scott subdivides the models once more into rational and natural categories according to time periods, rational earlier and natural later.

Open systems theories hold that (1) organizations are highly interdependent with environments; (2) boundaries are both permeable and variable; and (3) procurement of inputs and disposal of outputs are both uncertain matters and create dependencies that have profound effects on organizational functions.

Rational systems models treat organizations as intentionally created and arranged for the pursuit of explicit objectives, with overriding importance attached to goal specificity and to formalization of roles and rules. Natural systems models stress the importance and centrality of unplanned and spontaneous processes and events; organizations show themselves as composed of coalitions of participants who do not share consensus on goals but do share common interest in organizational survival; and "organically emerging" informal structures supplement or overcome more mechanically or intentionally arranged frameworks as the source of organizational behaviors and beliefs. As of 1980, says Scott (1981a), the prevailing posture of organizational thought had converged on the salience of environmental influences on organizational structures and process but remained divided over the pertinence of nonrational explanations of organizational adaptation and over the relative weight of goal attainment or system survival as an overriding value.

The relatively settled condition of open versus closed, but relatively unsettled status of rational versus natural, show themselves in the narratives on organizational thought in education presented by Bidwell and Abernathy (1979). They introduce a three-way cut (closed, control, and open) instead of a simple two-way cut (closed and open), which provides a number of useful insights about the presence or absence of an organizational "regulator."

Bidwell and Abernathy urge educational researchers and practitioners to apply organizational theory both cautiously and creatively, and especially to keep in mind that most closed and control systems models tend to ignore or discount the distinguishing characteristics of schools and school systems. (For another recommendation to look at the uniqueness of schools as organizations, see Bachrach & Mitchell, 1981.) Most educational approaches to consideration of productivity share two shortcomings of traditional organization theory: (1) they typically project closed or control systems views of schools and school systems; and (2) they rarely integrate explanations of classroom

structure and process with explanations of school or school district structure and process.

Bidwell and Abernathy say further that (1) schools are highly institutionalized, politicized, and disorganized; (2) considerations of technical rationality and efficiency play only a limited role in the ways schools are structured and operate, because educational technology is only poorly understood and the desired output is difficult both to produce and measure; (3) given these conditions, schools aim to maintain institutional legitimacy as much as to produce technical efficiency; (4) the boundary between educational organizations and their environments continually shifts and remains distinctly fluid, with many groups (parents, community organizations, political bodies, and government agencies) participating in variable amounts at various times; (5) definition of organizational membership remains ambiguous and uncertain; (6) educational organizations appear to try to shape their environments, not just passively wait to adapt or be shaped; (7) educational organizations look more like "organized anarchies" than tightly knit units; that is, they show signs of pluralistic power distribution, decentralized decision making, constant internal conflict, ambiguous goals, uncertain technology, and continuously shifting composition and membership; and (8) "loose coupling" prevails in a number of salient respects, even though tight coupling may show itself in other respects. In summary, Bidwell and Abernathy claim that open systems assumptions appear to describe education institutions better than other systems assumptions and characteristics. They conclude their argument with recommendations for a research agenda that avoids those disjunctions in levels of analysis that have seriously hampered previous work in education and in organizations generally. The Bidwell–Abernathy emphasis on methodical linking of macrostructure (school district and school) to microprocess (classroom teaching and learning) in an integrated explanatory framework squares with the call by Erickson (1977a, 1977b, 1979) to search the effects of organizational conditions.

Contingency Theory. Hanson (1979; Hanson & Brown, 1977) has argued vigorously in favor of adopting a contingency perspective in the study of educational institutions and in support of its salience to practicing administrators. In the two chapters of the text (5 & 9) in which he systematically develops the contingency approach, Hanson lays out the progression of his thought from earlier conceptual and empirical involvement with other perspectives (which include Hanson, 1972a, 1972b, 1975, 1976) to his advocacy and use of a contingency orientation (Hanson and Brown, 1977). He also acknowledges his debt to the earlier work of Lawrence and Lorsch (1969) and Derr and Gabarro (1972).

Predictable response to changing environmental circumstance is the central tenet of contingency theory. This perspective proposes a permeable boundary between organization and environment.

Willower (1980), for one, plays down the contribution thus far of contingency theory to describing and explaining organizational life in organizations. He asks whether contingency theory offers a set of explanatory concepts and generalizations or only an injunction to pay attention to environmental contingencies and associated organizational complexities.

Organized Anarchies and the Garbage Can Modality. A different concept of educational organizations has captured the imagination and attention of organizational analysts in and out of education (Cohen, March, & Olsen, 1972; Cohen & March, 1974; March & Olsen, 1976; Sproull, Weiner, & Wolf, 1978). The protagonists of this view argue that educational organizations share the characteristics of organized anarchies: unclear and diffuse goals, uncertain technology, uncertain outcomes, and fluid participation of members, patrons, and clients. Within organized anarchies, rational decision processes do not exist. Rather a "garbage can modality" of decision making prevails, in which participants, solutions, and problems tumble over and around each other in disorganized array, occasionally coming together in almost accidental fit. An important component of this perspective is the central place of amount and intensity of attention by particular participants in bringing preferred programs to the agenda table and in securing favorable action. The combined organized anarchy–garbage can view qualifies as an open-natural system model of organizational behavior. As such, this perspective represents a significant departure from the traditional paradigm, especially because of its singular emphasis on nonrational decision-making behavior.

Inquiry in the public schools has tended to draw heavily on the attention of administrators; that is, observing and reporting in minute detail exactly what administrators do, to permit drawing low-level inferences about the matters to which administrators actually pay attention. Measures of attention, in turn, yield indicators of matters and activities which administrators do and do not influence. In his survey of efforts to establish new paradigms in organizational analysis, Griffiths (1977) places March and Cohen between supporters of the *status quo* on one side and advocates of a phenomenological perspective on the other. He observes that the organized anarchy perspective does appear to explain pertinent dimensions of university decision making and notes that recent analyses of faculty behavior in and productivity of schools, colleges, and departments of education (Clark & Guba, 1976) agree with the formulation. However, he cautions that lower schools differ sufficiently enough from colleges and universities to restrict the broad application of this perspective.

Willower (1979b) presents a crisp summary of the organized anarchy–garbage can perspective and a sharp criticism. He locates the view along with two others (Marxist and phenomenologist) as "children of the times." In the garbage can case, the ideological strain appears in its slashing attack on rationality as representative of organizational life. Willower observes in this connection that a considerable amount of earlier study on authority and control actually reported nonrational behavior, even if the investigations employed frameworks that assumed rationality as a

condition. He aligns himself with others who reject the model as a faithful representation of organizational life, particularly in schools. Specifically, Willower proposes that schools are more organized than anarchic; that a number of discernible elements (formal and normative structures, which promote routinization and reduce variation) operate to counter elements that make for anarchy. Preoccupation with critique of rationality and emphasis on the features of anarchy understate the shifting interplay of organizing and anarchic forces. Nevertheless, Willower observes that the garbage can model has already demonstrated utility in educational organizations spanning schools and colleges; he predicts that it will catch hold, and he notes favorably that it does lend itself to test in the crucible of empirical inquiry. In his 1981 statement, Willower reports that the garbage can framework has shaped a number of school studies (e.g., the joint report by Hannaway & Sproull, 1979), and that the notions have helped to dispel the expectation that rationality actually characterizes organizational life.

Loose Coupling. Weick's presentation of educational organizations as loosely coupled systems has swept through the ranks of organizational analysts in education like wildfire, consuming large sections of the traditional paradigm (Weick, 1976).

The notion of coupling between levels, functions, offices, and persons is not a new one. In his 1965 essay on the school as a formal organization, Bidwell identified "structural looseness" as a singular characteristic, made necessary to provide sufficient teacher autonomy to cope with the inescapable variability among students that teachers face every hour of every day. The press from the bureaucratic side (the need to move cohorts in orderly fashion through progressive stages) confronts the professional press (the adaptation to variable needs, within which a nurturant orientation also surfaces) so as to yield internally loose articulation of units. In short, structural looseness and teacher autonomy have long appeared in the litany of organizational characteristics of schools. Lortie (1969, 1973, 1975) has regularly confronted the question of balance between control and autonomy.

What has Weick added that has commanded such widespread reaction and attention? Perhaps more important than any single substantive feature of his argument stands his expressed sentiment (with which the mid-1970s was ready to resonate) that preoccupation among organizational analysts with rationality in structure and process had created inclination to ignore not only the less rational structural properties and behaviors in organizations but also the extent to which loose coupling of organizational activities actually prevailed. Somewhat predictably, given the dispositions of students in educational administration to follow the leader (Boyan, 1981b), study of linkages in educational organizations moved toward accepting a presumption of looseness rather than empirically testing for it (Abramowitz & Tenenbaum, 1978). By 1979, Griffiths started to take issue with the notion of loose coupling on the grounds that observed variability in coupling overrides presumptions of loose coupling (Griffiths, 1979a). Willower (1980) also urges treating coupling as variable, allowing opportunities to see and describe organizational correlates of tight and loose instances. Willower (1981) attributed some of the growing popularity of the perspective to a fit between its emphasis on nonrational behavior in organizations with the pluralistic preference of many contemporary students of organizations. Davis (1977) concludes that Weick's arguments do not add much in the way of knowledge, and that the metaphor loses some value with any evidence of tight coupling. Spence, Takei, and Sim (1978) go much further; they label the language of loose coupling as analogous and acausal, figurative, one-directional, and dogmatic. They see the renaming of old concepts, and they accuse Weick of placing the very issue of labeling beyond debate; of asking others to seek enlightenment by adopting and believing his metaphor.

Institutional Myth and Symbol. Meyer and Rowan (1977, 1978) suggest that organizational structure may take shape without intent to control, coordinate, or implement specific activities. Formal structures for public institutions like schools arise and remain in existence to prove that they are legitimately and properly qualified to perform the functions and purposes for which the supporting public issued the charter. Society, say Meyer and Rowan, expects the school to perform a credentialing function; accordingly, the organizational structure must appear to the society as one that appropriately represents the fulfillment of that function. Tight coupling within that structure possesses the potential of revealing deficiencies and inconsistencies in the performance of the expected function. Thus, schools find it sensible and functional to decouple supervision from instruction, and instruction from measures of pupil performances. All of this rests on a foundation designated by Meyer and Rowan as the logic of confidence; namely, the assumption that all organizational participants perform regularly as expected.

Assessment of the Meyer–Rowan formulation varies across Davis, Spence et al., and Willower. Davis (1977) judges that the institutional approach generates useful questions and suggests helpful explanations for the study of organizations in the public as well as the private sector. Spence et al. (1978) speak of the work of Meyer and his associates as both elegant and sophisticated, but cite as egregiously ignored the importance of organizational rules and procedures in the exercise of direct and indirect control over teachers. Willower (1981) argues that supervision and instruction show as decoupled because teachers and administrators both understand and abide by the "rules of the game" (Willower, 1980) which govern classroom and school behavior. Willower (1981) also reminds the reader that even if decoupling appears characteristic of administrator-teacher relations and central office-building relations in respect to instruction, in other areas—e.g., budget and scheduling—the coupling may be much tighter.

Other Competitors to the Traditional Paradigm. The amount and quality of empirical study that the new perspectives have generated attest to their vitality. Several other developments also merit mention.

Phenomenology. Greenfield (1973, 1975, 1976, 1977, 1978, 1979, 1980) has argued vigorously for an emphasis on meaning as expressed existentially by participants rather than as interpreted "objectively" by observers. Greenfield endorses phenomenology philosophically and as a form of empirical inquiry. Early and regular challenge by Griffiths (1975, 1977, 1979a, 1979b) provoked an exchange which earned the label of the "Greenfield–Griffiths Debates." Given the grounds on which the antagonists staked their claims, little movement toward reconciliation appears likely.

Marxism. The Marxist position is that organizations in western societies serve primarily the purposes of the corporate state rather than participants, clients, or the public interest generally. The Marxist perspective has not yet penetrated organizational thought and inquiry in education, although its influence among both historians and economists of education suggests that the organizational life of schools may well become a focal point in the future.

Miscellaneous developments. Clark, McKibbin, and Malkas (1981) identify several other perspectives that may come to guide organizational analysis: (1) incentive system paradigm and marketplace model; (2) natural selection model (akin to a human ecology orientation noted by Scott, 1981a); (3) adaptive implementation; (4) collectivist perspective; (5) organizations as clans; (6) exchange model; (7) political economy model; and (8) negotiated order model. Clark (1981) concludes that the disturbances in the study of organizations have yielded skepticism and that the various challenges merit consideration. Clark attacks the goal-centered, rational decision-making model, which has long dominated thought and inquiry in organizational analysis.

Work Activities, Attention, and Ethnography. Three primary stimuli have contributed to a recent revival of interest in examining what administrators actually do. The first was the publication of Mintzberg's *The Nature of Managerial Work* (1973), which focused eyes on the utility of investigating work activities. The second was the set of studies of managerial attention prompted by the inquiries of Cohen, March, and Olsen (Cohen, March, & Olsen, 1972; Cohen & March, 1974; March & Olsen, 1976). Acclaim for the rich detail about school life yielded by a number of ethnographic studies (e.g., Wolcott, 1973; Jackson, 1968; Cusick, 1973) provided a third prod. Typically, ethnographic investigations and reports pertinent to the administration of educational institutions have attempted to infer meanings from the observed patterns of events against one dimension or another of a social system perspective (e.g., interaction of formal-informal organizations; influence of norms and expectations).

All three approaches—the first two new and the third revived—share in common a requirement to expend huge amounts of time in the study of a few individuals and cases. Accordingly, the quantity of instances for which reports of rich detail currently exist on administrative life remains small.

Summary. Bidwell and Abernathy (1979) and Scott (1981a) have helpfully categorized major developments in organizational theory to reveal the progression from loading on closed-rational systems models to open-natural systems models. Scott has indicated that open system views have captured the field, at least temporarily, whereas the outcome of the engagement between rational and natural systems adherents remains somewhat in doubt. Bidwell and Abernathy have argued for the appropriateness of employing open systems models in studying schools and have recognized the pertinence of attending to nonrational as well as rational bases of behavior in schools.

Four major competitors to the traditional paradigm in the study of school organization have appeared during the 1970s: (1) contingency theory; (2) organized anarchy–garbage can model; (3) loosely coupled systems; (4) institutional (myth and symbol) approach. All fit with the open system orientation, all but contingency theory fall in the natural system category. Despite questions raised about pertinence and applicability to school phenomena, each of the four departures has served as the conceptual framework for empirical work in educational institutions. A host of additional perspectives stand waiting in the wings for advocates to assemble. Almost all of the new perspectives share in common rejection of an orthodoxy which places rational pursuit of goals as central in organizational life. The creators, protagonists, and advocates of the alternative perspectives view organizations as fluid mixes of activities, purposes, and participants.

Also of moment during the 1970s appeared a powerful new methodology for studying school administrators' work life in rich detail (Mintzberg's work activities approach), a potentially useful variable around which to order data collected through intense observation (attention), and a remarkable revival of interest in ethnographic study of the organizational life of schools. The decade closed on the notes of (1) looking again, but much more carefully, at administrators and what they do, (2) identifying and making clear the meaning of the unique characteristics of schools as organizations, and (3) attempting to discern the effects of organizational arrangements and of administrator behavior.

Administrator Work and Effects

Study of the work of educational administrators draws data from one or a combination of three sources: (1) self-reports; (2) reports from others who presumably stand in a position to provide reliable information; and (3) direct observation. According to Sproull (1981a), the first approach typically yields unreliable estimates on the content of administrator activities; also, the missing data rate tends to be high. The second method nets the perceptions of

others (e.g., subordinates or superordinates) about the quality of the administrator's interpersonal behavior. (For a detailed exposition on issues of validity and reliability in using teachers' reports on principals for observing and assessing performance, see the Appendix in Gross and Herriott, 1965). The method of direct observation, says Sproull, offers a greater possibility for reliable and consistent data on managerial work. (See Mintzberg, 1973, for description of the methodology of "structured observation.") A singular drawback of direct, structured observation (and also of ethnographic methodologies) is the small number of cases that the observer can accommodate in any given period of time. Nevertheless, several investigators have turned to use of intensive and direct observation of education administrators because of its advantage in yielding more detailed data on the scope and content of managerial work in education.

Self-reports. Examples of the more customary survey analyses of school administrators, including self-reports on work, are found in Knezevich (1971); Abramowitz and Tenenbaum (1978); Byrne, Hines, and McCleary (1978); Gorton and McIntyre (1978); McCleary and Thomson (1979); Pharis and Zakariya (1979); Salley (1979); and Willower and Fraser (1980). Knezevich (1971) reported that superintendents work long hours (close to 60 per week) and are not strangers to controversy (including financial struggles; demand for innovations; changes in public, student, and employee values and behavior; spread of collective bargaining; pressure for reorganization and centralization). Problems that might prompt leaving the superintendency are community attacks on superintendents, labor negotiations and strikes, antagonism of the school board, low levels of financing, student unrest, and general social-cultural ferment. On these issues, as on other attitudes and orientations, considerable variability appeared in patterns of questionnaire responses, with size of school system appearing regularly as a discriminating factor. Superintendents reported the need for additional specialized assistance in more traditional areas, such as curriculum and instruction, rather than in more emergent areas, such as planning or systems analysis, and said they would like to sharpen their skills in human relations and public finance rather than to learn new, specialized management skills. Despite deep expressions of concern, approximately 85 percent of respondents perceived their status as educational leaders as equal to or better than it was ten years earlier, and 70 percent said they would seek the superintendency if they were to start their careers again. (Willower & Fraser, 1980, supply a similar picture in their report of fifty superintendents in Pennsylvania as of the late 1970s.)

On the principal side, both the National Association of Elementary School Principals (NAESP) and the National Association of Secondary School Principals (NASSP) conducted major surveys of their memberships. Pharis and Zakariya (1979) prepared the elementary school report; the secondary school report appeared in three volumes

(Vol. 1, Byrne et al., 1978; Vol. 2, Gorton & McIntyre, 1978; Vol. 3, McCleary & Thomson, 1979).

A particularly revealing feature of the NASSP volumes appears in the comparison of reports on attitudes and beliefs between participants in the 1977 survey and in a 1965 survey. Fourteen statements of basic beliefs on broad educational issues, on which principals reported their degree of agreement or disagreement, appeared in both surveys. Dramatic shifts occurred from the earlier to the later time period, with the 1977 group signifying agreement as compared to the 1965 signifying disagreement with five of the fourteen: (1) Hostile or disinterested youth should not be required to attend school. (2) Schools require too little academic work. (3) Schools should provide specific job training. (4) Schools should develop special programs for the talented. (5) Schools are not producing enough scholars in the field of human needs, energy, environment, and medicine. A sixth major shift also showed, this time from 1965 agreement to 1977 disagreement on the statement that court decisions concerning racial segregation are correct as they apply to the public schools. The authors of the summary volume (McCleary & Thomson, 1979) observe that not only have significant shifts in opinion taken place, but also that principals reveal substantial agreement among themselves (only two of the twenty items brought a close division of opinion).

McCleary and Thomson (1979) infer from both survey and nonsurvey data that the work of the secondary school principal has changed, and they cite from the survey new time demands (more time on the job in 1977, approximately fifty-six hours per week) and serious administrative road blocks: growing administrative detail, lack of time, and much variability in teacher competence. Other obstacles, not reported in 1965, include apathetic parents and problem students.

Secondary school principals in 1977, as in 1965 and in virtually every survey recorded, say that they do not spend their time as they would prefer to. Most of their time goes to management; they would like most of it to go to program development, planning, and professional development (faculty and their own); they would like to spend less time on student behavior problems and school district office activities. Still, like superintendents, they expressed overall satisfaction about their job status and conditions (McCleary & Thomson, 1979). They view the federal pressure for desegregation as relatively untroublesome, but federal pressure on Title IX (sex equity) and student rights as bothersome. They consider state requirements on compulsory attendance, evidence of accountability, and graduation standards as problems. Constraints at the local level include parental lack of interest, parental demands, and interest group pressures. The apparent contradiction in parental apathy and demands shows itself in strong preference among principals for limited and narrow participation by the public in program planning, administrative policy, and matters of educational process. From their central offices, principals want positive support (many report receiving such support), and they do not want policy and central office and school board "interference" in affairs at the school level. They want more autonomy and a broader scope of action.

Direct Observation. Wolcott (1973) has provided an extremely detailed and rich account of the life of an elementary school principal in a suburban community. He spent one full year directly observing the principal in the context of relationships with central office personnel, fellow principals, teachers and specialists, pupils and parents. He finished with serious questions about whether the position of principal can ever be one of instructional leader versus manager, or of change agent versus maintainer of social continuity. For a more recent ethnographic study, of five New Zealand principals, see Edwards (1979).

Students of educational administration, and other scholars interested in the work of educational administrators, discovered Mintzberg's concepts and methodologies at about the same time as Wolcott's study appeared and began to apply them seriously (Mintzberg, 1973). In the late 1970s and early 1980s, several Mintzberg-type studies of educational administrators reached completion and publication in the United States and abroad. These reports have added useful detail and insight about managerial activity in education and have helped to enlighten discussions about the effects and contributions of administrators to various dimensions of the educational program.

Larson, Bussom, and Vicars (1981) subjected the work activities of six superintendents to systematic study in an adaptation of the Mintzberg approach and employed his framework for data analysis and reduction. They identified a number of problems in transferring the Mintzberg analytical scheme directly to school conditions, but were able to adjust the category system readily enough to permit drawing useful comparisons between their findings and Mintzberg's report on other managers.

Of particular value from the study of Larson et al. comes the finding of extent of individual differences across the six superintendents in the way they spent their time, what they spent time on, and with whom. Comparison with three other direct observation studies of superintendents at work (Mintzberg, 1973; Kurke & Aldrich, 1979; Pitner, 1978) reveals still more variation in the proportion of time spent on various activities.

Duignan (1980) reports an investigation into the work life of eight superintendents in Alberta, Canada. His eight subjects spent approximately 70 percent of their working days in verbal contact with others (on the average twenty-six different contacts per day); about two-thirds of that time with central-office staff, school trustees, and school site administrators. Less than 14 percent went to teachers and students. Larson et al. also noted the concentration of personal interaction between superintendents and immediate subordinates, as have Pitner and Ogawa (1981). Duignan discusses his findings under five headings: (1) disjointed work—high incidence of interruption; (2) problem of time control—spending much time reacting to situations and events; (3) information broker—focal location in school system's informational network, with access to key informants within and without the system; (4) decision maker—more a facilitator, less an independent actor; and (5) executive or educational leader—primarily an executive, who engages in large amounts of verbal contacts with policy makers and system administrators and in small amounts with teachers and pupils.

Pitner and Ogawa (1981) have insightfully and skillfully weaved together the findings from their respective doctoral dissertations, and a subsequent investigation by the first author. On the side of work *per se,* the authors draw on Pitner's direct observations of three men in a midwestern state and three women in California. Findings come together under two main headings: superintending is communicating; superintendents experience the constraints of social and organizational structures, yet exert important organizational influence. These findings lead Pitner and Ogawa to draw a picture of the superintendent as mediator. Discrepancies with Duignan's (1980) report appear in respect to several particulars, but distributions of verbal contacts look remarkably similar: Duignan reported 67 percent of verbal contact spent with central office subordinates, trustees, site administrators; Pitner and Ogawa (1981) report 69 percent for virtually the same groups.

Of deeper significance, however, is the singular agreement between the respective investigators on the salience of communication generally. Both Duignan on one side and Pitner and Ogawa on the other use their data to document the strategic location of the superintendent in the web of verbal communication which affects the fortune of school districts. The report of Pitner and Ogawa (1981) on the functions of superintendent as mediator enriches Duignan's portrayal of a chief executive who performs as information broker. The two reports complement each other in useful fashion; both add depth and perspective to the portrait of variability painted by Larson et al. (1981); both suggest program interests on the part of superintendent which go beyond the actual amount of time allocated to educational activity *per se.*

Mintzberg-type studies of principals cover the work activities of school managers in both the United States and Australia. Willis (1980) reports on three secondary school principals in Australia; Martin and Willower (1981), on five in a northeastern U.S. commonwealth; Morris, Crowson, Hurwitz, and Porter-Gehrie (1981), on sixteen Chicago principals (see also Crowson & Porter-Gehrie, 1980); Sproull (1981a), on four principals and one community college chief. Peterson's (1978) analysis of the principal's tasks approximates but does not reach a full work activities treatment.

Willis (1980) organizes findings about work characteristics under three main headings: (1) variety, brevity, and fragmentation—confirmation is apparent; (2) invisibility—a weekly average of almost thirty-six hours of work (covering time at and away from school) takes place away from the eyes of faculty and staff; and (3) two orientations—

the data reveal a dual orientation, one internal and one external, indicating that Willis's principals (one from a state high school, one from an independent school, one from a Catholic school) serve an important linking function with the environment. Discussion of findings develops within the dichotomy between leadership and management, which has characterized literature on the principalship. Willis argues that the principals' external orientation satisfies fundamentally managerial requirements; the internal orientation, administrative requirements. The former attend primarily to adaptation; the latter, to maintenance and stability. His portrayal of external communication and internal translation match the perceptions developed by both Duignan and Pitner and Ogawa. Willis describes a model of the principalship, which encompasses twelve components, including reference to (1) work as susceptible to interruption, superficiality of treatment, shifting locations, and discontinuity; (2) activities as highly people-centered, with mostly one-on-one encounters; (3) work as significantly invisible; (4) external activities as constituting an important link with environmental regulators, customers, and competitors; (5) work as susceptible to personal orientations and personalities; and (6) work, at the core, as communication.

Martin and Willower (1981) also report that variety, brevity, and fragmentation characterize the managerial behavior of the five high school principals who participated in their study: over 80 percent of activities ranged between one and four minutes, with a modal time of one minute for some 3,730 tasks observed over the twenty-five days of observation. Interruptions occurred during 50 percent of all observed activities, requiring a polychronic disposition. Volume and pace were high: length of work week exceeded, on average, fifty hours; tasks per hour exceeded seventeen. Verbal interaction marked almost 85 percent of all activities and 64 percent of all time expended, with almost seven times as much face-to-face contact as telephone contact. Preferences for attending to current and pressing events (live action) versus reflective activity clearly prevailed. The five Martin–Willower principals differed notably from Willis's subjects in respect to proportion of time and activities devoted to external contacts, a difference likely attributable to variation in structural location. Martin and Willower report a distinctively heavy weighting of internal and external interaction; a total of 92.6 percent of all contacts occurred between principals and members of the organization they administered. They also report that, however much various factors may have contributed to erosion of the power base of principals in general, their subjects occupied focal positions in organizational governance and were generally in command of their respective situations. On the issue of instructional leadership, Martin and Willower offer an insightful conclusion: They note that their five principals spent, on average, 17.4 percent of time on instructional matters (consulting and evaluating, providing logistical and organizational maintenance discernibly related to instruction). They also observe, however, that the teaching staff clearly occupied a central position with respect to classroom instruction, which the principals both recognized and respected. Still, as far as the schoolwide instructional program was concerned, the principal both served as the only institutional overseer and retained final authority, generally passively enacted. In connection with these observations, Martin and Willower comment on the notion of loose coupling in educational organizations. They surmise that evidence of loose coupling prevails in the instructional area because of understandings about norms and expectations that hold for, and accordingly limit, autonomy in classrooms. Correspondingly, they note the presence of tight coupling in other educational task areas, such as organizational maintenance and logistics, schoolwide pupil control, and extracurricular activities.

Morris et al. (1981) explored the discretionary decision-making behavior of sixteen principals in the Chicago public schools. The investigators devote one chapter of their report exclusively to comparing the profiles of the elementary and secondary school principals in their study with the portrayal of managers offered by Mintzberg. Of particular interest is the projection of data for principals within Mintzberg's role rubric, which supported the following inferences:

1. For elementary principals—interpersonal role behavior, prominent (almost one-third of the managerial day); informational role, predominant (over one-half of the day); decisional role, limited (only 11 percent); subordinate behavior, representing activities when principals' immediate supervisor was enacting clearly superordinate behavior, virtually absent (one percent of time while principaling).
2. For secondary principals—interpersonal role (42 percent, higher than elementary); informational role (51 percent, slightly less pronounced than elementary); decisional role (six percent, about half as often as elementary); subordinate behavior (conspicuous by infrequency).

Morris et al. report, overall, considerable discomfort in laying the principals' behavior on Mintzberg's procrustean bed. They suggest that modification of the content of the various roles, which Mintzberg elaborated in his study of chief executives, appears necessary and appropriate in reporting and analyzing the behavior of middle managers such as principals. (See Martin & Willower, 1981, for a similar comment.)

On the other side, Morris et al. say enthusiastically that incorporation of the direct observation format enabled them to draw with considerable confidence the inference that a substantial amount of discretionary behavior prevails among elementary and secondary school principals in a large, apparently bureaucratic school district. They conclude that the way in which the principal manages himself, his relations with the environment of the system and the community, and his relations with the faculty give

definition to the school as a teaching and learning organization. Sproull (1981a) finds evidence of the following structural characteristics of managerial attention: local; extremely choppy, with many brief episodes; oral; unpredictable, with much interruption; as much other-directed as self-directed. She adds the following content characteristics: (1) within an overall instructional program allocation of approximately 23 percent of all activities, only 4 percent went directly to matters of teaching and learning; (2) about 22 percent of the days' activities implicated logistics (keeping track of people, material, and supplies); (3) some 20 percent attended to external requirements, typically imposed by a central office; (4) 11 percent involved social pleasantries, most often exchanged via brief conversations. (The distribution of the balance of 24 percent receives no mention.)

From her data on structure and character of managerial attention, Sproull concludes that (1) managers do not serve or are not asked to provide a technical resource function for teachers; (2) managers do not closely monitor or provide performance feedback on instructional activity; (3) managers display expertise on the location and status of people and supplies; and (4) managers serve as buffers between local sites and central offices, complying with requests and passing along information. Sproull estimates that central office personnel, and federal and state officials external to the system, should recognize the indeterminacy that may prevail in attempting to control or influence a particular program development in a given site. She also projects the difficulties which extant patterns of managerial attention in education pose for expectations that educational managers conduct meaningful evaluation of personnel and program.

Findings from direct observations suggesting that educational managers spend relatively small amounts of their time on instructional matters *per se*, because of other demands for their attention, set the stage for analysis of administrator effects on educational programs.

Administrator Effects. Two contradictory positions have developed on the question of amount and quality of influence that administrators exercise on the instructional program. March (1978) contends that the activities of administrators show only marginal association with the teaching activities of teachers and learning activities of learners. A completely diametric position appeared in textbooks and in literature of professional associations and in other scholarly observation and reports.

The negative position. The small proportion of time that educational managers devote to instruction argues against administrator effects on classroom processes. Investigators who draw their inferences from patterns of time and activity distributions typically do not place those patterns in an overall context introduced by observers like Martin and Willower (1981), who suggest that institutional norms and expectations carry much of the burden of coupling between supervision and instruction.

Hannaway and Sproull (1979) address the matter of linkages between central office and school sites. Hannaway collected work activity data from some fifty central office personnel; Sproull, from three high school principals in different districts. The authors assemble and present their findings as complementary evidence of relatively little interaction between central office personnel and school site managers, especially with respect to instruction. School managers influenced about 9 percent of all central office administrator work; overall, 2.47 percent of activities pertained to curriculum and instruction *per se,* with a range from 0.60 percent for nineteen upper-level administrators to 5.14 percent for eighteen administrators and supervisors in the district's division of instruction. Sproull's data, pertinent to coordination from the other side, reveal that district-level managers, on average, shaped or influenced only about 14 percent of the total work activities of her three high school principals, with a range from 2 percent to 20 percent; that on average, instruction *per se* accounted for only 2 percent of exchanges with a range from 0 to 5 percent. Both data sets provide support for the Meyer and Rowan (1977) argument that district-level managers seek information from schools that support the legitimacy of the organization, rather than seek information about personnel performance or program outcomes. Hannaway and Sproull conclude that managerial activities are only marginally related to the production activities of schools. They also conclude that "loose" management in instruction makes sense because teaching remains an unclear and uncertain technology. Alternatively, their conclusions may suggest the need to dig beyond the mechanics of counting work activities to achieve a deeper understanding of just how and why instructional activities take the shape and substance that they exhibit.

A different set of investigators, using a different framework and different methodology, reached approximately the same conclusions as Hannaway and Sproull (see Meyer et al., 1978). These investigators focused on the extent of agreement that they could find between central offices and school sites on reading programs in grades 1–3. The findings of Meyer et al. led them to conclude that (1) quite limited agreement exists between superintendents and principals in the same school districts on descriptions of typical district educational policies and procedures; (2) within a district, principals reveal a very low level of agreement as to the content and meaning of district regulations and educational policies; (3) rather limited levels of agreement appear between principals and teachers in the same schools on matters of policies and working arrangements; and (4) teachers within a given school exhibit relatively low levels of agreement in descriptions of school and classroom policies. Meyer et al. draw the conclusion that high segmentation, high decentralization, and distinctive decoupling characterize the organizational structure of school systems. They go further and, in keeping with the earlier Meyer and Rowan (1977) formulation, identify schools not only as loosely coupled in regard to educational work, but also as "institutionalized" in the sense of continuously seeking legitimacy, a condition that tight coupling between supervision and instruction could readily threaten or undermine.

Deal and Celotti (1980) offer another piece of evidence that documents looseness of linkages between administrator activity and instructional activity. They assessed the effects of district and school organizational structure, administrative policies, rules on individualized instruction, and team teaching. They found two primary sources of effect on individualized instruction; open space architecture and the influence of resources made available by a new statewide early childhood education program. Organizational and administrative features of the school (e.g., administrative style, evaluation policies, and schoolwide instructional policies) showed no discernible effects on individualized instruction. District-level characteristics appeared equally impotent. Results for team teaching proved virtually identical. The authors present a portrayal of the classroom as relatively autonomous, with organizational and instructional characteristics buffered from formal influence by principal, central office personnel, and community. Autonomy also appears to characterize schools within a district, the prevailing pattern looking very much like that reported by Meyer et al. For their colleagues, Deal and Celotti conclude that organizational and administrative arrangements and behavior at the school and district levels leave virtually unaffected the methods of classroom instruction and the way teachers work together in formal instructional teams. Further, various levels—classroom, school, and district—operate as independently from one another as do individuals within each level.

Given (1) the studies reported by Hannaway and Sproull, which have looked at educational organizations via a work-activities modality; (2) the evidence that other direct observations of administrator work has provided about proportion of attention that managers actually devote to instruction; (3) the findings and conclusions reached by Meyer et al.; and (4) the summary offered by Deal and Celotti, what support exists for the case that administrators do make a difference in the instructional activities of schools?

The positive position. Lipham (1981) and Rosenblum and Jastrzab (1980) document the positive influence of the principal on the educational operation of the school. They identify as prominent among the "effective school" observers Austin (1979); Averch (1971); Blumberg and Greenfield (1980); Brookover and Lezotte (1977); Brookover et al. (1979); Clark, Lotto, and McCarthy (1980); Edmonds (1979); Edmonds and Frederiksen (1978); Goldhammer et al. (1971); Henthorn (1980); Mangers (1978; see also California State Legislature, 1977); Olivero (1980); Rutter et al. (1979; and Wynne (1980). These observers cite the contribution of the principal as central in distinguishing schools of more effectiveness from schools of less effectiveness. As Lipham (1981) has put it, principal leadership has "invariably" emerged as the salient factor.

Lipham organizes his argument around eight domains

and issues: (1) working with faculty and community to choose and assess performance on a reasonable number of goals each year; (2) analyzing self and other value orientations, internally and in contact with the community; (3) maintaining a working and workable balance between centralization and decentralization, between school and central office, and within the school; (4) providing direction for the whole school while supporting the work of individuals within the school; (5) distinguishing across the what, who, and how of decision making; (6) demonstrating interest in and capability for shaping the instructional program by allocating the time and attention required; (7) assuming primary responsibility for instituting, implementing, nurturing, and sensibly planning for change; and (8) attending appropriately to school-community relationships in general. Although his data are high inference, his effort to identify behavioral differences offers more help than the listing of personal characteristics offered by Blumberg and Greenfield.

In summary, the literature that has directed itself at describing and explaining the conditions associated with effective schooling has identified the principal as a central factor in reaching effectiveness; has constructed at least one profile of apparently salient personal characteristics to describe principals who lead; and has assembled a set of behavioral statements that generally portray the effective principal.

Rosenblum and Jastrzab treat the literature on change as parallel to the literature on school effectiveness in the search for description and understanding of administrator effects. Early on, they note the shift in attention during the 1970s from central office to school site as the strategic locus for analysis of innovation. Pertinent literature includes Berman and McLaughlin (1975 and 1978), Gaynor (1977), Kent (1979), McLaughlin and Marsh (1978), Sarason (1971 and 1972), Small (1974). Also, relevant are Gross et al. (1971), Smith and Keith (1971), and the full set of essays in Herriott and Gross (1979). As in the case of effective schools, the literature portrays the strategic and pivotal location of the principal or program director in initiating and blocking, maintaining or terminating educational innovation. At the same time, conclude Rosenblum and Jastrzab, the principal does not count for all. As important as his or her posture may be, other factors also affect the life and death of change in schools.

Inquiry and exposition have, then, identified the post of school-site administrator or program head as source of substantial effect, documented and postulated. At the same time, as Rosenblum and Jastrzab perceptively note, the vagueness of treatments of the importance of the principal in promoting both school effectiveness and innovation leaves fundamentally unanswered the question of exactly which administrator behaviors consistently yield or occur in association with exactly what effects, how, and why. In brief, the extant literature on the centrality of the principal in school operation and performance has yet to dispel the darkness still surrounding the establishment of causal connections between patterns of administrator behavior and patterns of school or educational effects. A recent effort in this direction has come from Geske (1981), who suggests how school administrators could make a difference through their resource allocation behavior, a consideration which earlier claimed the attention of Thomas and his associates (Thomas, 1974; Thomas et al., 1978).

Literature that focuses specifically on superintendents offers about the same level of uncertain and unsettled insights on administrator effects as literature on principals. Cuban's (1976) perceptive treatment of three big city superintendents of schools suggests that determined executives can, indeed, introduce programs that shape educational activities, but even in these three cases the specific behaviors of the main actors show through only dimly. Evidence from Levy, Meltsner, and Wildavsky (1974) reveals that a new superintendent in Oakland (California) effected a substantial redistribution in allocation of teacher resources, but exactly how does not appear. Boyd's (1974) analysis of the educational and political behavior of superintendents suggests that too heavy a tilt toward the role of educational statesman can spell political disaster, but offers little insight on the dynamics of affecting program as such. Tyack's (1976) historical contribution to understanding conditions that shaped development of the superintendency, including personal orientations and values, addresses an altogether different pattern of questions and issues.

Commentary on Work and Effects. Direct observation studies have begun to produce mounds of data about administrator work that deserve careful refinement and processing lest the sheer volume of detail bury both reporters and readers before either group achieves useful enlightenment. Both direct observation studies and surveys have yielded contradictory findings and conclusions about the reality of administrator effect on the operation and performance of educational institutions. Time and circumstance appear opportune for major efforts to construct models of the managerial technology and the core technology of educational organizations, with an intent to discern actual and potential empirical association between the two.

Conclusions

The decade of the 1970s witnessed the growth of uncertainty and turbulence in the environment of educational institutions. Students of educational economics, politics, and policy documented and involved themselves in the unsettled conditions more than scholars of the internal administration of education. The latter, for the most part, drew on one dimension or another of the traditional paradigm, which has guided research in the domain for approximately the last quarter century. Meanwhile, emerging competitors to the traditional paradigm have commanded both uncritical and critical attention from students of educational institutions. Among the more hopeful of the new entries stand those views and associated methodologies that promise to enlighten the world of administrator work and the relationship between administrators' activities and organizational effects.

Norman J. Boyan

See also Administrator Preparation; Business Administration of Schools; Collective Negotiations; Comparative Education Administration; Financing Schools; Governance of Schools; Organization and Administration of Higher Education; School Personnel Policy.

REFERENCES

Abbott, M. Hierarchical impediments to innovation in educational organizations. In M. Abbott & J. Lovell (Eds.), *Change Perspectives in Educational Administration*. Auburn, Ala.: Auburn University, 1965.

Abramowitz, S., & Tenenbaum, E., with Deal, T. E., & Stackhouse, E. A. *High School '77: A Survey of Public Secondary School Principals*. Washington, D.C.: Department of Health, Education, and Welfare, National Institute of Education, 1978. (ERIC Document Reproduction Service No. ED 168 119)

Allison, G. T. *Essence of Decision: Explaining the Cuban Missile Crisis*. Boston: Little, Brown, 1971.

Alutto, J. A., & Belasco, J. A. Patterns of teacher participation in school system decision making. *Educational Administration Quarterly*, 1973, *9*, 27–41.

Anderson, B. D. Socio-economic status of students and school bureaucratization. *Educational Administration Quarterly*, 1971, *7*, 12–24.

Anderson, B. D. School bureaucratization and alienation from high school. *Sociology of Education*, 1973, *46*, 315–344.

Anderson, J. G. Bureaucratic rules: Bearers of authority. *Educational Administration Quarterly*, 1966, *2*, 7–34.

Anderson, J. G. The authority structure of the school: A system of social exchange. *Educational Administration Quarterly*, 1967, *3*, 130–148. (a)

Anderson, J. G. Bureaucratic rules: A final word. *Educational Administration Quarterly*, 1967, *3*, 7–10. (b)

Anderson, J. G. The teacher: Bureaucrat or professional? *Educational Administration Quarterly*, 1967, *3*, 291–300. (c)

Anderson, J. G. *Bureaucracy in Education*. Baltimore: Johns Hopkins Press, 1968.

Argyris, C. *Personality and Organization*. New York: Harper, 1957.

Austin, G. R. Exemplary schools and the search for effectiveness. *Educational Leadership*, 1979, *37*, 10–14.

Averch, H. A. *How Effective Is Schooling?* Santa Monica, Calif.: Rand Corporation, 1971.

Bachrach, S. B., & Mitchell, S. M. Toward a dialogue in the middle range. *Educational Administration Quarterly*, 1981, *17*(3).

Badcock, A. M. Combinations of effective leadership styles in Victorian state high schools. *Journal of Educational Administration*, 1980, *18*, 55–68.

Baldridge, J. V. *Power and Conflict in the University*. New York: Wiley, 1971.

Barnard, C. *The Functions of the Executive*. Cambridge, Mass.: Harvard University Press, 1938.

Becker, H. S. The career of the Chicago public school teacher. *American Journal of Sociology*, 1952, *57*, 470–477.

Becker, H. S. The teacher in the authority structure of the school. *Journal of Educational Sociology*, 1953, *27*, 128–141.

Belasco, J. A., & Alutto, J. A. Decisional participation and teacher satisfaction. *Educational Administration Quarterly*, 1972, *8*(1), 44–58.

Bendix, R. *Max Weber: An Intellectual Portrait*. New York: Anchor Books, 1962.

Berman, P., & McLaughlin, M. W. *Federal Programs Supporting Educational Change. Vol. 4: The Findings in Review*. Santa Monica, Calif.: Rand Corporation, 1975.

Berman, P., & McLaughlin, M. W. *Federal Programs Supporting Educational Change. Vol. 8: Implementing and Sustaining Innovations*. Santa Monica, Calif.: Rand Corporation, 1978.

Bidwell, C. E. The school as a formal organization. In J. G. March (Ed.), *Handbook of Organizations*. Chicago: Rand McNally, 1965.

Bidwell, C. E. Students and schools: Some observations on client trust in client-serving organizations. In W. R. Rosengren & M. Lefton (Eds.), *Organizations and Clients: Essays in the Sociology of Service*. Columbus, Ohio: Merrill, 1970.

Bidwell, C., & Abernathy, D. *Structural and Behavioral Theories of Organizations: A Bibliographic Review* (Working Papers Series No. 5.). Chicago: University of Chicago, Department of Education, Education Finance and Productivity Center, 1979.

Bishop, L. K., & George, J. R. Organizational structure: A factor analysis of structural characteristics of public elementary and secondary schools. *Educational Administration Quarterly*, 1973, *9*(3), 66–80.

Blau, P. M., & Scott, W. R. *Formal Organizations: A Comparative Approach*. San Francisco: Chandler, 1962.

Blumberg, A., & Greenfield, W. *The Effective Principal: Perspectives on School Leadership*. Boston: Allyn & Bacon, 1980.

Boyan, N. J. *A Study of the Formal and Informal Organization of a School Faculty*. Unpublished doctoral dissertation, Harvard University, 1951.

Boyan, N. J. *A Constitutional Perspective on Authority*. Paper delivered at the annual meeting of the American Educational Research Association, Los Angeles, April 1981. (a)

Boyan, N. J. Follow the leader: Commentary on research in educational administration. *Educational Researcher*, 1981, *10*(2), 6–13, 21. (b)

Boyd, W. L. The school superintendent: Educational statesman or political strategist. *Administrator's Notebook*, 1974, *22*(9).

Brennan, B. Principals as bureaucrats. *Journal of Educational Administration*, 1973, *11*, 171–178.

Bridges, E. M. Teacher participation in decision-making. *Administrator's Notebook*, 1964, *12*(9).

Bridges, E. M. Bureaucratic role and socialization. *Educational Administration Quarterly*, 1965, *1*(2), 19–28.

Bridges, E. M. A model for shared decision-making in the school principalship. *Educational Administration Quarterly*, 1967, *3*(1), 49–61.

Bridges, E. M. Subjective and objective aspects of demands for involvement. *Administrator's Notebook*, 1969, *17*(6).

Bridges, E. M. Administrative man: Origin or pawn in decision making. *Educational Administration Quarterly*, 1970, *6*(1), 7–25.

Bridges, E. M. Job satisfaction and teacher absenteeism. *Educational Administration Quarterly*, 1980, *16*, 41–56.

Bridges, E. M.; Doyle, W. J.; & Mahan, D. J. Effects of hierarchical differentiation on group productivity, and risk taking. *Administration Science Quarterly*, 1968, *13*, 305–319.

Brookover, W. B.; Beady, C.; Flood, P.; Schweitzer, J.; & Wisenbaker, J. *School Social Systems and Student Achievement.* New York: Praeger, 1979.

Brookover, W. B., & Lezotte, L. W. *Changes in School Characteristics Coincident with Changes in School Achievement.* East Lansing: Michigan State University, College of Urban Development, 1977.

Brown, J. S. Risk propensity in decision-making: A comparison of business and public school administrators. *Administrative Science Quarterly,* 1970, *15,* 473–481.

Brunetti, F. *The Teacher in the Authority Structure of the Elementary School: a Study of Open-space and Self-contained Classroom Schools.* Unpublished doctoral dissertation, Stanford University, 1970.

Bumbarger, C. A., & Thiemann, F. C. Behind the resource domino—Part I: Acquisition. *Journal of Educational Administration,* 1972, *10,* 3–18.

Byrne, D. R.; Hines, S. A.; & McCleary, L. E. *The National Survey.* Vol. 1 of *The Senior High School Principalship.* Reston, Va.: National Association of Secondary School Principals, 1978. (ERIC Document Reproduction Service No. ED 154 508)

Caldwell, W. E., & Lutz, F. W. The measurement of principal rule administration behavior and its relationship to educational leadership. *Educational Administration Quarterly,* 1978, *14*(2), 63–79.

California State Legislature, Office of the Legislative Analyst. *The School Principal: A Report Pursuant to Resolution Chapter 102 of 1977* (ACR 35, Report 77-26). Sacramento, Calif.: The Legislature, 1977.

Callahan, R. *Education and the Cult of Efficiency.* Chicago: University of Chicago Press, 1962.

Campbell, R. F.; Bridges, E. M.; & Nystrand, R. O. *Introduction to Educational Administration* (5th ed.). Boston: Allyn & Bacon, 1977.

Campbell, R. F., & Newell, L. J. *A Study of Professors of Educational Administration: Problems and Prospects of an Applied Academic Field.* Columbus: University Council for Educational Administration, 1973.

Carlson, R. O. Environmental constraints and organizational consequences: The public school and its clients. In D. E. Griffiths (Ed.), *Behavioral Science and Educational Administration: Sixty-third Yearbook of The National Society for the Study of Education* (Part 2). Chicago: University of Chicago Press, 1964.

Carver, F. D., & Sergiovanni, T. J. Complexity, adaptability, and job satisfaction: An axiomatic theory applied. *Journal of Educational Administration,* 1971, 9, *1,* 10–31.

Clark, D. L. Postscript: From orthodoxy to pluralism. In D. L. Clark, S. McKibbin, & M. Malkas (Eds.), *Alternative Perspectives for Viewing Educational Organization.* San Francisco, Calif.: Far West Laboratory for Educational Research and Development, 1981.

Clark, D. L., & Guba, E. G. *An Inventory of Contextual Conditions Affecting Individual and Institutional Behavior in Schools, Colleges, and Departments of Education* (RITE Occasional Papers). Bloomington: Indiana University, July 1976.

Clark, D. L.; Lotto, L. S.; & McCarthy, M. M. Factors associated with success in urban elementary schools. *Phi Delta Kappan,* 1980, *61,* 467–470.

Clark, D. L.; McKibbin, S.; & Malkas, M. (Eds.), *Alternative Perspectives for Viewing Educational Organizations.* San Francisco, Calif.: Far West Laboratory for Educational Research and Development, 1981.

Clear, D. K., & Seager, R. C. The legitimacy of administrative influence as perceived by selected groups. *Educational Administration Quarterly,* 1971, *7,* 46–63.

Clemson, B. Beyond management information systems. *Educational Administration Quarterly,* 1978, *14*(3), 13–38.

Clemson, B. Harnessing the computer in educational management. *Journal of Educational Administration,* 1980, *18,* 98–113.

Cohen, M. D., & March, J. G. *Leadership and Ambiguity: The American College President.* New York: McGraw-Hill, 1974.

Cohen, M. D.; March, J. G.; & Olsen, J. P. A garbage can model of organizational choice. *Administrative Science Quarterly,* 1972, *17,* 1–25.

Coleman, J. S. *The Adolescent Society.* New York: Free Press, 1961.

Coleman, P. *The Basic Value Dilemmas of the Educational Administrator in the Seventies.* Paper presented at the annual meeting of the Canadian Education Association, 1974. (ERIC Document Reproduction Service No. 108375)

Congreve, W. J. Administrative behavior and staff relations. *Administrator's Notebook,* 1957, *6*(2).

Conway, J. A. Test of linearity between teachers' participation in decision-making and their perception of schools as organizations. *Administrative Science Quarterly,* 1976, *21,* 130–139.

Conway, J. A. Power and participatory decision making in selected English schools. *Journal of Educational Administration,* 1978, *16,* 80–96.

Conway, J. A., & Ables, J. Leader-team belief system congruence and relationships to morale within teaching teams. *Educational Administration Quarterly,* 1973, *9*(2), 22–33.

Corwin, R. G. Professional persons in public organizations. *Educational Administration Quarterly,* 1965, *1*(3), 1–22.

Corwin, R. G. *Militant Professionalism: A Study of Organizational Conflict in High Schools.* New York: Appleton-Century-Crofts, 1970.

Corwin, R. G. Models of educational organizations. In F. N. Kerlinger & J. B. Carroll (Eds.), *Review of Research in Education* (Vol. 2). Itaska, Ill.: F. E. Peacock, 1974.

Crowson, R. L. Implementing accountability. *Administrator's Notebook,* 1974, *22*(5).

Crowson, R. L. *Educational Planning and Models of Decision-making.* June 1975. (ERIC Document Reproduction Service No. 131584)

Crowson, R. L., & Porter-Gehrie, C. The discretionary behavior of principals in large-city schools. *Educational Administration Quarterly,* 1980, *16*(1), 45–69.

Cuban, L. *Urban School Chiefs under Fire.* Chicago: University of Chicago Press, 1976.

Cunningham, L. L., & Gephart, W. J. (Eds.). *Leadership: The Science and the Art Today.* Itasca, Ill.: F. E. Peacock, 1973.

Cusick, P. A. *Inside High School: The Students' World.* New York: Holt, Rinehart & Winston, 1973.

Davis, M. R. *The Contribution of Loose Coupling.* Stanford, Calif.: Stanford University, Center for Research and Development in Teaching, May 1977.

Deal, T. E., & Celotti, L. D. How much influence do (and can) educational administrators have on classrooms? *Phi Delta Kappan,* 1980, *61,* 471–473.

Derr, C. B., & Gabarro, J. J. An organizational contingency theory for education. *Educational Administration Quarterly,* 1972, *8*(2), 26–43.

Doyle, W. J. The effects of leader achieved status on hierarchically differentiated group performance. *Administrator's Notebook,* 1969, *18*(1).

Doyle, W. J., & Ahlbrand, W. P. Hierarchical group performance and leader orientation. *Administrator's Notebook*, 1973, *22*(3).

Dufty, N. F. Some notes on resource allocation in tertiary institutions. *Journal of Educational Administration*, 1976, *14*, 220–235.

Dufty, N. F., & Williams, J. G. Participation in decision-making. *Journal of Educational Administration*, 1979, *17*, 30–38.

Duignan, P. Administration behavior of school superintendents: A descriptive study. *Journal of Educational Administration*, 1980, *18*, 5–26.

Duke, D. L.; Showers, B. K.; & Imber, M. *Teachers as School Decision-makers* (Research Report). Stanford: Institute for Research on Education Finance and Governance, 1979.

Duke, D. L.; Showers, B. K.; & Imber, M. Teachers and shared decision-making: The costs and benefits of involvement. *Educational Administration Quarterly*, 1980, *16*(1), 93–106.

Edmonds, R. Effective schools for the urban poor. *Educational Leadership*, 1979, *37*, 15–21.

Edmonds, R., & Frederiksen, R. *Search for Effective Schools: The Identification and Analysis of City Schools That Are Instructionally Effective for Poor Children.* Cambridge, Mass.: Center for Urban Studies, Harvard University, 1978.

Edwards, W. L. The role of the principal in five New Zealand primary schools: An ethnographic prospective. *Journal of Educational Administration*, 1979, *17*, 248–254.

Elboim-Bror, R. Organizational characteristics of the educational system. *Journal of Educational Administration*, 1973, *11*, 3–21.

ERIC Clearinghouse on Educational Management. Participative decision making. *Research Action Brief*, July 1977. Eugene: University of Oregon, The Clearinghouse.

Erickson, D. A. Moral dilemmas of administrative powerlessness. *Administrator's Notebook*, 1972, *20*(8).

Erickson, D. A. An overdue paradigm shift in educational administration, or how can we get that idiot off the freeway? In L. L. Cunningham, W. G. Hack, & R. O. Nystrand (Eds.), *Educational Administration: The Developing Decades.* Berkeley, Calif.: McCutchan, 1977. (a)

Erickson, D. A. (Ed.). *Educational Organization and Administration.* Berkeley, Calif.: McCutchan, 1977. (b)

Erickson, D. A. Research on educational administration: The state-of-the-art. *Educational Researcher*, 1979, *8*, 9–14.

Etzioni, A. *Modern Organizations.* Englewood Cliffs, N.J.: Prentice-Hall, 1964.

Fayol, H. *General and Industrial Management.* London: Sir Isaac Pitman & Sons, 1949.

Fiedler, F. E. *A Theory of Leadership Effectiveness.* New York: McGraw-Hill, 1967.

Fiedler, F. E., & Chemers, M. M. *Leadership and Effective Management.* Glenview, Ill.: Scott, Foresman, 1974.

Fletcher, L. The historical perspective of educational decision. *Journal of Educational Administration*, 1974, *12*, 71–82.

Follet, M. P. *Creative Experience.* New York: Longmans, Green, 1924.

Fraser, K. P. Supervisory behavior and teacher satisfaction. *Journal of Educational Administration*, 1980, *18*, 224–231.

Fuller, R., & Miskel, C. G. *Work Attachments and Job Satisfaction Among Public School Educators.* Paper presented at the annual meeting of the American Educational Research Association, 1972.

Garland, P., & O'Reilly, R. R. The effect of leader-member interaction on organizational effectiveness. *Educational Administration Quarterly*, 1976, *12*, 9–30.

Gates, P. E.; Blanchard, K. H.; & Hersey, P. Diagnosing educational leadership problems: A situational approach. *Educational Leadership*, 1977, *33*, 348–354.

Gaynor, A. K. Some implications of political systems theory for alternative demand processing mechanisms for public school systems. *Educational Administration Quarterly*, 1971, *7*(1), 34–45.

Gaynor, A. K. The study of change in educational organizations: A review of the literature. In L. L. Cunningham, W. G. Hack, & R. O. Nystrand (Eds.), *Educational Administration: The Developing Decades.* Berkeley, Calif.: McCutchan, 1977.

Gaziel, H. G. Role set conflict and role behavior in an education system: An empirical study of the Israeli General Inspector of Schools. *Journal of Educational Administration*, 1979, *17*, 58–67.

Gephart, W. J. Wrap-up. In L. L. Cunningham & W. J. Gephart (Eds.), *Leadership: The Science and Art Today.* Itasca, Ill.: F. E. Peacock, 1973.

Geske, T. C. School administrators can make a difference. *The Executive Review*, 1981, *2*(4).

Getzels, J. W. A psycho-sociological framework for the study of educational administration. *Harvard Educational Review*, 1952, *22*, 235–246.

Getzels, J. W., & Guba, E. G. Social behavior and the administrative process. *School Review*, 1957, *65*, 423–441.

Getzels, J. W.; Lipham, J. W.; & Campbell, R. F. *Educational Administration as a Social Process.* New York: Harper & Row, 1968.

Glasman, N. S. A perspective on evaluation as an administrative function in education. *Educational Evaluation and Policy Analysis*, 1979, *1*, 39–44.

Glasman, N. S., & Sell, G. R. Values and facts in educational administrative decisions. *Journal of Educational Administration*, 1972, *10*, 142–163.

Goldhammer, K.; Becker, G.; Withycombe, R.; Doyel, F.; Miller, E.; Morgan, C.; Deloretto, L.; & Aldridge, B. *Elementary Principals and Their Schools: Beacons of Brilliance and Potholes of Pestilence.* Eugene: University of Oregon, Center for the Advanced Study of Educational Administration, 1971.

Goodlad, J. I., & Klein, M. F. *Behind the Classroom Door.* Worthington, Ohio: Charles A. Jones, 1970.

Gordon, C. W. *The Social System of the High School: A Study in the Sociology of Adolescence.* Glencoe, Ill.: Free Press, 1957.

Gorton, R. A., & McIntyre, K. E. *The Effective Principal.* Vol. 2 of *The Senior High School Principalship.* Reston, Va.: National Association of Secondary School Principals, 1978.

Gracey, H. L. *Curriculum or Craftsmanship: Elementary School Teachers in a Bureaucratic System.* Chicago: University of Chicago Press, 1972.

Grassie, M. C., & Carss, B. W. School structure, leadership quality, and teacher satisfaction. *Educational Administration Quarterly*, 1973, *9*(1), 15–26.

Greenfield, T. B. Organizations as social inventions: Rethinking assumptions about change. *Journal of Applied Behavioral Science*, 1973, *9*, 551–574.

Greenfield, T. B. Theory about organization: A new perspective and its implication for schools. In M. Hughes (Ed.), *Administering Education: International Challenge.* London: University of London, Athlone Press, 1975.

Greenfield, T. B. Theory about what? Some more thoughts about theory in educational administration. *UCEA Review*, 1976, *17*(3), 4–9.

Greenfield, T. B. *Organization Theory as Ideology.* Paper presented at the annual meeting of the American Educational Research Association, 1977.

Greenfield, T. B. Reflections on organization theory and the truths of irreconcilable realities. *Educational Administration Quarterly*, 1978, *14*, 1–23.

Greenfield, T. B. Ideas versus data: How can the data speak for themselves? In G. L. Immegart & W. L. Boyd (Eds.), *Problem-finding in Educational Administration: Trends in Research and Theory*. Lexington, Mass.: Heath, 1979.

Greenfield, T. B. The man who comes back through the door in the wall: Discovering truth, discovering self, discovering organizations. *Educational Administration Quarterly*, 1980, *16*, 26–59.

Gregg, R. T. The administrative process. In R. F. Campbell & R. T. Gregg (Eds.), *Administrative Behavior in Education*. New York: Harper & Row, 1957.

Griffiths, D. E. Administration as decision-making. In W. Halpin (Ed.), *Administrative Theory in Education*. Chicago: University of Chicago, Midwest Administration Center, 1958.

Griffiths, D. E. *Administrative Theory*. New York: Appleton-Century-Crofts, 1959.

Griffiths, D. E. Administrative theory. In R. L. Ebel (Ed.), *Encyclopedia of Educational Research* (4th ed.). New York: Macmillan, 1969. (a)

Griffiths, D. E. A taxonomy based on decision-making. In D. E. Griffiths (Ed.), *Developing Taxonomies of Organizational Behavior in Educational Administration*. Chicago: Rand McNally, 1969. (b)

Griffiths, D. E. Some thoughts about theory in educational administration—1975. *UCEA Review*, 1975 *17*(1), 17.

Griffiths, D. E. The individual in organization: A theoretical perspective. *Educational Administration Quarterly*, 1977, *13*, 1–18.

Griffiths, D. E. Another look at research on the behavior of administrators. In G. L. Immegart & W. L. Boyd (Eds.), *Problem-finding in Educational Administration: Trends in Research and Theory*. Lexington, Mass.: Heath, 1979. (a)

Griffiths, D. E. Intellectual turmoil in educational administration. *Educational Administration Quarterly*, 1979, *15*, 43–65. (b)

Gross, N. C.; Giaquinta, J. B.; & Bernstein, M. *Organizational Innovation: A Sociological Analysis of Planned Educational Change*. New York: Basic Books, 1971.

Gross, N. C., & Herriott, R. E. *Staff Leadership in Public Schools*. New York: Wiley, 1965.

Guba, E. G. Reaction to "Suggestions for leadership research." In L. L. Cunningham & W. J. Gephart (Eds.), *Leadership: The Science and Art Today*. Itasca, Ill.: F. E. Peacock, 1973.

Gulick, L., & Urwick, L. (Eds.). *Papers on the Science of Administration*. New York: Columbia University, Institute of Public Administration, 1937.

Hacker, T. Management by objectives for schools. *Administrator's Notebook*, 1971, *20*(3).

Halpin, A. W. *The Leader Behavior of School Superintendents*. Columbus: Ohio State University, College of Education, 1956.

Hannaway, J., & Sproull, L. S. Who's running the show? Coordination and control in educational organizations. *Administrator's Notebook*, 1979, *27*(9).

Hanson, E. M. The emerging control structure of schools. *Administrator's Notebook*, 1972, *21*(2). (a)

Hanson, E. M. Structural and administrative decentralization in education: A clarification of concepts. *Journal of Educational Administration*, 1972, *10*, 95–103. (b)

Hanson, E. M. The modern educational bureaucracy and the pro-

cess of change. *Educational Administration Quarterly*, 1975, *11*(3), 21–36.

Hanson, E. M. The professional/bureaucratic interface: A case study. *Urban Education*, 1976, *11*, 313–332.

Hanson, E. M. *Educational Administration and Organizational Behavior*. Boston: Allyn & Bacon, 1979.

Hanson, E. M., & Brown, M. E. A contingency view of problem-solving in schools: A case analysis. *Educational Administration Quarterly*, 1977, *13*(2), 71–91.

Hayman, J. L., Jr. Educational management information systems for the seventies. *Educational Administration Quarterly*, 1974, *10*(1), 60–71.

Hemphill, J. K., & Coons, A. E. *Leader Behavior Description*. Columbus: Ohio State University, Personnel Research Board, 1950.

Hemphill, J. K.; Griffiths, D. E.; & Frederiksen, N. *Administrative Performance and Personality*. New York: Columbia University, Teachers College, Bureau of Publications, 1962.

Hencley, S. Impediments to accountability. *Administrator's Notebook*, 1971, *20*(4).

Henthorn, J. *Principal Effectiveness: A Review of the Literature*. Burlingame: Association of California School Administrators, 1980.

Hentschke, G. C. Reforms in urban school district policy-making. *Educational Administration Quarterly*, 1980, *16*(2), 77–99.

Herriott, R. E., & Gross, N. (Eds.) *The Dynamics of Planned Educational Change: Case Studies and Analysis*. Berkeley, Calif.: McCutchan, 1979.

Hill, M. Toward a taxonomy of bureaucratic behavior in educational organizations. In D. E. Griffiths (Ed.), *Developing Taxonomies of Organizational Behavior in Educational Administration*. Chicago: Rand McNally, 1969.

Hills, J. Some comments on James G. Anderson's "Bureaucratic rules: Bearers of organizational authority." *Educational Administration Quarterly*, 1966, *2*, 243–261.

Hills, J. On accountability in education. *Administrator's Notebook*, 1973, *21*(6).

Hills, J. On accountability in education. *Educational Administration Quarterly*, 1974, *10*(1), 1–17.

Holdaway, E. A. Facet and overall satisfaction of teachers. *Educational Administration Quarterly*, 1978, *14*, 30–47.

Hollon, C. J., & Gemmill, G. R. A comparison of female and male professors on participation in decision-making, job-related tension, job involvement, and job satisfaction. *Educational Administration Quarterly*, 1976, *12*, 80–93.

Holloway, W. H., & Niazi, G. A. A study of leadership style, situation favorableness, and the risk-taking behavior of leaders. *Journal of Educational Administration*, 1978, *16*, 160–168.

Hoy, W. K., & Miskel, C. G. *Educational Administration: Theory, Research, and Practice*. New York: Random House, 1978.

Hoy, W. K.; Newland, W.; & Blazovsky, R. Subordinate loyalty to superior, esprit, and aspects of bureaucratic structure. *Educational Administration Quarterly*, 1977, *13*, 71–85.

Hoy, W. K., & Rees, R. Subordinate loyalty to immediate superior: A neglected concept in the study of educational administration. *Sociology of Education*, 1974, *47*, 268–286.

Hoy, W. K.; Tarter, C. J.; & Forsyth, P. Administrative behavior and subordinate loyalty: An empirical assessment. *Journal of Educational Administration*, 1978, *16*, 29–38.

Hoy, W. K., & Williams, L. B. Loyalty to immediate superior at alternate levels in public schools. *Educational Administration Quarterly*, 1971, *7*(2), 1–11.

Hy, R. J., & Mathews, W. M. Decision-making practices of public service administrators. *Public Personnel Management*, 1978, *7*, 148–154.

Iannaccone, L. Informal organization of school systems (Chap. 14), leadership in Whitman (Chap. 15), and the stability of informal organization (Chap. 16). In D. E. Griffiths, D. L. Clark, D. R. Wynn, & L. Iannaccone, *Organizing Schools for Effective Education*. Danville, Ill.: Interstate, 1962.

Iannaccone, L. An approach to the informal organization of the school. In D. E. Griffiths (Ed.), *Behavioral Science and Educational Administration: Sixty-third Yearbook of the National Society for the Study of Education* (Part 2). Chicago: University of Chicago Press, 1964.

Iannaccone, L., & Cistone, P. J. *The Politics of Education*. Eugene: University of Oregon, ERIC Clearinghouse on Educational Management, 1974. (ERIC Document Reproduction Service No. ED 091 803)

Immegart, G. L. Suggestions for leadership research: Toward a strategy for the study of leadership in education. In L. L. Cunningham & W. J. Gephart (Eds.), *Leadership: The Science and Art Today*. Itasca, Ill.: F. E. Peacock, 1973.

Immegart, G. L. The study of educational administration, 1954–1974. In L. L. Cunningham, W. G. Hack, & R. O. Nystrand (Eds.), *Educational Administration: The Developing Decades*. Berkeley, Calif.: McCutchan, 1977.

Immegart, G. L., & Boyd, W. L. *Problem-finding in Educational Administration: Trends in Research and Theory*. Lexington, Mass.: Heath, 1979.

Inbar, D. E. Perceived authority and responsibility of elementary school principals in Israel. *Journal of Educational Administration*, 1977, *15*, 80–91.

Inbar, D. E. Organizational role climates: Success-failure configurations in educational leadership. *Journal of Educational Administration*, 1980, *18*, 232–244.

Inkpen, W. E.; Ponder, A. A.; & Crocker, R. A. Elementary teacher participation in educational decision-making in Newfoundland. *Canadian Administrator*, 1975, *14*(4), 1–5.

Isherwood, G. B., & Hoy, W. K. Bureaucratic structure reconsidered. *Journal of Experimental Education*. 1972, *41*, 47–50.

Isherwood, G. B., & Hoy, W. K. Bureaucracy, powerlessness, and teacher work values. *Journal of Educational Administration*, 1973, *11*, 124–138.

Jackson, P. M. *Life in Classrooms*. New York: Holt, Rinehart & Winston, 1968.

Johnson, G. A comment on "Rational decision-making in education: Some concerns." *Educational Administration Quarterly*, 1976, *12*(3), 103–109.

Kent, J. The management of educational change efforts in school systems. In R. E. Herriott and N. Gross (Eds.), *The Dynamics of Planned Educational Change: Case Studies and Analysis*. Berkeley, Calif.: McCutchan, 1979.

Kimbrough, R. B., & Nunnery, M. Y. *Educational Administration: An Introduction*. New York: Macmillan, 1976.

Knezevich, S. J. *Administration of Public Education* (3rd ed.). New York: Harper & Row, 1975.

Knezevich, S. J. (Ed.). *The American School Superintendent*. Arlington, Va.: American Association of School Administrators, 1971.

Kolesar, H. *An Empirical Study of Client Alienation in the Bureaucratic Organization*. Unpublished doctoral dissertation, University of Alberta, 1967.

Kuhlman, E., & Hoy, W. K. The socialization of professionals into bureaucracies: The beginning teacher in the school. *Journal of Educational Administration*, 1974, *8*, 18–27.

Kunz, D. W., & Hoy, W. K. Leadership style of principals and the professional zone of acceptance of teachers. *Educational Administration Quarterly*, 1976, *12*(3), 49–64.

Kurke, L. B., & Aldrich, H. E. *Mintzberg Was Right! A Replication and Extension of "The Nature of Managerial Work."* Paper presented at the annual meeting of the Academy of Management, 1979.

Larson, L. L.; Bussom, R. S.; & Vicars, W. M. *The Nature of a School Superintendent's Work* (Final Technical Report). Carbondale: Southern Illinois University, College of Business and Administration, Department of Administrative Sciences, 1981.

Lawrence, P. R., & Lorsch, J. W. *Organization and Environment*. Homewood, Ill.: Richard D. Irwin, 1969.

Levy, F. S., Meltsner, A. J., & Wildavsky, A. *Urban Outcomes: Schools, Streets, and Libraries*. Berkeley, Calif.: University of California Press, 1974.

Likert, R. *New Patterns of Management*. New York: McGraw-Hill, 1961.

Likert, R. *The Human Organization*. New York: McGraw-Hill, 1967.

Lipham, J. M. Leadership and administration. In D. E. Griffiths (Ed.), *Behavioral Science and Educational Administration: Sixty-third Yearbook of the National Society for the Study of Education* (Part 2). Chicago: University of Chicago Press, 1964.

Lipham, J. M. Making effective decisions. In J. A. Culbertson, C. Henson, & R. Morrison (Eds.), *Performance Objectives for School Principals*. Berkeley, Calif.: McCutchan, 1974.

Lipham, J. M. *Effective Principal, Effective School*. Reston, Va.: National Association of Secondary School Principals, 1981.

Lipham, J. M., & Hoeh, J. A., Jr. *The Principalship: Foundations and Functions*. New York: Harper & Row, 1974.

Lortie, D. C. The balance of control and autonomy in elementary school teaching. In A. Etzioni (Ed.), *The Semi-professions and Their Organization*. New York: Free Press, 1969.

Lortie, D. C. Observations on teaching as work. In R. M. W. Travers (Ed.), *Second Handbook of Research on Teaching*. Chicago: Rand McNally, 1973.

Lortie, D. C. *School Teacher*. Chicago: University of Chicago Press, 1975.

Lutz, F. W., & Evans, S. *The Union Contract and Principal Leadership in New York City Schools*. New York: Center for Urban Education, 1968.

MacKay, D. A. *An Empirical Study of Bureaucratic Dimensions and Their Relations to Other Characteristics of School Organization*. Unpublished doctoral dissertation, University of Alberta, 1964.

MacKay, D. A. Research on bureaucracy in schools: The unfolding of a strategy. *Journal of Educational Administration*, 1969, *7*, 37–44.

Maddock, J., & Hyams, B. Professional leadership within some South Australian high schools. *Journal of Educational Administration*, 1979, *17*, 51–57.

Mangers, D. *The School Principal: Recommendations for Effective Leadership*. Sacramento, Calif.: Task Force for the Improvement of Pre- and In-Service Training for Public School Administrators, 1978.

Mann, D. Public understanding and education decision-making. *Educational Administration Quarterly*, 1974, *10*(2), 1–18.

Mann, D. *Policy Decision-making in Education: An Introduction to Calculation and Control*. New York: Columbia University, Teachers College Press, 1975.

Mann, D. *The Politics of Administrative Representation: School*

Administrators and Local Democracy. Lexington, Mass.: Heath, 1976. (a)

Mann, D. *Prolegomenon to the Analysis of Non–decision-making.* Paper presented at the annual meeting of the American Educational Research Association, 1976. (b) (ERIC Document Reproduction Service No. ED 120 939)

March, J. G. Analytical skills and the university training of educational administrators. *Journal of Educational Administration,* 1974, *12,* 17–44.

March, J. G. American public school administration: A short analysis. *School Review,* 1978, *86,* 217–249.

March, J. G., & Olsen, J. P. *Ambiguity and Choice in Organizations.* Bergen: University Press of Norway, 1976.

March, J. G., & Simon, H. A. *Organizations.* New York: Wiley, 1958.

Marjoribanks, K. Bureaucratic orientations, autonomy, and the professional attitudes of teachers. *Journal of Educational Administration,* 1977, *15,* 108–113.

Marks, J. L. *On Decision-making Processes and Structures.* 1978. (ERIC Document Reproduction Service No. ED 162 690)

Martin, W. J., & Willower, D. J. The managerial behavior of high school principals. *Educational Administration Quarterly,* 1981, *17,* 69–90.

Martin, Y. M.; Isherwood, G. B.; & Lavery, R. E. Leadership effectiveness in teacher probationary committees. *Educational Administration Quarterly,* 1976, *12,* 87–99.

Martin, Y. M.; Isherwood, G. B.; & Rapagna, S. Supervisory effectiveness. *Educational Administration Quarterly,* 1978, *14,* 74–88.

Mayo, E. *The Human Problems of an Industrial Civilization.* Cambridge, Mass.: Harvard University, Graduate School of Business Administration, 1946.

McCamy, J. L. Analysis of the process of decision making. *Public Administration Review,* 1947, *7,* 41–48.

McCleary, L. E., & Thomson, S. D. *Summary Report.* Vol. III of *The Senior High School Principalship.* Reston, Va.: National Association of Secondary School Principals, 1979. (ERIC Document Reproduction Service No. ED 169 667)

McGivney, J. H., & Haught, J. M. The politics of education: A view from the perspective of the central office staff. *Educational Administration Quarterly,* 1972, *8,* 18–38.

McGregor, D. *The Human Side of Enterprise.* New York: McGraw-Hill, 1960.

McKague, T. LPC: A new perspective on leadership. *Educational Administration Quarterly,* 1970, *6,* 1–14.

McLaughlin, M. W., & Marsh, D. Staff development and school change. *Teachers College Record,* 1978, *80,* 69–94.

McNamara, J. F. Trend impact analysis and scenario writing: Strategies for specification of decision alternatives in educational planning. *Journal of Educational Administration,* 1976, *14,* 143–161.

Mellor, W. L. Structure and rationality in educational information-decision systems. *Journal of Educational Administration,* 1976, *14,* 119–125.

Mellor, W. L. Dynamic information systems in an educational environment. *Educational Administration Quarterly,* 1977, *13*(2), 92–107.

Meyer, J. W., & Cohen, E. G. *The Impact of the Open-Space School upon Teacher Influence and Autonomy: The Effects of an Organizational Innovation* (Technical Report No. 21). Stanford, Calif.: Stanford Center for Research and Development in Teaching, 1971.

Meyer, J. W., & Rowan, B. Institutionalized organization: Formal structure as myth and ceremony. *American Journal of Sociology,* 1977, *83,* 340–363.

Meyer, J. W., & Rowan, B. The structure of educational organizations. In M. W. Meyer & Associates (Eds.), *Environments and Organizations.* San Francisco: Jossey-Bass, 1978.

Meyer, J. W.; Scott, W. R.; Cole, S.; & Intili, J. K. Instructional dissensus and institutional consensus in schools. In M. W. Meyer & Associates (Eds.), *Environments and Organizations.* San Francisco: Jossey-Bass, 1978.

Miles, M. Some properties of schools as social systems. In G. Watson (Ed.), *Change in School Systems.* Washington, D.C.: National Training Laboratory, 1967.

Mintzberg, H. *The Nature of Managerial Work.* New York: Harper & Row, 1973.

Miskel, C. G. The motivation of educators to work. *Educational Administration Quarterly,* 1973, *9,* 42–53.

Miskel, C. G. Intrinsic, extrinsic, and risk propensity factors in the work attitudes of teachers, educational administrators, and business managers. *Journal of Applied Psychology,* 1974, *59,* 339–343. (a)

Miskel, C. G. *Public School Principals' Leader Style, Organizational Situation, and Effectiveness* (Final Report, National Institute of Education). Lawrence: University of Kansas, 1974. (b) (ERIC Document Reproduction Service No. ED 098 659)

Miskel, C. G. Principals' attitudes toward work and co-workers, situational factors, perceived effectiveness, and innovation effort. *Educational Administration Quarterly,* 1977, *13*(2), 51–70. (a)

Miskel, C. G. Principals' perceived effectiveness, innovation effort, and the school situation. *Educational Administration Quarterly,* 1977, *13,* 31–46. (b)

Miskel, C. G.; Fevurly, R.; & Stewart, J. Organizational structure and process, perceived school effectiveness, loyalty, and job satisfaction. *Educational Administration Quarterly,* 1979, *15,* 97–118.

Miskel, C. G., & Gerhardt, E. Perceived bureaucracy, teacher conflict, central life interests, voluntarism, and job satisfaction. *Journal of Educational Administration,* 1974, *12,* 84–97.

Miskel, C. G., Glasnapp, D., & Hatley, R. *Public School Teachers' Work Motivation, Organizational Incentives, Job Satisfaction, and Primary Life Interests* (Final Report, U.S. Office of Education). Washington, D.C.: Office of Education, 1972.

Miskel, C. G.; Glasnapp, D.; & Hatley, R. A test of the inequity theory for job satisfaction using educators' attitudes toward work motivation and work incentives. *Educational Administration Quarterly,* 1975, *11,* 38–54.

Miskel, C. G., & Heller, L. The educational work components study: An adapted set of measures for work motivation. *Journal of Experimental Education,* 1973, *42,* 45–50.

Moeller, G. H. Bureaucracy and teachers' sense of power. *Administration's Notebook,* 1962, *11*(3).

Moeller, G. H., & Charters, W. W. Relation of bureaucratization to sense of power among teachers. *Administrative Science Quarterly,* 1966, *10,* 444–465.

Mohrman, A. M., Jr.; Cooke, R. A.; & Mohrman, S. A. Participation in decision-making: A multidimensional perspective. *Educational Administration Quarterly,* 1978, *14*(1), 13–29.

Monk, D. H. A comprehensive view of resource allocation for education. *Administrator's Notebook,* 1979, *28*(3).

Morphet, E. L.; Johns, R. L.; & Reller, T. L. *Educational Organization and Administration* (3rd ed.). Englewood Cliffs, N.J.: Prentice-Hall, 1974.

Morris, V. C.; Crowson, R. L.; Hurwitz, E.; & Porter-Gehre, C.

The Urban Principal: Discretionary Decision-Making in a Large Educational Organization. Chicago: University of Illinois at Chicago Circle, College of Education, 1981.

Moyle, C. R. J. Principal leader behavior and shared decision-making. *Journal of Educational Administration,* 1979, *17,* 39–50.

Nias, J. Information and the management of innovation. *Journal of Educational Administration,* 1973, *11,* 79–87.

Olivero, J. *The Principalship in California: The Keeper of the Dream.* Newport Beach: Association of California School Administrators, 1980.

Owens, R. G. *Organizational Behavior in Education* (2nd ed.) Englewood Cliffs, N.J.: Prentice-Hall, 1981.

Packard, J. S.; Charters, W. W.; Duckworth, K. E.; & Jovick, T. D. *Management Implications of Team Teaching.* Eugene: University of Oregon, Center for Educational Policy and Management, 1978.

Parsons, T. Some ingredients of a general theory of formal organization. In A. W. Halpin (Ed.), *Administrative Theory in Education.* Chicago: University of Chicago, Midwest Administration Center, 1958.

Pellegrin, R. J. Schools as work settings. In R. Dubin (Ed.), *Handbook of Work, Organizations, and Society.* Chicago: Rand McNally, 1976.

Perrow, C. *Complex Organizations.* Glenview, Ill.: Scott, Foresman, 1972.

Peterson, K. D. The principal's tasks. *Administrator's Notebook,* 1978, *26*(8).

Pharis, W., & Zakariya, S. *The Elementary School Principal in 1978: A Research Study.* Arlington, Va.: National Association of Elementary School Principals, 1979.

Piele, P. K., & Hall, J. S. *Voting in School Financial Elections.* Eugene: University of Oregon, ERIC Clearinghouse on Educational Management, 1973. (ERIC Document Reproduction Service No. ED 082 282)

Pitner, N. J. *Descriptive Study of the Everyday Activities of Suburban School Superintendents: The Management of Information.* Unpublished doctoral dissertation, Ohio State University, 1978.

Pitner, N. J., & Ogawa, R. T. Organizational leadership: The case of the school superintendent. *Educational Administration Quarterly,* 1981, *17,* 45–65.

Pogrow, S. A low-complexity technology for developing computer simulations: Implications for decision-making. *Educational Administration Quarterly,* 1978, *14*(3), 39–60.

Punch, K. F. Bureaucratic structure in schools: Toward redefinition and measurement. *Educational Administration Quarterly,* 1969, *5,* 43–57.

Punch, K. F. Interschool variation in bureaucratization. *Journal of Educational Administration,* 1970, *8,* 123–134.

Punch, K. F., & Ducharme, D. J. Life-cycle leadership theory: Some empirical evidence. *Journal of Educational Administration,* 1972, *10,* 66–77.

Roethlisberger, F. J., & Dixon, W. J. *Management and the Worker.* Cambridge, Mass.: Harvard University Press, 1939.

Rogers, D. *110 Livingston Street.* New York: Random House, 1968.

Rosenblum, S., & Jastrzab, J., with Brigham, N., & Phillips, N. *The Role of the Principal in Change: The Teacher Corps Example.* Cambridge, Mass.: Abt Associates, 1980.

Rutter, M.; Maughm, B.; Mortimore, P.; & Outson, J., with Smith, A. *Fifteen Thousand Hours: Secondary Schools and Their Effects on Children.* Cambridge, Mass.: Harvard University Press, 1979.

Salley, C. Superintendents' job priorities. *Administrator's Notebook,* 1979, *28*(1).

Sarason, S. B. *The Culture of the School and the Problem of Change.* Boston: Allyn & Bacon, 1971.

Sarason, S. B. *The Creation of Settings and the Future Societies.* San Francisco: Jossey-Bass, 1972.

Saxe, R. W. *Educational Administration Today: An Introduction.* Berkeley, Calif.: McCutchan, 1980.

Schwille, J.; Porter, A.; & Gant, M. Content decision-making and the politics of education. *Educational Administration Quarterly,* 1969, *5,* 43–57.

Scott, W. R. Developments in organization theory, 1960–1980. *American Behavior Scientist,* 1981, *24,* 407–422. (a)

Scott, W. R. *Organizations: Rational, Natural, and Open Systems.* Englewood Cliffs, N.J.: Prentice-Hall, 1981. (b)

Sergiovanni, T. J. Factors which affect satisfaction and dissatisfaction of teachers. *Journal of Educational Administration,* 1967, *5,* 66–81.

Sergiovanni, T. J.; Buoluigame, M.; Coombs, D.; & Thurston, W. *Educational Governance and Administration.* Englewood Cliffs, N.J.: Prentice-Hall, 1980.

Sergiovanni, T. J., & Carver, F. D. *The New School Executive: A Theory of Administration* (2nd ed.). New York: Harper & Row, 1980.

Sergiovanni, T. J., & Elliot, D. *Educational and Organizational Leadership in Elementary Schools.* Englewood Cliffs, N.J.: Prentice-Hall, 1975.

Sergiovanni, T. J., & Starratt, R. J. *Supervision: Human Perspectives* (2nd ed.). New York: McGraw-Hill, 1979.

Sharples, B. Rational decision making in education: Some concerns. *Educational Administration Quarterly,* 1975, *11*(2), 55–65.

Sharples, B. Response to "A comment on 'Rational decision making: Some concerns.' " *Educational Administration Quarterly,* 1977, *13*(3), 105–109.

Shetty, Y. K., & Carlisle, H. M. An application of management by objectives in a university setting: An exploratory study of faculty reactions. *Educational Administration Quarterly,* 1974, *10,* 65–81.

Simon, H. A. *Administrative Behavior: A Study of Decision-making Processes in Administrative Organizations.* New York: Macmillan, 1945.

Simon, H. A. *Administrative Behavior: A Study of Decision-making Processes in Administrative Organizations* (2nd ed.). New York: Macmillan, 1957.

Skilbeck, M. Administrative decisions and cultural values. *Journal of Educational Administration,* 1972, *10,* 128–141.

Small, J. F. Initiating and responding to social change. In J. A. Culbertson, C. Henson, & R. Morrison (Eds.), *Performance Objectives for School Principals: Concepts and Instruments.* Berkeley, Calif.: McCutchan, 1974.

Smith, C. S. Resource allocation in education. *Journal of Educational Administration,* 1971, *9,* 135–150.

Smith, L. M., & Keith, P. M. *Anatomy of an Educational Innovation: An Organizational Analysis of an Elementary School.* New York: Wiley, 1971.

Smyth, W. J. Pupil control ideology and the salience of teacher characteristics. *Journal of Educational Administration,* 1977, *15,* 238–248.

Solomon, B. A comment on "The authority structure of the school." *Educational Administration Quarterly,* 1967, *3,* 281–290.

Spence, L. D.; Takei, Y.; & Sim, F. M. *Conceptualizing Loose*

Coupling: Believing Is Seeing, or the Garbage Can as Myth and Ceremony. Paper presented at the annual meeting of the American Sociological Association, 1978.

Sproull, L. S. Managing education programs: A micro-behavioral analysis. *Human Organization*, 1981, *40*, 113–122. (a)

Sproull, L. S. Response to regulation: An organizational process framework. *Administration and Society*, 1981, *12*, 447–440. (b)

Sproull, L. S.; Weiner, S. S.; & Wolf, D. B. *Organizing an Anarchy.* Chicago: University of Chicago Press, 1978.

Spuck, D. W. Reward structures in the public high school. *Educational Administration Quarterly*, 1974, *10*(1), 18–34.

Swan, B. A study of faculty staff reactions to three types of leadership. *Journal of Educational Administration*, 1980, *18*, 283–287.

Taylor, F. W. *The Principles of Scientific Management.* New York: Harper & Brothers, 1911.

Telfer, R. Agreement in perception of decision points by school staff, and the specificity of school policies in some New South Wales secondary schools. *CORE: Collected Original Resources in Education*, 1978, *2*, 1–4. (a)

Telfer, R. Decision congruence and the sex of school administrators. *Journal of Educational Administration*, 1978, *16*, 39–45. (b)

Thiemann, F. C., & Bumbarger, C. S. Behind the resource domino—Part II: Allocation. *Journal of Educational Administration*, 1972, *10*, 184–196.

Thomas, J. A. The productive school: A systems analysis approach to educational administration. New York: Wiley, 1971.

Thomas, J. A. Educational planning in school districts. *Administrator's Notebook*, 1974, *22*(7).

Thomas, J. A.; Kemmerer, F.; & Monk, D. H. Educational administration: A multi-level perspective. *Administrator's Notebook*, 1978, *27*(4).

Thompson, J. *Organizations in Action.* New York: McGraw-Hill, 1967.

Thornton, R. Organizational-professional commitment and supervision of the junior college teacher. *Educational Administration Quarterly*, 1971, *7*(2), 25–39.

Tronc, K. E. Leadership perceptions of the ambitious education. *Journal of Educational Administration*, 1970, *8*, 145–168.

Trusty, F. M., & Sergiovanni, T. J. Perceived needs deficiencies of teachers and administrators. *Educational Administration Quarterly*, 1966, *2*, 168–180.

Tucker, H. J., & Zeigler, L. H. *The Politics of Educational Governance.* Eugene: University of Oregon, ERIC Clearinghouse on Educational Management, 1980. (ERIC Document Reproduction Service No. ED 182 799)

Tyack, D. B. Pilgrim's progress: Toward a social history of the school superintendency, 1860–1960. *History of Education Quarterly*, 1976, *16*, 257–294.

van Geel, T. PPBES and district resource allocation. *Administrator's Notebook*, 1973, *22*(1).

Waller, W. *The Sociology of Teaching.* New York: Wiley, 1932.

Weatherley, R., & Lipsky, M. Street-level bureaucrats and institutional innovation: Implementing special education reform. *Harvard Educational Review*, 1977, *47*, 171–197.

Weick, K. E. Educational organizations as loosely coupled systems. *Administrative Science Quarterly*, 1976, *21*, 1–19.

Wiles, D. K. Politics and planning: A rationale for synthesis in educational administration. *Educational Administration Quarterly*, 1974, *10*(1), 44–59.

Williams, L. B., & Hoy, W. K. Principal-staff relations: Situational mediator of effectiveness. *Journal of Educational Administration*, 1971, *9*, 66–73.

Willis, Q. The work activity of school principals: An observational study. *Journal of Educational Administration*, 1980, *18*, 27–54.

Willower, D. J. Some comments on inquiries on schools and student control. *Teachers College Record*, 1975, *77*, 32–59.

Willower, D. J. Schools and pupil control. In D. A. Erickson (Ed.), *Educational Organization and Administration.* Berkeley, Calif.: McCutchan, 1977.

Willower, D. J. Ideology and science in organization theory. *Educational Administration Quarterly*, 1979, *15*, 20–42. (a)

Willower, D. J. Some issues in research on school organizations. In G. L. Immegart & W. L. Boyd (Eds.), *Problem-finding in Educational Administration: Trends in Research and Theory.* Lexington, Mass.: Heath, 1979. (b)

Willower, D. J. Contemporary issues in theory in educational administration. *Educational Administration Quarterly*, 1980, *16*, 1–25.

Willower, D. J. *Educational Administration: Some Philosophical and Other Considerations.* Paper presented at Conference for Lectures in Educational Administration, Welbourne, Australia, August 1981.

Willower, D. J.; Eidell, T. L.; & Hoy, W. K. *The School and Pupil Control Ideology* (Penn State Studies No. 24, 1st and 2nd eds.). University Park: Pennsylvania State University, 1967 and 1973.

Willower, D. J., & Fraser, H. W. School superintendents on their work. *Administrator's Notebook*, 1980, *28*(5).

Wolcott, H. F. *The Man in the Principal's Office: An Ethnography.* New York: Holt, Rinehart & Winston, 1973.

Wynne, E. A. *Looking at Schools: Good, Bad, and Indifferent.* Lexington, Mass.: Heath, 1980.

ADMINISTRATOR PREPARATION

Preparation for the role of educational administrator begins at the school level as teachers observe their supervisors and administrators. Those teachers who exhibit some leadership qualities and thus gain the attention of their superordinates (Griffiths et al., 1963) are, in turn, observed by their superiors and assessed informally in terms of their administrative potential. From the pool of more visible teachers, then, some are selected for further encouragement and actual informal training (Valverde, 1980). In this way teachers are introduced to the values and vocabulary of the superordinate group and given additional exposure to learning experiences and to central office leaders. In brief, most of the preparation for administrative practice that educators experience is informal in nature and obtained at the school and district site.

Once a teacher has decided to pursue a career in administration, however, further training of a more formal nature is required. This training, most often accomplished at a university in a graduate program in educational administration, affords a broader view of education systems, familiarity with a body of knowledge pertinent to various facets of administration, and an introduction to an array of conceptual, technical, and human relations skills. It is upon this phase of administrator preparation—the formal, preservice, university-based stage—that the major portion of this article focuses.

Having completed a certificate-oriented or degree-oriented program, the candidate is qualified to compete for appointment to an administrative position. Administrator preparation does not end, however, with the completion of a formal program. Practicing administrators continue to learn on the job as they encounter new experiences and develop strategies for confronting them (Argyris & Schön, 1974) and as they increase their contacts with successively higher echelons in the administrative hierarchy. In addition, the rapidly changing environment and the development of new technologies necessitate the continuation of learning through various types of in-service education. Continuing professional education will be considered in the latter portion of this essay. The concluding section considers emerging interests in the field.

University-based Preparation Programs

Educational administration, as a field of study distinguished from teacher education, is of relatively recent origin. The first doctorates in this field were granted in 1905 at Columbia University to Elwood Cubberley and George Strayer (Callahan, 1962), both of whom received their degrees in education but with special emphasis in administration. They then embarked upon teaching careers, Cubberley at Stanford and Strayer at Columbia, entailing the establishment of graduate programs in educational administration and the training not only of administrators but of numerous professors who, in turn, launched graduate programs at other institutions. In the seven decades since the field was founded, preparation programs have evolved considerably, as might be expected, in demographic features, contents, processes, and products.

Demographic Features. Currently, there are three levels of graduate programs in educational administration: master's programs, which might be directed toward Master of Arts (M.A.), Master of Science (M.S.) or Master of Education (M.Ed.) degrees; intermediate or sixth-year programs directed toward state certification or Education Specialist (Ed.S.) or Certificate of Advanced Study (C.A.S.) degrees; and doctoral programs, including Doctor of Education (Ed.D.) or Doctor of Philosophy (Ph.D.) degrees. This proliferation of programs parallels the explosive expansion in numbers of training institutions, students, and professors in this field since its inception.

Institutions and degrees. Culbertson (1972) traced the growth in the number of training institutions from 1940 to 1970 and projected further growth until 1980. According to his data the number of institutions offering administrator preparation programs tripled during that period, so that by 1972 there were about three hundred sixty such institutions in the United States. Growth in the number of intermediate programs was the most pro-

nounced, from fewer than ten such programs before 1941 to almost one hundred fifty by 1970, and continued growth to over two hundred of these intermediate programs was projected for the 1970–1980 decade. Mitchell and Hawley (1972) noted that there were approximately ninety universities offering doctorates in educational administration by 1950 and several hundred master's degree programs at that time. By 1970 there were about twelve hundred distinguishable state-accredited programs for educational leaders in the three hundred sixty or so institutions offering programs (Mitchell & Hawley, 1972).

The numbers of degree recipients have, of course, expanded concomitantly. In 1970/71 alone there were 7,702 master's degrees in educational administration and 707 in educational supervision awarded, according to data from the National Center for Educational Statistics (Knezevich, n.d.). At the doctoral level there were 957 degrees awarded in educational administration and 71 in educational supervision that year (Knezevich, n.d.). The growth in numbers of degree holders in this field is exemplified by the 449 doctorates awarded in 1956/57 compared to the 1,028 awarded in 1970/71, an increase of well over 100 percent in yearly productivity in the sixteen-year period.

Students. The types of students toward whom preparation programs are directed have changed substantially over the years. Initially designed for practicing superintendents of schools and superintendents planning to become professors, programs have become more varied and pertinent to a broader range of leadership positions. Master's programs are typically directed toward persons seeking or occupying building-level administrative and district-level supervisory positions; doctoral programs, on the other hand, tend to be geared for persons seeking those positions as well as district-level, regional-level or state-level administrative posts and for prospective professors and higher education administrators (Davis & Spuck, 1978). Some scholars have recommended further expansion of the range of positions and functions for which educational administrators are prepared, such as planning and "power brokerage" (Campbell, 1976), administration in nonschool settings (Culbertson, 1972), and "educational linking agentry" (Crandall, 1977).

The students in administrator preparation programs have generally been local people raised and educated in the vicinity of the preparing university (Mitchell & Hawley, 1972). The majority, even at the doctoral level, have full-time jobs and attend graduate school only on a part-time basis. They are predominantly Caucasian (about 84 percent at the doctoral level) and male (roughly 77 percent at the doctoral level), according to recent survey data (Davis & Spuck, 1978). The proportions of minority and female students show a marked increase over two decades ago, when only a negligible percentage of prospective administrators were in these groups. Some authors, including McIntyre (1966) and Weaver (1979), have noted that the quality of educational administration students, as measured by standardized tests and undergraduate grade point averages, is poor in comparison to the other professions.

Faculty. Like the students, professors of educational administration and supervision have become more numerous, more highly specialized, and more diverse over the years. Two major surveys conducted in the 1970s (Campbell & Newell, 1973; Silver & Spuck, 1978) provide ample information about the professoriate. In the mid-1970s there were approximately 6 full-time faculty members in each department of educational administration (Davis, 1978), or an estimated 2,411 full-time professors as well as numerous part-time faculty members in this field. Generally somewhat older than faculties in other fields, the professors in this field averaged 48 years of age in the earlier survey. About 50 percent of these faculty members held full professor rank in the mid-1970s, and only about 18 percent were at the assistant professor rank at that time. Whereas only 2 percent of educational administration professors were females in the earlier study, an estimated 10 percent of faculties were female in the mid-1970s. Minority group members constituted about 3 percent of faculty membership in 1972, and it can be assumed their proportional increase during the past decade has roughly paralleled that of women.

During the first half of this century, professors were typically drawn from the pool of superintendents, who taught about their experiences and drew upon prescriptive textbooks authored by their colleagues (Farquhar, 1977). Beginning in the 1950s a different breed of individuals entered the professorship—specialists in particular technologies or behavioral science disciplines, people who may not have had extensive field experience but who could bring technical or conceptual expertise to the education of administrators.

Influences upon growth. Some of the major forces that influenced this tremendous growth and diversification of preparation programs were the massive migrations of population to urban centers, the growth and increasing complexity of schools and school systems, advances in technical knowledge in business and industry, increasingly stringent certification requirements by the states, and changing cultural values. With the advent of mass production came both urban concentration, requiring large schools that could train the rural and foreign immigrants for gainful employment (Katz, 1971), and an esteem for expertise, especially scientific knowledge, that superceded the value given to culture and refinement in earlier eras. Symptomatic of the "cult of efficiency" and the rising social status of the "expert" was the establishment and increasing stringency of certification requirements initiated by state departments of education. Whereas early in the century these requirements usually entailed teacher training and administrative experience, they increasingly included graduate course work as the century progressed (University Council for Educational Administration, 1973). By the mid 1960s the states typically required completion of the

doctorate or seventy hours of graduate study to qualify for the superintendency (Farquhar, 1977) and between thirty and fifty graduate credit hours for the principalship. During the 1960s, with popular movements supporting cultural diversity and special interests, and with the availability of federal dollars to provide advanced and diversified educational opportunities, graduate programs were able to increase enormously and to attract more varied professors and students.

Currently graduate education seems to have reached a peak, and educational administration departments are likely to diminish in size as the decade progresses. The 1970s saw a downward trend in population size as well as spiraling inflation accompanied by increased unemployment; these factors have been associated with school closings, curtailment of programs, and district consolidations, all of which reduce the demand for administrators. In the early 1980s the national government's vow to reduce federal spending portends further reductions in the numbers and sizes of administrative preparation programs. Already, some state governments have undertaken assessments directed toward reducing the number of accredited doctoral programs in educational administration in public and private universities.

Program Content. The expansion of subject matter treated in preparation programs coincided approximately with the first three 25-year periods in this century. These three eras were respectively dominated by interest in scientific management, human relations, and behavioral science (Getzels, 1977).

Scientific management. According to Callahan (1962), the founders of the field of educational administration were imbued with the spirit of efficiency as articulated by outstanding industrial leaders. The types of efficiency studies conducted in business during the first quarter of this century were adapted to educational settings as district surveys and investigations directed toward increasing "productivity" while reducing costs. Thus, the content of preparation programs from about 1900 to about 1925 consisted of personal accounts, or "war stories," and prescriptions offered by experienced practitioners (Farquhar, 1977) as well as the findings of school surveys that were undertaken in great numbers (Callahan, 1962).

As the technologies for scientific management in business and industry became more sophisticated, these advances were reflected in preparation program content. They survive in contemporary programs in the form of courses dealing with systems analysis and with planning technologies such as Program Evaluation and Review Technique (PERT) and Management By Objectives (MBO). This type of technical content is found either in courses on specific technologies or in aspects of courses dealing with computer use, decision making, and school finance or business management (Bruno & Fox, 1973).

Human relations. Following the startling findings of the famous Hawthorne studies, which had been designed as scientific management research *par excellence*—

namely, that workers' productivity increased irrespective of experimental treatments applied (Roethlisberger & Dickson, 1939)—specialists in business management became increasingly interested in the human element in organizations. The Hawthorne research findings gave impetus to the development of the discipline of social psychology and the profession of industrial psychology, both of which emphasize the interdependence of individuals' personalities and of institutional structures in organizations, but not at the expense of the individual.

The orientation toward the human factor in business administration found its way into preparation programs in educational administration when readings by such leading authorities on management as McGregor, Argyris, and Maslow became incorporated into course content. Issues such as employee satisfaction and motivation, job enrichment, and personal growth and development were added to the curriculum of educational administration in the form of courses in "the human factor," sensitivity or leadership training experiences, and emphasis on the development of human relations skills. In the 1960s content drawn from the humanities was also added to many preparation programs (University Council for Educational Administration, 1973) to further broaden administrators' perspectives, help illuminate value dilemmas, and enhance leaders' creativity (Farquhar, 1970).

The human relations orientation, still prevalent in administrator preparation programs, is expressed in several forms: as courses devoted to such topics as organization development and human relations; as aspects of courses such as administrative theory and supervision; and as cognate or foundations courses in philosophy and the arts.

Behavioral science. The most recent movement in educational administration, roughly from 1950 to 1975, was triggered by advances in the growing social science disciplines and by developments in the philosophy of science, particularly the emergence of logical positivism as a widely accepted mode of knowledge production (Culbertson, 1980a). When many of the leading European philosophers of the Vienna Circle migrated to this country as a result of World War II and became established in major universities here, they impressed American scholars with the need for explanatory theories and methods of objective verification in the process of generating scientific knowledge about human phenomena.

The landmark event that first saw the role of theory in administrative research enunciated was the 1954 session of the National Conference of Professors of Educational Administration (NCPEA) in Denver (Halpin & Hayes, 1977). Scholars in behavioral science disciplines as well as those in educational administration participated, and the outcomes were numerous: a spirit of enthusiasm stimulating a series of conferences in the 1950s; major theory-oriented publications by such authors as Coladarci and Getzels (1955), Halpin (1958), and Griffiths (1959); and the establishment of the Cooperative Program in Educational Administration (CPEA) in 1950 at five (later expanded to eight) leading universities with support from the Kellogg Foundation (Culbertson & Shibles, 1973). Later, the CPEA was instrumental in founding the University Council for Educational Administration (UCEA) in 1959, also with Kellogg Foundation support, to foster the improvement of administrator preparation programs in education, primarily through the introduction of behavioral science content into these programs.

In the vanguard of the "theory movement," as this era has been called, were the University of Chicago and Harvard University, institutions that shared a commitment to integrating contributions from social science disciplines into preparatory programs for educational administrators (Cronin & Iannaccone, 1973). These universities, which trained numerous professors of educational administration as well as superintendents for major school districts, both drew faculty from behavioral science disciplines and sent students to social science departments for part of their course work. For the first time, the field of educational administration reached beyond the business management literature as scholars delved into sociology, psychology, anthropology, political science, and economics (Culbertson et al., 1973) for conceptual frameworks and theory-based empirical evidence relevant to the study of educational administration. As the professors who had been trained at these institutions began to populate the faculties of major universities, subject matter and research methods from the allied disciplines gained ascendancy in administrator preparation programs throughout the country.

Behavioral science content prevails in current programs in the form of courses devoted to administrative theory or organizational behavior as well as in the fairly widespread expectations that students complete cognate courses in behavioral science disciplines, conduct research in the hypothetico-deductive mode, and include in their dissertation committees a member of one of the allied discipline departments (Haller & Hickcox, 1973). Behavioral science content has also influenced various traditional educational administration courses in the form of theoretical content introduced into the study of school business and finance, school-community relations, supervision of instruction, and other areas.

Effects of program content. The existence of these three strands of emphasis in current preparation programs is demonstrated by recent findings that technical, human relations, and conceptual skills are treated with approximately equal emphasis, as perceived by students and professors in all program levels (Davis & Spuck, 1978). The same study also indicated that administrative theory, leadership, and decision making are the topics most heavily stressed at all program levels. On the other hand, curriculum development and instructional supervision tend to be stressed at the master's and intermediate levels, whereas educational law and business or finance are emphasized at the advanced intermediate and doctoral levels. Courses in research methods and statistics are also generally required, at introductory levels in M.A. programs and at advanced levels in Ph.D. and Ed.D. programs.

Whereas each of the three broad movements—scientific management, human relations, and behavioral science—inspired a zealous response at its inception and left residues that are still in evidence, no one of these strands holds preeminence today or still ignites a sense of mission and optimism in contemporary scholarship. Despite energetic efforts by leaders and followers of the behavioral science persuasion, the theory-based approach has never fully infiltrated major programs (Halpin & Hayes, 1977), nor has an integrated theory of administration emerged. During the 1970s dissertation research was still predominantly of the cross-sectional survey type, and hypothesis testing had not become the norm for the field (Immegart, 1977). The incorporation of behavioral science content was found to be somewhat more illusory than real (Haller & Hickcox, 1973). And by the late 1960s some disillusionment with behavioral science approaches was already being voiced (Farquhar, 1977).

Research issues. The literature on program content in educational administration is characterized by scant research (apart from a few survey studies) but much armchair philosophy. Some of the issues that have surfaced over the years have concerned common versus specialized learnings, needed competencies of the ideal practitioner, and the so-called theory versus practice dichotomy. While these issues have certainly not been resolved, recent literature indicates emerging trends in each of them. Current emphasis seems to focus upon the distinctiveness of educational organizations, as opposed to military, industrial, medical, and public service organizations (for example, Burlingame, 1976; Erickson, 1977), and on the common learnings requisite for various levels and functions of educational administration (for example, Hoy & Miskel, 1978). The competencies most frequently emphasized have been conceptual and analytical skills (e.g., Hills, 1975; Campbell, 1976; Silver & Hess, 1981), which the universities are best equipped to address (March, 1974). Of major concern in the current literature is an effort to generate "theories of practice" that incorporate both objective and subjective ways of knowing, both fact and value considerations, both "is" and "ought" dimensions of education within integrated frameworks for practice (e.g., Sergiovanni, 1981).

The most compelling influence on program content is derived from advances in knowledge and techniques in business and the academic disciplines, including philosophy and statistics as well as the behavioral sciences. In addition, the changing and ever expanding role of the educational administrator has affected program content, as the advent of collective negotiations, the introduction of new federal and state legislation, changes in family structures, and developments in information and communication technology have influenced the nature of school administration.

Program Processes. Two sets of processes are considered in this section: those associated with the teaching and learning of program content (instructional processes) and those associated with the mechanics of program design and implementation (technical processes).

Instructional processes. Although lecture and discussion in a classroom setting based on the use of the textbook remains the dominant mode of instruction (Davis & Spuck, 1978), other strategies and materials have found increasing use during the past two decades. For example, case studies and simulation or role playing are frequently used for instruction at all three program levels. Both of these strategies were promoted by efforts of UCEA, which inexpensively reproduced and distributed reality-base case materials during the past twenty years and which undertook, during the 1960s, the prodigious task of creating multimedia simulations of school systems (Culbertson & Coffield, 1960). By means of dissemination conferences held at numerous institutions across the country, conferences where the materials were displayed, demonstrated, and discussed, the simulations were introduced to most professors of educational administration and have since been widely used in administrator preparation programs.

A perennial problem in the training of professionals in applied fields, particularly those in the human services domain, is the infusion of sufficient realism into the instructional setting to enable the transfer of learning to the context of practice. Multimedia simulations of administrative situations are the most realistic of instructional materials. Gaynor and Duvall (1973) described the steps taken to intensify the realism of the UCEA simulations as (1) including taped and filmed interruptions along with in-basket items; (2) providing multiple perspectives on problem situations, using what is called a "Rashomon technique"; and (3) controlling access to information, so that persons enacting a given role might, as in reality, have no access to information that some other role players have.

Of more recent origin are computer simulations, such as a decision exercise developed at the University of Iowa (Webb, 1978) and a futuristic exercise developed at the University of Utah (Debenham, 1973). Other innovative instructional strategies used in administrator preparation include instructional modules (Van Meter, 1973; Davis, 1974), games and game theory (Horvat, 1968; Ohm, 1966), and laboratory exercises for the development of human relations skills (Wynn, 1972). Such teaching and learning devices clearly enhance the reality base of course content and add the spice of variety to the university setting. However, there is virtually no research evidence to support the effectiveness of any one of these approaches over others.

Field experiences of various types have long been associated with administrator preparation. These are opportunities for students to gain firsthand experience through interactions with practitioners, usually away from the university but with supervision by a professor. Sometimes called clinical or practicum program components, these experiences have included site visits, school surveys, implementation of organization development projects, in-depth case studies, and problem-oriented research (Cronin & Horoschak, 1973).

The most extensively discussed type of field experience is the internship, introduced to administrator preparation in the late 1940s as a sort of apprenticeship period (Farquhar, 1977). Ideas regarding the design, implementation and supervision of internships abound in the literature (e.g., Hencley, 1963; Sybouts, 1968; Cunningham & Nystrand, 1969; Ramsey & Lutz, 1973), but apart from a small-sample study by Ferreira (1970), little reported research exists on outcomes of the internship experience. Ferreira's findings suggest that the types of interactions students have during their internships will affect their attitudes on educational matters. In 1962 fewer than 50 percent of institutions offered internships, and relatively few students were involved in these experiences (Gregg, 1969). The pattern had not changed much by a decade later, when about 15 percent of students' time was reportedly devoted to field experiences (Davis & Spuck, 1978).

During recent years, emphasis on competencies and on minimum competency testing has had an impact on administrator preparation (Barrilleaux, 1972; Redfern, 1980). Several states have mandated competency-based graduate programs in educational administration, so that movement toward competency-based preparation was one of the most pronounced trends in administrator preparation during the mid-1970s (Silver, 1974, 1978b). Whereas many of these instructional changes have been more verbal than actual—for example, modifying program goal statements and course descriptions without altering program or course contents or strategies—some departments, most notably at the University of Utah (McCleary, 1972) and the University of Georgia (Payne, 1974–1975), have made major changes both in program design and in the structuring of field experiences.

In addition to course work, field experience, and original research, each of which underscores a different mode of learning, a full-time residency of one year or more at the doctoral level has traditionally been required to provide opportunities for intensive study and collegial interaction among students and professors. Practically all doctoral programs require a residency, most typically for one year (Trautmann, 1977), but the definitions of "residency" have loosened somewhat in recent years as sabbatical leaves for administrators have become rarer and as competition for students has sharpened. In some institutions "residency" is interpreted to mean course concentration during evenings and summers at the main campus.

Technical processes. The functioning of preparation programs is itself contingent upon numerous organizational processes and procedures. Of these processes, recruitment, selection, and evaluation are among the most important.

Recruitment and selection processes have been a point of contention for some time, since recruitment of students into programs usually has not been systematic, and admission standards typically have been low (Tyack & Cum-

mings, 1977). Authors have cited the relatively low social status of educational administrators and the questionable usefulness of preparation programs (Farquhar & Piele, 1972), among other factors, as causes of recruitment and selection problems. It appears that increasing competition for students in the 1980s will stimulate increased recruitment efforts (Silver, 1978b) but will perpetuate modest admission standards for some time to come. Authors have recommended recruiting individuals from other fields (Campbell, 1976), attracting teachers characterized as "constructive troublemakers" (Stout, 1973), and developing more clearly differentiated programs (Culbertson, 1972) as options for drawing talented individuals into educational administration.

Of the candidate data most often examined for doctoral program admission decisions—specifically, grade point averages, standardized test scores (on the Miller Analogies Test and/or the Graduate Record Examination), letters of recommendation, and previous career accomplishments (Trautmann, 1977)—transcripts and test results were found to be the best predictors of program completion, whereas résumés and letters of recommendation were found most useful in predicting career success (Thom & Hickcox, 1975).

Program evaluation has also been a contentious issue. Evaluation of schools, colleges, and departments of education is conducted by the National Council for Accreditation of Teacher Education (NCATE) and/or a regional association, such as the North Central Association (NCA), on a voluntary basis and by the state department of education on a mandatory basis in some states (Koff & Florio, 1977). An individual's certification to practice educational administration is contingent upon completion of an "approved program" in twenty-six of the states, and in many instances state approval rests upon accreditation by a regional or national association (University Council for Educational Administration, 1973). Therefore, as Koff and Florio (1977) noted, the voluntary accreditation associations will be accountable in the courts for assessment criteria and standards that bear "a reasonable relationship to needed job skills" (p. 23). Given the difficulties in demonstrating such a relationship empirically and the competing interests of various groups (teachers, administrators, professors, and parents) in this highly political arena, Koff and Florio recommended establishing a forum for the purpose of airing diverse views and attaining consensus about at least some of the criteria for accreditation of programs.

Self-evaluation of department programs by professors of educational administration by means of follow-up studies of graduates is conducted in about 70 percent of the programs, according to a recent survey (Silver, 1978a). However, the scientific validity of these assessments and the bases for determining program effectiveness are questionable, since there have been virtually no evaluative studies published. Because the relevance of preservice preparation to effectiveness in practice has not been demonstrated, it is difficult to sustain rigorous selection standards (Bridges & Baehr, 1971) or to establish a rationale for program changes or improvements.

Program Products. The two types of outcomes or products of preparation programs are persons qualified to assume administrative roles in education (or, in some instances, in other spheres of social life) and research conducted by students and professors.

Personnel. Several studies of the need for qualified educational administrators within states (e.g., Hooker, 1973) and nationally (e.g., Culbertson, 1972; Knezevich, n.d.) suggest that there is an "oversupply" of trained administrators. There are far more certified or credentialed people than there are positions for which advanced education has traditionally been required; and this situation is likely to be exacerbated in the 1980s. As Knezevich has noted, the certificate or degree represents a qualification to compete for an administrative position, not a guarantee of attaining one. If one assumes that the knowledge, skills, and attitudes acquired in a graduate program serve to enhance educators' capacities for leadership in any responsible position, from department supervisor through chief state school officer, then there is no circumstance such as an "oversupply." In fact, it seems likely that, despite less stringent state certification requirements during the past decade (University Council for Educational Administration, 1973), the competition for leadership appointments will serve to increase the range of positions for which advanced degrees are expected.

Research. Original research is required of students in about one-fourth of master's programs, one-half of intermediate programs, and virtually all doctoral programs (Davis & Spuck, 1978). Research advisors are generally selected or appointed to assist with students' research endeavors, and most often an oral defense before committee members or a broader review panel is required. In some programs, the research proposal must itself be "defended" before a review panel prior to data collection, and in some departments there are differential expectations for Ed.D. and Ph.D. projects, the latter generally requiring more theory-oriented research.

Research productivity of departments of educational administration has been studied periodically. Immegart (1977) has reported that there were about 310 studies reported per year in the 1950s, roughly 560 per year in the mid-1960s, and over one thousand per year in the mid-1970s. Of these, the majority (about 80 percent) have been dissertation studies, of which relatively few were reported in the research journals or professional periodicals. Research activity is distributed unequally across doctoral programs, with some institutions characterized as "high producers" and others as "low producers" in relation to the numbers of students receiving degrees (Clark & Guba, 1976). According to Immegart's analysis (1977) of research trends during the 1954–1974 period, inquiry became increasingly empirical, varied in methodology, concerned with instrumentation, and multivariate; however, studies generally continued to be cross-sectional, as opposed to longitudinal or experimental, and concerned with practical relevance, as opposed to theoretical or academic relevance.

Continuing Education

Like other applied professions, educational administration involves the continual upgrading of practical knowledge and skills through participation in professional associations and keeping abreast of the professional literature. Continuing professional education most often takes place through noncredit in-service programs and sometimes through credit-bearing external degree programs. These two types of preparation will be considered separately.

Noncredit Programs. National organizations such as the American Association of School Administrators, (AASA), the National Association of Elementary School Principals (NAESP), the National Association of Secondary School Principals (NASSP), the Association for Supervision and Curriculum Development (ASCD), and Phi Delta Kappa (PDK) have been the mainstay of continuing education through national and regional conventions, the conduct of workshops and seminars on topics of current interest, and the publication of practice-oriented periodicals, books, and monographs. These conventions, seminars, and publications are vehicles for making the latest research findings available in useful form, for familiarizing practicing administrators with recent innovations and political or legislative developments, and for enhancing some technical skills.

In addition to association programs are those programs designed and implemented within school districts or by district consortia and by state departments of education either at the state level or through regional service centers. The increasing prevalence of district-based in-service programs for school administrators and supervisors (as well as teachers) led to the formation of the National Staff Development Council in 1971 for the purpose of increasing districts' expertise in designing and implementing such programs (Kelley & Dillon, 1978). Frequently, universities provide research and staff development services for clusters of school districts through bureaus of educational research or school development councils. The National School Development Council, founded in 1969, serves the purpose of sharing experience and ideas for these services across universities (Frank & Mackett-Frank, 1980).

Numerous problems surround the conceptualization and implementation of in-service programs. The educational needs perceived by practicing administrators tend to be time-bound and place-bound, and even within a given district, the administrators' skills and knowledge bases differ (Lutz & Ferrante, 1972). Nevertheless, the perceived need for alternatives and supplements to traditional graduate programs is great (Usdan, 1976); therefore continuing education efforts supported by private, federal, state, regional, and local agencies will continue to multiply in the future.

External Degree Programs. As a result of some criticisms of graduate programs—for example, that they are resistant to change (Sroufe, 1975) and not sufficiently relevant to practice (Cowden & Jacobs, 1979)—and because of the difficulties in demonstrating the effectiveness of campus-based programs in enhancing practice, numerous "alternative" programs have come into being within the past ten years. These "external degree" or "campus-without-walls" programs offer Ed.D. degrees for working experience, independent study, and attendance at classes one weekend each month for two years as well as two weeks during two or three successive summers (Vonk & Brown, 1978).

According to critics of these programs (e.g., Ashworth, 1978; Vonk & Brown, 1978), admission standards are considerably lower than those for traditional graduate programs, dissertations are often waived in favor of on-the-job projects, and faculty are predominantly part-time and often without doctoral degrees. These programs depend upon the established universities for reputable scholars to teach part-time and for student access to library facilities.

Some effects of the development of these programs have been increases in the flexibility and individualization of the more traditional university programs, increases in the number of off-campus centers where degree candidates can complete some courses before maintaining residency at the main campus, and reductions in residency requirements. It will be incumbent upon the more established university-based programs to demonstrate their superior effectiveness more convincingly and upon school district leaders to determine legitimate credentials for increments and advancement in order to compete successfully with the less rigorous programs.

Emerging Interests

Three recent developments in the field of educational administration merit some consideration as the decade of the 1980s gains momentum. These are a growing interest in matters of global communication, a mounting concern with philosophical issues associated with the nature of knowing, and some evidence of increasing concern with generating knowledge having direct applicability to practice.

Global Education. In congruence with the emerging interest in "global education" on the part of educators, the field of educational administration has been establishing networks of increasingly global proportions. The Commonwealth Council for Educational Administration, for example, was founded in 1971 and has consistently maintained close relationships with the North American UCEA (Walker, 1972). Of more recent origin is the Interamerican Society for Educational Administration, founded in 1979 (Culbertson, 1980b; Sander, 1980). The study of educational administration has been burgeoning in Europe and elsewhere throughout the world during the past decade,

and it has become abundantly clear that the different nations have much learning to share. Informal talk has already begun about a worldwide council, and the likelihood is that such an organization will soon come into being.

Philosophical Issues. The sense of disillusionment with logical positivism that was fermenting by the late 1960s was brought to a head by a paper by Greenfield (1975), initially presented at the 1974 Third International Intervisitation Programme in England, in which many inadequacies of scientific approaches to the study of human organizations were exposed and phenomenological approaches propounded. That paper heralded a debate about the nature of knowing and the conduct of inquiry (Griffiths, 1975; Greenfield, 1976) that is still escalating as educational administration, like the behavioral disciplines themselves, searches for the meanings of knowing and explores new approaches to inquiry (Bates, 1980; Guba, 1978; Culbertson, 1981). One of the outcomes of this ferment is an increasing diversity of research methods, including attempts at qualitative ethnographic, naturalistic, phenomenological, and critical studies.

Research and Practice. A theme related to the current debate on research is a heightened interest in research as a guide to practice in school administration. Erickson's Vice Presidential Address at AERA (1979) emphasized the importance of research on the effects of schooling and of school variables not often examined in this field. Numerous recent studies have focused upon school factors associated with effectiveness (Clark, 1980), and the National Institute of Education has expressed specific interest in principals' effectiveness. It seems likely that new research strategies will evolve (Silver, 1981) that generate knowledge about what administrators can do to improve the effects of schooling.

Paula F. Silver

See also Administration of Educational Institutions; Evaluation of Teachers; Faculty Development; Licensing and Certification; Professions Education; Supervision of Teachers.

REFERENCES

Argyris, C., & Schön, D. A. *Theory in Practice: Increasing Professional Effectiveness.* San Francisco: Jossey-Bass, 1974.

Ashworth, K. H. The nontraditional doctorate. *Phi Delta Kappan,* 1978, *60,* 173–175.

Barrilleaux, L. Behavioral objectives for administrative internship: School principals. *Educational Administration Quarterly,* 1972, *8,* 59–71.

Bates, R. J. Educational administration, the sociology of science, and the management of knowledge. *Educational Administration Quarterly,* 1980, *16,* 1–20.

Bridges, E. M., & Baehr, M. E. The future of administrator selection procedure. *Administrator's Notebook,* 1971, *19,* 1–4.

Bruno, J. E., & Fox, J. N. *Quantitative Analysis in Educational Administrator Preparation Programs.* Columbus, Ohio: University Council for Educational Administration and ERIC/CEM, 1973. (ERIC Document Reproduction Service No. ED 082 270)

Burlingame, M. The federal role in the preparation of educational leaders. In N. Drachler & G. R. Kaplan (Eds.), *Training Educational Leaders: A Search for Alternatives.* Washington, D.C.: George Washington University, Institute for Educational Leadership, 1976, pp. 40–58.

Callahan, R. E. *Education and the Cult of Efficiency.* Chicago: University of Chicago Press, 1962.

Campbell, R. F. *Improving the Performance of Educational Administrators as Planners, Mediators, and Power Brokers.* Paper presented at the University Council for Educational Administration Career Development Seminar, University of Virginia, November 1976.

Campbell, R. F., & Newell, L. J. *A Study of Professors of Educational Administration: Problems and Prospects of an Applied Academic Field.* Columbus, Ohio: University Council for Educational Administration, 1973. (ERIC Document Reproduction Service No. ED 088 171)

Clark, D. L. An analysis of research, development, and evaluation reports on exceptional elementary schools. In Phi Delta Kappa, *Why Do Some Urban Schools Succeed?* Bloomington, Ind.: Phi Delta Kappa, 1980, pp. 171–190. (ERIC Document Reproduction Service No. ED 194 660)

Clark, D. L., & Guba, E. G. *An Institutional Self-report on Knowledge Production and Utilization in Schools, Colleges, and Departments of Education* (Research on Institutions of Teacher Education Occasional Papers Series). Bloomington: Indiana University, 1976.

Coladarci, A. P., & Getzels, J. W. *The Use of Theory in Educational Administration.* Stanford, Calif.: Stanford University, 1955.

Cowden, P., & Jacobs, F. The external degree and the traditions of diversity and competition. *Phi Delta Kappan,* 1979, *60,* 559–561.

Crandall, D. P. Training and supporting linking agents. In N. Nash & J. Culbertson (Eds.), *Linking Processes in Educational Improvement: Concepts and Applications.* Columbus, Ohio: University Council for Educational Administration, 1977, pp. 189–274. (ERIC Document Reproduction Service No. ED 141 902)

Cronin, J. M., & Horoschak, P. P. *Innovative Strategies in Field Experiences for Preparing Educational Administrators.* Columbus, Ohio: University Council for Educational Administration and ERIC/CEM, 1973. (ERIC Document Reproduction Service No. ED 082 271)

Cronin, J. M., & Iannaccone, L. The social sciences and the preparation of educational administrators at Harvard and Chicago. In J. A. Culbertson, R. H. Farquhar, B. M. Fogarty, & M. R. Shibles (Eds.), *Social Science Content for Preparing Educational Leaders.* Columbus, Ohio: Merrill, 1973, pp. 193–244.

Culbertson, J. A. *Alternative Strategies of Program Adaptation within the Future Time Frame of the Seventies.* Paper presented at the University Council for Educational Administration Career Development Seminar, University of Minnesota, October 1972.

Culbertson, J. A. *History and Theory of Educational Administration.* Paper presented at the University Council for Educational Administration Career Development Seminar, University of Wisconsin at Madison, March 1980. (a)

Culbertson, J. A. The Interamerican Society: An enlarged vista and new opportunity. *UCEA Review,* 1980, *21,* 2–3. (b)

Culbertson, J. A. Three epistemologies and the study of educational administration. *UCEA Review,* 1981, *22,* 1–6.

Culbertson, J. A., & Coffield, W. H. (Eds.), *Simulation in Adminis-*

trative Training. Columbus, Ohio: University Council for Educational Administration, 1960.

Culbertson, J. A.; Farquhar, R. H.; Fogarty, B. M.; & Shibles, M. R. (Eds.). *Social Science Content for Preparing Educational Leaders.* Columbus, Ohio: Merrill, 1973.

Culbertson, J. A., & Shibles, M. R. The social sciences and the issue of relevance. In J. A. Culbertson, R. H. Farquhar, B. M. Fogarty, & M. R. Shibles (Eds.), *Social Science Content for Preparing Educational Leaders.* Columbus, Ohio: Merrill, 1973, pp. 3–32.

Cunningham, L. L., & Nystrand, R. O. Toward greater relevance in preparation programs for urban school administrators. *Educational Administration Quarterly,* 1969, *5,* 6–23.

Davis, H. S. Preparing principals for action, leadership. *National Association of Secondary School Principals Bulletin,* 1974, *58,* 29–36.

Davis, W. J. Departments of educational administration. In P. F. Silver & D. W. Spuck (Eds.), *Preparatory Programs for Educational Administrators in the United States.* Columbus, Ohio: University Council for Educational Administration, 1978, pp. 23–51.

Davis, W. J., & Spuck, D. W. A comparative analysis of master's, certification, specialist, and doctoral programs. In P. F. Silver & D. W. Spuck (Eds.), *Preparatory Programs for Educational Administrators in the United States.* Columbus, Ohio: University Council for Educational Administration, 1978, pp. 150–177.

Debenham, J. Innovations in preparatory programs: Stimulating alternative futures in education. *UCEA Newsletter,* 1973.

Erickson, D. A. (Ed.). *Educational Organization and Administration.* Berkeley, Calif.: McCutchan, 1977.

Erickson, D. A. Research in educational administration: The state-of-the-art. *Educational Researcher,* 1979, *8,* 9–14.

Farquhar, R. H. *The Humanities in Preparing Educational Administrators.* Eugene: University of Oregon, ERIC Clearinghouse, 1970. (ERIC Document Reproduction Service No. ED 044 765)

Farquhar, R. H. Preparatory programs in educational administration, 1954–1974. In L. L. Cunningham, W. G. Hack, & R. O. Nystrand (Eds.), *Educational Administration: The Developing Decades.* Berkeley, Calif.: McCutchan, 1977, pp. 329–357. (ERIC Document Reproduction Service No. 140 422)

Farquhar, R. H., & Piele, P. K. *Preparing Educational Leaders: A Review of Recent Literature.* Columbus, Ohio: University Council for Educational Administration and ERIC/CEM, 1972. (ERIC Document Reproduction Service No. ED 069 014)

Ferreira, J. L. The administrative internship and role change: A study of the relationship between interaction and attitudes. *Educational Administration Quarterly,* 1970, *6,* 77–90.

Frank, F. P., & Mackett-Frank, M. A summary of trends in study council development, 1970–1990. *Catalyst for Change,* 1980, *10,* 12–18.

Gaynor, A. K., & Duvall, L. A. Role simulation and educational administration: Some issues and developments. *Journal of Educational Administration,* 1973, *11,* 60–68.

Getzels, J. W. Educational administration twenty years later, 1954–1974. In L. L. Cunningham, W. G. Hack, & R. O. Nystrand (Eds.), *Educational Administration: The Developing Decades.* Berkeley, Calif.: McCutchan, 1977, pp. 3–24.

Greenfield, T. B. Theory about organization: A new perspective and its implications for schools. In M. Hughes (Ed.), *Administering Education: International Challenge.* London: Athlone Press, 1975, pp. 71–99.

Greenfield, T. B. Theory about what? Some more thoughts about theory in educational administration. *UCEA Review*, 1976, *17*, 4–9.

Gregg, R. T. Preparation of administrators. In R. Ebel, *Encyclopedia of Educational Research* (4th ed.). New York: Macmillan, 1969, pp. 993–1004.

Griffiths, D. E. *Administrative Theory.* New York: Appleton-Century-Crofts, 1959.

Griffiths, D. E. Some thoughts about theory in educational administration. *UCEA Review*, 1975, *17*, 12–18.

Griffiths, D. E.; Benben, J. S.; Goldman, S.; Iannaccone, L.; & McFarland, W. J. *Teacher Mobility in New York City.* New York: New York University, School of Education, 1963.

Guba, E. G. *Methodological Rigor of Qualitative Inquiry.* Paper presented at the UCEA Graduate Student Seminar, Indiana University, November 1978.

Haller, E. J., & Hickcox, E. S. Incorporating the social sciences in administrator preparation programs: Some empirical evidence. In J. A. Culbertson, R. H. Farquhar, B. M. Fogarty, & M. R. Shibles (Eds.), *Social Science Content for Preparing Educational Leaders.* Columbus, Ohio: Merrill, 1973, pp. 33–58.

Halpin, A. W. *Administrative Theory in Education.* Chicago: University of Chicago, Midwest Administration Center, 1958.

Halpin, A. W., & Hayes, A. E. The broken icon, or, Whatever happened to theory? In L. L. Cunningham, W. G. Hack, & R. O. Nystrand (Eds.), *Educational Administration: The Developing Decades.* Berkeley, Calif.: McCutchan, 1977, pp. 261–297.

Hencley, S. P. (Ed.). *The Internship in Administrative Preparation.* Columbus, Ohio: University Council for Educational Administration and Committee for the Advancement of School Administration, 1963.

Hills, J. The preparation of administrators: Some observations from the "firing line." *Educational Administration Quarterly,* 1975, *11*, 1–20.

Hooker, C. P. The supply and demand of public school administrators. *Administrative Leadership* (Publication of the University of Minnesota), Division of Educational Administration, 1973, *8*. (ERIC Document Reproduction Service No. ED 079 809)

Horvat, J. *Professional Negotiations in Education.* Columbus, Ohio: Merrill, 1968. (ERIC Document Reproduction Service No. ED 017 065)

Hoy, W. K., & Miskel, C. G. *Educational Administration: Theory, Research, and Practice.* New York: Random House, 1978.

Immegart, G. L. The study of educational administration, 1954–1974. In L. L. Cunningham, W. G. Hack, & R. O. Nystrand (Eds.), *Educational Administration: The Developing Decades.* Berkeley, Calif.: McCutchan, 1977, pp. 298–328.

Katz, M. B. *Class, Bureaucracy, and Schools: The Illusion of Educational Change in America.* New York: Praeger, 1971.

Kelley, E., & Dillon, E. A. Staff development: It can work for you. *National Association of Secondary School Principals Bulletin,* 1978, *62*, 3.

Knezevich, S. J. *Doctorate Needs in Educational Administration During the 1970s and 1980s: A Preliminary Analysis.* Columbus, Ohio: University Council for Educational Administration, n.d.

Koff, R. H., & Florio, D. H. *Educational Policy and Accrediting Schools of Education.* Chicago: Roosevelt University, College of Education, 1977. (Mimeo)

Lutz, F. W., & Ferrante, R. *Emergent Practices in the Continuing Education of School Administrators.* Columbus, Ohio: University Council for Educational Administration and ERIC/CEM, 1972. (ERIC Document Reproduction Service No. ED 069 015)

March, J. G. Analytical skills and the university of educational administrators. *Journal of Educational Administration,* 1974, *12*, 17–44.

McCleary, L. The development of a competency-based individualized program. *UCEA Newsletter,* 1972, *14*, 2–4.

McIntyre, K. E. *Selection of Educational Administrators.* Columbus, Ohio: University Council for Educational Administration, 1966.

Mitchell, D. P., & Hawley, A. *Leadership in Public Education Study: A Look at the Overlooked.* Washington, D.C.: Academy for Educational Development, 1972. (ERIC Document Reproduction Service No. ED 075 896)

Ohm, R. E. Gamed instructional simulation: An exploratory model. *Educational Administration Quarterly,* 1966, *2*, 110–122.

Payne, D. A. *Results-oriented Management in Education: Project R.O.M.E.* (Final Report). Athens: University of Georgia, College of Education and Georgia State Department of Education, 1974–1975. (ERIC Document Reproduction Service No. ED 123 787)

Ramsey, M. A., & Lutz, F. W. The internship in school administration: A review of its history and conceptualization for the future. *Planning and Changing,* 1973, *4*, 135–143.

Redfern, G. B. *Evaluating Teachers and Administrators: A Performance Objectives Approach.* Boulder, Colo.: Westview, 1980.

Roethlisberger, F. J., & Dickson, W. J. *Management and the Worker.* Cambridge: Harvard University Press, 1939.

Sander, B. Interamerican cooperation in educational administration: A doorway to development. *UCEA Review,* 1980, *21*, 4–6.

Sergiovanni, T. J. *Theory of Practice in Educational Policy and Administration: An Hermeneutics Perspective.* Paper presented at the annual meeting of the American Educational Research Association, Los Angeles, April 1981.

Silver, P. F. Some apparent trends in preparatory programs for educational administrators. *UCEA Newsletter,* 1974, *15*, 20–25.

Silver, P. F. Some areas of concern in administrator preparation. In P. F. Silver & D. W. Spuck (Eds.), *Preparatory Programs for Educational Administrators in the United States.* Columbus, Ohio: University Council for Educational Administration, 1978, pp. 202–215. (a)

Silver, P. F. Trends in program development, 1974–1978. In P. F. Silver & D. W. Spuck (Eds.), *Preparatory Programs for Educational Administrators in the United States.* Columbus, Ohio: University Council for Educational Administration, 1978, pp. 178–201. (b)

Silver, P. F. The development of a knowledge base for the practice of educational administration. *Administrator's Notebook,* 1981, *29*, 1–4.

Silver, P. F., & Hess, R. The value of theory course work in enhancing students' conceptual complexity. *Journal of Educational Administration,* 1981, in press.

Silver, P. F., & Spuck, D. W. (Eds.). *Preparatory Programs for Educational Administrators in the United States.* Columbus, Ohio: University Council for Educational Administration, 1978.

Sroufe, G. E. Nova's Ed.D. program for educational leaders: Looking backward, looking forward. *Phi Delta Kappan,* 1975, *56*, 402–405.

Stout, R. *New Approaches to Recruitment and Selection of Educational Administrators.* Columbus, Ohio: University Council for

Educational Administration and ERIC/CEM, 1973. (ERIC Document Reproduction Service No. ED 075 888)

Sybouts, W. The internship in educational administration. *Journal of Educational Administration*, 1968, *6*, 173–176.

Thom, D. J., & Hickcox, E. S. The selection of new graduate students for an educational administration program. *Journal of Educational Administration*, 1975, *13*, 23–34.

Trautmann, R. D. Residence and admission requirements for the doctorate in administration at eighty-one institutions. *Phi Delta Kappan*, 1977, *59*, 208–209.

Tyack, D. B., & Cummings, R. Leadership in American public schools before 1954: Historical configurations and conjectures. In L. L. Cunningham, W. G. Hack, & R. O. Nystrand (Eds.), *Educational Administration: The Developing Decades*. Berkeley, Calif.: McCutchan, 1977, pp. 46–66.

University Council for Educational Administration. *The Preparation and Certification of Educational Administrators: A UCEA Commission Report*. Columbus, Ohio: UCEA, 1973. (ERIC Document Reproduction Service No. ED 079 839)

Usdan, M. D. The training task: Broadening the base. In N. Drachler & G. R. Kaplan (Eds.), *Training Educational Leaders: A Search for Alternatives*. Washington, D.C.: Washington University, Institute for Educational Leadership, 1976, pp. 11–27.

Valverde, L. Promotion socialization: The informal process in large urban districts and its adverse effect on non-whites and women. *Journal of Educational Equity and Leadership*, 1980, *1*, 36–46.

Van Meter, E. Theory in educational administration: An instructional module teaching approach. *Educational Administration Quarterly*, 1973, *9*, 81–95.

Vonk, H. G., & Brown, R. G. The external doctorate in education: Growing criticism and crisis. *Phi Delta Kappan*, 1978, *60*, 176–179.

Walker, W. G. UCEA's bright son at morning. The Commonwealth Council for Educational Administration. *Educational Administration Quarterly*, 1972, *8*, 16–25.

Weaver, W. T. In search of quality: The need for talent in teaching. *Phi Delta Kappan*, 1979, *61*, 29–32, 46.

Webb, L. D. *Title IX: Its Regulations, Implications, and Applications* (Computer Simulation). Columbus, Ohio: University Council for Educational Administration, 1978.

Wynn, R. *Unconventional Methods and Materials for Preparing Educational Administrators*. Columbus, Ohio: University Council for Educational Administration and ERIC/CEM, 1972. (ERIC Document Reproduction Service No. ED 069 013)

ADMISSION TO COLLEGES AND UNIVERSITIES

When we speak of college admissions in the United States, we mean a process that begins, for most students, toward the end of their secondary school years. The opportunity for postsecondary education is not limited to students in special secondary programs, as is the case in many European educational systems; thus the decision to attend college may be deferred until the last years of high school.

In many countries, attendance at a college or university is a privilege restricted to a small percentage of the population or to those who qualify for the academic secondary programs. Attending a college or university has become the expected educational pattern for the majority of United States students, because they are not locked in (or out of) postsecondary programs by virtue of their choices at the secondary level. Education beyond the high school years is now more the rule than the exception, particularly in view of the long-established relationship that has existed between level of educational attainment and earning power. Some (e.g., Trow, 1970), in fact have argued that the growth in enrollments and the movement toward universal higher education have "made enrollment in college increasingly obligatory for many students, and their presence there increasingly 'involuntary' " (p. 25). This same phenomenon has led other observers to label the postsecondary years "longer" rather than "higher" education (Machlup, 1971).

Prior to the early part of the twentieth century, both secondary and higher education offered an academic education to a small fraction of American youth (Trow, 1961). However, educators in secondary schools began to turn their attention from college preparation for a few, to job preparation and "citizenship" for many, and secondary school enrollments skyrocketed. College enrollments as a percentage of the relevant age-group remained small, however, about 15 percent as recently as 1940. But following World War II, enrollments in higher education institutions also began to increase dramatically, and by 1970, more than one-third of the 18–24 age-group attended college (Carnegie Commission, 1971). Today, approximately 40 percent of the 18–24 age-group attend college (Grant & Eiden, 1980). The most recently available figures on the percentage of high school graduates going on to college (Peng, 1977) indicate that approximately 54 percent of high school graduates enroll in college the following fall, a figure that might be slightly higher today.

It should be pointed out that although more than one-half of high school graduates go on to college the following fall—and an unknown (but probably substantial) number go on at some future date—the probability of college attendance is not uniform across the entire population of high school graduates (Peng, 1977). Two factors that affect the probability of college attendance are academic ability and socioeconomic status (SES). Inspection of Table 1 makes it clear that both academic ability and SES play a major role. Within each quarter of the distribution of ability (i.e., each row of the table), there is wide variation in the percentage of high school graduates going to college, and within each SES quarter (i.e., each column of the table), there is similar variation. The strong influence of academic ability and SES on college attendance indicated by these data has been confirmed by other investigators (e.g., College Entrance Examination Board, 1974; Flanagan, 1964; Sewell, 1971).

Selectivity. A common myth about admission to colleges and universities is that most colleges are very selec-

TABLE 1. *Percentage of students in the high school class of 1972 entering college by academic ability, socioeconomic status, and sex*

Academic ability in quarters	Socioeconomic status							
	Lowest quarter		Second quarter		Third quarter		Highest quarter	
	M	F	M	F	M	F	M	F
Highest quarter	53%	66%	70%	66%	81%	75%	85%	85%
Third quarter	36	28	47	46	57	50	69	65
Second quarter	22	22	31	25	35	29	41	44
Lowest quarter	16	14	16	13	20	21	30	38

SOURCE OF DATA: Peng, 1977.

tive, and that many of them annually turn away large numbers of applicants. In fact, however, the degree of selectivity among America's colleges and universities has been greatly exaggerated. As pointed out by the Carnegie Commission on Higher Education, "Most public and private institutions accept most if not all of the students who apply" (Carnegie Commission, 1973, p. 33). Based on the literal definition of "selectivity," the Carnegie Commission statement is supported by evidence. Of the high school graduates in the class of 1972 who applied to college, nearly 90 percent had been accepted by at least one institution by the end of their senior year (Hilton & Rhett, 1973). One might argue that high admission rates are the result of multiple applications, but 41 percent of the class of 1972 who applied for college admission had submitted only one application, and another 36 percent had applied to only two or three institutions. Furthermore, of the freshmen entering college during the three-year period 1975–1977, approximately 43 percent were attending the only college they had applied to, and approximately 20 percent had applied to only one other (Astin, King, & Richardson, n.d.).

Virtually one-third of the four-year institutions in this country admit more than 90 percent of their applicants (Hartnett & Feldmesser, 1980). Many are public institutions required by state law to accept all applicants who have graduated from an accredited secondary school within the state or who have graduated with some minimal evidence of academic attainment, such as achieving a passing grade point average or graduating in the top one-half of their class. More than one-half of the four-year institutions admit 80 percent or more of their applicants, and it has been estimated that fewer than 10 percent reject more than one-half of their applicants (Hartnett & Feldmesser, 1980). Institutions that admit fewer than one-half of the applicants collectively enroll no more than 10 percent of students entering four-year colleges each fall. Moll (1979) contends that "not more than forty private colleges enjoy the luxury of admitting one out of two of their candidates, and not more than a half-dozen private colleges admit one out of five applicants" (p. 5).

How is the myth of selectivity perpetuated? Part of the explanation is that the average percentage of applicants who are offered admission can be a misleading indicator of how difficult it is to get accepted to specific institutions. Students characteristically submit applications only to institutions where the abilities of enrolled students (as usually reflected in admissions test scores) appear to be much like their own. Because of this applicant self-selection, institutions could offer admission to most applicants, but still be "selective" in the sense that they offer admission only to those applicants judged capable of performing satisfactorily in what is a competitive academic environment. Another part of the explanation for how the myth of selectivity is perpetuated is that the relatively small number of selective institutions in the country are also among the most prestigious, and are the producers of some of the country's top talent in the arts and sciences. Their admissions policies are likely to generate an exaggerated interest that leads to general concern about acceptance rates. This concern about acceptance rates is stronger in some localities than in others. Gaining admission to college is not a problem for the nation's youth as a whole, but young people graduating from secondary schools in the Northeast do face different (and more difficult) college admission prospects. Since the vast majority of students attending college do so within their own state—85 percent, according to student migration statistics (Grant & Eiden, 1980)—it is clear that local or regional accessibility is an important factor. In some states (e.g., California, Michigan, Texas) the own-state enrollment figure is over 90 percent. In contrast, in six New England states (Maine, New Hampshire, Vermont, Massachusetts, Rhode Island, and Connecticut), the mean percentage of students attending college within their own state is only 72 percent.

A ranking of institutions in order of admissions test scores of their entering students, identified twenty-seven institutions in the highest "selectivity" category, of which seventeen were located in the Northeast (Astin & Lee, 1972). All private (or independent) institutions tend to be more selective than public ones (and private higher education has traditionally thrived in the Northeast). The public institutions of the Northeast are also more selective than public institutions in other parts of the country. For example, in 1978, the mean percentage of applicants accepted by the six New England state universities was 62 percent, whereas the mean acceptance rate at six contiguous midwestern state universities (Illinois, Iowa, Kansas, Nebraska, Missouri, and Oklahoma) was 82 percent (*College Handbook*, 1979). Thus, virtually all high school graduates who want to go to college in the Northeast, as well as graduates who hope to attend the proportionately small number of selective institutions in other parts of the country, do face a selective admissions situation. Although these students constitute only a small fraction of the total applying to colleges annually, they nevertheless represent a sizable number of applicants to the country's most prestigious colleges and universities. It is not surprising, then, that concern and interest have been expressed in how college admissions decisions are made, and what student qualities are considered in making those judgments.

Admissions Process. The college admissions process actually consists of a series of steps or stages through which both the student and college pass on the way from high school graduation to enrolling in a specific college. The importance of each stage varies substantially for both students and institutions, and warrants consideration here. The stages include exploration, recruitment, application, selection, notification, and enrollment.

Exploration. The first phase of the admissions process is one of mutual exploration. In a general sense, colleges define the type of student they wish to attract by the institutional goals they adopt. As Thresher (1966) has argued, institutional admissions policies must begin with a clear idea of what the college stands for. Some colleges seek students without regard for learning needs of the student or strengths of the college; others appear less interested in teaching students than in enrolling those already well educated, a practice prompting Thresher's observation that "it is easy for selection to become, to a degree, a substitute for education" (1966, p. 22).

Some students begin to think seriously about college, and pay attention to specific institutions early in their secondary school years, whereas others come to the process late in high school. Students form impressions about colleges from parents and peers, through the mass media (e.g., nationally televised athletic events), feedback from students already enrolled in college, and high school guidance personnel. During recent years, college guides have also become widely used sources of information, along with various computerized college data bases.

Recruitment. Often, first contact between student and college occurs when the college communicates with the student, perhaps by means of professionally designed pamphlets or brochures, to create a favorable image of the institution and attract an application. Marketing, at one time considered an inappropriate if not unethical practice, has become an acceptable aspect of college admissions work (College Entrance Examination Board,

1976), and will become more important as colleges face anticipated enrollment declines. Institutions will try to maintain steady enrollment figures during a period in which the available pool of students is dwindling and, in particular, colleges that look to tuition income as a major source of operating revenue will need to find more ways of recruiting students.

An example of how the recruitment process works is a service provided by the Admissions Testing Program of the College Entrance Examination Board (CEEB), known as the Student Search Service. When high school students take the SAT, they are requested to complete a biographical form that asks if they will permit the College Board to give the applicant's name and address to colleges that might be interested. Colleges then indicate to the College Board the characteristics of students whose names they would like to receive (e.g., all students living in a certain region of the country, those with SAT scores above a certain point, and those with certain curricular interests, etc). Prospective students (i.e., the test takers) subsequently receive recruitment materials from many institutions. Institutions likely to participate actively in recruiting students are most often private institutions, usually less selective, less prestigious ones. In addition, many admissions office personnel, in these same institutions, spend a considerable portion of their time traveling to secondary schools to meet guidance counselors and appear at "college nights" or "college fairs," where they can meet prospective students and their parents, and attempt to interest promising high school seniors in their college. In these and other ways college admissions personnel give far more time and attention to promoting a favorable image for the college (Burch, 1974), and to attracting students, than to the question of how to select the better-qualified ones from a surfeit of applicants (Knight & Johnson, 1981; Wolf, 1973).

In their recruiting efforts, of course, colleges must be realistic about the types of students they are likely to attract, and should also have informed estimates about the available pool of those students. As Doermann (1971) demonstrated, there simply are not that many students who are academically talented and financially advantaged. To the extent that colleges continue to compete with one another for the diminishing supply of able students of sufficient financial means, they are on a collision course in which some will not survive. For this reason, some critics have urged colleges to look forward "new clientele" for students, arguing that, in the long run, the search for new constituencies will be more useful to both the college and society than increased competition for students from a diminishing pool (Carnegie Commission, 1973; Cross, 1971).

Application. Since most students apply to only one or two colleges and are accepted there (Bean & Centra, 1973), the choice of applications is the single most important decision of subsequent college enrollment. Three factors influence this decision: cost, location, and image.

As indicated by data reported in Table 1, it is clear that SES is an important factor in determining whether or not high school graduates will attend college. Cost factors may or may not be important in student decisions about applying to specific institutions. For students of modest means, cost is important (Chapman, 1979; Doermann, 1971; Kendrick & Thomas, 1970; Sewell, 1971; Tierney, 1980; Tillery, Donovan, & Sherman, 1969). For this reason, numerous financial aid programs—often "packaged" to include direct scholarships, low-cost loans, part-time jobs, etc.—have been developed in recent years as a means of offsetting the financial burden for needy students. On the other hand, cost is less important to high-ability students, many of whom often apply to selective, prestigious (and generally expensive) colleges (Spies, 1973; 1978). For these students, who frequently come from families with relatively high incomes, factors such as the perceived quality of education appear to be far more important.

The influence of geographical proximity on student choice is not as consistent as cost. Some research (e.g., Medsker & Trent, 1965; Nelson & Poremba, 1980; Sewell, 1963) indicates that proximity is an important consideration, whereas others (e.g., Fenske, 1965; Tuckman, 1970) failed to find any direct or obvious relationship between college proximity and college-attendance plans. In a comprehensive review of literature dealing with the proximity question, Tinto (1973) concludes that proximity is important primarily for applicants of lower academic ability.

The image of a college, or the perception that a prospective student has of what a particular college is like, is a third factor influencing student choice. Most prospective students indicate that they look for colleges that are intellectually stimulating, friendly, staffed by excellent teachers, and that offer absorbing activities (Pace, 1966). Descriptions of colleges being considered are similar to descriptions of the "ideal" college (Baird, 1974). One difficulty is that prospective students rarely have much information about the colleges they are considering. This difficulty was recognized by Coleman (1970), who argued that prospective students were entitled to as much information about colleges, as colleges routinely collect from students, and recommended the "symmetry" principle in the flow of information between students and colleges. A similar recommendation has been recently made by a national task force on better information for students (El-Khawas, 1978).

In most cases, applying to college requires a good deal of paper work, careful coordination between the applying student and the secondary school office, and money. The paper work usually involves completion of a formal application (which often requires detailed personal history, interests, plans, etc.), forwarding of one's secondary school record, recommendations or "character references," admissions test scores (to be forwarded by the appropriate testing agency), and some form of biographical essay. Virtually all colleges now require an application fee of $20–$25, to defray expense of processing the application.

For needy applicants, the application fee can usually be waived.

Selection and eligibility. Most of the research in the area of college and university admissions has focused on the selection stage of the admissions process, particularly about the various factors institutions use in making judgments on student academic potential. The selection stage can be subdivided into two steps employed by most institutions: determination of applicant eligibility and applicant elimination.

To become eligible requires that the applicant has satisfied prerequisites. Virtually all institutions eliminate applicants who have not earned a diploma from an accredited secondary school. For some institutions, such as non-coed colleges and certain religious colleges, special characteristics might affect eligibility. Some public institutions might be required by law to accept all applicants who are residents of the state and graduates of an accredited high school, but deny admission to out-of-state applicants who did not graduate in the top one-half of their classes, or score above a certain level on standardized admissions tests, etc. A national survey of admissions officers conducted by the American Association of Collegiate Registrars and Admissions Officers (AACRAO) and the College Board found that nearly one-half of four-year public institutions were required to admit in-state high school graduates who had achieved some preestablished requirement; and one-fourth had percentage limits on out-of-state admissions (AACRAO/CEEB, 1980). At some schools, all eligible applicants are offered admission, whereas at many others, being regarded as admissible simply "qualified" the applicant for more careful consideration.

Those institutions that receive applications from more students than they can admit must find some rational means for making admissions decisions. The procedure must be fair to the applicants and helpful to the college in the sense that admitted students turn out to be successful, both academically and socially. In making admissions decisions, most colleges consider a variety of information about the applicant, but data obtained in a recent national survey indicate that the pattern of high school subjects completed, the academic performance in high school (as shown by grade average or class rank), and scores on one or more of the national standardized college admissions tests are the factors most frequently given serious consideration. These factors are seldom given equal weight for all applicants at any one institution. As Moll (1979) points out, most selective colleges first sort applicants into various subgroups, and judgment about the qualifications of individual students is then made by comparing the student with others in the subgroup. The same factors are considered (e.g., secondary school grades, test scores, etc.), but separate subgroup norms are used in evaluating the applicants. At most institutions, the subgroups include sons or daughters of alumni(ae), athletes, members of a minority group (which at some institutions might include male or female applicants), and students with special talents (e.g., music, drama, etc.). It is almost always the case that lower standards are used in making judgments about students in one of these various subgroups. Admission to the selective colleges is less difficult for the son or daughter of an alumnus, or for an athlete, for example.

Academic performance in high school is the single most important element in admissions decisions (AACRAO/CEEB, 1980). The emphasis on secondary school grades is not difficult to understand. For years, educational research has shown that the best indicator of performance on a given task is previous performance on the same or similar task. So it is with grades. In study after study, grades in high school have been consistently found to be the best predictor of academic performance during the first year in college. Findings from these studies have been summarized by Breland (1979). The level of grades attained in high school apparently indicates something about motivation as well as academic ability. Most colleges pay closer attention to grade average during the applicant's last two years of high school (allowing for the "late bloomer" phenomenon to appear), and occasionally to grade average in special courses.

The use of grades as an indicator of college academic potential is sometimes criticized because grading standards differ, sometimes dramatically, from one high school to another, and grades do not represent a common metric. Some argue that within one school grade averages can be misleading, since it is presumably more difficult to maintain a high grade average if the student is taking a "pre-college" curriculum (e.g., mathematics, science, foreign languages, various "honors" courses, etc.) than if taking non-college-preparatory courses. Although there is a certain amount of intuitive appeal to these arguments, grade average in high school remains the best predictor of first-year grades in college. This statement holds true for various subgroups and at various types of higher education institutions.

In response to concerns about effect of interschool variation in grading standards on the validity of secondary school records for predicting performance in college, Linn (1966) reviewed some possible techniques to adjust for interschool differences, as well as results of numerous empirical studies that employed adjusted grades to predict later achievement. He concluded that prediction improvement was "discouragingly small" (p. 326).

The value of high school grades as a predictor is changing, however; average grades in secondary school, as in college, have been on the rise for the past decade. One result of this "grade inflation" is that the range of mean secondary school grades has become narrower, and the grades are thus less accurate as a predictor of subsequent academic performance. Ramist (1981), found that the mean validity coefficients declined from .55, for studies carried out during 1964–1973, to .48 for studies conducted between 1974 and 1978. In contrast, the mean validity of high school rank-in-class as a predictor of performance in college rose slightly from .48 in older studies, to .49

in more recent ones. The predictive validity of rank-in-class is now equal to or slightly better than that of grade average, and if the grade inflation trend continues, the discrepancy in favor of rank-in-class might be expected to increase.

Over 90 percent of four-year institutions require that admissions test scores be submitted by applying students. At selective institutions, admissions tests have a real (if often controversial) role. Survey data indicate that although admissions officers rarely regard scores on one of the national standardized college admissions tests as the single most important element in admission decisions, a majority nevertheless regard test scores as a very important factor (AACRAO/CEEB, 1980).

The most widely used college admissions tests are those provided by the American College Testing Program and the College Entrance Examination Board. The American College Testing Program produces one college entrance examination (henceforth referred to as the ACT) that contains various subscores; the College Entrance Examination Board produces the Scholastic Aptitude Test (henceforth referred to as the SAT) with Verbal (V) and Mathematical (M) subscores, and separate achievement examinations in various disciplines. The scores represent a common metric, the only piece of information, in fact, that is uniform across all applicants. The fact that test scores represent a standard, objective measure is very appealing to those making judgments about individual differences and academic abilities. The tests also provide students with an alternate means of demonstrating academic ability.

Validities of ACT and SAT are essentially the same; the correlations with first-year college grades usually run around the high .30s or low .40s. The validity of test scores is rarely as high as those found for secondary school grade average, which tend to run in the high .40s to low .50s. A multiple predictor combining test scores and grades, yields a correlation in the mid-to-high .50s, indicating that the incremental validity of the tests, beyond what is already available with the high school record, is slight.

Validity coefficients for any predictor variable must be interpreted carefully, of course, for when prior selection has already taken place on the basis of the predictor variable, and the validity is thus based on this selected population, the obtained validity is always an underestimate of the true predictive value of the selection measure. In highly selective institutions, the correlation between test scores (or high school grades) and subsequent college performance can be misleadingly low. Though procedures for correcting correlations obtained in this manner are available, they are rarely used and, as a result, most of the validity data dealing with prediction of college performance represent conservative estimates of the usefulness of the measures in question.

Several factors have changed the way tests scores are interpreted by admissions officers. Disclosure laws have forced test publishers to release copies of tests, correct answers, and test statistics to examinees. Although only a small percentage of test takers request such information, publishers must develop new test forms for each administration. The effect of old-form release on new-form performance has not been fully assessed. Thus, the interpretation of scores will be more difficult. Two test takers successfully challenged the keyed correct answer on College Board examinations in the spring of 1981, and verified that errors do occur in the testing process, and that these errors occasionally penalize able students. The College Board is implementing a national disclosure policy in which copies of tests and correct answers are available to all interested examinees in a selected number of annual test-administrations.

Another factor influencing test-score interpretation is sensitivity of scores to short-term coaching. If coaching can be obtained only at a fee-charging school, it gives an unfair advantage to those who can afford to attend one of the coaching schools. The topic became a major issue after several studies (FTC, 1979; Slack & Porter, 1980) concluded that coaching greatly affects candidate performance on the SAT. More recently, Messick (1980) reported results of a comprehensive review of previous coaching studies, and a reanalysis of coaching-study data. He concluded that improvement in test scores is a function of time and effort expended by the examinee. In discussing the SAT, Messick suggested that since the time normally required to achieve score increases greater than 20 or 30 points approaches full-time schooling, the most reasonable preparation strategy appears to be enrollment in a secondary-school program emphasizing the development of thought as well as knowledge. Test scores can obviously be improved. The question is whether or not the amount of instruction required to yield substantial improvement can realistically be regarded as "coaching," rather than what we normally regard as schooling.

Interpretation is also affected by a steady decline in test scores over the past 15 years, (Beaton, Hilton, & Schrader, 1977). This decline has caused great concern among teachers, parents, educational researchers, and others, and let to speculation about numerous potential causes and correlates (CEEB, 1977).

Considering only the SAT, we know that declines have been substantial, (i.e., about 50 points on the verbal portion of the SAT and about 32 points on the mathematical portion between 1963 and 1977). Until about 1970, a large portion of score decline (probably somewhere between two-thirds and three-quarters) appears to have been the result of changes in the characteristics of those taking the tests; but the scores have continued to decline since 1970, even though the composition of population taking the SAT became considerably more stabilized with respect to its economic, ethnic, and social background during that period. The declines are not the result of statistical artifacts, such as tests having become "harder"—in fact, comparisons of studies suggest that more recent forms of the test might actually have been slightly "easier" than previous ones, thus implying that the true decline is perhaps greater than originally estimated. The declines are pervasive; that is, they have occurred at all SAT score levels, affecting high scorers and low scorers alike.

The causes of the score decline are not understood. Topics for conjecture include quality of high school teaching, influence of television, declining student motivation, grade inflation, and changes in the nature of students' course-taking behavior in secondary schools. It is unlikely that any single cause will be identified. This decline has meant that admissions officers have had to adjust their thinking about what constitutes a "good" score.

Numerous critics have argued that overreliance on traditional academic indicators is misguided, because they are only useful for predicting subsequent performance in school settings, but not particularly accurate for predicting performance in "real life" after college (Holland & Nichols, 1964; Hoyt, 1965; Wing & Wallach, 1971). These same critics have urged that more attention be given to other nonacademic, personal qualities in college admissions, because many such characteristics or behaviors stand (to some extent) as ends in themselves, and not merely useful predictors of further performance in school. Included here would usually be evidence of leadership potential, special talents and competencies, certain interests and goals, and previous noteworthy accomplishments and achievements. As Wing and Wallach (1971) point out, the relevance of such personal qualities as previous accomplishments, takes on particular importance in the admissions process at selective colleges, where traditional academic indicators for most applicants are in the upper range. In such cases, attempts to make fine distinctions among applicants on traditional indicators becomes extremely difficult, and turning to other qualities, such as previous attainments, seems both reasonable and desirable. A more recent and detailed case for considering personal qualities in college admissions has been made by Willingham (1980).

The usual means by which applicants inform colleges of their previous accomplishments and other personal qualities is the biographical questionnaire. Reservations often expressed about such self-reported information are whether or not the information is reliable and valid for predicting academic performance in college. With regard to the reliability question, the available evidence reinforces the reliability of self-report biographical information (Baird, 1976; Owens, 1976; Nicholson, 1970). With regard to the question of validity, self-report accomplishment data have been found to be related to both academic and nonacademic performance in college (Nichols & Holland, 1963; Wing & Wallach, 1971).

Other common methods of obtaining information about applicants' qualities include the personal statement, recommendations, and personal interviews. The problems of reliable assessment of personal characteristics by all of these methods are well known, which partially explains why they are apparently given so little emphasis at most institutions. Personal statements are frequently required for all applicants to some of the more selective institutions, and interviews are still required at many of these same institutions, particularly the private ones. And, personal recommendations are still a commonplace requirement, occupying much of the time of secondary school guidance personnel responsible for putting together the students' application packets, including teacher recommendations. However, use of this information for applicant elimination has not been systematically examined.

Notification. As indicated, some students apply to more than one institution at the same time. Therefore, the timing of the institution's admissions decisions can be very important to individual students, and is sometimes a source of confusion and controversy (Willingham & Breland, 1977). Many institutions, including the great majority of public ones, use what is called a "rolling admissions" plan, which simply means that applicants are notified of the institution's admission decision on a continuous basis throughout the year. The accepted students, in turn, are asked to inform the institution of their intentions regarding enrollment. Then, as some accepted students indicate their intention of enrolling elsewhere (or in some cases their decision not to enroll at all), the institution sends acceptance notices to other applicants on their waiting list. In this fashion, the rolling-admissions procedure continues until the institution is confident of having a complete freshman class. Rolling-admissions notification plans are usually found at less selective institutions where admissions decisions are usually based on straightforward credentials, and all eligible applicants (see previous discussion) are admitted until there are no more spaces in their class.

The more selective institutions, however, usually employ a uniform notification-date plan, in which decisions about all applicants (both those accepted and denied admission) are held for a single mailing, usually in the spring. Moreover, some schools take part in multiinstitutional arrangements by which all cooperating schools not only use the same notification date, but also request admitted students to inform them of their enrollment decision by some specified and agreed-upon date. The latter agreement is designed to eliminate what some admissions officers refer to as the "squeeze play," a practice used by some institutions in which they required accepted students to notify them of their intentions before the student has received word of acceptance or rejection from other institutions that he or she might have applied to.

Enrollment. As the final stage of the admissions process, students make their enrollment decision. For those students applying to (or accepted at) only one institution, there is really no decision to make at this point. For those receiving offers of admission to more than one institution, however, the applicant must again proceed through a choice-process similar to that discussed under the section on applications. Because some students (especially in the northeastern section of the country) submit multiple applications and receive multiple offers of admissions, the enrollment stage of the admissions process is very important,

particularly for the institutions. Since there will be more offers of admission than numbers of applicants, institutions usually extend offers of admission to more students than they can actually accommodate, recognizing that some admitted students—in some colleges a very substantial number—will choose to enroll elsewhere. In the jargon of admissions personnel, the percentage of accepted students who actually enroll is referred to as the admissions "yield" rate, an index which, along with number of applications received, is sometimes used as an informal measure of an institution's attractiveness among prospective students. The yield rate is very high among some institutions—Harvard and Radcliffe perhaps serving as the most noteworthy examples, where approximately three-fourths of accepted applicants actually enroll—but very low at others, often below 40 percent, even at institutions that have a reputation and image as being very selective. It is obviously important that admissions personnel understand and closely monitor their yield rate, because they must be careful to extend offers of admission to the right number of students; too many acceptances would mean overcrowded classrooms and dormitories; too few could cause serious financial difficulty, especially in those institutions whose operating revenue is derived largely from tuition income.

Comment. The past thirty years have seen vast changes in admissions to the undergraduate programs of American colleges and universities, in terms of numbers of people attending, as well as in the variety of student population. As several writers (Hodgkinson, 1978; Shulman, 1977; Willingham, 1980) have noted, the years from the early 1950s through 1965 could be characterized as a meritocratic period, when emphasis was placed on increasing selectivity, whereas the next fifteen years (roughly from 1965 until the present) could more accurately be viewed as an egalitarian period in college admissions. During this latter span many institutions established special admissions programs; large increases in financial aid became available, and, as a result, by the mid-1970s sizable gains in enrollment of disadvantaged minorities and women had been achieved. As Willingham (1980) points out, these two periods were certainly not distinct, and important aspects of the first period carried over into the second. Furthermore, there is reason to believe that certain aspects of each period will continue. But it is equally clear that as we begin the 1980s a new period of admissions is upon us, one that might be labeled the "pragmatic" era. The demographic trends already reported make it evident that institutional practices during the years ahead will place emphasis on recruitment and consumerism. The challenge for admissions personnel in the 1980s will be to deal effectively with pragmatic needs without yielding on meritocratic and egalitarian values.

Rodney T. Hartnett

See also Aptitude Measurement; Curriculum and Instruction in Higher Education; Effects of College Experience; Financial Aid to Students; Higher Education; Non-traditional Higher Education Programs.

REFERENCES

American Association of Collegiate Registrars and Admissions Officers and the College Entrance Examination Board. *Undergraduate Admissions: The Realities of Institutional Policies, Practices, and Procedures.* New York: College Entrance Examination Board, 1980.

Astin, A. W.; King, M. R.; & Richardson, G. T. *The American Freshman: National Norms for Fall, 1977.* Los Angeles: University of California Graduate School of Education, Laboratory for Research in Higher Education, n.d. (ERIC Document Reproduction Service No. ED 150 936)

Astin, A. W., & Lee, C. B. *The Invisible Colleges: A Profile of Small, Private Colleges with Limited Resources.* New York: McGraw-Hill, 1972.

Baird, L. L. The practical utility of measures of college environments. *Review of Educational Research*, 1974, *44*(3), 307–330.

Baird, L. L. *Using Self-reports to Predict Student Performance* (Research Monograph No. 7). New York: College Entrance Examination Board, 1976.

Bean, A. G., & Centra, J. A. Multiple college applications. *Journal of College Student Personnel*, November 1973.

Beaton, A. E.; Hilton, T. L.; & Schrader, W. B. *Changes in the Verbal Abilities of High School Seniors, College Entrants, and Scholastic Aptitude Test Candidates between 1960 and 1972* (Research Bulletin 77-22). Princeton, N.J.: Educational Testing Service, 1977.

Breland, H. M. *Population Validity and College Entrance Measures.* New York: College Entrance Examination Board, 1979.

Burch, C. H. Can a media tour help your image? *College Board Review*, Spring 1974, 91.

Carnegie Commission on Higher Education. *New Students and New Places.* New York: McGraw-Hill, 1971.

Carnegie Commission on Higher Education. *Continuity and Discontinuity.* New York: McGraw-Hill, 1973.

Centra, J. A. College enrollment in the 1980s: Projections and possibilities. *Journal of Higher Education*, 1980, *51*(1), 18–39.

Chapman, R. G. Pricing policy and the college choice process. *Research in Higher Education*, 1979, *10*(1), 37–57.

Coleman, J. S. The principle of symmetry in college choice. In *Report of the Commission on Tests.* New York: College Entrance Examination Board, 1970.

College Entrance Examination Board. *Equality of Educational Opportunity: Effects of Poverty and Minority Status.* New York: College Entrance Examination Board, 1974.

College Entrance Examination Board. *A Role for Marketing in College Admissions.* Paper presented at the Colloquium on College Admissions, Fontana, Wisconsin, May 1976. New York: College Entrance Examination Board, 1976.

College Entrance Examination Board. *On Further Examination: Report of the Advisory Panel on the Scholastic Aptitude Test Score Decline.* New York: College Entrance Examination Board, 1977.

College Handbook, 1979–1980 (17th ed.). New York: College Entrance Examination Board, 1979.

Cronbach, L. J. Equity in selection: Where psychometrics and political philosophy meet. *Journal of Educational Measurement*, 1976, *13*(1), 31–42.

Cross, K. P. *Beyond the Open Door.* San Francisco: Jossey-Bass, 1971.

Doermann, H. Lack of money: A barrier to higher education. In *Barriers to Higher Education.* New York: College Entrance Examination Board, 1971.

El-Khawas, E. H. *Better Information for Student Choice* (Report of the National Task Force on Better Information for Student Choice). Washington, D.C.: American Association for Higher Education, 1978.

Federal Trade Commission, Bureau of Consumer Protection. *Effects of Coaching on Standardized Admission Examinations: Revised Statistical Analysis of Data Gathered by Boston Regional Office of Federal Trade Commission.* Washington, D.C.: Federal Trade Commission, March 1979.

Fenske, R. *A Study of Post–High School Plans in Communities with Differing Educational Opportunities.* Unpublished doctoral dissertation, University of Wisconsin, 1965.

Flanagan, J. C. *Project Talent: The American High School Student.* Pittsburgh, Pa.: University of Pittsburgh, 1964.

Grant, W. V., & Eiden, L. J. *Digest of Educational Statistics, 1980.* Washington, D.C.: National Center for Educational Statistics, 1980.

Hartnett, R. T., & Feldmesser, R. A. College admissions testing and the myth of selectivity: Unresolved questions and needed research. *American Association of Higher Education Bulletin*, *32*(7), March 1980.

Hilton, T. L., & Rhett, H. Appendix B, Part 3. In *Final Report: The Base-year Study of the National Longitudinal Study of the High School Class of 1972.* Princeton, N.J.: Educational Testing Service, 1973.

Hodgkinson, H. L. Foreword. In H. Sacks (Ed.), *Hurdles: The Admissions Dilemma in American Higher Education.* New York: Atheneum, 1978.

Holland, J. L., & Nichols, R. C. Prediction of academic and extracurricular achievement in college. *Journal of Educational Psychology*, 1964, *55*, 55–65.

Hoyt, D. P. *The Relationship between College Grades and Adult Achievement: A Review of the Literature* (American College Testing Program Research Report No. 7). Iowa City, Iowa: American College Testing Program, 1965.

Kendrick, S. A., & Thomas, C. L. Transition from school to college. *Review of Educational Research*, 1970, *40*(1), 151–179.

Knight, B., & Johnson, D. Marketing higher education. *Educational Record*, 1981, *62*(1), 28–31.

Linn, R. L. Grade adjustments for prediction of academic performance: A review. *Journal of Educational Measurement*, 1966, *3*(4), 313–329.

Machlup, F. Longer education: Thinner, broader, or higher? *Proceedings of the 1970 Invitational Conference on Testing Problems.* Princeton, N.J.: Educational Testing Service, 1971.

Medsker, L., & Trent, J. *The Influence of Different Types of Higher Institutions on College Attendance from Varying Socioeconomic and Ability Levels.* Berkeley: University of California, Center for the Study of Higher Education, 1965.

Messick, S. *The Effectiveness of Coaching for the SAT: Review and Reanalysis of Research from the Fifties to the FTC.* Princeton, N.J.: Educational Testing Service, 1980.

Moll, R. *Playing the Private College Admissions Game.* New York: Times Books, 1979.

Nelson, R., & Poremba, G. *Reasons for Selecting the University of North Dakota by New Freshmen and College Transfer Students, 1979–1980* (Report prepared by the Division of Student Affairs). Grand Forks: University of North Dakota, 1980. (ERIC Document Reproduction Service No. ED 192 639)

Nichols, R. C., & Holland, J. L. Prediction of the first-year college performance of high-aptitude students. *Psychological Monographs*, 1963, *77*(7, Whole No. 570).

Nicholson, E. *Success and Admission Criteria for Potentially Successful Risks.* Providence, R.I.: Brown University, 1970.

Owens, W. A. Background data. In M. D. Dunnette (Ed.), *Handbook of Industrial and Organizational Psychology.* Chicago: Rand McNally, 1976.

Pace, C. R. *The Use of CUES in the College Admissions Process* (College Entrance Examination Board Report No. 2). Los Angeles: University of California, 1966.

Peng, S. S. Trends in the entry to higher education, 1961–1972. *Educational Researcher*, 1977, *6*(1), 15–18.

Ramist, L. Criterion-related validity of tests used in the College Board's admissions testing program. In *The College Board Admissions Testing Program.* Princeton, N.J.: Educational Testing Service, 1981.

Sewell, W. H. *The Educational and Occupational Perspectives of Rural Youth.* Report to the National Conference on Problems of Rural Youth in a Changing Environment, Madison, Wisconsin, September 1963.

Sewell, W. H. Inequality of opportunity for higher education. *American Sociological Review*, 1971, *36*(5), 795–796.

Shulman, C. H. *University Admissions: Dilemmas and Potential* (ERIC/Higher Education Research Report No. 5). Washington, D.C.: American Association for Higher Education, 1977. (ERIC Document Reproduction Service No. ED 146 826)

Slack, W. V., & Porter, D. The Scholastic Aptitude Test: A critical appraisal. *Harvard Educational Review*, 1980, *56*, 154–175.

Spies, R. R. *The Future of Private Colleges: The Effect of Rising Costs on College Choice.* Princeton, N.J.: Princeton University, Department of Economics, Industrial Relations Section, 1973.

Spies, R. R. *The Effect of Rising Costs on College Choice: A Study of the Application Decisions of High-ability Students.* New York: College Entrance Examination Board, 1978.

Thresher, B. A. *College Admissions and the Public Interest.* New York: College Entrance Examination Board, 1966.

Tierney, M. L. The impact of financial aid on student demand for public/private higher education. *Journal of Higher Education*, 1980, *51*(5), 527–545.

Tillery, D.; Donavan, D.; & Sherman, B. *SCOPE: Grade Eleven Profile, 1968 Questionnaire Selected Items.* New York: College Entrance Examination Board, 1969.

Tinto, V. College proximity and rates of college attendance. *American Educational Research Journal*, 1973, *10*(4), 277–293.

Trow, M. The second transformation of American secondary education. *International Journal of Comparative Sociology*, 1961, *2*.

Trow, M. Reflections on the transition from mass to universal higher education. *Daedalus*, 1970, *99*(1), 1–40.

Tuckman, H. *A Study of College Choice, College Location, and Future Earnings: Two Economic Models of Choice.* Unpublished doctoral dissertation, University of Wisconsin, 1970.

Willingham, W. W. The case for personal qualities in admissions. *College Board Review*, 1980, *116*, A1–A8.

Willingham, W. W., & Breland, H. M. The status of selective admissions. In *Selective Admissions in Higher Education* (A report of the Carnegie Council on Policy Studies in Higher Education). San Francisco: Jossey-Bass, 1977.

Wing, C. W., & Wallach, M. A. *College Admissions and the Psychology of Talent.* New York: Holt, Rinehart & Winston, 1971.

Wolf, J. S. Marketing admissions: Using modern business techniques in student recruiting. *College Board Review*, Fall 1973, *89*.

ADOLESCENT DEVELOPMENT

The term "adolescence" derives from the Latin verb *adolescere*, meaning "to grow into maturity." Thus it is "a process rather than a time period, a process of achieving the attitudes and beliefs needed for effective participation in society" (Rogers, 1981, p. 6). It may be interpreted in other ways as well—as a period in physical development, as a sociocultural phenomenon, as a chronological age span, as a transition period, or even abstractly as an attitude toward life.

Physically, adolescence is that period in life between the onset of puberty and the completion of bone growth. Physical adolescence embraces several distinct periods. Pubescence, sometimes called preadolescence, relates to the period of about two years preceding puberty and the physical changes during that period. The climax of pubescence, puberty, is distinguished by certain marks of sexual maturity: in boys by various signs, the most valid possibly being the presence of live spermatozoa (male reproductive cells) in the urine and in girls by the menarche, or first menses. The age of puberty is highly variable, with a span of as much as six years between early and late maturers (Lipsitz, 1979). Early adolescence, biologically, begins with the pubescent growth spurt and lasts until about a year after puberty, when the new biological functions are generally stabilized. Late adolescence is more difficult to define, continuing until physical growth is relatively complete, in the early twenties. Defined chronologically, or in terms of calendar years, adolescence embraces the period 12 or 15 years of age until 18 or 22.

There is no agreed-upon age when adulthood begins, an observation underscored by the states' widely varying minimum-age requirements for various functions such as driving a car or getting married. Chronological age alone is somewhat meaningless. Hence, society has developed "a social clock that is superimposed upon the biological clock, thus producing orderly and sequential changes in behavior and in self perceptions" (Neugarten, 1977, p. 63). All the "ages that an adolescent juggles—biological, social, emotional, intellectual and academic—make a mockery of chronological age" (Lipsitz, 1979, p. 4). A related concept, stage theory, suggests that the life span may be divided into relatively distinct periods, each with its distinctive characteristics, tasks, and privileges. Transitions between stages may span several years, each constituting "both an ending and a beginning, a departure and arrival, a death and rebirth, a meeting of past and future" (Levinson, 1977, p. 102). Adolescence is often viewed as a transition, a link between childhood and adulthood with no genuine essence of its own. Lipsitz (1979), however, objects to this notion. He sees adolescence as no more transitional than any other stage in life and with a significance of its own, and feels that it may not receive the attention it deserves if it is simply viewed as transient. Socially, adolescence is that span in an individual's life when society stops regarding an individual as a child but fails as yet to grant full adult status. Adolescence may also be viewed historically, through comparing youth of one age in history with youth in another; and phenomenologically, which involves considering adolescents' own points of view.

Adolescence is important for a variety of reasons. Even if it is not critical in the sense of constituting a crisis, it is critical in its significance. The sensitive-period hypothesis suggests that there are critical times when experiences have maximum effect. If these experiences occurred either earlier or later, they would presumably have less effect. Adolescence itself is critical in that attitudes, characteristics, and behaviors established during this time relate to those in the years ahead. In longitudinal research, which involves studying a population of subjects over a period of time, with follow-ups at intervals, it was found that life-style orientations initiated by the tenth grade produced patterns for overall modes of adjustment in the next stage of young adulthood (Newman, 1979). Thus, adolescence is a period for consolidating coping styles or characteristic ways of solving problems. Also during adolescence young people make the decisions that set patterns for the years that follow in work, loving relationships, friendship experiences, religious involvement, and academic orientation. The period is especially critical in defining sex-appropriate roles, establishing identity, and determining commitments to occupation, values, ideologies, and life-styles (Adams & Looft, 1977).

In one respect the significance of adolescence is perceived somewhat differently today. Formerly adolescence was perceived as a time of completing preparation for adulthood. Now human growth is no longer perceived as ceasing with adulthood but is seen as capable of continuing throughout life. Hence it is important to relate adolescence to the entire life cycle. Thus adolescence is perceived as representing the accumulated or emergent outcomes of all preceding life experience and as possessing "a certain directional thrust" that impinges on the future (Rosenfeld, 1977).

Adolescence research has its special methodologies and deficiencies. Logitudinal research helps us to appreciate the importance of adolescence in the total life cycle—how it builds on childhood experience and constitutes a transition to the future (Adelson, 1979). Other important methods for studying adolescence include the historical approach, which compares the characteristics of youth at different stages in history; anthropological research, which compares ways of living in different societies; and cross-cultural studies, which compare aspects of development in life in two or more countries or subcultures. Common deficiencies in research include a tendency to overgeneralize—to speak of *the* boy or *the* girl or *the* teenager—instead of realizing the importance of subcategories of adolescents and wide variations within each category. We should abandon the illusion that there is a single adolescent psychology, timeless and universal.

Personality.   There is considerable controversy over the extent to which adolescent personality is modifiable. In the Terman study, in which bright individuals have been followed for over six decades, time and again individuals proved not to be completely prisoners of their past (Goleman, 1980b). Such findings underscore adolescents' capacity for continuing growth. Nevertheless, certain characteristics apparent in youth tend to persist. Among Terman's subjects, those who had strong self-concepts in midlife also had had satisfactory self-concepts in early years (Goleman, 1980b). Early feelings, especially about oneself, proved to be particularly significant (Goleman, 1980a).

Much emphasis has been placed on the need for adolescents to establish an identity. However, little attention has been paid to their future identity. Still, the most important developmental change in later adolescence is an individual's relationship to the future (Winer, Schwartz, & Berger, 1977).

Physical Development.   Physically, the various aspects of growth proceed somewhat evenly but independently, and not collectively at any stage. That is, the amount of synchrony is relative. Thus skeletal and dental age are somewhat independent of each other, and the spurt in body development is not accompanied by as dramatic an increase in intellectual capacity (Tanner, 1978a).

Especially important now is the functioning of the endocrine glands. The pineal and thymus glands inhibit sexual development; the pituitary gland influences the operation of other glands affecting growth and metabolism; and the gonads (sex glands) are stimulated to produce mature ova and sperm as well as estrogen and androgen. Low levels of estrogen are found in both sexes until puberty; after this time the secretion of androgen in boys and estrogen in girls increases greatly.

The physical self is of greater concern in adolescence than perhaps in any other period of life except old age. Rapid physical changes intrude into the adolescent's awareness. Adolescents lose the security of familiar sensations, body, and features. They must adapt to such changes and to others' perceptions of them. They cannot be sexually neutral now, for they are viewed as sex objects (Rogers, 1981). Physical changes also symbolize the end of childhood and the beginning of maturity. Girls become especially concerned about weight. Overweight adolescents, especially girls, have poor images of their bodies and of themselves (Hendry & Gillies, 1978). For young adolescent boys, physical superiority symbolizes prestige and "the body is very much an instrument of the person" (Tanner, 1978b, p. 84). The acquisition of sports skills helps both sexes to learn skills important for their developmental level (Dozier et al., 1978).

Adolescents are generally healthy, but hazards do exist. They are particularly vulnerable to certain types of disease, accidents, and drug abuse. Accidents other than drowning are ranked first as cause of death among teenagers, accounting for 60 percent of deaths; drowning comes second and suicide is currently showing a sharp upward trend. Other special physical problems in adolescence relate to nutrition and fatigue, early and late maturation, and physical handicaps.

Of greatest social concern have been adolescents' drug

habits, especially in the consumption of marijuana and alcohol. By high school graduation over a third of all students have used some drug other than marijuana. Marijuana use rose considerably in the 1970s (Bachman & Johnston, 1979). The number of those who drink daily has remained stable over the past five years at around 6 percent, a figure that increases with the college experience. High school students who have smoked cigarettes from one to five years have already experienced pulmonary damage. Even healthy adolescents who smoke sustain increased heart rate and blood pressure and must exert greater effort to compete than do nonsmokers when undertaking physical tasks. Gradually, more serious effects of smoking will develop over the years (Katchadourian, 1977). Heavy drinking in youth can lead to heavy drinking later on; and many alcoholics who come for treatment in their thirties admit to dependence on alcohol from their early teens (Blume, 1975). The long-term effects of marijuana use are still controversial, one problem being that generalizations do not always hold for individuals (Scanlon, 1979).

Over the past few years drug use among youth has shown signs of declining. In college, especially, the incidence of smoking has dramatically declined; and alcohol consumption may have stabilized. A survey of drinking patterns on fifteen university campuses indicates no significant increase in the number of youths who have drink-related problems ("Student Spirits," 1979). Marijuana use remains popular, but young people are coming, increasingly, to question its safety. Of over 17,000 high school seniors surveyed in 1980, about half believed that regular marijuana smoking posed a great health risk, up from 35 percent in 1978 ("Youth on the Move," 1980).

Of special significance for adolescents is increasing emphasis on positive concepts of health. Many of them have undertaken their own personal health programs, especially jogging. Moderate exercise can be very helpful if it is not too strenuous (Scanlon, 1979). A hazard resulting from independent health plans is that some youth latch on to various diet and health fads without understanding them. Not much help is available from the medical profession, for although considerable scientific knowledge has been accumulated regarding children's health, there is much less concerning the special health problems of adolescents (Scanlon, 1979). Nevertheless, the effectiveness of health care in adulthood depends much on whether diseases and physical problems are identified early. An individual's overall health status tends to persist; hence youth's indifference to the future consequences of their health behaviors constitutes a challenge. The incidence of coronary disease is increasing among young adults, especially young women, perhaps because of the increasing use of contraceptive pills (Scanlon, 1979). In Terman's longitudinal study there was a continuity of health, as measured in adolescence, over the next five decades (Goleman, 1980b).

Mental Development. Mental development includes the acquisition of skills, attitudes, and interests. A broad range of skills is very helpful to adolescents in their adjustment. Motor skills are necessary for athletics and social adjustment; reading skills are basic to efficient learning. Individuals' attitudes modify their receptiveness to learning and decisions regarding everything they do in life. Adolescents' interests, which suggest favorable inclinations toward particular activities, are somewhat more egoistic, introspective, serious, social, and less active than those of children. Their interests focus on particular areas such as television, music, or hobbies. Adolescent male and female interests differ, young women being more interested in social, artistic, and domestic matters and young men in manual arts and outdoor pursuits (Matheny, Dolan, & Krantz, 1980).

There is general consensus about the pattern of mental growth from birth to adolescence. Intelligence grows rapidly at first and continues to increase at a declining rate into the teens. Most adolescents come to rely less on the concrete as they become capable of greater abstractions. They come to think about thinking, to generalize, to consider metaphors, to appreciate theories" (Lipsitz, 1979, p. 7). Exactly when intelligence peaks or when the plateau in adult intelligence transforms into decline is still at issue. In any case, some cognitive functions progress toward greater differentiation and others reach greater synthesis. This overall pattern obscures any fairly discrete stages, if any, that exist in mental development. Neither does it show how individuals of the same age vary nor how any particular individual's growth pattern will progress.

Nevertheless, intelligence quotient (IQ) and mental test scores in adolescence have proved to relate in various ways to adult outcomes. Women in Terman's group who demonstrated special mathematics abilities when young were more career-oriented than average and had more ambition and concern for excellence in work in their later adult years (Goleman, 1980b). Jencks (1979) reported only slight correlations between earlier IQs and successful performance in adulthood. From adolescence on, some individuals have ascending, and other descending, IQs. In the Terman group, individuals who were successful seemed to become brighter as they grew older, whereas among the less successful IQs increased less (Goleman, 1980b). Critics of intelligence tests insist that early results cannot predict an individual's capability in adulthood. They suggest that such tests be replaced or supplemented by measures of social intelligence, cognitive style, coping skills, learning potential, and electrical responses of the brain, and that entrance examinations to professional schools measure human dimensions, including sensitivity (Rice, 1979).

Emotional Development. Any particular individual's emotional pattern depends on both biological and sociological factors. The biological factors include body chemistry, general health, and degree of sympathetic or parasympathetic dominance. The influence of genetic factors is reflected in the early appearance of temperamental traits and resistance to environmental factors. Exactly what part puberty plays in emotion is debatable, although it is widely assumed to heighten emotionality.

From early infancy, individuals show characteristic

emotional patterns that persist over the years. Nevertheless, individuals and characteristics in the same individuals vary in their susceptibility to change. By adolescence basic emotional habits are well established. Intrapersonal and interpersonal factors contributing to youth's problems are having few friends, undeveloped social skills, lack of assertiveness, absence of someone with whom to share confidences, and lack of feelings of competence (Lipsitz, 1979).

One long-standing issue has been whether adolescence is characterized by any unusual storm and stress. It is sometimes argued that such stresses may be normal and even desirable, and that each life period has its own special stresses. Stress may be presumed to help adolescents clarify their values and, if satisfactorily resolved, helps them cope with future problems more effectively. Others cite symptoms of stress commonly associated with adolescence. In the past two decades the number of runaway adolescents has greatly increased, the most recent reliable projection being 600,000 in one year (Johnson & Carter, 1980). Lipsitz (1979) views adolescence as no more or less pathological than other stages in life. One-tenth of 1 percent of girls aged 10 to 14 have a baby, but 98 percent of unmarried girls aged 15 to 17 are not having them. The extremes in viewing adolescents range from "benign neglect to a crisis mentality" (p. 3). Most adolescents cope with this period remarkably well while attaining coping skills for the future.

Another issue concerns the relationship of adolescent emotion to later adjustment. Adelson (1979) believes that many forms of personal and social pathology appear first during adolescence, including depression, schizophrenia, and alcohol addiction.

Moral Development. Kohlberg's widely accepted model of moral development hypothesizes certain main stages. The first, or preconventional stage, involves relatively egocentric, self-centered concepts of right or wrong and is characteristic of earlier childhood. In the second stage of conventional morality, in late childhood, an individual identifies with the accepted standards of law and order. The next, or postconventional stage, involves more abstract reasoning and may produce conflict between personal and conventional standards (Kohlberg, 1975). A still higher stage involves coming to terms with the self and developing interpersonal commitments within a broader historical and social frame of reference (Kohlberg, 1977). Although adolescents are presumed to arrive at the postconventional stage, most adults remain at the conventional stage even by the age of 24. By that age only 10 percent of Kohlberg's middle-class male subjects had arrived at the personal principle phase, whereas 26 percent had reached the postconventional stage and still fewer the higher stage.

Kohlberg (1977) advocates programs in public schools specifically designed to elevate the level of moral reasoning. Critics of this theory argue that some behaviors embrace several stages at once, that regression does not always proceed in one way, and that Kohlberg's tests are

hardly valid indicators of how individuals will actually behave (Muson, 1979).

Over the past half century there has been little change in youth's religious views or basic morality (Caplow & Bahr, 1979). Present-day youth express somewhat more tolerance on civil rights issues, but there is little evidence of disintegration of traditional social values. Recent youth appear to be as patriotic, religious, and endowed with the Protestant ethic as their grandparents were at their age (Caplow & Bahr, 1979). In a national sampling of the attitudes of young people and their parents on eight traditional American values—saving money, hard work, competition, self-control, compromise, legal authority, private property, and organized religion—differences between the generations on seven of the eight were 9 percent or less. The only significant difference was in attitudes toward religion. Two-thirds of the young people thought religion was important to an individual, compared with 89 percent of their parents. The difference between college and noncollege youth was far greater than that between young people and their parents. In general, the college experience is a great divider in values and life-styles (Etzioni, 1978).

Adolescents' future goals are strongly focused on their private lives. A study of 17,000 high school seniors in 1980 indicated that almost three-quarters believed that a happy marriage and a good family life were very important. Almost 90 percent said that they wanted children, and about 80 percent of the young women and 60 percent of the young men cared very much or pretty much about latest records, clothes, and leisure activities ("Youth on the Move," 1981). In 1979, college freshmen over the country expressed considerable optimism regarding their personal future (Bachman & Johnston, 1979).

Youth's self-centeredness has been ascribed to an affluent society where they no longer have to bind their daily lives to the pursuit of success. The competitive pressures and complexities of modern life, combined with the success symbols that are available to almost everyone, have created an anomic condition, which produces self-oriented activity (Leger, 1980). Thus youth have withdrawn from expressing concern over society, because they feel helpless to control it, and express concern only about self. In the current mass society, youth's hedonism and escapism are symptomatic of having nothing to believe in: "no wars, no causes, no villains, no heroes" (Leger, 1980, p. 283).

Longitudinal research demonstrates the effect of the times on values. Youth who lived through the civil rights movement of the 1960s experienced quite different environments and different concepts of justice from those of earlier or later times. Today's youth are less willing to accept society's values without questioning than were those of the 1950s. They are now more concerned about their personal privacy and self-fulfillment ("Youth on the Move," 1980). In matters of religion, too, the new trend is personal, focused on self-development, and not strongly supported by social action ("Students Returning to Western Form of Worship," 1978).

Various suggestions have been made for upgrading youth's values. Discussing important issues in high school helps adolescents develop realistic values and achieve inner direction in a complex world ("Value of College Education," 1977). Youth may also be helped to reconcile values of work, duty, and tradition, as found in the Judeo-Christian ethic, with those of responsiveness and creativity stressed in existentialist philosophy (Scanlon, 1979). They may also be helped to understand how values vary among peoples of the earth. Various philosophers and educators have suggested formulas for moral education. Among them, Lawrence Kohlberg (1975) believes these programs should be cognitive, challenging, and related to an individual's stage of development.

Psychosexual Development. In adolescence psychosexual development has three main components: development of gender identity, development of sexual values and attitudes, and acquisition of sexual skills. These are presumed to develop according to stages. During the infancy period children are said to be narcissistic, gaining pleasure from their own bodies. In the second stage boys identify with their fathers, girls with their mothers. Each becomes attached to the parent of the opposite sex and jealous of the same-sex parent—the Oedipus complex in boys, the Electra in girls. In the third, or homosexual, stage of middle and late childhood, children associate mainly with members of their own sex; and in the final, heterosexual stage, beginning at puberty and continuing through life, they establish intimacy with someone of the other sex. However, these stages are conjectural, and in individual cases particular stages may be omitted altogether.

There is debate over whether there has been a sexual revolution among youth. Elias (1978) found today's adolescents to be more permissive in sexual behaviors and to discuss sex more naturally than their predecessors. He believes these changes indicate a healthy trend but do not constitute a sexual revolution. Meanwhile, the double sex standard, whereby sexes are judged by different codes of sexual morality, is weakening in some aspects but has not disappeared. Others describe changes in sex behaviors as dramatic. Youth are far more sexually experienced now than were their predecessors of the 1930s. Premarital intercourse has increased, especially for young women. Many young people are taking a life-style of sexual cohabitation without marriage with them into young adulthood, although in most cases they eventually marry. In 1950, of all couples ages 25 to 40 who lived together, 95 percent were married; by 1970 that number had declined to 80 percent (Scanlon, 1979).

Although youth have earlier sex experiences than formerly and the number of children born out of wedlock to teenagers is rapidly increasing, sex education is still remarkably haphazard and inadequate (Dickinson, 1978). Spanier (1978) reported that individuals who had not had sex education were neither more nor less likely to engage in premarital sex relations than those who had. Often such education comes too late. About 20 percent of babies born in the United States are to teenagers; and five in six of them are born to girls age 14 and younger (Finkel & Finkel, 1978). Ninety-five percent of teen mothers keep their babies today, compared with 10 to 12 percent some years ago (Connolly, 1978). Yet only 7 percent of girls under age 15 receive contraceptive advice, and rarely have they had instruction about childbirth or infant care (Dudley, 1979).

Boys receive even less assistance than girls. Among 421 high school boys, ages 12 to 19, only half of the questions asked about venereal disease and pregnancy were answered correctly. Their mean age for coitus was 12.8 years; thereafter sexual activity was about three times a month with one or two partners (Connolly, 1978). Wagner (1980) believes that males, along with females, should be encouraged to assume responsibility in matters of sexual expression, including contraception, abortion, and adoption.

Another special need is for better genetic education and counseling so that young people can learn of genetic defects and susceptibilities that might be transmitted to their offspring. They should also learn about precautions to be exercised by individuals with family histories of lung or breast cancer and be alerted to the dangers of drinking and smoking during pregnancy (Scanlon, 1979).

Sex roles. Youth's social sex roles, or behavior patterns appropriate for each sex, are based on biology but strongly modified by the culture (Hoffman, 1978). In general, the sexes have been affected by recent changes in women's role, but the precise influence of the women's movement is unclear. Girls continue to evaluate their sex roles lower than do boys, and students still support traditional sex roles in their more fundamental aspects. Nevertheless, Skovholt (1978) calls the change in sex role to be the "most viable evolutionary revolutionary movement" in the United States today. Women are invading many activities formerly dominated by men, whereas men are becoming more comfortable about their needs for dependency and intimacy. Adult males, in years to come, will have a richer life because they are coming to acknowledge their own feelings of tenderness, compassion, and gentleness (Skovholt, 1978).

Peer Culture. Peer groups—including gangs, crowds, and cliques—collectively constitute the peer culture, or adolescent society. There is some controversy over whether a true youth culture exists. Some observers perceive no real conflict between adult and youth culture. Others view it as somewhat independent of the larger society, with its own characteristic behaviors and values. In any case, teen cultures vary greatly according to social class, sex, and the times. Whether peer cultures in general have sound values is also a matter of dispute. Some research reveals them to be shallow in orientation; others report maturer values. They are viewed on the one hand as stifling individuality; on the other, as providing adolescents with support and security during initial ventures into the larger environment. Adolescents are somewhat open to others and thus gain important feedback concerning their own behavior. Adults find it more difficult to admit others to the inner core of the personality (Bensman & Lilienfeld, 1979). The discrepancy in evaluations of peer cultures may be due to the functions and character of the groups studied and to rapidly changing times (Kandel, 1978).

Counterculture. In recent years considerable attention has focused on alienated youth, or those who for some reason feel estranged from the larger society. "Countercultures," as alienated groups are termed, are a perennial phenomenon. These days only traces of the youth counterculture of the 1960s persist; yet they have left their mark on the present generation. Today's youth are sexually permissive without having the emotional bond that their predecessors of the 1960s had. Permissive sexual standards are the norm, but the emotional bond is gone (Leger, 1980).

A minority of youth continue to demonstrate their alienation from society. Among youth serious crime is rising at its most rapid pace ever, especially among girls. In the 1970s individuals under age 18 accounted for nearly half (43.3 percent) of all arrests for serious crimes (Lipsitz, 1979). Arrest of juveniles under 18 in the United States rose 27.5 percent from 1968 to 1977, and arrests for violent crimes rose 59.4 percent. Among girls under 18, arrests for such crimes rose 138.8 percent (Lipsitz, 1979). To date the relative importance of factors contributing to delinquency is still somewhat at issue, and the best methods of prevention debatable (Johnstone, 1978). Wynne (1978) attributes a considerable amount of youth's alienation to schools that have become larger and more bureaucratic, that focus on subject matter, and that foster activities that have little relevance to youth's present or future needs.

Nevertheless, college students surveyed in 1979 seemed relatively content with society. They were not unified by any major causes, such as those that youth espoused in the late 1960s (Rogers, 1981). In general they endorse the values of their elders, although opposing particular features of society ("Nation's Teenagers," 1977). Even the minority who were troublemakers as youth usually marry and become law-abiding adults, although a few remain troublemakers.

Family Experience. In some ways research on adolescents and the family still has a traditional ring. For youth, home continues to be an important base of security; and their future performance as parents tends to reflect their own experience in the family. Family relationships today are generally harmonious and the generation gap much narrower than formerly. Most parents still encourage the traditional sex roles—for example, by allowing boys more special privileges than girls and being more tolerant of their misbehaviors (Hart, 1978). Considerable debate persists about what constitutes optimal child rearing; however, longitudinal studies are yielding results that are throwing light on this question.

Other emphases on the family experience of youth are relatively new. Formerly attention focused mainly on the effect of parents on adolescents. More recently such relationships are viewed as interactive, with each affecting the other. Adolescents react to and react upon their parents, sometimes positively and sometimes negatively. Parents are coming to insist that they have rights that their children must respect. They are coming to retain benefits for themselves and are less likely to sacrifice all for their children.

Greater attention is also being paid to matters of family abuse, the most frequently abused children being 3-year-olds to 5-year-olds and 17-year-olds to 18-year-olds (Dudley, 1979). Eighteen out of every 100 children, most of them teenagers, sometimes assault their parents ("Battered Families," 1979).

An especially significant development is the increase in the numbers of youth reared in alternative or nonnuclear families, especially in one-parent households, headed by an unwed parent or one whose partner is not present because of divorce, death, or other reasons. Levine (1978) thinks the myth of the average family should be discarded and that educators should acknowledge the variety of family types in which children live. Already one in six children lives in a single-parent household, and 45 percent will do so before the age of 18 (Cornish, 1979).

Greater attention is also being paid to youth's future family role. Over the last decade or so, the family size that youth favor has declined. About half now want two children, 26 percent three, and 17 percent four (Juhasz, 1980). Male youth are coming to attach increasing importance to their future role in the family. Female youth still rank marriage and motherhood first among their future priorities, although most of them expect to combine career and marriage (Mash, 1978).

Vocation. A significant change has taken place in youth's attitudes toward work. They are showing greater interest in intrinsic work rewards and relatively less on making money and attaining high status (Miller & Simon, 1979). They still have a strong work ethic, only slightly less than the older generation, but they share in society's growing concern for constructive use of leisure time. Increasing emphasis is being placed on living a fuller, more human life and the more pleasant aspects of human experience. Thus leisure activities are gaining greater status than formally as part of the life-style ("Recreation for All," 1977).

The times have presented new, or modified old, problems of vocational decision. Youth are faced with the constantly accelerating pace of occupational obsolescence and innovation (Skovholt, 1978). They have few visible vocational role models and are confronted with the growing complexity and impersonality of the work world. Girls, especially, see few of their own sex in a great many occupations (Laska & Micklin, 1979).

Considerable emphasis is being placed on career choice and development in the schools. Adolescents are expected to develop a certain career maturity, including knowledge and attitudes about occupations (Krumboltz, Becker-Haven, & Burnett, 1979). They may approach this topic in terms of the life-span vocational career. In other nations the emphasis is on early occupational choice, but in the United States schools deliberately present a range of options and encourage postponement of irreversible decisions until late in their school careers (Tyler, 1981). Also, schools may prepare youth for on-the-job adjustment, including review of early career as a period of considerable exploration. Too often vocational education focuses mainly on first-time vocational choice and initial adjustment to jobs.

Often earlier experiences play an important part in later vocational career. In a longitudinal study of men aged 35 to 45, it was found that several novelists had begun writing in high school or earlier (Levinson, 1978). Jencks (1979) found that the leadership exhibited and the general educational attainment in grades 6 to 10 related to obtaining prestigious jobs in adulthood.

Environment and the Times. Youth are strongly affected by their environment. For example, peers become increasingly important after the transition to adolescence, especially in rural areas (Garbarino et al., 1978). In the homogeneous suburbs, youth have little opportunity for mixing with people who see things from varied viewpoints ("The Sheltered Life," 1978). Because of greater restrictions placed upon them, girls have less access than boys to the larger society (Hart, 1978).

Other factors relate to the times. Modern communication has greatly facilitated youth's acceleration of learning and understanding of the world's peoples ("Dangers and Hopes for Humanity," 1978). On the other hand, the speed of change has made it hard for youth to establish connections with past and future. The past is already out of date and the future unpredictable because of unexpected technological and sociological development. Youth have become suspicious of technology and fail to recognize that it can be utilized in either constructive or destructive ways ("Technology's Effect on American Society," 1978).

Academic Status. American youth's academic preparation for such a world has various deficiencies. In a cross-national test, including most countries in western Europe, Australia, New Zealand, Japan, Israel, and the United States, American 14-year-olds were third highest of the fifteen nations tested; however, in reading comprehension they fell in the lowest third (Tyler, 1981). Since the early 1960s fewer than half of American 14-year-olds have scored above-average on application of computational skills to quantitative problems, such as those encountered on automobile trips, in making purchases, or in computing taxes. The average science score of American high school seniors was lower than those of other modern nations, with students from New Zealand and Japan scoring far higher than the others (Tyler, 1981). In comparison with those from other advanced nations, American youth take citizenship for granted and have little concern about it.

The United States has also been least effective among the advanced nations in perfecting a smooth transition from school to work (Tyler, 1981). Neither the American students nor those in other countries were gaining the knowledge required for wise consumption. Other research disclosed that Scholastic Aptitude Test (SAT) scores of 1979 seniors had descended to record lows, continuing a decline that began in 1963. Their mean mathematics score dropped one point to 467, and the verbal score fell 2 points to 427. These declines have been blamed on everything from "television to Watergate to laxity in the schools" ("Oops! SAT Scores Still Falling," 1979, p. 155).

Teachers themselves perceive students' performance as inadequate. Three hundred veteran teachers in Minnesota, averaging seventeen years of service, noted significant changes in youth over two decades. They found today's students more outspoken and assertive and more concerned with instant gratification and the need to be entertained. Students were viewed as having shorter attention spans, being harder to please, having greater expectations, having less willingness to expend effort to learn, and being motivated more by external than internal rewards. Not one teacher saw them as possessing greater knowledge than in the past (Hedin & Conrad, 1980, p. 702).

The School's Performance. Some research raises questions about how well educators are doing their job. Nationally, the dropout rate for high school is about 25 percent (Lipsitz, 1979). Another problem has been school violence. In the year 1978 over 60,000 incidents of teachers being injured by students were reported (Handleman, 1980). School discipline is a major problem, reflecting trends toward growing desperation and disorder among teenagers and decreasing respect for authority (Rosow, 1979). Glasser (1978) concludes that the answer to the discipline problem is to give students a stake in the school through becoming involved in the school's activities and making decent grades.

Some of the evidence points to problems of motivation. A survey of more than 17,000 secondary school students disclosed that the general self-concept gradually increases with grade level but that academic self-concept declines slightly with increasing grade level. The question arises of whether lower-grade teachers do more than upper-grade teachers to help children feel good about their schoolwork. In this study, praise, encouragement, correction with guidance, and positive interaction decreased by almost 50 percent from early elementary grades until senior high school (Benham, Giesen, & Oakes, 1980). Teachers still relate to students "in a universalistic, not individualistic fashion, responding less to their emotional needs and more to the necessity for them to become task- and achievement-oriented" (Gump, 1978, p. 153). Also neglected is the importance of pupil-pupil interaction.

Tubbs and Bean (1981) conclude that "as life styles become more flexible the high school remains inflexibly standardized. . . . As social problems become more complex the high school curriculum focuses on discrete subject areas and minimal competence" (p. 399). Teachers themselves may be part of the problem. A great majority (95 percent) of Iowa science and social studies specialists agreed that teachers need help themselves in understanding the complexity and scope of major issues as well as strategies for teaching these issues (Blaga & Cooney, 1981).

Other critics believe that the quality of curriculum has declined. A comparison of American high schools in 1974 and 1979 indicated that teaching social issues and student involvement in community service and curriculum planning have decreased (Tubbs & Bean, 1981). Occasional schools required foreign language for graduation in 1974; by 1979 that requirement had all but disappeared. More vocational-career education, science, and basic-skills remedial courses are provided today than in 1974 but fewer in special subjects—for example, in art, music, and modern language.

Schools should also give more attention to subgroupings of youth, including different social classes, married youth, deviants, individualists, and dropouts. Also neglected are the very bright. The columnist James Kilpatrick (1979) argued that it is wrong for a state to spend $740 on each of 220,000 unprepared and handicapped students and only $40 per student on 70,000 of the gifted.

Some critics believe that teachers are inadequately prepared. Charles Frye, a California teacher, suggests that if a government agency were to manifest a fifteen-year decline, as students have done on achievement-test scores, the management would be closely scrutinized. Such has not been the case in education, whose establishment personnel, like the teachers they manage, have taken graduate education courses mostly lacking in content. Among teacher candidates taking graduate record examinations from 1964 to 1977, 81 percent of those applying to graduate schools of education were below average in the verbal section and 84 percent were below average in the quantitative. Fewer than 100 of the 4,365 made scores that might be called distinguished (Frye, 1979).

The schools may receive more negative criticism than they deserve. For one thing, background factors such as family, social class, and intellectual ability are important predictors of school success (Bachman, O'Malley, & Johnston, 1978). Besides, in the cross-national survey already cited (Tyler, 1981), the highest 5 percent of American young people achieved the same high scores reached in other industralized nations where advanced schooling is reserved for elite youth.

Upgrading Education.   Suggestions for improving adolescents' educational experience are varied. Adler (1979) stresses preparation for continuing to learn after formal schooling is terminated. He recommends a nonspecialized liberalized type of curriculum that introduces young people to the whole cosmos of learning, including basic ideas and pivotal points in civilization. Anderson (1979) identifies the main curriculum change as greater attention to the basics, especially in writing and core curriculum.

Goodlad (1979) believes this stress on going back to basics may enhance students' alienation because they will perceive schools as becoming even less relevant than before. Recently, growing attention has been paid to the school environment, including such phenomena as social climate and life space (Gump, 1978).

Anderson (1979) suggests that curricula be designed to promote youth's maturity. This concept involves acquiring firm preadult underpinnings, including healthy channels for emotion, learning to organize environments for maximum self-realization, establishing a sense of identity and rewarding life-styles, arriving at a rational moral code and philosophy of life, and developing the resourcefulness to deal with giant-sized problems. They must be prepared for uncertain futures that seem impossible or improbable today (Anderson, 1979). They must have the emotional stability and coping skills for dealing with ever changing and unusual problems.

Schools must also continuously update their curricula, anticipating what students will need in the future. Shane (1981) stresses the importance of commitment to something greater than oneself, without which nations do not maintain their moral character. An international panel of 135 distinguished scholars expressed a need for youth to appreciate the "unity or holistic quality of basic laws of nature" (Shane, 1981, p. 353). They should learn that human beings are significant environmental change agents and should avoid exploiting the planet. They should understand basic principles of science in a science-dominated world. At the same time, equity requires that youth comprehend the concepts of economic and social justice, and they should realize that human society is now global. They should appreciate the diversity of cultures and concepts of cultural relativism. Also important is knowing at least one language other than one's mother tongue for better cross-cultural communication. The panel complained that our schools have changed little.

To date, youth have emerged into adulthood with simplistic ideas about complex topics. They should learn to deal with vast problems, environmental complexity, alternative environments, and how to control them. They must learn to adapt to a complex mesh of cultures within cultures and, because of the world trend toward pluralism, to accommodate to varied groups and life-styles.

Dorothy Rogers

See also Junior High and Middle School Education; Life-Span Development; Physical Development; Preadolescent Development; Secondary Education; Sex Education.

REFERENCES

Adams, G. R., & Looft, W. R. Cultural change: Education and youth. *Adolescence,* 1977, *12*(46), 137–150.

Adelson, J. Adolescence and the generalization gap. *Psychology Today,* 1979, *12*(9), 33–37.

Adler, M. J. Education in a democracy. *American Educator,* 1979, *3*(1), 6–9.

Anderson, S. B. Educational measurement in a new decade. *College Board Review*, Summer 1979, *112*, 20–23.

Bachman, J. G., & Johnston, L. D. The freshmen, 1979. *Psychology Today*, 1979, *13*(4), 26–41.

Bachman, J. G.; O'Malley, P. M.; & Johnston, J. *Adolescence to Adulthood: Change and Stability in the Lives of Young Men.* Vol. 6 of *Youth in Transition.* Ann Arbor, Mich.: Institute for Social Research, 1978.

Battered families: A growing nightmare. *U.S. News and World Report,* January 15, 1979, pp. 60–61.

Benham, B. J.; Giesen, P.; & Oakes, J. A study of schooling: Students' experiences in schools. *Phi Delta Kappan,* 1980, *61*(5), 337–340.

Bensman, J., & Lilienfeld, R. Friendship and alienation. *Psychology Today,* 1979, *13*(4), 56–66, 114.

Blaga, J. J., & Cooney, T. M. Teachers need help on science-related social issues. *Phi Delta Kappan,* 1981, *62*(5), 400.

Blume, S. B. A psychiatrist looks at alcoholism. *Intellect,* 1975, *104*(2367), 27–30.

Caplow, T., & Bahr, H. M. Half a century of change in adolescent attitudes: Replication of a middle-town survey by the Lynds. *Public Opinion Quarterly,* 1979, *43*(1), 1–17.

Connolly, L. Boy fathers. *Human Behavior,* 1978, *7*(1), 40–43.

Cornish, E. The future of the family: Intimacy in an age of loneliness. *Futurist,* 1979, *13*(1), 45–59.

Dangers and hopes for humanity. *USA Today,* 1978, *107*(2401), 1–2.

Dickinson, G. E. Adolescent sex information sources: 1964–1974. *Adolescence,* 1978, *13*(52), 653–658.

Dozier, J. E.; Lewis, S.; Kersey, A. G.; & Charping, J. W. Sports groups: An alternative treatment modality for emotionally disturbed adolescents. *Adolescence,* 1978, *13*(51), 483–493.

Dudley, E. Rainbows and realities: Current trends in marriage and its alternatives. *Futurist,* 1979, *13*(1), 23–32.

Elias, J. E. Adolescents and sex. *Humanist,* 1978, *38*(2), 29–31.

Etzioni, A. Youth is not a class. *Psychology Today,* 1978, *11*(9), 20–21.

Finkel, M. L., & Finkel, D. J. Male adolescent contraceptive utilization. *Adolescence,* 1978, *13*(51), 443–451.

Frye, C. M. Who runs the schools? *Newsweek,* September 3, 1979, p. 13.

Garbarino, J.; Burston, N.; Raber, S.; Russell, R.; & Crouter, A. The social maps of children approaching adolescence: Studying the ecology of youth development. *Journal of Youth and Adolescence,* 1978, *7*(4), 417–428.

Glasser, W. Disorders in our schools: Causes and remedies. *Phi Delta Kappan,* 1978, *59*(5), 331–333.

Goleman, D. 1,528 little geniuses and how they grew. *Psychology Today,* 1980, *13*(9), 28–43.(a)

Goleman, D. Still learning from Terman's children. *Psychology Today,* 1980, *13*(9), 44–53.(b)

Goodlad, J. I. Can our schools get better? *Phi Delta Kappan,* 1979, *60*(5), 342–347.

Gump, P. V. School environments. In I. Altman & J. F. Wohlwill (Eds.), *Children and the Environment.* New York: Plenum Press, 1978.

Handleman, C. Teaching and academic standards today. *Adolescence,* 1980, *15*(59), 723–730.

Hart, R. *Children's Experience of Place: A Developmental Study.* New York: Irvington Press, 1978.

Hedin, D., & Conrad, D. Changes in children and youth over two decades: The perceptions of teachers. *Phi Delta Kappan,* 1980, *61*(10), 702.

Hendry, L., & Gillies, P. Body type, body esteem, school, and leisure: A study of overweight, average, and underweight adolescents. *Journal of Youth and Adolescence,* 1978, *7*(2), 181–195.

Hoffman, L. W. Changes in family roles, socialization, and sex differences. *Educational Horizons,* 1978, *57*(1), 10–18.

Jencks, C., interviewed by C. T. Cory. Making it: Can the odds be evened? *Psychology Today,* 1979, *13*(2), 35–39.

Johnson, R., & Carter, M. M. Flight of the young: Why children run away from their homes. *Adolescence,* 1980, *15*(58), 483–489.

Johnstone, J. W. C. Juvenile delinquency and the family: A contextual interpretation. *Youth and Society,* 1978, *9*(3), 299–313.

Juhasz, A. M. Adolescent attitudes toward childbearing and family size. *Family Relations,* 1980, *29*(1), 29–34.

Kandel, D. B. On variations in adolescent subcultures. *Youth and Society,* 1978. *9*(4), 373–384.

Katchadourian, H. *The Biology of Adolescence.* San Francisco: Freeman, 1977.

Kilpatrick, J. J. America's schools penalize the gifted child. *Miami Herald,* September 1, 1979, p. 7A.

Kohlberg, L. The cognitive-developmental approach to moral education. *Phi Delta Kappan,* 1975, *56*(10), 610–677.

Kohlberg, L. The implications of moral stages of adult education. *Religious Education,* 1977, *72*(2), 182–201.

Krumboltz, J. D.; Becker-Haven, J. F.; & Burnett, K. F. Counseling psychology. In M. R. Rosenzweig & L. W. Porter (Eds.), *Annual Review of Psychology* (Vol. 30). Palo Alto, Calif.: Annual Reviews, 1979, pp. 555–602.

Laska, S. B., & Micklin, M. The knowledge dimension of occupational socialization: Role models and their social influence. *Youth and Society,* 1979, *10*(4), 360–378.

Leger, R. G. Where have all the flowers gone? A sociological analysis of the origins and content of youth values of the seventies. *Adolescence,* 1980, *15*(58), 283–300.

Levine, J. A. Real kids versus "the average" family. *Psychology Today,* 1978, *12*(1), 14–15.

Levinson, D. J. The mid-life transition. *Psychiatry,* 1977, *40,* 96–112.

Levinson, D. J. Growing up with the dream. *Psychology Today,* 1978, *11*(8), 20–31, 89.

Lipsitz, J. S. Adolescent development: Myths and realities. *Children Today,* 1979, *8*(5), 2–7.

Mash, D. J. The development of life-style preferences of college women. *Journal of National Association of Women Deans and Counselors,* Winter 1978, pp. 72–76.

Matheny, A. P., Jr.; Dolan, A.; & Krantz, J. Z. Cognitive aspects of interests, responsibilities, and vocational goals in adolescence. *Adolescence,* 1980, *15*(58), 301–311.

Miller, P. Y., & Simon, W. Do youth really want to work? A comparison of the work values and job perceptions of younger and older men. *Youth and Society,* 1979, *10*(4), 379–404.

Muson, H. Moral thinking. Can it be taught? *Psychology Today,* 1979, *12*(9), 48–58, 67–68, 92.

Nation's teenagers becoming conservative. *Intellect,* 1977, *106*(2386), 1.

Neugarten, B. L. Personality and the aging process. In S. H. Garit (Ed.), *Readings in Aging and Death: Contemporary Perspectives.* New York: Harper & Row, 1977, pp. 72–77.

Newman, B. M. Coping and adaptation in adolescence. *Human Development,* 1979, *22,* 255–262.

Oops! SAT scores still falling: Verbal by two points, math by one in 1978–1979. *Phi Delta Kappan,* 1979, *61*(3), 155–156.

Recreation for all is latest goal in the cities. *U.S. News and World Report,* May 23, 1977, pp. 72–73.

Rice, R. R., & Marsh, M. The social environments of the two high schools: Background data. In J. G. Kelly (Ed.), *Adolescent Boys in High School: A Psychological Study of Coping and Adaptation.* Hillsdale, N.J.: Lawrence Erlbaum Associates, 1979, pp. 59–80.

Rogers, D. *Adolescents and Youth* (4th ed.). Englewood Cliffs, N.J.: Prentice-Hall, 1981.

Rosenfeld, A. The new SD: Life-span development. *Saturday Review,* October 1, 1977, pp. 32–33.

Rosow, J. M. The workplace: A changing scene. *Vocational Education,* 1979, *54*(2), 22–25.

Scanlon, J. *Young Adulthood.* New York: Academy for Educational Development, 1979.

Shane, H. G. Significant writings that have influenced the curriculum: 1906–1981. *Phi Delta Kappan,* 1981, *62*(5), 311–314.

The sheltered life. *Human Behavior,* 1978, *7*(10), 61.

Skovholt, T. M. Feminism and men's lives. *Counseling Psychologist,* 1978, *7*(4), 3–10.

Spanier, G. B. Sex education and premarital sexual behavior among American college students. *Adolescence,* 1978, *13*(52), 659–674.

Student spirits: A new look at drinking on campus. *Human Behavior,* 1979, *8*(1), 67.

Students returning to Western form of worship. *Intellect,* 1978, *106*(2396), 439.

Tanner, J. M. *Education and Physical Growth* (2nd ed.). London: University of London Press, 1978. (a)

Tanner, J. M. *Foetus into Man: Physical Growth from Conception to Maturity.* Cambridge, Mass.: Harvard University Press, 1978. (b)

Technology's effect on American society. *USA Today,* 1978, *106*(2396), 441–442.

Tubbs, M. P., & Beane, J. A. A second look at the U.S. high school. *Phi Delta Kappan,* 1981, *62*(5), 399–400.

Tyler, R. W. The U.S. versus the world: A comparison of educational performance. *Phi Delta Kappan,* 1981, *62*(5), 307–310.

Value of college education to jobless graduates. *Intellect,* 1977, *105*(2380), 210–211.

Wagner, C. A. Sexuality of American adolescents. *Adolescence,* 1980, *15*(59), 567–580.

Winer, J. A.; Schwartz, L. H.; & Berger, A. S. Sexual problems found in users of a student mental health clinic. *Journal of Youth and Adolescence,* 1977, *6*(2), 117–126.

Wynne, E. A. Behind the discipline problem: Youth suicide as a measure of alienation. *Phi Delta Kappan,* 1978, *59*(5), 307–315.

Youth on the move. *U.S. News and World Report,* 1980, *89*(26), 72–73.

ADULT DEVELOPMENT

Until very recently not much was known about the period of life that follows adolescence. The past decade, however, has seen a tremendous increase in both the scope and depth of our knowledge. This is particularly true concerning our understanding of adult cognitive development.

In spite of the progress made, research on adult development is still relatively incomplete. Firm answers to important questions are hard to come by. Oftentimes there is more published research on old age than on the middle-adult years.

The Senses. Our knowledge of sensory functioning in adulthood is among the most straightforward of the entire field. Research in this area has grown steadily, particularly in vision and hearing. Birren and Schaie, for example, devote four full chapters to research on sensation and perception in their handbook (1977).

Vision. Throughout the adult years a number of structural changes take place in the eye. First, the lens becomes thicker and less elastic. This process results in people becoming farsighted, as the ability to focus clearly on nearby objects diminishes. Although this gradual loss of accommodation, called presbyopia, begins early in life, the problem is most often noted after the age of 40. Second, the lens of the eye becomes progressively opaque, while at the same time the average size of the pupil diminishes. These changes often work at cross-purposes with each other (Fozard et al., 1977). The decreasing size of the pupil permits less light to reach the retina, while at the same time the clouding of the lens results in a scattering of available light. These two conditions are most notably a problem for older adults. Thus, although it may become necessary to increase average light levels as aging continues, the additional light may only cause new problems because of glare. Third, clouding of the lens is actually a yellowing of the lens. The yellow lens acts like a yellow filter, and color discrimination becomes increasingly difficult. Colors at the high end of the spectrum (blue, blue-green, and violet) are particularly difficult to discriminate; colors at the low end of the spectrum (orange and red) remain relatively unaffected. Finally, changes in clarity and elasticity of the lens have also been noted to affect depth perception (Fozard et al., 1977).

With increasing age, the ability to adapt to changing levels of illumination, called "dark adaption," is also affected. There are two points to consider in dark-adaption research. The first is the length of time necessary to reach maximum seeing ability in lowered light conditions, as upon entering a darkened movie theater, for example, or a darkened street after leaving a brightly lit office at night. The second consideration involves the maximum level of sensitivity that is ultimately reached. The evidence is abundantly clear that the maximum sensitivity reached declines throughout the adult years. In terms of the actual rate of adaption, evidence is less clear, but much of the research indicates that it does take longer to adapt to the dark as aging continues (McFarland et al., 1960).

Finally, "visual acuity," the ability to perceive fine details at a distance, declines with age, but most of the change takes place after the age of 40 (Fozard et al., 1977).

Hearing. Beginning with early adulthood, most men and women experience some hearing loss. The most often noted problem involves the progressive inability to hear high-frequency tones, a condition known as presbycusis. Normal hearing in young adulthood spans a frequency range of 20–20,000 Hz. But by mid-life, many individuals experience increasing difficulty in hearing tones above 7,000–10,000 Hz. For practical, everyday purposes, this decline is not terribly important until it begins to affect the range of tones involved in speech perception (500–2,000 Hz). Consonants such as *f, y, st, t, z, th,* and *sh* are most likely to be misperceived when ability to hear high tones is impaired (Corso, 1977). It also seems that males are more likely to suffer from high-frequency hearing loss than are females, probably because of such environmental factors as overexposure to very loud noises (Kart, Metress & Metress, 1978).

Olfaction and gustation. Although research in both olfaction and gustation has increased substantially during the past decade, it is still difficult to formulate any firm conclusions. Odor sensitivity appears to remain relatively stable throughout adulthood. There is evidence for decreased ability to taste in later life, but the evidence must be viewed with caution. Some support exists for decreased sensitivity to salty substances and increased aversion to bitter tastes. Engen (1977) concludes that changes of sensitivity to smells and tastes may be due to factors other than age, such as health status and smoking.

Touch and pain. As in the case of olfaction and gustation, it is difficult to draw any firm conclusions from available research on touch and pain, although a recent study by Thornbury and Mistretta (1981) does report substantial decline with age in touch sensitivity. In general, however, the changes reported depend more on differing methodologies, the part of the body being studied, and health of the subject than they do age.

Intelligence. No subject in the area of adult development has generated more research than the issue concerning stability of intelligence test scores across the life span. Although literature in this area is massive, great controversy remains. Perhaps the best way to disentangle some of this controversy is to look at different types of methodology used.

Cross-sectional studies. Most of the research concerning stability of intelligence has been cross-sectional. That is, individuals from different age-groups are compared with one another at the same point in time. The pattern resulting from most of these studies is sometimes referred to as "classic aging pattern." The argument is that intellectual growth continues up to the middle to late twenties, with substantial decline thereafter. Evidence for decline in adult intelligence-test scores dates back to the beginning of intelligence testing (Yoakum & Yerkes, 1920). In their now classic study, Jones and Conrad (1933) found that test scores on the Army Alpha declined steadily throughout middle to late adulthood. In his review of the cross-sectional literature, Botwinick (1977) reports that decline takes place for men and women, whites and blacks, for people of different economic statuses, and for people of high and low ability.

Many tests of adult intelligence are currently in use, but the one most often used today is the Wechsler Adult Intelligence Scale (WAIS). The WAIS consists of eleven subtests that measure verbal and performance ability. The verbal tests rely heavily on one's general knowledge and information store, and the performance tests require mainly problem-solving and reasoning skills. In addition, most verbal tests are untimed power tests, while most performance measures emphasize speed. Wechsler (1958), using cross-cultural data, argued that up to late middle age, verbal scores on the WAIS exhibit relatively little decline. Performance scores, particularly those that emphasize speed, show a much more accelerated decline. When Wechsler combined verbal and performance subtests to get a composite IQ, he argued that peak performance on the WAIS occurs in the twenties. Following that, a small decline begins in the thirties, with more rapid decline after the late fifties.

A major theory of intelligence was developed in the 1960s. Using factor analysis, Cattell (1963) defined two basic types of intelligence: fluid and crystallized. Fluid intelligence consists of abilities that depend on the physiological structure of the individual particularly on the central nervous system. It involves the capacity for acquiring new ideas, grasping relationships, and adapting to new conditions. Crystallized intelligence, on the other hand, involves the individual's general knowledge of the culture. It is the kind of information gained in school, and in one's day-to-day interaction and experience. Horn and Cattell (1967) argued that test scores measuring fluid ability correspond to performance scores on the Wechsler tests, in that each shows substantial decline with age. Crystallized intelligence scores are similar to verbal scores on the Wechsler, they argue, because both measures remain fairly stable with age, although some decline may occur.

Several reasons have been posited for the decline found in so many of the cross-sectional studies. Perhaps the oldest argument involves the role of speed. Few would disagree that as people age they become slower in their responses. This slowing down could affect scores on intelligence tests. But current controversy has revolved around whether decrease in speed is due to atrophy of muscles, senses, and peripheral nervous system or whether the problem lies with a central nervous system function. In short, the question is whether "output" or "thoughtput" is the limiting factor (Elias, Elias, & Elias, 1977).

One way to test for this distinction has been to compare scores on intelligence tests administered under speeded and nonspeeded conditions. The classic work in this area was performed by Doppelt and Wallace (1955). When they administered the WAIS with and without time limits to a group of older adults, they found almost no difference in scores between the two test conditions. Similar conclusions were more recently drawn by Storandt (1977). Since additional time does not seem to help older people on intelligence tests, Botwinick (1978) in his review, concludes that reported decline may be due to high-order cognitive processes in the central nervous system.

A second reason posited for the decline was presented by Demming and Pressey (1957). They argued that most intelligence tests used to assess adult intelligence were originally designed to predict success in school. Demming and Pressey (1957) constructed a test from information items that they felt was more closely related to the experiences of adults. They found a rise in scores through the middle and late years, even with people whose scores had declined on conventional tests. Unfortunately, further development of this work was cut short by Pressey's retirement two years later. At present, much additional research is needed to clarify the relevance of conventional intelligence tests with middle-aged and older adults.

A related area of work, however, has established a number of important facts. It is well known that level of formal education and intelligence test scores are correlated. It is also clear that the level of formal education reached by adults has increased steadily throughout the twentieth century. This change in educational attainment has significant implications for cross-sectional research. When people of different age-groups are compared, changes due to age become confounded with generational differences. Thus, the reported decline found in many cross-sectional studies may tell us as much about differing levels of educational attainment, as it does about developmental changes.

In an important study, Birren and Morrison (1961) analyzed the WAIS standardization data. Using scores for persons ranging in age from 25 to 64, they correlated age and education along with the eleven WAIS subtests. They reported that in predicting levels of adult intelligence, level of education was even more important than age. Although one should not conclude that educational attainment is the only variable on which people of different generations differ, it is certainly one of the most significant.

Longitudinal research. One way to avoid the problem of generational differences is through longitudinal research. In a longitudinal design, the same subjects are studied over a period of time. Two of the better-known longitudinal studies concerned with adult intelligence were conducted by Owens (1953, 1966). Owens located 127 males who had taken the Army Alpha as an entrance-exam requirement at Iowa State University in 1919. He tested them on the Alpha in 1950 when they were approximately 50 years old, and again in 1961 when they were in their early sixties. Owens did not report the decline that is often found with cross-sectional designs. In fact, he found an increase in total score up to age 50. There was a small decline in total score on the 1961 testing, but it was not significant. Some abilities, such as ability to solve arithmetic problems, did show decline in both testings, however. Other longitudinal studies have found similar results (Eisdorfer & Wilkie, 1973; Gilbert, 1973). From the longitudinal studies, one can conclude that there is decline in intellectual abilities, but the decline is not great until relatively late in life. Furthermore, the decline is mostly with perceptual-integrative and reasoning tasks, especially when speed is involved. Verbal skills are maintained except in advanced old age.

But the problem does not end here. Although cross-sectional studies artificially inflate age-changes, Botwinick (1977) argues that longitudinal studies may artificially deflate them. The problem involves the loss of subjects that inevitably occurs over extended periods of time. This loss of subjects is not random; persons of lower initial ability are least likely to continue across repeated testings. As a result, subjects remaining after the second or third testing begin to represent a select group.

Schaie (1965) and Kuhlen (1963) were among the first to argue that current research designs can distort age-related trends. Schaie (1965) recommends a third approach called "sequential analysis." Sequential analysis is a sophisticated approach designed to alleviate the problems inherent in both cross-sectional and longitudinal designs.

Up to now, several sequential studies have been reported. Examples include Schaie and Labouvie-Vief (1974), Schaie and Parham (1977), and Schaie and Strother (1968). Botwinick (1977) argues that general age-trends reported by these studies fall somewhere between the trends found with cross-sectional and longitudinal research.

The debate continues, however, and not everyone agrees that the final conclusions have been reached. Readers interested in this issue are encouraged to read the heated exchange in the *American Psychologist.* Horn and Donaldson (1976, 1977) took a strong position in favor of decline. In two other articles, Baltes and Schaie (1976) and Schaie and Baltes (1977) argued in favor of the plasticity and stability of intelligence.

Piagetian tasks. In addition to the traditional model of intelligence already discussed, there is a second competing model, the "Piagetian" approach. Although the bulk of work on Piagetian tasks has been done with children, interest in the past decade has been directed to the nature of concrete and formal operations in adulthood. One popular approach argues that adults regress in terms of these abilities; that is, after young adulthood, people often lose the ability to think in terms of formal operations. This regression may become so acute by late adulthood that concrete operational functioning may be affected as well.

In a review of published Piagetian research on adults, Papalia and Del Vento Bielby (1974) argued that, although some regression may be present in elderly adults, there are too many methodological problems in the literature to draw any final conclusions. More recent studies have also challenged the regression hypothesis. Tesch, Whitbourne, and Nehrke (1978) for example, found no differences in performance in an egocentrism task among subjects 33–83 years of age. It is important to point out, however, that many researchers outside the Piagetian camp (Arenberg, 1968; Hulicka, 1967) have commented on the difficulties of presenting older adults with complex problem-solving and learning tasks. These tasks involve abilities very similar to those demanded by formal operational tasks.

Learning. Adult learning is an area of growing interest with significant implications for education. The once popular belief that adults become less able to learn new things with age has given way to the notion that new learning is possible throughout life.

An important distinction in the work on adult learning is the difference between learning and performance. Learning can never be directly measured. What can be measured is performance, and from that we infer learning. Thus, when performance is poor, it does not necessarily mean learning has not occurred. Poor performance may be due to a number of other factors, such as available response time, motivational level of the learner, fatigue, and so forth.

In this regard, there is little doubt that a performance deficit occurs in adulthood, but there is much controversy about whether the decrement is due to difficulties in learning. Research performed with serial and paired-associate learning provides compelling evidence that fast pacing is related to performance deficits. A serial-learning task is a list of words to be remembered, whereas a paired-associate task refers to a set of word pairs. Both are sometimes referred to as verbal-learning tasks.

Fast pacing with these tasks includes two considerations. One is the length of time an individual is given to study the words; the second is the length of time given to respond to a question. In a paired-associate study, Monge and Hultsch (1971) reported that a limited amount of time in which to respond was harmful to a group of adult subjects, aged 40–66. This factor, however, did not hurt a group of younger adults, aged 20–39, nearly so much. But was a limited amount of study time also harmful? Monge and Hultsch said it was, but one age-group was not hampered any more than the other. The point was that, when response time was speeded, the older subjects could not express what they had learned.

The problem does not end here, however. Monge and Hultsch and others (Arenberg, 1965) have argued that even when older adults are permitted ample response time, their performance rate, although improved, is not equal to that of younger adults. More important, although response time accounts for much of performance decline on verbal-learning tasks, it does not account for all of this decline. On these tasks, older adults need more time to learn than their younger counterparts.

Another reason why performance deficits are seen on learning tasks is the apparent cautiousness of older adults. Canestrari (1963) was one of the first to observe that errors made by older adults on learning tasks are more likely to be errors of omission than of commission. In other words, they tend to skip items rather than make a wrong response. When adequate time is given to respond, the number of omission errors decreases markedly. The level of initial ability does not explain these omission errors of older learners (Silverman, 1963).

Yet another reason for decline in performance scores throughout adulthood may be differing levels of motivation. It is often presumed that adults, as they grow older, become less involved with learning tasks. Motivational

level seems to decline. The bulk of the evidence, however, does not support this contention.

Although there are many ways of defining motivation, one of the most typical views motivation as the general state of arousal, or involvement of an individual in a task. Studies of motivational level, have found older adults are often too aroused for the task. In one study, Powell, Eisdorfer, and Bogdonoff (1964) found physiological correlates of arousal increased steadily with age in a serial-learning task. Ross (1968) attempted to vary the level of "challenge" in the instructions preceding a paired-associates task. As instructions were changed from a supportive context to a challenging one, performance levels of older adults decreased markedly. Younger subjects remained unaffected. In effect then, the older adults had become too motivated for the task.

It is important to point out that most of the experiments dealing with motivational levels and learning tasks have been completed in laboratory environments. It is not yet clear whether the same motivational levels would be present in other settings.

Memory. Learning and memory are clearly related. Botwinick (1978) argues that learning has to do with how much information "gets in," and memory involves how this information gets "filed away." It is exceedingly difficult to separate learning and memory because memory is involved in the learning process and vice versa.

Models of memory. Atkinson and Shiffrin (1968) represent memory in terms of three memory-storage systems: (1) sensory memory, (2) short-term memory, and (3) long-term memory. As information enters the system, it is passed from one component to another. For a variety of reasons, some of the information gets lost in the process, and is not available for long-term storage. For example, short-term memory is limited in terms of both capacity and duration. For this reason, short-term memory may become over-loaded, and information will not be passed on. Memory researchers suggest ways of dealing with this problem. Rehearsal of information is one way that material in short-term store can be strengthened and transferred to long-term storage. Appropriate categorization of information is another way it can be accomplished.

Craik and Lockhart (1972) propose a different model of memory. They argue that the real issue in memory research is the level of processing that takes place. As depth of processing increases, forgetting decreases. The meaningfulness of new information plays an important role in this theory. Information that is more meaningful may proceed to a deeper level of analysis more quickly. Information that is less meaningful may not be processed so thoroughly.

Adult memory. Recent evidence concerning sensory memory indicates that information takes longer to process as age increases. An example of sensory memory is the afterimage experienced when a flash picture is snapped. As individuals age, it takes longer for a stimulus to "clear" the nervous system. When this happens, a stimulus may erase previous information not yet "read out" from the sensory store. This phenomenon is called "masking" (Klein & Szafrin, 1975). Because of masking, older adults may have fewer "bits" of information passed on from sensory registers to short-term store. In addition, the problems caused by masking become all the greater under speeded conditions (Elias, Elias, & Elias, 1977).

Much attention has been focused in recent years on the use of memory aids by adults of different ages. One particular kind of aid involves organizational strategies. The general conclusion here is that younger adults organize incoming materials in ways that improve performance and provide cues for recall. Hultsch (1974) argues that young adults tend spontaneously to categorize incoming information. Older adults do not, or at least are much less likely to do so. The real question has been whether older adults can benefit from instructions to use memory aids. Hultsch (1975) found that older adults do begin to categorize items from lists of words to be remembered, when told to do so. Moreover, they not only use the aid, but it greatly benefits their performance.

Closely related to these organizational strategies is a class of aids known as mediational techniques. The data on the use of mediators are not unlike those of categorization. The most common approach in the study of mediational techniques is to use paired-associate tasks. Mediators in this instance may be in the form of a mental picture used to connect word pairs, or in the form of verbal characteristics, such as a sentence, which also connects word pairs. In one study, Hulicka and Grossman (1967) compared older (mean age 74 years) with younger (mean age 16 years) participants and found that older adults improved considerably after being introduced to either verbal or visual mediators. Younger subjects were not helped nearly so much by this aid. It appears that the younger subjects were already using mediators even when they had not been told to do so. As in the case of categorization, mediators improved the older subjects' performance, but did not bring them up to the level of the young. More recently, a similar set of findings was reported by Treat and Reese (1976).

In both of these instances it appears that older adults are less likely than their younger counterparts to use memory aids. But they can use them when told to do so, and they do benefit from them markedly. Such results can be explained by both models of memory discussed earlier. In the first place, the use of categorization and mediators is an important consideration in whether information will be transferred from short-term to long-term storage. Second, such results are also consistent with the levels-of-processing model and suggest that, as adulthood progresses, individuals often do not process information at so high a level or so quickly as younger people do.

Recall and recognition memory. The majority of current evidence demonstrates that recall memory declines much more rapidly with age than recognition memory does (Botwinick, 1978). The two types of memory involve different processes. Recognition memory involves matching information in memory storage with information in the environment. It is the type of ability called for in multiple-choice tests. Recall memory, on the other hand, is the type of ability called into service on an essay test. On this type of task, information must not only be stored properly but must also be retrieved, or brought up from memory. The important distinction between the two types of memory is that recognition is thought not to involve retrieval, whereas recall memory involves both storage and retrieval.

Schonfield and Robertson (1966) argued that it is a breakdown in retrieval that explains the decline with age on recall-memory tasks. They did not believe that there was any problem with storage functions. More recently, Erber (1974) tempered this conclusion somewhat by arguing that some decline occurs with both storage and retrieval, but the problem with retrieval is greater. The general consensus then is that the actual storage of information is relatively unimpaired with age; the difficulty is bringing this information out of storage.

Another reason why these memory functions may decline with age is because of greater susceptibility to interference. Botwinick (1978) reports studies that found greater interference in recognition-memory tasks, and Rabbitt (1965) reported that older adults find it increasingly difficult to ignore irrelevent stimuli in a card-sorting task. The problem of interference may be present at all stages of the learning process, from the initial selection of materials to be attended to, through their ultimate retrieval from long-term storage. Agruso (1978), in a review of memory studies, argues that one way to alleviate the problem of interference is through overlearning of small sections of material.

Finally, the rate of memory search declines with age (Anders, Fozard, & Lillyquist, 1972). As the amount of material to be remembered increases, older adults find it takes more time to search their memory for correct information, even when it is called for only a short time after it has been acquired. Anders and Fozard (1973) argued that young adults search short-term memory at about twice the rate of older adults. They posited that the increase in search time may be due to the fact that, with age, there is more information to search through in memory.

Problem Solving. The work of problem solving stretches back to the earliest days of psychology. Although there have been many approaches to the study of problem solving, the current view is that it depends on a host of cognitive functions including learning, memory, and intelligence. It appears, then, that, as basic cognitive abilities decline, so does problem-solving ability.

This is generally thought to be so. Although verbal intelligence may not be closely related to problem-solving ability (Storck, Looft, & Hooper, 1972), adults with high IQs usually maintain the ability until late in life (Arenberg, 1974). Adults with low IQs, however, tend to decline in problem-solving ability.

One particular type of problem that adults find increasingly difficult is that involving abstraction. Arenberg (1968) reported that when the same problem was presented in both abstract and concrete formats, older adults performed much more successfully with the concrete format. Some have argued (Welford, 1958; Cijfer, 1966) that education is an important factor. Better-educated adults are more capable of thinking in abstract terms, even in old age, than their less-educated counterparts.

There are other difficulties that many adults have as they go about the process of solving problems. Welford (1958) found that older adults make more inquiries about a problem, but they have more difficulty using this information when it is needed later. Jerome (1962) added that many older adults tend to ask the same questions over and over again when given a problem-solving task. Such haphazard questioning leads many to become lost in a boggle of irrelevant information.

Cognitive style. One of the most frequently debated, and researched, cognitive styles in adulthood involves rigidity. The general stereotype has been that individuals become more rigid and inflexible with increasing age. If this is so, it would account for some of the difficulties adults have with problem solving.

But the evidence does not fully support the contention that adults become more rigid with age. One reason is that there may be several types of rigidity. Chown (1961) argued that there are five; Schaie (1958) found evidence for three. In any event, there is evidence that some types of rigidity do increase with age. Heglin (1956) reported that older adults find it increasingly difficult to change set in a learning situation. He argued that once an individual settles into a particular type of response mode in solving a problem, it becomes more difficult with age to shift to a new approach when the demands of the problem change. Schaie and Strother (1968) also report that adults find it increasingly more difficult to adjust readily to new situations.

It is interesting to note that support for increasing rigidity with age is also found in the literature of animal research. Goodrich (1972) found that older rats, when learning a maze, tend to make large numbers of perseverative errors. In other words, they tend to make the same errors over and over, and not benefit from experience.

In general, two sets of conclusions can be drawn from current evidence. First, there are great individual differences, and although some people do become more rigid with age, many others do not. Second, much evidence indicates that intelligence may be a factor. It appears that adults of high intelligence are least likely to become more rigid with age. Botwinick (1978) argues that the problem may actually be one of declining intelligence instead of increasing rigidity.

Creativity. One subset of our knowledge of problem solving is in the area of creativity. Over the past several decades, great interest has been placed on creativity research. Unfortunately, most of what we know about creativity in adulthood dates back many years.

Lehman (1953) made work on adult creativity his ca-

reer. His approach to studying the problem was to examine the lives of famous individuals in various fields. He used written histories of these people to note when, during the life span, their most notable achievements had been made. Lehman studied hundreds of fields and argued that high achievement occurs relatively early, generally no later than the middle thirties. He added that there is a marked decline in productivity following this peak.

A number of researchers challenged this analysis. Dennis (1966), for example, argued that Lehman's conclusions were misleading, because people of various longevities had been compared together. In so doing, Lehman blurred the fact that some people lived short lives and obviously made their contributions early. When Dennis controlled for longevity, peak productivity was found to come later, and the decline was more gradual than Lehman had predicted.

Kogan (1973) summarized the literature in this area. Part of the problem is that the mainstream of the literature on creative thinking in recent years has viewed creativity as process. That is, it has viewed creativity as a thinking style that is indigenous to all forms of creative output. The Lehman-Dennis work viewed creativity as product and is much more restricted. Clearly, more work needs to be done in this area.

Implications for Education. Adults, even in later life, have the capacity to learn new things and to benefit from formal education. Although the old arguments for decline are still with us, the new literature stresses that decline is not nearly so great as was previously believed. Furthermore, for the most gifted adults, there may be little or no decline, at least not until late in life.

Havighurst (1980) argues that our knowledge of adult development has moved from describing change to the explication of behavior change. We live in a society in which the average age of the population is increasing. Adult education will become a more important part of our educational process. But as Schaie and Willis (1978) state, the system will not only have to accommodate changing needs and capacities of the adult, but it will have to optimize the nature of that change as well.

Dennis Thompson

See also Adult Education; Aging; Life-Span Development; Parent Education.

REFERENCES

Agruso, V. M. *Learning in the Later Years.* New York: Academic Press, 1978.

Anders, T. R., & Fozard, J. L. Effects of age upon retrieval from primary and secondary memory. *Developmental Psychology,* 1973, *9,* 411–415.

Anders, T. R.; Fozard, J. L.; & Lillyquist, F. D. The effects of age upon retrieval from short-term memory. *Developmental Psychology,* 1972, *6,* 214–217.

Arenberg, D. Anticipation interval and age differences in verbal learning. *Journal of Abnormal Psychology,* 1965, *70,* 419–425.

Arenberg, D. Concept problem solving in young and old adults. *Journal of Gerontology,* 1968, *23,* 279–282.

Arenberg, D. A longitudinal study of problem solving in adults. *Journal of Gerontology*, 1974, *29*, 650–658.

Atkinson, R. C. & Shiffrin, R. M. Human memory: A proposed system and its control processes. In K. W. Spence & J. T. Spence (Eds.), *The Psychology of Learning and Motivation* (Vol. 2). New York: Academic Press, 1968.

Baltes, P. B., & Schaie, K. W. On the plasticity of intelligence in adulthood and old age. *American Psychologist*, 1976, *31*, 720–725.

Birren, J. E., & Morrison, D. F. Analysis of the WAIS subtests in relation to age and education. *Journal of Gerontology*, 1961, *16*, 363–369.

Birren, J. E., & Schaie, K. W. (Eds.). *Handbook of the Psychology of Aging*. New York: Van Nostrand, 1977.

Botwinick, J. Intellectual abilities. In J. E. Birren & K. W. Schaie (Eds.), *Handbook of the Psychology of Aging*. New York: Van Nostrand Reinhold, 1977.

Botwinick, J. *Aging and Behavior*. New York: Springer, 1978.

Canestrari, R. E., Jr. Paced and self-paced learning in young and elderly adults. *Journal of Gerontology*, 1963. *18*, 165–168.

Cattell, R. B. The theory of fluid and crystallized intelligence: A critical experiment. *Journal of Educational Psychology*, 1963, *54*, 1–22.

Chown, S. M. Age and the rigidities. *Journal of Gerontology*, 1961, *16*, 353–362.

Cijfer, E. An experiment on some differences in logical thinking between Dutch medical people, under and over the age of thirty-five. *Acta Psychologica*, 1966, *25*, 159–171.

Corso, J. F. Auditory perception and communication. In J. E. Birren K. W. Schaie (Eds.), *Handbook of the Psychology of Aging*. New York: Van Nostrand Reinhold, 1977.

Craik, F. J. M., & Lockhart, R. S. Levels of processing: A framework for memory research. *Journal of Verbal Learning and Verbal Behavior*, 1972, *11*, 671–684.

Demming, J. A., & Pressey, S. L. Tests "indigenous" to the adult and older years. *Journal of Counseling Psychology*, 1957, *2*, 144–148.

Dennis, W. Creative productivity between ages of twenty and eighty years. *Journal of Gerontology*, 1966, *21*, 1–8.

Doppelt, J. E., & Wallace, W. L. Standardization of the Wechsler Adult Intelligence Scale for older persons. *Journal of Abnormal and Social Psychology*, 1955, *51*, 312–330.

Eisdorfer, C., & Wilkie, F. Intellectual changes with advancing age. In L. F. Jarvik, C. Eisdorfer, & C. E. Blum (Eds.), *Intellectual Functioning in Adults*. New York: Springer, 1973.

Elias, M. F.; Elias, P. K.; & Elias, J. W. *Basic Processes in Adult Developmental Psychology*. St. Louis: Mosby, 1977.

Engen, J. Taste and smell. In J. E. Birren & K. W. Schaie (Eds.), *Handbook of the Psychology of Aging*. New York: Van Nostrand Reinhold, 1977.

Erber, J. T. Age differences in recognition memory. *Journal of Gerontology*, 1974, *29*, 177–181.

Fozard, J. L.; Wolf, E.; Bell, B.; McFarland, R. A.; & Podolsky, S. Visual perception and communication. In J. E. Birren & K. W. Schaie (Eds.), *Handbook of the Psychology of Aging*. New York: Van Nostrand Reinhold, 1977.

Gilbert, J. G. Thirty-five-year follow-up study of intellectual functioning. *Journal of Gerontology*, 1973, *28*, 68–72.

Goodrich, C. L. Learning by mature, young, and aged Wester Albino Rats as a function of test complexity. *Journal of Gerontology*, 1972, *27*, 353–357.

Havighurst, R. J. Life-span developmental psychology and education. *Educational Researcher*, 1980, *9*, 3–8.

Heglin, H. J. Problem-solving set in different age-groups. *Journal of Gerontology*, 1956, *11*, 310–317.

Horn, J. L., & Cattell, R. B. Age differences in fluid and crystallized intelligence. *Acta Psychologica*, 1967, *26*, 107–129.

Horn, J. L., & Donaldson, G. On the myth of intellectual decline in adulthood. *American Psychologist*, 1976, *31*, 701–709.

Horn, J. L., & Donaldson, G. Faith is not enough: A response to the Baltes-Schaie claim that intelligence does not wane. *American Psychologist*, 1977, *32*, 369–373.

Hulicka, I. M. Age differences in retention as a function of interference. *Journal of Gerontology*, 1967, *22*, 180–184.

Hulicka, I. M., & Grossman, J. L. Age-group comparisons for the use of mediators in paired-associate learning. *Journal of Gerontology*, 1967, *22*, 46–51.

Hultsch, D. Learning to learn in adulthood. *Journal of Gerontology*, 1974, *29*, 302–308.

Hultsch, D. Age differences in retrieval: Trace-dependent and cue-dependent forgetting. *Developmental Psychology*, 1975, *11*, 197–201.

Jerome, E. A. Decay of heuristic processes in the aged. In C. Tibbits & W. Donahue (Eds.), *Social and Psychological Aspects of Aging*. New York: Columbia University Press, 1962.

Jones, H. E., & Conrad, H. S. The growth and decline of intelligence: The study of a homogeneous group between the ages of ten and sixty. *Genetic Psychology Monographs*, 1933, *13*, 223–298.

Kart, C. S.; Metress, E. S.; & Metress, J. F. *Aging and Health: Biological and Social Perspectives*. Reading, Mass.: Addison-Wesley, 1978.

Klein, D. W., & Szafrin, J. Age differences in backward monoptic visual noise-masking. *Journal of Gerontology*, 1975, *30*, 307–311.

Kogan, N. Creativity and cognitive style: A life-span perspective. In P. B. Baltes & K. W. Schaie (Eds.), *Life-span Developmental Psychology: Personality and Socialization*. New York: Academic Press, 1973.

Kuhlen, R. S. Age and intelligence: The significance of cultural change in longitudinal versus cross-sectional findings. *Vita Humana*, 1963, *6*, 113–124.

Lehman, H. C. *Age and Achievement*. Princeton, N.J.: Princeton University Press, 1953.

McFarland, R. A.; Domey, R. G.; Warren, A. B.; & Ward, D. C. Dark adaptation as a function of age: I. A statistical analysis. *Journal of Gerontology*, 1960, *15*, 149–154.

Monge, R. H., & Hultsch, D. Paired-associate learning as a function of adult age and the length of the anticipation and inspection intervals. *Journal of Gerontology*, 1971, *26*, 157–162.

Owens, W. A. Age and mental abilities: A longitudinal study. *Genetic Psychology Monographs*, 1953, *48*, 3–54.

Owens, W. A. Age and mental abilities: A second adult follow-up. *Journal of Educational Psychology*, 1966, *57*, 311–325.

Papalia, D. E., & Del Vento Bielby, D. Cognitive functioning in middle- and old-age adults. *Human Development*, 1974, *17*, 424–443.

Powell, A. H., Jr.; Eisdorfer, C.; & Bogdonoff, M. D. Physiologic response patterns observed in a learning task. *Archives of General Psychiatry*, 1964, *10*, 192–195.

Rabbitt, P. An age decrement in the ability to ignore irrelevant information. *Journal of Gerontology*, 1965, *20*, 233–238.

Ross, E. Effects of challenging and supportive instructions in verbal learning in older persons. *Journal of Educational Psychology*, 1968, *59*, 261–266.

Schaie, K. W. Rigidity-flexibility and intelligence: A cross-sectional study of the adult life span from twenty to seventy years. *Psychological Monographs: General and Applied*, 1958, *72*, 1–26.

Schaie, K. W. A general model for the study of behavioral problems. *Psychological Bulletin*, 1965, *64*, 92–107.

Schaie, K. W., & Baltes, P. B. Some faith helps to see the forest: A final comment on the Horn and Donaldson myth of the Baltes-Schaie position on adult intelligence. *American Psychologist*, 1977, *32*, 1118–1120.

Schaie, K. W., & Labouvie-Vief, G. Generational versus ontogenetic components of change in adult cognitive behavior: A fourteen-year cross-sequential study. *Developmental Psychology*, 1974, *10*, 305–320.

Schaie, K. W., & Parham, I. A. Cohort-sequential analysis of adult intellectual development. *Developmental Psychology*, 1977, *13*, 649–653.

Schaie, K. W., & Strother, C. R. A cross-sequential study of age changes in cognitive behavior. *Psychological Bulletin*, 1968, *70*, 671–680.

Schaie, K. W., & Willis, S. L. Life-span development: Implications for education. In L. S. Shulman (Ed.), *Review of Research in Education* (Vol. 6). Itasca, Ill.: F. E. Peacock, 1978.

Schonfield, D., & Robertson, E. A. Memory storage and aging. *Canadian Journal of Psychology*, 1966, *20*, 228–236.

Silverman, I. Age and the tendency to withhold responses. *Journal of Gerontology*, 1963, *18*, 372–375.

Storandt, M. Age, ability level, and method of administering and scoring the WAIS. *Journal of Gerontology*, 1977, *32*, 175–178.

Storck, P. A.; Looft, W. R.; & Hooper, F. H. Interrelationships among Piagetian tasks, and traditional measures of cognitive abilities in mature and aged adults. *Journal of Gerontology*, 1972, *27*, 461–465.

Tesch, S.; Whitbourne, S. K.; & Nehrke, M. F. Cognitive egocentrism in institutionalized adult males. *Journal of Gerontology*, 1978, *33*, 546–552.

Thornbury, J., & Mistretta, C. Tactile sensitivity as a function of age. *Journal of Gerontology*, 1981, *36*, 34–39.

Treat, N. J., & Reese, H. W. Age, pacing, and imagery in paired-associate learning. *Developmental Psychology*. 1976, *12*, 119–124.

Wechsler, D. *The Measurement and Appraisal of Adult Intelligence*. Baltimore: Williams & Wilkins, 1958.

Welford, A. T. *Aging and Human Skill*. London: Oxford University Press, 1958.

Yoakum, C. S., & Yerkes, R. M. *Army Mental Tests*. New York: Henry Holt, 1920.

ADULT EDUCATION

Adult education is a field of study and a field of practice. Although the practice of adult education dates to ancient times, the formal study of adult education had its beginnings in this century. In fact, adult education as a field of study is so young, it has not yet developed an orthodoxy acceptable to all who would contribute to its growth.

The following description of the field of practice provides a context for our focus on the evolution of research in adult education. Practice is discussed in terms of the field's organizational forms, its programs, and its clientele.

The Nature of Practice. Adult education can be characterized as an amorphous, hybrid field, conceived by a variety of institutional parents. Diversity of both form and function is prevalent in the collage of organizations, programs, and clientele that constitute adult education. Its clientele are as varied as the individuals who compose the adult population, and its methods include all the arrangements between learner and mentor ever contrived by pedagogists and andragogists alike. Adult education activities take place in organizations with both primary and lesser interest in education and in a manner more diverse than in youth education, with the majority of activities taking place in institutions whose primary function is not education of adults. Although adult education has moved further into the informal processes than into the formal structures of institutions, one cannot overlook the relationship that exists between adult education and established institutions.

Schroeder (1980) defined adult education as "a developmental process used to link various agent and adult client systems for the purpose of establishing directions and procedures for adult learning programs" (p. 42). Unlike the singularity of institutional forms representative of youth education, the "agent systems" identified by Schroeder are myriad in form and function. His classification distinguished between "leadership systems" and "operating systems," each of which assumes particular functions with respect to practice. Leadership agent systems provide guidance to practice through establishment of broad goals and policies, allocation of resources, and generation of knowledge. Federal, state, and local governments, for example, provide leadership through such publicly funded programs as basic education for adults with less than a high school education and the programs of the Cooperative Extension Service, a 67-year-old adult education enterprise. Professional associations provide leadership to countless professional groups who conduct their individual enterprises of adult education. Private foundations, such as Kellogg, Carnegie, and Ford, have left their imprint on adult education practice. The Ford Foundation has funded development of residential centers for continuing education on university campuses. Finally, graduate programs in adult education provide leadership through their preparation of practitioners and their role in development of a knowledge base for research and practice.

What Schroeder calls "operating systems" constitute the largest number and more obvious forms of organizations involved in the practice of adult education. Included are elementary and secondary schools, community colleges, vocational-technical schools, and four-year colleges and universities. These are agencies whose primary purpose is to serve the educational needs of youth, but whose "secondary" functions include adult education. (In some cases, the *primary* purpose of higher education institutions is the education of essentially adult students.) Operating systems also include community service agencies, whose primary purpose is to serve the needs of a whole community or some segment of it. Examples are libraries, museums, social work agencies, correctional institutions, recreational centers, and health organizations. Again, education of adults is among the several functions performed by such agencies. Some agencies serve special interests, with adult education as a subordinate component of their operation. Examples are businesses and industries, religious organizations, and the military. Although adult education is subordinate among the priority of functions in such agencies, it is instrumental to their special interests. Finally, there are "pure-type" agencies, whose chief purpose is clearly that of educating adults. Proprietary schools, residential and nonresidential adult education centers, folk schools, and consulting firms are examples. These agencies are usually not subordinate to larger parent organizations and are characteristically autonomous in their operation.

The programs offered by these types of agencies were succinctly summarized by Knowles (1977), who suggested a typology of programs as a framework for development in the field of practice: (1) academic education, (2) education for the aging, (3) community development, (4) creative arts, (5) economic education, (6) fundamental and literacy education, (7) health education, (8) home and family life education, (9) human relations and leadership training, (10) intergroup education, (11) liberal adult education, (12) public affairs education, (13) adult recreation education, (14) science education, and (15) occupational education (pp. 252–253).

The diversity of adult education agency types and programs manifests itself in the equally varied clientele served. Cross (1981) depicted the clientele served as a "pyramid of learners" (p. 79), with the base consisting of self-directed learners and a smaller group in the middle, estimated at one-third or more of the population, participating in some form of organized instruction yearly. The tip of the pyramid consists of the relatively small proportion of adult learners who pursue college credit.

Social-class descriptors can be viewed from the same perspective. The base of the pyramid, the self-directed learners, is representative of the population as a whole (Cross, 1981), whereas those who participate in organized instruction show a consistency in social-class bias (e.g., the higher the level of educational attainment, the more likely they are to participate in learning activities) (p. 79). According to Cross, adult learners pursuing college degrees may come from "lower socioeconomic backgrounds than younger college students but are among the socioeconomically privileged in the pyramid of adult learners" (p. 80).

Participants in self-directed learning have often been excluded in previous studies of organized adult learning activities, leading Johnstone and Rivera (1965) to suggest that it "is probably the most overlooked avenue of activity in the whole field of adult education" (p. 37). Tough's seminal work, however, in self-directed learning (1971) has stimulated numerous other studies (e.g., Penland, 1977;

Peters & Gordon, 1974) suggesting that the phenomenon is virtually universal in scope. Estimates indicate that from 76 percent (Penland, 1977) to 100 percent (Coolican, 1974, 1975) of all adults conduct a minimum of one learning project annually. According to Cross (1981), "the typical adult spends about one hundred hours on each learning project, conducting five projects per year, for a total of five hundred hours per year" (pp. 63–64). Approximately 75 percent of the learning projects are primarily self-directed, and only 20 percent are planned by a professional (Tough, 1978). Inclusion of self-directed learners in studies on participation has diminished the differences between learners and nonlearners traditionally discussed in terms of participation in formal educational programs.

Motives for participation by adults in learning activities vary according to such factors as age, sex, occupation, and the stage of life being experienced by an adult. Most learners actually have more than one reason for choosing a learning activity, although their choices are usually practically motivated.

Cross's research revealed situational, institutional, and dispositional barriers to learning. Situational barriers arise at given times in an adult's life and include such problems as transportation and child care. Institutional barriers, such as inconvenient locations and schedules, exclude or discourage participation. Dispositional barriers are attitudinal in nature, such as the feelings of elderly individuals that they are too old to learn (Cross, 1981).

The field of practice needs a knowledge base if its agencies and practitioners are to make informed decisions regarding effective delivery of programs to their varied and changing clientele. Awareness of this need has given rise to a relatively new field of study in adult education.

Research. Concurrent with the dramatic increase in adult education programs and clientele in the past thirty years has been an equally dramatic rise in research activity related to adult education. Many of the programmatic changes and much of the growth in adult education as a field of study may be traced to earlier-mentioned funding by public and private sources and to the rise in number of graduate programs in adult education that occurred during the 1960s and 1970s (Long & Hiemstra, 1980).

Special federal legislation (e.g., the Adult Education Act of 1966), plus growing awareness of the need to prepare educators to deal with the educational needs of all adults, led more than sixty U.S. universities to add graduate programs in adult education or to increase the size of existing programs. Of the approximately 2,300 doctorates in adult education awarded since the 1930s, by far the majority have been earned since 1960.

Evolution. A study of the 1950 to 1970 volumes of the field's major research journal, *Adult Education*, revealed an increase in the number of authors affiliated with universities (Dickinson & Rusnell, 1971). Over the latter part of this same period, the number of professors of adult education increased from 24 in 1961 to over 150 in 1970. A review of the literature by Long (1977) showed that adult education professors did not limit their publications to *Adult Education,* however, and that a sample of 81 professors had published in over 300 journals (p. 184).

Not only have increasing numbers of professors published greater volumes of research reports, but their publication topics and their methodologies have changed as well. Dickinson and Rusnell (1971) discovered a steadily increasing emphasis on research-based articles, with a decreasing emphasis on program descriptions and statements of personal belief and experience (p. 177). Increasing attention was given to adult learning as a topic over the two decades covered in the study, and the research reported in *Adult Education* became more sophisticated in design and methodology. A later content analysis of articles in *Adult Education* by Long and Agyekum (1974) generally supported the Dickinson and Rusnell conclusions, with the additional observation that descriptive research was the dominant kind of research appearing in the journal. Dickinson and Blunt (1980) pointed out that, historically, survey research has constituted a major portion of adult education research, although its dominance may diminish as other methods become more appropriate to changing needs (p. 51). Grabowski (1980) pointed to the improving quality of doctoral dissertation research in adult education, resulting primarily from closer attention to "methods of research design that strengthen internal and external validity . . . knowledge of statistical analysis . . . [and] concern for improved theoretical structures" (p. 121).

We analyzed the content of articles appearing in *Adult Education* for Volumes 24 through the Volume 31, No. 2 issue, and compared them with the Dickinson and Rusnell analysis. The resulting increases and decreases in percentages of articles according to methodological types revealed a continuing trend similar to the previous results. The percentage of empirical studies, for example, was two and a half times as great as appeared in the twenty volumes covered by the Dickinson and Rusnell study. The percentage of interpretive reviews of literature doubled, as did the percentage of theoretical formulations. The percentage of historical studies nearly tripled, but the percentage of articles containing program descriptions fell from 25.2 percent to zero. The percentage of articles based on personal belief or opinion fell from 28.8 to 3 percent, excluding special issue-related articles in the "Forum" and "Critique" sections of recent issues of the journal.

In recent years, the percentage of articles devoted to adult learning has declined slightly, but the proportion of articles on program planning and administration, instructional methods, and education for special groups has increased. (These changes were also noted in the 1974 review by Long and Agyekum.) Greater attention also has been given in recent years to development of formal philosophies concerning the study and practice of adult education.

Article contents reported in the recent analyses indicate significant growth in the study of adult education. Although by no means abandoning their early concern with

definition of the field, scholars appear to have moved from that primitive phase of development into a kind of "technological refinement" marked by the increasing numbers of experimental studies, by theory-building efforts, and by studies that focus on special populations of adults.

Quality. The issue of quality of research has not diminished with the increased quantity of research activities in adult education. Still heard are claims that adult education research is mainly atheoretical (Boshier, 1979; Miller, 1967), is plagued by "chronic amateurism" (Griffith & Cristarella, 1979), and fails to address the most crucial needs of practicing adult educators (Krietlow, 1973). Boshier (1979) and Miller (1967) have placed blame on the predominance of *ex post facto* research (especially studies of participation by adults in education) and called for more experimental research. Griffith and Cristarella (1979) have placed no small measure of the onus on "the characteristics of the researchers who claim to be employing methodologies which are (erroneously) blamed for poor research" (p. 38). Krietlow (1975) cited institutional pressures and the exigencies of federal funding as contributing to the inappropriateness of much research in adult education.

In spite of these criticisms of adult education theory and research, promising advances have been made in recent years. Among the theorists, Boshier, for example, has conducted thematic research in participation, with the aim of developing a theory of adult motivation for participation in education. Boshier's theory is that motives for participation are related to social, psychological, and other variables and that motivational orientations are surface manifestations of psychological states, with the latter being related to age and socioeconomic factors (Boshier, 1977). Miller's approach (also aimed at a model of motivation for learning) is to incorporate theory from sociology and psychology into a force-field analysis of why people participate in education and why there are differences between social classes in what they expect from participation. Miller's immediate concern was to provide a conceptual framework for studying participation in education. Unfortunately, few empirical studies have utilized his framework since its publication in 1967. In a related attempt, however, Rubenson (cited in Cross, 1981) has been successful in utilizing current research findings and theoretical modes developed by others to arrive at a framework for analyzing adult motivation to participate in education. His "expectancy-valance model" draws upon works by Lewin, Tolman, McClelland, and Atkinson, who are interaction theorists. The uniqueness of Rubenson's model lies in the emphasis placed on perceptions of would-be learners regarding external forces operating in their environment, as opposed to the emphasis placed by other theorists on the influence of the external factors themselves.

Miller, Boshier, and Rubenson share the determination to explain the factors operating in an adult and the environment vis-à-vis the act of participation. The encouraging aspect of their efforts is that they have approached their work from a rigorous conceptual base, notwithstanding the enormous difficulties inherent in testing their constructs. Boshier (1977), for example, has labored to develop a measure of the variables in his model through developing and testing his Education Participation Scale. What is also common among these attempts at theorizing about adult behavior is that each author has depended heavily upon the behavioral sciences in his theory-building efforts and each has attempted to reformulate the supporting concepts into models that would explain the dynamics of adult behavior in learning environments. The goal of each has been to extend the knowledge base in adult education through further research, but to do so within a rigorously developed framework. To the extent that they are successful, they will challenge their own and others' criticisms of the atheoretical nature of research in the field.

Methodological issues. Any discipline has its advocates of one method of research against all others. Adult education is no exception, as some of its scholars claim that respectability comes at the price of doing more experimental research. Moderates in the field, however, plead for a "catholicity of outlook" regarding methods of inquiry; for example, Apps (1972) called for a definition of research that is not limited to empirical inquiry. He suggested other avenues to knowledge creation, to include "thinking, synthesizing, sensing, and accepting." Farmer (1980) and Forest (1972) echoed Apps's view that adult educators may be caught up in the belief that empiricism or "scientism" is the only defensible framework for research, at the expense of other useful approaches.

Knowles (1973) sought to lend perspective to the methodology issue by proposing a taxonomy of "developmental needs for research" in adult education. Knowles's thesis is that scholars in adult education can increase their understanding of appropriate methodologies by contrasting the field's growth and state of the art with that of similar fields and their research needs. He examined his own experience in the fields of social work, recreation, and adult education and postulated that a field of social practice may have developmental needs that change through its stages of maturation. For adult education, he proposed the following phases of developmental needs: (1) definition of the field, (2) differentiation of the field, (3) standard setting, (4) technological refinement, (5) respectability and justification, and (6) understanding the dynamics of the field. Knowles saw these phases as overlapping and somewhat "spiral" in nature, so that research relevant to an advanced phase could be under way, alongside research relevant to an earlier phase (pp. 298–303). Knowles's framework has not been tested; however, the content analyses discussed previously indicate that certain patterns of development appear to be forming in the study of adult education, and these patterns roughly parallel the phases of development proposed by Knowles.

Conclusions. Adult education as a field of study and practice has made considerable progress during the past thirty years. Its recent history is characterized by rapid growth in programs and in number of adult participants.

Educators have discovered the fact that adults continue to learn outside formal institutional auspices, and such institutions as colleges and universities have come to depend upon the growing numbers of older students on and off their campuses.

The study of adult education is beginning to come of age, as reflected in the almost geometric rise in number of research reports relevant to education of adults and in the growth in sophistication of design and methodology in adult education research. The knowledge base has grown to the point that adult educators are beginning to understand the dynamics of a field scarcely defined only a few years ago. More important, the current knowledge base should provide an impetus of its own, such that future growth in research should be even faster and more productive than in past years. The research needs of this complex field of practice will never be completely met, but the uncertainty of purpose once characteristic of this youthful field of study is no longer as problematic to scholars whose intent is to reduce the complexity itself.

John M. Peters
Betty B. Banks

See also Adult Development; Distance Education; Experiential Education; Independent Study; Labor and Education; Life-Span Development; Nontraditional Higher Education Programs; Parent Education.

REFERENCES

Apps, J. W. Toward a broader definition of research. *Adult Education*, 1972, *23*, 59–64.

Boshier, R. Motivational orientations revisited: Life-space motives and the educational participation scale. *Adult Education*, 1977, *28*(2), 75–88.

Boshier, R. A conceptual and methodological perspective concerning research on participation in adult education. In J. A. Niemi (Ed.), *Viewpoints on Adult Education Research*. Columbus: Ohio State University, National Center for Research in Vocational Education, 1979.

Boshier, R. Motivational orientations revisited: Life-space motives and the educational participation scale. *Adult Education*, 1977, *28*(2), 75–88.

Coolican, P. M. *Self-planned Learning: Implications for the Future of Adult Education. Syracuse, N.Y.:* Syracuse University Research Corporation, Educational Policy Research Center, 1974. (ERIC Document Reproduction Service No. ED 095 254)

Coolican, P. M. *Self-planned Learning: Implications for the Future of Adult Education. An Addendum to the 1974 Paper.* Washington, D.C.: U.S. Office of Education, Division of Adult Education, 1975.

Cross, K. P. *Adults as Learners.* San Francisco: Jossey-Bass, 1981.

Dickinson, G., & Blunt, A. Survey research. In H. B. Long, R. Hiemstra, & Associates. *Changing Approaches to Studying Adult Education.* San Francisco: Jossey-Bass, 1980.

Dickinson, G., & Rusnell, P. A content analysis of adult education. *Adult Education*, 1971, *21*(3), 177–185.

Farmer, J. *The Conduct of Inquiry Relative to Adult and Continuing Education.* Symposium conducted at Adult Education Research Conference, Vancouver, May 1980.

Forest, L. B. *Beyond Scientific Empiricism in Adult Education Research.* Paper presented at Adult Education Research Conference, Chicago, April 1972.

Grabowski, S. M. Trends in graduate research. In H. B. Long, R. Hiemstra, and Associates, *Changing Approaches to Studying Adult Education.* San Francisco: Jossey-Bass, 1980.

Griffith, W. S., & Cristarella, M. C. Participatory research: Should it be a new methodology for adult educators? In J. A. Niemi (Ed.), *Viewpoints on Adult Education Research.* Columbus: Ohio State University, National Center for Research in Vocational Education, 1979.

Johnstone, J. W., & Rivera, R. J. *Volunteers for Learning.* Hawthorne, N.Y.: Adline, 1965.

Knowles, M. S. *The Adult Learner: A Neglected Species.* Houston: Gulf Publishing, 1973.

Knowles, M. S. *The Adult Education Movement in the United States* (Rev. ed.). New York: Holt, Rinehart & Winston, 1977.

Krietlow, B. W. Federal support to adult education: Boon or boondoggle? *Adult Education,* 1973, *23,* 115–131.

Long, H. B. Publication activity of selected professors of adult education. *Adult Education,* 1977, *17*(3), 173–186.

Long, H. B., & Agyekum, S. K. Adult education, 1664–1973: Reflections of a changing discipline. *Adult Education,* 1974, *24*(2), 99–120.

Long, H. B., & Hiemstra, R. *Changing Approaches to Studying Adult Education.* San Francisco: Jossey-Bass, 1980.

Miller, H. L. *Participation of Adults in Education: A Force-field Analysis.* Boston: Boston University, Center for the Study of Liberal Education for Adults, 1967. (ERIC Document Reproduction Service No. ED 011 996)

Penland, P. *Individual Self-planned Learning in America.* Washington, D.C.: U.S. Office of Education, 1977.

Peters, J. M., & Gordon, R. S. *Adult Learning Projects: A Study of Adult Learning in Urban and Rural Tennessee.* Knoxville: University of Tennessee, 1974.

Schroeder, W. L. Typology of adult learning systems. In J. M. Peters & Associates, *Building an Effective Adult Education Enterprise.* San Francisco: Jossey-Bass, 1980.

Tough, A. *The Adult's Learning Projects: A Fresh Approach to Theory and Practice in Adult Learning* (Research and Education Series No. 1). Toronto: Ontario Institute for Studies in Education, 1971.

Tough, A. Major learning efforts: Recent research and future directions. In *The Adult Learner: Current Issues in Higher Education.* Washington, D.C.: American Association for Higher Education, 1978.

AESTHETIC EDUCATION

Aesthetic education, unlike the fields of art education, music education, dance education, and theater education, is not a field that has an organized professional constituency or that claims a distinctive or secure place among subjects in the school curriculum. Aesthetic education is, rather, an area of study and practice in which members of diverse fields have a common interest. Aesthetic education is defined by a set of shared concerns and by a few journals. There is no national organization of aesthetic educators, no specialized programs in universities preparing aesthetic educators, and no departments in universities or colleges that focus exclusively on the problems of aesthetic education. Yet despite these voids there is a recognition on the part of those whose allegiance is to the individual fine arts fields that there is something called aesthetic education, something that transcends the parameters of each of the individual fine arts.

Definition. The term "aesthetic" did not have much currency in the philosophic literature until Baumgarten made it prominent in his *Aesthetica,* published in 1755. Although part of the Greek distinction between *noesis, poesis,* and *aesthesis* (Onion, 1978), it was not until the 1800s that it became a standard part of the lexicon of philosophy.

Aesthetics, as one of the major branches of philosophic study, parallels epistemology, axiology, ontology, and logic. In general terms, aesthetics is that branch of philosophic study that deals with the philosophy of art. Yet, in its more liberal sense aesthetics deals with feeling. Just as that which is "anesthetic" depresses feeling, that which is aesthetic heightens it. Its connection with the fine arts is therefore obvious: the fine arts are regarded as generative of feeling, and they cultivate, as Santayana (1936) put it seventy-five years ago, "the sense of beauty."

The term "aesthetic" is also distinctive in two other ways. First, its connotation is different from that of art. "Aesthetic" does not, as "art" does, suggest the making of something. It is, rather, related to the experience secured from things already made. Art has connotations of *tekhne* (Onion, 1975), a Greek term implying the application of skill in the making of expressive form. "Aesthetic" is more closely associated with the experience or appreciation of such form. In this sense, it is both less manual and more intellectual and sensory in character.

Second, aesthetics is to be distinguished from criticism. As a branch of philosophy, aesthetics is done by aestheticians, people who are primarily interested in defining and discussing the nature of art. Their intellectual problems focus most centrally on the question "What is art?" (Tolstoy, 1930) or, more recently, "When is art? (Goodman, 1977). The questions they ask are philosophic questions; and although individual works of art might be referred to in the course of their work, they are used as instrumentalities through which their more general philosophic interests are served.

For critics of the fine arts the opposite practice ensues. Although critics might use concepts in aesthetics and aesthetic theory, these concepts are used primarily as vehicles to illuminate the qualities of individual works of art or of artistic styles or schools. These distinctions are, of course, not hard and fast. They are a matter of emphasis and degree and there clearly are writers who function midway between the aesthetician and the critic.

As for aesthetic education, it is a relative newcomer to American education. Although there has been interest in the field of art education in cultivating skills of art appreciation, an interest that began in the 1920s with the picture study movement (Dobbs, 1972), aesthetic education as a distinctive area of study and practice within education is a product of the mid-1950s. It was only as recently as 1966 that the *Journal of Aesthetic Education* was first published. It is interesting to note that the founder of the American Society of Aesthetics, Thomas Munro, was himself deeply engaged in education. As Curator of Education at the Philadelphia Museum of Art from 1931 to 1967 he was one of the first to take seriously the educational mission of the American art museum. In addition, he developed an active research program for the study of children's art at the Philadephia Museum in the early 1930s (Rawlins, 1981). The point here is that aesthetics as a distinctive form of philosophic study was given great impetus in the United States by an educator. It was only later that aesthetic *education* became itself a subject of inquiry by those in the fields of art, philosophy, and education. Thus aesthetic education involves a group of scholars and educational practitioners whose primary professional roots are in the fields of art, music, dance, and theater education as well as in the fields of philosophy, psychology, and curriculum who see in aesthetics the more general issues underlying their work. These issues focus upon a number of problems or conceptions: epistemological, educational, axiological, historical. Some of the issues with which scholars are concerned are purely theoretical; others are related to the kinds of practice in education that should be emphasized, given a commitment to aesthetic education. The work of these scholars has yielded three distinctive conceptions that guide the manner in which aesthetic education is provided.

Major Conceptions.   One conception of aesthetic education regards it as the product of the kind of learning secured in each of the individual fine arts. The argument runs something like this: each of the fine arts is a distinctive language having its own structure, syntax, vocabulary, and history. To be able to secure the kinds of meaning that each art form makes possible, an individual must become literate in that particular form. Once literate, kinds of experience unique to that art form are possible. One is therefore aesthetically educated when multiple forms of literacy are achieved. These forms of literacy are best achieved by studying or practicing each art form in a way that maintains its integrity. This is more likely to occur if those who know the particular art form best teach it. Furthermore, it is taught best in a curricular situation in which each art form is given adequate time and attention. Thus the ends of aesthetic education are best achieved when each of the fine arts is well taught in a supportive curricular situation as an independent discipline. In this view integrative approaches to the teaching of fine arts are believed to dilute the quality and distinctiveness of each (Kaufman, 1966).

A second conception of aesthetic education argues that all of the arts have both common and distinctive features. If there were no common features they would not be called

the arts; if there were no distinctive features, either music or the visual arts would be redundant. Because both the similarities and the differences among the arts are of central importance in an adequate conception of aesthetic education, it is important to provide a curriculum in which these differences and similarities can be examined. This is best achieved in a single course that integrates the fine arts; that encourages students to compare and contrast the qualities of each of them; and that, more often than not, will be taught by more than one teacher. Thus, in this view of aesthetic education, collaborative teaching is important since few teachers are likely to possess the skills necessary for effectively teaching several art forms. In this approach, the curriculum would be especially designed to heighten students' perception of the ways in which different arts express meaning. It would also help them appreciate the common structural features that all the arts possess: the fact that all of the arts are composed form, that they all convey feeling or mood, that they all represent human intention, that they all, to some degree, reflect the times and cultures in which they were created. Aesthetic education is best achieved when an integrated program of study is designed to foster such outcomes.

A third conception of aesthetic education, and by far the most general, was first advanced by Sir Herbert Read (1958) in his influential book *Education through Art*. In this view aesthetic education is best regarded as an effort to enable all students to become artists, not artists in those realms limited to the conventional fine arts but rather in all realms in which things are made, including the realms of ideas. According to Read, the major aim of education is the creation of artists.

Given the view that Read has advanced, all subjects constituting the curriculum have potential for aesthetic education, not only with respect to the specifically constructive activities within those fields but also by enabling students to appreciate their aesthetic aspects. Mathematics, history, geography, physics, as well as literature, the visual arts, music, dance, and theater are forms created by man. To the extent to which these forms are well made, they have aesthetic properties. The major aim of education is to help students acquire the skills necessary for the creation of such forms—and of course the inclination to do so. Another educational aim is to help them learn how to experience the aesthetic qualities of forms already made. Given this view, aesthetic education is not to be restricted to a special part of the school day or to a particular subject in the school curriculum; it is intended to be all-pervasive. As Read (1958) wrote, "Our aim is not two or more extra periods. We demand nothing less than the whole 35 into which the child's week is now arbitrarily divided. We demand, that is to say, a method of education that is formally and fundamentally aesthetic" (p. 220).

Of these views, the last, Read's, is least well understood and least implemented in schools. To create an educational program in which teachers and curriculum developers intentionally aim at the achievement of such goals would require a major revolution in teacher training as well as in the schools. The ambition is a lofty one, relatively few teachers are familiar with Read's work, and, perhaps more important, at the time of this writing such aims are not likely to be well received given the largely instrumental attitude towards schooling that is currently most pervasive.

As for the other two conceptions, the first view is of course the one that requires the least amount of reorganization in schools and in the relevant professional fields. Those who have been trained in a particular fine arts field tend to have a proprietary interest in maintaining its autonomy. Efforts to create collaborative undertakings require skills and attitudes that many teachers do not possess. Such efforts are often regarded with suspicion or as a threat to the integrity of their particular discipline. As a result, although there have been some collaborative efforts by those in the fields of art and music education, these efforts have been exploratory rather than programmatic and aim more at increasing political strength than at restructuring the curriculum.

One movement related to the aims of aesthetic education, which began to develop about 1975, is that of "the arts in general education." Given its initial thrust by the John D. Rockefeller III Fund, "all the arts for all the children" has been its rallying cry. This development in arts education has focused upon providing seed money to school districts to develop programs in the arts for children and adolescents, programs that are justified not only in terms of what the arts themselves have to contribute but also because the proponents of this program argue that the arts contribute significantly to better reading, writing, and mathematics skills. The position taken has been to emphasize the instrumental function of the arts in meeting the aims of general education in nonart areas. At the same time when budgets for educational programs are limited, some school districts have viewed this orientation to the arts as an opportunity to replace individual arts consultants with a single art consultant, thus saving substantial amounts of money. In California, for example, the number of visual art consultants employed in the approximately eleven hundred school districts in the state was 438 in 1975 (Nash, 1976). As of 1980 there were about 30. As a result, many supervisors and consultants in the fine arts have viewed with suspicion the move toward arts education. They have wondered, and understandably, whether it was motivated by a sound educational rationale or was essentially a means of reducing expenditures.

Despite the arts in education movement in some American schools, the major theoretical rationales for aesthetic education have been the three identified earlier: aesthetic education as the result of effective but distinct and separate fine arts programs; the development of specially designed courses that would integrate the arts so that students could better appreciate their similarities and differences; and aesthetic education as the ability to appreciate and produce the well-made form, whether in the fine arts or in any other subject in the school curriculum.

Philosophical Views. The aims or rationales that have thus far been discussed are educational in character. But on what basis is the aesthetic justified in education? And how do such justifications enter educational rationales? Four philosophical views of the function of arts in human experience can be identified as related to the educational justifications for aesthetic education. One of these is epistemological, a second is experiential, a third is moral, and a fourth perceptual.

Epistemological. The epistemological view is perhaps best exemplified by the work of Suzanne Langer. Langer (1957) argues that there are two basic ways in which people come to know or to express what they know. One of these is discursive, the other nondiscursive. Discursive modes of expression provide the most reliable knowledge about empirical matters and are epitomized by scientific language: it is propositional and formal. The rules through which its elements are combined are public and codified. Scientific discourse is best used to describe the facts of the world, but discursive knowledge—that form of knowledge embodied in propositions—is of little use in dealing with the life of feeling. It cannot portray accurately the character of particular events or the feelings we have about them. It is precisely in this realm that nondiscursive knowledge is paramount.

Given these views of the unique functions of discursive and nondiscursive forms, it is the arts on which we must depend to understand what the life of feeling provides. Hence the claim that the arts, and therefore aesthetics, have to educational resources rests upon education's more general aim as the expansion of human understanding. If one major aim of education is to foster the growth of understanding, to enable people to know, then it appears obvious that the neglect of the aesthetic in education will constitute a neglect of enormous magnitude. Furthermore, neglect of the aesthetic is one that cannot be replaced by other modes of knowing: it is literally unique.

Given this view, that the aesthetic makes knowledge of the life of feeling possible, one of the major justifications for the arts in education is one that rests upon arguments from epistemology.

Experiential. A second philosophical view of the nature of the aesthetic argues that the virtues of the aesthetic are not primarily found in their cognitive contributions but in the fact that they provide people with unique forms of human experience, that such experience is intrinsically valuable, that it represents the apotheosis of living, and that education as a process concerned with the improvement of life ought to develop the abilities needed to have such experience (Dewey, 1934). Perhaps the most influential spokesman for this view is John Dewey, for whom the concept of the aesthetic (Dewey, 1934) is rooted in man's biological nature. The living creature has a dynamic relationship with his environment. That environment contains forms specifically made for our apprehension. Such forms are capable of enabling people who are competent to deal with them to have very special forms of experience.

Although aesthetic experience is possible, in principle, in virtually any encounter an individual has with the world, it is in the arts that such encounters are intentionally activated. But because art forms are complex and often subtle, relating to them meaningfully requires tuition. It is here that aesthetic education becomes particularly relevant. As the means through which such skills are developed, it has a primary role to play in enabling people to achieve the quintessence of experience, the experience that is art.

Moral. A third view argues that the arts cultivate appetites and express and develop values. Far from being neutral or simply innocuous pleasures for the senses, the arts are powerful motivators and shapers of thought. Since human actions are to a large degree motivated by how people feel and what they believe as contrasted to what they know, vehicles that shape feeling and belief are of considerable consequence from a moral point of view. Possibly the most powerful of such vehicles are the arts. It is through them that we come to feel in certain ways. It is through them that we are persuaded to hold certain values. From the commercial that sells beer on television, to the interior of St. Peter's in Rome, to the pageantry of the Nazi party's Nuremburg rallies, the arts have been used to shape feelings, beliefs, and opinion. Because education is itself a moral undertaking, neglect of the arts in education has two important vices. First, such neglect would deprive education of one of the most powerful tools it has available for developing interests and allegiance to moral values: educators must have certain values in order to educate. The arts can be used to support such values. Second, neglect of the arts in education leaves students vulnerable to values that might be antithetical to those that are educational. Thus attention to the arts in education both directs and protects. It points students toward those virtues worth achieving and it innoculates them against those values that are likely to lead them away from virtue. Perhaps the classic statement of this view of the power of the arts to shape moral disposition is found in Plato's *Republic*, Book X (Cornford, 1951), and in Leo Tolstoy's *What Is Art?* (1930).

Perceptual. A fourth view represents the function of the aesthetic in human experience as the vehicle for bringing to consciousness aspects of reality that would otherwise be missed. One tradition in which this view is embedded is phenomenology (Sparling, 1977). The other is Bullough's work (1912) on aesthetic distance. The argument develops in this way. Much of what we experience is contaminated by preconceptions that interfere with the direct reception of the qualitative world. As a result we make contact with the world only partially. Our language and our expectations, our forms of socialization, and our habits often interfere with our ability to experience the multitude of qualities that surround us. For example, the fact that we know that the protruding form in the center of the face is a nose may interfere with our visual perception of its unique qualities: its shape, its color, its texture. To miss these qualities is to miss experiencing the fundamental reality that

the form possesses. To secure such experience, and hence to achieve a particular level of consciousness, we must "bracket out" names that interfere, stock responses, inappropriate habits, and other features that contaminate our direct perception of the world. Aesthetic education is a primary means through which the ability to experience such qualities directly can be secured. Since education ought to heighten human consciousness, and since aesthetic education is uniquely qualified to contribute to the achievement of such an end, it should occupy a central role in the school curriculum. It is through aesthetic education that our senses are refined, which in turn shape our consciousness, and through a sensitive consciousness the experience of reality in its purest form is attained.

What we have examined thus far are four philosophical views of the function of the aesthetic in human experience. These functions inform us about the life of feeling. They make the quintessence of human experience possible, they shape our moral nature, and they teach us how to experience reality. One or more of these philosophic views have been used to justify aesthetic education within the context of general education.

Research. But what of research in aesthetic education? What does it have to tell us that is relevant to the improvement of practice in this field? Research in aesthetic education per se is not plentiful. The reasons are not difficult to discern. First, those interested in aesthetic education are, by and large, trained in fields in which the skills necessary for doing empirical quantitative research are not generally developed. Most of the articles and books pertaining to aesthetic education are conceptual in character: they are discussions of issues, they attempt to provide rationales, they aim at making useful distinctions, or they talk about the type of research that might be undertaken. Typically they do not themselves report the results of quantitative empirical inquiry, which is usually regarded as the paradigm to be used in educational research.

A second reason for the paucity of research in aesthetic education is that those who are trained in empirical research methods are either uninterested in aesthetic education or find it difficult to study it empirically. Aesthetic education is, after all, concerned in part with that form of experience we call aesthetic. Aesthetic experience does not lend itself to the kind of empirical research methods that many empiricists are able to use. Thus, those most interested and informed about aesthetic education tend to be least skilled in research, whereas those most skilled in research tend to be least interested in aesthetic education.

What kinds of questions might be asked about aesthetic education? What are the central problems to which empirical research might be addressed? Questions to be asked include:

1. Is there a developmental period in which attention to the aesthetic characteristics of objects or events is most likely to be productive?

2. What types of pedagogical methods are most likely to yield the kinds of outcomes valued by those in aesthetic education?

3. In what ways do aesthetic modes of expression make it possible for students to convey what cannot be conveyed through more conventional modes of expression?

4. Is there a pattern of interest in aesthetic properties or aesthetic experience during the human life cycle?

5. To what extent do these modes of thinking developed in an effective aesthetic program transfer to fields typically regarded as nonaesthetic?

Studies of aesthetic sensitivity. Let us turn now to what has been done in the field. Although the foregoing questions are important ones, they in no way exhaust the particular problems that individual investigators deem significant. For example, in a study conducted by Anderson (1969), the relationship between aesthetic sensitivity and previous experience in art was studied. The specific question asked was, "To what extent does a traditional art curriculum, one that largely emphasizes the making of art products, increase students' aesthetic sensibilities, a process that might best be cultivated in programs that emphasize the critical aspects of art, rather than the productive?" (p. 11). Anderson compared secondary school students who had won recognition in art in the Scholastic Awards Competition with students in classes in which award winners were enrolled and with students who had not enrolled in art classes in high school. Anderson found that experience in art classes was, in general, significantly related to scores on the Child Test of Aesthetic Sensitivity, although the magnitude of the correlation was small. Since statistically significant correlations between aesthetic sensitivity and the number of art courses taken were found, Anderson speculates that courses that are specifically designed to develop such sensitivities would be even more effective and yield even higher correlations. Although one might not be surprised that more experience in art is likely to be related to aesthetic sensitivity, few studies demonstrating such relationships exist. The paucity of such research is due, in part, to the scarcity of measures on aesthetic sensitivity. Most of the published measures were developed in the 1930s and 1940s and are often not regarded as valid indicators of what they purpose to measure. A second reason for the paucity of research in this area is due to the "obviousness" of the question. Few people question whether exposure to courses in art affect the sensibilities; they assume that they do.

Another study along similar lines was conducted as a doctoral dissertation by Day. (1973) Day wanted to know if the appreciation and attitudes of junior high school students toward art style could be extended through a planned instructional program. To answer this question Day conducted an experimental study in eight secondary school art classrooms. Through the use of two specially designed visual art tests and a curriculum designed to expand students' ability to perceive, recognize, and judge

style in visual art, Day attempted to find out if such abilities were also related to students' art preference. It is conceivable that although the ability to detect subtle differences in visual form might be fostered through especially designed curriculum, preferences for such forms, even in significant works of art, might not be developed. Day found that students in the control group had very stable art preferences and art judgments: they did not significantly alter their ability to perceive style or their preferences for visual form over a two-month period. The experimental group, however, did expand its art preferences and its ability to perceive, recognize, and judge art style significantly, from both a statistical and educational point of view.

Although it is not possible to provide a detailed description of the study here, it is significant because through the development of a specially designed curriculum, which is quite feasible to employ in a typical secondary school art classroom, students can be helped to see more subtleties in works of art than they would learn to see in more typical classroom conditions; and, perhaps even more important, their preferences for the works they have learned to see can be significantly increased. This suggests that the study not only succeeded in developing abilities related to discrimination skills and to the understanding of art history, but that it also heightened the students' aesthetic experience, causing them to want more of the same.

Project Zero. Perhaps the most extensive array of studies of aesthetic sensitivity has been conducted by researchers associated with Project Zero at Harvard University (Gardner, 1971; Perkins & Leondar, 1977). Gardner (1972), the co-director of the project, has been particularly productive in this area. In a study of children's sensitivity to painting styles, subjects age 6, age 11 and age 14 were shown postcard size reproductions of pictures painted by the same artist and asked to select the one reproduction in a set of four that was painted by the artist that had painted the pair of pictures they had seen earlier. Gardner found that older children performed better than younger children largely because older children are able to disregard subject matter when identifying painting style in order to pay attention to form, which, in this task, is a critical feature.

Style discrimination is, of course, not a necessary condition for having aesthetic experience. One might well be able to detect stylistic differences and still miss "the art" in the picture. Yet research of this kind is important in learning what it is that children of various ages are or are not able to do. It is in this sense that studies of discrimination or concept formation may contribute to the development and improvements of educational programs in aesthetic education.

In another study, Gardner attempted to determine how children conceptualize the arts: what they knew about the arts and what ideas they had of their importance, their sources, or the kinds of meanings that they provide (Gardner, Winner, & Kircher, 1975). For example, did children know where art came from? Did they think that people liked art? How did they think art was made? Gardner and his associates found that the younger the child the more likely it would have misconceptions about the arts. Furthermore, they found that the views of art that young children have were likely to be more concrete and mechanistic; that is, "The child focused on the mechanisms of producing a work, the scenery and actions involved in its production, and the technical limitations, such as the size of the canvas or the amount of paint available" (p. 64). The younger students (6 to 8 years of age) tended to be legalistic, that is, concerned with rules about what in art is allowed and not allowed and more animistic than their older counterparts.

As children matured (from about 8 to 11 years of age) they tended to believe that artists were interested in achieving realism, and they tended to be literal in their responses to art. As children matured further (ages 14 to 15) their views of art became more complex and more cognitive. Although not totally free from misconceptions about art, they were more tolerant of relativism in aesthetic judgment and displayed "an understanding of the difficulty involved in artistic creation" (p. 65).

Studies such as these exemplify much of the work done by the Project Zero group and are important indicators of the various abilities children can display at various stages of development on matters relevant to aesthetic education. But these studies, by and large, are more descriptive than experimental in character and have their own degrees of methodological imperfection. For example, in a critique of Project Zero's work, Lovano-Kerr and Rush (1980) state that "Project Zero researchers seldom mention either the educational environment of the subjects or other research on the efficacy of teaching the visual arts" (p. 22). Perhaps even more important, what is needed in research relevant to aesthetic education, in addition to descriptive studies, are studies of an experimental kind that provide guidance to curriculum developers and teachers concerning what might be done in the classrooms to change attitudes toward the arts, to develop sensitivity to the expressive aspects of the arts, and to perceive the relationship between the aesthetic characteristics found in works of art and those found in the environment at large. A great deal of research describing developmental trends simply provides empirical evidence that as children get older, they grow up.

Cross-cultural studies. Cross-cultural studies of children's aesthetic sensitivities are also rare. One of the few studies undertaken is by Harris, de Lissovoy, and Enami (1975). Interested in the extent to which children in grade 1, grade 4, grade 7 and grade 10 would be able to select from a pair of slides of objects projected on a screen the one of the two regarded as aesthetically better by experts, Harris and his associates found that fourth-grade children living in Japan and in the United States had the highest percentage of agreement with judges, that the percentage of students who agreed with expert judges declined in

grade 4 and grade 7, and had a slight but statistically significant increase in grade 10. They found, further, that Japanese students tended to receive scores indicating higher degrees of agreement with experts when the works to be judged for aesthetic quality were objects made in their own culture rather than Western origin. The researchers concluded that in cross-cultural studies of aesthetic sensitivity, it is important to use forms with which the population is familiar. Yet, in an earlier study of sensitivity to aesthetic quality conducted by Child and Iwao (1966), it was found that American potters and those Japanese potters who had no contact with the Western world tended to attain higher levels of agreement concerning aesthetic qualities found in pottery than did American potters and American college students. Thus, the question of the extent to which aesthetic qualities override cultural expectations still remains problematic.

In another study of children's sensibilities to aesthetic qualities Eysenck (1972) concluded that "maturation was probably more influential than teaching in producing 'correct' judgments. . . . The fact that differences between art and non-art students are quite small (. . . suggests that formal teaching does not play much part in the genesis of aesthetic response" (p. 9).

Consistent with his emphasis on the genetic influence on human performance, Eysenck tends to discount instruction and emphasize the features over which teachers and others have no control. This is done in spite of the fact that no connection was made or even examined between what art students studied and the abilities assessed by the modified version of the Graves Design Judgment Test, an instrument that Eysenck used in his own research. It may very well be that genetic factors do affect aesthetic judgment, but education seeks to optimize whatever capabilities individuals have, and this is precisely the area in which curriculum and teaching have such a crucial role.

Cognitive development. One potential benefit of aesthetic education in programs that engage children in the creation of aesthetic objects has to do with the contribution that such activities might make to the child's general cognitive development. To what extent, if any, does the medium with which one works cultivate particular mental skills that can be used in situations other than the ones in which the skills were initially applied or developed? In short, does work in the arts influence thinking abilities that are relevant to nonarts areas? The results of a variety of studies (Brigham, 1978; Ives, 1979; Ives & Pond, 1980) suggest that such development indeed occurs. The kinds of skills that one employs in coping with a task is influenced not only by the problem as formally stated but by the materials with which one works and by the extent to which the problem posed is nestled in a field or task that permits or encourages fantasy and speculation. Hence, problems in the arts cultivate intellectual skills that differ significantly from those posed in fields in which denotation or convention is prominent and in which rules through which elements are to be related to each other are codified and prescribed. The import of studies by Ives and Pond, Gardner, Brigham, and others is especially significant for those who need an instrumental justification for aesthetic education in the schools. Many who make educational policy have a difficult time justifying the allocation of scarce resources to aesthetic education or to the arts. However, these same individuals are often receptive to such programs when they can be linked to educational outcomes that they do value highly. Although for those committed to the intrinsic values of aesthetic education such justifications are less than satisfying, the support gained for aesthetic education programs because of the contributions they make to the child's general cognitive development is not trivial, even if the major aims of aesthetic education go unappreciated.

Summary. Earlier, this entry described three major orientations to aesthetic education that can be found in the literature. From the review of research in the field it is apparent that studies of aesthetic education, as distinct from those pertaining to the arts, are extremely rare. The vast majority of studies focus upon forms of learning, performance, and experience that are related to the arts: the development of aesthetic sensitivity, the ability to perceive formal aspects of works of art, attitude toward and conceptions of the arts, the more general cognitive consequences of works in the arts. In one sense, this is not surprising. Aesthetic education has historically been linked to the arts. Yet, as I have already indicated, there are other, more general views of what aesthetic education should be. For example, the view that Read (1958) has advanced is a very attractive one. The idea that all subjects have their potentially aesthetic aspects, that the process of bringing form into existence, whether it is within the fine arts *per se* or in the sciences, mathematics, or other fields is a powerful one. It is an idea that seems intuitively correct, especially if one listens to the aesthetic descriptors that practitioners of the sciences, mathematics, and other "nonaesthetic" fields use when talking about their work. Yet, schools are not organized to exploit the aesthetic aspects of such fields. Teachers are not prepared to do so. And curricula are not designed to bring about such realizations. Hence, that these potentially important aspects of aesthetics education should be absent in the research literature is understandable. Yet this area of study appears to be particularly important at a time in educational practice when instrumental orientations tend to override those that are consummatory in character. Study and work in fields with the intention of helping students secure intrinsic forms of satisfaction is not a salient orientation at present. Yet, if students are to secure those satisfactions that are likely to lead them to continue to study and work in the fields with which they come in contact, aesthetic motivations and satisfactions will be extremely important. In this sense, the broader view of aesthetic education can be said to reside at the very heart of education. It is through aesthetic motives that inquiry is undertaken in its own terms. Research has scarcely touched this aspect of aesthetic education. It is this neglected domain in which

the agenda for research needs most to be built, and it is in this area that aesthetic education might make its most important contribution to those who attend our schools.

Elliot W. Eisner

See also Art Education; Dramatic Arts Education; Literature; Museums; Music Education.

REFERENCES

Anderson, F. Aesthetic sensitivity, previous art experience, and participation in the scholastic art awards. *Studies in Art Education,* 1969, *10*(3), 4–13.

Baumgarten, A. G. *Aesthetics.* Frankfurt, Germany: Nachdruckder Ausgabe, 1750.

Brigham, D. Art and learning: Partners in the learning process. *Studies in Art Education,* 1978, *19*, 25–32.

Bullough E. Psychical distance as a factor in art and as aesthetic principle. *British Journal of Psychology,* 1912, *5*, 87–98.

Child, I., & Iwao, S. Comparison of aesthetic judgments by American experts and by Japanese potters. *Journal of Social Psychology,* 1966, *68*, 27–33.

Cornford, F. M. (Trans.). *The Republic of Plato.* New York: Oxford University Press, Clarendon Press, 1951.

Day, M. *Teaching for Art Appreciation: A Study of the Effects of Instruction on High School Students Art Preferences and Art Judgments.* Unpublished doctoral dissertation, Stanford University, 1973.

Dewey, J. *Art as Experience.* New York: Minton, Balch, 1934.

Dobbs, S. *Paradox and Promise: Art Education in the Public Schools.* Unpublished doctoral dissertation, Stanford University, 1972.

Eysenck, H. J. The development of aesthetic sensitivity in children. *Journal of Child Psychology and Psychiatry,* 1972, *13*, 1–10.

Gardner, H. Children's sensitivity to musical styles. *Merrill-Palmer Quarterly,* 1971, *19*, 67–77.

Gardner, H. Style sensitivity in children. *Human Development,* 1972, *15*, 325–338.

Gardner, H., Winner, E., & Kircher, M. Children's conceptions of the arts. *Journal of Aesthetic Education,* 1975, *9*(3), 60–77.

Goodman, N. When is art? In D. Perkins & B. Leondar (Eds.), *The Arts and Cognition.* Baltimore: Johns Hopkins University Press, 1977.

Harris, D.; de Lissovoy, V.; & Enami, J. The aesthetic sensitivity of Japanese and American children. *Journal of Aesthetic Education,* 1975, *9*(4), 81–96.

Ives, W. *The Visual Arts and Cognitive Development: An Annotated Bibliography.* Urbana: University of Illinois, ERIC Clearinghouse on Elementary and Early Childhood Education, 1979. (ERIC Document Reproduction Service No. ED 170 025)

Ives, W., & Pond, J. The arts and cognitive development. *High School Journal,* 1980, *63*(8), 335–340.

Kaufman, I. *Art and Education in Contemporary Culture.* New York: Macmillan, 1966.

Langer, S. *Problems of Art.* New York: Scribner, 1957.

Lovano-Kerr, J., & Rush, J. Project Zero: *The Evaluation of Visual Arts Research during the Seventies.* Unpublished manuscript, Indiana University, 1980.

Nash, L. The politics of arts education in California. In E. Eisner (Ed.), *The Arts, Human Development, and Education.* Berkeley: McCutchan, 1976, 149–159.

Onion, C. F. *The Oxford Dictionary of English Etymology.* New York: Oxford University Press, Clarendon Press, 1978.

Perkins, D., & Leondar, B. (Eds.). *The Arts and Cognition.* Baltimore: Johns Hopkins University Press, 1977.

Rawlins, K. *The Educational Metamorphosis of the American Art Museum.* Unpublished doctoral dissertation, Stanford University, 1981.

Read, H. *Education through Art* (3rd ed.). New York: Pantheon Books, 1958.

Santayana, G. *The Sense of Beauty.* New York: Scribner, 1936.

Sparling, L. *Phenomenology and the Social World: The Philosophy of Merleau-Ponty and Its Relation to the Social World.* Boston: Routledge & Kegan Paul, 1977.

Tolstoy, L. *What Is Art?* (Aylmer Maude, Trans.). New York: Oxford University Press, 1930.

AFFECTIVE EDUCATION

Concern for students as persons—for their mental health and self-development, for their interpersonal skills and potential roles in society, and for their joy in learning—these are the kinds of concerns that define affective education. They have a familiar ring when one reads in Cremin (1961) about the history of progressive education in America, and the more recent developments seem to be a natural outgrowth of that history. Teachers and students in the mid-sixties and early seventies might have thought that affective education was a spontaneous development. Catchwords such as "open classrooms," "alternative schools," "psychological education," "personal growth," "values education," "group dynamics," "classroom management," "mental imagery," "confluent education," and "student-directed learning," among many others, were new and very popular. Now that the excitement has died down, it is easier to reflect on their connection to educational and psychological theory prevalent at the time.

Theory and Beginnings. Cremin chronicled the demise of the progressive education movement in the mid-fifties, but showed how Dewey's philosophy dating back to the late 1800s had a pervasive permanent effect—causing a shift away from a narrow focus on the content of schooling and toward an emphasis on students as persons. From a comparative, comprehensive study of two traditional and two modern schools of the fifties, Minuchin et al. (1969) in descriptions of the modern elements convey a sense of affective education in its initial forms. Cohen (1973) has described how the launching of *Sputnik* in 1957 reversed the trend to some extent by emphasizing a renewed but temporary concern solely for intellectual content. The larger picture he described is one in which American education, rooted in changes begun near the turn of the century, is given greater responsibilities for the physical, recreational, vocational, social, and emotional needs of children as well as for their intellectual development.

Summerhill (Neill, 1960) tells of an English private school with a radical philosophy emphasizing the emotional development of children; the school is a bold experiment in providing greater educational freedom for students. The book was widely acclaimed, and served as a standard for arguing against repressive school environments. From a study of American education, Silberman (1970) produced an extensive critique of schools in the sixties. It served as a starting point for many of the changes that followed.

Many other books criticized the schools. Quite a few were based on the authors' experiences as teachers and their attempts to nurture both the emotional and intellectual needs of children. To do so always required bucking the system, and this literature suggested a wide spectrum of possibilities. Holt (1964) analyzed how children responded to traditional teaching and found ways to make learning more realistic. Kohl (1967) found himself confronted with a hostile ghetto classroom and courageously re-created it into an energetic, interactive, and productive environment. Dennison (1969) tells the story of a small school in New York city that was formed as a haven of escape from repressive classrooms. Reports of the British infant school seemed to provide a sure model for filling in what was missing (Featherstone, 1971). Books like these encouraged the creation of open classrooms and alternative schools, and in these experimental environments affective education developed.

The progress of educational research only vaguely paralleled the changes that were happening in the everyday world of students and teachers. Even so, supporting theory and evidence were steadily accumulating. Dissatisfaction with behaviorism as an adequate explanation for the psychology of learning made Piaget's research on cognitive development particularly compelling; the philosophy of the British infant schools was substantially influenced by it. Although by no means a mainstay of affective education, Furth's interpretations (1970) did show clearly how Piaget significantly expanded the meaning of intellectual objectives. Bruner (1966) argued the importance of thinking over and above rote learning, and saw affective components such as curiosity, need for competence, and identification—intrinsic motivation—as central to education. Underlying this argument was the assumption that children had a natural desire to learn, and that, if allowed to flourish, that alone could productively guide students' endeavors. This assumption was a major precept for many open classrooms, and research on exploratory behavior in children (Berlyne, 1970) provided some evidence for its validity.

The appearance of a taxonomy of cognitive educational objectives (Bloom, 1956) was a logical response, and it was followed in 1964 by an affective taxonomy (Krathwohl, Bloom, & Masia). These taxonomies helped to clarify expanding expectations in the school community for educating the whole child. In a review entitled "The teaching of affective responses," Kahn and Weiss (1973) firmly established the centrality of affective education, covering a full range of possibilities including learner and teacher characteristics, classroom climate, instructional strategies, and the nature of the curriculum. Finally it was becoming clearer that, planned or not, education is affective. Thelen (1960) was early to perceive its significance, affirming a view of education as an inquiry involving all human dynamics.

The contributions of psychological theory are more marked because of major developments that were happening in the early sixties. Many psychologists were not only dissatisfied with behaviorism, but also with the influence of Freud (whom Neill considered his mentor) and mainstream psychology in general. The leadership of Maslow (1962, 1968, 1971) was instrumental in establishing a third force, humanistic psychology. Buhler (1971) recognizes many dimensions to this approach, but the dominant concept is self-actualization. Postulated as a need, it is every human's potential road to creative self-fulfillment. Self-actualization could be seen as the main goal of humanistic psychology, and it underlies most of the goals and techniques of affective education.

Other psychological theories and approaches have also been influential on affective education. For example, a recent edition (Combs, Richards, & Richards, 1976) of a phenomenological approach to psychology by Snygg and Combs (1949) proposes that each individual person's perception of reality determines behavior. This focus on individuality is an important part of the concept of self-actualization. In another work, support is drawn from the existentialist writings of the fifties, applied to psychotherapy, and used to argue for the fundamental rightness of personal choice (May, 1967). Yet a radically different but significant influence is the field of group dynamics stemming from the work of Kurt Lewin and the famous Lewin, Lippitt, and White (1939) study on styles of leadership. Without the current emphasis on groups, it is hard to imagine the practical aspects of humanistic psychology or affective education. Less can hardly be said about what grew out of Rogers's concept of client-centered therapy (Rogers, 1951). His *Freedom to Learn* (1969) directly converted therapists' techniques into skills for educators; teachers, Rogers says, need to be facilitators who are authentic, accepting, and empathic.

Defining Affective Education. The task of defining affective education is difficult because of the broad range of phenomena involved—new kinds of school environments, the evolution of affective educational objectives, and the birth of humanistic psychology. Buhler (1971) called for a consistent definition of humanistic psychology, and many who define affective education would agree. For example, Heath (1972) enumerates four basic tenets: (1) education of affects, (2) experiential learning, (3) learning as organismic experience, and (4) nurturance of our social being. Rossiter (1976) lists five maxims: (1) develop the whole person, (2) treat students as persons, (3) foster interaction that leads to self-actualization, (4) know yourself as a teacher, and (5) do not teach by formula. It is

no surprise that even though the lists overlap, they are never the same. Affective education and humanistic education are used interchangeably, but beyond this there are always differences.

Using Herbert's suggestions (1977), affective education can be considered a process of becoming; and a description of the variety of programs that facilitate this process can serve as a more realistic means of definition. Brown's survey (1975) of developments across the country reveals wide differences in programs and models. In an attempt to organize the models, Miller (1976) lists seventeen separate approaches, ranging from a focus on mental health to consciousness expansion. Affective education involves a wide spectrum of options and possibilities, made possible by changes in the schools, new kinds of curricula, and educational approaches that aim to bridge the gap between affective and cognitive learning.

Changes in the schools. Open classrooms were the most visible changes that occurred in schools in response to the events of the last twenty years. Kohl's experience led to the writing of *The Open Classroom* (1969), a book suggesting how one might be created by other interested teachers. Rathbone (1972) has described and examined the ways in which this kind of classroom facilitates child-centered learning. Straight rows of desk chairs are replaced by interest areas, work tables, chairs in small groupings, and individual learning spaces. Students move from place to place depending on what they are doing. The arrangements are constantly changing and the schedule is flexible. Students are not all learning the same subject at the same time. Learning is done individually, in small groups and only occasionally as an entire class, and children of widely different ages are found working together. Self-directed learning is considered optimal and intrinsic motivation essential. The primary goal of open classrooms is not necessarily affective education; but an analysis by Miles (1975) has revealed that there tends to be greater planned emphasis on affective priorities than in the traditional classroom.

Hein (1975) and Elkind (1977) argued that cognitive objectives receive higher priority in the open classroom than in affective education programs as a whole. However, evidence from two reviews of research (Gatewood, 1975; Horwitz, 1979) suggests that cognitive and affective objectives are mutually obtainable in the open classroom. Among scores of studies, there are positive and negative results, and those revealing no differences. But on balance, there is no less achievement in the open environments; and not infrequently, affective factors such as self-concept, attitude toward school, creativity, independence, and curiosity show measurable advantage. This does not mean that open classrooms are better than traditional ones. The definitions of openness and the evaluative criteria are too varied to result in conclusive evidence. But the evidence does point to still unclarified aspects of open classroom teaching that might help to attain affective objectives. For example, in a study of ten schools where there were mixed results,

Lukasevich and Gray (1978) found higher achievement for traditional methods and higher self-concept for open environments. This led them to suggest that the level of openness could be the critical variable.

Alternative schools. The concept of the open classroom also led to the establishment of entirely new, alternative schools. Graubard reported that there were possibly six hundred "outside-the-system" schools in 1972, excluding public programs and progressive schools that existed prior to 1960. Using a more general definition, Deal and Nolan (1978) cited five thousand such schools from a report in 1975. In some cases, a central space is used as a resource area—a learning center—for all of the students in the building, and the open classroom becomes an open school. Some are "free" schools primarily based on Neill's philosophy; some are politically motivated; and others are primarily influenced by ideals of progressive education. Deal and Nolan refer to them in a conceptual framework with picturesque names: the filling station, the greenhouse, the school as a tool, and the school as a marketplace. Many alternative schools are small and not unlike the one-room schoolhouses of earlier America. There are also large-scale efforts such as the Parkway Program of the Philadelphia Public School System, which draws upon the city's cultural resources and attempts a school-without-walls (Bremer & von Moschzisker, 1971).

How permanent are these changes in the schools? Graubard (1972) and Deal and Nolan (1978) agreed that alternative schools tend to be very unstable. Surely many of those in the original counts no longer exist. The same is true for open classrooms. And there is no evidence that any noticeable number of new ones are being established. In addition, Kepler and Randall (1977) indicated how unchecked individualization in an open classroom can even subvert affective objectives when instructional materials foster the control of students' learning by curriculum makers. Indeed, some affective programs of the sixties and seventies may not be viable options today. However—as Cremin similarly observed about the effects of progressive education—classroom environments in general are probably much more supportive of child-centered learning and affective development than they were twenty years ago because of them. Equally important is Tewksbury's cogent argument that (1976) choice through alternative programs is a major development in American education. Questioning the value of open classrooms and alternative schools is no longer as productive as utilizing the techniques they have provided in affective education programs.

New Kinds of Curricula. Many new and different programs have been created for affective education. They are as varied as is the full range of human emotional growth.

Mental health. School programs for mental health respond to concerns about the prevention of mental illness. Mental health programs can include personal growth goals, but the ideal of promoting total health is the main focus. Such concerns motivate research on the link between poor mental health and failure in school. For example, a recent study by Butkowsky and Willows (1980) associated learned helplessness, a newly developing variable, with poor reading ability. And using programs aimed at combating depressive symptoms in adolescents, Butler et al. (1980) demonstrated how role playing improves classroom behavior. The results of these studies buttress the need for mental health programs.

The curricula are not unique programs in affective education; but rather share a common underlying goal. Meant primarily for high school students, psychological education is the most formalized approach to mental health programming (Mosher & Sprinthall, 1970; Sprinthall, 1980). It is often a course in psychology and, its objectives are intended to promote intellectual and emotional development. A study by Lindberg, Bartell, and Estes (1977) found improved attitudes toward teachers, other students, and oneself. A study by Smith and Troth (1975) found improvements in achievement motivation. Mainly because the definition of psychological education lacks precision, such studies are not definitive—but they are encouraging. At the elementary level, the mental health focus is promoted by school counselors. Sometimes the counselors work directly with children in classrooms; at other times they facilitate teacher and parent leadership. For example, Kilmann et al. (1979) described affective activities that significantly improved the reading skills of a targeted group of underachievers. Such a program might be considered a pragmatic approach to affective education. As Gumaer (1976) pointed out in his opposition to a merely crisis role for counselors, the goal of mental health programs ought to be problem prevention and the development of emotional skills.

Personal growth. One of the most important facets of affective education is personal growth. With the aim of self-actualization in mind, even for young children, hundreds of activities have been designed to promote the development of self. Besides the texts and handbooks written for humanistic psychology in general, there are especially helpful ones directly related to education. A partial list from Hendricks and Wills (1975) and Hendricks and Roberts (1977) includes exercises for emotional centering, for relaxing the mind and the body, for expanding perception, for working with dreams, for learning body movement, and for learning to take responsibility, in addition to energizing, intuition, and quieting activities. Canfield and Wells offer *One Hundred Ways to Enhance Self-concept in the Classroom* (1976). Other books, such as Thayer (1976), have even more of a variety, but typically the crossover into other areas of affective education is greater.

The more immediate goal of personal-growth programs is to help students succeed in school. How well they succeed has not been widely researched, and published curricula incorporating the exercises and activities, when evaluated, do not necessarily pass muster. A review of studies of four such programs (Medway & Smith, 1978) produced only a little positive evidence, and another study of one of the same four programs (Hudgins, 1979) revealed no effects. Following Purkey's advice (1978), however, much of the effort is directed toward helping students build better self-concepts, and the research in this area is instructive. Although the causal relationship is unclear, Purkey feels that a relation between self-concept and success in school is fairly well established. Recent research (Ames & Felker, 1979; and Calsyn & Kenny, 1977) suggests that there is a dynamic interaction between students' actual level of achievement, their sense of personal responsibility for success, and deliberate attempts to enhance self-concept. The possibility of helping children gain skills for fulfilling their potential in school and beyond is what makes personal growth a fertile area of affective education.

Values education. Curricula for values education often generate the most controversy. Many people feel that values education is more appropriately the job of the family or the church. However, arguing that it includes important secular tasks for the schools, Kohlberg (1973) and Simon, Howe, and Kirschenbaum (1978) have been responsible for the creation of two major programs. Kohlberg's interest is moral development. Influenced by Dewey and Piaget, he has proposed hierarchical moral stages through which a person's learning must pass. Instructional materials that confront children with a series of increasingly challenging moral dilemmas are meant to teach skills for coping independently with issues of personal value. Simon, Howe, and Kirschenbaum's approach—values clarification—is intended to help students develop values and to better understand the ones they have. The authors have generated scores of activities for teachers to use in their classrooms. They emphasize choosing freely, weighing alternatives, and the importance of sharing and acting upon values. Others, such as Hawley and Hawley (1975), draw upon these two approaches, add some, and integrate them into broader versions of affective teaching.

Irrespective of curricular decisions, as in most areas of affective learning, children develop their values willy-nilly; the issue at stake, however, is whether or not the school should take an active role. Values education works least well for children of parents who feel that it is wrong to tamper with fundamental values. Freiberg and Foster (1979) argue that there are some basic skills, such as problem solving and learning to evaluate, listen, and question, that teachers can facilitate without unduly influencing their students. From a research standpoint, although moral development and values clarification programs cannot do all that is claimed, pertinent evidence indicates that they can improve moral reasoning and positively influence classroom behavior (Lockwood, 1978). New refinements will surely be introduced, but the appropriateness of values education still remains, not surprisingly, mainly a question of values. Bricker's discussion (1972) of the common belief that teachers ought to be neutral demonstrates the difficulty of the question; teachers of affective education would

characteristically want to share their values, and yet an important norm in our culture demands that they do not.

Group dynamics. Social interaction is an essential part of everyone's affective learning. It is no less so in the classroom, where it may be developed by means of group dynamics. Many group activities are an integral part of designs for fostering personal growth. Many of these, and others, are meant to help the entire classroom group become a positive, interactive unit that can constructively further its own goals. Another use of small groups is to facilitate cognitive learning. There are texts that assist teachers' understanding of group processes (Schmuck & Schmuck, 1979), that provide techniques for the development of classroom groups (Stanford, 1977), and that give direction for the analysis of group interaction (Hunter, 1972). From a study of group membership in twenty-five elementary school classrooms, Zeichner (1978) concluded that "the quality of a student's group membership is related to his or her emotional health and academic performance." He adds, "It is my belief that significant improvements in the quality of education will only occur if attention is paid to the social dynamics of classroom groups" (p. 563).

Research has centered on the use of small groups in the classroom, and cooperation has been a significant variable. Johnson and Johnson (1974, 1978) distinguished practical differences between cooperative, competitive, and individualistic learning. The distinction is reminiscent of Lewin's work on democratic, authoritarian, and laissez-faire leadership styles, and they argued that alternating learning modes can be utilized, depending on the teacher's goals. However, from extensive reviews of research, they concluded, along with Sharan (1980) and Slavin (1980), that significant advantages exist in cooperative learning because cognitive and affective objectives can most often be achieved simultaneously. The evidence decidedly supports the need for the use of effective classroom groups.

Classroom Management. Teacher authority is not easy to establish when priority is given to affective objectives. No matter how humanistic a teacher wants to be, somewhere down the line, basic issues of classroom management will arise. The need for boundaries is always present, and the question of discipline can come up at any time. Difficulties with the abuse of freedom are echoed from Dewey (1938) to Neill (1966) to Maslow (1979). Each of them felt compelled to clarify that freedom must not be confused with license.

Traditionally, punishment is the antidote for misbehavior, but affective educators argue that there are more effective means. Reviewing models of discipline, Blume and Blume (1979) felt that communication between teacher and student is the most essential factor—particularly the type of communication that encourages students to maintain a sense of responsibility for their actions. This theme is made practical in different ways. An approach by Dreikurs, Grunwald, and Pepper (1971) is based on the notion that all behavior is purposive; dealing with misbehavior means helping students understand their motivations. Glasser (1969) offers another approach in his book *Schools without Failure*. The key for him is the problem of negative self-perceptions. Yet another approach is *T.E.T.: Teacher Effectiveness Training* by Gordon (1974), based on systematic, cooperative problem solving. Each approach includes an entire body of techniques, although there is some overlap, such as in the use of discussion and role playing. Drawing upon the full breadth of these concepts, Hipple (1978) creatively proposes fifteen possibilities for humane discipline.

There is little research directly related to affective approaches to classroom management. However, studies by McClure, Chinsky, and Larcen (1978) and Elrado and Caldwell (1979), for example, provide evidence for the potential of role playing in the development of classroom social skills. And a study by Shiffler, Lynch-Sauer, and Nadelman (1977) reveals how important affective education can be for classroom management. Naturalistic observations of two informal elementary classrooms revealed a positive relationship between a measure of self-concept and task-oriented behavior as well as a negative relationship with nondirected behavior.

Confluent Education. The connection between affective and cognitive learning, the source of their interdependence in human brain function, is a consistent theme in affective education. Brown (1971) adopts the theme as the main tenet of an approach he calls "confluent education." Sometimes the term is used as a synonym for "affective education," but Brown (1975) says it is something more. The advantage of conceptualizing a confluent education is that it accommodates variability and need include only the kinds of affective curricula that a teacher or a school system may choose. What is considered critical is recognition of the confluence of affect and cognition in all learning processes.

The interdependency of affective and cognitive learning is documented in a recent study of hierarchical order by Hurst (1980). Using an individualized learning task, she found the two learning domains interwoven in a test of their sequential importance to the task. Although it has been difficult to document that changes in self-concept affect achievement (Scheirer & Kraut, 1979), direct facilitation of achievement by affective variables has been found. For example, in a review of several studies, Condon (1978) found a relationship between affective measures such as interest and curiosity, and improvements in reading; and in an experimental study, Brett (1978) demonstrated the positive effects of young children's circle activities on reading readiness.

There is much material available for facilitating confluent education. Influenced by Perls and the techniques of Gestalt therapy, the exercises and activities bring feelings and subject matter into the here-and-now in ways that are helpful and appealing. Castillo's (1978) book includes scores of activities covering such topics as sensory awareness, imagination, communication, trust, aggression, art, language, science, reading, and mathematics. Lederman (1969) relates how, with a special rocking chair in her class, she helps students to translate feelings, particularly angry ones, into energy for learning. Culler and Phillips (1979) offer activities for the reduction of mathematics anxiety. Actually, the influence of confluent education's principles on instructional materials is probably as significant as the changes that have occurred in the classroom environment. Materials today are generally much more interesting than they used to be. This is exemplified by a wonderful catalogue of science activities, *The Whole Cosmos* (1977) by Abruscato and Hassard, where learning is definitely a confluence of affective and cognitive domains.

Mental imagery. The significance of mental imagery as an educational tool has recently gained recognition. It is not new, and Higbee (1979) points out that in the form of visual mnemonics it has been known to be an aid to learning for centuries. Developments in recent years have greatly expanded the potential of mental imagery and make it one of the most fascinating areas of affective education. New breakthroughs in research on the brain (Chall & Mirsky, 1978) have revealed two kinds of learning—one associated with the left hemisphere of the brain, and one with the right. The left functions in a more orderly and logical manner; the right functions in a more intuitive and holistic manner. Ornstein (1972) concludes that both mental functions require critical attention, and it is generally accepted that both are an integral part of intellectual and personal learning. Imagery, a right-brain function, is understood to be an indispensable help to left-brain functioning.

Although a large body of experimental research exists on mental imagery and a considerable number of teaching activities rely on the use of imagination, there is little overlap between the two areas of developmental work. The experimental research has focused on how verbal and visual imagery facilitate learning. A review by Pressley (1977) included paired-associate learning, recognition, recall, and prose learning. Levin (1976) clarified differences that result from pictures which are imposed images in contrast to self-induced images. Drawing on these variables, a study by Levin et al. (1979) provided a practical example for teaching foreign languages through imagery. There is little doubt that the techniques will eventually be useful in the classroom. On the other hand, the work of Assagioli (1965) has influenced the development of activities for training children's imagination for the primary goal of self-development. Assagioli has argued that the guided use of imagination is a powerful tool for personal change; his underlying assumption is that realistic action can be heavily influenced by carefully constructed fantasies. Many of the personal growth activities utilize guided fantasies (e.g., Hendricks & Roberts, 1977), and a particularly clever book on the topic is *Put Your Mother on the Ceiling* by de Mille (1973). Using imagination training to help students write better papers more freely for their English class, Wedin (1977) gives a hint about how the two areas—experimental research and teaching activities—might come together.

Student-directed learning. Another approach that crosses all aspects of affective education is the emphasis on student-directed learning. The degree of student direction is variable, but the need to give students some responsibility for their own learning is accepted. Gibbons et al. (1980) have analyzed the characteristics of twenty recognized individuals who became expert without formal training, and they conclude that active, experiential learning is an essential ingredient for the fulfillment of personal potential. Discussing the relationship of student direction and humanistic education, Wells (1980) says, "If one considers the behaviors . . . which characterize self-directed learners, it seems clear that opportunities which encourage students to work in these ways should lead to more fully functioning and more self-realizing persons" (p. 45). In a study of college students, Allender and Silberman (1979) also found different kinds of student-directed learning equally useful. Measures of student involvement and levels of inquiry were significantly affected by what was differentiated as teacher-directed, group-guided, and individually oriented student direction.

Several avenues of research clarify how students' personal responsibility for learning is related to confluent education. Thomas's review (1980) discussed the ways in which degree of student control over learning heightens the affective prerequisites of academic achievement. From an experimental investigation, Owings et al. (1980) have shown, for example, that knowing how to monitor and regulate learning strategies distinguishes successful from less successful students. This may be connected with what Flavell (1979) has termed "metacognition." That is, effective learning depends on a host of conscious monitoring processes involving attention, perception, motivation, memory, problem solving, imagination, among others. Yet another aspect is seen in a study of locus of control. Arlin and Whitley (1978) found that students who perceive that they are partly managing their own learning tend to accept more personal responsibility for academic successes and failures.

It is common to misconstrue this evidence by thinking that no important role for teachers exists. Quite to the contrary, the teacher's leadership is essential. Silberman, Allender, and Yanoff (1976) have explained how the structure of student direction must involve carefully designed classroom activities including adequate resources, cooperative planning, and clear boundaries. Many problems arise without this kind of preparation (Allender, 1978). But with appropriate planning, student-directed learning, along with other confluent strategies, can be an important vehicle of affective education.

Research Directions. Weinberg (1974) has argued articulately that a humanistic orientation brings with it new ways of looking at education. Affective goals typically increase students' alternatives, and the study of this kind of teaching and learning, to be relevant, has to incorporate

the additional range of options. Innovative orientations also sometimes require new research methodologies. Much of what has been done is tied to a research paradigm that views academic achievement as the principle dependent variable. This is partly a result of the difficulties of noncognitive measurement; but in an insightful overview of such variables as affects, attitudes and beliefs, interests, motives and needs, curiosity, temperament, social sensitivity, coping strategies, cognitive styles, creativity, and values, Messick (1979) has shown that the situation is changing. An instrument based on Anderson and Walberg's (1974) work on open classrooms is one example. Fraser (1979) modified and refined their Learning Environment Inventory, and has proposed it for monitoring the effects of innovations in classroom learning environments, and for identifying these effects on students' cognitive and affective learning.

Research on affective education can benefit from several existing methodological developments. Because of the holistic nature of humanistic goals, ethnographic models and other kinds of observation are particularly appropriate. Jackson's informal observations of classroom life (1968) produced a classic study, and it has had an impact on the subsequent course of affective education. McDermott (1977) feels that social relations as a context for learning in schools can be studied in this way. There is also a history of systematic observation methods (e.g., Amidon & Hunter, 1966; Flanders, 1970) that have been useful in studying the interrelationship of cognitive and affective variables in the classroom. Particularly cogent is the distinction made by these researchers between a teacher's direct and indirect influence. Their methods have been coupled with the use of microteaching—training techniques that involve role playing, videotaping, and feedback. Sadker, Sadker, and Strain (1977) have demonstrated the effectiveness of microteaching in building a teacher's affective skills. These examples can only be suggestive. The methods of educational research are always changing, and it seems that they are now more closely linked to affective classroom factors. This means that there are more options open to the creative researcher.

Limitations and potential. Innovative programs are accompanied by raised hopes for solving long-standing problems; yet limitations are inherent in any new approach to education, if for no other reason than that the high expectations are hardly ever in line with the practical achievements. Worse yet, there is no coordinated way to stop the occasional misuse of developing programs. Divoky (1975) has marshaled evidence to show that affective education is not appropriate for classroom instruction, and has gathered illustrations of invasion of personal privacy that are indeed convincing. Au (1977) was supportive of confluent education, but still sees critical avenues for misuse: the dangers of anti-intellectualism, technique orientation, manipulation, freedom without responsibility, and preoccupation with self in the absence of sensitivity to others. The limitations of all brands of education are not so dissimilar, and the accomplishments of affective programs and approaches have to be judged in a total educational context. Most importantly, it would seem that the goals of the educational community—children, teachers, administrators, and parents—have to overlap sufficiently to allow for the potential that there is.

Goodlad (1978) has suggested that back-to-back movements are a normal part of the rebound in education from the soft and tender to the hard and tough, and then back again. He feels that such swings have been helpful in the continuing dialogue for improvement of American education and that our country's schools have not changed so much with each swing as one would imagine. According to this view, the techniques of affective education mainly contribute more options for the classroom teacher. It remains to decide how much emphasis to place on content and subject learning as opposed to nurturing the growth of each student as a person. Natko (1979) clarifies the many conflicting needs arising in the classroom. The resolution of these conflicts is necessarily the task of teachers, and they relate cogently to the limitations of affective education.

The immediate potential of affective education consists of what teachers can do in their classrooms; its far-reaching potential depends more upon what the educational community sets out to accomplish. At the community level, leadership of school administrators is a key factor. Lorch (1975) has argued that schools can be administered "confluently" and presents a set of principles for doing so. Ranging from making the school a place where feelings and emotions can be expressed constructively to facilitating the exercise of responsibility by everyone involved, the principles are meant to integrate academic goals and personal growth. Another offshoot of humanistic psychology, organizational development embodies this approach to administration on a larger scale. A review by Fullan, Miles, and Taylor (1980) has indicated that it is an extensive field in and of itself. "A change strategy for organizational self-development and renewal, which has been used . . . over the past twenty years, starting in business organizations and moving to public agencies and schools" (p. 121). It is clear that such organizational efforts often result in school communities reaching their goals more effectively on a variety of fronts at the same time.

Affective education, in all its many dimensions, can be viewed as itself a strategy for change, and can be used to attack problems that plague schools today. The abuse of drugs and alcohol, the difficulties of integration and mainstreaming, outright vandalism, among other problems, are commonly faced by teachers and administrators. Traditional approaches to education do not focus on these issues, and much more seems to be needed than varying degrees of punishment. For example, regarding problems of racial integration, survey data (Slavin & Madden, 1979) and observational data (Serow & Solomon, 1979) both suggest that cooperative learning groups are likely to ease

tensions and build better intergroup relations. There is also evidence that interdependent group learning improves educational achievement, especially for minorities (Lucker et al., 1976). Studies such as these suggest that great potential exists in all of affective education areas—mental health, personal growth, values education, group development, classroom management, confluent education, mental imagery, and student-directed learning—for solving the pressing everyday problems of schools. Continued exploration is bound to be fruitful.

Some potential benefits of affective education is outside the typical goals that people set for schooling. Transpersonal education is the prime example, with objectives that include the realization of higher states of consciousness, the pursuit of personal paths to self-discovery, and the recognition of inner wisdom (Clark, 1974). It is sometimes argued that transpersonal education is outside the pale of affective education. For example, Ryback (1978) feels that transpersonal education is more value-free and less systematic, more intrapersonal and psychic, placing greater emphasis on mastering as opposed to actualizing the self; experience exists for its own sake, not necessarily for positive growth. As exemplified by Hendricks and Fadiman (1976), transpersonal learning activities are not totally different from other affective activities, but there is decidedly a greater influence from Eastern thought and practices. A delightful article, however, by Seiler and Renshaw (1978), entitled "Yoga for Kids," shows how transpersonal approaches can be a realistic part of affective education. Its charming photographs show how breathing exercises, meditation, and simple yoga postures can lead children toward calmness and quietness.

Methods of Evaluation. Underlying and overriding each approach to education are methods of evaluation. How students, teachers, and schools are evaluated significantly influences their intentions and actions. A discussion of this issue by Deutsch (1979) points out how competition for grades, our dominant cultural norm for evaluation, works against positive attitudes among students for each other's successful achievement. The relationship between teacher and students is subject to similar negative pressures. Difficulties also arise from traditional strategies for teacher appraisal (Hoyle, 1977). In general, norm-referenced criteria, particularly if they are focused solely on only a few cognitive objectives, necessarily have a limiting effect on broad affective objectives. Suggesting new possibilities for humanistic evaluation, Joyce (1975) has emphasized the importance of self-evaluation as well as attitudes on the part of teachers that encourage students to fulfill their individual potential. Special care is needed not to foster in children negative images of their abilities and potential. Looking at the problem broadly, Nash (1979) has proposed a humanistic interpretation of accountability that has organizational, interpersonal, and personal dimensions. According to this view, successful affective evaluation includes planning, goal setting, and learning as a cooperative venture of students, teachers, administrators, and parents.

Jerome S. Allender

See also Drug Abuse Education; Emotional Development; Experiential Education; Games and Simulations; Group Processes; Mental Health; Moral Development; Social Development.

REFERENCES

Abruscato, J., & Hassard, J. *The Whole Cosmos: Catalogue of Science Activities.* Santa Monica, Calif.: Goodyear, 1977.

Allender, J. S. *Structuring Freedom to Learn.* (Center for the Study of Psychoeducational Processes Monograph). Philadelphia: Temple University, 1978.

Allender, J. S., & Silberman, M. L. Three variations of student-directed learning: A research report. *Journal of Humanistic Psychology,* 1979, *19,* 79–83.

Ames, C., & Felker, D. W. Effects of self-concept on children's causal attributions and self-reinforcement. *Journal of Educational Psychology,* 1979, *71,* 613–619.

Amidon, E., & Hunter, E. *Improving Teaching: The Analysis of Classroom Verbal Interaction.* New York: Holt, Rinehart and Winston, 1966.

Anderson, G. J., & Walberg, H. J. Learning environments. In H. J. Walberg (Ed.), *Evaluating Educational Performance: A Sourcebook of Methods, Instruments, and Examples.* Berkeley, Calif.: McCutchan, 1974.

Arlin, M., & Whitley, T. W. Perceptions of self-managed learning opportunities and academic locus of control: A causal interpretation. *Journal of Educational Psychology,* 1978, *70,* 988–992.

Assagioli, R. *Psychosynthesis: A Manual of Principles and Techniques.* New York: Penguin Books, 1965.

Au, W. Confluent education: A critical evaluation. *Confluent Education Journal,* 1977, *5,* 54–75.

Berlyne, D. E. Children's reasoning and thinking. In P. H. Mussen (Ed.), *Carmichael's Manual of Child Psychology* (3rd ed.). New York: Wiley, 1970.

Bloom, B. S. (Ed.). *Cognitive Domain. Handbook I of Taxonomy of Educational Objectives.* New York: McKay, 1956.

Blume, R. A., & Blume, D. M. Better discipline through communication. *Journal of Humanistic Education,* 1979, *3,* 15–19.

Bremer, J., & Moschzisker, M. von. *The School without Walls: Philadelphia's Parkway Program.* New York: Holt, Rinehart & Winston, 1971.

Brett, A. The influence of effective education on the cognitive performance of kindergarten children. *Child Study Journal,* 1978, *8,* 156–173.

Bricker, D. C. Moral education and teacher neutrality. *School Review,* 1972, *80,* 619–627.

Brown, G. I. *Human Teaching for Human Learning: An Introduction to Confluent Education.* New York: Viking Press, 1971.

Brown, G. I. The training of teachers for affective roles. In K. Ryan (Ed.), *Teacher Education: The Seventy-Fourth Yearbook of the National Society for the Study of Education* (Part II). Chicago: University of Chicago Press, 1975.

Bruner, J. S. *Toward a Theory of Instruction.* Cambridge, Mass.: Harvard University Press, 1966.

Buhler, C. Basic theoretical concepts of humanist psychology. *American Psychologist,* 1971, *26,* 378–386.

Butkowsky, I. S., & Willows, D. M. Cognitive-motivational characteristics of children varying in reading ability: Evidence for learned helplessness in poor readers. *Journal of Educational Psychology,* 1980, *72,* 408–422.

Butler, L.; Miezitis, S.; Friedman, R.; & Cole, E. The effects of two school-based intervention programs on depressive symptoms in preadolescents. *American Educational Research Journal,* 1980, *17,* 111–119.

Calsyn, R. J., & Kenney, D. A. Self-concept of ability and perceived evaluation of others. Cause or effect of academic achievement? *Journal of Educational Psychology,* 1977, *69,* 136–145.

Canfield, J., & Wells, H. C. *One Hundred Ways to Enhance Self-concept in the Classroom: A Handbook for Teachers and Parents.* Englewood Cliffs, N.J.: Prentice-Hall, 1976.

Castillo, G. A. *Left-handed Teaching: Lessons in Affective Education* (2nd ed.). New York: Holt, Rinehart & Winston, 1978.

Chall, J. S., & Mirsky, A. F. (Eds.). *Education and the Brain: The Seventy-seventh Yearbook of the National Society for the Study of Education* (Part II). Chicago: University of Chicago Press, 1978.

Clark, F. V. Rediscovering transpersonal education. *Journal of Transpersonal Psychology,* 1974, *6,* 1–7.

Cohen, S. The elementary school in the twentieth century: A social context. In J. I. Goodlad & H. G. Shane (Eds.), *The Elementary School in the United States: The Seventy-second Yearbook of the National Society for the Study of Education* (Part II). Chicago: University of Chicago Press, 1973.

Combs, A. W.; Richards, A. C.; & Richards, F. *Perceptual Psychology: A Humanistic Approach to the Study of Persons.* New York: Harper & Row, 1976.

Condon, M. W. F. Consideration of affect in comprehension: The person belongs in reading. *Viewpoints in Teaching and Learning,* 1978, *54*(3), 107–116.

Cremin, L. A. *The Transformation of the School: Progressivism in American Education, 1876–1957.* New York: Random House, Vintage Books, 1961.

Culler, S., & Phillips, L. B. A confluent approach to math anxiety. *Confluent Education Journal,* 1979, *9,* 1–12.

Deal, T. E., & Nolan, R. R. Alternative schools: A conceptual map. *School Review,* 1978, *87,* 29–49.

de Mille, R. *Put Your Mother on the Ceiling: Children's Imagination Games.* New York: Penguin Books, 1973.

Dennison, G. *The Lives of Children: The Story of the First Street School.* New York: Random House, Vintage Books, 1969.

Deutsch, M. Education and distributive justice: Some reflections on grading systems. *American Psychologist,* 1979, *34,* 391–401.

Dewey, J. *Experience and Education.* New York: Macmillan, 1938.

Divoky, D. Affective education: Are we going too far? *Learning: The Magazine for Creative Teaching,* 1975, *4*(2), 20–27.

Dreikurs, R.; Grunwald, B. B.; & Pepper, F. C. *Maintaining Sanity in the Classroom: Illustrated Teaching Techniques.* New York: Harper & Row, 1971.

Elardo, P. T., & Caldwell, B. M. The effects of an experimental social development program on children in the middle childhood period. *Psychology in the Schools,* 1979, *16,* 93–100.

Elkind, D. Humanizing the curriculum. *Childhood Education,* 1977, *53,* 179–182.

Featherstone, J. *Schools Where Children Learn.* New York: Liveright, 1971.

Flanders, N. A. *Analyzing Teaching Behavior.* Reading, Mass.: Addison-Wesley, 1970.

Flavell, J. H. Metacognition and cognitive monitoring: A new area of cognitive-developmental inquiry. *American Psychologist*, 1979, *10*, 906–911.

Fraser, B. J. Assessment of learning environment in elementary-school classrooms. *Elementary School Journal*, 1979, *79*, 297–300.

Freiberg, H. J., & Foster, D. Who should facilitate values education? *Journal of Teacher Education*, 1979, *30*(3), 37–40.

Fullan, M.; Miles, M. B.; & Taylor, G. Organization development in schools: The state of the art. *Review of Educational Research*, 1980, *50*, 121–183.

Furth, H. G. *Piaget for Teachers*. Englewood Cliffs, N.J.: Prentice-Hall, 1970.

Gatewood, T. E. How effective are open classrooms? A review of the research. *Childhood Education*, 1975, *51*, 170–179.

Gibbons, M.; Bailey, A.; Comeau, P.; Schmuck, J.; Seymour, S.; & Wallace, D. Toward a theory of self-directed learning: A study of experts without formal training. *Journal of Humanistic Psychology*, 1980, *20*, 41–56.

Glasser, W. *Schools without Failure*. New York: Harper & Row, 1969.

Goodlad, J. I. The trouble with humanistic education. *Journal of Humanistic Education*, 1978, *2*, 8–29.

Gordon, T. *T.E.T.: Teacher Effectiveness Training*. New York: Peter H. Wyden, 1974.

Graubard, A. The free school movement. *Harvard Educational Review*, 1972, *42*, 351–373.

Gumaer, J. Affective education through the friendship class. *School Counselor*, 1976, *23*, 257–263.

Hawley, R. C., & Hawley, I. L. *Human Values in the Classroom: A Handbook for Teachers*. New York: Hart, 1975.

Heath, D. H. Affective education: Aesthetics and discipline. *School Review*, 1972, *80*, 353–372.

Hein, G. E. Humanistic and open education: Comparison and contrast. *Journal of Education*, 1975, *157*(3), 27–38.

Hendricks, G., & Fadiman, J. (Eds.). *Transpersonal Education: A Curriculum for Feeling and Being*. Englewood Cliffs, N.J.: Prentice-Hall, 1976.

Hendricks, G., & Roberts, T. B. *The Second Centering Book: More Awareness Activities for Children, Parents, and Teachers*. Englewood Cliffs, N.J.: Prentice-Hall, 1977.

Hendricks, G., & Wills, R. *The Centering Book: Awareness Activities for Children, Parents, and Teachers*. Englewood Cliffs, N.J.: Prentice-Hall, 1975.

Herbert, P. C. The Association for Humanistic Education: A process of becoming. *Journal of Humanistic Education*, 1977, *1*, 2–4.

Higbee, K. L. Recent research on visual mnemonics: Historical roots and educational fruits. *Review of Educational Research*, 1979, *49*, 611–629.

Hipple, M. L. Classroom discipline problems? Fifteen humane solutions. *Childhood Education*, 1978, *54*, 183–187.

Holt, J. *How Children Fail*. New York: Dell, 1964.

Horwitz, R. A. Psychological effects of the "open classroom." *Review of Educational Research*, 1979, *49*, 71–85.

Hoyle, J. R. Teacher evaluation: A humanistic approach for administrators. *Journal of Humanistic Education*, 1977, *1*, 71–82.

Hudgins, E. W. Examining the effectiveness of affective education. *Psychology in the Schools*, 1979, *16*, 581–585.

Hunter, E. *Encounter in the Classroom: New Ways of Teaching*. New York: Holt, Rinehart & Winston, 1972.

Hurst, B. M. An integrated approach to the hierarchical order of the cognitive and affective domains. *Journal of Educational Psychology*, 1980, *72*, 293–303.

Jackson, P. W. *Life in Classrooms*. New York: Holt, Rinehart & Winston, 1968.

Johnson, D. W., & Johnson, R. T. Instructional goal structure: Cooperative, competitive, or individualistic. *Review of Educational Research*, 1974, *44*, 213–240.

Johnson, D. W., & Johnson, R. T. Cooperative, competitive, and individualistic learning. *Journal of Research and Development in Education*, 1978, *12*(1), 3–15.

Joyce, J. F. Humanistic education through an analysis of evaluation practices. *Journal of Education*, 1975, *157*(3), 39–53.

Kahn, S. B., & Weiss, J. The teaching of affective responses. In R. M. W. Travers (Ed.), *Second Handbook of Research on Teaching*. Chicago: Rand McNally, 1973.

Kepler, K., & Randall, J. W. Individualization: The subversion of elementary schooling. *Elementary School Journal*, 1977, *77*, 358–363.

Kilmann, P. R.; Henry, S. E.; Scarbro, H.; & Laughlin, J. E. The impact of affective education on elementary school underachievers. *Psychology in the Schools*, 1979, *16*, 217–223.

Kohl, H. R. *Thirty-six Children*. New York: New American Library, 1967.

Kohl, H. R. *The Open Classroom: A Practical Guide to a New Way of Teaching*. New York: New York Review Book, 1969.

Kohlberg, L. The contribution of developmental psychology to education: Examples from moral education. *Educational Psychologist*, 1973, *10*, 2–14.

Krathwohl, D. R.; Bloom, B. S.; & Masia, B. B. *Affective Domain. Handbook II of Taxonomy of Educational Objectives*. New York: McKay, 1964.

Lederman, J. *Anger and the Rocking Chair: Gestalt Awareness with Children*. New York: Viking Press, 1969.

Levin, J. R. What have we learned about maximizing what children learn? In J. R. Levin & V. L. Allen (Eds.), *Cognitive Learning in Children: Theories and Strategies*. New York: Academic Press, 1976.

Levin, J. R.; Pressley, M.; McCormick, C. B.; Miller, G. E.; & Shriberg, L. K. Assessing the classroom potential of the keyword method. *Journal of Educational Psychology*, 1979, *71*, 583–594.

Lewin, K.; Lippitt, R.; & White, R. K. Patterns of aggressive behavior in experimentally created "social climates." *Journal of Social Psychology*, 1939, *10*, 271–299.

Lindberg, R. E.; Bartell, S.; & Estes, G. Measured outcomes of involvement in the classroom. *School Counselor*, 1977, *24*, 148–156.

Lockwood, A. L. The effects of values clarification and moral development curricula on school-age subjects: A critical review of recent research. *Review of Educational Research*, 1978, *48*, 325–364.

Lorch, T. M. Administering schools confluently. *Confluent Education Journal*, 1975, *2*, 18–34.

Lucker, G. W.; Rosenfield, D.; Sikes, J.; & Aronson, E. Performance in the interdependent classroom: A field study. *American Educational Research Journal*, 1976, *13*, 115–123.

Lukasevich, A., & Gray, R. F. Open space, open education, and pupil performance. *Elementary School Journal*, 1978, *79*, 108–114.

Maslow, A. H. *Toward a Psychology of Being*. Princeton, N.J.: Van Nostrand, 1962.

Maslow, A. H. *Toward a Psychology of Being* (2nd ed.). Princeton, N.J.: Van Nostrand, 1968.

Maslow, A. H. *The Farther Reaches of Human Nature*. New York: Viking Press, 1971.

Maslow, A. H. Humanistic education. *Journal of Humanistic Psychology,* 1979, *19,* 13–25.

May, R. *Psychology and the Human Dilemma.* Princeton, N.J.: Van Nostrand, 1967.

McClure, L. F.; Chinsky, J. M.; & Larcen, S. W. Enhancing social problem-solving performance in an elementary school setting. *Journal of Educational Psychology,* 1978, *70,* 504–513.

McDermott, R. P. Social relations as contexts for learning in school. *Harvard Educational Review,* 1977, *47,* 198–213.

Medway, F. J., & Smith, R. C., Jr. An examination of contemporary elementary school affective education programs. *Psychology in the Schools,* 1978, *15,* 260–269.

Messick, S. Potential uses of noncognitive measurement in education. *Journal of Educational Psychology,* 1979, *71,* 281–292.

Miles, D. T. Affective goals in open education. In B. Spodek & H. J. Walberg (Eds.), *Studies in Open Education.* New York: Agathon Press, 1975.

Miller, J. P. *Humanizing the Classroom: Models of Teaching in Affective Education.* New York: Praeger, 1976.

Minuchin, P.; Biber, B.; Shapiro, E.; & Zimiles, H. *The Psychological Impact of School Experience.* New York: Basic Books, 1969.

Mosher, R. L., & Sprinthall, N. A. Psychological education in secondary schools: A program to promote individual and human development. *American Psychologist,* 1970, *25,* 911–924.

Nash, P. A humanistic perspective. *Theory into Practice,* 1979, *18,* 323–329.

Natko, J. Overcoming need conflict in the classroom. *Journal of Humanistic Education,* 1979, *3,* 31–33.

Neill, A. S. *Summerhill: A Radical Approach to Child Rearing.* New York: Hart, 1960.

Neill, A. S. *Freedom—Not License!* New York: Hart, 1966.

Ornstein, R. E. *The Psychology of Consciousness.* New York: Viking Press, 1972.

Owings, R. A.; Petersen, G. A.; Bransford, J. D.; Morris, C. D.; & Stein, B. S. Spontaneous monitoring and regulation of learning: A comparison of successful and less successful fifth graders. *Journal of Educational Psychology,* 1980, *72,* 250–256.

Pressley, M. Imagery and children's learning: Putting the picture in developmental perspective. *Review of Educational Research,* 1977, *47,* 585–622.

Purkey, W. W. *Inviting School Success: A Self-concept Approach to Teaching and Learning.* Belmont, Calif.: Wadsworth, 1978.

Rathbone, C. H. Examining the open education classroom. *School Review,* 1972, *80,* 521–549.

Rogers, C. R. *Client-centered Therapy: Its Current Practice, Implications, and Theory.* Boston: Houghton Mifflin, 1951.

Rogers, C. R. *Freedom to Learn.* Columbus, Ohio: Merrill, 1969.

Rossiter, C. M., Jr., Maxims for humanizing education. *Journal of Humanistic Psychology,* 1976, *16,* 75–80.

Ryback, D. On the difference between transpersonal and humanistic education. *Journal of Humanistic Education,* 1978, *2,* 84–87.

Sadker, M.; Sadker, D.; & Strain, P. The development of affective skills: New directions for microteaching. *Journal of Humanistic Psychology,* 1977, *17,* 59–68.

Scheirer, M. A., & Kraut, R. E. Increasing educational achievement via self-concept change. *Review of Educational Research,* 1979, *49,* 131–149.

Schmuck, R. A., & Schmuck, P. A. *Group Processes in the Classroom* (3rd ed.). Dubuque, Iowa: Brown, 1979.

Seiler, G., & Renshaw, K. Yoga for kids. *Elementary School Guidance and Counseling,* 1978, *12,* 228–238.

Serow, R. C., & Solomon, D. Classroom climates and students' intergroup behavior. *Journal of Educational Psychology,* 1979, *71,* 669–676.

Sharan, S. Cooperative learning in small groups: Recent methods and effects on achievement, attitudes, and ethnic relations. *Review of Educational Research,* 1980, *50,* 241–271.

Shiffler, N.; Lynch-Sauer, J.; & Nadelman, L. Relationship between self-concept and classroom behavior in two informal elementary classrooms. *Journal of Educational Psychology,* 1977, *69,* 349–359.

Silberman, C. E. *Crisis in the Classroom: The Remaking of American Education.* New York: Random House, 1970.

Silberman, M. L.; Allender, J. S.; & Yanoff, J. M. (Eds.). *Real Learning: A Sourcebook for Teachers.* Boston: Little, Brown, 1976.

Simon, S. B.; Howe, L. W.; & Kirschenbaum, H. *Values Clarification: A Handbook of Practical Strategies for Teachers and Students* (Rev. ed.). New York: Hart, 1978.

Slavin, R. E. Cooperative learning. *Review of Educational Research,* 1980, *50,* 315–342.

Slavin, R. E., & Madden, N. A. School practices that improve race relations. *American Educational Research Journal,* 1979, *16,* 169–180.

Smith, R. L., & Troth, W. A. Achievement motivation: A rational approach to psychological education. *Journal of Counseling Psychology,* 1975, *22,* 500–504.

Snygg, D., & Combs, A. W. *Individual Behavior: A New Frame of Reference for Psychology.* New York: Harper & Brothers, 1949.

Sprinthall, N. A. Psychology for secondary schools: The sabertooth curriculum revisited? *American Psychologist,* 1980, *35,* 336–347.

Stanford, G. *Developing Effective Classroom Groups: A Practical Guide for Teachers.* New York: Hart, 1977.

Tewksbury, J. L. Alternative programs in public elementary schools. *Theory into Practice,* 1976, *15,* 134–141.

Thayer, L. (Ed.). *Affective Education: Strategies for Experiential Learning.* La Jolla, Calif.: University Associates, 1976.

Thelen, H. A. *Education and the Human Quest.* New York: Harper & Brothers, 1960.

Thomas, J. W. Agency and achievement: Self-management and self-regard. *Review of Educational Research,* 1980, *50,* 213–240.

Wedin, W. Locating the center through fantasy. *Confluent Education Journal,* 1977, *5,* 48–53.

Weinberg, C. Social science and humanistic education. In C. W. Gordon (Ed.), *Uses of the Sociology of Education: The Seventy-third Yearbook of the National Society for the Study of Education* (Part II). Chicago: University of Chicago Press, 1974.

Wells, J. D. Self-directed learning and the humanistic educator. *Journal of Humanistic Education,* 1980, *4,* 44–45.

Zeichner, K. M. Group membership in the elementary school classroom. *Journal of Educational Psychology,* 1978, *70,* 554–564.

AFFIRMATIVE ACTION

See Black Education; Equity Issues in Education; Women's Education.

AGING

Since the reviews by Pressey (1960) and by Havighurst (1969) for previous editions of the *Encyclopedia of Educational Research,* the study of adult development and aging—gerontology—has grown rapidly. Geriatrics, the study of the medical aspects of aging, has advanced as well. Some of the efforts have pinpointed the roles of education (Johnson et al., 1980; Peterson & Bolton, 1980; Sprouse, 1976; Sullivan, 1981); but in all areas of this multidisciplinary and interdisciplinary field, much remains to be learned and applied to human affairs.

Part of the stimulus for the rapid development of gerontology has come from increased awareness of changing age distributions of populations and from the rising appreciation of the positive potentials of age and of aging. The issues for American society at the level of policy were examined, for instance, in the 1981 White House Conference on Aging: the broad areas of economic security, physical and mental health, social well-being, older Americans as a "growing natural resource," creating an age-integrated society within social institutions, and research (Barberis, 1981). Certainly education, at all levels, can and should perform important functions in helping to resolve these issues, building on what is already known about aging and the aged. (See, for example, the reviews of Birren & Schaie, 1977; Binstock & Shanas, 1976; Eisdorfer, 1980; Eisdorfer & Lawton, 1973; Finch & Hayflick, 1977; and Poon, 1980.)

The Aging Process. Aging may be seen as a complex process of continuities and changes occuring over time throughout the entire life span. This principle defines aging as an ongoing movement or a series of complex actions that take place over the entire course of life. It emphasizes the idea that one cannot understand any period in life without considering what goes on before and what may follow that period. It suggests that aging begins at conception or birth and ends at death and that aging does not begin at a specific chronological age, including the almost traditional point of demarcation—age 65 (Riley, 1979). From such a point of view it follows that aging is to be considered as a process and not simply a stage in life.

This premise is based upon the notion that growing up and growing old bring about continuities in some characteristics or processes and at the same time bring on changes in many aspects of behavior (Brim & Kagan, 1980). That there are both continuities and discontinuities in behavior throughout the life span provides opportunity to observe "consistent maturity" of adults and also their capacity for "dynamic change and adaptability." We do include the potential of positive change. It provides a framework for developing abilities in adults, including abilities of persons in late adulthood (Britton & Britton, 1972; see also Knox, 1977).

The definition presented here contrasts with other ideas about aging. Biologists have often considered aging only as *deteriorative* changes—ones that are universal, intrinsic, and progressive and that contribute to the increased probability of death (Strehler, 1977). Birren and Renner (1977), on the other hand, explicitly attempt to define aging so as to permit "the study of the incremental as well as the decremental changes in functions which occur over the life span." To them aging refers to "the regular changes that occur in mature genetically representative organisms living under representative environmental conditions as they advance in chronological age" (p. 4). Thus, they emphasize study of the selective reductions or the selective increments in functions occurring in adult life, including the reorganization of functions and structures.

Such a definition does not preclude the examination of certain age groups or specific populations or periods in the life cycle. Thus we can study the needs and special circumstances surrounding those persons who have retired, for example, or those changing careers in midlife. Although much of the available information about aging refers to those aged 65 and over, we want to emphasize the *process* of aging over the arrival at or passage of some particular birthday.

Organismic View. Aging involves the whole person and that person's health, personality, and intellectual capacity, as well as social and economic competence; changes in one area may bring about changes in another. One of the prime principles of human development and aging is that these processes involve the "wholeness" of the individual. This idea obviously deals with fundamental human nature, and it stresses that as whole living organisms, persons are more than the sum of their separate parts and that their functioning as human beings cannot be explained as resulting from independent elements. This is an organismic view of human beings, in contrast to a mechanistic perspective (Reese & Overton, 1970). It appears to hold as much for the old as for the young.

Thus, aging is seen as a biological, social, and psychological process involving these separate processes in some form together. The individual person's functioning may be studied in partitive fashion, and often this is necessary and desirable; it is nonetheless necessary and desirable to see those separate functions in the context of the whole person and also to perceive the parts in interaction with each other. For instance, poor health may affect one's capacity to work and earn a living; how one's employer, one's family, and friends view the person's sickness and health may change how they view the person's character and personality, which may also affect how that person views himself or herself.

Retirement from an active work life also demonstrates the totality of a functioning person. Retirement is not a discrete and separate event or process. How it is perceived is interlocked with one's health, age, sex, personal, and family financial circumstances, and one's self-esteem. The retirement experience may well be a function of whether it was taken by one's own choice or was mandatory. What alternative activities and social interactions are available and desired may also be relevant. How all of these tie in with one's occupational, family, and personal life cycles also gives meaning to retirement (Atchley, 1976; Carp, 1966; Havighurst et al., 1969). Thus the whole person is involved.

Individual Differences. Aging individuals differ greatly from each other and in their capacities to deal with the exigencies of aging. In thinking about aging and the aged, it seems natural to deal with averages, common tendencies, or normative data. This principle is a reminder that typically individuals vary around a norm and that we should consider not only the norms but also the variations in aging. This principle is a caution against accepting stereotypes about aging.

Individual differences—or what some refer to as interindividual differences, as contrasted with intraindividual differences (Baltes & Willis, 1977)—may be seen in all aspects of aging: the biological, social, and psychological. A few such differences should serve to illustrate the point; in some cases the apparent long-term impact of differences has been demonstrated as well.

Perhaps the most vivid presentation of the variations in aging involving several domains were the studies of forty-seven healthy aged men begun by Birren et al. (1963) and followed up by Granick and Patterson (1971). In the first publication, the data on hemotology and chemistry showed such a lack of homogeneity among the subjects that the investigators divided them into two subgroups— one that represented "optimally healthy aged" and one that contained men showing "definite evidence of disease . . . though completely asymptomatic" (Birren et al., 1963, p. 37). Variation was also shown in other functions such as mental abilities and psychomotor responses. The follow-up showed that initially low scores on certain of the tests were associated with earlier death (Granick, 1971).

Personality research, too, has shown that individuals differ much from each other in aging (Neugarten, 1977). In particular, the analysis of data from the growth studies at the University of California at Berkeley (Maas & Kuypers, 1974) showed individual differences among "normal" men and women, their life-styles, antecedent conditions, and personality patterns. Similarly personal and lifestyle variations between and among older adults were revealed in the work of Williams and Wirths (1965). Britton and Britton (1972) also showed individual patterns of aging in a longitudinal study of older community residents, illustrated by some men and women who improved in their personal functioning, some who declined, and some who simply maintained their patterns over the nine years of the study.

In research dealing with the impact of social change, Elder (1974) studied life experiences following the Depression of the 1930s. He was able to demonstrate linkages between family deprivation and behavior of the subjects as children and later as adults. This research underscores the desirability of the search for correlates and antecedents of individual differences. Perspectives from cross-national and cross-cultural research also support the proposition of individual differences and the description of correlative factors. (See Goody, 1976; Palmore, 1975; Shanas et al., 1968.)

Age Strata. Aging occurs within a context of several age strata, which over the life course may or may not interact with each other: they may (or may not) share common attitudes and values, they may compete with each other for society's resources, and they may support and be supported by each other; many factors appear to explain such variations. Almost any society at a given point in history consists of persons of different ages—infants, children, youth, and young, middle-aged, and older adults, and these age groups often differ and are similar in their behavior (Riley, 1976). To explain variations among age strata, social scientists have focused upon three sets of factors: age—developmental or maturational factors; those associated with the time in history when the individuals were born and lived—cohort factors; and differences associated with the particular timing of the behavioral assessment in relation to the individual's circumstances—nonnormative or period-specific factors. These sets of factors logically interact with each other; and together they have important implications for design and method for empirical research (Baltes & Willis, 1979; Bengtson & Cutler, 1976).

The extent and manner of interaction between and among cohorts or generations are directly relevant to processes of intergenerational socialization, of the young as well as of the adult portions of the population. How closely young adults see their needs served when the elderly are served may be a function of such interaction and the extent of sharing of attitudes and values by each other.

Discussions of the so-called generation gap have stimulated examination of how conscious different age strata in the population are of themselves as age groups and of their capacity to exercise political power. How different generations may vary in their economic and political and social views may have impact on many practical matters. The current and future costs of benefit programs, such as pensions and health care for the elderly, illustrate the potential rivalry between and among age groups. This kind of issue is not unlike discussions in communities of the costs and benefits of public education and recreational and work programs for the young. Riley (1976) has commented that "partitions of the population by age acquire meaning as age strata only as they index socially significant aspects of people and roles" (p. 191; see also Bengtson & Cutler, 1976; Estes, 1979).

The concept of aging in relation to age strata is useful in another way. Kahn (1979) has used the metaphor of a "convoy," suggesting that "each person . . . (moves) . . . through life surrounded by a set of significant other people to whom that person is related by giving or receiving of social support" (p. 84). An individual's convoy at any point in time consists of the set of persons on whom he or she relies for support and those who rely on him or her for support. Kahn suggested that analyses could then be made of the structure and characteristics of the social convoy, the adequacy of the education and support it provides, and the ways in which a convoy may change over the life course.

Families and Care. The family is the primary unit providing social and psychological and often financial support and physical care for the aging and the aged. The family provides the "binding force for our social system" (Allen, 1979, p. 21); it serves as a "key resource in maintaining a sense of well-being" (Hendricks & Hendricks, 1981, p. 302). "In a rapidly changing world, the family becomes more important, not less important; kinship ties may assume different, but no less valuable, meanings to the individual" (Streib & Shanas, 1965, p. 8). The family is seen, then, as a social institution of continuing significance for individuals throughout the entire life span, and this is no less true for individuals in the latter part than in the early phases of life. This principle stems from a desire to dispel the widespread myth (Hendricks & Hendricks, 1981) that "the elderly are abandoned by their families to face life's challenges solely through their own devices" (p. 332). (See also Stack, 1979; Uzoka, 1979).

The nuclear family—the immediate family consisting of parents and their children—is a common form in modern society, and it is often seen as having no place for its more distant kin, including the elders. Evidence is available, however, showing that in the vast majority of cases, the nuclear family is *not* isolated from the older generations. In fact, the "kin network" functions to provide mutual support, help, and service being given to and by one generation for the others, as well as to and by siblings (Sussman, 1965).

This kind of evidence points to the existence of a "modified extended family structure" in modern, industrialized societies, in which family members live independently, but within relatively short distances, and interact selectively with each other (Atchley & Miller, 1980; Shanas, 1979; Streib, 1973; Troll, 1971; see also Streib & Beck, 1980). The preference to live alone and to remain self-sufficient as long as it is physically and financially possible seems to be a long-standing pattern, and these preferred patterns of living are reflected in the demography of the aging (Long Term Care Committee, 1981; Soldo, 1980; Sussman, 1976).

In a classic study dealing with the health of older people, Shanas (1962) surveyed older community residents regarding whom they would turn to for assistance in making arrangements for long-term care. Whereas nearly 5 percent said there was no one they would turn to, approximately 60 percent of the older people named a son or daughter who would be responsible; almost 10 percent named a nonrelative. In four-fifths of the cases, Shanas also interviewed the responsible persons named for helping with extended care, who tended to be daughters more often than sons, and most of them were middle-aged persons already involved with many family responsibilities.

Older people also looked to them for financial help, but more often than not it was expected that primary responsibility for financial assistance should be assumed by government through income maintenance programs.

Community and Family Support. The family is often unable to provide adequate total care and support of its elders; the community, in its local and wider sense, must provide supplemental support and care as needed. In traditional agrarian societies, the family was expected to fulfill several functions beyond procreation: it was expected to serve as an economic unit, supplying food, clothing, and shelter for its members; as a protective force, providing its members with health care and security from adversaries; and as an educational agent, socializing the young, transmitting and teaching its members the traditions, beliefs, values, and attitudes held by the group. The old were repositories of the "wisdom" of the culture. In modern industrial societies, many of these functions have been assumed by other agencies and institutions, and modernization itself has been viewed theoretically as a process leading toward dependency and lowered status of the old (Cowgill, 1974).

Families are still a real resource, as Tobin and Kulys (1980) have said, functioning "to assist elderly members by showing concern, giving affection, giving instrumental aids to support independent living, linking to bureaucratic services, and sharing care-giving with friends and service providers" (pp. 370–371). Care of impaired elderly is a more burdensome task for families to assume, leading often to family members seeking services outside the family. Practitioners have become aware of the need to facilitate family care giving, including the process which leads to an elder's entering a long-term care facility.

In recent years the development of services outside the family has been guided somewhat by the "entitlements" listed for older citizens by the Older Americans Act of 1965, as amended and reauthorized (*Older Americans Act of 1965, As Amended,* 1979). The objective of that act was to develop service systems that would facilitate maximum independence and dignity in a home environment, remove barriers to economic and personal independence, and improve the availability of care for the vulnerable elderly. The intent was to back up families in their roles as care givers and to assure the needed services and facilities that would assist older people to secure "equal opportunity," for example, to adequate income, good health, and "freedom, independence, and the free exercise of individual initiative in planning and managing their own lives" (*Older Americans Act of 1965, As Amended, 1979,* p. 3).

It is important to point out, additionally, that not all older persons have "family." Sussman (1976) estimated proportions of the population according to family type, using a taxonomy linking functional capacity of the family "network" and various family forms. He estimated that some 19 percent of the United States population exists as families of "other single, widowed, separated or divorced adults" (p. 230). As to living arrangements *per se,* census data for 1976 showed, for example, that 42.8 percent of women and 18.4 percent of men aged 75 and over were living alone (Soldo, 1980).

Social and health services have been designed to augment personal means and to provide some of the supplemental resources needed by the elderly and their families. Some are public services, such as the Social Security system, provisions for financing health by means of Medicare and Medicaid, and housing and rent supplements. Other services are directed toward the homebound, such as homemaker service, home-health aides, or home-delivered meals. Other services focus upon the more ambulatory elderly and include transportation, job placement, congregate meals, and recreation. Still others provide more specialized service, for those needing counseling, or protective, custodial, or hospice care. A critical and contrasting view regarding services for the aging is apparent in a 1981 Reagan administration policy statement calling for a "new outlook on aging," with "less Government spending and 'intrusion' and more self-reliance among the elderly" (Weaver, 1981, p. A16).

Beattie (1976) has provided a description of a number of human services along with some perspectives on social planning and on manpower, training, and research. He concluded that new organizational forms will develop that combine environmental, social, health, educational, and recreational functions.

Life Satisfaction.   There are multiple patterns of aging and a variety of criteria for "success" and life satisfaction in aging. Both Rosow (1974) and Neubeck (1978) have commented upon the richness and complexity of aging and upon the vagueness and unregulated ways that society uses to usher its members into old age. This suggests that persons who are trying to adapt to old age "successfully" receive ambiguous and sometimes conflicting messages as to what cultural behaviors are expected in order to age successfully. Clearly, there is no one social standard for satisfactory aging, and individuals, too, have differing criteria for their own personal success.

In 1961 the idea was advanced (Cumming & Henry, 1961) that successful aging occurs when individuals and the society they live in *disengage* from each other. The reasoning was that since death is inevitable, the individual and society are protected by such a process—the individual safeguarded, for example, by being able to quit working when he or she no longer feels competent to do so and the society sheltered by having time to replace its workers; such mutual withdrawal constitutes success. This view was contrasted with one in which the successful individual continues his or her activity into old age, not unlike activity at earlier periods (Havighurst, 1973).

These "theories" have generated considerable research, which has shown that success may be associated with either pattern of aging, the personality acting as a mediating agent (Neugarten, 1973). In their study of successful aging, Lemon, Bengtson, and Peterson (1972) also found that ac-tivity in and of itself had little relationship to whether people were satisfied with life.

Among their subjects, Britton and Britton (1972) found evidence that "though constitutional, group membership, role and situational factors undoubtedly influenced the patterns of adjustment of individuals, their influence appeared to be indirect" (p. 73). While physical health would seem to influence adjustment in later life, the investigators found good health to be associated with both decline and improvement over the nine-year period. They suggested that their subjects used mediating capacities of the self, thus enabling them to perceive, evaluate, and interpret concrete facts, events, and circumstances in ways that made them acceptable to themselves. Whereas others might categorize them as successful or unsuccessful agers, they could still see that their personal integrity was intact. Britton and Britton (1972) added that "a desirable goal for our society . . . (should be) to increase the range of acceptable behaviors" (p. 169).

Other investigators have shown the varieties of patterns of aging that may be more or less successful. Reichard, Livson, and Petersen (1962) delineated several patterns in men, which they labeled as "mature," "rocking chair," and "armored" types; less successful were "angry" men and the "self-haters." The research of Williams and Wirths (1965) and of Maas and Kuypers (1974) also demonstrates the varieties of success patterns. The reader should also refer to the reviews of Chown (1977) on "morale, careers, and personal potentials" and of Neugarten (1977) on "personality and aging."

Physical-Social Environment.   Aging is influenced by the degree of match between the individual's capabilities and the demands of the physical-social environment. The person's living situation and the "fit" between that situation and the capacities he or she has to fulfill individual needs affects the satisfaction derived in the process.

Lawton and Nahemow (1973) describe a model, building on an "environmental docility" hypothesis suggested by Lawton and Simon (1968), as a way to view differential changes in vulnerability to the environment. This model conceived outcomes in terms of adaptational level and positive versus negative affect. The writers assumed that the most adaptive outcome and most positive affect will occur when the "demand quality" of the environment is within the range of the individual's "competence"—particularly where demand quality approaches the maximum capacity of the individual.

Thus, this conception suggested evaluation of the impact of specific environments upon specific elderly according to their capacity to meet their needs and derive satisfaction from their surroundings. It predicts that as environmental demands exceed a given level, no level of personal competence can allow a positive outcome. Likewise, at certain levels of demand, or press, the environment will be stimulating, and at press levels much below competence level, the outcome will be negative, the person then becoming "bored" and "unchallenged." The important consideration is the fit between the needs and abilities of the person and the degree of support and challenge offered by the environment (Lawton, 1977).

Whereas Lawton and his colleagues have applied this model most often to the physical environment, considering issues of housing design, the conception is also useful in assessing the capacity of the individual's social system, for instance, the capability of members of the individual's household or of neighbors or friends to complement or compensate for various levels or types of individual competence. Thus, if an individual could not negotiate the distance to the grocery, one's spouse or housemate might compensate for that deficiency. This compensatory principle is similar to the "social reconstruction syndrome" of Kuypers and Bengtson (1973; Bengtson, 1973), in which various interventions could be planned as means of increasing competence.

In a different context, hypotheses about the critical status of certain periods in individual's lives and about how environmental effects may change have been advanced by Britton and Britton (1972, pp. 167–168). Their propositions pertained to possible effects of environmental conditions during an individual's decline, when circumstances are ambiguous, when competency is in question, and when expectations of self and others are most unclear.

Other discussions of the transactions of persons with living environments have been provided by Howell (1980), Kahana (1975), Parr (1980), and by Windley and Scheidt (1980). The last review defines eleven environmental attributes, such as sensory stimulation, accessibility, and meaning, which may be useful as qualitative indicators in appraising the harmony between an individual's environment and his or her own competence. In her discussion of housing and living environments of older people, Carp (1976) underscored the need "to understand the complex interplay of physical and social environment with the characteristics of the resident" (p. 245) and emphasized the desirability of involving planners, designers, administrators, users, and researchers in utilizing knowledge to create optimum living environments for the elderly.

Now we will turn to some of the implications of these principles for the broad area of education.

Educational Implications. Here education is to be considered in its broadest sense, encompassing all of learning and teaching, in formally and informally organized settings, in and out of schools, as organized by consumers or as carried out on a one-to-one basis. Education is seen as a lifelong process, a point emphasized by Gross (1977) and by the title of a White House "mini conference" held in 1980 (see *Lifelong Learning for Self-Sufficiency*, 1980). It is intended to assist people of all ages to adapt to and manage the constant change within themselves as well as change in the larger culture. Thus, education must address the needs of all people.

One impressive feature of our times is the fact that we live in a society requiring that we learn constantly. Within recent decades and at an increasing rate, new learning has become an essential condition for participating in the world around us as well as for personal development. Change is transforming all aspects of living for people of all ages (White House Conference on Aging, 1973). In effect, education must be thought of as being as continuous as change itself; it has become a necessity for all persons regardless of age.

The following statements are some aims suggested by the principles we have outlined, in keeping with our broad definition of education: (1) educational opportunities should be available for persons throughout the total life cycle, not just "school-aged" young people; (2) education should provide opportunities for intergenerational communication and development of understanding of individual and intergenerational similarities and differences; (3) education should assist adults throughout their life careers in modifying their performance in family, occupation, community, and personal roles, consistent with their abilities, interests, and motivations; (4) education should be available to help members of the families of older persons as well as other care givers; (5) educational practitioners should assist adults in learning according to sound knowledge of adult learners and of the processes of learning and teaching; (6) education should be available for the general public about the processes of aging and about the aged; (7) education should be provided to prepare and to update service personnel at all levels to enable them to provide the best possible care for the elderly who need it; (8) educational institutions should assume responsibility for developing society's capacity and leadership in building knowledge through research and in disseminating and utilizing knowledge about all aspects of aging.

These goal statements raise many questions concerning philosophy and practice of education as well as regarding programs for the aging. Some of the resources for dealing with the issues are already in place. Some will need to be developed. We believe policies and operations for such education can and must be formulated to accommodate the needs of an aging population.

Joseph H. Britton
Jean O. Britton

See also Adult Development; Adult Education; Life-Span Development.

REFERENCES

Allen, C. M. Defining the family for post-industrial public policy. In D. P. Snyder (Ed.), *The Family in Post-industrial America: Some Fundamental Perceptions for Public Policy Development.* Boulder, Colo.: Westview Press, 1979.

Atchley, R. C. *The Sociology of Retirement.* Cambridge, Mass.: Shenkman, 1976.

Atchley, R. C., & Miller, S. J. Older people and their families. In C. Eisdorfer (Ed.), *Annual Review of Gerontology and Geriatrics* (Vol. 1). New York: Springer, 1980.

Baltes, P. B., & Willis, S. L. Toward psychological theories of aging and development. In J. E. Birren & K. W. Schaie (Eds.),

Handbook of the Psychology of Aging. New York: Van Nostrand Reinhold, 1977.

Baltes, P. B., & Willis, S. L. Life-span developmental psychology, cognitive functioning, and social policy. In M. W. Riley (Ed.), *Aging from Birth to Death: Interdisciplinary Perspectives.* Boulder, Colo.: Westview Press, 1979.

Barberis, M. America's elderly: Policy implications. *Population Bulletin* (Policy Supplement), 1981, *35*(4). Washington, D.C.: Population Reference Bureau.

Beattie, N. M. Aging and the social services. In R. H. Binstock & E. Shanas (Eds.), *Handbook of Aging and the Social Sciences.* New York: Van Nostrand Reinhold, 1976.

Bengtson, V. L. *The Social Psychology of Aging.* Indianapolis: Bobbs-Merrill, 1973.

Bengtson, V. L., & Cutler, N. E. Generations and intergenerational relations: Perspectives on age groups and social change. In R. H. Binstock & E. Shanas (Eds.), *Handbook of Aging and the Social Sciences.* New York: Van Nostrand Reinhold, 1976.

Binstock, R. H., & Shanas, E. (Eds.). *Handbook of Aging and the Social Sciences.* Van Nostrand Reinhold, 1976.

Birren, J. E.; Butler, R. N.; Greenhouse, S. W.; Sokoloff, L.; & Yarrow, M. R. *Human Aging: A Biological and Behavioral Study.* Washington, D.C.: U.S. Government Printing Office, 1963.

Birren, J. E., & Renner, V. J. Research on the psychology of aging: Principles and experimentation. In J. E. Birren & K. W. Schaie (Eds.), *Handbook of the Psychology of Aging.* New York: Van Nostrand Reinhold, 1977.

Birren, J. E., & Schaie, K. W. (Eds.). *Handbook of the Psychology of Aging.* New York: Van Nostrand Reinhold, 1977.

Brim, O. G., Jr., & Kagan, J. (Eds.). *Constancy and Change in Human Development.* Cambridge, Mass.: Harvard University Press, 1980.

Britton, J. H., & Britton, J. O. *Personality Changes in Aging: A Longitudinal Study of Community Residents.* New York: Springer, 1972.

Carp, F. M. Housing and living environments of older people. In R. H. Binstock & E. Shanas (Eds.), *Handbook of Aging and the Social Sciences.* New York: Van Nostrand Reinhold, 1976.

Carp, F. M. (Ed.). *The Retirement Process.* Bethesda, Md.: National Institutes of Health, 1966. (ERIC Document Reproduction Service No. ED 058 545)

Chown, S. M. Morale, careers, and personal potentials. In J. E. Birren & K. W. Schaie (Eds.), *Handbook of the Psychology of Aging.* New York: Van Nostrand Reinhold, 1977.

Cowgill, D. O. Aging and modernization: A revision of the theory. In J. F. Gubrium (Ed.), *Late Life: Communities and Environmental Policy.* Springfield, Ill.: Thomas, 1974.

Cumming, E., & Henry, W. E. *Growing Old: The Process of Disengagement.* New York: Basic Books, 1961.

Eisdorfer, C. *Annual Review of Gerontology and Geriatrics* (Vol. 1). New York: Springer, 1980.

Eisdorfer, C., & Lawton, M. P. (Eds.). *The Psychology of Adult Development and Aging.* Washington, D.C.: American Psychological Association, 1973.

Elder, G. H., Jr. *Children of the Great Depression: Social Change in Life Experience.* Chicago: University of Chicago Press, 1974.

Estes, C. L. *The Aging Enterprise: A Critical Examination of Social Policies and Services for the Aged.* San Francisco: Jossey-Bass, 1979.

Finch, C. E., & Hayflick, L. (Eds.). *Handbook of the Biology of Aging.* New York: Van Nostrand Reinhold, 1977.

Goody, J. Aging in nonindustrial societies. In E. Shanas & R. Binstock (Eds.), *Handbook of Aging and the Social Sciences.* New York: Van Nostrand Reinhold, 1976.

Granick, S. Psychological test functioning. In S. Granick & R. D. Patterson (Eds.), *Human Aging II: An Eleven-year Follow-up Biomedical and Behavioral Study.* Washington, D.C.: U.S. Government Printing Office, 1971.

Granick, S., & Patterson, R. D. (Eds.), *Human Aging II: An Eleven-year Follow-up Biomedical and Behavioral Study.* Washington, D.C.: U.S. Government Printing Office, 1971.

Gross, R. *The Lifelong Learner.* New York: Simon & Schuster, 1977.

Havighurst, R. J. Adulthood and old age. In R. L. Ebel (Ed.), *Encyclopedia of Educational Research* (4th ed.). New York: Macmillan, 1969.

Havighurst, R. J. Social roles, work, leisure, and education. In C. Eisdorfer & M. P. Lawton (Eds.), *The Psychology of Adult Development and Aging.* Washington, D.C.: American Psychological Association, 1973.

Havighurst, R. J.; Munnichs, J. M. A.; Neugarten, B.; & Thomae, H. (Eds.), *Adjustment to Retirement: A Cross-national Study.* Assen, Netherlands: Van Gorcum, 1969.

Hendricks, J., & Hendricks, C. D. *Aging in Mass Society: Myths and Realities* (2nd ed.). Cambridge, Mass.: Winthrop, 1981.

Howell, S. C. Environments and aging. In C. Eisdorfer (Ed.), *Annual Review of Gerontology and Geriatrics* (Vol. 1). New York: Springer-Verlag, 1980.

Johnson, H. R.; Britton, J. H.; Lang, C. A.; Seltzer, M. M.; Stanford, E. P.; Yancik, R.; Maklan, C.; & Middlesworth, A. B. Foundations for gerontological education. *Gerontologist,* 1980, *20* (Part 2).

Kahana, E. A congruence model of person-environment interaction. In P. G. Windley & G. Ernst (Eds.), *Theory Development in Environment and Aging.* Washington, D.C.: Gerontological Society, 1975.

Kahn, R. L. Aging and social support. In M. W. Riley (Ed.), *Aging from Birth to Death: Interdisciplinary Perspectives.* Boulder, Colo.: Westview Press, 1979.

Knox, A. B. *Adult Development and Learning.* San Francisco: Jossey-Bass, 1977.

Kuypers, J. A., & Bengtson, V. L. Competence and social breakdown: A social-psychological view of aging. *Human Development,* 1973, *16,* 37–49.

Lawton, M. P. The impact of the environment on aging and behavior. In J. E. Birren & K. W. Schaie (Eds.), *Handbook of the Psychology of Aging.* New York: Van Nostrand Reinhold, 1977.

Lawton, M. P., & Nahemow, L. Ecology and the aging process. In C. Eisdorfer & M. P. Lawton (Eds.), *The Psychology of Adult Development and Aging.* Washington, D.C.: American Psychological Association, 1973.

Lawton, M. P., & Simon, B. B. The ecology of social relationships in housing for the elderly. *Gerontologist,* 1968, *8,* 108–115.

Lemon, B. W.; Bengtson, V. L.; & Peterson, J. A. An exploration of the activity theory of aging: Activity types and life satisfaction among in-movers to a retirement community: *Journal of Gerontology,* 1972, *27,* 511–523.

Lifelong Learning for Self-sufficiency: Report of a Miniconference Endorsed by the 1981 White House Conference on Aging, November 12–14, 1980. Washington, D.C.: Institute of Lifetime Learning, 1980.

Long Term Care Committee. *The Need for Long Term Care—Information and Issues: A Chartbook of the Federal Council on Aging.* Washington, D.C.: U.S. Government Printing Office, 1981.

Maas, H. S., & Kuypers, J. A. *From Thirty to Seventy.* San Francisco: Jossey-Bass, 1974.

Neubeck, G. Getting older in my family: A personal reflection. *Family Coordinator,* 1978, *27,* 445–447.

Neugarten, B. L. Personality change in late life: A developmental perspective. In C. Eisdorfer & M. P. Lawton (Eds.), *The Psychology of Adult Development and Aging.* Washington, D.C.: American Psychological Association, 1973.

Neugarten, B. L. Personality and aging. In J. E. Birren & K. W. Schaie (Eds.), *Handbook of the Psychology of Aging.* New York: Van Nostrand Reinhold, 1977.

Older Americans Act of 1965, As Amended: History and Related Acts (OHDS: 79-20170). Washington, D.C.: Department of Health, Education, and Welfare, Administration of Aging, July 1979.

Palmore, E. *The Honorable Elders: A Cross-cultural Analysis of Aging in Japan.* Durham, N.C.: Duke University Press, 1975.

Parr, J. The interaction of persons and living environments. In L. W. Poon (Ed.), *Aging in the 1980s: Psychological Issues.* Washington, D.C.: American Psychological Association, 1980.

Peterson, D. A., & Bolton, C. R. *Gerontology Instruction in Higher Education.* New York: Springer, 1980.

Poon, L. W. (Ed.). *Aging in the 1980s: Psychological Issues.* Washington, D.C.: American Psychological Association, 1980.

Pressey, S. L. Adulthood and old age. In C. W. Harris (Ed.), *Encyclopedia of Educational Research* (3rd ed.). New York: Macmillan, 1960.

Reese, H. W., & Overton, W. F. Models of development and theories of development. In L. R. Goulet & P. B. Baltes (Eds.), *Life-span Developmental Psychology: Research and Theory.* New York: Academic Press, 1970.

Reichard, S.; Livson, F.; & Petersen, P. G. *Aging and Personality: A Study of Eighty-seven Older Men.* New York: Wiley, 1962.

Riley, M. W. Age strata in social systems. In R. H. Binstock & E. Shanas (Eds.), *Handbook of Aging and the Social Sciences.* New York: Van Nostrand Reinhold, 1976.

Riley, M. W. (Ed.). *Aging from Birth to Death: Interdisciplinary Perspectives.* Boulder, Colo.: Westview Press, 1979.

Rosow, I. *Socialization to Old Age.* Berkeley, Calif.: University of California Press, 1974.

Shanas, E. *The Health of Older People: A Social Survey.* Cambridge, Mass.: Harvard University Press, 1962.

Shanas, E. The family as a social support system in old age. *Gerontologist,* 1979, *19,* 169–174.

Shanas, E.; Townsend, P.; Wedderburn, D.; Friis, H.; Milhøj, P.; & Stenhouwer, J. *Old People in Three Industrial Societies.* New York: Atherton Press, 1968.

Soldo, B. J. America's elderly in the 1980s. *Population Bulletin,* 1980, *25*(4). Washington, D.C.: Population Reference Bureau.

Sprouse, B. M. (Ed.). *National Directory of Educational Programs in Gerontology* (1st ed., prepared by the Association for Gerontology in Higher Education). Washington, D.C.: U.S. Government Printing Office, 1976.

Stack, C. B. Extended familial networks: An emerging model for the twenty-first–century family. In D. P. Snyder (Ed.), *The Family in Post-industrial America: Some Fundamental Perceptions for Public Policy Development.* Boulder, Colo.: Westview Press, 1979.

Strehler, B. L. *Time, Cells, and Aging* (2nd ed.). New York: Academic Press, 1977.

Streib, G. F. Facts and forecasts about the family and old age. In G. F. Streib (Ed.), *The Changing Family: Adaptation and Diversity.* Reading, Mass.: Addison-Wesley, 1973.

Streib, G. F., & Beck, R. W. Older families: A decade review. *Journal of Marriage and the Family,* 1980, *42,* 937–956.

Streib, G. F., & Shanas, E. Social structure and the family: Generational relations—An introduction. In E. Shanas & G. F. Streib (Eds.), *Social Structure and the Family: Generational Relations.* Englewood Cliffs, N.J.: Prentice-Hall, 1965.

Sullivan, E. N. (Ed.). *National Directory of Educational Programs in Gerontology* (3rd ed.). Washington, D.C.: Association for Gerontology in Higher Education, 1981.

Sussman, M. B. Relationships of adult children with their parents. In E. Shanas & G. F. Streib (Eds.), *Social Structure and the Family: Generational Relations.* Englewood Cliffs, N.J.: Prentice-Hall, 1965.

Sussman, M. B. The family life of old people. In R. H. Binstock & E. Shanas (Eds.), *Handbook of Aging and the Social Sciences.* New York: Van Nostrand Reinhold, 1976.

Tobin, S. S., & Kulys, R. The family and services. In C. Eisdorfer (Ed.), *Annual Review of Gerontology and Geriatrics: 1980* (Vol. 1). New York: Springer-Verlag, 1980.

Troll, L. E. The family of later life: A decade review. *Journal of Marriage and the Family,* 1971, *33,* 263–290.

Uzoka, A. F. The myth of the nuclear family: Historical background and clinical implications. *American Psychologist,* 1979, *34,* 1095–1106.

Weaver, W. Administration's view on aged arouses criticism at conference. *New York Times,* June 23, 1981, p. A16.

White House Conference on Aging. *Toward a National Policy on Aging: Proceedings of the 1971 White House Conference on Aging* (Vol. 2). Washington, D.C.: U.S. Government Printing Office, 1973. (ERIC Document Reproduction Service No. ED 072 346)

Williams, R. H., & Wirths, C. G. *Lives through the Years: Styles of Life and Successful Aging.* New York: Atherton Press, 1965.

Windley, P. G., & Scheidt, R. J. Person-environment dialectics: Implications for competent functioning in old age. In L. W. Poon (Ed.), *Aging in the 1980s: Psychological Issues.* Washington, D.C.: American Psychological Association, 1980.

AGRICULTURAL EDUCATION

Agricultural education in the public schools has involved instruction in classrooms, laboratories, the homes and home farms of students, and the work place. The unique aspects of agricultural education have included, but have not been limited to, supervised occupational-experience programs, the intracurricular Future Farmers of America (FFA) organization, the teacher as a community agricultural leader, problem solving as an approach to teaching and learning, and continuing education for adults.

Warmbrod (1980) reviewed the changes that occurred in federally funded and state funded vocational agriculture programs from the 1970/71 year to the 1977/78 year and reported the following significant findings.

• Total enrollment in vocational agriculture increased 19 percent, from 845,100 to 1,006,500 persons enrolled.

- Enrollment in secondary school vocational agriculture programs increased 27 percent, from 562,100 to 715,300. In 1970/71, 3 percent of all students were enrolled in vocational agriculture; in 1977/78, 3.8 percent of all public school secondary students were enrolled in vocational agriculture.
- Enrollment in postsecondary agricultural education programs increased 102 percent, from 28,400 to 57,500.
- Enrollment in adult vocational agriculture programs decreased 8 percent, from 254,500 to 233,700.
- The percentage of the total enrollment in vocational agriculture that is female increased by 398 percent. In 1970/71, 4 percent of the total enrollment was female; in 1977/78, 17 percent of the total enrollment was female.
- Enrollment in secondary school production agriculture programs remained stable, with 339,500 students in 1970/71 and 341,400 students in 1977/78. Enrollment in nonfarm specialties increased by 68 percent, from 222,600 to 373,900 students. In 1970/71, 40 percent of all secondary school vocational agriculture students were enrolled in nonfarm programs; in 1977/78, 52 percent were enrolled in nonfarm programs.

The volume of research activity in agricultural education during the period since the last edition of this encyclopedia has precluded an exhaustive review. Mannebach (1980) identified 344 completed research studies in the three-year period between 1974 and 1977. In the year 1977/1978, Mannebach (1978) identified an additional 140 studies. Cheek (1979) discovered 165 studies that were completed in the 1978/1979 year. The research committee of the Agricultural Education Division of the American Vocational Association has each year assumed responsibility for publishing a compilation of completed research (e.g., Mannebach, 1977; McCracken 1975; McCracken, 1976). The compilation has annually been distributed to each university department offering instruction in agriculture education. The research in agriculture education has also been reviewed and synthesized periodically since 1966. Warmbrod and Phipps (1966) wrote the first major comprehensive review and synthesis. Their work was updated in 1970 by Carpenter and Rodgers (1970) and more recently by Newcomb (1978). Readers who desire a more comprehensive and historical treatment of research in agriculture education should examine these reviews as well as previous editions of the *Encyclopedia of Educational Research* (e.g., Swanson & Persons, 1969).

Emphasis in this treatise has been placed on studies that illustrate research issues and areas that have been of concern to the profession.

Philosophy and Objectives. The philosophy and objectives that guided research and program development in agricultural education underwent significant revision in the early part of the 1960s. Before this time, emphasis had been on preparing students for the work of the farm or farm home. During the early 1960s the profession ac-

cepted responsibility for preparing students to explore and enter occupations relating to agricultural production; agricultural business, supply, and service; agricultural mechanics; horiculture; agricultural products processing; agricultural resource conservation; forestry; and in some states, even other areas related to the plant and animal sciences. In the late 1960s the profession adapted to the career education movement; providing programs for career awareness, career orientation and exploration, and career preparation. Agriculture education was offered in some states at the seventh-grade and eighth-grade levels with the stated purpose of providing career orientation and exploration. Programs were also expanded at the thirteenth and fourteenth grade levels, in postsecondary institutions, for students to prepare for middle management and technical-level occupations. Adult education in agriculture has remained an important component of the program.

Much debate has occurred concerning the extent to which agriculture education should be job-specific. Warmbrod and Phipps (1966) reported that before 1917, agriculture in the public schools was primarily an informational or general education subject. However, by 1950, because of federal financial assistance for vocational education, there had been a gradual reduction of courses that were not vocational in purpose (pp. 1, 2).

Carpenter and Rodgers (1970) suggested that "job-specific vs. broader-based occupational education geared to individual needs and interests of students is the most critical issue concerning vocational education in recent times. Much has been written by agricultural educators about the need for providing students with a basis for upward mobility beyond their entry occupations in agriculture" (p. 3).

Edin (1979) asked 155 teachers in nineteen Minnesota secondary vocational centers to rate the relative importance of three goals—occupational exploration, preparation for advanced training, and placement in job—in their teaching. Exploration was the goal rated highest by the teachers. When the students taught by these teachers were asked what was the most important reason for attending the secondary vocational center, about half said preparation for a job or for further education. Although employment and further education (Copa, 1980) are important areas to examine when assessing the outcomes of secondary vocational agriculture education, they are by no means the only reasons teachers and students come together in these programs (p. 4).

Espenschied (1961) found that parents did not value vocational preparation highest among the outcomes of vocational agriculture, but rather changes in their child's work habits, interests, attitudes, and character attributes that contribute to success in any occupation.

More recently there has been a tendency (Carpenter & Rogers, 1970) to offer basic courses in principles of plant and animal sciences in the ninth and tenth grades, with more specialized offerings such as horticulture and agricultural mechanics in later years (p. 3). As persons become more concerned about training-related placement, more emphasis is being placed on job-specific educational programs.

Cross (1981) reflected this trend in agricultural education when he restated the sixteen theorems of Charles A. Prosser as the basis for vocational education in agriculture. He stressed vocational education as training for a specific job in a specific work environment and prophesied that agricultural education as a profession would be successful to the extent that it subscribed to the sixteen theorems.

There remains considerable debate concerning the extent to which vocational agriculture should be job-specific. Few question a high degree of specialization in postsecondary agriculture education. Also, most would agree that any agriculture offered at the eighth grade or below should be exploratory in nature. The controversy continues, however, concerning the nature of offering in grades 9 through 12. The answer may be that for some students agriculture education will be viewed as preparation for a range of career options. For others, such education may be for a specific occupational objective. The programs will continue to be expected to serve both types of students.

Research Issues. The research committee of the Agricultural Education Division of the American Vocational Association appointed a subcommittee in 1975 to ascertain the professional concerns that might provide a basis for establishing research priorities. The identified concerns (Richardson, Shinn, & Stewart, 1977, p. 25), in priority order, were curriculum development, funding, teacher evaluation, teacher shortage, evaluation, teacher certification, supervision and administration, adult education, manpower needs, the FFA, research, postsecondary program, and urban program development.

Mannebach (1980) evaluated the extent to which studies reported between 1974 and 1977 related to the identified areas of concern. Fifty-two percent of the studies were related to the first five areas of concern. Eighty-seven of the 344 studies (25 percent) related to curriculum development, the number-one area of concern.

Peripheral but important findings in the Mannebach (1980) study were data that revealed that the reported agriculture education research was being conducted in only thirty-five of the fifty states and that researchers in a few states conducted and reported most of the research of the profession. Ohio, Oklahoma, Pennsylvania, Iowa, and Virginia accounted for 57 percent of the reported studies. West Virginia, Minnesota, New York, and Indiana, along with the previously mentioned states, accounted for 75 percent of the research reported during that three-year period (p. 20).

Mannebach (1980) also discovered that 78 percent of the reported research had been conducted by graduate students, with the remaining 22 percent conducted as staff studies (p. 22). A possible explanation for this situation

might be that there has been little funding for continuing or programmatic research in agriculture education.

Brown (1980) stated that "too much of our research effort is motivated by research dollars in ancillary areas instead of by identified problems in agricultural education" (p. 2). He proposed research led by senior members of the profession, that would programmatically focus on major problems of the profession and would be conducted on a regional or national basis over a significant period of time.

Programmatic research efforts have been conducted in institutions that have continuing support. The most notable source of continuing support has been the agricultural experiment stations with Hatch Act funds. State departments of education have also supported research with federal vocational education funds. However, in many states, researchers have been expected to conduct research on the priority areas of concern of vocational education in general, which may have had little specific applicability to agriculture education.

Curriculum Development. In recent years, more research has been conducted on curriculum development than on any other area of professional concern (Mannebach, 1980). The research has resulted in progress toward implementation of competency-based core curriculum concept in many states (Amberson, 1980; Bishop, 1980; Christiansen, 1980; Hemp, 1980; Lee, 1980a; Marvin, 1980; McCormick, 1980). The development of competency-based core curricula has been seen as a logical extension of the competency studies completed during the late 1960s and 1970s. Numerous studies were concucted to identify specific competencies needed by workers in various agricultural enterprises.

Competency studies. The most comprehensive project was completed by McClay (1978). He coordinated research to identify and evaluate competencies in 196 production agriculture and agribusiness occupations. Sixty-two researchers representing forty universities in thirty-five states assisted with portions of the study. McCracken and Yoder (1975) conducted occupational surveys in twenty-eight occupations in an attempt to develop a common core of basic skills for agriculture and natural resources. They concluded that the diversity of agricultural enterprises resulted in common skills that lacked meaning for many specific occupations. A common core was found to be more feasible for each of the instructional program areas within vocational agriculture (e.g., horticulture, agricultural mechanics) than across all instructional program areas. Richardson and Brown (1978) investigated a possible common core curriculum for grades 9 and 10 to prepare students to enter specialized programs at higher grade levels. The procedure involved a project advisory committee, which recommended the content.

Burnett (1980) conducted a study to compare alternative methods of ascertaining task inventory information. The Position Analysis Questionnaire was found to identify generic competencies that had more applicability across occupations. This procedure also thoroughly identified tasks relating to human relations, communications, and personal skills. The task inventory procedure, the one generally used in vocational education competency identification research, specifically identified tasks unique to each occupation. Twelve occupational surveys relating to the feed, seed, grain, and fertilizer industries were reported.

Thomas (1979) surveyed teachers in selected western states to determine if their rating of competencies agreed with a national sample of workers (McClay, 1978) on selected animal science skills. The teachers and the workers rated competencies differently. Teachers tended to rate competencies according to their ability to perform them. It was concluded that teachers should be prepared to teach competencies rated high by workers.

The implementation of the competency-based core curriculum concept was evaluated in a Nebraska study (Blezek & Dillon, 1980). Teacher materials provided by the project were used by a majority of the teacher respondents. The planned use, however, was nearly twice the actual use. Teachers felt a need to supplement the core with local information.

Concerns about the curriculum. While the profession has been making steady progress in implementing a competency-based core curriculum, words of caution have been expressed in philosophical dialogue. Marvin (1980) indicated the recommended first step in curriculum planning is to "survey the community," a step missing in a state-imposed core. He also verified the results of the study by McCracken and Yoder (1975) by concluding that a common core becomes difficult to identify across the instructional program areas in vocational agriculture. He questioned whether the developers of a core are more qualified than the local teacher in establishing what should be taught.

Lancelot (1944), one of the early leaders in problem-solving teaching, stated: "Knowledge, notwithstanding its great value to people generally, is not to be regarded as an end in education, but simply as a means to other ends which lie beyond. *It is those ends which are valuable,* rather than the knowledge, itself; and, unfortunately, pupils can, and often do, acquire knowledge without attaining the ends at all." (p. 21). Lancelot further defined the desired ends as interests; ideals and purposes; understandings; abilities, skills, and habits; and emotional responses and attitudes. He, realizing that the specific content would soon become dated, advocated teaching students a process by which they could continue to learn. Stewart (1950) was in agreement with Lancelot in advocating that what was to be learned was to be drawn from and built upon the experiences of the students. He also agreed with Lancelot in suggesting that the content of the curriculum was a vehicle by which manipulative ability, reasoning ability, judgment ability, and creative ability and the related un-

derstandings, interests, ideals, appreciations, and attitudes might be taught.

Hemp (1980) built a case for the core curriculum approach. He summarized the traditional approach of a teacher developing a local course of study based on community needs and then suggested a statewide core curriculum as a better approach. The reasons he gave were (1) the increased mobility of students; (2) lack of farm experience by students; (3) competency studies providing a basis for a core; (4) the need for exploration of a broad range of agricultural occupations, not just those available locally; (5) the possibility of delaying specialization for postsecondary instruction; (6) the minimum-competency movement in education; (7) articulation among educational levels; and (8) the help provided a teacher by having a specified curriculum.

Hampson, Newcomb, and McCracken (1977) identified competencies relating to leadership and personal development. It was suggested that these competencies be taught in agricultural education because of their importance, not only in the entry-level job but also for advancement in one's profession and relating to others throughout life. This area was found to be missing from most of the occupation-specific competency studies.

Research in the curriculum area has sufficiently identified competencies performed by agricultural workers. Research is needed to enable such information to be combined with other inputs to curriculum decision making in the design of relevant courses of study. The extent to which the course of study will be based on local needs as opposed to a statewide core will continue to be a subject of debate within the profession.

Program Components. Research relating to supervised occupational-experience programs, the FFA, and the summer program will now be discussed

Agricultural educators have been in general agreement that supervised occupational experience (SOE) programs are an integral component of the vocational agriculture curriculum. These programs have been theoretically and logically justified by the concept of learning by doing. The SOE of students may involve farming or off-farm agricultural experience. It may be an entrepreneurship project, a cooperative education employment experience, or in some cases, supervised laboratory experience.

Morton and McCracken (1979) investigated the relationship between scope and profitability of SOE and achievement of students in vocational agriculture. Positive relationships were found between achievement test scores and several other variables: quality as measured by scope and profitability; opportunity to engage in SOE; cumulative grade point average; and the number of instructor project visits. A positive relationship between quality and achievement remained when grade point average, years of vocational agriculture, and opportunity were statistically controlled.

McMillion and Auville (1976) found the variable most

associated with successful SOE was "teacher assists with fairs and shows." The teacher's having a part-time job was negatively associated with successful SOE.

Iowa State University has been the location of the most programmatic effort in SOE perception research. Benefits students derive from vocational agriculture as perceived by parents (Rawls and Williams, 1979) and students (Williams, 1979) were investigated. SOE was perceived as more beneficial to students in production agriculture than to students preparing for agribusiness. Rawls (1981) concluded that parents who were engaged in farming as an occupation felt that they provided their children with greater assistance in developing and conducting SOE than parents who were engaged in either agribusiness or nonagricultural occupations (p. 40). A factor analysis of benefits vocational agriculture students derive from SOE, as perceived by parents, revealed three clusters of benefits (Rawls, 1980): work attitude, occupational development, and human relations skills (p. 17).

There has been concern in the profession that SOE has received less emphasis in recent years. Miller (1980) reported in a North Carolina study that vocational agriculture teachers expected 58 percent of their students to have an SOE program. Less time in 1977 was devoted to SOE supervision than in 1972, with 42 percent of the teachers *not* making visits to students on a regular basis. Iverson (1980), in a survey of program graduates from ten southern states, found that 40 percent did not have an SOE project during each year they were enrolled (p. 20). These findings were alarming in view of the traditional expectation that *all* students would have an SOE and that teachers would supervise the SOE of their students by making regular periodic visits. Research findings show SOE to be of high educational value. There has been a trend toward less SOE by teachers. A reversal of the trend is needed to ensure the quality of this important program component.

Lee (1980b) stated: "If we expect to have good supervised occupational experience programs, we must provide teacher time and support for them. We must make use of many alternatives, such as school-based experiences and new strategies in placement. We must conduct significant research which documents the role of SOE in our program. We must have pilot and exemplary programs to experiment with new approaches in SOE. In short, considerable study is needed of the SOE area" (p. 8).

The FFA. The FFA has served as an intracurricular laboratory for students to participate in leadership and personal development activities (Hampson, Newcomb, & McCracken, 1977). Researchers and other leaders have questioned whether the organization has kept pace with the changes that have occurred in other aspects of the program.

Pfister (1978) conducted a study to determine the attitudes of first-year vocational agriculture teachers toward the FFA as an instructional technique, changing aspects of the FFA, and training received and needed for FFA

work. The aims and purposes of the FFA were less accepted by women and by those in the nontraditional areas of vocational agriculture. It was concluded that FFA possesses a rural image. Student participation in FFA was examined by Coffey (1978), Pettis (1977), and Slocombe (1979). Nonfarm students had less participation in project work but did participate in FFA activities in Oklahoma. In Virginia, FFA members, when compared with vocational agriculture students who were nonmenbers, were more likely to attend rural schools, be children of farmers, and respect farmers and farming. Welton (1971) suggested more appropriate activities for those who were planning agribusiness careers, improvement of the image students have of FFA, and changes in contests and awards. He found that in the Central and Southern Regions, nearly nine of ten vocational agriculture students were FFA members; however, in the Pacific Region, only five out of every ten were members. Blackledge (1972) found that instructors with a lower percentage of students who were FFA members taught more students, had a greater percentage of female students and nonfarm students, conducted a less traditional program, held higher academic degrees, had more years of experience, and spent less time on the FFA. Adviser attitude toward the FFA was found to be related to participation in FFA during student teaching and type of school where employed (Gilliam, 1979).

Research relating to the FFA has been descriptive in nature and nontheoretical in emphasis. If indeed the FFA is a laboratory for practice of essential competencies, the organization should become more instead of less intracurricular. Research is needed to ascertain the value added by the FFA in preparing students for employment.

Summer programs. Vocational agriculture has been a year-round instructional program. The nature of agricultural work has necessitated summer instruction. Because summer programs are not common throughout public education, researchers have conducted studies to obtain data for program justification and improvement. Cepica and Stockton (1980) reported certain commonalities prevalent among teachers who have outstanding twelve-month programs. These teachers were normally highly visible people, possessing good communication skills. They were operating programs that actively involved both in-school and adult students. Successful teachers were concerned with instructing in-school youth, the FFA, adult and young farmer education, facility improvement, program and instruction planning, community service and public relations, and professional development.

Preliminary data in a study of Florida teachers employed for either ten or twelve months (Arrington & McCracken, 1981) indicated that a strong relationship existed between length of teacher contract and the scope of student SOE programs. The summer program (Cepica & Irwin, 1979) was viewed as important by Texas teachers, administrators, teacher educators, and state staff. An Iowa study (Hilton, 1979) also found teachers and administrators rating the summer program as important but differing on the priority they placed on selected summer activities and allocation of teacher time to activities. Cepica (1979) conducted a study in Oklahoma in which he also found some disagreement between administrators and teachers in ranking selected summer program activities. Teachers tended to rank working with students higher, and administrators preferred that teacher time be devoted to public relations and "paperwork" types of activities. Holmes (1979) examined attitudes of principals and teachers in Florida and found general agreement on the importance of activities and teacher time perceived as desirable for various activities.

Additional research is needed to determine the value added by summer programs. Do summer programs make a difference in student learning, in SOE program development, and in the FFA as a laboratory for leadership and personal development? Are summer activities equally important for each of the instructional program areas (e.g., agricultural mechanics and horticulture)?

Postsecondary and Adult Education. Postsecondary education (grades 13 and 14) in agriculture experienced over a 100 percent enrollment growth during the 1970s. In contrast, enrollment in adult education in agriculture has declined slightly (Warmbrod, 1980, p. 6). Postsecondary educational institutions received attention in the vocational education legislation of the 1960s and 1970s and were undergoing development as a result. Adult education in agriculture had been a part of the production agriculture program since the Smith-Hughes Act of 1917. Little new emphasis, with a few notable exceptions, was being placed on adult education during the period covered by this entry.

Postsecondary education. Erpelding (1976, 1977) reported that there were 1,334 postsecondary agriculture programs in 1975 and 1,640 in 1977. By 1977 enrollment was reported as 92,656, with 1,903 full-time faculty employed. There were 1,171 part-time faculty in 1976 and 1,585 in 1977. About 450 institutions offered postsecondary education in agriculture at lower than baccalaureate level (Newcomb, 1978, p. 47).

The articulation between secondary and postsecondary programs of agricultural education was studied in Iowa (Byler & Williams, 1978) and in Minnesota (Arfstrom, 1977). In Iowa, articulation activities were reported in the categories of curriculum development, teaching, and communications. The process involved conducting a workshop to develop guidelines for articulation, completing research to identify articulation needs, and conducting a conference to plan articulation procedures. The Minnesota study utilized a testing procedure to determine the knowledge possessed by students at the time of entry into the postsecondary institution.

Several studies (Byler & Lindahl, 1977; Erpelding, 1972; Jensen, 1974; Lindahl, 1977; Schlicting, 1972) have reported the professional education competencies needed by postsecondary agriculture instructors and their in-service education needs. The recommendations resulting from the studies suggested formats and possible content for in-service teacher education.

A national postsecondary student organization has been inititated. No research on this recent development has yet been reported. The organization is separate from the FFA organization, having its own board of directors.

University researchers have given emphasis to secondary programs in choosing problems for study. Several fruitful areas for research exist in postsecondary agricultural education. Possible subjects include the role and value of occupational internships, the contributions of the postsecondary student organization, and the administration and funding of institutions.

Adult education. Warmbrod (1980) reported that adult enrollment in agricultural education declined during the 1970s. The expansion of adult education in the off-farm areas of agriculture has not kept pace with the decline in adult and young farmer enrollment. Also, the traditional expectation that secondary instructors also teach adults has become somewhat unrealistic in view of the other requirements of their job description. Purcell and Hemp (1975) studied adult programs in Illinois and found that the number of such courses declined from 485 in 1959/60 to 86 in 1972/73. Reasons given by teachers for the decline were low reimbursement from the state, inadequate pay for teachers, lack of teacher time, and the increase in adult education offerings in community colleges.

Miller (1979) maintains that "any school district that can justify a high school program of vocational agriculture . . . can undoubtedly justify a continuing education program " (p. 101). However, because fewer teachers have been willing to teach both secondary students and adults, full-time and part-time adult programs have been expanding whereas adult instruction as an extra duty has been declining.

Teacher Tenure. Research relating to the work of the vocational agriculture teacher has received considerable attention. Much of this research has been spurred by the continuing shortage of certified teachers. There has been an interest in factors relating to the attractiveness of teaching as a profession and to the variables of morale and satisfaction. Some have been concerned that the position of vocational agriculture teaching is too demanding and that the requirements ought to be more realistic.

In Indiana, Moore and Camp (1979) determined the extent of agreement between teachers and administrators about why vocational agriculture teachers left the profession. There was agreement that long hours, inadequate salary, and having different long-range occupational goals were contributing factors. Teachers rated high the item "Students in class who should not be in vocational agriculture." Administrators rated the item "Unable to get the students to learn as desired" higher than former teachers did.

Knight (1978) found in an Ohio study that the highest-ranked of forty-five factors relating to the decision to leave teaching were (in order) "long-range occupational goal was something different from teaching vocational agriculture," "had students in class who should not have been in vocational agriculture," "inadequate advancement opportunities," "long hours," and "inadequate salary."

The reasons why former teachers reentered teaching in thirteen southern states were studied by McMillion (1978). Forty-nine of ninety-six responded to a questionnaire in which they listed one or two reasons for returning. Teachers in other jobs lacked a sense of accomplishment and did not enjoy being gone from home because of job responsibilities. The economics of retirement benefits, business conditions, and loss of job were found to be important in decisions to return.

Dickens (1978) used questionnaires and telephone interviews to examine why Ohio teachers remained in the profession. Thirteen factors relating to security and retirement benefits, variety of work, feeling of accomplishment, enjoyment in teaching, independence, students, association with agriculturalists, and rural life were identified.

Olson (1979) studied North Dakota teachers and found that they derived satisfaction from serving others, observing student growth and development, working in agriculture, and being innovative and varying the work being done.

In Oklahoma, White (1979) found tangible factors to be less important than intangible factors to those who chose to remain in teaching.

Teachers who planned to leave teaching and those who planned to remain rated identical factors in a Kansas study (Reilly, 1979). The two groups significantly differed on the following factors: (1) "Helping students to mature and learn is satisfying to me as a teacher," (2) "I like living in the community of the size and type in which I live," (3) "Most students in my school respect teachers," and (4) "The achievements of my students in FFA competition more than compensate me for the extra hours I spend training them."

It was interesting to note that similar factors might appear as reasons teachers remain in the profession and as reasons they leave the profession. This would suggest that research is needed to make better predictions about the qualities that would enable people to find teaching satisfying. One must also consider whether some turnover might indeed be healthful for the profession.

Sex Equity.   Recent emphasis on sex equity in the nation and in vocational education appears to have resulted in some research being initiated in this area in agricultural education. Ries (1980) related the perception of sex bias among female high school and university students to the desire to teach vocational agriculture. She also related the perception of sex bias among female production agriculture teachers with their job satisfaction. A consistent negative relationship was found between perception of sex bias and the desire to teach vocational agriculture. Those who perceived more bias were less interested in teaching. A negative relationship was also found between perception of sex bias and job satisfaction of female production agricul-

ture teachers. Perception of bias among community personnel and parents was more negatively correlated with job satisfaction than perception of bias among school personnel and students. Moore (1979) found that 38 percent of the female vocational agriculture teachers contacted in a nationwide survey indicated that they had been discriminated against in their efforts to find a teaching job. The women applied for 2.4 jobs, received 2.0 interviews, and were offered 1.3 jobs. Males applied for 2.1 jobs, had 1.7 interviews, and were offered 1.6 jobs.

Klein (1979) studied the impact of admitting females to vocational agriculture in Idaho. Instructors supplied information indicating that females were more active in FFA and in communication skills. No negative influences were found. A Montana study (Shelhamer, 1979) also found females to be more active than males in FFA.

Kluckman (1979) examined the differences between male and female teachers in career choice, work satisfaction, and career plans. Participants were from California, Florida, Ohio, New York, and Virginia. Differences were found in the three variables. Males were generally more committed to an agricultural career than were females.

Equity research should continue in agricultural education. Such research should also examine other subpopulation groups, such as minorities and handicapped students.

Planning and Management.   Studies in planning and management include those relating to manpower needs, advisory committees, supervision, and standards. During the 1960s a multitude of local and state manpower studies were conducted to justify the need for agribusiness educational programs to prepare students for off-farm agriculture. Few studies have been conducted in the 1970s as programs have been established and have stayed in operation. Thuemmel (1975) assessed the agricultural manpower situation in Michigan and found educational programs to be inadequate to meet current and projected needs. He also found many students with agricultural interest not enrolled in agricultural education programs. An Arizona study (Zurbrick, 1979) identified 33,555 employed people in the state who required a knowledge of and skill in agriculture. This was an increase over previous studies.

Programs of vocational education in agriculture have been expected to have citizens' advisory committees to assist in developing a community-based program. Research, though sparse, has indicated that advisory committees have not been functioning as effectively as their advocates desired. Abd-Rahman (1980) concluded that 30 percent of the committees met less frequently than once a year. He also found that nearly one-half of the Ohio teachers did not report having an active committee. Similar findings were reported by McGhee and Becker (1979) in Florida. A large percentage of programs did not have an advisory committee. Teachers were of the opinion that committees were not essential.

Additional research and in-service education for teachers concerning the use of advisory committees are needed if the expectation of legislation and the profession is to be realized in this area of lay-citizen involvement.

Barrick (1978) suggested state supervisors' major responsibility was the improvement of local programs by assisting in determining needs, establishing goals, identifying ways and means, evaluating progress, and rewarding success. In a later study Barrick and Warmbrod (1981) studied the degree of authority and the degree of direct contact with vocational agriculture programs by state supervisors. Thirty states had supervisors who worked exclusively with vocational agriculture programs, and in twenty states supervisors had multiple program responsibility. Householder (1978) studied the perception in Ohio of the role of the local supervisor of vocational agriculture. He found a lack of consensus among the groups surveyed about the supervisor's actual and expected role. It was generally agreed, however, that the local supervisor should perform tasks primarily in curriculum, instruction, and personnel administration.

The National Standards Project conducted by Iowa State University (1977) validated a preliminary set of standards and developed a plan for dissemination and implementation. The standards that were developed were common to all programs, specific to the secondary level, specific to the postsecondary level, specific to administration and supervision, specific to teacher education, and specific to adult education. A number of states reviewed the standards and adopted a revised set for use in program management.

Evaluation. Followup studies have been the major focus of those who seek to evaluate the effectiveness of vocational agriculture programs. The theory has been that former students who do well in employment and life help to prove the efficacy of the instructional program. Warmbrod (1970) cautioned that evaluative studies that are intended to investigate relationships between outcomes and inputs do not necessarily result in conclusions denoting cause-effect relationships (p. 3).

A significant number of local and state follow-up studies have been reported. The most comprehensive recent study was reported by Iverson (1980). The research was conducted to "determine the role of vocational agriculture/agribusiness programs in the occupational success of graduates from the Southern Region" (p. 11). The current status of graduates, graduates' perceived value of various program components, and program completers' reactions to recent program changes were obtained. Graduates of the 1973/74 school year from every tenth-listed agriculture department in ten states were sampled. A 40.2 percent response rate yielded 1,252 usable responses. The external validity of the research, as is true with much survey research, is questionable, because one simply does not know how the 60 percent who did not respond differ from the 40 percent who did. Also, one does not know the extent to which success of graduates can be attributed to having enrolled in vocational agriculture. The remainder of the

school curriculum, parents, and many other factors influence the degree of one's success.

Copa (1980), though aware of the problems with follow-up studies, conducted an evaluation in Minnesota to study the question "Does vocational agriculture at the secondary school level make a difference?" (p. 1). The question was discussed by examining context issues, data issues, findings, and conclusions. The discussion of context issues emphasized that vocational agriculture has been a small part of an individual's total schooling, that students have sought vocational agriculture for different purposes, that students who have left high school choose a job rather than a career, that agricultural work has remained undefined, and that the home and other factors have assisted in preparing students for employment.

Who is a vocational agriculture student? Copa (1980) indicated that the amount of time devoted to vocational agriculture may be related to a student's objectives. Enrolling in a vocational agriculture class for one hour a day for one school year may serve an exploratory function. Additional hours and years were found to result in a greater likelihood of continuing in an agricultural career. Researchers should carefully define who is and is not a vocational agriculture student for follow-up purposes.

The sex differences in the Minnesota study provided information for further research on sex equity. Women were less likely to choose agricultural careers than men. Also, students of lower academic rank in the class were less likely to choose agricultural careers. Copa, by having the high schools collect the data, was able to obtain an 85 percent response rate.

Warmbrod (1974) stressed that occupational preparation is a goal of the entire high school program, not just of vocational education courses. Also, some students take vocational agriculture for the practical arts and avocational values of the skills and abilities they learn. Any specific part of the curriculum will show little impact on post–high school success. Also, general education skills, socioeconomic and personal characteristics of students, economic conditions and employment practices are factors that must be considered when studying occupational success.

J. David McCracken

See also Home Economics Education; Rural Education; Trade and Industrial Education; Vocational Education.

REFERENCES

Abd-Rahman, Z. *Functions of Agricultural Advisory Committees in Selected Ohio High Schools.* Unpublished master's thesis, Ohio State University, 1980.

Amberson, M. The competency-based core curriculum: Innovative and accountable. *Agricultural Education Magazine,* April 1980, *52*(10), 4–5.

Arfstrom, G. *Systematic Approach to Articulation in Agricultural Occupations Programs.* Unpublished master's thesis, University of Minnesota, 1977.

Arrington, L., & McCracken, J. D. *Relationship of Vocational Agriculture Teacher Summer Employment to Student Super-*

vised Occupational Experience and School FFA Program Activities. Unpublished manuscript, 1981. (Available from J. D. McCracken, Ohio State University, 2120 Fyffe Road, Columbus, Ohio 43210).

Barrick, K. Supervisors can help improve programs. *Agricultural Education Magazine,* October 1978, *51*(4), 75.

Barrick, K. R., Jr., & Warmbrod, J. R. *The Relationship between State-level Administrative Structure and the Role of State Supervisors of Vocational Agriculture.* Columbus: Ohio State University, Department of Agricultural Education, 1981. (ERIC Document Reproduction Service No. ED 195 712)

Bishop, D. From job to classroom and back again. *Agricultural Education Magazine,* April 1980, *52*(10), 12–14.

Blackledge, D. *A Study to Determine Selected Factors Which Influence the FFA Membership of Vocational Agriculture Students.* Unpublished master's thesis, Kansas State University, 1972.

Blezek, A. G., & Dillon, R. A summary of an evaluation of the first year of the Nebraska vocational agriculture core curriculum. *Journal of the American Association of Teacher Educators in Agriculture,* July 1980, *21*(2) 35–40.

Brown, R. A. *Improving Research in Agricultural Education.* Paper presented at the seventh annual National Agricultural Education Research Meeting, New Orleans, December 1980.

Burnett, M. F. *Tasks and Job Requirements of Skilled Technical and Managerial Agri-business Positions.* Unpublished doctoral dissertation, Ohio State University at Columbus, 1980.

Byler, B. L., & Lindahl, T. S. *Professional Education In-service Needs of Agriculture Instructors in Iowa Post-secondary Area Vocational Schools.* Ames: Iowa State University, Department of Agricultural Education, 1977.

Byler, B. L., & Williams, D. L. Promoting articulation between secondary and post-secondary vo-ag programs. *Agricultural Education Magazine,* May 1978, *50*(11), 245, 247, 255, 263.

Carpenter, E. T., & Rodgers, J. H. *Review and Synthesis of Research in Agricultural Education* (2nd ed.). Columbus: Ohio State University, National Center for Research in Vocational Education, June 1970. (ERIC Document Reproduction Service No. ED 040 275)

Cepica, M. J. A comparison of the summer programs of Oklahoma vocational agriculture teachers and administrator perceptions of selected aspects of the summer program. *Journal of the American Association of Teacher Educators in Agriculture,* March 1979, *20*(1), 18–25.

Cepica, M. J., & Irwin, J. F. *Development of Guidelines for Summer Vocational Agriculture Programs in Texas.* Lubbock: Texas Tech University, 1979.

Cepica, M. J., & Stockton, J. Observations of summer programs of vocational agriculture. *Agricultural Education Magazine,* June 1980, *52*(12), 4–5.

Cheek, J. G. *Summaries of Research and Development Activities in Agricultural Education, 1978–1979.* Gainesville: University of Florida, Department of Agricultural and Extension Education, December 1979.

Christiansen, J. E. What is a competency-based core curriculum in vocational agriculture? *Agricultural Education Magazine,* April 1980, *52*(10), 6–7, 14.

Coffey, D. M. *Factors Associated with Membership and Non-membership Status of Black Tenth Graders from Former NFA States.* Unpublished doctoral dissertation, Virginia Polytechnic Institute and State University, 1978.

Copa, G. H. *Assessing the Employment and Further Education Effects of Secondary Vocational Agriculture Programs.* Key-

note address presented at the Central States Research Conference on Agricultural Education, Kansas City, July 1980.

Cross, I. What are our roots? *Journal of the American Association of Teacher Educators in Agriculture,* March 1981, *22*(1), 2–8.

Dickens, J. W. *Why Vocational Agriculture Teachers Enter and Remain in the Teaching Profession.* Unpublished doctoral dissertation, Ohio State University at Columbus, 1978.

Edin, S. *Attitudes of Minnesota Secondary Vocational Center Training: Relationships Relevant to Student and Instructor Characteristics, Perceptions, Opinions, and Plans.* Unpublished doctoral dissertation, University of Minnesota, 1979.

Erpelding, L. H., Jr. *Professional Education Competency Needs of Teachers of Vocational-Technical Programs in Post-secondary Schools.* Unpublished doctoral dissertation, Kansas State University, 1972.

Erpelding, L. H., Jr. *Status of Post-secondary Education in Agriculture, Agribusiness, Natural Resources, and Environmental Occupations, 1976.* Columbus: Ohio State University, Department of Agricultural Education, 1976.

Erpelding, L. H., Jr. *Status of Post-secondary Education in Agriculture, Agribusiness, Natural Resources, and Environmental Occupations, 1977.* Columbus: Ohio State University, Department of Agricultural Education, 1977.

Espenschied, R. F. Major findings of a study of parental attitudes toward vocational agriculture (Doctoral dissertation, University of Illinois, 1961). *Dissertation Abstracts,* 1962, *22*(10), 3467.

Gilliam, C. M. *Attitudes of Virginia Vocational Agriculture Teachers toward the Future Farmers of America (FFA).* Unpublished doctoral dissertation, Virginia Polytechnic Institute and State University, 1979.

Hampson, M. N.; Newcomb, L. H.; & McCracken, J. D. *Essential Leadership and Personal Development Competencies Needed in Agricultural Occupations as Identified by Agriculture Leaders in Ohio.* Columbus: Ohio State University, Department of Agricultural Education, Columbus, 1977.

Hemp, P. E. Building a case for the core curriculum in agriculture. *Journal of the American Association of Teacher Educators in Agriculture,* November 1980, *21*(3), 2–4, 66.

Hilton, J. W. *Perceptions of Vocational Agriculture Instructors and Superintendents Concerning Vocational Agriculture Summer Programs in Iowa.* Unpublished doctoral dissertation, Iowa State University, 1979.

Holmes, T. L. *Perceptions of Principals and Vocational Agricultural Instructors toward Selected Summer Program Activities in Florida.* Unpublished master's thesis, Iowa State University, 1979.

Householder, L. D. Local supervision in ag education. *Agricultural Education Magazine,* October 1978, *51*(4) 82–83.

Iowa State University. *Standards for Quality Vocational Programs in Agricultural/Agribusiness Education.* Ames: Iowa State University, 1977.

Iverson, M. The role of vocational agriculture in the occupational success of graduates: A southern region study. *Journal of The American Association of Teacher Educators in Agriculture,* July 1980, *21*(2), 11–20, 47.

Jensen, R. *A Professional Function-Task-Competency Approach to Curriculum Development for Wisconsin Post-secondary Agricultural Instructors.* Unpublished doctoral dissertation, University of Wisconsin, 1974.

Klein, T. E. *A Study of the Impact of Admitting Female Students to the High School Vocational Agriculture and FFA Programs in Idaho.* Unpublished master's thesis, University of Idaho at Moscow, 1979.

Kluckman, D. M. *Traditional and Nontraditional Career Role Vocational Agriculture Teacher Perception of Career Choice, Work Satisfaction, and Career Plans.* Unpublished doctoral dissertation, Oregon State University at Corvallis, 1979.

Knight, J. A. Why vocational agriculture teachers in Ohio leave teaching. *Journal of the American Association of Teacher Educators in Agriculture*, November 1978, *19*(3) 11–17.

Lancelot, W. H. *Permanent Learning. A Study in Educational Techniques.* New York: Wiley, 1944.

Lee, J. S. Basic competency programs: Are there any dinosaurs? *Agricultural Education Magazine*, April 1980, *52*(10), 3–4. (a)

Lee, J. S. Time to take inventory in agricultural education. *Journal of the American Association of Teacher Educators in Agriculture*, March 1980, *21*(1), 2–12. (b)

Lindahl, T. J. *Employment Qualifications of Post-secondary Instructors of Agriculture in Iowa Area Schools.* Unpublished doctoral dissertation, Iowa State University, 1977.

Mannebach, A. J. (Ed.). *Summaries of Research and Development Activities in Agricultural Education, 1976–1977.* Storrs: University of Connecticut, Department of Higher, Technical, and Adult Education, 1977.

Mannebach, A. J. (Ed.). *Summaries of Research and Development Activities in Agricultural Education, 1977–1978.* Storrs: University of Connecticut, Department of Higher, Technical, and Adult Education, 1978.

Mannebach, A. J. An analysis of the impact of agricultural education research on identified professional concerns. *Journal of the American Association of Teacher Educators in Agriculture*, March 1980, *21*(1), 19–25.

Marvin, P. Pros and Cons: Should we adopt a statewide curriculum? *Agricultural Education Magazine*, April 1980, *52*(10), 11–12.

McClay, D. R. *Identifying and Validating Essential Competencies Needed for Entry and Advancement in Major Agriculture and Agribusiness Occupations* (Final report). Washington, D.C.: U.S. Department of Health, Education, and Welfare, May 1978.

McCormick, F. G. Implementing a competency-based curriculum. *Agricultural Education Magazine*, April 1980, *52*(10), 8–10.

McCracken, J. D. (Ed.). *Summaries of Research and Development Activities in Agricultural Education, 1974–1975.* Columbus: Ohio State University, Department of Agricultural Education, 1975.

McCracken, J. D. (Ed.). *Summaries of Research and Development Activities in Agricultural Education, 1975–1976.* Columbus: Ohio State University, Department of Agricultural Education, 1976.

McCracken, J. D., & Yoder, E. *Determination of a Common Core of Basic Skills for Agribusiness and Natural Resources.* Columbus: Ohio State University, Department of Agricultural Education, 1975.

McGhee, M. B., & Becker, W. J. *Advisory Committees for Agribusiness and Natural Resources Education in the State of Florida.* Gainesville: University of Florida, October 1979.

McMillion, M. B. *Why Agriculture Teachers Return to Teaching.* Blacksburg: Virginia Polytechnic Institute and State University, 1978.

McMillion, M., & Auville, M. *Factors Associated with the Success of Supervised Farming Programs of Virginia High School Students.* Blacksburg: Virginia Polytechnic Institute and State University, 1976.

Miller, L. E. Adult education: Growth for vocational agriculture in the eighties. *Agricultural Education Magazine*, November 1979, *52*(5), 101, 119.

Miller, T. R. The changing status of supervised occupational experience in vocational agriculture in North Carolina. *Journal of the American Association of Teacher Educators in Agriculture*, March 1980, *21*(1) 13–18.

Moore, G. E. *Perceptions of Vocational Agriculture Teachers Concerning Sex Discrimination in the Teaching of Agriculture.* West Lafayette, Ind.: Purdue University, 1979.

Moore, G. E., & Camp, W. G. Why vocational agriculture teachers leave the profession: A Comparison of perceptions. *Journal of the American Association of Teacher Educators in Agriculture*, November 1979, *20*(3) 11–18.

Morton, R. H., & McCracken, J. D. *Supervised Occupational-experience Programs and Achievement of Students in Vocational Agriculture.* Columbus: Ohio State University, Department of Agricultural Education, 1979.

Newcomb, R. H. *Agricultural Education: Review and Synthesis of the Research.* Columbus: Ohio State University, ERIC Clearinghouse on Adult, Career, and Vocational Education, 1978. (ERIC Document Reproduction Service No. ED 164 979)

Olson, J. M. *Reasons Why North Dakota Secondary Vocational Agriculture Instructors with Three or More Years of Teaching Experience Have Remained in Teaching.* Unpublished master's colloquium paper, North Dakota State University at Fargo, 1979.

Pettis, B. J. *A Comparison between Non-farm and Farm Students in Relation to Course Enrollment and Involvement in Selected Activities in the Future Farmers of America.* Unpublished master's thesis, Oklahoma State University at Stillwater, 1977.

Pfister, J. A. *Attitudes of First-year Vocational Agriculture Teachers toward Using FFA as an Instructional Technique.* Unpublished master's thesis, University of Maryland at College Park, 1978.

Purcell, A., & Hemp, P. *A Study of Adult Programs in Agriculture Conducted in Illinois High Schools, 1972–1973.* Urbana: University of Illinois, 1975.

Rawls, W. Parental perceptions of benefits vocational agriculture students derive from supervised occupational experience. *Journal of the American Association of Teacher Educators in Agriculture*, November 1980, *21*(3), 14–17.

Rawls, W. Relationship between parents' occupation and selected factors related to student supervised occupational experience. *Journal of the American Association of Teacher Educators in Agriculture*, March 1981, *22*(1), 35–40.

Rawls, W. J., & Williams, D. L. Parental perceptions of vocational agriculture supervised occupational-experience programs in Iowa. *Journal of Vocational Education Research*, Spring 1979, *4*(2), 31.

Reilly, P. W. *An Analysis of Factors Which Encourage Vocational Agriculture Teachers in Kansas to Remain in Teaching.* Unpublished master's thesis, Kansas State University at Manhattan, 1979.

Richardson, W. B., & Brown, C. E. *Common Content Core for Agribusiness Education Programs.* West Lafayette, Ind.: Purdue University, 1978.

Richardson, W. B.; Shinn, G. C.; & Stewart, B. R. Concerns of the agricultural education profession: Implications for teacher education. *Journal of the American Association of Teacher Educators in Agriculture*, November 1977, *18*(3), 19–26.

Ries, A. E. *Relationship of Perceived Sex Bias and the Decision of Women to Teach Production Agriculture.* Unpublished master's thesis, Ohio State University at Columbus, 1980.

Schlicting, H. *Identifying Professional and Technical Needs of Post-secondary Teachers of Agriculture.* Unpublished master's thesis, Montana State University, 1972.

Shelhamer, C. V. *Educational and Demographic Changes in Secondary Vocational Agriculture and Home Economics in Montana as a Result of Title IX.* Unpublished master's thesis, Montana State University at Bozeman, 1979.

Slocombe, J. W. *A Study to Determine the Relationship of Selected Factors on FFA Membership of Vocational Agriculture Students.* Unpublished master's thesis, Kansas State University at Manhattan, 1979.

Stewart, W. F. *Methods of Good Teaching.* Columbus, Ohio: Author, 1950.

Swanson, G., & Persons, E. Agricultural education. In R. L. Ebel (Ed.), *Encyclopedia of Educational Research* (4th ed.). New York: Macmillan, 1969.

Thomas, L. G. *Vocational Agriculture Teachers' Opinions Relative to Selected Animal Science Competencies.* Unpublished doctoral dissertation, Colorado State University, 1979.

Thuemmel, W. L. *Agribusiness and Natural Resources Education in Michigan: Manpower Needs, Competencies Needed, and School Program Characteristics.* East Lansing: Michigan State University, 1975.

Warmbrod, J. R. Evaluating outcomes: Some problems of interpretation. *Journal of the American Association of Teacher Educators in Agriculture,* September 1970, *11*(2), 1–10.

Warmbrod, J. R. *The Liberalization of Vocational Education.* Danville, Ill.: Interstate Printers & Publishers, 1974.

Warmbrod, J. R. Agricultural education in the 1980's. *Agricultural Education Magazine,* January 1980, *52*(7), 6–8.

Warmbrod, J. R., & Phipps, L. J. *Review and Synthesis of Research in Agricultural Education.* Columbus: Ohio State University, National Center for Research in Vocational Education, August 1966. (ERIC Document Reproduction Service No. ED 011 562)

Welton, R. *Relationship of Student Characteristics and Program Policies to Participation in FFA.* Unpublished doctoral dissertation, Ohio State University, 1971.

White, J. D. *Identification and Comparison of Factors Influencing Oklahoma Vocational Agriculture Instructors to Remain in the Profession.* Unpublished doctoral dissertation, Oklahoma State University at Stillwater, 1979.

Williams, D. L. Benefits received from supervised occupational-experience programs as perceived by students. *Journal of The American Association of Teacher Educators in Agriculture,* July 1979, *20*(2), 33–40.

Zurbrick, P. R. *Agricultural Employment in Selected Areas of Arizona* (Research Report 277). Tucson: University of Arizona, Agricultural Experiment Station, 1979.

ALTERNATIVE SCHOOLS

With good reason, the previous edition of the *Encyclopedia of Educational Research* (1969) contained no article on alternative schools. Knowledgeable observers pinpoint the beginnings of what has become a significant movement in American public education to any time from the early to late 1960s, although unlabeled antecedents of alternative schools existed as early as the 1930s (e.g., the Bronx High School of Science). Fantini (1973) did a good deal of the early writing on the topic and envisioned much of the potential gains that optional or alternative schools could bring to the public sector.

In the 1960s, alternative schools seemed to be springing up on every street corner; most were privately funded free schools to the left of center ideologically. The Parkway Program, in Philadelphia, which is generally identified as the first autonomous, public alternative school, opened its doors in 1969. It was followed shortly by Metro, in Chicago, and the St. Paul Open School in Minnesota. Duke (1978) and Smith, Barr, and Burke (1976) outline the history of the rapid development of alternative schools since that time. One reason for the rapid growth of alternative schools is that, unlike other reform strategies, they need not cost more than conventional schools (Theroux, 1974).

Definition and Criteria. Defining alternative schools and even counting them are not simple matters. In a study of alternative schools in Indiana, Smith and Coppedge (1974) reported that at least one small school system labeled its only school as an alternative. Numerous schools that violate widely accepted characteristics of alternative schools, such as free choice and distinctiveness of program, nevertheless answer to that name. Also, terms like "open," "informal," "free," and "alternative" are sometimes used to describe not only programs that students freely elect but also those to which they are arbitrarily assigned. Some research that applies to the latter settings has been included in this review when it seemed to augment similar research in free-choice settings. There is, however, a large body of literature on open education that was omitted here because of space limitations. Counting schools is also difficult because some schools are short-lived and new schools are continually opening. Numerous state legislatures, for example, have enacted various forms of enabling or mandatory legislation to stimulate the widespread formation of alternatives, resulting in the "overnight" sprouting of dozens of schools. These and other factors contribute to a movement in flux, one impossible to portray accurately with any degree of certainty.

The roles of state legislatures and state departments of education in encouraging the formation of alternative schools are an interesting but, sadly, undocumented area of the literature. No one, to the authors' knowledge, has attempted the huge task of summarizing this diffuse and relatively inaccessible body of information.

Smith, Barr, and Burke (1976) have identified three indispensable criteria of public alternative schools: (1) that students attend by choice; (2) that the school or program be responsive to unmet local needs; and (3) that the student body reflect the racial and socioeconomic mix of the community. Schools ideologically to the left and right of conventional school programs, such as open schools and back-to-basics schools respectively, can meet these criteria.

Other criteria have been proposed by Deal (1975), Ellis (1975), and Parrett (1979), but many of them seem more appropriate for schools on the left side of the ideological spectrum alone. Even the term "alternative school" is controversial to the extent that it connotes criticism of conventional schooling. As a result, many educators, attempting to emphasize the concept of free choice among equally valid conceptions of schooling, substitute the term "optional schools." In a project funded by the National Institute of Education, Raywid (1980) is developing scales of nine dimensions of schooling to identify ideal or pure types of optional or alternative schools.

Surveys by the National Alternative Schools Program (Wolf, Walker, & Macklin, 1974) and the National School Boards Association (1976) helped describe alternative schools in the public sector. Using the latter and other sources, Smith (1978) concluded that at least one-third of the nation's 1,600 school systems had one or more alternative schools in operation. He estimated that this figure increased to 80 percent when only the larger school districts (over twenty-five thousand students) were considered; and that over ten thousand public alternative schools were in operation in 1978, serving about 2 million young people, or 5 percent of the elementary and secondary school population.

Alternative schools are typically small in size with only a small percentage of schools exceeding two hundred students. In fact, smallness and the informality it fosters are generally considered prime virtues of these schools. The range of existing schools is extremely diverse. Many, perhaps most, of the first schools formed focused on middle-class, often college-bound students. The concept was quickly applied to various "dis" populations (e.g., the disaffected, the disadvantaged, the disruptive, the underachieving, the pregnant, and the dropout-prone). That segment of the spectrum has expanded rapidly. Developing estimates from several sources, Arnove and Strout (1980) concluded that one-third of all alternative schools were serving such students. Using nine categories, Barr (1975) identified continuation schools with individualized programs (20%), learning centers with specialized resources (18%), schools-within-schools that make frequent use of the community (17%), and open schools with integrated curricula (15%) as the most frequently encountered types of alternative schools. A more recent phenomenon is the rapid development of traditional, back-to-basics alternatives. Thus, a complete range of schools from free schools to military academies now exists in the public sector. The gamut includes schools for the fine and performing arts, maternity schools for pregnant students, behavior modification schools, street academies, and Montessori schools, to name only a few.

A variety of these schools may be found in major cities. Clusters of alternatives are sometimes specifically designed to function as one element in a larger desegregation effort by attracting students of two or more racial or ethnic groups to a school with specialized curricula or resources; such schools have been appropriately termed "magnet schools" (Estes & Waldrip, 1978; McMillan, 1980).

Educational Environment.   All the evidence indicates that alternative schools are, indeed, unusual environments. Since they have fewer rules (Duke, 1978), perhaps significantly less rule-breaking behavior occurs in them than in conventional schools (Perry & Duke, 1978). The rules that do exist are clearer, and in contradiction to the prevailing stereotype, open settings have higher levels of order and organization than do conventional schools (Trickett, 1978). Gluckstern (1974) identified seven environmental characteristics and twelve personality factors in examining forty-three alternative programs. His analysis suggests that alternative education environments constitute a significant deviation from the traditional school structure.

The differences in environment run deep. Dreeben (1968) postulated that schools receive young children accustomed to the norms of the family and prepare them for the norms that govern formal institutions by the schools' adopting the latter norms themselves. Alternative schools, however, do not; rather they seem to operate by norms similar to, but not identical with, the norms of family (Swidler, 1976). Alternative-school teachers tend to substitute bonds of affection for authority and to treat students as "whole people" rather than as performers of discrete tasks. Perhaps, as a result, students under their tutelage prefer sharing to competing. Fizzell (1975) concluded that the differences between alternative and conventional schools were so great that the behaviors that evidenced success in one type of setting evidenced failure in the other.

Studies regularly find that students like alternative schools (Barr, Colston, & Parrett, 1977; Duke & Muzio, 1978; Swidler, 1976). Using a new instrument, grounded in the Maslow needs hierarchy (1954), Smith, Gregory, and Pugh (1981) found that the lowest-scoring of seven alternative schools was superior to the highest-scoring of six conventional schools. The thirteen schools were evaluated on meeting students' needs for social interaction and a sense of belonging, for esteem and a sense of accomplishment, and for personal growth and self-actualization. Furthermore, the teachers in the alternative schools were significantly more satisfied with their success in those areas than were their conventional-school colleagues. Interestingly, the two groups of schools differed little in meeting students' needs for order, safety, security, and control.

Studies of Organizational Structures and Processes. The number of studies conducted on the organizational structures and processes of alternative schools is striking, because alternative schools scarcely constitute complex organizations.

Nirenberg (1977) compared the response of alternative-school teachers with those of teachers in conventional schools in the same sociopolitical environment. He found significant differences in administrative climate, in teachers' sense of power, in degree of bureaucratization, and in degree of teachers' autonomy—all in favor of the alternative schools.

Cusick, Martin, and Palonsky (1976), reviewing results from four separate studies (Cusick, 1973; Cusick & Ayling, 1972; Martin, 1975: Palonsky, 1974), examined the reciprocal relationship between student behavior and the organizational structures of schools. They concluded that the organizational structure of comprehensive high schools results in a large amount of school time when students are required to do little other than be in attendance and be minimally compliant. In the one alternative-school setting examined, the staff developed a variety of strategies designed to form a new social group composed of both students and teachers, in the process developing a system of rewards and a system of normative behavior that valued high student involvement and academic achievement. Thus, the alternative program substituted internal cohesion for external authority as a device for controlling student (and teacher) behavior, a finding congruent with Swidler's work (1976).

Using case studies of two alternative schools, Deal (1975) identified a four-stage model of the development of these schools: a euphoric stage (living out fantasies); a psychic upheaval stage (early conflicts with reality); a dissatisfaction stage (disappointment); and a resolution stage (dissolution of the school or reversion to conventional practices or stability). In another case study, Singleton, Boyer, and Dorsey (1972) portrayed the "structure crisis" at a private, midwestern, free-school alternative. They describe the refusal of students to attend classes that they and the staff had initiated, and the group's failure to find a substitute for individual student autonomy. Among the potential explanations, the research identified (1) both groups' ambivalence about power and the staff's failure to assert its leadership; (2) the participants' feelings that any structuring of the group would encourage competition rather than the highly valued norm of cooperation; (3) a general agreement among the staff and students of the primacy of personal experience; and (4) the participants' failure to engage in critical dialogue because of an overemphasis on tolerance.

In an interesting conceptual article, Argyris (1974), a respected organizational theorist, postulated that "people may be 'programmed' by our culture to behave in ways that cancel out their uniqueness and reduce their effectiveness in groups" (p. 429). According to Argyris, people so programmed construct organizations that protect their incompetence. He terms this extension of the Peter principle—that people protect their levels of incompetence once they have reached them—"Model I theories-in-use." He further suggests that many qualities of alternative schools, including the developmental tendency to revert to conventional forms, are due to the fact that the participants hold "theories-in-use" that will not permit the schools to succeed as atypical governance models.

Student participation in the life of the school and especially in its governance, a trait of many alternative schools, is described in two separate case studies (Center for New Schools, 1972; McKinney, 1978.) In each study, the researchers found that many students—indeed probably most of them, did not want to get involved in long governance meetings unless a significant crisis had emerged to pique their interest. One explanation of this phenomenon involved Etzioni's instrumental and expressive realms of organizational activity (1965). Except for crisis situations or when aroused by what they considered an improper decision, students were generally more interested in controlling the expressive realm rather than the instrumental. An additional explanation, extended by McKinney, is that the alternative school did not evolve its own positive ideology but constructed its identity only in reaction to what it viewed as the negative features of the conventional school. McKinney termed this failure to develop a positive institutional identity "retarded ideology."

Educational Effects. Research comparing learning gains in alternative and conventional schools is scant. Some of the research collected in evaluations of individual schools is difficult to generalize to other populations. Several studies, comparing gains in formal and informal but not necessarily alternative-school settings, provide the best evidence of these effects. In the lower grades—what one might call the basic skills years—the weight of the evidence suggests that structured settings result in higher academic achievement (Bane, 1972; Bennett, 1976; Minuchin, Biber, Shapiro & Zimiles, 1969; Wright, 1975). This advantage appears to be especially true for very young, disadvantaged children (Bane, 1972). At least some of this difference seems to be attributable to test-taking ability (Minuchin et al., 1969). Young children taught in informal settings appear to be at a disadvantage in situations requiring speed and concentrated effort (e.g, formal test taking). These same children, however, proved strikingly superior to conventionally trained cohorts on a test requiring a cooperative group effort. The informally trained children's work was described as vigorous, relevant, self-propelled, effective, and technically accurate, whereas the conventionally trained children's effort was described as tense, competitive, rigid, and noninvolved.

Some shift occurs in the results for older students. Here several other factors appear to intervene. The disaffection, absenteeism, psychological withdrawal, and disruptive behavior that characterize some adolescents' responses to conventional schooling seem to decrease the school's ability to induce learning. Additionally, suspected differences in test-taking ability between conventional and alternative students might be expected to moderate with time. Whatever the causes, most comparisons of academic achievement in the high school years yield either no significant differences or mixed results (Barr, Colston, & Parrett, 1977; Duke & Muzio, 1978; McPartland & Epstein, 1977; Swidler, 1976). Moreover, it becomes apparent that only in the domain of the standardized achievement test is the relative success of alternative schools at all suspect.

Many alternative high schools make frequent use of their communities. Smith and Barr (1976) detail the many variations of the theme of learning-from-the-real-world that alternative schools have developed. Variously termed "action learning"; "walkabout"; or "experienced-based," "community-based," or "experiential" learning, these forays into the real world make new demands on teachers (Bontempo, 1979) and students (Shoup, 1978), but little hard evidence of the outcomes of their efforts exist.

One justification for alternative schools is that legitimate differences in learning styles need to be accommodated by different learning environments. Building on the work of Baker (1976), Parrett (1979) found that alternative school and conventional school teachers reported teaching styles significantly different from each other. The data he collected from students corroborated these results.

Schools strive to accomplish goals beyond academic achievement. They universally want their students to behave reasonably; to enjoy the schooling endeavor; to learn that they are worthwhile people; and to find sufficient satisfaction in learning to be motivated to engage in it. In these areas, alternative schools display considerable success. In summarizing the evaluations of six alternative programs, Barr, Colston, and Parrett (1977) found that students in these programs consistently had more favorable attitudes toward themselves, their teachers, and their schools than was true of conventional school students. Duke and Muzio (1978) reported similar positive results in their review of nineteen school evaluations, but they cautioned against reading too much into these usually unsystematically collected data. Two well-constructed studies (Strathe & Hash, 1979; Reddy, Langmeyer, & Asch, 1978) reported favorable improvements in the self-concepts of alternative school students. Barr, Colston, and Parrett (1977) and Heinle (1976) indicated that programs reporting attendance data showed decreases in dropouts and increases in school attendance.

When one considers that many alternative schools serve previously disruptive students, the low incidence of discipline problems in these schools is indeed remarkable (Barr, Colston, & Parrett, 1977; Duke & Perry, 1978; Perry & Duke, 1978). A promising application of the concept is in the arena of delinquency prevention. Alternatives that serve delinquent students have been in operation a comparatively short time. Little hard evidence of their impact exists yet. Arnove and Strout (1978) found gains in basic academic and social skills, improved self-concept, and increased acceptance by others. On the negative side, they reported finding negative labeling of students, disproportionate percentages of minority students, academic tracking, and tight social control. Little (1979) made some useful distinctions between conventional programs intended to control individual disruptive students (e.g., by using suspensions, expulsion, isolation, and compensatory education) and alternative education approaches that attempt to alter the total school environment to make it possible for more students to succeed.

Gold (1978) theorizes that "delinquent behavior is a manifestation of a psychological defense against threats to self-esteem and a substantial number of those threats originate in school experiences" (p. 290). He hypothesizes that an alternative program run by warm, accepting teachers who significantly increase the proportion of delinquent youths' successful, rather than unsuccessful, experiences will be effective. Hawkins and Wall (1980) identified some elements of typical alternative education approaches that promise to prevent the sort of behavior leading to delinquency; to increase achievement and success experiences; and to increase attachment to school and teachers while decreasing attachment to delinquent peers. The elements included an individualized system of instruction; a realistic, attainable system of rewards; a goal-oriented learning environment; and a small-sized, attentive, and supportive environment. Many researchers point to the need for more research on the impact of alternative schools on delinquency; several have already begun that effort in this new area.

Policy Implications. At least three policy implications emerge from the research that has been done. First, alternative schools appear to be an effective response to the mounting pressures placed on comprehensive high schools by an increasingly pluralistic society. They have proven to be a workable mechanism for bringing the sort of choice and variety to public education that has heretofore been available only in the private sector. Second, alternative schools are being used, with considerable success, to solve some of society's most serious youth-related problems. Most apparent is their success in reducing crime and violence in schools and providing environments that both teachers and students view as highly supportive and responsive. Third, considerable speculation about the potential of alternative schools to deal effectively with the problems of highly talented students exists in the literature, but little research has been done in schools serving this population. The observation that many programs for gifted and talented students in conventional schools employ the sort of interdisciplinary, individualized learning typical of the regimen available to *all* students in many alternative schools lends credence to that speculation.

Conclusions. The most obvious conclusion emerging from a review of research on alternative schools is that little research has been carried out on the topic. Much of the research that has been done is of limited value for three reasons. First, most of the research employs the institutional case study, typically focused on one or two schools. While useful, particularly for generation of hypotheses, data from case studies are limited in their capacity to be generalized. Second, much of the research has been carried out by young researchers, often in doctoral dissertations that are handicapped by time and money constraints. Third, there are relatively few studies that include comparisons of alternative and conventional students' academic achievement. Although the goals of alternative and conventional schools differ in focus and emphasis, common areas of agreement, such as the teaching of basic skills, do exist.

A national assessment of alternative schools in the public

sector is long overdue. Although two descriptive surveys (Wolf et al. 1974; National School Boards Association, 1976) have been reported in the literature, their results are not widely disseminated. Moreover, the former is, at this writing, seven years old, and the latter reports few details of its research design and methodology.

Most studies—some of them quite carefully crafted—reflect favorably on alternative schools. They reveal programs that meet student needs; reduce rates of delinquency, crime, vandalism, absenteeism, and tardiness; and enhance self-concept, social skills, and attitudes toward school. Specific causal variables have not been identified, but the concepts of choice, small size, informality, and student empowerment are frequently mentioned as reasons for what must, on balance, be called a successful innovation in American education.

Thomas B. Gregory
Gerald R. Smith

See also Affective Education; Change Processes; Experiential Education; Private Schools; Secondary Education.

REFERENCES

Argyris, C. Alternative schools: A behavioral analysis. *Teachers College Record*, 1974, *75*, 429–448.

Arnove, R. F., & Strout, T. *Alternative Schools for Disruptive Youth*. Arlington, Va.: Document Reproduction Service of ERIC, 1978. (ERIC Document Reproduction Service No. ED 162 413)

Arnove, R. F., & Strout, T. Alternative schools for disruptive youth. *The Educational Forum*, 1980, *44*, 453–471.

Baker, T. *An Investigation of Teachers' and Students' Perceptions of Instructional Practices in Selected Conventional and Alternative Public Schools*. Unpublished doctoral dissertation, Indiana University, 1976.

Bane, M. J. Open education. *Harvard Educational Review*, 1972, *42*, 273–281.

Barr, R. D. The growth of alternative public schools: The 1975 ICOPE report. *Changing Schools*, 1975, *12*, 2–10.

Barr, R. D.; Colston, B.; & Parrett, W. H. The effectiveness of alternative public schools: An analysis of six school evaluations. *Viewpoints*, July 1977, *54*(4), 1–30.

Bennett, N. *Teaching Styles and Pupil Progress*. London: Open Books, 1976.

Bontempo, B. T. *A Study of Experience-based Learning in Alternative Public High Schools: Implications for a New Role for Educators*. Unpublished doctoral dissertation, Indiana University, 1979.

Center for New Schools. Strengthening alternative high schools. *Harvard Educational Review*, 1972, *42*, 313–350.

Cusick, P. A. *Inside High School*. New York: Holt, Rinehart & Winston, 1973.

Cusick, P. A., & Ayling, R. J. *An Exploratory Study of the Formal and Informal Relationships between White and Black Students in a Racially Mixed Urban Secondary School* (Report to United States Office of Education, Grant OEG 5–72–00369509, Project No. 1–E–179). Washington, D.C.: U.S. Government Printing Office, 1972. (ERIC Document Reproduction Service No. ED 095 245)

Cusick, P. A.; Martin, W.; & Palonsky, S. Organizational structure and student behavior in secondary school. *Curriculum Studies*, 1976, *8*, 3–14.

Deal, T. E. An organizational explanation of the failure of alternative secondary schools. *Educational Researcher*, 1975, *4*, 10–16.

Dreeben, R. *On What Is Learned in School*. Reading, Mass.: Addison-Wesley, 1968.

Duke, D. L. Looking at the school as a rule-governed organization. *Journal of Research and Development in Education*, 1978, *11*, 116–126.

Duke, D. L., & Muzio, I. How effective are alternative schools?: A review of recent evaluations and reports. *Teachers College Record*, February 1978, *79*, 461–483.

Duke, D. L., & Perry, C. Can alternative schools succeed where Benjamin Spock, Spiro Agnew, and B. F. Skinner have failed? *Adolescence*, Fall 1978, *13*, 375–392.

Ebel, R. (Ed.). *Encyclopedia of Educational Research* (4th ed.). New York: Macmillan, 1969.

Ellis, J. *The Creation of a Conceptual Framework for Alternative Schools through the Case Study Method*. Unpublished doctoral dissertation, Columbia University, 1975.

Estes, N., & Waldrip, D. R. *Magnet Schools: Legal and Practical Implications*. Piscataway, N.J.: New Century Education Corporation, 1978.

Etzioni, A. Organizational control structure. In J. G. Marsh (Ed.), *Handbook of Organizations*. Chicago: Rand McNally, 1965.

Fantini, M. D. *Public Schools of Choice: A Plan for the Reform of American Education*. New York: Simon & Schuster, 1973.

Fizzell, R. *Reschooling Society*. Unpublished doctoral dissertation, Northwestern University, 1975.

Gluckstern, S. M. *Assessment of Educational Environments: The Public Alternative School and Its Students*. Unpublished doctoral dissertation, University of Massachusetts, 1974.

Gold, M. Scholastic experiences, self-esteem, and delinquent behavior: A theory for alternative schools. *Crime and Delinquency*, July 1978, *24*, 290–308.

Hawkins, J. D., & Wall, J. S. *Alternative Education: Exploring the Delinquency Prevention Potential* (Office of Juvenile Justice and Delinquency Prevention Document No. J26.27:ED8). Washington, D.C.: U.S. Government Printing Office, 1980.

Heinle, F. W. *Evaluation of an Alternative School Program: Affective Change and Cognitive Achievements of Eleventh- and Twelfth-Grade Students*. Unpublished doctoral dissertation, University of Southern California, 1976.

Little, A. D. *Alternative Education Options* (Office of Juvenile Justice and Delinquency Prevention Document No. J26.2:ED8). Washington, D.C.: U.S. Government Printing Office, 1979. (ERIC Document Reproduction Service No. ED 178 792)

Martin, W. *A Participant Observation Study of an Open Experimental Curriculum Operating in a Public Secondary School*. Unpublished doctoral dissertation, Michigan State University, 1975.

Maslow, A. *Motivation and Personality*. New York: Harper & Brothers, 1954.

McKinney, W. L. Governance and development of an alternative school. In G. Willis (Ed.), *Qualitative Evaluation*. Berkeley, Calif.: McCutchan, 1978.

McMillan, C. B. *Magnet Schools: An Approach to Voluntary Desegregation*. Bloomington, Ind.: Phi Delta Kappa, 1980.

McPartland, J. M., & Epstein, J. L. Open schools and achievement: Extended tests of a finding on no relationship. *Sociology of Education*, 1977, *42*, 133–144.

Minuchin, P.; Biber, B.; Shapiro, E.; & Zimiles, H. *The Psychological Impact of School Experience: A Comparative Study of Nine-year-old Children in Contrasting Schools.* New York: Basic Books, 1969.

National School Boards Association. *Research Report: Alternative Schools.* Evanston, Ill.: National School Boards Association, 1976.

Nirenberg, J. A comparison of the management systems of traditional and alternative public high schools. *Educational Administration Quarterly,* 1977, *13,* 86–104.

Palonsky, S. B. *A Participant Observer Investigation of the Students and Their Social World in an Urban, Integrated, and Innovative High School.* Unpublished doctoral dissertation, Michigan State University, 1974.

Parrett, W. H. *An Investigation of Teachers' and Students' Perceptions of Instructional Practices in Nationally Recognized Alternative Schools and Their Conventional Counterparts.* Unpublished doctoral dissertation, Indiana University, 1979.

Perry, C. L., & Duke, D. L. Lessons to be learned about discipline from alternative high schools. *Journal of Research and Development in Education,* 1978, *11*(4), 78–90.

Raywid, M. A. *Alternative Education in American Secondary Schools: Nature, Extent, Effectiveness, Responsiveness.* Unpublished research proposal to the National Institute of Education. Hempstead, N.Y.: Hofstra University, 1980.

Reddy, W. B.; Langmeyer, D.; & Asch, P. A. S. Self-concept, school self-image, satisfaction, and involvement in an alternative high school. *Psychology in the Schools,* January 1978, *15,* 66–71.

Shoup, B. J. *Living and Learning for Credit.* Bloomington, Ind.: Phi Delta Kappa, 1978. (ERIC Document Reproduction Service No. ED 174 595)

Singleton, S.; Boyer, D.; & Dorsey, P. Xanadu: A study of the structure crisis in an alternative school. *Review of Educational Research,* 1972, *42,* 525–531.

Smith, G. R., & Coppedge, F. L. Alternative schools in Indiana. *Indiana School Boards Association Journal,* 1974, *20,* 8–11.

Smith, G. R.; Gregory, T. B.; & Pugh, R. C. Meeting student needs: Evidence for the superiority of alternative schools. *Phi Delta Kappan,* April 1981.

Smith, V. H. A decade of alternative schools and what of the future? *National Association of Secondary School Principals Curriculum Report,* October 1978, *8*(1), 1–12.

Smith, V. H., & Barr, R. D. Where should learning take place? In W. Van Til (Ed.), *Issues in Secondary Education.* Chicago: University of Chicago Press, 1976.

Smith, V. H.; Barr, R. D.; & Burke, D. *Alternatives in Education.* Bloomington, Ind.: Phi Delta Kappa, 1976.

Strathe, M., & Hash, V. The effect of an alternative school on adolescent self-esteem. *Adolescence,* 1979, *65,* 185–189.

Swidler, A. What free schools teach. *Social Problems,* 1976, *24,* 214–227.

Theroux, J. B. *Financing Public Alternative Schools.* Unpublished doctoral dissertation, University of Massachusetts, 1974.

Trickett, E. J. Toward a social-ecological conception of adolescent socialization: Normative data on contrasting types of public school classrooms. *Child Development,* 1978, *49,* 408–414.

Wolf, T. E.; Walker, M.; & Macklin, R. A. *Summary of the National Alternative Schools Program Survey, 1974.* Unpublished report, University of Massachusetts, 1974.

Wright, R. J. The affective and cognitive consequences of an open education elementary school. *American Educational Research Journal,* 1975, *12,* 449–468.

AMERICAN INDIAN EDUCATION

The history of Indian education has been shaped by the concepts of survival, recognition, land acquisition and control, assimilation, and participation in decision making. These concepts generated the corresponding national policies of cooperation through trading and hunting, treaty making, removal and settlement, termination of federal responsibility of services, and self-determination. The educational practices resulting from these policies are complex, contradictory, confusing, and characterized throughout history by the common belief that the formal education of American Indians has been a failure.

The early colonists depended upon Indian nations for survival. Cooperation through trading and hunting allowed many colonists to survive harsh winters. Later, as a developing country, the United States viewed Indian nations as a threat to the union. Indian tribes were recognized as sovereign nations and entered into treaties with the United States. Approximately four hundred treaties were negotiated from 1778 to 1871. Although land acquisition was their primary goal, many treaties promised to educate Indian children. Treaties and subsequent executive orders, congressional acts, and court decisions formed the legal basis for federal recognition and responsibility for Indian education.

From the beginning, formal education was used as a tool to civilize, Christianize, and transmit the European life-style to the Indian. The assimilative attempt to remove Indians from their tribal and family members, religion, language, and homeland by placing them in distant schools to learn non-Indian ways gained wide support during the 1700s and 1800s. These total educational institutions, or boarding schools, were first established by missionaries in the 1600s and flourished in the 1800s, when the federal government increased its involvement and responsibility by developing an educational system for American Indians. This approach was viewed as a solution to the "Indian problem"; in reality, however, the boarding school system became the problem. Tribal and family disorganization, the breakdown of tribal culture, lack of involvement by Indian parents in the education of their children, and students' emotional, psychological, and mental anguish were the results of boarding school education.

Educational practice shifted away from boarding schools to day schools, and away from Bureau of Indian Affairs (BIA) education to public education in the early 1900s. By 1912, more Indian children were attending public schools than federal schools. Even though the policy of attending public schools continues into the 1980s, the instructional approach in teaching Indian students has varied over time: the 1930s saw attention given to culturally related materials; the 1950s witnessed the federal government's policy of termination of services to Indian people and a move away from Indian-related curriculum; the 1960s and 1970s have seen a revival of "Indianness" in the classroom. A detailed history of Indian education is found in reports by a U.S. congressional committee (Senate Committee on Labor and Public Welfare, 1969) and the American Indian Policy Review Commission (1976).

Population. American Indians can be described as young, increasing in number, and increasingly more urban. The 1970 census reported a total Indian population of 792,730 compared to 523,591 in 1960. More than half of the 1970 population live in the states of Arizona, California, New Mexico, North Carolina, and Oklahoma. In 1972 the birthrate for Indians was 31.7 per 1,000 population compared to 15.6 for the United States as a whole. Given this rate, a conservative estimate of Indian population for the 1980 census will be about 1,050,000. The median age of the Indian was 20.4 in 1970, compared to 28.1 for the United States population. The population is becoming more urban. The 1960 census reported that 30 percent of the Indian population lived in urban areas, compared to 44.6 percent in 1970.

In 1980 the BIA reported 227,777 Indian students, age 5 to 18, from federally recognized tribes attending school. The count includes 225 federally sponsored schools, 78 of which are boarding schools. Fifty-one contract schools are also included. If the broad definition of "Indian" in the Indian Education Act of 1972 is used, the number of students attending public schools increases significantly from the BIA estimated count of 175,000 to over 400,000. An additional 20,000 students are attending colleges and universities. As a result of federal funds, most college and university students have received their degrees in law, medicine, engineering, natural resources, and business administration. Approximately 42,000 Indians are enrolled in adult education programs.

Policy and Practice Issues. Before identifying and discussing significant issues, it is important to recognize and respect two facts basic to an understanding of Indian education. First, great diversity exists within and among Indian tribes. There are over two hundred sixty federally recognized tribes, each with its own language, religion, and cultural heritage. In order to avoid the problem of stereotyping the Indian, generalities are to be used with caution, and allowances provided for tribal differences. Second, American Indians differ from other minority groups in the United States, both legally and culturally. The legal difference stems from the formal government-to-government relationship established through treaties, executive orders, congressional acts, and court decisions. Culturally, the American Indian has a deep sense of religion that is tied to the earth and based upon a relationship to all living things.

Legislation. Indian education has come under constant criticism over the past four hundred years. Phraseology such as "mental genocide," "a change in the point of view is needed," and "a national tragedy, a national challenge" has been used to describe Indian education policy and practice. An equally consistent recommendation for improving the condition of Indian education has been to develop and implement educational policies that allow for Indian involvement in and control of education programs.

Current legislation that directly affects Indian education mandates parental involvement and local control. The Johnson-O'Malley Act of 1934, the Indian Education Act of 1972, the Self-determination and Education Assistance Act of 1975, and the Indian-controlled Community College Assistance Act of 1978 are examples of legislation that promote Indian involvement and control. Public Law 95-561, or the Educational Amendments of 1978, require the Bureau of Indian Affairs to undergo changes that will allow more control and decision-making authority to reside in local school boards.

In addition, "set-aside" provisions exist in legislation. Examples include the Education for all Handicapped Children Act and the Vocational Education Act, which transfer funds to the BIA for use with American Indian students. Indian students also benefit from Impact Aid programs because they live on federally affected lands; Title I of the Elementary and Secondary Education Act programs because they are termed disadvantaged; or the Title VII bilingual program because they have limited English proficiency (U.S. Congress, House Committee on Education and Labor, 1975). Indian education legislation is further complicated by entitlement versus discretionary programs, basic versus supplementary financial support, and conflicting eligibility criteria for services. The legislation and delivery systems are products of political actions and individual and organizational interest rather than of a carefully planned approach to Indian education. These haphazard, piecemeal, individualized solutions lead to charges of overlap, duplication, and inconsistency in the delivery of services. Many tribes, schools, and organizations experience administrative nightmares because of this situation. Proposal development, reporting, and other paperwork detract attention from actual student educational attainment.

Indian-controlled schools. Criticism and failure of BIA and public school education led to an alternative approach to educating Indian students. In 1966, Rough Rock Demonstration School paved the way for Indian-controlled schools. In 1975 the passage of the Indian Self-Determination and Education Assistance Act provided authority for tribes to contract with the BIA to conduct or administer all or part of any Indian program conducted by the Department of Interior. Since 1975, approximately fifty Indian-controlled or contract schools have been established; however, the move to gain control through contracting has not proceeded with the anticipated growth. The practice of local control through contracting brings its own set of problems. Administrative concerns such as difficult contract negotiations, late funding, paperwork, reporting, funding for construction, personnel, and fiscal and program accountability are the more common problems.

Education as a priority. Another major policy issue concerns the importance placed on education by parents and tribes. A common recommendation for improving Indian education calls for involvement of parents and community in the educational process of their children. The Indian Education Act of 1972 and Public Law 95-561, the Educational Amendments of 1978, both require such involvement. The result has been significant, with more parents actively involved in the education of their children today than at any other time in history; however, even with the progress, the effort to get parents involved remains a major concern. The long history of noninvolvement has had its impact; a large-scale educational process is needed to inform parents of the importance of involvement, provide them with basic program information, and develop their skills to influence schools.

Tribes need to place more emphasis upon education. Historically, tribes have not given a high priority to education when allocating resources; natural resources, including water and land rights, have received higher priority. Some tribes, like the Navajo, have developed strong departments of education in the tribal structure to oversee, coordinate, and develop programs, and to provide educational leadership and direction. This approach is viewed as a way of developing tribal capabilities in education and of making education a priority within the tribal structure. The opportunity to pursue this approach is available through Indian Education Act funds.

Classroom materials. Indian education has come under sharp attack because of the claims that school systems use curriculum and teaching methods that are irrelevant to Indian students. The policy of self-determination has resulted in attempts to develop materials that are based on the child's culture; however, two basic problems are apparent. First, materials are developed locally, with very little dissemination; consequently, it appears that little is being done nationally in the area of curriculum development. Second, apart from Indian-controlled schools, much development of curriculum material and teaching strategies takes place outside regular school programs. Efforts are supported by supplementary funds and are usually considered marginal to the school's basic education program. The challenge lies in integrating these materials and teaching strategies into the regular school program. This is especially critical in urban areas or classrooms in which Indian students are in the minority. Although there are strong indications that supplementary programs are successful in increasing student retention and academic achievement, empirical data are not available.

Educator attitudes and expectations have been identified as detrimental to the academic success of Indian students. However, preservice and in-service training in Indian education and special education personnel training programs have helped to bring about better understanding and respect for the Indian student.

Research and Evaluation. Research and evaluation have been neglected in Indian education. Policy development and implementation have tended to be political and reactionary, failing to build on research and evaluation findings and recommendations. The diverse nature of In-

dian education influences research and evaluation efforts; for example, a national student dropout rate is difficult to determine when the rate varies depending upon the tribe and school sampled.

National studies have accounted for a large part of the research and evaluation efforts in Indian education. The Meriam Report (Meriam et al., 1928), the first comprehensive study of Indian affairs, suggested that the "first and foremost need in Indian education is a change in point of view," rejecting the removal of Indian children from their home environment in favor of an approach that would allow upbringing in their home and family settings. A series of studies (U.S. Senate, Committee on Labor and Public Welfare, 1969; Havighurst, 1970; McKinley, Bayne, & Nimnicht, 1970; American Indian Policy Review Commission, 1976) were critical of Indian education and offered recommendations for its improvement. Brophy and Aberle (1966) investigated the status of American Indians in light of House Concurrent Resolution 108, which set forth a policy of terminating the special relationship Indians have with the federal government.

Other studies have focused upon specific areas in Indian education. ACKCO (1974) and National Association for the Advancement of Colored People (NAACP) (1971) reported on the impact of federal funds in public school districts. Doctoral dissertations have addressed many varied aspects of Indian education. Examples include Peregoy (1979) on educational and occupational expectations; Leitka (1973) on higher education; Cata (1977) on literature; and Ramirez (1980) on teacher orientation and sense of autonomy.

Congressional actions continue to support research and evaluation activities in the field of Indian education; amendments to laws and their implementation support research and evaluation efforts. In 1980, the Office of Indian Education (OIE), Department of Education, established five regional resource and evaluation centers to assist local projects in evaluation as well as other areas of accountability. Part of the difficulty in this area results from the fact that American Indians have not been actively involved in research and evaluation because of their preoccupation with delivery of educational services to Indian students. The OIE centers will help develop evaluation skills among Indian people.

For the 1980s, research and evaluation is a priority area in Indian education. The bleak economic conditions of the late 1970s and early 1980s have led to the need for hard impact data to justify future budget and program growth in Indian education.

Important research questions in Indian education address the effectiveness of supplementary programs, bilingual programs, parental involvement, and different teaching methods; and they examine the relations between cultural activities and basic skill development.

An analysis of Indian education shows that progress is being made, but much remains to be done. The policy of self-determination and Indian control had resulted in increased parental involvement, greater control by tribes and communities, better teaching and counseling techniques, relevant curriculum, and an increase in the number of Indian people prepared as professional educators. The coming decade will see greater accomplishments, but not before Indian education encounters some difficult questions and problems.

John W. Tippeconnic III

Gerald E. Gipp

See also Culture and Education Policy; Equity Issues in Education; Multicultural and Minority Education; Racism and Sexism in Children's Literature.

REFERENCES

ACKCO, Inc. *So That All Indian Children Will Have Equal Educational Opportunity.* Boulder, Colo.: ACKCO, Inc., 1974.

American Indian Policy Review Commission. *Report on Indian Education* (Prepared as part of the final report to the American Indian Policy Review Commission). Washington, D.C.: U.S. Government Printing Office, 1976.

Brophy, W. A., & Aberle, S. *The Indian: America's Unfinished Business.* Norman: University of Oklahoma Press, 1966.

Cata, J. O. *The Portrait of American Indians in Children's Fictional Literature.* Unpublished doctoral dissertation, University of New Mexico, 1977.

Havighurst, R. J. The education of Indian children and youth. In *National Study of American Indian Education* (Series 4, No. 6). Chicago: University of Chicago, 1970.

Leitka, E. *A Study of Effectiveness of Existing Native American Studies Programs in Selected Universities and Colleges.* Unpublished doctoral dissertation, New Mexico State University, 1973. (ERIC Document Reproduction Service No. ED 073 901)

McKinley, F.; Bayne, S.; & Nimnicht, G. *Who Should Control Indian Education?* Berkeley, Calif.: Far West Laboratory for Educational Research and Development, 1970. (ERIC Document Reproduction Service No. ED 042 538)

Meriam, L., et al. *The Problem of Indian Administration.* Baltimore: Johns Hopkins Press, 1928.

National Association for the Advancement of Colored People Legal Defense and Educational Fund, Inc. *An Even Chance.* Annandale, Va.: Graphics Four, 1971. (ERIC Document Reproduction Service No. ED 047 867)

Peregoy, R. M. *Educational and Occupational Expectations of High School Students on the Flathead Indian Reservation.* Unpublished doctoral dissertation, Montana State University, 1979.

Ramirez, B. A. *Professional and Bureaucratic Orientations and Sense of Autonomy between Teachers in Public and Bureau of Indian Affairs Schools in the Navajo Nation.* Unpublished doctoral dissertation, Pennsylvania State University, 1980.

U.S. Congress, House, Committee on Education and Labor. *A Compilation of Federal Education Laws.* Washington, D.C.: U.S. Government Printing Office, 1975. (ERIC Document Reproduction Service No. ED 108 311)

U.S. Congress, Senate, Committee on Labor and Public Welfare, Special Subcommittee on Indian Education. *Indian Education: A National Tragedy—A National Challenge.* (S. Rept. 1969). 91st Cong., 1st sess., 1969.

ANALYSIS OF VARIANCE AND COVARIANCE

Analysis of variance (ANOVA) is a statistical inference technique that expands the processes used to test the equality of two means (via t tests) into a test of the equality of K means (via a mean square ratio contrasted with an F distribution). ANOVA permits an experimenter to manipulate two or more factors in an experiment and to come to conclusions about the effects of each factor and the possibility that one factor may influence the effects of the other factor (an interaction).

Analysis of covariance (ANCOVA) is a related technique that attempts to reduce the error term in an ANOVA design by "partialing out" the variation in the criterion, Y, that can be predicted by a linear regression from a covariate, X. The covariate should be a measure that is obtained on each subject before the experiment is conducted. Although some researchers have the illusion that covariance can be used to salvage a wrecked experiment, or a pseudoexperiment, clear interpretations can be obtained only when subjects (or several classes) have been randomly assigned to treatment groups, just as in an analysis of variance.

This article, which assumes some familiarity with ANOVA and ANCOVA, covers two major topics. One is a versatile system for describing various designs for experimental studies that does not depend on the agricultural labels that were established with the earlier applications of ANOVA methodology. Then it discusses the more versatile, but more abstract, approach, using the general linear model (GLM). With the invention of sophisticated statistical packages on high-speed computers, GLM has now become practical.

Terminology and Representation of Designs. In the behavioral sciences most experimental designs can be represented by only two basic terms: nested and crossed. We shall assume that subjects or pupils are the random unit in the following discussion, although classes or schools could be substituted.

If a level of factor A occurs within only one level of factor B, then we say A is nested in B. Symbolically, this may be represented as A in (B). [Computer programs BMDP8V (Dixon & Brown, 1977) and SAS PROC GLM (Helwig, 1979) merely use $A(B)$; the extra "in" is a redundancy that helps the neophyte remember that the first term is nested in the second.] Thus the independent group t test with twenty subjects randomly divided into two groups of ten each may be represented as RS_{10} in (A_2). Typically only random factors (here denoted by the prefix R) are nested under fixed treatments (denoted by the absence of an R). The ANOVA of RS_n in (A_J), where $J > 2$, is an exact extension of the t test for independent groups and has the same assumptions. One assumption is that the observations, Y_{ij}'s, are normally distributed, but both the t test and the ANOVA are robust to violations of this assumption when used with n's needed to yield decent power, say, $n_j > 20$. The other assumption is that of homogeneous cell variances. Both the t test and the ANOVA are robust to violations of this assumption only with equal n's of moderate size (Pratt, 1964).

Two factors are crossed if each level of each factor appears with each level of the other factor, or symbolically, $A*B$. If ten random subjects take both a pretest and posttest, we may call the tests two levels of factor A. Inasmuch as each subject took both a pretest and a posttest, subjects are crossed with A, so the design may be written as $RS_{10}*A_2$. To test $H: \mu_1 - \mu_2 = 0$ for this situation, we would use the dependent t test. The more general extension, RS_n*A_J, $(J > 2)$, is often referred to as a repeated measures design. The dependent t test with $n > 20$ is practically an assumption-free test since the only assumption needed in the derivation is that the $D_i = Y_{1i} - Y_{2i}$ are normally distributed, and again the test is robust to violations of this assumption with decent size n's. Formulas for the dependent t statistic are

$$t_0 = \frac{\overline{D}}{\sqrt{s_D^2/n}} = \frac{\overline{Y}_1 - \overline{Y}_2}{\sqrt{(s_1^2 + s_2^2 - 2s_{12})/n}},$$

where s_{12} is the covariance of the Y_1 and Y_2 columns or

$$[\Sigma(Y_{1i} - \overline{Y}_1)(Y_{2i} - \overline{Y}_2)]/(n-1) = r_{12}s_1 s_2.$$

However, in the extension of the relatively assumption-free t test to its more general ANOVA counterpart, a very restrictive condition is needed that is often grossly violated in dependent behavioral data. With many levels of A we will have a variance-covariance (VCV) matrix with the variances of each column on the diagonal and the covariances on the off-diagonals. In this design the proper mean square (MS) ratio is $MS_A/MS_{RSA} = MS_A/MS$ interaction. Unfortunately, to show that this MS ratio is distributed as F with the usual degrees of freedom, df, of $df_u = (J - 1)$ in the numerator and $df_d = (J - 1)(n - 1)$ in the denominator requires the circularity assumption that $s_D^2 = s_j^2 + s_{j'}^2 - 2s_{jj'}$ is a constant for all pairs $(j \neq j')$ (Huynh & Feldt, 1970; Rouanet & Lepine, 1970). (This assumption can be stated in a slightly more general form that is slightly less demanding. However, this more general form involves mastery of contrasts, so it is avoided here in the interests of simplicity and length.) When this assumption is violated, the risk of Type I error (FWI) on the omnibus $F = MS_A/MS_{RSA}$ usually is much larger than the nominal level of significance, α. Fortunately, there is an index, $\hat{\epsilon}$, of the degree of deviation from this condition in the sample VCV matrix that can be used to produce adequate control of the familywise risk of Type I error (FWI) simply by multiplying the usual df by this index (Box, 1954; Huynh & Mandeville, 1979; Winer, 1971, p. 283). In general, $1/df_u \leq \epsilon \leq 1.0$; when the circularity assumption is met, $\epsilon = 1.0$. Regrettably many journal articles present repeated measure designs that fail to attend to this problem. For example, Jennings and Wood (1976) have stated that 84 percent of the articles published in *Psychophysiology* in

1975 that used repeated measure factors seem to have ignored this assumption. One suspects it is little better in educational articles. To protect us from a surplus of Type I errors (and hence unreplicatable results) reviewers and editors should insist that authors either use the conservative test with $\epsilon = 1/(df_u$ of numerator MS) or compute $\hat{\epsilon}$ from the sample data and use it to yield a good approximate test. One of the virtues of the ANOVA series computer programs (Games, 1975a) is that they will yield these $\hat{\epsilon}$ values. (Another approach is via multivariate analysis, but that is beyond the scope of the present article.)

These two basic designs may be combined in many ways to form more complex designs. Designs in which two or more experimental factors are completely crossed are called factorial designs. Thus an RS_{10} in (A_3*B_4) design would have twelve independent groups in the twelve cells formed by crossing A and B, for a total of 120 subjects and 120 data values. Similarly, repeated measures designs may be extended, for example, $RS_{10}*A_3*B_4$. This also has 120 data points but only ten subjects, since each subject would yield twelve data points, one in each of the twelve cells. For this design three different $\hat{\epsilon}$'s should be computed, $\hat{\epsilon}_A$, $\hat{\epsilon}_B$, and $\hat{\epsilon}_{AB}$ (Mendoza, Toothaker, & Crain, 1976).

Finally, it is possible to combine the two basic types of ANOVA. For example, if 30 students are included in each treatment A_j but each student is tested five times on the material being learned (B_5), then the design would be $[RS_{30}$ in $(A_3)]*B_5$ (Winer, 1971, p. 518). Designs that include subjects nested under one factor but crossed with another factor are sometimes called mixed designs (Myers, 1979, chap. 8). However, mathematical statisticians usually describe an $RS*A$ design as a mixed design because it has one random factor *(RS)* and one fixed factor *(A)*. One virtue of the nesting and crossing notation is that it avoids the confusion caused by the use of different terminologies in different sciences. In typical texts all designs discussed up until chapters on Latin squares in Kirk (1968), Myers (1979) and Winer (1971) can be described easily in this fashion. Latin squares cannot be so described because they (and several other advanced designs) are incompletely crossed. Such designs assume, often erroneously, that certain interactions are zero. ANOVA will handle completely crossed designs up to a complexity of $[RS_n$ in $(A*B*C*D)]*J*K*L*M$. BMDP8V (Dixon & Brown, 1977) will handle designs with up to ten factors, and is the most flexible program on hierarchical designs, that is, designs with more than one level of nesting. For example, one might have $Rsubjects_{30}$ in $[Rclasses_5$ in $(A_3)]$ with two layers of nesting for a total of fifteen classes, each with thirty students, or 450 students in all. A common mistake is to analyze such a study as an RS_{150} in (A_3) design. Myers (1966, pp. 216–218) shows how this mistake may greatly inflate the risk of a Type I error if there are substantial differences among classes.

General Linear Model. Related to the topics of ANOVA and ANCOVA are computer programs for the general linear model. Both ANOVA and ANCOVA can be considered special cases of the GLM. However, these computer programs are more difficult to use than some ANOVA computer programs with which one merely specifies the design and the programs automatically generate the proper F tests. Because the GLM programs are more flexible, they place more responsibility on the user, who must specify the proper model, the error term to be used for each test, and so on. Assumptions such as the circularity ($\epsilon = 1.0$) assumption are not dealt with at all by these programs. It is suggested that users strive for equal n's in most designs and use the simpler ANOVA programs where possible. The GLM programs are like surgeons' scalpels; only if the user has excellent training are they a valuable tool. However, ANCOVA is best accomplished on these GLM programs. It is a complicated technique and the GLM approach makes it clear to the user what ANCOVA is doing, which is not true when using hand calculation formulas (e.g., Winer, 1971, p. 773).

As an example of ANCOVA on a GLM program, the following discussion uses the Statistical Analysis System (SAS) Procedure GLM (Helwig, 1979). Table 1 illustrates input in a design with five subjects nested in each of three treatments, with two covariates available on each subject. First the data are read in from cards. If the data set is small, use PROC PRINT to check that all of the data were read correctly by the computer. If the data set is massive, use PROC UNIVARIATE instead. With something as complex as ANCOVA, it is desirable either to do several different runs and make sequential decisions to find a model that is a reasonable approximation to the truth, or to run several different models in one run knowing that many of the models will be discarded. The latter policy is followed in Table 1.

The first step in any ANCOVA should be to check the assumption of homogeneous slopes of the covariates for the three A groups. This is done in Job 1 by checking the F's for the $A*X1$ and $A*X2$ terms. SAS PROC GLM by default gives two sets of sums of squares (SS). The first set (SS1) gives SS with only preceding variables partialed out. In Job 1, SS1 would give SS(reg $X1$), then SS(reg $X2/X1$), meaning the regression SS of $X2$ when $X1$ has already been partialed out of both Y and $X2$; then SS(reg $A/X1$, $X2$), the usual "adjusted treatment effect SS of ANCOVA"; then SS(reg $A*X1/X1$ $X2$ A); then SS(reg $A*X2/X1$ $X2$ A $A*X1$). The other default SS, SS4, gives each SS with *all* other terms in the model partialed out. Thus the first term would be SS(reg $X1/X2$ A $A*X1$ $A*X2$).

For homogeneous slopes, both SS(reg $A*X1/$ . . .) and SS(reg $A*X2/$ . . .) should be nonsignificant. In this case arguments could be made for using either SS1 or SS4.

Heterogeneous slopes in an ANCOVA are roughly equivalent to an interaction in a treatment-by-blocks design (Myers, 1979, chap. 6). To proceed to the ANCOVA when you have important heterogeneity in the slopes is equivalent to attending only to the main effects of A when you have a substantial $A*$Blocks interaction. Assuming that the foregoing F values are clearly nonsignificant (say

TABLE 1. *An example using SAS PROC GLM on an RS_n with X_1X_2 in (A_3) design*

```
// EXEC SAS  } Job control language needed to load
//SYSIN DD *  } SAS & say here come the data.
TITLE RS5 WITH OBSERVATIONS ON TWO COVARIATES
IN (A3);
DATA COVAR;
  INPUT A  X1  X2  Y   ;CARDS;
       1  15  10  18
       .
       .
       1  35  46  49
       2  14  18  24
       .
       .
       2  19  16  21
       3  14  51  38
       .
       .
       3  12  18  26
PROC PRINT;
PROC UNIVARIATE;
PROC GLM; CLASSES A;
  TITLE2 Job 1-FULL MODEL WITH HETERO SLOPES TEST
  ON X1 & X2;
  MODEL Y=X1 X2 A A*X1 A*X2/CLM P;
  LSMEANS A/STDERR PDIFF;
PROC GLM; CLASSES A;
  TITLE2 Job 2-COV MODEL ASSUMING HOMOGENEOUS
  SLOPES ON BOTH X1 & X2;
  MODEL Y=X1 X2 A/CLM P SOLUTION;
  LSMEANS A/STDERR PDIFF;
PROC GLM; CLASSES A;
  TITLE2 BE SURE TO USE SS4 ON A FROM HERE ON OUT;
  TITLE3 JOB 3 COV ASSUMING HOMOGENEOUS SLOPES
  ON X2, HETERO ON X1;
  MODEL Y=X2 A X1 (A)/CLM P SOLUTION;
  LSMEANS A/STDERR PDIFF;
PROC GLM; CLASSES A;
  TITLE 3 JOB 4 COV ASSUMING HOMOGENEOUS SLOPES
  ON X1, HETERO ON X2;
  MODEL Y=X1 A X2(A)/CLM P SOLUTION;
  LSMEANS A/STDERR PDIFF;
PROC GLM; CLASSES A;
  TITLE3 JOB 5 FULL MODEL WITH HETEROGENEOUS
  SLOPES ON BOTH X1 & X2;
  MODEL Y= A X1(A) X2(A)/SOLUTION CLM P;
  LSMEANS A/STDERR PDIFF;
/*
```

$p > .20$) and unimportant, you may proceed to Job 2 and report your LSMEANS output. One limitation of SAS PROC GLM is that the PDIFF option compares all pairs of adjusted means and reports only *post hoc* per-comparison risks of Type I errors *(p)*. Thus PDIFF is equivalent to running all possible *t*'s, and the family wise risk of Type I (FWI) error rises rapidly as the number of treatments rises (Games, 1971, pp. 537–541). To control FWI a conservative approximate procedure would be to compute the number of contrasts, $g = (J)(J-1)/2$, and then use $\alpha_r = \alpha/g$ as the critical value that p must be less than to be significant.

It is important that the user specify LSMEANS when employing PROC GLM. If MEANS is specified you will obtain descriptive means that are completely unaffected by the two covariates and are unrelated to the COV summary table you report. The LSMEANS that you obtain are the predicted values of Y for the grand mean of the X's, $[\overline{X}1.. \& \overline{X}2..]$, or exactly the so-called adjusted means of ANCOVA. This also holds for the later outputs.

If one of the two covariates yields significant and important differences in the slopes, then either Job 3 or Job 4 can be used. Here the LSMEANS are of less interest, since the model tells you that there are different regression lines for one of the covariates (say $X1$). The LSMEANS then merely give you the difference between the different $X1$ regression lines at the $\overline{X}1..$ point, and there are both smaller and larger differences at different values of $X1$. In this case you should use the regression weights that are given when you ask for SOLUTION, and plot the several regression lines just as you usually plot the means if you have an $A*$BLOCK interaction in ANOVA. The P OPTION yields predicted Y values for every $[X1_i \ X2_i]$ value in the data, and the CLM option yields a $1-\alpha$ confidence interval for the mean of the Y's for the subpopulation that has that particular $[A \ X1 \ X2]$ value. A very conservative test for the equality of these predicted means of $A1$ versus $A2$ is to see if the confidence intervals overlap, and if they do *not* overlap, to declare the difference significant. A more accurate test is available via SAS PROC GLM options, which cannot be covered here.

Job 5 concludes the run with a solution that has heterogeneous slopes for both $X1$ and $X2$. This is analogous to an $A*$Blocks1$*$Blocks2 design with two blocking variables in which you find two significant two-factor interactions, $A*$Block1 and $A*$Block2. Again both sets of heterogeneous regression lines should be plotted, and the LSMEANS output is not of much interest. Some researchers suggest that we check to see if there is the equivalent of a three-factor interaction in the data by including an additional term $A*X1*X2$ in Job 1. It is also possible to use curvilinear trend lines by defining additional terms in the data input step. For example, $X1SQ = X1**2$, include these in the model and even have $A*X1SQ$ and $A*X2*X1*X1SQ$, etc. In short, GLM procedures are so flexible that they can generate thousands of models, and it is up to the user to decide which of these models is a reasonable approxima-

tion of the truth. Although there may be three or four relatively simple models that can well describe the data, there often are 300 or 400 ways of doing things on GLM programs that do not make sense, or are not internally consistent.

The present GLM example was relatively simple because there was only one experimental factor *(A)*, and because subjects were nested only, not crossed with any experimental factors. When repeated measure designs, or mixed designs such as [RS_n in $(A*B)]*J*K$, are required, the GLM programs usually are expensive and entail large amounts of computer storage because the matrix for such a design includes a vector for every subject and every subject interaction.

The other feature of GLM programs that appeals to many users is the fact that on designs with nested subjects it is possible to have nonproportional n's (unbalanced designs). In the past ten years a number of articles dealing with such designs have appeared but unfortunately many of these articles were confused and confusing. For anyone who wishes to analyze unbalanced designs several publications are available that will explain the issues involved (Appelbaum & Cramer, 1974; Carlson & Timm, 1974; Games, 1975b; Herr & Gaebelein, 1978; Hosking & Hamer, 1979). After reading these articles most users undoubtedly will be impressed with the great virtue of simplicity in balanced designs. At the Pennsylvania State University the committee on statistical computer programs (1980) has agreed on the following statement: "The change from the simplicities of balanced data of the complexities of unbalanced data should not be entered into lightly. The hypothesis tested and the estimates obtained are all considerably more complex. The user should know what he is doing, and/or hire expert statistical help before adopting these (GLM) programs."

This article has described "nested" and "crossed" as two general terms useful for describing a variety of experimental designs. The article has further illustrated the GLM approach to ANCOVA, using SAS. Although the details would differ from Table 1, if you have SPSS or BMDP available at your computer the same general approach could be used. Finally, a warning about the complexities of unbalanced designs is given, with references that should be understood by anyone undertaking such an analysis.

Paul A. Games

See also Information Management and Computing; Multivariate Analysis; Statistical Methods.

REFERENCES

Appelbaum, M. I., & Cramer, E. M. Some problems in the nonorthogonal analysis of variance. *Psychological Bulletin*, 1974, *81*, 335–343.

Box, G. P. E. Some theorems on quadratic forms applied in the study of analysis of variance problems: II. Effect of inequality of variance and correlation of errors in the two-way classification. *Annals of Mathematical Statistics*, 1954, *25*, 484–498.

Carlson, J. E., & Timm, N. H. Analysis of nonorthogonal fixed-effects designs. *Psychological Bulletin*, 1974, *81*, 563–570.

Dixon, W. J., & Brown, M. B. (Eds.). *BMDP-77 Biomedical Computer Programs, P-series*. Berkeley and Los Angeles: University of California Press, 1977.

Games, P. A. Multiple comparisons of means. *American Educational Research Journal*, 1971, *8*, 531–565.

Games, P. A. Computer programs for robust analyses in multifactor analysis of variance designs. *Educational and Psychological Measurement*, 1975, *35*, 147–152. (a)

Games, P. A. Confounding problems in multifactor AOV when using several organismic variables of limited reliability. *American Educational Research Journal*, 1975, *12*, 225–232. (b)

Helwig, J. T. (Ed.). *SAS User's Guide*. Raleigh: SAS Institute, Inc., 1979.

Herr, D., & Gaebelein, J. Nonorthogonal two-way analysis of variance. *Psychological Bulletin*, 1978, *85*, 207–216.

Hosking, J. D., & Hamer, R. M. Nonorthogonal analysis of variance programs. *Journal of Educational Statistics*, 1979, *4*, 161–188.

Huynh, H., & Feldt, L. S. Conditions under which mean squares in repeated measurements designs have exact *F*-distributions. *Journal of the American Statistical Association*, 1970, *65*, 1582–1589.

Huynh, H., & Mandeville, G. K. Validity conditions in repeated measures designs. *Psychological Bulletin*, 1979, *86*, 964–973.

Jennings, J. R., & Wood, C. C. The ϵ-adjustment procedure for repeated measures analyses of variance. *Psychophysiology*, 1976, *13*, 277–278.

Kirk, R. E. *Experimental Design: Procedures for the Behavioral Sciences*. Belmont, Calif.: Brooks/Cole, 1968.

Mendoza, J. L.; Toothaker, L. E.; & Crain, B. R. Necessary and sufficient conditions for *F* ratios in the $L \times J \times K$ factorial design with two repeated factors. *Journal of the American Statistical Association*, 1976, *71*(356), 992–993.

Myers, J. L. *Fundamentals of Experimental Design*. Boston: Allyn & Bacon, 1966.

Myers, J. L. *Fundamentals of Experimental Design* (3rd ed.). Boston: Allyn & Bacon, 1979.

Pennsylvania State University Committee on Statistical Programs. *Guide to Available Analysis of Variance (AOV) and Covariance (COV) Programs*. University Park: PSU Computation Center, June 1980. (Mimeo)

Pratt, J. W. Robustness of some procedures for the two-sample location problem. *Journal of the American Statistical Association*, 1964, *59*, 665–680.

Rouanet, H., & Lepine, D. Comparison between treatments in a repeated-measures design: ANOVA and multivariate methods. *British Journal of Mathematical and Statistical Psychology*, 1970, *23*, 147–163.

Winer, B. J. *Statistical Principles in Experimental Design* (2nd ed.). New York: McGraw-Hill, 1971.

ANTHROPOLOGY

Anthropology is easily the most ambitious of the sciences concerned with human behavior. It is characterized by an extreme eclecticism both of subject and of approach to subject. It includes within its domain four traditional fields of interest: physical anthropology, the study of the physical characteristics of *Homo sapiens;* archaeology, the study of the residues of the human past; linguistics, the study of ways of speaking in all human societies; and cultural anthropology, the study of contemporary (people alive today) human societies and behaviors. Each of these four fields is composed of numerous schools and theoretical strands that challenge the new student to keep track of the diversity with which one is faced. (In this entry I exclude anthropological linguistics from the discussion since it is dealt with in other entries in this encyclopedia, and I exclude physical anthropology and archaeology because of their limited relevance to education.) What disciplines—in both senses of the term—this diversity is the orientation that people are part of one human species. Anthropology is devoted to its study. Wherever, whenever, and whatever humans have done or are doing is grist for the anthropoligist's mill. Given this breadth of subject matter, the diversity and eclecticism that characterize the discipline should not be unexpected.

In addition to or concomitant with the diversity mentioned above, anthropology has developed differently in different countries. Within cultural anthropology in the United States, anthropology has grown in ways different from those found in other countries, for example, England and France. American anthropology by comparison with those two traditions is a sprawling and, to some, bewildering accumulation of diverse theoretical themes as well as diverse subjects for study. On something as simple as the concept of culture, which most nonanthropologists in the social sciences associate with anthropology, there is such diversity that some anthropologists do not even use the term. Books could be and have been written simply on an inventory of the various definitions of "culture" (Kroeber & Kluckhohn, 1952). Space does not allow a complete review here. Culture is, of course, an abstraction. As distinct from a group of people, you cannot see culture any more than you can see evolution or gravity. This is one reason why so many definitions exist. Another is that our definition is purposely broad so as to include more in the study of culture than it excludes.

Although American anthropologists use the term "culture" frequently and indeed took their definition from a nineteenth-century Englishman, E. B. Tylor, the term is almost totally absent in today's British literature of the discipline. In the British literature one encounters "society" but rarely "culture." By focusing their attention on society the British anthropologists are declaring their interest in behavior, seeking regularities of social interactions or human behaviors. They are less interested in people's feelings, attitudes, values, or beliefs than in how these attitudes, values, or beliefs are translated into action.

Instead, the Americans, and to a certain degree the French as well, focus on "culture," by which they mean "society" as it is understood in England, plus the value systems of that society, plus the individual and/or shared attitudinal belief and value systems that support it. This view leads inevitably to a concern for the relationship between the individual and culture, the main theoretical antecedent of anthropological research in education. It is therefore not accidental that the study of anthropology and education has developed in the United States.

Before delving further into the history of cultural anthropology within America, we turn next to a discussion of culture. Culture is a much misunderstood concept. In colloquial usage one talks about a "cultured person" as someone who enjoys, for example, fine art, classical music, and elegant crystal. This "high" culture conceptualization provokes misunderstanding of anthropological usages of the term. Whereas the colloquial usage is highly value-laden (both ways—in Neil Simon's play *The Odd Couple* Felix is "cultured" and is proud of it, while Oscar is not and is proud of it), the anthropological usages are not. Clyde Kluckhohn, for example, formulated a definition with which many anthropologists agree: "Culture consists of patterns, explicit and implicit, of and for behavior acquired and transmitted by symbols, constituting the distinctive achievements of human groups. . . . Culture systems may, on the one hand, be considered as products of action, on the other as influences upon further action" (Kluckhohn, 1965, p. 73). In such usages everyone is by definition cultured if he or she grew up interacting with other people. Culture is not high or low; cultures are diverse. The urban Nigerian is no more cultured than the rural Nigerian, any more than the urban New Yorker is more cultured than the rural farmer. The content of some cultures may be more complex, but the difference is one of quantity, not quality.

A final note on culture. For some, culture is primarily a descriptive concept. It is considered a product of human action: observe the action and you can label the culture. For others, culture is an explanatory concept; culture is seen as influencing further action. "He is a Hopi" is a statement that is essentially little more than a use of the culture concept as a way of categorizing humans into discrete units. It is often important for anthropologists to do so. The second use, as an explanatory concept, treats culture as a functional rather than a status characteristic. "He behaves that way because he is Hopi" is an example of the latter. Such explanations are usually unsatisfactory because they are a shorthand representation of much more complicated phenomena that the theoretical structures described below are designed to elucidate.

The diversity within anthropology is so great that to some the field seems a collection of "shreds and patches" without structure or shape. We turn now to an alternative view that attempts to delineate structure and shape for this discipline whose influence upon educational research is increasing rapidly.

Historical Development. Franz Boas is accorded the traditional position as founder of American anthropology. As a trained physicist, his concern was typical of nineteenth-century natural science after Darwin. Like Darwin he was concerned with the collection and understanding of facts. Theories emerged after the facts and were actually simply ways to explain them. Later, sophisticates might argue that theory determines the facts one collects, indeed, that if theory building must await completion of fact collection, the theory can never be built since facts are produced by addressing theories with appropriate methods to produce data appropriate to what is studied. It follows that the more scientists generate facts, the more facts there are to gather. Despite the naiveté of his position, Boas's influence on his students was profound. Indeed, it was Boas's fate to be responsible for both the strength and the weakness of early American anthropology: its commendable empiricism and concern for salvaging descriptions of native cultures before they disappeared and (unlike Darwin) its inablity to generate one theory powerful enough to produce understanding and adequately direct further inquiry.

Boas's own, now extreme, position must be understood as a timely caution based in reaction to the speculative theory building of the nineteenth century. While pure Boasian thought did not characterize the discipline for long, because of its influence in the development of anthropology as a university discipline in the United States, it was a powerful determiner of the image formed for anthropology by other disciplines. The reputation of anthropologists as essentially ethnographers (producers of description and not theory) is a picture drawn largely from Boas or his students.

In actual fact Boasian skepticism did not characterize the discipline for long. To be sure, Lewis Henry Morgan and the other nineteenth-century "armchair theorists" were dismissed—and quite forcefully too (Lowie, 1920). But theoretical concerns quickly resurfaced. Wissler's theory of diffusion as explanation of social change in North America was an important early theory, and it was respected by the Boasians because of its heavy empirical base (Wissler, 1923). Boas's own *The Mind of Primitive Man* is not merely a refutation of the thought of others but also a powerful statement of a postulated psychic unity of human beings that survives to the present day (Boas, 1911). Anthropology also inherited the social Darwinism of the nineteenth century, which in the United States led to a concern for ecology and what were later to emerge as the ecologically oriented theories of Julian Steward and his followers. In the twenties Malinowski introduced Freudian theory to anthropology, and for better or worse psychoanalytically oriented theory dominated anthropological studies of childhood and personality into the seventies. Marxism or neo-Marxism came into play at various times, although Marx himself was treated badly or ignored by early twentieth-century anthropologists in the United States because of his reliance on the discredited L. H. Morgan for his theory and mid-twentieth-century anthropologists seemed unwilling to be publicly associated with Marxism. Boas's student Margaret Mead introduced American psychological theories of adolescence, and his student Douglas Haring wrote a theoretical treatment entitled *Or-*

der and Possibility in Social Life. (Haring & Johnson, 1940). Overtly a theoretical book, it is still characteristically Boasian, in that descriptive data "without interpretive comment" are presented before the theory-building section.

No discipline could survive without theoretical structures. All researchers, anthropologists or not, are theorists first and foremost. Boas himself was not against theory, but was rather against bad theory: bad in the sense of being inadequate to address known facts, and worse, often contradicted by such facts. His naive solution to the problem was to say to not build theory until after the facts are in. His advice, taken literally, would have put an end to scientific inquiry. Within the discipline its form was eventually abandoned for its substance. After all, the descriptive data presented by Haring and Johnson (1940) were collected with some idea in mind, and the researchers selected from all the available descriptions certain facts, with their theory at least implicitly guiding what they selected.

But others follow the form of Boas and not the substance. They never reach the theory, as even Mead and Haring did. They argue that anthropology must be essentially atheoretical and descriptive. This view is a misunderstanding not only of science in general, but of anthropology in particular. Parenthetically, it is a fault of educational researchers who have mastered the methods of anthropology but not its theory. To pursue this point it will be necessary to make explicit the link between theory building and ethnography. These educational ethnographers (they are often not trained anthropologists) are the ones who have recently come under implicit criticism by Hymes (1980), whose argument is that the promise of anthropology and education lies in ethnology, not ethnography. Ethnography is at heart idiographic, as Radcliffe-Brown defined it: "In an idiographic inquiry the purpose is to establish as acceptable certain particular or factual propositions or statements" (Radcliffe-Brown, 1952, p. 1). Ethnology, on the other hand, is nomothetic: "A nomothetic inquiry, on the contrary, has for its purpose to arrive at acceptable general propositions. . . . In anthropology, . . . the term ethnography applies to what is specifically a mode of idiographic inquiry, the aim of which is to give acceptable accounts of . . . peoples and their social life. . . . The ethnographer derives [one's] . . . knowledge, or some major part of it, from direct observation of or contact with the people about whom . . . [one] writes, and not, like the historian, from written records [alone]" (Radcliffe-Brown, 1951, p. 2). Ethnological studies, on the other hand, imply comparative generalization and are overtly theoretical albeit built upon the facts of ethnographic inquiry.

Ogbu offered a further distinction, between macroethnography and microethnography. In a macroethnographic educational inquiry, for example, the researcher goes beyond description of a particular school to examine such broader issues as how schooling is linked to other institu-

tions and "how societal forces, including beliefs and ideologies of the larger society, influence the behaviors of participants in the schools" (Ogbu, 1981, p. 13). These are comparisons within a culture. We can use the label "macroethnography" for ethnological inquiries whose comparisons do not cross cultural boundaries but are made with other levels and other institutions within the same culture.

Interestingly, although known for its ethnography, anthropological research related to education has been from the beginning ethnological. Whiting's pioneering study of the Kwoma was an overt effort to apply Hull/Dollard learning theory to derive an understanding of education in a New Guinea tribe; thus it was the application of a general theory to specific ethnographic data (Whiting, 1941, reprint 1979). Pettit's powerful study of education in native North America was a bold attempt to synthesize the ethnographic data on North American societies and build conclusions upon them for the purpose of general understanding (Pettit, 1946). Although Pettit's work was more overtly comparative than Whiting's, encompassing an entire continent rather than one tribe, Whiting's strong theoretical orientation forced his data into a comparative perspective implicit in the theory itself. Of course Whiting then turned to studies that were both theoretical and explicitly and broadly comparative, in his classic study of child training and personality in seventy-five societies (Whiting & Child, 1953). Spindler's concern for education as cultural transmission was broadly comparative, examining cultural systems in which a wide variety of teaching and learning techniques are utilized (Spindler, 1967). Suffice it to say here that the pioneers of the field were overtly ethnological.

Only recently, as large numbers of ethnographic studies have been done with little attention to theoretical or comparative issues, has an imbalance been created which some of today's researchers find disturbing. It is almost as if, for some researchers, anthropology is synonymous with ethnography alone. As Hymes has said, "An emphasis on the ethnological dimension takes one away from immediate problems and from attempts to offer immediate remedies, but it serves constructive change better in the long run. Emphasis on the ethnological dimension links anthropology of education with social history through examination of the ways in which larger forces for socialization, institutionalization and reproduction of an existing order are expressed and interpreted in specific settings. The longer view seems a surer footing." (Hymes, 1980, p. 5).

Hallmarks. The first hallmark of anthropological approaches to education and one that emerges directly from the previous discussion is the insistence that educational phenomena be examined in a cross-cultural framework. As such, anthropologists are not content with mere ethnography of one setting, but wish to place particular settings and behaviors in cross-cultural frames either implicitly or explicitly. Such comparisons are usually broader than those found within "comparative education" because that field is usually limited to societies with Western-influenced schools, whereas the anthropological inquiry is broad enough to include comparison across all human cultures. When studies of education in the United States do occur (and they do with ever increasing frequency, such research is at least implicitly put into some cross-cultural or cross-ethnic frame. The work is therefore ultimately ethnologic.

The second hallmark of anthropological approaches to education is the methodology brought to bear on the problems researched. Cultural, social, psychological, and other branches of anthropology herein described all share a dedication to the efficacy of a variety of techniques subsumed under the label "participant observation." By participant observation we mean not one technique but rather a mélange of strategies aimed at producing an accurate model of the behaviors of particular people (including the related problems of how people justify their behaviors to themselves and how they describe them to others). Participant observation is often—and wrongly—called a qualitative methodology when in fact it is a blending of qualitative and quantitative techniques and always has been (see Hymes, 1977). Participant observation is usually carried out in explicit or implicit combination with other strategies designed to elicit different sorts of data. Various subgroups in anthropology have developed their own ancillary methods in response to specific problems each has chosen to solve. Psychological anthropology, for example, has emphasized the importance of systematic observation and recording of data, collection of life and family histories, use of adaptations of the psychologist's assessment techniques, and so on. Participant observation does remain central in anthropological approaches to education, and this means the work is at base ethnographic.

A third orientation that sets anthropology apart from other disciplines studying education is that it takes a broad view of education, insisting that it not be confused with just schooling. This approach is due to the number of ethnographic studies showing education by parents or peers when no schools are present as well as to the prevalence of theoretical orientations stressing that education must encompass both formal and informal learning. Anthropologists' definitions of education have been so broad as to encompass nearly everything that is learned by a person through a lifetime, whereas definitions used by educators have occasionally been so narrow as to be limited to what a child learns through the formal curriculum of a school. The breadth of anthropologists' definitions of education is due in part to the eclecticism that characterizes the discipline itself, as well as to the orientation of the particular theoretical models that have been brought to bear on education.

Theoretical Orientations. We turn now to an overview of the current theoretical approaches in anthropology that have been used in, or are most likely to be useful to, an anthropology of education. Comitas and Dolgin (1978), in a summary of an extensive report on anthropology and education for the National Academy of Education, argued that the "approaches to anthropological inquiry with cur-

rent significance in the United States would perforce include the following [theoretical perspectives]: structural-functionalism (in its various modern guises); psychological anthropology; Weberian theory; neo-Weberian theory (associated particularly with Talcott Parsons and his students); ethnoscience; ethology; interactionalism and ethnomethodology; cultural ecology; structuralism; phenomenology; symbolic theory; and Marxist theory (in its several guises)" (Comitas and Dolgin, 1978, p. 169). They also point out that, although several of the approaches are congruent and in fact combinable, others are partially or wholly contradictory. I do not have space here to describe all the major trends in detail, but it is necessary to review some of them.

For many educators, cultural transmission is the most familiar approach, but the term can also, and more properly, be understood as the anthropological definition of education itself. "Culture transmission" examines the means by which, and the forms through which, values and attendant behavior are taught within the specific content of the societal, cultural, or group value system. The study of cultural transmission originated in a subbranch of anthropology labeled "culture and personality," a field concerned with the relationship between the individual and the culture. Preeminent in the field of culture and personality were issues that were easily related to education. How did a culture transmit itself from generation to generation (enculturation)? How do individuals adjust to change within their own lifetime (if the change is due to culture contact, acculturation)? Indeed the very label "cultural transmission," makes its ancestry clear. Further developments, however, that led to a relabeling of "culture and personality" as "psychological anthropology" or "cross-cultural human development" or more specialized fields like "cognitive anthropology" were slow to come to anthropology and education. These perspectives were designed to correct certain limitations of the older approaches, some of which continued in the culture transmission field. Most notable among these improvements was the reemphasis that socialization is not a simple transmittal from one generation to another, but a dynamic process through which differentiation and change can occur; that not all members of a culture are identical, and that these within-culture differences are worthy of study. This orientation, first articulated by Wallace, emphasized that one generation is not a replica of the last, nor is each individual a carbon copy of his other neighbor (Wallace, 1961). Indeed, the job of culture is to successfully organize such individual diversity for its own survival. The diversity that Wallace addressed goes beyond discontinuities betweeen statuses or institutions (see Spindler, 1967). It is a diversity of behaviors acceptable within such patterns.

A second limitation of the cultural transmission approach was that, as Ogbu suggested (1981), cultural transmission studies of formal education focus almost entirely on school, classroom, home, and playground and ignore other societal institutions. Although it is recognized that schooling is just one type of cultural transmission, the field has focused on persons who have direct contact with children and ignored such indirect influences as social class. It has also generally ignored the possibility of adult learning.

Anthropologists concerned with psychological anthropology had meanwhile turned their attention to a systematic examination of cross-cultural variations in learning, socialization, and social change. As Harrington (1979) viewed the field, psychological anthropology has a goal of explaining the diversity of human cultures and how cultures, and hence their diversity, are maintained over time. The latter explanation lies in the abiliy of the culture to transmit itself from one generation to another and, in the process, to grow and incorporate change. Psychological anthropology offers perspectives on three areas critical to an anthropology of education: perception and cognition, socialization, and social change. In studies of perception and cognition—the learning process itself—we must be concerned with what individuals learn, what they can be aware of (which is a precondition to learning), and what they do with their perceptions. Taken together, studies of perception and cognition describe how people experience their world and think about it (Harrington, 1979) and how these processes occur or vary in all human societies. Through socialization individuals become members of particular groups, learning ranges of actions and beliefs which are acceptable or possible, how to perceive "reality," and how to change aspects of it. Socialization is conceptualized not as a filling of an empty vessel but as a dynamic process by which individuals learn to structure reality in ways that enable them to sort out and make sense of the diverse stimuli that form their environment and to behave in ways congruent with others' expectations of them in the social process. Students of socialization are sometimes criticized for taking a conservative view of the world by seeing societies as if they were in equilibrium or static. This view, however, is not due to the socialization model itself, but rather to the view of society held by some authors. In discussions of socialization, cultures are often treated as stable. But if one defines society as made up of factions in competition for scarce resources, socialization approaches would need to account for the ways people learn to participate in such competing systems (see Harrington, 1979, chap. 2). In research on sociocultural change, psychological anthropologists have studied acculturative processes and change in various societies, including the effects of change upon individual actors. Within psychological anthropology studies of culture change have included change due to contact across cultures (acculturation) as well as change generated within cultures owing to revolutionary or revitalizing forces (Wallace, 1961).

As Comitas and Dolgin (1978) have pointed out, social anthropology, including structural-functional theory, provides tools for describing the social structures that mediate between the more global concepts of society and the individual and that offer the frames within which individuals' choices are constrained in particular social contexts. Before the psychological anthropologist can study learning processes, the social anthropologist's tools are necessary to lay out the frames within which learning occurs and the behaviors they encompass. There has been a heavy commitment to analysis of social structure since Firth defined it (1964) as the establishment of precedents and the providing and limiting of the range of alternatives. In contrast, "social organization" involves the decisions individuals actually make among sets of possible actions, yielding information about the systematic ordering of social relations. This emphasis has been particularly noticeable in studies that view classrooms as social structures. But this is only one imbalance. Under the rubric of "social anthropology" is included a rich diversity of theoretical perspectives not all of which have been fully developed as they apply to education: structural-functional theory, Weberian and neo-Weberian theory, structuralism, and Marxist theory in its various guises. Linkages through social anthropology to sociology of education have been limited, although historically the field shares much with sociology. (This situation parallels an interesting pattern in that psychological anthropologists have been more likely to work collaboratively with psychologists than with educational psychologists.)

Symbolic anthropology is related to aspects of both psychological and social anthropology. It is concerned with codes through which meaning originates, is expressed, defined, and changed, and is shared through interaction and communication. It attempts to ascertain the systems of symbolic forms that educators and students use to act and define educational environments. Through the analysis of symbols, linkages between educational institutions and other institutions can be examined and underlying structures revealed. The use of the concept of symbol is close to Bion's notion of transformations, in which various realities are transformed into symbolic forms that give them meaning (Bion, 1965). We include in symbolic anthropology ethnoscience, or inquiries into classification systems and logic in other cultures; interactionalism, or studies of symbolic interaction; phenomenology; and symbolic theory.

Implications for Policy. The stuff of anthropology can bear directly on educational policy, and the number of applied anthropologists doing research in education and involved in planning educational programming around the world increases rapidly. The job facing educators is often similar to the main-line anthropological skills of description, generalization, and synthesis. The tools of ethnography, the concepts of ethnology, and the broad definition of what is educative provide a basis for educational programming properly grounded in knowledge about needs, goals, and opportunities of individuals. Although anthropology is thoroughly grounded in the particular—how this school, this classroom, this child can be affected—it is wedded to a general frame in which specific knowledge can be generalized and made useful in other settings. Policy makers are often wary of anthropology because ethnography can be a time-consuming and expensive methodology, but this is a misunderstanding of the full potentialities of the discipline.

Although some have criticized the field for taking so long to collect data that there can be limited policy impact, it seems that a more reasoned criticism might equally address the tendency of policy makers to intrude on the basis of their own perceptions of others' needs, and to implement without adequate knowledge of the impact of general policy on the particular people involved or of such people's own perceptions of their needs. The major effects of the discipline to date have been indirect, one might argue: correction of culture-bound practices in assessment, use of knowledge about how change happens in complex organizations, assumptions about the meaning of change. But the real test of the usefulness of anthropology to education will wait for incorporation of the full range of what anthropology has to offer into the habits of the education policy maker/researcher. As Comitas and Dolgin pointed out, the ultimate testing of any policy can take place only in a world where people actually live. "In abstracting from reality the anthropologist, like other social scientists, selects some parts for study (and then reexamines them against actual behaviors and activities). . . . This procedure is conceptually similar to one long employed by those formulating action programs and by those responsible for policy implementation . . . [but] is a research task uniquely suited to the interests and strengths of anthropology" (Comitas & Dolgin, 1978, p. 176).

It is in fact the great strength of anthropology that it strives to deal simultaneously with the particular and the general. Policy that is concerned only with general rules often falls down in the translation of the general into specific times and places. Policy generated totally from particular problems is of dubious utility in other settings. It is the anthropologists' unique perspective that enables them to see both the general and the particular. As Arensberg argued years ago, anthropologist' views of particular communities allow them a perspective that examines how the general laws of the larger society are translated into action at the local level (Arensberg & Kimball, 1965). Indeed, Arensberg and Kimball argued that it is only at the community level that such an examination can be made. Congress, for example, may think it has successfully implemented desegregation in schools by mandating certain criteria in terms of percentages of students who are black or white or so on in each school. But the ethnography of a particular school shows that within each grade there is one all-white class and the rest of the classes are all-minority. Is this integration? Or take an evaluation of a federally funded program, such as Title I. Such evaluations have taken place on the basis of the effect of the program on the child, without ever bothering to observe whether in fact the particular programming that was funded was implemented. The real potential of anthropology for policy makers is that it makes it possible, by following established methodological and disciplined procedures, to examine the particular cases as tests of the need for, and efficacy of, policies made at other levels, and that it does so through direct observation of and involvement with those themselves most affected by the policies.

Charles C. Harrington

See also Culture and Education Policy; Ethnography; Family Studies; Sociology of Education.

REFERENCES

Arensberg, C., & Kimball, S. *Culture and Community*. New York: Harcourt, Brace, 1965.

Bion, W. R. *Transformations*. New York: Basic Books, 1965.

Boas, F. *The Mind of Primitive Man*. New York: Macmillan, 1911.

Comitas, L., & Dolgin, J. On Anthropology and education: retrospect and prospect. *Anthropology and Education Quarterly*, 1978, *9*, 165–180.

Firth, R. *Essays on Social Organization and Values*. London: The Athlone Press, 1964.

Haring D., & Johnson, M. *Order and Possibility in Social Life*. New York: Richard R. Smith, 1940.

Harrington, C. *Psychological Anthropology and Education*. New York: AMS Press, 1979.

Hymes, D. Qualitative/quantitative research methodologies in education: A linguistic perspective. *Anthropology and Education Quarterly*, 1977, *8*, 165–176.

Hymes, D. Educational ethnology. *Anthropology and Education Quarterly*, 1980, *11*, 3–8.

Kluckhohn, C. *Culture and Behavior*. New York: Free Press, 1965.

Kroeber, A., & Kluckhohn, C. *Culture*. Vol. 47 of Papers of the Peabody Museum, Cambridge, Mass., 1952.

Lowie, R. *Primitive Society*. New York: Liveright, 1920.

Ogbu, J. School ethnography: A multilevel approach. *Anthropology and Education Quarterly*, 1981, *12*, 3–29.

Pettit, G. Primitive education in North America. *University of California Publications in American Archaeology and Ethnology*, 1946, *43*, 1–182.

Radcliffe-Brown, A. *Structure and Function in Primitive Society*. Glenroe, Ill.: Free Press, 1952.

Spindler, G. The transmission of culture. In A. Beals, G. Spendler, & L. Spindler (Eds.) *Culture in Process*. New York: Holt, Rinehart & Winston, 1967.

Wallace, A. *Culture and Personality*. New York: Random House, 1961.

Whiting, J. *Becoming a Kwoma: Teaching and Learning in a New Guinea Tribe*. New York: AMS Press, 1979. (Originally published, New Haven: Yale University Press, 1941.)

Whiting, J., & Child, I. *Child Training and Personality*. New Haven: Yale University Press, 1953.

Wissler, C. *Man and Culture*. New York: Thomas Y. Crowell, 1923.

APTITUDE MEASUREMENT

For the past eighty years psychologists have been using various labels such as "intelligence," "aptitude," and "ability" to identify a construct (or set of constructs) that seems to be useful in helping to predict various kinds of behaviors. The tests designed to measure this construct (or set of constructs) vary to some extent because of different definitions of the construct. For purposes of discussion aptitude measurements can be grouped into three categories: (1) tests that give a general measure of aptitude, (2) tests that give measures of multiple aptitudes, and (3) tests that are measures of specific aptitudes. But first we will discuss the use of various terms and present some definitions.

Terminology and Definitions. The terms "aptitude," "ability," "intelligence," and "achievement" are used interchangeably by some, although others suggest that subtle shades of meaning distinguish them. The first three terms are considered to have the most meaning in common.

The distinction between the terms "aptitude" and "intelligence" is not at all clear, but intelligence is generally thought of as a broader construct. Cleary et al. (1975) define intelligence as "the entire repertoire of acquired skills, knowledge, learning sets, and generalization tendencies considered intellectual in nature that are available at any one period in time" (p. 19). "Aptitude as a construct refers to psychological characteristics of individuals that predispose and thus predict differences in later learning under specified instructional conditions" (Snow, 1980, p. 41). To the extent the constructs differ, the operational definitions of the terms should differ. Most writers would feel the task of establishing construct validity for a test labeled an intelligence test would be more challenging than establishing the construct validity of an aptitude test. Because the tests designated as "intelligence tests" generally do not have a high degree of construct validity for most definitions of intelligence, most current test experts would prefer to use the term "aptitude." Because these tests are most useful in predicting school success, many believe the phrase "scholastic aptitude test" is the most honest and descriptive (Anastasi, 1976; Cronbach, 1970; Mehrens & Lehmann, 1980). The term "intelligence" is also more apt to connote innateness than does the term "aptitude"; and since what is measured by any current test is at least partly subject to environmental influences, the term "aptitude" may be less likely to be misinterpreted (Cronbach, 1970; Mehrens & Lehmann, 1980). Michael (1960) suggested that "ability" would be preferred to "aptitude" in most situations, but that many people in the testing field use the term "ability" when prediction of future success is the primary purpose of the test. Anastasi (1980) has said that if she could eliminate four words from the tester's vocabulary she would choose "intelligence," "aptitudes," "abilities," and "achievement." If she had to retain one term, it would be "abilities." The basic reason for wishing to eliminate the terms is their acquisition of too many connotative meanings.

Test publishers seem generally to agree with those who prefer to use the terms with a more narrow meaning. Thus they have modified the titles of their tests, moving in general away from the terms "intelligence" and "aptitude" and toward the use of the term "ability." For example, the Otis-Lennon School Ability Test was previously referred to as the Otis-Lennon Mental Ability Test. The Cognitive Abilities Test was previously called an intelligence test, and the Short Form Test of Academic Aptitude was previously called a mental maturity test (Lennon, 1980). Yet, as Lennon (1980) points out, "there is a certain equivocation or ambivalence on the part of their [the tests] authors as to whether the tests continue to be intelligence or mental ability tests, or should be regarded only as measures of school learning ability" (p. 3).

As mentioned, aptitude, ability, and intelligence are probably considered more similar to each other than they are to achievement. Whether aptitude and achievement should be thought of as separate concepts has been the subject of much debate. Kelley (1927) defined the jangle fallacy as "the use of two separate words or expressions covering in fact the same basic situation, but sounding different, as though they were in truth different" (p. 64). He believed that intelligence and achievement tests were examples of the jangle fallacy. Many other psychologists from his time to the present have also believed that the two types of tests are quite similar. Carroll (1974), however, notes that we must distinguish between aptitude as a *construct* and *indicants* of aptitude. He states that "it is difficult to see why there should be any great difficulty in distinguishing between aptitude and achievement as *concepts*. . . . if aptitude for a learning task is measured prior to an individual's engaging in a task, and if achievement on the task is measured after a given amount of exposure to the learning task, the concepts of aptitude and achievement are operationally distinguishable" (p. 287).

Whether or not, or to what extent, the measures of aptitude and achievement differ is more debatable. Kaiser (1974), for example, believes that the measures might well be different based upon what he admits are two very nonscientific sources: "I have been writing test items . . . for more than 20 years, and I know damn good and well when I am writing an achievement item. . . . Over the years I have consulted with approximately 40 million teachers . . . and all of them, without exception, firmly believe that achievement relative to aptitude can be measured; indeed, they claim to measure it all the time. . . . Can 40 million teachers be wrong? Not completely, is my guess" (pp. 345–346).

There is certainly no hard-and-fast rule that allows us to distinguish an achievement test from an aptitude test by cursory examination of the test format. Furthermore, both tests do measure behavior, and the behavior measured is acquired rather than innate. However, aptitude and achievement tests do frequently differ along several dimensions: (1) general aptitude tests typically have broader coverage than achievement tests; (2) achievement tests are more closely tied to particular school subjects; (3) achievement tests typically measure recent learning, whereas aptitude tests sample learning from all times in the individual's past; (4) studies generally show that aptitude tests have higher heritability indexes than achievement tests; and (5) the purpose of aptitude tests is to predict future performance; the purpose of achievement tests is to measure the present level of knowledge or skills.

Aptitude and achievement tests are sometimes classified according to the degree to which the tasks within a test are dependent upon formal school learning. This distinction is a matter of degree. Some aptitude tests are more like achievement tests than others. As the test tasks become more and more dependent upon specific educational instruction, the test becomes more and more an achievement test. Being more dependent on specific school instruction, achievement tests are more environmentally influenced than aptitude tests.

Cronbach (1970) suggests that aptitude tests can be arranged along a continuum. Tests at one extreme are strictly measures of the outcomes of education; these resemble achievement tests in content and usefulness. Tests at the other extreme are those whose scores are fairly independent of specific instruction. In general, the more content-oriented an aptitude test, the more useful it is in predicting future school success in the same content area, but the less useful it is in predicting general future learning.

In summary, several possible distinctions have been suggested between aptitude tests and achievement tests. If the author's purpose is to develop a predictive instrument, it will no doubt be called an aptitude test. If the purpose is to develop an instrument to measure past performance, it will be called an achievement test. For the latter goal the test items will be based on past school instruction; for the former goal that may or may not be the case. However, regardless of what an author calls a test, its uses may vary. Many achievement tests, like aptitude tests, are used to predict. This is ordinarily quite appropriate.

General Scholastic Aptitude Tests. General scholastic aptitude tests are used primarily for two broad purposes: (1) educational decision making of various types in the elementary and secondary schools, and (2) admissions decisions for higher education. Tests for the first general purpose are given most frequently at the middle and upper elementary grades. For the second purpose, tests are given to high school juniors or seniors and to college students if they desire to apply for graduate or professional schools.

Many tests, designed to give a measure of general scholastic aptitude, actually give scores on two (or more) subtests. These may be given such titles as verbal and nonverbal scales or language and performance scales. It is always hard to know just when to consider a test a measure of general aptitude and when to consider it a measure of multiple aptitudes. The classification is not solely dependent upon the number of subscores. The author's definition of aptitude and the method of constructing the tests are primarily what determines the classification.

The tests used for elementary and secondary school decision making would in many cases contain items that measure verbal abilities (e.g., vocabulary, opposites, sentence completion); reasoning abilities (e.g., analogies, classifica-

tion, number series, inference); quantitative skills; information; and memory (Lennon, 1980).

The tests used for higher education admission decisions measure many of the same skills, but at a much higher level. The two tests most commonly used in undergraduate college admission decisions are the ACT Assessment Program and the Scholastic Aptitude Test (SAT). The former contains subtests in English, mathematics, social studies, and natural sciences. The Scholastic Aptitude Test reports verbal, mathematical, and English scores.

Tests such as the Graduate Record Examination (GRE) Aptitude Test and the Miller Analogies Test are used to assist in graduate admission decisions. The GRE Aptitude Test provides two scores: verbal and quantitative; the Miller Analogies test provides only one.

Tests also exist that are designed to assist in admission decisions for professional schools. Examples are the Law School Admission Test (LSAT) (two scores: aptitude and writing ability) and the Medical College Admission Test (MCAT) (six scores: biology, chemistry, physics, science problems, reading skills analysis, and quantitative skills analysis). Most measurement experts would probably classify these tests as specific aptitude tests rather than measures of general scholastic aptitude since they are designed to predict performance in a particular type of professional training.

Aptitude Test Use in Public Schools. The results of the tests given in the elementary schools are used in instructional, guidance, administrative, and research decision making. We will not discuss the various decisions in detail (see Mehrens & Lehmann, 1980). The two types of use that are most debated are using scholastic aptitude tests for homogeneous ability grouping and using them for placement into special education classes such as those for the mentally retarded. We will not discuss the latter controversy here because typically individually administered tests are used for that decision.

Homogeneous ability grouping. Those who are opposed to the use of scholastic aptitude tests for homogeneous ability grouping are actually opposed to the decision being made rather than opposed to the use of scholastic aptitude test data to help make the decision.

If the policy, right or wrong, is to group on the basis of ability, it is appropriate to use an aptitude test to help decide who should be placed in what group. Some have argued that tests are unfair to different subgroups, and therefore the test results should be ignored when doing ability grouping. However, although one should not use test data alone, Findley (1974) reported that Kariger has shown that such a process would result in less separation of upper and lower socioeconomic status (SES) students than would result from the use of other factors in addition to test scores—for example, teacher grades, study habits, citizenship and industry, and social and emotional maturity. As Findley (1974) explains, "stereotypes of upper and lower SES children held by school personnel result in further separation between groups than the tests alone would warrant" (p. 25). This example is not meant to advocate ability grouping or decisions made only upon test data. It does suggest that blaming tests for what may be considered harmful social separation is inappropriate.

Teacher expectancies.   A argument that has occasionally been voiced against the use of aptitude tests for instructional purposes is that teachers will use low aptitude scores as an excuse for not attempting to teach students. Unfortunately, it is probably true that some teachers have this attitude. Aptitude test scores should be used in helping teachers form realistic expectations of students; they should not be used to help teachers develop fatalistic expectations.

Although measurement specialists would not condone—in fact, would condemn—teachers who develop fatalistic attitudes toward the learning abilities of their students, they do not think that aptitude tests should be made the scapegoat. We admit this potential misuse of tests. There is little evidence, however, to suggest that teachers' attitudes toward the learning potential of their students are unduly influenced by test results. A 1973 teachers opinion poll of National Education Association members shows, for example, that six teachers in ten thought that group IQ test scores predicted poorly or not at all the ability of physically handicapped pupils. Three teachers in four thought the test predicted poorly or not at all the ability of socially or culturally different pupils. However, seven in ten thought the tests predicted very well or fairly well the ability of pupils other than the handicapped (Teacher Opinion Poll, 1974). Obviously, the teachers sampled in this poll were not (as a group) overinfluenced by test results. Goslin (1967), in a comprehensive survey of teachers' opinions about tests, found that less than one-fourth of the teachers felt that abilities measured by aptitude tests are more important than other qualities for predicting school success.

Discovery of talent.   One area in which aptitude testing is being used increasingly is in the discovery of talent. At the time of this writing, there is a growing awareness of the importance of providing appropriate educational experiences for the gifted. Aptitude tests are certainly one of the tools used to identify the gifted and talented. They are especially useful among youth who have been educationally deprived since aptitude tests are less influenced by specific educational experiences than are achievement tests.

College Admission Testing.   Many colleges have limited resources and cannot admit everyone who applies. In general, college admission officers have felt that their job was to admit those who have the greatest probability of success in college. The criterion for judging success has typically been grades. Time and again it has been shown that high school grades are the best single predictor of college grades, that scholastic aptitude tests are the second best predictors, and that the two predictors combined in a multiple regression equation give a significantly better prediction than either one alone. The average correlation

between high school performance and first-year college grades is around .50 to .55. When scholastic aptitude tests are added as a predictor, the multiple correlation is raised from .05 to .10 points (Astin, 1971; Hills, 1964). Research suggests that biographical data, interviews, references, personality variables and work samples have seldom added any practical precision to the prediction process (Hills, 1971). Thus, research clearly shows that if the admissions staff wishes to admit students on the basis of predicted success in college, scholastic aptitude tests are useful.

Some people are opposed to the use of scholastic aptitude tests in college admissions decisions. It is sometimes unclear whether they oppose the notion of selecting college students on the basis of predicted success in college or whether they oppose the use of scholastic aptitude tests in assisting in that prediction. If the former, that is a philosophical point and should be argued separately from the issue of whether tests help in predicting success. If the latter, they should read the research literature. As Samuda (1975) states, "the evidence about college entrance tests as predictors is no longer a subject of legitimate dispute. The studies have been widespread, they number in the thousands, and the results are consistent. By and large, the higher the test scores, the more successful the students are in college" (p. viii). In fact, there is also evidence that academic aptitude at time of college admission is significantly related to occupational level later in life (Lewis, 1975).

Some of the specific concerns about using scholastic aptitude tests in college admission are (1) that they have potential bias, (2) that they are coachable, (3) that they are overemphasized in the decision-making process, and (4) that the cutoff score is or can be set inappropriately.

Bias.   Scholastic aptitude tests have often been severely criticized for their "cultural biases." This term has been defined in so many ways, however, that one can never be completely sure of the meaning of the criticism. There are three common interpretations of cultural bias. To some, a test is considered culturally biased if different subgroups obtain different mean scores on the test. To others, a test is culturally biased if it measures different constructs (or achievements) for different subcultures. Still others consider the issue of cultural bias in terms of differential prediction equations and/or different selection ratios or success ratios (see Flaugher, 1978, for a nontechnical summary discussion).

Many measurement experts prefer the third definition, since it focuses upon the fair use of tests rather than upon the tests themselves. With respect to the first two definitions regarding the tests themselves, nonmeasurement specialists who are critics of testing are more likely to use the first definition (e.g., tests are unfair to blacks if the mean score for blacks is lower than the mean score for whites). Measurement specialists are more likely to prefer the second definition to the first: a test is biased if it measures something different in different subcultures. Now, a test biased in the second sense will probably (but not necessarily) be biased in the first sense. The logic is much less compelling in the opposite direction.

Clearly the second kind of bias is bad. It leads to incorrect and harmful inferences to assume that children are inadequate in one area when in fact they have been measured (unknowingly) on something else. Test constructors try to avoid building tests that will have such biases. Research evidence (Jensen, 1980) tends to indicate that publishers are generally quite successful in minimizing this kind of bias, but they surely have not eliminated it (Williams, 1974).

With respect to the third definition of fair use, Cleary (1968) has offered the following definition: "A test is biased for members of a subgroup of the population if, in the prediction of a criterion for which the test was designed, consistent nonzero errors of prediction are made for members of the subgroup. In other words, the test is biased if the criterion score predicted from the common regression line is consistently too high or too low for members of the subgroup. With this definition of bias, there may be a connotation of "unfair," particularly if the use of the test produces a prediction that is too low" (p. 115). Even this precise definition is an incomplete guideline. Hunter and Schmidt (1976) define three mutually incompatible ethical prositions in regard to the fair and unbiased use of tests, present five statistical definitions of test bias, and show how they are related to the three ethical positions. These positions are (1) unqualified individualism, (2) qualified individualism, and (3) quotas. The unqualified individualism position in employment would be to give the job to the person best qualified to serve. According to this position it would be unethical not to use whatever information increases the predictive validity of performance even if such information is sex or ethnic group membership. The unqualified individualist interprets "discriminate" to mean treat unfairly, and to refuse to recognize a difference between groups would result in unfair treatment. The qualified individualist believes it is unethical to use information about race, sex, and so on, even if it were scientifically valid to do so. "The qualified individualist interprets the word *discriminate* to mean *treat differently*" (Hunter & Schmidt, 1976, p. 1054). The quota position is that the ethical response is to give every well-defined group (e.g., black, white; male, female; Protestant, Catholic, Jew) its "fair share" of desirable positions. "The person who endorses quotas interprets *discriminate* to mean *select a higher proportion of persons from one group than from the other group.*" (Hunter & Schmidt, 1976, p. 1054)

The Cleary definition (1968) is an example of unqualified individualism; and according to her definition, unreliable tests are biased against whites and in favor of blacks with respect to predicting performance in college (Cleary, 1968; Hills, 1964; Hills & Gladney, 1966; Hills, Klock, & Lewis, 1963; Kallingal, 1971; Munday, 1965; Pfeifer & Sedlacek, 1971; Silverman, Barton, & Lyon, 1976; Stanley & Porter, 1967; Temp, 1971). Findley and Bryan (1971) found much the same thing in reviewing the research on different tests used in the elementary grades. This overprediction would be a test bias in one sense of the word, but certainly not unfair to the minority groups. Thomas and Stanley (1969) have clearly shown that scholastic aptitude tests are better than high school grades for predicting college grades of black students. This is the reverse of findings for white students. Stanley (1971), in a thorough review of predicting college success of the educational disadvantaged, urged a reversal of the then current trend of waiving test scores in admitting disadvantaged applicants. He felt that the more disadvantaged an applicant, the more objective information one needs about him.

Thorndike (1971) and Darlington (1971) have argued for different approaches, which Hunter and Schmidt show to be forms of quota setting. Darlington suggests that the term "cultural fairness" be replaced with the term "cultural optimality," which would include a subjective policy-level decision on the relative importance of two goals: maximizing test validity and minimizing test discrimination.

The entire spring 1976 issue of the *Journal of Educational Measurement* was devoted to the topic of bias in selection. Peterson and Novick (1976), in a detailed evaluation of the existing models for culture-fair selection, ultimately conclude that "the concepts of culture fairness and group parity are neither useful nor tenable. . . . The problem, we think, should be reconceptualized as a problem in maximizing expected utility" (see Hunter, Schmidt, & Rauschenberger, 1977). Novick and Ellis (1977) argue that "an acceptable solution must (1) be based on statistical decision theory, which emphasizes the concept of utility rather than fairness to groups; (2) address individuals as individuals without regard to race, sex, or ethnic origin, except under narrowly delineated conditions carefully defined; (3) take direct account of individual disadvantage in providing compensation; and (4) employ more effective methods than those of group parity when race, sex, or ethnic origin are required as classifiers" (p. 307).

Coaching. Critics of scholastic aptitude tests have claimed that students can be coached to do better on such tests and that therefore the tests are unfair (since some individuals have more access to coaching than others) and invalid (since coaching shows that the tests are not measuring "a student's capacity to learn") (Slack & Porter, 1980). Rebuttals to this position suggest that it is useful to distinguish between short-range coaching effects and more extended instructional effects; that short-range coaching effects have not, in general, proven to be very powerful; and that instructional effects do not invalidate scholastic aptitude tests because they are not intended to be measures of capacity impervious to education but, rather, measures of developed abilities (Jackson, 1980). Messick (1980), in a comprehensive look at the coaching issue, makes many cogent points; a few of them are paraphrased here as follows. (1) The interpretation of the results of research on coaching is equivocal because of the absence of randomization in the studies. The results could be due to self-selection factors. (2) Coaching studies have not addressed the question of whether increased scores reflect ability improvements or increased "test-wiseness." (3) Since scholastic aptitude tests measure developed abilities acquired gradually through both instruction and experience, one should expect high-quality instruction to result in improved scores. (4) The soundest mode of preparation for scholastic aptitude tests would be a secondary school program emphasizing the development of thought and knowledge.

Influence upon admissions decisions.   The issue here is twofold: how much are scholastic aptitude tests weighted in admissions decisions, and how much should they be? Neither question can be answered unambiguously. Certainly many colleges do not weigh scholastic aptitude tests at all. Students are not required to take any such test to get into many colleges. Of course, there are colleges that are more selective and do consider scholastic aptitude test results in their admission decisions. Competitive graduate and professional schools also typically consider such tests (GRE, LSAT, MCAT) in admissions decisions. The weight placed upon the test scores varies considerably from college to college, but most colleges would probably count the test scores as less important than other variables such as previous grades. How much such tests should be weighted is both a philosophical and mathematical question. Any time selection decisions are made, some individuals get admitted and some do not. If resources are limited, who "deserves" the limited resources is a policy question. If it is believed that admission to a college having limited enrollment should be based upon predicted academic success, if test scores increase the predictive accuracy (they do), and if the admissions offices use the test scores correctly in a regression equation (or set of regression equations, differentiated according to ethnicity, sex, or whatever other demographic variable would increase predictive efficiency) to help predict success, then measurement specialists would argue that the test was weighted correctly given the policy decisions.

Cutoff score.   Most colleges using scholastic aptitude tests do not set a minimum cutoff score (Lerner, 1980). Of course, eventually decisions get made, but they are based upon a predicted criterion using several predictor variables. As mentioned above, this is usually based upon a linear multiple regression equation. For very selective schools, it has been argued that scholastic aptitude scores are not linearly related to the criterion and that one should set a cutting score on the aptitude test at the point where the curve's slope approaches zero and randomly (or quota) select among individuals who exceed this score. This issue is highly related to the previous one, and "answers" depend upon both philosophical and empirical considerations. The empirical consideration is whether, in fact, the relationship is nonlinear and approaches zero slope for the top predictor scores. The philosophical considerations are similar to those in the previous issue. Who should be admitted is always, in the final analysis, a philosophical or policy issue. (It is, of course, also a legal issue. In general,

the courts have said that one cannot discriminate on the basis of race, religion, nationality, or sex, but there have been some legal decisions which have permitted discrimination in favor of minorities.)

Multifactor Aptitude Tests.   Many psychologists and educators believe it worthwhile to obtain measures of several (six to twenty) fairly broad aspects of one's aptitude. For example, many schools administer a multifactor aptitude test at some stage of a student's school career.

One aspect that has led to the increased popularity of multifactor aptitude tests is the vocational and educational counseling movement. The discovery of differential abilities within a person should certainly facilitate vocational and educational counseling. But does it? Some argue that identification of differential abilities is helpful in counseling only to the extent that this knowledge allows us to predict differentially how well an individual will be able to perform in various educational curricula or vocational tasks. The degree to which multifactor tests enable us to predict differentially is an important aspect in determining their usefulness.

In general, the data indicate that multifactor aptitude tests are not very good for differential prediction. This is not solely because of test inadequacies in subdividing intellect into its component subparts. The problem is that the criteria (for example, job success) are not solely dependent upon certain differential aptitudes. Thus, although we may be able to obtain measures of numerical ability and verbal ability that are distinct, there simply is not any criterion that differentially demands one aptitude and not the other. Therefore, there is little evidence of differential predictive validity. Whether this makes the test no more useful than the less expensive and less time-consuming test of general scholastic aptitude depends upon the degree to which one believes that a more precise description is useful in counseling, regardless of whether it increases predictability. As with any belief, there are differences of opinion on this. It is not a belief easily subjected to scientific verification.

The three most widely used multifactor aptitude tests are probably the Differential Aptitude Test (DAT), the General Aptitude Test Battery (GATB), and the Armed Services Vocational Aptitude Battery (ASVAB). The DAT is used primarily in the public schools for future vocational and educational planning. The GATB is used primarily by the United States Employment Serivce in vocational counseling and job placement. The ASVAB is used to stimulate interest in various military service opportunities. In general, the first two tests are considered to be more psychometrically sound than the latter. More detailed information about the tests can be found in Buros (1978) or in a basic measurement textbook such as Mehrens and Lehmann (1980).

Special-aptitude Tests.   A special aptitude is usually defined as a person's developed ability to acquire proficiency in a specified type of activity. Special-aptitude tests were developed primarily for help in making vocational and educational selection decisions as well as for counseling. Compared to multifactor aptitude tests, they are probably more useful in selection (or placement) decisions by an institution and generally less useful in personal counseling for individual decision making.

Although many kinds of special-aptitude tests could be mentioned in this section, we will not discuss any particular test because all readers will not be interested in the same areas. There are tests of vision and hearing, mechanical aptitude tests, clerical and stenographic aptitude tests, and musical and artistic aptitude tests. Those interested in a more thorough coverage of any test or area of testing should turn to books such as those by Anastasi (1976) or Cronbach (1970). We briefly discuss aptitude tests for specific courses and professions and tests of creativity.

Specific courses and professions. Aptitude tests developed for particular school subjects such as algebra and foreign languages have been used in the past to help individual pupils with their curricular choice. In recent years, however, this practice has diminished. Research has shown that such tests generally do not significantly increase the predictive validity over what can be obtained by a general mental ability test, the relevant subscores on multifactor aptitude tests, or achievement test batteries. Because these latter tests are usually given in the schools, it may well be a waste of time and money to administer special-aptitude tests.

Many special-aptitude tests, such as the Law School Admission Test and the Medical College Admission Test, have been developed in recent years for use in various graduate and professional schools. We have already addressed their uses under the discussion of general scholastic aptitude tests. These tests are designed to be of appropriate difficulty (harder than general aptitude tests for adults) and emphasize the abilities of importance to the particular profession.

Creativity. Although research findings are somewhat equivocal, there is some evidence to indicate that creativity is a distinct ability from intelligence or general scholastic aptitude. Research seems to indicate that whereas a person has to be reasonably intelligent to be creative, the converse does not hold. Butcher (1968) reports good correspondence between general aptitude and creativity test scores up to an IQ score of around 120, but above that there is little relationship between intelligence and creativity. In other words, a reasonably high level of intelligence appears to be a necessary but not sufficient condition for creativity. Although the majority of psychologists subscribe to the notion that creativity is something beyond (or different from) general intelligence or scholastic aptitude, the problem is that it is difficult to agree on constructual definitions of creativity, let alone operational definitions. Even if we could agree on an operational definition, it would be difficult to indicate validity for the measure because of the absence of an adequate criterion measure. Does creativity imply a creative process or a creative product? Or does the former lead to the latter? Is a creative

person one who comes up with a variety of unique ideas or one who has a variety of unique good ideas? That is, is there simply a quantity criterion or also a quality criterion for judging creativity? If a person is asked, as in the Torrance Tests of Creative Thinking, to name as many uses of a cardboard box as one can think of, how should the results be scored? Torrance has created a scoring scheme, but it is doubtful if all would agree with it. As has been pointed out, the distinction between creative and asinine ideas is often hard to make. Most people feel that the production of a large number of unworkable ideas is of little use, and to measure this type of creativity is a waste of time.

We feel that more research on attempts to measure creativity and to investigate its correlates is warranted. Enough evidence is now available to suggest that creativity is something unique and not necessarily correlated with ability to perform well in an academic setting. (However, it is a misconception that creative children do poorly in schoolwork. Research shows that, as a group, creative children do quite well in school.) There are many potential benefits available if the construct of creativity can be effectively isolated and measured. Creative people are important for an advancing society. If creativity can be further understood, if the identification of creative people becomes possible, and if creativity can be taught in the schools, society is sure to benefit.

At the present time there are few creativity tests on the market. The tests that do exist should be considered only as research instruments, and much more work is needed in the area before we can really feel comfortable with the results that these tests give us. Fortunately, this entire area is being carefully investigated, and it is possible that psychologists will soon have more adequate tests available. For further reading on this interesting topic, refer to Crockenberg (1972), Getzels and Jackson (1962), Guilford (1967), Hudson (1966), Torrance (1962, 1965), and Wallach and Kogan (1965).

William A. Mehrens

See also Achievement Testing; Admission to Colleges and Universities; Individual Differences; Intelligence; Intelligence Measurement; Measurement in Education; Norms and Scales; Prediction Methods.

REFERENCES

Anastasi, A. *Psychological Testing* (4th ed.). New York: Macmillan, 1976.

Anastasi, A. Abilities and the measurement of achievement. In W. B. Schrader (Ed.), *New Directions for Testing and Measurement: Measuring Achievement; Progress Over a Decade* (No. 5). San Francisco: Jossey-Bass, 1980.

Astin, A. W. *Predicting Academic Performance in College.* New York: Free Press, 1971.

Buros, O. K. (Ed.). *The Eighth Mental Measurements Yearbook.* Highland Park, N.J.: Gryphon Press, 1978.

Butcher, H. J. *Human Intelligence: Its Nature and Assessment.* New York: Harper & Row, 1968.

Carroll, J. B. Fitting a model of school learning to aptitude and achievement data over grade levels. In D. R. Green (Ed.), *The Aptitude-Achievement Distinction.* Monterey, Calif.: CTB/McGraw-Hill, 1974.

Cleary, T. A. Test bias: Prediction of grades of Negro and White students in integrated colleges. *Journal of Educational Measurement,* 1968, *5,* 115–124.

Cleary, T. A.; Humphreys, L. G.; Kendrick, A. S.; and Wesman, A. Educational uses of tests with disadvantaged students. *American Psychologist,* 1975, *30,* 15–41.

Crockenberg, S. B. Creativity tests: A boon or boondoggle for education. *Review of Educational Research,* 1972, *42,* 27–46.

Cronbach, L. J. *Essentials of Psychological Testing* (3rd. ed.). New York: Harper & Row, 1970.

Darlington, R. B. Another look at "cultural fairness." *Journal of Educational Measurement,* 1971, *8,* 71–82.

Findley, W. G. Ability grouping. In G. R. Gredler (Ed.), *Ethical and Legal Factors in the Practice of School Psychology.* Harrisburg: Pennsylvania State Department of Education, 1974.

Findley, W. G., & Bryan, M. M. *Ability Grouping: 1970 Status, Impact, and Alternatives.* Athens, Ga.: University of Georgia, Center for Educational Improvement, 1971. (ERIC Document Reproduction Service No. ED 060 595)

Flaugher, R. L. The many definitions of test bias. *American Psychologist,* 1978, *33*(7), 671–679.

Getzels, J. W., & Jackson, P. W. *Creativity and Intelligence.* New York: Wiley, 1962.

Goslin, D. A. *Teachers and Testing.* New York: Russell Sage, 1967.

Guilford, J. P. *The Nature of Human Intelligence.* New York: McGraw-Hill, 1967.

Hills, J. R. Prediction of college grades for all public colleges of a state. *Journal of Educational Measurement,* 1964, *1,* 155–159.

Hills, J. R. Use of measurement in selection and placement. In R. L. Thorndike (Ed.), *Educational Measurement* (2nd ed.). Washington, D.C.: American Council on Education, 1971.

Hills, J. R., & Gladney, M. B. *Predicting Grades from Below Chance Test Scores* (Research Bulletin 3-66, Office of Testing and Guidance). Atlanta: Board of Regents of the University System of Georgia, 1966

Hills, J. R.; Klock, J. C.; & Lewis, S. *Freshman Norms for the University System of Georgia, 1961–1962.* Atlanta: Board of Regents of the University System of Georgia, Office of Testing and Guidance, 1963.

Hudson, L. *Contrary Imaginations.* New York: Schocken Books, 1966.

Hunter, J. E., & Schmidt, F. L. Critical analysis of the statistical and ethical implications of various definitions of test bias. *Psychological Bulletin,* 1976, *83*(6), 1053–1071.

Hunter, J. E.; Schmidt, F. L.; & Rauschenberger, J. M. Fairness of psychological tests: Implications of four definitions for selection utility and minority hiring. *Journal of Applied Psychology,* 1977, *62*(3), 245–260.

Jackson, R. The Scholastic Aptitude Test: A response to Slack and Porter's "critical appraisal." *Harvard Educational Review,* 1980, *50*(3), 382–391.

Jensen, A. R. *Bias in Mental Testing.* New York: Free Press, 1980.

Kaiser, H. F. The Chaldeans speak: An interpretive summary. In D. R. Green (Ed.), *The Aptitude-Achievement Distinction.* Monterey, Calif.: CTB/McGraw-Hill, 1974.

Kallingal, A. The prediction of grades for black and white students at Michigan State University. *Journal of Educational Measurement,* 1971, *8,* 263–266.

Kelley, T. L. *The Interpretation of Educational Measurement.* Yonkers-on-Hudson, N.Y.: World Book, 1927.

Lennon, R. T. The anatomy of a scholastic aptitude test. *Measurement in Education,* 1980, *11*(2), 1–8.

Lerner, B. The war on testing: David, Goliath, and Gallup. *The Public Interest,* Summer 1980, 119–147.

Lewis, J. The relationship between academic aptitude and occupational success for a sample of university graduates. *Educational and Psychological Measurement,* 1975, *35,* 465–466.

Mehrens, W. A., & Lehmann, I. J. *Standardized Tests in Education* (3rd ed.). New York: Holt, Rinehart & Winston, 1980.

Messick, S. *The Effectiveness of Coaching for the SAT: Review and Reanalysis of Research from the Fifties to the FTC.* Princeton, N.J.: Educational Testing Service, 1980.

Michael, W. B. Aptitudes. In C. W. Harris (Ed.), *Encyclopedia of Educational Research* (3rd ed.). New York: Macmillan, 1960.

Munday, L. Predicting college grades in predominantly Negro colleges. *Journal of Educational Measurement,* 1965, *2,* 157–160.

Novick, M. R., & Ellis, D. D., Jr. Equal opportunity in educational and employment selection. *American Psychologist,* 1977, *32*(5), 306–320.

Peterson, N. S., & Novick, M. R. An evaluation of some models for culture-fair selection. *Journal of Educational Measurement,* 1976, *13,* 3–30.

Pfeifer, C. M., Jr., & Sedlacek, W. E. The validity of academic predictors for black and white students at a predominantly white university. *Journal of Educational Measurement,* 1971, *8,* 253–262.

Samuda, R. J. *Psychological Testing of American Minorities.* New York: Dodd, Mead, 1975.

Silverman, B. I.; Barton, F.; & Lyon, M. Minority group status and bias in college admissions criteria. *Educational and Psychological Measurement,* 1976, *36*(2), 401–407.

Slack, W. V., & Porter, D. The Scholastic Aptitude Test: A critical appraisal. *Harvard Educational Review,* 1980, *50*(2), 154–175.

Snow, R. E. Aptitude and achievement. In W. B. Schrader (Ed.), *New Directions for Testing and Measurement: Measuring Achievement—Progress over a Decade* (No. 5). San Francisco: Jossey-Bass, 1980.

Stanley, J. C. Predicting college success of the educationally disadvantaged. *Science,* February 1971, *171,* 640–647.

Stanley, J. C., & Porter, A. C. Correlation of Scholastic Aptitude Test scores with college grades for Negroes versus whites. *Journal of Educational Measurement,* 1967, *4,* 199–218.

Teacher Opinions Poll. *Today's Education,* 1974, *63*(2), 4.

Temp, G. Validity of the Scholastic Aptitude Test for blacks and whites in thirteen integrated institutions. *Journal of Educational Measurement,* 1971, *8,* 245–252.

Thomas, C. L., & Stanley, J. C. Effectiveness of high school grades for predicting college grades of black students: A review and discussion. *Journal of Educational Measurement,* 1969, *6,* 203–216.

Thorndike, R. L. Concepts of cultural fairness. *Journal of Educational Measurement,* 1971, *8,* 63–70.

Torrance, E. P. *Guiding Creative Talent.* Englewood Cliffs, N.J.: Prentice-Hall, 1962.

Torrance, E. P. *Reward Creative Behavior.* Englewood Cliffs, N.J.: Prentice-Hall, 1965.

Wallach, M. A., & Kogan, N. *Modes of Thinking in Young Children.* New York: Holt, Rinehart & Winston, 1965.

Williams, R. L. Stimulus/Response: Scientific racism and IQ—The silent mugging of the black community. *Psychology Today,* 1974, 7(12), 32, 34, 37–38, 41, 101.

ARCHIVES AND RECORDS MANAGEMENT

Historians of education and related fields have a strong and continuing interest in access to documents and papers that are the elements of the American past. School records in particular are central to research in the social and political context of education. The proper management and storage of school records and other educational materials and their organization into responsible and accessible archive repositories have become an increasing concern to researchers.

Archives. Generally speaking, archives are considered to be agencies responsible for selecting, preserving, and making available for public examination historically relevant records, papers, collections, and manuscripts of an organization, institution, or individual. Archives may exist in a variety of settings and have an assortment of functions. Consider these examples. Early in America's development as a nation, the federal government established an archive called the Library of Congress, today known as the National Archives. All fifty states have established state archives, and many cities, such as Philadelphia, Detroit, Boston, and New York City, have created city archives. A great number of America's smaller and intermediate communities have established archive programs through historical societies, county governments, or local museums. Colleges and universities almost without exception have established archive programs. Finally, businesses, such as U.S. Steel, IBM, and Corning Glass; specialty museums, such as the National Baseball Hall of Fame and the Whaling Museum Society; and state court systems, such as the one found in Massachussets, have sought to secure their role in the American past by establishing business, museum, and legal archives. In all, according to varied sources, some 12,000 archive repositories are known to exist in all states, the District of Columbia, and American territories.

To help researchers sift through this range of organizations, several national guides or directories to American archives and their holdings have been compiled. Hamer (1961) edited a volume entitled *Guide to Archives and Manuscripts in the United States,* which was intended as a guide to assist researchers to find archives or manuscripts containing the information in which they are interested. Barely a decade later, the Library of Congress began to produce annually the first of a fourteen-volume series known as the *National Union Catalog of Manuscript Collections* (NUCMC). Collectively this series has reported on the holdings of 1,000 repositories and is published annu-

ally. In addition, the Modern Language Association has described collections of approximately 500 repositories in *American Literary Manuscript Repositories* (Robbins et al., 1977). The National Historical Publications and Records Commission prepared the *Directory of Archives and Manuscript Repositories in the United States* (1978), which to date is the most comprehensive guide to archives available, in that it lists the locations and briefly describes the holdings of 2,675 repositories. Finally, the Society of American Archivists in 1980 published a guide to archives found in institutions of higher education entitled *Directory of College and University Archives in the United States and Canada* (1980).

The location and identification of documents and papers oriented to American education are obviously of interest to scholars and researchers in that field, but at present no comprehensive national guide to historical materials in American education has been prepared or published. However, the State Archives in Wisconsin has published a guide, specifically related to the education papers and manuscripts found in their holdings, entitled *Resources for Research in the History of Education Collections at the State Historical Society of Wisconsin* (Curti, 1967).

Guides to historical materials of a specific nature, such as *Women's History Sources: A Guide to Archives and Manuscript Collections in the United States* (Hinding, 1979) and *Descriptive Inventory of the Archives of the City and County of Philadelphia* (Daly, 1970), can be valuable sources of information to social and educational historians examining their indexes for references to education-related topics. For example, the women's guide has 500 references to documents relating to women and education. Many other specialty-finding aids certain to have references to educational documents have been published in recent years, such as *Guide to Materials on Latin America in the National Archives of the United States* (Harrison, 1974), *Preliminary Guide to the Special Collections of Indiana State University* (1975), *Descriptive Inventory of the Archives of the State of Illinois* (Irons and Brennan, 1978), and *Immigrant Archives: Guide to Manuscript Holdings* (1976). Furthermore, the Society of American Archivists, in their journal, *The American Archivist,* provides reviews of published guides and is often a good source for more information about educational materials in America's archives.

A significant number of institutions of higher education have published guides to materials in their repositories, such as the following: *Guide to the Archives of the University of Pennsylvania from 1740 to 1820* (Dallett, 1978) *A Guide to the Michigan State University Archives and Historical Collections* (Honhart, 1976), *A Descriptive Guide to the Harvard University Archives* (Elliott, 1974), and *A Descriptive Guide to the Holdings of the University Archives and Manuscripts Collection: Texas A & M University* (1974).

Researchers should also be aware that state archives frequently publish a newsletter or journal reviewing their holdings and collections and describing efforts to store, classify, and acquire records. For example, the State of Florida Archives produces *Archives and History News,* and the State Archives of Illinois publishes *For the Record.* Such periodicals as these offer the researcher sources of information concerning educational materials in the various state repositories.

Records Management. Given the important function of archives, it is reasonable to expect that preservation and orderly transition of documents, papers, and other materials about the American past to responsible and appropriate archive repositories would be of paramount concern to historical researchers. This transferring of documents to archives can occur in either a haphazard or a planned manner. An example of the haphazard method is a prominent person in a local community (perhaps a judge or the mayor) selecting documents believed to be of historical value from personal and administrative files and donating them to a local historical society for preservation and public use. On the other hand, when an institution such as a government agency, a college or university, a school district, a business, or a museum develops a policy creating a records management program, then it is interested in the planned method of document preservation and storage. Formally, then, records management is recognized to be that area of an institution's general administrative structure concerned with economy and efficiency in the creation, use, and disposition of records. For example, federal and state governments probably have better-defined policies directing the use and disposition of government reports, correspondence, forms, and directives into federal and state archives than any other type of institution in this country.

The importance of the transfer of historical materials into repositories has prompted social and educational historians to become increasingly concerned with the development by local school districts, in cooperation with local historical societies, or records management and records disposition programs. In 1979 a symposium convened at the Pennsylvania State University to address this growing concern included historians, school personnel, and archivists. The proceedings, edited by Best and Alterman (1979) and entitled *Symposium on a National Inventory of Historical Materials in American Education,* explore in detail the issues and problems associated with historical archives and records management programs for local school districts.

A central problem pointed out by archivists at this meeting was the necessity for local districts of records management programs to coordinate with state, county, or university archivists to ensure an orderly transition of materials. Archivists also pointed out that several twentieth-century factors would have to be taken into account when considering the establishment of records management programs: the poor quality of paper used in most records and documents produced within the last five decades, the massive volume of paperwork that has come with computer use

and spreading bureaucracies, and the vast amount of non-paper documents, such as tape and video recordings. These recent factors, they suggested, would create general storage problems for archives because low funds and high energy costs have forced archives to cut back on vital climate controls necessary for proper storage of these new, more fragile materials.

Finally, it was stated that the major professional problem confronting archivists will be decisions on what to save and what to discard, a problem of appraisal and arrangement. For example, ten years ago when archivists were arranging papers related to labor history, they were not too concerned with membership or dues lists. While they did not throw them away, they were not particularly concerned about their inclusion in the development of the collection. But with the current research emphasis on social and family histories, these items have come to be considered essential. The determination, by either archivists or historians, of what future research needs might or should be, will continue to be an extremely difficult but important task.

Historians attending the symposium presented their professional concerns regarding archive and records management problems for local school districts. Several points were made clear. First, policies governing educational materials would perhaps lessen the amount of documents lost or destroyed each year. Second, organization of materials would help the researcher identify relevant materials and thus contribute to clearer historical judgments; even the knowledge of which materials were inaccessible would help in this matter. Third, responsible policies in records management programs would reduce subjective judgments currently being made by administrators and clerical staff as to what to save for historical purposes.

Historians pointed out two central issues that need consideration in order for the records management program of any local school district to be effective. First, since administrators in most school districts have little sense of the specific historical value of their materials, the participation of historians in the formulation of archival policies for school districts is essential. The task of determining what to save and what to discard should be a shared responsibility and not left to school administrators alone. Second, archivists should consult with historians to ensure that the arrangement of materials be kept useful and flexible in meeting current and future research needs.

Most local school districts do not have well-defined or comprehensive policies concerning preservation of educational materials for historical purposes. Frequently, school districts leave preservation decisions to principals, teachers, school superintendents, and administrators. This can lead to boxes of documents that are either misplaced or put in basements or attics and thus are exposed to hazards such as fire and dampness. Although school administrators are legally bound to preserve student academic records carefully long after students leave the schools, they do not do the same for other educational materials. Documents are often misplaced, lost in fires, abandoned when a school district reorganizes, or simply thrown away. The problem, of course, is that documents as years go by can easily be misplaced or destroyed even with the best intentions of school officials to preserve them.

School officials, historians, and archivists need to join together in an effort to produce responsible archive and records management programs for local school districts. Researchers wishing to pursue this problem have a wide variety of sources to consult, such as the following: *Modern Archives and Manuscripts: A Select Bibliography* (Evans, 1975; "Writings on Archives, Historical Manuscripts, and Current Records," an annual bibliography appearing in each summer issue of the *American Archivist* (1938–); *Archives* (1949–), the quarterly journal of the Society of Archivists of Great Britain; *Archivaria* (1975–), the semi-annual journal of the Association of Canadian Archivists; *American Jewish Archives* (1948–), the journal of the Jewish Institute of Religion; *Gazette des archivistes français* (1947–), the journal of the Association des Archivistes Français; *Alternative Archivist* (1977–), the journal of the Federation of Alternative Libraries; *Caribbean Archives* (1973–present), the journal of the Caribbean Archives Association; *Georgia Archives* (1972–), published by the Society of Georgia Archivists; *College and University Archives: Selected Readings* (Committee on College and University Archives, 1979); "Management of Archives and Manuscript Collections for Librarians in *Drexel Library Quarterly* (Lytle, 1975); and *Records Management Quarterly* (1967–), the journal of the American Records Management Association.

In addition, the Society of American Archivists has published numerous monographs with special themes that are a valuable resource for research in records management and archives. Particularly useful is the Basic Manual Series (Fleckner, 1977) on archives and manuscripts, which clearly delineates the principles of appraisal, arrangement, accessioning, referencing, security, surveys, and exhibits. To help the nonarchivist become familiar with common archive terms, the society has published a booklet entitled *A Basic Glossary for Archivists, Manuscript Curators, and Records Managers* (Rofes et al., 1974).

It should be noted that the society's quarterly journal, *The American Archivist* (1938–), is perhaps the richest source for research in archive and records management. This journal provides bibliographies; articles on a variety of topics, including local and state programs or holdings, library collections, surveys and inventories, records management, ethnic interests, programs in foreign countries, public records, and modernization; reports on the various divisions or committees of the society, such as the Records Management Division and the Division of College and University Archives; general news and information concerning new collections, openings, and accessions; and reviews. A ten-year index has been published.

The proper management of educational records into accessible and responsible archives and knowledge about the location of educational records currently stored in America's repositories are crucial to historical and social research and education. It should be noted that little effort has been made by archives to publish guides to historical materials in American education, nor have local school districts done much to develop appropriate records management programs. Minimal research has been conducted in this area, despite its recognition as a significant concern to history and education.

Richard C. Alterman

See also Historiography; Information Management and Computing; Libraries.

REFERENCES

Alternative Archivist. Kitchener, Ont.: Federation of Alternative Libraries, 1977–.

American Archivist, The. Chicago: Society of American Archivists, 1938–.

American Jewish Archives. Cincinnati: Hebrew Union College, Jewish Institute of Religion, 1948–.

Archivaria. Ottawa: Association of Canadian Archivists, 1975–.

Archives. London: British Records Association, 1949–.

Archives and History News. Tallahassee, Fla.: Department of State, Division of Archives, 1970–.

Best, J. H., & Alterman, R. *Symposium on a National Inventory of Historical Materials in American Education.* University Park: Pennsylvania State University, 1979. (ERIC Document Reproduction Service No. ED 190 055)

Caribbean Archives. Basse-Terre, Guadeloupe: Caribbean Archives Association, 1973–.

Committee on College and University Archives (Eds.). *College and University Archives: Selected Readings.* Chicago: Society of American Archivists, 1979.

Curti, M., et al. (Comps.) *Resources for Research in the History of Education Collections at the State Historical Society of Wisconsin.* Madison: State Historical Society of Wisconsin, 1967.

Dallett, F. J., *Guide to the Archives of the University of Pennsylvania from 1740 to 1820.* Philadelphia: University of Pennsylvania Archives, 1978.

Daly, J. *Descriptive Inventory of the Archives of the City and County of Philadelphia.* Philadelphia: Department of Records, 1970.

Descriptive Guide to the Holdings of the University Archives and Manuscript Collection: Texas A & M University. College Station: Texas A & M University Library, 1974.

Directory of Archives and Manuscript Repositories in the United States. Washington D.C.: National Historical Publications and Records Commission, 1978.

Directory of College and University Archives in the United States and Canada. Chicago: Society of American Archivists, 1980.

Elliot, C. A. (Comp.). *A Descriptive Guide to the Harvard University Archives.* Cambridge, Mass.: Harvard University Library, 1974.

Evans, F. B. *Modern Archives and Manuscripts: A Select Bibliography.* Chicago: Society of American Archivists, 1975.

Fleckner, J. A. *Archives and Manuscripts: Surveys* (Basic Manual Series). Chicago: Society of American Archivists, 1977.

For the Record. Springfield: State Archives of Illinois, 1976–.

Gazette des archivistes français. Paris: Association des Archivistes Français, 1947–.

Georgia Archives. Atlanta: Society of Georgia Archivists, 1972–.

Hamer, P. M., *A Guide to Archives and Manuscripts in the United States.* Washington, D.C.: National Historical Publications and Records Commission, 1961.

Harrison, J. P. *Guide to Materials on Latin America in the National Archives of the United States,* Washington, D.C.: National Archives, 1974.

Hinding, A., et al. (Eds.). *Women's History Sources: A Guide to Archives and Manuscript Collections in the United States* (2 vols.). New York: R. R. Bowker, 1979.

Honhart, F. L. (Ed.), *A Guide to the Michigan State University Archives and Historical Collections.* East Lansing: Michigan State University, 1976.

Immigrant Archives: Guide to Manuscript Holdings. Minneapolis: University of Minnesota Library, 1976.

Irons, Victoria, & Brennan, Patricia C. *Descriptive Inventory of the Archives of the State of Illinois,* Springfield: Illinois State Archives, 1978.

Lytle, R. H. (Ed.). Management of archives and manuscript collections for librarians. *Drexel Library Quarterly,* January 1975, *11*(4).

National Union Catalog of Manuscript Collections. Washington, D.C.: Library of Congress. Issued annually.

Preliminary Guide to the Special Collections of Indiana State University. Terre Haute: Indiana State University, 1975.

Records Management Quarterly. Bradford, R.I.: Association of Records Managers, 1967–.

Robbins, J. A. (Ed.), et al. (Comps.). *American Literary Manuscripts.* Athens: Modern Language Association, University of Georgia Press, 1977.

Rofes, W. L., et al. (Eds.). A basic glossary for archivists, manuscript curators, and records managers. *American Archivist,* July 1974, *37*(3).

Writings on archives, historical manuscripts, and current records. *The American Archivist.* A summary issued annually in the summer.

ARITHMETIC

The reappearance of "arithmetic" as an article, independent of "mathematics" as reviewed a decade ago by Willoughby (1969), reflects the impact of the back-to-basics movement in the 1970s. Commonly associated with this movement has been competency in the skills of reading, arithmetic, and communications. The changing of the name from "arithmetic," as reviewed by Buswell (1960) to "elementary mathematics" was a signal in the 1960s to provide the child with a continuous mathematical experience by means of the spiral curriculum and to perceive mathematics as an integrated discipline. Indeed, elementary mathematics gives at least nominal recognition of mathematics as a unified system of ideas, ranging from primitive, abstract number notions to highly complex abstractions. Arithmetic, a branch of mathematics, is the study of number; a base-ten numeration system; of algorithms, based on the four basic operations (addition, sub-traction, multiplication, and division), and the use of these ideas and skills in problem solving.

In the perspective of the roots from which they have emerged, this article is an effort to capture the trends and developments in arithmetic research in the 1970s, an era of assessment, accountability, and cost effectiveness. In particular, it focuses on the research studies that have been responsive to multisocietal needs and expectations in a rapidly changing and growing age of science and technology.

In retrospect, three broad concerns have prevailed throughout the history of arithmetic: utility, problem solving, and qualities inherent in mathematics. Since the colonial period, social utility has been a determiner of arithmetic in school mathematics in the United States. Although most early colonists did not depend on the arithmetic instruction of the schools for needs of commerce, the instruction that was given by tutors, teachers, or textbooks was primarily that of providing rules to be memorized and applied in solving problems with a minimum of understanding of these rules. Colburn's *Intellectual Arithmetic* in 1820 was the first significant development in content and methodology (Buswell, 1960). Many of Colburn's ideas continued to be used in the textbooks of Joseph Ray, sometimes known as the "McGuffey of mathematics." Thirty-eight different arithmetics and nineteen algebras were published under his name (Morusett & Vinsonhaler, 1965). In his book, *Practical Arithmetic,* which was published in 1877, Ray noted that changes in content were made in response to changes in modes of transacting business, including money, billing, weights and measures, metric system, discounts, exchange, insurance and taxes, partnership, and square and cube roots. As noted by Buswell (1960), near the end of the previous century, arithmetic had oscillated between the influence of the Grube method, (which subscribed to the slow introduction of natural number ideas and the presentation of all four operations at the outset) and the extremes of spiral organization, with the content load becoming so heavy and teaching so formal that the Committee of Ten, in 1893, and the Committee of Fifteen, in 1895, recommended radical changes in teaching and that arithmetic be both "abridged and enriched." In response to these recommendations, the theory of social utility was used in reducing the content.

In the 1920s, there was a shift from social applications to qualities inherent in mathematics. The outcomes of this interest were the organization of the subject in terms of successive skill units, followed by a greater stress for drill in these skills, supported by the "law of exercise." Furthermore, the expansion of the school population resulting from compulsory education laws encouraged a "watering down" of content. As noted by Willoughby (1969), Thorndike and his stimulus-response approach to teaching arithmetic became the predominant method of instruction for attaining the important goals of speed and accuracy of computation.

In the late 1930s, the excessive emphasis on drill was

halted by the advocation of an interest in teaching arithmetic for meaning. Mathematics educators began to emphasize meaningful learning, and a plea was made for emphasis on a comprehensive understanding of the whole situation rather than on isolated parts. Brownell (Buswell, 1951) made a marked contribution toward clarifying the distinction between social meaning and mathematical meaning by proposing that "meaningful arithmetic" should be meaning of arithmetic. Brownell (1947) stated that these meanings must be taught so that they make sense to those who learn them. Since that time there has been increasing interest in the mathematical, as contrasted with the strictly social, objectives of arithmetic, supported by research that found advantages of learning with understanding as contrasted with learning by drill (Brownell & Moser, 1949; Dawson & Rudell, 1955; Van Engen & Gibb, 1956).

Meaning theory continued to have much impact on the arithmetic curriculum of the 1950s (DeVault & Weaver, 1970) and to set the stage for the "new math" of the 1960s. Another stimulus for reform was attributed to professional mathematicians. They were eager for schools to reflect those positive features of mathematical programs. As expressed by Van Engen (1965), arithmetic taught in the schools should relate more closely to the ideas that mathematicians find most useful and powerful. Arithmetic programs should not only be concerned with computation, measurement, and social business applications, but should also provide for a meaningful concept of number, an understanding of numeration systems, and a systematic approach to problem solving.

In the 1960s, the program was no longer named "arithmetic" but was usually called elementary mathematics. The four basic operations of whole numbers, fractions, decimals, and "bland" applications to a variety of verbally stated problems were retained. During that decade, however, curriculum improvement projects were supported to provide redirections not only to arithmetic but to the improvement of school mathematics and science programs. Among those projects with direct concern for arithmetic and/or the elementary school were the Madison Project, the Experimental Teaching of Mathematics in the Elementary Schools, the University of Illinois Arithmetic Project, the Greater Cleveland Mathematics Project, the School Mathematics Study Group, the Minnesota Mathematics and Science Teaching Project (Minnemast), and Patterns in Arithmetic Project. Common goals that appeared across these projects were emphases on structure and organization of mathematics, the elements of pure and socially applied mathematics, and the method of discovery. They also were the impetus for new content that appeared in the curriculum in topics concerning sets, systems of numeration, properties of operations, bases other than base ten, selected geometry concepts, and organizing and interpreting data.

As noted by Willoughby (1969), two major longitudinal studies were under way. A portion of one study, the National Longitudinal Study of Mathematical Abilities (NLSMA) compared curricular effects on arithmetic achievement. Carry and Weaver (1969) concluded that "scales classified as computation yielded contrast patterns generally different from scales classified as comprehension" (p. 167). Their results strongly indicated that comprehension of mathematical concepts was at least as important as computational skill for the ability to solve problems.

In the late 1960s, however, Clark (1965) and Rappaport (1965) noted that since 1957 the content of arithmetic was becoming heavy again, much as it was prior to 1900. Glennon (1966) agreed with this assessment and noted that, prior to 1957, research was on the learning process. He indicated that there was a movement again toward the needs of the learner. Thus, the 1970s were approached with some disenchantment of the perceived results of the efforts to improve not only arithmetic but school mathematics.

Foundations of Research. Theories of psychology have long been and continue to be an active force on the content and learning/teaching of arithmetic. Shulman (1970) stated that instruction in arithmetic has been quite sensitive to shifts in psychological theories. Prior to 1900, the use of a deductive system in order to make arithmetic a "science of number" was viewed as exercising specific psychological faculties associated with mental discipline and faculty psychology (Jones and Coxford, 1970). Mental discipline was retained as a goal of education for more than thirty years. Based on their research to test the validity of the concept of mental discipline, E. L. Thorndike and R. S. Woodworth (1901) concluded that this idea could not be supported. Thorndike continued to develop his theory of connectionism or stimulus-response (S-R) bond theory and, in 1922, published his *Psychology of Arithmetic.* His theory resulted in identifying each small segment of the curriculum as disjointed from all other segments. Evidence of this skill analysis still pervades the organization of arithmetic. Judd (1927), in his "Psychological Analysis of the Fundamentals of Arithmetic," demonstrated the expectations of automatic transfer if emphasis were placed on meaning. Yet, Judd's theory was unable to counteract the S-R approach. Influenced by the pragmatism of James, Dewey advocated education as reorganizing and reconstructing experiences to increase ability to direct subsequent experience (Ratner, 1928).

In his "Psychology of Learning in Relation to the Teaching of Arithmetic," Buswell (1951) classified the major general categories of psychology related to arithmetic as either "association theories" or "field theories." These two general theories have provided foundations for research focused either on products of learning (association theories) or on processes of learning (field theories). As noted by Shulman (1970), psychology has "harbored opposing camps" on learning theory. Research on arithmetic has been based on theories from both camps. Skinner's (1968) operant conditioning provided support for research in programmed learning and computer-assisted instruction. The task analysis of subordinate capabilities that are prerequisite to the attainment of a given objective follows Gagné's hierarchical structure of learning, extending to subsequent research for validation of learning hierarchies (Gagné, 1977). Bruner's learning-by-discovery, highly influenced by the theories of Piaget and Plato, has provided a body of theory and research, advocating discovery teaching and emphasis on the processes of learning. Ausubel's (1968) concept of instructional sequence reflects positions of both Gagné and Bruner. He advocates a carefully guided, expository sequencing and the initiation of the sequence at a higher point on the hierarchy, his principle of the advance organizer. The developmental stage theory of Piaget has been of special interest to researchers as well as to curriculum designers since the early 1960s.

More recently, Carpenter (1980) reviewed the research in cognitive development as it related to the area of arithmetic and mathematics. Although cognitive development may be viewed in many different ways, he draws a useful distinction between two viewpoints. One is based on an organismic model represented by the work of Piaget (Flavell, 1963) and his followers, and the other is a mechanistic model espoused by Gagné. In comparing and contrasting the two points of view, Carpenter lists attributes of the organismic model as (1) study of how the child processes information; (2) process-oriented; (3) integrated, cognitive systems; (4) active participation in construction of knowledge; and (5) qualitative changes. He lists attributes of the mechanistic model as (1) specific knowledge that a child possesses; (2) product orientations; (3) chainlike associations; (4) reactive participation in organizing knowledge; (5) environment; generality; and (6) quantitative changes. It seems that many low-level skills in arithmetic (for example, memorization of the basic facts) are best described by mechanistic models; higher levels of mathematical thinking seem to lend themselves easily to an organismic analysis. Many mathematics educators find it inviting to develop an eclectic approach. For example, White (1965) maintains that children undergo a change in behavior at about six years of age. Thus, the mechanistic model is valid for the early years, and the organismic model is more applicable to the later years. Kohlberg (1968) and Uznadze (1966) also attempt to forge a compromise between the two models to explain simple and complex behavior.

Skemp (1971), a mathematician-turned-psychologist because of his concern with the problems that intelligent and hard-working students have with mathematics, notes that there seems to be emerging from research a qualitative difference between two kinds of learning: habit, or rote memorizing, and learning that involves understanding, or intelligent learning. Later Skemp (1977) drew a distinction between "relational" and "instrumental" understanding, which has been extended by Byers and Herscovics (1977) to include intuitive and formal understanding and a tetrahedral model for determining how these levels of understanding interact, by reinforcing or hindering each other. Further integration of these different theoretical models requires more research.

Research on arithmetic has employed different psychological modes to describe the behavior of students related to learning arithmetic. In this context, studies have sought answers to content, sequences, readiness, and alternative instructional strategies.

The report by Coleman et al. (1966) has been widely used as a basis for research, incorporating socioeconomic status as a factor in designing studies in arithmetic achievement. Also, factors of ethnic, cultural and sex differences, as they relate to student learning and achievement in arithmetic, have received much interest in research on arithmetic.

Research Support. During the 1970s, two federal agencies, the National Science Foundation (NSF) and the National Institute of Education (NIE), provided financial support for research and development in arithmetic as well as in other areas of mathematics. It has not always been a simple matter, however, to determine what amount of a specific project has been devoted to arithmetic.

Based on a letter from Joseph Lipson (director of the Division of Science Education Development and Research), the nature of the NSF funding changed considerably during the 1970s. Most of the financial support during the early part of the period went to large-scale curriculum development efforts that were completing their work at that time. These projects included the School Mathematics Study Group, directed by Edward G. Begle, and the Unified Science and Mathematics for Elementary Schools, directed by Earl Loman.

From 1977 to 1980, federal funding for arithmetic supported mainly smaller projects, and much less was done in curriculum development. Research during this period included studies of manipulative aids, counting, early number concepts, whole number concepts, calculators, and problem solving. Development projects included work in mental errors in arithmetic, use of the microcomputer to teach basic skills, and use of arithmetic in applications. Three areas that have received considerable attention are the development of early number concepts, rational number concepts, and problem solving. Recent development, however, has focused on applications and the use of information technology in the teaching of arithmetic.

The NIE also has provided support for research, focusing on number, numeration, rational numbers, problem solving, and learning difficulties in mathematics. Included in some of the studies are the factors associated with cultural background and language, particularly for Mexican Americans, American Indians, and blacks.

With concern for competency in mathematics, including arithmetic as well as other areas of learning, the National Assessment of Educational Progress (NAEP) has completed two assessments (1973 and 1979). The first effort was supported by the Education Commission of the States through the National Center for Education Statistics in the Department of Health, Education and Welfare, and the NIE (NAEP, 1979). The second assessment was supported by the NIE.

As reported by Higgins, Kasten and Suydam (1979), all fifty states and the District of Columbia have supported minimum competency testing and/or assessment in mathematics through state legislatures, state departments or boards of education, or through local education agencies. As they acknowledge, it is most difficult to get an accurate indication of the levels of achievement across the states.

The commitment to financial support of research in arithmetic as well as for education in general (primarily through tax monies) is an indication of the commitment and influence of the public for excellence in education. The trend toward increased accountability for determining the cost-effectiveness of tax dollars is not surprising, however.

Research on Arithmetic Teaching.   The era of back-to-basics, concern for the educationally deprived and minority groups, desegregation, mainstreaming, rapid advances in computer technology, mathematical literacy, and escalation of open-door colleges have been a few of the many forces that have given direction to research in arithmetic during the 1970s. Consequently, there has been much diversity in research.

Trends.   As reported by Suydam and Osborne (1977), research on arithmetic has continued to pursue teaching approaches, learning of specific content within arithmetic, content organization, and achievement evaluation. Newer areas of research emerging during the 1970s have included organizational patterns; specification of objectives; attitudes and self-concepts; physical, psychological, and social characteristics; sex differences; socioeconomic differences; grouping procedures; audiovisual devices and, more specifically, calculators and computers. It might be said that Aiken (1970, 1971) set the tone for these new focuses in his recommendations for research to include topics of language, perception, sex differences, interest, attitudes, and other sociocultural factors as they relate to mathematics learning.

Not only has there been a shift in the problems studied, but also a change of intent on the problems. Earlier research placed emphasis upon "what children can do—the products of learning." More recent studies have turned to what processes children use in learning or doing arithmetic, with increased interest in underlying reasons for student errors in arithmetic.

In addition to changing emphasis in research on arithmetic, federal agencies have demanded better accountability of the financial support that has been provided for research and development. The Conference Board of the Mathematical Sciences appointed the National Advisory Committee on Mathematical Education (NACOME) to provide an overview of mathematics education in the schools, to synthesize reactions, and to make recommendations for the future. This committee (1975) observed that the innovations of the 1960s had not fulfilled their promises, and that the intent of these innovations had not made

it to the classrooms. Contrary to articles in journals of education and the popular press, most teachers continued to emphasize what they knew best and what they felt they could teach—computational skills with whole numbers, fractions, and decimals. Three topics frequently identified in arithmetic as "new math" have virtually disappeared: sets as a unifying idea, other number bases, and subtractive division.

To provide a retrospective look at science, mathematics, and social science education, the NSF awarded three proposals for independent but related studies using different methodological approaches and drawing on different data bases. These studies were a status study by Suydam and Osborne (1977); a national survey of curriculum and instructional practices by Weiss (1978), and case studies of the actions and perceptions of teachers and students by Stake and Easley (1978). Perspectives from the three national surveys as they relate to the elementary grades have been made by Fey (1979). Not particularly pleasing findings, reported by Gibney and Karas (1979), were that (1) whatever the new math was (and perceptions vary), it didn't "take" in most elementary school classrooms; (2) a large proportion of time available for teaching mathematics is consumed by noninstructional activities; (3) there is no one way to organize school and classrooms and no one mode of instruction that will promote achievement; (4) teachers frequently do not differentiate instruction to meet individual needs; (5) the textbook is the primary determinant of curriculum; and (6) neither attitudes nor achievement are as poor at the elementary level as headlines proclaim.

According to the NAEP report (1979), computational achievement with whole numbers is high, although achievement on fractions and on decimals is less satisfactory. Of concern are the low scores for problem solving and student difficulty in applying computational skills in solving problems.

Based on the results of the NSF status reports, the National Council of Teachers of Mathematics (NCTM, 1981) conducted a Priorities in School Mathematics Project (PRISM) to collect information on current beliefs and reactions held by six groups in the mathematics education community, school principals, presidents of school boards, and presidents of parent-teacher organizations, in an effort to ascertain curriculum changes in the 1980s. Four of the nine content strands in this study that related to arithmetic are whole numbers; fractions and decimals; ratio, proportion, and percent; and problem solving. This study also was deemed to be useful in implementing NCTM's *Agenda for Action* 1980. The essence of the recommendations pertaining to arithmetic in this agenda were that problem solving should be the focus of school mathematics in the 1980s at all levels; basic skills should be defined to encompass more than computational facility; mathematics programs should take full advantage of the power of calculators and computers at all grade levels; the success of programs and student learning should be evaluated by a wider range of measures than conventional testing; a greater range of options should be available to accommodate the diverse needs of the student population; a high level of professionalism on the part of teachers should be established; and stronger public support for mathematics instruction should be called for. The effectiveness of the implementation of these recommendations can be expected to have impact on arithmetic teaching and learning in the 1980s.

Research findings. As noted in trends of research, there has been a diversity in topics. A general summary of findings is useful.

Studies have attempted to look at the relationship of language skills to achievement in mathematics, including arithmetic. (Lamberg & Lamb, 1980; Aikens, 1972a; Beilin, 1976; Skypeck, 1981; Earle, 1976; Geeslin, 1977). In general, these studies have shown that the ability to operate in mathematics and, more specifically, in arithmetic situations is closely related to language arts skills such as reading and writing. The results have been supportive of earlier studies, such as that of Chase (1960), in which it was determined that a primary factor in problem-solving ability for arithmetic was the ability to note details in reading.

There have been many studies of sex-related differences in mathematics (Stafford, 1972; Sherman, 1977; Fennema, 1974; Fennema & Sherman, 1977; Aiken, 1971; Callahan & Glennon, 1975; Fennema, 1975). As reported in a review of 38 studies by Fennema (1974), no significant differences were found between boys' and girls' mathematics achievement before or during early elementary years. If apparent in the upper-elementary and early high school years, any differences were between levels of cognitive tasks. Boys were favored when the tasks were at higher cognitive levels, and girls were favored when tasks were at lower cognitive levels. Data from the National Assessment of Educational Progress (NAEP, 1975) indicate that neither sex has a clear advantage in computational ability.

Mathematics educators and teachers believe that attitude toward mathematics is related to achievement. Research indicates, however, that only a slight causal influence on how much arithmetic is learned can be attributed to positive or negative attitudes toward arithmetic. It has been found that relatively definite attitudes are developed by the time children are nine years of age and that there is no evidence that the content or mathematics program has particularly influenced attitudes. Aiken (1970) concluded from his thorough review of research that children's attitudes appear to become increasingly less positive as they progress through school; more recent studies continue to support this conclusion (Aiken, 1972b; Knaupp, 1973; Suydam, 1975; Suydam & Weaver, 1970, 1975). Whether self-concept is significantly related to mathematics achievement has not been ascertained (Koch, 1972; Moore, 1972; Hunter, 1974; Phelan, 1974; Zander, 1973).

Socioeconomic factors appear to account for much of the variance in mathematics achievement. Students from high socioeconomic levels tend to achieve better than students from low socioeconomic levels. Also, students from urban areas tend to achieve slightly better than do students from rural areas (Suydam & Osborne, 1977; NAEP, 1975).

Team teaching, modular scheduling, special teachers, and other organizational patterns have been used as alternatives to the self-contained classroom, which remains the predominant pattern. As noted by Suydam and Osborne (1977), there seems to be more rationale for effective organizational patterns than evidence. Based on the reviews of research by Suydam (1972, 1974) and Suydam and Weaver (1970, 1975), there appears to be no one organizational pattern for increasing student achievement in arithmetic. Perhaps the most predominant implication from this body of research is that good teachers can be effective regardless of the school organizational pattern.

Walbesser and Eisenberg (1972) and Duchastel and Merrill (1973) have reviewed the research comparing the effects of achievement between groups having knowledge or no knowledge of behavioral objectives prior to instruction. In an analysis of these reviews and additional studies, Begle (1979) found that about one-half of the studies supported significant effects favoring behavioral objectives. In only one study did the provision of objectives have a negative effect on learning.

The greatest change in testing has been the increasing use of criterion-referenced tests, as behavioral objectives were emphasized. In the 1970s, however, there was less concern for the form of the objectives than for the intention (Suydam & Osborne, 1977). Instructional objectives and test items compare favorably on content involving knowledge of computation, although there is need for more attention to the testing of higher-order objectives.

Current research on number has shifted from assessing children's attainment of number to an attempt to explain the development of basic number concepts. This redirection has received much of its theoretical support from the work of Piaget. However, Brainerd (1973a, 1973b) takes issue with Piaget's contention that concepts of cardinality (how many) and ordinality (which one) of number develop simultaneously. In his review of research on number, Brainerd (1976) proposes to change early number instruction to an ordinal approach rather than the currently accepted cardinal approach (Davydov, 1975; Gelman; 1972a, 1972b, 1977; Ginsburg, 1977a, 1977b). The sequence of development of different number skills has not been established clearly. Klahr and Wallace (1976) cite evidence to suggest that children perceive directly the number of elements in small sets before they count. Yet, Gelman (1972a, 1972b, 1977) asserts that counting precedes directly perceiving or subitizing.

Research on addition, subtraction, multiplication, and division of whole numbers can be classified into two categories: those studies related to basic facts and those studies on algorithms. In their review of basic skills, Suydam and Dessart (1980) note that open subtraction sentences have been found more difficult to solve than open addition sentences; sentences with the operation sign on the right-hand side of the equals sign are more difficult than those with the operation sign on the left-hand side; sentences with numbers between twenty and one hundred are more difficult than those within the context of basic facts; and childrens' methods of solving open sentences vary both within and between types (Aims, 1971; Engle & Lerch, 1971; Groen & Poll, 1973; Grouws, 1972, 1974; Grouws & Good, 1976; Weaver, 1971, 1972, 1973). Research on algorithms has identified both strengths and weaknesses of each algorithm, the use of manipulative material or other concomitants that may affect or facilitate the teaching of particular algorithms. Some indicate that one algorithm may be better for one type of learner and another for other learners (Dashiell, 1975; Hiker, 1976; Hutchings, 1973; Kratzer & Willoughby, 1973; Wheatley, 1976). The lack of extension or replication of studies in this area does not lend strong support for the findings of individual studies.

General results of research on rational numbers, reviewed by Suydam and Dessart, support the rule-first sequence as promoting higher-skill achievement, but a model-first sequence leads to better understanding. There have been mixed findings with respect to teaching methods, but the use of materials has been found superior to the nonuse of materials (Choate, 1975; Ellerbruch, 1976; Novillis, 1976; Phillips & Kane, 1973; Uprichard & Phillips, 1977; Stenger, 1972; Colburn, 1974; Green, 1970).

Research on decimals has been sparse with mixed results. Wilson (1969, 1972), however, found no significant differences in fraction-decimal and decimal-fraction sequences.

Lester (1980) reviewed the recent research in problem solving in mathematics, categorizing it into four sections: (1) subject variables (characteristics of the learner); (2) task variables (the problem itself); (3) process variables (problem-solving behavior); and (4) instructional variables (environmental factors). Studies relating characteristics of the problem solver to processes used have found that good problem solvers exhibit (1) good overall mathematics achievement; (2) good verbal and general reasoning ability; (3) strong spatial ability; (4) a positive attitude; (5) resistance to distraction; (6) field independence; (7) divergent thinking; (8) confidence; (9) lack of anxiety; (10) flexibility; (11) lack of rigidity; and (12) ability to cope with uncertainty (Dodson, 1972; Meyer, 1978; Kantowski, 1974; Moses, 1977; Putt, 1978; Trimmer, 1974).

Studies made of the problem to be solved have found that the problem syntax, computational errors, and the amount of information are the crucial aspects of a problem task (Linville, 1970; Knifong & Holtan, 1976; Jerman, 1974; Caldwell, 1978; Lester, 1978). Kilpatrick (1968) identified processes used in problem solving to be (1) drawing a figure; (2) using successive approximations; (3) questioning the evidence; (4) questioning the uniqueness of the solution; (5) using deductions; (6) using an equation; (7) using

trial-and-error; and (8) checking the solution. The most powerful processes seem to be trial-and-error and successive approximations. Studies have attempted to develop instruments to be used in refining protocol analysis procedures (Kantowski, 1977; Krutetskii, 1976; Smith, 1973; Vos, 1976; Proudfit, 1977). Results of clinical studies have found that students can be taught to solve problems, to ask questions that assist in understanding the problem, and to use specific strategies, although it may limit their flexibility (Kantowski, 1977; Putt, 1978).

The decade of the 1970s was clearly a time of rapid development and advancement for the electronic calculator. Its impact on arithmetic instruction has been noted by several reports (NACOME, 1975; NCTM, 1980). In reviewing thirty-four studies conducted across elementary, secondary, and college students, Roberts (1980) concluded that the general results seem to show that (1) computation benefits accrue from the calculator; (2) accuracy and efficiency accompany calculator usage; (3) improvement in conceptual areas has been minimal; and (4) hypothesized changes in general attitudes towards mathematics have not been supported. Also, Roberts suggests that calculator research shift to looking for positive effects rather than negative effects. For example, he proposes that students use the calculators on the criterion tasks. Also, he suggests that educators look for the unique and specific possibilities for calculator use.

Methodological problems. The problems encountered in doing research on arithmetic teaching and learning are numerous, yet similar in nature to those involved in other areas of educational research. Not only are there problems with research design, but also the desire to describe human phenomena in such a way as to be useful to society.

Many of the problems inherent in the search for quality research in arithmetic are identified by White (1980). There is the important matter of sampling. Errors in this category include (1) failure to identify the population from which the sample will be drawn; (2) using procedures that result in a biased sample; (3) choosing an incorrect sample size; (4) misinterpretation of results by using only a portion of the elements sampled; and (5) failure to randomize the sample into groups.

The second category concerns the matter of instrumentation. Errors in this category include (1) misinterpretation of test scores; and (2) unreliable tests. The third category deals with statistical methods in research: (1) failure to consider interactive effects; (2) failure to use relevant information to formulate hypotheses; and (3) use of inappropriate statistical methods (such as t tests instead of an F test, or univariate analyses when multivariate methods are appropriate).

Closely related to these errors has been the concern of researchers in education for the replicability of research results; that is, is it possible to obtain consistent results across studies over time? Of primary importance is the possibility of recreating the experiment so as to bias the result. Variables investigated in this regard have been the teacher variable (Will a different teacher affect results?), reorganization of subjects (Are subjects treated differently and, if so, will the results be different?), and class size or room size (Will physical arrangements have an effect on the results?).

The search for pertinent variables in arithmetic and teaching has given rise to a methodological controversy in educational research. On one hand, there is a desire to control such variables through randomization, matching of students and statistical methods, and other experimental procedures. In this way, there is an attempt to "sterilize" the results and obtain "pure" results, which answer a well-formulated, precise set of questions.

Vos (1980) discusses the pros and cons of the experimental approach. In the context of a recent study he conducted, Vos illustrates the problems associated with experimental studies. Initially, there are several pitfalls to be considered. (1) Are there unrealistic demands in a classroom setting? (2) Will the results make a significant contribution to the profession? (3) Are there other uncontrollable variables to be considered?

Major steps involved are (1) formulating the research idea; (2) designing the study; (3) implementation (2 and 3 may be improved through the use of a pilot study); (4) interpretation of results (experimenter bias may be a problem here); and (5) future plans for research (this gives the researcher the chance to speculate on possible improvements for future projects). By considering these in sequence, the reader can see the demands made by a quality experimental design and determine that well-designed research is a challenge for any educator.

At the other end of the continuum is the position of the researcher who uses clinical observations in arithmetic research studies (Nelson, 1980a, 1980b). This technique tends to forego traditional controls in favor of a more naturalistic view of the learning and teaching environment. Often in this type of study, no specific research hypotheses are formulated to be later tested through statistical procedures. Much like the experimental study, pilot work is helpful in designing and implementing the study. As data are collected, there is an effort to systematize protocols. When there is deviation from usual behavior, validated descriptions of phenomena are provided. Analysis and interpretation of results are often time-consuming and do not always yield generalizable results because of the difficulties inherent in developing a scheme for analysis. At the same time, unexpected results may lead to new descriptions about behavior related to arithmetic. In addition, such studies may lead to future research on the observed behaviors as well as on the newly developed statistical and interpretive procedures.

The methodological problems discussed have been related to either the logistics of the classroom (students, materials, etc.) or the particular methods used to conduct research. The final problem to be discussed is further removed from the process itself. The topic of concern is government involvement in the research process. In June 1976, the U.S. Department of Health, Education, and Welfare (HEW) issued the final rules to implement the 1974 Buckley Amendment. The Buckley Amendment, also known as the Family Educational Rights and Privacy Act, was written to provide protection for the families and children used in the educational research process (Buckley, 1976). In addition to this legislation, which could hinder access to student records used in research, Public Law 93-348, as amended, has mandated that institutions of higher learning set up procedures for guaranteeing the protection of human subjects. In many cases, there is a review of the proposed research at several levels of administration, with effects that can be quite time-consuming and frustrating to the researcher. Because of the effort expended in covering all the legal bases, it is becoming very difficult to conduct research in the public schools. As a result, many researchers are turning to the use of private schools and/or their own college classes. Although this practice is legitimate, the professional field may suffer by limiting its population of subjects for study. Furthermore, these choices of samples for study may be composed of subjects who are atypical and thus lead to problems with generalizability.

These unsettled questions are only some of the problems facing the researcher in arithmetic. Each educational researcher has several more to add. The important thing to remember is that there is no one simple method of research. In Bauersfeld's comments to the Third International Congress on Mathematical Education, he said, "Mathematics educators and teachers have to learn . . . how to deal with a variety of methods for research and teaching. . . . He [the mathematics teacher] should not reduce complexity by following current modes of research or public opinions, nor should he get lost in a poorly oriented pragmatism. He has to develop his own self-concept" (Bauersfeld, 1977, pp. 242–243). Thus, the researcher on arithmetic continually accepts the challenge to overcome these persistent problems when embarking on a research effort.

Public Opinion.   Reports of decline on test scores and pressure for a back-to-basics educational approach have resulted in emphasis on assessment and accountability for the learning of arithmetic on the part of children and youth. Much of this controversy was sparked by disagreement over the value and effectiveness of innovations in curriculum and instruction that were supported by the NSF, the United States Office of Education, and the NIE. The NSF conducted three status studies in the mid-1970s in response to the many questions of "for whom, for what, and how" that were raised concerning the curricula.

The issue of back-to-basics prevailed throughout the 1970s. Most people have thought of the basics as being "the three *R*'s"—reading, writing, and arithmetic. For a number of years, George Gallup has polled the citizenry about American education. In one poll during the 1970s, over 80 percent of the people acquainted with the back-to-basics movement responded in favor of it. For many, this movement was interpreted to be, in practice, the bare-bones techniques of computation. Though emphasis on acquiring such basic skills is at the heart of the educational process, there has been much concern on the part of the mathematics education community that such an approach itself becomes the curriculum and leads to the tendency to teach only those things for which students can be tested for purposes of demonstrating minimum competency.

Policy makers and leaders in government, industry, and business have had a continuing concern that the United States be the world leader in science and technology, especially as these fields become increasingly complex. It was in response to both this concern for leadership and to the international situation of the 1950s that an all-out effort was made to develop curricula that could properly educate potential scientists and engineers, who could ensure that the United States would be first to reach the moon. Conceived during the 1940s and born in 1950, the NSF was preparing to meet this goal when the nation became concerned about our scientific capacity. When the rockets lifted off, the measures taken were deemed successful by most citizens.

According to the results of NAEP reports, students at all levels can add, subtract, multiply, and divide now as well as they always have, but there is a sharp decline in their ability to deal with any items that would require understanding and interpretation beyond the rudimentary arithmetic skills. There also is concern that minority groups, including women, are not receiving the appropriate early education in arithmetic that would lead to continuing in the field of mathematics.

As the 1970s drew to a close, there was recurring concern for leadership in science and technology, but not in altered curricula for potential mathematicians and scientists, as in the 1960s. The new concern is for the non-mathematics student who must be prepared to enter fields in industry, business, and government in which mathematical knowledge is basic to skilled employment.

E. Glenadine Gibb
Charles E. Lamb

See also Comparative School Achievement; Mathematical Behavior of Children; Mathematics Education; Metric Education.

REFERENCES

Aiken, L. R., Jr. Attitudes toward mathematics. *Review of Educational Research*, 1970, *40*, 551–596.

Aiken, L. R., Jr. Intellective variables and mathematics achievement: Directions for research. *Journal of School Psychology*, 1971, *9*, 201–212.

Aiken, L. R., Jr. Language factors in learning mathematics. *Review of Educational Research*, 1972, *42*, 359–385. (a)

Aiken, L. R., Jr. Research on attitudes toward mathematics. *Arithmetic Teacher*, 1972, *19*, 229–234. (b)

Aims, B. D. A study of selected relationships between solution time and five characteristics of arithmetic drill problems (Doctoral dissertation, Memphis State University, 1970). *Dissertation Abstracts International*, 1971, *31*, 4373A.

Ausubel, D. P. *Educational Psychology: A cognitive view*. New York: Holt, Rinehart & Winston, 1968.

Bauersfeld, H. Research related to the mathematical learning process. In H. Athen and H. Kunle (Eds.), *Proceedings of the Third International Congress on Mathematical Education*. Karlsruhe, F.R.G.: 3rd ICME, 1977.

Begle, E. G. *Critical Variables in Mathematics Education: Findings from a Survey of the Empirical Literature*. Washington, D.C.: Mathematical Association of America, and the National Council of Teachers of Mathematics, 1979. (ERIC Document Reproduction Service No. ED 171 515)

Beilin, H. Linguistic, logical, and cognitive models for learning mathematical concepts. In A. Osborne (Ed.), *Models for Learning Mathematics*. Columbus, Ohio: ERIC, 1976.

Brainerd, C. J. Judgements and explanations as criteria for the presence of cognitive structures. *Psychological Bulletin*, 1973, *79*, 172–179. (a)

Brainerd, C. J. Neo-Piagetian training experiments revisited: Is there any support for the cognitive-developmental stage hypothesis? *Cognition*, 1973, *2*, 349–370. (b)

Brainerd, C. J. Analysis and synthesis of research on children's ordinal and cardinal number concepts. In R. A. Lesh (Ed.), *Number and Measurement*. Columbus, Ohio: ERIC, 1976.

Brownell, W. A. The place of meaning in the teaching of arithmetic. *Elementary School Journal*, 1947, *47*, 257–258.

Brownell, W. A., & Moser, H. E. *Meaningful versus Mechanical Learning: A Study in Grade Three Subtraction*. Durham, N.C.: Duke University Press, 1949.

Bruner, J. S. *The Relevance of Education*. New York: W. W. Norton, 1971.

Buckley, T. *Family Educational Rights and Privacy Act and H.E.W. Guidelines*. Washington, D.C.: Department of Health, Education, and Welfare, 1976. (ERIC Document Reproduction Service No. ED 129 143)

Buswell, G. T. The psychology of learning in relation to the teaching of arithmetic. In N. B. Henry (Ed.), *The Teaching of Arithmetic: Fiftieth Yearbook of the National Society for the Study of Education* (Part 11). Chicago: University of Chicago Press, 1951.

Buswell, G. T. Arithmetic. In C. W. Harris (Ed.), *Encyclopedia of Educational Research* (3rd ed.). New York: Macmillan, 1960.

Byers, V., & Herscovics, N. Understanding school mathematics. *Bulletin of the Association of Teachers of Mathematics*, 1977, No. 81.

Caldwell, J. H. Cognitive development and difficulty in solving word problems in mathematics (Doctoral dissertation, University of Pennsylvania, 1977). *Dissertation Abstracts International*, 1978, *38*, 4637A.

Callahan, L. G., & Glennon, V. J. *Elementary School Mathematics: A Guide to Current Research* (4th ed.). Washington, D.C.: Association for Supervision and Curriculum Development, 1975. (ERIC Document Reproduction Service No. ED 116 966)

Carpenter, T. P. Research in cognitive development. In R. Shumway (Ed.), *Research in Mathematics Education*. Reston, Va.: National Council of Teachers of Mathematics, 1980. (ERIC Document Reproduction Service No. ED 187 563)

Carry, L. R., & Weaver, J. F. Patterns of mathematics achievement in grades four, five, and six: X-Population. In J. W. Wilson, L. S. Cohen, & E. G. Beglef (Eds.), *NLSMA Report No. 10*. Stanford, Calif.: School Mathematics Study Group, 1969.

Chase, C. I. The position of certain variables in the prediction of problem-solving in arithmetic. *Journal of Educational Research*, 1960, *54*, 9–14.

Choate, S. A. The effect of algorithmic and conceptual development for the comparison of fractions (Doctoral dissertation, University of Michigan, 1975). *Dissertation Abstracts International*, 1975, *36*, 1410A.

Clark, J. R. Perspective in programs of instruction in elementary mathematics. *Arithmetic Teacher*, 1965, *12*, 604–611.

Colburn, T. G. The effect of a ratio approach and a regional approach on equivalent fractions and addition/subtraction for pupils in grade four (Doctoral dissertation, University of Michigan, 1973). *Dissertation Abstracts International*, 1974, *34*, 4688A.

Coleman, J. S.; Campbell, E. Q.; Hobson, C. J.; McPartland, J.; Mood, A. M.; Winfeld, F. D.; & York, R. L. *Equality of Education Opportunity*. Washington, D.C.: U.S. Government Printing Office, 1966. (ERIC Document Reproduction Service No. ED 012 275)

Dashiell, W. H. An analysis of changes in affect and changes in both computational power and computational stamina occurring in primary and elementary school children after instruction in Hutching's low fatigue addition algorithms, practice with unusually large samples, and exposure to one of two alternative performance options (Doctoral dissertation, University of Maryland, 1974). *Dissertation Abstracts International*, 1975, *35*, 7740A.

Davydov, V. V. On the formation of an elementary concept of number by the child. In J. W. Wilson (Ed.), *Analysis of Reasoning Processes: Soviet Studies in the Psychology of Learning and Teaching Mathematics* (Vol. 13). Palo Alto, Calif.: School Mathematics Study Group, 1975.

Dawson, D. T., & Ruddell, A. K. The case for the meaning theory in teaching arithmetic. *Elementary School Journal*, 1955, *55*, 343–349.

DeVault, M. V., & Weaver, J. F. Forces and issues related to curriculum and instruction, K–6. In National Council of Teachers of Mathematics, *A History of Mathematical Education in the United States and Canada: Thirty-second Yearbook*. Washington, D.C.: National Council of Teachers of Mathematics, 1970.

Dodson, J. W. *Characteristics of Successful Insightful Problem Solvers* (NLSMA Report No. 31). Stanford, Calif.: School Mathematics Study Group, 1972.

Duchastel, P. C., & Merrill, P. F. The effects of behavioral objectives on learning: A review of the empirical studies. *Review of Educational Research*, 1973, *43*, 53–69.

Earle, R. A. *Teaching Reading and Mathematics*. Newark, Del.: International Reading Association, 1976.

Ellerbruch, L. W. The effects of the placement of rules and concrete models in learning addition and subtraction of fractions in grade four (Doctoral dissertation, University of Michigan, 1975). *Dissertation Abstracts International*, 1976, *36*, 6441A–6442A.

Engle, C. D., & Lerch, H. H. A comparison of first-grade children's abilities on two types of arithmetical practice exercises. *School Science and Mathematics*, 1971, *71*, 327–334.

Fennema, E. Sex differences in mathematics achievement: A review. *Journal for Research in Mathematics Education*, 1974, *5*, 126–139.

Fennema, E. Mathematics, spatial ability, and the sexes. In E. Fennema (Ed.), *Mathematics Learning: What Research Says About Sex Differences*. Columbus, Ohio: ERIC Clearinghouse for Science, Mathematics, and Environmental Education. 1975.

Fennema, E., & Sherman, J. Sex-related differences in mathematics achievement, spatial visualization, and affective factors. *American Educational Research Journal*, 1977, *14*, 51–71.

Fey, J. T. Mathematics teaching today: Perspectives from three national surveys. *Arithmetic Teacher*, 1979, *27*, 10–14.

Flavell, J. H. *The Developmental Psychology of Jean Piaget*. Princeton, N.J.: Van Nostrand, 1963.

Gagné, R. M. *The Conditions of Learning* (3rd ed.). New York: Holt, Rinehart & Winston, 1977.

Geeslin, W. E. Using writing about mathematics as a teaching technique. *Mathematics Teacher*, 1977, *70*, 112–115.

Gelman, R. Logical capacity of very young children: Number invariance rules. *Child Development*, 1972, *43*, 75–90. (a)

Gelman, R. The nature and development of early number concepts. In H. Reese (Ed.), *Advances in Child Development and Behavior* (Vol. 7). New York: Academic Press, 1972. (b)

Gelman, R. How young children reason about small numbers. In N. J. Castillan, D. P. Pisoni, & G. R. Ports (Eds.), *Cognitive Theory* (Vol. 2). Hillsdale, N.J.: Lawrence Erlbaum Associates, 1977.

Gibney, T., & Karas, E. Mathematics education: 1955–1975—A summary of the findings. *Educational Leadership*, 1979, *36*, 356–369.

Ginsberg, H. *Children's Arithmetic: The Learning Process*. New York: Van Nostrand, 1977. (a)

Ginsberg, H. The psychology of arithmetic thinking. *Journal of Children's Mathematical Behavior*, 1977, *1*, 1–89. (b)

Glennon, V. J. Research need in elementary school mathematics education. *Arithmetic Teacher*, 1966, *13*, 363–368.

Green, G. A. A comparison of two approaches, area and finding a part of, and two instructional materials, diagrams, and manipulative aids, on multiplication of fractional numbers in grade five (Doctoral dissertation, University of Michigan, 1969). *Dissertation Abstracts International*, 1970, *31*, 676A–677A.

Groen, G. J., & Poll, M. Subtraction and the solution of open sentence problems. *Journal of Experimental Child Psychology*, 1973, *16*, 292–302.

Grouws, D. A. Differential performance of third-grade children in solving open sentences of four types (Doctoral dissertation, University of Wisconsin, 1971). *Dissertation Abstracts International*, 1972, *32*, 3860A.

Grouws, D. A. Solution methods used in solving addition and subtraction open sentences. *Arithmetic Teacher*, 1974, *21*, 255–261.

Grouws, D. A., & Good, T. L. Factors associated with third- and fourth-grade children's performance in solving multiplication and division sentences. *Journal for Research in Mathematics Education*, 1976, *7*, 155–171.

Higgins, J. L.; Kasten, M.; & Suydam, M. V. *Assessing Mathematical Achievement*. Columbus, Ohio: ERIC Clearinghouse for Science, Mathematics, and Environmental Education, 1979. (ERIC Document Reproduction Service No. ED 184 809)

Hiker, D. L. The effects of increasing additional skill on self-concept in children (Doctoral dissertation, University of Maryland, 1976). *Dissertation Abstracts International*, 1976, *37*, 3078B.

Hunter, M. L. Group effect on self-concept and math performance (Doctoral dissertation, California School of Professional Psychology, Los Angeles, 1973). *Dissertation Abstracts International*, 1974, *34*, 5169B.

Hutchings, L. B. An examination, across a wide range of socioeconomic circumstances, of a format for field research of experimental numerical computational algorithms, an instrument for measuring computational power under any concise numerical addition algorithm, two experimental numerical addition algorithms, and equivalent practice with the conventional addition algorithm (Doctoral dissertation, Syracuse University, 1972). *Dissertation Abstracts International*, 1973, *33*, 4768A.

Jerman, M. E. Problem length as a structural variable in verbal arithmetic problem. *Educational Studies in Mathematics*, 1974, *5*, 109–123.

Jones, P. S., & Coxford, A. F. Introduction. In P. S. Jones & A. F. Coxford (Eds.), *A History of Mathematics Education in the United States and Canada*. Washington, D.C.: National Council of Teachers of Mathematics, 1970.

Judd, C. H. Psychological analysis of the fundamentals of arithmetic. In F. Bobbitt (Ed.), *Curriculum Investigations*. Chicago: University of Chicago Press, 1927.

Kantowski, E. L. *Processes Involved in Mathematical Problem-solving*. Unpublished doctoral dissertation, University of Georgia, 1974.

Kantowski, M. G. Processes involved in mathematical problem-solving. *Journal of Research in Mathematics Education*, 1977, *8*(3), 163–180.

Kilpatrick, J. Analyzing the solution of word problems in mathematics: An exploratory study (Doctoral dissertation, Stanford University, 1967). *Dissertation Abstracts International*, 1968, *28*(11), 4380A.

Klahr, D., & Wallace, J. G. *Cognitive Development: An Information-processing View*. Hillsdale, N.J.: Lawrence Erlbaum Associates, 1976.

Knaupp, J. Are children's attitudes toward learning arithmetic really important? *School Science and Mathematics*, 1973, *73*, 9–15.

Knifong, J. D., & Holtan, B. An analysis of children's written solutions to word problems. *Journal for Research in Mathematic Education*, 1976, *7*(2), 106–112.

Koch, D. R. Concept of self and mathematics achievement (Doctoral dissertation, Auburn University, 1972). *Dissertation Abstracts International*, 1972, *33*, 1081A.

Kohlberg, L. Early education: A cognitive developmental view. *Child Development*, 1968, *39*, 1013–1062.

Kratzer, R. O., & Willoughby, S. S. A comparison of initially teaching division employing the distributive and Greenwood algorithms with the aid of a manipulative material. *Journal for Research in Mathematics Education*, 1973, *1*, 95–128.

Krutetskii, V. A. *The Psychology of Mathematical Abilities in Schoolchildren*. Chicago: University of Chicago Press, 1976.

Lamberg, W. J., & Lamb, C. E. *Reading Instruction in the Content Areas*. Skokie, Ill.: Rand McNally, 1980.

Lester, F. K. Mathematical Problem-solving in the elementary school: Some educational and psychological considerations. In L. L. Hatfield & D. A. Bradbard (Eds.), *Mathematical Problem-solving: Papers from a Research Workshop*. Columbus, Ohio: ERIC Clearinghouse for Science, Mathematics, and Environmental Education, 1978.

Lester, F. K. Research on mathematical problem-solving. In R. Shumway (Ed.), *Research in Mathematics Education*. Reston, Va.: National Council for Teachers of Mathematics, 1980. (ERIC Document Reproduction Service No. ED 187 563)

Linville, W. J. The effects of syntax and vocabulary upon the difficulty of verbal arithmetic problems with fourth-grade students (Doctoral dissertation, Indiana University, 1969). *Dissertation Abstracts International*, 1970, *30*, 4310A.

Meyer, R. A. Mathematical problem-solving performance and in-

tellectual abilities of fourth-grade children. *Journal for Research in Mathematics Education*, 1978, *9*(5), 334–348.

Moore, B. D. The relationship of fifth-grade students' self-concepts and attitudes toward mathematics to academic achievement in arithmetical computation, concepts, and application (Doctoral dissertation, North Texas State University, 1971). *Dissertation Abstracts International*, 1972, *32*, 4425.

Morusett, L. N., & Vinsonhaler, J. (Eds.). *Mathematical Learning* (Monograph of the Society for Research in Child Development, Serial No. 99, No. 1). Chicago: University of Chicago Press, 1965.

Moses, B. E. *The Nature of Spatial Ability and Its Relationship to Mathematical Problem-solving*. Unpublished doctoral dissertation, Indiana University, 1977.

National Advisory Committee on Mathematical Education. *Overview and Analysis of School Mathematics: Grades K–12*. Washington, D.C.: Conference Board of the Mathematical Sciences, 1975. (ERIC Document Reproduction Service No. ED 115 512)

National Assessment of Educational Progress. *Mathematics Fundamentals: Selected Results from the First National Assessment of Mathematics* (Report No. 04-MA-01). Washington, D.C.: U.S. Superintendent of Documents, 1975.

National Assessment of Educational Progress. *Mathematical Knowledge and Skills: Selected Results from the Second Assessment of Mathematics* (Report No. 09-MA-02). Washington, D.C.: U.S. Superintendent of Documents, 1979.

National Council of Teachers of Mathematics. *An Agenda for Action: Recommendations for School Mathematics of the 1980s*. Reston, Va.: The Council, 1980. (ERIC Document Reproduction Service No. ED 186 265)

National Council of Teachers of Mathematics. *Priorities in School Mathematics: Executive Summary of the PRISM Project*. Reston, Va.: The Council, 1981.

Nelson, D. Case study 2: Clinical research. In R. Shumway (Ed.), *Research in Mathematics Education*. Reston, Va.: National Council of Teachers of Mathematics, 1980. (a) (ERIC Document Reproduction Service No. ED 187 563)

Nelson, D. *Studying Problem-solving Behavior in Early Childhood* (Lecture Series Award Monograph). Edmonton: University of Alberta, Faculty of Education, 1980. (b)

Novillis, L. F. An anlysis of the fraction concept into a hierarchy of selected subconcepts and the testing of the hierarchical dependencies. *Journal for Research in Mathematics Education*, 1976, *7*, 131–144.

Phelan, E. J. Achievement, self-concept, creativity, and attitude toward school of students in formal and informal education programs (Doctoral disseration, Fordham University, 1974). *Dissertation Abstracts International*, 1974, *35*, 1400A–1401A.

Phillips, E. R., & Kane, R. B. Validating learning hierarchies for sequencing mathematical tasks in elementary school mathematics. *Journal for Research in Mathematics Education*, 1973, *4*, 141–151.

Proudfit, L. *The Development of a Process Evaluation Instrument (Technical Report V) Mathematical Problem-solving Project*. Bloomington, Ind.: Mathematics Education Development Center, 1977.

Putt, I. J. *An Exploratory Investigation of Two Methods of Instruction in Mathematical Problem-solving at the Fifth-grade Level*. Unpublished doctoral dissertation, Indiana University, 1978.

Rappaport, D. Historical factors that have influenced the mathematics program for the primary grades. *School Science and Mathematics*, 1965, *65*, 23–25.

Ratner, J. *The Philosophy of John Dewey*. New York: Henry Holt, 1928.

Roberts, D. M. The impact of electronic calculators. *Review of Educational Research*, 1980, *50*, 71–98.

Sherman, J. Effects of biological factors on sex-related differences in mathematics achievement. In L. H. Fox, E. Fennema, & J. Sherman (Eds.), *Women and Mathematics: Research Perspectives for Change*. Washington, D.C.: National Institute of Education, 1977.

Shulman, L. S. Psychology and mathematics education. In E. G. Begle (Ed.), *Mathematics Education: Sixty-ninth Yearbook of the National Society for the Study of Education* (Part 1). Chicago: University of Chicago Press, 1970.

Skemp, R. *The Psychology of Learning Mathematics*. Baltimore: Penguin Books 1971.

Skemp, R. Relational understanding and instrumental understanding. *Mathematics Teaching*, 1977.

Skinner, B. F. *The Technology of Teaching*. New York: Appleton-Century-Crofts, 1968.

Skypeck, D. H. Teaching mathematics: Implications from a theory for teaching the language arts. *Arithmetic Teacher*, 1981, *28*, 13–17.

Smith, J. P. *The Effect of General versus Specific Heuristics in Mathematical Problem-solving Tasks*. Unpublished doctoral dissertation, Columbia University, 1973.

Stafford, R. E. Hereditary and environmental components of quantitative reasoning. *Journal of Educational Research*, 1972, *42*, 183–201.

Stake, R. E., & Easley, J. (Eds.). *Case Studies in Science Education* (Vols. 1 and 2). Urbana: University of Illinois, 1978.

Stenger, D. J. An experimental comparison of two methods of teaching the addition and subtraction of common fractions in grade five (Doctoral dissertation, University of Cincinnati, 1971). *Dissertation Abstracts International*, 1972, *32*, 3676A.

Suydam, M. N. *A Review of Research on Secondary School Mathematics*. Columbus, Ohio: ERIC Clearinghouse for Science, Mathematics, and Environmental Education, 1972. (ERIC Document Reproduction Service No. ED 065 313)

Suydam, M. N. *A Categorized Listing of Research on Mathematics Education K–12, 1964–1973*. Columbus, Ohio: ERIC Information Analysis Center for Science, Mathematics, and Environmental Education, 1974. (ERIC Document Reproduction Service No. ED 097 225)

Suydam, M. N. Research on some key non-cognitive variables in mathematics education. In *Schriftenreihe des IDM*. Beilefeld, Germany: Universität Beilefeld, Institut für Didaktik der Mathematik, 1975.

Suydam, M. N., & Dessart, D. J. Skill learning. In R. J. Shumway (Ed.), *Research in Mathematics Education*. Reston, Va.: National Council of Teachers of Mathematics, 1980. (ERIC Document Reproduction Service No. ED 187 563)

Suydam, M. N., & Osborne, A. *The Status of Pre-college Science, Mathematics, and Social Science Education: 1955–1975*. Vol. 2 of *Mathematics Education*. Columbus: Ohio State University, Center for Science and Mathematics Education, 1977.

Suydam, M. N., & Weaver, J. F. *Using Research: A Key to Elementary School Mathematics*. University Park: Pennsylvania State University, 1970.

Suydam, M. N., & Weaver, J. F. *Using Research: A Key to Elementary School Mathematics*. Columbus, Ohio: ERIC Clearinghouse for Science, Mathematics, and Environmental Education, 1975.

Thorndike, E. L., & Woodworth, R. S. The influence of improvement in one mental function upon the efficiency of other functions. *Psychological Review*, 1901, *8*, 247–261, 384–395, 553–564.

Trimmer, R. G. *A Review of the Research Relating Problem-solving and Mathematics Achievement to Psychological Variables and Relating These Variables to Methods Involving or Compatible with Self-correcting Manipulative Mathematics Materials*. Unpublished manuscript, 1974.

Uprichard, A. E., & Phillips, E. R. An intraconcept analysis of rational number addition: A validation study. *Journal for Research in Mathematics Education*, 1977, *8*, 7–16.

Uznadze, D. N. *The Psychology of Set*. New York: Plenum, 1966.

Van Engen, H. *Foundations of Elementary School Arithmetic*. Chicago: Scott, Foresman, 1965.

Van Engen, H., & Gibb, E. G. *General Mental Functions Associated with Division*. Cedar Falls: Iowa State Teachers College, 1956.

Vos, K. The effects of three instructional strategies on problem-solving behaviors in secondary school mathematics. *Journal for Research in Mathematics Education*, 1976, *7*(5), 264–275.

Vos, K. Case study 3: Experiment. In R. Shumway (Ed.), *Research in Mathematics Education*. Reston, Va.: National Council of Teachers of Mathematics, 1980. (ERIC Document Reproduction Service No. ED 187 563)

Walbesser, H. H., & Eisenberg, T. A. A review of research on behavioral objectives and learning hierarchies. In *Mathematics Education Reports*. Columbus: Ohio State University, ERIC Clearinghouse for Science, Mathematics, and Environmental Education, 1972. (ERIC Document Reproduction Service No. ED 059 900)

Weaver, J. F. Some factors associated with pupils' performance level on simple open addition and subtraction sentences. *Arithmetic Teacher*, 1971, *18*, 513–519.

Weaver, J. F. The ability of first-, second-, and third-grade pupils to identify open addition and subtraction sentences for which no solution exists within the set of whole numbers. *School Science and Mathematics*, 1972, *72*, 679–691.

Weaver, J. F. The symmetric property of the equality relation and young children's ability to solve open addition and subtraction sentences. *Journal for Research in Mathematics Education*, 1973, *4*, 45–56.

Weiss, I. *Report of the 1977 National Survey of Science, Mathematics, and Social Studies Education*. Research Triangle Park, N.C.: Research Triangle Institute, 1978.

Wheatley, G. H. A comparison of two methods of column addition. *Journal for Research in Mathematics Education*, 1976, *7*, 145–154.

White, A. L. Avoiding errors in educational research. In R. J. Shumway (Ed.), *Research in Mathematics Education*. Reston, Va.: National Council of Teachers of Mathematics, 1980. (ERIC Document Reproduction Service No. ED 187 563)

White, S. H. Evidence for hierarchical arrangement of learning processes. In L. P. Lipsett & C. C. Spiker (Eds.), *Advances in Child Development and Behavior* (Vol. 2). New York: Academic Press, 1965.

Willoughby, S. S. Mathematics. In R. L. Ebel (Ed.), *Encyclopedia of Educational Research* (4th ed.). New York: Macmillan, 1969.

Wilson, G. H. A comparison of decimal-common fraction sequence for fifth-grade arithmetic (Doctoral dissertation, University of Arizona, 1969). *Dissertation Abstracts International*, 1969, *30*, 1762A.

Wilson, G. H. Decimal common fraction sequence versus conventional sequence. *School Science and Mathematics*, 1972, *72*, 589–5920.

Zander, B. J. J. Junior high students view themselves as learners: A comparison among eighth-grade students (Doctoral dissertation, University of Minnesota, 1973). *Dissertation Abstracts International*, 1973, *34*, 2254–2255A.

ART EDUCATION

Since the late nineteenth century, the social sciences have been the model for inquiries into making art, responding to art, and teaching and learning art. Thus, the knowledge perspective adopted has, until recently, been close to that of the natural sciences. The arts themselves, however, have continued their even longer alignment, both attitudinally and linguistically, with the humanistic tradition. As a result, a split has arisen between the way artists and students of art live, work, and learn, and the way inquiries into the wide spectrum of artistic and aesthetic phenomena are conducted.

It might be said that the 1950s were a decade in which art education was discovering its "scientific" voice; that the 1960s found that voice; and that the 1970s questioned that voice, even while extending it, admitting openly to knowledge interests of wider scope. Sociocultural, philosophical, critical, qualitative, microethnographic, phenomenological, historical, political, and hermeneutic orientations appear with increasing frequency during the 1970s.

In the third edition of this encyclopedia, Beittel (1960) applied a strictly empirical-analytical-scientific rule both in determining what should be included and how it should be interpreted. Eisner (1969c) faced with the same task ten years later, gave slightly more attention to philosophical and historical studies, although he defined art education itself as a "technology of instruction," thereby ascribing to the research reported a control or delivery function incongruent with the more humanistically oriented studies included. In a still later research report on the teaching of art, Eisner (1973) excused Read (1945) and Lowenfeld (1947) for their prescientific, mythic inheritance, which operated against their understanding of a scientific attitude toward art education research. At the end of the decade, Engel (1978), at a federally funded research conference on cognition and the arts, persisted in defining art education as a "technology of instruction."

Scope of Art Education. The 1960s saw a burgeoning of empirical-analytical-scientific research in art education. At The Pennsylvania State University, where the largest concentration of doctoral theses for this period is found, sixty-five of seventy-five doctoral theses are "scientific," and the remaining ten are "humanistic." Of ninety-five doctoral theses at the same university for the 1970s, however, thirty-four are "scientific," and sixty-one are "humanistic."

For comparative data from art education as a whole, I examined and categorized 232 articles published in *Studies in Art Education* between 1969 and 1980. Exactly 50 percent of these fall within "scientific," 50 percent within "humanistic," and the distribution is fairly uniform throughout the decade (Table 1). (It should be noted that "methodological-theoretical" and "critical-interpretive" articles are placed under "humanistic." I leave to the reader the problem of how to resolve differing reviews of *Studies in Art Education* of this same period; for example, Rush and Kratochwill (1981) classify 77 percent of the articles as what is here called "scientific.")

The 1970s saw a number of theorists within art education and in surrounding fields change or extend their knowledge orientations. Eisner (1976), Beittel (1973), Aoki (1978), L. M. Smith (1978), for example, found themselves questioning a purely scientific ground for knowledge. For

TABLE 1. *Percent distributions in content categories of 232 articles classified from* Studies in Art Education, *1969–1980*

Scientific (Empirical-Analytical)	1969–72	1973–76	1977–80	Total
Descriptive	12.1%	10.3%	6.9%	29.3%
Test construction	1.3	0.4	1.0	2.6
Experimental	4.7	5.2	8.0	18.1
Subtotal: Scientific	18.1	15.9	16.0	50.0
Humanistic (Historical-Hermeneutic)				
Methodological-theoretical	3.9%	3.0%	5.6%	12.5%
Critical-interpretive	7.3	6.9	6.9	21.1
Historical	2.2	2.6	3.4	8.2
Philosophical	2.2	2.6	3.4	8.2
Subtotal: Humanistic	15.6	15.1	19.3	50.0
Total	33.7	31.0	35.3	100.0

a broader epistemological analysis, however, it has been necessary to look outside education, art, and art education. The works of Pepper (1942), Weiss (1958), Steiner (1981), and Habermas (1971a) all look toward a pluralistic view of knowledge. Habermas has cogently argued, from a critical perspective on the history and sociology of knowledge, that all forms of knowledge serve human interests, and are therefore never above historical and political entanglements.

No one of the above thinkers, however, provides a theory for the partitioning of knowledge interests that would make a reviewer completely comfortable in classifying the diversity of studies the 1970s include. This inadequacy stems partly from the fact that researchers themselves are variously sophisticated about the metaphysical and epistemological assumptions under which they operate, and partly from the fact that the language worlds of theorists do not neatly fit one with the other. Suffice it to say here that I intend to reflect a pluralistic attitude toward knowledge, while honoring the local coloration of each study cited. This attitude is not so much eclecticism as a reflection of the present amorphous state of the art of research in art education.

Broad Perspectives. A number of books of wide scope and pervasive influence appeared during the 1970s. Two of these are from Europe. Gadamer's *Truth and Method* (1975) addresses the limitations of natural science as applied to cultural areas. Gadamer criticizes modern aesthetic theory for its effort to differentiate the experience of art from the general quality of our existential life-world. Art is knowledge to Gadamer, and the experience of a work of art is sharing in this knowledge. There is always a historical, dialectic, linguistic, and applied (or hermeneutic) aspect to his thought.

The other landmark book from the Continent is Dufrenne's *The Phenomenology of Aesthetic Experience* (1973). Dufrenne is more structural and "scientific" than Gadamer. The standpoint adopted in his phenomenology is that of the spectator rather than of the creator. Dufrenne approaches aesthetic experience through a theory of perception, emphasizing the central role of feeling and reflection. His book is not purely phenomenological, but existential and ontological as well.

Hausman's *A Discourse on Novelty and Creation* (1975) also deserves mention for its theoretical scope and cogency. In examining the problem of novelty and creation, Hausman proposes three models of intelligibility: (1) conceptual understanding; (2) aesthetic understanding; and (3) fundamental paradox that includes both of the other forms of understanding in an "indeterminate vacillation." This third model "is more like a way of regarding a paradoxical world. It is a way of being cognitively open to a world apprehended as an unbounded metaphor" (p. 154). In comparing the other two models of intelligibility, Hausman says: "Just as there is the possibility of finding a restricted explanation in terms of efficient causality by circumscribing creative acts, there is the possibility of

constructing a teleological understanding . . . which acknowledges recalcitrant discontinuities" (pp. 154–155).

Here also might be mentioned Feldman's *Becoming Human through Art* (1970). This is a book that brings a broad humanistic tradition to the educative aspects of art experience, wherein the art educator is seen as that professional who acts most purely on the connection between life and art.

Epistemological Issues. This section concentrates on writings that explore a broadened knowledge base in studying artistic and aesthetic phenomena. Within the arts, Bamberger (1978), Olson (1978), and Gruber (1978) argue for a balance between intuitive and formal knowing, for enlarging the functions of knowledge to include the aesthetic, and for addressing positive emotional life in all its complexity.

Child (1973) contrasts humanistic psychology with "the research tradition," ending with a plea for cross-fertilization of "hard" and "soft" research methods. B. Smith (1978) examines humanism and behaviorism in psychology, concluding that we need to incorporate both causal and interpretative perspectives to understand behavior and selfhood. To Farson (1978), humanistic and artistic learnings have intrinsic value, are nonlinear in character, and are not simple determinants of observable behavior.

Efland (1979) proposes alignments between aesthetic and psychological theory: mimetic/behaviorist; pragmatic/cognitive; expressive/psychoanalytic; and objectivist/Gestalt. Wieder (1975) tries to undercut the split between "hard" (nomothetic, precise, reductionist) and "soft" (idiographic, subtle, complex) approaches to inquiry by recommending a "tough" orientation, where "inquiry should rest on an explicit epistemological basis" (p. 24). Similarly, Beittel (1979b) has called for pluralistic epistemological openness and pointed to the fit between hermeneutic philosophy and concerns for unity of truth, language, and method in art education.

Bradley (1976) says, "Education in the arts is clearly an aperspective enterprise, a nurturing toward the acceptance of the sacred condition, and a preparation for the rites of passage required to move in and out of its time suspension" (p. 52). This access to deep structure he sees as most closely tied to performance-participation in the arts.

Working pluralistically, Allport (1965) applied an existential, a depth-psychological, and a structural-dynamic methodology to the same case material; and Stapleton (1976) did a pluralistic interpretation of the drawing serial of one artist, using Pepper's four "world hypotheses" (Pepper, 1942).

Contrary to such scope, Engel (1978) sees only one defensible methodology—a neocognitive, positivistic, technological one. Similarly, Hardiman and Zernich (1977b) assume that "we are interested in discovering uniformities or psychological laws for human behavior in the visual arts" (p. 21), and restrict the broad universe of inquiry to a particular kind of research. Against such specialization,

Beittel and Novosel-Beittel (1978) have proposed an experiment–case-study combination, where humanistic and scientific orientations, as irreconcilable knowledge modes, are jointly applied to the study of body-mind changes associated with sustained immersion in the arts.

Sociology and politics of knowledge. One sign of maturation in art education is the appearance of theory and research related to ideology critique, policy studies, sociocultural and transcultural factors, and research on women in the arts. Research is not seen as a broad panacea to society's ills. Kovel (1976), for example, takes an ironic view of extant therapies, reminding us that, no matter what the therapy, it "only hopes to mobilize our imaginative powers to deal with the real contradictions of life. There may be little solace in such a view, which promises no 'true self,' gleaming with authenticity, striding out from the rubble of neurosis" (p. 259).

Habermas (1971a) and White (1973) remind us that all knowledge is guided by human interests; that all history has its political ideology concealed within its interpretive bent. Efland (1978) points out that whether, consciously or not, we identify with Plato, Aristotle, Kant, Schiller, or Dewey, this kind of identification strongly affects how we relate the arts to education.

R. A. Smith (1975), in critically examining the "efficiency movement" in education, shows how it contains "the social rhetoric of the more politically conservative segments of American Society." Habermas (1971b) contends that information from the empirical sciences can enter the social life-world only in the expansion of our technological control. "Thus, such information is not on the same level as the action-orienting self-understanding of social groups" (p. 52). R. A. Smith (1973, 1977, 1978) has repeatedly raised the issue of policy determination in the arts as related to political and sociological forces. The rise of "arts management" professionals shows that this issue is not just academic. McFee (1969, 1971) has long researched the sociocultural context of art education. McFee and Degge (1977) hope "to equip children of varied cultural backgrounds to cope in the mainstream of the society without causing them to devalue their own cultural background" (p. 10). Foley and Templeton (1970) attempt a sociological analysis of the role of the art teacher.

Rosario (1978) studies how aesthetic meanings are acquired through actual schooling. Shaw (1978) documents how curricular intention can be transmitted into its opposite by the contextualization of ideas into hardware and delivery systems. Eisner (1969b) shows that spatial development in drawings is related to socioeconomic status. Korzenik (1979) explores "socialization and drawing," and Wilson and Wilson (1977) report that children learn to draw from their exposure to the drawings of others, who, in turn, were similarly influenced earlier.

Chalmers (1971, 1978) adopts a sociological and anthropological perspective toward the teaching of art history. Mann (1979) sees artistic taste as pluralistic, reflective of individual and social class sensibilities. Wolff (1975) says

that the sociology of art "as a branch of the sociology of knowledge, shares the theoretical orientation of the latter as well as its problems of method and philosophy" (p. 129). According to her, Habermas's hermeneutic sociology (1970) plots a course from positivism through phenomenology, linguistic analysis, and hermeneutics, culminating in a revised materialism-functionalism that relates knowledge to language, work, and authority, thus including the multidimensional determinants of thought.

There have been a number of studies on the women's art movement (e.g., Sandell, 1979). Collins (1978, 1979) examines integrationist, separatist, and pluralistic approaches to the changing status of women, offering her own "androgynous value system" as a corrective to the polarizations and politics of the present plight of women in the arts and in art education.

Organization of Research Efforts. Logan (1975) generously attributes much of the growth in art education between the years 1955 (see Logan, 1955) and 1975 to the influence of research. Certain it is that a great proliferation of published research marks the decade under review. Davis (1977), in summarizing research trends in art education between 1883 and 1972, scanned 544 published manuscripts, finding that 30 percent of the total fell within the fifty-seven years marked off from 1883 to 1939, while 70 percent fell within 1940–1972. Although his is a narrower definition of research than that of this article, it can be assumed from all evidence that this proliferation has intensified since 1972, and that it would be close to exponential in its expansion if a still broader definition were employed. Torrance (1980), for example, says that there are over 1,000 references to his creativity tests alone. That the arts touch the larger populace is shown by Farrell's survey (1975) of public-arts involvement. He reports that 71 percent of the adult population (or 103.3 million people) attended at least one live performance of dance, music, or theater, or one museum, in the twelve-month period prior to being surveyed.

The two highest categories reported in Hawkins's ten-year totals of *Studies in Art Education* fell within what he called "methodological" (52 percent) and "philosophical" (37 percent) (1975). Some surveys, such as Wieder's of three decades of research on child art (1977), are critical as well. White (1977), in his historical review of doctoral program growth and dissertation research in art education, 1893–1974, concludes that "the majority of published research within art education appears to be the direct result of doctoral investigations rather than research activities conducted subsequent to those tutorial studies" (p. 17).

Hardiman and Zernich (1977b) examined "psychologically oriented dissertations in art education" from 1970 to 1974 and concluded, pessimistically, "if one were to eliminate all of the research in art education which has been done during the past decade, the practice of teaching art in the elementary and secondary schools would be largely unaffected" (p. 25). These same authors (Hardiman

& Zernich, 1975) conducted a survey ranking graduate schools in art education, showing the top ten to be, in order, The Pennsylvania State University, Ohio State University, Stanford University, University of Indiana, University of Illinois, Columbia Teachers College, New York University, University of Oregon, Pratt Institute, and Cranbrook Academy of Art.

Hoffa (1970) analyzed federally funded research conferences in art education. He felt that "the conferences have proven disappointing catalysts for further research."

Smith and Smith (1978) coordinated a valuable reference tool, *Research in the Arts and Aesthetic Education: A Directory of Investigators and Their Fields of Inquiry.* Areas of interest and expertise, and representative publications are listed for each investigator.

Critiques. Chapman (1979) felt that in our research " 'utility' must be measured by the significance of the issue or problem in the context of teaching and learning in art, the soundness of the inquiry, and consequently the *trust* we can place in the knowledge" (p. 4). Erickson (1979) said, "Strict adherence to a scientific model for art education research unnecessarily restricts inquiry methods which might be employed to shed light on the art teaching/learning situation" (p. 12). Koh (1979) stressed differences in theoretical, empirical, normative, and practical knowledge, stating that much of our research ignores these distinctions. Eisner (1979b) described recent developments in educational research that affect art education: (1) concern with the process of educational practice as well as with consequences; (2) concern with the wholeness or organicity of a situation; (3) "recognition that the billiard ball model of human behavior is basically wrong" (p. 12); (4) concern with the "qualitative"; and (5) "the change from the expectation that it would be possible to secure enduring generalizations to expectations that are considerably more modest" (p. 13).

Jourard (1968) invited laymen "who are studied by or consult psychologists to ask for as much transparency as the professionals ask of them." Silverman said: "There is no reason why research cannot be multi-dimensional; some empirical; some humanistic. We limit ourselves in research by asking only those questions which can be answered by statistics" (cited in Murphy & Jones, 1976, p. 7).

Norris (1977) alluded to "the heart of the problem with research in art education: confusion about what is, what ought to be, and the relation between the two" (p. 35). Leonhard and Colwell (1976) warn, "Reducing an art to the degree of simplicity necessary for research may result in a loss of the essence of the art" (p. 65). Clark (1975), in analyzing nine popular textbooks in art education, found most references were to Dewey and to expression theories, with a neglect of contemporary theory of art and art criticism.

Interdisciplinary models. Morris and Stuckhardt (1977) have theorized about the study and meaning of art attitudes. In an earlier study, Morris (1975) stated that the main objective of his proposed alternative methodol-

ogy for research into attitudes is "to characterize an individual through the revelation of a personal system of aesthetic attitudes and values" (p. 30).

Burton (1973) explored synesthesia in constructing a theory of aesthetic education based on the development of the awareness of the self. In a broadly conceived effort, Clark and Zimmerman (1978) proposed a model for visual arts education based on four professional roles: artist, art critic, art historian, and aesthetician. Their model ranges from unskilled and naive entering behaviors to fully realized "ideal end states" and "professional roles." Role descriptions are given for each exemplar, in both naive and sophisticated terms, and the strands within each role are delineated.

Lanier (1977) explored the politics of experience within the profession through "the five faces of art education." In an alliterative mood, he identified these as (1) magicians, mystics, manipulators; (2) mechanics; (3) merchants; (4) muckrakers; and (5) mosaicists.

Bradley (1975) proposed an alternative to the individualistic, begin-from-the-start state of art education research. Using examples from England and America as touchstones, he defined the organizational and knowledge advantages of team research.

In one of the few models to take seriously the advantages of pluralism in methodology and epistemology, Sevigny (1977, 1978) designed and tested an alternative methodology for the study of classroom life. He called his multiple perspective "triangulated inquiry." He employed ethnomethodological orientation, multiple case studies, multiple data-collection strategies, and multiple analytical strategies. His was one of few studies that were theoretically based and that used open, qualitative designs without specified *a priori* hypotheses.

Further discussion of alternative, interdisciplinary, and pluralistic theories and methods occur under phenomenological and qualitative inquiry in art education within this article.

Responding and appreciating. Janes (1970) and Johansen (1979) have theorized about response modes. Johansen plots the dialogical interaction, in teaching, of art criticism (theoretical knowing) and art appreciation (qualitative knowing). He proposes a model to show how these concepts combine synergistically in "impression," "expression," and "commitment" within the art-learning context. Wilson (1970) compared the response statements of art teachers, art critics and historians, and non–art-trained individuals about *Guernica.* He found art teachers deficient in critics' and historians' language usages.

Ecker (1973) analyzed children's talk about art. He learned the importance of "listening" in a phenomenological manner to the world of the child. Beittel (1979a) sketched out an art education theory on qualitative responding to art. In an effort to establish a "unit character" and definitional center, he called the "extended qualitative immediate present the end of responding to art" (p. 39), feeling that to study this theory necessitated a "hermeneutic phenomenology of dialogue concerning authentic responding to art" (p. 40).

Descriptive studies. Kensler (1971) organized the final report covering a preconference education-research training program for descriptive research in art education. There are valuable methodological chapters in this report, for example, Dale B. Harris's "Observation: The Basis for Teaching and Research" and "Varieties of Observation." In "Some Values of Case Studies," Beittel took a minority view by stressing that case studies have other than preliminary, protoscientific uses, seeing them more as irreducible ends of knowledge closer to phenomenology, where philosophical questions about the experience of art can be raised.

Getzels and Csikszentmihalyi (1968, 1976) reported their conclusions on value orientations of art students as determinants of artistic specialization, finding different characteristics within art education, art, and design majors. Getzels summarized his longitudinal study of "problem finding" in art: "If [research] has any influence on education it will be to call attention to 'problem-finding,' which has hitherto been neglected. As Einstein said regarding creative science, and the same thing holds for art, 'The formulation of a problem is often more important than its solution' " (Murphy & Jones, 1976, p. 7).

In a descriptive study of the relationship between years of art training and the use of aesthetic judgment criteria among high school students, Wilson (1972) made use of Pepper's world views as applied to art criticism (Pepper, 1942). MacGregor (1972) developed and tested a "perceptual index" for use in art teaching. The index was based on major contributions to perceptual research, and phrased in children's language. He later used this index to describe response strategies of elementary school children (MacGregor, 1975).

Historical studies. Central figures in art education in this century have been reevaluated. Simons (1972), McWhinnie (1972), and Michael (1981) have taken a reflective and historical look at Lowenfeld's influence on the field, whereas Parsons (1970) examined Read's positions on art and intellect. Chapman (1971) and Efland (1971) reappraised Barkan's influence (1955) and extended the base he laid down for art education into the 1970s.

Munson (1971) presented and analyzed the little-known theory of the visual arts which was developed by Gustav Britsch. In this theory, the history of art and human development are seen as progressive achievements in the subordination of nature to unified mental concepts.

Qualley (1970) compared "spontaneous" and "divergent" art strategies to historical analyses of style, showing antecedents for these empirically derived constructions in art history theory. Saunders (1976) explored "the 200-year war" between art and industrial art. Packard (1976) found contributions and solutions for art education in the thought of Jane Addams. Keel (1976) analyzed the turn-of-the-century challenge to art education formulated by Fred Burk and the child study movement.

As a theoretical and analytical work, White's *Metahistory* (1973) deserves further study. He developed a four-dimensional model with which he interpreted great nineteenth-century German historians. His four dimensions, each with four levels, are (1) mode of employment (romance, tragedy, comedy, satire); (2) mode of argument (formist, organicist, mechanistic, contextualistic); (3) mode of ideological implication (anarchism, conservatism, radicalism, liberalism); and (4) figurative language trope (metaphor, metonymy, synecdoche, irony).

Developmental studies. McFee and Degge (1977) criticized developmental theory in art: "To adequately develop a theory of child development in art, cognitive, perceptual, cultural and environmental factors must be considered, as well as biologically encoded development patterns. It is questionable whether it is possible to separate encoded from learned patterns, as learning starts at least at birth" (p. 361).

Kratochwill, Rush, and Kratochwill (1979) supported this view with experimental findings that challenge the assumption that developmental factors are the primary influences on the character of children's art. Wilson (1974) did a case study of the "super-heroes of J. C. Holz" and proposed an outline for a theory of child art, in which he suggested that our unreflecting strictures on copying need to be reexamined.

Kaplan (1979) questioned value-free, natural developmentalist positions and stated that "the liberation of the self is what is meant by full human development" (p. 107). He feels that such a position is tenable without belief in an immanent law, individual or social, that necessitates such development.

From a more natural, developmentalist perspective, however, Gardner, in *The Arts and Human Development* (1973), believed that the artistic process complements the cognitive, intellectual, and socialized accent in theorists such as Piaget. He arrived at an unexpected conclusion on the relationship between the mature artist and the young child engaged in artistic practice: "the child of 7 or 8 has, in most respects, become a participant in the artistic process and he need not pass through any further qualitative reorganizations" (p. vi). Thus, the stages for artistic development, apart from those of the critic, do not pass through those stages Piaget found "crucial for the scientist engaged in hypotheticodeductive thought" (p. vii). Gardner drew from wide sources, including biographies and case studies. Other studies supported the view of his book (Gardner & Gardner, 1970, 1973; Gardner, 1974).

Cross studies. Anderson (1979) and Eisner (1979a) discussed methods, problems, issues, and prospects associated with cross-cultural inquiries in the arts. Wilson and Wilson (1979), comparing figure structure, figure action, and framing in drawings by American and Egyptian children, stressed the central role that culture plays in artistic development. In a study rare for its approach, Lewis (1974) replicated J. S. Clark's 1896–97 study to sort out maturational as opposed to instructional-environmental influences on children's spatial representations. She found that children of earlier periods moved more directly into pictorial representations, and that contemporary children move more rapidly into mixed representations (symbolic and representational together) and stay there longer.

Experimental studies. I found almost twice as many descriptive and measurement studies as experiments within this time period (the 1970s). A number of the experiments reviewed are hard to describe because they contain many operational details, but do not report what theoretical base such details reflect. Two studies reported little evidence in their findings for "prevailing brain lateralization notions" (Dorothy & Reeves, 1979) or "the double-dominance model of hemisphere specialization" (Doerr, 1980).

Staying closer to theory, Hysell (1973) tested Ausubel's "advance organizer" model in the development of aesthetic perception (Ausubel, 1960). He found that teaching points of focus increased the number of aesthetic elements the learner perceived in art works. Pariser (1978) compared the effects of two methods of teaching drawing skills. He concluded that both perceptual cues and graphic conventions contribute to the child's drawing repertoire.

Hardiman and Zernich (1977a) studied the influence of style and subject matter on the development of children's art preferences. They found that degree of realism had the most potent impact on preference judgments and reported no significant differences between students at Piaget's concrete operations level and those at the stage of formal operations, thus supporting Gardner's earlier claim that factors other than those touched on by Piaget are at work in children's aesthetic development. (It should be noted that Hardiman and Zernich studied preferences and not critical ability.)

All in all, we can conclude that the earlier faith of many thinkers in the field in experiments has been justified neither by numbers of actual experiments engaged in nor by far-reaching significance in their outcomes. Energy and attention have apparently shifted elsewhere.

Psychological studies. Many book-length treatments of psychological studies appeared during the 1970s. Kreitler and Kreitler (1972) presented one of the most general works in this category. Its comprehensiveness is limited in two ways: it does not include the making of art, and it ignores developmental aspects. In including internal and external behavior, the authors take on a quasi-phenomenological position. Their theory is eclectic and rests on a concept of psychological homeostasis or balance and on a concept of tension, its arousal, and relief. But they also see the homeostatic as insufficient to account for all human behavior. To account for all human behavior, they turn to "cognitive orientations," or to the problem of "meaning," stating that "the theory of cognitive orientation assumes behavior to be directed by what a person knows and believes, by his judgments and evaluations, by his views about himself, others, and the world" (p. 23). Within

cognitive orientation, they identify (1) the common reality (shared perceptions); (2) the archaeological reality (genetic, autobiographical, partially unconscious sources); (3) normative reality (what ought to be); and (4) prophetic reality (what might exist in the future). Their treatment of symbolization and symbols is inclined to psychologize the responder to art by explaining away his or her response through homeostasis and cognitive orientation.

In a different vein, Arnheim's *Visual Thinking* (1969) treats visual perception itself as eminently cognitive, for "artistic activity is a form of reasoning, in which perceiving and thinking are indivisibly intertwined" (p. v). In discussing the abstraction of shape, Arnheim departs sharply from the British empiricists. We do not abstract by extracting properties found in common in an array of particulars (leading to what he calls the "container concept"). Rather, we proceed more interpretively, differentiating departures from an initially grasped underlying structure (what he calls "type concepts"). This distinction is repeated when he discusses "intuitive cognition" and "intellectual cognition." The former is a "highly complex field process, of which, as a rule, very little reaches consciousness," while the latter is linear. He goes so far that he sees words as most useful when they support thought, as it "operates in a more appropriate medium, such as visual imagery" (p. 232). Language thus reinforces the "container concept"—the classifiable, conservative, and static—whereas productive thinking is broad and flexible, closer to the "type concept" and to visual thinking. In general, he ignores structuralist, transactional, phenomenological, and hermeneutic approaches to language, but he reinstates the subject of images at the core of thinking. Another book, Weber's *The Psychology of Art* (1969) purports to approach the subject from an existential-phenomenological approach.

Extending the perspective of these books beyond art is Csikszentmihalyi's *Beyond Boredom and Anxiety* (1977). The author talks of "deep play," "flow experience," patterns of these in everyday life, and of the "politics of enjoyment." He points toward "personal causation" and "intrinsic motivation" as factors essential to understanding the human being in context. Berlyne's *Aesthetics and Psychobiology* (1971) takes a psychoscientific approach to experimental aesthetics, particularly based on his own work in arousal, exploratory, and motivational behavior related to stimulus patterns and conditions.

Barron's *Artists in the Making* (1972) is a broad compilation of test, performance, and interview data concerning the personality, interests, creativity, and inner life of art students in higher education in America. The assessment methods used project a more reductive and static image than the process that the title suggests. His in-depth interpretation of writers (with whom he personally identifies) is more successful in this regard.

Cognitive approaches. Goodman, Perkins, and Gardner (1972), in their funded research "Project Zero," turn from norms of value in the arts in the social, historical, and educational sense, because they flatly define the inherited literature of art education on the whole as "unrewarding." They turn instead to Piaget, perceptual and developmental psychology, the less mentalistic brands of cognitive psychology, and especially to Goodman's theory of symbols as outlined in his *Languages of Art* (1968). As reviewers Murphy and Jones (1976) described it, Project Zero "has spread its net wide and avoided any single psychological approach. Thus it takes judicious account of the psychoanalytic tradition, which concentrates on the motivation of the artist and the audience (exemplified by Otto Rank), and the Gestalt School, which focuses on 'certain laws of perception' (exemplified by Arnheim), as well as many others including the psychophysical and the behavioristic" (pp. 21–22).

A number of researchers have felt the impact of this project. Korzenik (1974), in her analysis of role taking and children's drawings, concluded that "comprehensible pictures are a result of the drawing-child's awareness of the viewer and that he is performing . . . by eliminating alternative interpretations, narrowing the possibilities of what may be read from a particular graphic configuration" (p. 23).

Silvers (1978) warned that definitions of cognition often point to a purely unidimensional, scientific epistemology. When we speak of knowing, knowledge, understanding, and experiencing, we already, she believes, make most cognitive theorists squirm. Silvers says that ambiguity, nonparaphrasability, polysemy, amplification, and conflicting interpretations need not necessarily be deterrents to a cognitive view of art.

More narrowly conceiving of empirical research as the only route to knowledge, Hochberg (1978) theorized about "visual art and the structures of the mind." For him "both training and some extrinsic motive (social, substantive, or other) are preconditions for the aesthetic response as it is manifested in art" (p. 171). Further, he says: "In the natural course of learning both verbal and non-verbal signs and symbols, . . . meaning is acquired mostly by context. . . . Learning by context means entering the situation with sufficient knowledge about the other components to define the new one" (Hochberg, 1978, p. 165).

Wilson and Wilson (1977, 1978) presented their "iconoclastic view of the imagery sources of young people" and reported how graphic symbols are "recycled." The authors feel that the raw materials of "real life" do not simply pass into artistic symbols and schemata. They treat the various arts in a structuralist mode, assuming them to be "essentially closed structures with complex sets of rules governing their various elements" (1978, p. 103). Their inquiry focuses on how symbols are transmitted within an art form; on "mythic images"; and on interactions between visual and verbal symbolic modes. They also consider the arts as ways of making a world.

In a response to Wilson and Wilson, Gross (1978) pointed out that the arts are neither exclusively self-fecundating nor life-bound. The recycling machinery works both ways, he feels, confounding our sense of the symbolic and the real, mixing up the maps and the territories.

Packard (1973) attempted to single out new variables for fruitful inquiry into children's art. She identified a creative tempo personality dimension as measured by the time a child takes to solve art problems.

Two books worthy of separate mention in this section are Perkins and Leondar's *The Arts and Cognition* (1977), and Madeja's *Arts and Aesthetics: An Agenda for the Future* (1977). Both of these edited compilations argue for a broad and inclusive approach toward a cognitive psychology of art. Perkins and Leondar argue that "a cognitive approach to the arts entails reconsidering and reconstructing many traditional attitudes" (p. 4). Their book is organized around (1) cognition, the act of knowing—how all human activity occurs relative to a knowledge base and to how a situation is understood—(2) the view that our reactions, though dependent on knowledge, are also ways of knowing; and (3) that cognition includes *knowing how* as well as *knowing that*. Key chapters by Goodman and by Gardner appear in this anthology.

Philosophical studies. In addition to a drift toward social and political aspects of knowledge, there has been a marked transition toward the philosophical. This influence from philosophy is broader than the more positivistic, operational, analytical one of the earlier times. Dennis (1970) and Gunter (1971) have reinterpreted the art philosophies of Dewey and Langer, respectively. Barger and Helgesen (1977) systematically looked at "aesthetic valuation" in idealism, realism, and environmentalism. To these three they relate Allport's three psychological systems: (1) reactive (behavioristic); (2) reactive-depth (psychoanalytic); and (3) process-becoming (Gestalt, existential).

R. A. Smith (1970, 1971) has edited two books on aesthetic education, in one of which (1971) aesthetics is presented both as research and as ground for other research. Marshall (1972) has written on "critical thought about the esthetic and art education." Tsugawa (1972) has related "art, knowledge, and love" to art education.

Bradley (1977, 1981) has explored imagery, visual memory, and instructional memory-training "games" for "mnemonics in art." Like Bachelard (1969), Bradley argues for the primacy and autonomy of the image in art, showing how it leaves "visceral traces" in the work.

MacGregor (1970) relates three concepts of art criticism to art teaching. Geahigan (1980), Sharer (1980), and Mittler (1973) likewise contribute to relationships between art criticism and art education.

Works broadly written in the area of existential, phenomenological, and hermeneutic studies are Greene's *Teacher as Stranger* (1973); Vandenberg's *Being and Education* (1971); Yates's *The Art of Memory* (1974); Iser's *The Act of Reading* (1978), and Spiegelberg's *Doing Phenomenology* (1975). In a critical mood, Wingerter (1973) referred to "pseudo-existential writings in education" (p. 240), whereas Gordon (1973) asked "Would Martin Buber endorse the Buber model?" (p. 240). Casey (1976) showed how Western thought, in striving for imageless thinking, has written imagining out of philosophy.

Bachelard (1969) dwelled at the image level without leaping into concepts. His "poetics of space" illustrates his insight that, in the phenomenology of the imagination, the image works through variation (or expansion), as opposed to reflection on how objects are constituted in the mind (or reduction). Clear phenomenological descriptions appear in Van den Berg's *A Different Existence* (1972). He says that one of phenomenology's main characteristics" is that it does not offer a fine theory but, rather, gives a plausible insight" (p. 4).

W. J. Madenfort (1972) and D. Madenfort (1973, 1974) theorized about sensuous experience and illustrated the many ways in which the immediacy of sensuous experience enters into aesthetic education. Flannery (1973) has written supportively in this vein as well. Kuspit (1974), Thompson (1973), and Stumbo (1970, 1973) have also utilized phenomenological methods in their research into aesthetic experience.

DeFurio (1974, 1979) has contextualistically and phenomenologically explored responses to art. Day (1976, 1979, 1981) has done phenomenological inquiry into visual imagery and metaphor and into dreams. Jordan (1980) and Giopulos (1979, 1981) combined hermeneutic, phenomenological, and literary orientations in their studies of the life-world of the potter.

Novosel (1976) and Novosel-Beittel (1978, 1979a), the latter author basing her theory on Hausman's earlier-cited discourse on novelty and creation (1975), developed a "structural-existential" model for confronting the paradox of how creative acts can be viewed as both determined and free. Novosel-Beittel (1979b) also theorized concerning how hermeneutic phenomenology opens up "access to privileged disclosure" according to "the metaphysics of relationship" in a place "where the desirable becomes existential."

Ott (1967) presented six "pointers" toward a phenomenology of dialogue. Says he, "The model and basic structure of every hermeneutic event is the dialogue" (p. 14).

Ricoeur (1963, 1978) proposed a possible collaboration of structuralism and hermeneutics. Says he, however: "It is the function of hermeneutics to make the comprehension of the other . . . coincide with the comprehension of oneself and of being" (1963, p. 617).

In a conference on phenomenological description in art education (Victoria & Sacca, 1978), papers were presented by Wagner (1978) on phenomenology in art; by Aoki (1978) on pluralistic curriculum research methodology; and by Beittel (1978) on qualitative description of the qualitative. Elsewhere, Zurmuehlen (1980) critically reviewed phenomenology in doctoral research, ending with a plea for the attempt "to integrate the Husserlian and Heideggerian phenomenologies of the other" (p. 9).

Mason (1980) and Brooks (1980) both applied to advantage, in greatly different contexts, hermeneutic phenomenology to live "texts" of art experience. Rosine (1980) followed Heidegger and Gadamer to show how the creation of art is the basic model for artistic inquiry.

Qualitative inquiry. Kaelin (1969) and Eisner (1969a) showed how instructional objectives do not honor the qualitative nature of art education. Pohland (1972) argued that "participant observation" is a viable methodology for research in art education.

Beittel (1972a, 1972b) proposed a case methodology for study of the drawing process and the drawing series true to artistic phenomenological experience. He also proposed (1973) "alternatives for art education research" through the use of a special participant observer and privileged access to the creating artist's stream of consciousness in a nurturant setting.

L. M. Smith (1978) has done a comprehensive review and analysis on the "evolving logic of participant observation, educational ethnography, and other case studies." He attempts a patterned analysis of qualitative research at four levels of abstraction: (1) data; (2) descriptive narrative; (3) theoretical; and (4) metatheoretical. A number of efforts have been made to apply participant observation to art education (e.g., Bersson, 1978; Sevigny, 1977, 1978; Willis, 1978). Stake (1975) has also collected together essays on evaluating the arts in education.

To Steiner (1981), many so-called qualitative methods are not truly qualitative. Participant observation, for example, in which observers "note important themes and formulate hypotheses," really applies universals and is therefore a "theoretical" and, to her, a "quantitative" approach. If Steiner is right, such methods more likely merely enlarge the range of qualitative phenomena that can be quantified.

Van Manen (1978, 1978–1979, 1979) studies qualitative features of educational experience through the "constitutive phenomenology" of the Dutch Utrecht School. This method explores concrete life-world experiences in search of the "ground structures" or "essences" that these are theorized to embody. His view has something in common not only with Husserlian and Heideggerian phenomenology, but also with depth psychology and the "deep structure" of linguistics. Similarly, Van Dusen (1973) believes that all experiences, particularly those which are highly qualitative or deal with "fringe phenomena," are autosymbolic in character.

Eisner (1972, 1974, 1976, 1979c) has written extensively on the use of qualitative methods for evaluation in the arts. Vallance (1975) and Alexander (1977, 1980) have used art criticism and connoisseurship as models for educational description, evaluation, and criticism.

Steiner (1981), in a critique of Eisner (1979c), says that art criticism, as a model, clashes with the concept of qualitative method, because criticism entails judgment, criteria, and the application of universals, thus becoming "theoretical" and "quantitative." Says she: "the task of relating the artistic inquiry model to educational design is advanced by making appreciation, literary discourse and qualitative problem solving part of the methodology of design along with the extant methodology with its extension through participant observation or criticism" (p. 114).

We thus return to the issue of epistemological pluralism raised earlier in this review, to the wide-net approach, for example, of Sevigny (1978) and Aoki (1978). We also return to the examples set by Ricoeur (1978), Van den Berg (1972), and Bachelard (1969), who show us firsthand the meaning of ostensive language and of a phenomenology of the artistic imagination.

                                                        Kenneth R. Beittel

See also Aesthetic Education; Creativity; Museums.

REFERENCES

Alexander, R. R. Educational criticism of three art history classes (Doctoral dissertation, Stanford University, 1977). *Dissertation Abstracts International*, 1978, *38*, 5195A. (University Microfilms No. 78-2125)

Alexander, R. R. Mr. Jewel as a model: An educational criticism of a high school art history class. *Studies in Art Education*, 1980, *21*(3), 20–30.

Allport, G. W. *Letters from Jenny*. New York: Harcourt, Brace, 1965.

Anderson, F. E. Approaches to cross-cultural research in art education. *Studies in Art Education*, 1979, *21*(1), 17–26.

Aoki, T. T. Toward curriculum research in a new key. In J. J. Victoria & E. J. Sacca (Eds.), *Presentations on Art Education Research: Phenomenological Description—Potential for Research in Art Education* (No. 2). Montreal: Concordia University, 1978, pp. 47–69.

Arnheim, R. *Visual Thinking*. Berkeley: University of California Press, 1969.

Ausubel, D. P. The use of advance organizers in the learning and retention of meaningful verbal learning. *Journal of Educational Psychology*, 1960, *51*, 267–272.

Bachelard, G. *The Poetics of Space* (M. Jolas, Trans.). Boston: Beacon Press, 1969.

Bamberger, J. Intuitive and formal musical knowing: Parables of cognitive dissonance. In S. J. Madeja (Ed.), *The Arts, Cognition, and Basic Skills*. St. Louis: CEMREL, Inc., 1978, pp. 173–209.

Barger, R. N., & Helgesen, G. S. Aesthetic valuation: Systematic survey and humanistic thesis. *Review of Research in Visual Arts Education*, 1977, *7*, 12–20.

Barkan, M. *A Foundation for Art Education*. New York: Ronald Press, 1955.

Barron, F. *Artists in the Making*. New York: Seminar Press, 1972.

Beittel, K. R. Art. In C. W. Harris (Ed.), *Encyclopedia of Educational Research* (3rd ed.). New York: Macmillan, 1960, pp. 77–87.

Beittel, K. R. A case methodology for the study of the drawing process and the drawing series (Project No. 1-C-024, Grant No. OE 9-3-71-0087). State College: Pennsylvania State University, 1972. (a)

Beittel, K. R. *Mind and Context in the Art of Drawing*. New York: Holt, Rinehart & Winston, 1972. (b)

Beittel, K. R. *Alternatives for Art Education Research: Inquiry into the Making of Art*. Dubuque, Iowa: Brown, 1973.

Beittel, K. R. Qualitative description of the qualitative. In J. J. Victoria & E. J. Sacca (Eds.), *Presentations on Art Education Research: Phenomenological Description—Potential for Research in Art Education* (No. 2). Montreal: Concordia University, 1978, pp. 91–113.

Beittel, K. R. Toward an art education theory on qualitative responding to art. *Review of Research in Visual Arts Education*, 1979, *10*, 33–40. (a)

Beittel, K. R. Unity of truth, language, and method in art education. *Studies in Art Education*, 1979, *21*(1), 50–56. (b)

Beittel, K. R., & Novosel-Beittel, J. Mind-body changes accompanying sustained immersion in art experiences. In J. J. Victoria & E. J. Sacca (Eds.), *Presentations on Art Education Research: Phenomenological Description—Potential for Research in Art Education* (No. 2). Montreal: Concordia University, 1978, pp. 106–111.

Berlyne, D. E. *Aesthetics and Psychobiology*. New York: Appleton-Century-Crofts, 1971.

Bersson, R. D. The use of participant observation in the evaluation of art programs. *Studies in Art Education*, 1978, *19*(2), 61–67.

Bradley, W. Team research as an alternative model. *Studies in Art Education*, 1975, *16*(3), 5–11.

Bradley, W. The forgotten protasis of experience. In P. Edmonston (Ed.), *Penn State Papers, Art Education: An Anthology of Faculty Papers*. University Park: Pennsylvania State University, Department of Art and Music Education, 1976, pp. 45–54.

Bradley, W. Some aspects of visual memory. *Viewpoints*, 1977, *5*(1), pp. 83–90.

Bradley, W. Evocative images. *Studies in Art Education*, 23(1), 1981.

Brooks, C. A. *The Meaning of Childhood Art Experience: A Dialectical Hermeneutic*. Unpublished doctoral dissertation, Pennsylvania State University, 1980.

Burton, D. E. A theory of aesthetic education based on the development of the awareness of the self (Doctoral dissertation, Pennsylvania State University, 1973). *Dissertation Abstracts International*, 1973, *35*(1). (University Microfilms No. 74-15, 999)

Casey, E. *Imagining: A Phenomenological Study*. Bloomington: Indiana University Press, 1976.

Chalmers, F. G. Towards a theory of art and culture as a foundation for art education (Doctoral dissertation, University of Oregon, 1971). *Dissertation Abstracts International*, 1971, *32*, 3000A. (University Microfilms No. 72-912)

Chalmers, K. A. Teaching and studying art history: Some anthropological and sociological considerations. *Studies in Art Education*, 1978, *20*(1), 18–25.

Chapman, L. H. A second look at *A Foundation for Art Education*. *Studies in Art Education*, 1971, *13*(1), 40–49.

Chapman, L. H. The utility of research. *Studies in Art Education*, 1979, *20*(2), 3–4.

Child, I. L. *Humanistic Psychology and the Research Tradition: Their Several Virtues*. New York: Wiley, 1973.

Clark, G. A., & Zimmerman, E. A walk in the right direction: A model for visual arts education. *Studies in Art Education*, 1978, *19*(2), 34–49.

Clark, S. H. Modern theoretical foundations of appreciation and creation in art education textbooks, 1960–1970. *Studies in Art Education*, 1975, *16*(3), 12–21.

Collins, G. C. Reflections on the head of Medusa. *Studies in Art Education*, 1978, *19*(2), 10–18.

Collins, G. C. Women and art: The problem of status. *Studies in Art Education*, 1979, *21*(1), 57–64.

Csikszentmihalyi, M. *Beyond Boredom and Anxiety*. San Francisco: Jossey-Bass, 1977.

Davis, D. J. Research trends in art and art education: 1883–1972. In S. J. Madeja (Ed.), *Arts and Aesthetics: An Agenda for the Future*. St. Louis: CEMREL, Inc., 1977, pp. 109–147.

Day, E. S. A study of dreams and dreaming and the transformation of dream themes into drawings and paintings (Doctoral dissertation, Pennsylvania State University, 1976). *Dissertation Abstracts International*, 1977, *37*, 4073A. (University Microfilms No. 76-29626)

Day, E. S., Jr. Toward a phenomenology of dream imagery and metaphor. *Art Education*, 1979, *32*(7), 15–17.

Day, E. The phenomenology of visual imagery and metaphor. *Journal of the Ohio Art Education Association*, 1981, *20*(1), 11–23.

DeFurio, A. G. A contextualistic interpretation of aesthetic response: The contribution of the experiential domain and idiosyncratic meaning (Doctoral dissertation, Pennsylvania State University, 1974). *Dissertation Abstracts International*, 1975, *36*, 1249A. (University Microfilms No. 75-19743)

DeFurio, A. G. Toward aesthetic response. *Art Education*, 1979, *32*(7), 8–11.

Dennis, L. Dewey's brief for the fine arts. *Studies in Art Education*, 1970, *11*(3), 3–8.

Doerr, S. L. Conjugate lateral eye movement, cerebral dominance, and the figural creativity factors of fluency, flexibility, originality, and elaboration. *Studies in Art Education*, 1980, *21*(2), 5–11.

Dorothy, R., & Reeves, D. Mental functioning, perceptual differentiation, personality, and achievement among art and non-art majors. *Studies in Art Education*, 1979, *20*(2), 52–63.

Dufrenne, M. *The Phenomenology of Aesthetic Experience*. Evanston, Ill.: Northwestern University Press, 1973.

Ecker, D. Analyzing children's talk about art. *Journal of Aesthetic Education*, 1973, *7*, 58–73.

Efland, A. D. The transition continued: The emergence of an affective revolution. *Studies in Art Education*, 1971, *13*(1), 13–25.

Efland, A. D. Relating the arts to education: The history of an idea. *Studies in Art Education*, 1978, *19*(2), 5–13.

Efland, A. D. Conceptions of teaching in art education. *Art Education*, 1979, *32*(4), 21–33.

Eisner, E. W. Instructional and expressive educational objectives: Their formulation and use in curriculum. In R. E. Stake (Ed.), *Instructional Objectives* (AERA Monograph Series on Curriculum Evaluation, No. 3). Chicago: Rand McNally, 1969, pp 1–31. (a)

Eisner, E. W. The drawings of the disadvantaged: A comparative study. *Studies in Art Education*, 1969, *11*(1), 5–19. (b)

Eisner, E. W. Art education. In R. Ebel (Ed.), *Encyclopedia of Educational Research* (4th ed.). New York: Macmillan, 1969. (c)

Eisner, E. W. Emerging models for educational evaluation. *School Review*, 1972, *80*(4), 573–590.

Eisner, E. W. Research on teaching the visual arts. In R. M. W. Travers (Ed.), *Second Handbook of Research on Teaching*. Chicago: Rand McNally, 1973, pp. 1196–1209.

Eisner, E. W. Toward a more adequate conception of evaluation in the arts. *Art Education*, 1974, *27*, 2–5.

Eisner, E. W. Educational connoisseurship and educational criticism: Their forms and functions in educational evaluation. *Journal of Aesthetic Education*, 1976, *10*, 135–150.

Eisner, E. W. Cross-cultural research in arts education: Problems, issues, prospects. *Studies in Art Education*, 1979, *21*(1), 27–35. (a)

Eisner, E. W. Recent developments in educational research affecting art education. *Art Education*, 1979, *32*(4), 12–15. (b)

Eisner, E. W. *The Educational Imagination: On the Design and Evaluation of School Programs*. New York: Macmillan, 1979. (c)

Engel, M. An informal framework for cognitive research in arts education. In S. J. Madeja (Ed.), *The Arts, Cognition, and Basic Skills*. St. Louis: CEMREL, Inc., 1978, pp. 23–30.

Erickson, M. An historical explanation of the schism between research and practice in art education. *Studies in Art Education*, 1979, *20*(2), 5–13.

Farrell, J. Research and the arts. *Studies in Art Education*, 1975, *16*(2), 37–41.

Farson, R. The technology of humanism. *Journal of Humanistic Psychology*, 1978, *18*(2), 5–35.

Feldman, E. B. *Becoming Human through Art*. Englewood Cliffs, N.J.: Prentice-Hall, 1970.

Flannery, M. Aesthetic education. *Art Education*, 1973, *26*(5), 10–14.

Foley, R. R., Templeton, D. E. Conflict, craftsmen, and professionals: A sociological view of the art teacher. *Art Education*, 1970, *23*(2), 8–13.

Gadamer, H. G. *Truth and Method*. New York: Seabury Press, 1975.

Gardner, H. *The Arts and Human Development*. New York: Wiley, 1973.

Gardner, H. Metaphors and modalities: How children project polar adjectives onto diverse domains. *Child Development*, 1974, *45*, 84–91.

Gardner, H., & Gardner, J. Developmental trends in sensitivity to painting style and subject matter. *Studies in Art Education*, 1970, *12*(1), 11–16.

Gardner, H., & Gardner, J. Developmental trends in sensitivity to form and subject matter in paintings. *Studies in Art Education*, 1973, *14*(2), 52–56.

Geahigan, C. Metacritical inquiry in arts education. *Studies in Art Education*, 1980, *21*(3), 54–67.

Getzels, J. W., & Csikszentmihalyi, M. The value-orientations of art students as determinants of artistic specialization and creative performance. *Studies in Art Education*, 1968, *10*(1), 5–16.

Getzels, J. W., & Csikszentmihalyi, M. *The Creative Vision: A Longitudinal Study of Problem Finding in Art*. New York: Wiley, 1976.

Giopulos, P. Play as transformation: A potter's world. *Art Education*, 1979, *32*(7), 12–14.

Giopulos, P. Potting as a phenomenon: Movement and choice stimulate transformation (Doctoral Dissertation, Pennsylvania State University, 1981). *Dissertation Abstracts International*, in press.

Goodman, H.; Perkins, D.; & Gardner, H. *Basic Abilities Required for Understanding and Creation in the Arts* (Project No. 9-0283, Grant No. CE G-0-9-310283-3721(010)). Cambridge, Mass.: Harvard University Graduate School of Education, 1972.

Goodman, N. *Languages of Art*. Indianapolis: Bobbs-Merrill, 1968.

Gordon, H. Would Martin Buber endorse the Buber model? *Educational Theory*, 1973, *23*(3), 215–223.

Greene, M. *Teacher as Stranger*. Belmont, Calif.: Wadsworth, 1973.

Gross, L. A response to Wilson and Wilson. In S. J. Madeja (Ed.),

The Arts, Cognition, and Basic Skills. St. Louis: CEMREL, Inc., 1978, pp. 110–113.

Gruber, H. E. Emotion and cognition: Aesthetics and science. In S. S. Madeja (Ed.), *The Arts, Cognition, and Basic Skills.* St. Louis: CEMREL, Inc., 1978, pp. 134–146.

Gunter, M. Langer's semantic view of the nonverbal arts: Its meaning for art education. *Studies in Art Education,* 1971, 12(2), 34–41.

Habermas, J. *Zür Logik der Sozialwissenchaften.* Frankfurt: Suhrkamp Verlag, 1970.

Habermas, J. *Knowledge and Human Interests.* Boston: Beacon Press, 1971. (a)

Habermas, J. *Toward a Rational Society.* Boston: Beacon Press, 1971. (b)

Hardiman, G. W., & Zernich, T. A ranking of graduate schools in art education: An exploratory survey. *Art Education,* 1975, 28(4), 26.

Hardiman, G. W., & Zernich, T. Influence of style and subject matter on the development of children's art performances. *Studies in Art Education,* 1977, 19(1), 29–35. (a)

Hardiman, G. W., & Zernich, T. Strategies for research in art education. *Review of Research in Visual Arts Education,* 1977, 7, 21–29. (b)

Hausman, C. R. *A Discourse on Novelty and Creation.* The Hague: Martinus Nijhoff, 1975.

Hawkins, G. W. Technology as an influence in art education literature. *Studies in Art Education,* 1975, 16(1), 38–44.

Hochberg, J. Visual art and the structures of the mind. In S. S. Madeja (Ed.), *The Arts, Cognition, and Basic Skills.* St. Louis: CEMREL, Inc., 1978, pp. 151–172.

Hoffa, H. *Analysis of Recent Research Conferences in Art Education.* Bloomington: Indiana University Foundation, 1970.

Hysell, D. M. Testing an advance organizer model in the development of aesthetic perception. *Studies in Art Education,* 1973 14(3), 9–17.

Iser, W. *The Act of Reading.* Baltimore: Johns Hopkins University Press, 1978.

Janes, H. E. Conceptual modes of children in responding to art objects. *Studies in Art Education,* 1970, 11(3), 52–60.

Johansen, P. An art appreciation teaching model for visual aesthetic education. *Studies in Art Education,* 1979, 20(3), 4–14.

Jordan, Lawrence. On the journey of claying (Doctoral dissertation, Pennsylvania State University, 1980). *Dissertation Abstracts International,* 41(9), pp. 3760A–4197A.

Jourard, S. M. *Disclosing Man to Himself.* New York: Van Nostrand, 1968.

Kaelin, E. G. Are "behavioral objectives" consistent with social goals of aesthetic education? *Art Education,* 1969, 22(8), 4–11.

Kaplan, B. Art in human development. In D. Pariser & R. Staley (Eds.), *Presentations in Art Education Research: Aesthetics and Culture* (No. 5). Montreal: Concordia University, 1979, pp. 105–113.

Keel, J. Child study, Fred Burk, and art education: Notes on a turn-of-the-century challenge. *Art Education,* 1976, 29(1), 25–29.

Kensler, G. (Ed.). *Observation: A Technique for Art Educators* (Health, Education, and Welfare Project No. 0EG-0-70-2849). Washington, D.C.: National Art Education Association, 1971.

Koh, J. A preface for inquiries into art education. *Studies in Art Education,* 1979, 20(2), 14–17.

Korzenik, D. Role-taking and children's drawings. *Studies in Art Education,* 1974, 15(3), 17–24.

Korzenik, D. Socialization and drawing. *Art Education,* 1979, 32(1), 26–29.

Kovel, J. *A Complete Guide to Therapy.* New York: Pantheon Books, 1976.

Kratochwill, C. E.; Rush, J. C.; & Kratochwill, T. R. The effects of descriptive social reinforcement on creative responses in children's easel painting. *Studies in Art Education,* 1979, 20(2), 29–39.

Kreitler, H., & Kreitler, S. *Psychology of the Arts.* Durham, N.C.: Duke University Press, 1972.

Kuspit, D. B. A phenomenological approach to artistic intention. *Art Forum,* 1974, 48–54.

Lanier, V. The five faces of art education. *Studies in Art Education,* 1977, 18(3), 7–21.

Leonhard, C., & Colwell, R. J. Research in music education. *Review of Research in Visual Arts Education,* 1976, 5, 65–84.

Lewis, H. P. Spatial relations in children's drawings: A cross-generational comparison. *Studies in Art Education,* 1974, 15(3), 49–56.

Logan, F. *The Growth of Art.* New York: Harper, 1955.

Logan, F. M. Update '75. Growth in American art education. *Studies in Art Education,* 1975, 17(1), 7–16.

Lowenfeld, V. *Creative and Mental Growth.* New York: Macmillan, 1947.

MacGregor, N. Concepts of criticism: Implications for art education. *Studies in Art Education,* 1970, 11(2), 27–33.

MacGregor, R. The development and validation of a perceptual index for utilization in the teaching of art. *Studies in Art Education,* 1972, 13(2), 11–18.

MacGregor, R. Response strategies adopted by elementary school children to items in a perceptual index: An exploratory study. *Studies in Art Education,* 1975, 16(3), 54–61.

Madeja, S. S. (Ed.). *Arts and Aesthetics: An Agenda for the Future.* St. Louis: CEMREL, Inc., 1977.

Madenfort, D. Educating for the immediately sensuous as unified whole. *Art Education,* 1973, 26(7), 6–11.

Madenfort, D. The aesthetic as immediately sensuous: An historical perspective. *Studies in Art Education,* 1974, 16(1), 4–17.

Madenfort, W. J. Aesthetic education: An education for the immediacy of sensuous experience. *Art Education,* 1972, 25(5), 10–14.

Mann, D. A. Architecture, aesthetics, and pluralism: Theories of taste as a determinant of architectural standards. *Studies in Art Education,* 1979, 20(3), 15–29.

Marshall, H. J. Critical thought about the esthetic and art education. *Art Education,* 1972, 25(2), 15–18.

Mason, R. M. Interpretation and artistic understanding (Doctoral dissertation, Pennsylvania State University, 1980). *Dissertation Abstracts International,* in press.

McFee, J. K. Urbanism and art education in the U.S.A. *Art Education,* 1969, 22(6), 16–18.

McFee, J. K. Children and cities: An exploratory study of urban-, middle-, and low-income neighborhood children's responses in studying the city. *Studies in Art Education,* 1971, 13(1), 50–69.

McFee, J. K., & Degge, R. M. *Art, Culture, and Environment.* Belmont, Calif.: Wadsworth, 1977.

McWhinnie, H. J. Viktor Lowenfeld: Art education for the 1970s. *Studies in Art Education,* 1972, 14(1), 8–14.

Michael, J. A. Viktor Lowenfeld: Pioneer in art education therapy. *Studies in Art Education,* 1981, 22(2), 7–19.

Mittler, G. A. Experiences in critical inquiry: Approaches for use in the art methods class. *Art Education,* 1973, 26(2), 16–21.

Morris, J. W. An alternative methodology for researching art attitudes and values. *Studies in Art Education*, 1975, *17*(1), 24–31.

Morris, J. W., & Stuckhardt, M. H. Art attitude: Conceptualization and implication. *Studies in Art Education*, 1977, *19*(1), 21–28.

Munson, R. S. The Gustav Britsch theory of the visual arts. *Studies in Art Education*, 1971, *12*(2), 4–17.

Murphy, J., & Jones, L. *Research in Arts Education: A Federal Chapter* (HEW Publication No. (OE) 76-02000). Washington, D.C.: U.S. Department of Health, Education, and Welfare, Office of Education, 1976. (ERIC Document Reproduction Service No. ED 157 816)

Norris, R. Research in art education. *Review of Research in Visual Arts Education*, 1977, *6*, 34–52.

Novosel, J. The structural existentiality of arting: Inquiry into the nature óf the creative process (Doctoral dissertation, Pennsylvania State University, 1976). *Dissertation Abstracts International*, 1977, *37*, 6906A. (University Microfilms No. 77-9712)

Novosel-Beittel, J. Inquiry into the qualitative world of creating: The S-E model. *Studies in Art Education*, 1978, *20*(1), 26–36.

Novosel-Beittel, J. On meditative thinking in the creation of art. *Art Education*, 1979, *32*(7), 6–8. (a)

Novosel-Beittel, J. Where the desirable becomes existential. Canadian Society for Education through Art, *Annual Journal*, 1979, *9*, 39–44. (b)

Olson, D. R. The arts as basic skills: Three cognitive functions of symbols. In S. S. Madeja (Ed.), *The Arts, Cognition, and Basic Skills*. St. Louis: CEMREL, Inc., 1978, pp. 59–81.

Ott, H. Hermeneutics and personhood. In S. R. Hopper & D. L. Miller (Eds.), *Interpretation: The Poetry of Meaning*. New York: Harcourt, Brace & World, 1967, pp. 14–33.

Packard, S. Creative tempo in children's art production. *Studies in Art Education*, 1973, *14*(3), 18–26.

Packard, S. Jane Addams: Contributions and solutions for art education. *Art Education*, 1976, *29*(1), 9–12.

Pariser, D. A. Two methods of teaching drawing skills. *Studies in Art Education*, 1978, *20*(3), 30–42.

Parsons, M. J. Sir Herbert Read on art and intellect. *Studies in Art Education*, 1970, *11*(3), 9–19.

Pepper, S. C. *World Hypotheses: A Study in Evidence*. Berkeley: University of California Press, 1942.

Perkins, D., & Leondar, B. *The Arts and Cognition*. Baltimore: Johns Hopkins University Press, 1977.

Pohland, P. Participant observation as a research methodology. *Studies in Art Education*, 1972, *13*(3), 4–15.

Qualley, C. A. A comparison of spontaneous and divergent strategies to historical analyses of style. *Studies in Art Education*, 1970, *12*(1), 17–24.

Read, H. *Education through Art*. New York: Pantheon Books, 1945.

Ricoeur, P. Réponses à quelques questions. *Esprit*, 1963.

Ricoeur, P. *The Philosophy of Paul Ricoeur*. Boston: Beacon Press, 1978.

Rosario, J. On the child's acquisition of aesthetic meaning: The contribution of schooling. In G. Willis (Ed.), *Qualitative Evaluation*. Berkeley, Calif.: McCutchan, 1978, pp. 208–228.

Rosine, G. L. The speculative mode of being in the work of art (Doctoral dissertation, Pennsylvania State University, 1980). *Dissertation Abstracts International*, in press.

Rush, J. C., & Kratochwill, T. R. Time-series strategies for studying behavior change: Implications for research in visual arts education. *Studies in Art Education*, 1981, *22*(2), 57–67.

Sandell, R. Feminist art education: An analysis of the women's art movement as an educational force. *Studies in Art Education*, 1979, *20*(2), 18–28.

Saunders, R. J. Art, industrial art, and the two-hundred-years war. *Art Education*, 1976, *29*(1), 5–8.

Sevigny, M. J., Jr. A descriptive study of instructional interaction and performance appraisal in a university studio-art setting: A multiple perspective (Doctoral dissertation, Ohio State University, 1977). *Dissertation Abstracts International*, 1978, *38*, 6477A. (University Microfilms No. 78-6199)

Sevigny, M. J. Triangulated inquiry: An alternative methodology for the study of classroom life. *Review of Research in Visual Arts Education*, 1978, *8*, 1–16.

Sharer, J. W. Distinguishing justifications and explanations in judgments of art. *Studies in Art Education*, 1980, *21*(2), 38–42.

Shaw, F. S. In search of congruence. In G. Willis (Ed.), *Qualitative Evaluation*. Berkeley, Calif.: McCutchan, 1978, pp. 229–249.

Silvers, A. Show and tell: The arts, cognition, and basic modes of referring. In S. S. Madeja (Ed.), *The Arts, Cognition, and Basic Skills*. St. Louis: CEMREL, Inc., 1978, pp. 31–50.

Simons, A. P. Viktor Lowenfeld and social haptics. *Art Education*, 1972, *25*(6), 8–15.

Smith, B. Humanism and behaviorism in psychology: Theory and practice. *Journal of Humanistic Psychology*, 1978, *18*(1), 27–36.

Smith, L. M. An evolving logic of participant observation, educational ethnography, and other case studies. In L. Shulman (Ed.), *Review of Research in Education* (No. 6). Chicago: F. E. Peacock, 1978, pp. 316–377.

Smith, R. A. The new policy-making company in aesthetic education. In R. A. Smith, *Aesthetic Education Today*. Columbus: Ohio State University, Division of Art Education, 1973.

Smith, R. A. A policy analysis and criticism of the Artist-in-Schools Program of the National Endowment for the Arts. *Art Education*, *30*(5), 12–19.

Smith, R. A. Justifying policy for aesthetic education. *Studies in Art Education*, 1978, *20*(1), 37–42.

Smith, R. A. (Ed.). *Aesthetic Concepts and Education*. Urbana: University of Illinois Press, 1970.

Smith, R. A. (Ed.). *Aesthetics and Problems of Education*. Urbana: University of Illinois Press, 1971.

Smith, R. A. (Ed.). *Regaining Educational Leadership: Critical Essays on PBTE/CBTE, Behavioral Objectives, and Accountability*. New York: Wiley, 1975.

Smith, R. A., & Smith, C. M. *Research in the Arts and Aesthetic Education: A Directory of Investigators and Their Fields of Inquiry*. St. Louis: CEMREL, Inc., 1978.

Spiegelberg, H. *Doing Phenomenology*. The Hague: Martinus Nijhoff, 1975.

Stake, R. (Ed.). *Evaluating the Arts in Education: A Responsive Approach*. Columbus, Ohio: Merrill, 1975.

Stapleton, D. J. Ontological inquiry in art education: Hermeneutic interpretation of a drawing serial (Doctoral dissertation, Pennsylvania State University, 1976). *Dissertation Abstracts International*, 1977, *37*, 6906A. (University Microfilms No. 77-9776).

Steiner, E. The qualitative arts in educational inquiry. *Aesthetic Education*, 1981, *15*(1), 107–115.

Stumbo, H. W. Changes in meaning that follow phenomenological analysis. *Studies in Art Education*, 1970, *12*(1), 50–60.

Stumbo, H. W. A high school art curriculum in which phenomenological analysis was the dominant component. *Art Education*, 1973, *26*(2), 23–27.

Thompson, S. R. Complexity in perception: An explanation in phenomenological terms by psychology, with some parallels in aesthetic philosophy. *Studies in Art Education*, 1973, *14*(2), 3–12.

Torrance, E. P. Creative intelligence and an agenda for the eighties. *Art Education*, 1980, *33*(7), 8–14.

Tsugawa, A. Art, knowledge, and love. *Art Education*, 1972, *25*(5), 3–9.

Vallance, E. J. Aesthetic criticism and curriculum description (Doctoral dissertation, Stanford University, 1975). *Dissertation Abstracts International*, 1975, *36*, 5795A. (University Microfilms No. DAH76-05820)

Vandenberg, D. *Being and Education: An Essay in Existential Phenomenology*. Englewood Cliffs, N.J.: Prentice-Hall, 1971.

Van den Berg, J. H. *A Different Existence*. Pittsburgh, Pa.: Duquesne University Press, 1972.

Van Dusen, W. *The Natural Depth in Man*. New York: Harper & Row, 1973.

Van Manen, M. Objective inquiry into structures of subjectivity. *Journal for Curriculum Theorizing*, 1978, *1*(1), 44–64.

Van Manen, M. An experiment in educational theorizing: The Utrecht School. *Interchange*, 1978–1979, *10*(1), 48–66.

Van Manen, M. The phenomenology of pedagogic observation. *Canadian Journal of Education*, 1979, *4*(1), 5–16.

Victoria, J. J., & Sacca, E. J. (Eds.). *Presentations on Art Education Research: Phenomenological Description—Potential for Research in Art Education* (No. 2). Montreal: Concordia University, 1978.

Wagner, H. R. Phenomenology in art. In J. J. Victoria & E. J. Sacca (Eds.), *Presentations on Art Education Research: Phenomenological Description—Potential for Research in Art Education* (No. 2). Montreal: Concordia University, 1978, pp. 7–27.

Weber, J. P. *The Psychology of Art*. New York: Delta Press, 1969.

Weiss, P. *Modes of Being*. Carbondale: Southern Illinois University Press, 1958.

White, D. W. An historical review of doctoral program growth and dissertation research in art education, 1893–1974. *Studies in Art Education*, 1977, *19*(1), 6–20.

White, H. *Metahistory*. Baltimore: Johns Hopkins University Press, 1973.

Wieder, C. G. Alternative approaches to problems in art education. *Studies in Art Education*, 1975, *17*(1), 17–24.

Wieder, C. G. Three decades of research on child art: A survey and a critique. *Art Education*, 1977, *30*(2), 4–11.

Willis, G. (Ed.). *Qualitative Evaluation*. Berkeley, Calif.: McCutchan, 1978.

Wilson, B. Relationships among art teachers', art critics', and historians' statements about *Guernica*. *Studies in Art Education*, 1970, *12*(1), 31–39.

Wilson, B. The relationship between years of art training and the use of aesthetic judgmental criteria among high school students. *Studies in Art Education*, 1972, *13*(2), 34–43.

Wilson, B. Super-heroes of J. C. Holz: Plus an outline of a theory of child art. *Art Education*, 1974, *27*(8), 2–9.

Wilson, B., & Wilson, M. An iconoclastic view of the imagery sources of young people. *Art Education*, 1977, *30*(1), 5–12.

Wilson, B., & Wilson, M. Recycling symbols: A basic cognitive process in the arts. In S. S. Madeja (Ed.), *The Arts, Cognition, and Basic Skills*. St. Louis: CEMREL, Inc., 1978, pp. 89–109.

Wilson, B., & Wilson, M. Figure structure, figure action, and framing in drawings by American and Egyptian children. *Studies in Art Education*, 1979, *21*(1), 36–43.

Wingerter, J. R. Pseudo-existential writings in education. *Educational Theory*, 1973, *23*(3), 240–259.

Wolff, J. *Hermeneutic Philosophy and the Sociology of Art*. London: Routledge & Kegan Paul, 1975.

Yates, F. *The Art of Memory*. Chicago: University of Chicago Press, 1974.

Zurmuehlen, M. Affirmation and study: Phenomenology in doctoral research. *Review of Research in Visual Arts Education*, 1980, *12*, 1–12.

ASIAN-AMERICAN EDUCATION

"Asian Americans" are Americans whose ancestors are from Asian countries. In practice, their exact definition is confusing, varying with whom one consults and when. For example, the 1970 census included Southeast Asians, East Asians, and Oceanics under "Asian Americans," but did not include Western Asians (Gee, 1976). In recent years, the term "Asian Americans" has come to mean Americans from East or Southeast Asian countries (excluding people from the Soviet Union). People of Hawaiian ancestry or from the Pacific Islands are called "Pacific Americans."

Asians in the United States. The history of Asian Americans began in 1850, when Chinese came to California during the gold rush. From 1850 to 1924, large numbers of Chinese, Japanese, and Filipinos and a small number of Koreans came to the United States, usually to the West Coast and Hawaii. They provided the cheap labor that made possible the phenomenal economic growth of the American West. Asian immigration was categorically ended by the U.S. Congress in a series of legislative acts. First, the Chinese Exclusion Act of 1890 forbade immigration of Chinese laborers (Coolidge, 1969). Then, in 1924, the National Origin Act effectively excluded Japanese and other Asians (Ichihashi, 1932). Filipinos were allowed into the United States because of their country's status as a U.S. colony; however, in 1934, the Tydings-McDuffie Act limited Filipino immigration to fifty per year (Lasker, 1969). Because of these measures and other programs encouraging Asian Americans to move back to their home countries, the total Asian population in the United States actually declined between 1924 and 1965. U.S. immigration policy toward Asians, however, underwent a major shift in 1965, when the Immigration and Nationality Act was amended and set annual quotas of 20,000 immigrants for each country and 170,000 for the eastern hemisphere (U.S. Commission on Civil Rights, 1980). Immigration from Asian countries resumed.

The 1970 census estimated the Asian-American population to be 1,663,000, slightly over .8 percent of the total population. A review of immigration records (Immigration and Naturalization Service, 1976) shows that 25 percent of these Asian Americans immigrated between 1960 and 1970. These records also show that between July 1970 and September 1976 there were 800,875 immigrants from Asian countries, a number equal to 48 percent of the total Asian-American population in 1970. In addition, the influx of refugees from Indochina added a minimum of 150,000 people per year to the Asian-American population. These figures illustrate the drastic increase and change in the nature of the Asian-American population in the United States. The 1980 census results, to be released in 1982, will provide a more up-to-date account of this trend.

Educational Needs. Asian Americans have always been thought of as a model minority, and few researchers have examined the educational needs or problems of Asian-American children (Kitano, 1980). The few studies that addressed Asian Americans found that they were achieving at the national norm (Mayeske et al., 1973; Backman, 1972; Lesser, Fifer, & Clark, 1965; Stodolsky & Lesser, 1967). However, these studies must be examined carefully, since they are based on data collected before or immediately after the passage of the Immigration and Nationality Act of 1965. The population has since increased drastically, and the backgrounds of these new immigrants are different from those that were then already in the United States. Also, these studies mainly use Chinese and Japanese as samples, although the present Asian-American population is more diverse and consists of many more groups.

In fact, the increasing number of Asian-American students in U.S. schools, especially in large urban centers, poses tremendous problems for educators (Sung, 1977). The linguistic and cultural backgrounds of Asian-American students have influenced their knowledge, concepts, and methods of learning. In addition, immigrant students have been influenced by the curricula, teaching methods, and other pedagogical practices of their native countries. These facts have to be examined and identified by researchers before appropriate curricula and pedagogy can be designed to meet the needs of Asian-American students. The lack of research on the educational concerns of Asian Americans has left educational practitioners with no guidance.

Language instruction. One of the difficulties encountered by Asian Americans in school is the need for English proficiency. A survey conducted in 1976 (published in 1979) by the National Center for Education Statistics found that 90 percent of foreign-born Asian Americans were living in households whose dominant languages were other than English. Many of these Asian Americans were school-age children, who encountered grave difficulties in classrooms where instruction was given in English. In 1970, Chinese parents brought the *Lau* v. *Nichols* (414 U.S. 563, 1974) suit against the San Francisco Unified School District, claiming that the schools were not providing equal educational opportunity for Chinese students instructed in a language they did not understand. The case went to the U.S. Supreme Court. In 1974, the Court mandated the San Francisco Board of Education to rectify the problem and to provide services that met the special linguistic

needs of Chinese students (Teitelbaum & Hiller, 1977).

The plaintiff in *Lau* had originally asked for bilingual education as the specific remedy. This plea was dropped when the case went to the U.S. Supreme Court. According to its advocates, bilingual education will (1) teach the content subjects in a language the students understand, while they acquire English language proficiency, (2) use a culturally relevant curriculum to facilitate learning and to increase student self-concept, and (3) maintain the students' home languages through classroom instruction. Envisioned as results of bilingual education are children who communicate competently in English and their home languages, who operate successfully in both the mainstream society and their home environment, and who are proud of their cultural background.

The *Lau* decision of 1974 highlighted the modern bilingual-education movement in public schools. However, some forms of bilingual education can be traced back many decades in Asian-American communities. Private schools were established in the early 1900s by most major Chinese and Japanese immigrant communities. Most of these schools offered bilingual instruction and were established because Asian students were barred at that time from attending public schools. After those students were integrated into the public schools, some private schools became language schools with the sole purpose of maintaining language and culture. Students attended these schools after regular school hours or on weekends. Although most Japanese language schools ceased to exist during World War II, Chinese language schools have continued to the present. Korean language schools have also flourished during the last ten years (Chu, 1980).

The notion of bilingual education is controversial and has been under attack in recent years. Critics argue that if students are instructed in their home language, they will not learn the English language. This argument gained momentum when a widely criticized evaluation study found that Spanish-speaking students in bilingual programs had lower English proficiency than students in regular programs (American Institute of Research, 1978). Some critics dislike the additional cost of implementing bilingual programs, and others fearful of encouraging separatism, object to the idea of an ethnic group maintaining its language and culture. The pros and cons of bilingual education provide a wealth of topics for educational researchers. Few of these topics have been researched, very few relating to Asian Americans. Since bilingual education is based on several assumptions regarding community aspirations (e.g., the desire for bilingualism), bilingual education can mean different things to communities or ethnic groups with different aspirations. Researchers should be careful when applying findings based on a particular group to other language groups.

Research Needs. One factor that has led to the paucity of research on Asian-American educational issues is that few Asian-American researchers, those who are most likely to possess the necessary insights, engage in such research activities. The educational research community, subscribing in part to the conception that Asian Americans do not have any educational problems, has not recognized this research area. Institutions of higher education seldom recruit scholars who specialize in Asian-American educational issues as faculty members. Thus, many Asian-American educators are diverted into other mainstream research activities. This situation is self-perpetuating, because the lack of faculty members interested in Asian-American educational problems makes difficult the training of other researchers in this area. The lack of research on Asian-American educational problems is further compounded by the fact that federal and other programs that support educational research seldom include this area of research in their research agendas and that rarely are Asian Americans sought out in minority-recruitment programs.

Recent programs at the National Institute of Education have included Asian Americans as a target group in the effort to promote Asian-American educational researchers. Although their effects have yet to be studied these programs indicate a shift in attitudes among federal agencies and institutions. The educational problems of Asian Americans have begun to be acknowledged. However, a more concerted effort among all educational organizations is required to meet the special needs of the rapidly increasing numbers of Asian-American students in public schools.

Summary. The large number of immigrants from Asian countries since 1965 has led to a drastic increase in the Asian population. This trend will continue if the U.S. immigration policy does not revert to one favoring European immigration. Schools, especially those in large urban centers, have encountered a surge in the Asian-student population. Since these students have brought to the schools their unique language and cultural backgrounds, traditional school curricula may not meet their needs. To design and implement appropriate programs for these students, much research and experimentation are needed. Bilingual education is one attempt to serve the special needs of these students. The programs have been under criticism, and how they benefit Asian students has yet to be systematically studied.

Support from educational organizations, governmental agencies, and private foundations is needed to encourage research on educational issues concerning Asian-American students. Such research findings will guide and direct the practitioner toward how best to serve the increasing number of Asian-American children.

Sau-lim Tsang

See also Culture and Education Policy; Equity Issues in Education; Multicultural and Minority Education; Racism and Sexism in Children's Literature.

REFERENCES

American Institute of Research. *Evaluation of the Impact of ESEA Title VII Spanish/English Bilingual Program.* Los Angeles: California State University, National Dissemination and Assessment Center, 1978.

Backman, M. E. Patterns of mental abilities: Ethnic, Socio-economic, and sex differences. *American Educational Research Journal,* 1972, *9,* 1–12.

Chu, H. *The Contributions and Needs of Korean Saturday Schools.* Paper presented at the annual conference of the National Association for Asian and Pacific American Education, Washington, D.C., April 1980.

Coolidge, M. R. *Chinese Immigration.* New York: Arno Press, 1969.

Gee, E. (Ed.). *Counterpoint.* Los Angeles: University of California, Asian-American Studies Center, 1976. (ERIC Document Reproduction Service No. ED 147 378)

Ichihashi, Y. *Japanese in the United States.* Stanford, Calif.: Stanford University Press, 1932.

Immigration and Naturalization Service. *1976 Annual Report.* Washington, D.C.: U.S. Government Printing Office, 1976.

Kitano, M. K. Early education for Asian-American children. *Young Children,* 1980, *35,* 13–26.

Lasker, B. *Filipino Immigration.* New York: Arno Press, 1969.

Lesser, G. S.; Fifer, G.; & Clark, D. H. Mental ability of children from different social-class and cultural groups. *Monographs of the Society for Research in Child Development,* 1965, *30* (4, Whole No. 102).

Mayeske, B. W.; Okada, T.; Beaton, A. E., Jr.; Cohen, W. M.; & Wisler, C. E. *A Study of the Achievement of Our Nation's Students.* Washington, D.C.: U.S. Government Printing Office, 1973. (ERIC Document Reproduction Service No. ED 085 629)

National Center for Education Statistics. *Bulletin No. 144.* Washington, D.C.: National Center for Education Statistics, 1979.

Stodolsky, S. S., & Lesser, G. S. Learning patterns in the disadvantaged. *Harvard Educational Review,* 1967, *37,* 546–593.

Sung, B. L. *Gangs in New York's Chinatown.* New York: City College of New York, Department of Asian Studies, 1977. (ERIC Document Reproduction Service No. ED 152 894)

Teitelbaum, H., & Hiller, R. J. *Bilingual Education: Current Perspective, Law.* Arlington, Va.: Center for Applied Linguistics, 1977. (ERIC Document Reproduction Service No. ED 144 378)

U.S. Commission on Civil Rights. *The Tarnished Golden Door: Civil Rights Issues in Immigration.* Washington, D.C.: U.S. Government Printing Office, 1980.

ASSESSMENT

See Evaluation of Programs; Measurement in Education.

ATTENDANCE POLICY

Attendance policy, dependent as it is on a definition of compulsory school age, becomes compulsory school attendance policy. Schooling is not mentioned in the United States Constitution; neither is the right to be educated recognized in the Constitution. Therefore, schooling was left to the states. By 1918 all states, beginning with Massachusetts in 1852 and ending with Mississippi in 1918, had enacted laws requiring children to attend school for a varied range of years.

During the last few years poor attendance has become an increasingly serious problem in the schools, especially the secondary schools, and has been identified by superintendents and principals as one of the most troubling student problems. Some large city schools have reported absentee rates as high as 50 percent per day (Thomson & Stanard, 1975). Teachers, counselors, and administrators have been forced to spend more time on the details of managing attendance. When time is taken away from the primary instructional duties for which these educators are employed, the quality of teaching and learning in the schools eventually suffers.

This examination of attendance policy will focus on (1) development of attendance policies; (2) enforcement of state attendance laws; (3) effective attendance policies; and (4) current attacks on compulsory attendance.

Development of Attendance Policies. For centuries in many countries of the world laws were established requiring school attendance by some part of the population. Such laws were found as early as 2000 B.C. in Babylon's Code of Hammurabi. In 1907 Japan became the first Asian country to pass compulsory attendance laws. Comenius' reforms, designed to supply the state with great minds, depended on government support. Luther's advocacy of free, universal education influenced Protestantism toward the principle of education as a function of the state. The Anglican church was the state's educational agency in England; and the Poor Law of 1601 required pauper children to be apprenticed and taught the rudiments. These examples indicate that in most countries with histories of legally mandated schooling, the issue of compulsory education was intertwined with humanitarian concerns, child labor laws, and the goals of church and state.

Prussia became the first country in Europe to establish compulsory education, demanding that the masses be taught their duties to the state; control was centered in a department of education. The United States was the next to establish compulsory education. The major question facing young America was this: can a democracy with universal suffrage exist if its people are not literate? Elementary compulsory education was established, in part, to guarantee the success of the experiment in democracy; and only the government could compel parents to send their children to school (Mulhern, 1946).

U.S. development. In New England the principle of government ownership and operation of schools was firmly established. Massachusetts, where the first attendance laws were passed, was an authoritarian society; there were laws to regulate every part of life, including relations between church and state, compulsory monogamy, and imbibing spirits. Rhode Island, the exception to this authoritarian pattern, did not pass compulsory education laws. In 1691 Massachusetts passed a law requiring a town of fifty families to provide a schoolmaster to teach its children to read and write; towns of one hundred families were also required to have a grammar school. Any town that did not enforce the law was fined. Thus, the town, a subdivision of the state, became the unit of local school administration (Parker, 1981).

Compulsory education developed later in the South than in other parts of the country. The planter aristocracy represented a widely scattered population, not clustered in towns, and financially able to educate its own children. Southern colonists, unlike their New England counterparts, were not involved in building a new social order; therefore, they did not see education as a way to force a new social design upon their youth (Edwards & Richey, 1963).

After the Civil War, urbanization accompanied rapid economic expansion. Immigrants who had to learn to adjust to American society increased the number of children to be socialized. The growing heterogeneity of natural origins and religions strengthened the dominant middle-class fear that the stability of their society was in jeopardy (Abbott, 1938). Attendance laws were contested by ethnic, religious, and family interest groups.

Passage of compulsory education laws implied the ability to enforce attendance. However, early laws establishing schools were weak and written without mentioning schools, schooling, or attendance. Enforcement was left to the schools. In general, educators were not enthusiastic about enforcing the laws because they did not want unwilling students who would be in attendance only because of legal coercion.

Prior to 1920, state control of education was weak. State departments usually consisted of only two people, one of whom was the state superintendent, who had little power. Neither was federal control strong; the United States Commissioner of Education was chiefly a collector of statistics. Consequently, control of schools remained local (Richardson, 1980).

Paralleling the growth in schooling legislation was legislation to remove children from the labor force, an important factor in expanding education (Deffenbaugh & Keesecker, 1935). In 1813 Connecticut passed the first state law requiring owners of mills to provide instruction in reading, writing, and arithmetic to children who worked in factories (Umbeck, 1960; Felt, 1965). All states now have child labor laws.

The Fair Labor Standards Act of 1940 outlawed child labor in industries engaged in interstate commerce. A student who left school before the mandated age could not be employed until the age of 18 (Tibble, 1970). During the years since the passage of that act, fewer employment opportunities have existed for 14- to-18-year-olds. Education or training requirements for many jobs have increased, and social pressure to stay in school has also increased. Society expects secondary school attendance to the point that students who leave school have been labeled "dropouts."

Enforcement of State Attendance Laws. Each state in its education code defined compulsory school age (usually from age 6 or age 7 to age 14 or age 18), ordinarily guaranteeing nine years of schooling. Laws required compulsory attendance of residents of a school district and also of nonresidents who were being supported by residents of the district. Most codes required an affidavit or some other legal proof of responsibility for nonresident children (Lawyers' Committee for Civil Rights Under Law, 1974).

Scope of codes. Laws of each state have spelled out the conditions for maintaining and operating a school for a specified time, a specific number of days each year, generally 180 days, 36 weeks, or 9 months. Some states have required "regular" or "continuous attendance," while others called for attendance "during the full term." Five states do not specify the time; one exceeds the usual 180 days (Steinhilber & Sokolowski, 1966).

Public school codes have spelled out penalties for violation of compulsory attendance requirements, which regulate every parent, guardian, or person in a parental relation who is in charge or control of any child of compulsory school age. Any who fail to comply with the provisions for compulsory school attendance may be convicted and sentenced to pay a fine for the benefit of the school district in which the offending person lives. Dollar amounts were generally spelled out for the first offense along with increases for succeeding offenses, plus court costs. In default of payment the offender may be sentenced to county jail for a stated period, in Pennsylvania, for example, for five days. These offenses have usually been considered misdemeanors (Francis, 1970).

Codes control nonpublic school attendance; attendance at such a school must be deemed to be the equivalent of public school attendance. In 1981 Nebraska Supreme Court upheld the state's power to impose upon private schools attendance and other standards that relate to the quality of education. *(Education USA, 1981)*

Every compulsory attendance law contains exemptions within the compulsory age limits. All states recognize the right to be instructed in nonpublic schools. All states except one exempt those certified as physically and mentally unable to profit from or to complete minimum requirements. Other causes for exemption are distance from school, seasonal work at home, sickness or other insurmountable conditions, lawful employment before reaching the school-leaving age, or completion of the minimum requirements before the mandated age. Some laws even spell out temporary excuses, such as music lessons or religious instruction (Umbeck, 1960).

Parts of the law and the required record-keeping exist less for registering attendance than for providing information to determine state reimbursement to a school district. Some state laws require information about average daily membership as the basis for reimbursement, whereas others require average daily attendance. These are financial incentives for administering attendance.

Data collecting procedures that incorporate use of the computer have reduced to an extent some of the time spent in compiling absentee lists; however, the fact that computer procedures require precise language could lead to the requirement of more rules specifying attendance enforcement.

In order to control attendance, accurate and up-to-date data on those who are supposed to attend school must be available. Therefore, a continuous census is necessary, recording individuals from the time of birth, or the age span of 0 to 18 years, in order that the school may know when to expect how many for how long. The more efficient the census, the more effective the administration of attendance. It is difficult for a school district to identify children within its jurisdiction who are of compulsory age but are not enrolled in school. (Umbeck, 1960)

Truancy. The school is responsible for providing instruction and informing parents when their child is absent. The state prescribed attendance, but enforcing attendance was the responsibility of parents and students.

Compulsory schooling can be equated with state truancy laws. Every truancy statute imposes criminal penalties on the parents or guardians who do not see that a child for whom they are responsible receives the amount of education required by the state law for the required age ranges. In early enforcement, if a parent or master did not teach a child whatever the law required, the child was taken away from the parent or guardian and apprenticed to someone who would carry out the law.

Attendance officers are hired to enforce the law. Titles of these officers have varied as society's attitudes and values have shifted. Sometimes they have been known as visiting teachers, attendance teachers, and truant officers, and more recently as student advocates. Baltimore, Maryland, faced with an absentee rate of 30,000 per day, hired 100 new, young, often unemployed, truant officers to work all year round as tutors, counselors and primarily as student advocates as a means to combat the big impersonal system which may be a factor in the high rate of absenteeism.

In many states laws have invested attendance officers with the powers of police officers, thereby enabling them to make arrests in enforcing attendance laws. Jurisdiction of attendance officers may be included in attendance policies to that students and parents will have no doubt about their responsibilities.

School districts, whose primary purpose is instruction (teaching and learning), must allocate funds for enforcing attendance laws that could be used for instructional purposes. At least one state, New Mexico, reduced expenses when it changed attendance regulations by requiring that school boards and the governing authorities of private schools only initiate enforcement action. The parent or guardian is first notified. If the student continues to be absent, then the school notifies Children's Court; the child then is subject to provisions of the Children's Code, which requires that the state provide assistance and take whatever action is appropriate in each incident.

Suspension and expulsion. Some codes have spelled out procedures for suspension and expulsion. Generally states are concerned with due process or procedures for expulsion or suspension, not with reasons for the actions. Expansion of due process as related to the classroom came with the Supreme Court decision, *Goss* v. *Lopez*, 1975, in which the court ruled in a 5 to 4 decision that students are entitled to an informal hearing before a suspension of ten days or less. This decision made it clear that more elaborate procedures would be required for more serious charges. Schools now have rules requiring formal hearings and appeals if severe penalties are considered (Flygare, 1981).

In states lacking statutes relating to suspension and expulsion, an injunction can be obtained to block such action when it is threatened on the ground that the school district lacks statutory authority to expel or suspend. For every action there must be a law supporting it (Vaughn, 1970).

Effective Attendance Policies. Attendance policy is based upon an assumption that the school staff provides appropriate and interesting learning experiences. Programs of instruction should be interesting and challenging to students who are forced to attend and should meet the needs and abilities of students. When an ineffective program of studies does contribute to absenteeism, generally a careful examination will reveal it to be only one of many causes of the problem. Even schools with a flexible and wide-ranging program of studies and related activities have attendance problems.

The National Association of Secondary School Principals (NASSP) maintains an up-to-date file of attendance policies of secondary schools across the United States that have developed effective ways to control attendance. The schools that report improvement in attendance have developed attendance policies that are strictly observed. These policies originate in large and small schools, urban and rural, but they have several features in common.

Effective approaches. First, these schools consider all nonattendance as "absence" and do not use the labels "excused" or "unexcused." Second, these schools establish a maximum number of allowable absences for a specified time period, typically ten per semester, for which course credit will be granted. Third, a five- or six-member appeal board consisting of teachers, students, and administrators, reviews records of students who have more than the maximum allowable number of absences. These boards consider any special circumstances related to excessive absence before deciding to withhold course credit. Fourth, effective school districts make clear in letters to parents and in student publications that no credit will be given for courses if more than ten class absences are reported. Explanations for required attendance are provided, suggesting that full participation is necessary for full education. Labs, oral reports, and discussions require participation; and work completed by test does not compare with the interaction and learning that occur in a classroom.

Some schools use several approaches to reduce absences, such as operating alternative schools or programs for the chronic truant, exempting students with good attendance from formal examinations, lowering grades, telephoning the home of each absentee or the office of working parents, suspending or expelling, establishing coordination between the school and court personnel, or mailing attendance reports home on a weekly or monthly basis.

Reports from a Napa, California, experimental school attendance policy which allowed for a maximum of twelve absences with possible dropping from class with 13; and notified parents in writing of the fourth, eighth and twelfth absences, indicated that absences were reduced by approximately 50 percent from an average of 8 to 10 percent in 1972–1974 to 4.5 percent in 1975 (Fotinos, 1975).

Research. Little research has been done on reasons for poor attendance, even though the problem has been increasing and thus increasingly interfering with the education process. In 1980 the National Education Association (NEA) Representative Assembly directed the NEA to help states study the causes of truancy and other patterns of school nonattendance and to find means of identifying and treating irregular student attendance practices. Earlier, in its 1980 Representative Assembly, the NEA had adopted a resolution that identified student "rights" but had added comparable student "responsibilities," which included regular school attendance along with conscientious effort in classrooms and adherence to school rules and regulations (National Education Association, 1980).

Studies can be cited that show that no relation exists between delinquency, compulsory school attendance laws, and child labor laws; but in a Sacramento, California, study where attendance was strictly enforced, and truants returned to school for counseling and modified instruction, the juvenile crime rate was claimed to have dropped approximately 40 or 50 percent. In South Carolina enrollments were studied for the year before and after the repeal of the state's compulsory attendance law. It was concluded that the law had little or no effect on attendance, but the compulsory attendance law was reenacted anyway in 1967.

Effective policies are ones that have been well publicized and are consistently enforced with immediate follow-up of each absence.

Current Attacks on Compulsory Attendance. Although there have been attacks on the concept of compulsory attendance even before the first laws were enacted, the 1970s and 1980s brought increasingly vigorous debate along with proposals for drastic changes. Suggestions range from elimination of all compulsion, leaving social, economic, and cultural incentives to assure retention in school, to lowering of the required entrance age and raising of the required leaving age. Critics pointed out that the state in its attempt to protect the public interest is responsible for professional licensing, but it is only in education that an individual is compelled to use the services of one or more specifically licensed practitioners.

The high rate of disorder, violence, and vandalism, especially in large and urban schools, that developed in the 1960s though previously unknown, generated additional criticism. Many critics began to question what they perceived to be the custodial function of the school. Compulsory attendance laws force youth to attend school until an arbitrary age; thus the school becomes an organization responsible for managing or controlling some clients who are involuntary members, who for one-third of the day are in school, told what to do and when to do it while there. Any organization, that is forced to assume a custodial role with involuntary members must develop methods of social control and soon may evolve into a holding operation for the uninterested (Moralla, Williams, & McGrath, 1980).

In the past students did not question teachers' authority. The prevailing attitude was a willingness to accept the rules of the school, since both the family and society in general were authoritarian. By the 1960s and 1970s both society and the family had become more democratic, whereas the school continued to be authoritarian, revealing a rare resistance to change.

Children and youth now accustomed to less authority in family life expect institutions outside the family to be more permissive also, and they resist authority. A confrontation results: students as they perceive their rights versus school authority. As a "right," students expect an explanation for every rule. Academic success is no longer a priority for many students; grades or other evidence of approval are not appropriate to youth who are just marking time, waiting to become responsible adults.

For most of a typical day, high school youth are segregated from society in a separate youth culture, where a strong peer pressure operates. If the peer group's values are consistent with what the peer group perceives the school's authority to be, there is no problem or confrontation.

Learning is not facilitated by compulsory attendance. Therefore, the custodial atmosphere, in which unwilling learners are forced to be in school, will not help them to learn; the unwilling learner may, in fact, seriously interfere with learning in a regular classroom.

Much has been written about student alienation, its causes, and suggested cures, without enough attention to its relation to compulsory attendance and how students are actually involved during the school day (Keniston, 1965; Schiamberg, 1973). In some schools where students have been included in making decisions that influence their school lives, such as developing attendance policy, vandalism has been reduced. Generally it is the students who are enrolled in a school who are responsible for the acts of vandalism committed at their schools. For some youth, involvement in meaningful activities, in assuming responsibility for their behavior, has changed their attitude toward school attendance.

Constitutionality and student rights. The constitutionality of compulsory education laws has been widely debated throughout the history of American education, but never so hotly as in the decade of the 1970s. Until recently, whenever the question of constitutionality had gone to the courts, the courts had confirmed the principle of the states' enforcement of school attendance. One case concerned the attempt by Oregon in 1922 to prohibit private schools, thereby forcing all children to attend public schools. The Supreme Court struck the law down during the following year (Rickenbacker, 1974).

The *Tinker* v. *Des Moines* landmark decision of 1969 specifically provided to students the constitutional right to nondisruptive symbolic speech in school by declaring that juveniles have rights in public institutions and in the justice system (Flygare, 1981). This dramatic decision initiated the era of student rights and called for a wide range of changes in a school's operating procedures. Many knowledgeable educators have contended that this decision reaffirmed that students are persons under the Constitution in school as well as out of school and thereby have fundamental rights that the state must respect. This argument contends that the freedom that this decision gave to youth wiped out *in loco parentis* and made compulsory schooling unconstitutional.

The Amish decision in 1972, ending their long battle against compulsory schooling above the eighth grade, suggested that compulsory attendance may be unconstitutional. Based on the Amish decision, a Florida judge ruled that an Indian father did not have to send his five youngest children to school; the judge had previously ruled that Florida's compulsory attendance law impinged on fundamental rights protected by the free enterprise clause of the First Amendment. Thus, in this example, Chief Justice Burger's majority opinion in the Amish decision influenced a later decision about compulsory education, suggesting that Burger's decision had undermined the importance of compulsory education (Katz, 1976).

Lowering the school-leaving age. At about the time "student rights" became a slogan as well as a dominant concern, the age of majority was lowered from 20 years to 18 years of age. With these drastic changes in laws governing youth came renewed attacks on compulsory attendance. The most prestigious challenge to the old attendance laws came from the National Commission on the Reform of Secondary Education, financed by the Charles F. Kettering Foundation to examine the directions of secondary education. The most powerful of the commission's thirty-two recommendations was the one stating the student's right not to be in formal schooling after the age of 14. Most states still require schooling until ages 16 or 18.

Reasons cited by the commission for recommending the lower school-leaving age were: earlier physical and social maturing; the Tinker decision making compulsory education unconstitutional; problems resulting from attendance by students who do not want to be in school; and the high absence rate. It must be pointed out that the commission did distinguish between compulsory school attendance and compulsory education; they favored the continuation of compulsory education.

The National Education Association (NEA) and the American Federation of Teachers (AFT) opposed lowering the school-leaving age. The National Association of Secondary School Principals warned that chaos would result and recommended meaningful options for all students. Washington provided for flexibility in waiving compulsory attendance. However, many educators who disagreed with lowering the school-leaving age to 14 admitted that compulsion is not consistent with the values of current young adults and also recognized the need for more learning options.

Some educators predicted that should the laws be changed, a rush of 14-year-olds to leave school would result. Yet the experience in California with an "early-out" examination did not create upheaval. Students younger than the leaving age of 18 who passed an examination and had their parents' permission to leave school could do so, with a certificate of proficiency. Only 2 percent of the 16- and 17-year-olds took the test; of this group only 45 percent passed. The best students did not opt for early leaving, which had been another administrator fear.

When South Carolina legislators began a study of the feasibility of eliminating grade 12, the Student Advisory Council to the state superintendent rejected any attempt to eliminate the twelfth grade.

Age of majority. Compulsory attendance age determines a school's legal responsibility for requiring youth of the specified age to be in school. Schools are obligated to report to the courts those of compulsory age who do not comply. Others outside the age attend school by choice, unforced by law. However, should they be 18, the age of majority, or above, and attend by choice, these students, too, are subject to all the policies that govern the school, including attendance. Options frequently provided for the older students are work-study and off-campus programs, which operate within the governing policies of the school.

Some policies and procedures have been changed to adapt to the age of majority—for example, excuses for absence. If the age of majority means freedom from parental control, parents' written excuses cannot be required. However, an adult is expected to be responsible for his own behavior, which means accepting a school's conditions for attendance. Procedures need to be examined and those modified that no longer require parental approval for majority-age students. New circumstances require new procedures. Freedom in being an adult calls for new responsibilities.

Policy Considerations. In the present circumstances, marked by student rights, the lowered age of majority, less authoritarian family and society, and earlier physical and social maturation of youth, the current debate about school attendance can be summarized by the question: does school attendance have to be forced?

No one really knows how many years of common, universal schooling should be required. Laws of the fifty states reflect this lack of agreement. There is no consensus on the ideal age for completing the educational process. Learning never ceases. The acceptable school age in the 1980s ranges from the very young to the old. Demands have increased for lowering the mandated entrance age to include what has been called the preschool or nursery age, generally 4 years old. Head Start and increased day care programs have contributed to this demand.

Rapid increase in voluntary request for education by older citizens, evidenced in one way by the growth of community college attendance, has been interpreted as a demand for raising the age for state-supported schooling. Community college education is generally state-supported in part. Increased enrollment in formal schooling on the part of older Americans has destroyed the typical 18- to 21-year-old college student profile. In the 1970s studies of community college attendance policies first appeared in the professional literature (Kelso, 1978). Voluntary request for schooling suggests the need to reduce punitive measures to control attendance among adults, even young adults who are guaranteed rights and are legally responsible for their behavior.

Young people in the present mandated age range vary widely in all learner characteristics, far more widely than did youth during the early period of compulsory education. As heterogeneity in the school population increased, there was a need for changing the amount of schooling from which students can benefit; however, amount of time spent in school remains the usual criterion for completion of schooling. School policy has largely ignored the research in child growth and development that has emphasized earlier maturation and its implication for schooling. Learners require improved counseling; more individualization of schedules and activities, including work-study and independent study; earlier career orientation; and new options for obtaining the high school diploma.

Any decision about age for schooling should be made on educational grounds; that is, it should be determined by information about learners and learning, preferably based on study and research, rather than by political, economic, or social beliefs. Progress in learning should be more important than the number of years spent in school (Grieder, 1972).

Americans cannot ignore the expansion and development of their country. Neither can Americans forget the investment they have made through the years in providing schooling for all the children of all the people and the laws they enacted to force the children and youth to partake. The investment resulted in higher wages, greater purchasing power for the poor, and new products created by educated minds (Tibble, 1970).

Some argue that compulsory attendance is justified in our society if for no other reason than it provides driver training and free meals for the needy. History suggests a stronger justification. The school is the first formal institution outside the family that all children encounter. It has been argued that a child needs some structure or ceremony through which he becomes a participant in society, and that the school represents such a structure or ceremony; this has been true of children in all ages and cultures of the past and continues to be so (Ihle, 1978).

Court decisions reflecting societal changes in values and attitudes have resulted in the altered status of youth. Voluntary attendance among older learners has increased. Young children's experiences in preschool programs have pointed up the value of early learning. Yet, attendance laws have not been repealed or substantially revised. And there seems to be little interest on the part of educators or state governments to repeal or even change attendance regulations. A recent study of Michigan superintendents indicated that the group polled strongly opposed home instruction and no required attendance. A large number admitted that compulsory attendance laws were not effective in producing high-quality education. Nevertheless, about three-fourths of those polled favored a leaving age of 16 or higher. There was no support for changing the attendance law; the most notable change these superintendents would favor was lowering the entrance age from 6 to 5 (Furst & Cruise, 1980).

Attendance policies, especially as they relate to young adults, need to be changed. The policies must incorporate the recent Supreme Court decisions about student rights, the new status of responsibilities of young adults brought about by the court decisions. Procedures must be updated to allow young adults to take on the responsibilities, new to them, required by adult status. However, since Americans do not have a feasible alternative to compulsory attendance, it should not be eliminated until enough study and research can indicate what would happen without it.

If school codes are not changed, as study and the wishes of the people warrant, at least flexibility in exemptions to attendance can be incorporated into the codes to meet the new needs, some of which are not now anticipated. When the viable alternative is put forth, laws can be repealed; or, under new circumstances, compulsory attendance may become so insignificant an issue that laws will not matter.

Margaret Gill Hein

See also Behavior Problems; Instructional Time and Learning; Promotion Policy; State Influences on Education; Truants and Dropouts.

REFERENCES

Abbott, G. *The Child and the State* (Vol. 1). New York: Greenwood Press, 1938.

Deffenbaugh, W. S., & Keesecker, W. W. *Compulsory School Attendance Laws and Their Administration*. Washington, D.C.: U.S. Government Printing Office, 1935.

Education USA. Nebraska keeps control of private schools. Arlington, Va.: National School Public Relations Association, 1981, *23*, 186.

Edwards, N., & Richey, H. G. *The School in the American Social Order*. Boston: Houghton Mifflin, 1963.

Felt, J. P. *Hostages of Fortune: Child Labor Reform in New York State*. Syracuse, N.Y.: Syracuse University Press, 1965.

Flygare, T. J. Schools and the law. *Phi Delta Kappan*, 1981, *62*, 390–391.

Fotinos, T. *Napa High School Attendance Policy: An Experiment to Reduce Unnecessary School Absences* (Project description, unpublished). Napa, Calif., 1975.

Francis, S. N. *Pennsylvania School Law: Public School Code of 1949 Annotated* (Article XIII, Pupils and Attendance, Vol. 2, 61–90, Cleveland: Burk-Baldwin, 1970. (ERIC Document Reproduction Service No. ED 119 353)

Furst, L. G., & Cruise, R. J. Michigan superintendents look at compulsory attendance laws. *Phi Delta Kappan*, 1980, *61*, 494.

Grieder, C. Are students spending too much time in school? *Nation's Schools*, 1972, *90*, 12.

Ihle, R. An argument for compulsory schooling. *Today's Education*, 1978, *67*, 45–47.

Katz, M. S. *A History of Compulsory Education Laws*. Bloomington, Ind.: Phi Delta Kappa Educational Foundation, 1976. (ERIC Document Reproduction Service No. ED 119 389)

Kelso, G. *Student Attendance Policies at El Centro College: Their Rationales and Results*. (Unpublished doctoral dissertation, Nova University, 1978.

Keniston, K. *The Uncommitted: Alienated Youth in American Society*. New York: Harcourt Brace, 1965.

Lawyers' Committee for Civil Rights under Law. *A Study of State Legal Standards for the Provision of Public Education*. Washington, D.C.: National Institute of Education, 1974. (ERIC Document Reproduction Service No. ED 122 461)

Moralla, J. A.; Williams, J. S.; & McGrath, J. H. Schools: Antiquated systems of social control. *Educational Forum*, 1980, *45*, 77–93. (ERIC Document Reproduction Service No. ED 157 191)

Mulhern, J. *A History of Education*. New York: Roland Press, 1946.

National Education Association. *Handbook 1980–1981*. Washington, D.C.: NEA, 1980.

Parker, F. Ideas that shaped American schools. *Phi Delta Kappan*, 1981, *62*, 314–319.

Richardson, J. G. Variations in data of enactment of compulsory school attendance laws: An empirical inquiry. *Sociology of Education*, 1980, *53*, 153–163.

Rickenbacker, W. F. (Ed.). *The Twelve-Year Sentence*. Lasalle, Ill.: Open Court, 1974.

Schiamberg, L. B. *Adolescent Alienation*. Columbus, Ohio: Merrill, 1973.

Steinhilber, A. W., & Sokolowski, C. J. *State Law on Compulsory Attendance*. Washington, D.C.: U.S. Department of Health, Education and Welfare, Office of Education, 1966.

Thomson, S., & Stanard, D. School attendance and absenteeism. *Practitioner*. Reston, Va.: National Association of Secondary School Principals, March, 1975.

Tibble, J. W. (Ed.). *The Extra Year: The Raising of the School-Leaving Age*. London: Routledge & Kegan Paul, 1970.

Umbeck, N. R. *State Legislation on School Attendance and Related Matters: School Census and Child Labor*. Washington, D.C.: U.S. Department of Health, Education, and Welfare, Office of Education, 1960.

Vaughn, J. G. *The Pupil's Day in Court: Review of 1969* (Annual Compilation). Washington, D.C.: National Education Association, 1970. (ERIC Document Reproduction Service No. ED 070 151)

ATTITUDE MEASUREMENT

The study of attitudes has been of practical concern to researchers in such diverse fields as health, conservation, merchandising, and public opinion polling, as well as in project evaluation and educational research. A wide variety of practical problems and theoretical concerns have therefore been identified, and techniques for coping with problems have come from many disciplines. Hence, the research literature outside education has been examined for helpful viewpoints and practical suggestions.

Since measurement of attitudes has developed independently of the different theoretical positions taken with respect to attitude formation and change, no attempt has been made to summarize these theoretical positions (Fishbein & Ajzen, 1975; Insko, 1967; Kiesler, Collins, & Miller, 1969; Sherif, Sherif, & Nebergall, 1965). Nor has any attempt been made to review the research on specific instruments, such as the widely used Minnesota Teacher Attitude Inventory (1951), for which Buros (1978) reports 361 research studies. Nor was the extensive research literature on the measurement of the self-concept (Shavelson, Hubner, & Stanton, 1976) or need achievement (Atkinson, 1974; Atkinson & Feather, 1966), or internal-external locus of control (Rotter, 1966) included.

In the two most recent reviews under the heading "Attitude and Attitude Change" in the *Annual Review of Psychology* (Cialdini, Petty, & Cacioppo, 1981; Eagly & Himmelfarb, 1978), the renewed interest in attitudinal phenomena, after a decade of low interest, has been noted. As research on attitudes has become recognized as more important, greater concern is being shown for the improvement of attitude measures. As in any other field, research on attitudes can be only as effective as the measuring instruments available.

Concepts. According to Fisher (1977), the concept of attitude has had more definitions than any other concept in social psychology. Perhaps in an effort to simplify the construct of attitude to one that could be studied by methods then available, the pioneers in attitude measurement tended to define the term "attitude" narrowly (Lemon, 1973), in terms of the intensity of affect for or against a psychological object (Thurstone, 1928).

Attitudes cannot be observed but must always be inferred from behavior. The process of measuring attitudes, therefore, can be conceptualized as consisting of three stages: (1) identification of the types of behavior samples that are acceptable as a basis for making inferences, (2) collection of the samples of behavior, and (3) treatment of the behavior samples so as to convert findings about them into a quantitative variable (Summers, 1970). Although a great deal of research has been done on the third aspect (attitude scaling), insufficient attention has been given to the acceptability of behavior samples and to the procedures by which such samples are obtained.

Cook and Selltiz (1964) recognize the affective, cognitive, and behavioral-intention aspects of attitude; they consider the affective component of attitude to be its central aspect. They define attitude as an underlying disposition that enters, along with many other influences, into the determination of a variety of behaviors toward the attitude object, or class of objects, including statements of belief and feelings about the attitude object and approach-avoidance actions with respect to it. When behaviors, or behavioral intentions, are included in the definition of "attitude," they are of the type from which one could infer favorable or unfavorable feelings.

In a reanalysis of data from an earlier study (Fishbein & Ajzen, 1975), Bagozzi and Burnkrant (1979) found strong supporting evidence for three factors corresponding to the three hypothesized components of attitude (affective, cognitive, and behavioral).

Self-report Techniques. Thurstone (1928) first developed procedures by which one could select from a pool of attitude statements those that were more relevant and unambiguous and arrange them in a scale that would have interval properties, although many writers have debated whether Thurstone scales represent measurement at the interval level or whether scores from these scales must be considered ordinal measures (e.g., Bruvold, 1975; Petrie, 1969).

Consensual-location scaling. Thurstone's early work (1927) involved the method of paired comparisons, which becomes time-consuming if a large number of attitude statements are to be evaluated. Shoemaker (1971) developed a simpler adaptation of this approach.

The equal-appearing-intervals method, which became Thurstone's recommended method, is fully described in a monograph by Thurstone and Chave (1929), which became the standard handbook for this approach. The procedure involves (1) formulating a large number of statements reflecting a wide range of attitudes toward a social object (e.g., the church); (2) selecting and editing approximately 100 brief statements; (3) submitting these statements to a large number of judges, who are asked to sort them into eleven groups on a continuum, ranging from "least favorable" to "most favorable"; (4) calculating the median scale value for each statement (consensus on its location on the attitude continuum); (5) eliminating as ambiguous those items on which judges' ratings varied widely; (6) eliminating items on the basis of the criteria of irrelevance; and (7) selecting approximately twenty items (ten positive and ten negative), evenly graduated along the attitude continuum. When the shorter scale is then administered to research subjects, the respondents simply check the statements with which they agree. (The individual's score is the median scale value of the statements checked.)

Thurstone's method has been criticized because of the large amount of work involved and the probability that judges' scale ratings might be affected by their own attitudes (Seiler & Hough, 1970). Later research has revealed that if careful instructions are given, judges' biases do not seriously distort their ratings (Bruvold, 1975).

Summated ratings. Likert (1932) developed an approach to attitude measurement that eliminated the need for having a large group of judges. The method of "summated ratings" soon became popular and has remained so. The first steps, as in the Thurstone method, involved assembling a large number of statements and submitting them to editorial review. The next step, however, involved administering the preliminary form of the inventory to 100 to 200 subjects who indicated *their own* reactions to each statement on a five-point scale (from "strongly agree" to "strongly disagree"). A balanced number of positive and negative statements were included, with the scale values being reversed for negative statements. This arrangement assures that respondents' scores are not influenced by a position set and are less likely to be influenced by a response set to agree or disagree, without regard to item content (Couch & Keniston, 1961).

Item discrimination indices were then used to select the items that discriminated best between the high-scoring and low-scoring groups (with respect to total score). Perhaps twenty items (ten negative and ten positive) were selected for the final form. Although a homogeneous inventory has been developed by this method, the items have not been scaled. In the years since Likert introduced this method, many refinements have been suggested (Andrich, 1978; Dubois & Burns, 1975; Spector, 1976); computer programs have also been developed to obtain item correlations with total score and to develop subscales by means of item factor analysis (Aiken, 1975; Kohr, 1971). On the other hand, many investigators have developed Likert-type scales, ignoring the procedures recommended for selecting items and for increasing scale homogeneity (Gardner, 1975; Triandis, 1971).

In addition to their greater ease of construction, Likert scales have been shown to be more reliable than Thurstone scales of the same length (Seiler & Hough, 1970); the reasons for this difference will be discussed later. The major empirical studies comparing the Thurstone and Likert techniques have been summarized by Seiler and Hough (1970).

Cumulative scaling. Guttman's scalogram technique (Guttman, 1944, 1947, 1950; Guttman & Suchman, 1947) was introduced in order to develop unidimensional scales, so constructed that the respondent who endorsed an item would (with a probability of .90 or higher) endorse all items that were lower on this cumulative scale. Later research has shown that only rarely do attitude inventories meet Guttman's standards (Lemon, 1973). Although Guttman recommended having at least ten items, few Guttman scales have more than eight, and many are even shorter. The typically small number of items has led to two types of inadequacy: (1) the ability to make fine distinctions among respondents is diminished by the narrow score range, and (2) since the items are often widely spaced on the attitude continuum, the fact that the reproducibility requirements are met does not guarantee that the scale is unidimensional. Another problem is that since the items are selected empirically, the ones surviving the reproducibility test may not be representative of the attitude domain. This risk, which is faced in all methods of attitude scaling, is accentuated because of the small number of items (Lemon, 1973). Refinements in Guttman scaling procedures have been reviewed by Dotson and Summers (1970).

One of the simpler methods of scalogram analysis, adaptable for use with a computer, has been developed by Toby and Toby (1954); procedures for multiple scalogram analysis were later developed by Lingoes (1963).

Combination of methods. The three approaches to attitude measurement already discussed were combined by Edwards and Kilpatrick (1948) in their method of scale construction. Their scale discrimination technique involved selecting the most discriminating items from each group of statements to which judges had assigned similar scale values (by the Thurstone method). This procedure not only utilized Thurstone scaling procedures but also retained Likert's procedures for screening items on the basis of their discriminating power, as well as Likert's use of a large number of response categories.

Each of the alternative forms developed by this method was found to have an adequate reproducibility coefficient. The interest in combining Thurstone and Likert procedures has continued (Andrich, 1978a; 1978b).

Other self-report techniques. No attempt will be made to discuss specific attitude measures. An extensive collection of unpublished attitude scales that are available for use by researchers has been assembled by Shaw and Wright (1967). Information about recently developed measures of both attitudes and values has been compiled by Robinson and Shaver (1973). A collection of sixteen measures of school-related attitudes has been compiled by Knapp (1972).

One of the most popular and least expensive procedures for studying attitudes is the mail survey. Its limitations, however, are great, because of the typically low percentage of return and the distortion in findings that inevitably results from biased sampling. There is a vast and growing literature on means of improving responses to mail surveys (Blumberg, Fuller, & Hare, 1974; Carpenter, 1975; Dillman & Frey, 1974; Eisinger et al., 1974; Erdos & Morgan, 1970; Fuller, 1974; Hinrichs, 1975; Sheth & Roscoe, 1975).

Interviews may be tightly structured, with interviewers trained to ensure comparability of data, or they may have little structure, with the order and wording of questions adjusted in any way that will encourage spontaneous conversation regarding the attitude object(s). The lower degree of structure may be needed in areas in which cultural norms are changing; it may also be valuable in the exploratory phase of an investigation—for example, to make sure that one is including all aspects of an attitude domain in a structured instrument being developed, or to facilitate phrasing stimulus questions in terminology appropriate to the group being studied. The use of such procedures as the "funnel technique," the "inverted funnel technique," and "probe questions" are explained by Kahn and Cannell (1957).

The training of interviewers should be thorough so that they can establish rapport, convince the subjects of the confidentiality of interview data, and obtain comparable results. It is often advisable to have interviews recorded, with the interviewee's permission; transcriptions can then be coded by persons trained in the assignment of behavior elements to categories; also, a measure of intercoder consistency can be obtained. It is important that persons coding the transcripts be uninformed concerning the purpose of the study and concerning the subjects' memberships in different subgroups.

Q-sort methodology, pioneered by Stephenson (1953), involves the subjects' sorting of attitude statements on cards, just as in Thurstone's method. However, the subjects give their own reactions to the content, sorting statements into piles in accordance with specific sets of instructions (e.g., "most like me" or "most like my ideal"); also the number of cards to be sorted into each pile is specified (so that the final distribution approximates a normal frequency distribution). Like other forced-choice procedures, the Q-sort yields ipsative scores (which reflect *intra*individual differences). Kerlinger's study of political attitudes (1972) provides a good example of the application of Q-methodology. Although Stephenson recommended factor analysis as the method of choice for analyzing Q-sort data, Maguire (1973) recommends other methods of data analysis.

The semantic differential technique (SD), designed to measure connotative meanings of concepts (Osgood, Suci, & Tannenbaum, 1957), has been frequently used in the measurement of attitudes (Osgood, 1967). The scales can be easily constructed and group-administered. The scales for any specific attitude object would consist of a series of relevant bipolar adjectives, each pair typically separated by a 7-point graphic scale. The respondent is asked to indicate where along each of these continua (between the paired adjectives) the attitude object lies. Usually a set of bipolar adjectives for a single concept is placed on a page, with the concept heading the page. The concepts chosen for rating vary with the problem; in a study of attitudes toward school, the attitude objects would include "teacher," "principal," "tests," "homework," "assembly," "report card," and the like. One can discover through factor analysis of responses which concepts have similar connotations.

The bipolar adjectives should be (1) representative of the attitude domain and (2) appropriate to the attitude objects as well as to the population being studied. In selecting adjective pairs, investigators can supplement their own ideas by using Roget's Thesaurus, combining the literature in the field (not neglecting the popular literature), and asking knowledgeable persons to list adjectives that describe the selected concepts (Maguire, 1973). If the re-

search involves study of attitude change over a short period of time, two equivalent forms should be constructed (Heise, 1970).

Response sets. A tendency for respondents to react in terms of the format of an item, regardless of specific content, is called "response set." The need for balancing positive and negative items with similar content, in order to reduce the "acquiescence response set" has already been mentioned. This response set (tendency to agree) tends to be especially marked among young children (Kolson & Green, 1970; Sabers, Reschly, & Meredith, 1974).

When inferences about attitudes are based on self-report measures, they may be inaccurate because of the subject's desire and ability to present a socially desirable self-picture. The purpose of questionnaires and interviews is often transparent, and respondents who wish to make a good impression can easily do so, either to impress the examiner or interviewer or to preserve their own self-image.

One of the simplest ways to deal with social desirability (SD) set is to make the purpose of the inventory less obvious—for example, by including many filler items unrelated to the purpose. Building rapport with respondents, appealing for honest responses to aid in scientific research, and emphasizing that there are no right or wrong answers may also be helpful. Rationalizations can be built into some items. Or questions can be worded to imply that the respondent holds certain views or engages in certain kinds of behavior (e.g., "When did you first . . . ?").

Scott and Rohrbach (1977) list five methods for identifying fakable items and/or reducing the likelihood of faking: (1) establishing rapport and convincing subjects that they should give honest responses; (2) correlating item responses with a measure of social desirability (Schuessler, Hittle, & Cardascia, 1978); (3) constructing attitude measures with a forced-choice format; (4) using a "suppressor scale," such as a "lie factor" scale, to correct scores; and (5) selecting items that do not lose validity under conditions where faking is probable.

To correct for the subject's tendency to mark extreme positions on a Likert-type scale, or for his tendency to mark the middle or neutral position, one can provide matched pairs of items, one referring to the attitude object under study and the other referring to some control object. Then the respondents' replies can be scored in terms of discrepancies between their reactions to the target and control objects (Westie, 1953).

Observation of Behavior. Observation of behavior is a reactive technique in that subjects' behavior may be altered by their awareness of being observed. In some laboratory schools and clinics, it is possible to observe subjects through one-way-vision screens; in such situations, observation may be a nonreactive process, with behavior being uninfluenced by the observation.

If observers are recording and/or classifying behaviors, errors attributable to inadequate precision in defining categories, inadequate training of observers, and individual biases of observers should be minimized. Observers should not know the purpose of the investigation or the subgroups to which individuals belong.

When one observes in a natural setting, a problem is the low frequency of occurrence of the behaviors under study; for instance, there may be few opportunities to observe attitudes toward different types of leaders (democratic, autocratic, etc.). For this reason, researchers may turn to specially designed or contrived situations.

Contrived situations may be difficult to design and standardize; their use tends to be time-consuming and therefore costly; certainly a tryout of a proposed situational test in a pilot study should illuminate (through the use of postexperimental interviews with subjects) the degree to which the staged situation was convincing and should make possible wiser decisions about further use (Cook & Selltiz, 1964). Also, there remain questions about whether inferences from behavior in contrived situations can be generalized to real-life situations. These questions are unique to each study, relating to the age and sophistication of subjects, as well as to the similarity of the contrived to the real-life situation.

Cook and Selltiz (1964) indicate that specially designed situations can be of three types: (1) presenting subjects with standardized situations that seem unstaged (e.g., being asked to sign a petition in behalf of an instructor whose tenure is threatened by membership in a radical party, or being asked to pledge money to help migratory workers); (2) asking the subject to play a role in an admittedly staged situation but with the stated intention of evaluating creativity or acting ability; (3) asking for sociometric choices among individuals, some of whom are members of the object group. All three approaches are designed to make it easier to respond in ways that might be considered socially undesirable. If responses are expected to have real consequences, the anticipation of such consequences may outweigh the subject's wish to make a good impression.

The use of disguised situations makes it imperative that the names of subjects not be recorded in the data files; moreover, after the observation, the true purpose of the situational test and the ways in which the data are to be used should be explained fully to the subjects. In fact, the ethical problems inherent in the use of disguised measures have led to the formulation of a statement of principles concerning their use in research (Anastasi, 1976; *Ethical Principles in the Conduct of Research with Human Participants*, 1972; Lemon, 1973).

Partially Structured Stimuli. In using partially structured stimuli, such as pictures that might be interpreted in various ways, it is assumed that respondents will perceive and interpret the stimulus so as to project their own characteristic attitudes into the interpretation. Subjects may be asked to describe a photographed character or scene, or to tell a story about a relevant picture that could be interpreted in more than one way. Only very general instructions are given, which might imply that the respondent's storytelling, imagination, or creativity is being studied. Since the instructions used with partially structured stimuli are very important to the validity of the study, they should be tried out in advance with representative subjects.

Specially developed pictures, similar to those used in the Thematic Apperception Test (Murray, 1943), are often used (Williams et al., 1975). Proshansky (1943) developed slides that were very briefly exposed. Following each slide, the subjects were allowed only two and a half minutes to write about what they had seen. The slides were used with groups already identified as markedly pro-union and anti-union. In this study of attitudes toward labor, the findings did reveal perceptual distortion in the direction of the attitudes that one would expect in these groups. Adaptations of the Rosenzweig Picture Frustration Study (Rosenzweig, 1948–1964) have been used in the study of social attitudes (Kidder & Campbell, 1970). Doll play can be used with younger children (Lerner & Schroeder, 1975).

Several research studies have found low but significant correlations between the results of partially structured measures and scores on self-report measures (Cook & Selltiz, 1964). Data from partially structured stimuli are more difficult to summarize than data from self-report inventories; however, they reveal the content of the individual's bias.

The sentence-completion method (in which sentence stems likely to evoke attitudinal responses are presented to subjects) is one of the least disguised of the methods involving partially structured stimuli (Kidder & Campbell, 1970). Requesting immediate responses reduces the individual's tendency to be on guard. Interspersing sentence stems that are irrelevant to the attitude object(s) under study may help to obscure the focus of the instrument. Sometimes the incomplete sentences are worded in the third person as one way of putting the examinee off guard; however, the assumption that people will reveal their own attitudes in response to third-person stems may not be justified (Friesen, 1948).

Performance in Objective Tasks. The techniques described as "objective tasks" are especially useful when there is a high probability of respondents faking on self-report measures. The findings from the use of such indirect measures also help to validate, or question the validity of, findings from self-report approaches (Campbell, 1950; Kidder & Campbell, 1970).

In Hammond's error-choice technique (1948), the assumption is made that if respondents are given a test of information in which they must guess, any systematic bias in attitude will influence test performance (Hammond, 1948). In an information test on labor and management, respondents in Hammond's study were asked to choose between two alternatives, equally wrong, that varied in opposite directions from the correct answer. In trying out this test, and a similar one concerning the Soviet Union, presenting them as an information test in one setting and as an attitude measure in another, Hammond (1948) was able to demonstrate how responses changed when the purpose of the instrument was not disguised.

Studies comparing subjects' differential memory for details of pictures, or their differential memory of information that supported "pro" and "anti" views on an issue, have yielded inconsistent evidence. Research studies have not supported the use of memory tests as valid measures of attitudes (Lemon, 1973). For other measures of objective task performance, the reader is referred to Kidder and Campbell (1970).

Physiological Measures. Physiological measures have been used to study attitudes when individuals are likely to be unwilling or unable to report their honest reactions. A recent review of research using physiological measures in the study of attitudes has been prepared by Cacioppo and Sandman (1980).

Most physiological measures reflect only the arousal level of subjects and not the direction (favorable or unfavorable) of their attitude. However, in some areas, it can be assumed that the range of attitudes in a certain group of subjects is from neutral to strongly unfavorable. On the basis of this assumption, one can infer that the greater the physiological reaction, the more unfavorable the attitude (Cook & Selltiz, 1964).

Unobtrusive Measures. The techniques discussed in this report have varied considerably in the extent to which they would be described as "reactive": i.e., the extent to which the responses of participants are influenced by their awareness of being studied. A 1966 publication that presented a number of novel methods utilizing "unobtrusive" or "nonreactive" measures had considerable influence on social science research (Webb et al., 1966). It called for a multiple-indicator approach in the social sciences and for greater use of methods unaffected by the subjects' awareness of being studied. A new edition of this book superseded this earlier edition (Webb et al., 1981).

Examples of unobtrusive measures include erosion measures (e.g., the differential rate of replacement of tiles in front of different museum exhibits, or the differential wear on several dictionaries purchased for the school library at the same time); accretion measures (e.g., the number of liquor bottles in the trash); archival records (e.g., birth records from which attitudes can be inferred by studying the male/female ratios of last-born children in families); conversation sampling; observation in contrived situations that appear natural (e.g., signing petitions, volunteering, pledging money, etc.). The use of several of these methods involves ethical questions, which the authors do consider.

Importance of a Multi-indicator Approach to Research Studies. If a single measure or several measures of the same type are used to measure attitudes, it becomes impossible to distinguish the amount of variance due to the attitude as distinguished from that attributable to the characteristic errors inherent in that method (e.g., social

desirability and acquiescence response sets with self-report inventories, or halo effect and generosity error with rating scales). Each approach has its own typical sources of error. By using a variety of methods, one can make sounder inferences and can have a broader base of support for those inferences than is possible through the use of any single data source, in which method and trait variance are confounded. One's inferences are less likely to be distorted by response bias or other method-related errors. Moreover, as will be explained later, use of multiple indicators makes possible construct validity studies of attitude measures.

Multidimensional Scaling. Although educators with immediate concerns, such as project evaluation, continue to make almost exclusive use of self-report questionnaires, investigators who are studying attitude formation and change, as well as attitude structure, have directed their attention to multidimensional scaling (MDS).

MDS was developed by Torgerson (1958); his approach, called "similarity analysis," made possible the mapping of psychological structures, based on the respondents' judgments of psychological distances between attitude objects. Van der Kamp (1973) performed a similarity analysis on attitudes toward the church, which are multidimensional.

MDS may be used to search for conceptual structures or to map individual attitude structures (Schroder, Driver, & Streufert, 1967). When the distances plotted are between attitude objects or between attitude statements, the map is one of conceptual structure; if the distances are between subjects studied, the map is designed to discover the attitudes on which they agree and differ (Ross, 1970; Schroder, Driver, & Streufert, 1967).

Shepard (1962a; 1962b) developed a method of MDS called "proximity analysis," which is based on *relative* distances—i.e., rank orders of perceived distances between pairs of elements. Proximity analysis is an iterative procedure; it begins with the construction of an initial map, which is either arbitrary or very approximate, and repeatedly adjusts the map to achieve a better fit with the data. Alternative maps are produced, from which the investigator may choose. Kruskal (1964) developed an improved measure of "stress" or "lack of fit."

A method for the multidimensional scaling of dichotomous (two-choice) items (as in Thurstone and Guttman scales) has been developed by Krus and Bart (1974); it is related to the multivariate extension of Guttman's (1944, 1966) scalogram analysis, developed by Coombs (1950) and derived from ordering theory (Airasian, Madaus, & Woods, 1975).

Validity and Reliability. Many sources of invalidity of attitude measurement have already been discussed. Since most attitude measures are transparent, respondents are quite capable of faking their responses. Response sets, notably social desirability and acquiescence, can and do affect the validity of attitude scale scores; methods of reducing response sets have already been presented. The three major types of validity (content, criterion-related, and construct) will now be considered. Attention will be focused on self-report instruments, since studies regarding the validity of other methods have been infrequent. Moreover, an attempt will be made to consider factors affecting the validity of each method as it is presented.

Content validity. Attitude measurement involves sampling an attitude domain and then generalizing, from scores obtained on that sample, to the attitude domain. For example, if one wishes to generalize about students' attitudes toward school, one should make sure that the statements selected for the attitude scale are representative of the different elements in that domain. Hartke (1979) recommends that one formulate a table of specifications as one would for an achievement test. Initially the author(s) should identify all possible facets that should be included; then statistical procedures (for example, factor analysis of item responses) (Steiner & Barnhart, 1972; Wiechmann & Wiechmann, 1973)—can be used to group related items into subgroups, as well as to eliminate those items that are not relevant to any of the factors or dimensions identified. To ensure comprehensive coverage of the attitude domain, students could be asked to describe their school in short essays, interviews, responses to incomplete sentences, and so on; the literature on student attitudes toward school could be studied, not neglecting the popular literature. A comprehensive and representative sample of the complete attitude domain is the goal. If that goal is achieved, one can make sample-to-domain inferences, and the attitude measure will have satisfactory content validity. On the other hand, if certain aspects of the school environment are omitted or overemphasized, the instrument will not have satisfactory content validity.

Predictive validity. Perhaps the greatest challenge to the validity of attitude measurement has been the disappointing results of the earlier research studies on the ability to predict behavior from attitude scores (Fishbein, 1967; Wicker, 1969). Later, better-designed studies yielded more positive findings concerning attitude-behavior relationships. In a review of these later studies (Cialdini, Petty, & Cacioppo, 1981), it was emphasized that attitude scores predict behavior when the attitudinal and behavioral measures show a high degree of correspondence (Ajzen & Fishbein, 1977); that attitudes tend to be better predictors when measured under high-commitment conditions (i.e., when subjects thought that they would be performing the behaviors); that attitude scales with many affective items tend to predict behavior better than scales that were more cognitively oriented (Bagozzi & Burnkrant, 1979); and that attitude scales predict multiple-act criteria much better than single elements of behavior (Bagozzi & Burnkrant, 1979).

Very high correlations between attitude and behavior should not be expected; attitude is only one of many factors affecting behavior. To the degree that the behavioral criterion involves multiple acts over a period of time, this improvement in the validity of the criterion will result in higher attitude-behavior relationships. However, since many factors (both personal and situational) affect behavior, one should be suspicious of very high correlations. For example, some of the high correlations obtained between attitudes and behavior may have resulted from the pervasive effects of social norms, which have influenced behavior in *both* the test and the social situation.

When normative influences and attitudes are in opposition, one tends to obtain more valid responses with techniques that tap behavior less likely to be under conscious control. When there is the greatest conflict of attitudes with social norms, the investigator may need to use physiological measures (least under conscious control); as the pressure from social norms decreases, attitudes may be expressed in such indirect measures as information tests (error-choice technique) and reasoning tasks. As the strength of normative pressure decreases further, attitudes will be expressed in partially structured, or projective, measures; with still less normative pressure, in transparent verbal questionnaires.

Criterion-related validity can also be estimated by the known-groups method; for example, scores on attitudes toward labor unions can be used to predict union membership versus membership in business-management organizations (Bohrnstedt, 1970). Another way in which the validity of an attitude scale can be checked is by comparing responses obtained on an attitude scale with responses obtained through interviews (Labaki, 1973).

Construct validity. If an investigator measures two or more attitudes, each by two or more methods, the data can be analyzed to provide evidence on the construct validity of the measures. All possible intercorrelations of trait-method units are combined into a multitrait-multimethod matrix (MTMM). Convergent validity is shown by agreement among different measures of the same attitude; and discriminant validity is shown by low correlations between measures of different attitudes. For illustrative studies involving the use of the MTMM approach (Campbell & Fiske, 1959), the reader is referred to Aiken (1975), Arlin & Hills (1974), Kothandapani (1971), Lerner & Schroeder (1975), and Roshal, Frieze, & Wood (1971).

To apply the MTMM method in a research study in education, one might assess "attitudes toward school" and "attitudes toward authority" by means of an attitude scale, by a semantic differential measure, and by a partially structured stimuli, such as incomplete sentences. In order to have evidence of convergent validity, the correlations among the three measures of "attitudes toward school" must be significantly higher than any other correlations in the matrix. Discriminant validity is also important. The correlations between measures of "attitudes toward school" and "attitudes toward authority" should be lower than the intercorrelations among the different measures of "attitudes toward school." If the correlations with "attitudes toward authority" were too high, one might question whether the "attitudes toward school" measures were too heavily loaded with items concerned with the students' relationships to authority figures. If measures of two differently named attitudes correlate too high, there may be so much overlap that the two measures should be combined into a measure of a single attitude, which could then be renamed (e.g., "attitude toward school authority figures"). Or the homogeneity of each scale might be improved by a factor analysis of items (Steiner & Barnhart, 1972), which might result in reassignment of items to make each scale a better measure of the construct it claims to measure.

Progress is definitely being made toward greater sophistication in the measurement of attitudes. Aiken (1980) indicates with approval that the trend is away from the use of unidimensional scales, as evidenced by the development of multidimensional scaling (Torgerson, 1958; van der Kamp, 1973), latent structure analysis (Lazarsfeld & Henry, 1968), and latent partition analysis (Hartke, 1979; Wiley, 1967). Examples of well-designed construct validity studies are Arlin & Hills (1974), Kerlinger (1972), and Kothandapani (1971).

Reliability. Adequate information on the reliability of many attitude scales is not available (Shaw & Wright, 1967). The reliability of an attitude scale should be checked on a sample of the subjects included in a specific study unless the manual presents reliability data on a clearly similar group.

Several factors can affect the reliability of an attitude measure: testing conditions, number of response categories, and response sets. Reliability is lower whenever testing conditions affect respondents in different ways—for instance, in a test-retest condition, in which some but not all subjects have had their interest in politics stimulated by the administration of a scale of political attitudes. The larger number of response categories on Likert scales may largely explain their reliability coefficients being consistently higher than those for Thurstone scales with the same number of items. Increasing the number of response categories beyond five, however, has usually not resulted in increased reliability (Masters, 1974; Matell & Jacoby, 1971, 1972), for subjects do not use the additional categories to any great extent. The presence of response sets may contribute to spuriously high reliability coefficients, because the response set affects individuals' scores on both test and retest, on both forms, or on both halves of a test (Bohrnstedt, 1970).

Because attitude scales are reactive measures, the test-retest method is not recommended. Measures of equivalence are important; the use of a single score to summate the subject's responses to several items is based on the assumption that the scale is unidimensional. If parallel forms are available, alternate-forms reliability coefficients should be obtained. However, most attitude scales do not have alternate forms. Hence, since the test-retest method is inadvisable, the Kuder-Richardson method (which measures internal consistency in responses among all items) is the preferred method (Bohrnstedt, 1970).

Researchers and project evaluators who are interested in measuring attitude change face special problems of the low reliability of test scores, as well as pretest sensitization. The low reliability of measures of change was demonstrated by Cronbach and Furby (1970). The probability of sensitizing subjects through use of a pretest is also important in studies of attitude change. The use of a post-test-only research design or of a Solomon design (Solomon & Lessac, 1968) is recommended (Ary, Jacobs, & Razavieh, 1979).

Use of attitude inventories in program evaluation. A series of eight guidebooks for program evaluation has been developed by the Center for the Study of Evaluation (University of California, Los Angeles). This program kit (Morris, 1978) was developed over a three-year period and field-tested at 151 sites. Volume 5, on the measurement of attitudes, contains many suggestions of practical value to project evaluators (Henerson, Morris, & Fitz-Gibbon, 1978).

A number of evaluation models, guidebooks, and new instruments have been developed in large-scale school evaluation programs; these are now in the public domain, available through the Educational Resources Information Center (ERIC) system. A few examples of available materials will be given.

Damico (1979) developed a handbook on the measurement of pupils' attitudes toward schools. Smith and Ernst (1978) have studied two practical problems inherent in school evaluation programs: (1) the bias introduced by teacher administration of school attitude inventories and (2) the high cost of having such measures administered by outside test administrators. They found that when fifth-grade students (utilizing specially prepared tape cassettes) administered the inventory "My Class," the results obtained were in closer agreement with those obtained by outside test administrators than were results obtained with teacher administration. After trying out each of the three methods of administration in thirty classrooms, the staff recommended that student administration (with the aid of cassettes) be used in the future.

Under the auspices of the National Study of School Evaluation, three attitude inventories have been developed: Teacher Opinion Inventory, Student Opinion Inventory, and Parent Opinion Inventory. These inventories are now available for distribution on a nonprofit basis (National Study of School Evaluation, 1974, 1975, 1976). For each inventory, a manual has been prepared, which describes development of the inventory and provides instructions for administration, scoring, and interpretation, as well as data from reliability and validity studies.

Since interest in attitude measurement has been recently increasing and since highly qualified researchers are now turning their attention to this field, it would seem advisable for any project evaluator to request a focused search of the ERIC system whenever the project includes appraisal of pupil progress toward attitudinal objectives. The ERIC system includes journal articles, dissertations, and convention papers, as well as research conducted in research-and-development centers, school districts, and universities. Each year will bring new advances in the measurement of attitudes.

Georgia S. Adams

See also Affective Education; Emotional Development; Individual Differences; Interests Measurement; Measurement in Education; Motivation; Personality Assessment.

REFERENCES

Aiken, L. R. A program for computing rank correlations from ordered contingency tables. *Educational and Psychological Measurement*, 1975, *35*, 181–183.

Aiken, L. R. Attitude measurement and research. In D. A. Payne (Ed.), *Recent Developments in Affective Measurement*. San Francisco: Jossey-Bass, 1980.

Airasian, P. W.; Madaus, G. F.; & Woods, E. M. Scaling attitude items in a comparison of scaling analysis and ordering theory. *Educational and Psychological Measurement*, 1975, *35*, 809–819.

Ajzen, I., & Fishbein, M. Attitude-behavior relationships: A theoretical analysis and review of empirical research. *Psychological Bulletin*, 1977, *84*, 888–918.

Anastasi, A. *Psychological Testing* (4th ed.). New York: Macmillan, 1976.

Andrich, D. A binomial latent trait model for the study of Likert-style attitude questionnaires. *British Journal of Mathematical and Statistical Psychology*, 1978, *31*(1), 84–98. (a)

Andrich, D. Scaling attitude items constructed and scored in the Likert tradition. *Educational and Psychological Measurement*, 1978, *38*, 665–680. (b)

Arlin, M. N., & Hills, D. Comparison of cartoon and verbal methods of school attitude assessment through multitrait-multimethod validation. *Educational and Psychological Measurement*, 1974, *34*, 989–995.

Ary, D., Jacobs, L. C., & Razavieh, A. *Introduction to Research in Education* (2nd ed.). New York: Holt, Rinehart & Winston, 1979.

Atkinson, J. W. Motivational determinants of intellective performance and cumulative achievement. In J. W. Atkinson, J. O. Raynor, D. Birch, et al. *Motivation and Achievement*. New York: Wiley, 1974.

Atkinson, J. W., & Feather, N. T. *A Theory of Achievement Motivation*. New York: Wiley, 1966.

Bagozzi, R. P., & Burnkrant, R. E. Attitude organization and the attitude-behavior relationship. *Journal of Personality and Social Psychology*, 1979, *37*(6), 913–929.

Blumberg, H. H.; Fuller, C.; & Hare, A. P. Response rates in postal surveys. *Public Opinion Quarterly*, 1974, *38*, 112–123.

Bohrnstedt, G. W. Reliability and validity assessment in attitude measurement. In G. F. Summers (Ed.), *Attitude Measurement*. Chicago: Rand McNally, 1970.

Bruvold, W. H. Judgmental bias in the rating of attitude statements. *Educational and Psychological Measurement*, 1975, *35*, 605–611.

Buros, O. K. (Ed.). *The Eighth Mental Measurements Yearbook* (Vol. 1). Highland Park, N.J.: Gryphon Press, 1978.

Cacioppo, J. T., & Sandman, C. A. Psychophysiological functioning, cognitive responding, and attitudes. In R. E. Petty, T. M. Ostrom, & T. C. Brock (Eds.), *Cognitive Responses in Persuasion*. Hillsdale, N.J.: Lawrence Erlbaum Associates, 1980.

Campbell, D. T. The indirect assessment of social attitudes. *Psychological Bulletin*, 1950, *47*, 15–38.

Campbell, D. T., & Fiske, D. W. Convergent and discriminant validation by the multitrait-multimethod matrix. *Psychological Bulletin*, 1959, *56*, 81–105.

Carpenter, E. H. Personalizing mail surveys: A replication and reassessment. *Public Opinion Quarterly*, 1975, *38*, 614–620.

Cialdini, R. R., Petty, R. E., & Cacioppo, J. T. Attitude and attitude change. *Annual Review of Psychology*, 1981, *32*, 357–404.

Cook, S. W., & Selltiz, C. A. A multiple-indicator approach to attitude measurement. *Psychological Bulletin*, 1964, *62*, 36–55.

Coombs, C. H. Psychological scaling without a unit of measurement. *Psychological Review*, 1950, *57*, 145–158.

Couch, A., & Keniston, K. Agreeing response set and social desirability. *Journal of Abnormal and Social Psychology*, 1961, *62*, 175–179.

Cronbach, L. R., & Furby, L. How should we measure "change"? Or should we? *Psychological Bulletin*, 1970, *74*, 68–80.

Damico, S. B. *The Measurement of Pupils' Attitudes toward Achievement: A Handbook for Teachers*. Gainesville, Fla.: Educational Research and Development Council, 1979. (ERIC Document Reproduction Service No. ED 159 193)

Dillman, D. A., & Frey, J. H. Contribution of personalization to mail questionnaire response as an element of a previously tested method. *Journal of Applied Psychology*, 1974, *59*, 297–301.

Dotson, L. E., & Summers, G. P. Elaboration of Guttman scaling techniques. In G. F. Summers (Ed.), *Attitude Measurement*. Chicago: Rand McNally, 1970.

DuBois, B., & Burns, J. A. An analysis of the meaning of the question-mark response category in attitude scales. *Educational and Psychological Measurement*, 1975, *35*, 869–884.

Eagly, A. H., & Himmelfarb, S. Attitudes and opinions. *Annual Review of Psychology*, 1978, *29*, 517–554.

Edwards, A. L., & Kilpatrick, F. P. A technique for the construction of attitude scales. *Journal of Applied Psychology*, 1948, *32*, 374–384.

Eisinger, R. A.; Janicki, W. P.; Stevenson, R. L.; & Thompson, W. L. Increasing returns in international mail surveys. *Public Opinion Quarterly*, 1974, *38*, 124–130.

Erdos, P. L., & Morgan, A. J. *Professional Mail Surveys*. New York: McGraw-Hill, 1970.

Ethical Principles in the Conduct of Research with Human Participants. Washington, D.C.: American Psychological Association, 1972. (ERIC Document Reproduction Service No. ED 075 467)

Fishbein, M. Attitudes and the prediction of behavior. In M. Fishbein (Ed.), *Readings in Attitude Theory and Measurement*. New York: Wiley, 1967.

Fishbein, M., & Ajzen, I. *Belief, Attitude, Intention, and Behavior: An Introduction to Theory and Research*. Reading, Mass.: Addison-Wesley, 1975.

Fisher, R. J. Toward the more comprehensive measurement of intergroup attitudes: An interview and rating scale procedure. *Canadian Journal of Behavioral Science*, 1977, *9*, 283–294.

Friesen, E. P. The incomplete-sentences technique as a measure of employees' attitudes. *Personnel Psychology*, 1948, *43*, 38–48.

Fuller, C. Effect of anonymity on return rate and response bias in a mail survey. *Journal of Applied Psychology*, 1974, *59*, 292–296.

Gardner, P. L. Attitude measurement: A critique of some recommended research. *Educational Research*, 1975, *17*, 101–109.

Guttman, L. A basis for scaling qualitative data. *American Sociological Review*, 1944, *9*, 139–150.

Guttman, L. The Cornell technique for scale and intensity analysis. *Educational and Psychological Measurement*, 1947, *7*, 247–280.

Guttman, L. The problem of attitude and opinion measurement. In S. A. Stouffer et al. (Eds.) *Measurement and Prediction*. Princeton, N.J.: Princeton University Press, 1950.

Guttman, L. Order analysis and correlational matrices. In R. B. Cattell (Ed.), *Handbook of Multivariate Experimental Psychology*. Chicago: Rand McNally, 1966.

Guttman, L. & Suchman, E. A. Intensity and a zero point for attitudinal analysis. *American Sociological Review*, 1947, *12*, 55–67.

Hammond, K. R. Measuring attitude by error-choice: An indirect method. *Journal of Abnormal and Social Psychology*, 1948, *43*, 38–48.

Hartke, A. R. The development of conceptually independent subscales in the measurement of attitudes. *Educational and Psychological Measurement*, 1979, *39*, 585–592.

Heise, D. R. The semantic differential and attitude research. In G. F. Summers (Ed.), *Attitude Measurement*. Chicago: Rand McNally, 1970.

Henerson, M. E.: Morris, L. L.; & Fitz-Gibbon, C. T. How to measure attitudes. Beverly Hills, Calif.: Sage, 1978.

Hinrichs, J. R. Factors related to survey response rates. *Journal of Applied Psychology*, 1975, *60*, 249–251.

Insko, C. A. *Theories of Attitude Change*. New York: Appleton-Century-Crofts, 1967.

Kahn, R. L., & Cannell, C. F. *The Dynamics of Interviewing*. New York: Wiley, 1957.

Kerlinger, F. N. A Q-validation of the structure of social attitudes. *Educational and Psychological Measurement*, 1972, *32*, 987–995.

Kidder, L. H., & Campbell, D. J. The indirect testing of social attitudes. In G. F. Summers (Ed.), *Attitude Measurement*. Chicago: Rand McNally, 1970.

Kiesler, C. A.; Collins, E. E.; & Miller, N. *Attitude Change: A Critical Analysis of Theoretical Approaches*. New York: Wiley, 1969.

Knapp, J. (Comp.) *An Omnibus of Measures Related to School-based Attitudes*. Princeton, N.J.: Educational Testing Service, 1972.

Kohr, R. L. Item analysis and scoring program for summated rating scale. *Educational and Psychological Measurement*, 1971, *31*, 769–770.

Kolson, K. L., & Green, J. J. Response set bias and political socialization research. *Social Science Quarterly*, 1970, *51*, 527–538.

Kothandapani, V. Validation of feeling, belief, and intention to act as three components of attitude and their contribution to prediction of contraceptive behavior. *Journal of Personality and Social Psychology*, 1971, *19*(3), 321–333.

Krus, D. J., & Bart, W. M. An ordering theoretic method of multidimensional scaling of items. *Educational and Psychological Measurement*, 1974, *34*, 325–335.

Kruskal, J. B. Multidimensional scaling by optimizing goodness of fit to a nonmetric hypothesis. *Psychometrika*, 1964, *29*, 1–27.

Labaki, F. G. The development of a scale for measuring the attitudes of middle school and high school students toward geometry (Doctoral dissertation, State University of New York at Buffalo, 1973). *Dissertation Abstracts International*, 1973, *34*. (University Microfilm No. 73–23, 860)

Lazarsfeld, P. F., & Henry, N. W. *Latent Structure Analysis*. Boston: Houghton Mifflin, 1968.

Lemon, N. *Attitudes and Their Measurement*. New York: Wiley, 1973.

Lerner, R. M., & Schroeder, C. Racial attitudes in young white children: A methodological analysis. *Journal of Genetic Psychology*, 1975, *127*, 3–12.

Likert, R. A technique for the measurement of attitudes. *Archives of Psychology*, 1932, *140*.

Lingoes, J. C. Multiple scalogram analysis: A set-theoretical model for analyzing dichotomous items. *Educational and Psychological Measurement*, 1963, *23*, 501–524.

Maguire, T. O. Semantic differential methodology for the structuring of attitudes. *American Educational Research Journal*, 1973, *10*, 295–306.

Masters, J. R. Relationship between number of response categories and reliability of Likert-type questionnaires. *Journal of Educational Measurement*, 1974, *11*, 49–53.

Matell, M. S., & Jacoby, J. Is there an optimal number of alternatives for Likert scale items?: Reliability and validity (Study 1). *Educational and Psychological Measurement*, 1971, *31*, 657–674.

Matell, M. S., & Jacoby, J. Is there an optimal number of alternatives for Likert scale items? Effects of testing time and scale properties. *Journal of Applied Psychology*, 1972, *56*, 506–509.

Minnesota Teacher Attitude Inventory. New York: Psychological Corporation, 1951.

Morris, L. L. (Ed.). *Program Evaluation Kit* (8 vols.). Beverly Hills, Calif.: Sage, 1978.

Murray, H. A. *Thematic Apperception Test*. Cambridge, Mass.: Harvard University Press, 1943.

National Study of School Evaluation. *Student Opinion Inventory*. Arlington, Va.: Author, 1974. (ERIC Document Reproduction Service No. ED 155 184)

National Study of School Evaluation. *Teacher Opinion Inventory*. Arlington, Va.: Author, 1975. (ERIC Document Reproduction Service No. ED 155 185)

National Study of School Evaluation. *Parent Opinion Inventory*. Arlington, Va.: Author, 1976. (ERIC Document Reproduction Service No. Ed 155 183)

Osgood, C. E. Cross-cultural comparability in attitude measurement via multilingual semantic differentials. In M. Fishbein (Ed.), *Readings in Attitude Theory and Measurement*. New York: Wiley, 1967.

Osgood, C. E.; Suci, G. J.; & Tannenbaum, P. H. *The Measurement of Meaning*. Urbana: University of Illinois Press, 1957.

Petrie, B. M. Statistical analysis of attitude-scale scores. *Research Quarterly*, 1969, *40*, 434–437.

Proshansky, H. M. A projective method for the study of attitudes. *Journal of Abnormal and Social Psychology*, 1943, *38*, 393–395.

Robinson, J. P., & Shaver, P. R. *Measures of Social Psychological Attitudes* (Rev. ed.). Ann Arbor: University of Michigan, Institute for Social Research, 1973.

Rosenzweig, S. *Rosenzweig Picture Frustration Study*. St. Louis, Mo.: Author, 1948–1964. (Available from S. Rosenzweig, 8029 Washington St., St. Louis, Mo.)

Roshal, S. M.; Frieze, I.; & Wood, J. T. A multitrait-multimethod validation of measures of student attitudes toward school, toward learning, and toward technology in sixth-grade children.

Educational and Psychological Measurement, 1971, *31*, 999–1006.

Ross, J. Multidimensional scaling of attitudes. In G. Summers (Ed.), *Attitude Measurement*. Chicago: Rand McNally, 1970.

Rotter, J. B. Generalized expectancies for internal versus external control of reinforcements. *Psychological Monographs*, 1966, *80*(1, Whole No. 609).

Sabers, D.; Reschly, D.; & Meredith, K. *Age Differences in Degree of Acquiescence on Positively and Negatively Scored Attitude-Scale Items*. Paper presented at the annual meeting of the National Council for Measurement in Education, 1974. (ERIC Document Reproduction Service No. ED 091 446).

Schroder, H. M.; Driver, M. J.; & Streufert, S. *Human Information Processing*. New York: Holt, Rinehart & Winston, 1967.

Schuessler, K.; Hittle, D.; & Cardascia, J. Measuring responding desirably with attitude-opinion items. *Social Psychology*, 1978, *41*, 224–235.

Scott, O., & Rohrbach, I. Comparison of five criteria for identifying fakable items on an attitude inventory. *Journal of Experimental Education*, 1977, *45*(3), 51–55.

Seiler, L., & Hough, R. L. Empirical comparisons of the Thurstone and Likert techniques. In G. F. Summers (Ed.), *Attitude Measurement*. Chicago: Rand McNally, 1970.

Shavelson, R. J.; Hubner, J. J.; & Stanton, J. C. Self-concept: Validation of construct interpretations. *Review of Educational Research*, 1976, *46*, 407–441.

Shaw, M. E., & Wright, J. M. *Scales for the Measurement of Attitudes*. New York: McGraw-Hill, 1967.

Shepard, R. N. The analysis of proximities: Multidimensional scaling with an unknown distance function (Part 1). *Psychometrika*, 1962, *27*, 125–140. (a)

Shepard, R. N. The analysis of proximities: Multidimensional scaling with an unknown distance function (Part 2). *Psychometrika*, 1962, *27*, 219–246. (b)

Sherif, C.; Sherif, M.; & Nebergall, R. *Attitude and Attitude Change: The Social Judgment-Involvement Approach*. Philadelphia: Saunders, 1965.

Sheth, J. N., & Roscoe, A. M. Impact of questionnaire length, follow-up methods, and geographical location on response rate to a mail survey. *Journal of Applied Psychology*, 1975, *60*, 252–254.

Shoemaker, D. M. Application of item-examinee sampling to scaling attitudes. *Journal of Educational Measurement*, 1971, *8*, 279–282.

Smith, H. W., Jr., & Ernst, N. S. *Controlling Teacher Bias in Attitude toward School Measures*. 1978 (ERIC Document Reproduction Service No. ED 157 922)

Solomon, R. L., & Lessac, M. S. A control-group design for experimental studies of developmental processes. *Psychological Bulletin*, 1968, *70*, 145–150.

Spector, P. E. Choosing response categories for summated rating scales. *Journal of Applied Psychology*, 1976, *61*, 374–375.

Steiner, R. L., & Barnhart, R. B. Development of an instrument to assess environmental attitudes utilizing factor analytic techniques. *Science Education*, 1972, *56*, 427–432.

Stephenson, W. *The Study of Behavior: Q Technique and Its Methodology*. Chicago: University of Chicago Press, 1953.

Summers, G. F. Introduction. In G. E. Summers (Ed.), *Attitude Measurement*. Chicago: Rand McNally, 1970.

Thurstone, L. L. A law of comparative judgment. *Psychological Review*, 1927, *34*, 273–286.

Thurstone, L. L. Attitudes can be measured. *American Journal of Sociology*, 1928, *33*, 529–554.

Thurstone, L. L., & Chave, E. J. *The Measurement of Attitude*. Chicago: University of Chicago Press, 1929.

Toby, J., & Toby, M. A method of selecting dichotomous items by cross-tabulation. In M. Riley, J. W. Riley, J. Toby, et al. (Eds.), *Sociological Studies in Scale Analysis*. New Brunswick, N.J.: Rutgers University Press, 1954.

Torgerson, W. S. *Theory and Methods of Scaling*. New York: Wiley, 1958.

Triandis, H. C. *Attitudes and Attitude Change*. New York: Wiley, 1971.

van der Kamp, L. J. T. Thurstone revisited: Multidimensional similarity scaling of attitude toward the church. *Educational and Psychological Measurement*, 1973, *33*, 577–585.

Webb, E. J.; Campbell, D. T.; Schwartz, R. D.; & Sechrest, L. *Unobtrusive Measures: Nonreactive Research in the Social Sciences*. Chicago: Rand McNally, 1966.

Webb, E. J.; Campbell, D. T.; Schwartz, R. D.; & Sechrest, L. *Nonreactive Measures in the Social Sciences* (2nd ed.). Boston: Houghton Mifflin, 1981.

Westie, F. R. A technique for the measurement of race attitudes. *American Sociological Review*, 1953, *18*, 73–78.

Wicker, A. W. Attitudes versus action: The reliability of verbal and overt behavior responses to attitude objects. *Journal of Social Issues*, 1969, *25*(4), 41–78.

Wiechmann, G. H., & Wiechmann, L. A. Multiple factor analysis: An approach to attitude validation. *Journal of Experimental Education*, 1973, *41*, 74–84.

Wiley, D. E. Latent partition analysis. *Psychometrika*, 1967, *32*, 183–193.

Williams, J. E.; Best, D. L.; Boswell, D. H.; Mattson, L. H.; & Graves, D. J. Preschool racial attitude measures (Part 2). *Educational and Psychological Measurement*, 1975, *35*, 3–18.

ATTITUDES TOWARD THE HANDICAPPED

Attitudes or affective reactions to handicapped individuals or groups or to issues involving the handicapped may be examined utilizing historical sources as well as recent behavioral science research strategies. The evidence includes structured and unstructured, qualitative and quantitative studies of verbal expressions as well as observed overt behavior. Although the literature generally provides some empirical support for a number of widely held hypotheses, there are numerous exceptions and limitations that must also be addressed. Among the commonly stated propositions in this field are that attitudes toward the handicapped are very unfavorable, that they are improving, that being labeled handicapped has very negative consequences, and that contact with handicapped persons leads to more favorable attitudes. Each of these assumptions is examined below.

Unfavorable Attitudes.   Most investigations involving comparisons of handicapped and nonhandicapped persons find that the handicapped are less preferred. This includes sociometric choices within regular elementary classrooms (for example, "Who would you like to sit next to?") and "social distance" measures among college students (for example, "Would you be willing to marry someone who is epileptic?"). The magnitude of this negative effect, however, varies with the nature and severity of the handicap, prior contact with persons so handicapped, and specific training in the field. Furthermore, when the attitude is to a specific, known handicapped person rather than to the whole class of persons, personal characteristics of the individual tend to determine reactions more strongly than does the handicap itself.

Research on reactions of the general public, professionals, and the potential employers all indicate considerable variation in willingness to interact with, employ, and teach handicapped persons, depending on the nature and severity of the handicap.

Hierarchy of response to handicaps. An example of an attitude study that provides evidence on a hierarchy of handicaps is found in an investigation by Shears and Jensema (1969), who asked ninety-four normal adults to rank ten "anomalies" in terms of perceived severity and then had them indicate their degree of acceptance of each condition according to a series of situations varying in "social distance" from "would marry" to "would live in the same country." Regarding both severity of handicap and willingness to accept persons with the condition, the most positive reaction was to the amputee, blind, and wheelchair conditions; intermediate reactions were to the harelip, stutter, and deaf-mute conditions, followed by a more negative reaction to the cerebral palsied; the most unfavorable reactions were to the mentally ill, retarded, and homosexual conditions.

A number of investigators have been interested in employer bias and have asked potential employers to evaluate persons with a range of disabilities. Thus, in Rickard, Triandis, and Patterson's study (1963) of 105 personnel directors and school administrators, they reported that ex-tubercular persons were preferred, followed by wheelchair handicapped, then deaf; the epileptic was the least preferred. In a similar study, Nikoloff (1962) asked 197 principals to evaluate the employability of handicapped persons as teachers. Blind or deaf persons were judged to be less employable than persons with speech handicaps, who were, in turn, less employable than those with an artificial leg or crutches.

It appears that the ordering of handicaps varies with the specific handicaps (and labels) presented, the evaluating audience, and the questions they are asked. Similar variations occur when we examine teachers' preferences for different types of students. Thus, whereas Shotel, Iano, and McGettigan (1972) found that teachers preferred the learning disabled to the emotionally disabled, and felt least favorable toward the educable mentally retarded student, Warren, Turner, and Brody (1964) reported the educable retarded student to be more acceptable than the brain injured; and Combs and Harper (1967) found that psychotic disorders were interpreted more negatively by teachers than retarded or neurological syndromes.

Although the diversity of findings makes generalization difficult, it appears that the more severe a handicap and the more problems it creates in relationships with the nonhandicapped, the less favorable the reaction.

Attitude improvement. Although it is popularly believed that natural reactions to the handicapped are destructive, the primitive societies and earlier civilizations destroyed or abandoned handicapped infants, and that until very recently, mentally and physically handicapped persons were seriously abused, evidence reveals far less consistency of response than is assumed. Thus, Berkson (1977) shows that nonhuman primates may react protectively rather than aggressively to defective infants. Similarly, Edgerton (1970) reports that an examination of evidence from non-Western societies demonstrates the lack of simple, predictable, negative reactions to the handicapped. Diverse cultural norms include everything from infanticide to exalted religious status, and informal reactions include both cruelty and protectiveness.

Historical trends in the West are also inconsistent, ranging from widespread infanticide approved and practiced in classical Greece for all who appeared imperfect at birth to the creation of special roles such as the court fool, the "seer," the blind musician or poet, and the licensed beggar in medieval and renaissance society. Later, in the seventeenth and eighteenth centuries residential isolation evolved as a strategy for dealing with the handicapped in urban settings, both as a punitive approach, in the case of work houses, and as an educational or therapeutic program, in the case of the special schools that evolved from enlightenment philosophy.

More recently, residential institutions that were founded as optimistic schools or hospitals became methods of segregating the undesirable, and they have been attacked for their overcrowding and abuse of residents. Similarly, special day schools and special classes have served both to educate and to segregate and have come into disfavor for their negative features. If we are to treat social actions as signs of public attitude, it appears that attitudes toward the handicapped include both hostile and supportive elements and that the relative dominance of these components has varied from culture to culture and over time in a complex and unpredictable way. What appears consistent is that handicapped persons have generally been treated much like other lower status or disfavored groups. Female infants in classical Greece, illegitimate children in medieval through seventeenth-century Europe, the poor in eighteenth-century Europe, and Jews in twentieth-century Nazi Germany all shared similar fates with the handicapped.

Effects of Handicap Labels. Since attitudes and stereotypes about handicaps so often include negative evaluations, it is generally assumed that being labeled or recognized as handicapped results in negative consequences for individuals so labeled. Certainly there is evidence that persons prefer to avoid being characterized as handicapped if they can. Thus, Goffman (1963) has discussed at length the attempts of the nonvisibly handicapped to "pass" as normal. Similarly, Edgerton (1967) and Jones (1972) have described how persons who have been classified as mentally retarded attempted to avoid recognition.

Despite the negative reputation of such labels as "mentally retarded," the evidence of their negative consequences is limited (MacMillan, Jones, & Aloia, 1974; Guskin, 1978). Thus, although the label by itself has consistently negative connotations (e.g., Gottwald, 1970), results are variable when other information about an individual is presented along with the label. For example, when films or videotapes of a child are presented along with information that the child is mentally retarded, one child may be seen as more subnormal with the label than without it, whereas there is no such effect for another child (Guskin, 1962). Gottlieb (1974) has shown that the label may not have an effect if the videotapes show clear instances of competence or incompetence. On the other hand, if the videotapes show instances of aggressive behavior, negative reactions may be accentuated by the "retarded" label (Gottlieb, 1975).

A number of studies have examined the consequences of handicap information upon the actual interaction of persons. In one set of investigations, Robert Kleck and his associates (Kleck, 1975) examined the effects of a simulated disability (amputee in wheelchair) upon the way others interacted both verbally and nonverbally with the person. It was found that verbal statements by the nondisabled seemed to be biased in favor of the disabled, but nonverbal measures such as galvanic skin response (GSR) and interaction distance suggested less comfort with the disabled. Other studies have examined the effects of handicap information on performance of the other person. Jones (1970) found no influence of a simulated blind person on the other's performance, although the other person thought his own performance had been impaired. Farina and Ring (1965), studying the influence upon a cooperative game of persons thinking their partner was mentally ill, found that perceiving the co-worker as mentally ill enhanced performance. However, it led the labeling person to prefer to work alone and to blame the mentally ill partner for inadequacies in their joint performance.

In another study, Farina et al. (1976) had college students interact on a learning task with someone they thought was either mentally ill, mentally retarded, or normal. The student was to administer shocks when the learner made errors. It was found that "mentally retarded" confederates were administered less intense shocks and of less duration than either the "mentally ill" or "normal" confederates. Thus, we can see that whereas awareness of a person's handicap may influence the way others interact with him, the consequences need not be negative.

The complexity of labeling effects may also be seen in a series of studies by Farina and his associates (Farina, Felner & Boudreau, 1973; Farina & Hagelauer, 1975; Farina, Murray, & Groh, 1978) examining the effects of labeling a person as an ex-mental patient upon job interviews.

It was found that men reacted very negatively to male former mental patients and only slightly negatively to female ex-patients. Women accepted both male and female ex-patients. Thus, for some labels, both the characteristics of the person labeled and the reactor may influence the effect obtained.

Many have argued that the effects of labeling are so negative that diagnostic categories and special education programs that label children should be eliminated (e.g., Hobbs, 1975a, 1975b). Typically, some variant of the labeling theory of deviance (Mercer, 1973; Rains et al., 1975) is invoked. Once labeled, the person is seen as accepting the label, being treated by others in a manner consistent with the label, and ultimately coming to behave in accord with others' expectations. This may be a useful model for conceptualizing possible effects of labels, but it is by no means a statement of fact about the consequences of specific labeling experiences on specific persons. Instead, the effects are variable in magnitude and direction, depending upon a number of different factors, including the behavior and characteristics of the persons labeled. Furthermore, we have very little data about the ways in which handicap labels operate in classrooms, although we know that handicapped children are less liked than their peers. Other data suggest that teachers and peers respond to differences in behavior and appearance more consistently and strongly than to differences in labels and that the latter tend to be ignored when they are inconsistent with observed behavior.

Contact and Attitudes. Changes in laws as well as in educational and social policies have greatly increased the integration of the handicapped into schools, classrooms, and the larger community. Many believe that this will lead to more favorable reactions, but both theory and research indicate that this is an oversimplified view. The most promising conditions for acceptance occur when the handicapped individuals with whom one has contact are of equal status to the nonhandicapped and demonstrate few of the negative characteristics of the stereotype of their group. That this is not always easy to establish is clear from the extensive evidence on mildly retarded children integrated into regular classes, which consistently finds them to be less well accepted than their nonretarded classmates (Gottlieb & Corman, 1981). It is difficult for even mildly retarded children to "pass" when integrated into an academically demanding situation. The situation for the more severely handicapped is even more difficult. Equal status and "normality" cannot be readily attained.

When we examine regular teachers' attitudes toward integrated handicapped children or towards the integration itself, the results again do not suggest a simple positive reaction. Teachers often are unfavorable to such integration, and those who are initially positive may become less favorable after experience with mainstreaming. Baker and Gottlieb (1980), who have reviewed the literature in the area of mental retardation, suggest that "important components of regular teachers' attitudes toward the integration of retarded children [are]: (1) their knowledge of retarded children's academic and social behaviors, (2) their feelings about their own competence to teach retarded children, (3) their expectations of receiving assistance in teaching retarded pupils from valued supportive services, (4) their beliefs concerning the advantages and disadvantages of different educational placements for retarded children, and (5) their attitudes toward other teaching-related matters" (p. 11).

Attitude Improvement. We have seen that contact or integration by themselves are no guarantee of acceptance of handicapped individuals. However, considerable evidence is accumulating that contact can be structured in such a way that more favorable attitudes result (Donaldson, 1980). Two studies carried out in school settings illustrate this. Ballard et al. (1977) found that mildly retarded children integrated into regular classes were more accepted by their nonhandicapped peers when classroom activities were structured around small cooperative groups. Voeltz (1980) found that willingness to interact with handicapped children increased as a result of carefully designed contact experiences with severely handicapped children who had been integrated into their school.

Other methods of controlled exposure to handicaps that have been explored are the use of the mass media, such as children's television (Guskin et al., 1979), and stimulation activities (Clore & Jeffrey, 1972; Guskin, 1973), although findings have not been consistent.

Conclusions. Research concerning attitudes toward the handicapped allows us to conclude that attitudes toward handicapped persons are, in general, less favorable than toward nonhandicapped individuals. However, the magnitude of negative reactions varies with the severity and type of handicap. Attitudes have varied considerably from culture to culture and time period to time period, but there does not appear to be a progression associated with either time or "civilization." Reactions to the handicapped do seem to be related to reactions toward other lower status and dependent individuals such as children, minorities, and the poor. Although reactions to handicap and associated labels may be negative and formal treatment programs may have unfortunate consequences, reactions to individual handicapped persons appear to be more influenced by the behavior and competence of the person than by knowledge of the handicap. Contact, as in integration of the handicapped, may not lead to acceptance of the handicapped by the public, by teachers, or by peers. Nevertheless, attitudes toward handicapped persons can be improved if exposure to the handicapped is carefully structured to reduce stereotypes and interpersonal tension and to foster equal status or otherwise satisfying contacts.

Samuel L. Guskin
Reginald L. Jones

See also Deinstitutionalization of the Handicapped; Equity Issues in Education; Handicapped Individuals; Legislation; Special Education.

REFERENCES

Baker, J. L., & Gottlieb, J. Attitudes of teachers toward mainstreaming retarded children. In J. Gottlieb (Ed.), *Educating Mentally Retarded Children in the Mainstream.* Baltimore: University Park Press, 1980, pp. 3–23.

Ballard, M.; Corman, L.; Gottlieb, J.; & Kaufman, M. J. Improving the social status of mainstreamed retarded children. *Journal of Educational Psychology*, 1977, *69*, 605–611.

Berkson, G. The social ecology of defects in primates. In S. Skolnikoff & F. Poirier, *Primate Bio-social Development.* New York: Garland, 1977, pp. 189–204.

Clore, G. L., & Jeffrey, K. M. Emotional role-playing, attitude change, and attraction toward a disabled person. *Journal of Personality and Social Psychology*, 1972, *23*, 85–95. (ERIC Document Reproduction Service No. ED 050 393)

Combs, R. H., & Harper, J. L. Effects of labels on attitudes of educators toward handicapped children. *Exceptional Children*, 1967, *33*, 399–403.

Donaldson, J. Changing attitudes toward handicapped persons: A review and analysis of the literature. *Exceptional Children*, 1980, *46*, 504–514.

Edgerton, R. B. *The Cloak of Competence: Stigma in the Lives of the Mentally Retarded.* Berkeley: University of California Press, 1967.

Edgerton, R. B. Mental retardation in non-Western societies: Toward a cross-cultural perspective on incompetence. In H. C. Haywood (Ed.), *Sociocultural Aspects of Mental Retardation.* New York: Appleton-Century-Crofts, 1970, pp. 523–559.

Farina, A.; Felner, R. D.; & Boudreau, L. A. Reactions of workers to male and female mental patient job applicants. *Journal of Consulting and Clinical Psychology*, 1973, *41*, 363–372.

Farina, A., & Hagelauer, H. D. Sex and mental illness: The generosity of females. *Journal of Consulting and Clinical Psychology*, 1975, *43*, 122.

Farina, A.; Murray, P. J.; & Groh, T. Sex and worker acceptance of a former mental patient. *Journal of Consulting and Clinical Psychology*, 1978, *46*, 887–891.

Farina, A., & Ring, K. The influence of perceived mental illness on interpersonal relations. *Journal of Abnormal Psychology*, 1965, *70*, 47–51.

Farina, A.; Thaw, J.; Felner, R. D.; & Hust, B. E. Some interpersonal consequences of being mentally ill or mentally retarded. *American Journal of Mental Deficiency*, 1976, *80*, 414–422.

Goffman, E. *Stigma: Notes on the Management of Spoiled Identity.* Englewood Cliffs, N.J.: Prentice-Hall, 1963.

Gottlieb, J. Attitudes toward retarded children: Effects of labeling and academic performance. *American Journal of Mental Deficiency*, 1974, *79*, 268–273.

Gottlieb, J. Attitudes toward retarded children: Effects of labeling and behavioral aggressiveness. *Journal of Educational Psychology*, 1975, *67*, 581–585. (ERIC Document Reproduction Service No. ED 108 437)

Gottlieb, J., & Corman, L. Attitudes toward mentally retarded children. In R. L. Jones (Ed.), *Attitudes and Attitude Change in Special Education*, Reston, Va.: Council for Exceptional Children, 1981.

Gottwald, H. Public awareness about mental retardation. *Research Monograph.* Reston, Va.: Council for Exceptional Children, 1970. (ERIC Document Reproduction Service No. ED 041 440)

Guskin, S. L. The perception of subnormality in mentally defective children. *American Journal of Mental Deficiency,* 1962, *67,* 53–60.

Guskin, S. L. Simulation games for teachers on the mainstreaming of mildly handicapped children. *Viewpoints,* 1973, *49,* 85–95.

Guskin, S. L. Theoretical and empirical strategies for the study of the labeling of mentally retarded persons. In N. R. Ellis (Ed.), *International Review of Research in Mental Retardation* (Vol. 9). New York: Academic Press, 1978, pp. 127–158.

Guskin, S. L.; Morgan, W.; Cherkes, M.; & Peel, D. *Deafness and Signing on Sesame Street: Effects on Understanding and Attitudes of Pre-schoolers.* New York: Children's Television Workshop (One Lincoln Plaza, N.Y. 10023), 1979.

Hobbs, N. *The Future of Children: Categories, Labels, and Their Consequences.* San Francisco: Jossey-Bass, 1975. (a)

Hobbs, N. (Ed.). *Issues in the Classification of Children* (Vols. 1 & 2). San Francisco: Jossey-Bass, 1975. (b)

Jones, R. L. Learning and association in the presence of the blind. *New Outlook,* 1970, *64,* 317–324.

Jones, R. L. Labels and stigma in special education. *Exceptional Children,* 1972, *38,* 553–564. (ERIC Document Reproduction Service No. ED 054 279)

Kleck, R. Issues in social effectiveness: The case of the mentally retarded. In M. J. Begab & S. A. Richardson, *The Mentally Retarded and Society: A Social Science Perspective.* Baltimore: University Park Press, 1975, pp. 181–195.

MacMillan, D. L.; Jones, R. L.; & Aloia, G. F. The mentally retarded label: A theoretical analysis and review of research. *American Journal of Mental Deficiency,* 1974, *79,* 241–261.

Mercer, J. R. *Labeling the Mentally Retarded.* Berkeley: University of California Press, 1973.

Nikoloff, O. M., II. Attitudes of public school principals toward employment of teachers with certain physical disabilities. *Rehabilitation Literature,* 1962, *23,* 344–345.

Rains, P. M.; Kitsuse, J. I.; Duster, T.; & Freidson, E. The labeling approach to deviance. In N. Hobbs (Ed.), *Issues in the Classification of Children* (Vol. 1). San Francisco: Jossey-Bass, 1975, pp. 88–100.

Rickard, T. E.; Triandis, H. C.; & Patterson, C. H. Indices of employer prejudice toward disabled applicants. *Journal of Applied Psychology,* 1963, *47,* 52–55.

Shears, L. M., & Jensema, C. J. Social acceptability of anomalous persons. *Exceptional Children,* 1969, *36,* 91–95.

Shotel, J. R., Iano, R. P., & McGettigan, J. F. Teacher attitudes associated with the integration of handicapped children. *Exceptional Children,* 1972, *38,* 677–683.

Voeltz, L. M. Children's attitudes toward the handicapped. *American Journal of Mental Deficiency,* 1980, *84,* 455–464.

Warren, S. A.; Turner, D. R.; and Brody, D. S. Can education students' attitudes toward the retarded be changed? *Mental Retardation,* 1964, *2,* 235–242.

B

BASIC EDUCATION

See Curriculum History; Elementary Education.

BEHAVIOR PROBLEMS

Children and youth with behavior problems represent a major concern to educators. The passage of Public Law 94-142, the Education for All Handicapped Children Act of 1975, guaranteed these children free and appropriate education in the least restrictive environment. Both this law and the acceptance of the educational system's role as a major socializing force responsible for promoting the academic, social, and emotional growth of students have had a profound impact on educators (Biber, 1976; Joint Commission on the Mental Health of Children, 1973; Bower, 1967; Deno, 1978). These children, historically isolated or barred from school, are currently placed throughout the full range of educational settings, from regular classrooms to residential centers.

Regardless of the setting, however, children with behavior problems continue to be extremely difficult to understand, teach, and manage in the classroom. In addition, it is widely acknowledged that they are currently being underserved. Grosenick and Huntze (1979) summarize Bureau of Education for the Handicapped (BEH) national statistics for the seriously emotionally disturbed as follows: 2 percent of all children and youth aged 3 to 21 require special education because of their emotional disturbance; we can determine from this figure and from the figures for the number of children and youth currently being served that there are approximately 741,000 seriously disturbed children and youth not receiving special education (p. 9). Other populations identified as underserved are adolescents with behavior problems (Halpern, 1979); the mildly and moderately disturbed and socially maladjusted (Raiser & VanNagel, 1980; Yard, 1977; Meyen & Moran, 1979) and incarcerated youth (Johnson, 1979).

Needs assessment activities (*Update*, 1979) indicate that there is an urgent demand on the part of parents, teachers, and other professionals for more information, research, and delivery of services to children with behavior problems. Special educators are striving to meet the demand, and their efforts are resulting in many exciting new directions in conceptualizing these children and methods for meeting their needs.

The most frequently used terms in the literature for children with behavior problems are "emotionally disturbed" and "behavior-disordered." Although these terms have different meanings (Hewett & Taylor, 1980; Saunders, 1974), preference is given to the term "behavior-disordered" in the following discussion because of its focus on behavior and its frequent use in educational literature.

Current Issues. The field of special education for children with behavior disorders is undergoing intense self-evaluation and rapid change. Many of the traditional assumptions regarding the definition, assessment, diagnosis, and treatment of children with behavior disorders are being reevaluated.

Historically, approaches toward understanding and treating behavior-disordered children were rooted in specific conceptual models. The major conceptual models of the 1960s—behavioral, psychodynamic, biophysical, sociological, and ecological—were presented in detail in the publications of the Conceptual Project in Emotional Disturbance (Rhodes & Tracy, 1972a, 1972b). Each of the models was based on a different formulation of who these children were, how they got that way, and how to deal with them. Proponents of each model expended much energy attempting to argue the validity of their model over the other models. The net outcome for the educator was to produce a greater appreciation of theory but more confusion regarding teaching the intervention techniques.

195

Current thinking involves a movement away from the adherence to discrete conceptual models toward a more integrated approach that is based on selecting the most appropriate method for a specific student to achieve a particular goal. Over the past decade, the field has become more functional than theoretical, more specific than general, and more inclusive than exclusive. Professional energies have gone into expanding services and struggling with bureaucratic issues around legal responsibilities; new roles and relationships with regular teachers, parents, principals, and community agencies; program accountability; and the problem of vanishing financial support.

Assessment. The complexity of defining emotional disturbance and behavior disorders is addressed by Wood and Lakin (1979). The conclusion of this review emphasizes that the definition of emotional disturbance and behavior disorders must be directed toward the goal of effectively meeting the academic, social, and emotional needs of children in order to be of any value in an educational setting. This means that all future identification of behavior-disordered children must transcend the restrictions of individual theoretical models and be stated in functional descriptive terms that relate to educational programming.

Past definitions, based on the psychodynamic and behavioral models, have placed the locus of the problem within children or on their behaviors. Over the past ten years, there has been growing acceptance of the ecological theorists' position that behavior occurs in a social context and that the source of the problem may exist entirely apart from the child or in the interaction between the child and the environment (Hobbs, 1966; Rhodes, 1967). Wood (1979) differentiates between behavior that is disturbed, disordered, and disturbing. He indicates that " 'disturbing' directs our attention to the effects of one person's behavior on the thoughts and feelings of one who observes that behavior"; if the behavior is disturbing to the observer, he or she may *judge* the person's behavior to be disordered or *infer* that the person's thoughts and feelings are disturbed (pp. 3–4). Kauffman (1980) summarizes this current attitude toward definition in stating that "there is no clear, unambiguous definition of *emotional disturbance* . . . disordered behavior is what we choose to make it; it is not an objective thing that exists outside our arbitrary sociocultural rules" (p. 524).

The acknowledgment of the role that social context plays in the determination of whether or not a pupil is viewed as disturbed or disordered has resulted in greater sensitivity to the distinction between individual difference and deviance. More specifically, diverse cultural and socioeconomic backgrounds (Whelan, 1978) and individual variables such as sex, maturational level, intelligence, and learning style (Stainback & Stainback, 1980) are being regarded as valuable differences among individuals, to be appreciated for their uniqueness rather than to be labeled deviant (Rhodes, 1980). In essence, the view of certain children once considered deviant or abnormal is giving way to the position that normalcy is relative (Rhodes, 1980) and that all children are unique and should be treated accordingly (Stainback & Stainback, 1980). This is not to say that emotional disturbance and behavior disorders do not exist. The point is that not all children who are different are disturbed or disordered. For educational purposes, there are more functional ways of describing all children in terms of their abilities to function effectively within the established norms of specific settings.

There is widespread agreement that a meaningful educational definition of the disturbed or disordered child must, in fact, be a description that (1) identifies the problem, (2) describes the problem behavior, (3) indicates in which setting the problem behavior occurs, (4) indicates to whom the behavior is problematic, (5) identifies means by which the "disturber" is differentiated from others, and (6) specifies what directions should be taken to intervene properly in the problem (Wood, 1979, pp. 7–8). This type of definition or educational description has positive implications for educators because it not only elicits a more usable description of the total nature of the problem but also suggests a course of action for interventions.

The above criteria for definitions have further implications for current thinking regarding educational diagnostic and assessment procedures. Traditional diagnostic procedures, which have too frequently served only to label children as handicapped and in need of special services in separate settings, are being abandoned in favor of descriptions that are more useful in educational settings. Long, Morse, and Newman (1976) discuss both the value in education of describing pupils in terms of their strengths and weaknesses rather than using labels and diagnostic stereotypes and the need to set individualized expectations for pupils based on individual differences. Whelan (1978) discusses emotionally disturbed children in terms of excesses and deficits, stating that a "history of behavior excesses and deficits observed in a child can illuminate and provide targets or objectives for instructional activities" (pp. 333–334).

Saunders (1974) points out that differential diagnostic procedures are more reflective of the medical model and are of questionable value to educators. He proposes "functional diagnosis" as a preferable alternative, stating that it is prescriptive in application—that is, it is diagnosis that is "employed to develop specific programming based upon the assessment of current functioning, using the assessed level as a starting point in treatment" (p. 16).

Stainback and Stainback (1980) discuss the direct assessment and intervention model as an approach that is gaining favor among professionals. According to the authors, the "mystique of the diagnostic/labeling procedure in education is being broken down and replaced with more direct and functional methods for identification of programming needs" (p. 242). This model involves "the assessment of a child's behavior (e.g., academic, social, emotional, physical) in the natural setting in which he typically interacts"

(p. 243). The assessment data are then used to build a program based on the child's needs. The authors point out that one of the advantages of this approach is that it focuses on "individual characteristics and needs rather than normative comparisons and disability groupings," and that this focus "facilitates maintenance in the natural setting by avoiding labeling and subsequent segregation associated with it" (p. 244).

Many definitions have been proposed in attempts to meet the above criteria. Among those most frequently cited in the literature are the definitions of Ullman and Krasner (1969), Graubard (1973), Kauffman (1977), and Bower (1969). Bower's definition is of special significance, because it has become, with slight modification, the basis for the definition of "seriously emotionally disturbed" under Public Law 94-142 (Department of Health, Education, and Welfare, 1977, p. 42478).

Intervention. The shift from the specific conceptual models of the 1960s toward more integrated and educationally relevant conceptualizations of behavior-disordered children has led to significant new directions with regard to intervention approaches.

The specific intervention strategies advocated under each of the conceptual models (Rhodes & Tracy, 1972b) have not been rejected. On the contrary, Morse (1977) indicates that what has happened is a "broadening of the concepts of intervention . . . moving from a rather restrictive dynamic point of view to an inclusion of behavioristic and other learning approaches and to a greater appreciation of the ecological factors" (p. 158). As Morse illustrates, combinations of intervention approaches taken from each of the models can be effective when the main priority is the matching of the specific intervention strategy with the type of problem the child has. He concludes that with this individualized approach, "the method does not predominate, the child predominates" (p. 159).

Morse's line of thought is in keeping with the concept of educational descriptions discussed previously and with the mandate of Public Law 94-142 that an individualized educational plan (IEP) be developed, specifying the interventions to be initiated to help each handicapped child (Department of Health, Education, and Welfare, 1977, p. 42490).

Space limitations prohibit a comprehensive review of all the intervention strategies currently being used, but it is important to mention a few approaches that are particularly significant and deserving of further investigation by the reader. Among these are the developmental-therapy approach developed by Wood (1975), the structured approach to educational intervention developed by Gallagher (1979); the orchestration-of-success approach presented by Hewett and Taylor (1980); and the current revival of interest in the life space interview, which was first discussed by Redl and Wineman (1957) and which is covered comprehensively by Fagen and Long (1981).

One significant development in intervention ap-

proaches currently receiving much attention is the employment of self-control instructional strategies to teach children with behavior problems ways of controlling their own behaviors. Meichenbaum (1977) defines self-control as "behavior initiated by the individual, where such behavior is relatively free from external constraints" (p. 7). Fagen and Long (1979) define self-control as "the capacity to flexibly and realistically direct and regulate personal action or behavior so as to effectively cope with a given situation" (p. 68).

Three cognitively oriented techniques designed to teach children self-control are identified by Polsgrove (1979): self-instruction, problem solving, and modeling-rehearsal. Self-instruction techniques involve teaching individuals to make suggestions to themselves to guide their own behavior in a manner that is similar to being guided by another individual (Rosenbaum & Drabman, 1979). The belief is that children can be taught to make verbal statements to themselves that enable them to control their behavior. The problem-solving technique is designed to teach children effective strategies for understanding and coping with the various problem situations they encounter. Examples of popular applications of this technique include the classroom meeting described by Glasser (1969), the conflict-management curriculum (Palomares & Logan, 1975), the five-phase problem-solving process discussed by D'Zurilla and Goldfried (1973), and finally the self-control curriculum developed by Fagen, Long, and Stevens (1975). The role that modeling plays in children's learning is well documented (Bandura, 1971). Children imitate the behaviors of their teachers and peers in the classroom. The modeling-rehearsal strategy for teaching children self-control involves systematically presenting situations in which children observe a model and rehearse that model's behavior. Models may be teachers, peers, or older students and may be observed in real life or on videotapes. O'Leary and Dubey (1979), Rosenbaum and Drabman (1979), and Polsgrove (1979) provide comprehensive reviews of the application and effectiveness of these and other self-control instructional techniques. In summary, cognitive self-control strategies are gaining in popularity. In general, the research, while not conclusive, indicates that there is sufficient value to this approach to warrant its use and further investigation.

Conclusions. Special education for emotionally disturbed and behavior-disordered children has made strides over the past ten years toward more effective and educationally relevant ways of conceptualizing and supporting children with behavior problems. The major thrust behind this growth is the efforts of special educators to provide quality programming for which they are held, and hold themselves, accountable. Hewett and Taylor (1980) provide an excellent concluding statement of the growth that has taken place in the field of special education for children with behavior problems as they make the point that, over the past twelve years, "the emotionally disturbed child has come to be viewed more and more as a child with a learning problem teachers can do something about and only secondarily as a complex psychiatric casualty" (preface).

Anthony Werner
Nicholas J. Long

See also Behavioral Treatment Methods; Discipline; Drug Abuse Education; Handicapped Individuals; Mental Health; Preadolescent Development; Special Education; Truants and Dropouts.

REFERENCES

Bandura, A. *Psychological Modeling: Conflicting Theories.* Chicago: Aldine-Atherton, 1971.

Biber, B. Mental health and the school environment. In *The Report of Task Force II to the Joint Commission on Mental Health of Children.* New York: Harper & Row, 1976, pp. 128–158.

Bower, E. M. Three rivers of significance to education. In E. Bower & W. Hollister (Eds.), *Behavioral Science Frontiers in Education.* New York: Wiley, 1967, pp. 5–45.

Bower, E. M. *Early Identification of Emotionally Handicapped Children in School* (2nd ed.). Springfield, Ill.: Thomas, 1969.

Deno E. *Educating Children with Emotional and Behavior Problems.* Minneapolis: University of Minnesota Press, National Support Systems Project, 1978.

Department of Health, Education, and Welfare; Office of Education. Education of handicapped children: Implementation of Part B of the Education of the Handicapped Act (Part 2). *Federal Register, 42*(163), August 23, 1977, pp. 42474–42518. (ERIC Documents Reproduction Service No. ED 144 294)

D'Zurilla, T. J., & Goldfried, M. R. Problem-solving and behavior modification. *Journal of Abnormal Psychology,* 1973, *78,* 107–126.

Fagen, S. A., & Long, N. J. A psychoeducational curriculum approach to teaching self-control. *Behavioral Disorders,* 1979, *4*(2), 68–82.

Fagen, S. A., & Long, N. J. (Eds.). *Pointer,* 1981, *25*(2).

Fagen, S. A.; Long, N. J.; & Stevens, D. J. *Teaching Children Self-control.* Columbus, Ohio: Merrill, 1975.

Gallagher, P. A. *Teaching Students with Behavior Disorders: Techniques for Classroom Instruction.* Denver: Love, 1979.

Glasser, W. *Schools without Failure.* New York: Harper & Row, 1969.

Graubard, P. S. Children with behavioral disabilities. In L. M. Dunn (Ed.), *Exceptional Children in the Schools: Special Education in Transition* (2nd ed.). Holt, Rinehart & Winston, 1973.

Grosenick, J. K., & Huntze, S. L. *National Needs Analysis in Behavior Disorders: A Model for a Comprehensive Needs Analysis in Behavior Disorders.* Columbia: University of Missouri, 1979.

Halpern, A. S. Adolescents and young adults. *Exceptional Children,* 1979, *45*(7), 518–523.

Hewett, F. M., & Taylor, F. D. *The Emotionally Disturbed Child in the Classroom: The Orchestration of Success.* Boston: Allyn & Bacon, 1980.

Hobbs, N. Helping disturbed children: Psychological and ecological strategies. *American Psychologist,* 1966, *21,* 1105–1115.

Johnson, J. L. An essay on incarcerated youth: An oppressed group. *Exceptional Children,* 1979, *45*(7), 566–571.

Joint Commission on the Mental Health of Children. Report of Task Force VI. In *Social Change and the Mental Health of Children.* New York: Harper & Row, 1973.

Kauffman, J. M. *Characteristics of Children's Behavior Disorders.* Columbus, Ohio: Merrill, 1977.

Kauffman, J. M. Where special education for disturbed children is going: A personal view. *Exceptional Children,* 1980, *46*(7), 522–527.

Long, N. J.; Morse, W. M.; & Newman, R. (Eds.). *Conflict in the Classroom* (3rd ed.). Belmont, Calif.: Wadsworth, 1976.

Meichenbaum, D. Teaching children self-control. In B. B. Lahey & A. E. Kazdin (Eds.), *Advances in Clinical Child Psychology* (Vol. 1). New York: Plenum Press, 1977, pp. 1–33.

Meyen, C. L., & Moran, M. R. A perspective on the unserved mildly handicapped. *Exceptional Children,* 1979, *45*(7), 526–530.

Morse, W. C. Serving the needs of individuals with behavior disorders. *Exceptional Children,* 1977, *44*(3), 158–164.

O'Leary, S. G., & Dubey, D. R. Applications of self-control procedures by children: A review. *Journal of Applied Behavior Analysis.* 1979, *12*(3), 449–465.

Palomares, U. H., & Logan, B. *A Curriculum on Conflict Management.* La Mesa, Calif.: Human Development Training Institute, 1975.

Polsgrove, L. Self-control: Methods for child training. *Behavioral Disorders,* 1979, *4*(2), 116–130.

Raiser, L., & Van Nagel, C. The loophole in Public Law 94-142. *Exceptional Children,* 1980, *46*(7), 516–520.

Redl, F., & Wineman, D. *The Aggressive Child.* New York: Free Press, 1957.

Rhodes, W. C. The disturbing child: A problem of ecological management. *Exceptional Children,* 1967, *33,* 637–642. (ERIC Document Reproduction Service No. ED 135 121)

Rhodes, W. C. Beyond theory and practice: Implications in programming for children with emotional disabilities. *Behavioral Disorders,* 1980, *5*(4), 254–263. (ERIC Document Reproduction Service No. ED 135 120)

Rhodes, W. C., & Tracy, M. L. (Eds.). *Conceptual Models.* Vol. 1 of *A Study of Child Variance.* Ann Arbor: University of Michigan, 1972. (a)

Rhodes, W. C., & Tracy, M. L. (Eds.). *Interventions.* Vol. 2 of *A Study of Child Variance.* Ann Arbor: University of Michigan, 1972. (b)

Rosenbaum, M. S., & Drabman, R. S. Self-control training in the classroom: A review and critique. *Journal of Applied Behavior Analysis,* 1979, *12*(3), 467–485.

Saunders, B. The diagnosis, management, and treatment of emotional disturbance and behavior disorders in children. In B. Saunders (Ed.), *Approaches with Emotionally Disturbed Children.* Hicksville, N.Y.: Exposition Press, 1974, pp. 3–24.

Stainback, S., & Stainback, W. Some trends in the education of children labelled behaviorally disordered. *Behavioral Disorders,* 1980, *5*(4), 240–249.

Ullman, L. P., & Krasner, L. *A Psychological Approach to Abnormal Behavior.* Englewood Cliffs, N.J.: Prentice-Hall, 1969.

Update. Newsletter of the Council for Exceptional Children, 1979, *11*(1).

Whelan, R. J. The emotionally disturbed. In E. L. Meyen (Ed.), *Exceptional Children and Youth: An Introduction.* Denver: Love, 1978, pp. 322–358.

Wood, F. H. Defining disturbing, disordered, and disturbed behavior. In F. H. Wood & K. C. Lakin (Eds.), *Disturbing, Disordered, or Disturbed? Perspectives on the Definition of Problem*

Behavior in Educational Settings. Minneapolis: University of Minnesota, 1979, pp. 3–16.

Wood, F. H., & Lakin, K. C. (Eds.). *Disturbing, Disordered, or Disturbed? Perspectives on the Definition of Problem Behavior in Educational Settings.* Minneapolis: University of Minnesota, 1979.

Wood, M. M. (Ed.). *Developmental Therapy: A Textbook for Teachers as Therapists for Emotionally Disturbed Young Children.* Baltimore: University Park Press, 1975.

Yard, G. J. Definition and interpretation of Public Law 94-142: Is behavior disorders a question of semantics? *Behavioral Disorders,* 1977, *2*(4), 252–254.

BEHAVIORAL TREATMENT METHODS

Behavioral treatment is designed to eliminate or reduce the difference between appropriate and inappropriate behavior. The term "behavior," as used in this context, refers to all overt and covert acts, including speaking, writing, and computing, as well as nonverbal movements. The behavior most often analyzed and treated is that which is observable to others, but internal events are sometimes analyzed (Skinner, 1953) and treated (Rimm & Masters, 1979).

Behavioral treatment methods have been applied to developing a wide range of appropriate behaviors including those in basic written language and mathematics (e.g., Holt, 1971; Lovitt, Guppy, & Blattner, 1969; McKenzie et al., 1968), oral language and speech (e.g., Sailor, Guess, & Baer, 1973; Bricker & Bricker, 1970; McReynolds, 1970), self-care skills (e.g., Azrin & Foxx, 1971; Song & Gandhi, 1974; Martin et al., 1971), social-emotional behavior (e.g., Patterson, 1976; Wolf, Risley, & Mees, 1964; Burchard & Tyler, 1965), self-control (e.g., Rubin, Schneider, & Dolnick, 1976), thoughts and feelings about oneself (e.g., Krop, Calhoon, & Verrier, 1971), hyperactivity (e.g., O'Leary et al., 1976), and physiologically based disorders (e.g., Alexander et al., 1973). In fact, a perusal of the published literature on exceptional persons reveals that virtually every human problem has been analyzed and treated behaviorally.

Characteristics. Those who use behavioral treatment differ about its defining characteristics (Thoreson, 1980). In general, however, behavioral treatment rests on several important assumptions. First, behavior therapists assume that behavior is the focus of treatment rather than a symptomatic manifestation of underlying pathological states, traits, and processes. Second, they assume that the reasons for current behavior can be found in the individual's learning history, in the current environment, and in that person's biology. Third, and very importantly, behavior therapists assume that all behavior changes as a result of consistent alterations in the individual's environment. Finally, behavioral treatment is characterized by a heavy emphasis on evaluating treatment effects by repeated direct observation and recording of problem behavior before, during, and after treatment.

Behavioral treatments are based primarily on two sets of principles (cf. Ferster, Culbertson, & Boren, 1975; Reynolds, 1968). One set governs changes in "operant behavior," or voluntary behavior, and the other governs "respondent behavior" or reflexive behavior. An additional set of principles is sometimes invoked under the heading of "social learning theory," which gives special emphasis to modeling, imitation, and covert verbal mediation in governing behavior change (Bandura, 1977). The number of major principles required to explain most behavior change is quite small (Reynolds, 1968); however, the number of different treatment procedures that use behavioral principles is very large (Rimm & Masters, 1979). Furthermore any one of these general therapeutic procedures can be implemented in a variety of ways to reduce behavior problems experienced by a particular individual.

Behavioral treatments are often classified as procedures to increase behavior, decrease behavior, or maintain behavior and sometimes as procedures to produce generalization or discrimination. "Modeling" (prompting), "shaping," "chaining" (task analysis), and "reinforcement" are the primary procedures used to teach new behavior or to increase the strength of operant behavior. "Extinction," "timeout from reinforcement," "response cost," "punishment," "reinforcement of low-rate or other behaviors," and "overcorrection" are common techniques for decreasing operant behaviors. Schedules of reinforcement can be arranged to teach behavior that is resistant to extinction or that will be maintained at a level considered appropriate.

How a specific behavioral problem is treated depends on whether operant or respondent principles are used to analyze it. For example, an exceptional student who participates too little in group activities might be treated through desensitization or assertiveness training, if the problem is seen to be one of respondently conditioned fear and anxiety elicited by social stimuli. On the other hand, praise and attention, tokens, or a contingency contract, might be used if the problem is viewed as the student's receiving insufficient reinforcement for participation.

Programs for Exceptional Students. The history of behavioral treatment is long and complex (Kazdin, 1978). In that history, it is common to find applications of behavioral principles and methods to individuals whose behavior made them exceptional. Initial applications to individual behavior in institutional settings (e.g., Fuller, 1949; Lindsley, 1956; Allyon, 1963) were soon followed by more complete day-long treatment programs (Allyon & Azrin, 1965). At the same time, behavioral principles led to a reconceptualization of the nature of exceptionality and human development (Bijou, 1959, 1963). Eventually, demonstrations that behavioral treatments can help even the most profoundly handicapped people learn contributed to landmark litigation (e.g., *Pennsylvania Association for Re-*

tarded Children, 1971) and legislation (Public Law 94-142, 1975). In the late 1960s, then, and throughout the 1970s, behavioral treatments were elaborated and became common elements in educational programs for exceptional students. Eventually, the analysis of behavior became a comprehensive approach to working with mildly, moderately, severely, and profoundly handicapped students (cf. White & Haring, 1976; Snell, 1978; Berdine & Cegelka, 1980). Evidence now exists that behavioral approaches may serve as well to improve instruction in basic skills in regular school programs (Carnine & Silbert, 1979). The result has been not only to influence the definition of what constitutes appropriate educational programming for exceptional students but also to influence the definitions of exceptionality in common texts (Hewett & Forness, 1974; Smith & Neisworth, 1975) and to redefine the roles, responsibilities, and competencies of special education personnel (cf. McKenzie et al., 1970; Deno, 1972).

Issues Raised. The development of behavioral treatment procedures has been accompanied by a wide variety of issues regarding their use. A few of the more salient issues are presented here.

Standards for defining exceptional behavior. Behavioral treatment requires, first, that a behavior that differs from someone's standards or expectations be identified. An issue that typically arises whenever treatment is considered is who have the right to impose their standards of behavior on the individual who is to be treated. In the education of exceptional students, the issue seems less intense in cases of severe and profound handicapping conditions that make behavioral differences from normative development extreme. Nevertheless, questions concerning what behaviors should be changed, if any, are just as controversial when a person cannot stand, walk, and talk in a residential treatment-facility as when a student stands, walks, and talks more than a classroom teacher desires. Although attempts to resolve the question often involve application of normative standards for behavior and what some have termed "social validation" (Kazdin, 1977), the argument for "pluralism" (i.e., consulting more than one set of values) in setting standards applies equally well to educating exceptional students as it does to educating cultural minorities. At the present time, in education of the exceptional, the issue regarding whose standards ought to define behavior as different is resolved procedurally through the rules and regulations of Public Law 94-142. The result is a definition of exceptional behavior that is based more firmly on civil rights than on pathology (Gliedman & Roth, 1980).

Focus on symptoms. An issue related to problem identification is whether behavioral treatment focuses on change in "surface behavior" rather than on underlying causes for that behavior. To some extent, resolution of the issue rests on theoretical differences and assumptions regarding human nature. As long as one believes behavior is a manifestation of unobservable states of mind and emotion, focusing on changing behavior rather than on those

states or dispositions may seem superficial. In contrast, if one accepts behavioral difference as the problem, whatever the cause of that difference, then resolution of that difference is the treatment goal. The issue finds its analogue in other realms of human service, including medicine, where treatment may be based on reducing the current problem rather than on discovering causes of that problem. A sometimes fruitful approach to resolving the difference has been to view etiology as useful in preventing behavior problems and to view reducing current behavior problems as necessary for treatment. A second partial resolution of the issue may rest on the success of "cognitive behavior therapy," which is based on the traditional principles and methods of behavioral treatment but focuses on altering thoughts and feelings as a basis for treatment (Thoreson, 1980). The cognitive behavioral approach may provide a common ground for resolving conceptual differences, since it emphasizes the importance of both inner events and self-control, major tenets of traditional therapy. Cognitive behavior therapy has been criticized by behavioral and nonbehavioral therapists alike (Thoreson, 1980), however, and its contribution to reducing professional differences remains to be determined (Messer & Winokur, 1980). Finally, as with the issue concerning whose standards for behavior should apply when identifying behavioral difference, the decision to focus educational treatment on overt behavior rather than on covert processes is a decision that must be embedded within the procedural protections of the law.

Ethics of treatment. A major criticism of behavioral treatment is that certain commonly used procedures may be morally wrong because (1) they indirectly teach students to work for extrinsic gain (as in token economics), (2) they involve depriving the individuals of their rightful acquisition or possession of goods and services (as with response cost and deprivation), (3) they include deliberate and systematic use of aversive consequences for behavior (as with overcorrection and various punishment techniques), and (4) they teach caregivers to respond in mechanistic and inhumane ways to the behavior of others (as when social reinforcers are withheld or deliberately made contingent on desired behavior rather than "spontaneously" provided). Ethical criticisms of behavior treatment are so widespread that most books on behavioral treatment include chapters devoted exclusively to the nature of these criticisms and the counterarguments for those criticisms (Sulzer-Azaroff & Mayer, 1977; Axelrod, 1977). Like the issue of whether behavioral treatment focuses on symptoms rather than on underlying causes, the resolution of many of the ethical issues rests on one's assumptions about human development. If, as behaviorally oriented psychologists contend, behavior increases and decreases in accordance with behavioral principles, then the use of behavioral procedures in treatment is not a matter of choice, but a necessity. Since behavioral treatments are based on the principles (laws) that govern behavior change, effective utilization of the principles in treatment is required if some change is to occur. Not using such treatments is akin to not using physiological principles in medical treatment. Given this position, the only choice is whether to treat at all, not how to treat. In fact, however, the issue is more complex, since any treatment procedure can be operationalized in a multitude of ways. Potential reinforcers must be selected from a variety of alternatives, such as food, objects, activities, attention, or praise. To increase an exceptional student's participation in a group may mean choosing between having the student earn a cracker or giving the student the opportunity to play with a friend.

Ethical criticisms are often raised as a consequence of what may seem like a choice between simple alternatives. The issues may be even more complicated when electric (faradic) shock is used to eliminate self-destructive behavior, such as head banging, since there are many who feel inflicting pain on another person, no matter how effective in eliminating behavior, is not justifiable. Efforts have been made by state welfare agencies to develop policies and regulations concerning the use of aversive control procedures, and state educational agencies typically have regulations concerning the use of corporal punishment. Such policies and regulations change, however, as the attitudes of society change and officials are elected or appointed who reflect these changes in legislative and legal decisions. In the face of transitory policy and regulation, the rights of individuals seem best protected by affording everyone, no matter how atypical, the basic civil rights guaranteed under the Constitution and by ensuring that parents and legal guardians have necessary counsel.

Efficiency and effectiveness of treatment. Since a defining characteristic of behavioral treatment is that reliable and valid records of problem behavior be obtained before, during, and after treatment to provide a data base for evaluating treatment effects, an increased proportion of teacher time must be devoted to measurement and record keeping. If successful treatment requires more extensive data collection, teachers must not only be trained in what data should be collected and how to interpret those data, but they must also be afforded the time and the resources required to do so. In the education of exceptional persons, it is common to find that the more difficult the person is to teach, the more intense the data collection requirements. One solution to these problems may be to employ paraprofessionals in data collection and analysis, in much the same way that medicine employs laboratory technicians and paramedics. A second solution may be the increased use of small-computer technology in educational programs. Whatever the solution, both professionals and clients are apt to find increased emphasis on defining the quality of special education programs in terms of recorded changes in the behavior of students rather than in terms of either the type of curriculum and instruction provided or the staff-student ratios.

A second apparent inefficiency in behavioral treatment is the increased amount of time that teachers must devote to arranging and managing the delivery of reinforcing consequences for behavior. Teachers traditionally direct most of their attention to identifying curriculum tasks and to telling or showing students what, when, where, and how to do those tasks. Motivating students to perform curriculum tasks more often involves exhortation, persuasion, and incitement that it does ensuring that reinforcers succeed behavior. Exceptional students often learn little or nothing unless clear consequences occur immediately after desired behavior. For severely handicapped students, this fact may be true because ordinary communication cannot be used to bridge delays between behavior and its natural or logical consequences. For less severely handicapped students, clear, immediate consequences may be required because their environmental history has been one of failure and punishment when working on curriculum tasks and in classroom participation. Whatever the reason, teachers of exceptional children will find that the time involved in arranging and managing the immediate consequences of behavior changes their role.

At present, there is general agreement that behavioral techniques can alter the form and frequency of behavior. Disputes about treatment effectiveness revolve, instead, around the durability and generalization of the treatment effects. The issue arises because behavior changed in the treatment setting may revert to previous levels outside that setting. Behavior therapists have tended to view this outcome as consistent with predictions from behavioral principles. They have argued that either generalization training must be incorporated into treatment or nontreatment settings must be altered in ways that support behavior acquired in treatment settings. Efforts in cognitive behavior therapy to increase self-control through verbal rehearsal and self-instruction are sometimes identified as potentially improving generalization (Meichenbaum & Cameron, 1974). Like other promising behavioral treatments, however, continued empirical testing will likely determine the fulfillment of that promise.

Stanley L. Deno

See also Behavior Problems; Correctional Education; Deinstitutionalization of the Handicapped; Mental Health; Psychological Services; Rehabilitation Services; Special Education.

REFERENCES

Alexander, A. B.; Chai, H.; Greer, T. L.; Miklich, D. R.; Renne, C. M.; & Cardoso, R. R. The elimination of chronic cough by response suppression shaping. *Journal of Behaviour Therapy and Experimental Psychiatry,* 1973, *4,* 75–70.

Allyon, T. Intensive treatment of psychotic behavior by stimulus satiation and food reinforcement. *Behaviour Research and Therapy,* 1963, *1,* 53–61.

Allyon, T., & Azrin, N. H. The measurement and reinforcement of behavior with psychotics. *Journal of the Experimental Analysis of Behavior,* 1965, *8,* 357–383.

Axelrod, S. *Behavior Modification for the Classroom Teacher.* New York: Holt, Rinehart, & Winston, 1977.

Azrin, N., & Foxx, R. M. A rapid method of toilet training the institutionalized retarded. *Journal of Applied Behavioral Analysis*, 1971, *4*, 89–99.

Bandura, A. *Social Learning Theory*. Englewood Cliffs, N.J.: Prentice-Hall, 1977.

Berdine, W. H., & Cegelka, P. T. *Teaching the Trainable Retarded*. Columbus, Ohio: Merrill, 1980.

Bijou, S. W. Learning in children. *Monographs of the Society for Research in Child Development*, 1959, *24*(5, Serial No. 74).

Bijou, S. W. Theory and research in mental (developmental) retardation. *Psychological Record*, 1963, *13*, 95–110.

Bricker, W. A., & Bricker, D. D. Development of receptive vocabulary in severely retarded children. *American Journal of Mental Deficiency*, 1970, *74*, 599–607.

Burchard, I., & Tyler, V. The modification of delinquent behavior through operant conditioning. *Behavior Research and Therapy*, 1965, *2*, 245–250.

Carnine, D., & Silbert, J. *Direct Instruction Reading*. Columbus, Ohio: Merrill, 1979.

Deno, E. N. (Ed.). *Instructional Alternatives for Exceptional Children*. Reston, Va.: Council for Exceptional Children, 1972. (ERIC Document Reproduction Service No. ED 074 678)

Ferster, C. B.; Culbertson, S.; & Boren, M. C. P. *Behavior Principles* (2nd ed.). Englewood Cliffs, N.J.: Prentice-Hall, 1975.

Fuller, P. Operant conditioning of a vegetative human organism. *American Journal of Psychology*, 1949, *62*, 587–590.

Gliedman, J., & Roth, W. *The Unexpected Minority: Handicapped Children in America*. New York: Harcourt Brace Jovanovich, 1980.

Hewett, F., & Forness, S. *Education of Exceptional Learners*. Boston: Allyn & Bacon, 1974.

Holt, G. L. Effect of reinforcement contingencies in increasing programmed reading and mathematics behaviors in first-grade children. *Journal of Experimental Child Psychology*, 1971, *12*, 362–369.

Kazdin, A. E. Assessing the clinical or applied significance of behavior change through social validation. *Behavior Modification*, 1977, *1*, 427–452.

Kazdin, A. E. *History of Behavior Modification*. Baltimore: University Park Press, 1978.

Krop, H.; Calhoon, B.; & Verrier, R. Modification of the "self-concept" of emotionally disturbed children by covert reinforcement. *Behavior Therapy*, 1971, *2*, 201–204.

Lindsley, O. R. Operant conditioning methods applied to research in chronic schizophrenia. *Psychiatric Research Reports*, 1956, *5*, 118–139.

Lovitt, T. C.; Guppy, T. C.; & Blattner, J. E. The use of a free time contingency with fourth-graders to increase spelling accuracy. *Behavior Research Therapy*, 1969, *7*, 151–156.

Martin, G. L.; Kehoe, B.; Bird, E.; Jensen, V.; & Darbyshire, M. Operant conditioning in dressing behavior of severely retarded girls. *Mental Retardation*, 1971, *9*(3), 27–30.

McKenzie, H. S.; Clark, M.; Wolf, M. W.; Kothera, R.; & Benson, C. Behavior modification of children with learning disabilities using grades as tokens and allowances as back-up reinforcers. *Exceptional Children*, 1968, *34*, 745–752.

McKenzie, H. S.; Egner, A. N.; Knight, M. F.; Perelman, P. F.; Schneider, B. M.; & Garvin, J. S. Training consulting teachers to assist elementary teachers in the management and education of handicapped children. *Exceptional Children*, 1970, *37*, 137–143.

McReynolds, L. V. Contingencies and consequences in speech therapy. *Journal of Speech and Hearing Disorders*, 1970, *35*, 12–24.

Meichenbaum, D., & Cameron, C. The clinical potential of modifying what clients say to themselves. In M. J. Mahoney & C. E. Thoreson (Eds.), *Self-Control: Power to the Person*. Monterey, Calif.: Brooks/Cole, 1974, pp. 263–290.

Messer, S. B., & Winokur, M. Some limits to the integration of psychoanalytic and behavior therapy. *American Psychologist*, 1980, *35*, 818–827.

O'Leary, K. D.; Pelham, W. E.; Rosenbaum, A.; & Price, G. H. Behavioral treatment of hyperkinetic children: An experienced evaluation of its usefulness. *Clinical Pediatrics*, 1976, *15*, 510–515.

Patterson, G. R. The aggressive child: Victim and architect of a coercive system. In E. J. Mash, L. A. Hamerlynch, & L. C. Handy (Eds.), *Behavior Modification and Families*. New York: Brunner/Mazel, 1976, pp. 267–316.

Pennsylvania Association for Retarded Children, Nancy Beth Bowman et al. v. Commonwealth of Pennsylvania, Davis H. Kurtzman et al. Court Action No. 71–42 (June 18, 1971).

Public Law 94-142, *Education of All Handicapped Children Act of 1975* (S.G.). 94th Cong., 1st sess., 1975.

Reynolds, G. S. *A Primer of Operant Conditioning*. Glenview, Ill.: Scott, Foresman, 1968.

Rimm, D. C., & Masters, J. C. *Behavior Therapy: Techniques and Empirical Findings*. New York: Academic Press, 1979.

Rubin, A.; Schneider, M.; & Dolnick, M. The turtle technique: An extended case of self-control in the classroom. *Psychology in the Schools*, 1976, *13*, 449–453.

Sailor, W.; Guess, D.; & Baer, D. M. Functional language for verbally deficient children: An experimental program. *Mental Retardation*, 1973, *11*(3), 27–35.

Skinner, B. F. *Science and Human Behavior*. New York: Macmillan, 1953.

Smith, R. M., & Neisworth, J. T. *The Exceptional Child*. New York: McGraw-Hill, 1975.

Snell, M. E. (Ed.) *Systematic Instruction of the Moderately and Severely Handicapped*. Columbus, Ohio: Merrill, 1978.

Song, A. Y., & Gandhi, R. An analysis of behavior during the acquisition and maintenance of phases of spoon-feeding skills of profound retardates. *Mental Retardation*, 1974, *12*,(1), 25–28.

Sulzer-Azaroff, B., & Mayer, G. R. *Applying Behavior Analysis Procedures with Children and Youth*. New York: Holt, Rinehart & Winston, 1977.

Thoreson, C. *The Behavior Therapist*. Monterey, Calif.: Brooks/Cole, 1980.

White, O. R., & Haring, N. G. *Exceptional Teaching: A Multimedia Training Package*. Columbus, Ohio: Merrill, 1976.

Wolf, M. M.; Risley, T. R.; & Mees, H. L. Application of operant conditioning procedures to the behavior problems of an autistic child. *Behavior Research and Therapy*, 1964, *1*, 305–312.

BILINGUAL EDUCATION

Although many educational theories or programs have evoked controversy among educators, teachers, and the public, probably few of them have aroused such passionate attacks and defenses as has bilingual education. Since language must be used to teach students, and since language includes social and cultural values, teaching children in a language other than English will inevitably catch the attention of an English-speaking public. Although bilingual education is not a new phenomenon in education, it is only in the past ten or so years that the controversy surrounding it has escalated to its current level. The debate for the eighties appears to focus on the question of whether bilingual education is sufficiently effective to accomplish the goals of providing children with equal opportunity for education, however limited their knowledge of English.

Glazer (1981) describes three different models that have been used by schools faced with numbers of immigrant children: positive hostility, official disinterest, and positive reinforcement. The model of positive hostility was found when laws forbade the use of any language but English in the schools, when children were punished for not speaking English, and when their language and backgrounds were ridiculed. Whether such officially outlawed practices still exist, no one speaks in favor of them. The model of official disinterest has a great deal of support. The United States, despite the non–English-speaking millions of people who emigrated, remained an English-speaking nation. Newspapers, churches, schools, and organizations using non-English languages flourished with little official notice either to encourage or hamper their use. Maintaining the switch to English; newspapers and schools disappeared, and churches and organizations moved into English. The positive reinforcement model is probably the dominant one among educators whom Glazer (1981) defines as those who think and write about schools and about education, but not among teachers, administrators, and school boards. There are simple educational as well as political arguments for the policy of positive encouragement, while the arguments on the other side are less well formulated.

Glazer sees the pressure for bilingualism and biculturalism coming from the Mexican-American and Puerto Rican communities; he does not see the same pressure coming from the several groups of Asian immigrants or from immigrants from other Latin American countries who see the schools as an assimilating agency. The issue is one in which educational arguments on either side will not determine the outcome, but one which will be settled in elections, in fights over legislation, and in the courts.

Historical Perspective. Bilingual education is almost as old as formal education itself and can be traced to the third century B.C. when Akkadian-speaking children in ancient Mesopotamia learned the unrelated Sumerian language for use in special formal, literary, and administrative contexts. European countries have had bilingual-education programs for centuries and have considered bilingual education as a form of elite education (Ferguson, 1977).

Probably every nation in the world has had some bilingual population served by bilingual education. Since the status of bilingualism varies from country to country, practices that succeed in one country may not necesarily succeed in another country (Andersson & Boyer, 1970).

During the period from 1830 to 1848, bilingual-education programs flourished in many localities in the United States. An Ohio law passed in 1839 allowed youth who wished to study in the German language to attend a German school. An 1840 amendment to the Cincinnati city charter mandated German schools for students who wished to learn German or German and English. Both Catholic and Protestant parochial German or German-English schools were established during this period; after 1848 public schools used German as the language of instruction either alone or with English. Midwestern school districts with German populations wanted to hire a German teacher without regard for the statutes. An 1872 Oregon law permitted monolingual German schools, and an 1887 Colorado law allowed bilingual public schools. The Missouri superintendent of public instruction complained in his 1887/88 report that in many German communities schoolteachers taught in German, thereby depriving American children of an education in English and necessitating their learning German. In 1889 he urged that the law specify the language of instruction for the public schools so that citizens would not have to initiate legal action to have their children taught in English. Similar situations prevailed in other states and territories. In the 1880s three factors weakened the German-English schools. The first attack was against teaching German in the public schools; the second attack focused on German Catholic schools, where nationality problems were intertwined with ecclesiastical problems; and the third attack was directed against Lutheran schools, when an 1889 law prescribed English as the language of instruction in nonpublic schools (Kloss, 1966).

The literature on the consequences of becoming bilingual goes back to the early twentieth century, according to Lambert (1977). The tone of the writings on the value of bilingualism was pessimistic through the 1930s, but it has been optimistic since the 1960s. Many of the early studies regarded negative findings, partly because factors such as social class background and educational opportunities were not controlled.

In an effort to meet the educational needs of the 21,000 Cuban refugee children arriving in Miami, the schools of Dade County, Florida, established a bilingual program in the Coral Way School in Miami in 1963. Half of the instruction was presented in Spanish by Cuban teachers, and half in English by American teachers (Rojas, 1966). An evaluation of achievement in language arts and mathematics revealed that the bilingual program was as effective as the regular program in English (Andersson & Boyer, 1970). Evidence accumulated since 1963 has revealed that children enrolled in the bilingual-education program have continued to achieve as well or better than children in the regular English program (Robinett, 1981).

Probably the most comprehensive treatment of bilingual education is found in the five-volume *Bilingual Education: Current Perspectives* (1977). Federal support for bilingual education began when the Elementary and Secondary Education Act (ESEA) of 1965 was amended by

Title VII, the Bilingual Education Act of 1968, which recognized that children whose native language was not English needed instructional treatment different from that given to native English speakers (Saville & Troike, 1971).

Learning and Socialization Issues. A cursory review of two hundred years of official documents reveals that English has been the national language of the United States. Many immigrants found it necessary to learn English to become assimilated into the dominant society. Other non–English-speaking groups did not move to the United States, but were incorporated into it—native Americans, the Spanish in territory formerly Mexican, Acadian-French transplanted to Louisiana, and Puerto Ricans. Some speech communities have maintained their linguistic and cultural identity for generations. Children from unassimilated minorities face discouraging prospects unless problems concerning the language relations between majority institutions and minority groups are overcome. Saville-Troike (1973) details the language problems of several groups of bilingual children.

Language planning is usually considered an organized search for solutions to language problems at the national level. Paulston's model (1974) distinguishes between language cultivation, which deals with matters of language, and language policy, which deals with matters of society and nation. Determination, development, and implementation are all involved in both language cultivation and language policy. Official language choice and commitment to bilingual education, such as the Title VII Bilingual Education Act, are examples of determination. Development includes curriculum development and teacher training. Implementation attempts to achieve goals such as textbook distribution in both languages or even mass-media communication in both languages.

Language learning theory has implications for language planning. Teachers in bilingual-education programs need training in second language teaching in order to understand the linguistic difficulties of their students as well as the non–English-speaking child's socioeconomic and cultural background. What is known about language learning theory indicates that sociolinguistic problems must be studied in a sociolinguistic and anthropological framework.

Bilingual education results from societal factors, not from linguistic theory. If the sociohistorical, cultural, and political-economic factors that lead to bilingual education are not accounted for, the consequences of the education will be neither understood nor assessed (Paulston, 1977). Di Pietro (1973) also states that societal factors need to be considered when making decisions about bilingual education.

In an extensive review, Blanco (1977) found that most writers support the cognitive and affective purposes of bilingual education rather than its linguistic aspect. Although the linguistic dimension is both basic and necessary to the concept of bilingual education, the goal is not to teach language but rather to enable children to acquire knowledge and skills through the language they know, and at the same time to learn English. If children of limited English-speaking ability progress more effectively with initial instruction in their native language, bilingual education can be justified. This assumption raises issues of a psychological nature concerning the interrelations between the child's proficiency in the two languages, cognitive development, and academic progress (Cummins, 1977).

Relating cognitive development theories to bilingualism is proposed by DeAvila and Duncan (1979) on the grounds that metacognition or metalinguistic awareness is not tied to any single language or set of sociocultural circumstances. The potential advancement of bilingual children should manifest itself in superior performance on general ability tasks such as intelligence, although variables such as cultural bias and variations in relative language proficiency may obscure the head start. Comparing monolingual and bilingual populations on verbal IQ without ensuring the linguistic proficiency equivalence of the groups, or comparing groups on verbal measures when the groups have not been equated for verbal proficiency, is questionable and probably invalid. Many studies that apply Piagetian constructs to the study of bilingualism have not controlled for the relative linguistic proficiency of the comparison groups and therefore support a negative view of bilingualism.

Legal Issues. Judicial actions have had a profound effect on bilingual education in the United States in mandating that non–English-speaking students must be offered educational programs that allow them an opportunity to learn. A number of judicial decisions have been handed down in the past several years. Teitelbaum and Hiller (1977) consider the 1974 *Lau* v. *Nichols* case the landmark in bilingual education because it brought to the courts the issue of whether non–English-speaking students receive an education free from unlawful discrimination when instructed in English, a language they do not understand.

In the *Lau* v. *Nichols* case, both the plaintiff and the San Francisco Unified School District agreed that 1,790 Chinese students suffered educationally because they received no services that met their linguistic needs. The plaintiffs claimed that the lack of programs for the linguistic minority students violated both Title VI of the Civil Rights Act and the equal protection clause of the Fourteenth Amendment. Their claims of educational exclusion were rejected by the federal district court, which ruled that the students' rights to an equal educational opportunity had been satisfied by the education offered to other students in the San Francisco District. The Ninth Court of Appeals affirmed, ruling that use of English does not constitute unlawful discrimination. However, the Supreme Court rejected the rulings of the lower courts that offering the same services to all students met the strictures of the equal protection clause and Title VI, instead relying on the Title VI regulations and guidelines that speak to equality in the offering and receipt of benefits. The Supreme Court decision did not mandate bilingual education programs. Justice Douglas wrote that there were several options and directed the San Francisco Board of Education to apply its expertise to the problem and rectify the situation.

Although the *Lau* ruling did not mandate bilingual education, two other decisions, *Serna* v. *Portales Municipal Schools* and *Aspira of New York, Inc.* v. *Board of Education of the City of New York* did mandate bilingual programs. The *Rios* v. *Read* decision amplified the holding of *Lau* and discussed the school's responsibilities by stating that the simple provision of programs without demonstrating the quality of those programs was insufficient. A fourth decision, *Otero* v. *Mesa County Valley School District*, rejected all claims of national origin discrimination and found no *Lau* violations.

In the *Cintron* v. *Brentwood Union Free School District*, the district court held that the plan for students of limited English-speaking ability must be bilingual and bicultural with instruction by competent bilingual teachers in the subject matter of the curriculum. In the 1978 *Guadalupe Organization, Inc.* v. *Tempe Elementary School District Number 3*, the district court ruled against a group of Mexican-American and Yaqui children who sought to compel the Tempe district to provide non–English-speaking students with bilingual-bicultural education. The Ninth Court of Appeals, in affirming the decision, found that the district fulfilled its equal protection duty to the children when it adopted measures, short of bilingual education, to cure their language deficiencies ("Bilingual Education: A Review of Cases," 1980).

Two cases that raised issues of native American bilingualism, *Sinajini* v. *San Juan School District* and *Denetclarence* v. *Board of Independent School District Number 22.*, ended in consent decrees, but neither case was concerned exclusively with bilingual education. The spread of bilingual education in reservation schools has resulted not so much from litigation related to bilingualism as from the efforts of the Indian nations, both in and out of court, to establish and strengthen their political sovereignty.

The basis of the controversy over court-ordered bilingual programs is the effort to balance the command that unlawful discrimination must be swiftly and effectively remedied against the Supreme Court's admonition that judges are not educators (Teitelbaum & Hiller, 1977). The major impetus for bilingual education in the United States came as a result of the *Lau* decision and other legal decisions. Educational implications of the *Lau* ruling focus on the matter of providing educational programs that allow non–English-speaking students an opportunity to learn. The question asked of researchers in bilingual education is whether bilingual education programs help students to achieve in academic areas.

Studies of Educational Effects. Although many articles about bilingual education have been published in journals, the number of reported studies on bilingual education is small. The ESEA Title VII Bilingual Education Program was established by Congress in 1968 to meet the needs of students of limited English-speaking ability and to enable them to achieve competence in English. The first national evaluation of this federally funded program was begun in 1974. The American Institutes for Research (AIR) study had as its goal the evaluation of the impact of the Title VII program rather than the evaluation of individual projects.

The American Institutes for Research study. The Spanish-English bilingual projects evaluated were in either their fourth or fifth year of funding in the fall of 1975. The performance of students in the Title VII projects was contrasted with that of comparable students not enrolled in such projects. The four areas of student achievement assessed were English language arts, mathematics, student attitudes, and Spanish language arts. Tests in each of the areas were administered to each child in the language deemed most appropriate by the child's teacher. Approximately 74 percent of the third-graders and three-fourths of the fourth-graders, fifth-graders and sixth-graders were judged by their teachers to be either English monolingual or English-dominant bilingual. Investigators found that generally less than one-third of the students in the Title VII classroom were there because of their need for English instruction as judged by the classroom teacher. Thirty-five percent of the Hispanic students were in second-grade Title VII classrooms because of their need for English instruction.

One goal of the impact study was to determine educational practices in the Title VII projects. In response to the question of what happened to the Spanish-dominant children after they were able to function in English, 86 percent reported that students remained in the bilingual project; 8 percent reported that students were transferred to an English classroom with some Spanish language follow-up; and 5 percent that students were transferred to an English classroom with no Spanish language maintenance. Danoff (1978) said that the findings reflected Title VII project activities that were counter to the transition approach strongly implied by the authorizing legislation; project goals were more consistent with the maintenance approach. The majority of the teachers and aides in the projects were bilingual; 67 percent of the teachers and 90 percent of the aides said they used both Spanish and English in the home, and 50 percent of the teachers and 66 percent of the aides said they were proficient in both languages.

Analysis of the second-grade through sixth-grade sample from fall 1975 to spring 1976 showed that the Title VII program did not appear to have a significant impact on student achievement in English language arts and mathematics. Comparisons, across grades, of total Title VII and non–Title VII students revealed that the Title VII students were performing in English less well than the non–Title VII students. In mathematics, both groups performed at about the same level. On national norms, Title VII students were at about the 20th percentile in English reading and about the 30th percentile in mathematics.

Participation in the program did not bring about a more positive attitude toward school and school-related activities. The extent of grouping—forming smaller subgroups of students within the class for instructional purposes— was significantly and positively related to gains in English, math, Spanish as a second language, and overall gains in student achievement. Apparently the more groups or the more individualized the instruction in mathematics, the greater were the gains. There was a consistent positive relationship between number of small groups and gains in Spanish as measured by second-language test scores; the greater the number of different groups and regrouping of the same students, the greater the gains in student achievement.

There was no consistent relationship across grades between any of the gains in student achievement or attitudes and the proportion of Hispanic students in the classroom. The degree to which English was used in the home and neighborhood had no consistent relationship to gains in student test scores in English, Spanish, or mathematics, or in attitudes across grades. Apparently neither overall teaching qualifications of teacher and teacher aide, nor bilingual teaching qualifications, nor bilinguality had much relationship across grades to student gain in English reading, English as a second language, mathematics, and Spanish reading; nor did these factors contribute to a more positive attitude on the part of the students toward school and school-related activities, English usage, or Spanish usage.

Santa Fe Title VII program. The findings of the AIR study aroused considerable discussion among both opponents and proponents of bilingual education. In a response to the study, Leyba (1978) reported a study of the Title VII bilingual education program in the Santa Fe schools in which the findings were at variance with three of the AIR conclusions. He noted that the project was identified by AIR as one of seven exemplary bilingual programs because of its sound evaluation and reporting system. The Santa Fe Title VII students showed, over time, increasing capability in English skills, mathematics, and especially reading. These students, over time, outperformed the non–Title VII Students in reading and mathematics. The AIR study reported that, compared to national norms, the Title VII Hispanic students performed at the 20th percentile in English reading and at the 30th percentile in mathematics. Over time, the Santa Fe Title VII students surpassed and/or matched national norms in reading and mathematics.

French immersion programs. Lambert, Tucker and their associates have reported extensively on immersion programs in Canada. In one study, (Bruck, Lambert, & Tucker, 1977) two forms of French immersion programs were studied by comparing two groups of seventh-grade students. The early French immersion program of one group included instruction in French in kindergarten and grade 1, with English introduced in the second and third grades, and both languages used after grade 3. The second group followed a traditional curriculum with a French-as-a-second-language component through grade 6 and then went into a one-year intensive French immersion program.

The data revealed that the level of French proficiency of the students in the early immersion program exceeded that of the students in the later immersion program. Intelligence test results indicated that the early immersion students represented a much broader range of scholastic and intellectual abilities than did the self-selected students in the later immersion program. The study did not address such questions as whether later immersion programs are suitable for all children or suitable only for children from relatively high IQ, upper-middle-class homes. The investigators warned that replication of the study is essential before concluding that either early or later immersion programs are viable alternatives for parents.

Cziko, Lambert, and Gutter (1980) noted the increase since 1965 in popularity of French immersion programs throughout Canada that have been extensively evaluated and found to be effective in fostering development of French language skills, with no detrimental effects on English language development or an academic or cognitive development. Findings of affective consequences were considerably less consistent. Cziko, Lambert, and Gutter (1980) studied the validity and usefulness of multidimensional scaling methodology (MDS) for determining students' perceptions of ethnolinguistic group differences attributable to background and school language program. Ethnic dissimilarity judgments of both Anglophone and Francophone children were compared to determine the way in which English-speaking and French-speaking Canadians perceived each other. They also explored the relationship between French immersion programs and students' perceptions and attitudes.

There was a consistent pattern in the final MDS configurations of the four groups of fifth-grade and sixth-grade English-speaking and French-speaking students, which the investigators interpreted as a reflection of the force of early socialization in Canada, where deep and real differences exist between English Canadians and French Canadians. Cziko, Lambert, and Gutter (1980) found that experience with the other group's language appeared to reduce the English-Canadian–French-Canadian gulf to a significant degree; they concluded that although nonschool factors may have contributed to the findings, the early immersion experience appears to have reduced the social distance between English Canadians and French Canadians, especially bilingual French Canadians.

Finnish immigrant children in Sweden. A study of Finnish immigrant children in Sweden at preschool and junior levels was conducted over an eight-year period at the University of Lund. Its purpose was to give Finnish immigrant children with home languages other than Swedish educational and developmental opportunities on a level with those of Swedish children so that the Finnish immigrant children could become functionally bilingual. The term "functional bilingualism" implies that nonnative Swedish speakers can cope with various language situations as well as children who are native Swedish speakers.

Four groups of children were studied continuously in school achievement and linguistic and general development. The instructional model included a two-year, Finnish-speaking preschool and a two-year junior level or elementary school. Children spent three hours each day in the Finnish-speaking preschool with a "slice" of Swedish language instruction daily. The Finnish children who were integrated into Swedish parallel classes at the junior level were taught both in Finnish and Swedish, and initial reading and writing instruction was in Finnish. Since the model was aimed at a transition to regular Swedish instruction at grade 4, the number of Swedish-speaking periods was increased between grades 1 and 3.

The bilingual model that evolved in the project increased the prospects of the Finnish children becoming functionally bilingual. The identity of the children's first language was not a crucial factor in their educational achievement; their social environment and intellectual ability did more than purely linguistic factors to determine their success at school. The development of the immigrant children's Swedish proficiency was not a direct result of their level of first language proficiency. Instruction in the first language did not have a negative effect on the children's command of Swedish ("Models for the Bilingual Instruction of Immigrant Children," 1980).

Bilingual education programs usually operate on the assumption that teachers must not only be bilingual but must also know how to teach in both languages. The teacher's degree of proficiency in both languages and its relationship to student achievement generally has not been examined. In a study of teachers' Spanish proficiency and its relationship to student achievement, teachers' and aides' scores on a Spanish proficiency test were found to be significantly related to student gains in English. A subsequent study focused on the relationship of teaching behavior to student reading in Spanish and found a relationship between performance on the Teachers' Spanish Proficiency Test and pupil gains in reading (Merino, Politzer, & Ramirez, 1979).

Evaluation. Because little research has been conducted on the role of language input in language learning, characteristics of teachers' language and teaching behavior in third-grade and fifth-grade classes in both immersion and French schools in Montreal were examined by Hamayan and Tucker (1980). The two categories of teaching behaviors studied were general teaching strategies and reactions to students' errors. The extent to which each teaching strategy occurred did not vary as a function of group or grade level although some strategies such as questioning were used more frequently than others. The extent to which errors were ignored or corrected varied with linguistic group and grade level; the tendency to correct more of the errors of younger, second language learners than of younger, native language speakers was attributed to differences in teachers' expectations.

Troike (1978) blames the lack of federal funding for the very limited amount of research data available for determining the effectiveness of bilingual education. Of 150 evaluation reports surveyed by the Center for Applied Linguistics, only seven met minimal criteria for acceptability. Surveys by Dulay and Burt (cited in Troike, 1978) and by Zeppert and Cruz (1977) revealed similar findings. Despite the lack of research and inadequate program evaluation reports, Troike maintains that enough evidence exists that quality bilingual programs can meet the goals of providing equal educational opportunity for students for non–English-speaking backgrounds and cites twelve unpublished evaluations of Title VII programs as evidence. Two studies, one Navajo and one Spanish, are important in suggesting that bilingual instruction has a cumulative effect that probably will not be evident in short-term yearly evaluations.

In the study on the achievement of Finnish immigrant children in Sweden, Skuttnab-Kangas and Toukomaa (1976) found that if children immigrated to Sweden when they were of preschool or primary level age, they fell within the lower 10 percent of Swedish children in Swedish language skills. However, if they were 10 to 12 years of age when they immigrated and had had five to six years of education in their native language in Finland, they were much more likely to approach the norms of Swedish children when both were tested in Swedish. Achievement in mathematics, chemistry, and physics correlated highly with Finnish language skills. Similar anecdotal observations have been made of children immigrating from Mexico to the United States after sixth grade who acquire English quickly and soon outperform Chicano students who have been in U.S. schools since first grade. The results of the Finnish study constitute evidence that immersing children in another language before the age of 10 exerts a destabilizing effect on the development of their native language as a tool for cognitive organization, and they may fail to acquire the ability to use the second language for such purposes, becoming semilingual, or not fully competent to carry out complex cognitive operations in either language.

Although the findings of the Finnish study that the best educational solution might be to provide instruction in the child's native language for the first five grades appear to contradict the results of immersion programs for English speakers in Canada reported by Lambert and Tucker, Troike says that the probable explanation derives from the fact that both Finnish and Chicano children belong to dominated minorities. As they begin their education, such students are subjected to various forms of discrimination as well as disvaluation of their language and culture during a critical development period, whereas students who escape this experience quickly overcome the language barrier and are able to function successfully in their second language.

The difference may be ascribed to "subtractive versus additive bilingualism," as Lambert (1980) calls it. The social and cultural status of groups may be responsible. Children from middle-class supportive homes whose language and culture are not threatened have the greatest success in immersion programs. The Finnish research shows that children's competence in their native language declines sharply when they begin school in a second language, a situation characteristic of most linguistic minority groups in the United States.

Bilingual Education for Adults. Although bilingual-education programs are provided in elementary and secondary school, few such programs are available for adults. Adult basic education programs may include English as a Second Language (ESL) programs for adults, but adult bilingual-education programs are rare. One federally funded program for adults, bilingual vocational training authorized by Public Law 93-380, provides both job training and job-related ESL instruction. Evidence accumulated during the past five years reveals that the bilingual vocational training model has worked well with adults who had previously experienced failure because of their lack of English (Berry & Feldman, 1980). Although the funding level has been low ($2,800,000 each year), with few projects funded each year, some 7,200 unemployed or underemployed adults have received training during the five-year period. Many of these adults had been on welfare; few received unemployment benefits because they had never held jobs previously in the United States.

The significant difference between bilingual vocational training and bilingual-education programs is that bilingual vocational training combines ESL with skill training. Bilingual vocational training involves close day-to-day cooperation between the vocational teacher and the ESL teacher; often the ESL teacher attends the vocational class in order to determine the English requirements of the occupation that the trainee needs to learn. Job-related ESL differs from academic ESL in that the English learned by the trainees must be essential to the particular jobs for which they are being trained. Since programs propose to teach both English and an occupational skill in a nine-month period at the maximum, instruction must be concentrated. The individual proposing to acquire skills that will lead to employment must acquire certain specified job-related language skills required to function in an occupational environment (Galvan & Gunderson, in preparation).

One bilingual vocational training project that has accomplished its objective of training extremely limited English-speaking Chinese for employment in the restaurant industry is conducted by the China Institute in America. A continuous follow-up of former trainees reveals that of the 496 individuals trained during the five years of program operation, 95 percent have been employed in the restaurant industry, and none of them has gone on welfare. Thirty-one are restaurant owners, and the average salary of the trainee on a first job in June 1980 was $13,500 (*Bilingual Vocational Training Program,* 1980).

Social and Cognitive Effects. Some educators believe that although insufficient evidence exists to justify bilingual education on the basis that such programs help students to achieve academically, there are social values in bilingual education that serve to justify the programs. Others feel that the advantage of learning two languages outweighs the lack of increased academic achievement in bilingual-education programs.

Over 180 studies were evaluated on the basis of research design by Zeppert and Cruz (1977), who found that most of the reviews of bilingual-education research focused on historical, geographic, or treatment perspectives and did not include a systematic assessment of the quality and applicability of the research to a discussion of the effects of bilingual education on student performance. They established six criteria for excluding studies that demonstrated one or more methodological weaknesses and rejected 105 of 108 project evaluations and 67 of 76 research studies.

The few studies not rejected showed a significant positive or nonsignificant effect on student performance. A nonsignificant effect was not considered to be a negative finding since students in bilingual classes learn at the same rate as students in monolingual classes, demonstrating that learning in two languages does not interfere with a student's academic and cognitive performance. Since students in bilingual classes have the advantage of learning a second language and culture without impeding their educational progress, Zeppert and Cruz postulated that a nonsignificant finding could be interpreted as a positive effect of bilingual education. They concluded that the research they examined was not contradictory with regard to the effects of bilingualism and bilingual education on student performance, and supported the use of a child's native language as a medium of instruction.

The role of language in bilingual classrooms is particularly significant because of the deliberate attempts to manipulate the use of two languages in the instructional process. Ramirez (1979) looked at sixteen studies concerned with the role of language in bilingual classrooms and found that the studies on classroom discourse concentrated on language use without relating it to school performance. Only one study related language-use patterns to pupil gains in English oral comprehension.

Garcia (1979) studied the language-use patterns of a small sample of mothers and children in a bilingual preschool in which a Spanish immersion program was implemented during free-play sessions to test the influence of immersion techniques in the preschool situation. The preschool considered bilingualism to be its most important function; the subjects from a low socioeconomic background described their homes as bilingual. Findings indicated that while mothers—who served on a rotating basis as teachers—used both languages, children used English primarily, especially during free play sessions. Results of criterion-reference tests revealed that children were acquiring curriculum material in both languages. Although both mothers' and children's use of Spanish increased substantially during free-play sessions when immersion procedures were used, there were no changes in use of English outside the free-play situation during the immersion period. There appeared to be no substitution effect; English did not suffer as a result of the increase in Spanish, and the children's Spanish usage never increased to high levels.

The relationship between degree of bilingualism and cognitive functioning was investigated by assessing the English-Spanish proficiency of four groups of Hispanic children in grades 1 and 3 in rural and urban communities. Findings revealed a positive, monotonic relationship between degree of relative linguistic proficiency and cognitive functioning; the more proficient the children were in both languages, the better they performed on dependent measures (Duncan & DeAvila, 1979).

Although the literature on immersion programs for English-speaking children in Canada reports educational values, Lambert (1980) considers the most exciting aspect of such programs to be the opportunity for children to open their minds and make fairer evaluations of an otherwise foreign and possibly threatening out-group and to realize that peaceful, democratic coexistence among members of distinctive ethnolinguistic groups calls for more than learning one another's languages. He recommends that immersion schooling should be conducted in the home language of the ethnolinguistic-minority child for three to four years or until the child's language can flourish on its own; then the child should begin bilingual or entirely English instruction. The plan, however, will work only if the mainstream child is simultaneously developing skills in and appreciation for at least one of these languages and its associated culture, and if no time is taken from developing competence in the content subjects of science, mathematics, and language arts.

The president of the Carnegie Corporation in his 1979 annual report called attention to the controversy surrounding bilingual education. He speculates that three factors are responsible for the passionate debate about bilingual education. First, public perceptions about the record of accomplishment, particularly the lack of evaluation studies, have led critics to conclude that the concept, as opposed to the implementation, is unsound. Second, the apparent departure of bilingual education from the traditional language policy of the schools challenges assumptions and practices about cultural assimilation. Third, Pifer (1980) says that these two concerns probably would not be as great if bilingual education were not so closely associated in the minds of large segments of society with Hispanic Americans and seen as a strategy for realizing their

social, political, and economic aspirations. Pifer concludes that justification of the continuation of the bilingual-education experiment can come only with solid evidence that the technique is a means of achieving academic goals.

Federal Role. The Supreme Court in the *Lau* v. *Nichols* decision affirmed the responsibility of local school districts to comply with Title VI of the 1964 Civil Rights Act as well as the Department of Health, Education, and Welfare's (HEW's) regulations and guidelines requiring school districts to take affirmative action so that non–English-speaking children have equal access to educational opportunities offered to all other children. The under secretary of HEW discusses the Department's position on bilingual education, stating that the federal role was to assist states and local educational agencies in building their capacities to meet the needs of non–English-speaking and limited English-speaking children, and was not a service role to supplant state and local educational efforts. The under secretary (Carlucci, 1974) said in 1974 that the law (P.L. 93-380) clearly stated that the goal of federal bilingual programs is to demonstrate effective ways of providing instruction for children of limited English-speaking ability to enable them, while using their native language, to achieve competence in English so that they might enjoy equal educational opportunity. The goal is not to require cultural pluralism. The department position on bilingual education clearly was to support transitional rather than maintenance programs.

HEW published remedies to be used by schools in implementing the *Lau* decision. However, proposed rules were not published until August 1980 and required schools to teach children with little or no English in their native language so that they would not fall behind their classmates in academic instruction. The proposed rules received a great deal of attention in the popular press. The *Education Daily* reported on October 22, 1980, that the proposed rules had caused a rift between education and civil rights groups; educators complained that the proposed rules were too strict and infringed on local control of education, and civil rights groups criticized them as too weak and full of waivers. Although the Department of Education had planned to publish final rules in December 1980, Congress barred the department from issuing them for six months. The proposed rules were withdrawn by the secretary on February 2, 1981.

In 1976 the school system of Fairfax, Virginia, was told by the Office for Civil Rights that its ESL program for non-English-speaking children violated Title VI of the 1964 Civil Rights Act. However, on December 30, 1980, the Department of Education withdrew its objections and advised the school system that since the children in the ESL program were performing well as evidenced by test scores, the system did not have to provide bilingual classes for students of limited English-speaking ability.

Support as well as requirements for bilingual education come not only from the federal government but also from the states. More than half of the states and territories either require or permit bilingual-education programs.

Future Research. Cummins (1980) says that research has had very little impact on policy decisions in bilingual education because of the invalid theoretical assumptions with which the research findings have been approached. Researchers have not conceptualized the construct of language proficiency and its cross-lingual dimensions. Analysis of the development of language proficiency in bilingual children is of central importance in building a rationale for bilingual education and determining who needs it, why it is needed, and how children are identified. Cummins differentiates between what he terms "cognitive-academic language proficiency" (CALP), which refers to the dimension of language proficiency related to literacy skills, and "basic interpersonal communicative skills" (BICS), which refers to cognitively undemanding manifestations of language proficiency in interpersonal situations or natural communications.

Placing bilingual children in different types of instructional programs should not only be based on natural communication (BICS) tasks, but the development level of first and second language CALP should also be considered. The linguistic mismatch hypothesis is inadequate for determining entry criteria for bilingual programs since it focuses only on surface differences between first and second language, and not only ignores CALP but also the sociocultural determinants of minority children's poor academic performance. The exit policy based on the assumption that mainstreaming minority children out of a bilingual program into an English program will promote development of English literacy skills more effectively than a bilingual program is contrary to empirical research showing that minority children in bilingual programs tend to reach grade norms in English reading only in the later grades of elementary school (Cummins, 1980).

Perhaps the most important thing that can be said about bilingual education is that a great deal of research needs to be conducted. Troike (1978) has noted that the state of the art remains distressingly primitive. While the guarded conclusion of many educational researchers often suggests replication or further study of any particular problem or topic, this conclusion is overwhelmingly true of bilingual-education research. Longitudinal studies, as tightly controlled as possible, to determine the effects of bilingual education on student achievement are needed; they would address the matter of cumulative effect suggested by Troike (1978). The assertion that children in bilingual programs receive educational, psychological, social, and cultural benefits must be reinforced by hard data.

Studies in bilingual education have examined a single component of the program instead of looking at a total program with all the necessary components in place. Language development in bilingual education must be based on the principles of language development and psycholinguistics, and the language development base should focus on the purpose of language use in school. Although ESL is assumed to be a part of a bilingual program, the very important role of ESL within bilingual education has not been studied. The amount of native language maintenance necessary in transitional bilingual programs should be examined.

In a comprehensive review of research, Blanco (1977) says that although there is insufficient research documenting the effects of bilingual education, there is no research to substantiate the claim that bilingual education and bilingualism are harmful. Moreover, the available research indicates that bilingual education is either beneficial or neutral in terms of scholastic achievement, giving the student the added advantage of exposure to two languages.

It is claimed that bilingual education not only removes impediments that stand in the way of non–English-speaking children in school but also provides them with educational programs that enable them to compete with language-majority children. If this claim is to hold, data must be generated to substantiate it and to demonstrate conclusively that bilingual-education programs work.

Doris V. Gunderson

See also Culture and Education Policy; English Language Education; Hispanic-American Education; Language Development; Multicultural and Minority Education; Second Language Acquisition.

REFERENCES

Andersson, T., & Boyer, M. *Bilingual Schooling in the United States.* Austin, Tex.: Southwest Educational Development Laboratory, 1970. (ERIC Document Reproduction Service No. ED 039 527)

Berry D. W., & Feldman, M. A. *Evaluation of the Status and Effects of Bilingual Vocational Training* (Final report). Washington, D.C.: Kirschner Associates, Inc., 1980. (ERIC Document Reproduction Service No. ED 192 625)

Bilingual Education: Current Perspectives (5 vols.). Arlington, Va.: Center for Applied Linguistics, 1977. (ERIC Document Reproduction Service Nos. ED 142 074, ED 142 073, ED 144 378, ED 146 822)

Bilingual education–A review of cases. *Education Times*, September 1980, *1*(35), 6.

Bilingual Vocational Training Program for Chinese Chefs. New York: China Institute in America, 1980.

Blanco, G. The education perspective. In *Bilingual Education: Current Perspectives* (Vol. 4). Arlington, Va.: Center for Applied Linguistics, 1977, pp. 1–66.

Bruck, M.; Lambert, W. E.; & Tucker, G. R. Alternative forms of immersion for second language teaching. *Journal of the National Association for Bilingual Education*, 1977, *1*(3), 33–48.

Carlucci, F. *Departmental Position on Bilingual Education.* Washington, D.C.: Department of Health, Welfare, and Education, 1974. (Mimeo)

Cummins, J. Psycholinguistic evidence. In *Bilingual Education: Current Perspectives* (Vol. 4). Arlington, Va.: Center for Applied Linguistics, 1977, pp. 78–89. (ERIC Document Reproduction Service No. ED 146 822)

Cummins, J. The entry and exit fallacy in bilingual education.

Journal of the National Association for Bilingual Education, 1980, *4*(3), 25–59.

Cziko, G. A.; Lambert, W. E.; & Gutter, R. French immersion programs and students' social attitudes: a multidimensional investigation. *Journal of the National Association for Bilingual Education,* 1980, *4*(2), 19–33. (ERIC Document Reproduction Service No. ED 184 341)

Danoff, M. N. *Evaluation of the Impact of ESEA Title VII Spanish/English Bilingual Education Program: Overview of Study and Findings.* Palo Alto, Calif.: American Institutes for Research, 1978. (ERIC Document Reproduction Service No. ED 154 634)

DeAvila, E., & Duncan, S. E. Bilingualism and the metaset. *Journal of the National Association for Bilingual Education,* 1979, *3*(2), 1–20.

DiPietro, R. J. Bilingualism and bidialectalism. In R. P. Fox (Ed.), *Essays on Teaching English as a Second Language.* Champaign, Ill.: National Council of Teachers of English, 1973, pp. 35–42. (ERIC Document Reproduction Service No. ED 061 824)

Duncan, S. E., & DeAvila, E. A. Bilingualism and cognition: some recent findings. *Journal of the National Association for Bilingual Education,* 1979, *4*(1), 15–50.

Ferguson, C. A. Linguistic theory. In *Bilingual Education: Current Perspectives* (Vol. 2). Arlington, Va.: Center for Applied Linguistics, 1977, 43–52. (ERIC Document Reproduction Service No. ED 142 073)

Galvan, M. M., & Gunderson, D. V. *Bilingual Vocational Education: Five Years.* In preparation for National Conference on Research in English, 1981.

Garcia, E. E. Bilingualism and schooling environments. *Journal of the National Association for Bilingual Education,* 1979, *4*(1), 1–13.

Glazer, N. Ethnicity and education: Some hard questions. *Phi Delta Kappan,* 1981, *62*(2).

Hamayan, E. V., & Tucker, G. R. Language input in the bilingual classroom and its relationship to second language achievement. *Teachers of English to Speakers of Other Languages Quarterly,* 1980, *14*(4).

Kloss, H. German-American language maintenance efforts. In J. A. Fishman (Ed.), *Language Loyalty in the United States.* The Hague: Mouton, 1966, pp. 206–252.

Lambert, W. E. The effects of bilingualism on the individual: Cognitive and sociocultural consequences. In P. A. Hornby (Ed.), *Bilingualism: Psychological, Social, and Educational Implications.* New York: Academic Press, 1977, pp. 15–27.

Lambert, W. E. The two faces of bilingual education. *Focus.* Rosslyn, Va.: National Clearinghouse for Bilingual Education, August 1980, *3*(3), pp. 1–4.

Leyba, C. F. *Longitudinal Study of Title VII Bilingual Program: Santa Fe Public Schools.* Los Angeles: California State University, National Dissemination and Assessment Center, 1978. (ERIC Document Reproduction Service No. ED 161 275)

Merino, B. J.; Politzer, R.; & Ramirez, A. The relationship of teachers' Spanish proficiency to pupils' achievement. *Journal of the National Association for Bilingual Education,* 1979, *3*(2), 21–37.

Models for the bilingual instruction of immigrant children. *School Research Newsletter.* Stockholm: National Board of Education, 1980. (ERIC Document Reproduction Service No. ED 196 529)

Paulston, C. B. *Implications of Language Learning Theory for Language Planning: Concerns in Bilingual Education.* Arling-ton, Va.: Center for Applied Linguistics, 1974. (ERIC Document Reproduction Service No. ED 102 866)

Paulston, C. B. Research. In *Bilingual Education: Current Perspectives* (Vol. 2). Arlington, Va.: Center for Applied Linguistics, 1977, pp. 87–126. (ERIC Document Reproduction Service No. ED 142 073)

Pifer, Alan. *Bilingual Education and the Hispanic Challenge.* Reprinted from 1979 Annual Report, Carnegie Corporation, 1980. (ERIC Document Reproduction Service No. ED 190 336)

Ramirez, A. G. Language in bilingual classrooms. *Journal of the National Association for Bilingual Education,* 1979, *4*(3), 61–79.

Robinett, R. Personal communication. March 10, 1981.

Rojas, P. The Miami experience in bilingual education. *On Teaching English to Speakers of Other Languages* (Series II). Champaign, Ill.: National Council of Teachers of English, 1966, pp. 43–45. (ERIC Document Reproduction Service No. ED 034 202)

Saville, M. R., & Troike, R. C. *A Handbook of Bilingual Education* (Rev. ed.). Washington, D.C.: Teachers of English to Speakers of Other Languages, 1971. (ERIC Document Reproduction Service No. ED 035 877)

Saville-Troike, M. *Bilingual Children: A Resource Document.* Arlington, Va.: Center for Applied Linguistics, 1973. (ERIC Document Reproduction. Service Nos. ED 102 867 and ED 082 584)

Skuttnab-Kangas, T., & Toukomaa, P. *Teaching Migrant Children's Mother Tongue and Learning the Language of the Host Country in the Context of the Socio-cultural Situation of the Migrant Family.* Helsinki: Finnish National Commission for UNESCO, 1976.

Teitelbaum, H., & Hiller, R. J. Bilingual education: The legal mandate. *Harvard Educational Review,* 1977, *24*(2), 138–170.

Troike, R. C. *Research Evidence for the Effectiveness of Bilingual Education.* Arlington, Va.: National Clearinghouse for Bilingual Education, 1978. (ERIC Document Reproduction Service No. ED 159 900)

Troike, R. C., & Perez, E. At the crossroads. In *Bilingual Education: Current Perspectives* (Vol. 5). Arlington, Va.: Center for Applied Linguistics, 1978, pp. 63–81.

Zeppert, L. T., & Cruz, B. R. *Bilingual Education: An Appraisal of Empirical Research.* Berkeley, Calif.: Bay Area Bilingual Education League/Lau Center, 1977. (ERIC Document Reproduction Service No. ED 153 758)

BIOLOGICAL BASIS OF LEARNING

See Cognition and Memory; Learning; Neurosciences.

BLACK EDUCATION

Black education must be put in historical perspective and looked at in the context of the discrimination and ignorance perpetuated by the American public school system since its beginnings.

Historical Background. American educational policy for slave children was "compulsory ignorance" (Simpson,

1865). In 1740, South Carolina adopted the first compulsory ignorance law in America, which stated that any person who taught slaves to write or employed slaves as scribes would, for every offense, forfeit the sum of £100. (Klingberg, 1941).

Such laws or stronger ones were adopted in one state after another. In 1823, Mississippi outlawed any gathering of six or more Negroes for educational purposes. An 1830 law in Louisiana prescribed imprisonment of from one to twelve months for anyone teaching a slave to read or write (Woodson, 1919). Virginia adopted laws in 1819 and 1831 forbidding meetings to instruct Negroes. Compulsory ignorance laws of North Carolina, enacted in 1831 and 1832, precluded slaves freed after those dates from learning to read and write. In spite of this, some slaves attempted to educate their children in secret schools. "Clandestine schools were in operation in most of the large cities and towns of the South where such enlightenment of the Negroes was prohibited by law" (Woodson, 1936, p. 319). In the Deep South, however, in such states as Alabama and Mississippi, there is virtually no evidence that secret schools for slaves existed during this period. In 1834, James G. Birney, a slaveholder turned abolitionist, reported that day schools for free Negroes existed in Lexington and Louisville, Kentucky, but that no slaves were enrolled (Birney, 1834).

Of special note is the comparison between the education of slaves and that of free Negroes during the period 1800–1860. The ratio of slaves to free Negroes was 9:1 during this time. (U.S. Bureau of the Census, 1960). Since the free Negroes' educational future lay outside the planters' direct authority, the regulation of their education was a matter of legislation and public administration. "Free Negroes in the South gained their education through one or more of the following: (1) public schools, (2) secret and other private schools, (3) Sabbath schools, (4) apprenticeship, and (5) special treaty requirements" (Weinberg, 1977, p. 15). "Free Negroes in the sixteen slave states, but concentrated in the upper South and border states, enrolled 4,114 children in public schools in 1850 and only 3,661 ten years later" (Woodson, 1919, pp. 237–240).

In the North on the eve of the Civil War, there were 250,000 free blacks, concentrated primarily in a small number of urban centers. These black communities were distinctive in that they were organized and had as their major purpose to search for educational opportunities for their children. Although black life in the North was distinctly better than in the South (because of greater physical mobility and increased communication by the black and abolitionist press), black children in general were excluded from the public schools. Nowhere in the North was systematic and widespread schooling provided for blacks. New England provided public schools, but few free black children attended them. Except for places like New Bedford, Massachusetts, where schools were never segregated by race, the New England states, especially Connecticut, were inhospitable to black people (Richards, 1970). Although the 1784 Rhode Island Emancipation Bill made it compulsory to teach freed Negro children to read and write, the provision was not enforced. An Ohio law for a common school system, passed in 1829, explicitly excluded Negro children. In Pennsylvania, blacks' right to vote, which had been exercised for many years, was withdrawn in 1838. Thereafter, black children were excluded from Pennsylvania public schools.

Despite racism and discrimination, black parents in the North established private schools for their children. Such schools existed in Philadelphia as early as 1797. The African free schools operated in cities such as Portland, Maine; Boston, Massachusetts; New Haven, Connecticut; and New York City (*Freedom's Journal*, 1827; cited in Dann, 1971). Because of the poverty of blacks, these schools could offer only a minimal program even though they were aided from time to time by white abolitionists. The schools lacked materials and books, operated for only a short time during the year, and were located in basements and spare rooms. The obvious answer to these problems was public funds, but white society did not acknowledge widely the necessity of educating black children and was therefore unwilling to provide public funds. Black children were physically attacked, and black schools were burned. Blacks attempting to educate their children were faced with hostility and racism.

From 1845 to 1860 the most pressing problem for blacks in the North was segregation and discrimination in the public schools. This segregation included segregation inside formally nonsegregated schools. Black opposition to segregation was community-wide. There were mass meetings, black boycotts, and court cases in such places as Boston, Massachusetts, and Buffalo and Rochester, New York.

Exclusion of black children from school continued after the Civil War until 1867, when blacks were given equal rights in accord with the Fourteenth Amendment. The amendment appeared to insure the status of blacks as free citizens, since no state would dare deny opportunities to blacks. Thus, by 1870 every southern state had created a public school system financed by a state fund. In the South blacks attended regularly and in large numbers, and by 1880 a third of all black children in the United States were enrolled in public schools.

Still, numerous efforts were made to evade the new constitutional requirements. It was popular for states to establish dual systems financed by separate taxes paid by each racial group. Since whites were far wealthier than blacks, inequality in the schools was ensured. By the end of the 1870s, expenditures that had been almost equal in 1875 had become markedly unequal (Du Bois, 1901). In 1883 in Kentucky (*Claybrook* v. *Owensboro,* 16 Fed. R. 302) and in 1886 in North Carolina (*Puitt* v. *Commissioners,* 94 N.C. 519), blacks brought suit against the state, arguing that disparities in financial support of education for black and white children violated the equal protection requirement of the Fourteenth Amendment to the Constitution. The decisions in these cases *appeared* to promote equality of treatment of black and white children; however, equal treatment of the races was required only with respect to allocation of school funds by the state, while local government agencies were left unregulated. There were other cases, but in general the Fourteenth Amendment became the framework for planned educational deprivation administered in the name of states' rights.

Between 1896 and 1899 the U.S. Supreme Court approved the principles of compulsory segregation and the near inviolability of state control of education. In both *Plessy* v. *Ferguson* (163 U.S. 537, 1896), in which the Court ruled that racial separation in public facilities was constitutional so long as the separate facilities were equal, and the *Cumming* case in 1899 (*Cumming* v. *County Board of Education,* 175 U.S. 545), where the Court found no constitutional violation when a Georgia school board closed down the black high school but continued to operate the white one, the Supreme Court created the legal base for segregated schools. After 1900, black schools fell far behind white schools, and by 1950 the difference in expenditures had grown from 50 percent to 300 percent. Minor gains by black schools came through campaigns by fledgling organizations such as the Urban League and through organized protests mounted by the National Association for the Advancement of Colored People (NAACP). But the pattern of inequality and segregation reinforced during Reconstruction was strengthened in the early twentieth century South. Whites operated the public schools as though they were private property, forcing blacks to create private schools as their public schools.

From 1865 to 1950 in the North, there were numerous court cases involving black children, but few resulted in the improvement of everyday practices. The overwhelming majority of black children attended separate schools. Although in some states there were laws forbidding segregation (Illinois in 1874 and New Jersey in 1881), black children were systematically excluded and/or segregated. Moreover, the legal challenges of black parents were virtually always turned away by the states.

In the 1920s many blacks moved to cities, and for the first time in American history the majority of black school-age children were no longer on farms but in urban areas. Improved schooling did not automatically result from this migration. As blacks moved to the cities, housing became more segregated, and in time the schools followed this pattern. The concentration of blacks in certain residential areas was a fact of American life both in the North and in the South. In the South it had no consequence with regard to schooling: assignment to a school was based on race, not residence. In the North both race and place were considered. From 1865 to 1920 northern courts approved the use of residence as the assignment criterion for white children and race as the assignment criterion for black children. Whites attended the nearest school, and blacks attended the black school, wherever it was located. By 1960 American cities and public schools had become highly segregated. Where black children did attend non-

segregated schools, they were subjected to many cruelties and many forms of discrimination.

Midcentury marked a turning point in the history of black America and black education, with the emergence of black leaders such as A. Philip Randolph of the Brotherhood of Sleeping Car Porters, Whitney Young of the Urban League, Roy Wilkins of the NAACP, and Martin Luther King, Jr., of the Southern Christian Leadership Conference. Their leadership was supported by the involvement of unprecedented numbers of blacks. As a result, the fight for equality became national in scope. There was a persistent black initiative that forced a reformulation of public policies in education. In 1954 the Supreme Court ruled:

In the field of public education the doctrine of "separate but equal" has no place. Separate educational facilities are inherently unequal. . . . We hold that the plaintiffs and others similarly situated . . . are, by reason of the segregation complained of, deprived of the equal protection of the laws guaranteed by the Fourteenth Amendment. (*Brown* v. *Board of Education* (I), 347 U.S. 483 at 495, 1955.)

Although the case of *Brown* v. *Board of Education* (1955) had structural weaknesses, black parents supported by black organizations seized the chance for equal education. Nevertheless, the nation was still reluctant to move toward equality of opportunity. The result was a mass movement of protesting blacks led by Martin Luther King, Jr., during the early 1960s. Blacks in the North and in the South participated in the movement.

The Civil Rights Act of 1964 was a direct result of the black revolution of the 1960s. In November 1965, President Johnson asked the United States Commission on Civil Rights to report on race and education. The report (United States Commission on Civil Rights, 1967) confirmed that "American public education remains largely unequal in most regions of the country, including all those where Negroes form any significant proportion of the population. . . . the great majority of American children attend schools that are largely segregated—that is, almost all of their fellow students are of the same racial background as they are" (Coleman et al., 1966).

Title IV of the Civil Rights Act authorized the United States Commissioner of Education to help schools desegregate. The attorney general was empowered to bring about lawsuits to institute desegregation. Black parents in the North had been suing school boards for more than a century concerning overt discrimination. No such case had ever been considered by the Supreme Court. Following the *Brown* decision, northern school boards and their attorneys formulated a legal doctrine that asserted a sharp distinction between *de jure* and *de facto* segregation. One was conscious in design, while the other was neutral and impersonal. The *de facto* doctrine was weak, and the most serious blows to school boards in the North came from court decisions that found their districts guilty of *de jure* segregation.

In 1964, at the time that the Civil Rights Act was

drafted, school desegregation was seen exclusively as a southern problem, and the solution was seen as the development of desegregation plans based on pupil reassignment. By 1970, however, most southern school districts were desegregated physically, and attention began to focus on *de facto* segregation in the North (McConany, 1978). The focus on the North emerged as two interrelated shifts in the civil rights movement influenced attitudes toward racial issues. The first was a shift from the South to the rest of the nation. As long as the civil rights movement remained principally in the South, northern whites were real, even if somewhat reluctant, allies of the blacks. The second shift was from issues of freedom to those of equality. Northerners began to see the civil rights movement as a threat (i.e., as a demand for equality rather than for freedom), and this dampened the enthusiasm of their support, helped to create antiblack feelings, and stimulated the advocacy of laissez-faire doctrines of government and "traditional" values.

Clearly, the most controversial issue associated with desegregation is busing. Although two-thirds of the American public approve of desegregated schools, over two-thirds of the public concurrently oppose busing as a means to achieve desegregated schools. An interesting point of view is that of Scherer and Stanski (1979), who believe that school desegregation should be viewed as a process rather than as an event. To view school desegregation as an event is to see the racial mixing of students as a straightforward, lockstep procedure aimed only at racial balance. In contrast, to look at school desegregation as a process is to have a phenomenological view of desegregation as part of the evolution of race relations in American society as a whole, as well as in the schools.

Although a number of researchers and individuals actually engaged in working toward desegregation contend that courts have tended to view desegregation as an event rather than as a process, there is evidence that courts have also viewed desegregation in the broader context. *Millikin II* (97 S. Ct. 2749, 1977), the Supreme Court's second Detroit decision, is a case in point. This decision was characterized by von Euler and Parham (1978) as a landmark case that set judicial precedent because it addressed educational concerns in the context of school desegregation. In brief, desegregation efforts can address the broader issues of quality education.

Role of Testing. The issue of quality education that was raised by the struggle to integrate the public schools leads us to examine other issues important to black education. One of the most controversial and complex issues has been educational and psychological testing, particularly as it affects the assessment of individual intelligence. It is ironic that the nation that gave birth to the world's first system of common schools found few defenders of that system to champion the cause of minority children, especially black children. Belief in the intellectual inferiority of blacks was extremely common both among the politicians who created legislation for education and among

the educators who created the system of education. Two outstanding examples of believers in black inferiority are Thomas Jefferson and Horace Mann. Jordan (1968) points out that Jefferson, more than any other person, framed the terms of the debate on mental capacity. "Comparing them by their faculties of memory, reason, and imagination, it appears to me, that in memory they are equal to whites; in reason much inferior, . . . and that in imagination they are dull, tasteless, and anomalous" (Jefferson, 1955, [1787], pp. 138, 139). In 1851, Mann wrote: "In line, I suppose the almost universal opinion to be, that, in intellect, the blacks were inferior to the whites; while in sentiment and affection, the whites were inferior to the blacks." (cited in Weinberg, 1977, p. 31). These beliefs are embedded in the history of the education of black children. The defense of segregated schools in particular was based on the belief that black children were different. Historically, the belief in the intellectual inferiority of blacks was the basis for their treatment in the area of education.

During World War I, testing shifted from individual to group tests, and the most frequently quoted data came from comparisons between black and white army recruits. A special committee appointed by the American Psychological Association developed the test known as the Army Alpha. Although the Army Alpha made little attempt to measure abilities independent of prior education, it quickly came to be regarded as an accurate measure of innate mental ability. The test items on the Army Alpha presented many problems to the black soldiers, and the Army Beta, a nonverbal test parallel to the Alpha, was even worse (Guthrie, 1981).

Since black psychologists were practically nonexistent during the 1920s, black educators had to lead the protest against the psychological testing movement. Most black educators belonged to the American Teachers Association (ATA) because they had been denied membership in southern National Education Association (NEA) chapters. Criticism of and discontent with the psychological testing of black children were inevitable. White behavioral scientists were unrestricted in administering tests in their search for group differences in IQ, and black educators and psychologists attacked the findings, which were based on questionable measuring instruments and influenced by the arrogance found among white researchers. The most vocal critic was Horace Mann Bond, a black educator who warned black people about the conclusions reached by white psychological examiners. Bond (1927) called for action by blacks against propaganda suggesting that the Negro is intellectually and physically inferior to others in society. He criticized the practice of generalizing on the basis of comparisons of unequal social groups.

From 1930 to 1960 only a few black students of psychology filtered through northern universities. It was not until the 1960s that a growing body of black professionals—through publications and black caucuses at professional meetings—challenged researchers in the fields of psychology, education, and mental health to reassess their roles in perpetuating biased attitudes and practices and to take a fresh look at long-standing presuppositions. Among the black caucuses that became formalized groups are the Association of Black Psychologists and the American Educational Research Association's group, Research Focus on Black Education.

The controversy over the intellectual inferiority of blacks resurfaced in the late 1960s when some social scientists reacted to the civil rights and black liberation movements by attempting to find scientific justification for racial intellectual inferiority. The controversy quickly became enmeshed in the tangle of political and social philosophies (Miller, 1974). Although the controversy concerned claims of racial differences in intelligence (Jensen, 1969), the issues clearly included testing, research, education, and public policy (Plotkin, 1974). A number of studies were widely publicized by the mass media. In 1969, Jensen asserted that intelligence is inherited and that whites inherit conceptual intelligence, while blacks are genetically capable of rote associative learning only. Herrnstein (1971) held that intelligence is inherited and high-paying jobs are held by persons of higher intellect. Therefore, higher social status can be traced to genetic endowment. Jencks (1972) dismissed schooling as irrelevant to the reduction of differences between blacks and whites in achievement. These studies met severe criticism (Deutsch & Deutsch, 1974).

Testing continues to be the most important issue affecting the education of black children. The function of assessment and the impact of testing on students are still not clearly understood. Educators and social and behavioral scientists, however, have changed their thinking on the major issues regarding testing. The heredity-versus-environment argument no longer receives the attention that it did in the early 1970s. The controversies and problems revolve around state education competency tests, standardized tests versus criterion-referenced tests, and the notion that schools should be held accountable for student learning and achievement. A National Institute of Education (1979) report on testing research suggests that educational tests are used in American education to hold teachers, schools, and school systems accountable; to make decisions concerning individual students; to evaluate educational innovations and experimental projects; and to provide guidance to teachers in the classroom. According to the report, major criticisms of tests include the following: (1) tests are not sensitive to the full range of student cultural backgrounds, and scoring is thus unfair to minority students; (2) tests have limited use in holding educators accountable; (3) tests limit classroom teaching; and (4) tests are too narrow to provide fair evaluations of new approaches to teaching. Contemporary literature on testing is primarily concerned with the use of tests, the effects that tests have on students in the classroom, accountability, competency testing and test items, and truth-in-testing laws.

Equal Educational Opportunity. An important issue in black education is that of equal educational opportunity.

This notion has changed radically in recent years and is likely to change further (Coleman, 1974). Although the concept of equal educational opportunity appears to have been accepted by American society, there has been and still is considerable controversy over some of the assumptions and interpretations made by social scientists and politicians. The report by Coleman et al. (1966) is a landmark in the history of social science, signaling a new relationship between social research and social policy (Grant, 1973). The report had its origins in the Civil Rights Act of 1964, amended section 402. The major findings of the study were that (1) schools account for only small differences in achievement, (2) achievement among minority groups is more dependent on schooling than it is among white children, and (3) a strong relationship exists between the achievement of Negro pupils and the educational backgrounds and aspirations of their fellow students. The report caused a stir of reactions from the press, from the United States Office of Education, and from researchers, educators, and politicians. From the very beginning and through the presidencies of Kennedy, Johnson, and Nixon, the report was influential in shaping social policy. Depending on how the findings were interpreted, the report was attacked, supported, or questioned. Daniel Moynihan had an early interest in the report because it seemed to confirm his theories about the importance of focusing on the family as the indicator of effectiveness of social policy (Moynihan & Mosteller, 1971). Moynihan pointed to the findings of the report in a number of articles and eventually advised a national policy of benign neglect for blacks, which became President Nixon's message on educational reform in March 1970. Thus, ironically, Moynihan probably had more to do with the way the report was received, analyzed, and used as an instrument of social policy than had Coleman himself (Grant, 1973).

A consequence of the difference of opinion on equality of opportunity was a change from assessing schools in the traditional way—looking at the quality of the plant, facilities, and the credentials of professional personnel—to measuring the performance of children who attend the school (Dyer & Rosenthal, 1971). This change in thinking was a product of the National Assessment Program and was reflected in the enactment of the Elementary and Secondary Education Act of 1965 and the Emergency School Aid Act of 1972, as well as in the Coleman report. This legislation included requirements that school systems assess by objective means their effect on student achievement (Miller, 1974). Despite the conclusions of the Coleman report that the socioeconomic status and therefore the race of a pupil's classmates is an important determinant in his academic achievement, the matter was disputed. Social scientists seemed to be at odds as they continued to attack the reliability of the Coleman report and the Moynihan and Mosteller studies, as well as the data on which they were based.

Deficit theory. Although desegregation and school achievement are important issues, there are other areas of concern in the education of black children. In the 1960s and 1970s a plethora of researchers and writers expounded on the notion that black students began school with deficits which resulted from both family and low socioeconomic circumstances. This is frequently called the "deficit theory." Generally, the proponents of this notion were white researchers and writers. The theory was elaborated in a variety of books, for example, *The Culturally Deprived Child* (Riessman, 1962). Researchers conducted many studies of contrasts between black and white achievement and aspirations, based on parental occupation, hue of skin, and age of children. Self-concept became the most frequently studied variable in investigations involving black children. In general, these studies concluded that black children had a negative image of themselves. A number of studies reported that black youths had lower academic and vocational aspirations as a result of their depressed social and personal conditions (Ausubel & Ausubel, 1963). In the 1970s, however, a number of researchers, particularly blacks, pointed to the fact that social scientists and researchers in the past had all but ignored the input of broad social factors on black or any other children.

Teacher expectation. Teacher expectation is another controversial issue related to the education of black children. A series of studies examined what has been called the "Pygmalion effect," a term applied to broadly analogical events in which the subject has a directing hand in producing the response he or she wishes from another person. The question is "Do students tend to fulfill expectations that teachers have for them, whether positive or negative?" Numerous research studies were carried out to evaluate this notion of teacher influence on student achievement. Most of these studies followed the work of Rosenthal and Jacobson (1968). Three formal studies of teacher expectancy in an interracial setting were reported. The findings suggested that black students were given less and ignored more, praised less and criticized more. In addition, gifted black children are the least praised and most criticized, even when compared with their nongifted black counterparts (Rubovits & Maehr, 1973; Johnson, 1974). In another study it was found that teachers related to the black children more negatively than to the white children and that the black children tended to be characterized more often as dull, passive, and unfriendly (Coates, 1972). To biased teachers, talented minority students contradict the stereotype that supposes an incapacity to learn. These studies supported the findings of the numerous other studies that pointed up the important role of teacher expectations in the classroom.

Race of the teacher. Given the history of black education, the question of the effect of the race of the teacher takes on special significance. Initially, the question made little sense. During the era of statutory segregation, black teachers were restricted to working in black schools. In the North, as late as the 1940s and 1950s most black teachers were in elementary schools. Few taught in high schools except those attended by a sizable number of black chil-

dren. In general, black children were taught by white teachers. During the 1960s, blacks charged that the largely white staff of public schools was insensitive to black children and uninterested in teaching them. Moreover, it was contended that black teachers were better prepared to teach black children.

It is important to note that most teachers are white, even in areas where minority students represent the bulk of the student population. In New York City, for example, only 18 percent of the teachers are members of minority groups. This is typical of large inner-city areas. Contemporary efforts to overcome this general disparity have been only moderately successful. In general, blacks contend that minority communities should have meaningful input in the staffing decisions of the schools where their children are being educated. Central to this demand is the desire to establish school employment as a possible career for black children.

Project Head Start. The War on Poverty, instituted by President Lyndon Johnson in 1964, included Head Start, which became an important factor in the education of black children. Blacks embraced Head Start as a compensatory educational program for low-income preschoolers and their families; they saw it as having the potential of substantially alleviating, if not eliminating, the causes of poverty. Head Start aimed at stimulation of children's social and cognitive development, provision of health services, and encouragement of parental involvement with children and in the community. Head Start programs were initiated in low-income communities all over the country and represented a major effort on the part of government to make up for the long history of unequal educational opportunities for blacks.

Unfortunately, the program stimulated another controversy in the history of educational policy. An evaluation (Cicirelli, 1967) of the effectiveness of the Head Start Program concluded that it had only a few weak and fleeting effects. The study argued that whatever gains were made in the program were lost when Head Start children returned to their regular schools. Largely as a result of this study, the criterion of success for an educational program became defined as cognitive development that is maintained by children long after they leave the program (Datta, 1976). The findings were extensively criticized on methodological grounds and by blacks who argued that it was not that the Head Start programs were weak, but that the schools to which the children returned were ineffective; thus, gains made by children were not capitalized on in the regular school.

The report also had a profound effect on the educational policies of the Nixon administration, which began to dismantle many antipoverty programs. Since that time, a number of researchers have concluded that early-intervention programs do provide benefits that endure. The Consortium on Developmental Continuity (1977), which consisted of twelve investigators who conducted experimental preschool intervention programs in the early and mid-1960s, contributed significantly to that assessment. The members pooled their data and collected common follow-up data in 1976 and 1977. The findings indicated that the preschool program directed by Consortium members had substantial and lasting effects on the school performance of low-income children. Children in the programs were more likely to meet the minimum requirements of their schools. They were also more likely to score higher on standardized math achievement tests in the fourth grade. In addition, the gains in intelligence scores achieved by children in preschool programs were maintained for at least three years after leaving the program (Consortium for Longitudinal Studies, 1978).

Black Higher Education. The history of blacks in higher education mirrors the history of their problems and progress in elementary and secondary education. Black higher education is characterized by the traditionally black colleges and universities that have successfully educated black youth for more than a century. These black schools have accepted students regardless of their level of preparedness and tailored their instruction according to their needs. Hence, black colleges reversed the tradition of exclusiveness that characterized higher education in general and originated the practice, if not the concept, of open enrollment. The original purpose of black schools was to mold former slaves and their children into people with the self-respect, dignity, and learning necessary for survival.

An early difference of opinion about the proper focus of black higher education was characterized by a running debate between Tuskegee's founder, Booker T. Washington, and W. E. B. Du Bois, who questioned whether vocational education was more efficacious than liberal arts training. Washington contended that vocational training suited the masses, while Du Bois advocated the development of a talented tenth to teach and lead other blacks. Whatever its focus, black higher education was strongly opposed by the white South. State legislatures and local school boards tended to ignore black efforts to establish schools, while some whites resorted to such drastic measures as beating teachers, burning black schools, and intimidating black students and their parents. Despite these vicious acts, most black colleges survived. Today, although black schools constitute only 3 percent of all United States colleges, they award close to 40 percent of the baccalaureates conferred on blacks in the United States.

In the North, as in the South, the pattern of racial discrimination was established among the foremost colleges and universities. In the early 1900s, misgivings about admitting blacks on the part of such universities as Harvard, Cornell, Columbia, and Chicago were not only held on academic grounds but were also concerned with the desirability of social contact between black and white students. Black enrollment in universities was highly concentrated. In 1928 approximately 1,200 of the 2,200 Negro college students in the North attended just ten institutions (*Crisis*, 1928). In 1947 the President's Commission on Higher Education sparked a national debate regarding discrimination and exclusionary enrollment practices in higher education with respect to blacks. The report, however, did not call for any legal action.

The maintenance of all-white faculties was a policy of northern colleges and universities. In 1940 only two or three black persons were employed in northern institutions of higher education. In 1940–1941, a national survey found no blacks holding tenured positions in any American universities except for those who taught at black institutions. There were efforts to improve the situation on the part of foundations that encouraged universities to employ more black staff members. The situation changed very slowly, but the numbers continued to rise, and by 1958 there were 200 blacks who taught in white institutions. By 1960 about 3 percent of all college instructors were black.

The lack of black faculty was primarily the result of exclusionary policies by white institutions. White faculty members protested the hiring of black faculty and suggested that white students would withdraw if blacks were appointed. However, black professors who were appointed were generally accepted by white students. This was not the case, however, with the white professors, who proved to be a problem for black professors.

The small number of black faculty in higher education is related to blacks' problems in obtaining a graduate education. The black schools in the South were in many cases prevented from offering graduate programs by the insufficiency of the funds supplied by southern state legislatures. In the North, blacks were discouraged from enrolling in certain courses and in certain fields at the graduate level. Such exclusion was common in fields that involved graduate professional work, particularly in medicine. Even today, most black physicians obtain their degrees from one of three colleges: Meharry Medical College and Fisk University in Nashville, Tennessee, or Howard University in the District of Columbia. In other graduate fields quota systems were widely applied in the North, while in the South blacks were completely excluded from the graduate schools. Those who sought advanced training were obliged to go North. Out-of-state scholarships were available to blacks who wished to take graduate or professional courses at northern universities. Many of these students obtained the doctoral degree; as late as the mid-1960s, such students were matriculating at some of the major northern universities. Northern white universities were, for the most part, willing to accept these students, but primarily in fields such as education. Entry into the professional schools has been a different matter, and it continues to be a problem for black students. It was not until black aspirants to graduate schools turned to the courts to seek relief that access to many of these fields became available (Weinberg, 1977).

In the late 1960s and early 1970s, black professionals began to find their way into largely white institutions of higher education. In the fields of education and social science there was a dramatic increase in the number of blacks holding professorships. Yet the number of black professors compared to the number of white professors remained small.

A specific problem for black professors is how to become involved in the research community and in setting educational policy that affects blacks. The major studies affecting blacks in America have been conducted by white social scientists and educators. The problem was highlighted in a report (Wright, 1979) by the National Advisory Committee on Black Higher Education and Black Colleges and Universities. The report suggested that the findings, conclusions, and recommendations and the way the problems are formulated, the hypotheses selected, and the inferences drawn are influenced by the researchers' concerns, biases, and beliefs, an observation made by Gunnar Myrdal in 1944. Black social scientists and educators undoubtedly also bring their concerns, biases, and beliefs to research on public-policy questions relating to the educational needs of blacks; however, these are very different from those of whites' and will lead, perhaps, to different recommendations for dealing with the stubborn educational problems that confront blacks.

It is obvious that the primary reason for the limited amount of research by blacks is the relatively small number of blacks who are adequately trained in the social sciences. Blacks are grossly underrepresented among the holders of the doctoral degree. While the number of doctoral degrees awarded blacks has increased significantly in recent years, it still amounts to less than 4 percent of the annual total. Another limiting factor has been the fact that research has not offered blacks promising careers. Thus, even those with the necessary training have found teaching and administration more inviting.

Black professionals in higher education have pointed out that black colleges and universities and black researchers have found little support for their programs and for research. A number of circumstances, perhaps including inadequate black representation on advisory boards and peer review procedures, have led federal agencies to give black colleges an extremely small portion of the funds needed to increase the pool of black researchers and to stimulate research by blacks.

Conclusions. Closing the educational gap between whites and minorities (in this case, blacks) is crucial to the achievement of a sound, just society. Although some progress has been made, the goal of equalizing educational opportunities has not been fully achieved. A major reason illustrated by this discussion is that American educational policy in such areas as school desegregation and equal educational opportunity is often affected by the relationship between research and the prevailing climate of opinion. The relationship between politics and educational policy is more than a coincidence. Researchers have become political advocates and caused controversies that have impeded progress in black education. The relationship between researchers and politicians ought to be carefully examined. Researchers can walk away from a policy that

fails and go back to the drawing board, a luxury that politicians do not enjoy. This underscores the risk of too close a relationship between research and policy making.

If those who wield political power are to make use of research, and they should, the research should be neutral, both in fact and in appearance. This has not been the case in those areas that affect the education of black children. The history of black education is characterized by the denial of schooling by the dominant society in the North and in the South and by the constant struggle by blacks for the right to learn and the right to be taught in an equal, nonsegregated setting. The claim that blacks are intellectually incapable of learning makes no sense when seen against the background of white attempts to deny them equal opportunities to learn. As Weinberg (1977) stated: "Whites seemed to fear not that Negroes could not learn but that they would" (p. 39). The thirst for learning and the drive to achieve it survived in the face of slavery and compulsory ignorance laws, just as it will survive in the face of restrictive public policies.

LaMar P. Miller

See also Culture and Education Policy; Equity Issues in Education; Multicultural and Minority Education; Racism and Sexism in Children's Literature; Urban Education.

REFERENCES

Ausubel, D. P., & Ausubel, P. Ego development among segregated Negro children. In H. A. Passow (Ed.). *Education in Depressed Areas.* New York: Columbia University, Teachers College, 1963.

Birney, G. *Liberator,* October 4, 1834.

Bond, H. M. Some exceptional Negro children. *Crisis,* October 1927, *34*(8), 257–259, 278, 280.

Brown v. *Board of Education* (I), 347 U.S. 483 (1955).

Cicirelli, V. (Ed.). *The Impact of Head Start: An Evaluation of Head Start on Children's Cognitive and Affective Development.* Washington D.C.: Office of Economic Opportunity, U.S. Department of Commerce, June 1967.

Coates, B. White adult behavior toward black and white children. *Child Development,* 1972, *43*, 143–154.

Coleman, J. S. The concept of equality of educational opportunity. In E. W. Gordon & L. P. Miller (Eds.), *Equality of Educational Opportunity.* New York: AMS Press, 1974.

Coleman, J. S.; Campbell, E. O.; Hobson, C. J.; McPartland, J.; Mood, A. M.; Weinfield, D.; & York, R. L. *Equality of Educational Opportunity.* Washington, D.C.: U.S. Government Printing Office, 1966. (ERIC Document Reproduction Service No. ED 012 275)

Consortium for Longitudinal Studies. *Lasting Effects after Preschool* (Final report). Denver: The Education Commission of the States, October, 1978.

Consortium on Developmental Continuity. *The Persistence of Preschool Effects* (Final report). Washington D.C.: U.S. Department of Health, Education, and Welfare, October, 1977. (ERIC Document Reproduction Service No. ED 175 523)

Crisis, August, 1928.

Dann, M. E. (Ed.). *The Black Press, 1827–1890: The Quest for National Identity.* New York: Putnam, 1971.

Datta, L. E. The impact of the Westinghouse/Ohio evaluation on the development of Project Head Start: An examination of the immediate and long-term effects and how they come about. In C. Abt (Ed.), *The Evaluation of Social Programs.* Beverly Hills, Calif.: Sage, 1976.

Deutsch, M., & Deutsch, C. P. Intelligence, heredity, and environment: The critical appraisal of an outmoded controversy. *New York University Education Quarterly*, 1974, *5*(2), 4–12.

Du Bois, W. E. B. (Ed.). *The Negro Common School.* Atlanta: Atlanta University Press, 1901.

Dyer, H. S., & Rosenthal, E. *State Educational Assessment Program: An Overview.* Princeton, N.J.: ERIC Clearing House on Tests, Measurement, and Evaluation, 1971. (ERIC Document Reproduction Service No. ED 058 309)

Grant, G. Shaping social policy: The politics of the Coleman Report. *Teachers College Record*, 1973, *75*, 17–54.

Guthrie, R. V. IQ testing: Some historical perspectives. *Generator*, Spring 1981, *11*(2), 1–11.

Herrnstein, R. IQ. *Atlantic Monthly*, September 1971, pp. 43–64.

Jefferson, T. *Notes on Virginia* (William Peden, Ed.). Chapel Hill: North Carolina University Press, 1955. (Originally published, 1787.)

Jencks, C. (Ed.). *Inequality: A Reassessment of the Effect of Family and Schooling in America.* New York: Basic Books, 1972.

Jensen, A. R. How much can we boost IQ and school achievement? *Harvard Education Review*, 1969, *39*, 1–123.

Johnson, E. B. *Teacher Influence in the Desegregated Classroom: Factors Mediating the School Desegregation Experience.* Unpublished manuscript, 1974.

Jordan, W. D. *White over Black.* Chapel Hill: N.C.: University of North Carolina Press, 1968.

Klingberg, F. J. *The Appraisal of the Negro in Colonial South Carolina: A Study in Americanization.* Washington, D.C.: Associated Publishers, 1941.

McConany, J. Paper presented at the meeting of the American Political Science Convention, New York, September 3, 1978.

Miller, L. P. (Ed.). *The Testing of Black Students.* Englewood Cliffs, N.J.: Prentice-Hall, 1974.

Moynihan, D. P., & Mosteller, F. (Eds.). *On Equality of Educational Opportunity.* New York: Random House, Vintage Books, 1971.

Myrdal, G. *An American Dilemma: The Negro Problem and Modern Democracy.* New York: Harper & Brothers, 1944.

National Institute of Education. *Teaching, Testing, and Learning.* Washington, D.C.: The Institute, October 1979.

Plotkin, L. Research, education, and public policy: Heredity versus environment in Negro intelligence. In L. P. Miller (Ed.), *The Testing of Black Students.* Englewood Cliffs, N.J.: Prentice-Hall, 1974.

Richard, L. L. *Gentlemen of Property and Standing: Anti-abolition Mobs in Jacksonian America.* New York: Oxford University Press, 1970.

Riessman, F. *The Culturally Deprived Child.* New York: Harper & Row, 1962.

Rosenthal, R., & Jacobson, L. *Pygmalion in the Classroom: Teacher Expectations and Pupils' Intellectual Development.* New York: Holt, Rinehart & Winston, 1968.

Rubovits, C., & Maehr, L. Pygmalion black and white. *Journal of Personality and Social Psychology*, 1973, *25*, 210–218.

Sherer, J., & Stanski, J. J. Coping with desegregation: Individual strategies and organizational compliance. In M. L. Wax (Ed.), *When Schools are Desegregated: Problems and Possibilities for Students, Educators, Parents, and the Community.* New York: Academic Press, 1979.

Simpson, J. *Liberator,* August 11, 1865.

U.S. Bureau of the Census. *Historical Statistics of the United States: Colonial Times to 1957.* Washington, D.C.: U.S. Government Printing Office, 1960.

U.S. Commission on Civil Rights. *Racial Isolation in the Schools.* Washington, D.C.: U.S. Government Printing Office, 1967. (ERIC Document Reproduction Service No. ED 015 970)

von Euler, M., & Parham, D. L. *The Citizen's Guide to School Desegregation Law.* Washington, D.C.: National Institute of Education, 1978. (ERIC Document Reproduction Service No. ED 160 689)

Weinberg, M. *A Chance to Learn: The History of Race and Education in the United States.* Cambridge, England: Cambridge University Press, 1977.

Woodson, C. G. *The Education of the Negro Prior to 1861* (2nd ed.). Washington, D.C.: Associated Publishers, 1919.

Woodson, C. G. *The African Background Outlined: Or Handbook for the Study of the Negro.* New York: Negro Universities Press, 1968. (Originally published, 1936.)

Wright, S. J. *The Black Educational Policy Researcher: An Untapped National Resource.* Washington, D.C.: National Advisory Committee on Black Higher Education and Black Colleges and Universities, December 1979.

BLINDNESS

See Visual Impairment.

BUSINESS ADMINISTRATION OF SCHOOLS

As a service and support function of the field of school administration, school business administration in elementary and secondary schools is effective to the degree that predetermined goods and services are made available to pupils and teachers in a timely manner (Jordan, 1969a). Although responsibilities may vary among school districts, school business administration usually encompasses financial management and planning, facility planning, management, and operation; school food-service programs; and related activities.

Financial management and planning activities include supervision of the receipt and expenditure of school funds and development of budgets and long-term fiscal plans for the school district. Responsibilities for facilities may include interpretative and liaison roles in school-facility planning and direct control of all facility maintenance. Risk management or insurance programs are an integral part of the efforts to secure maximum efficiency and economy in the operation of facilities. Purchasing and property management are also among the typical functions of the business office. Service and support activities, like food services and transportation, may be assigned to the school business office because they are also support activities for the instructional program. Many school districts have assigned management and operation of the information systems office to the school business administrator (Educational Research Service, 1966), but this position is not uniformly accepted as best practice (Glasscock & McKeown, 1977). Other activities related to school business administration include personnel management and collective bargaining.

School business administration should be as responsive to the needs of school personnel as other facets of school administration for the success of the instructional process depends upon the availability of human and material resources. The activities of school business administration should be flexibly defined rather than highly standardized because effective school business administration should be responsive to changes in the instructional program and shifts in service requirements. The decade of the 1970s caused a shift in the focus of school business administration. No longer are expanding resources available to meet the increasing needs of an ever larger number of students. Decremental planning rather than incremental planning has become the management challenge. Now the school business administrator must shift attention to the demands for increased accountability and strive to develop the most efficient assignment of declining resources to a smaller number of clients with more diverse and expensive needs.

Earlier reviews by Knezevich and DeKock (1960), Griffith (1964), and Jordan (1969b) have noted that solutions derived from research are often not available to solve current problems because the emphasis has been on status reports and suggestions for improving practices rather than on carefully designed research projects. Research in school business administration has not been sufficiently comprehensive in scope or rigid enough in design to provide adequate directions for evaluation or revision of administrative practices. There is a need for carefully designed research, with attention given to the systematic gathering and interpretation of data and the use of a sufficient sample to permit generalization.

Financial Management and Planning. A survey of school business officers (Walters, 1978) indicated that fiscal accounting and financial planning were the top priority areas for school business administrators. In this context, fiscal management includes budgeting, preparation of reports on revenues and expenditures, and collection, custody, investment, and disbursement of funds. In a comprehensive treatment, Tidwell (1974), defined public school accounting as the information base for administrative decisions and the information source for groups as diverse as parents and bond-rating companies.

Guidance for public elementary and secondary school accounting techniques has been provided by the federal government. Impetus for financial accounting on an educational program basis has been provided by *Financial Accounting for State and Local School Districts* (United States Office of Education, 1980); this primary source for generally accepted accounting principles for school systems provides guidance for the implementation of program accounting and cost center budgeting. These accounting and budgeting techniques are an integral part of a program-planning, budgeting, and evaluation system (PPBES). Designed to assist school administrators in resource-allocation decisions, PPBES for local school districts is a budgetary technique that emphasizes inputs and outputs and consideration of various alternatives with presentation of costs and potential benefits to assist the decision-making process (Association of School Business Officials, 1971). A further modification of PPBES, zero-based budgeting (ZBB) has been viewed as a useful management tool (Hodel & Gruendel, 1980). In order to reach decisions on resource allocations under ZBB, goals and objectives should be operationally defined, performance levels measured, alternative means for accomplishing objectives reviewed, and associated costs analyzed.

Most school business administrators were first involved in fiscal management and resource allocation during a period of incremental planning and budgeting, but the challenge in the 1980s is to participate in an integrated decision-making process and to provide sound fiscal planning during a period of rising unit costs, stable or declining enrollments, and declining resources. Little research is available to assist the school business administrator in making wise allocation decisions during a period of decline. Notable exceptions are found in a California State Department of Education study (1979) that reported the impact of Proposition 13 on California local school districts; in a study (Reyes, 1979) of the design and application of a simulation model for financial forecasting in New Mexico school districts; and in Wolfe's study (1976) that combined cost and production functions to determine where cutbacks could be made in resource allocation.

Linear programming, program evaluation and review techniques *(PERT)*, and time series analysis are other tools that permit more complex and detailed analyses and more systematic planning in local school districts. Although the application of these techniques is quite advanced in private-sector, profit-centered accounting and management, research on the application of these tools to education is limited, especially in the milieu of tax or revenue limitations like Proposition 13 in California. Even though Guthrie (1980) cautioned that educational researchers have been too quick to accept private-sector conceptual schemes and theoretical models, some of these research and management techniques may enable decision makers to allocate and utilize resources more effectively.

Facility Planning, Management, and Operation. The focus of facilities planning and management in school business administration has shifted to reflect complex changes in education: monitoring of facilities by federal, state, and local governments to ensure compliance with health and safety requirements; accessibility for the handicapped; increased energy efficiency; reduction of security and vandalism problems; adequacy of current instructional programs; and planning techniques for closing or converting excess space in one area and constructing new facilities in another. Perkins and Brubacher (1980) indicated that the trend in facilities planning is to provide alternative uses for unneeded facilities, and Day (1980) reported that efficient and cost-effective uses for vacant school buildings include leasing them to community organizations and service groups as well as sharing them with day care centers or senior citizens groups. Tarran (1979) found twenty-three factors that can be used to determine if it is cost-effective to close school buildings. Whittenberg's study (1980) on the relationship between energy costs and school-building design is illustrative of research that can have utilitarian value for planners. The study reviewed the diverse practices in energy consumption and cost per square foot for alternative mechanical and lighting systems in buildings, detailed conclusions relate to cost-efficient and energy-efficient design of school buildings.

State constitutional and statutory provisions dictate varying practices for financing the new construction and renovation of school facilities. In a report on the factors influencing interest rates on the sale of school district bonds to finance school-facility construction or renovation, Engelage (1978) identified five factors: average maturity of the issue, use of a prospectus, type of sale, market index, and time of sale. These factors differ from those reported by Furno (1965), indicating a shift in the bond market and the importance of current research to guide fiscal management practices in local school districts.

Risk Management. The need to minimize financial loss and reduce costs has resulted in school business administrators' giving greater attention to risk management or insurance programs of local school districts. Webb (1979) indicated that, as insurance rates have risen dramatically in the last two decades, local school districts have sought alternative solutions to minimize insurance costs but maintain adequate protection. Four broad insurance options are available: typical commercial insurance programs; state-operated insurance programs; self-insurance at the district level; or no insurance, with assumption of losses as they occur. Preventive risk management has become more important as commercial rates have increased; among the factors that should be included in a loss control program are loss prevention, loss reduction, and loss avoidance (California Association of School Business Officials, 1979). Golz (1980) identified factors that reduce the costs of insurance through use of commercial companies, and Stokes (1980) concluded that district consortia for risk management can be successful when the number of districts is sufficiently large to spread the risk. Earlier studies by Linn (1976) and Schaerer (1964) focused on individual school districts and concluded that school districts should have adequate financial ability, enrollments, and geographic size before considering self-insurance programs. Stokes (1980) discusses examples of creative alternatives used by local school districts to prevent financial disaster and also illustrates the need for continuing research.

Property Management. To the traditional property management challenges for the school business administrator—supply management, property accounting, and purchasing—has been added the use or disposal of surplus property. Recent studies include Knapp's report (1979) on techniques used by forty-three school districts to dispose of surplus property and Shoaf's discussion (1979) of techniques for property control. Staffing flexibility options were stressed by Fredenburg (1980) in a three-year project to determine if the employment of a full-time or part-time purchasing agent was economically justified in small school districts.

Additional Management Areas. Other areas of management include school food service, transportation, data processing, and personal management. Typical of the research problems in school business areas were those encountered by Garvue (1971) in a national study of school food-service programs. Data for interstate comparisons were either not available, not comparable, or inconsistent. Findings noted that improvements were needed in fiscal accounting and personnel practices and that increased use was being made of private contractors to provide school food-service programs.

Much of the recent research on pupil transportation has been related to energy-efficient and cost-efficient operation. McKeown (1978) reported the development of a cost-efficiency-oriented transportation formula that can be used to identify school districts operating transportation programs at cost-efficient levels. Jordan and Hanes (1978) provided data on the increasing proportion of school budgets that are being required for pupil transportation among the states. Temple (1977) and Simpson (1978) presented state-of-the-art energy-savings ideas that translate into resource savings. State summary data for expenditures and operation of school transportation programs are published annually ("School Bus Statistics," 1981).

Continuing technological developments in electronic data processing have decreased the costs of computers and computer applications. Even the smaller school districts now have access to advanced technology that can be used to allocate resources and secure current fiscal information. Constantly expanding uses include data processing to monitor school funds (IBM Data Processing Division, 1980), computerized energy-monitoring devices (Honeywell, 1980), and computer applications for extracurricular activities (Costerison, 1980). Most information, however, deals with current practices and does not provide research-based guidance for the policy maker.

The shift in focus for the school business administrator is most clearly illustrated by the increased participation in collective bargaining with employee organizations. Byrd (1979), in a study of collective bargaining and teacher strikes in the period from 1949 to 1979, found that thirty-six states had passed collective bargaining statutes since 1960 and concluded that continued use of strikes could be anticipated. Carlton (1976) presented a detailed description of the collective bargaining process and procedures for grievance and impasse solution. Grogan (1979) emphasized that the most important preparation for negotiation is adequate research, not only on the financial situation of the school district but also on the techniques and methodology of collective bargaining.

Policy Implications. Typical school business administration research efforts have consisted of reporting current practices, with limited analysis. In contrast to ethical and moral concerns about the use of experimental research techniques with students under alternative instructional arrangements, experimental studies of alternative approaches to various school business administration practices will likely be met with minimal resistance. Business practices from private and public-service agencies conceivably could be transferred or adapted to education without interfering with the desired level of support for the instructional program. Interest in alternatives will likely increase as fiscal resources become more limited and costs increase for essential components of the instructional process.

K. Forbis Jordan
Mary P. McKeown

See also Administration of Educational Institutions; Administrator Preparation; Comparative Education Administration; Financing Colleges and Universities; Financing Schools.

REFERENCES

Association of School Business Officials. *Educational Resources Management System.* Park Ridge, Ill.: The Association, Research Corporation, 1971. (ERIC Document Reproduction Service No. ED 061 595)

Byrd, W. L. *Teacher Collective Bargaining and Strikes in Public Elementary and Secondary Education.* Unpublished doctoral dissertation, St. Louis University, 1979.

California Association of School Business Officials. *Loss Control Supplement to the Administration of School District Risk Management Programs* (School Business Administrators Publication No. 1), Sacramento, Calif., 1979. (ERIC Document Reproduction Service No. ED 180 077)

California State Department of Education. *A Study of Local Government Impacts of Proposition 13.* Sacramento: California State Department of Education, 1979.

Carlton, P. W. *Ground Rules, Contract Language, Grievances and Impasse Resolution.* Proceedings of the Collective Bargaining Clinic, Virginia Polytechnic Institute and State University, 1976. (ERIC Document Reproduction Service No. ED 128 940)

Costerison, D. Home-style computer application for extracurricular activities. *School Business Affairs,* 1980, *46,* 35.

Day, W. C. Efficient and cost-effective uses of vacant school buildings. *School Business Affairs,* 1980, *46,* 21, 27.

Educational Research Service. *The Status and Function of the Local School Business Administrator* (Circular No. 8), Washington, D.C.: National Educational Association, 1966. (ERIC Document Reproduction Service No. ED 013 478)

Engelage, J. R. Factors influencing interest rates on the sale of school bonds. *School Business Affairs,* July 1978, *44*(7), 229.

Fredenburg, P. Is a purchasing agent needed in semirural school districts? *School Business Affairs,* 1980, *46*(9), 24–25.

Furno, O. The cost of borrowing money. *School Management,* 1965, *9,* 105–107.

Garvue, R. J., Flanagan, T. G., & Castine, W. H. *School Food Service and Nutrition Education* (National Educational Finance Project, Study No. 8). Gainesville, Fla., 1971.

Glasscock, D., & McKeown, M. Participative management in data processing resource allocation. In *CAUSE 1976.* Boulder, Colo.: College and University Systems Exchange, 1977.

Golz, W. C., Jr. Minimize the risk in risk management. *School Business Affairs,* April 1980, *46*(5), pp. 10, 11, 39, 40.

Griffith, W. Organizational character of educational facility planning and business management. *Review of Educational Research,* 1964, *34,* 470–484.

Grogan, J. L. The salary and fringe benefit package. *School Business Affairs,* January 1979, *45*(1), pp. 22, 23, 36.

Guthrie, J. W. An assessment of educational policy research. *Educational Evaluation and Policy Analysis,* 1980, *2*(5), 41–56.

Hodel, R., & Gruendel, G. Budgeting: A management approach for the eighties. *School Business Affairs,* February 1980, *46*(2), 24–25.

Honeywell, Inc. Building management systems team up with thermostats to save energy. *School Business Affairs,* November 1980, *46*(11), 33–34.

IBM Data Processing Division. Computer systems give local districts a daily budgeting tool. *School Business Affairs,* November 1980, *46*(11), 33.

Jordan, K. F. *School Business Administration.* New York: Ronald Press, 1969. (a)

Jordan, K. F. School business administration. In R. L. Ebel (Ed.), *Encyclopedia of Educational Research* (4th ed.). New York: Macmillan, 1969. (b)

Jordan, K. F., & Hanes, C. E. A survey of state pupil transportation programs. *School Business Affairs,* May 1978, *44*(5), 133–136.

Knapp, H. School closings and surplus property. *School Business Affairs,* March 1979, *45*(3), 20.

Knezevich, S. J., & DeKock, H. C. Business administration, public schools. In C. W. Harris (Ed.), *Encyclopedia of Educational Research* (3rd ed.). New York: Macmillan, 1960, pp. 161–173.

Linn, H. H. *School Business Administration.* New York: Ronald Press, 1956.

McKeown, M. P. An efficiency-oriented funding formula for pupil transportation. *Journal of Educational Finance,* Fall 1978, *4*(2), 225–233.

Perkins, B. & Brubacher, C. W. Current trends in school facility planning. *School Business Affairs,* December 1980, *46*(12), 24–29.

Reyes, R. V., Jr. *The Design, Test, and Evaluation of an Educational Dynamics Simulation Model for Public School District Financial Forecasting.* Unpublished doctoral dissertation, New Mexico State University, 1979.

Schaerer, R. W. Self-insurance. *Proceedings of the Association of School Business Officials,* 1964, *50,* 384–387.

School bus statistics. *School Bus Fleet,* December–January 1981, pp. 64–67.

Shoaf, L. Advantages of using an equipment control system. *School Business Affairs,* March 1979, *45*(3), 22–23.

Simpson, W. Five ways to improve gas mileage. *School Bus Fleet,* August–September 1978, pp. 47, 49, 51–52.

Stokes, S. A. *Utilization of School District Consortia for the Purpose of Risk Management.* Unpublished doctoral dissertation, University of Southern California, 1980.

Tarran, D. G. *The Benefits and Costs Associated with the Closure of Public School Facilities in the State of Washington.* Unpublished doctoral dissertation, University of Washington, 1979.

Temple, L. Improved fuel economy, lower maintenance costs benefits of diesel power. *School Bus Fleet,* October–November, 1977, pp. 12–16.

Tidwell, S. B. *Financial and Managerial Accounting for Elementary and Secondary School Systems.* Park Ridge, Ill.: The Association, Research Corporation, 1974.

United States Office of Education. *Handbook II; Financial Accounting for State and Local School Districts* (Rev. ed.). Washington, D.C.: USOE, 1980.

Walters, D. L. Accounting and financial planning: Top priorities for school business administration. *Proceedings of the Association of School Business Officials,* 1978, *64.* (ERIC Document Reproduction Service No. ED 163 604)

Webb, L. D. Taking the risk out of risk management. *School Business Affairs,* April 1979, *45*(4), 16, 17, 40.

Whittenberg, R. W. *A Study of the Cost and Quantity of Energy Used in School Buildings.* Unpublished doctoral dissertation, Brigham Young University, 1980.

Wolfe, B. *A Cost-effective Analysis of Reductions in School Expenditures.* Madison: University of Wisconsin, Institute for Research on Poverty, November 1976.

BUSINESS EDUCATION

The phrase "business education" has many meanings. In this article it will be used to refer to collegiate programs preparing teachers of business subjects and office workers desiring administrative and management positions; and, in the secondary and postsecondary (community colleges and vocational-technical) schools, "to vocational objectives—preparation for initial office . . . occupations, and to nonvocational objectives—general or basic business, consumer, and economic information and understandings applicable to all persons as part of general education, as well as beginning typewriting and, in the view of some, beginning bookkeeping" (West, 1969, p. 105). Occasionally, the term refers to collegiate programs in business administration and management; however, since that application of the term is limited, and because of space restrictions, that aspect of the term will not be covered here.

After a review of enrollment patterns, student characteristics, and occupational trends in the fields for which students are being prepared, attention will be given to research completed since the 1969 *Encyclopedia of Educational Research* that relates to issues affecting policy decisions, followed by research in the subject areas within business education.

Enrollment Patterns. During 1972/73, the last year for which statistics are available on enrollment in specific courses, business education accounted for 34.2 percent of the total public secondary school enrollments, grades 7 to 12 (U.S. Department of Health, Education, and Welfare, 1975). Only six subject areas (which tend to be required)

ranked higher. As most business education courses are taught in grades 9 to 12, enrollments are probably underrepresented in these figures. By specific subject, Typewriting I was the largest (10.6 percent), followed by general business (3.2 percent), personal typewriting (2.8 percent), bookkeeping I (2.6 percent), typewriting II, III, IV (2.5 percent), shorthand I (2.1 percent), business arithmetic (1.9 percent), and business law (1.2 percent). Business education's share of total enrollments has dropped about 5 percent each decade since 1948/49 (Grant & Eiden, 1980, p. 48).

Business education is the third-largest of the federally aided vocational education programs, accounting for 21.4 percent of the enrollments in 1978 (Grant & Eiden, 1980, p. 168). Business education accounts for the largest number of adult education enrollments: 19.4 percent in 1978 (Dearman & Plisko, 1980, p. 254).

In 1977/78, business and distributive teacher education graduates accounted for 3.5 percent of the bachelor's degrees in education, 1.4 percent of the master's, and 0.8 percent of the doctor's—with women accounting for 79.4 percent, 76.5 percent, and 34.9 percent, respectively (Grant & Eiden, 1980, p. 121).

Occupational Trends. Of all occupational categories, clerical workers will grow the most from 1978 to 1990, from 16.9 to 21.7 million workers (or an increase of 29 percent) (Bureau of Labor Statistics, 1980, p. 21). Although there has been some decline in employment in office machine operators, file clerks, and stenographers, the "electronic office" has increased the need for computer and peripheral equipment operators and dictation machine transcribers. At the same time, because of the increasing paper flow and desire for personal contact, the demand for secretaries and receptionists will grow (Bureau of Labor Statistics, 1980, p. 21). Despite the growth potential in this area, future prospects for employment are not clear. Already there are major shortages of workers in these fields because of the relatively low wages paid and the high level of skill required. This discrepancy has led some to refer to the clerical area as the "pink collar ghetto"—one of every five clerical workers is a secretary, and almost all secretaries are women. Through the combined use of dictation machines and word-processing equipment, the employment of stenographers (with a knowledge of shorthand) "has been severely reduced," and "fewer jobs will be available than in the past" (Bureau of Labor Statistics, 1980, p. 90).

Erickson (1971) analyzed the basic components of office work across subject areas using a critical incidents technique. The components occurring in over 25 percent of the jobs were communicating with others (90 percent); sorting, filing, and retrieving (71 percent); typewriting (49 percent); and checking, computing, and verifying (47 percent).

Teacher Education. Where are teacher education programs in business education housed? Langford, Sink, and Weeks (1978) found that 45 percent of business education programs are in business administration schools without AACSB (American Assembly of Collegiate Schools of Business) accreditation; 25 percent in education with AACSB; 17 percent in education without AACSB; and 13 percent in business administration with AACSB. More business content was required and there was better coverage of the common body of knowledge when the programs were housed in AACSB business administration schools.

Johnson's survey (1979) found that teachers felt themselves to be least competent to teach business mathematics, business law, and cooperative office education. In evaluating competency-based modular preservice programs, Bryan (1979) found that individualized modules rather than lecture and discussion yielded no differences in achievement or attitude and led to higher scores on performance tests.

Sex Equity. Because so much of business education enrollment, and subsequent employment, is female, questions of sex equity are important. Kuiper (1978) found that young married women seek employment in clerical positions for both economic need and for self-fulfillment but do not aspire to management positions. Potential conflicts between home and career demands were being resolved successfully. The greatest potential stress was seen as tension between home-task satisfaction and job advancement.

Sexual harassment is one office stress encountered. Baldridge (1979) determined that 62 percent of the randomly selected respondents had experienced verbal harassment and 32 percent had experienced unwanted physical contact. These figures are lower than those found in earlier studies (Safran, 1976; Working Women's United Institute, 1975), which used self-selecting samples. Gilchrist's work (1980) substantially supports this finding. Gramling (1980) found that men also experience sexual harassment, from both men and women—36.6 percent have experienced verbal harassment and 18.3 percent unwanted physical contact.

In examining teacher attitudes, Thomas (1975) found that male teachers more than women, white teachers more than black, and medium-income teachers more than low-income and high-income tended to support stereotypic roles for women. McLean, Kleven, and McLean (1978) found considerable evidence of sexism in general business textbooks, even after publishers had developed guidelines that were used in revisions.

Other Issues. Little research has been done in business education in the area of special needs: no research on physical handicaps, gifted students, mainstreaming, racial equity, and so on was located. Erickson (1975a) found that students from low socioeconomic backgrounds were almost always associated with the poorest typewriting performances, based on both speed and accuracy in straight-copy timings. Santiago-Perez (1979) found that students in Puerto Rico who used specifically designed materials in Spanish performed better on straight-copy speed than

students using the regular adopted materials. No differences on accuracy were found. Low self-concept, according to Jackson (1978), is associated with being male, being nonwhite, having a low income, and having a history of low grades.

With increasing emphasis on competency-based programs some attention has been given to evaluating individualized learning. Lambrecht (1975) examined student course completions and student and teacher attitudes toward individualization in business education in Wisconsin postsecondary schools. Wide variations were found in completion rates, scheduling patterns, and degrees of individualization. Students seemed to do best with previous instruction, scheduled time for classes with laboratory facilities available for extra work, pretesting and advanced placement, remedial adjuncts, student selection of course-unit progression, and personally developed course outlines.

Typewriting. Several reviews of research in typewriting exist (McLean, 1978b; Robinson et al., 1979; West, 1974; West, 1982). Several studies (e.g., Balsley, 1977; Ober, 1974) identified current typing practices in the business world, often contradicting common classroom practices. Sales of manual typewriters are so small they are not even reported in Standard & Poor's 1980 report. Erickson (1971) and Ober (1974), among others, have routinely shown that more than half of the real-world copy is either handwritten or typed with handwritten corrections.

The research, summarized by McLean (1971), presents a wide range of correlations between straight-copy and production speed and accuracy, depending on the stage of training, task, test material features, and test conditions. On the average, the results show that beyond novice typists, for whom speed correlations are very low, straight-copy speed correlates with production speed at about .6; for accuracy, at about .3. Keystroking is only a part of production typewriting, with other components being decision making, correction, and machine manipulation. West (1972) compared two groups of students—one with minimal straight-copy comparisons—but found those with minimal straight-copy drill performing 50 percent higher in production typewriting quality. Since production-type tasks are those performed on the job and for personal use, the focus of classroom instruction should clearly be directed to production drill rather than to straight-copy drill.

While the evidence is somewhat inconclusive (Hamed, 1972; Schmidt, 1975), it would appear that massed practice is necessary during beginning stages of instruction, followed by spaced practice at later stages. The research also presents inconsistencies relative to repetitive practice of straight-copy material (Mach, 1971; Weise, 1975). For several reasons, however, extensive, rather than repetitive, practice is to be preferred. DeLoach (1968) found no differences among the groups following typewriting instruction to youngsters in grades 3, 5, and 7, supporting the feasibility of elementary school instruction. Class size (whether under thirty or over sixty) appears to have no end-of-year differences in stroking skills, production skills, or associated information (Good, 1970). Because of the large number of errors found on the second reading of a typescript (Wong, 1971), it is important for accuracy in evaluation to proofread student papers at least twice. Olson (1978) developed a prognostic test to predict straight-copy typewriting performance. The research also supported earlier research relative to the ease of certain stroking combinations.

Erickson (1975b) found that student speed declined consistently as straight-copy difficulty increased. Accuracy was not consistently affected by differences in copy difficulty. West (1980) found average straight-copy error rates to be "rather more than two errors per minute at all levels of school training, as well as among applicants for employment and employees" (p. 224). Errors tend to go up, not down, as skill (measured by speed) increases. In schools where heavy emphasis is given to accuracy, accuracy figures are not better but speed scores are much lower.

West and McLean (1968) found net-words-per-minute and error cutoff methods of evaluating straight-copy typewriting to lower both reliability and validity. Scoring for gross words per minute and errors separately is justified.

McLean (1971) established that there were clear differences in the difficulty level of various production typing tasks based on identifiable characteristics—an important consideration in evaluation and establishing office standards. McLean, Kranz, and Magnuson (1980) also identified the most frequently occurring production errors in typing letters (omission of reference initials—82 percent) and tables (braced headings over two columns incorrectly centered and table not vertically centered—70 percent each).

Bookkeeping and Accounting. West (1977) made an extensive survey of employers to determine job requirements. His conclusions raise serious questions about typical secondary school bookkeeping curricula: computerization has reduced the need to understand bookkeeping concepts; prior school training was seldom a requirement for entry-level employment; on-the-job training prevailed; the recordkeeping curriculum appears to be nonfunctional; the terminology of school instruction often varies from that found on the job; the job duties and job-responsibility levels of those with no school training were indistinguishable from those with only high school training; responsibility and advancement depended heavily on work experience, less on postsecondary education, and not discernibly on high school bookkeeping training; journal and ledger work was carried out by experienced, not novice, employees; and high school instruction beyond the trial balance was "totally unjustifiable." Reap (1980) reviewed several task analyses and textbooks, supporting West's conclusions. Of the 150 job tasks of the "real world," only 36 were

found in high school textbooks. Fifty-two percent of textbook volumes contained information not found on the task lists.

Shorthand. Research studies, with their educational implications, are reviewed in Gallion (1980) and VanHuss, Lambrecht, and Christensen (1980). How important is shorthand? Williamson and Houghton (1978) found that 46 percent of businesses in Idaho always or sometimes required shorthand skill at the entry level, while 45 percent required the use of voice dictation equipment. Yet the most common response to frequency of shorthand use was one to two hours per week, and shorthand was not even listed as a transcription source used several times a day. In contrast, machine dictation was the most frequent response to the source used several times a day.

Several studies focused on a comparison of performance among several types of shorthand. The dropout problem in shorthand and the declining willingness of students to commit two years to learning a shorthand skill have contributed to the development of alternative symbolic systems (notably, Century 21) and alphabetic systems (most research appears to focus on Forkner), in addition to the traditional (in the United States) symbolic system, Gregg. In an extensive study Lambrecht compared the attitudes (1980) and achievement (1978) among students in Century 21, Forkner, and Gregg. Forkner students performed best at the end of the first year. By the end of the second year, achievement was higher for Gregg, except on transcription rate, which was higher for Forkner. There were no differences in withdrawals during the first year. In their comparison of Gregg and Century 21, Durso and Blair (1978) found that Century 21 students scored significantly better than Gregg on fourteen of eighteen criterion measures. There were no differences in accuracy. Even at the low dictation rate of sixty words per minute, the Century 21 students had an accuracy rate of only 90.6 percent and the Gregg students had 86.9 percent.

Other shorthand studies examined methodological practices in shorthand instruction. Gilmore (1976) determined that students who had been exposed to a chalkboard presentation and a programmed approach to learning theory made fewer theory errors, transcribed more rapidly from dictation, and made fewer transcription errors than students learning from traditional methods. Students with low socioeconomic backgrounds did better with the programmed approach, while students from middle to upper backgrounds did better with a traditional approach. McLean (1978a) examined the relationships among straight-copy and production typewriting performance, shorthand transcription performance, and demographic data. The only significant correlations were between transcription time and straight-copy gross speed, and between transcription and production time. Shorthand transcription appears to be a unique task requiring specific-focus instruction.

Accuracy of shorthand outlines (and the subsequent emphasis on theory testing) has long been a controversial point. While VanHuss, Lambrecht, and Christensen (1980, p. 63) summarize a number of studies showing high correlations between theory knowledge and transcription accuracy, Levine (1980) hypothesized that the slight advantage in accuracy may come at the expense of speed development.

Business and Economic Education. Jones (1975) analyzed the contents of textbooks in general business, consumer economics, business principles and management, business law, and economics. A two-semester basic business course, a two-semester advanced basic business course, and a one-semester course in business management principles were recommended.

For assessment of consumer competencies, Stanley (1976) developed a test for grades 8 to 12 and gathered normative data. Using the Test of Understanding in Personal Economics, Kim (1977) found no differences among students enrolled in three different general college courses at the University of Minnesota, and Duff (1977) found that secondary students who had completed a basic business course, when compared with students who had not taken the course, scored higher on consumer concepts, worker concepts, and citizen concepts. Whitney (1979) found basic business skill deficiencies in 65 percent to 93 percent of students tested. Surprisingly, students with two business subjects did no better than students with no business courses.

Capstone Courses. "Capstone courses" are defined as integrating courses offered at the conclusion of a student's high school program. Typically, students choose from among office procedures (an in-class, one-hour-per-day, textbook-centered and teacher-centered experience), co-operative office education (one hour a day in class and half a day in a supervised, career-related, paid job), and a simulated model office (an in-class, block-time replication of the "real world" using work flow materials).

Seven studies examining the effectiveness of capstone courses were reviewed, and the results were remarkably similar: no consistent pattern of superiority emerged. Where one program appeared to produce students with higher scores on one variable, scores on other variables in other programs counterbalanced this finding. In addition, in comparison with norm groups of employed workers and with their own performance at the beginning of the year, students in all three programs appeared to be receiving effective education for entry-level employment (Beta Eta Chapter, 1977; Gould, Jackson, & Hopkins, 1978; and Church, 1979; Gould, Jackson, & Hopkins, 1978; Hopkins & McLean, 1978; McLean, 1975; Pitko, 1975).

Management and Administration. A detailed listing of tasks performed by administrative office managers, along with demographic data, are presented by Quible (1974). McQueen (1980) identified the five most important areas for administrative office managers and middle managers: oral communications, basic managerial functions, written communications, employee motivation, and employee supervision.

Career expectations and opportunities reveal some frustrating evidence about job placement of students entering the work force from this degree program. While Sullivan (1980) found that 67 percent of the graduates at Michigan State University were satisfied or very satisfied with their choice of major, it was also evident that an office administration degree was inappropriate for those wishing to move beyond secretarial positions in business. The respondents recommended more emphasis in the business administration core (59 percent). Goodrich's findings (1977) were similar.

Word Processing. Claffey (1981) found that the concept of word processing differed in each of the fifteen firms used in his case studies. The satisfactions of the personnel in word-processing centers came from the work itself, whereas those of the administrative assistants came from dealing with other people and answering questions. Skills needed for word processing included sound understanding of English grammar and spelling, human relations skills, keyboarding skills, proofreading skills, and an understanding of the logic behind text-editing equipment.

Job satisfaction of correspondence secretaries (i.e., those who do the keystroking) is directly related to supervisory style, intensity, and personality (Mitchell, 1980). Kutie (1977) compared the job satisfaction of traditional secretaries, administrative support coordinators, administrative support secretaries, word-processing operators, word-processing lead operators, and word-processing supervisors. Job satisfaction scores were highest for administrative positions and traditional secretaries and lowest for the specialized positions with restricted tasks.

Lewis (1979) examined the impact of word processing. While 46 percent of input prior to word processing was from personal handwriting, with shorthand dictation (19 percent) and machine dictation (24 percent) following, machine dictation became number one (63 percent) after its introduction, followed by handwriting (26 percent) and shorthand dictation (5 percent). Users were much more likely to use dictation equipment when training was provided. Fried (1978) found that scores on a spelling test were the best predictors of transcription quality.

Data Processing. Johnson (1978) surveyed computer-operations managers and found that upward career paths exist for all operations workers except data entry; wide variations in standards, input processes, and sophistication of systems exist; and basic requirements for employment include high school education, skill in operating business machines, clerical aptitudes, and, preferably, one year of prior work experience. Several managers required a four-year college education.

Lambrecht and McLean (1977) surveyed data-processing teachers in secondary schools, postsecondary technical institutes, and two-year community colleges in two states. Recommendations were made for in-service and preservice education. Teacher background and program characteristics were also identified.

Gary N. McLean

See also Career Education; Marketing and Distributive Education; Trade and Industrial Education; Vocational Education.

REFERENCES

Baldridge, K. *Sexual Harassment of Women in Office Positions in Minneapolis/St. Paul.* Unpublished master's paper, University of Minnesota at Minneapolis, 1979.

Balsley, I. W. *Current Transcription Practices in Business Firms* (Monograph 130) Cincinnati: South-Western, 1977.

Beta Eta Chapter, Delta Pi Epsilon, & Hamed, C. A comparison of traditional capstone office occupations courses with intensive office occupations block programs based on selected work values of twelfth-grade students in Ohio. *Delta Pi Epsilon Journal,* 1977, *19*(2), 1–6.

Bryan, F. S. Adapting a competency-based model for preparing vocational business teachers in the traditional class. *NABTE Review,* 1979, *6,* 34–38.

Bureau of Labor Statistics, U.S. Department of Labor. *Occupational Outlook Handbook: 1980–1981 Edition.* Washington, D.C.: U.S. Government Printing Office, 1980.

Church, O. Aspirations, needs, and perceptions by occupation and sex of office personnel, students, and teachers. *Delta Pi Epsilon Journal,* 1979, *21*(3), 20–33.

Claffey, G. F. Word processing: Case studies of 15 selected business firms (Volumes I and II). *Business Education Forum,* 1981, *35*(5), 29–34.

Dearman, N. B., & Plisko, V. W. *The Condition of Education: 1980 Edition.* Washington, D.C.: U.S. Government Printing Office, 1980. (ERIC Document Reproduction Service No. ED 188 304)

DeLoach, R. L. C. A study of fine motions by learners of touch typewriting at three levels of physical development (Doctoral dissertation, University of Michigan, 1968) *Dissertation Abstracts,* 1968, *29*(3), 831-A. (University Microfilm No. 68-13,300)

Duff, T. B. Measurement of personal economic understandings developed in basic business. In *Robert E. Slaughter Research Award Studies 1977* (Research Report No. 6). New York: McGraw-Hill, Gregg Division, 1977, pp. 3–7.

Durso, M. W., & Blair, R. C. A comparative study of achievement of 393 high school students enrolled in first year Century 21 and Gregg shorthand. *NABTE Review,* 1978, *5,* 96–103.

Erickson, L. W. *Basic Components of Office Work: An Analysis of 300 Office Jobs* (Monograph 123). Cincinnati: South-Western, 1971.

Erickson, L. W. Effects of socio-economic background factors on typewriting speed and accuracy. *NABTE Review,* 1975, *3,* 107–112. (a)

Erickson, L. W. Effects of straight-copy difficulty on the speed and accuracy of second-year high school typing students. *NABTE Review,* 1975, *3,* 102–106. (b)

Fried, N. E. The contribution of typewriting speed, spelling, and proofreading skills to transcription abilities of IBM magnetic keyboard operators (Doctoral dissertation, Ohio State University, 1978). *Dissertation Abstracts,* 1978, *39*(5), 2704-A. University Microfilms No. 78-19,595)

Gallion, L. M. *Teaching Shorthand* (Rapid Reader No. 4). St. Peter, Minn.: Delta Pi Epsilon, 1980. (ERIC Document Reproduction Service No. ED 187 940)

Gilchrist, O. A. *Sexual Harassment of Women in Office Positions in Fargo/Moorhead.* Unpublished master's paper, Moorhead State University, 1980.

Gilmore, M. C. A comparison of a traditional approach and a programmed approach to developing shorthand skill in inner-city schools. *Robert E. Slaughter Research Award Studies 1976* (Research Report No. 5). New York: McGraw-Hill, Gregg Division, 1976, pp. 1–6.

Good, G. A. Effect of class size on skills acquired in typing (Doctoral dissertation, Pennsylvania State University, 1970). *Dissertation Abstracts,* 1970, *31*(6), 2704-A. (University Microfilm No. 70-24,160)

Goodrich, E. A. Office administration majors' career expectations and opportunities. *Delta Pi Epsilon Journal,* 1977, *19*(3), 16–30.

Gould, K. R.; Jackson, A. L.; & Hopkins, C. R. A comparison of typewriting skills in cooperative office education, model office and office procedures. *Delta Pi Epsilon Journal,* 1978, *20*(3), 30–38.

Gramling, D. L. *Sexual Harassment of Men in Office Positions in Minneapolis/St. Paul.* Unpublished master's paper, University of Minnesota, 1980.

Grant, M. V., & Eiden, L. J. *Digest of Education Statistics, 1980.* Washington, D.C.: U.S. Government Printing Office, 1980.

Hamed, C. J. Massed versus spaced practice in the development of production typewriting ability. *Business Education Forum,* 1972, *27*(1), 57–58.

Hopkins, C. R., & McLean, G. N. Comparative effectiveness of three capstone office education courses using in-class measures. *Delta Pi Epsilon Journal,* 1978, *20*(2), 12–22.

Jackson, B. The self-concepts of business education students at the secondary level. *Delta Pi Epsilon Journal,* 1978, *20*(4), 1–11.

Johnson, M. F. Job specifications for the computer productions operations and skill-related data-processing job cluster. *Delta Pi Epsilon Journal,* 1978, *20*(1), 1–12.

Johnson, V. J. Factors emanating from analyses of competencies. *NABTE Review,* 1979, *6,* 45–49.

Jones, L. E. A study of the content in selected textbooks for the commonly offered basic business courses in secondary schools. In *Robert E. Slaughter Research Award Studies 1975* (Research Report No. 3). New York: McGraw-Hill, Gregg Division, 1975, pp. 9–19.

Kim, P. Y. Personal economic understanding and college business and economics courses. *Delta Pi Epsilon Journal,* 1977, *19*(2), 22–35.

Kuiper, S. Work values and problem perceptions of young married women in clerical occupations. *Delta Pi Epsilon Journal,* 1978, *20*(2), 23–39.

Kutie, R. C. An analysis of the job dimensions of word processing secretaries, administrative support secretaries, and traditional secretaries, and the correlation of these job dimensions with job satisfaction factors. In *Robert E. Slaughter Research Award Studies 1977* (Research Report No. 6). New York: McGraw-Hill, Gregg Division, 1977, pp. 8–11.

Lambrecht, J. J. Observations on first attempts to "individualize." *Delta Pi Epsilon Journal,* 1975, *17*(2), 1–14.

Lambrecht, J. J. First- and second-year shorthand achievement for Century 21, Forkner and Gregg shorthand. *Delta Pi Epsilon Journal*, 1978, *20*(4), 12–26.

Lambrecht, J. J. Assessment of attitudes of first-year Gregg and Forkner shorthand students. *NABTE Review*, 1980, *7*, 15–19.

Lambrecht, J. J., & McLean, G. N. Content and methodology background and perceived competencies of data-processing teachers. *NABTE Review*, 1977, *4*, 25–29.

Langford, T. E.; Sink, C. V.; & Weeks, R. R. The business education department in a college of business administration. *NABTE Review*, 1978, *5*, 9–15.

Levine, B. A. The relationship between theory testing and transcription skill in Gregg shorthand (Doctoral dissertation, New York University, 1979). *Dissertation Abstracts*, 1979, *40*(2), 825-B. (University Microfilms No. 80-27459)

Lewis, S. D. The effect of word processing on business letter writing. *Delta Pi Epsilon Journal*, 1979, *21*(2), 26–32.

Mach, K. A. The effects of repetitive and nonrepetitive practice on straight-copy speed and accuracy achievement on first-semester beginning typewriting. (Doctoral dissertation, University of North Dakota, 1971). *Dissertation Abstracts*, 1971, *33*(1), 231-A. (University Microfilms No. 72-19423)

McLean, G. N. Difficulty indices for office-typing tasks (Doctoral dissertation, Columbia University Teachers College, 1971) *Dissertation Abstracts*, 1972, *32*(9), 5122-A. (University Microfilms No. 72-8827)

McLean, G. N. Effectiveness of model office, cooperative office education, and office procedures courses based on employee satisfaction and satisfactoriness eighteen months after graduation. In *Robert E. Slaughter Research Award Studies 1975* (Research Report No. 3). New York: McGraw-Hill, Gregg Division, 1975, pp. 1–8. (Also published in *Delta Pi Epsilon Journal*, 1977, *19*(4), 21–28.)

McLean, G. N. The relationship between typewriting performance and shorthand transcription skills. *Delta Pi Epsilon Journal*, 1978, *20*(1), 20–25. (a)

McLean, G. N. *Teaching Typewriting* (Rapid Reader No. 3). St. Peter, Minn.: Delta Pi Epsilon, 1978. (b)

McLean, G. N.; Kleven, B. D.; & McLean, L. H. Sexism in general business texts. *Journal of Business Education*, 1978, *53*(5), 215–217.

McLean, G. N.; Kranz, P. R.; & Magnuson, J. C. Identifying form errors in production typing. *Business Education Forum*, 1980, *35*(1), 16–17.

McQueen, H. Pre-employment training needed for middle management positions in selected Tennessee industrial firms. *Delta Pi Epsilon Journal*, 1980, *22*(3), 28–38.

Mitchell, R. B. An investigation of job satisfaction among correspondence secretaries and the impact of supervision. *Delta Pi Epsilon Journal*, 1980, *22*(1), 32–40.

Ober, B. S. An analysis of the business working papers typed by beginning office workers. (Doctoral dissertation, Ohio State University, 1974). *Dissertation Abstracts*, 1975, *35*(8), 4968-A. (University Microfilms No. 75-03156)

Olson, N. J. Design and validation of a straight-copy typewriting prognostic test using kinesthetic sensitivity. In *Robert E. Slaughter Research Award Studies 1978* (Research Report No. 7). New York: McGraw-Hill, Gregg Division, 1978, pp. 3–8. (Also published in *Delta Pi Epsilon Journal*, 1980, *22*(3), 13–27.)

Perkins, C. D. *Sex Discrimination and Sex Stereotyping in Vocational Education*. Washington, D.C.: U.S. Government Printing Office, 1975.

Pitko, A. J. Interaction effects of office education programs, community size, and teacher attitude on the attitudes held by high school office education students toward office employment. *Delta Pi Epsilon Journal*, 1975, *17*(2), 15–27.

Quible, Z. K. Use of participative management in supervising office employees. *Delta Pi Epsilon Journal*, 1974, *16*(4), 13–22.

Reap, M. C. Job tasks of the beginning accounting and bookkeeping worker compared with the content of the high school accounting and bookkeeping curriculum. *Delta Pi Epsilon Journal*, 1980, *22*(1), 10–19.

Robinson, J. W.; Erickson, L. W.; Crawford, T. J.; Beaumont, L. R.; & Ownby, A. C. *Typewriting: Learning and Instruction*. Cincinnati: South-Western, 1979.

Safran, C. What men do to women on the job—A shocking look at sexual harassment. *Redbook Magazine*, November 1976, *149*, 217–224.

Santiago-Perez, A. A comparison of student achievement in beginning typewriting in high schools in Puerto Rico using special Spanish materials versus those currently adopted. *Delta Pi Epsilon Journal*, 1979, *21*(3), 1–19.

Schmidt, R. A. *Motor Skills*. New York: Harper & Row, 1975.

Standard & Poor's Industry Surveys. *Office Equipment Systems and Services—Basic Analysis*. May 15, 1980 (Section 2), 028.

Stanley, T. O. The development of the test of consumer competencies. In *Robert E. Slaughter Research Award Studies 1976* (Research Report No. 5). New York: McGraw-Hill, Gregg Division, 1976, pp. 7–10. (Also published in *Delta Pi Epsilon Journal*, 1977, *19*(3), 1–15.)

Sullivan, V. Self-reports of advancement opportunities by graduates of a traditionally female collegiate program. *NABTE Review*, 1980, *7*, 29–33.

Thomas, E. G. Perceptions of business teachers and business education majors regarding the roles of women. *Delta Pi Epsilon Journal*, 1975, *18*(1), 30–46.

Thomas, E. G. The effect of office practice classes on student knowledge and attitudes. *Delta Pi Epsilon Journal*, 1976, *18*(3), 28–39.

U.S. Department of Health, Education, and Welfare, Office of Education. *Summary of Offerings and Enrollments in Public Secondary Schools, 1972/73*. Washington, D.C.: U.S. Government Printing Office, 1975. (ERIC Document Reproduction Service No. ED 114 977)

VanHuss, S. H.; Lambrecht, J. J.; & Christensen, E. L. *Shorthand: Learning and Instruction*. Cincinnati: South-Western, 1980.

Weise, B. Using repetition and alternating levels of practice in beginning typewriting. *Balance Sheet*, 1975, *57*(3), 108–109, 111–112, 139.

West, L. J. Business education. In R. L. Ebel (Ed.), *Encyclopedia of Educational Research* (4th ed.). New York: Macmillan, 1969, pp. 105–116.

West, L. J. Reversed instructional procedures for vocational typing tasks. *Delta Pi Epsilon Journal*, 1972, *14*(2), 28–36.

West, L. J. *Implications of Research for Teaching Typewriting* (2nd ed., Research Bulletin No. 4) St. Peter, Minn.: Delta Pi Epsilon, 1974. (ERIC Document Reproduction Service No. ED 107 884)

West, L. J. Survey of bookkeeping job activities in relation to the high school bookkeeping curriculum. *Delta Pi Epsilon Journal*, 1977, *17*(1), 1–34.

West, L. J. Accuracy standards for straight copy timings. *Journal of Business Education*, 1980, *55*, 223–224.

West, L. J. *Acquisition of Typewriting Skills* (2nd ed.). New York: Harcourt Brace Jovanovich, 1982.

West, L. J., & McLean, G. N. An evaluation of error cutoff scoring in straight-copy typewriting tests. *Business Education Forum,* 1968, *23*(2), 10–12.

Whitney, E. P. A report on the survey of basic business survival skills. *Delta Pi Epsilon Journal,* 1979, *21*(1), 23–40.

Williamson, D., & Houghton, E. L. Shorthand skills required by business administrators. *NABTE Review,* 1978 *5,* 89–93.

Wong, S. M. A study to compare the effects of three different methods of reading copy when proofreading straight paragraph copy materials by first-year typewriting students (Doctoral dissertation, Oregon State University, 1971). *Dissertation Abstracts,* 1971, *32*(4), 2004-A. (University Microfilms No. 71-25074)

Working Women's United Institute. *Sexual Harassment on the Job: Results of a Preliminary Survey.* New York: The Institute, 1975. (Mimeo)

BUSING

See Black Education; Judicial Decisions; Transportation of Students; Urban Education.

CAREER EDUCATION

Any movement in education can logically be expected to pass through the following stages: (1) an idea stage; (2) a conceptual development stage; (3) a try-out–implementation–refinement stage; (4) an evaluation stage; (5) a research stage; and (6) a substantive body of knowledge–further refinement stage. Unlike most other topics included in the *Encyclopedia of Educational Research*, career education has, to date, not advanced beyond the evaluation stage. Thus, this article necessarily differs in format and content from many others.

Although historical antecedents to career education extend back many years (Herr, 1972), the formal movement itself is generally acknowledged to have begun only in 1971 (Herr, 1975). The first formal book on career education appeared in 1972 (Hoyt et al.). The first reported attempt to obtain any kind of national consensus, with respect to meaning of the term "career education," was reported in a policy paper in the mid-1970s (Hoyt, 1975). The first attempt to define the career education treatment in terms amenable to systematic evaluation did not appear in print until 1977 (Hoyt).

By 1980, the three basic goals of the career education movement had been identified: (1) to change the educational system through inserting a "careers" emphasis throughout the curriculum; (2) to increase community–education system linkages in ways that make career education a community effort rather than an effort of the education system alone; and (3) to provide persons with a set of ten general employability-adaptability-promotability skills required to adjust to change in the occupational society (Hoyt, 1980). The contents of this article are organized around these three basic goals.

A "Careers" Emphasis. The most obvious indicator of career education's ability to change the educational system through a "careers" emphasis is seen by simply noting that it has survived for a full decade. Brodinsky (1979), after noting that the average life of an educational reform movement is about three years, pictured career education as "alive and doing well" after a full decade, and as the decade's "moderate success story." Evidence of future probable acceptance is a study reported by the National School Boards Association (NSBA) (1980). In that study, a national sample of superintendents and school board members rated career education as the single topic "most deserving" of more attention among 16 topics introduced during the 1970s. Further, of 31 areas identified in that NSBA survey, career education ranked third among those judged likely to receive increased interest and financial support during the 1980–1985 period.

A second indicator is the number of national professional organizations and associations in education that have endorsed career education. The Education Commission of the States (1979b) has identified and reported such endorsements from 19 national groups. In addition to these 19 organizations, Hoyt (1980) has identified 13 other national educational associations that have formally endorsed career education. Thus, a total of 32 national organizations and associations in education have, to date, endorsed career education.

Attitude surveys regarding career education can be viewed as a third indicator of the extent to which career education can influence education change. From the beginning of the career education movement, such attitude surveys have produced generally favorable results. This was true even as early as 1971–1972 (Brickell, 1972). In 1974, an extensive study of fifty locations (one in each state) found that well over one-half of all teachers and counselors surveyed indicated that it was important to include career education in the curriculum (Development Associates, 1975). A representative nationwide sample of local school districts surveyed during the 1974/75 school year found that 80–95 percent of respondents rated each of career education's nine learner outcomes as somewhere between "important" and "absolutely necessary" (McLaughlin, 1976).

Efforts to study and summarize large numbers of attitude surveys regarding career education have been similarly positive. For example, a survey of ten attitude studies conducted in ten different states concluded that students respond positively to career education regardless of grade level or type of program (National Advisory Council for Career Education, 1976). After an extensive review of the literature, Herr (1977) summarized by saying, "Surveys of parents, teachers, and students about the goals or intent of career education tend to be positive with almost no exceptions" (p. 61). These positive findings continue to be generated, as illustrated in a study of 1,598 students, parents, educators, and business persons in the Deer Park Independent School District of Deer Park, Texas, where it was concluded that all types of respondents—and especially educators—shared a strong desire to see the concept of career education implemented in the school system (Grant, 1979). Similar strong support was found in a 1979 survey of 20 chief state school officers, with the report concluding that 15 of the 20 felt career education was "very important" or "extremely important," whereas only one said it was "not very important" (Hansford, 1979).

A fourth—and the most empirical—indicator is found in data regarding the extent to which career education has been implemented in school systems throughout the nation. Implementation activities during the first half of the decade have been documented extensively by Herr (1975) and summarized by High (1976). Much of the literature concerning the decade's implementation activities has been cataloged by Hall and High (1979).

The first—and, to date, only—national survey of career education implementation activities was conducted during the 1974/75 school year (McLaughlin, 1976). This survey included 900 representative school districts, selected without regard to actual career education programs. The results indicated that career education was gradually being considered and implemented throughout the country. Although 60 percent (about 9,000) of the nation's 16,000 school districts were estimated to have begun career education implementation efforts, only 3 percent (about 480) had taken what were regarded then as five essential steps demanded by a comprehensive career education effort. There were clear differences in extensiveness of implementation efforts between school districts with clear career education policies as opposed to those without such policies. The most prevalent implementation activity was staff development. The researchers estimated that, in terms of comprehensive implementation, career education had come about 15 percent of the way by the end of the 1974/75 school year.

A second extensive effort to survey career education implementation activities was conducted by the American Institutes for Research, in May and June of 1980, for purposes of a rapid-feedback evaluation concerning implementation of the first year of the Career Education Incentive Act (Steel et al., 1980). This survey involved 31 local and intermediate school districts within nine states. The states were located in nine different geographic regions and represented high, medium, and low levels of state support for career education at the time of the 1974/75 nationwide survey. State-level results from these nine states found that chief state school officers in six states were actively promoting career education implementation; five state legislatures had passed legislation endorsing career education; four state boards of education had adopted formal resolutions of approval; and seven states had appropriated funds to support implementation. All nine states reported that implementation activities had increased since receipt of Public Law 95-207 (Career Education Incentive Act) funds. At the local school-district level, only school districts receiving Public Law 95-207 grants were surveyed. All reported their superintendents had endorsed career education. Roughly 58 percent of the teachers in these districts were estimated to be using a "careers" emphasis regularly in their teaching, while 62 percent of elementary school counselors and 78 percent of secondary school counselors in these school districts were involved.

Finally, a fifth indicator can be found by examining state legislation for career education. By the 1974/75 school year, nine state legislatures had enacted some form of career education legislation (McLaughlin, 1976). Jesser (1979) reported finding fifteen states that had enacted specific career education legislation, and three more that had included career education in broader education-reform legislation during the 1970s. A study by the Education Commission of the States (1979a) identified 21 states with some form of career education legislation by the end of 1978.

The fiscal year 1980 annual reports, submitted by the 47 states participating in Public Law 95-207, indicated that approximately 2,000 of the nation's 16,000 school districts were using comprehensive career education as a vehicle for changing education to include a "careers" emphasis. Thus, after a full decade of existence, it seems safe to say that career education has made some progress toward meeting this goal.

Community–Education System Linkages. The 1974–1975 national survey of K–12 career education found that increasing the involvement of the work community in educational policymaking and as an instructional resource was a key ingredient for extensive career education implementation (McLaughlin, 1976). This study found that those learner activities most frequently rated effective for career education were those that brought students together with individuals in the work world.

The 1980 rapid-feedback evaluation study conducted by the American Institutes for Research found that about one-half of the nine states examined were devoting some leadership funds to promoting collaborative relationships with business, labor, industry, professional, government, civic, or community groups (Steel et al., 1980). In seven of the nine states included in this study, business, labor, and community groups had conducted or assisted in the conduct of workshops or other implementation support activities, and, in six states, such groups had prepared or disseminated instructional materials for use in career education. All but two of the 24 local school districts visited in this study reported some business–community organization participation in their career education efforts.

The Education Commission of the States (1979b) has identified 25 business, labor, industry, and government organizations that have endorsed the career education concept and/or adopted formal policy statements in support of career education. An earlier monograph identified 11 national business, industry, and community organizations with national career education efforts in place (Hoyt, 1976). A comprehensive review of organized labor's involvement in career education has been prepared (Hoyt, Bommarito, and Schulman, 1978), as has a monograph describing concrete examples of community involvement in K–12 career education efforts (Hoyt, 1979). It seems safe to say that very marked and substantial progress toward meeting the goal of community–education system linkages has taken place.

General Employability Skills. To most persons, the crucial evaluation question is "What benefits accrue to recipients when the career education treatment is applied"? Thus, it seems appropriate to devote most of this article to examining this question. The two obviously great deterrents to providing adequate answers are (1) that the newness of career education forces us to limit reported results to short-range, intermediate criteria (rather than to have results of a developmental-longitudinal effort assessing during the adult years populations exposed to career education during the K–12 school years); and (2) that wide variation exists in definition of what constitutes the career education treatment, thus leading to the inability to specify what is being evaluated.

In order to organize evaluation studies for presentation here, three basic organizational schemes have been used. First, following a classification scheme proposed by Tuckman and Carducci (1974), only quantitative studies involving (1) experimental-control subjects with pretesting and posttesting; (2) experimental-control subjects with posttesting only; or (3) experimental subjects only with pretesting and posttesting, are included. Tuckman and Carducci refer to other studies, most of which deal with processes of career education rather than student outcomes, as "case studies." Although acknowledging that, almost without exception, such case studies produce results pointing to the success of career education, they emphasize that such results must be interpreted with caution. For this reason, case studies have been eliminated from this review. That such case studies are commonplace in career education is illustrated by Hamilton and Mitchell (1978), who reported that, when they examined 257 career education evaluation reports for possible submission to the Depart-

ment of Education's Joint Dissemination Review Panel (JDRP), only 64 had quantitative data and included both experimental and control subjects.

Second, in attempting to find a common unit for use in reporting results, Bonnet's definition of an "outcome study" as consisting of "the assessment of one outcome objective at one grade level" was adopted (Bonnet, 1977). Where there were doubts regarding the exact number of "outcome studies" contained in a single evaluation report, the lowest possible number was used. Thus, it seems likely that the total number of "outcome studies" is actually greater than reported here.

Third, the evaluation studies, reported during the decade, were divided into three basic time categories: (1) those taking place from 1971 through early 1976; (2) those taking place at the end of the 1975/76 school year; and (3) those career education evaluation studies that, during the decade, successfully passed through JDRP review and were certified as "education programs that work." This was done primarily so that evaluation studies in the early part of the decade, those at the midpoint of the decade, and those near the end of the decade could be contrasted.

The evaluation studies reported here, which took place during the 1971 to early 1976 period, have been reviewed and summarized in six separate reports: Tuckman and Carducci (1974); National Advisory Council for Career Education (1976); Enderlein (1976); Datta et al. (1976); Bhaerman (1977); and Herr (1977). Duplications omitted, these six reports reviewed a total of 209 individual evaluation studies. These 209 studies, in turn, contained a total of 351 "outcome studies" as defined by Bonnet.

The evaluation studies at the end of the 1976/76 school year are summarized by Bonnet (1977). She limited her investigation to 81 federally funded career education demonstration projects that terminated in the summer of 1976. Thirty-two were three-year projects funded under Part D of Public Law 90-576, whereas the remaining 49 were one-year projects funded under Section 406 of Public Law 93-380. Of the 81 project reports, Bonnet identified 45 concerned with student outcomes, which, in total, contained 512 "outcome studies" as Bonnet defined that term. The large number of one-year studies clearly distinguishes this set from the other two.

Of the 14 studies identified as JDRP-approved, 11 were approved during the 1978–1980 period. Each had to submit compelling evidence to convince the evaluation experts who compose the JDRP that positive answers could be given to each of the following questions: (1) Is there evidence that something happened? (2) Is the evidence credible? (3) Did something happen often enough that effects as large as those observed would be likely to happen again? (4) Did something of such magnitude happen that the effects are educationally significant? (5) Did the something that happened often enough, in sufficient size, also occur under circumstances that are likely to be reproducible? and (6) Can what happened be attributed to the treatment? These 14 studies, which are identified in the reference list as "submissions to the JDRP," produced a total of 121 "outcome studies" as defined by Bonnet.

Taking the "outcome studies" for these three sets of evaluation reports, we can summarize the number producing statistically significant positive results, the number with no statistically significant differences, and the number favoring the control pupils, as opposed to the experimental pupils, for each of the ten general employability-adaptability-promotability skills that Hoyt (1980) has identified.

Basic academic skills. The first employability skill of career education concerns the basic academic skills of reading, oral and written communication, and mathematics. The assumption made is that, by infusing a "careers" emphasis into the teaching-learning process, pupils will be motivated to increase their academic achievement.

During the 1971 to early 1976 period, using a conservative approach to identify outcome studies, a total of 46 outcome studies were clearly identified. Of these, 40 are summarized in the Bhaerman report (1977), and 6 in the remaining reports covering this period. Of the 46 identified outcome studies, 19 produced statistically significant differences at the .05 level favoring the career education treatment, 27 produced no statistically significant differences, and none produced results favoring control (non–career education) over experimental (career education) pupils.

During the 1975/76 midyear of the decade, Bonnet's analysis located 43 outcome studies, 10 of which produced statistically significant differences at the .05 level in favor of career education, with an additional 10 outcome studies showing positive, but not statistically significant, differences in means favoring experimental (career education) over control (non–career education) pupils. Of the remaining 23 outcome studies, all of which showed no difference or negative differences between means, Bonnet did not identify which ones, if any, were statistically significant.

Of the 14 JDRP-approved projects, 2 included study of the effect of a career education treatment on increases in basic academic skills (Cobb County, 1973; Lincoln County, 1973). These 2 studies produced a total of 4 outcome studies. Of these, 2 produced statistically significant differences favoring experimental (career education) over control (non–career education) pupils; two found no statistically significant differences; and no one study found control pupils exceeding experimental pupils in basic academic-skill gains.

Thus, during the decade, using conservative means to identify outcome studies, a total of 93 outcome studies assessing the impact of career education on gains in basic academic skills were identified. Almost all were conducted at the elementary school level. Of these, a total of 31 produced statistically significant differences at the .05 level favoring pupils who had been exposed to a career education treatment through infusion of a "careers" emphasis into the teaching-learning process. No statistically significant studies were found favoring control (non–career education) over experimental (career education) pupils. It is

concluded that career education can, but does not always, serve to improve pupil acquisition of basic academic skills at the elementary school level. Furthermore, there is no reason to believe that, when a "careers" emphasis is infused into the teaching-learning process, pupil academic skills will be lowered.

Skills in practicing good work habits. The second employability skill of career education is practicing good work habits, for example, being punctual, doing one's best, completing assignments on time. The assumption made is that, if teachers emphasize and reward the practice of good work habits in the classroom, such skills will be learned by pupils.

During the 1971 to early 1976 period, using a conservative approach to identify outcome studies, 10 outcome studies were clearly identified. Of these, 6 produced statistically significant differences favoring the career education treatment, 3 produced no statistically significant differences, and 1 produced statistically significant differences favoring control (non–career education) over experimental (career education) pupils. These studies were spread over the K–12 levels.

During the 1975/76 midyear of the decade, Bonnet's analysis located 45 outcome studies, 4 of which produced statistically significant differences at the .05 level in favor of career education, with an additional 16 showing positive, but not statistically significant, differences in means favoring experimental (career education) over control (non–career education) pupils. Of the remaining 25 outcome studies, all of which showed no difference or negative differences between means, Bonnet did not identify which ones, if any, were statistically significant.

None of the 14 JDRP-approved studies investigated the effectiveness of career education in improving pupil skills in practicing good work habits.

Thus, during the decade, using conservative means to identify outcome studies, a total of 55 outcome studies assessing the impact of career education on increasing pupil skills in the practice of good work habits were identified. Of these, a total of 10 produced results statistically significant at the .05 level favoring the career education treatment, one produced results favoring the control group, and the remainder produced no statistically significant differences between experimental (career education) and control (non–career education) pupils as reported by the authors. It is concluded that, based on evidence available to date, it is possible, but unlikely, that a career education treatment in the classroom will increase pupil skills in practicing good work habits. It is further concluded that there is almost no reason to believe that a career education treatment will act to decrease or depress pupil skills in practicing them.

Skills in developing meaningful work values. The third employability skill of career education concerns skills in developing and using personally meaningful work values. The assumption made is that, given a "careers" emphasis during the K–12 educational experiences, pupils will increase their desire to work. The kinds of measures used in assessing this skill are predominately ones measuring the extent to which pupils hold positive attitudes toward work.

During the 1971 to early 1976 period, using a conservative approach to identify outcome studies, a total of 52 outcome studies were clearly identified. Of these, 30 produced statistically significant results favoring a career education treatment, 21 produced no statistically significant differences between experimental (career education) and control (non–career education) pupils, and one produced results favoring control over experimental pupils. These studies were conducted at various grade levels, covering early elementary school through senior high school.

During the 1975/76 midyear of the decade, Bonnet's analysis located 44 outcome studies, 5 of which produced statistically significant differences at the .05 level in favor of career education, with an additional 25 showing positive, but not statistically significant, differences in means favoring experimental (career education) over control (non–career education) pupils. Of the remaining 14 outcome studies, all of which showed no difference or negative differences between means, Bonnet did not identify which ones, if any, were statistically significant.

Of the 14 JDRP-approved studies, 4 assessed results in the general domain of work values (Akron Public Schools, 1978; Ceres Unified School District, 1978; Ontario-Montclair School District, 1978; Pima County Public Schools, 1978). These 4 studies produced, using conservative estimates, a total of 12 outcome studies. Of these, 9 favored experimental (career education) over control (non–career education) pupils; three showed no statistically significant differences; and none favored control over experimental pupils.

Thus, during the decade, using conservative means to identify outcome studies, a total of 108 outcome studies assessing the impact of career education on increasing favorable pupil attitudes toward work—and so, indirectly, work values—were identified. These studies were conducted at various grade levels throughout the K–12 school system. Of these 108 outcome studies, 44 produced statistically significant results favoring the career education treatment, whereas an additional 25 showed positive, but not statistically significant, differences in means favoring the career education treatment. Only 1 of the 108 outcome studies showed statistically significant results favoring control (non–career education) over experimental (career education) pupils, far less than would have been expected by chance alone. It is concluded that a career education treatment is likely to produce increases in positive pupil attitudes toward work, even though such a treatment does not always do so. Further, it is extremely unlikely that a career education treatment will cause pupils to view work in a negative attitudinal sense.

Skills in understanding private enterprise. The fourth employability skill of career education concerns skills in basic understanding and appreciation of the pri-

vate enterprise system. The assumption is that, if pupils are exposed to the American system of private enterprise, through both cognitive and experiential approaches, they will increase in both their knowledge of and appreciation of that system.

During the 1971 to early 1976 period, using a conservative approach to identify outcome studies, a total of only 4 outcome studies bearing directly on this skill were identified. All 4 produced results showing statistically significant differences favoring experimental (career education) over control (non–career education) pupils. Bonnet's mid-decade analysis of studies conducted at the end of the 1975/76 school year included no outcome studies bearing on this employability skill. Of the 14 JDRP-approved studies, 4 (Akron Public Schools, 1978; Ceres Unified School District, 1978; Ontario-Montclair School District, 1978; Pima County Public Schools, 1978) produced a total of 12 outcome studies bearing directly on this employability skill. Of these 12 outcome studies, 10 produced results showing statistically significant differences favoring experimental (career education) over control (non–career education) pupils, whereas 2 of the 12 showed no statistically significant differences.

Thus, during the decade, using conservative means to identify outcome studies, a total of 16 outcome studies assessing the impact of career education on increasing pupil understanding and appreciation of the private enterprise system were identified. Of these 16 outcome studies, 14 produced statistically significant differences favoring pupils exposed to career education, when compared to pupils not exposed to career education. Two produced no statistically significant differences. None produced results favoring control (non–career education) over experimental (career education) pupils. The relatively small number of outcome studies identified during the decade indicates that the career education treatment has often not included an emphasis on this employability skill. In spite of the small number of outcome studies, it is concluded that the career education treatment, when including an emphasis on providing students with basic understanding and appreciation of the private enterprise system, is highly likely to do so.

Skills in self-understanding and understanding career interests and aptitudes. The fifth employability skill of career education concerns skills in self-understanding and understanding of educational-occupational opportunities. Here, only that part dealing with increasing student self-understanding of career interests and aptitudes is considered. The remaining portion of this skill is reported in the following section. The assumption made is that pupils exposed to the career education treatment will gain in understanding of their individual career interests and aptitudes.

During the 1971 to early 1976 period, using a conservative approach to identify outcome studies, a total of 73 outcome studies were clearly identified. Of these, 42 produced statistically significant results favoring a career education treatment, 28 produced no statistically significant differences, and 3 produced results favoring control (non–career education) pupils over experimental (career education) pupils. Most of these studies were conducted at the secondary school level.

During the 1975/76 midyear of the decade, Bonnet's analysis located 106 outcome studies, 9 of which produced statistically significant results favoring a career education treatment, with an additional 52 showing positive, but not statistically significant, differences in means favoring experimental (career education) over control (non–career education) pupils. Of the remaining 45 outcome studies, all of which showed no difference or negative differences between means, Bonnet did not identify which ones, if any, were statistically significant.

Of the 14 JDRP-approved projects, 8 included assessment of increases in pupil self-understanding in their evaluations (Akron Public Schools, 1978; Ceres Unified School District, 1978; Cobb County Public Schools, 1973; Coloma Community School District, 1978; District of Columbia Public Schools, 1980; Ontario-Montclair School District, 1978; Pima County Public Schools, 1978; Southwest Iowa Learning Resources Center, 1978). These eight studies, using conservative estimates, produced a minimum of 21 outcome studies. All 21 produced statistically significant results favoring a career education treatment.

Thus, during the decade, using conservative means to identify outcome studies, a total of 200 outcome studies assessing the effectiveness of career education on increasing pupil self-understanding of career interests and aptitudes were identified. Of these 200 outcome studies, 72 produced statistically significant results favoring the career education treatment, and an additional 52 produced differences in means favoring experimental (career education) over control (non–career education) pupils. Only 3 of the 155 outcome studies, where possible negative effects could be identified, found control (non–career education) pupils exceeding experimental (career education) pupils in self-understanding skills. The relatively negative findings reported by Bonnet at middecade are not confirmed by the studies conducted either during the 1971 to early 1976 period, or the 1978–1980 period. It is concluded that a career education treatment can—and is very likely to—increase pupil self-understanding of career interests and aptitudes.

Skills in understanding career opportunities. The assumption made here is that the career education treatment will result in increasing pupil understanding of possible educational and occupational opportunities available to them.

During the 1971 to early 1976 period, using a conservative approach to identify outcome studies, a total of 110 outcome studies were identified. Of these 76 produced statistically significant results favoring the career education treatment, 32 failed to find statistically significant differences, and 2 studies found control (non–career education) pupils exceeding experimental (career education)

pupils in terms of gains in understanding of educational and occupational opportunities. These studies were conducted at various grade levels of the K–12 school system.

During the 1975/76 midyear of the decade, Bonnet's analysis located 167 outcome studies, 46 of which produced statistically significant results favoring the career education treatment, with an additional 79 showing positive, but not statistically significant, differences in means favoring experimental (career education) over control (non–career education) pupils. Of the remaining 42 outcome studies, all of which showed no difference or negative differences between means, Bonnet did not identify which ones, if any, were statistically significant.

Of the 14 JDRP-approved projects, 12 (the two exceptions being Cogent Associates, 1978, and Highline Public Schools, 1978) included study of career education's effectiveness in improving pupil understanding of educational and/or occupational opportunities. These 12 studies, using conservative estimates, produced a minimum of 34 outcome studies. Of these, all 34 yielded statistically significant results favoring experimental (career education) pupils over control (non–career education) pupils.

Thus, during the decade, using conservative means to identify outcome studies, a total of 311 outcome studies assessing the effectiveness of career education in increasing pupil understanding of educational and/or occupational opportunities were identified. Of these, 156 produced statistically significant results favoring the career education treatment, whereas in another 79 whose results were not statistically significant, mean scores of experimental (career education) pupils exceeded those of control (non–career education) pupils. In only 2 of the 269 outcome studies where possible negative effects could be identified were results favoring control pupils over experimental pupils found. It is concluded that career education can (and is extremely likely to) result in increasing pupil understanding of educational and/or occupational opportunities.

Career decision-making skills. The sixth employability skill of career education is career decision-making skill. The assumption made is that, given systematic assistance in tentative career decision making during the elementary and secondary school years, pupil ability to undertake acceptable career decision-making procedures will be increased.

During the 1971 to early 1976 period, using a conservative approach to identify outcome studies, a total of 43 outcome studies were identified. Of these, 26 produced statistically significant results favoring the career education treatment, whereas the remaining 17 found no statistically significant differences. None of them found statistically significant differences favoring control (non–career education) over experimental (career education) pupils. These studies were conducted primarily at the secondary school level.

During the 1975/76 midyear of the decade, Bonnet's analysis located 100 outcome studies, 23 of which produced statistically significant results favoring the career education treatment, with another 47 studies showing positive, but not statistically significant, differences in means favoring experimental (career education) pupils over control (non–career education) pupils. Of the remaining 30 outcome studies, all of which showed no difference or negative differences between means, Bonnet did not identify which ones, if any, were statistically significant.

Of the 14 JDRP-approved projects, 7 included study of career education's effectiveness in improving pupils' career decision-making skills (Akron Public Schools, 1978; Ceres Unified School District, 1978; Coloma Community School District, 1978; District of Columbia Public Schools, 1980; Ontario-Montclair School District, 1978; Pima County Public Schools, 1978; University of California at Los Angeles, 1973). These seven studies, using conservative estimates, produced a minimum of 21 outcome studies. Of these, 19 yielded statistically significant results favoring experimental (career education) pupils over control (non–career education) pupils, whereas the remaining 2 found no statistically significant differences to exist. None favored control over experimental pupils.

Thus, during the decade, using conservative means to identify outcome studies, a total of 164 outcome studies assessing effectiveness of career education in equipping pupils with career decision-making skills were identified. Of these, 68 produced statistically significant results favoring the career education treatment, whereas in another 47 whose results were not statistically significant, mean scores of experimental (career education) pupils exceeded those of control (non–career education) pupils. In none of the 134 outcome studies where possible negative effects could be identified did results favor control over experimental pupils. It is concluded that career education can— and frequently does—result in increasing pupil career decision-making skills.

Job-related skills. The seventh employability skill of career education concerns job-seeking, job-finding, job-getting, and job-holding skills. The assumption made is that, given systematic assistance in acquiring such skills through some combination of cognitive and experiential learning, pupil knowledge, with respect to how to seek, find, get, and hold a job, will be increased.

During the 1971 to early 1976 period, using a conservative approach to identify outcome studies, a total of 13 outcome studies were identified. Of these, 8 produced statistically significant results favoring the career education treatment, whereas the remaining 5 found no statistically significant differences. None found statistically significant differences favoring control (non–career education) over experimental (career education) pupils. These studies were conducted primarily at the secondary school level.

During the 1975/76 midyear of the decade, Bonnet's analysis located 6 outcome studies, 1 of which produced statistically significant results favoring the career education treatment, with an additional 2 studies showing positive, but not statistically significant, differences in means

favoring experimental (career education) pupils over control (non–career education) pupils. Of the remaining 3 outcome studies, all of which showed no difference or negative differences between means, Bonnet did not identify which ones, if any, were statistically significant.

Of the 14 JDRP-approved projects, 2 included study of career education's effectiveness in improving pupils' job-seeking, job-finding, job-getting, and job-holding skills (Akron Public Schools, 1978; Ceres Unified School District, 1978). These 2 studies, using conservative estimates, produced a minimum of 5 outcome studies. Of these, 3 showed statistically significant differences favoring experimental (career education) pupils over control (non–career education) pupils, whereas the remaining 2 found no statistically significant differences to exist.

Thus, during the decade, using conservative means to identify outcome studies, a total of 24 outcome studies assessing career education's effectiveness in equipping pupils with job-seeking, job-finding, job-getting, and job-holding skills were identified. Of these, 12 produced statistically significant results favoring the career education treatment, whereas none were identified that produced statistically significant results favoring control over experimental pupils. It is concluded that, although career education can and sometimes does succeed in equipping pupils with job-seeking, job-finding, job-getting, and job-holding skills, an insufficient number of studies have been conducted to date to justify an assertion that success is the likely outcome of a career education effort. It is further concluded that relatively little attention has been focused on the evaluation of this career education employability skill to date, in terms of the studies reviewed here.

Skills in productive use of leisure. The eighth employability skill of career education is skill in making productive use of leisure time through unpaid work, including both volunteerism and work within the home-family structure. The assumption made is that a bona fide career education treatment will provide students with both the interest and the motivation to engage in unpaid work leading to productive use of leisure time.

Of the total of 984 outcome studies conducted during the decade that are reviewed here, only one, which was included in Bonnet's middecade analysis, addressed this employability skill. That single study, although showing positive results, failed to produce statistical significance. It is concluded that, based on these 984 outcome studies, there is no evidence to justify an assertion that career education can provide pupils with skills in making productive use of leisure time. Further, there appears to be a great need to increase attention toward supplying pupils with such skills as part of a comprehensive career education treatment.

Skills in overcoming bias. The ninth employability skill of career education is skill in overcoming bias and stereotyping that deter full freedom of career choice for all persons. The assumption made is that, if pupils can be provided with accurate information bearing on this topic, their attitudes will be changed in ways that reflect a more nonstereotyped perception of the occupational society.

None of the 1971 to early 1976 studies, or of the studies included in Bonnet's mid-decade analysis, addressed this skill. However, of the 14 JDRP-approved studies, 3 centered primary attention on this topic (Cogent Associates, 1978; Cogent Associates, 1980; Highline Public Schools, 1978). These 3 studies, each of which involved experimental-control pupils in elementary school settings with pretest and posttest comparisons, produced a total of 12 outcome studies. All 12 of the outcome studies yielded statistically significant results favoring experimental (career education) over control (non–career education) pupils.

Because of the careful way in which each of these three studies was conducted, and the consistency and impressive nature of their results, it is concluded that a career education treatment can help elementary school pupils overcome sex bias and stereotyping in ways that allow them to view careers as open to both women and men. Further, these studies indicate the need to focus increased attention on providing pupils with such skills as part of a comprehensive career education treatment.

Skills in humanizing the work place. The tenth employability skill of career education is the ability to humanize the work place for oneself in such a way that a person can find personal dignity, meaning, and satisfaction in her or his occupation. The assumption made is that, through career education, pupils can be prepared to accomplish this goal.

Of the 984 outcome studies reviewed in this article, not one included this skill as one to be assessed. It is, therefore, concluded that no evidence exists at present to justify career education's claim that such skills can be delivered to youth as part of a comprehensive career education effort.

Summary of Employability Skills. Using Bonnet's definition of "outcome study," a total of 984 outcome studies are included in this review of career education employability skills during the 1971–1980 period. Of these 984 studies, 419 produced statistically significant results favoring the career education treatment. These 419 outcome studies included 301 involving experimental-control pupil comparisons and 118 involving precomparisons and postcomparisons of only experimental pupils. Because Bonnet's analysis did not include data regarding the number of statistically significant outcome studies favoring control pupils, the need exists to look separately at (1) a combination of the 1971 to early 1976 studies, and the 14 JDRP-approved studies; and (2) Bonnet's middecade analysis at the end of the school year 1975/76.

A total of 472 outcome studies are included in the 1971 to early 1976 studies and the 14 JDRP-approved studies. Of these 472 studies, 321 produced statistically significant differences favoring the career education treatment. Of the 372 of these 472 outcome studies involving experimen-

tal-control group comparisons, statistically significant differences favoring control over experimental pupils were found in only six instances.

Of the 512 outcome studies included in Bonnet's mid-decade analysis, 247 involved experimental-control pupil comparisons whereas 265 involved precomparisons and postcomparisons of only experimental pupils. Of the 247 outcome studies involving experimental-control comparisons, 53 produced statistically significant differences favoring experimental (career education) pupils over control (non–career education) pupils, whereas an additional 85 found positive, but not statistically significant, differences in means favoring experimental pupils over control pupils. Of the 265 outcome studies involving precomparisons and postcomparisons of only experimental pupils, 192 showed positive (posttest over pretest) differences in means, and in 45 of these 192 studies, the differences were statistically significant. A majority of Bonnet's studies, unlike the other two groupings used here, involved only a one-year treatment period.

Conclusion. Evidence reviewed here covers the 1971 to 1980 period and concentrates on evaluative, rather than research, data. In terms of the two basic process goals of career education, the evidence reported leads to the conclusion that career education made good progress during the 1971–1980 period in both (1) changing the education system through inserting a "careers" emphasis throughout the K–12 curriculum and (2) increasing community–school system linkage efforts in the work-education relationships domain. In both of these major areas, it appears obvious that career education enjoyed considerable success during its first full decade of existence—the decade of the 1970s.

Available evidence is mixed with respect to career education's ability to deliver its ten claimed employability skills to K–12 pupils. Evidence is strong that career education can provide pupils with (1) skills in understanding and appreciating the private enterprise system; (2) skills in understanding their own career interests and aptitudes and in understanding educational-occupational opportunities; and (3) skills in overcoming bias and stereotyping. Evidence is promising, but certainly not yet conclusive, that career education can provide pupils with (1) basic academic skills; (2) skills in developing and using personally meaningful work values; (3) career decision-making skills; and (4) job-seeking, job-finding, job-getting, and job-holding skills. Evidence is largely lacking to justify career education's claims that it can provide pupils with (1) skills in practicing good work habits; (2) skills in making productive use of leisure time; or (3) skills in humanizing the work place for oneself. There is no evidence that a career education treatment can be expected to have a negative effect on development of any of these ten employability skills in K–12 pupils.

The contents of this article have demonstrated that, even during its first decade of existence, evaluation of effectiveness has been a high priority of the career education movement. Further, the evidence must generally be regarded as more positive than negative in nature. There is some reason to believe that progress has been made in meeting, to some extent, the goals of career education during the decade of the 1970s. Serious problems remain.

First, this article makes clear the fact that evidence concerning career education's acceptability is more convincing than is evidence regarding its effectiveness. The long-run survival of career education will depend on its ability to make its acceptability and its effectiveness equally convincing. In these times of budget constraints in education that cause various educational movements to compete against each other for limited dollars, it is hoped that more than the political pressures of the past will be brought to bear in the decision-making process. Instead of political lobbying, it is hoped that each program will be judged on merit—"merit" defined as a combination of (1) documented need and (2) documented evidence of effectiveness in meeting that need. Career education has not yet achieved the ideal balance here. At the same time, it is safe to conclude that, compared with many other aspects of education that still base their pleas for financial assistance on purely political lobbying efforts, career education has come closer to achieving this balance.

Second, there is great need for the exact nature of the career education treatment to be more carefully defined by those who evaluate its effectiveness. Research has proved frustrating in those many instances where it could not be discerned, with any degree of exactness, what the evaluators meant by the career education treatment. Equally serious is the need for evaluators of career education to specify, with equal exactness, the treatment given to control groups of pupils. Until both are stated in more exact and measurable terms, the question of career education's effectiveness will continue to be difficult to answer.

Third, the comparison of studies included in Bonnet's review, when contrasted with the other two groupings of studies included here, makes it abundantly clear that evaluations of career education should cover more than a one-year period. The developmental nature of career education demands longitudinal studies covering a period of several years. Too few studies of this nature have, to date, been undertaken.

Fourth, this article has been limited to studies of career education's effectiveness in K–12 school settings. Yet, the career education concept has the potential for effectiveness in all facets of postsecondary education. There is a great need to undertake and to report on career education evaluation studies at these levels.

Fifth, the studies reported here have been limited to use of intermediate, rather than ultimate, criteria. There are two basic problems involved. One concerns itself with the fact that, in the long run, the effectiveness of career education will surely be measured, not by the extent to which pupils possess employability skills, but rather by what they do with such skills as adult workers. Such data are, of course—given career education's limited life to date—still unavailable. It is time that systematic, long-range evaluative studies be launched and aimed at including such data in their final reports. The second problem is that, so long as only short-run intermediate criteria of effectiveness are used, it is quite likely that alternative delivery systems may well be able to demonstrate at least as much effectiveness in meeting these criteria as can career education. Longitudinal studies are badly needed.

Finally, although obviously far from complete, evaluation of career education has now reached the stage where it is time to move systematically toward research investigations in career education. There is now a fair, although obviously still incomplete, basis for believing that career education works. It is time now to begin systematic study of which career education methods work better than others for given populations under a variety of different conditions. It is expected that the coming decade will witness a marked effort to move in this direction.

Kenneth B. Hoyt
Sidney C. High

See also Career Guidance; Interests Measurement; Vocational Education.

REFERENCES

Akron Public Schools, Ohio. *Akron Career Development Program: Submission No. 78–181 to the Joint Dissemination Review Panel.* Unpublished manuscript, 1978. (ERIC Document Reproduction Service No. ED 170 499)

Bhaerman, R. D. *Career Education and Basic Academic Achievement: A Descriptive Analysis of the Research.* Washington, D.C.: U.S. Office of Education, 1977. (ERIC Document Reproduction Service No. ED 140 032)

Bonnet, D. G. *What Does Career Education Do for Kids? A Synthesis of 1975–1976 Evaluation Results.* Crawfordsville, Ind.: New Educational Directions, Inc., 1977. (ERIC Document Reproduction Service No. ED 143 831)

Boston Mountains Educational Cooperative, Arkansas. *Project CAP; Career Awareness Program: Submission No. 78–178 to the Joint Dissemination Review Panel.* Unpublished manuscript, 1978. (ERIC Document Reproduction Service No. ED 170 501)

Brickell, H. M. *Attitudes toward Career Education: A Report of an Initial Study of Pupil, Staff, and Parent Opinions in Atlanta, Hackensack, Jefferson County, Los Angeles, Mesa, and Pontiac.* New York: Institute for Educational Development, 1972. (ERIC Document Reproduction Service No. ED 068 636)

Brodinsky, B. Something happened: Education in the seventies. *Phi Delta Kappan,* 1979, *61*(4), 238–241.

Ceres Unified School District, California. *Project CERES: Career Education Responsive to Every Student: Submission No. 78–182 to the Joint Dissemination Review Panel.* Unpublished manuscript, 1978. (ERIC Document Reproduction Service No. ED 170 502)

Cobb County Public Schools, Georgia. *Occupational and Career Development Project: Submission No. 74–7 to the Joint Dissemination Review Panel.* Unpublished manuscript, 1973. (Available from Executive Secretary, Joint Dissemination Review Panel, U.S. Department of Education, Washington, D.C. 20202)

Cogent Associates, New Jersey. *Project HEAR; Human Educa-*

tional Awareness Resource: Submission No. 78–185 to the Joint Dissemination Review Panel. Unpublished manuscript, 1978. (Available from Executive Secretary, Joint Dissemination Review Panel, U.S. Department of Education, Washington, D.C. 20202)

Cogent Associates, New Jersey. *Project Opening the Doors: Submission No. 80–36 to the Joint Dissemination Review Panel.* Unpublished manuscript, 1980. (Available from Executive Secretary, Joint Dissemination Review Panel, U.S. Department of Education, Washington, D.C. 20202)

Coloma Community School District, Michigan. *Project CDCC; Career Development Centered Curriculum: Submission No. 78–168 to the Joint Dissemination Review Panel.* Unpublished manuscript, 1978. (ERIC Document Reproduction Service No. ED 169 245)

Datta, L. E.; Arterbury, E. H.; Rapley, F.; Spieth, P. E.; Ruff, R. D.; & High, S. C., Jr. *Career Education: What Proof Do We Have That It Works?* Washington, D.C.: U.S. Office of Education, 1976. (ERIC Document Reproduction Service No. ED 151 516)

Development Associates, Inc. *An Evaluation of Vocational Exemplary Projects: Executive Summary and Final Report.* Washington, D.C.: Author, 1975. (ERIC Document Reproduction Service No. ED 109 475)

District of Columbia Public Schools. *Career Education Resource Center Program: Submission No. 80–4 to the Joint Dissemination Review Panel.* Unpublished manuscript, 1980. (Available from Executive Secretary, Joint Dissemination Review Panel, U.S. Department of Education, Washington, D.C. 20202)

Education Commission of the States. *An Overview of State Career Education Laws.* Denver: The Commission, 1979. (a) (ERIC Document Reproduction Service No. ED 166 544)

Education Commission of the States. *Collaboration in State Career Education Policy Development: The Role of Business, Industry, and Labor.* Denver: The Commission, 1979. (b) (ERIC Document Reproduction Service No. ED 166 542)

Enderlein, T. E. *A Review of Career Education Evaluation Studies.* Washington, D.C.: U.S. Office of Education, 1976. (ERIC Document Reproduction Service No. ED 141 584)

Grant, L. T. A comparative study of attitudes of students, parents, educators, and business leaders toward selected concepts of career education (Doctoral dissertation, University of Houston, 1979). *Dissertation Abstracts International,* 1979, *40,* 1223-A. (University Microfilms No. 7919365)

Hall, L. A., & High, S. C., Jr. *Bibliography on Career Education.* Washington, D.C.: U.S. Office of Education, 1979. (ERIC Document Reproduction Service No. ED 177 368)

Hamilton, J. A., & Mitchell, A. M. *Identification of Evaluated Exemplary Activities in Career Education, K–12: Final Technical Report.* Palo Alto, Calif.: American Institutes for Research, 1978. (ERIC Document Reproduction Service No. ED 162 097)

Hansford, B. W. *The Implementation of Career Education as Perceived by Selected Chief State School Officers.* Washington, D.C.: U.S. Office of Education, 1979. (ERIC Document Reproduction Service No. ED 177 364)

Herr, E. L. *Review and Synthesis of Foundations for Career Education.* Columbus: Ohio State University, 1972. (ERIC Document Reproduction Service No. ED 059 402)

Herr, E. L. *The Emerging History of Career Education: A Summary View.* Washington, D.C.: National Advisory Council for Career Education, 1975. (ERIC Document Reproduction Service No. ED 122 011)

Herr, E. L. *Research in Career Education: The State of the Art.*

Columbus: Ohio State University, 1977. (ERIC Document Reproduction Service No. ED 149 177)

High, S. C., Jr. Career education: A national overview. *School Science and Mathematics Journal,* 1976, *76*(4), 276–284.

Highline Public Schools, Washington. *Project Equality: Submission No. 78–180 to the Joint Dissemination Review Panel.* Unpublished manuscript, 1978. (ERIC Document Reproduction Service No. ED 170 503)

Hoyt, K. B. *An Introduction to Career Education: A Policy Paper of the U.S. Office of Education.* Washington, D.C.: U.S. Government Printing Office, 1975. (ERIC Document Reproduction Service No. ED 130 076)

Hoyt, K. B. *Community Resources for Career Education.* Washington, D.C.: U.S. Office of Education, 1976. (ERIC Document Reproduction Service No. ED 130 118)

Hoyt, K. B. *A Primer for Career Education.* Washington, D.C.: U.S. Office of Education, 1977. (ERIC Document Reproduction Service No. ED 145 252)

Hoyt, K. B. *Community Involvement in the Implementation of Career Education.* Washington, D.C.: U.S. Office of Education, 1979. (ERIC Document Reproduction Service No. ED 189 315)

Hoyt, K. B. Career education: A report card for the 1970's and some predictions for the decade of the 1980's. *Journal of Career Education,* 1980, *7*(2), 82–96.

Hoyt, K. B.; Bommarito, P. A.; & Schulman, M. *Career Education and Organized Labor.* Washington, D.C.: U.S. Office of Education, 1978. (ERIC Document Reproduction Service No. ED 164 983)

Hoyt, K. B.; Evans, R. N.; Mackin, E. F.; & Mangum, G. L. *Career Education: What It Is and How to Do It.* Salt Lake City, Utah: Olympus, 1972.

Jesser, D. L. *Existing and Emerging Legislation for Career Education at the State Level.* Washington, D.C.: U.S. Office of Education, 1979. (ERIC Document Reproduction Service No. ED 170 539)

Lincoln County Public Schools, West Virginia. *Lincoln County Exemplary Project in Career Education: Submission No. 73–2 to the Joint Dissemination Review Panel.* Unpublished manuscript, 1973. (Available from Executive Secretary, Joint Dissemination Review Panel, U.S. Department of Education, Washington, D.C. 20202)

McLaughlin, D. H. *Career Education in the Public Schools, 1974–1975: A National Survey.* Washington, D.C.: U.S. Office of Education, 1976. (ERIC Document Reproduction Service No. ED 122 165)

National Advisory Council for Career Education. *The Efficacy of Career Education.* Washington, D.C.: The Council, 1976. (ERIC Document Reproduction Service No. ED 130 092)

National School Boards Association. *What Priority for "Global Education"? An NSBA Survey of School Board Members and School Superintendents.* Washington, D.C.: The Association, 1980.

Ontario-Montclair School District, California. *Project MATCH; Matching Attitudes and Talents to Career Horizons: Submission No. 78–167 to the Joint Dissemination Review Panel.* Unpublished manuscript, 1978. (ERIC Document Reproduction Service No. ED 170 504)

Pima County Public Schools, Arizona. *Pima County Developmental Career Guidance Project: Submission No. 78–177 to the Joint Dissemination Review Panel.* Unpublished manuscript, 1978. (ERIC Document Reproduction Service No. ED 170 500)

Southwest Iowa Learning Resources Center, Iowa. *Project Discovery: Submission No. 78–161 to the Joint Dissemination Review*

Panel. Unpublished manuscript, 1978. (Available from Executive Secretary, Joint Dissemination Review Panel, U.S. Department of Education, Washington, D.C. 20202)

Steel, L.; Jung, S. M.; McBain, S. L.; & Kingi, M. *Implementation of the Career Education Incentive Act: Interim Report on the Rapid Feedback Evaluation.* Palo Alto, Calif.: American Institutes for Research, 1980. (ERIC Document Reproduction Service No. ED 194 800)

Tuckman, B. W., & Carducci, J. A. *Evaluating Career Education: A Review and Model.* Washington, D.C.: National Institute of Education, 1974. (ERIC Document Reproduction Service No. ED 102 212)

University of California at Los Angeles. *Allied Health Professions Project: Submission No. 73–1 to the Joint Dissemination Review Panel.* Unpublished manuscript, 1973. (Available from Executive Secretary, Joint Dissemination Review Panel, U.S. Department of Education, Washington, D.C. 20202)

CAREER GUIDANCE

Education in virtually every nation of the world is undergoing rapid and dramatic change. In the past decade, nation after nation has implemented policies and legislation designed to reconceptualize the content of curricula and to expand or to change the focus of the guidance mechanisms available to children and youth (Herr & Watts, 1981; Watts & Ferreira-Marques, 1978).

The reasons for reshaping education and guidance to meet specific national needs and goals vary. However, common to all of these national movements are (1) growing linkages between education and work; (2) concern for rising rates of youth unemployment; (3) the need to create labor forces that are functionally literate, capable of engaging in the growing complexity of technological applications to work tasks, and emotionally committed to productive effort; (4) shifts in proportions of women leaving the home and entering the work force; (5) alarm that large numbers of students are not mastering the school-to-work transition because they lack the attitudes, skills, or personal goals that constitute employability; and (6) awareness that the major questions concerning the implementation of technology are not technical, but human questions.

Nations differ in how they respond to such concerns or conditions. Some nations have infused all subject matter with career development concepts or work-related examples. Other nations have expanded occupational-specific skill-training, work-practices, work-study, or apprenticeship programs. These educational emphases are variously titled career(s) education, vocational education, functional education, life-long education. What seems to be common to each is an expanded place for career-guidance programs and services in meeting educational goals (Herr, 1978a).

Definition. There are different definitions of career guidance. In general, such definitions agree that "career guidance" is a set—preferably, a systematic program—of processes, techniques, or services designed to assist an individual to understand and to act on self-knowledge and knowledge of opportunities in work, education, and leisure and to develop the decision-making skills by which one can create and manage one's career development.

Within this context, McDaniel (1978) has defined career guidance as an organized program to assist an individual to assimilate and integrate knowledge, experience, and appreciation related to (1) self-understanding; (2) understanding the work society and those factors that affect its constant change, including worker attitude and discipline; (3) awareness of the part leisure may play in a person's life; (4) understanding of the multitude of factors to be considered in career planning; and (5) understanding the information and skills necessary to achieve self-fulfillment in work and leisure.

The term "career guidance" represents the array of intervention strategies designed to facilitate individual career development. The term "career development" describes the lifelong behavioral processes, and the influences upon them, which lead to work values, choice of occupation(s), creation of a career pattern, work satisfaction and adjustment, decision-making style, self-identity and career identity, and role integration. Conceptual and research insights into career development map out the behavioral domains to which the types of intervention represented by career guidance should be directed. Career guidance may include the development of job-search or interview skills, placement into a chosen occupation, and follow-through to ensure effective placement. It ordinarily includes individual counseling; assessment of aptitudes, interests, and career maturity; information retrieval and analysis; and specific instruction in decision making, goal setting, and evaluation.

Career guidance can exist independently of career education, but the same cannot be said of the latter. "Career education" tends to use the teaching-learning process as its principal intervention modality. By frequently infusing all types of subject matter with examples and concepts that connect the subject matter to its application in various work tasks and settings career education tends to provide information and reality testing that career-guidance techniques can help the individual to personalize. Clearly, many of the goals of career education overlap with those of career guidance, but the principal intervention modalities differ.

History. Contemporary views of career guidance have evolved from earlier models of vocational guidance. The founder of vocational guidance is generally considered to be Frank Parsons (1909), who established the Vocations Bureau in Boston and wrote *Choosing a Vocation.* Parsons urged that it is "better to choose a vocation than merely to hunt a job," and suggested that the proper way to achieve this goal is to have "first, a clear understanding of yourself, aptitudes, abilities, interests, resources, limitations, and other qualities; second, a knowledge of the requirements and conditions of success, advantages, and disadvantages, compensation, opportunities, and prospects in different lines of work; third, true reasoning on the relations of these two groups of facts" (Parsons, 1909, p. 5).

In some ways, Parsons's early formulation of content and process in vocational guidance has changed little through the years. Until the early 1970s, for example, almost all vocational guidance in the lower schools was based on his model. Vocational guidance was generally provided only at a single point in time (usually late in one's schooling) by means of a one-to-one counseling mode. The counseling was usually Parsonsian, with somewhat more sophistication provided by later advances in the theory, instrumentation, and practice of trait-and-factor psychology. The development of more elegant individual-assessment procedures, such as the increasing number of aptitudes that can be measured and the provision of more representative norm groups, was coupled with enhanced analysis of occupational requirements. The result was a narrow matching of person and job: round pegs in holes and square pegs in squares. In general, there was little recognition of the fact that individuals change, and the world of work does not stay the same. Trait-and-factor psychology is basically a static phenomenon; vocational guidance requires a more dynamic framework. Furthermore, a trait-and-factor approach to vocational guidance in its classic form recognizes neither the importance of values in career choice nor the essentially developmental nature of that choice.

In the late 1960s and early 1970s, these restricted notions of vocational guidance gave way to the broader concept of career guidance. Career guidance is much more psychologically oriented than its precursor. It integrates the personal, educational, and vocational aspects of guidance, rather than treats them as discrete entities. It focuses on an individual's self-understanding and self-acceptance in relation to educational and occupational alternatives. Career guidance embraces a time frame that extends from earliest family influences to and including retirement.

Since the emphasis in a career-guidance model is developmental, the school counselor is concerned with more than an immediate choice of training or job. Some of the important variables in career guidance include such dimensions as personal values, the clarity of self-concept, personal planfulness, and exploratory activities related to choice options. Also of paramount concern are variables such as decision-making skills, life-styles, leisure, free choice, individual differences, and coping with change.

Vocational guidance tends to use as its principal unit of concern the differences in work activity across occupations and how these differ in requirements for individual characteristics. Prime considerations in career guidance are not only occupational differences reflected in immediate choices but also the larger concept of continuity of purposeful behavior in immediate, intermediate, and distant choices. Thus, such individual goal setting takes into account contingency planning; interactions of educational and occupational choices across time; planning for se-

quences of occupations, jobs, and positions; and integration of family and work roles as primary units of concern.

An occupational approach (vocational guidance) tends to reinforce the idea that there is only one right occupational choice for each person; a career approach tends to help people consider the fact that most people have multiple choices that can be made now and in the future if they are aware of their values and preferences, their strengths and weaknesses, and the interplay of educational, occupational and personal factors that shape a career. In short, an occupational approach tends to be most concerned with the *content* of a choice that is immediately before the person; a career approach is, instead, principally concerned with the *process* of choice and the power that people have to shape that process if they understand it. In practice, it is likely that both approaches are needed by many people and thus are blended in the more comprehensive career-guidance approach.

Developmental, Remedial, and Systematic Delivery Models.   Given this background, there is general agreement that both developmental and remedial career-guidance delivery systems should be in place in the schools. The "developmental model" attempts to provide all students in career guidance with structured experiences that are sequential, integrated, and programmatic—it is an attempt to systematically educate students to the career-related knowledge, attitudes, and skills they will need in the future as they plan educational programs and select and plan for work. These experiences are coordinated by the school counselor. A major issue for career guidance in the secondary school is the fact that school counselors have many other functions besides career guidance. Thus, career guidance is not always given the emphasis or the resources that are required to meet the needs of all students. Frequently, then, although the goal of career guidance is a developmental one, the actual practice is remedial.

If ultimate career choice is the result of a developmental process, and if interventions occur at various chronological points to enhance that process, then there must be developmental tasks of a career nature that need to be mastered at each level. These tasks are the subject matter of career guidance, and they have been described in a number of documents (Crites, 1974; Gysbers et al., 1973; Super et al., 1963; Tennyson et al., 1980). Important work in expanding knowledge of career development and the effects of career-guidance interventions on it has continued in many institutions. Of particular interest is the work of Super and his associates at Teachers College, Columbia University; Holland and his associates at Johns Hopkins and at the University of Maryland; Crites at the University of Maryland; Tennyson, Hansen, and Borow at the University of Minnesota; Gysbers and his associates at the University of Missouri; and, Herr and Cramer at Pennsylvania State University and the State University of New York at Buffalo. Although many other persons can be cited, these educators are engaged in continuing research and publication about both career development and career guidance.

In contrast to the developmental model of career guidance is the "remedial model." This model assumes that individuals have failed to master the appropriate career-related developmental tasks and that they are therefore suffering from deficiencies in their behavioral repertoires. The counselor intervenes at these crisis points and attempts to accelerate the process that leads to career maturity. Usually, counselors resort to using a modified trait-and-factor model by assessing a student's cognitive and affective characteristics as related to work and helping him or her survey the world of work to find occupations appropriate to those characteristics. The decision-making processing of these data, however, relies much more heavily on considering the importance of values, especially work values, to the career choice. Typically, three or four individual sessions or four to ten group sessions are considered sufficient to produce this accelerated career-guidance experience.

The delivery method of current preference in career guidance, whether one is providing developmental interventions or remedial assistance, is a "systematic model." Although there are minor variations in a systematic approach, each has common elements. One element is conducting a needs analysis. In career guidance, most needs are universal, but a small proportion are parochial or unique to a given setting. Consequently, the developmental tasks of career development provide the catholic needs, and local needs arise in small proportion because of the peculiar characteristics of a given community. A second element is the translation of these needs, once identified, into behavioral objectives or student outcomes; that is, specific statements are formulated to describe what students are expected to do, think, feel, know, and so on, as a result of the career-guidance program. A third element in a systematic approach to career guidance involves devising activities to achieve these objectives. These activities include individual and group counseling, assessment, field trips, gaming and simulation, and a large variety of proven techniques. After the counselor has selected these activities, materials are chosen to implement them, for example, interest inventories, decision-making workbooks, and films and video tapes about different forms of work or job search strategies. Finally, an evaluation is conducted to determine how closely the objectives have been achieved as a result of the activities and materials provided.

Evaluations in career guidance are, of necessity, short-term and confined to measurement of the attainment of immediate and intermediate behavioral objectives. The ultimate evaluation of career guidance is, of course, entry into and successful performance in and satisfaction with an occupation and a life-style. These criteria can be assessed only after a protracted time span, with the complication of all sorts of intervening experiences. Consequently, we tend to call a career decision good if the

individual making it has demonstrated mastery of the requisite knowledge, skills, and attitudes deemed necessary for making a good decision.

Status of Research. Although the research in career guidance is less comprehensive and less rigorous than some observers desire, an empirical base describing the effects of career guidance is rapidly enlarging. Aggregated positive findings about the effects of different types of career-guidance intervention have been reported in relation to a wide range of criterion variables. These include self-esteem and self-concept, decision making, information seeking, career planning, career maturity, transition to work, work adjustment, interview skills, job satisfaction, and school achievement. Such criterion variables have been studied in relation to populations that differ in age, race, and educational level. Several comprehensive analyses of such research are now available (Crites, 1978; Bhaerman, 1977; Herr, 1976, 1977, 1978b; Herr & Cramer, 1979; Hilton, 1979; Pinson, 1980).

Stating that a research base favoring career guidance is available and growing is not to argue that there are not weaknesses and problematic issues in it. There are. For example, career-development theory and research are not yet effectively addressed to sex differences in career behavior. There are relatively few systematic analyses of race or ethnic differences in career development. Attention has not been given to the career development of gay persons or the congenitally versus the adventitiously handicapped populations. With respect to career-guidance strategies, relatively little attention has been given to the comparative effects of different intervention strategies on the same type of presenting problem. Although career-guidance programs have been studied in relation to outcome variables, virtually no component analyses have been accomplished to determine which program aspects are making the primary contributions to the outcomes. In such cases, the specificity of treatment effects is lost. Most of the research about career-guidance interventions tend to be one-shot, one-group approaches, not longitudinal approaches. Rather than provide comparison or control groups, analysis is often made of pre-post changes in the same group. In such cases, as in others, it is difficult to be confident that career guidance rather than halo effect, maturity, or other rival explanations produce the outcomes. A further issue in much of the existing research is the expectancy effect. Given the relative lack of specific process or content description in many current research studies, it is difficult to know whether such groups have equal expectations for change and thus are meaningful tests of different treatment effects.

The importance of career guidance in American education has been affirmed in various pieces of federal legislation. Its importance has also been reinforced in several national studies of guidance and counseling priorities as viewed by parents, teachers, administrators, and students (Prediger, Roth, & Noeth, 1973). The conceptual mortar and the repertoire of intervention skills constituting models of career guidance are being refined and evaluated. Issues and weaknesses in the research base exist, but the research base itself is expanding. In sum, it appears that the role of career guidance in meeting educational objectives of student choice and planning is an enduring one.

Edwin L. Herr
Stanley H. Cramer

See also Career Education; Counseling; Interests Measurement; Psychological Services.

REFERENCES

Bhaerman, R. D. *Career Education and Basic Academic Achievement: A Descriptive Analysis of the Research.* Washington, D.C.: U.S. Government Printing Office, 1977. (ERIC Document Reproduction Service No. ED 140 032)

Crites, J. O. Career development processes: A model of vocational maturity. In E. L. Herr (Ed.), *Vocational Guidance and Human Development.* Boston: Houghton Mifflin, 1974, pp. 296–320.

Crites, J. O. Career counseling: A review of major approaches. In J. M. Whiteby & A. Resnikoff (Eds.), *Career Counseling.* Belmont, Calif.: Wadsworth, 1978, pp. 18–56.

Gysbers, N.; Moore, E. J.; Magnuson, C.; Peters, C.; & Sturgis, B. *Elements of an Illustrative Guide, Career Guidance, Counseling and Placement for State Departments of Education.* Columbia: University of Missouri, 1973. (ERIC Document Reproduction Service No. ED 092 767)

Herr, E. L. *The Relationship of Guidance and Counseling to National Educational, Occupational, and Social Priorities.* Washington, D.C.: American Personnel and Guidance Association, 1976.

Herr, E. L. *Research in Career Education: The State of the Art* (Information Series No. 106). Columbus, Ohio: ERIC Clearinghouse on Career Education, 1977. (ERIC Document Reproduction Service No. ED 149 177)

Herr, E. L. Career development concepts and practices: Some international perspectives. *Counseling and Human Development,* 1978, *11*(1), 1–8. (a)

Herr, E. L. Research in guidance. In G. Walz & L. Benjamin (Eds.), *Imperatives in Guidance.* Ann Arbor, Mich.: ERIC-CAPS, 1978, pp. 63–112. (b) (ERIC Document Reproduction Service No. ED 167 940)

Herr, E. L., & Cramer, S. H. *Career Guidance through the Life Span: Systematic Approaches.* Boston: Little, Brown, 1979.

Herr, E. L., & Watts, A. G. Implications of youth unemployment for career education and counseling. *Journal of Career Education,* 1981, 7(3), 184–202.

Hilton, T. L. *Confronting the Future: A Conceptual Framework for Secondary School Career Guidance.* New York: College Entrance Examination Board, 1979.

Holland, J. L. *Making Vocational Choices: A Theory of Careers.* Englewood Cliffs, N.J.: Prentice-Hall, 1973.

McDaniel, C. The practice of career guidance and counseling. *INFORM,* 1978, 7(1), 1–2, 7–8.

Parsons, F. *Choosing a Vocation.* Boston: Houghton Mifflin, 1909.

Pinson, N. M. *The Contribution of Guidance and Counseling to the Employability of Youth.* Washington, D.C.: American Personnel and Guidance Association, February 1980. (Mimeo)

Prediger, D. J.; Roth, J. D.; & Noeth, R. J. *Nationwide Study of Student Career Development: Summary of Results.* Iowa City, Iowa: American College Testing Program, 1973. (ERIC Document Reproduction Service No. ED 083 383)

Super, D. E.; Starishevsky, R.; Matlin, N.; & Jordaan, J. P. *Career Development: Self-Concept Theory.* New York: College Entrance Examination Board, 1963.

Tennyson, W. W.; Hansen, L. S.; Klaurens, M. K.; & Antholz, M. B. *Educating for Career Development.* Washington, D.C.: National Vocational Guidance Association, 1980. (ERIC Document Reproduction Service No. ED 118 812)

Watts, A. G., & Ferreira-Marques, J. *Guidance and the School Curriculum.* Paris: UNESCO, 1978.

CASE STUDY METHODS

See Ethnography.

CATHOLIC SCHOOLS

Catholic education embraces a system of diverse church-related institutions from kindergarten through the postdoctoral level. Quantitatively, it represents a substantial minority in the total system of American education; qualitatively it represents a distinctive approach to the meaning of education.

There are 4 million students in Catholic schools today. Over 3.2 million attend 9,600 elementary and secondary schools operated by local parishes or dioceses. Another 530,000 of them attend 250 colleges and universities sponsored largely by religious congregations of men and women operating under state charters and independent boards of trustees. American Catholic schools are a segment of a pluralistic, decentralized national system of mass education, both public and private, that is unique in the world.

At the elementary and secondary levels, the Catholic student population represents 11 percent of the total number of students in school; 89 percent of American students attend public or non-Catholic private elementary and secondary schools. At the postsecondary level, Catholic colleges and universities represent 30 percent of the 800 church-related institutions, 17 percent of the 1,500 independent institutions, and 8 percent of the total 3,000 postsecondary institutions. Their student bodies constitute 4 percent of the total college and university student population in the United States.

During the last decade, enrollment in Catholic colleges and universities has increased; in secondary and elementary schools it has declined. Postsecondary enrollment grew by 19 percent from 1972 to 1978, outpacing the rate of growth of other independent colleges and universities, though lagging far behind the growth rate of public institutions. At the secondary school level, students have declined from 1 million to 846,000, and over 500 high schools have closed. At the elementary level, enrollments have dropped by 1.3 million, and almost 1,800 schools have closed.

Institutionally, Catholic schools resemble their secular, non-Catholic religious, and public counterparts in faculty, curriculum structure, organization, and activities. Their distinctiveness is found in their motivating spirit and in the explicitness of their underlying value system. The essential characteristic of a Catholic school is the centrality of Christian value system not only of individuals within the school system but of the community as a corporate whole.

Catholic education has been shaped historically by external developments in education in the United States and by the internal desire of the church to evangelize and catechize. The first influence has provided the form; the second influence provides the motivation. Faculty and administration have created its curricula. The practices of other school systems, public and private; professional education associations; and government policy have set its economic and political limits. Catholic church sponsorship has determined its ultimate purpose. In the last two decades these three institutional influences have led to substantial changes in the Catholic educational system.

Internal Changes.   The chief internal engine of religious change has been the Second Vatican Council (1962–1965). Pope John XXIII opened the windows of the church to the world; the council declared the church a universal sign of salvation rather than a parochial shelter for those already saved. Though the council looked at education only peripherally, its new thrust of mission had a major impact on all Catholic educational institutions. The council motifs of service, unity of people, dignity of persons, freedom, and community were both inspirational and disturbing to a school system that cherished the ideals but had not yet figured out a way to achieve them in a rapidly changing world.

Two major pronouncements from the National Conference of Catholic Bishops (NCCB) specified the mandates of the Second Vatican Council and applied them to the contemporary American scene.

The first was a pastoral letter, *To Teach as Jesus Did,* issued in 1972 (published, 1973) for the elementary and high schools. It argued that Catholic schools should be unique, contemporary, and oriented to service. It prescribed a pattern of academic superiority, religious formation of the student, and openness to community service.

The second major pronouncement of the NCCB was the first pastoral letter of the U.S. bishops ever to be addressed to the higher education community. Issued in 1980, *Catholic Higher Education and the Pastoral Mission of the Church* reaffirmed the church's commitment to higher education on the grounds that (1) it "can help elevate the human family to a better understanding of truth, goodness and beauty and to the formation of judgments which embody universal values" (p. 378); (2) it "educates men and women to play responsible roles in the contemporary world" (p. 379); (3) it is "indispensable to the pluralism

that has characterized American education" (p. 378). It called on Catholic colleges and universities to manifest clearly their identity and mission, to promote academic excellence, to emphasize Christian humanism in the curriculum, and to integrate learning and living by developing a community of faith. Reflecting the sensitive mood of the NCCB to "the signs of the times," the bishops stated that "academic freedom and institutional independence are essential components of educational quality and integrity; commitment to the Gospel and the teachings and heritage of the Catholic Church provide the inspiration and enrichment that make a college fully Catholic" (p. 380).

These two NCCB documents have furnished general guidelines for school operations amid heavy pressures for adaptation and change. The mandate to the secondary and elementary schools has led to significant attempts at a renewal of religious education curricula and, more recently, to experimentation with faculty development programs and student service requirements. The pastoral letter to the colleges and universities is of too recent origin for us judge its full impact. But even before it appeared there was growing among school leaders a more serious interest in the question of the religious identity of the institution. The quest for greater intellectual quality had been first recognized as a priority by a minority of the American bishops in the late nineteenth century (Bohr, 1977). It was reemphasized by Catholic scholars in the decade of the 1950s and led to a wide upgrading of faculty and academic programs.

The struggle for citizenship rights for disadvantaged students characterized the early 1970s. Today the issues of religious identity and mission are in the forefront of concern. The pastoral letter has given recognition, perhaps more than impetus, to that interest.

Underlying both letters was an acknowledgment of the declining numbers of religious men and women teachers and the consequent necessity for sharing the spiritual insight and commitment of the founding religious orders with a large number of laymen and laywomen. Though the efforts have been tentative and the results uneven, the development of lay-religious collaborative efforts is opening up new possibilities for building community and raising new questions of basic spirituality. Many Catholic leaders believe that these areas of concern will be the top priority for the future.

External Changes.   More than ever before, American schools in recent years have been confronted with forces beyond their internal control. The rise of mass education and the desire for universal access, the clamor for measurable results and standardization by professional associations, the increasingly dominant role of government in education, and the steady erosion of capital, both human and material, by inflation have engulfed U.S. schools. Most educational institutions underwent substantial changes in the 1970s.

All schools, public and private, secular and church-related, have been affected by the external political, social, and economic forces. Church-related schools faced the same challenges as others and had some distinctive challenges of their own: constitutional questions of church-state relationships, value orientations of curriculum, preservation of religious identity in the face of growing homogeneity and secularism, entanglement of government in religious affairs, an insistence on the right to dissent from conformity, and rationalization of the educational effort.

In addition to facing the external problems of other higher educational institutions, Catholic schools were hit hard by the almost simultaneous growth in demand for greater student access to their schools and a major decline in the number of teaching priests, sisters, and brothers. The change raised questions not only of financial viability but of religious mission as well. The dilemma of providing greater outreach while preserving the essential religious identity of the enterprise remains unresolved. It has become the central issue of the 1980s.

In many instances, the response of the Catholic schools has been imitative of their secular educational counterparts; in some important social and religious cases, it has been distinctive.

Minorities. The response of the Catholic school system to the growing demand for universal student access has been similar to that of the American educational system as a whole. The demand for access did not originate in the schools. Rather, it arose from an aroused public opinion backed by government insistence. Schools, therefore, have found the objective of greater minority representation a difficult one to achieve. Church-related schools that wanted to admit more disadvantaged students discovered that little government subsidy was available to support their efforts. After strenuous litigation, government funds became available at the postsecondary level in the mid-1960s. With this assistance, Catholic schools have taken in more than the average share of minority students. The twenty-eight Jesuit colleges and universities for example, which represent 10 percent of all Catholic colleges and universities and 30 percent of the student population, increased their minority undergraduate population by 5,000 students from 1972 to 1978. Today minorities represent 13 percent of the total undergraduate enrollment in those schools.

At the high school and elementary school levels, even without the support of federal financial funds for the disadvantaged, student minority populations account for 18 percent of the students. The private high school, subject to declining enrollments in the first half of the decade, is in fact enjoying a resurgence of interest today. Recent studies by Coleman (1981) suggest that the discipline of a school and a sense of community are key factors in learning and, therefore, in success. Since most parents of minority students seek to have their offspring enter the mainstream of education and move upward, the objectives of these parents and the private schools tend to coincide. Thus Catholic schools, especially those in urban centers

that have traditionally served disadvantaged and upwardly mobile clientele, are finding new applicants for the system among minority groups who are replicating this pattern.

Disadvantaged students do well in Catholic secondary schools. Greeley's studies (1981) conclude that the academic outcomes of Catholic secondary education for minority groups are impressively superior to the academic outcomes of public education for the same groups. Research is currently underway to assess the consequences of this trend on the educational system itself.

Public Policy. The formation of public policy and the search for public funding have only recently been placed on the agenda of Catholic educators. For the first century of their existence, Catholic schools were financed largely by parents, students, and friends, and Catholic school leaders shunned major participation in governmental affairs. But the emergence of mass education after World War II and the active intervention of government as patron and power changed much of that.

The colleges and universities were the first segment of the Catholic system to adapt to the new external circumstances. Catholic leaders formed professional associations to organize for action and to articulate their interests before the public. The Association of Catholic Colleges and Universities, representing 211 institutions, and the Association of Jesuit Colleges and Universities, representing 28, both opened offices in Washington in the early 1970s. When blocked by litigation, they carried their citizenship claims to the Supreme Court. In a series of significant verdicts (*Tilton* v. *Richardson*, 1971; *Hunt* v. *McNair*, 1973; *Roemer* v. *Maryland Board of Public Works*, 1976), they won rights to federal and state funds. That litigation established citizenship rights for Catholic colleges and universities and opened the possibility of broader public support. It also brought greater demands for accountability, greater homogeneity of effort, and the threat of entanglement of government in religion.

Anticipated action in the public forum prompted internal restructuring of the institutions. Independent boards of trustees mushroomed in the 1970s as sponsoring religious congregations sought broader financial and community support and moved to incorporate the institution separately from the sponsoring congregation. Lay people were added to the boards, frequently becoming a majority. These efforts further widened the basis of support for the institutions and guaranteed a continuity for the work, but they made the institution vulnerable to a threat of lessened independence and a charge of secularization. Research is not yet available to evaluate the consequences of these changes of the last decade. Data from the Council for Financial Aid to Education (1980) suggest that during the 1970s Catholic colleges and universities improved their financial support, from both public and private sources, at a better rate than other independent colleges, but the cost to individuality or independence has not yet been systematically assessed.

Recent suits for public recognition of church-related

schools are coming from such denominations as the Mormons, the Jehovah's Witnesses, the Amish, the Unification Church, and the Church of Scientology rather than from Catholic or Protestant mainline churches. For them, the line of challenge today on educational issues is not with the government but with their own governing bodies.

Although postsecondary Catholic schools have succeeded in obtaining some federal support, elementary and secondary schools have repeatedly been denied public funds. On the day in 1971 that the Supreme Court upheld the right of colleges and universities to receive federal funds (*Tilton* v. *Richardson*) it rejected the claims of the Catholic high and elementary schools (*Lemon* v. *Kurtzman; DiCenso* v. *Robinson*). The rejection was more than symbolic. Despite strong efforts on the part of the United States Catholic Conference of Bishops and the establishment of a Washington office of the National Catholic Education Association (NCEA), little headway has been made for public aid to education. The constitutional questions and opposition by a strong public school lobby have been too formidable for a quick or clear solution.

With the change of presidential administrations in 1981, new efforts to obtain financial relief for parents who want to send their children to private schools were begun. Coalitions of private school educators sought to have Congress pass a tuition tax-credit program. A prolonged and bitter debate was the prospect as the 97th Congress opened in January 1981.

As the new decade begins, Catholic colleges and universities find themselves beneficiaries of a major government program of student financial aid that is firmly set in place. The secondary and elementary schools are at the beginning of a new struggle. Both are under a cloud of new limitations on government spending and declining student populations.

Religious Issues. Catholic schools at all levels have faced religious questions of identity and mission. The Second Vatican Council called for an upgrading of religious education and new sophistication in theological studies. Mass education demanded new organizational forms and new ministries to the religiously illiterate and indifferent. The shortage of religious vocations raised questions of religious identity and forced a new consideration of the roles of religious and laypersons in the institutions. A stated rejection by the schools of both scientific positivism and secular humanism, along with the rise of interest in spirituality and cults, challenged religious educators to reevaluation and renewal.

At the secondary and elementary school levels, renovations of curriculum and teaching methods are introduced. Diocesan-wide boards of education, as opposed to parish boards, were created to draw on wider resources and knowledge. In 1973 the NCEA published a handbook written by Elford, *The Catholic School in Theory and Practice*, as a self-study guide to help local institutions review the mission of their schools. It organized workshops around the country on school renewal. It directed two national

symposia, one in 1967 and one in 1976, to bring national attention to the questions of setting priorities and reorganizing school structures. It is currently directing a curriculum-process pilot project in forty elementary and high schools that emphasizes the relationship of learning to cognitive, affective, and behavioral experiences. The Jesuit Secondary Education Association of forty-seven high schools is simultaneously conducting reflective-retreat-type sessions called "colloquia on the ministry of teaching" for religious and lay faculty in their schools. These colloquia aim at greater collaboration in school work and deeper meaning in each individual's contribution. They have been highly popular and will probably be implemented on a wider basis in the years ahead.

At the college and university level, which is more diffuse in its structure, more diverse in its operations, and richer in local resources, response to the issues of theological education, religious-lay collaboration, and community of faith have been more locally initiated.

In the past decade, the large universities have strengthened their graduate programs in theology and have greatly expanded faculty in that area. New graduate institutes in religious education, designed to prepare teachers for the secondary and elementary schools, have been started. Endowed chairs in theology, both from a Catholic and an ecumenical perspective, have begun to appear on campuses. Religious congregations have worked through elaborate programs of self-analysis and long-range planning.

The campus ministry, a relatively new phenomenon on the Catholic college campus, has grown steadily in the past decade. Until the late 1960s, pastoral and religious needs of students were handled by the community as a whole. But with the rapid expansion of both faculty and staff, the need for a more concentrated pastoral orientation became evident. Today a campus ministry is part of the campus hierarchy, usually located within the student development area, or, in some cases, reporting directly to the president of the institution. A national professional organization, the Catholic Campus Ministry Association, serves as a forum and placement office for this ministry. Campus ministry's major problems today are finding adequately prepared personnel and devising a closer integration of their pastoral emphasis with the primary academic work of the college.

A Catholic college or university shares the concept of community of learners with all other educational institutions. It shares with church-related colleges the concept of a community built explicitly on a religious faith. Beyond those common notes, it seeks to realize a community built on a specifically Catholic faith. This implies not only individual commitment but also, in some way, an institutional commitment to the reality of building a community bonded by both reason and faith. This distinctive aspect of the Catholic college and university has been the subject of growing speculation and experimentation in the last five years. It is perceived as being closely related to such diverse issues as religious identity, the mission of the institution, religious-lay collaboration, the role of women in the enterprise, and the need for a deeper lay spirituality. A task force of the Association of Catholic Colleges and Universities is currently seeking to define and explore the characteristics of a community of faith while looking for evidences of the existence of such communities at individual institutions. The work is only in its infancy.

Management and Leadership. Catholic educators have appropriated to themselves many of the behavioral and managerial techniques of modern organizational theory. The schools have become more professionally and efficiently managed as they move away from a paternalistic to a managerial pattern of governance. Progress is evidenced in better long-range planning, more sophisticated personnel procedures, tighter budgeting, more efficient fund raising and student recruitment, more responsiveness to community relations, and greater openness to ecumenical relationships. Even contraction (under pressure from declining population trends), budget constraints, and runaway inflation have been managerially controlled.

Education leaders have tended to become managers in this environment of rapid change. University presidents, diocesan superintendents, and school principals see themselves more and more as administrators, not as educational leaders. Few prominent Catholic college or university educators have achieved national prominence. Few superintendents write for the national professional journals.

Maycock and Glatthorn (1980) in their research on the self-perceptions of Catholic school superintendents conclude that superintendents "define themselves primarily as administrators, not as educational leaders" (p. 47). The authors recommend that the NCEA "develop special programs to increase superintendents' awareness of their leadership role in curriculum, supervision and instruction and to develop the skills needed for such leadership functions" (p. 47).

As the national social environment shifts from one of Christian pluralism to one of religious pluralism, Catholic educators in a postmanagerial age will be challenged to be leaders, as well as managers of the educational enterprise. What the prerequisities and skills of that leadership might be remain on the agenda of the future.

William McInnes

See also Private Schools; Religion and Education.

REFERENCES

Bartel, E. *Enrollment, Finances, and Student Aid at Catholic Colleges.* Washington, D.C.: Association of Catholic Colleges and Universities, 1980.

Bohr, D. *Evangelization in America.* New York: Paulist Press, 1977.

Coleman, J. *Public and Private Schools.* Chicago: National Opinion Research Center, 1981. (ERIC Document Reproduction Service No. ED 197 503)

Council for Financial Aid to Education. *Voluntary Support of Education, 1978–1979.* New York: The Council, 1980.

DiCenso v. *Robinson,* 403 U.S. 602 (1971).

Elford, G. *The Catholic School in Theory and Practice.* Washington, D.C.: National Catholic Education Association, 1973.

Greeley, A. *Minority Students in Catholic Secondary Schools.* Chicago: National Opinion Research Center, 1981.

Hunt v. *McNair,* 413 U.S. 734 (1973).

Lemon v. *Kurtzman,* 403 U.S. 602 (1971).

Maycock, L., & Glatthorn, A. NCEA and the development of the post-conciliar Catholic school. *Momentum,* 1980, *11*(4), 7–46.

National Conference of Catholic Bishops. *To Teach as Jesus Did: A Pastoral Message on Catholic Education.* Washington, D.C.: United States Catholic Conference, 1973.

National Conference of Catholic Bishops. Catholic higher education and the pastoral mission of the Church. *Origins,* 1980, *10*(24), 378–384.

Roemer v. *Maryland Board of Public Works,* 44 LW 4939 (1976).

Tilton v. *Richardson,* 20 U.S. 701 (1971).

CAUSAL MODELING

Causal modeling refers to a group of quantitative techniques designed to help a researcher to draw causal inferences from nonexperimental data. The importance of these techniques to educators seems likely to increase substantially; for if educational research is to advance further as a valid policy science, it must grapple more effectively with problems of causality. Even if a particular educational means is ethical and cheap, and the value of the goals is high, science must remain skeptical and test claims that, indeed, the means bring about the goals in question. Simply finding statistical relations is not enough; it is well known that correlation does not establish causation. Nevertheless, many educators and researchers noncritically accept certain relations as indicating a specific causal pattern. One might, for example, assume that teaching behavior and student motivation cause learning rather than considering learning as a cause, all three factors to jointly affect one another, or all three to be influenced by other causal factors. Since correlations among educational goals and means abound, it may be argued that, because of its scarcity, knowledge about their causal relations is one of the greatest values that research can bring to educational policymaking.

Purposes. Controlled experiments in which classes are assigned to educational treatments by randomized procedures were designed, of course, to probe causality, and have contributed much to the natural and behavioral sciences. Agriculture and medicine, for example, benefit enormously from the more confident identification of effective, time-efficient or cost-efficient techniques that experiments permit. Experiments, however, may be difficult to execute and may be somewhat contrived and possibly unethical in education. Nevertheless, it is easy to exaggerate the importance of such shortcomings, since they can often be overcome (Cook & Campbell, 1979); further, it may be even more inefficient and unethical to continue administering programs whose comparative effectiveness remains to be proven.

Causal-modeling techniques provide an alternative to the experimental method (e.g., Kenny, 1979). They cannot establish causality as can experiments, since imposing a causal structure upon correlational data can never prove the validity of that causal structure. Rather, the causal-modeling approach can be used to establish the plausibility of a causal structure and to compare that structure with alternative causal structures. In this way, deficient models can be discarded as they are found to be inadequate. Thus, it is extremely important to develop causal models that have both theoretical and prior empirical support, for only with such models are valid inferences likely to be drawn. Maximal benefits can be realized when theoretically derived models are tested across several data sets, employing the different data sets to refine the models as well as to discount alternative models.

Because causal-modeling techniques can only be used to examine plausibility of patterns of causal relationships, they will not replace experimental methods. Nevertheless, they have a definite place in research methodology since they complement experiments in requiring less intervention in natural settings, encouraging theoretical explanation, and taking explicit account of measurement and other errors. Causal modeling together with experimentation and case studies should converge in principle on valid causal inferences, and all three should be encouraged. Findings that are robust across methods should have the highest degree of credibility.

Among the statistical methods, causal-modeling techniques are relatively new and complex, and may present formidable conceptual and computational problems. The older of two distinct mainstreams of causal models, developed around 1950 and known as "simultaneous-equation systems" or "structural regressions" in econometrics, offers a variety of alternative techniques, none of which stands out as clearly superior (Kmenta, 1971). The second, "maximum-likelihood analysis of covariance structures" (Bentler, 1980; Jöreskog, 1978), with origins primarily in psychometrics and confirmatory factor analysis, can involve a great deal of conceptual effort and substantial amounts of computer time; it remains newer and less frequently demonstrated than ordinary least-squares regression and econometric models.

Causal-modeling techniques, however, may be elegantly and usefully thought of as a general class of statistical techniques that includes more familiar and traditional procedures as special cases. Just as generalized regression or the general linear model includes the *t* test, correlation, univariate and multivariate analysis of variance and covariance, and, in many practical instances, nonparametric techniques as well (Ahlgren & Walberg, 1975), causal modeling includes all these and, in addition, can free the researcher from often untenable assumptions such as one-way causal directionality and the absence of measurement

error. Thus, causal modeling offers a realistic, powerful, and widely applicable approach to the study and improvement of educational practice and policy.

The plan of the remainder of this article, accordingly, is first to provide an overview of path analysis, which may be characterized as providing variants of ordinary least-squares regression with explicit causal orderings and which deals only with measured (or manifest) variables. This brief overview serves to introduce more powerful causal techniques that subsume path analysis as a special case and that deal with unmeasured (or latent) as well as measured variables. The more powerful techniques are far more complex. For example, they require identification of all parameters; that is, there must be enough information in the data to estimate uniquely each parameter of a model (e.g., Jöreskog, 1978; Kmenta, 1971). The primary focus of this article is on psychometric rather than econometric approaches to causal modeling for three reasons: psychometric methods are more familiar to educators; the econometric approach is widely discussed in econometric textbooks published after 1960 (e.g., Kmenta, 1971; see also Anderson, 1978; James & Singh, 1978); and the psychometric approach to causal modeling explicitly separates measurement and causal-specification errors, a useful distinction in educational research.

Path Analysis. Sewell Wright, a geneticist interested in exploring the strength of genetic linkages across generations, developed path analysis as the first quantitative technique designed to allow researchers to examine their notions about causality without manipulating variables. According to Wright (1921), path analysis is a "method of measuring the direct effect along each separate path in such a system and thus of finding the degree to which variation of a given effect is determined by each particular cause. The method depends upon the combination of knowledge of the degree of correlation among the variables in a system with such knowledge as may be possessed of the causal relations" (p. 557). Wright (1934), however, later pointed out that "the method of path coefficients is not intended to accomplish the impossible task of deducing causal relations from the values of correlation coefficients. It is intended to combine the quantitative information given by the correlations with such qualitative information as may be at hand on causal relations to give a quantitative interpretation" (p. 193). Thus, Wright clearly stated that path analysis techniques are not intended to develop theory in the absence of conceptual clarity but, instead, to examine the plausibility of well-conceived but unproven theories. His statement is equally true for all the causal modeling techniques described in this article.

The logic underlying path analysis can most easily be demonstrated through an example. Consider a case in which there are four variables (circles appearing in Figure 1). "Ability" and "adult acceptance" are viewed as causes; their antecedents are not of interest in the present model. Such variables are called "independent" or "exogenous." "Peer acceptance" and "school achievement," variables

FIGURE 1. *"Causal" model depicting interrelations of ability, adult acceptance, peer acceptance, and school achievement*

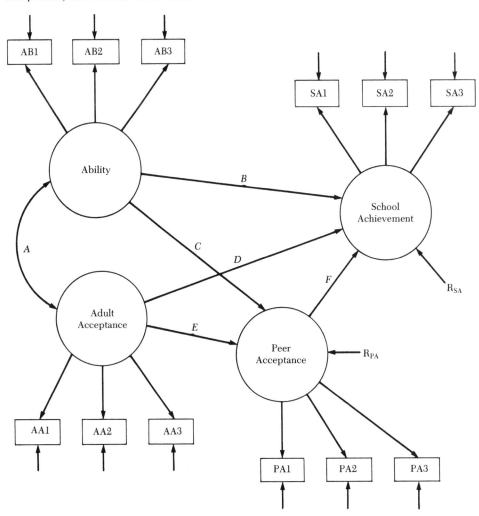

whose causes are being examined, are termed "dependent" or "endogenous." Peer acceptance is viewed as an intermediate or mediating variable, since it is both a cause and an effect; school achievement is exclusively a criterion variable.

Upon inspection, the advantages of path analysis over regression become apparent. Rather than focusing simply upon predictors of achievement, the path model explicitly postulates causal relations between the exogenous variables and the mediating variables. Thus, one could talk of "direct (causal) effects" of the exogenous variables upon achievement (the paths B and D that go directly to achievement) as well as the mediated or "indirect (causal) effects," which pass through some mediating variable or variables (in this case, the paths $C–F$ and $E–F$). Recent work has provided rules and algorithms for partitioning correlations into direct and indirect causal effects as well

as spurious and other noncausal components (e.g., Alwin & Hauser, 1975).

Although path analysis explicitly shows the presumed causal flow pictorially, it assumes (1) one-way causal flow, which may not capture the complexity of real-world causality; and, even more importantly, (2) no measurement error, a problem since nearly all measures in educational research possess measurement error. An approach to the first problem is to measure the variables repeatedly so that the dynamics of the causal process can be examined longitudinally. It is, of course, difficult to measure students repeatedly because of problems such as subject attrition, the time required, and validity problems. In addition, this approach exacerbates the second problem, assuring the presence of nonrandom measurement error, correlated across occasions, which violates least-squares regression assumptions. Thus, path analysis is perhaps most valuable because it provides the introduction to and groundwork for causal inference. The remainder of this article examines an approach designed to overcome the weaknesses of path analysis.

Analysis of Structural Equation Models. The approach to be described, known as "maximum-likelihood analysis of structural equations" (MLASE), is at present the best known and most widely used technique for simultaneously estimating all unknown parameters in causal models containing latent variables (Bentler, 1980). These estimates, derived through full-information procedures, make use of all information in the data about each parameter (e.g., Jöreskog, 1978). The value of such a solution is maximized when the logic of factor analysis is applied to causal modeling. Besides containing measurement error, variables in education may be imprecise or biased measures of the latent variable they are designed to tap. For example, a measure of social class may assess occupational status, income, educational attainment, or some other aspect of social status. Clearly, however, none of the measures is thought of as equivalent to social class. Rather, social class is considered to be reflected in some way in each of the various measures. It might well be thought of as the common part of all of the measures, namely, the latent or structural factor or dimension that underlies and is responsible for what is common among the manifest or observed measures (often called "indicators"). Structural analysis of multiple measures of the dimensions of interest can reduce problems resulting from biased or imprecise measurement of the dimension to be defined. Further, the crucial relations in the model become those interrelating structural dimensions rather than manifest measures.

The framework for the MLASE approach is provided by confirmatory factor analysis techniques in which the factor structure of the measures is defined *a priori*. The virtues of the approach can be summarized as follows: nonrandom as well as random error is allowed; measures do not have to be pure indicators of theoretical variables; all parameters are estimated simultaneously; confidence intervals can be generated for all estimated parameters; and an overall goodness-of-fit test can easily be computed.

A computer program called Linear Structural Relations (LISREL), now available at many universities and other institutions, provides an approach for solving models using MLASE (Jöreskog & Sörbom, 1978). The general model is applicable to virtually all types of causal models (manifest, latent, recursive, nonrecursive, with random and nonrandom error), and produces a goodness-of-fit test, residuals, and derivatives, which help assess the fit of the model as well as how the model could be improved. The LISREL model can be thought of as having two parts. A measurement model relates measures to their underlying dimensions, estimates error components (which contain unique true-score variance plus measurement error), and interrelates error terms. A structural model interrelates the underlying dimensions (Maruyama and McGarvey, 1980,

provide a description of how LISREL can be used). Note that Figure 1 is a multiple-indicator model in which measures are depicted by rectangles and the underlying dimensions by circles. The structural model contains the paths interrelating the underlying variables (circles) that are of substantive or policy interest.

There are a number of other important features of LISREL. First, it can be used to examine competing theoretical models (e.g., Bentler & Bonett, 1980); information about parameter significance and derivatives of fixed parameters also can help refine and clarify theoretical models. Second, recent refinements of LISREL allow cross-population comparisons to be made by means of simultaneous analyses of data from two or more populations. Varying the restrictions imposed in parameter estimation allows tests to be made of the comparability of data from different populations (for example, comparing achievement processes of males with those of females). Third, the program implicitly tests for parameter identification (e.g., Jöreskog, 1978).

The above description is too brief to explain the methodology in complete detail but does acquaint readers with the underlying logic, value, flexibility, and features of causal-modeling techniques. Such techniques clearly advance the analysis of nonexperimental data. Despite their sophistication, however, they neither develop theory nor are sufficient by themselves to determine causality. As noted earlier, at best they can (1) confirm plausibility of a hypothesized causal structure; (2) allow deficient models to be discarded; or (3) suggest ways in which a causal model may be deficient, thereby helping refine the model before its plausibility is tested on additional data sets.

Geoffrey M. Maruyama
Herbert J. Walberg

See also Path Analysis; Regression Analysis; Statistical Methods.

REFERENCES

Ahlgren, A., & Walberg, H. J. Regression analysis. In D. Amick & H. J. Walberg (Eds.), *Introductory Multivariate Analysis.* Berkeley, Calif.: McCutchan, 1975.

Alwin, D. F., & Hauser, R. M. The decomposition of effects in path analysis. *American Sociological Review,* 1975, *40,* 37–47.

Anderson, J. G. Causal models in educational research: Non-recursive models. *American Educational Research Journal,* 1978, *5,* 81–97.

Bentler, P. M. Multivariate analysis with latent variables: Causal modeling. *Annual Review of Psychology,* 1980, *31,* 419–456.

Bentler, P. M., & Bonett, D. G. Significance tests and goodness-of-fit in the analysis of covariance structures. *Psychological Bulletin,* 1980, *88,* 588–606.

Cook, T. D., & Campbell, D. T. *Quasi-experimentation.* Chicago: Rand McNally, 1979.

James, L. R., & Singh, B. K. An introduction to the logic, assumptions, and basic analytic procedures of two-stage least squares. *Psychological Bulletin*, 1978, *85*, 1104–1122.

Jöreskog, K. G. Structural analysis of covariance and correlation matrices. *Psychometrika*, 1978, *43*, 443–477.

Jöreskog, K. G., & Sörbom, D. *LISREL IV: Estimation of Linear Structural Equation Systems by Maximum-likelihood Methods.* Chicago: National Educational Resources, 1978.

Kenny, D. A. *Correlation and Causality.* New York: Wiley, 1979.

Kmenta, J. *Elements of Econometrics.* New York: Macmillan, 1971.

Maruyama, G., & McGarvey, B. Evaluating causal models: An application of maximum-likelihood analysis of structural equations. *Psychological Bulletin*, 1980, *87*, 502–512.

Wright, S. Correlation and causation. *Journal of Agricultural Research*, 1921, *20*, 557–585.

Wright, S. The methods of path coefficients. *Annals of Mathematical Statistics*, 1934, *5*, 161–215.

CERTIFICATION

See Licensing and Certification; Teacher Certification.

CHANGE PROCESSES

As Robert Burns wrote, some time ago, "The best-laid schemes o' mice and men/Gang aft agley." This wide-ranging assessment has been well supported by evaluation studies, sponsored by the U.S. Office of Education (USOE), to ascertain whether the federally funded educational projects aimed at changing and improving the American educational system were attaining some of their intended purposes. The federal programs and outcomes, especially a set of four change-agent programs, serve as a metaphor of the history and results of most of the disparate change projects and hopes, governmental and nongovernmental, launched in the United States. This is not to say that nothing was achieved; there were outcomes, but few that were sought or intended.

Federal Education Programs. Except for legislation in 1921 to aid vocational education, the federal government had not intervened, until the 1950s, in the schools. Education had been and remained exclusively a state preserve and responsibility. But, as a result of the Supreme Court's ruling in May 1954 regarding the unconstitutionality of separate but equal schools for nonwhites and whites, the congressional and executive branches of the government set in motion a series of legislative initiatives. The first in 1958, the National Defense Education Act (NDEA), was given added impetus by the Soviet Union's launching of *Sputnik*. That piece of legislation was followed by many others throughout the 1960s and 1970s. These laws aimed at changing and improving the nation's schools, their outcomes, and their products. Special attention was paid to economically and socially disadvantaged learners. Before

too long, Congress legitimately sought to determine whether the federally devised programs and expenditures were making a difference. Evaluation and research groups were commissioned by USOE to assess earlier federal programs, such as the 1965 Elementary and Secondary Education Act (ESEA), Title I; Head Start; Follow Through; and similar programs.

In the 1970s, the federal government funded an evaluation study of a group of four "change-agent" programs in primary and secondary schools. This assessment was conducted between 1973 and 1978. The analysis of the change-agent projects was not confined to determining what outcomes resulted, but aimed to find out what factors impeded or enhanced educational change and innovation. The programs studied were the ESEA, Title III (Innovative Projects), and ESEA, Title VII (Bilingual Projects; Vocational Education, Part D, Exemplary Programs; and Right-to-Read Programs).

The Rand Corporation was given the task of evaluating the programs. The resulting eight-volume report, with appendices, entitled *Federal Programs Supporting Educational Change* exemplified by volumes I, V, VII, and VIII (Berman & McLaughlin, 1974, 1977, 1978; Berman et al., 1975), constitutes an impressive document on the basis of its rationale, national scope, probing for extent of implementation of projects and of change processes, methodology, thoroughness, and potential contribution to change theory in education. Volumes I through V describe the first phase of the Rand evaluation study. The basic finding was that a school district's adopting a change project funded by the federal government did not mean that the project would be implemented, if at all, in the manner intended. Results from the evaluation of the final phase were in the same negative vein. Projects were rarely implemented; the few that were did not continue innovations after funding ended (Berman & McLaughlin, 1977). Innovative developments were not exported or disseminated to other schools or school districts.

It seemed reasonable to expect, because of the more than twenty years (1958–1978) of effort and the millions of dollars expended for change and improvement in educational personnel and institutions, that there would have been a considerable harvest of positive developments and outcomes. Such was not the case.

Examples of these "nonevents," as someone labeled the unsuccessful programs, governmental and nongovernmental, that produced no or minimal expected results include the New York City schools' experimental elementary programs (Warren, 1978); the Ford Foundation's "Lighthouse" program (Ford Foundation, 1972); and, last but not least, *Federal Programs Supporting Educational Change* (Berman & McLaughlin, 1978), beginning in the late 1950s and blossoming through the 1960s and 1970s up to the 1980s.

There were and continued to be change programs initiated by individuals, school districts, and educational agencies other than the types listed above. In most instances, the outcomes were not what had been projected, were not usually continued, and were rarely disseminated to other educational sites or institutions. The findings by Westinghouse Learning Corporation and Ohio University (1969) and Wargo et al. (1972) were consistently negative, regardless of who funded the innovative projects and who evaluated them.

Ineffectualness of projects. The reason for this negative finding is, in part, the fact that change theory for educational settings is incomplete and therefore inadequate. Another more telling reason is that change models and theory drawn from industry and business have generally been applied, and they appear to be inapplicable, to educational situations, personnel, and agencies.

Boyd and Immegart (1979) deplored the pressures put on educational settings, preschool through university, to adopt efficiency and evaluation techniques from the commercial and business world—as if schools were factories. The same assessment (Berman et al., 1975) is that schools and educators cannot be helped, or evaluated either, on the basis of theories of planned change developed for market-pressured entities. No marketplaces exist, as yet, where schools can display their wares, services, and goods as better than those of "competitors." Since schools are publicly supported, they will neither cease to operate nor lose clients as a result of implementing or not implementing change.

In addition to difficulties arising from inappropriate models and inadequate theory to guide implementation of innovations, all change projects were hindered by other problems. Some of these uncovered by the Rand evaluative study included:

1. Use of inadequate and inappropriate evaluative instruments by local educators and schools.
2. Failure of communication between funding agency and host school or district concerning desired outcomes and preferred procedures.
3. Belief by funding agency that agreement to take funds for an innovative project meant it would be implemented by the recipient school or district.
4. Innocence or unawareness by initiating and funding agency of the large measure of autonomy exercised by local educators and schools once a project was funded.
5. Failure of funding agency and host education agencies to attain "mutual adaptation" or understanding of, and accommodation to, each other's plans, purposes, and procedures.
6. Nonuse of recognized change-agent strategies and skills that are essential in planning, initiating, implementing, and evaluating change projects.

The most telling factors affecting the implementation and outcomes of any change project arose from the properties of the community, the citizenry, and the schools and their personnel. The variables included tenuous but potent issues such as taxpayers' and parents' concern; relations and interactions and politicking within the school's board of directors or school board; morale and concerns of teachers; and ambitions and risk-avoidance tendencies of principals and superintendents.

To cut the Gordian knot of complexities, Mann (1978) suggested that there were five strategies of change. They include forcing, buying, persuading, manipulating and reinforcing, innovation. After pointing out the assets and liabilities of each, he recommends the strategy of buying change. It relies on the premise drawn from political science that self-interest is a highly reliable motivator of change. His "modest proposal": pay educators and schools for improvements in student achievement above a predicted or targeted level.

Models and Theories of Change. Attempts to produce innovation in education and change in individuals are based largely upon theories and hypotheses grounded in social psychology. The models are built upon notions of how people learn, ingest ideas and information, and develop attitudes, concepts, coping and inquiry skills. By nurturing changes in and by individuals through referent groups with which they identify, innovation and development occur in organizations and institutions. The resultant change processes encompass concepts, strategies, and principles that contribute to and explain innovation phenomena.

The concepts include motivation, self-image, self-efficacy, and communication, both verbal and nonverbal. Strategies encompass behaviors such as focused attending, listening, questioning; challenging ideas and assumptions; fulfilling roles and functions; matching experiences to needs of individuals or a group; and nurturing a sense of adequacy for coping and problem solving. Psychological principles take in such factors as individual uniqueness, autonomy, trust in others, congruence of behaviors, and credibility.

This frame of reference has its roots in the philosophy of Dewey (1915, 1963) and the psychological theory and research of Lewin (1947, 1948, 1957). Both insisted on the integration of theory and practice, and both acted upon the aphorism credited to Lewin that there is "nothing so practical as a good theory." Both appreciated the immense difficulties of altering existing institutions—especially educational ones. They saw education as a problem-solving enterprise based upon scientific method. Ecker, Johnson, and Kaelin (1969) succinctly restate this dictum: "The business of science is still to solve human problems" (p. 588).

Lewin and Dewey pointed out the necessity of active participation of learners, the targets of change, in the planning, development, and implementation of alterations in perceptions, information, attitudes, and behaviors. Contemporary scholars Bennis, Benne, and Chin (1969), Havelock (1973), Johnson and Johnson (1975), and Schmuck and Schmuck (1976) reaffirm this viewpoint.

Socio-psychological theory. Lewin's $B = f(P \times E)$—behavior is a function of interaction between person and environment—has influenced much of the social psychological research, both past and present. It prompted the study by Lewin, Lippitt, and White (1939) on social climate and the research of the creative band of scholars whom Lewin attracted around him. The research of Anderson and Brewer (1945) and of Anderson, Brewer, and Reed (1946a, 1946b) in systematic observation of teachers' behaviors had its roots in Lewin's seminal research, as did much of the Chicago Group's with Thelen (1949, 1950), Thelen and Withall (1949), and Thelen et al. (1951).

A tide of concepts and constructs has been emerging to enhance and enlarge the theory developing since the 1940s. These include research and theory contributions by Kohlberg (1968, 1969, 1971a, 1971b) and Kohlberg and Turiel (1971) to understanding stages of moral development; and complementing Kohlberg's findings are the contributions of Piaget regarding stages of cognitive development (1952, 1955, 1962, 1963, 1964, 1971). Rest (1974) has highlighted the impressive fit of Kohlberg's and Piaget's formulations. In addition, there are the achievement motivation theories of Atkinson (1957, 1964) and Atkinson and Feather (1966); Mager and McCann's learner-controlled instruction (1963); Rotter's construct "locus of control" (1966); and Alschuler's analyses (1968) of learners' achievement when they set their goals and procedures and evaluate the results themselves. The contribution by de Charms (1968) of learners desiring a sense of being "origins" of their goals and behaviors rather than "pawns" of others' decisions and demands added to the developing learning and change theory. There is an interesting parallel between de Charms' statement of the motivational and learning benefits human beings derive from perceiving themselves as origins, not pawns, and the "conscientization" formulation for oppressed peoples (Freire, 1970), whereby they become self-aware and politically conscious that they, in concert with like-minded cohorts, can change their environment and themselves.

Weiner (1970, 1972) and Weiner et al. (1971) investigated individuals' perceptions of the causality of events, actions, and outcomes involving themselves and others. This paradigm postulated causal attributions arising from effort and ability—two factors accessible to and controllable by the individual—and two factors, luck and difficulty of task, neither of which is learner-controlled. The interplay of these variables in perceptions of causality was a crucial determinant in learning, motivation, performance, and persistence.

The threads of achievement motivation, locus of control, and attribution theory interweave to influence, predict, and explain the differential probabilities in the learning and achievement of human beings. A form of motivation dubbed "continuing motivation" (Maehr, 1976) is viewed as a skill to be developed. Individuals would return to and take up work on tasks that had been interrupted and were unfinished. In order to achieve closure they return to continue and complete the task. The long-term results would be a pattern of continuing motivation and learning as perceived by Gross (1977) and Tough

(1978). This "Zeigarnik effect" (1927) is related to intrinsic motivation and persistence (Zeigarnik, 1927).

The work of Bandura and Walters (1963) and Bandura (1974, 1977a, 1977b, 1978) has integrated and rounded out current and prior thinking on the role of the learner in the process of learning and change. The concepts of self-efficacy (sense of personal competence to attain goals) and self-system (the total person including self-awareness of skills, knowledge, interests, and needs) in association with the constructs of social learning (individuals interacting and learning with and from others) and modeling (enactment or implementation of a skill, attitude, ability, or behavior to be emulated) have contributed to sociopsychological theory. A recent contribution (Bandura, 1978) is a reinterpretation or reformulation of the $B = f(P \times E)$ formula, wherein the triad is viewed as functioning in three-way interactions that trigger reciprocal reactions.

Behavior modification model. A major theory for behavioral change and innovation in education is that of Skinner (1948, 1953, 1968, 1969, 1971). The basic thesis of behavior modification is that human beings, along with all other living organisms, are inexorably and inescapably controlled by their environment. The appropriate response to this situation for human organisms is to comprehend how external forces such as the environment, including one's fellow human beings, affect one's responses and behavior. It then is possible to initiate moves for coping with, fending off, and utilizing those impingements to enhance one's control over and influence upon the surrounding activities and effects. Since the bases of human behavior are known, they can be codified into laws and principles. These can guide and inform individuals of the reasons for and predictability of their own and everybody else's actions. Thus, behavior is controllable because the stimulus and its antecedents are known and observable.

Insofar as one appreciates the impact of the environment and its origins, one can manage it, including other persons, in one's own best interests as well as others' interests. As long as one remains uninformed of the facts, one is at the mercy of the environment. Yet, Skinner contends, the solution is at hand: utilize the principles that govern behavior, apply behavioral technology such as positive or negative reinforcement in the ensuing situation, change occurs, and new behaviors emerge. This paradigm offers individuals, through knowledge of principles and laws that govern human behavior, the opportunity to employ their knowledge for their own and others' benefit. This knowledgeability is attained by submitting to behavior modification procedures that include reinforcers, alternative prescribed schedules, stimuli, and contingencies.

The system seems autonomous. The aim of the learner or the person with knowledge of the laws governing behavior is to ally herself or himself with a process that encompasses all that we are and do. Conscious capitalizing on and achieving synchronization with the enormous potency of the controlling environment is the goal. If the learner or individual lacks the knowledge of the laws of behavior, someone who does possess the knowledge has to persuade and shape the behaviors and thinking of the uninformed person and move her or him into synchronization with environmental forces. This is when the behavioral specialist enters to serve as a catalyst to change another's tactics and behaviors without being changed himself or herself. This is a familiar paradigm that guides the operations of educators, schools, and administrators of many schools.

The behavior modification model basically is a sophisticated explanation and legitimization of the stimulus-response, educator-controlled paradigm that flourishes in the bulk of American classrooms and schools, primary grades through graduate school. Any teacher (Hanley, 1970) to whom one might describe it would say: "I've been doing those things in my classroom for years" (p. 597).

Operant conditioning of learners in schools (Sulzer & Mayer, 1972) involves positive and negative reinforcement, nurturing new behaviors, establishing contingencies, implementing behavior modification programs, and assessing results. Current and continuing behavioral research was assayed by Hartley and Davies (1976), Robin (1976), and McLaughlin (1976) and progress and problems were cited.

Alternative school model. A frontal attack for achieving change has been the emergence and spread of alternative schools or "free" schools (liberated schools). The concepts and principles undergirding these programs were enunciated by Rogers (1969), Postman and Weingartner (1969), Illich (1971), Freire (1970), Kozol (1972), Gross (1977), and Horwitz (1979). "Free" schools, colleges, and universities are usually under the aegis of a traditional school board or university board of trustees. These alternative programs support cohort-aided or peer-aided study, instruction, and learning, and encourage self-directed undertakings and investigations in informal, group-oriented, loosely structured settings. Furthermore, the proponents and implementers of free education proselytize by modeling and implementing their methods.

Alternative educational institutions are sufficiently numerous and operational to organize associations and publish directories. If all the alternative public schools that call themselves by that label were tallied, they probably would comprise a list of ten thousand schools or more. The number of free universities is about two hundred. As indicated, they are nested within but not subservient to the administration of their host institutions. Alternative schools assess student progress on the basis of student performance in and outside of school; draw on community human resources and facilities; and use fewer traditional methods to evaluate achievement.

Alternative, open, or free schools were planned and established to serve the needs and goals of normal students who resisted the competitive, teacher-dominated, and joyless regimen of traditional schools. The learners were encouraged to make choices and work at self-selected topics and problems in consultation with parents, educators, and peers. The school's and parental inputs were complemented by a wealth of human resources plus cultural and educational facilities in the community.

Evaluation of Theory and Change. Happily, concurrent with the development of socio-psychological learning theory and change models, there were contributions to evaluation by Scriven (1966, 1967), Stake (1967), Cohen (1970), Rosenshine (1970a, 1970b), and Rosenshine and Furst (1973). They reexamined and redefined evaluative criteria and reinforced the rationale undergirding measurement and evaluation of tenuous personality variables, such as attitudes, self-perceptions, needs, and appreciations. Scriven differentiated between process-oriented and product-oriented evaluation. Process assessments measure environmental, instructional, and interpersonal influences upon educational aims. Product measurements assess the final outcomes. Process evaluation, with soundings taken from time to time of procedures, materials, and emerging outcomes, was labeled "formative." Final product or outcomes assessment was tagged "summative." Formative evaluation enables materials revision and redirection of procedures. Summative evaluation offers a final outcome report and recommendations. The two types of measures differ with respect to focus but not with respect to methods. Stake (1970) underlined the role that judgment plays in educational assessment and highlighted the aspect of fallible data. Other social scientists are faced with similar challenges and have experimented with methods that may be applicable to education. Along with needs assessment goes the necessity that evaluators search for and comprehend what the clients (learners and parents) expect of the educational system. Cohen (1970) explored the import of federal and state education programs for social change and deplored transfer to the local communities and educational agencies of the task of evaluating program impacts. The resultant evaluation proved either inadequate or nonexistent. In addition there was confounding of treatment classes with related programs, problems with sample size, insufficient classroom observation, and student background measures.

Coates and Thoreson (1976), Glaser (1976), Berman and McLaughlin (1974), Mayer (1975), and Miles (1980) stress the need for explicit empirical data collected in naturalistic settings regarding behavioral interactions, instructional processes, learning events, and specific strategies in order to know (Miles, 1980) "what is really going on" (p. 126).

Systematic observation. The assessment by Melby (1936) of the enormous gap between theory and classroom practice still holds true when data are collected for analysis and description of classroom interactions and events. In fact, because of the plethora of research tools to systematically observe and record classroom procedures and interpersonal interactions (Withall, 1960, 1963; Rosenshine & Furst, 1973), the concern can be stated now with even stronger conviction. Incredible as it may seem, the major figures who ought to be key participants in setting goals, procedures, and evaluation processes—the learners and their interactions with peers—have been, until recently, slighted and ignored in that process. Scholars such as Kirkland (1971), Boyd and Immegart (1979), Mann (1978), and Paolitto (1976) and others have felt impelled to, as it were, remind everyone that learners are the primary clients and focus of the whole educational enterprise. That should imply their full involvement in helping determine goals, procedures, and standards.

The plea for greater individualization of education and instruction is one indication of appreciation of the centrality of students in the system (Flanagan, 1970). The learners, whether we like it or not, inevitably individualize and draw unique meanings from their learning. Educators can only individualize instruction to match or complement the individualized learning of their clients (Maas & Kleiber, 1975).

In collating the number of instruments available for studying classroom events and processes, Rosenshine and Furst (1973) identified at least 120. Simon and Boyer (1970) provide explicit descriptions of 92.

Because of the existence of a pool of observational tools, staff development and personnel preparation programs have been mounted. They are guided largely by the writing and research of Goldhammer (1969) and Cogan (1972). The term that they and others use, "clinical supervision," is prefaced by the word "peer" (Skoog, 1980). Appropriate psychological, threat-reducing strategies are being underscored to mitigate the concerns attached to the words "observation" and "supervision" (Withall & Wood, 1979).

Higher education. Lack of theory to ground change processes in education impedes progress in organizational and staff development in higher education (Dill & Friedman, 1979). Integrating, or at least sorting out, the multitude of variables involved in organizational change demands a multidisciplinary approach. Four vantage points from which to systematically analyze and study innovations in higher learning have been delineated by Gamson (1974). However, identification of valuable frames of reference does not reduce complexities (Heiss, 1973; Havelock & Havelock, 1973). Studies compiling empirical data are necessary to help explicate educational innovation and facilitate further data-based investigations (Lindquist, 1978; Radnor, Feller & Rogers, 1978).

Organizational development. Organizational development (OD) (Fullan, Miles, & Taylor, 1980) is a procedure to help organizations develop and change. The methodology and model was constructed for business and industrial settings. Transferring the strategy to educational settings has been accompanied by a large number of difficulties and problems (Blumberg, 1976; Derr, 1976). The difficulties included such issues as poor understanding of organizational development processes by educators, probabilities of successful implementation in educational settings standing at .5 or less, and consensus of assessments of OD in schools that valid, data-based studies are virtually unavailable. Despite this bleak picture, Fullan, Miles, and Taylor (1980) optimistically state that "organizational develop-

ment is a useful strategy for school improvement" (p. 178).

Figure and ground variables. Miles's comprehensive analysis (1980) of the issues and problems facing public schools and educators encapsulates most of the complex questions, data, and dilemmas with which the American educational system, including higher education, is struggling to cope.

The analysis prepared for the National Institute of Education delineated the huge range of problems accompanying school operation and school change. These were telescoped into nine "dilemmas," including "core task versus survival emphasis," (educating students versus ensuring survival of schools), "environmental dependence versus autonomy" (community and governmental decision makers settling issues versus local education agencies settling issues); centralized (at the district level) versus "shared influence" (including teachers, learners, and principals). Concomitant "regularities" were specified for each of the nine dilemmas. These regularities were related to "claimed antecedents" (causes of regularities) and "knowledge gaps" that worked against solution of each dilemma.

The report culminated with a proposed research agenda for school improvement:

1. Collect more "directly descriptive" data on, for example, teachers' autonomy and their instructional strategies and educators' definitions of goals.
2. Engage in more "contingent analyses" to determine, for example, when teacher involvement will pay off; what aspects of routinization are related to implementation of change.
3. Employ "comparative analysis" with naturally occurring variations and "intervention evaluation" where variables are experimentally manipulated.
4. Treat "innovativeness" and "effectiveness" as dependent variables.

The report was tagged by its author as a "mapmaking journey" that may advance understanding of American schools and help in efforts "to support them, operate them, study them and improve them" (Miles, 1980, p. 130). An enormous sweep of issues, variables, and problems was critically examined and incisively analyzed.

Goals of Education. Educators, traditional or innovative, have identified goals in terms of the needs, expectations, and roles that human beings strive to fulfill. Dewey has suggested that the responsibility of educators and education is to help people to perform better what they have to do throughout their lives. One way of defining this responsibility would be to specify the major roles that all individuals have to assume as human beings: member of a nuclear or extended family, as child, partner or spouse, and parent; citizen of a community, country, and the world; consumer and conserver of the world's products and resources; recreator, using leisure time for healthful, challenging, self-fulfilling, and service activities; worker and producer of goods and services for personal income and society's needs.

Bruner (1960) has suggested that some major goals of education aim at helping learners to develop problem-solving skills, fundamental concepts to guide and manage their lives, and their own body of organized facts and principles for everyday use.

Within the framework of a cooperative goal structure, Johnson and Johnson (1974) hypothesize that competencies such as the following can be aimed at and achieved by learners: problem-solving skills, ready retrieval of information to be used for problem solving; competence in social relations, communication, and empathetic ability; positive attitudes toward information, the learning process, and fellow learners; positive self-attitudes; and development of interpersonal skills and behaviors based upon intrinsic motivation. They further hypothesize that cooperative goal structures promote group cohesiveness and *esprit de corps*, effective communication, mutual helpfulness, and divergent and risk-taking thinking and actions.

The aspect of goals and goal setting that is troubling is that the beneficiaries of these goals—learners and their guardians, or parents—have very little direct opportunity or say in setting them. The purposes of education are primarily determined by professional educators and curriculum experts. Competency-based education, for instance, is founded upon this procedure and rationale.

The slighting of the learners with respect to participation in identifying and choosing goals and methods to attain them prevents their involvement and commitment as well as their self-attribution for and consummation of the skills, concepts, ideas, and coping abilities subsumed under the term "goals." If some of the tenets of Dewey, Lewin, Weiner, Atkinson, de Charms, Bandura, and others can be implemented through change processes in education, learners, their guardians, and society at large will all benefit.

John Withall
Norman D. Wood

See also Evaluation of Programs; National Development and Education; New Technologies in Education.

REFERENCES

Alschuler, A. S. *How to Increase Motivation through Climate and Structure* (Working Paper No. 8). Cambridge, Mass.: Harvard Graduate School of Education, Achievement Motivation Development Project, 1968.

Anderson, H. H., & Brewer, H. M. Studies of teachers' classroom personalities: I. Dominative and socially integrative behavior of kindergarten teachers. *Applied Psychology Monograph of the American Psychological Association* (No. 6). Stanford, Calif.: Stanford University Press, 1945.

Anderson, H. H.; Brewer, J. E.; & Reed, M. F. Studies of teachers' classroom personalities: II. Effects of teachers' dominative and integrative contacts on children's classroom behavior. *Applied Psychology Monograph of the American Psychological Association* (No. 8). Stanford, Calif.: Stanford University Press, 1946. (a)

Anderson, H. H.; Brewer, J. E.; & Reed, M. F. Studies of teachers' classroom personalities: III. Follow-up studies of the effects of dominative and integrative contacts on children's behavior. *Applied Psychology Monograph of the American Psychological Association* (No. 2). Stanford, Calif.: Stanford University Press, 1946. (b)

Atkinson, J. W. Motivational determinant of risk-taking behavior. *Psychological Review*, 1957, *64*, 359–373.

Atkinson, J. W. *An Introduction to Motivation*. Princeton, N.J.: Van Nostrand, 1964.

Atkinson, J. W., & Feather, N. T. (Eds.) *A Theory of Achievement Motivation*. New York: Wiley, 1966.

Bandura, A. *Psychological Modeling: Conflicting Theories*. New York: Lieber-Atherton, 1974.

Bandura, A. Self-efficacy: Toward a unifying theory of behavioral change. *Psychological Review*, 1977, *84*, 191–215. (a)

Bandura, A. *Social Learning Theory*. Englewood Cliffs, N.J.: Prentice-Hall, 1977. (b)

Bandura, A. The self-esteem in reciprocal determinism. *American Psychologist*, 1978, *33*, 344–358.

Bandura, A., & Walters, R. H. *Social Learning and Personality Development*. New York: Holt, Rinehart & Winston, 1963.

Bennis, W. G.; Benne, K. D.; & Chin, R. (Eds.). *The Planning of Change* (2nd ed.). New York: Holt, Rinehart & Winston, 1969.

Berman, P.; Greenwood, P. W.; McLaughlin, M. W.; & Pincus, J. *Executive Summary*. Vol. 5 of *Federal Programs Supporting Educational Change* (R-1589/5-HEW). Santa Monica, Calif.: Rand Corporation, 1975. (ERIC Document Reproduction Service No. ED 108 331)

Berman, P., & McLaughlin, M. W. *A Model of Educational Change*, Vol. 1 of *Federal Programs Supporting Educational Change* (R-1589/1-HEW). Santa Monica, Calif.: Rand Corporation, 1974. (ERIC Document Reproduction Service No. ED 099 957)

Berman, P., & McLaughlin, M. W. *Factors Affecting Implementation and Continuation*. Vol. 7 of *Federal Programs Supporting Educational Change* (R-1589/7 HEW). Santa Monica, Calif.: Rand Corporation, 1977. (ERIC Document Reproduction Service No. ED 140 432)

Berman, P., & McLaughlin, M. W. *Implementing and Sustaining Innovations*. Vol. 8 of *Federal Programs Supporting Educational Change* (R-1589/8-HEW). Santa Monica, Calif.: Rand Corporation, 1978. (ERIC Document Reproduction Service No. ED 159 289)

Blumberg, A. OD's future in schools—Or is there one? *Education and Urban Society*, 1976, *8*, 213–226.

Boyd, W. L., & Immegart, G. L. Education's turbulent environment and problem-finding: Lines of convergence. In G. L. Immegart & W. L. Boyd (Eds.), *Problem-finding in Educational Administration*. Lexington, Mass.: Heath, 1979.

Bruner, J. *The Process of Education*. Cambridge, Mass.: Harvard University Press, 1960.

Coates, T. J., & Thoreson, C. E. Teacher anxiety: A review with recommendations. *Review of Educational Research*, 1976, *46*, 159–184.

Cogan, M. L. *Clinical Supervision*, Boston: Houghton Mifflin, 1972.

Cohen, D. Politics and research: Evaluation of social action programs in education. *Review of Educational Research*, 1970, *40*, 213–239.

de Charms, R. *Personal Causation: The Internal Affective Determinants of Behavior*. New York: Academic Press, 1968.

Derr, C. B. OD won't work in schools. *Education and Urban Society*, 1976a, *8*, 227–241.

Dewey, J. *The School and Society*. Chicago: University of Chicago Press, 1915.

Dewey, J. *Experience and Education*. New York: Macmillan, 1963.

Dill, D. D., & Friedman, C. P. An analysis of frameworks for research on innovation and change in higher education. *Review of Educational Research*, 1979, *49*, 411–435.

Ecker, D. W.; Johnson, T. J.; & Kaelin, E. F. Aesthetic inquiry. *Review of Educational Research*. December 1969, *39*, 577–592.

Flanagan, J. C. *Project PLAN: The Basic Role of Guidance in Individualizing Education*. Paper presented at the American Personnel and Guidance Association Convention, New Orleans, March 1970. (ERIC Document Reproduction Service No. ED 038 676)

Ford Foundation. *A Foundation Goes to School: The Ford Foundation Comprehensive School Improvement Program, 1960–1970*. New York: Office of Reports, 1972. (ERIC Document Reproduction Service No. ED 071 190)

Freire, P. *Pedagogy of the Oppressed*. New York: Seabury Press, 1970.

Fullan, M.; Miles, M. B.; & Taylor, G. Organizational development in schools: The state of the art. *Review of Educational Research*, 1980, *50*, 121–183.

Gamson, Z. F. *Course Outline: G804, Sociological Approaches to Collegiate Innovation* (Course Syllabus). Ann Arbor: University of Michigan, Winter 1974.

Glaser, R. Components of a psychology of instruction: Toward a science of design. *Review of Educational Research*, 1976, *46*, 1–24.

Goldhammer, R. *Clinical Supervision*. New York: Holt, Rinehart & Winston, 1969.

Gross, R. *The Lifelong Learner*. New York: Simon & Schuster, 1977.

Hanley, E. M. Review of research involving applied behavior analysis in the classroom. *Review of Educational Research*, 1970, *40*, 597–625.

Hartley, J., & Davies, I. K. Pre-instructional strategies: The role of pretests, behavioral objectives, overviews, and advance organizers. *Review of Educational Research*, 1976, *46*, 239–265.

Havelock, R. G. *The Change Agent's Guide to Innovation in Education*. Englewood Cliffs, N.J.: Educational Technology Publications, 1973.

Havelock, R. G., & Havelock, M. C. *Educational Innovation in the United States*. Ann Arbor, Mich.: Center for Research on Utilization of Scientific Knowledge, 1973. (ERIC Document Reproduction Service No. ED 091 865)

Heiss, A. *An Inventory of Academic Innovation and Reform*. New York: McGraw-Hill, 1973.

Horwitz, S. Exploration of *Self-directed Learning in Theory and as Facilitated by Learning Networks and Free Universities*. Honors thesis in Liberal Arts, Pennsylvania State University, College of Liberal Arts, 1979.

Illich, I. *Deschooling Society*. New York: Harper & Row, 1971.

Johnson, D. W., & Johnson, R. T. Instructional goal structure: Cooperative, competitive, or individualistic. *Review of Educational Research*, 1974, *44*, 213–240.

Johnson, D. W., & Johnson, R. T. *Learning Together and Alone*. Englewood Cliffs, N.J.: Prentice-Hall, 1975.

Kirkland, W. C. The effects of tests on students and schools. *Review of Educational Research*, 1971, *41*, 303–350.

Kohlberg, L. Early education: A cognitive developmental view. *Child Development*, 1968, *39*, 1013–1062.

Kohlberg, L. *Stages in the Development of Moral Thought and Action*. New York: Holt, Rinehart & Winston, 1969.

Kohlberg, L. The concepts of developmental psychology as the central guide to education. In M. Reynolds (Ed.), *Psychology and the Process of Schooling in the Next Decade*. Minneapolis: University of Minnesota, Audio-visual Extension, 1971. (a)

Kohlberg, L. Stages of moral development as a basis for moral education. In C. Beck, E. Sullivan, & D. Crittendon (Eds.), *Moral Education*. Toronto: University of Toronto Press, 1971. (b)

Kohlberg, L., & Turiel, E. Moral development and moral education. In G. Lesser (Ed.), *Psychology and Educational Practice*. Glenview, Ill.: Scott, Foresman, 1971.

Kozol, J. Free schools. *Saturday Review*, March 4, 1972.

Lewin, K. Frontiers in group dynamics: Concept, method, and reality in social science, social equilibria, and social change. *Human Relations*, 1947, *1*, 5–41.

Lewin, K. *Resolving Social Conflicts*. New York: Harper & Brothers, 1948.

Lewin, K. *Field Theory in Social Sciences*. New York: Harper & Brothers, 1957.

Lewin, K.; Lippitt, R.; & White, R. Patterns of aggressive behavior in experimentally created "social climates." *Journal of Social Psychology*, 1939, *10*, 271–299.

Lindquist, J. *Strategies for Change*. Berkeley, Calif.: Pacific Soundings Press, 1978.

Maas, J. B., & Kleiber, D. A. *Directory of Teaching Innovations in Psychology*, Washington, D.C.: American Psychological Association, 1975. (ERIC Document Reproduction Service No. ED 127 209)

Maehr, M. Continuing motivation: An analysis of a seldom-considered educational outcome. *Review of Educational Research*, 1976, *46*, 443–462.

Mager, R. F., & McCann, J. *Learner-controlled Instruction*. Palo Alto, Calif.: Varian Associates, 1963.

Mann, D. The user-driven system and a modest proposal. In D. Mann (Ed.), *Making Change Happen?* New York: Teachers College Press, Columbia University, 1978, pp. 285–307.

Mayer, R. E. Information-processing variables in learning to solve problems. *Review of Educational Research*, 1975, *45*, 525–541.

McLaughlin, T. F. Self-control in the classroom. *Review of Educational Research*, 1976, *46*, 631–660.

Melby, E. O. Supervision. *Review of Educational Research*, 1936, *6*, 324–336.

Miles, M. B. *Common Properties of Schools in Context: The Backdrop for Knowledge Utilization and "School Improvement."* New York: Center for Policy Research, 1980.

Paolitto, D. P. The effect of cross-age tutoring on adolescence: An inquiry into theoretical assumptions. *Review of Educational Research*, 1976, *46*, 215–237.

Piaget, J. *The Origins of Intelligence in the Child*. New York: International Universities Press, 1952.

Piaget, J. *The Language and Thought of the Child*. New York: Harcourt, Brace & World, 1955.

Piaget, J. *Play, Dreams, and Imitation in Childhood*. New York: Norton, 1962.

Piaget, J. *The Child's Conception of the World*. Paterson, N.J.: Littlefield, Adams, 1963.

Piaget, J. Development and learning. *Journal of Research in Science Teaching*, 1964, *2*, 176–186.

Piaget, J. *Science of Education and the Psychology of the Child*. New York: Viking Press, 1971.

Postman, N., & Weingartner, C. *Teaching as a Subversive Activity*. New York: Dell, Delacorte Press, 1969.

Radnor, M.; Feller, I.; & Rogers, E. *The Diffusion of Innovations: An Assessment* (Report to the National Science Foundation). Evanston, Ill.: Northwestern University, 1978.

Rest, J. Developmental psychology as a guide to value education: A review of "Kohlbergian" programs. *Review of Educational Research*, 1974, *44*, 241–259.

Robin, A. L. Behavioral instruction in the college classroom. *Review of Educational Research*, 1976, *46*, 631–663.

Rogers, C. R. *Freedom to Learn.* Columbus, Ohio: Merrill, 1969.

Rosenshine, B. Evaluation of instruction. *Review of Educational Research*, 1970, *40*, 279–300. (a)

Rosenshine, B. The stability of teacher effects upon student achievement. *Review of Educational Research*, 1970, *40*, 647–662. (b)

Rosenshine, B., & Furst, N. F. The use of direct observation to study teaching. In R. M. W. Travers (Ed.), *Second Handbook of Research on Teaching.* Chicago: Rand McNally, 1973.

Rotter, J. B. Generalized expectancies for internal versus external control of reinforcement. *Psychological Monographs*, 1966, *80*(1).

Schmuck, R. A., & Schmuck, P. A. *Group Processes in the Classroom* (2nd ed.). Dubuque, Iowa: Brown, 1976.

Scriven, M. *The Methodology of Evaluation* (Social Science Education Consortium Publication No. 110.) Boulder: Social Sciences Education Consortium, University of Colorado, 1966.

Scriven, M. The methodology of evaluation. In R. E. Stake (Ed.), *Perspectives of Curriculum Evaluation* (American Educational Research Association Monograph Series on Curriculum Evaluation, No. 1). Chicago: Rand McNally, 1967.

Simon, A., & Boyer, E. G. *Mirrors for Behavior.* Philadelphia: Research for Better Schools, 1970. (ERIC Document Reproduction Service No. ED 042 937)

Skinner, B. F. *Walden Two.* New York: Macmillan, 1948.

Skinner, B. F. *Science and Human Behavior.* New York: Macmillan, 1953.

Skinner, B. F. *The Technology of Teaching.* New York: Appleton-Century-Crofts, 1968.

Skinner, B. F. *Contingencies of Reinforcement: A Theoretical Analysis.* New York: Appleton-Century-Crofts, 1969.

Skinner, B. F. *Beyond Freedom and Dignity.* New York: Knopf, 1971.

Skoog, G. Improving college teaching through peer observation. *Journal of Teacher Education*, March-April 1980, *31*, 23–25.

Stake, R. E. (Ed.). *Perspectives of Curriculum Evaluation* (American Educational Research Association Monograph Series on Curriculum and Evaluation No. 1). Chicago: Rand McNally, 1967.

Stake, R. E. Objectives, priorities, and other judgment data. *Review of Educational Research*, 1970, *40*, 181–212.

Sulzer, B., & Mayer, G. R. *Behavior Modification Procedures for School Personnel.* New York: Dryden Press, 1972.

Thelen, H. A. Group dynamics in instruction: Principle of least group size. *School Review*, 1949, *57*, 139–148.

Thelen, H. A. Educational dynamics: Theory and research. *Journal of Social Issues*, 1950, *6*, 2–96.

Thelen, H. A., & Withall, J. Three frames of reference: A description of climate. *Human Relations*, 1949, *2*, 159–176.

Thelen, H. A.; Withall, J.; Flanders, N. A.; Rehage, K. J.; Perkins, H. V.; Glidewell, J. C.; & Singletary, J. Experimental research toward a theory of instruction. *Journal of Educational Research*, 1951, *45*, 89–136.

Tough, A. Major learning efforts: Recent research and future directions. *Adult Education*, 1978, *28*, 250–263.

Wargo, M. J.; Tallmadge, G. K.; Michaels, D. D.; Lipe, D.; & Mor-

ris, S. J. *ESEA Title I: A Re-analysis and Synthesis of Evaluation Data from Fiscal Year 1965 through 1970: Final Report.* Palo Alto, Calif.: American Institutes for Research, March 1972. (ERIC Document Reproduction Service No. ED 059 415)

Warren, C. The non-implementation of EEP: All that money for business as usual. In D. Mann (Ed.), *Making Change Happen?* New York: Teachers College Press, Columbia University, 1978, pp. 150–180.

Weiner, B. New concepts in the study of achievement motivation. In B. Maher (Ed.), *Progress in Experimental Personality Research* (Vol. 5). New York: Academic Press, 1970, pp. 67–109.

Weiner, B. Attribution theory, achievement motivation, and educational process. *Review of Educational Research*, 1972, *42*, 203–216.

Weiner, B.; Frieze, I.; Kukla, A.; Reed, L.; Rest, S.; & Rosenbaum, P. M. *Perceiving the Causes of Success and Failure.* New York: General Learning Press, 1971.

Westinghouse Learning Corporation and Ohio University. *The Impact of Head Start: An Evaluation of the Effects of Head Start Experience on Children's Cognitive and Affective Development.* Springfield, Va.: Clearinghouse for Federal Scientific and Technical Information U.S. Dept. of Commerce, June 1969. (ERIC Document Reproduction Service No. ED 036 321)

Withall, J. Research tools: Observing and recording behavior. *Review of Educational Research*, 1960, *30*, 496–512.

Withall, J., & Lewis, W. W. Social interaction in the classroom. In N. L. Gage (Ed.), *Handbook of Research on Teaching.* Chicago: Rand McNally, 1963.

Withall, J., & Wood, F. H. Taking the threat out of classroom observation and feedback. *Journal of Teacher Education*, 1979, *30*, 55–58.

Zeigarnik, B. Über das behalten von erledigten, und unerledigten handlungen. *Psychologische Forschung*, 1927, *9*, 1–85.

CHARACTER EDUCATION

See Citizenship Education; Discipline; Moral Development; Moral Education; Religion and Education.

CHILDREN'S LITERATURE

See Literature; Textbooks.

CHRISTIAN SCHOOLS

See Catholic Schools; Private Schools; Protestant Education; Religion and Education.

CITIZENSHIP EDUCATION

Citizenship education is influenced directly and indirectly by religious, economic, social, and political institutions, particularly the family, mass media, and schooling. The focus here is upon the citizenship education role of elementary and secondary schools in the United States and includes interpretations of citizenship education, prevailing school programs and practices, evidence regarding the effects of school experiences on students' political dispositions, and policy implications.

Historical Perspective. Conceptions of citizenship and citizenship education in the United States are usually traced from Plato and Aristotle through Rousseau and Locke to Jefferson, Mann, Dewey, and the "Cardinal Principles." In seventeenth-century England, citizenship meant the personal and perpetual relationship of allegiance between subject and king. In contrast, the English colonists and their successors viewed citizenship in terms of contractual membership in and allegiance to a national political community, where authority resides in the citizenry (Kettner, 1978). The initial aim of citizenship education in the United States was the creation of a national identity, which was to be attained by fostering commitment to democratic value claims and national loyalty. In addition to patriotism, basic literacy and religious morality were promoted in the name of "civic education," largely by means of repetitive reading and spelling exercises and school rituals.

During the nineteenth-century, the purpose of citizenship education changed from contributing to the establishment of a national character and community to a more encompassing socialization of young people. Once the nation's political identity had been formed, it was to be perpetuated and celebrated, buttressed by knowledge of government structure and function and by commitment to selected value claims (such as hard work, honesty and integrity, individual effort and property, and compliance with legitimate authority). Controversial issues, political analysis, and participatory skills were ignored in nineteenth-century civics texts (Belok, 1978). Generally, this pattern persists in twentieth-century civics texts.

A broader conception of citizen socialization is reflected in (1) school programs and practices intended to Americanize immigrants in the late nineteenth- and early twentieth-centuries; (2) community civics programs, which appeared in the 1920s and 1930s to increase the relevance of citizenship education for young people and to improve the local community; and (3) programs reflecting various forms of defensive chauvinism during the post–World War II period.

Citizenship education seems to have been overshadowed by other concerns during the 1960s. However, by the mid-1970s, citizenship education was experiencing a revival (Butts, 1980), apparently in response to a widely perceived need for a renewed sense of political community—for an antidote to widespread public apathy and cynicism.

Review of the historical development of citizenship education in the United States suggests that the realm of citizenship education has been dramatically extended. What Butts (1980) calls "the civic role of public education" has expanded from promoting basic literacy and politically relevant learning to promoting acculturation, usually to some version of dominant American culture (Edelman,

1976). Students are now expected not only to accept prevailing democratic political principles but also to adopt certain economic and and social norms. Civic education has become citizenship education, and in the process, citizenship education has become a slogan.

Meanings. "Citizenship education" is a slogan that has widespread appeal largely because it suggests that essential national interests are being promoted. A slogan can serve as a summary statement—a shorthand way of representing a cluster of assumptions, descriptions, and courses of action. Citizenship education represents assumptions about learning and ways of achieving desired goals. It usually refers to education for good citizenship; however, education for good citizenship does not indicate the nature of good citizenship or an appropriate education.

Citizenship education could be interpreted as relevant only for aliens who wish to become naturalized citizens and who therefore are expected to demonstrate "a knowledge and understanding of the history, principles, and form of government of the United States" as determined by the Justice Department's Immigration and Naturalization Service. Conversely, citizenship education could be construed as appropriate for all citizens, encompassing most if not all of general education.

Citizenship education is more meaningfully viewed as democratic political education. Primarily civic or political in nature, it addresses public affairs and is not directly concerned with personal or social activities (Kelly, 1979). Its goal is to sustain and refine a democratic political community—a group of people who share both a commitment to certain principles, such as freedom, justice, equality, due process, diversity, personal contribution to the public well-being, human rights, and dignity (Butts, 1980)—as well as an involvement in governing processes based on mutual consent, wherein "we the people" are the ultimate source of legitimate power and authority. The referent political community can be local, national, or global in scope. In the school context, it is most often national.

The subject matter of citizenship education consists of the complex, interactive relationship between individuals and the democratic political community. This relationship involves democratic value commitments, formal and informal political processes, and responsible participation in public affairs, including critical scrutiny of truth claims, institutions, public officials, and political operations (Cherryholmes, 1980; Engle, 1977; Giroux, 1980; Shaver, 1977). The school's role in citizenship education includes both formal programs and the implicit curricula (school policies and routines or practices) that, in effect, encourage some ideas and behaviors and discourage others.

Forms of Citizenship Education. The distinctions among illusory, technical, and constructive schooling proposed by Popkewitz, Tabachnick, and Wehlage (1981) provide a useful means of analyzing citizenship education programs and practices. Their empirically based conceptualization extends Litt's more general distinctions among civic education models (1965) and has the particular advantage of highlighting important aspects of citizenship education across school settings and content emphases.

An illusory form of citizenship education incorporates a limited range of political content and learning activities. Consideration of citizen participation, for example, most often is restricted to voting. There is little or no provision for the integration of content across topics or for adaptation to student interests. It is assumed that students cannot handle much content or variety in activities, that relationships are too difficult for them to grasp, and that their interests are usually not worth pursuing. Learning activities stress rote memorization, unrelated to students' experiences, under the assumption that knowledge is static and that conscientious students will accept predetermined right answers. The students' role is a passive one. It is further assumed that students must be properly socialized before they can benefit from substantive learning opportunities, and discipline and ritual are emphasized. For example, students might regularly recite the Pledge of Allegiance but rarely if ever engage in examination of the concepts of republic, liberty, and justice. Proper behavior—cooperation with school and teacher demands, attention to assigned tasks—and espousal of democratic norms take precedence over meaningful political learning. Overall, illusory citizenship education reflects a conformist political orientation and is inconsistent with the interpretation of citizenship education employed here.

Technical citizenship education offers a carefully preplanned series of activities intended to yield measurable competencies that can be checked off as students demonstrate mastery of them, often by completing work sheets. The range of political content is limited to discrete skills and bits of information. If there is time left after prescribed activities have been completed, integration of content and student interests might be pursued. For example, one assigned task might have students list the rights guaranteed by the First Amendment, and another might have students describe two ways in which citizens can participate in government and influence political decision making. Later, students might discuss the relationship between First Amendment guarantees and political participation, but such discussion would be considered an extra activity. Official learning (what counts for grades) tends to be mechanical and unrelated to students' experiences; knowledge is standardized, and right answers are predetermined. The student's role is moderately active insofar as students are expected to strive to attain the objectives set for them—within the bounds of explicit discipline and management procedures that are intended to promote efficiency. Technical citizenship education reflects a political orientation that would likely support change in the interests of efficient management but would not otherwise question the status quo.

With constructive citizenship education, students are encouraged to pursue their own interests, engage in a variety of activities, and examine a broad range of political content and possibilities. Comprehension rather than memorization is sought, with content being integrated and related to students' experiences. Constructive citizenship education assumes that knowledge is tentative, that there are multiple ways of learning and knowing, and that different perspectives ought to be considered. For example, along with political structures and processes, students might examine the meanings of justice and the proper limits of government. The student role is an active one; learning activities are designed to foster students' exercise of rights and responsibilities, and students are expected to demonstrate independence and initiative. In sum, constructive citizenship education reflects a questioning orientation, one that encourages critical examination of the political system as well as effective participation in public affairs.

The characteristics and assumptions that distinguish the three forms of citizenship education illustrate dimensions of various school programs and practices—(for example, from passive to active student roles, and from little political content to discrete segments of political content to a range of integrated political content). These dimensions might well be considered when developing school programs and practices and when designing citizenship education research.

Research. Research that is relevant to the school's role in citizenship education spans a range of topics and modes of inquiry. Historical studies, surveys of state mandates and school programs, and textbook analyses have been cited previously. In this section, attention is directed to studies of the relationship between school or classroom factors and students' political knowledge, beliefs, and participatory behavior.

School and classroom studies. Studies conducted by Goldenson (1978) and Litt (1963) are illustrative of citizenship education research that examines facets of schooling in addition to the formal curriculum. These studies also reflect a concern for active and informed democratic citizenship, and they indicate the value of research that investigates how citizenship education is conducted and how it is mediated by students. In contrast to the assumption that students are passive recipients of citizenship education, mediation assumes student initiative in processing information and interpreting experience.

Litt's study (1963) of the effects of a high school civic education course upon students' political attitudes is noteworthy for its use of multiple data sources. In an effort to describe and explain changes in students' political attitudes in three different socioeconomic status (SES) communities after completion of a one-semester civic education course, Litt analyzed the textbooks used, interviewed community leaders including teachers and school administrators characterized as "potential civic and education influentials," and administered questionnaires to students. Five dimensions were examined: political chauvinism; democratic creed (especially the rights of minorities to influence government policy); political participation; political process (as opposed to a mechanical view of government function); and politics as the resolution of group conflict. In one school in each community, the attitudes of students in a civic education course were assessed at the beginning and at the end of the semester, as were the attitudes of an equivalent group of students who did not take the course.

Although the textbooks were quite similar to the positions of the various community leaders with respect to the five dimensions, there were important differences among the communities. Citizen participation received more emphasis in the upper-middle-class and lower-middle-class communities than in the working-class community. Attention to partisan political processes and conflict resolution was evident only in the higher SES community. Both before and after taking a civic education course, students in the higher SES community displayed the most positive attitudes, and they were the only ones to modify their perception of politics to include power interactions and conflict resolution. Students in the lower SES communities were offered a more passive and idealistic-consensual political education, and they tended to perceive political activity more mechanistically and harmoniously. On all dimensions except political chauvinism, differences between students in the upper-middle-class and working-class communities were greater after completion of a civic education course. The three schools appeared to reinforce and perpetuate community differences and to encourage students to adopt different citizen roles. Unfortunately, few studies have further explored the relationships among school and community citizenship education characteristics, processes, and outcomes.

In evaluating the effects of an experimental curriculum unit on senior high school students' attitudes toward civil liberties, Goldenson (1978) investigated attitude change in relation to teacher credibility as perceived by students—the extent to which students saw their teachers as fair, knowledgeable, concerned, interesting, and lucid. Not only was attitude change supportive of civil liberties associated with involvement in the experimental curriculum, but positive attitude change was greater when teachers were rated high on credibility. Further, low teacher credibility was associated with negative attitude change in the experimental group. Generally, students' perceptions of teacher credibility appeared to mediate the effects of the experimental curriculum.

Most of the recent school and classroom research relevant to citizenship education has been concerned with political socialization. Focusing upon the national political community, these studies have used written questionnaires and oral interviews to examine young people's sociopolitical knowledge, beliefs, and behavior. The outcomes of particular interest are students' knowledge of government structure and function; support for the national government (for example, beliefs about public officials); commitment to democratic values (for example, tolerance for diversity, dissent, and conflict); feelings of political cynicism and efficacy; and interest and participa-

tion in conventional political activity (such as voting and letter writing). The independent variables most often examined are demographic characteristics such as age, sex, race or ethnicity, and SES.

This school and classroom research has been reviewed by Ehman (1980), among others (e.g., Jennings & Niemi, 1974; Massialas, 1969, 1975; Patrick, 1977; Weissberg, 1974). Ehman's review encompasses empirical studies conducted in United States and Canadian schools. He concluded that the formal curriculum effectively transmits political knowledge, particularly to lower SES students, but does not substantially influence political attitudes or participation. School and classroom climate and student participation in extracurricular and school governance activities, however, do significantly influence political attitudes and participation. Similar conclusions were reached by Massialas (1975) in an earlier review, which included textbook analyses and studies conducted in other nations.

More specifically, school and classroom research offers the following tentative conclusions.

1. Schooling is an important means of transmitting political information to young people, and its importance in this regard increases from elementary to high school. It is less influential in shaping political attitudes and behavior, although it appears to be more important for racial minorities and lower SES groups than for higher-status groups.

2. Conventional civics and government courses have a negligible impact upon students' political attitudes and participation, with the exception of racial minorities. It may be that the regular curriculum is redundant or otherwise irrelevant for many students. The use of repetitive worksheets, emphasis on political facts, and engagement in patriotic rituals tend to be negatively related to student's political knowledge and democratic beliefs (Torney, Oppenheim, & Farnen, 1975), whereas some specially designed curricula have been found quite effective in enhancing students' political knowledge, beliefs, and behavior (Farquhar & Dawson, 1979; Patrick, 1977; Wiley & Superka, 1977). Citizenship education curriculum materials tend to present a simplistic and idealized picture of the United States that is inconsistent with political realities, other sources of political information (media), and citizenship objectives with respect to critical scrutiny and decision making. There is little evidence concerning the effects of such curriculum materials upon students, although it might reasonably be inferred that they contribute initially to positive feelings toward the political system and later to cynicism (Massialas, 1969, 1975).

3. Teacher attitudes and credibility are moderately but positively related to students' political attitudes, particularly for lower-SES students.

4. An open classroom climate, in which controversial issues are freely discussed and students believe that they can influence classroom procedures and events, shows a consistently strong, positive relationship with political and participatory attitudes, including higher political efficacy and trust and lower political cynicism and alienation. It appears that such a climate is more likely to provide experiences and models supportive of active democratic citizenship. Open climates appear to characterize a small proportion of the classrooms studied. Instead, teachers tend to promote a nonreflective political orientation (unquestioning loyalty, obedience) and to discourage change-oriented participatory behavior. Sociopolitical conflict and issues perceived as controversial and likely to offend local community groups are rarely examined in social studies classes (Shaver, Davis, & Helburn, 1979).

5. Participation in school governance and extracurricular activities is positively related to students' political attitudes, as is school organization pattern and governance climate. Less authoritarian school environments that afford varied opportunities for meaningful student participation are associated with positive political attitudes and behavior.

6. School context variables, including school size and socioeconomic and racial or ethnic composition, are related to students' political attitudes and participatory behavior.

Overall, the research suggests that school milieu and the manner in which citizenship education is conducted has as much or more impact upon students, particularly upon their political beliefs and participatory behavior, than do the specific topics and activities included in the formal program. A dominant impression is that citizenship education in the elementary grades tends to be illusory whereas citizenship education in secondary schools tends to be technical in nature, particularly in lower-SES communities. There is a need for systematic field studies to extend understanding of school and community factors that might facilitate constructive citizenship education.

In addition to the research already reviewed are state, national, and international surveys of young people's political knowledge, beliefs, and participatory behavior, for example, the National Assessment of Educational Progress (NAEP). These surveys, which, for the most part do not directly consider school or classroom factors, are of interest because of the interpretation of citizenship they offer and the possible impact of their findings upon school policies and programs.

National assessment. The National Assessment of Educational Progress (NAEP), established in 1964, is a periodic, nationwide census of 9-year-olds, 13-year-olds, and 17-year-olds in ten areas, including citizenship education. The NAEP defines citizenship in terms of the following objectives: understanding the main structure and functions of local, state, and national government in the United States; showing concern for the well-being and dignity of other people; supporting justice and the rights of all individuals; comprehending international and world problems; dealing rationally with public issues and decisions; and participating in democratic civic improvement. In contrast to earlier NAEP citizenship objectives, the objectives for the 1980s assessment define citizenship in broader

than national terms, compare political institutions and processes in the United States with those of other nations, and pay somewhat more attention to the nation's legal system and political process (National Assessment of Educational Progress, 1980).

Overall, the NAEP interpretation of citizenship is a broad one, encompassing social as well as public spheres of activity. Generally supportive of the sociopolitical status quo, the NAEP objectives do accommodate conventional, legal-constitutional citizen activity directed toward undefined civic improvement and greater justice.

Although NAEP objectives assume that schools can and should have a substantial influence on students' socially and politically relevant knowledge, skills, beliefs, and participatory behavior, NAEP citizenship scores cannot be taken as indicators of school effects or citizenship education effectiveness because the scores are not directly related to specific school factors. Also, most 9-year-olds (fourth-graders) have not yet had formal instruction in United States history or government, and most 13-year-olds (eighth-graders) have had formal instruction in United States history but not in civics or government. Assuming that formal school instruction can make a difference, it is not likely that NAEP scores for 13-year-olds and especially for 9-year olds reflect this influence. (For a critical interpretation of the first citizenship and social studies assessments, see Fair, 1975.)

Five topics are addressed in NAEP's *Changes in Political Knowledge and Attitudes, 1969–1976* (National Assessment of Educational Progress, 1978): constitutional rights, respect for others, government structure and function, political processes, and international affairs. Overall, the political knowledge and attitude scores of 13-year-olds and 17-year-olds declined by about 3 percent (7 percent for 17-year-olds' knowledge). Generally, scores on recognition and valuing of constitutional rights and respect for others declined less than scores on understanding government structure and function and political process.

In *Education for Citizenship: A Bicentennial Survey* (National Assessment for Educational Progress, 1976), the results of the 1975/76 assessment are summarized as follows: "Thirteen-year-olds and 17-year-olds express similar social and political attitudes . . . these change very little during their secondary education. Their respect for the human rights of all Americans, regardless of race, sex, color, religious or political beliefs, is high, as is their estimation of the importance of participation in the political process. However, during their secondary school years students acquire a great deal of information about politics, and this new knowledge increases their interest in the political process and, presumably, their effectiveness as citizens" (p. 1).

The 1975/76 citizenship assessment also included several items requesting 13-year-olds' and 17-year-olds' perceptions of their political education experiences in school. Two of these items, frequency of classroom discussion about political issues and frequency of studying how to acquire and analyze information about political issues, were examined in relation to students' total citizenship scores (all knowledge and attitude items). In both cases, the relationship was positive. Sixty-three percent of the 17-year-olds and 48 percent of the 13-year-olds reported classroom discussions of domestic government and politics "at least three or four times a month"; corresponding figures for classroom discussion of international politics and global problems were 61 percent and 46 percent, respectively. Sixty-six percent of the 17-year-olds said that they had studied how to acquire information about political issues and to analyze the values and alternatives involved in political issues at least "in some degree" (National Assessment for Educational Progress, 1976, pp. 34–35).

Other political education results suggest that student's perceptions of classroom climate and citizenship education curricula have changed somewhat during the last decade. In 1975/76, students seemed to perceive classroom climate as more open and citizenship education curricula as more relevant than they did previously.

Policy Implications. How one views the democratic political community influences the implications to be drawn from citizenship education research. If, for example, the political community is seen as an electoral democracy in which the majority of citizens elect representatives to govern for them and take little or no active part in politics or government until the next election, then citizenship education that promotes national loyalty and provides information about elections and voting would be sufficient for most citizens. However, such a conception of citizenship education would be inadequate if the political community is seen as (1) a representative democracy where citizens not only elect but monitor their representatives, holding them accountable and influencing policy-making processes; or (2) a participatory democracy where citizens are directly involved in all phases of policy making and implementation (Weissberg, 1974).

Although Torney, Oppenheim, & Farnen (1975) suggest that there may be an "inherent contradiction" in citizenship education attempting to encourage an informed citizenry that is both supportive of the prevailing political system and engaged in critical examination and responsible political participation, citizen support and critical activism are not necessarily incompatible. One can support democratic principles and at the same time work to change specific political institutions so that they might better reflect the democratic values they are intended to embody and sustain. The relationship between political support and criticism is but one of several manifestations of the continuing tension between pluralism and unity characteristic of a democratic society, a tension that contributes to the vitality of such a society (Cornbleth, Gay, & Dueck, 1981).

Continuing challenges for citizenship education policy involve clarifying purposes and priorities, seeking consistency between stated aims and actual programs and practices, and overcoming obstacles to constructive citizenship education. Among the current obstacles are (1) the efforts of special interest groups to impose their particular conception of political morality on citizenship education; (2) back-to-basics and minimum competency movements that neglect citizenship education concerns; and (3) economic pressures that limit resources (including time and personnel) allocated for citizenship education programs and research. There also seems to be a prevailing inertia that mitigates against widespread, substantive reform of citizenship education—an inertia maintained in part by inadequate dissemination of research findings that might stimulate change (Browne, 1973).

In view of these constraints as well as nonschool influences on young people's political dispositions, the following seem to be reasonable expectations for citizenship education.

1. Schools would focus on what they can do best, namely, provide opportunities for students to acquire realistic information and to develop practical reasoning and political action skills (Cleary, 1971; Ehman, 1979). Citizenship education programs would incorporate and extend students' experiences and interests. They would offer up-to-date information about informal political processes as well as formal government structure and function: this includes examination of the continuing tensions and not infrequent conflicts between democratic principles (for example, between individual freedom and contribution to the public well-being as illustrated by controversy surrounding nonvoluntary military service) and between subgroups within the political community (for example, the controversy between liberals and conservatives surrounding the nature of good citizenship).

2. The implicit curriculum of the school and classroom would not contradict the democratic principles that the formal curriculum seeks to promote. Teachers and other school personnel would be positive models; school and classroom environments would reflect, if not exemplify, a democratic political community; and students would be able to intelligently choose from among several ways of being a good citizen.

3. Citizenship education research would further explore the relationship between aspects of schooling and politically relevant learning by means of intensive case studies, including systematic observation of school and classroom events, as well as descriptive surveys. There is much more to be learned, for example, about school experiences that seem to affect students' political dispositions.

In conclusion, although citizenship education does not now appear to have a substantial influence upon most students' political dispositions, schooling has the potential to play a more significant and positive citizenship education role in the future.

Catherine Cornbleth

See also Affective Education; Moral Development; Moral Education; Social Sciences Education.

REFERENCES

Belok, M. V. The instructed citizen: Civic education in the United States during the nineteenth century. *Paedagogica Historica,* 1978, *18,* 257–274.

Browne, W. P. Citizenship education: Policy and practice in the elementary grades. *Education,* 1973, *94,* 149–159.

Butts, R. F. *The Revival of Civic Learning.* Bloomington, Ind.: Phi Delta Kappa, 1980.

Cherryholmes, C. H. Social knowledge and citizenship education: Two views of truth and criticism. *Curriculum Inquiry,* 1980, *10,* 115–141.

Cleary, R. E. *Political Education in the American Democracy.* Scranton, Pa.: Intext, 1971.

Cornbleth, C.; Gay, G.; & Dueck, K. G. Pluralism and unity. In H. D. Mehlinger & O. L. Davis, Jr., (Eds.), *The Social Studies: Eightieth Yearbook of the National Society for the Study of Education* (Part 2). Chicago: University of Chicago Press, 1981.

Edelman, L. F. Basic American. *Nolpe School Law Journal,* 1976, *6,* 83–122.

Ehman, L. H. Implications for teaching citizenship. *Social Education,* 1979, *43,* 594–596.

Ehman, L. H. The American school in the political socialization process. *Review of Educational Research,* 1980, *50,* 99–119.

Engle, S. H. *The Search for a More Adequate Definition of Citizenship Education.* Paper presented at the annual meeting of the National Council for the Social Studies, Cincinnati, November 1977. (ERIC Document Reproduction Service No. ED 148 720)

Fair, J. (Ed.) *National Assessment and Social Studies Education.* Denver: Education Commission of the States, 1975. (ERIC Document Reproduction Service No. ED 111 748)

Farquhar, E. C., & Dawson, K. S. *Citizen Education Today: Developing Civic Competencies* (Report of the Citizen Education Staff). Washington, D.C.: Office of Education, 1979. (ERIC Document Reproduction Service No. ED 186 350)

Giroux, H. A. Critical theory and rationality in citizenship education. *Curriculum Inquiry,* 1980, *10,* 329–366.

Goldenson, D. R. An alternative view about the role of the secondary school in political socialization: A field-experimental study of the development of civil liberties attitudes. *Theory and Research in Social Education,* 1978, *6,* 44–72.

Jennings, M. K., & Niemi, R. G. *The Political Character of Adolescence: The Influence of Families and Schools.* Princeton, N.J.: Princeton University Press, 1974.

Kelly, G. A. Who needs a theory of citizenship? *Daedalus,* 1979, *108*(4), 21–36.

Kettner, J. H. *The Development of American Citizenship, 1608–1870.* Chapel Hill: University of North Carolina Press, 1978.

Litt, E. Civic education, community norms, and political indoctrination. *American Sociological Review,* 1963, *28,* 69–75.

Litt, E. Education and political enlightenment in America. *Annals of the Academy of Political and Social Science,* 1965, *361,* 32–39.

Massialas, B. G. Citizenship education and political socialization. In R. L. Ebel (Ed.), *Encyclopedia of Educational Research* (4th ed.). New York: Macmillan, 1969.

Massialas, B. G. Some propositions about the role of the school in the formation of political behavior and political attitudes of students: Cross-national perspectives. *Comparative Education Review,* 1975, *19,* 169–176.

National Assessment of Educational Progress. *Education of Citizenship: A Bicentennial Survey.* Denver: Education Commission of the States, 1976. (ERIC Document Reproduction Service No. ED 135 705)

National Assessment of Educational Progress. *Changes in Political Knowledge and Attitudes, 1969–1976.* Denver: Education Commission of the States, 1978. (ERIC Document Reproduction Service No. ED 166 123)

National Assessment of Educational Progress. *Citizenship and Social Studies Objectives.* Denver: Education Commission of the States, 1980. (ERIC Document Reproduction Service No. ED 186 330)

Patrick, J. J. Political socialization and political education in schools. In S. A. Renshon (Ed.), *Handbook of Political Socialization: Theory and Research.* New York: Free Press, 1977.

Popkewitz, T. S.; Tabachnick, B. R.; & Wehlage, G. *School Reform and Institutional Life: A Case Study of Individually Guided Education.* Madison: University of Wisconsin Press, 1981.

Shaver, J. P. (Ed.). *Building Rationales for Citizenship Education.* Washington, D.C.: National Council for the Social Studies, 1977. (ERIC Document Reproduction Service No. ED 147 218)

Shaver, J. P.; Davis, O. L., Jr.; & Helburn, S. W. *An Interpretive Report on the Status of Pre-collegiate Social Studies Education based on Three NSF-funded Studies.* In National Science Foundation, *What Are the Needs in Pre-college Science, Mathematics, and Social Studies Education? Views from the Field.* Washington, D.C.: U.S. Government Printing Office, 1979. (ERIC Document Reproduction Service No. ED 164 363)

Torney, J. V.; Oppenheim, A. N.; & Farnen, R. F. *Civic Education in Ten Countries.* New York: Wiley, 1975.

Weissberg, R. *Political Learning, Political Choice, and Democratic Citizenship.* Englewood Cliffs, N.J.: Prentice-Hall, 1974.

Wiley, K. B., & Superka, D. P. *Evaluation Studies on "New Social Studies" Materials.* Boulder, Colo.: Social Science Education Consortium, 1977. (ERIC Document Reproduction Service No. ED 137 146)

CLASS SIZE

See Classroom Organization; Instruction Processes.

CLASSROOM ORGANIZATION

During the past two decades, educators have continued to search for more appropriate means of organizing schools and classrooms for instruction. Heathers (1969) saw the 1960s as the beginning era for individualized instruction and predicted its growth for the 1970s. To a limited degree, this prediction has materialized, although the majority of the schools are still as they were in previous decades. Most elementary schools continue to be organized with age-level self-contained classes in the primary grades and departmentalized classrooms at the upper-grade level, whereas high schools continue to be organized by subject areas with several curriculum tracks (academic, general, vocational). There are many factors that account for this continuation, including costs associated with new methods and procedures, lack of adequate dissemination and communication processes, ambivalent results of comparisons of methods, and satisfaction with current practices (Sussman, 1977). However, even with the continuation of age-level and subject matter organization, some changes have taken place, both within buildings and within classrooms.

Any discussion of classroom organization must begin with some attention to building and district policies and procedures (Barr & Dreeben, 1977; Dahllöf, 1971). In nearly all school districts, major instructional decisions that affect the classroom are made at the district level. Teacher salaries and salary schedules are set, numbers of teachers and other personnel are established, supervisory and administrative arrangements are determined, types and numbers of programs for special students are instituted, and resources for equipment, supplies, facilities, and transportation are allocated. At the building level, decisions about assignments of students to teachers, specific curricula to be followed, allocation of space, schedules for special teachers, assignment of paraprofessionals, and general operating procedures for the school also affect the classroom. At the classroom level, then, teachers must select an organization limited by the constraints imposed while remaining consistent with and compatible with the policies and procedures of the school and the district. These differing policies and situations may explain some of the inconsistencies in the results of research comparing various classroom organizations (Bidwell & Kasarda, 1975), but it still appears that the most viable level at which to aggregate data for most schools is at the classroom level (Barr & Dreeben, 1977). It is at this level that the decisions, the resources, and the interaction with the person primarily responsible for instruction have their impact on a student.

One of the decisions usually delegated to the building-level administrator, after the special students have been provided for, is the assignment of students to instructional groups. Heathers (1969) and others (Coleman et al., 1966; Rosenbaum, 1980) have reported that the prevailing practice for over a century has been to group students into grade-level classes, either in heterogeneous or homogeneous groups for instruction. For both types of grouping there are different procedures used for the assignment of students to classes. In assigning students heterogeneously, some administrators assign the students randomly, whereas others attempt to ensure heterogeneity by stratifying the groups on several variables, such as race, sex, ability, and age. Rosenbaum (1980) terms the two most common types of homogeneous grouping "grouping by ability" (achievement) and "grouping by curriculum." Ability grouping includes groups that are formed by teachers' judgment of achievement and ability, results obtained from intelligence and achievement tests, or combinations of test results and teacher judgment. Curriculum grouping is exemplified by groups created for the academic, general, and vocational curricula in the high school. Other less commonly used grouping strategies include grouping students by personal-social characteristics, subject-by-subject achievement grouping, and multiage or multigrade-level

grouping. When considering all schools, elementary and secondary, the most common practice is some form of homogeneous grouping (Rosenbaum, 1980).

Over the past twenty years, the practice in the elementary schools of grouping students by both age and ability has decreased (Anderson, 1973; Heathers, 1969; Rosenbaum, 1980). However, there is a question as to whether the magnitude of the decrease reported reflects the actual conditions or administrative concerns for reporting practices (Rosenbaum, 1980). Although such grouping practice has been under criticism for some time, the more recent concerns about *de facto* segregation in desegregated schools and educating the handicapped in "least restrictive environment" (P.L. 94-142) have further reduced its popularity.

At the secondary level, the most common practice of grouping students has been curriculum grouping, that is, grouping students by academic, general, and vocational curricula. Although this practice continues, the practice of "tracking," or subdividing students by ability or achievement level within and between the curriculum groups, has decreased. As with the elementary school, this decrease may not be as great as reported (Rosenbaum, 1980). At the secondary level, in addition to the perceived unpopularity of ability and achievement tracking, there seems also to exist some confusion as to what actually happens as a result of curriculum grouping. An examination of the conditions that prepare students for each group, the reasons the students give for selecting a particular curriculum, and the factors used by counselors in encouraging students to select a particular track indicate that there is little difference between curriculum grouping and ability-achievement grouping (Bowles & Gintis, 1976; Brophy & Good, 1974; Haller & Davis, 1980; Jencks, 1972; Rist, 1970; Rosenbaum, 1976; Schafer & Olexa, 1971). According to Rosenbaum (1980), this "confusion and ambiguity about grouping is widespread and it stems from America's highly charged ambivalence about grouping" (p. 362).

At least part of the cause of the ambivalence toward grouping can be attributed to the conflicting results obtained by the various studies on this topic. The studies present mixed results, regardless of the dependent variable(s) selected: achievement (Barr & Dreeben, 1977; Heathers, 1969; Jencks, 1972; Rist, 1970; Rosenbaum, 1980); self-concept (Rosenbaum, 1980); attitudes toward others (Rosenbaum, 1980); and social behavior (Brophy & Good, 1974; Rosenbaum, 1980). The conflicting data about the social consequences relating to ability grouping further compound the confusion caused by the examination of the outcomes variables. During an era of concern for equal rights, social justice, and equality of opportunity, educators have become defensive about practices that might not be in agreement with these concerns. On the surface, it appears that curriculum grouping is one such practice. This would be so if socioeconomic status really does influence grouping, as some believe it can. Rosenbaum (1980), in attempting to answer the question "Are curriculum selections meritocratic or class-biased?," concluded, after reviewing six major works, that no consensus can be reached. Four of these reports indicated that curriculum selections are not class-biased, whereas two indicated that they are. In addition to the studies reported by Rosenbaum, there are studies by Bowles and Gintis (1976), Jencks (1972), and Schafer and Olexa (1971) that suggest a relationship between socioeconomic status and placement in curriculum group, whereas Haller and Davis (1980) found no such relationship. Thus, the confusion continues and the doubts persist.

One position that tends to remain unchallenged concerning grouping is that regardless of the grouping procedures used—ability or curriculum—the variability of students in any group is great and the overlap between groups is usually considerable (Anderson, 1973; Barr & Dreeben, 1977; Heathers, 1969; Westbury, 1977). A second position that has not been tested is the contention that, for ability groups and curriculum groups, there is little mobility of students from group to group and what mobility does exist is mostly downward. Regardless, then, of the pros and cons for ability or curriculum grouping, these two characteristics should be enough to discourage such practices. As might be expected, these characteristics contributed to the search for alternative organizational arrangements.

Single-teacher Classrooms. Because students generally are assigned to a single classroom teacher for instruction, it is now the responsibility of teachers to select a classroom organizational structure that satisfies their needs and the needs of students. In the primary grades, where the self-contained classroom is most in evidence (Anderson, 1973; Heathers, 1969), the organization employed is usually in-class achievement grouping—for example, the blue birds, the green birds, and the red birds or the Pirates, the Dodgers, and the Cardinals or some other clearly named groups that the students know as the best, the average, and the substandard. This same practice often continues within classrooms at the upper grades of the elementary school and at the middle school when departmentalization is employed. The research on the effects of this type of achievement grouping also indicates mixed results. In some cases, it indicates significant differences in achievement, favoring grouped over nongrouped classes, while others show no difference between the two organizational methods (Barr & Dreeben, 1977). However, the complexity of the variables and the number of intervening variables not controlled in the various studies make a comparison of the results questionable and conclusions open to criticism. Similar to whole-class findings, analyses of interclass achievement grouping show considerable overlap of abilities between the groups. When mobility does take place between groups, the movement is to a lower group. At least partly because of the uncomfortableness associated with grouping, educators continue the search for instructional practices that can be employed within a single teacher's classroom while still operating within the constraints of the building organization and

the building architectural plan. So far, strategies to accomplish this outcome have included (1) whole-class lecture and discussion; (2) utilization of learning packets for independent study either of specific units or of specific skills that can be conveniently removed from the rest of curriculum; (3) use of academic games; (4) tutoring (by adults and by peers); (5) computer-assisted instruction; (6) small-group instruction (when groups are flexible and change routinely); and (7) cooperative learning strategies.

In general, the research reports on these strategies are of an evaluative nature, tending to explore the conditions under which a particular strategy—for a limited set of outcomes and for a limited set of learning activities—is effective. With this as the basic purpose of the research in this field, then, the synthesis of such research will describe the internal effectiveness of each strategy and not the comparison of one strategy with another (Berliner & Gage, 1976). Teachers tend to use a variety of these strategies within a single classroom depending upon the subjects being taught, the characteristics of the students, and the learning outcomes desired.

Before we leave the organizational structure represented by a single teacher responsible for a group of students for an extended period of time (year or term), some attention should be given to the research on the comparisons of the two most common techniques used: self-contained organization and departmental organization. As Heathers (1969) reported in his review of classroom organizations for the 1960s, the trend in the 1950s and 1960s in elementary and middle schools was to return to departmentalization—at the upper-grade levels, at least. One reason given for this movement is associated with teacher preference. A majority of teachers "did not feel adequately prepared, either in knowledge of subject matter or of teaching methods, to teach all of the major subjects" (Heathers, 1969, p. 561). There are few research reports on the pros and cons of departmentalization, possibly indicating an acceptance of this practice by educators. Another indication of the general agreement on the need for departmentalization as students advance through the grades is the level of content specialization required for teaching certificates in early childhood, elementary–middle school, and secondary school. An occasional article still appears, such as the one by Lamme (1976), indicating the advantage of one organization over the other, but these articles are rare.

Team Teaching. One of the most common alternative staffing practices to self-contained and departmentalization plans is team teaching (Anderson, 1973; Sterns, 1976). Sterns (1976) reports that the percentage of elementary schools utilizing some form of team teaching had increased from 15 to 43 percent over the ten-year period 1962–1972, while the percentage of secondary schools reporting its use in 1972 was 35 percent (p. 375). Team teaching is an organizational arrangement of two or more educational personnel involved in regular cooperative planning and instruction for all or part of the instructional program offered to the same students on a regular basis for an extended period of time (Charters, 1976; Heathers, 1969; Sterns, 1976). The key to determining whether or not a particular grouping of teachers is a team in the team-teaching sense is whether there is regular (daily or weekly) planning and whether there are shared instructional responsibilities for the same group of students. In elementary schools, team members are usually responsible for most of the content areas for the same group of students. Students may be regrouped at any time; teachers may be responsible for different groups or different functions at any time; and different emphasis may be given to different content areas at any time. At the secondary level, teams are usually responsible for a single subject or possibly two subjects for a group of students studying the same or closely related topics, for example, American history, world history, biology, English, and social studies, and algebra. A description of the theory and practice of team teaching can be found in most educational books describing classroom organization patterns (Beggs, 1964; Pumerantz & Galano, 1972).

The variety of team-teaching organizational patterns has been reported by Heathers (1969) and Sterns (1976). Teams vary in size from two or three teachers to eight or ten teachers. They vary in composition as well, some consisting exclusively of teachers and others involving paraprofessionals, resource teachers, master teachers, counselors, and administrators. Teams also vary as to their basic function, some being formed to redistribute instructional responsibilities, others to change the basic managerial system, and still others to do both (Charters, 1976). There are other variations: one grade or many grades, one subject area or many subject areas, single-subject assignments to teachers to multiple-subject assignments, small-group instructional responsibilities for some staff and large-group responsibilities for others, and lecture and discussion responsibilities for some and laboratory or independent study responsibilities for others. Teams vary from school to school and often within the same school, depending on situational needs and the educational personnel involved (Sterns, 1976).

As might be expected, with the many variations in team-teaching systems that exist and the often different purposes for which teaming is established, the research on comparisons between team teaching and other organizational patterns is inconclusive. Summaries of the research on student outcomes for both the elementary and secondary schools (Armstrong, 1977; Sterns, 1976), along with studies not included in these works, tend to substantiate this expectation (Begle et al., 1975). They indicate no superiority of one organizational pattern over another. As might be expected, most of the studies included in these reports indicate that the teachers (or team members) prefer team teaching to other alternatives. This finding probably reflects the self-selection process that takes place either at the time of the original decision to create teams or in later hiring.

Research on managerial changes within a school brought about by team teaching has been of interest to the Center for Educational Policy and Management in Eugene, Oregon (Charters, 1976). The Management Implications of Team Teaching (MITT) project has examined the changes in the elementary school work system and in the structure of its managerial system. Teachers in teams continue to work in self-contained or departmentalized classrooms much the same as before. In a similar manner, there is no reason to expect that the managerial system will change in every instance. The MITT project team examined changes over time in schools using a particular organizational and instructional team-teaching model (Klausmeier, 1977). The project team examined the organizational structure of the schools prior to implementation of team teaching and twice during implementation. Their findings indicate that some schools change the managerial system by changing the number of people involved in decision making, planning, and so on, but not by changing the work system, whereas some schools do the opposite. Most teams are formed by grade level, and the team shares the instruction for a selected subset of students in a restricted number of subjects. Although experimental schools are gradually adopting team teaching, it is not fully implemented by the end of the first year (Charters, 1976).

Team teaching is an effective organizational pattern for administering several innovative programs: Individually Guided Education (IGE); Individually Prescribed Instruction (IPI) (Lindvall & Bolvin, 1967); Primary Education Project (PEP) (Resnick, Wang, & Rosner, 1975); and Program for Learning in Accordance with Needs (PLAN) (Flanagan et al., 1975). The changes in the instruction and delivery systems of these programs seem to necessitate joint planning for the student day, as well as cooperative decision making on most matters affecting instruction. The interdependence of teachers desired by these systems, though not always obtained, is usually required for their optimum implementation.

Tutoring. A second type of staffing change that has affected classroom organization is the use of tutors. With the advent of modified and innovative instructional procedures and the frequent need to adapt existing educational programs to restricted space, teachers and school staff have utilized tutors. The variety of tutoring programs is nearly as great as the number of schools in this country. Some tutors are paid employees assigned to work with a teacher, with a team of teachers, or with a special project, such as the federal Title I projects. There are programs of volunteer adult tutors serving in much the same capacity as the paid ones. The volunteers might be parents, college students, retired persons, or community residents. There are special projects, often funded, to establish organizations for tutors, such as special retired-person projects, in which tutors are assigned by the project staff to work with a school or group of schools for specific purposes. The availability of these outside people permits teachers to modify their instructional activities and to establish a different classroom organization. The utilization of such tutors adds dimensions to the teacher's management function: the management of adult personnel as well as the management of student activities.

A second type of tutoring employed is peer tutoring, or student tutoring. Peer tutoring is usually performed by students in the same class or group who have already mastered a particular skill, set of skills, or other designated activity. Instructional schemes such as Bloom's Mastery Learning (Bloom, 1968) require the use of peer tutors if other types of tutors are not available. Other schemes, such as IPI, PEP, PLAN, IGE, and the Korean Educational Development Institute Elementary–Middle School Project (KEDI E–M Project) (Masoner et al., 1980), are designed to encourage their use as part of the total management system.

Student tutoring is tutoring usually conducted in the same school, the older students tutoring the younger ones or students taking a lower-level course in the same content area. Some programs are arranged within the school so that the tutors are assigned to a particular teacher for a few specified hours in the week and the teacher is responsible for the activities of the tutor and the pupil. Other programs are organized to provide direct service to the student needing help by providing a time and place for the tutor and pupil to meet to work on weaknesses identified by the two of them. In high schools in particular, there may be a specified time in the day, such as immediately before school, in which many pairs of tutors and pupils meet in a common room, such as the cafeteria, under the supervision of a teacher, club adviser, or administrator.

Recognizing the multiple ways and means in which tutoring takes place, the variety of purposes—both instructional and managerial—for which it is used, and the varying skills of the tutor, one must not expect much consensus when examining the benefits acquired by the pupil. Ellson (1976), in a review of the results of tutoring programs, has concluded that tutoring by nonprofessionals is successful when it involves "intensive training and supervision by professionals for instructional tutoring situations," or when "the tutor [is] provided highly structured programs that the tutors are required to follow in detail" (p. 165).

An instructional strategy somewhat related to peer tutoring in that it involves students working together in a helping way is cooperative learning. Slavin (1980) defines cooperative learning as a classroom technique "in which students work on learning activities in small groups and receive rewards or recognition based on their group's performance" (p. 315). Although cooperative learning in small groups has been used by educators for many years for project work, games, and similar situations, it has taken on new emphasis during the past decade. Contributing to this resurgence are the development and refinement of games and simulation and the search for appropriate classroom practices to facilitate desegregation and mainstreaming.

Cooperative-learning or team-learning methods require some changes in the classroom instructional process, which affects in turn the management of that classroom (Sharon, 1980). These techniques require a decentralization of control. The classroom is changed from a large group to five or six groups, depending upon the class size. In this situation, the teachers have to relinguish their authority, which is transferred to each of the groups. There are changes in the instructional process. Large-group study and individual or independent study give way to small-group strategies. Finally, there is usually a change in the reward system. Either individual rewards are eliminated and substituted for by group rewards or group and individual rewards are combined (Slavin, 1980). Sharon (1980), in his review of team-learning techniques, separates them into two major categories: peer tutoring and group investigation. Under peer tutoring, he has included the Jigsaw Method, Teams-Games-Tournaments (TGT), and Student Teams–Achievement Divisions (STAD); under group investigation, he has included the Group-Investigation Model (G-I). Sharon's classification is helpful in that it provides a general framework for describing two different ways of dividing student tasks. In peer-tutoring techniques, each student in the group is responsible for learning a particular subset of materials or tasks and for teaching these to other members of the group. In this way each has contributed to the total outcome of the group and the full range of information acquired by each member of the group. The group-investigation technique emphasizes group planning, shared data-gathering, and reporting of each student to the group. Then the group, through discussion, arrives at an interpretation of all the data reported. In both types of cooperative learning, the groups usually represent a cross section of ability, sex, and race. In discussing the effects on classroom organization, Sharon (1980) reports that for peer tutoring, "the class functions as an aggregate of teams which are uncoordinated or engage in a uniform task," whereas for group investigation "the class functions as a 'group of groups' with between-group coordination and division of labor and tasks" (p. 264).

The results of cooperative learning studies, as summarized by Johnson, Skon, and Johnson (1980), Sharon (1980), and Slavin (1980), indicate promise for these techniques in the classroom. In comparison studies with more conventional methods and a few with individualized classrooms, the results for achievement tend to favor the cooperative-learning techniques. Sharon (1980), Slavin (1980), and Slavin and Madden (1979) report positive findings on group cohesiveness and race-reaction variables. A similar finding for handicapped students mainstreamed in regular classrooms was reported by Johnson, Rynders, and Johnson (1979). As a minimum, those schools currently involved in desegregation or mainstreaming should seriously investigate the various models now available that describe the procedures for implementing cooperative-learning techniques.

Mastery Learning. A concept that has taken on new or renewed emphasis over the past decade is mastery learning. Block (1980) defines mastery learning as (1) a theory that any teacher can help virtually all students to learn excellently, and (2) an effective set of individualized-instruction practices that consistently help most students to learn excellently (p. 66). As in instructional strategy, mastery learning is designed to provide the needed time for each student to reach mastery, thus increasing the percentage of students who successfully complete tasks and reducing the dispersion of student achievement within a class. Barr and Dreeben (1977), in discussing mastery learning, have distinguished between its principles and its instructional arrangements: "Mastery learning strategies are based on pedagogical principles that pertain to three conditions at the level of the individual student: aptitude, ability to understand instruction, and perseverance; and two conditions at the classroom or school level: quality of instruction, and time allowed for learning" (Barr & Dreeben, p. 116). The instructional arrangements usually accompanying mastery learning consist of four phases: "preinstructional assessment," usually measuring prerequisite knowledge; "initial teaching," most often involving group instruction; "remediation," usually involving individualized materials or tutoring; and "certification of mastery," managing the task or content to some predetermined criterion level (Block, 1980). Mastery learning as a concept involving a specified set of instructional objectives, the specification of some criteria of mastery for an objective or set of objectives, and the variable time permitted students to reach the criteria can be found embedded in many other instructional systems (Barr & Dreeben, 1977; Block, 1980; Lindvall & Bolvin, 1967; Masoner et al., 1980; Talmage, 1975). Many of these are individualized systems providing limited time and opportunities for group instruction. Mastery learning as a system tends to rely on considerably more group instruction; because of this reliance, it requires the teacher to plan both the organization of the instructional content and the organization of the time and conditions under which the instruction is given.

Barr and Dreeben (1977), in reviewing the effects of the mastery-learning system, raised questions about class composition, classroom instruction, and the management of time. These questions were (1) Do such methods work with cognitively heterogeneous groups of students? (2) What do teachers do or what are they supposed to do during the remediation phase? and (3) Does the system provide the time for students, including the slower students, to reach mastery within the time spans that schools can realistically allot to the task? Partial or probable answers to their concerns appear in reports describing a large-scale project carried out by the Korean Educational Development Institute (KEDI) known as the Elementary–Middle School (E–M) Project (Masoner et al., 1980). The E–M Project of KEDI—although it contains other components in its system, such as instructional television, instructional radio, a team teaching plan, and other organizational elements—follows the basic model of mastery learning. Through the tryout periods of the project, students, including students who in the United States would be in special classes for the mentally retarded, were heterogeneously assigned to age-level classes of fifty to sixty students per teacher. The teacher was given a guide, which specified the units to be covered, the time allotted per unit, the objectives for each unit, and the mastery-level test with the specified criteria to be used. Bolvin, reporting in Masoner et al. (1980), found that the teachers did use the preinstructional-assessment procedures as recommended but did not have sufficient time to bring all students to the recommended level of proficiency before beginning a new unit. Next, after employing the group-instructional procedures as recommended, the students were divided into three categories: mastery, near-mastery, lack of mastery. Generally, mastery students served as tutors for the near-mastery and some of the lack-of-mastery students, while the teachers concentrated their efforts with the lower group. To increase the time available for instruction, students were required to work on their weaknesses at home and during one special period or more set aside for this work each week, again supervised by the teachers. Thus, there were two ways of getting additional time for remedial work. As a result of these efforts, 60 to 80 percent of the students in a given class were able to reach the mastery and near-mastery criteria for each unit. In nearly all units for grades 2 to 6, the percentage of mastery students in the E–M schools exceeded the percentage for the control schools.

In studies comparing cognitive and affective outcomes for mastery-learning students in other systems, Block (1980) states that there is little question that mastery-learning ideas and practices promote student growth. He goes on to claim that mastery learning is more effective, more efficient, and better liked by the students. Because of the problems of comparison of any two classrooms, schools, or systems, some caution is warranted in accepting these findings (Barr & Dreeben, 1977).

Individualized Instruction. Individualized instruction systems emerged in the 1960s for three interrelated reasons: the developments that had taken place in learning and instruction; the establishment of national educational research and development centers and regional laboratories; and the dissatisfaction with the existing educational system. Educators had long recognized the need to adapt instruction to the needs of the individual learner. Grouping practices, tracking schemes, project work, independent study, nongraded systems, dual-purpose plans, continuous progress plans, and remedial schemes had all been attempts to modify instruction to adapt to student differences.

Although developers and implementers of individualized systems now generally accept the principles of adaptiveness, programs differ in their adherence to these principles and in approaches to providing for them. Currently there is a wide variety of individualized systems in use, with many differences in scope, degree, and method. Some programs provide for one subject area, such as reading or mathematics, whereas others include three, four, or more subjects. Differences in degree of individualization provided for are reflected in the adequacy, quality, and timeliness of student assessment; the learning options available and their appropriateness for student needs; the system for data collection and summarization; and the degree to which a student has control over time for learning. Programs differ as to methods employed to facilitate individualization of instruction. Some programs provide assessment instruments or procedures for using them, whereas others only suggest ways to assess; some provide computer systems for data collection; some require aides or paraprofessionals, and others involve only the student and teacher; and some begin with group instruction and then individualize, whereas others individualize from the beginning of each unit. Some of the differences between the systems can be attributed to their current stage of development, subject areas involved, level of education provided for, and varying points of view about school and classroom organization.

In spite of these differences, there are elements common to most of the individualized systems (Bolvin & Glaser, 1971; Glaser, 1977). These are (1) redefinition of school time to provide the opportunity to vary time for students to complete tasks and reach planned outcomes; (2) well-defined and well-structured curricula that provide necessary sequencing and multiple options for learning to facilitate student progress; (3) procedures for assessing student readiness, needs, characteristics, and accomplishments to assist in student and teacher decision making; (4) availability of instructional materials and other resources to facilitate learning that are open and accessible to students and can provide a variety of paths for attaining the desired mastery; (5) individual lesson plans for each student that address the tasks to be accomplished, estimated time for accomplishment, appropriate materials and resources, and the criterion of accomplishment expected; (6) strategies for information feedback to permit periodic monitoring of progress and to facilitate decision making; (7) reorganization of the school environment to permit greater flexibility in assignments of staff, utilization of facilities, and reallocation of time.

The implementation of individualized programs designed to address these guidelines has had its effects on school and classroom organization. Systems such as Individually Prescribed Instruction (IPI), Primary Education Project (PEP), Program for Learning in Accordance with Needs (PLAN), and Individually Guided Education (IGE), have necessitated role changes for principals, teachers, and other staff. Of the many functions that principals perform, the one most affected by the adoption of individualized programs is that of instructional decision making. Because of the flexibility required within the school for time, facilities, and resources—including human resources—many

decisions must now be shared decisions. These include decisions on placement of students; curricula; selection, use, and location of materials; allocation of space; techniques and resources for data gathering and reporting; and allocation of time. To provide an organization permitting this interaction, some form of team teaching has been adopted.

The Wisconsin Research and Development Center for Cognitive Learning's IGE model has gone the furthest in specifying organizational changes necessary as a part of its system. One component of the IGE system is the multiunit organizational-administrative arrangement. Each school is organized into multiage "units" responsible for the education of 100 to 150 students, coordinated by a unit leader and staffed by teachers, paraprofessionals, student teachers, or interns. The unit leader serves with other unit leaders and the principal on a school instructional improvement committee (IIC). This committee, working with the principal, is responsible for coordinating, planning, and managing the instructional program of the school. Representatives of each of the school IICs serve on a systemwide program committee with representatives from other schools and staff members of the central office. The three groups—the unit, the building committee, and the systemwide committee—are responsible for planning, decision making, and evaluation at the three respective levels, as well as for communication between levels and between the school and community (Klausmeier, 1976). Although functions of all professionals change, the only new position within this structure is the unit leader. This individual is a teacher and an instructional leader of the unit (Sorenson, Rossman, & Barnes, 1976). With the exception of the building and sometimes district responsibilities, the unit leader functions much the same as a team leader in many team-teaching situations.

In individualized systems, the major change at the classroom level is that the teacher is no longer the primary determiner of what the classroom organization is. Because classroom organization is dependent upon instructional decisions, the organizational scheme is then established at the level where instructional decisions are made.

The more closely a school begins to provide for the seven elements common to individualized systems, the more difficult it becomes for a teacher to provide the desired learning options needed for any one group of students. Teachers must share space, equipment, materials, personnel, and information as planned in the IGE unit. The decisions that the teacher must make between what is optional for each student in the group and what it is possible to provide are dependent upon the resources available at any given time.

The classroom organization for an individual teacher now changes from week to week or from day to day, depending upon the decisions of the team. It appears, then, that the more appropriate level to discuss the school organization in these situations is the team level, for it is the team that has the most immediate and direct impact on the student. It is at this level that certain decisions are made: which students will study what; when a student should repeat an activity or progress to the next unit; what optional learning strategies can be available, for whom, and when; which team members will work with which students and how; and many others of more or less importance.

It should be pointed out, however, that this change in classroom organization from the classroom to the team is still an anticipated one and not a reality in many instances. Charters (1976), Leinhardt (1977), and many others describing the implementation of a particular individualized program have noted that the classroom organization for the same program may vary from school to school. These differences are due to the type of organization the school was utilizing prior to implementing the new system, the numbers of students and teachers, the number of content areas included at a given time, the length of time the program has been in operation, and the quality and quantity of instructional materials and resources available. For this reason, many developers and implementers of individualized systems have developed checklists or implementation guides to assist the schools, developers, and outside evaluators in assessing the degree of implementation. Such checklists and guidelines are helpful to teachers and administrators in understanding their current organization in light of an expected one. It is recognized that some variations are possible and anticipated; however, organizational structures that limit the flexibility of the system generally have a negative impact on student outcomes (Lindvall & Cox, 1970). Often the complexities of the systems and the lack of clarity or understanding of the interrelatedness of the components of the system result in modification by the users that destroys the intent of the original model.

The characteristic of adapting and modifying instructional systems and instructional concepts is indicative of the problems associated with individualized education. In retrospect, it appears that the choice of the term "individualized" has added to the problems. Some educators relate it to independent study; some to individual pacing; some to individual diagnosis; some to attainment of individual outcomes; some to a host of other characteristics; and some to selected combinations. Regardless of the number of these characteristics included in a program, school, or classroom, the users refer to their programs as "individualized." The differences in reference points between theorists and practitioners further compound the problem. While a theorist may be explaining or examining the effects for learning, the practitioner may be interpreting the results for classroom operation. Because there are no simple solutions to these problems of interpretation and misinterpretation, developers, disseminators, and implementers must take pains in describing in detail what they mean when discussing individualized instruction.

The research on individualized-instruction programs is ambiguous, regardless of whether the studies are conducted by independent evaluators or by the sponsoring institution (Block, Stebbins, & Proper, 1977; Otto, 1977; Resnick, Wang, & Rosner, 1975; Romberg, 1977; Rosenshine, 1976; Soar, 1973; Stallings & Kaskowitz, 1974; Stebbins et al., 1977). Generally, the results show no real difference in student achievement when different organizational patterns are compared and different subject areas combined. They indicate some improvement in student attitudes toward school under individualized conditions and usually no difference in attitudes toward teachers. Teachers tend to find the work more difficult and tiring, and at the same time they find teaching more challenging and rewarding. One of the negative results of individualized programs is the initial and ongoing costs of implementation. When the cost factor is considered with the ambivalent research results reported, practitioners are hesitant to adapt fully developed systems as their first step toward individualizing instruction. More recently, this trend seems to be changing, particularly for the Wisconsin IGE model (Smith, 1979).

Conclusions. The majority of schools still practice some form of age, ability, achievement, or curriculum grouping, with some teachers and administrators supporting its practice. On the other hand, individualization has become increasingly important, and educators at least pay lip service to the concept. However, individualization and grouping are not mutually exclusive. Many schools organized for individualization still use age-level or grade-level grouping and still employ grouping and group instruction for many content areas. When we examine what has happened and is happening to adapt and modify individualized instruction for the schools, we may confidently anticipate its continued growth in the immediate years ahead. At the same time, we expect teachers and administrators to hold on to the practices of self-contained classrooms for the primary grades and the curriculum grouping with departmentalization in the high school, thus preserving much of the classroom organization as it exists today. The more flexible arrangements appear to be the trend for the upper elementary and middle school years.

There are two unrelated school-organizational changes that will have an impact on the character of the schools in the immediate years ahead. These are the mainstreaming of students previously educated in special classrooms and the establishment of "magnet" schools within a district. The mainstreaming of special students will probably encourage teachers and administrators to retain the existing organization in hopes of holding to a minimum the adjustment problems that may be caused by mainstreaming. The establishment of "magnet" schools to provide optional educational settings for parents and students to select will continue the grouping practice of the past as well as provide newer techniques. At the secondary level, the options appear to be more specialization and more curriculum groupings, not less.

In summary, it is anticipated that individualized-instructional programs with more options, greater flexibility, and team organization will increase in the middle years of schooling. The organizational structure for the early elementary and high school years will continue as a classroom structure, with individualization or adaptation for learners being the responsibility of the teacher within the particular classroom.

John O. Bolvin

See also Group Processes; Independent Study; Individualized Systems of Instruction; Instruction Processes; Instructional Time and Learning; Systems Design in Instruction.

REFERENCES

Anderson, R. H. Organizing and staffing the school. In J. Goodland & H. Shane (Eds.), *The Elementary School in the United States: Seventy-second Yearbook of the National Society for the Study of Education.* Chicago: University of Chicago Press, 1973.

Armstrong, D. G. Team teaching and academic achievement. *Review of Educational Research,* Winter 1977, *47,* 65–86.

Barr, R., & Dreeben, R. Instruction in classrooms. In L. S. Shulman (Ed.), *Review of Research in Education* (Vol. 5). Itasca, Ill.: F. E. Peacock, 1977.

Beggs, D. W., III (Ed.). *Team Teaching: Bold New Venture.* Indianapolis: Unified College Press, 1964.

Begle, E. G.; Pence, B.; Ng, K.; & Davis, M. *Review of the Literature on Team Teaching in Mathematics* (Working Paper No. 3). Stanford, Calif.: Stanford University Teacher Corps, 1975.

Berliner, D. C., & Gage, N. L. The psychology of teaching methods. In N. L. Gage (Ed.), *The Psychology of Teaching Methods: Seventy-fifth Yearbook of the National Society for the Study of Education.* Chicago: University of Chicago Press, 1976.

Bidwell, C. E., & Kasarda, J. D. School district organization and student achievement. *American Sociological Review,* 1975, *40,* 55–70.

Block, G.; Stebbins, L.; & Proper, E. *Education as Experimentation: A Planned Variation Model. In Effects of Follow-Through Models* (Vol. 4B). Cambridge, Mass.: Abt Associates, 1977. (ERIC Document Reproduction Service No. ED 148 491)

Block, J. H. Promoting excellence through mastery learning. *Theory into Practice,* June 1980, *19,* 66–74.

Bloom, B. S. *Human Characteristics and School Learning.* New York: McGraw-Hill, 1968.

Bolvin, J. O., & Glaser, R. Individualizing instruction. In D. Allen & E. Seifman (Eds.), *The Teacher's Handbook.* Glenview, Ill.: Scott, Foresman, 1971, pp. 270–279.

Bowles, S., & Gintis, H. *Schooling in Capitalist America.* New York: Basic Books, 1976.

Brophy, J., & Good, T. *Teacher-Student Relationships: Causes and Consequences.* New York: Holt, Rinehart & Winston, 1974. (ERIC Document Reproduction Service No. ED 091 495)

Brown, S. W., & Wunderlich, K. W. *The Effect of Open-Concept Education and Ability Grouping on Achievement Level Concerning the Teaching of Fifth-grade Mathematics.* Paper presented at the annual meeting of the American Educational Research Association, San Francisco, 1976. (ERIC Documentation Reproduction Service No. ED 128 197)

Charters, W. W., Jr. *Work System Change in the Unitized Schools: Some Through-time Findings.* Eugene: Oregon University, Center for Educational Policy and Management, 1976. (ERIC Document Reproduction Service No. ED 124 520)

Coleman, J. S.; Campbell, E. Q.; Hobson, C. J.; McPartland, J.;

Mood, A. M.; Weinfeld, F. D.; & York, R. L. *Equality of Educational Opportunity.* Washington, D.C.: U.S. Government Printing Office, 1966. (ERIC Document Reproduction Service No. ED 012 275)

Dahlöff, U. S. *Ability Grouping, Content Validity, and Curriculum Process Analysis.* New York: Teachers College Press, 1971.

Ellson, D. G. Tutoring. In N. L. Gage (Ed.), *The Psychology of Teaching Methods: Seventy-fifth Yearbook of the National Society for the Study of Education.* Chicago: University of Chicago Press, 1976.

Flanagan, J. C.; Shanner, W. M.; Brudner, H. J.; & Marker, R. W. An individualized instructional system: Program for Learning in Accordance with Needs (PLAN). In H. Talmage (Ed.), *Systems of Individualized Education.* Berkeley, Calif.: McCutchan, 1975.

Glaser, R. *Adaptive Education: Individual Diversity and Learning.* New York: Holt, Rinehart & Winston, 1977.

Haller, E. J., & Davis, A. Does socioeconomic status bias the assignment of elementary school students to reading groups? *American Educational Research Journal,* Winter 1980, *17,* 409–418.

Heathers, G. Grouping. In R. L. Ebel (Ed.), *Encyclopedia of Educational Research* (4th ed.). New York: Macmillan, 1969, 559–570. (ERIC Document Reproduction Service No. ED 026 135)

Jencks, C. *Inequality.* New York: Basic Books, 1972. (ERIC Document Reproduction Service No. ED 077 551)

Johnson, R.; Rynders, J.; & Johnson, D. W. Interaction between handicapped and nonhandicapped teenagers as a function of situational goal structuring: Implications for mainstreaming. *American Educational Research Journal,* 1979, *16,* 161–167.

Johnson, W.; Skon, L.; & Johnson, R. Effects of cooperative, competitive, and individualistic conditions on children's problem-solving performance. *American Educational Research Journal,* 1980, *17,* 83–93.

Klausmeier, H. J. Individually guided education. *Journal of Teacher Education,* 1976, *27,* 199–205.

Klausmeier, H. J. Instructional programming for the individual student. In H. J. Klausmeier; R. Rossmiller; & M. Saily (Eds.), *Individually Guided Elementary Education.* New York: Academic Press, 1977, pp. 56–76.

Lamme, L. L. Self-contained to departmentalized: How reading habits changed. *Elementary School Journal,* 1976, *76,* 209–218.

Leinhardt, G. Program evaluation: An empirical study of individualized instruction. *American Education Research Journal,* 1977, *14,* 277–293. (ERIC Document Reproduction Service No. ED 131 092)

Lindvall, C. M., & Bolvin, J. O. Programmed instruction in the schools: An application of programming principles in "Individually Prescribed Instruction." In P. C. Lange (Ed.), *Programmed Instruction: Sixty-sixth Yearbook of the National Society for the Study of Education.* Chicago: University of Chicago Press, 1967.

Lindvall, C. M., & Cox, R. C. *Evaluation as a Tool in Curriculum Development: The IPI Evaluation Program.* Chicago: Rand McNally, 1970. (ERIC Document Reproduction Service No. ED 036 198)

Masoner, P.; Bolvin, J.; Grady, W.; Kim, R.; Lee, S.; Spaulding, S.; & Watson, P. *Analytical Case Study of the Korean Educational Development Institute.* Washington, D.C.: American Association of Colleges for Teacher Education, 1980.

Otto, W. The Wisconsin Design: A reading program for individually guided education. In H. J. Klausmeier; R. A. Rossmiller;

& M. Saily (Eds.), *Individually Guided Elementary Education: Concepts and Practices.* New York: Academic Press, 1977.

Pumerantz, P., & Galano, R. W. *Establishing Interdisciplinary Programs in the Middle School.* West Nyack, N.Y.: Parker, 1972.

Resnick, L. B.; Wang, M. C.; & Rosner, J. *Adaptive Education for Young Children: The Primary Education Project.* Pittsburgh, Pa.: University of Pittsburgh, Learning Research and Development Center, 1975.

Rist, R. Student social class and teacher expectation: The self-fulfilling prophecy in ghetto education. *Harvard Educational Review,* 1970, *40,* 411–451.

Romberg, T. A. Developing mathematical processes: The elementary mathematics program for Individually Guided Education. In H. J. Klausmeier; R. A. Rossmiller; & M. Saily (Eds.), *Individually Guided Elementary Education: Concepts and Practices.* New York: Academic Press, 1977, pp. 77–107. (ERIC Document Reproduction Service No. ED 142 648)

Rosenbaum, J. E. *Making Inequality: The Hidden Curriculum of High-school Tracking.* New York: Wiley, 1976. (ERIC Document Reproduction Service No. ED 139 857)

Rosenbaum, J. E. Social implications of educational grouping. In D. C. Berliner (Ed.), *Review of Research in Education* (Vol. 8). Itasca, Ill.: F. E. Peacock, 1980.

Rosenshine, B. Classroom instruction. In N. L. Gage (Ed.), *The Psychology of Teaching Methods: Seventy-fifth Yearbook of the National Society for the Study of Education.* Chicago: University of Chicago Press, 1976, pp. 335–371.

Schafer, W., & Olexa, C. *Tracking and Opportunity.* Scranton, Pa.: Chandler, Intext, 1971.

Sharon, S. Cooperative learning in small groups: Recent methods and effects on achievement, attitudes, and ethnic relations. *Review of Educational Research,* 1980, *50,* 241–271.

Slavin, R. E. Cooperative learning. *Review of Educational Research,* 1980, *50,* 315–342.

Slavin, R. E., & Madden, N. A. School practices that improve race relations. *American Educational Research Journal,* 1979, *16,* 169–180. (ERIC Document Reproduction Service No. ED 170 437)

Smith, B. O. Individually Guided Instruction (IGE) and teacher education. *Journal of Teacher Education,* 1979, *30,* 17–19.

Soar, R. Final report. *Follow-through Classroom Process Measurement and Pupil Growth (1970–1971).* Gainesville: University of Florida, College of Education, 1973. (ERIC Document Reproduction Service No. ED 106 297)

Sorenson, J.; Rossman, P. A.; & Barnes, D. The unit leader and educational decision making. *Journal of Teacher Education,* 1976, *27,* 224–228.

Stallings, J. A., & Kaskowitz, D. H. *Follow Through Classroom Observations Evaluation 1972–1973.* Menlo Park, Calif.: Stanford Research Institute, 1974. (ERIC Document Reproduction Service No. ED 104 969)

Stebbins, L.; St. Pierre, R.; Proper, E.; Anderson, R.; & Cerva, T. *An Evaluation of Follow Through* (Vol. 4A). Cambridge, Mass.: Abt Associates, 1977.

Sterns, H. N. Team teaching: Cooperative organizational concept. In S. E. Goodman (Ed.), *Handbook on Contemporary Education.* New York: R. R. Bowker, 1976.

Sussman, L. *Tales Out of School: Implementing Organizational Change in the Elementary Grades.* Philadelphia: Temple University Press, 1977.

Talmage, H. (Ed.). *Systems of Individualized Education.* Berkeley, Calif.: McCutchan, 1975.

Westbury, I. *The Curriculum and the Frames of the Classroom.* Paper presented at the annual meeting of the American Educational Research Association. New York, 1977. (ERIC Document Reproduction Service No. ED 141 959)

CLASSROOM PHYSICAL ENVIRONMENT

The image of the classroom is such a familiar one in our culture that its potential impact on the instructional process has long remained unexamined. But curricular movements of the past fifteen years such as the open classroom/integrated day, and managerial concepts such as team teaching and flexible scheduling have focused considerable attention on the physical context in which learning takes place. These developments have also stimulated an awareness that classroom physical environments can have significant social consequences. Accordingly, researchers have begun to investigate the role that the physical setting can assume in the creation of new types of learning environments.

For the purposes of this review, classroom physical environment is defined as the interior space, including furnishings and props, where instruction principally takes place in the school. Much of the research on classroom environments has been quite recent and, as might be expected, has focused on new, unconventional settings such as open plan schools and open classrooms. These two terms are sometimes confused and are also worth defining. "Open plan" refers to a type of construction that makes possible the creation of large, partition-free interior spaces to permit maximum flexibility of use. "Open classrooms" are the physical realization of a particular set of ideas about how children learn—for example, by direct interaction with materials, by making choices, or by following their natural interests. Open classrooms have often been established within conventional self-contained classroom space.

The attention of researchers has also focused primarily on elementary and preschool settings. Given the more creative ways in which classroom space is typically used with younger children, this pattern is easily understandable. In addition, research on classroom physical environments has been largely nontheoretical, concentrating on the development of techniques for measuring environments and on the description of behavior patterns in different types of settings.

Given the objectives of this volume, only a highly selective introduction to the available research on classroom physical environments is appropriate. For more detailed treatments the reader is referred to Weinstein (1979) and Gump (1978), who comprehensively review the research on classrooms, to Phyfe-Perkins's overview of preschool environments (1980), and to Prescott and David (1976) and Moore et al. (1979) for an examination of day care settings. Moore, Lane, and Lindberg (1979) have also compiled an extensive bibliography on children and the physical environment. Two more general collections of papers concerning learning environments are Coates (1974) and David and Wright (1975).

The available research literature on classroom physical settings can be organized into three overlapping areas: efforts at environmental assessment and evaluation; observational studies focusing on person-environment interactions; and, experimental and quasi-experimental investigations of environmental interventions.

Environmental Assessment and Evaluation. Studies in this area are directed toward the systematic description of environments (assessment) and the evaluation of the "effectiveness" of particular environments (generally defined in terms of student outcomes). One approach to assessment has been the direct measurement of objective physical attributes of a setting by outside observers. Such work fits generally within the "human factors" engineering perspective that has characterized much of traditional architectural research. A prime example was the pioneering work of Harmon (1951), who conducted a series of investigations in the 1940s on the "functional geometry" of the classroom, which he characterized in terms of objective measures of lighting, seating, and wall decoration. Britain's Building Performance Research Unit (1972) took the notion of objective measurement a step further, subjecting data on a wide range of physical features of comprehensive schools to a quasi-economic analysis in an effort to arrive at an "optimized" layout for instructional space. In the United States, similar but smaller scale analysis of "building performance" was conducted by Rabinowitz (1975).

The direct measurement approach has been utilized by other investigators to focus directly on substantive instructional issues. The most sophisticated rating scale available for classroom space is that developed by Prescott and her associates (Kritchevsky, Prescott, & Walling, 1968; Prescott et al., 1975) for the assessment of day-care environments. It includes ratings of attributes such as organization, complexity of materials, intrusion/seclusion, and softness, which add up to a total space-quality score. Ross and Gump (1978) have defined two indices—"openness quotient" and "percent of containment"—as a way of quantifying the degree of architectural openness of classroom space, a potentially important device for cross-setting comparisons.

In contrast to the direct assessment of aspects of the physical setting, other studies have adopted indirect techniques which focus on the perceptions and opinions of building users. Most of the indirect assessments of classroom space have centered on user satisfaction, a complex issue in view of the large amount of variation typically observed in the responses of individuals to built environments. For example, in Giles and Tedrick's survey (1975) of twenty-nine open-plan schools, there was considerable disagreement among building users on such concrete issues as the level of distraction, adequacy of storage space

for students, and appropriate temperature level. User satisfaction can probably be defined most realistically in terms of trade-offs—the achievement of desired priorities in exchange for an acceptable level of negative return—rather than by a generalized acceptance of a particular setting. This would suggest that indirect assessment of classroom settings could be improved considerably by augmenting general attitude measures with trade-off questions to hone in on user preferences for specific features.

Efforts to evaluate the "effectiveness" of classroom physical environments have most frequently been directed toward open-plan schools. Given the substantial public investment in such schools, it is not surprising that many of the evaluation studies have been commissioned by school boards. Most of these studies (George, 1975) appear to suggest that the open physical environment alone should stimulate new teaching practices and significant student outcomes, a rather demanding criterion of effectiveness.

The available evidence offers no definitive verdict on the open-plan concept, but many of the studies were of such questionable quality that a summary of results is difficult to compile. Many of the evaluations were conducted only once, often during the first year of a school's operation. Most of the studies also failed to control for program or curricular variation and relevant antecedent variables or to clearly define variations in the physical setting itself.

However, two noteworthy evaluation efforts are those of Beck (1979) and Traub et al. (1976). Both not only made an effort to control for each school's curricular emphasis, but distinguished between a limited number of different types of open-plan environments as well. Both also looked at noncognitive as well as cognitive student outcomes across a number of schools (120 for Beck, 30 for Traub et al.). Although noting that there was considerable variation within the school types, the Beck study found that, on the average, students in conventional schools significantly outscored open-plan students on mathematics and reading achievement tests. Noncognitive outcomes such as attitude to word school and locus of control showed no relationship to the physical setting. The degree of "openness" of teaching strategy reported by the teachers was unrelated to both achievement and affective outcomes.

In contrast, the Traub et al. evaluation found no consistent relationship between architecture and achievement outcomes. Moreover, they observed that students in open-plan schools displayed more positive attitudes toward school, their teachers, and themselves, and also rated higher on independence. Teachers in the open-plan settings were also more positive about their work and interacted more with other teachers and the principal than did their peers in conventional schools.

The contradictory findings of these two large-scale studies neatly illustrate the difficulty, if not futility, of trying to establish a reliable causal connection between standardized pencil-and-paper outcome measures and the physical environment, particularly when measured in such a simple categorical fashion. It is doubtful whether even the most ardent advocates of open-plan construction would claim that the building alone could significantly affect children's test scores. In order to fully understand the potential impact of the environment, it is important to examine those social and instructional variables that intercede between the architectural shell and educational outcomes. It is here that systematic observation can play an important role.

Systematic Observation. The studies just reviewed concentrated on the measurement of fairly static properties of the classroom setting. In contrast, systematic observation provides a more dynamic view of environment-behavior transactions—that is, how the environment works its occupants. Accordingly, observational studies have been more concerned with the careful documentation of patterns of student and teacher behavior in different settings than with student outcomes. Such observational evidence has helped to focus the attention of investigators on those aspects of classroom life where the physical environment is most likely to make a difference. Zifferblatt (1972) for example, attributed differences in task attention span and student disruptiveness that he observed in a third-grade open classroom to spatial arrangements such as the placement of desks and of barriers between work areas.

Most of the available observational studies that have concentrated on the physical setting have examined life in open-plan schools. Gump (1974) observed individual children in open-plan and traditional design schools to determine the number and type of behavior settings they occupied in the course of a day. The open-plan environment was more active than the traditional, with more variety and stimulation. Students entered more sites in the open setting, but they spent less time in instructional "segments" where their own pacing was central. They generally spent more time following segment conditions (e.g., teachers' directions) than traditional school students, particularly in the primary grades. Another concomitant of more frequent site changes was greater transition or non-substantive time in the open school, accounting for as much as 40 percent of non-recess time in one open-school period.

In another "shadow" study of individual children in open and traditional plan schools, Burnham (1970) included a variant of Flanders' Interaction Analysis (1970) to record the child's overt behaviors at ten-minute intervals. He noted that in the open environment, children were more likely to be observed initiating activities reflecting their personal interests, engaging in cooperative planning with teachers and fellow students, exercising personal responsibility, and examplifying a "spirit of inquiry."

Although such studies as these suggest readily observable differences in behavior patterns between schools of open and more traditional architecture, the results are by no means unequivocal. As Durlak, Beardsley and Murray (1972) observed, some ostensibly "traditional" schools supported more open patterns of activity while some "open" environments housed traditional programs. Gump (1974) also noted few differences in behavior patterns between schools for children in intermediate (fifth and sixth) grades in his sample.

Rivlin and Rothenberg (1976) utilized a more longitudinal approach to examine the issue of fit between behavior and environment. They observed in two elementary schools using an open-classroom approach within traditional school buildings, mapping furniture arrangements and behavior patterns across a school year. Although furniture arrangements showed considerable stability, patterns in the teachers' use of space were more striking.

Despite the fact that teachers differed in style and in the use of their rooms, there was an overwhelming tendency to concentrate their time in limited locations. They tended to remain in the front center portion of the room, a zone which permitted proximity to the blackboard (whether used or not) and to the room's only entrance. As a consequence of the teachers' relative immobility, the children tended to concentrate their work in areas in or near the teacher zones, resulting in an uneven use of available space. Ironically, in interviews, the teachers complained most about inadequate space and storage while children felt the lack of private, quiet spaces.

Gump and Ross (1977) documented the process of accommodation of a traditional program and open physical milieu in a newly built open-plan elementary school over a period of two years. Their observations revealed a general closing off of the open space and a reassignment of certain potentially distracting activities to more enclosed spaces in order to better serve the traditional program. Class areas were shielded from distraction with tall, vision-blocking furniture, and additional low furniture was used to mark territories and control traffic.

Another issue, which observational studies have only begun to address, involves the behavior of special subgroups of children with regard to the physical environment. For example, Kinsman and Berk (1979) give evidence that the sex-typed nature of young children's play can be influenced by environmental structures. Simply removing the dividers separating the block and housekeeping areas in a nursery school resulted in more mixed-sex play groups, with girls in particular expanding and enriching their activities in the "opposite sex" environment of the block corner.

Williamson and Le Resche (1975) observed children identified by their teachers as "problems" or "nonproblems" in an open-plan elementary school. From their data on location of the children in the room and their interaction with others, some patterns emerged; "problem" children were characterized by extensive use of the sides and back edges of the room, high mobility, and the lack of a well-defined home range.

Observational studies have identified some general differences between settings as well as potential problems such as the inordinate amount of transitional or unengaged time recorded in some open-plan schools. Observational analyses also pointed out aspects of environment-behavior transactions that were otherwise not apparent, such as the consequences of the uneven or inefficient use of classroom space. However, many of the investigations that compared behavior patterns between schools have failed to control for process variables such as curriculum or social climate. The limited time frame of most studies also leaves some questions unanswered. For example, would the disruptive influence of the open setting in new open-plan schools lessen after the building had been occupied for several years, with or without extensive additional interior partitioning? In order to more effectively disentangle the contribution of the physical setting from that of other "person" and "process" variables, more controlled experimental manipulations of environmental attributes are desirable.

Experimental and Quasi-experimental Studies. The most coherent body of literature on experimental manipulations of the classroom physical environment addresses the effects of levels of density on young children's behavior (Smith & Connolly, 1976; Evans, 1978). Although it is not uncommon in a traditional schoolroom to allow only 20–25 square feet of floor space per student for a sedentary curriculum, experimental evidence indicates that the space requirements of more active early childhood programs are substantially greater. High density conditions (comparable to those in an average classroom) have been found to result in increased aggression (Hutt & Vaizey, 1966; Loo & Kennelly, 1979), decreased social interaction (Hutt & Hutt, 1970; Loo, 1972) and to non-involvement (Shapiro, 1975).

Rohe and Patterson (1974) systematically varied both density and the types of material resources available in a day-care classroom. As density was increased, a corresponding increase was observed in aggressive, destructive, and unoccupied behavior. As the amount of physical resources increased, cooperative, constructive, and relevant participation also increased, and irrelevant participation decreased. The most negative interaction among children occurred under the "high density/low resources" condition, indicating that the effect of density results from more than the amount of available space; it is also linked to the arrangement of that space and the types of resources provided. Rohe and Patterson define the optimal day-care environment as one of low density (at least 48 square feet per child) and high resources. If high density is unavoidable, they suggest increasing the amount and quality of materials to provide activity options.

Other quasi-experimental manipulations focused on the arrangement of spatial elements. Weinstein (1977) collected baseline data on the activities and locations of students in a second third-grade open classroom. These data were then shared with the teacher, who assisted in identifying priorities for change, such as the uneven distribution of children across the room, girls' avoidance of the science and math areas, and the infrequent use of manipulative

materials. The physical environment was then rearranged to support desired patterns of behavior. After the passing of a familiarization period, repeat observations revealed a significant shift in the predicted direction. Students entered areas of the room they had previously avoided and target behaviors such as the manipulation of materials increased noticeably.

Phyfe-Perkins (1979) utilized design intervention to modify the behavior of children in a day-care classroom who were low on constructive play and task-oriented activities and high on waiting and unoccupied behaviors compared to children in a similar center. A quiet area was defined, the materials in the woodworking and manipulative areas were supplemented and reorganized, and the room was rearranged to eliminate disruptive traffic patterns. After these changes were made, levels of task-focused behavior and constructive play increased significantly. There was no reduction in waiting or unoccupied behavior, however, a finding the author attributed to the large amount of time the children spent in teacher-led group activities.

The sole example of systematic environmental intervention in a secondary school is Evans and Lovell's study (1979) of an open-plan alternative high school. Initial observations revealed problems with distraction, class interruptions, high noise levels, and poor traffic flow. Sound-absorbent partitions of variable height were introduced to redirect traffic away from class areas and to more clearly demarcate class boundaries. Several smaller, isolated areas were also created to increase opportunities for privacy. As predicted, environmental modifications resulted in significantly reduced classroom interruptions and increased substantive, content questioning in class meetings.

Although the number of experimental and quasi-experimental studies has been limited, their results have tentatively identified a number of areas in which arrangement of the physical environment can influence behavior. Other than density and level of resources, noteworthy examples are display and accessibility of materials, clear demarcation of boundaries between subsettings, and the provision of private places. Many other dimensions of classroom physical environment remain to be explored.

Conclusions. Research on classroom physical environments is an emergent field that as yet, constitutes but a minor tributary to the mainstream of educational research. The quantity of research directly addressing the physical setting has been limited, and hampered by a lack of more sophisticated methods of measuring environmental factors. Certainly the simple distinction between "open plan" and "traditional" doesn't begin to capture the most important physical differences between those settings, and no one has attempted to map the universe of "average" classrooms. Yet instruments such as Prescott's (1975) day-care environmental inventory demonstrate that more detailed measurement of "social and curricular" aspects of the physical environment is possible.

From a naive model of environmental determinism, research on physical settings has moved toward a concern with person-environment fit. This view suggests that "effects" of the environment are most likely to be observed in the interaction between setting, instructional methods, and persons. Recent observational studies concerning the use of classroom space by special groups of students tentatively confirm this notion. As more investigators turn their attention to the physical setting and, equally important, as studies of instruction begin to incorporate environmental variables, we will come closer to realizing the potential of classrooms as true "learning environments."

Thomas G. David

See also Media Use in Education; New Technologies in Education; School Plant and Facilities.

REFERENCES

Beck, T. M. *An Australian Study of School Environments.* Paper presented at the meeting of the American Educational Research Association, San Francisco, 1979. (ERIC Document Reproduction Service No. ED 172 357)

Building Performance Research Unit. *Building Performance.* New York: Wiley, Halsted, 1972.

Burnham, B. *A Day in the Life: Case Studies of Pupils in Open Plan Schools.* Toronto: York County Board of Education, 1970.

Coates, G. J. (Ed.). *Alternative Learning Environments.* Stroudsberg, Pa.: Dowden, Hutchinson & Ross, 1974.

David, T. G., & Wright, B. D. (Eds.). *Learning Environments.* Chicago: University of Chicago Press, 1975.

Durlak, J. T.; Beardsley, B. E.; & Murray, J. S. Observation of user activity patterns in open and traditional plan school environments. In W. Mitchell (Ed.) *Environmental Design: Research and Practice.* Los Angeles: Environmental Design Research Association, 1972. (ERIC Document Reproduction Service No. ED 079 828)

Evans, G. W. Crowding and the developmental process. In A. Baum & Y. M. Epstein (Eds.), *Human Response to Crowding.* Hillsdale, N.J.: Lawrence Erlbaum Associates, 1978.

Evans, G. W., & Lovell, B. Design modification in an open-plan school. *Journal of Educational Psychology,* 1979, *71,* 41–49.

Flanders, N. A., *Analyzing Teacher Behavior.* Reading, Mass.: Addison-Wesley, 1970.

George, P. S. *Ten Years of Open Space Schools: A Review of the Research.* Gainesville: University of Florida, Florida Educational Research and Development Council, 1975.

Giles, T. E., & Tedrick, G. D. What students think about open-area schools. *Orbit,* 1975, *6,* 27–28.

Gump, P. V. Operating environments in schools of open and traditional design. *School Review,* 1974, *82,* 49–67.

Gump, P. V. School environments. In I. Altman & J. F. Wohlwill (Eds.), *Children and the Environment.* New York: Plenum Press, 1978.

Gump, P. V., & Ross, R. The fit of milieu and programme in school environments. In H. McGurk (Ed.), *Ecological Factors in Human Development,* New York: North-Holland, 1977.

Harmon, D. B. *The Co-ordinated Classroom.* Grand Rapids, Mich.: American Seating Company, 1951. (ERIC Document Reproduction Service No. ED 020 621)

Hutt, C., & Vaizey, M. J. Differential effects of group density on social behavior. *Nature,* 1966, *209,* 1371–1372.

Hutt, S. J., & Hutt, C. *Direct Observation and Measurement of Behavior.* Springfield, Ill.: Thomas, 1970.

Kinsman, C. A., & Berk, L. E. Joining the block and housekeeping areas: Changes in play and social behavior. *Young Children,* 1979, *35,* 66–75.

Kritchevsky, S.; Prescott, E.; & Walling, L. *Planning Environments for Young Children: Physical Space.* Washington, D.C.: NAEYC, 1968.

Loo, C. The effects of spatial density on the social behavior of children. *Journal of Applied Social Psychology,* 1972, *2,* 372–382.

Loo, C., & Kennelly, D. Social density: Its effects on behaviors and perceptions of preschoolers. *Environmental Psychology and Nonverbal Behavior,* 1979, *3,* 131–146.

Moore, G. T.; Lane, C. G.; Hill, A. B.; Cohen, U.; & McGinty, T. *Recommendations for Child Care Centers.* (Report R79-2) Milwaukee: University of Wisconsin–Milwaukee, Center for Architecture and Urban Planning Research, 1979.

Moore, G. T.; Lane, C. G.; & Lindberg, L. *Bibliography on Children and the Physical Environment.* (Report R79-3). Milwaukee: University of Wisconsin–Milwaukee, Center for Architecture and Urban Planning Research, 1979. (ERIC Document Reproduction Service No. ED 184 696)

Phyfe-Perkins, E. *Application of the Behavior-Person-Environment Paradigm to the Analysis and Evaluation of Early Childhood Education Programs.* Unpublished doctoral dissertation, University of Massachusetts, 1979.

Phyfe-Perkins, E. Children's behavior in preschool settings: A review of research concerning the influence of the physical environment. In L. G. Katz (Ed.), *Current Topics in Early Childhood Education.* Norwood, N.J.: Ablex Publishing, 1980.

Prescott, E., & David, T. G. *The Effects of the Physical Environment on Day Care.* Washington, D.C.: U.S. Office of Child Development, 1976.

Prescott, E.; Jones, E.; Kritchevsky, S.; Milich, C.; & Haselhoef, E. *Assessment of Child-rearing Environments: An Ecological Approach.* Pasadena, Calif.: Pacific Oaks College, 1975.

Rabinowitz, H. Z. *Buildings in Use Study.* (Report R75-1) Milwaukee: University of Wisconsin–Milwaukee, Center for Architecture and Urban Planning Research, 1975. (ERIC Document Reproduction Service No. ED 135 106)

Rivlin, L. G., & Rothenberg, M. The use of space in open classrooms. In H. M. Proshansky, W. H. Ittelson, & L. G. Rivlin (Eds.), *Environmental Psychology: People and Their Physical Settings* (2nd ed.). New York: Holt, Rinehart & Winston, 1976.

Rohe, W., & Patterson, A. H. The effects of varied levels of resources and density on behavior in a day care center. In D. H. Carson (Ed.), *Man–Environment Interactions.* Washington, D.C.: Environmental Design Research Association, 1974.

Ross, R., & Gump, P. V. Measurement of designed and modified openness in elementary school buildings. In S. Weidemann & J. R. Anderson (Eds.), *Priorities for Environmental Design Research.* Washington, D.C.: Environmental Design Research Association, 1978.

Rothenberg, M., & Rivlin, L. G. *An Ecological Approach to the Study of Open Classrooms.* Paper presented to the conference on Ecological Factors in Human Development, University of Surrey, Guilford, U.K., 1975. (ERIC Document Reproduction Service No. ED 132 209)

Shapiro, S. Preschool ecology: A study of three environmental variables. *Reading Improvement,* 1975, *12,* 236–241.

Smith, P. K., & Connolly, K. J. Social and aggressive behavior in preschool children as a function of crowding. *Social Science Information,* 1976, *16,* 601–620.

Traub, R.; Weiss, J.; Fisher, C.; & Khan, Y. *Openness in Schools: An Evaluation Study* (Research in Education Series 5). Toronto: Ontario Institute for Studies in Education, 1976.

Weinstein, C. S. Modifying student behavior in an open classroom through changes in the physical design. *American Educational Research Journal,* 1977, *14,* 249–262.

Weinstein, C. S. The physical environment of the school: A review of the research. *Review of Educational Research,* 1979, *49,* 577–610.

Williamson, P., & Le Resche, L. *Use of Space in an Architecturally Open Plan Elementary School.* Paper presented at the annual conference of the Environmental Design Research Association, Lawrence, Kans. 1975.

Zifferblatt, S. M. Architecture and human behavior: Toward increased understanding of a functional relationship. *Educational Technology,* 1972, *12,* 54–57.

COGNITION AND MEMORY

This article reviews some of the historical factors leading to the establishment of the new field of cognitive psychology in the 1960s. Cognitive psychology is basically a set of research techniques that capitalize on recent developments in the field of computer science. This field not only provides the technology for new experimental paradigms in cognition but also provides a general model of the human mind as information processor. Such a model has been applied in some detail to the field of memory, and this article includes a discussion of research that substantiates features of the prevailing models of memory.

Cognition

Cognition is the act of knowing. The analysis of the act and its components is the core of psychologists' and educators' attempts to understand the mind and its development. "Cognition" is a troublesome term to define in psychology because it has no clear referent; it is defined narrowly by some as merely "awareness" (e.g., Guilford, 1967) and is defined so broadly by others as to include all higher mental processes (perception, thinking, attention, language, reasoning, problem solving, creativity, and memory). For others (e.g., Hunt, 1976) intelligence cannot be understood apart from cognition. The analysis of cognition or knowing is complicated at the outset by the kind of difficulty Augustine describes in his analysis of time: "Yet what more familiar word do we use in speech than *time?* Obviously when we use it, we know what we mean, just as when we hear another use it, we know what he means. What then is time? If no one asks me, I know; if I want to explain it to a questioner, I do not know" (*Confessions,* Book 11, section 14). Still, it is fair to say that psychology has always been about cognition even if it did not use the term until the last two decades.

Early Theoretical Models. When William James (1890) proposed the new discipline of psychology as "the science of mental life," it was clear then, as it is now, that the mind was the proper object of study for the new field. The science James and others inaugurated before the turn of the century was more a hope for a science than a science, since the available research methodologies amounted to little more than having people report the activities of their own minds. This "introspective method" yielded little information that met the scientific criterion of replicability, although over the years matters improved on this account as researchers learned that replicability could be achieved by carefully contriving and controlling the situations in which the introspections occurred (Lachman, Mistler-Lachman, & Butterfield, 1979).

Throughout its relatively short history as an experimental science, psychology, which had no theoretical model of its own for the mind, borrowed major concepts and models from other disciplines. Borrowing initially from atomic theory and Lockean epistemology, psychologists searched for the mental atoms that were bonded by the principles of association (proximity, temporality, similarity) first laid down by Aristotle. These efforts to identify the atomic structure of the mind gave way somewhat, under the influence of the theory of evolution, to considerations of the mind's functions rather than its structure. Whatever the mind's structure, what it does requires explanation. Until quite recently the question of the structure of the mind was answered inevitably by the postulation of association mechanisms and structures that mediated or stood between a stimulus and a person's response to it. Examination of the functions of mind in the survival of our species through learning and problem-solving mechanisms dominated psychological research until the 1960s, particularly in America.

During the same period, the rapid advances of field theory in physics found their counterparts in the Gestalt psychologies of perception. The invention of topology in mathematics led again to considerations of structure, this time to the "topological" structures of personality. More recently the Bourbaki group of logicians provided Piaget with a model for the development of children's reasoning, and advances in linguistic theory by Chomsky supported the contemporary notion of the mind as an innate system of plans and rules underlying our competence to know things, particularly language.

Learning Theories. The work of Piaget, although largely ignored in the United States until the 1960s, and the work of Chomsky paved the way for the contemporary study of cognition. American psychology, in particular, from World War I until 1960 was dominated by a behaviorist approach, which focused on learning and held that a science of mind is not possible except insofar as it is a science of behavior. Furthermore, the principal theoretical factor in the explanation of a behavior is the consequence of the behavior, whether it is reinforced positively or negatively. The work of Piaget, for example, showed that a child's acquisition of certain logical-mathematical ideas (such as, if $A = B$ and $B = C$, then $A = C$) is not so simply explained by reinforcement principles. For example, it proves difficult—some say impossible—to teach a child, using reinforcement procedures, that A has to equal C, given their relationship to B. Chomsky and others showed that the language a child acquires, particularly during the first two years, seems entirely too complicated to be shaped simply by environmental contingencies that follow upon a child's babblings. Instead, a child's language competence seems to be generated by elaborate rules that it simply does not have time to master if the rules are acquired in accordance with prevailing learning theories.

When the post-*Sputnik* curriculum reforms were mandated, many psychologists and educators turned away from the learning theories, with their emphases on reinforced associations between stimuli and responses, toward the study of cognition that was emerging as a new approach to the study of the higher mental processes.

Information-processing Model. What convinced psychologists that the new approach, a renewed attack on so-called cognitive processes, would succeed when the earlier attempts to specify the mind's inner workings had failed to win scientific support was the development of computer programs. Thus another model was borrowed, this time from computer engineering. It was the model of a mind as an information processor that did many of the things computers did (e.g., accept information, manipulate and transform it, store it, and retrieve it). The fact of computers, as Neisser (1976) points out, gave psychologists reassurance that cognitive processes were as real as the muscular and glandular responses that constitute behaviors. Moreover, the development of programs—artificial intelligence programs—that did things people do in ways that were indistinguishable from the ways people did them reinforced the belief that cognitive processes could be understood by the development of computer programs simulating human higher-order behavior (such as playing chess, proving theorems, writing poems, diagnosing illnesses, or landing airplanes). A computer program that plays chess as well as a person offers a good theory about what the person could be doing when he or she plays chess—whether he or she is aware of it or not.

Whereas the model of the mind as a computer nourished theories of cognitive psychology, the empirical need to support these theories with precise measures of the flow of information through the mind generated new research techniques and paradigms. Most of these avoided the need for introspection by carefully constructing tasks for research subjects and precisely timing a person's responses to various tasks (Posner, 1978) or by tracking a person's eye movements (Cohen, 1978). Newell (1973) cataloged fifty-nine cognitive research paradigms, for example.

These techniques, coupled with models of the mind as an information processor, constitute the approach to the science of the mind known as "cognitive psychology."

When cognitive psychologists have analyzed the reading process or the way in which basic arithmetical operations are or can be carried out, educators have been quick to see the implications for the sequencing of curricular information (Farnham-Diggory, 1978; Shavelson, 1981; Siegler, 1981). Although the "cognitive" approach is not without its critics, it can point to a number of achievements. The most significant have been in the general field of memory, and are treated in the latter portion of this article.

Throughout the 1960s and 1970s cognitive psychologists created several models of the mind (Lachman, Mistler-Lachman, & Butterfield, 1979). These models all separated the act of knowing into its component processes, some of which could be reduced to well-established neurophysiological events. The models all stressed mental processes over mental content. These processes are actions that depend upon biological features and that take place in real time. On the other hand, the contents of cognition, such as symbol systems and knowledge, are acquired culturally, not biologically, and have meaning that is independent of time, as Blumenthal (1977) has noted. Although processes create content, each is independent; for example, a person's ability to do large-scale mental arithmetic is limited by process constraints that have no counterpart in the content of arithmetic itself.

The cognition models were rarely developmental, that is, they attempted to specify the cognitive capacity of mature persons only. The models defined only the end point of cognitive development, and developmental psychologists have just begun the systematic exploration of changes in information processing over the life span (Siegler, 1981). They have also taken up the question of the child's cognition of cognition (called "metacognition") and have found generally that children's ideas about the workings of their own minds are consistent with their developing knowledge about everything else.

The models stress psychological function over neurophysiology insofar as behavioral phenomena would be true and meaningful regardless of the neural actions that may "cause" them. Although model builders have been constrained by neurophysiological findings, most notably by split-brain research and clinical neurology literature on hemispheric dominance (Cohen, 1977; Glass, Holyoak, & Santa, 1979), few features of the models can be reduced directly to brain events. Since the complex, interconnected firings of 14 billion cells may preclude in principle the prediction of cognitive events in any case, neurophysiological fidelity may not be a significant criterion for adequate cognitive models.

Features. By and large, cognition models over the last two decades have shared a set of common features. The components of knowing were thought to be serially connected, although parallel functioning sometimes is thought to occur during the initial knowing stages. Information from the environment has been generally thought to receive some processing independent of attention given to it. This information is collected or aggregated in sensory buffers or collectors for brief periods (0.75 seconds). The buffers cause input delays and are needed in any system in which the capacity to receive information exceeds the capacity to process it. Most of the information or experience created in the buffer is lost, but with attentional processing some of it is transferred to a short-term memory store, where the information quickly decays (in about 5 to 18 seconds) unless it is continually attended to and reinstated. Here it is recognized or identified for what it is through an interaction of higher-level and lower-level processing, and sometimes it is recoded in verbal form. Some of the information in the limited short-term store can be shifted with rehearsal and study to a relatively unlimited long-term store where it can be maintained without conscious attention more or less indefinitely.

New cognitive methodologies. This oversimplified sketch of the dominant information-processing models is expanded and critiqued in many current texts (e.g., Anderson, 1980; Cohen, 1977; Glass, Holyoak, & Santa, 1979). Despite the tremendous technological progress brought about by the new cognitive methodologies, such as mental chronometry, eye-movement tracking, and computer simulation, actual advances in our knowledge of cognition have been slight (Cohen, 1977). Empirical findings are constantly challenged by new experiments (Glass, Holyoak, & Santa, 1979), and specific theoretical models are so rapidly invented and discarded that firm summaries of the field are not possible.

As early as 1976, Neisser warned that the optimism generated by new cognitive methodologies may have been premature: "Lacking in ecological validity, indifferent to culture, even missing some of the main features of perception and memory as they occur in ordinary life, such a psychology could become a narrow and uninteresting specialized field. There are already indications that this may be happening. The proliferation of new techniques is no longer encouraging; it has become oppressive" (p. 7). Despite these cautions, the contribution of new cognitive methodologies to an understanding of one major component of mental functioning, namely, memory, can be elaborated as an illustration of their power.

Memory

Memory refers to the active mental process by which knowledge is (1) coded or represented, (2) stored, (3) retrieved or accessed, and (4) integrated with previously stored information.

General models of memory have been proposed by a number of psychologists, most notably by Atkinson and Shiffrin (1968, 1971) and Waugh and Norman (1965). Figure 1 presents an oversimplified schematic representation of one general model. More technical accounts occur in Kintsch (1977), and less technical accounts are found in Klatzky (1975) and Loftus and Loftus (1976).

The model shown in Figure 1 claims that information is first processed in one of the "sensory stores," in which all the information impinging upon the sense organs is held. However, information in this store decays quickly (within one second) and would be irrevocably lost if, in the next processing stage, some of the information in the sensory store were not transferred to a "short-term memory (STM) store." This store has a limited capacity, and information in it decays quickly, usually within five to eighteen seconds. However, one of the characteristics of short-term memory is a "rehearsal buffer." Information in this buffer may be maintained indefinitely by rehearsal (e.g., repeating the information to oneself over and over again). Since STM has limited capacity, information not rehearsed or directly transferred to the next storage phase is lost and irretrievable. This next phase, the "long-term memory (LTM) store," has unlimited capacity. It is in LTM that our knowledge of the world resides, including our knowledge of language; mathematics; what happened to us yesterday, last week, and ten years ago; or the names and telephone numbers of our friends. The longer information is maintained in STM, the more of that information can be transferred to LTM. It is thought that information may be retrieved directly from STM while being rehearsed, or from LTM through various "retrieval strategies" to be discussed shortly.

Although the model is compartmentalized into discrete boxes, the memory system functions as a whole with no clear distinctions between where or when short-term memory ends and long-term memory begins. The system is one in which raw sensory information is coded and transformed into more and more stable and permanent forms of information, permitting integration with previously stored information. Thus, the boxes in Figure 1 do not describe separate memory systems as such but rather different levels or types of encoding.

The sensory memory stores hold a trace of sensory information long enough to be coded into a form that can be processed by the other stores in the system. The duration of the sensory trace can be measured by electrical activity in the brain that persists after termination of the stimulus and by the duration of such mental phenomena as visual aftereffects. Information in sensory store can be lost not only through decay but through the entrance of new information into the system. Without such a provision for discarding old images, we would constantly experience simultaneous, overlapping images.

Sensory Memory. Research on sensory memory was begun by Sperling (1960) in order to determine how much information could be seen during a brief exposure. The eye does not scan its visual field in one continuous motion, nor can it remain fixed or motionless. Instead, there are a series of short periods of fixation and movements ("saccades") of the eye, and it is only during the periods of fixation, which last approximately three hundred milliseconds, and between saccades (about three per second) that visual information is registered. It has been well established (Cattell, 1885; McDougall, 1904) that if a display of items, such as letters or numbers, are presented tachisto-

FIGURE 1. *Schematic representation of the memory system*

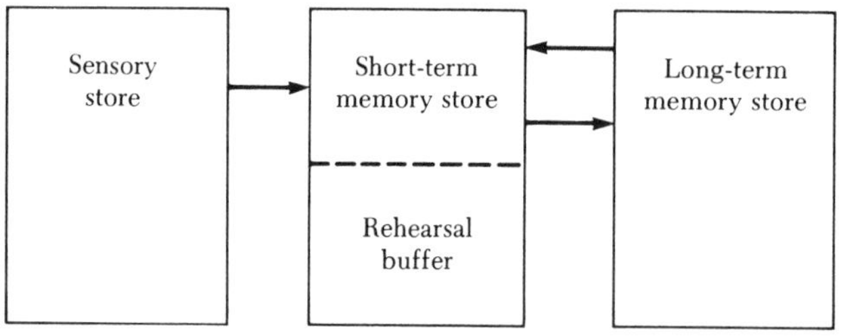

scopically for a period of about fifty milliseconds, subjects can identify only four or five items, regardless of the number of items in the display (the "span of apprehension"). However, subjects report that the four or five items make up only a subset of the items they actually saw; but in the process of recall, by the time they reported four or five items the others were forgotten.

To determine the number of items that could have been seen during these brief exposures if the problem of forgetting or trace decay during recall were eliminated, Sperling presented subjects with twelve digits or letters arranged in three rows of four items for fifty milliseconds and asked subjects to recall the items in only one row. Since the subjects did not know which row they would be asked to recall, it was assumed that performance would have been just as good on the recall of either of the other two rows. Thus, the average percent correct on the row recalled would equal the average percent correct for the entire array, if forgetting during the act of recall did not occur. Sperling found that rather than four or five items recalled, subjects could report about nine items. Using other procedures to delay trace decay in sensory store, subjects were estimated to be able to report up to sixteen items; and there is no reason to believe that this is the upper limit. Similar results have been obtained for auditory sensory store (Darwin, Turvey, & Crowder, 1972), with the exception that visual sensory memory lasts for about one second, but auditory sensory memory lasts for about four seconds. Thus, researchers have concluded that sensory information remains available for a short period after stimulus termination, thereby permitting encoding and consolidation to be completed in sensory store, which seems to be of large, perhaps unlimited capacity.

If these conclusions are correct, how is the large amount of information in sensory memory transferred to the limited capacity of STM? The answer seems to involve selective attention on the part of the individual, who may choose to attend to information important for the task at hand, preserving only this information for further processing while filtering out the other information. Thus, at a cocktail party only one of several simultaneous conversations is selectively attended to. Numerous models of this selective attention process have been proposed (Broadbent, 1971; Deutsch & Deutsch, 1963; Neisser, 1967).

Pattern recognition. The question of how information attended to in sensory store is transferred to STM involves the transformation of sensory information into recognizable and meaningful forms. This extremely complex topic, called "pattern recognition," is not very well understood but is of particular importance to educators since it is a critical component in the mastery of reading skill.

Since meaning is stored in long-term memory, pattern recognition must involve both sensory and long-term memory converging in short-term memory. In oversimplified terms, the general model of pattern recognition claims that the information in the sensory store is compared to information stored in LTM, which is coded in such a way that direct comparisons are possible. After comparisons are made between information in the sensory store and LTM codes, a decision is made regarding the best match. These comparisons are most likely conducted simultaneously (Neisser, 1964). The LTM codes may be "templates," "prototypic examplars," or "lists of critical features." At the present time, the last appear to offer the most promising model of how the match is made.

Short-term Memory. Once the sensory information is encoded by pattern recognition, it is available in short-term memory store, sometimes also called "primary memory." STM is distinguished from the sensory store by its limited capacity, its longer duration, and the nature or level of encoding. While it was initially believed that a major difference between STM and LTM was that information loss in STM was a function of trace decay and information loss in LTM was a function of interference, it is now generally recognized that simple trace decay accounts for only a small portion of the loss in STM and that loss in both STM and LTM is primarily a function of interference (Keppel & Underwood, 1962; Reitman, 1971; Waugh & Norman, 1965).

Retention and capacity. The first systematic study of retention duration in STM was carried out by Peterson and Peterson (1959). On each trial a "consonant trigram," such as ZVL or KMB, was presented, followed by a three-digit number. Subjects were instructed to count backward by threes from this number until a red light appeared, at which time they were to recall the consonant trigram. On different trials the counting backward lasted for three, six, nine, twelve, or eighteen seconds ("retention intervals"). The counting backward was assumed to prevent the subject from continuously rehearsing or repeating the trigram to himself. After three seconds about 20 percent of the subjects forgot the trigram, and by eighteen seconds approximately 90 percent of them forgot it. Murdock (1961) found the same results for both consonant trigrams and three real words. Even when Murdock presented just one real word, there was some forgetting after only eighteen seconds. Thus, in the absence of rehearsal, STM is of short duration and is a function of the number of units to be remembered.

The most common way of measuring the capacity of STM is a memory span procedure in which a subject is presented a string of items (digits are most common) and asked to repeat as many as he can. The capacity of STM is then defined as the maximum number of items in a string that can be recalled. This is a common task on mental-ability tests. Regardless of the nature of the items in the string (digits, letters, words, or phrases), memory span remains surprisingly constant—seven, plus or minus two, items. Miller (1956) argued that STM appears to be able to hold about seven items, or seven "chunks" of information. Thus, by reorganizing discrete items into categories, classes, or chunks, the capacity of STM may in fact be exceedingly large. These organizational chunks may be as large as sentences or idea units representing the meaning of entire paragraphs or chapters. It should be clear that ability to organize information into chunks must involve the active participation of LTM, just as LTM must be involved in pattern recognition. The information code in STM is most often acoustic (e.g., Conrad, 1964), but there is ample evidence that visual and semantic codes may also be used (e.g., Posner & Mitchell, 1967; Shulman, 1972).

Since STM has a limited capacity of seven, plus or minus two, chunks of information, it is clear that for new information to enter STM, existing information in it must be either transferred to LTM or dropped from further processing. If not, no new information can enter. The individual actively controls this process, and according to the task demands, decides what information is relevant and must be maintained and what information is irrelevant and may be dropped.

Rehearsal. Information is maintained in STM by the active process of "rehearsal." Rehearsal has two functions. First, it can be used to maintain information in STM (maintenance rehearsal), and, second, it is the mechanism by which information is transferred to LTM (elaborative rehearsal). For example, if you must look up a phone number in a directory that you cannot bring to the telephone, and you cannot write it down, you will most likely read the phone number, repeat it to yourself, and keep repeating it until you reach the phone and dial the number. If you have no further use for the number, it will be forgotten almost immediately after dialing. Thus, rehearsal serves the purpose of maintaining information in STM only as long as needed. However, if you believe that you will need a number frequently, you will continue to rehearse until

it is transferred to LTM and becomes a part of your permanent memory of phone numbers.

A great deal of evidence exists that the greater the amount of rehearsal, the greater the long-term retention. When subjects are asked to rehearse out loud and are later given a recall task, recall is a function of the number of rehearsals. However, maintenance or rote rehearsal does not appear to be sufficient for transfer of information to LTM. Such transfer requires more elaborate encoding of information. Maintenance rehearsal provides the opportunity for elaborative rehearsal to take place.

Long-term Memory.   The two primary characteristics of LTM are (1) that information is relatively permanent; (2) that information is stored in an organized fashion.

For storage in LTM "elaborative" rehearsal appears necessary. By elaborative rehearsal is meant the active deeper level of information processing that involves semantic, imaginal, and affective treatment of information. The notion of levels of processing (e.g., Craik & Lockhart, 1972) suggests that the more elaborately information is rehearsed, the better the long-term retention. Thus, rehearsal that involves the subject's elaborate imaging of information, or construction of semantic associations or logical categories related to information already in LTM, is more likely to be effective for transferring information from STM to LTM. Also, the more varied the rehearsed encodings, the more probable it is that information will be stored in LTM (Melton, 1970).

Organization.   The most notable characteristic of LTM is that the information stored in it is organized. The organization is varied and complex. There may in fact be two long-term memories (Tulving, 1972). One, called "semantic memory," contains all the information we possess for using language. This includes information about words and their meanings, the rules of syntax and phonology, and all the facts about our world that are not dependent on a particular time or place. The second is "episodic memory" and includes autobiographical information that is coded temporally. For example, the rules of addition (such as the fact that $2 + 5 = 7$) are part of semantic memory. The fact that yesterday you added $2 + 5$ would be part of your episodic memory since it is temporally coded. Thus, episodic memory is constantly changing, and information may be transferred from episodic to semantic memory, although the mechanism for such transfer is not well understood. Forgetting is more likely to occur for information in episodic memory, since the temporal code is often lost as information is transferred from episodic to semantic memory. Thus, it is more likely that you will forget that yesterday you added $2 + 5$ than it is that you will forget the rule that allows you to add $2 + 5$. In addition to semantic information, acoustic information is also stored in LTM (Nelson & Rothbart, 1972). However, STM is apparently more sensitive to acoustic information, whereas LTM is more sensitive to semantic information (Loftus & Loftus, 1976).

Apart from "chunking," which occurs in both STM and

LTM, "mnemonics" provide another form of LTM organization. Such devices as "Thirty days hath September, April . . ." are powerful organizational aids in both the acquisition and retention of information. In addition, when learning a list of randomly ordered words, subjects tend to order those words by conceptual categories when they recall them later. For example, when subjects are presented a sixty-item list of words composed of fifteen instances of four conceptual categories (such as animals, vegetables, and so forth) in random order, they recall clusters or groups of words by category rather than according to the random order in which they were presented. Even when the words appear unrelated, subjects tend to impose some subjective organization and will recall in the same way on successive trials a list with certain words clustered together.

Retrieval. The basic purpose of such organizations for memory are that they provide retrieval cues, which tell us where to go in memory to find what we are looking for, and thus help us to limit the amount of search through our memory. Without such cues it would be nearly impossible to find relevant information; it would be like looking for a word in a randomly ordered dictionary. Thus, in organizing memory by, for example, conceptual categories, we can access the proper category and search for the relevant information in that category. Retrieval fails and thus forgetting occurs when the retrieval cue is not accessible or when we choose an inappropriate cue. Similarly, research on meaningful prose material reveals that the stored information is organized by "idea units" or "gist of meaning" rather than verbatim memory of the text (Bransford & Franks, 1971; Sachs, 1967). The theme or gist is stored much like a retrieval cue, from which particulars of the text or experience are then reconstructed.

Network models. The question of the structure of semantic memory has received much attention. Although there are several models of this structure, including network models, set-theoretical models (Meyer, 1970), and semantic feature models (Smith, Shoben, & Rips, 1974), at the present time network models appear to be the most powerful in terms of the range of memory phenomena they can account for. Collins and Quillian first suggested a network model in 1969. The model assumes that concepts are hierarchically organized into subordinate and superordinate relations. Thus, the concept "robin" is subordinate to the concept "bird," which, in turn, is subordinate to the concept "animal." The common attributes of all members of a concept are stored with the superordinate concept, but only the particular attributes of each member of the class are stored directly with it. Thus, within a network, the concept "bird" has stored with it the attribute that all birds have wings, whereas only the subordinate concept "robin" has "red breast" stored with it. All related concepts are connected in the hierarchical network, with the distance between concepts in the network a function of their relatedness. One implication of this model is that retrieval of information concerning the relationship be-

tween two concepts should be a function of the distance between concepts in the network. Thus, it should take less time to decide whether all robins are birds than it would to decide whether all robins are animals. It should also be easier to answer the question "Does a robin have a red breast?" than the question "Does a robin fly?" since the memory search enters at "robin" and quickly finds "red breast" attached to it, whereas "flying" is not attached directly to "robin" and the search must continue up the hierarchy until it reaches the concept "bird." Experiments generally confirm this expectation, but it is also clear that there must be some built-in redundancy in the network in order that very common attributes may be stored at both the superordinate and subordinate levels (Conrad, 1972). Although a number of problems exist with network models, as well as with alternate models, it is abundantly clear that semantic memory is organized according to the relationships between concepts and the attributes that define them.

Although information-processing models have allowed psychologists to gain substantial insight into mental processes such as memory, only the surface has been scratched, and, as in all science, more questions have been raised than answered. For educators, the implications of this model are substantial. For curriculum development, the implications rest on the ability to design curricula that maximize the potential storage of information in meaningful and organized ways consistent with the organizational properties of human memory. For teaching children how to learn, the implications involve the teaching of potentially useful and powerful strategies for efficient and meaningful storage and retrieval of information as well as the different strategies applicable to different purposes of information processing.

Frank B. Murray
Ludwig Mosberg

See also Cognitive Development; Intelligence; Language Development; Learning; Psychology.

REFERENCES

Anderson, J. *Cognitive Psychology and Its Implications.* San Francisco: Freeman, 1980.

Atkinson, R. C., & Shiffrin, R. M. Human memory: A proposed system and its control processes. In K. W. Spence & J. T. Spence (Eds.), *The Psychology of Learning and Motivation: Advances in Research and Theory* (Vol. 2). New York: Academic Press, 1968.

Atkinson, R. C., & Shiffrin, R. M. The control of short-term memory. *Scientific American,* 1971, *225,* 82–90.

Blumenthal, A. *The Process of Cognition.* Englewood Cliffs, N.J.: Prentice-Hall, 1977.

Bransford, J. D., & Franks, J. J. The abstraction of linguistic ideas. *Cognitive Psychology,* 1971, *2,* 331–350.

Broadbent, D. E. *Decision and Stress.* New York: Academic Press, 1971.

Cattell, J. M. Über die Zeit der Erkennung und Benennung von

Schriftzeichen, Bildern, und Farben. *Philosophische Studien,* 1885, *2,* 635–650.

Cohen, G. *The Psychology of Cognition.* New York: Academic Press, 1977.

Cohen, K. Eye activity in the study of the reading process In F. B. Murray (Ed.), *Models of Efficient Reading.* Newark, Del.: International Reading Association, 1978. (ERIC Document Reproduction Service No. ED 163 408)

Collins, A. M., & Quillian, M. R. Retrieval time from semantic memory. *Journal of Verbal Learning and Verbal Behavior,* 1969, *8,* 240–247.

Conrad, C. Cognitive economy in semantic memory. *Journal of Experimental Psychology,* 1972, *92,* 149–154.

Conrad, R. Acoustic confusions in immediate memory. *British Journal of Psychology,* 1964, *55,* 75–84.

Craik, F. I. M., & Lockhart, R. S. Levels of processing: A framework for memory research. *Journal of Verbal Learning and Verbal Behavior,* 1972, *11,* 671–684.

Darwin, C. J.; Turvey, M. T.; & Crowder, R. G. An auditory analogue of the Sperling partial report procedure: Evidence for brief auditory storage. *Cognitive Psychology,* 1972, *3,* 255–267.

Deutsch, J. A., & Deutsch, D. Attention: Some theoretical considerations. *Psychological Review,* 1963, *70,* 80–90.

Farnham-Diggory, S. How to study reading: Some information-processing ways. In F. B. Murray & J. J. Pikulski (Eds.), *The Acquisition of Reading.* Baltimore: University Park Press, 1978.

Glass, L.; Holyoak, K.; & Santa, J. *Cognition.* Reading, Mass.: Addison-Wesley, 1979.

Guilford, J. *The Nature of Human Intelligence.* New York: McGraw-Hill, 1967.

Hunt, E. Varieties of cognitive power. In L. Resnick (Ed.), *The Nature of Intelligence.* Hillsdale, N.J.: Lawrence Erlbaum Associates, 1976.

James, W. *The Principles of Psychology.* New York: Henry Holt, 1890.

Keppel, G., & Underwood, B. J. Proactive inhibition in short-term retention of single items. *Journal of Verbal Learning and Verbal Behavior,* 1962, *1,* 153–161.

Kintsch, W. *Memory and Cognition.* New York: Wiley, 1977.

Klatzky, R. L. *Human Memory: Structure and Processes.* San Francisco: Freeman, 1975.

Lachman, R.; Mistler-Lachman, J.; & Butterfield, E. *Cognitive Psychology and Information Processing.* Hillsdale, N.J.: Lawrence Erlbaum Associates, 1979.

Loftus, G. R., & Loftus, E. F. *Human Memory: The Processing of Information.* Hillsdale, N.J.: Lawrence Erlbaum Associates, 1976.

McDougall, R. Recognition and recall. *Journal of Philosophic and Scientific Methods,* 1904, *1,* 229–233.

Melton, A. W. The situation with respect to the spacing of repetitions in memory. *Journal of Verbal Learning and Verbal Behavior,* 1970, *9,* 546–606.

Meyer, D. E. On the representation and retrieval of stored semantic information. *Cognitive Psychology,* 1970, *21,* 242–300.

Miller, G. A. The magical number seven, plus or minus two: Some limits on our capacity for processing information. *Psychological Review,* 1956, *63,* 81–97.

Murdock, B. B. The retention of individual items. *Journal of Experimental Psychology,* 1961, *62,* 618–625.

Neisser, U. Visual search. *Scientific American,* 1964, *210,* 94–102.

Neisser, U. *Cognitive Psychology.* New York: Appleton-Century-Crofts, 1967.

Neisser, U. *Cognition and Reality.* San Francisco: Freeman, 1976.

Nelson, T. O., & Rothbart, R. Acoustic savings for items forgotten from long-term memory. *Journal of Experimental Psychology,* 1972, *93,* 357–360.

Newell, A. You can't play Twenty Questions with nature and win. In W. G. Chase (Ed.), *Visual Information Processing.* New York: Academic Press, 1973.

Peterson, L. R., & Peterson, M. J. Short-term retention of individual verbal items. *Journal of Experimental Psychology,* 1959, *58,* 193–198.

Posner, M. I. *Chronometric Explorations of Mind.* Hillsdale, N.J.: Lawrence Erlbaum Associates, 1978.

Posner, M. I., & Mitchell, R. F. Chronometic analysis of classification. *Psychological Review,* 1967, *74,* 392–409.

Reitman, J. S. Mechanisms of forgetting in short-term memory. *Cognitive Psychology,* 1971, *2,* 185–195.

Sachs, J. Recognition memory for syntactic and semantic aspects of connected discourse. *Perception and Psychophysics,* 1967, *2,* 437–442.

Shavelson, R. Teaching mathematics: Contributions of cognitive research. *Educational Psychologist,* 1981, *16,* 23–44.

Shulman, H. G. Semantic confusion errors in short-term memory. *Journal of Verbal Learning and Verbal Behavior,* 1972, *11,* 221–227.

Siegler, R. Information-processing approaches to development. In P. Mussen (Ed.), *Manual of Child Psychology.* New York: Wiley, 1981.

Smith, E. E.; Shoben, E. J.; & Rips, L. J. Structure and process in semantic memory: A featured model for semantic decisions. *Psychological Review,* 1974, *81,* 214, 241.

Sperling, G. The information available in brief visual presentations. *Psychological Monographs,* 1960, *72,* 1–29.

Tulving, E. Episodic and semantic memory. In E. Tulving & W. Donaldson (Eds.), *Organization of Memory.* New York: Academic Press, 1972.

Waugh, N. C., & Norman, D. A. Primary memory. *Psychological Review,* 1965, *72,* 89–104.

COGNITIVE DEVELOPMENT

The study of cognitive development concerns changes with age in relation to the system of what we know and changes in the way in which that system interacts with other facets of behavior (Flavell, 1977; McCall, 1981; Wohlwill, 1973). Characteristics of human intellectual functioning such as thinking, planning, knowing, relating, classifying, creating, and problem solving have been traditionally labeled as cognitive processes. More recent views have broadened this characterization to include attention, perception, memory, imagery, and motor learning, among others. These processes are not solely intellectual but are clearly influenced by or under the control of higher-order intellectual processes. Further, affective facets of life are linked through beliefs, attitudes, judgments, and values, with the cognitive apparatus and therefore cannot be excluded from a consideration of cognitive influences.

Much of cognitive development takes place through

the interaction of biology (nature) and environment (nurture) in informal ways (McCall, 1981). The brain grows, and thinking capacity changes. Biological characteristics limit what the child can do and learn and the contribution that formal education can make; they limit the assumed malleability of the child. Conversely, children are not the static products of the environment, for they are equipped with powerful intellectual capacities for thought, including the ability to acquire the first language and a developing ability to handle logical operations.

Maturation, formally defined as growth due to biological factors, occurs as a consequence of both nature and nurture. As a result of the interaction of inherent capacities and environmental experiences, specific cognitive abilities develop, each of which is intimately involved with a variety of other intellectual, social, motor, and emotional changes.

As a consequence of such interactions, one's knowledge is not simply a copy of the world but is some representation of objects and events. Every activity results in a transformation constructed from whatever cognitive, emotional, or motor interactions the person has had with a given object or event. Even the simple interaction involved in the infant's pushing and pulling an object will eventually result in a transformation, a notion of cause-effect relations.

Developmental changes occur through the process of adaptation, which begins in infancy (where cognitive development primarily involves physical experience) and continues through adulthood (where cognitive development is primarily represented by symbolic structures such as those represented in language and mathematics).

The two components of adaptation are the processes of assimilation and accommodation. Through assimilation the information provided by an activity is transformed to become compatible with whatever knowledge structures (schemata) are already available. Even though more sophisticated conceptualizations might be more adaptive in the long run, they may not be possible at a given immature level of development. The clearest representation of schema usage is play, where the primary aim of make-believe games is to duplicate behaviorally the products of the imagination (Piaget, 1969). No change in the form of knowledge is required.

Assimilation never occurs without some degree of accommodation (and vice versa). Through accommodation new knowledge taken into the schema of existing knowledge changes the character of the schema itself; in short, accommodation results in schema change. Thus, a different point of view, a different interpretation, or a new way of thinking is required, resulting in progressive changes not only in *what* the individual knows but, just as important, in the *ways* of knowing. The general course of accommodation moves from the inherent structures involving the reflexes, through perceptual organization of information, to logical or symbolic organizations (structural knowledge). Imitation is predominantly an accommodative activity (Piaget, 1969).

The consequences of the interplay of the two components of adaptation is a progressive change in the person's schemata, or knowledge structures.

Always there is equilibrium between the two processes, regardless of the level of development. An event that cannot be understood by sheer assimilation demands accommodation if equilibrium (balance) is to be achieved. Equilibrium is more readily achieved from middle childhood to maturity than in infancy and early childhood, since the person is better able to avoid the distortions of reality, the subjectivity, that results from such characteristics as egocentrism and centration. Children remaining centered on their own viewpoint and actions, on a single perspective when a relation between two or more elements is required, are unequipped to accommodate. With increasing decentration, there is a corresponding increase in ability to separate oneself from an event and to view it objectively.

Cognitive development occurs linearly (continuously) when the fundamental nature of the facet of the mental function remains unchanged and the growth is quantitative (Emmerich, 1964; Wohlwill, 1973). To examine cognitive growth in linear terms, one or more abilities or achievements (e.g., vocabulary, arithmetic, digit-span memory) would be operationally defined and the ability to handle progressively larger quantitative or qualitatively related units of similar information would be measured over the age range.

Applications have been made to mental development in the form of intelligence tests and normative studies. These approaches have failed to take into account the active participation of children in their interaction with environment. (However, it should be recognized that this criticism is not intrinsic to linear assumptions.)

Cognitive development is also discontinuous. That is, the fundamental character of a function changes qualitatively from one level of development to another, as, for example, it is assumed to do in Piaget's stage theory of development, to be described below. Stage theories assume first that knowledge is represented as structures or relations among elements rather than as discrete attributes such as vocabulary or arithmetic facts. Second, the mode of representation changes from one level of development to the next. Third, cognitive structures develop in an orderly (invariant) sequence through cognitive maturity. Finally, the structures develop out of the interaction of the activities of the developing child with the environment, out of the child's commerce with the environment, rather than emerging automatically with sheer maturation.

Stages. The course of cognitive growth can be exemplified in Piaget's description of the periods of cognitive development, where the interest is in species-general functions of mental development. Space does not permit a complete description of the details of each period, of the wealth of examples available, or of the experimental evidence in support of (or contradicting) some of Piaget's conclusions (see Flavell, 1977, and Piaget & Inhelder,

1969, on which the present description is based). The chronological ages (CA) typically designated for the four major periods of development are the sensorimotor (CA: 0–2 years), preoperational (CA: 2–7 years), concrete operational (CA: 7–11 years), and formal operational (CA: 11–15 years) thought. The chronological ages shown are approximate ranges. Some children reach a given stage earlier or later than shown, and children in milieus other than the United States may take a longer or shorter time to reach a given period.

Sensorimotor period. As the name implies, the sensorimotor period is one in which the infant employs the capacities (primarily reflexes) with which it is born. The initial reflexive behavior and general motor patterns give way to increasing differentiation and employment of symbolic behavior. Thus, the first characteristics of "intelligent" behavior probably begin to be manifested at about 12 to 18 months (Piaget & Inhelder, 1969, p. 5).

Continual interaction with the environment is motivated by intrinsic motives including curiosity, being effective, and competence, all of which are components of effectance motivation. Situations involving novelty, conflict, puzzlement, or other cognitive disturbances that cannot be immediately assimilated result in accommodation in order that the new and existing information be brought into alignment by compensatory responses.

There is general agreement that the stage boundaries in this period occur at about 2, 8, 13, and 21 months of age (Fischer, 1980; McCall, Eichorn, & Hogarty, 1977; Piaget, 1966 [1954]). Initially (CA: 0–1 month), behavior is primarily reflexive and assimilative. The exercise of the reflexes allows new responses such as sucking one's thumb to be incorporated into the schema already available. However primitive such extensions appear, they provide the humble precursors of intelligence.

Later (CA: 1–4 months), clear manifestations of acquired behavior are observed. The early fortuitous accident of thumb-to-mouth is now extended into a coordinated activity involving coordination of vision and prehension. Activity, although part of a generalized schema, cannot be used yet to achieve a specific objective. Visual pursuit (tracking) can be initiated by a moving object, but when it is out of sight the infant is no longer interested. This is the stage in which the "first habits" of the child have their origin.

In the next phase (CA: 4–8 months) the vision-prehension coordination is extended to other objects in the environment. Objects are identifiable on the basis of a few clues—for example, the identification of a doll hidden partially behind a screen or of the source of an action by location of a sound. Circularity of behavior is characteristic of this stage; in other words, behavior that produces a different, novel, or interesting result is repeated. Circular reactions allow for variability to occur, provide a sense of competence in being able to achieve a successful result, and provide the basis for awareness of one's abilities through reality testing.

The third phase (CA: 8–12 months) shows definite coordination of two schemata (mental structures or skills that the person uses to understand new events). For example, the infant at this age will deliberately strive for an object that is out of reach or look for an object that has disappeared. Some perseverance is noted here, however, since if the infant has once found an object in one place and you hide it in a second place, the infant will look for it where it was first hidden. An important development in this phase is that of object constancy and permanence—the realization that objects continue to exist even though they are removed from view. In the beginning of the fourth phase (CA: 12–18 months), some degree of inventiveness is exhibited. For example, if the baby sees an object out of reach but attached to a string, the baby will pull the string to retrieve the object instead of approaching the object. The final boundary of this stage (CA: 18–24), as described by Piaget and Inhelder (1969), marks the completion of the previous stages. In the initial part of the fourth stage, an object viewed through the partial opening of a matchbox is seen as attainable, but the means are not immediately available. Through groping and experimentation, the opening is eventually made larger and the object is reached. In the final part of the fourth stage, the same result would be achieved immediately by deferred imitation. The child now transfers knowledge acquired from having seen a similar end achieved by a different means, such as having seen an object retrieved by opening a desk drawer.

At the culmination of the sensorimotor period, the child is able to use symbolic behavior. Through combinations of mental representations, new means to ends can be achieved and used, even though they are temporally removed from the original source. And the first manifestations of pretense or symbolic play make their appearance.

Preoperational period. The cognitive capabilities of the preschool child take on considerably different qualities from those in the earlier, sensorimotor, period. The primary mark of this change is a noticeable difference in the child's ability, even at 2 years of age, to use the semantic (meaning) components of symbol systems. Piaget (Piaget & Inhelder, 1969) calls this new ability the semiotic function, because it refers to the use of symbols as a general class rather than the use of only the symbols of the language system. Growth in the semiotic function facilitates dealing with objects and events that are not physically present.

Several new behavior patterns emerge in this period. Although they do not appear in any particular temporal order (i.e., they appear more or less simultaneously), they do differ in complexity. These behaviors are deferred imitation, symbolic play, drawing or direct graphic representation, mental imagery, and verbal evocation of events that are not present at the time.

As a result of these changes, the child's ability to communicate grows. The child can gather information and transmit it to others, accomplishments that permit rapid learning. He or she can respond to the commands of others, control others verbally, make demands or requests of others, instruct, be instructed, and the like. (However, see the discussion of perspective taking, below, for qualifications.)

Language, too, can be used to control one's own behavior. Speech, at first impulsive, gradually gives way to its primary semantic function: conveying meaning. Luria (1961) suggests that this accomplishment, for the purpose of self-regulation, proceeds through three stages: Initially (about 2–3 years of age) behavior is controlled solely by the verbal commands of another person. Later, at about 3–5 years, the child's own overt speech regulates the action called for, and, finally, at 4 or 5 years of age, behavior is regulated by internal speech (thinking). Accordingly, the self-regulatory facet of language becomes less impulsive and more semantic, eventually requiring only covert rather than overt expression. Self-regulation is achieved by other forms of symbols (such as gestures, lights, and sounds), as well (Flavell, 1977). Children around 4 years of age were found, for example, to inhibit their own responses for a given time period by employing distractions, falling asleep, or other ploys that obviously do not have the same qualities as direct overt speech (Mischel, Ebbesen, & Zeiss, 1972).

Concrete operations period. The changes occurring with the transition to a new period are not jumps, as may seem to be implied. Changes occur gradually during a given period, each period containing vestigial reminders of earlier periods. These points will become more apparent in the following description of the concrete operations period, which corresponds roughly to the elementary school years.

Children enter this period with several cognitive skills related to their growing knowledge. Language and other symbol systems are skillfully used to communicate both to peers and adults and for self-regulation of behavior. Invariants (identity of objects) are dealt with on a qualitative basis. Differentiations can be made among groups of people, a necessary requirement for perspective taking. Memory improves. Nevertheless, these capabilities evolve gradually. For example, children of 4 or 5 can easily find their way back home from a place nearby. Yet when given *miniatures* of objects that are located along this path, they are unable to place them in a way that forms a spatial representation. What is represented in sensorimotor activity thus has not yet achieved the status, but clearly is a necessary precursor, of a coordinated mental representation. During this period the child begins to think accurately and to separate the intuitive from the logical. Judgments are based on observations rather than guesses. The child is able to draw conclusions, to relate observations to classes of objects, and to count, all of which are important for testing reality.

The task traditionally used to represent the changes occurring in the concrete operations period is the conservation task. For example, one of two identical glass containers, equally filled with water, is poured into a tall thin cylindrical container. The child is then asked if there is now more, less, or the same amount as in the original. In the preoperational (i.e., the preschool) period, the response usually is that there is more or less water in the new container but rarely the same. On the other hand, the child who is in the concrete operations period responds that the volumes are the same and does so without equivocation or hesitation.

The conservation task requires that the child deal with the initial state, the intervening process of transformation, and the final state. A characteristic of the concrete operations period is ability to handle such considerations concurrently, provided the materials can be perceived directly. However, the child is unable to deal with verbal statements of hypothetical problems or statements that require mental manipulations of three or more premises.

The child's performance on the conservation tasks reflects progressive changes in cognitive ability. First, preoperational children deal primarily with what they perceive, the initial and final state. The operational child, makes inferences about what happens in the transition. Second, the preoperational child centers on one dimension—in the example of the glass containers, either on height, in which case there is said to be "more," or on width, in which case there is less. Operational children take into account the changes in both height and width; they decenter and are able to examine the relation between the two dimensions. Third, the preoperational child's judgments are based on qualitative characteristics of what is perceived, whereas the operational child's judgments are based on the identity of the numerical, quantitative, relationships (Bearison, 1969). Finally, the preoperational child sees the initial and final states as being irreversible. The operational child is aware of the principles of inversion and compensation; more height but less width is interchangeable with less height and more width, and the act of pouring does not make a difference. The complete sequence, for the operational child is seen to be reversible. Nevertheless, reversibility is a complex structure and may not appear clearly in the child's behavior until late in the operational period (Gelman & Weinberg, 1972).

Conservation in several kinds of tasks emerges in approximately the following order (Piaget & Inhelder, 1969): number, area, length, mass, and volume. In all these tasks, children in the concrete operations period are no longer depending on sheer perceptual differences. They know what constitutes a problem and what does not. They can engage in proof by quantitative means without regard for irrelevant apparent differences.

More skills than conservation are acquired during the concrete operations period. Seriation, for example, progresses gradually. Progressively longer sticks at first cannot be coordinated into a single ascending series; later, the task is performed systematically by first selecting the smallest stick, then adding to it the smallest stick of the group left, and so on, until the series is completed. The relation of the person's schemata to memory can be seen clearly in one of Piaget's interesting observations regarding seriations. Upon reproducing, by drawing, a series of progressively larger sticks, the preoperational child tends to draw the sticks in groups of the same size, or sets of small and large sticks, rather than as a uniformly ascending series. However, when asked six months later to draw from memory the earlier presentation, the child draws the representation accurately. Thus, changes in one part of the system—for example, the knowledge structure—can affect another part of the system, such as memorial capacity.

The ability to classify follows a similar orderly pattern. When given a set of wooden beads, eight of which are green and two of which are yellow, the child is asked, "Are there more wooden beads or more green beads?" The child's response in the preoperational period is usually "more green beads." He does not see the inclusion property of green and yellow within the set of wooden beads. The understanding of the relation between the subset and the entire class is achieved at about the age of eight.

The understanding of numbers, an important concept in a technological society, grows concomitantly with classification and seriation. It occurs when numbers of objects can be separated from their spatial arrangement. Earlier, in the preoperational period, the child believed that two rows, with equal numbers of objects in each, are not numerically equivalent when one of the rows is spread out.

Flavell (1977) summarized from several sources some of the skills that are acquired in understanding numbers (see also Gelman, 1978b; Schaeffer, Eggleston, & Scott, 1974). A brief account of that summary will be presented. One skill to be developed in the use of numbers is "subitizing," or the ability to recognize, spontaneously, the number of objects simply by perceiving an array. However, with increased understanding the older child, as with the adult, recognizes that when the number of objects is increased, estimates of numbers based on perceptions are untrustworthy and one must resort to counting.

Counting is an important numerical skill that is acquired early. It first appears as an exercise in which the numbers are rattled off without meaning. Then counting is used for other things, such as determining equivalency of small sets and later for adding and subtracting objects from arrays and the like.

During the middle-childhood period the child learns that numbers have both cardinal (e.g., there are ten objects in a row and ten is a larger set than nine) and ordinal (e.g., the object at the end is the tenth object and 10 is higher in the number set than is 9) properties. Children in middle childhood can use either written or arabic forms of numerals. They can also make corresponding sets, based on the use of numbers, with different objects by either counting off the number of objects in each set or placing them in one-to-one correspondence. They can compare set sizes, using "more than" and "less than" accurately to denote differences. In keeping with these skills, the child learns the basic rules by which the number system operates and the basis for counting (i.e., that each succeed-

ing number is higher than the present one, or the rule $N = n + 1$).

Each of the number skills described undergoes subtle changes. In the early stages of counting, for example, children have difficulty in just touching each of a series of objects once in turn (Potter & Levy, 1968). Later, in counting, they may skip a number, or may forget the number of the last object named (Wang, Resnick, & Boozer, 1971). In sum, the child does not learn arithmetic skills in isolation but learns the understandings that accompany them as well (e.g., that the spatial arrangement is not an indicator of the number of items in a row), again illustrating that cognitive development in any area is a gradual accrual of many functions rather than a sudden appearance of a single important function at a given age (Gelman, 1972).

The list of structures mentioned or described above as illustrative of accomplishment during the concrete operations period is impressive. Yet it still is only a partial listing. Among these are other acquisitions, including notions of time, velocity, causality, space, and motion. Other realms of growth during this period, which touch on cognitive development, include the social, moral, and affective facets of the child's life.

Formal operations period. The final stage, that of mature thought, is initiated in the preadolescent period and continues throughout adolescence. The child who has successfully accomplished the cognitive tasks involved in the concrete operations period can now begin to use formal operations. Thus, the adolescent can think logically about abstract and hypothetical concepts, as well as about concrete situations. In the formal operations period, objects no longer need to be present in order for the reasoning about them to occur; the problems can be context-free. Since symbolic representations can be employed, it is possible for the person to combine objects, ideas, and events that otherwise would seem disconnected or impossible, to arrive at a reasonable solution. Assumptions rather than concrete objects can be acted upon. Symbols without referential meaning can be manipulated. Several statements can be related in systematic, logical fashion. Operations can be employed for performing logical combinations, whether of objects, propositions, or variables, to arrive at conclusions.

The two reversibilities of inversion and reciprocity (compensation), which made their initial appearance in the middle-childhood period, now function in dynamic relation to each other. One schema in which processes appear is that of proportionality. In the concrete operations period, for example, the lever principle involves simply the understanding that to achieve equilibrium, two objects, placed initially at opposite ends of a lever, are moved individually toward or away from the fulcrum. On the other hand, at the formal operations period, the solution can be arrived at by employing the logic of inverse proportionality between hypothetical or real values for the variables of weight and length. The operations of inversion and compensation become incorporated into other schemata (structures) critical to logical thinking, including sets, equilibriums, transformations, probabilities, and double reference systems. Thus, both hypothetical and proportional reasoning are characteristic of the formal operations period. Formal operations provide the underpinnings of scientific thought, in which one must formulate and test hypotheses systematically and in which all possible alternative outcomes are considered.

There is considerable uniformity across peoples within and across cultures in achievement of the concrete operations period. There is much less uniformity in manifestations of the types of thinking involved in the formal operations period, whether one considers cognitive development (Flavell, 1977) or mature levels of moral development (Kohlberg, 1969).

What Develops?   The facets of cognition that develop with maturity are as yet undefined. Current targets for investigation can be broadly classified as changes in capacity, changes in strategies, and changes in the form of knowledge acquired. (Siegler, 1978). Representative of these classes are the Piagetian structures, some of which have been identified earlier in this entry. Other changes include memory development, perceptual development, schema development, concept development, metamemory, and perspective-taking abilities. The last five areas will be discussed briefly below. The reader will recognize that these are the more specific components of the species-general behaviors represented in the stage theories described above.

Perceptual development.   Perceptual development is an essential forerunner of cognitive development. What is "seen" or "heard" will determine how one reacts; conversely, "What is seen or heard depends on what one already knows." All information around us cannot be used; there is too much of it. Accordingly, there must be a selection. What is selected and what categories are constructed depend on the perceived context (Bransford & McCarrell, 1974) and the higher-order (general) knowledge of the perceiver (Pittenger, Shaw, & Mark, 1979). The percept is a source of data-driven input (external stimulation), but it, in turn, is influenced by conceptual-driven input (what one knows).

Some of the changes that occur in perceptual development are changes in information pickup, selective attention, and differentiation (Rosinski, 1977). Information pickup, in visual perception, refers to the ability to control eye movements for information. The construction of the eye does not permit seeing all parts of a large display simultaneously. Only parts of it are seen at a time. In the adult, the parts that are seen are determined by expertly controlled movements. The total is then "constructed," giving the subjective impression that the whole is seen. Young infants have only restricted control of eye movements, with minimal fine control. With older children, the eye movements become more directed and systematic. In addition to control of eye movements, more specific information is used with increasing age, an important re-

quirement for reading, listening, and extraction of meaning (Gibson, 1969).

What is selectively attended to also undergoes changes. Children may at first attend to all the information, but with experience only information that is relevant for a given purpose is identified. Similarly, with increasing age there is a corresponding differentiation of what is attended to for given purposes. Differentiation occurs on the basis of how the person organizes or uses the organization of incoming information, whether in the form of auditory, textual, or pictorial material. Older children can come to identify and use organization economically, whereas they neglected it or used it inefficiently in earlier years (Gibson & Levin, 1975).

The developmental changes that occur in perception represent the increasing use of what one knows; from sheer perception (dependence on immediate experience) in the early years to conception (the use of conceptual higher-order information) in the later years (Wohlwill, 1962). Such changes can be traced in the dimensions of the growing independence from the need for redundancy, distractibility by irrelevant information, and the requirement that events must be located in close temporal-spatial relationships for them to be integrated.

In the process of perceptual learning, as in other learning, three levels of change can be identified: first, distinctive features among alternative events are identified; second, some characteristics of events come to have invariant properties, such as the converging of lines in the perception of perspective; and, third, individual events become organized into higher-order structures such as sentences, story plots, and musical compositions (Gibson & Levin, 1975).

Schemata.   A critical variable affecting perception and cognition is the knowledge one has already acquired. This point is central to Piaget's theory, in which such knowledge is represented in the form of schemes, an organization of mental structures at a given level of development. Current theories have incorporated the facts, concepts, and organization of knowledge as significant determiners of behavior. The term "schema," traceable to both Piaget (1966 [1954]) and Bartlett (1932), has been commonly applied to such knowledge structures (also see Ausubel, 1962). These orientations encompass the stored consequences and interpretations of experiences (Rumelhart & Ortony, 1977) and thereby represent the current world view of the person.

The schema is not a mere collection of facts, images, abstractions, or other residues of experience but is highly organized. It has been demonstrated that even young, preschool children can, with some limitations, use cause-effect relations (Bullock & Gelman, 1979), classification processes (Rosch et al., 1976), temporal order (Brown, 1976), semantic regularities (Piaget's semiotic function), and the like; all of which are constituents of the knowledge structures.

The cognitive capacities of even the young infant include basic (most typical) categorization levels (see Mervis & Rosch, 1981), a necessary prerequisite to differentiation of the schemata. Young infants show this ability in experimental situations for some kinds of categories as early as 10 months. At about 3 years they can sort objects into basic levels but not subordinate or superordinate categories. At around 5 years their final categorization of a borderline exemplar (for example, a chicken may not be classified, initially, as a bird) is similar to the adult's categorization but only after considerable "pendulum" cognitive activity of hesitation and vacillation (Nelson & Nelson, 1978). Thus, basic representative examples (for example, a robin as a prototype bird) of a concept are learned first, followed by learning of less representative examples.

Schemata function as conceptual input to interact with, and therefore modify the interpretation of, data input (i.e., external stimuli such as visual or auditory stimuli). They enter into attending, perceiving, remembering, comprehending, reading, and performing motor skills (Fischer, 1980). They form the basis within these functions in determining what is attended to, what is learned, what kinds of inferences are made, and what is recalled. All these functions have been implied in the Piagetian notions of accommodation and assimilation. To illustrate, an early study by Piaget (1926) led to the conclusion that children had difficulty in remembering. This conclusion was drawn from the observation that when retelling stories, children's descriptions were inaccurate, scrambled, and generally poor. The reasons were attributed to the child's egocentrism and lack of understanding of temporal relations.

Thus, the preoperational child was considered to be insufficiently mature to use logical or temporal order for mediating performance where reversibility is required (Beilin, 1975; Brown & Murphy, 1975; Piaget & Inhelder, 1969).

Although the views about children's use of schema are unresolved at this writing, there is a growing body of evidence to show that children, under some circumstances, do understand and use the sequences involved in temporal order (Beilin, 1975; Gelman, 1978a, 1979). A set of observations (Schank & Abelson, 1977) of a single child over a period of years indicates some progressive changes in the structure of story scripts (schemata for the general events, and their order, in narratives). At about 3 years of age, the child treated a story as a series of relatively routine events, each of which was equally important. A year later the story was treated as a series of episodes much like those in the scripts of the adult.

Also contrary to Piaget's finding of the child's memory as inadequate (Piaget, 1968), a recent study (Mandler & Johnson, 1977) shows that first-graders, fourth-graders, and college students recall a story in the same way. Setting and outcomes are most likely to be recalled, and the reactions of the characters are least likely to be recalled. Most important, however, is that children can recall accurately stories with structures that are consistent with their schemata (Stein & Glenn, 1979). Children 3 and 4 years old can remember the events in such stories very well on an immediate recall task, whether the events are placed initially in an arbitrary or in a logical order (Brown, 1976). However, on a delayed recall task, recall of the arbitrary arrangement was poor. Nevertheless, the children's responses contained attempts to provide an order, even though it did not correspond to the original one. Thus, young children's schemata permit simple arrangements of events into orderly sequences but are not sufficiently developed to facilitate long-term retention of that order (also see McClure, Mason, & Barnitz, 1979).

In general, there is progressive growth in schemata. Children as young as 4 or 5 years do have adultlike schemata for stories (Poulsen et al., 1979). Nevertheless, when processing demands depart radically from traditional formats or from the age level of the child, the ability of the child to employ the appropriate schema or to maintain it over long periods of time appears to be limited (Spiro, 1981).

Metacognition. Both children's and adult's schemata undergo changes; voids are filled in, new relationships are incorporated, and the schemata are extended. In the adult, changes occur in part on the basis of decisions concerning where the changes are to be made—for example, whether one's abilities limit the extent of the change, whether the task difficulty requires different motivation levels, and whether some strategies are more useful than others. Since information provided by external reality is transformed for storage, the central mechanism must be capable of planning and evaluating its operations (Brown, 1977, 1978). Such a control system, comprising, in part, metacognitions, should provide for (1) sensitivity to capacity limitations; (2) knowledge of general criteria for effective completion of a task and of rules, short cuts, and the like for proceeding; (3) ways of identifying the nature of problems to be solved; (4) monitoring an orderly sequence of procedures for completing a task; and (5) continual checking of the value or effectiveness of routines used against criteria to be achieved.

Metacognitions are held about people, tasks, and strategies (Flavell, 1978, 1979; Flavell & Wellman, 1977). The person variables are knowledges about oneself or others; about their ways of understanding, qualities of their capacities, and limitations on their abilities. The task variables include cognitions about how problems can vary in difficulty, how much information may be available under certain circumstances, and appraisal of the difficulty or ease with which a task can be performed. The strategy variables constitute a large category encompassing all the child must learn about the voluntary activities that are available for attending, perceiving, listening, coding information, retrieving information, and all the other processes involved in learning and comprehending (Kreutzer, Leonard, & Flavell, 1975).

Children have more metacognitive deficits, because of their lack of experience, than do adults (Flavell & Wellman, 1977). Growth of metacognitive knowledge apparently begins in the unconscious mode being automatically acquired and then is followed by a stage in which there is increased conscious self-regulation and self-monitoring in the use of that knowledge and in the acquisition of new knowledge (Brown & DeLoache, 1978; Vygotsky, 1962).

Brown and DeLoache (1978) summarize a number of studies to show that development trends occur in three areas of reading: extracting main ideas from texts, visual scanning, and retrieval of information from storage. In these accomplishments the trend is one of increasing refinement, of sensitivity to and awareness of the demands of the task, of knowledge about one's own problem-solving potential, and of appropriate strategies for improving performance. Other areas in which metacognition has been studied in children's development include the comprehension of nonverbal communication, memory development (Miller & Bigi, 1979), perception (Flavell, et al., 1981a), communication and comprehension (Flavell, 1977), referential communication (Markman, 1977, 1979), problem solving (Brown & DeLoache, 1978), and reading (Di Vesta, Hayward, & Orlando, 1979; Meyers & Paris, 1978).

Expertise in the use of metacognitions is developed through increased experience with nonspecific activities (strategies) such as attending, searching, or remembering—in fact, with any structures, including the Piagetian structures. Furthermore, parents and teachers provide help in this development by defining the child's goals and arranging problems so that children deal with simpler sequences. They also provide instruction in such strategies as predicting, monitoring, and self-testing (Brown, Campione, & Barclay, 1978). Such strategies, when deliberately taught, have been found to remain a year later and even to undergo increased refinement. Some evidence (Butterfield, Wambold, & Belmont, 1973) also indicates that memory training of retarded adolescents can result in improved recall surpassing that of their normal counterparts. (See also Campione & Brown, 1977, for related studies with educable mentally retarded children.)

Concept development. Current definitions suggest that concepts are organized sets of diverse objects or events that are nameable (Nelson, 1977). They differ from such Piagetian structures as invariance, causality, order, and conservation, which are logical organizations but are not identified by name.

Concepts are functionally important parts of the schemata. They allow simplification of the infinite variety of single events by grouping those that are similar in some fashion. They allow classification of a novel experience, object, or event. They permit predictability of the consequences or functions of objects classified in a given category. Concepts once named facilitate learning, memory, and communication. Thus, they constitute the major subsumers or anchors (Ausubel, 1962) at basic, subordinate, and superordinate levels of knowledge structures (schemata). Undoubtedly, there are among human beings universal basic-level processing tendencies to conceptualize. Basic-level processes are characteristically those processes that the person uses without conscious effort and are used with a degree of efficiency, by the end of the sensorimotor period (Flavell & Wellman, 1977). They appear to control basic-level categorization (the formation of natural categories) (Mervis & Rosch, 1981).

Basic-level categories or concepts are those that meet the requirements of having the common properties of similar motor patterns, similar configurations, and a recognizable image for all members of a category (e.g., chair versus furniture) (Rosch et al., 1976). Further, they can be named by common words in the language, are named spontaneously, and can be identified by a general configuration, a prototype, without analysis of specific attributes. In sign language, for example, only single signs are used for basic-level categories such as chair or bird, whereas multiple signs are used for superordinate or subordinate categories (Newport & Bellugi, 1978).

This characterization implies that even infants must begin to categorize if they are to interact efficiently with the potentially infinite variety of events or objects they will encounter. Nonetheless, all events initially experienced are necessarily novel for the infant (Nelson, 1977). With increasing experience and perceptual memory accompanying experience, there is the emergence of familiarity, of recurrence of events with characteristic similarities such that predictions of the properties of novel events can be made. It was once believed that children were unable to form categories before the age of 5–7 years. New experimental techniques have provided evidence to contradict this earlier conclusion. (By measuring time spent by the infant in examining novel objects, it can be implied that increased examination time of an object from a novel category reflects the recognition that the object belongs in a new category rather than a familiar one and, therefore, must be examined.) By such procedures it has been shown (Cohen & Strauss, 1979) that infants as young as 10 months can easily form basic-level categories.

Rosch et al. (1976) were unable to demonstrate discernible trends in the use of basic-level categories from 3 years of age to adulthood. The changes occurred primarily at the fifth-grade level in the ability of children to use superordinate classifications. Accordingly, it can be seen that the development of basic-level categories precedes development of categories at other levels (Rosch et al., 1976).

In the formation of a category, representativeness is important; not all members of a category are equally representative, as was once assumed (e.g., see Bourne, Dominowski, & Loftus, 1979); category membership is first established for the most representative exemplars, the prototype, and last for the least representative exemplars (Mervis & Pani, 1980; Rosch, 1975).

Along with early development of basic-level categories comes the development of scripts (Nelson, 1977). Scripts are not concepts, but they are similar to concepts in that they represent organization of events. The organization is based on spatial-temporal relations, which permit the prediction of the occurrence of events (e.g., the child could have a script of the major events related to "attending nursery school"). As with structures, scripts generally are not named, whereas concepts always are. However, the importance of scripts in concept development is that they provide one of the frameworks within which concepts are placed.

Other basic trends in the development of concept categories can be identified (see Mervis & Rosch, 1981). Infants' behavior reflects the beginning of conceptual development. Given a new toy, they will find it novel or interesting and begin to identify its attributes by the means available to them, by throwing, biting, hitting, or selecting it because of its brightness or color (Nelson, 1977). Botanical labels are learned first for basic-level categorizations and later for the superordinate or subordinate levels (Doughtery, 1978, cited in Mervis & Rosch, 1981). Young children prefer to process information holistically rather than to separate the specific attributes, although they are capable of doing so (Kemler & Smith, 1979; Mervis & Rosch, 1981). Adults, on the other hand, tend to view the attributes as separable rather than integral dimensions of the object. With development, concepts become increasingly related to one another in hierarchical organization. In an earlier tradition (Bruner, Olver, & Greenfield, 1966; Vygotsky, 1962), the development sequence was described as proceeding from "heaps" of unrelated objects, to complexes or pseudoconcepts based on fragmentary attributes that partially defined the full meaning of the concept, to true concepts as superordinate sets of relations. Even when children form "heaps," one should recognize that they are employing the basic process of grouping events; there is at least a beginning of the metacognition that objects can be put into categories and that those things in a category are somehow related.

Gelman (1978a, 1979) has reviewed a great deal of evidence to show that young children are capable of classification ability. Her evidence indicates that the appearance of inability to employ rules for classification may be attributed to (1) the lesser inclination of children to define the organization of materials the way the adult requires them to, (2) the inability of children to access a given level of organization (i.e., the organization may be available but cannot be used spontaneously), (3) being presented with too many diverse examples for a category, some of which are not good examples, and (4) the children's use of a strategy that is inconsistent with adult expectations about what strategy ought to be used.

Perspective taking and egocentricism. To study perspective taking, Piaget (Piaget & Inhelder, 1956) had young preschool children become familiar with a model of three mountains. They were then asked to select, from several pictures, the one picture that represented the scene viewed by a doll located opposite the child. Regardless of the doll's position, the children always picked the same view, the one seen from their own positions. Earlier

studies on how individuals perceive their environment are currently being extended to how people use, represent, and manipulate representations (cognitive maps) of their spatial environments (see Liben, Patterson, & Newcombe, 1980).

The presumed inability to consider different perspectives has been attributed to the child's egocentrism, or the inability to recognize that another's viewpoint is different from one's own. Egocentrism, in these terms, appears in other facets of behavior, including the early phases of the development of moral judgment and values, reasoning, rules of play, reality judgments, and communication.

With increasing age, clear-cut changes in perspective taking occur. In communicating (Piaget, 1926), for example, the preschool child must come to consider the status and abilities of the listener. The evolution of this ability from egocentric speech (Piaget, 1926) is initiated in the form of echolalia, a form of speech that seems to exist solely for the speaker's benefit without regard for the listener's needs and without intent to communicate. A later phase (4 to 6 years of age) in egocentric speech finds children conversing in a collective monologue: several interacting children each with a different topic of conversation and seemingly unresponsive to the conversations of others. At approximately 6 years of age, socialized speech emerges; the listener's needs are taken into account, and conversations are truly interactive and responsive.

Following Piaget's lead (1926), Krauss and Glucksberg (1969) studied the ability of children at different age levels to use referential communication; that is, the ability to communicate through language alone which objects (targets or referents) are being talked about from among a set of alternatives, an activity that makes severe demands on perspective taking. Objects of uncommon shapes were used, and the communicator and recipient of the message were separated by an opaque barrier. The studies confirmed the earlier findings. Whether speaking to other children or to adults, the children's communication included their encoding ability (again indicating insufficient knowledge rather than capacity). The labels assigned to the complex objects were based on self-encodings. Thus, the listener was unable to identify the target object, although the children, on a later test, could associate their own object labels with the same objects. Similarly, when culturally uniform labels are used for common objects, the children had no difficulty in communicating the referent's characteristics. Often, when the children were asked why the listener did not perform the task correctly, they would blame the listener for her inadequacy (an incorrect metacognition) (Robinson & Robinson, 1977). The young child, as listener, too, may not have acquired the metacognitions that (1) the communication helps in delineating the alternatives, (2) one must question the speaker when information is left out, or (3) that one must be sensitive to gross inadequacies in the message (Markman, 1979). Similar difficulties arise in reading when children in middle childhood are found to have difficulty in another form of perspective taking, that of separating the more important underlying themes in stories from those less important (Brown & Smiley, 1977).

Gelman's (1978a, 1979) compelling reviews of the evidence lead her to conclude that when tasks are appropriately matched to children's knowledge, they can and do take the listener or observer into consideration. When a preschool child explained the workings of a toy to a 2-year-old, the utterances were short, syntactically simple, and intended to direct and monitor the observer's attention. Explanations to an adult, on the other hand, were longer, more complex sentences were used, and the content was oriented toward using the adult as a resource. Similar sensitivities to age differences were observed in choices of toys for younger and older children, in predictions about adults' and 2-year-olds' motor and memorial abilities, about information that would be known or not depending on the circumstances, in visual-perspective-taking tasks, and in sensitivity to needs of different people (e.g., blindfolded people).

Task difficulty contributes to the egocentric-like appearance of perspective taking in the preschool years. Experience eventually contributes to the child's understanding of and sensitivity to the makeup of stimuli (i.e., the referent-nonreferent arrays from which targets are selected for reporting); what listeners with different characteristics know and do not know; feedback provided by the listener; and the role of the listener (Glucksberg, Krauss, & Higgins, 1975). With development the young child learns that to communicate about objects is to describe their differences, and there is an increase in the child's ability to encode complex situations and to interpret peculiar transformations in tasks that occur from a different perspective (Flavell et al., 1981b; Flavell et al., 1980).

Summary. The current study of cognitive development considers the relative effects of maturation and experience on the role of the schemata in the acquisition of new knowledge. The mental representations at each level of development are used in perceptions and comprehension of new events. Both influence the products of those perceptions, which, in turn, have an influence on schema change. Thus, the schemata, perceptions, and products comprise an interactive whole.

A major issue raised by this view pits the acquisition of knowledge against the sheer aggregation of information. How best to achieve real knowledge involves a consideration of several facets of the educative process (see Kohlberg & Mayer, 1972). Certainly readiness is important, but readiness is defined in terms of what schemata are available, how children at different levels of development process information and by what strategies.

The conditions for maximization of schema change need to be identified. Maturation affects the very young child's development most, whereas experience is most influential in the development of the older person. Yet the more firmly schemata are established, the more resistant they are to change because of attempts to make the new infor-

mation consistent with what is known. The best conditions for schemata change may be those suggested by Bruner (1960), Ausubel (Ausubel, Novak, & Hanesian, 1978), and Collins (1977): the gentler discovery method and the harsher Socratic dialogue. Nevertheless, there is still the need to identify precisely where and under what conditions such methods are advantageously used compared with other methods, such as the didactic.

The nature of enrichment must be specified. None of the evidence suggests that attempts at drastic acceleration from one stage to another should be attempted as an optimal procedure. Other forms of enrichment are implied, either integrative or elaborative. Integrative enrichment links many ideas and experiences around a common conceptual or categorical representation. Elaborative enrichment retains the essential character of a structure and links that structure to other concepts or categories (e.g., across disciplines in the most extreme case). These ends are not achieved by downward extensions of more advanced education but rather by breadth of experience at a given level of development.

As more is learned about what develops, the nature of the curriculum may be questioned. There may be attempts to incorporate more process-oriented or cognitive-developmental objectives with the goal of high transferability, rather than the current emphasis on behavioral objectives aimed at immediate outcomes (Kohlberg & Mayer, 1972). Process-oriented curricula do not neglect content but rather provide for continuity in development by consideration of the relationship of content to be acquired to the capacities and abilities represented by the schemata of the person, structures acquired, and processing strategies available and employable by the person at successive stages of development. Indeed, inadequate knowledge and inefficient strategies have been identified as important sources of apparent or presumed lower intellectual levels (Bransford, 1979) or memorial capacity (Chi, 1978). The resolution of the issues implied by present knowledge of cognitive development may require informed dialectical analysis, since applied research has not yet advanced to the point of providing clear-cut answers.

Francis J. Di Vesta

See also Cognition and Memory; Intelligence; Language Development; Learning; Neurosciences.

REFERENCES

Ausubel, D. P. A subsumption theory of meaningful verbal learning and retention. *Journal of General Psychology*, 1962, *66*, 213–224.

Ausubel, D. P.; Novak, J. D.; & Hanesian, H. *Educational Psychology: A Cognitive View* (2nd ed.). New York: Holt, Rinehart, & Winston, 1978.

Bartlett, F. C. *Remembering.* Cambridge, England: Cambridge University Press, 1932.

Bearison, D. J. Role of measurement operations in the acquisition of conservation. *Developmental Psychology*, 1969, *1*, 653–660.

Beilin, H. *Studies in the Cognitive Basis of Language Development.* New York: Academic Press, 1975.

Bourne, L. E., Jr.: Dominowski, R. L.; & Loftus, E. F. *Cognitive Processes.* Englewood Cliffs, N.J.: Prentice-Hall, 1979.

Bransford, J. D. *Human Cognition: Learning, Understanding, and Remembering.* Belmont, Calif.: Wadsworth, 1979.

Bransford, J. D., & McCarrell, N. S. A sketch of a cognitive approach to comprehension: Some thoughts about understanding what it means to comprehend. In W. B. Weimer & D. S. Palermo (Eds.), *Cognition and the Symbolic Processes.* New York: Wiley, 1974.

Brown, A. L. The construction of temporal succession by preoperational children. In A. D. Pick (Ed.), *Minnesota Symposium on Child Psychology* (Vol. 10). Minneapolis: University of Minnesota Press, 1976.

Brown, A. L. Development, schooling and the acquisition of knowledge about knowledge: Comments on Chapter 7 by Nelson. In R. C. Anderson, R. J. Spiro, & W. E. Montague (Eds.), *Schooling and the Acquisition of Knowledge.* Hillsdale, N.J.: Lawrence Erlbaum Associates, 1977.

Brown, A. L. Knowing when, where, and how to remember: A problem of metacognition. In R. Glaser (Eds.), *Advances in Instructional Psychology.* New York: Halsted Press, 1978.

Brown, A. L.; Campione, J. C.; & Barclay, C. R. *Training Self-checking Routines for Estimating Test Readiness: Generalization from List Learning to Prose Recall* (Technical Report No. 94). Champaign-Urbana: University of Illinois Center for the Study of Reading, 1978. (ERIC Document Reproduction Service No. ED 158 226)

Brown, A. L., & DeLoache, J. S. Skills, plans, and self-regulation. In R. S. Siegler (Ed.), *Children's Thinking: What Develops?* Hillsdale, N.J.: Lawrence Erlbaum Associates, 1978.

Brown, A. L., & Murphy, M. D. Reconstruction of arbitrary versus logical sequences by preschool children. *Journal of Experimental Child Psychology,* 1975, *20,* 307–326.

Brown, A. L., & Smiley, S. S. Rating the importance of structural units of prose passages: A problem of metacognitive development. *Child Development,* 1977, *48,* 1–8.

Bruner, J. S. *The Process of Education.* Cambridge, Mass.: Harvard University Press, 1960.

Bruner, J. S.; Olver, R. R.; & Greenfield, P. M. (Eds.) *Studies in Cognitive Growth.* New York: Wiley, 1966.

Bullock, M., & Gelman, R. Preschool children's assumptions about cause and effect: Temporal ordering. *Child Development,* 1979, *50,* 89–96.

Butterfield, E. C.; Wambold, C.; & Belmont, J. M. On the theory and practice of improving short-term memory. *American Journal of Mental Deficiency,* 1973, *77,* 654–669.

Campione, J. C., & Brown, A. L. Memory and metamemory development in educable retarded children. In R. V. Kail, Jr., & J. W. Hagen (Eds.), *Perspectives on the Development of Memory and Cognition.* Hillsdale, N.J.: Lawrence Erlbaum Associates, 1977.

Chi, M. T. H. Knowledge structures and memory development. In R. Siegler (Ed.), *Children's Thinking: What Develops?* Hillsdale, N.J.: Lawrence Erlbaum Associates, 1978.

Cohen, L. B., & Strauss, M. S. Concept acquisition in the human infant. *Child Development,* 1979, *50,* 419–424.

Collins, A. Processes in acquiring knowledge. In R. C. Anderson, R. J. Spiro, & W. E. Montague (Eds.), *Schooling and the Acquisition of Knowledge.* Hillsdale, N.J.: Lawrence Erlbaum Associates, 1977.

Di Vesta, F. J.; Hayward, K. G.; & Orlando, V. P. Developmental trends in monitoring text for comprehension. *Child Development,* 1979, *50,* 97–105.

Dougherty, J. W. D. Salience and relativity in classification. *American Ethnology,* 1978, *5,* 66–80.

Emmerich, W. Continuity and stability in early social development. *Child Development,* 1964, *35,* 311–332.

Fischer, K. W. A theory of cognitive development: The control and construction of hierarchies of skills. *Psychological Review,* 1980, *87,* 477–531.

Flavell, J. H. *Cognitive Development.* Englewood Cliffs, N.J.: Prentice-Hall, 1977.

Flavell, J. H. Metacognitive development. In J. M. Scandura & C. J. Brainerd (Eds.), *Structural-Process Theories of Complex Behavior.* Alphen aan den Rijn, The Netherlands: Sijthoff & Noordhoff, 1978.

Flavell, J. H. Metacognition and cognitive monitoring: A new area of cognitive-developmental inquiry. *American Psychologist,* 1979, *34,* 906–911.

Flavell, J. H.; Everett, B. A.; Croft, K.; & Flavell, E. R. Young children's knowledge about visual perception: Further evidence for the Level one to Level two distinction. *Developmental Psychology,* 1981, *17,* 99–103. (a)

Flavell, J. H.; Flavell, E. R.; Green, F. L.; & Wilcox, S. A. The development of three spatial perspective rules. *Child Development,* 1981, *52,* 356–358. (b)

Flavell, J. H.; Speer, J. R.; Green, F. L.; & August, D. L. *The Development of Comprehension Monitoring and Knowledge about Communication.* Palo Alto, Calif.: Stanford University, 1980. (Mimeo)

Flavell, J. H., & Wellman, H. M. Metamemory. In R. V. Kail & J. W. Hagen (Eds.), *Perspectives on the Development of Memory and Cognition.* Hillsdale, N. J.: Lawrence Erlbaum Associates, 1977.

Gelman, R. Logical capacity of very young children: Number invariance rules. *Child Development,* 1972, *43,* 75–90.

Gelman, R. Cognitive development. In M. R. Rosenzweig & L. W. Porter (Eds.), *Annual Review of Psychology* (Vol. 28). Palo Alto, Calif.: Annual Reviews, Inc., 1978. (a)

Gelman, R. Counting in the preschooler: What does and does not develop. In R. S. Siegler (Ed.), *Children's Thinking: What Develops?* New York: Wiley, 1978. (b)

Gelman, R. Preschool thought. *American Psychologist,* 1979, *34,* 900–905.

Gelman, R., & Weinberg, D. H. The relationship between liquid conservation and compensation. *Child Development,* 1972, *43,* 371–383.

Gibson, E. J. *Principles of Perceptual Learning and Development.* New York: Appleton-Century-Crofts, 1969.

Gibson, E. J., & Levin, H. *The Psychology of Reading.* Cambridge, Mass.: MIT Press, 1975.

Glucksberg, S., Krauss, R.; & Higgins, E. T. The development of referential communication skills. In F. D. Horowitz (Ed.), *Review of Child Development Research* (Vol. 4). Chicago: University of Chicago Press, 1975.

Kemler, D. G., & Smith, L. B. Accessing similarity and dimensional relations: Effects of integrality and separability on the discovery of complex concepts. *Journal of Experimental Psychology: General,* 1979, *108,* 133–150.

Kohlberg, L. *Stages in the Development of Moral Thought and Action.* New York: Holt, Rinehart & Winston, 1969.

Kohlberg, L., & Mayer, R. Development as the aim of education. *Harvard Educational Review,* 1972, *42,* 449–496.

Krauss, R. M., & Glucksberg, S. M. The development of communication: Competence as a function of age. *Child Development,* 1969, *40,* 255–266.

Kreutzer, M. A.; Leonard, C.; & Flavell, J. H. An interview study of children's knowledge about memory. *Monographs of the Society for Research in Child Development,* 1975, *40*(1, Serial No. 159).

Liben, L. S.; Patterson, A. H.; & Newcombe, N. *Spatial Representation and Behavior Across the Life Span.* New York: Academic Press, 1980.

Luria, A. R. *The Role of Speech in the Regulation of Normal and Abnormal Behavior.* New York: Pergamon Press, 1961.

Mandler, J. M., & Johnson, N. J. Remembrance of things parsed: Story structure and recall. *Cognitive Psychology,* 1977, *9,* 111–151.

Markman, E. M. Realizing that you don't understand: A preliminary investigation. *Child Development,* 1977, *48,* 986–992.

Markman, E. M. Realizing that you don't understand: Elementary school children's awareness of inconsistencies. *Child Development,* 1979, *50,* 643–655.

McCall, R. B.; Eichorn, D. H.; & Hogarty, P. S. Transitions in early development. *Monographs of the Society for Research in Child Development,* 1977, *42*(3, Serial No. 171).

McCall, R. B. Nature-nurture and the two realms of development: A proposed integration with respect to mental development. *Child Development,* 1981, *52,* 1–12.

McClure, E.; Mason, J.; & Barnitz, J. Story structure and age effects on children's ability to sequence stories (Technical Report No. 187). Champaign: University of Illinois Center for the Study of Reading, 1979. (Eric Document Reproduction Service No. ED 170 732)

Mervis, C. B., & Pani, J. R. Acquisition of basic object categories. *Cognitive Psychology,* 1980, *12,* 496–522.

Mervis, C. B., & Rosch, E. Categorization of natural objects. In M. R. Rosenzweig & L. W. Porter (Eds.), *Annual Review of Psychology* (Vol. 32). Palo Alto, Calif.: Annual Reviews, Inc., 1981.

Meyers, M., & Paris, S. G. Children's metacognitive knowledge about reading. *Journal of Educational Psychology,* 1978, *70,* 680–690.

Miller, P. H., & Bigi, L. The development of children's understanding of attention. *Merrill-Palmer Quarterly,* 1979, *25,* 236–250.

Mischel, W.; Ebbesen, E. G.; & Zeiss, A. R. Cognitive and attentional mechanisms in delay of gratification. *Journal of Personality and Social Psychology,* 1972, *21,* 204–218.

Nelson, K. Cognitive development and the acquisition of concepts. In R. C. Anderson, R. J. Spiro, & W. E. Montague (Eds.), *Schooling and the Acquisition of Knowledge.* Hillsdale, N.J.: Lawrence Erlbaum Associates, 1977.

Nelson, K. E., & Nelson, K. Cognitive pendulums and their linguistic realization. In K. E. Nelson (Ed.), *Children's Language.* New York: Gardner Press, 1978.

Newport, E. L., & Bellugi, U. Linguistic expression of category levels in a visual gestural language. In E. Rosch & B. B. Lloyd (Eds.), *Cognition and Categorization.* Hillsdale, N.J.: Lawrence Erlbaum Associates, 1978.

Piaget, J. *The Language and Thought of the Child.* New York: Harcourt, Brace, 1926.

Piaget, J. *The Origins of Intelligence in Children.* New York: International Universities Press, 1966. (Originally published, 1954.)

Piaget, J. *On the Development of Memory and Identity.* Barre, Mass.: Clark University Press and Barre Publishers, 1968.

Piaget, J. *The Child's Conception of Time.* London: Routledge & Kegan Paul, 1969.

Piaget, J., & Inhelder, B. *The Child's Conception of Space.* London: Routledge & Kegan Paul, 1956.

Piaget, J., & Inhelder, B. *The Psychology of the Child.* New York: Basic Books, 1969.

Pittenger, J. B.; Shaw, R. E.; & Mark, L. S. Perceptual information for the age level of faces as a higher-order invariant growth. *Journal of Experimental Psychology: Human Perceptual Performance,* 1979, *5,* 478–493.

Potter, M. C., & Levy, E. I. Spatial enumeration without counting. *Child Development,* 1968, *39,* 265–272.

Poulsen, D.; Kintsch, E.; Kintsch, W.; & Premack, D. Children's comprehension and memory for stories. *Journal of Experimental Child Psychology,* 1979, *28,* 379–403.

Robinson, E. J., & Robinson, W. P. Children's explanations of communication failure and the inadequacy of the misunderstood message. *Developmental Psychology,* 1977, *13,* 156–161.

Rosch, E. Cognitive representations of semantic categories. *Journal of Experimental Psychology: General,* 1975, *104,* 192–233.

Rosch, E.; Mervis, C. B.; Gray, W. D.; Johnson, D. M.; & Boyes-Braem, P. Basic objects in natural categories. *Cognitive Psychology,* 1976, *8,* 323–439.

Rosinski, R. R. *The Development of Visual Perception.* Santa Monica, Calif.: Goodyear, 1977.

Rumelhart, D. E., & Ortony, A. The representation of knowledge in memory. In R. C. Anderson, R. J. Spiro, & W. E. Montague (Eds.), *Schooling and the Acquisition of Knowledge.* Hillsdale, N.J.: Lawrence Erlbaum Associates, 1977.

Schaeffer, B., Eggleston, V. H.; & Scott, J. L. Number development in young children. *Cognitive Psychology,* 1974, *6,* 357–379.

Schank, R. C., & Abelson, R. P. *Scripts, Plans, Goals, and Understanding.* Hillsdale, N.J.: Lawrence Erlbaum Associates, 1977.

Siegler, R. S. (Ed.). *Children's Thinking: What Develops?* New York: Wiley, 1978.

Spiro, R. J. Prior knowledge and story processing: Integrations, selection, and variation. *Poetics: The International Review for the Theory of Literature,* in press.

Stein, N. C., & Glenn, C. C. An analysis of story comprehension in elementary school children. In R. O. Freedle (Ed.), *New Directions in Discourse Processing.* Norwood, N.J.: Abler, 1979.

Vygotsky, L. S. *Thought and Language.* Cambridge, Mass.: MIT Press, 1962.

Wang, M. C.; Resnick, L. B.; & Boozer, R. F. The sequence of development of some early mathematics behaviors. *Child Development,* 1971, *42,* 167–178.

Wohlwill, J. From perception to inference: A dimension of cognitive development. *Monographs of the Society for Research in Child Development,* 1962, *27,* 87–112.

Wohlwill, J. *The Study of Behavioral Development.* New York: Academic Press, 1973.

COLLECTIVE NEGOTIATIONS

Schooling in the United States is highly labor-intensive, employing over 4.2 million persons and devoting three-fourths or more of expenditures to personnel costs. Bilateral negotiation between schools and employee unions has become the dominant mode for establishing wages and working conditions for these employees. Thus collective negotiations have become the core of much of the interactions between school staff and management. The central elements of labor-management relations—the negotiation process, the agreement, and its administration—are therefore subjects of direct interest in education policy development, governance, and research.

State of Education Negotiations

Negotiations are subjects of interest in their own right as well as in terms of how they affect the educational processes in the schools. Labor-management relations are complex and costly, involving most of the school staff at one time or another. The direct and indirect costs, as well as the potential for improved operation or disruption, have stimulated the study of collective negotiation itself, independent of its effects on the rest of the organization, which may be substantial.

The state of collective negotiation—its history, development, and policy setting—is treated in the following section. Subsequent sections deal with the process, impacts on schooling, and prospects for further development and evolution of the process.

The Bargaining Process. Bargaining has grown rapidly from a rare, low-visibility process in the early 1960s to a pervasive presence in school operation. Using the existence of a formal written agreement as an indicator of collective negotiations, a 1964 survey found only 19 agreements in force in schools and only 419 in a follow-up two years later (Wildman & Burns, 1968). This grew to 1,531 agreements in schools in 1966–1967 (Burton, 1979, p. 31). Over 16,000 collectively negotiated agreements covering school employees were reported in 1979, involving 49 percent of the school districts and 60 percent of the full-time employees (U.S. Bureau of the Census, 1980).

Public education is among the government functions with the greatest amount of bargaining activity at the state and local level. Only among local firefighters is a higher proportion of employees organized and covered by bargaining agreements than among teachers (U.S. Bureau of the Census, 1980).

When a more inclusive indicator of activity is used—presence of a collective interaction, whether or not it produces a formal written agreement—bargaining appears to be even more extensive. Negotiations over wages and working conditions extend to more than three out of four school districts. Approximately 90 percent of the school districts with over 1,000 students, surveyed in 1976, reported some collective interaction with a teacher organization (Cresswell & Murphy, 1980, p. 31). Bargaining activity is, of course, most extensive in those thirty-two states with statutes mandating or providing for public school bargaining (see summary of state policies below).

The level of activity among school employees other than teachers is probably somewhat lower than among teachers, but is more difficult to estimate. There has been some penetration of union activity into the ranks of middle managers. Approximately 21 percent (10,000) of the public school administrators in middle ranks are engaged in some form of collective negotiations with school boards (Cooper, 1979). Organization and bargaining among classified (nonprofessional) school employees is roughly coextensive with teacher activity. However, nonteaching employees are not as thoroughly organized as teachers (44.9 percent as opposed to 67.5 percent of teachers: U.S. Bureau of the Census, 1980). In some cases teacher aides are part of the teacher organization, in other districts they form a separate unit. Most state policies, however, provide for separate bargaining units for teaching and nonteaching personnel. The nonteaching personnel are typically members of general public employee unions rather than teacher organizations.

Employee Organizations. The rapid growth of bargaining activity in schools has been directly paralleled by the growth of employee membership in bargaining organizations. This growth has proceeded by two different but related processes: the transformation of the National Education Association (NEA) into a bargaining organization; and the growth of the American Federation of Teachers (AFT) through organization of new locals, often recruiting members away from the NEA. This competition and interaction has been a central part of the dynamics of teacher union growth.

That the growth of teacher unionism has been explosive is clear; the reasons for it are not. In 1965 the AFT had approximately 100,000 members and was not growing rapidly; the NEA as a national association counted over 1 million members, but was opposed to bargaining. Five years later the AFT had grown to over 200,000 members, and the NEA had changed its policy to support bargaining and strikes by teachers. By 1979 the combined membership of the NEA and AFT was over 2 million, representing 90 percent of the teaching work force in public schools (Burton, 1979; Cresswell & Murphy, 1980).

Some of this growth is accounted for by simple expansion of the teaching work force. In the 1965–1979 period, the number of public school teachers increased from 1.7 to 2.2 million (up 26 percent), and all public and private teachers increased from 1.9 to 2.4 million (up 23 percent). This is, of course, substantial growth, but not by comparison with the preceeding ten years, which had seen the virtual doubling of the number of teachers and pupils in elementary and secondary schools. By 1965 the rapid growth in enrollment had slowed considerably, but the period of rapid growth of the teacher organizations was just beginning (U.S. Department of Education, 1980; U.S. Bureau of the Census, 1980).

Part of this growth can be understood in terms of the competition between the two major teacher organizations. Much of the increase in the size of the AFT in the late 1960s and into the 1970s came at the expense of the NEA;

the AFT organized locals formerly affiliated with the NEA. The competition was costly to both organizations and led to serious merger negotiations in the 1970s. Several local unions did merge, led by the Flint, Michigan, local in 1969 and the state-level mergers in Florida and New York. However, the merger talks were generally fruitless, and the mergers were not uniformly successful; the New York merged units voted to disaffiliate with the NEA in 1976, and the Florida merger split as well.

The competition has had two apparent effects. Under the spur of the militancy and organizing success of the AFT, the NEA transformed itself into a bargaining organization. At its 1960 convention the membership soundly defeated a motion to insert the word "negotiation" into the association's policy on salary determination. By 1968 the membership had endorsed negotiations and moved to the support of strikes by teachers and other public employees (Cresswell & Murphy, 1980). The competition also spurred more aggressive organizing efforts.

There was also a parallel but somewhat less spectacular growth in the organization of the public sector generally. Between 1965 and 1979 the proportion of state and local government employees in bargaining organizations grew from less than 30 percent to over 50 percent (U.S. Bureau of the Census, 1974 and 1980). This indicates a general climate of greater acceptance of public employee unionism, which supported the unionization of teachers (Engel, 1976; Gershenfeld, 1979).

This climate of public acceptance was reflected in public policy as well. Prior to 1965 only Wisconsin had implemented a statute giving bargaining rights to public employees. In the 1965–1967 period six more states added similar statutes, and by 1979 thirty-three states had a bargaining statute for public employees; thirty-one of them covering teachers (Ross, 1980; Schneider, 1979).

The sustained growth in membership of teacher organizations during the late 1960s and early 1970s began to falter in the late 1970s. The labor market for teachers was slackening because of declining enrollments. Both the NEA and AFT lost membership from layoffs and attrition. In response the AFT moved to organize nonteaching employees. The NEA initially signed an agreement limiting competition with the American Federation of State, County, and Municipal Employees (AFSCME), which represents many nonteaching school employees. But the NEA has since increased efforts at organizing nonteachers. There has also been a reaction against the NEA's militancy by some of its members, leading to the formation of the National Association of Professional Educators (NAPE), primarily in the southern states (Burton, 1979; Government Employee Relations Report, 1980). Competition between the two main organizations and splinter groups is likely to continue in the face of unsuccessful merger efforts and declining enrollments.

Organization for Negotiations. An activity as pervasive and complex as collective negotiations in education requires a large and complex organization structure. Organi-

zations of employees, managers, negotiators, and school board members exist at the national, state, and local levels, and take an active part in labor-management relations and all related activities. These organizations reflect both their role in the negotiation system and their historical origins.

All but a small number of organized teachers are affiliated with either the American Federation of Teachers, AFL-CIO (500,000 members) or the National Education Association (1,887,000 members). The National Education Association (NEA) grew from a combination of state associations into a national one providing general support to teachers and, for much of its history, administrators. The American Federation of Teachers (AFT) grew by acquiring local organizations, primarily in the larger school systems. Thus the membership of the AFT is mostly in large, urban, or suburban school systems; the NEA members are found more in suburban and rural districts (Doherty, 1980). The NEA maintains a large national staff for research and political activities. Its state affiliates have research and political staffs, as well as an extensive system of field representatives who provide bargaining and related services directly to local organizations. The AFT structure, by contrast, is typical of labor unions, with larger national and local staffs and fewer at the state level.

State and local associations appear to be the main organizational support for administrator bargaining units. The AFT created an American Federation of Educational Administrators in 1976 to support its organizing efforts. The NEA, however, does not support the organizing of administrators at the national level. State administrator organizations have begun to offer negotiation support services to local administrator bargaining units.

The national and state affiliate structure of the NEA is reflected in the structures of the two major associations involved in negotiations on the management side: the National School Boards Association and the American Association of School Administrators (AASA). Each has state affiliates that provide management and bargaining support services to local school boards and administrators. In addition there are national associations for elementary and secondary school administrators, an Association of Educational Negotiators, and a council of negotiators within the AASA. AASA also operates a National Academy for School Executives that offers training in labor-management relations for school managers. Thus on both management and labor sides, there are roughly parallel organizational structures reflecting the alignments of parties to the bargaining process providing a variety of support services to local members.

Public Policy toward Negotiations

For public elementary and secondary schools the governing policy framework is at the state level. As a result, there is considerable variety in the policy arrangements. Statutes providing a specific framework for public schools and other public employees have been enacted in thirty-three states; thirty-two cover school employees (Ross, 1980). Three states have prohibitions against formal collective negotiation of agreements for public employees. The remaining states have a mix of permissive statutes and court decisions that allow some form of negotiated agreement in the public schools.

The public policy framework for private schools is quite ambiguous. Private, nonreligious schools come under the jurisdiction of the National Labor Relations Act (NLRA), provided the National Labor Relations Board (NLRB) chooses to assert jurisdiction. The NLRB has, however, usually declined to assert jurisdiction over employers who have no significant impact on interstate commerce. Religious elementary and secondary schools are in a legal limbo, since the ruling of the U.S. Supreme Court that the National Labor Relations Act does not apply to religious-associated schools (Gill, 1980; *NLRB* v. *Catholic Bishop of Chicago,* 440 U.S. 490, 1979). Thus for most private schools, there is no directly applicable body of controlling public policy.

Although the details of public policy at the state level differ considerably, there is a common core of issues, reflecting the basic sources of conflict in the structure of labor-management relations (see Creswell & Spargo, 1980). The four main ones are (1) What is the duty of the employer to recognize and negotiate with an employee organization? (2) What will be negotiated? (3) Who will be the parties to the bargain (i.e., how will the employees be organized into bargaining units and who will represent the public)? and (4) How will impasses be resolved? Those states with statutes for public employee bargaining generally place a positive duty to bargain on the employer. The employer is thus required to meet with a duly-recognized employee organization and negotiate in good faith (i.e., with the intention to reach agreement). Statutes typically prescribe a method and criteria for deciding which employees shall be grouped together for the purposes of bargaining (bargaining unit determination). They also specify what subjects are to be bargained (scope of negotiations). Policies for impasse resolution include third-party intervention (mediation, fact-finding, arbitration) and regulations or penalties (or both) for strikes.

Public and Private Sector. The central policy issues in public employee labor relations derive from the question of how to balance the duty of the government to govern against the rights of the employees. This is parallel to the problem of balance in the private sector: the property rights of employer against the rights of the employees. Much public sector policy has developed around this theme in the context of existing private sector precedent and practice. Assumptions about similarities and differences between the two sectors have affected the degree to which policy and experience from the private side can be applied to the public.

The question of the public interest has been central, giving rise to two conflicting points of view. The first is that public union activity and bargaining is a threat to the public interest because of the power of the public unions to distort government decision making and substitute the pursuit of their private interests for the efficient functioning of government (Wellington & Winter, 1971; Summers, 1974). The second is that the public interest is served by peaceful labor relations and the recognition of rights for public employees roughly parallel to those of private sector workers (Burton & Krider, 1975; Barbash, 1980). In this view, the role of policy is to promote balance, and state government should be neutral regarding bargaining in schools. In the first point of view it is clearly assumed that differences between public and private sector bargaining are sufficiently large to justify different public policies for the sectors. The second clearly grows from the premise that since the two sectors are quite similar, the same basic policy can apply to both. The question of differences between the public and private sectors thus becomes central to the logic of labor policy development.

The case for the uniqueness of the public sector rests on legal, economic, and political grounds. Public school boards have a grant of authority from the legislature to operate schools in the public interest. Delegating that authority through negotiations may be considered illegal. Moreover schools are governed by education and civil service codes that may be incompatible with negotiated contracts. State courts have often found that the existence of a bargaining statute can provide the authority to negotiate or that the power to bargain may be implicit in the education code. In either case statutes may limit or deny a school board's authority to bargain.

Economic distinctions can be drawn between private and public employers because the latter do not operate in a competitive market; they are monopolies. The absence of competitive constraints allows the public employer, under union pressure, to make concessions not in the public interest, such as excessive wage settlements, surrender of control, etc. Moreover public sector strikes have the potential to disrupt vital services for which there are no alternative sources.

Politically, public employers may also be considered vulnerable. Employee unions can be potent political agents, with more resources and incentives to influence employers than other interest groups (Wellington & Winter, 1971). One source of vulnerability is that public employers are not single firms with monolithic management hierarchies, but rather are complex overlapping government jurisdictions; for example, school boards, county or regional units, courts, legislative bodies, and state departments of education all have some control. Thus public management often has difficulty maintaining a solid position, and unions have multiple access points to influence bargaining outcomes. This is commonly referred to as multilateral bargaining, and it is considered one of the key differences between public and private employment.

Taken together, these arguments suggest the need for a policy structure designed to protect public management.

Such a policy would restrict the scope of bargaining, prohibit strikes, and provide alternative impasse procedures. Even bargaining itself may be prohibited. If, however, the alternative view is held, markedly different policy implications emerge.

That alternative emphasizes the diversity and balance in both public and private sectors (Horton, Lewin, & Kuhn, 1976). Not all public services are essential or monopolistic (e.g., schools, parks, refuse collection). Alternatives exist and interruptions can be inconvenient but not necessarily dangerous to public health and safety. Courts have, in fact, been reluctant to issue injunctions against public school strikes on the grounds of a threat to public safety (Graber & Colton, 1980). Moreover, although product markets do not always exist for public services, political constraints, in the form of public resistance to taxes or defeat of school board members, can curb management tendencies to make concessions. Resources to balance power do exist in the environment of both public and private employers (Juris & Roomkin, 1978). So it is not so much an absence of constraints on public employers as a variety of political and economic ones.

What constitutes illegal delegations of authority can also vary widely. Specific elements of negotiated agreements may be illegal because of conflicts with school codes, civil service systems, or other statutes; others may not be, depending on state court rulings. Balance between employer and employee interests can be constructed on an issue-by-issue basis.

The multilateral nature of public employment takes many forms, and is present as well in several private employment situations. School boards and municipal governments are quite autonomous in many states, with many of the characteristics of independent employers. By contrast, large corporations may have several, widely separated levels of management involved in bargaining and have substantial government regulation as well (e.g., airlines and utilities).

Rather than emphasizing the public-private distinction, particular features of the bargaining relationships and its context may be considered. Within each sector the variety of economic and political constraints, legal structures, and bargaining history, is at least as great as the differences between sectors. From this second point of view, policy should provide for balance and diversity, rather than build on an assumption of public sector uniqueness.

The state of policy for public school bargaining reflects the general lack of agreement as to whether the public sector is unique and the particular efforts of states and localities to solve the day-to-day problems of bargaining conduct. The four main problem areas—duty to bargain, scope, impasses, and bargaining unit composition—deserve special attention.

Scope of Bargaining. The legal definition of what must and may be bargained—scope—remains one of the least orderly and most complex topics in public labor relations. The complexity of the scope issue arises in part from the multiplicity of approaches defined, positions taken, and decisions made by state courts, labor agencies, and the bargaining parties themselves (Schneider, 1979). These approaches are derived in large measure from state labor statutes, or where statutes are absent, by standards set by state courts. Thus, the basic concept of scope has developed at the state level. The basic language of most statutory and court definitions of scope has come, however, from the NLRA: bargaining must take place over "wages, hours, and other terms and conditions of employment." Interpretation of the meaning of this phrase has caused the greatest conflict and legal activity. Those items that are considered to fall within these limits of "other terms and conditions of employment" are mandatory items. Those items that may not be bargained, generally because they are covered by existing statute or case law, or are explicitly within the mission of the employer, are prohibited. Those items falling somewhere between mandatory and prohibited items are permissive items that may be bargained.

Certain state statutes specify where individual items fall with regard to bargainability. In those states where statutes do not provide a specific itemization, further interpretation is up to the parties; upon dispute, the courts or state labor agencies make a determination.

The courts and state labor agencies have based their bargainability decisions primarily on one of the two following rationales. One approach examines the link between the disputed item and the language of "wages, hours, and other terms and conditions of employment." Those items seen as related would be termed mandatory. A second approach is based on impact balancing in which an attempt is made to balance competing interests of the disputing parties, that is, the effect on individual teachers versus the effect on the operation of the school (Bowles, 1978, p. 658). If bargaining an item would not adversely affect the operation of the school, then it would be deemed a mandatory or permissive item.

Despite differing approaches by state agencies and the courts, some trends are becoming evident in the pattern of decisions and legislation emerging on the issue of scope (Kerchner, 1978). One is a gradual broadening of scope at the bargaining table (discussed in the following section). A second is that legislation has tended to narrow scope by specifying the meaning of "terms and conditions of employment" or otherwise setting aside a management preserve (Schneider, 1979, p. 211). Finally, the courts and agencies, despite differing approaches, are finding most topics within the scope of bargaining, unless there is a direct connection to basic policy or service (Gershenfeld, Loewenberg, & Ingster, 1977).

Parties to the Bargaining. State policy structures generally include criteria for how employees are to be grouped for bargaining (patterned after the NLRA in most cases). Professionals may not ordinarily be in the same unit as nonprofessionals. Supervisors may not be in the same unit as teachers ordinarily, but may form their own organization and bargain in most states. Employees with confidential access to information critical to management's bargaining strategy and those directly involved in labor relations may not organize or bargain (Hayford & Sinicropi, 1976). Principals and assistant principals have organized in many of the large school systems (Cooper, 1979). Where they have done so, they are subject to the same policy as teachers.

Strike and Impasse Resolution. Along with scope, policy issues of strike and impasse are central to the power relationship between the parties. Common to all state policy is the posture that strikes by teachers and other public employees are contrary to the public interest. In all but eight states, that leads to a prohibition against strikes; those eight provide a modified right to strike, after impasse resolution procedures have been exhausted. The remaining states with bargaining statutes provide some structure of procedures to resolve impasses without the strike, usually mediation, fact-finding, and arbitration. Those states without statutory structures generally prohibit strikes, with employers free to seek injunctions ordering strikers back to work.

The effect of the statutory environment on impasse behavior is difficult to evaluate. Strike activity is lower, proportionately, in the public sector than in the private, so the restrictions could be said to be effective. However, an increase of strike actions in state and local government has occurred along with an increase of public employee bargaining legislation designed to control them. The number of work stoppages in local government grew rapidly from 42 in 1965 to 446 in 1975. The number leveled off briefly then rose sharply to 536 in 1979 (U.S. Department of Labor, 1981). This is the same period in which most of the current legislation was drafted. Of the 1979 strikes, 315 were in education, accounting for 62.6 percent of the days idle.

Strike policy does not, however, seem to be closely related to strike activity (Colton, 1978; Perry, 1977; Burton & Krider, 1975). Instead, strikes in schools and other local government agencies seem to be products of the economic, political, and legal environments, the organizational context of bargaining, the interpersonal relationships and characteristics of the bargainers, and the history of the relationship (Kochan, 1979, p. 163–164). Policy is only one feature of this complex of causes.

In spite of this complexity there is some evidence of a connection between statutory strike policy and strike activity; the existence of bargaining legislation is positively, though weakly, related to occurrences of strikes (Perry, 1977; Burton & Krider, 1975). It is not clear, however, which is cause and which is effect. Passage of bargaining statutes is associated with increase in strike activity in some states, but not uniformly (Colton, 1978). The nature of statutory policy can be as much a reaction to strikes as a cause of them.

The existence of specific strike penalties in bargaining legislation does not appear to affect strike incidence either.

Statutory penalties do, however, appear to affect the outcomes of bargaining. Both the comprehensiveness (Gerhart, 1976) and the growth of contracts (McDonnell & Pascal, 1979) seem to be restricted by the existence of strike penalties. Strike penalties, if enforced, would be expected to reduce employee bargaining power and produce such effects.

It is not clear, however, that there is consistent enforcement of these penalties. Injunctions do not regularly lead to penalties, and dismissals or suspensions are often rescinded (Gray & Dyson, 1976). Enforcement and standards for antistrike injunctions are spotty (Graber & Colton, 1980). More detailed examination of state politics in California (Geiger, 1979) and Florida (Williams, 1979) yielded similar negative findings for the effects of strike and impasse policies. This raises the question of the efficiency of statutory impasse resolution mechanisms overall.

Procedures for dispute resolution—mediation, fact-finding, arbitration—are designed as alternatives to strikes. Mediation involves a neutral party, chosen by both sides, who acts informally to resolve impasses. Mediators work privately, through persuasion and facilitating communication, but they have no formal authority or power over the parties. In fact-finding, a neutral party conducts formal hearings, collects data, and makes public some specific recommendations, which are not usually binding but are supposed to bring pressure toward a settlement and provide an objective basis for one. In arbitration of bargaining impasses (known as interest arbitration), a neutral party (or panel of three) has the authority to make a binding award, resolving the impasse. Mediation and fact-finding are often compulsory steps in a statutory sequence of procedures required of the parties once impasse is reached. In those states that allow strikes, the impasse procedures must be exhausted before the strike is legally sanctioned. Compulsory arbitration as a final impasse step for school bargaining is currently required in three states (Connecticut, New Jersey, Wisconsin) and voluntary in New York. Some form of mandatory arbitration for other employees, particularly police and fire protection, is found in 19 states, and is prohibited in 3 (Ross, 1980; U.S. Department of Labor, 1979).

Arbitration provisions take several forms. In conventional arbitration the substance of the award is left to the arbitrator(s). A variation called "final-offer arbitration" requires the arbitrator(s) to choose as the award one party's final or "last best offer." Each party's offers may be treated as a package or issue by issue. Restricting the award to final offers is intended to provide an incentive for the parties to bargain more effectively before reaching impasse.

All of these procedures are intended to protect the public interest by reducing strikes. However, procedures that in doing so interfere with the free conduct of bargaining are not consistent with the public interest either. Impasse procedures are effective, therefore, to the degree that they provide an alternative to strikes without unduly distorting or inhibiting bargaining, or fostering excessive dependence on the procedures (the so-called chilling and narcotic effects). In the private sector, most reliance is placed on the free conduct of bargaining, including strikes with use of mediation only. The public sector, by contrast, depends heavily on statutory impasse procedures. Their effectiveness is therefore a central policy question.

The evidence on effectiveness is quite mixed. The use of arbitration and other impasse procedures does seem to lead to small additions in teacher salary settlements, up to two percent (Lipsky & Drotning, 1977). Similar results were found for other public employees (Kochan & Baderschneider, 1978; Doherty & Gallo, 1979; Stern et al., 1975). But the overall results are small and, in the case of teachers (Lipsky & Drotning, 1977), not consistent over time. Thus if the use of these impasse procedures does distort bargaining outcomes, the effects are not large or consistent. Lipsky and Drotning (1977) also found some evidence that the parties learn to exploit the procedures over time, and the comparative advantage diminishes.

Evidence of impasse procedures "chilling" the bargaining process is also mixed. The chilling effect is inferred from greater recourse to the procedures. On this basis there is reason to suspect chilling for some firefighters (Wheeler, 1978), Canadian federal services (Anderson & Kochan, 1977), New York police and fire employees (Kochan & Baderschneider, 1978), and generally in Massachusetts (Lipsky & Barocci, 1978). But no evidence of chilling was found in a later study in New York (Doherty & Gallo, 1979), Michigan (Wolkinson & Stieber, 1976; Feuille, 1977), Wisconsin (Feuille, 1977; Olson, 1978), Hawaii (Klauser, 1977), or Iowa (Gallagher & Pegnetter, 1979). When there is evidence of chilling, it appears to be less under final-offer arbitration than conventional arbitration (Stern et al., 1975; Holden, 1976; Feuille, 1975, 1977; Lipsky & Barocci, 1978). Studies of the arbitration process itself suggest that many of these variations are a result of impact of structural details of the arbitration process on the behavior of participants (Weitzman & Stochaj, 1980).

An increase in the use of impasse procedures over time might suggest a growing dependency or narcotic effect. This does not appear to happen in public employment. Reductions over time in the use of impasse procedures is reported by Lipsky and Drotning (1977), Lipsky and Barocci (1978), and Olson (1978). Some support for the dependency hypothesis is found in Feuille and Dworkin (1979) and Anderson and Kochan (1977), but the support is weak and not tied directly to school bargaining. If anything, the results suggest support for the suggestion of Lipsky and Drotning (1977) that the parties learn about the use of procedures fairly rapidly and thus cannot continue to exploit them. There is, however, strong evidence that the size of the bargaining unit is important in impasse incidence and the use of impasse procedures; larger units have much higher rates of impasse and procedure use (Kochan, 1979).

Dynamics of Negotiations. Negotiation is a dynamic phenomenon in two ways. It is first of all a process, a set of activities that occur in working out a particular written agreement and its administration. It is a process with its own characteristics, one that connects to school operations and governance. Moreover the description and understanding of that process have evolved over the history of bargaining in schools; that evolution is a second aspect of bargaining dynamics. There is good reason to believe that the negotiation process itself has changed and will continue to change.

Negotiations in the organization. Negotiations take place between individuals who represent two groups within the organization; that is, it is a basically bilateral, representative process. There are, of course, multilateral aspects to the process (discussed in the following sections), but only two parties sign the agreement: the school district represented by the board and the employee organization, each through their individual representatives. The role of the participants is best understood as a boundary spanning role. That is, they are members of their own organizations, but the main activity of bargaining takes place on the boundary between their own and the other organization (Adams, 1976; Kochan & Wheeler, 1975; Walton & McKersie, 1965). The individuals who participate in bargaining usually have other organizational roles as well, and the subjects of bargaining have important implications for much of the rest of the school system. So there are definite links between the process and the organizational context in which it occurs, as well as with the larger political and economical environment.

Organizational linkages. Collective negotiations of employee agreements can be seen as part of the overall processes of organizational decision and negotiation, along with budgetmaking, personnel hiring and promotion, program structuring, etc. The manager can be viewed as a coordinator of bargains, handling and balancing the different arenas and demands in order to maintain power (Chamberlain, Cullen & Lewin, 1980). Thus every decision or concession in collective negotiations can affect the balance with other arenas. Bargaining can increase the decision-making power of teachers and other employees (McDonnell & Pascal, 1979; Goldberg & Harbatkin, 1970) or result in greater centralization, depending on the power relationship. Similarly the organizational role of school principals can be reduced in power, leading them to organize to expand their participation and power (Cooper, 1979). Although the particular manifestations of bargaining linkages and impacts are difficult to predict, it does appear that greater formalization of most organizational relations is a common result (Mitchell et al., 1981; Perry, 1979).

Participants in negotiations. As bargaining has evolved from a rare to a commonplace phenomenon in schools, the patterns of participation have changed, as have the roles of participants. During bargaining's early growth period (around 1965), the school superintendent was the dominant management figure; ten years later the superintendent was still central, but the involvement of others had increased. Bargaining was becoming an organizational specialization on the management side (Cresswell & Murphy, 1980). As would be expected, the larger the district, the more likely it is that negotiations are handled by a management specialist and less likely that board members will be directly involved. With the growth of field staffs within the NEA and AFT affiliates, the number of bargaining specialists among the teaching ranks has grown as well, although historical comparisons are not available.

The relationship between an individual's role in the organization and in the bargaining process has been the subject of considerable speculation, but little systematic attention, in school settings. General theories of the bargaining process suggest that the negotiator be a specialist, separated to some degree from the main authority of the organization. The bargaining role requires the incumbent to make concessions, control information flow, absorb hostility, and generally maintain flexible commitments (Walton & McKersie, 1965; Rubin & Brown, 1975). The role also requires some specialized skills in acting, communication, and strategy. These considerations suggest that lay persons (e.g., board members) or those with central authority (e.g., superintendent) not be negotiators. Since authority in employee organizations is less centralized, this is less of a concern for them.

However, because the subjects of bargaining are major organizational matters, the negotiator cannot function well if far removed from the control of the organization. This explains why superintendents have retained close connection with bargaining, and why specialists perform the task only in coordination with top management.

The professionalization of bargaining on the management side has been matched to a large degree on the employee side. Teacher union officers may have support from labor professionals working for the state or national organization or from hired consultants. Large locals have their own full-time staff (McDonnell & Pascal, 1979). The result is an arrangement producing smoother negotiations, more opportunities for cooperative effort, less acrimony, and fewer errors leading to impasse.

School board members' participation on bargaining teams has diminished. This is due to the growing professionalization of the process and to particular problems of their behavior. Board members often lack the discipline and professional skill to handle the emotional pressure of negotiation. The result can be angry outbursts and loss of control of the process, with the possibility of impasse, or spillover of hostility beyond the negotiations (see McDonnell & Pascal, 1979; Cresswell & Simpson, 1977).

Negotiating process. Bargaining can be described in terms of four main elements identified by Walton and McKersie (1965). Simple exchange of concessions on a *quid pro quo* basis is called "distributive bargaining"; one side's gain is the other's loss. Problem solving wherein both can gain is called "integrative bargaining." Resolving differ-

ences among the members of each side and sustaining their support requires "intraorganizational bargaining." Finally, tactics used to change an opponent's perceptions and feelings are called "attitudinal structuring."

These elements, essentially as described by Walton and McKersie (1965), are reported in school bargaining (McDonnell & Pascal, 1979; Mitchell et al., 1981). Distributive issues—such as wages, benefits—are the dominant causes of impasses in schools, as in most other negotiations (U.S. Dept. of Labor, 1979). Integrative activity is involved on matters of complex working conditions and policy participation (e.g., instructional policy committees). There are major differences, however, in some aspects of intraorganizational bargaining and additional structuring.

The multilateral nature of school management and negotiations complicates intraorganizational bargaining on that side. So-called end run tactics are common, where the employees attempt to influence bargaining through local political activity, such as electing school board members, influencing public opinion, etc. (McDonnell & Pascal, 1979; Perry, 1979). While not regularly successful, the opportunity for the employees to use these tactics is part of the process.

The main additional element in school negotiations seems to revolve around the legitimacy of the process. Attitudes about legitimacy seem to be so deeply felt that they change only slowly in response to experience and bargaining tactics. Perry (1979) reports that much of the ideological conflict over legitimacy observed in 1967 was gone in 1977. However, in districts with less experience, these attitudes still appear. A unique aspect of school negotiations is that the changes in attitudes toward greater legitimacy come often via political processes. So the interaction of local politics with bargaining is central to the process.

Negotiations and politics. Two related questions are integral to understanding the political aspects of negotiations: (1) Does bilateral negotiation with employee unions distort or interfere with democratic control of public institutions?, and (2) Are the conduct and outcomes of collective negotiations constrained or controlled by the political governance mechanisms of schools? These questions are just alternative ways of asking how collective negotiations can be consistent with the pursuit of the public interest by government acting in the political system.

The questions are also at the root of much of the ideological conflict in negotiations. The legitimacy of bargaining in government rests in part on the assumption that unions will not run roughshod over their employers and exploit the process for purely selfish ends. Those who do not accept this assumption reject the bargaining rights of public employees and resist negotiations, or at least advocate strong legal restrictions on the process. The basic argument was presented in the previous discussion of the policy context. At this point the question is how do political interactions work.

The predominant body of research indicates that political controls do in fact operate in public bargaining in a way roughly analogous to the market constraints in the private sector. Even in the beginnings of widespread school bargaining, evidence in the work of Perry and Wildman (1971) indicates some political controls. A follow-up ten years later found little evidence of direct public participation in bargaining, but concluded that "[political] constraints operate primarily through normal political channels" (Perry, 1979, p. 7). This same finding is supported in studies by McDonnell and Pascal (1979), Schick and Couturier (1977), and Cresswell and Simpson (1977), in a review of the literature by Cohen (1979), and particularly by Mitchell et al., (1981).

This last study (Mitchell et al., 1981) found specific political mechanisms for public exercise of influence. Major conflicts, first over the legitimacy of negotiation and secondly over excessive employer concessions, appear to occur in sequence, separated by periods of relatively low conflict. These conflicts were resolved through the normal political mechanisms of school governance: board elections, superintendent turnover, etc. In short, formal public participation in school politics appears as the mechanism for resolving major conflicts and setting negotiation parameters. In the periods between major conflicts the process is more private. Teacher organizations continue to attempt to exert influence outside negotiations by political or other means. But these are not regularly or markedly successful. Teacher organization's political activity is more intense and generally more successful at the state level. Public participation therefore focuses not on bargaining *per se* but on normal school governance.

Participation and privatization. The power associated with negotiations also accounts for the participation or attempted participation of a number of other actors. There has been considerable controversy over the supposed private nature of bargaining, the notion that because bargaining is bilateral and private, it is antidemocratic when performed in public institutions, and that the structure of the process prevents others with legitimate interests from having a meaningful role (Cheng, Hamer, & Barron, 1979). Evidence from case studies in various bargaining settings, however, indicates that public participation in bargaining or public influence can be substantial. Even though participation *per se* was light, Mitchell et al. (1981) found citizen influence to be an important factor in bargaining. Public participation through elected politicians is also documented by Schick and Couturier (1977) and Englert (1981) in Philadelphia and by Peterson (1976) in Chicago.

This controversy raises a larger question of how the bargaining environment affects the process. Some studies of the bargaining process (Perry, 1979; Derber & Wagner, 1979) suggest that the economic environment is the stronger determinant of outcomes; that the political constraints are less important. This perspective is consistent with some of the studies of salary determinants discussed subse-

quently. It is not consistent, however, with the evidence from other studies of school bargaining, such as Mitchell et al. (1981), Schick and Couturier (1977), and McDonnell and Pascal (1979), which show political concerns and participation as more important. The contradictory evidence may be a consequence of perspective. An examination of economic constraints alone would not show the political process by which they are translated into bargaining concerns, nor would a study of the political process show how economic concerns shape political objectives. Both are probably important aspects of bargaining dynamics.

Effects on Schools

Research on the impact of collective negotiation on schools is clustered into developments that directly concern the working environment and those that capture changes in teachers as a population. Three aspects of the working environment relate directly to teachers: compensation, work loads, and participatory rights in policy decisions. A fourth concerns the school as an institution. Effects on the population that have been analyzed include profile characteristics (age, sex, experience, education) and attitudes (morale, satisfaction).

Compensation Bargaining Effects. The absolute wage gains for unionized teachers have been minimal, with most studies reporting 1–5 percent increases from bargaining (Thornton, 1971; Lipsky & Drotning, 1973; Baird & Landon, 1972; Holmes, 1976). The variation in percentages is partially attributable to the methodology employed in the research and to the unit of analysis; that is, effects on individual wage gains, district wage gains, or state-level analysis. The greater increases appear in studies of individual gains, the least from an aggregate state analysis.

Absolute wages are not the only mode in which compensation gains can be made, although wage increases are the most visible evidence. Teachers receive increments for service, up to some limit, as well as differential increases for earning academic credit. Wage gains achieved through changes in the latter forms of salary structure account for relatively higher monetary benefits than across-the-board salary increases (Perry & Wildman, 1970; Lipsky & Drotning, 1973). This can be accomplished by increasing the magnitude of dollar amounts or increasing the frequency of increments. The incentive for pursuing incremental increases may be to mask the cost implications of wage demands (Gustman & Segal, 1978).

Bargaining may also affect the distribution of gains among teachers. Several studies report disproportionate gains for certain subgroups of the teaching population. Kasper (1973) and Thornton (1971) found that individuals at the higher end of salary scales have been more advantaged as a group. Teachers with small pensions benefited most by bargaining on this issue (Gustman & Segal, 1977). Holmes (1979) found that bargaining leveled the discrepancies in wages between male and female teachers and between elementary and secondary teachers. These results show that although the effect of bargaining on absolute wages is small, it has had a substantial impact on salary structure and the distribution of gains within the teaching community.

Work Load Bargaining Efforts. The scope of bargaining on work-load issues encompasses three areas: class size, contact hours, and definition of duties. Of these, the most discernible changes have been in the limitation of duties and responsibilities of teachers (Perry, 1979; Mitchell et al., 1981). The potential for heated negotiations over reducing or regulating class sizes has been mitigated somewhat by the large costs of changes in class sizes (Perry, 1979). During an interval of vigorous cost containment efforts, unions have recognized that choices must be made between negotiating salary increases and standardizing class size, since both items have substantial cost implications.

The impact of bargaining over contact hours refers to the length of the school year and day as negotiated within the statutory constraints. The tendency over a twenty-year period has been to reduce instructional contact time to the minimum, aside from the influence of bargaining: a decrease from an average of 1,000 to 900 hours between 1955 and 1975 (Doherty, 1980). Perry (1979) found that in addition to a general decline in contact hours over the ten-year period he studied, districts had reduced the school day by 30–35 minutes by active bargaining efforts. Minimizing the work day was a pattern found in the districts studied by Mitchell et al. (1981) as well.

Marked changes in work load have resulted from negotiating definitions of responsibilities, especially extra duties of the teacher (Mitchell et al., 1981). The negotiated factors include teacher preparation time, duty-free lunch periods, mandatory extracurricular and supervision times, professional released time for faculty meetings, report card preparation, and parent conferences. Unions have been successful in contractually defining the teaching duties to exclude extracurricular and supervision responsibilities from work loads (McDonnell & Pascal, 1979; Mitchell et al., 1981; Perry, 1979). These activities now require districts to hire additional staff or provide remuneration for teachers who participate voluntarily. Teacher preparation time is a regular provision in contracts, as is also released time for conferences and faculty meetings. Negotiations over preparation time can involve both work-load issues and contests over management's authority versus professional prerogative. Specifically the issue has been the question of who controls and directs the use of preparation time. Results of bargaining this issue have tended to favor increased teacher control.

The overall pattern of many of these issues suggests a change in the style of how a teaching job is defined. Mitchell et al. (1981) describe it as a change from outlining minimum expectations to prescribing maximum requirements. The contract can thus become the source

of defining just how much teacher time and effort is expended.

Rights Efforts. Efforts to bargain for the right to participate in policy formation have concentrated on three areas: procedures for promotion and evaluation, layoffs, and transfers. These issues are consistently addressed in contract negotiations, most likely because they pertain to job security and to protection of employees from arbitrary management actions. Contractual provisions have been won that guarantee teacher participation in such decisions. This second outcome is notable since it defines seniority as the basis for promoting and retaining staff, a value that is typical of labor contracts but somewhat inconsistent with the preferences for quality and ability adhered to by educational professionals (Perry, 1979).

Prior to the early 1970s few contracts contained provisions that limited management autonomy over promotion and layoff. Since then collective bargaining has had a potent effect on both the presence and strength of these provisions (McDonnell & Pascal, 1979; Perry, 1979). On balance, the negotiation of limits to management's discretion in these central personnel matters indicates a shift in control and autonomy away from managers. The areas in which teachers have increased control are not, however, usually ones of educational policy, but rather directly tied to working conditions. Except through affecting the amount of time involved, negotiations appear to have little effect on classroom behavior. The main effect appears to be an increase in teacher autonomy (McDonnell & Pascal, 1979; Mitchell et al., 1981).

Achievement. The impacts of collective bargaining directly on pupil achievement have not been well documented. Bargaining would be expected to have an impact upon the age, sex, education, and experience of teachers through salary structure changes and the growing importance of seniority. It would be reasonable to expect that wage advantages for teachers at the higher end of the scale, increases in differentials for those with more graduate education, and contractual protection for more senior staff would lead to older, more educated, more experienced, and more expensive teaching staffs. Eberts and Pierce (1980) found that unionized districts do in fact retain staffs of this type.

Teachers with these characteristics would be expected to produce higher pupil achievement, based on research on education production (Levin, 1980; Bridge, Judd, & Moock, 1979; Summers & Wolfe, 1977). Eberts and Pierce (1980) found some support for this; principally that negotiation relates to higher teacher education levels, and those in turn produce higher achievement. Contractual provisions for teacher aides, class sizes, and teacher preparation periods also relate to higher achievement. However, the effects of negotiations on pupil-teacher ratios and teacher experience are not reflected in achievement. Bargaining seems to promote more traditional classroom arrangements, which promote more homogeneous achievement.

Enrollment decline may also influence the configuration of teaching staffs. There are two direct effects on staff sizes as a result of enrollment decline, depending on the magnitude of the decrease. In a milder decline, hiring of young, inexperienced teachers is curtailed. In a more severe situation, where reduction in force is necessary, the most senior staff is retained. Both situations contribute to the movement towards an older, more experienced teaching staff. This would not be expected to influence pupils' achievement substantially in light of the findings of Eberts and Pierce (1980); but other research on teacher productivity suggests some decrement in achievement (see especially Bridge, Judd, & Mooch, 1980).

Finance and Budget.   Since negotiations deal with the principal resources of schools, a strong relation to finances and budgets would be expected. The evidence of interaction is consistent, but not as strong as the volume of resources involved would indicate.

Budgets are affected. Negotiating districts do spend more both overall and on instruction (McDonnell & Pascal, 1979; Barro & Carroll, 1975), with greater union power related to higher salaries, benefits, and pupil expenditures (Eberts & Pierce, 1980). The magnitude of the effects are generally small (maximum of $72 per pupil) but more pronounced in districts with declining enrollments.

Trade-offs among negotiated items are revealed in budgets as well. McDonnell and Pascal (1979) report trade-offs are common among financial items, but much less common between financial and nonfinancial ones. Eberts and Pierce (1980), however, found evidence of both types, including salary trade-offs with fringe benefits, class size, job security, and arbitration clauses.

Financial decisions are related to negotiations as well. Budget flexibility is diminished (McDonnell & Pascal, 1979). Budget decisions are coordinated with negotiations and can often control budget choices (Perry, 1979). In environments of fiscal adversity, however, economic constraints tend to control negotiations (Derber & Wagner, 1979). The importance of the economic environment is also reflected in the finding by Gallagher (1979) that negotiated compensation increases are financed out of tax increases where wealth is higher, but out of budget reallocation in less wealthy areas (see also Straussman & Rodgers, 1979).

Clearly negotiations interact with other financial decisions in schools, but there is little evidence that labor concerns dominate. Even where there are large increases in outside funds, they do not go proportionately into teacher salaries (Kirst, 1977). Instead negotiations can be seen as just one among a cluster of major influences in school finance.

Negotiations, Policy, and Diversity

Elementary and secondary education in the United States is a diverse enterprise, with certain common struc-

tures and themes. It is not surprising, then, that collective negotiations in the schools should have the same appearance. The autonomy of local school boards and administrators to design and operate schools, although somewhat restricted by state and federal laws, has produced a system reflecting local circumstances. The common practices of teaching and learning emerge in forms and styles adapted to particular needs. The same appears true of collective negotiations. A process and set of norms developed in the private sector has been adapted to the particulars of public education, while retaining its basic character.

The basic character is that of bilateral negotiations between an employer and an employee organization leading to an enforceable written agreement on wages, hours, and working conditions. Bargaining takes place in a legal framework designed to promote free play of the process, with superordinate government in a neutral role.

The particular adaptations to schools and the public sector generally include legislated impasse procedures, limits to scope, public access to and occasional participation in the process, and multilateral bargaining. In particular, teacher bargaining in school systems has gone further than other areas in negotiating details of operation and participation in policy. This is not surprising, however, in light of the history of teacher professionalism and activity in school governance.

There is little reason to believe that there has been a generalized dominance of school governance by unions. Instead, a dynamic of shifting advantage seems to have emerged, responsive to the press of the economic and political setting of the school. Even where bargaining is illegal, management dominance is unlikely, given the history of informal negotiations between teachers and school systems.

Given the diversity of the system itself and the apparent robustness and flexibility of bargaining as a part of governance, certain directions for policy are indicated. Close regulation and standardization of negotiations through policy seems disadvantageous. State policy continues to adapt to changing conditions; no stable or universally applicable model exists. Federal policy has adapted to the wide diversity in the private sector by, in large part, avoiding close regulation and rigid standards. Serious attention must also be given to the role of the public. Although direct, continuous participation is not desirable, neither is exclusion. Policy makers have yet to find effective mechanisms for appropriate involvement. The long-term prospect of enrollment declines places additional burdens on negotiations. Policy initiatives to soften the impacts on employees are indicated; for example, early retirement systems, retraining, and placement assistance.

Overall, collective negotiations has been neither as detrimental or revolutionary as its critics feared nor as effective as its advocates wished. It has, of course, had an enormous impact on schools, but that impact is merged with and conditioned by the other forces that shape schooling. The understanding of collective negotiations in schools must rest, therefore, on seeing it both as a distinctive process and as part of the larger phenomenon of school governance.

Anthony M. Cresswell

See also Academic Freedom and Tenure; Administration of Education Institutions; Governance of Schools; School Personnel Policies.

REFERENCES

Adams, S. J. The structure and dynamics of behavior in organizational boundary roles. In M. D. Dunnette (Ed.), *Handbook of Industrial and Organizational Psychology.* Chicago: Rand McNally, 1976.

Anderson, J. C., & Kochan, T. A. Impasse procedures in the Canadian federal service: Effects on the bargaining process. *Industrial and Labor Relations Review,* 1977, *30*(3), 283–301.

Baird, R. N., & Landon, J. H. The effects of collective bargaining on public school teachers' salaries. *Industrial and Labor Relations Review,* 1972, *25*(3), 410–417.

Barbash, J. Commentary. In G. Somers (Ed.), *Collective Bargaining: Contemporary American Experience.* Madison: Industrial Relations Research Association, 1980.

Barro, S. M., & Carroll, S. J. *Budget Allocation by School Districts: An Analysis of Spending for Teachers and Other Resources* (R-1797-NIE). Santa Monica, Calif.: Rand, 1975. (ERIC Document Reproduction Service No. ED 122 451)

Bowles, J. Defining the scope of collective bargaining for teacher negotiation: A study of judicial approaches. *Labor Law Journal,* 1978, *29*(10), 649–665.

Bridge, R. G.; Judd, C. M.; & Moock, P. R. *The Determinants of Educational Outcomes: The Impact of Families, Peers, Teachers, and Schools.* Cambridge, Mass.: Ballinger, 1979.

Burton, J. F., Jr. The extent of collective bargaining in the public sector. In B. Aaron, J. R. Grodin, & J. L. Stern, (Eds.), *Public Sector Bargaining.* Washington, D.C.: Bureau of National Affairs, 1979.

Burton, J. F., Jr., & Krider, C. E. The incidence of strikes in public employment. In S. Hamermesh (Ed.), *Labor in the Public and Nonprofit Sectors.* Princeton, N.J.: Princeton University Press, 1975.

Chamberlain, N. W.; Cullen, D. E.; & Lewin, D. *The Labor Sector* (3rd ed.). New York: McGraw-Hill, 1980.

Cheng, C. W.; Hamer, I.; & Barron, M. A framework for citizen involvement in teacher negotiations. *Education and Urban Society,* 1979, *11*(2), 219–240.

Cohen, S. Does public employee unionism diminish democracy? *Industrial and Labor Relations Review,* 1979, *32*(2), 189–195.

Colton, D. L. Collective bargaining laws and teacher strikes. *Journal of Collective Negotiations in the Public Sector,* 1978, *7*(3), 201–212.

Cooper, B. S. Bargaining for school administrators four years later. *Phi Delta Kappan,* 1979, *61*(2), 130–131.

Cresswell, A. M.; Murphy, M. J.; with Kerchner, C. T. *Teachers, Unions, and Collective Bargaining in Public Education.* Berkeley, Calif.: McCutchan, 1980.

Cresswell, A. M., & Simpson, D. Collective bargaining and conflict: Impacts on school governance. *Educational Administration Quarterly,* 1977, *13*(3), 49–69.

Cresswell, A. M., & Spargo, F. *Impacts of Collective Bargaining Policy in Elementary and Secondary Education: A Review of Research and Methodology; Recommendations for New Research.* Denver: Education Commission of the States, 1980. (ERIC Document Reproduction Service No. ED 193 806)

Derber, M., & Wagner, M. Public sector bargaining and budget-making under fiscal adversity. *Industrial and Labor Relations Review,* 1979, *33*(1), 18–23.

Doherty, R. E. Public education. In G. Somers (Ed.), *Collective Bargaining: Contemporary American Experience.* Madison: Industrial Relations Research Association, 1980.

Doherty, R. E., & Gallo, M. E. *Compulsory Interest Arbitration in New York State: Experience under the 1977 Amendments.* Ithaca, N.Y.: Cornell University, New York State School of Industrial and Labor Relations, 1979. (Mimeo)

Eberts, R. W., & Pierce, L. C. *The Effects of Collective Bargaining in Public Schools.* Eugene: University of Oregon, Center for Educational Policy and Management, 1980. (ERIC Document Reproduction Service No. ED 197 493)

Engel, R. A. Teacher negotiation: History and comment. In A. M. Cresswell & M. J. Murphy (Eds.), *Education and Collective Bargaining.* Berkeley, Calif.: McCutchan, 1976.

Englert, R. M. *Teacher Negotiations and Third-Party Involvement in Philadelphia in 1980: A Case Study and Comparative Analysis.* Paper presented at the American Educational Research Association Annual Meeting, Los Angeles, 1981.

Feuille, P. Final offer arbitration and the chilling effect. *Industrial Relations,* 1975, *14*(3), 302–310.

Feuille, P. Final offer arbitration and negotiating incentives. *Arbitration Journal,* 1977, *32*(3), 203–220.

Feuille, P., & Dworkin, J. B. Final offer arbitration and intertemporal compromise: Or, it's my turn to win. In *Proceedings of the Thirty-first Annual Meeting of the Industrial Relations Research Association, 1978.* Madison: IRRA, 1979.

Gallagher, D. G. Teacher negotiations, school district expenditures, and taxation levels. *Educational Administration Quarterly,* 1979, *15*(1), 67–82.

Gallagher, D. G., & Pegnetter, R. Impasse resolution under the Iowa multistep procedure. *Industrial and Labor Relations Review,* 1979, *32*(3), 327–338.

Geiger, M. Right to strike and the rodda act: A shift in bargaining power. *Pacific Law Journal,* 1979, *10*(2), 971–990.

Gerhart, P. F. Determinants of bargaining outcomes in local government labor negotiations. *Industrial and Labor Relations Review,* 1976, *29*(3), 331–351.

Gershenfeld, W. J. Public employee unionization: An overview. In M. K. Gibbons, R. D. Helsby, J. Lefkowitz, & B. Z. Tener (Eds.), *Portrait of a Process: Collective Negotiations in Public Employment.* Fort Washington, Pa.: Labor Relations Press, 1979.

Gershenfeld, W. J.; Loewenberg, J. J.; & Ingster, B. *Scope of Public-sector Bargaining.* Lexington, Mass.: Heath, 1977.

Gill, J. C., Jr. Jurisdiction of the National Labor Relations Board over parochial schools. *Tulane Law Review,* 1980, *54*(3), 786–797.

Goldberg, A. J., & Harbatkin, L. The teachers union chapter in the elementary school. *Teachers College Record,* 1970, *71*(4), 647–654.

Government Employee Relations Report. *Special Report: Teachers and Labor Relations, 1979–1980.* Washington, D.C.: Bureau of National Affairs, 1980.

Graber, E., & Colton, D. *The Limits of Effective Legal Action: The Use of the Labor Injunction in Teacher Strikes.* Paper presented at the Annual Meeting of the Law and Society Association, Madison, Wis., 1980.

Gray, D. A., & Dyson, B. Impact of strike remedies in public-sector collective bargaining. *Journal of Collective Negotiations in the Public Sector,* 1976, *5*(2), 125–132.

Gustman, A. L., & Segal, M. Interstate variations in teachers pensions. *Industrial Relations,* 1977, *16*(3), 335–344.

Gustman, A. L., & Segal, M. Teachers' salary structures: Some analytical and empirical aspects of the impact of collective bargaining. In *Proceedings of the Thirtieth Annual Meeting of the Industrial Relations Research Association, 1977.* Madison: IRRA, 1978.

Hayford, S. L., & Sinicropi, A. V. Bargaining-rights status of public-sector supervisors. *Industrial Relations,* 1976, *15*(1), 44–61.

Holden, L. T., Jr. Final-offer arbitration in Massachusetts: One year later. *Arbitration Journal,* 1976, *31*(1), 26–35.

Holmes, A. B. Effects of union activity on teachers' earnings. *Industrial Relations,* 1976, *15*(3), 328–332.

Holmes, A. B. Union activity and teacher salary structure. *Industrial Relations,* 1979, *18*(1), 79–85.

Horton, R. D.; Lewin, D.; & Kuhn, J. W. Some impacts of collective bargaining on local government: A diversity hypothesis. *Administration and Society,* 1976, *7*(4), 497–516.

Juris, H. A., & Roomkin, M. *Education Collective Bargaining: Sui Generis?* Paper presented at the annual meeting of the American Educational Research Association, Toronto, 1978. (ERIC Document Reproduction Service No. ED 153 366)

Kasper, H. On the effect of collective bargaining on resource allocation in public schools. *Economic and Business Bulletin,* 1973, *23*(3), 834–841.

Kerchner, C. T. From Scopes to scope: The genetic mutation of the school control issue. *Educational Administration Quarterly,* 1978, *14*(1), 64–79.

Kirst, M. W. What happens at the local level after school-finance reform? *Policy Analysis,* 1977, *3*(3), 301–324.

Klauser, J. E. Public-sector impasse resolution in Hawaii. *Industrial Relations,* 1977, *16*(3), 283–289.

Kochan, T. A. Dynamics of dispute resolution in the public sector. In B. Aaron, J. R. Grodin, & J. L. Stern (Eds.), *Public-sector Bargaining.* Washington, D.C.: Bureau of National Affairs, 1979.

Kochan, T. A., & Baderschneider, J. Dependence on impasse procedures: Police and firefighters in New York State. *Industrial and Labor Relations Review,* 1978, *31*(4), 431.

Kochan, T. A., & Wheeler, H. N. Municipal collective bargaining: A model and analysis of bargaining outcomes. *Industrial and Labor Relations Review,* 1975, *29*(1), 46–66.

Levin, H. Educational production theory and teacher inputs. In C. E. Bidwell & D. W. Windham (Eds.), *The Analysis of Educational Productivity (Vol. 2: Issues in Microanalysis).* Cambridge, Mass.: Ballinger, 1980.

Lipsky, D. B., & Barocci, T. A. Final-offer arbitration and public safety employees: The Massachusetts experience. In *Proceedings of the Thirtieth Annual Meeting of the Industrial Relations Research Association, 1977.* Madison: IRRA, 1978.

Lipsky, D. B., & Drotning, J. E. The influence of collective bargaining on teachers' salaries in New York State. *Industrial and Labor Relations Review,* 1973, *27*(1), 18–35.

Lipsky, D. B., & Drotning, J. E. The relation between teachers' salaries and the use of impasse procedures under New York Taylor Law: 1968–1972. *Journal of Collective Negotiations in the Public Sector,* 1977, *6*(3), 229–244.

McDonnell, F., & Pascal, A. *Organized Teachers in American Schools.* Santa Monica, Calif.: Rand Corporation, 1979.

Mitchell, D. E.; Kerchner, C. T.; Erck, W.; & Pryor, G. The impact of collective bargaining on school management and policy. *American Journal of Education* 1981, *89*(2), 147–188.

Olson, C. A. Final-offer arbitration in Wisconsin after five years in *Proceedings of the Thirty-first Annual Meeting of the Industrial Relations Research Association.* Madison: IRRA, 1978.

Perry, C. R. Teacher bargaining: The experience in nine systems. *Industrial and Labor Relations Review,* 1979, *33*(1), 3–17.

Perry, C. R., & Wildman, W. A. *The Impact of Negotiations in Public Education.* Worthington, Ohio: Jones, 1970.

Perry, J. L. Public policy and public employee strikes. *Industrial Relations,* 1977, *16*(3), 273–282.

Peterson, P. *School Politics: Chicago-style.* Chicago: University of Chicago Press, 1976.

Ross, D. *Cuebook II: State Education Collective-bargaining Laws.* Denver: Educational Commission of the States, 1980.

Rubin, J. Z., & Brown, B. R. *The Social Psychology of Bargaining and Negotiation.* New York: Academic Press, 1975.

Schick, R. P., & Couturier, J. L. *The Public Interest in Government Labor Relations.* Cambridge, Mass.: Ballinger, 1977.

Schneider, B. V. H. Public-sector labor legislation: An evolutionary analysis. In B. Aaron, J. R. Grodin, & J. L. Stern (Eds.), *Public-sector Bargaining.* Washington, D.C.: Bureau of National Affairs, 1979.

Stern, J. L.; Rhemus, C. M.; Loewenberg, J. J.; Casper, H.; & Dennis, B. D. *Final Offer Arbitration.* Lexington, Mass.: Heath, 1975.

Straussman, J. D., & Rodgers, R. Public sector unionism and tax burdens: Are they related? *Policy Studies Journal,* 1979, *8*(3), 438–448.

Summers, A. A., & Wolfe, B. L. Do schools make a difference? *American Economic Review,* 1977, *67*(4), 639–652.

Summers, C. W. Public employee bargaining: A political perspective. *Yale Law Journal,* 1974, *83,* 1156–1200.

Thornton, R. J. The effects of collective negotiations on teachers' salaries. *Quarterly Review of Economics and Business,* 1971, *11*(4), 37–46.

U.S. Bureau of the Census, Census of Governments. *Labor Management Relations in State and Local Government: 1973.* Washington, D.C.: U.S. Government Printing Office, 1974.

U.S. Bureau of the Census, Census of Governments. *Labor Management Relations in State and Local Government: 1979.* Washington, D.C.: U.S. Government Printing Office, 1980.

U.S. Department of Education, National Center for Educational Statistics. *The Condition of Education, 1980.* Washington, D.C.: U.S. Government Printing Office, 1980. (ERIC Document Reproduction Service No. ED 188 304)

U.S. Department of Labor, Bureau of Labor Statistics. *Work Stoppages in Government, 1979.* Washington, D.C.: U.S. Government Printing Office, 1981.

U.S. Department of Labor, Labor-Management Services Administration. *Summary of Public-sector Labor Relations Policies.* Washington, D.C.: U.S. Government Printing Office, 1979.

Walton, R. E., & McKersie, R. B. *A Behavioral Theory of Labor Negotiations.* New York: McGraw-Hill, 1965.

Weitzman, J., & Stockaj, J. M. Attitudes of arbitrators toward final-offer arbitration in New Jersey. *Arbitration Journal,* 1980, *35*(1), 25–40.

Wellington, H. H., & Winter, R. K., Jr. *The Unions and the Cities.* Washington, D.C.: Brookings Institution, 1971.

Wheeler, H. N. How compulsory arbitration affects compromise activity. *Industrial Relations*, 1978, *17*(1), 80–84.

Wildman, W. A., & Burns, R. K. *Teacher Organizations and Collective Action: A Review of History and Survey of School District Activity, 1964–1965*. Vol. 1 of *Collective Action by Public School Teachers*. Washington, D.C.: U.S. Department of Health, Education, and Welfare, Office of Education, 1968.

Williams, A. S. Alternatives to the right to strike for public employees: Do they adequately implement Florida's constitutional right to collectively bargain? *Florida State Law Review*, 1979, *7*(3), 475–504.

Wolkinson, B. W., & Stieber, J. Michigan fact-finding experience in public sector disputes. *Arbitration Journal*, 1976, *31*(4), 225–247.

COLLEGES AND UNIVERSITIES

See Effects of College Experience; Higher Education; Organization and Administration of Higher Education.

COMMUNITY CONTROL OF SCHOOLS

See Governance of Schools; Home-School Relationships; Local Influences on Education; School Boards.

COMMUNITY EDUCATION

See Adult Education; Experiential Education; Labor and Education; Parent Education.

COMPARATIVE EDUCATION

Comparative education can be likened to a mosaic consisting of several pieces of knowledge that do not constitute a clearly integrated pattern. Instead, the field presents a collage of diverse trends, schools of thought, and methods. Therefore, a comprehensive review of the literature, within the limits of this article, becomes virtually impossible. To make this task more manageable, we have used the following criteria. (1) We have excluded all textbooks of a general nature (e.g., King's latest edition of *Other Schools and Ours*, 1979); all descriptive material, such as the Around-the-World country studies by the U.S. Department of Education, and all similar reports and publications; and all studies or statements dealing exclusively with methodological concerns, such as Holmes's *Comparative Education* (1981). (2) We have limited ourselves to English-language sources in the West. (3) We have been guided by what has been published in the comparative education literature and not by research in other comparative fields.

This article, more than a summary of research, is also an effort to interpret the main currents of such research. In the search for an interpretive framework, we have often come across two major analytic categories or paradigms: "functional" and "radical." This two-dimensional framework can be used most effectively in conceptualizing and interpreting comparative education research. The article is organized under the following rubrics: (1) functional paradigm, (2) radical paradigm, (3) social relations, (4) political relations, (5) economic relations, (6) development education, (7) effects of schooling, and (8) curriculum and pedagogy.

Functional Paradigm. Among the several theoretical and methodological strands that were woven into the conceptual tapestry of comparative education and provided interpretive guidelines for a substantial volume of research in the 1960s and much of the 1970s, functionalism may be said to be the most salient and the most pervasive. Some general tenets of the functionalist framework—namely, education does not function *sui generis;* it is interrelated with other social and political institutions; and it can best be understood if examined in its social context—have been espoused by most educational comparativists. Certainly such features can be found in many of the well-known works in the field, especially the classic historical studies of Kandel (1933, 1955) and Hans (1950).

In contrast, however, to the "historical" functionalism of Kandel and Hans, the more recent branches, for example, "sociological" or "technological" functionalism, in comparative education are characterized by the following traits: (1) efforts to ground the study of education in scientific, empirical (mostly quantitative) methods and techniques; (2) a quest for "invariant" and "timeless" relationships and thus the assumption that it is possible to develop a theory of education; (3) focus on the actual role of schooling in social, political, and economic processes, as in socialization (including political socialization), social selection or social differentiation, recruitment of elites, social or national integration, human resource development, and the like; (4) a view of educational change as essentially "reformist" or "adaptive," that is, a process of adaptation of educational structures and forms to changes in other sectors or subsystems of the social order; and (5) a vision of the modern society—"meritocratic," "democratic," and "expert"—toward which socioeducational developments should strive (Hurn, 1978; Foster, 1977; Karabel & Halsey, 1977).

The rise of the functional paradigm in comparative education coincided with a variety of other intellectual currents: the prevalent school of American sociology (Parsons, Merton), British social anthropology (Malinowski, Radcliffe-Brown), human-capital theory and its corollaries (Schultz, Harbison, and Myers), theories of development and modernization (Levy, Lerner, Rostow, McClelland, and Black), and the political culture and systems analysis schools of thought in political science (Coleman, 1965; Easton 1965). At the same time, functionalism and social theories of educational change or modernization, as well as policy recommendations based on functionalist analyses, were a response to the socioeconomic and political conditions of the times and were reinforced by institutional and/or individual support from governments, foundations, and international organizations for promotion of their own policy interests.

Radical Paradigm. "Radicalism," or the "radical paradigm," refers to approaches, attitudes, or interpretive theories that view schools as instruments of elite domination or ideological mechanisms that reproduce and perpetuate the hegemonic interests of particular groups; arenas of social conflict; essentially repressive and inegalitarian institutions; and places that inculcate class-related values and attitudes rather than cognitive and technical skills.

To understand school-society relationships and the role of schooling, according to the radical paradigm, one must inquire into the power structure of a society and the social relations of production. It follows, therefore, that educational change presupposes radical transformation of socioeconomic and power relations and institutions—in short, of society itself (Hurn, 1978; Karabel & Halsey, 1977).

In contrast to functionalism, statements and interpretations of radicalism have appeared in the comparative education literature rather recently (mostly in the last ten years). Their intellectual roots may be traced to, among others, conflict theorists (Weberian or Neo-Marxist), dependency theorists, and the so-called new sociologists. At the same time, as with functionalism, the radical paradigm was influenced by the social and political context of the 1960s and 1970s: growing social and educational unrest, along with dissipation of optimism about the benefits of schooling, the liberals' efforts at educational reform, and the humane and democratic nature of existing institutions generally.

Social Relations. The functionalist framework of analysis in the emerging new comparative education of the 1960s and afterward was most apparent in productive research on the social relations of education, particularly the links between educational systems and systems of social stratification, the role of education in social development and modernization, and theories of educational change.

Functional comparative education focusing on macro-socioeducational themes flourished especially at the University of Chicago Comparative Education Center. It is evident in the works of all scholars and students who have been associated at one time or another with the center, particularly C. A. Anderson, P. Foster, and M. J. Bowman. The Chicago school has been especially concerned with the important role of the economy and the occupational structure in educational diffusion, educational structures, and even the curriculum. Elsewhere, Kazamias and Schwartz (1977) have noted that the conceptualization of educational change, as a process of "functional transformation" or adaptation of institutional patterns, in the Chicago

school can be reconstructed from Foster's Ghana study (1965) as follows:

1. A differentiated economic and occupational structure makes certain demands on the schools; it rewards differentially the various types of education.
2. Individuals respond by seeking the types of education that will reward them in ways demanded by the occupational structure; that is, the individual's perception of what schooling is for is determined by the occupational structure.
3. Thus a functional equilibrium is sought and maintained between schools and the economy; and as the economy changes, so does the school.

On the instrumental side of this socioeducational coin, the contributory value of education for purposes of development and modernization, the Chicago group was less sanguine and more cautious than the contemporary, ardent developmentalists—a dimension of the issue that is treated more extensively elsewhere.

Reflecting trends in the social sciences (notably sociology) and spurred by liberal democratic and welfare state socioeducational reformism (with its emphasis on democracy in education, education as a citizenship right, and social equity, comparative education pursued with greater methodological rigor, conceptual sophistication, and even ideological fervor such themes as (1) the structure and context of educational opportunities and inequalities; (2) the mechanisms of educational selection and discrimination; (3) the ways education bears on social ascent, status, and life chances; and (4) the ways education is influenced by family background and social provenance (what the English sociologists Karabel and Halsey, 1977, referred to as "political arithmetic").

The main course of comparative research in this socioeducational and political sphere paralleled the mainstream of social science inquiries with respect to conceptual framework, ideology, and types of questions examined. Early writings on Western-developed and Western-developing societies by persons identified with the field of comparative education, such as C. A. Anderson, P. Foster, G. Z. Bereday, T. Husén, M. Eckstein, and A. Kazamias and B. Massialas, looked into problems of educational *access* and educational *selection*, that is into the question "Who gets what in education and how much?" gauged in terms of socioeconomic and demographic background of students (occupational and social-class family characteristics, place and region of residence). Invariably, the findings in Western, more advanced societies showed differential patterns of social recruitment and a prevalence of what came to be known as the "iron law of educational selection," namely that children whose parents belonged to upper-status occupational or social-class groups and had higher levels of education and income were comparatively more successful in selective examinations, were overrepresented in high-status schools and universities, and generally had higher levels of educational attainment than their lower-status counterparts (Kazamias & Massialas, 1965; Husén, 1972; Bereday, 1977).

Differential patterns of educational access and disparities in educational provision were also observed in less developed countries (Foster, 1965; Kazamias, 1966). In some of these countries, however (e.g., in Africa), as Foster (1977) pointed out, one must be cautious in applying the same stratification terms (e.g., social class) as in more advanced societies, for "there are multiple bases of social differentiation including race, ethnicity, occupation, regional origin, lineage and sex" (p. 215).

Similar types of comparative research continued into the 1970s and were also undertaken on a large scale by international organizations (Organization for Economic Cooperation and Development [OECD], 1975). At the same time, however, conceptual framework, focus of investigation, and ideological perspective had shifted. Here comparative education writings made references to the findings of two influential American sociological studies: the Coleman Report (Coleman et al., 1966) and Jencks's *Inequality: A Reassessment of the Effects of Family and Schooling in America* (Jencks et al., 1972). Both studies, it should be remembered, went beyond examination of access to education and examined influences on educational results.

In *Educational Policies for the 1970's* Frankel and Halsey noted that in the past decade there had been a gradual change in the meaning of "equality of educational opportunity" from "equality of access to education" to "equality of achievement" (OECD, 1971). Social influences on educational achievement in Western developed societies were also studied comparatively by Husén (1975) and Neave (1976). The extent to which the Coleman and Jencks theses applied to the less developed countries was discussed by Foster (1977) and Farrell (1974); a study by Heyneman (1976) compared influences on academic achievement in Uganda "and more industrialized societies" and concluded that "the relationship between socioeconomic status and academic achievement appears weaker in less industrialized societies" (p. 210).

In conceptualization and approach, the type of comparative literature reviewed previously displayed methodological characteristics and ideological assumptions of the functional paradigm described earlier and, not infrequently, of "methodological empiricism" (Karabel & Halsey, 1977; Kazamias & Schwartz, 1977). Implicit in most of these works is a liberal and progressive educational reformism in the conception and policy ramifications of equality of opportunity (Husén, 1975) as well as of educational change. As a general rule these writings eschew radical socioeconomic solutions to educational problems, which are viewed as internal maladjustments or dysfunctions in an essentially sound and benign liberal democratic polity.

Radical interpretations of the social relations of schooling, and radical criticisms of the liberal doctrines of equality of opportunity, compensatory education policies, and other liberal reforms were more frequent in comparative education writings of the last decade (Husén, 1975; Levin, 1978; Paulston, 1977; Zachariah, 1975, 1979).

Political Relations. Functionalism in comparative education has characterized the conceptual framework and methodological approach of studies that examined the relations between education and the political system and the role of the school in political development or modernization. In this regard, much of the research has been guided by the influential works of social scientists (Coleman, 1965; Easton, 1965).

Coleman considered education (primarily formal education) to perform three important functions in the political system: socialization of children and youth into the political culture; selection, recruitment, and training of political elites; and political integration or nation building of groups of people.

Easton elaborated on the concept of the political system, which he defined as "those interactions through which values are authoritatively allocated for a society." His political-system idea constituted a departure from older concepts such as state, government, and nation in that it included both formal and informal governmental institutions as well as the political beliefs and acts of citizens as individuals and as groups; it signified interdependence of its parts; and it implied the notion of boundary between the system and its environment (that is, some parameters define political acts and distinguish them from economic or social acts).

Numerous studies since 1965 on the political dimensions of education have focused on the key areas of the functionalist framework as outlined here: political socialization, political recruitment, and the role of formal education in political integration.

Political socialization. In political socialization research, effort is directed toward examining the various social agents, especially the family and the school, in order to determine their relative impact on the individual's political knowledge and attitudes. Results have been rather inconclusive, more so in the case of formal education and the schools than in the case of the family. Almond and Verba (1963) and Hess and Torney (1967) found that "manifest teaching about Government" and the school in general are effective instruments in political socialization. Such conclusions have been challenged consistently since the mid-1960s, however. Niemi (1973), for example, found that "the effects of the school are highly variable—depending at least on the quality of the teacher, the class material, the social and political composition of the school and classroom, particular circumstances of time and place, and even interactive effects such as the correspondence between what is taught in the classroom and what is informally taught outside of school" (p. 131). Massialas (1972), who looked at fourteen studies in a number of countries,

concluded that "the impact of the conventional civics curriculum on any of the political socialization indices (e.g.,
political efficacy, expectations for political participation,
even political knowledge) is negligible" (p. 251). In almost
no country does the school create conditions for students
to learn the skills needed to participate effectively in political life.

Contrary to the functionalist socialization argument,
which assumes internalization of consensus values, Hess
(1968) himself in another statement on the subject argued
that in the United States, at least "the schools have contributed to divisions within society by teaching a view
of the nation and its political processes which is incomplete
and simplistic, stressing values and ideals but ignoring social realities" (p. 531). Similar ambivalences and contradictions about the role of the schools in development of political awareness and in citizenship training generally have
been noted by other writers, especially from England, who
prefer to use the narrower term "political education"
rather than "political socialization" (Entwistle, 1971).

Summarizing the literature on one focus of the socialization research, that of "democratic political socialization,"
Merelman (1980) put it simply: "Schooling has yet to demonstrate its contribution to the child's development of
democratic values" (p. 319).

Political elites. Another way in which education has
been perceived to relate functionally to the political system has been through its role in selection, training, and
recruitment of political elites. Frey's important work on
the significance of education in the recruitment of Turkish
political elites (1965) represents a type of literature that
sought to ascertain this political function of schooling by
examining the educational background of political leaders.
A series of studies, using historical, anthropological, and
sociological approaches, as reported by Wilkinson (1969),
established links between education (both formal and nonformal) and access to political leadership positions. At the
same time, these studies provided evidence to indicate
that education cannot escape many of the constraints imposed by the general culture of the society; for example,
the education received by the immobile societies of the
Incas and the Aztecs was highly differentiated among the
social orders, whereas such mobile societies as the various
tribes of Plains Indians were more meritocratic and provided opportunities for all to occupy elite positions.

Political integration. Two aspects of the functional
relationship between education and nation building or political integration usually discussed in the literature are
the elite-mass gap, or the vertical dimension of political
integration, and the international, ethnic, or regional division, or the horizontal dimension (Coleman, 1965).

Education has a tendency to perpetuate and reinforce
existing inequalities either through its allocative functions
(e.g., it assigns individuals to perform certain roles in society) or through its legitimation functions (e.g., it legiti-
mates the authority of elites). In this respect, Bock (1976)
argued that formal as contrasted with informal education

often accentuates problems of political integration and nation building in developing countries.

As in the case of elite-mass relations, education by and
large tends to reinforce or accentuate existing inequalities
based on ethnicity, religion, language, or place of residence. Primarily as a result of colonial policies, disintegra-
tive educational privileges exist in such countries as Nigeria, Sri Lanka, Indonesia, and the Philippines, where
ethnic, regional, and denominational privileges occur together, or Rwanda and Burundi (ethnic privileges), or the
Sudan and Lebanon (regional and sectarian privileges)
(Hanf et al., 1975). The evidence suggests that, in most
Afro-Asian states where the degree of political integration
is related to ethnic, linguistic, and religious heterogeneity,
"formal education reproduces, aggravates, and, in many
cases, even causes the heterogeneity and inequality that
exist" (Hanf et al., 1975, p. 76).

Massialas (1977) took exception to the theoretical framework espoused by most researchers in these fields. Undue
emphasis on political systems has colored our perception
of what education does and can do for individuals, their
families, and their communities. We repeatedly discard
whole school programs or introduce new ones based on
the extent to which they relate to the political system.
If the school created political activists who would question
the authorities in the political system and introduce major
demands into the system, then (as per systems theory)
the school would be thought of as dysfunctional since it
did not promote stability and continuity of the system either directly or through diffuse support. Extending this
theoretical frame to research narrowed the scope of the
research agenda; that is, only systems-relevant questions
were asked. The topic of students, teachers, and other
key school actors serving as change agents because of their
schooling received virtually no attention in the literature.
As a result, we have accepted almost on faith that the
school, regardless of its program, serves only to certify
individuals for occupational placement in society. We need
to change the conservative, theoretical framework to a
dynamic one that focuses on the individual and the community (mainly sociopsychological and psychoanalytic
frameworks) and uses both qualitative and quantitative
data-gathering techniques.

Politics of education. The literature reviewed previously, cast in the conceptual and ideological mold of functionalism, provided a new perspective on the study of the
intersection of school and polity. It was certainly different
in its theoretical approach, methodology, and types of
problems studied from that of the historical-functional approach of the earlier classic comparative work of Kandel
and Hans (Kazamias, 1975). At the same time, it by no
means defined the sphere of investigations into the political relations of education. Comparative educators continue
to be concerned with the political factors that affect patterns and policies of schooling, administration and control
of education, educational decision making, the church-
state-school issue, educational change or reform, in short,

with the politics of education. As in most other domains of comparative education, research trends and schools of thought on education as an arena of public controversy, political conflict, and public policy have been more analytic and more empirically based and less descriptive or hortatory than before. At the same time, certain aspects of the politics of education have attracted the attention of conflict or critical theorists as well as of the so-called new sociologists, the sociologists of knowledge, whose influence had already penetrated comparative education. These developments are most saliently manifested in the fast-growing and, from methodological and ideological standpoints, increasingly sophisticated area of the politics of educational reform.

In a recent critical review of the literature, Merritt and Coombs (1977) pointed to some important strides in conceptualization and comparative treatment of the politics of educational reform, as found, for example, in works by Peterson (1973), Heidenheimer (1974), and Herndon (1974). At the same time, they noted that the single-system case study continues to characterize the majority of scholarly productivity and that even excellent comparative studies lack an adequate explanatory theoretical framework. They urged studies that "select a variable upon which systems differ and then set about accounting for the difference across a number of systems" (Merritt & Coombs, 1977, p. 252).

An interesting and enlightening socioeducational controversy, which has recently found strong echoes in comparative education, has centered in the nature, limits, and possibilities of liberal educational reform. In this connection, comparativists and theorists of schooling who have espoused some variant of the radical paradigm have been critical of scholio-centric reforms and the claims made on their behalf by liberal educational reformers. Apple (1978), for example, argued that "educational reform needs to be grounded in an analysis of the complex relationship among knowledge, ideology, economics and power" (p. 386). In another vein, Levin (1978) examined the comprehensive-school reforms in Western Europe and concluded that comprehensive schools are faced with an impossible dilemma. On the one hand, they are called upon to increase individual opportunities for social mobility (claims of equity), and, on the other, they must produce labor for the unequal work role of monopoly capitalism. The main message of the antireformist literature is that school-centered reforms by themselves cannot resolve social and economic problems. Because schools serve to reproduce the political, social, and economic relations of a society, they will change only when such relations themselves change (Carnoy & Levin, 1976).

Economic Relations. A third major socioeducational domain to which the research and policy interests of comparativists in education have been increasingly and rather productively turned in recent decades was the economic and more broadly developmental relations of schooling. The lines of inquiry into this topic displayed similar methodological and conceptual characteristics as well as similar ideological trends and countertrends to those already examined. Varieties of the functionalist framework, such as technological functionalism, guided theoretical research into human resource development (Karabel & Halsey, 1977) and action research in educational planning, whereas methodological empiricism provided the rationale for certain methods and techniques. Functionalist characteristics were likewise manifested in the widespread concern with what came to be known as development education.

Education as investment. One major stream of research that flowed into the pool of comparative education knowledge on the economic aspects of schooling sprang from the human-capital theory associated with the works of Schultz, Becker, Denison, and others in the early 1960s. Looking at education as a form of productive investment rather than pure consumption, the human-capital theory provided the conceptual apparatus for several lines of investigation. Among them, the most widely discussed in the comparative education literature were rates of return to education, relationships between education and economic growth, and manpower requirements and educational needs relationships, or the "forecasting approach" (Hansen, 1977; Sobel, 1978).

Rates of return to education. Rate-of-return studies examine the relationships between education and earnings and evaluate education as an investment by comparing costs incurred with individual and social benefits derived. Among the most prolific and better-known rate-of-return researchers, those work has also penetrated the comparative education literature, are Psacharopoulos (1973, 1975) and Carnoy (1972). Some of the main generalizations from the Psacharopoulos comprehensive comparative analysis of fifty-three rate-of-return studies for thirty-two developed and developing countries around the world (Psacharopoulos, 1973) illustrate the type of education-earnings relationships encountered in the literature: (1) the payoff (private and sound rates of return) from investment in education is generally higher in developing than in more advanced countries; (2) benefits from investment in primary schooling tend to be the highest; (3) returns to human capital are higher than those to physical capital in the less developed countries, but are approximately equal to the returns on physical capital in advanced countries; (4) human-capital differentials can explain per capita income differentials better than can differences in physical capital; (5) benefits from investment in formal vocational education were substantially lower than those in secondary general academic schools in two of the three countries studied.

Education for economic growth. The economic benefits of education were also buttressed by studies that examined the impact of schooling on economic growth and development (Adams, 1977; Hansen, 1977). This research tributary, whose main theoretical source was also the human-capital theory, flowed especially into the comparative education literature that dealt with educational developments and educational planning in the emerging Third World countries (Adams & Bjork, 1971). The sources of poverty and economic backwardness (low productivity and low per capita income, primitive technology, and overwhelmingly agricultural economies) were seen to reside in inadequate reservoirs of human skill development as well as in values, attitudes, and motivations—in short, in inadequate education and training.

It followed, therefore, that the best way to remedy what was perceived to be internal maladjustments of the system, and to bring about economic prosperity and efficiency, was through more and better schooling, and schooling of the functional type—technical and vocational education. This educational gospel of economic national salvation received considerable empirical support from comparative researchers and was epitomized in Harbison and Myers's widespread aphorism, "Education is the key that unlocks the door to modernization" (Harbison & Myers, 1964, p. 181). Correlational empirical studies linking educational and economic growth indices were paralleled by a frenzy of economic and human resource development plans that gave educational requirements high priority (Adams, 1977).

The human-capital theory and its planning corollaries struck a responsive chord in such international organizations and agencies as OECD, the U.S. Agency for International Development (AID), and the World Bank, which readily supported research projects or provided consulting services to various countries (OECD, 1965; World Bank, 1980). Such lines of inquiry, and their underlying theoretical and ideological assumptions, did not go unchallenged. Criticism and reservations about the rate-of-return and labor-forecasting approaches, as well as about unqualified belief in the economic value of education, especially vocational schooling, appeared in the literature concurrently with words of praise (Sobel, 1978; Foster, 1975, 1977; Adams, 1977). More strident attacks have recently come from radical economists, dependency theorists, and, more broadly, comparative educators who place more emphasis upon social justice and a more equitable distribution of social goods than upon economic efficiency and mere accumulation of wealth (Carnoy, 1975).

Regardless of the numerous criticisms and attacks, the human-capital theory as an explanation of education and economic development has had and continues to have a major impact upon the thinking, analytical approach, and vocabularies of economists, educators, and planners (Sobel, 1978; World Bank, 1980).

Development Education.   Economic growth, although basic, denotes but one dimension of the social process of development toward which education was believed to contribute. Another aspect of this process is the political, discussed earlier. Still, neither exhausts the education-for-development research and thinking that characterized a substantial body of comparative education literature in the 1960s and 1970s. An important strand in this literature pertained to the role of education in the broad and multifa-

ceted process of sociocultural transformation or modernization. The perspectives from which this process was examined employed concepts and techniques from a variety of disciplines or areas (education, sociology, cultural anthropology, social psychology, economics, and politics). Whatever the approach or focus of research and thinking in this field, it was pervaded by optimism about the instrumental-developmental value of education in all spheres of social activity and public policy as well as in personal life and relationships (Adams, 1977; Inkeles & Smith, 1974). Although this optimism largely evaporated in the 1970s, certain organizations, such as the World Bank, continued to place heavy faith in the positive role of education for social and personal development (World Bank, 1980). Further research on individual and social modernity found grounds to criticize the functionalist and evolutionary assumptions of the modernization theorists. Drawing mostly from Neo-Marxist and other conflict theorists (Bowles & Gintis, 1976), a new school of thought emerged that infiltrated the literature in comparative education. Generally known as the "dependency school," this school of thought advocated, for example, that the inequalities in developing countries are due to dependency preconditions inherited from colonial times, the neocolonial postindependence period, and the present capitalist-dominated direction of development (*Comparative Education Review*, 1975).

Effects of Schooling.   One aspect of education that earlier comparative studies did not explore systematically in its social and pedagogical context was the actual *effectiveness* of schooling in accomplishing the educational tasks it sets for itself. Creditable answers to such related questions as "What do schools actually do?" "What do children learn at school?" and "What influences what in school outcomes?" have been important missing links in the chain of reasoning regarding cross-national judgments about educational systems and the setting of priorities in educational policy decisions. In certain respects, of course, concerns with the social, economic, and political functions of education, of the type discussed previously, addressed themselves to school outcomes. What has been conspicuous in the literature, however, has been the paucity of hard data on cognitive learning or on academic achievement of students in all levels and types of schools.

The single most ambitious and certainly in many respects most impressive research undertaking that sought to chart a course toward filling the learning-outcomes void in comparative education was the empirical survey initiated and carried out by an international consortium of researchers known as the Council for the International Evaluation of Educational Achievement, later called the International Association for the Evaluation of Educational Achievement (IEA). The IEA project sought to assess quantitatively the academic productivity or present-day effectiveness of the educational systems of twenty-one countries by studying the relationship between input factors (school structures, teacher and pupil characteristics, classroom pedagogical practices, students' socioeconomic background) and output factors (measurable achievement in various subjects of the curriculum, such as mathematics, reading comprehension, literature, science, civics education, and English and French as foreign languages) (Husén, 1967; *Comparative Education Review*, 1974). In a review of the methodology and some of the main findings of the IEA studies, Eckstein (1977) observed that "home background . . . stands out as an internationally strong variable in explaining variations in achievement" and "few of the directly school related variables seemed to bear any straightforward, universal relationship to achievement variance with the exception of 'opportunity to learn' " (p. 351). The study revealed the gaps that exist between developed and developing countries, especially in educational provision and student achievement.

The IEA survey has been praised for its rigorous design, its empirical base and analysis, and its catholicity of perspective. At the same time, some of the very same aspects of the project that drew accolades from several social science quarters and from comparative educators have also been the focus of controversy and criticism. A recent accounting of the project by Husén (1979), one of its architects, brought out some often-cited shortcomings: undue emphasis on quantitative methods as supplied to achievement tests to validate certain hypotheses, limitations of the input-output model, absence of qualitative analyses, and generally heavy reliance on a positivist research paradigm.

Husén's critical observations (1979) are appropriate in conceptualizing and assessing the theoretical *cum* methodological and the ideological research framework of other scientific comparative investigations that seemed to be *de rigueur* in the seventies. Certainly this could be true of all so-called educational production function studies, which, like the IEA survey, examined the relationships between educational inputs and outputs (Hansen, 1977; Alexander & Simmons, 1975; Schiefelbein, 1975).

Curriculum and Pedagogy. In 1972 Kazamias deplored the fact that comparative education had not dealt adequately with the internal aspects of education, with the relations of educational knowledge, and with the nature and processes of classroom interaction—in short, with the predominantly pedagogical dimensions of schooling. Five years later, Springer (1977) echoed the same concern, but added that in three fields relevant to pedagogy, comparative education had made some contributions. She identified these as follows: broad-scale information about national education systems (e.g., the work done by King, 1973); collaboration with international and national government agencies (here the coordination of requirements for academic school-leaving certificates in France, Germany, and Holland is mentioned; and research conducted by individuals or teams of experts, such as Susan M. Shafer's "The Socialization of Girls in Secondary Schools of England and the Two Germanies," and Val D. Rust's "Teacher Control in Pre-Schools of Los Angeles, London, and Frankfurt." In this connection we should also mention the well-

known IEA surveys, examined earlier, as well as some recent, scattered efforts: curriculum changes in Greece (Kazamias, 1978), student learning in Uganda (Heyneman & Jamison, 1980), curriculum tracking in Israel (Nachmias, 1980), and basic education in Egypt (Joint Egyptian-American Survey Team, 1979).

Although work in comparative education has continued to center in the external socioeconomic and political aspects of schooling, some promising stirrings have become evident along the lines suggested by Foley (1977), Hayman (1979), Kazamias (1972), Massialas (1977), Singleton (1977), and Springer (1977). The theoretical and methodological orientation of studies that examine the internal aspects of schooling has drawn less from the functional paradigm and methodological empiricism and more from conflict theories, from the so-called new sociology school, from anthropological works of inquiry (participant observation, intensive interviewing), and from ethnographic analyses (Foley, 1977).

Andreas Kazamias
Byron G. Massialas

See also Comparative Education Administration; Comparative School Achievement; Economics and Education; International Education; National Development and Education.

REFERENCES

Adams, D. Development education. *Comparative Education Review*, 1977, *21*, 296–310.

Adams, D., & Bjork, R. M. *Education in Developing Areas*. New York: McKay, 1971.

Alexander, L., & Simons, J. *The Determinants of School Achievement in Developing Countries: The Educational Production Function* (Staff Working Paper No. 201). Washington, D.C.: World Bank, 1975.

Almond, G. A., & Verba, S. *The Civic Culture: Political Attitudes and Democracy in Five Nations*. Princeton, N.J.: Princeton University Press, 1963.

Apple, M. Ideology, reproduction, and educational reform. *Comparative Education Review*, 1978, *22*, 367–387.

Bereday, G. Z. Social stratification and education in industrial countries. *Comparative Education Review*, 1977, *21*, 195–210.

Bock, J. The institutionalization of nonformal education. *Comparative Education Review*, 1976, *20*, 346–367.

Bowles, S., & Gintis, H. *Schooling in Capitalist America*. London: Routledge & Kegan Paul, 1976.

Carnoy, M. The rate of return to schooling and the increase in human resources in Puerto Rico. *Comparative Education Review*, 1972, *16*, 68–86.

Carnoy, M. The role of education in a strategy for social change. *Comparative Education Review*, 1975, *19*, 393–402.

Carnoy, M., & Levin, H. M. *The Limits of Educational Reform*. New York: McKay, 1976.

Coleman, J. *Education and Political Development*. Princeton, N.J.: Princeton University Press, 1965.

Coleman, J. S.; Campbell, E. Q.; Hobson, C. J.; McPartland, J.; Mood, A. M.; Weinfeld, F. D.; & York, R. L. *Equality of Educational Opportunity*. Washington, D.C.: U.S. Government Printing Office, 1966.

Comparative Education Review (Special issue on What Do Children Know? Intercultural Studies in Educational Achievement). 1974, *18*(2).

Comparative Education Review (Educational development: A symposium). 1975, *19*(3), 375–433.

Easton, D. *A Systems Analysis of Political Life.* New York: Wiley, 1965.

Eckstein, M. A. Comparative study of educational achievement. *Comparative Education Review*, 1977, *21*, 345–357.

Entwistle, H. *Political Education in a Democracy.* London: Routledge & Kegan Paul, 1971.

Farrell, J. A review of Jencks' *Inequality. Comparative Education Review*, 1974, *18*, 430–435.

Foley, D. E. Anthropological studies of schooling in developing countries: Some recent findings and trends. *Comparative Education Review*, 1977, *21*, 311–345.

Foster, P. J. *Education and Social Change in Ghana.* Chicago: University of Chicago Press, 1965.

Foster, P. J. Dilemmas of educational development: What we might learn from the past. *Comparative Education Review*, 1975, *19*, 375–392.

Foster, P. J. Education and social differentiation in less developed countries. *Comparative Education Review*, 1977, *21*, 211–229.

Frey, W. *The Turkish Political Elite.* Cambridge, Mass.: MIT Press, 1965.

Hanf, T.; Ammann, K.; Dias, P.; Fremerey, M.; & Weiland, H. Education: An obstacle to development? *Comparative Education Review*, 1975, *19*, 68–87.

Hans, N. *Comparative Education.* London: Routledge & Kegan Paul, 1950.

Hansen, W. L. Economics and comparative education: Will they ever meet? And if so, when? *Comparative Education Review*, 1977, *21*(2-3), 230–246.

Harbison, F., & Myers, C. A. *Education, Manpower, and Economic Growth: Strategies of Human Resource Development.* New York: McGraw-Hill, 1964.

Hayman, R. Comparative education from an ethnomethodological perspective. *Comparative Education.* 1979, *15*, 241–249.

Heidenheimer, A. The politics of educational reform: Explaining different outcomes of school comprehensive attempts in Sweden and West Germany. *Comparative Education Review*, 1974, *18*, 388–410.

Herndon, A. *Education in the Two Germanies.* Oxford: Basil Blackwell, 1974.

Hess, R. O., Political socialization in the schools: Discussion. *Harvard Educational Review*, 1968, *38*, 528–536.

Hess, R. O., & Torney, J. V. *The Development of Political Attitudes in Children.* Chicago: Aldine, 1967.

Heyneman, S. P. Influences on academic achievement: A comparison of results from Uganda and more industrial societies. *Sociology of Education*, 1976, *49*, 200–211.

Heyneman, S. P., Jamison, D. T. Textbook availability and other determinants of student learning in Uganda. *Comparative Education Review.* 1980, *24*, 206–220.

Holmes, B. *Comparative Education: Some Consideration of Method.* London: Allen & Unwin, 1981.

Hurn, C. J. *The Limits and Possibilities of Schooling: An Introduction to the Sociology of Education.* Boston: Allyn & Bacon, 1978.

Husén, T. (Ed.) *International Study of Achievement in Mathematics: A Comparison of Twelve Countries* (Vols. 1 and 2). New York: Wiley, 1967.

Husén, T. *Social Background and Educational Career.* Paris: Organization for Economic Cooperation and Development, 1972.

Husén, T. *Social Influences on Educational Attainment.* Paris: Organization for Economic Cooperation and Development, 1975.

Husén, T. An international research venture in retrospect: The IEA surveys. *Comparative Education Review*, 1979, *23*, 371–385.

Husén, T.; Sagerlind, I.; & Liljefors, R. Sex differences in science achievement and attitudes. *Comparative Education Review*, 1974, *18*, 292–304.

Inkeles, A., & Smith, D. H. *Becoming Modern.* Cambridge, Mass.: Harvard University Press, 1974.

International Studies in Evaluation (Vols. 1–9). New York: Wiley, 1973–1976.

Jencks, C.; Smith, M.; Acland, H.; Bane, M.; Cohen, D.; Gentis, H.; Heyns, B.; & Michaelson, S. *Inequality: A Reassessment of the Effects of Family and Schooling in America.* New York: Harper Colophon Books, 1972.

Joint Egyptian-American Survey Team. *Basic Education in Egypt.* Washington, D.C.: Human Resources Management, Inc., 1979.

Kandel, I. L. *Comparative Education.* Boston: Houghton Mifflin, 1933.

Kandel, I. L. *The New Era in Education: A Comparative Study.* Boston: Houghton Mifflin, 1955.

Kandel, I. L. Methodology of comparative education. *International Review of Education*, 1959, *5*(3), 273.

Karabel, J., & Halsey, A. H. (Eds.) *Power and Ideology in Education.* New York: Oxford University Press, 1977.

Kazamias, A. M. *Education and the Quest for Modernity in Turkey.* London: Allen & Unwin, 1966.

Kazamias, A. M. Comparative pedagogy: An assignment for the seventies. *Comparative Education Review*, 1972, *16*, 406–411.

Kazamias, A. M. Editor's note. *Comparative Education Review* (Special issue on Politics and Education). 1975, *19*(1), 1–4.

Kazamias, A. M. The politics of educational reform in Greece: Law 309/1976. *Comparative Education Review*, 1978, *22*, 21–45.

Kazamias, A. M., & Massialas, B. G. *Tradition and Change in Education: A Comparative Study.* Englewood Cliffs, N.J.: Prentice-Hall, 1965.

Kazamias, A. M., & Schwartz, K. Intellectual and ideological perspectives in comparative education. *Comparative Education Review*, 1977, *21*(2/3), 153–176.

King, E. J. *Other Schools and Ours* (4th ed.) New York: Holt, Rinehart & Winston, 1973.

Langton, K. P. *Political Socialization.* New York: Oxford University Press, 1969.

Levin, H. M. The dilemma of comprehensive school reforms in Western Europe. *Comparative Education Review*, 1978, *22*, 434–451.

Massialas, B. G. *Education and the Political System.* Reading, Mass.: Addison-Wesley, 1969.

Massialas, B. G. The inquiring activist. In B. G. Massialas (Ed.), *Political Youth, Traditional Schools: National and International Perspectives.* Englewood Cliffs, N.J.: Prentice-Hall, 1972.

Massialas, B. G. Education and political development. *Comparative Education Review*, 1977, *21*, 274–295.

Merelman, R. M. Democratic politics and the culture of American education. *American Political Science Review*, 1980, *74*, 319–331.

Merritt, R. L., & Coombs, F. S. Politics and educational reform. *Comparative Education Review*, 1977, *21*, 247–273.

Nachmias, C. Curriculum tracking: Some of its causes and consequences under a meritocracy. *Comparative Education Review*, 1980, *24*, 1–20.

Neave, G. *Patterns of Equality*. London: National Foundation for Educational Research Publishing Co., 1976.

Niemi, R. G. Political socialization. In J. N. Knudson (Ed.), *Handbook of Political Psychology*. San Francisco: Jossey-Bass, 1973.

Organization for Economic Cooperation and Development. *The Mediterranean Regional Project: Country Reports*. Paris: OECD, 1965.

Organization for Economic Cooperation and Development. *Educational Policies for the 1970's: General Report*. Paris: OECD, 1971.

Organization for Economic Cooperation and Development. *Education, Inequality, and Life Chances*. Paris: OECD, 1975.

Paulston, R. Social and educational change. Conceptual frameworks. *Comparative Education Review*, 1977, *21*, 370–395.

Peterson, P. The politics of educational reform in England and the United States. *Comparative Education Review*, 1973, *17*, 160–179.

Psacharopoulos, G. *Returns to Education: An International Comparison*. San Francisco: Jossey-Bass, 1973.

Psacharopoulos, G. *Earnings and Education in OECD Countries*. Paris: Organization for Economic Cooperation and Development, 1975.

Schiefelbein, E. Repeating: An overlooked problem of Latin American education. *Comparative Education Review*, 1975, *19*, 468–487.

Selby, H. Elite selection and social integration: An anthropologist's view. In R. Wilkinson (Ed.), *Governing Elites: Studies in Training and Selection*. New York: Oxford University Press, 1969.

Singleton, J. Education and ethnicity. *Comparative Education Review*, 1977, *21*, 329–344.

Sobel, I. The human capital revolution in economic development: Its current history and status. *Comparative Education Review*, 1978, *22*, 278–304.

Springer, U. Education, curriculum, and pedagogy. *Comparative Education Review*, 1977, *21*, 358–369.

Symposium on educational reform in Greece. *Comparative Education Review*, 1978, *22*, 1–98.

Wilkinson, R. (Ed.). *Governing Elites: Studies in Training and Selection*. New York: Oxford University Press, 1969.

World Development Report, 1980. Washington, D.C.: World Bank, 1980.

Zachariah, M. *Those Who Pay the Piper Call the Tune*. Paper presented at the annual meeting of the Comparative and International Education Society, San Francisco, March 1975.

Zachariah, M. Comparative education and international development policy. *Comparative Education Review*, 1979, *23*(3), 341–354.

COMPARATIVE EDUCATION ADMINISTRATION

Comparative education administration as a specific area of study is rather new. Both World War I and World War II were followed by increasing concern among the more economically developed nations about education as a way of rebuilding and achieving well beyond prior expectations. Democratization for secondary and later higher education was demanded. The easy faith in democracy as the normal and natural political system was challenged and tested by the growth of fascism and communism. The technology of production, distribution, and communication had vast new implications for society and government. In the newly developing nations, an unprecedented awakening brought with it—along with high expectations—a somewhat naive belief in government power and the efficacy of planning and a desire to borrow and achieve economic advancement quickly while preserving traditional social and cultural values. There were also enough persons in economically developed nations who were pleased to prescribe solutions. Thus the world scene was rather fertile for comparisons, transfer, borrowing, and for international education. The decade of the seventies has witnessed considerable lowering of expectations.

Definition. Comparative education administration is the systematic study and determination of similarities and differences of legal bases, powers of authorities and individuals, theories of control (inspection, supervision, administration), and policies and procedures of the educational service of two or more societies or nations. Closely related to comparative public administration, comparative education administration is an important aspect of comparative education. It is a difficult field of study since it requires a relatively valid knowledge and understanding of at least two societies, of their concepts of education and schooling, and of relevant historical, political, economic, and social factors. Frequently the comparison may involve the writer's tendency to overvalue or undervalue his own society. Additional barriers to understanding the social fabric and the administrative policies and procedures of another society are linguistic and cultural factors. However, explicit attempts at comparison are generally preferable to studies in which implied assumptions and comparisons predominate. Studies of a single society not involving comparison do not come within the scope of this article.

The article focuses on the defensibility of comparative education administration; problems of methodology; studies in comparative elementary and secondary education administration; and studies in comparative higher education administration. Special attention is given to higher education, since it is the level at which there has been sharply increased activity in the 1970s and in which methodological developments may be illustrated.

Defensibility. The study of comparative education administration may be readily defended on the basis of knowledge for its own sake. It is also justified by the desire of one society to have knowledge of other societies in order to select more intelligently and responsibly from various alternatives among educational and administrative practices. Much can be learned from others even though there is recognition that borrowing may itself be highly questionable. Furthermore, educators can learn very much about their own systems by examining them from the vantage point of others. All of these justifications become stronger as the interdependence of nations and the need for international cooperation and development increases. Perhaps the nature of the administrative role in many organizations may reduce breadth of vision rather than expand it, but expansion is imperative. The study of comparative education administration is an important aid to that expansion.

Problems of Methodology. Research methodology has been difficult and uncertain in both the areas of comparative education and educational administration. Early studies in comparative education were historical and broadly descriptive. Those in administration were largely of practice. In its methods, comparative education administration must rely on a number of other disciplines, such as history, philosophy, political science, psychology, sociology, and economics. Few, if any, significant educational problems can be attacked in terms of a single discipline. Consider, for example, such problems as the role of the school principal in different societies, the power of the administrator, the role of the teacher, and the limitations of bureaucracy.

Bereday (1964) states that there has been "some brilliant qualitative writing" and much presentation of "pedagogical facts without an attempt at analysis and comparison" (Preface, p. ix). His introduction to the systematic study of comparative education offers a survey of education in a single country at the same time that it combines materials from more than one country. It also embodies the mechanics of analysis and fusion that result in comparison. This book is one of a number of methodological studies that appeared in the sixties reflecting the growth of available cross-national data; the desire to move beyond the historical, broadly descriptive approach; the borrowing from or use of related disciplines; and the employment of empirical methods, theory, and theoretical models. In the early seventies, the UNESCO Institute for Education in Hamburg sponsored a meeting of experts in the field to review the directions of research. *Relevant Methods in Comparative Education* (Edwards, Holmes, & Van de Graaff, 1973) is a report of the papers presented at that meeting. It is a valuable presentation and analysis of changing trends, problems, issues, and expectations.

The field of research in educational administration has had equally difficult problems in defining its methodology. Attention has centered upon methodology especially in the United States. Those involved have struggled to escape normative practice as the central guideline. For a decade or more they have sought to establish a theoretical base and to learn from related disciplines; while there have been advances achievement has not been in line with expectations and the search continues. At the same time interest in cross-national studies of administration has increased. For example, papers by Culbertson (1980) and Getzels (1980) confront the problems. Getzels (1980) states, "The cross-national perspective permits, as no other method can, the comparative examination of cultural factors in the differences and similarities of administrative behavior in the operation of the school; the relation between the administrative structure and the ecology of the school; and the interaction between the administration of the school and the communities of education" (p. 375).

Elementary and Secondary Education Studies. The literature on comparative education administration is large if one considers the attention given to administration in many treatises on comparative education and if one recognizes the many studies that may deal largely with one nation but implicitly involve comparison because of the author's nationality or interest in more than one society. Even if attention is given only to studies that explicitly consider the many aspects of administration (legal, structural, behavioral, financial), there are numerous studies. Attention here is given only to a few such studies, to the identification of a few issues or problems, and to suggested bibliographical materials. Consideration is also largely restricted to the American and European scenes and to materials in the English language. There are also important resources in other areas and languages.

Any consideration of comparative education administration in the twentieth century must recognize the significant contribution of Kandel. Kandel (1933) devoted a long chapter to administration of education, analyzing practice in six countries. Five years later (1938), he described nations that administer education according to four major purposes: for conformity, for solidarity, for adaptation, and for efficiency. His deep concern with and contributions to the study of education administration are well established even if his work and that of others at that time reflected too large an emphasis upon national characteristics and traits and may have insufficiently recognized the difficulty of delineating them. Furthermore, comparative educators, along with other educators at that time, had too melioristic a belief in certain values and were overly optimistic regarding the impact of formal schooling (Kazamias & Massialas, 1965).

Kazamias and Massialas (1965) developed a system for analysis of the structure of educational systems (administration, control, and organization of schools) in three Western developed countries, two non-Western societies, and three economically developing societies. All countries are described in terms of administration and control and are briefly analyzed in relation to traditional factors and change. Attention is devoted to the expansion of education, the equalization of educational opportunity, centralization and decentralization, and democratization.

Reller and Morphet (1962) presented an overview of education administration in sixteen countries from different continents and in various stages of economic development. They also examined briefly educational purposes and their implications for administration; noted trends in organization and administration; and discussed problems of control (processes, decision making, centralization, and decentralization). Given the limited definitive study that had been devoted to comparative education administration, the treatment was necessarily exploratory.

Planning in education was widely and optimistically employed in the sixties and early seventies and should be noted here, because it very frequently involved staff members from more than one society. Whether explicitly or not, considerable cross-national study was carried on. Educational planning was especially apparent in newly developing societies—but also in other societies aware of specific issues or problems and seeking blueprints for action. Weiler (1980) identified some assumptions about educational planning that were made in this period. They include belief that education furthers economic development through meeting manpower needs; that "baseline information on the present and target information on the future can be ascertained with sufficient reliability to serve as an adequate basis for a realistic and valid planning operation"; and that "the future is subject to being influenced or manipulated" (pp. 306–311). He further observed that educational planning has been conservative (reproducing the existing); hierarchial (involving too largely those in the administrative hierarchy); too largely committed to growth; neglectful of implementation; and given to "oversimplifying causal relations." He calls for the writing of a critical history of educational planning and for "enlightened humility" regarding the contribution it can and should make to the educational service.

Comparative metropolitan educational administration remains a relatively undeveloped field because little direct attention has been given to comparative education administration and because education is seen by many as a national or state service, not a metropolitan one. There are no volumes in the field of education comparable to those of Robson and Regan (1972) or Walsh (1969) on local government in metropolitan areas of the world. However, some steps in the study of comparative metropolitan educational government have been taken by the *World Yearbook of Education* (1970), McKelvey (1973), and Eckstein and Noah (1973). Probably the regions most explored or described have been London, Toronto, and similar regions organized on a metropolitan base in the United States.

Consideration of metropolitan areas leads almost certainly to the issue of pluralism, since metropolitan areas in many countries contain substantial minority groups or segmental cleavages that may be religious, ideological, linguistic, regional, cultural, racial, or ethnic. Relatively little work has been done regarding education administration in nations with many cleavages. In his treatment of "consociational democracy," Lijphart (1977) offers an optimistic view of pluralistic societies achieving stability and democracy. He also offers significant bases for examining educational service and its administration in segmented countries and metropolitan areas.

In recent years some attention has been given to the role and preparation of education administrators in different societies. A large part of the credit for this development goes to the University Council for Educational Administration, which has sponsored four international intervisitation programs beginning in 1966. It began by focusing on the English-speaking world, and it gradually extended its activity to other areas. The fourth intervisita-

tion program focused on the administrator as mediator, trends in education administration, and contemporary issues in training education administrators (Farquhar & Housego, 1980).

Husén (1979) identifies cross-nationally the criticisms, crises, and trends of formal education and then raises a number of questions that must be considered as educational systems are reshaped. He gives special attention to formal education at the secondary level. Drawing especially upon the experiences of the industrialized Western societies, he identifies such issues as (1) the expansion of the organizational machinery, with growth of the hierarchy of decision makers, convergence of more power to the top, "proliferation of time-consuming channels for the transaction of business," increased centralization—even though the "in" words are participation and grassroots involvement; (2) the reconciliation of models of organization (the bureaucratic, the technical, the human relations); (3) the "dilemma between meritocracy and participatory democracy"; (4) the "conflict between the goal rhetoric and system and regulations agreed to by the central officials" of the government agencies and teacher unions or associations; and (5) policy regarding the educational system as a selector and distributor of status versus equality of opportunity and self-realization—with legal and administrative machinery a growing source of controversy (pp. 54, 112–126).

Recent decades have witnessed much growth in the literature on comparative education, including some slight growth in studies devoted more explicitly to comparative education administration. Much of this literature is found or referred to in the *Times Educational Supplement, Comparative Education Review* (especially the annual bibliography in the February issue), *Comparative Education*, and UNESCO publications. The return of the *World Yearbook of Education* in 1979 after a five-year lapse may also result in some volumes on or related to administration.

Higher Education Studies. Higher education expanded and changed in an unprecedented way during the 1960s and 1970s both in the industrialized world and in developing nations. Universities become politicized in the fundamental sense that they influenced economic and social policy. Research at or closely linked to universities was recognized as being socially and economically significant. All this activity was the result of population growth, the growth of expectation, and the growth of and demand for knowledge.

Much of the development in higher education was related to the problems or issues in a given nation and therefore was not seen as demanding a comparative perspective. However, there was enough commonality in concerns and enough demand for study and change or the consideration of alternatives that a substantial number of explorations in comparative higher education were undertaken. Further, it appeared that crises in higher education in one country influenced development in others to a considerable degree.

National agencies and growth of studies. Altbach (1979) notes that various national agencies studying higher education recognized the importance of a comparative perspective. Thus the Carnegie Commission on Higher Education in the United States sponsored two volumes dealing with higher education in foreign countries (Burn et al., 1971; Ben-David, 1977) and commissioned foreign scholars to write on selected issues; and the Committee on Higher Education in Great Britain (1963) issued a volume on higher education in other countries. In Japan there was also considerable interest in higher education in other countries, reflected in translations of works into Japanese and visits of Japanese administrators abroad. The Association of Private Universities of Japan, for example, has offered a number of travel seminars to selected countries for administrators of higher education during the last decade. Commissions studying higher education in the Third World have frequently had directors or members from other nations.

The extent of the literature on comparative higher education is revealed by the fact that Altbach (1979) lists almost five hundred items. Most of these books and articles pertain to developments since 1960. Some of them deal largely with one nation, but many have a genuine comparative aspect. The growth of literature in this field is also reflected in the development of organizations, their decision to focus upon comparative higher education, and the publication of periodicals in the field. Notable examples are the Organization for Economic Cooperation and Development (OECD), the International Council for Educational Development (ICED), the International Association of Universities (IAU), the Max Planck Institute, and the *London Times Higher Education Supplement.*

The last decade has produced considerable literature on higher education in individual countries as well as some significant comparative material. This period has also produced studies of higher education administration, again frequently pertaining to a single country. No attempt is made here to review the range of studies on comparative higher education, which nearly always contain some materials pertaining to administration, nor to studies of individual countries. Instead, attention is focused upon a few studies that present trends in selected issues and illustrate approaches to the comparative study of administration. Special attention is devoted to a study of power—one of the important ways to glimpse actors and processes in administration.

Studies in power. In *Academic Power: Patterns of Authority in Seven National Systems of Higher Education* (Van de Graaff et al., 1978), Clark states that on fundamental aspects of academic power, the research in higher education has been especially weak. Most studies have focused very limited attention on governance either within the university or in terms of relations to the state. In this study the case study is used because of the lack of research, the need for "intensive exploration," and the desirability of attempting to understand the whole and relations among the parts. From these case studies "modest generalizations" may be formulated based upon more adequate descriptive data (preface, pp. vi–vii).

In *Academic Power: Patterns of Authority in Seven National Systems of Higher Education,* academic power in Germany, Italy, France, Sweden, Great Britain, United States, and Japan is analyzed. The analysis is founded on two major concepts: the degree of structural hierarchy and the extent of cohesion or unity in decision making. Degree of hierarchy is used "to characterize the steepness or flatness of organization" ranging from an authoritarian structure to a collegial or democratic one (Van de Graaff et al., 1978, p. 2). Unity or cohesiveness of decision making is used to show "the extent to which a level of organization can adopt, implement, and enforce a coherent or uniform policy." A typology developed by Warren (1967) is employed to characterize structures from highly cohesive to "free social choice." Thus attention is focused upon the inclusiveness and locus of decision making (Van de Graaff et al., 1978, p. 3).

The six levels of organization in each of the seven chapters analyzing countries are (1) the institute or department, (2) the faculty (in the European meaning; in the United States, the college or school), (3) the university, (4) the multicampus system, (5) state or provincial government, and (6) national government. The cross-national analyses following the national case studies reveal the multitude, difficulty, and complexity of the problems associated with attempts at the study of comparative higher education administration. Goldschmidt (1978) observes that higher education has grown from relatively small, "loosely coordinated groupings" to massive systems with struggles between teaching staffs and institutions as well as among governmental authorities, interest groups, and market forces (p. 147).

Regarding decision making, Goldschmidt observes that in almost every case, power shifts from lower to higher levels; government has become more important; within the universities, bureaucracies devoted to administration and planning, staffed by full-time administrators, have expanded and gained significant responsibility for implementing policy decisions; policy processes have become increasingly formalized; and whereas the locus of decision making has tended to rise, there has been a contrary trend toward delegation of certain responsibilities to lower levels (p. 159).

Administrative structures in countries and institutions have expanded with more full-time administrators, and more formalized communication and decision making, along with attempts to decentralize in certain areas and to extend participation to junior academic staff, students, and nonacademic staff. Structural reform has been forced on institutions by legislation, ministerial policy making, and market forces.

Important organizational problems remain for all systems: the place of traditional universities as the shift from elite to mass higher education occurs; the reconciliation of the need to provide mass higher education and to concentrate resources for research and scholarly training; the consequences of large-scale institutions for the locus of decision making, and bureaucratization and formalization of policy making and administration.

Clark (1978) notes the important differences in the ways in which authority is distributed and in the nature of the authority exercised at various levels in the nations studied. Further, these systems of higher education "are among the most complex social enterprises ever evolved" (p. 164). In an effort to assist in an analysis and understanding of these systems, he offers the following concepts of academic authority as starting points for the analyst: personal rulership (professorial); collegial rulership (professorial); guild authority; professional authority; charismatic authority; trustee authority (institutional); bureaucratic authority (institutional); bureaucratic authority (governmental); political authority; and systemwide academic oligarchy.

Focusing on the organizational structure of power and authority, Clark (1978) makes an important contribution to future research with four approaches to an analysis of academic authority (pp. 179–187).

1. *Levels of analysis.* Any defensible comparison requires determination and analysis of levels. What in the United States is comparable to the Ministry of Education in France or Germany? What are the limitations of any such comparison? With a schema of organization, the bases for decision making and the exercise of authority in any aspect of the system can be examined, and the different levels at which decision making occurs can be delineated and the interrelationships of levels determined. Thus through levels analysis the determination of roles and the exercise of authority can be described and the total system envisioned.

2. *Integration and differentiation analysis.* This analysis facilitates consideration of integration and coordination of various forces and of various levels of systems that are complex and loosely coupled as well as those that are highly bureaucratized. It recognizes the growing number and complexity of organizations, the role of expertise, relations among those involved, the power of professional interest groups "with privileged access by virtue of position within public bureaus" (p. 182).

3. *Developmental analysis.* This may involve the study of historical factors regarding the organization, its development, and its institutionalization. It also includes consideration of international practices and influences, borrowing or transferring of organizational forms or roles, adapting and implementing of structures and relationships.

4. *Interest analysis.* This approach focuses upon who governs and how. It involves a recognition that structure and its control by groups are of great importance and that these matters are genuinely related to tradition, beliefs, vested rights, assumptions. Thus the analysis of interests in educational organizations relates closely to politics.

Higher education finance. The comprehensive study of academic power does not attempt to get into the question of higher education finance. The British University Grants Committee (UGC) has been studied and regarded by many as a model for effecting a proper balance between needed central control and institutional autonomy. It has not, however, been borrowed successfully in many cases, probably because of the widely differing political, social, and educational circumstances.

A study by Glenny (1979) on funding provides substantial comparative data on France, Greece, Italy, Spain, Sweden, and the United States. The study was based upon a previous comprehensive study of budget practices and related matters in seventeen states of the United States. It provides comparative information on (1) the formal policies, formulas, and guidelines for allocating public funds among the different types of colleges, institutions, and universities considered a part of higher education; (2) the central agencies, ministries, and other offices that review, recommend, or make decisions on the allocation of funds; (3) the methods by which such agencies differentiate allocations among types of programs and levels of students and when possible, the criteria used to reflect qualitative differences in programs and institutions; and (4) the major educational and social issues that impinge directly on either the budget process or budget outcomes.

Glenny (1979) presents case studies of five nations varying considerably in political and economic development. His analysis involves trends and issues regarding who gets what and how. Attention is paid to political and social settings, economic conditions, confidence in higher education, political influence, organization for budgeting, and forms, formulas, and formula bases. Consideration is also given to the roles of students and faculty in formulating public policy on funding higher education.

Other issues. In his analysis of research trends in comparative higher education, Altbach (1979) identifies six key issues believed to be important in most nations: planning, the professoriate, governance, university-society relations, student activism, and higher education in the Third World. Although each of these areas relates rather closely to or has important implications for higher education administration, attention here is focused only on governance and university-society relations. A number of general analyses have been made of university governance, especially on the American scene (e.g., Corson, 1975). Ashby (1973) notes the challenges to university organization in different cultures. However, the literature pertaining to governance that is explicitly comparative is limited. The same is true regarding university-society relations, although the growth of governmental action and the demand for accountability have in many nations challenged the autonomy of the university and the power of the professoriate and the chair holder. The Yale University Institute for Social and Policy Studies must be recognized for direct comparative work (e.g., Van de Graaff, 1980).

It should be noted that the amount of work focused sharply on comparative education administration or aspects of it remains extremely limited. Further, as Reller and Morphet (1962) note, "The educational systems of the world constitute a tremendous though relatively unused laboratory for the study of educational administration" (p. 425). A base now exists for highly significant development. Possibly the field of comparative public administration may serve as a guide.

As work in the study of comparative education administration advances, it is to be hoped that a strongly culturalist interpretation of the distinctive values and social organization of each society may be avoided, as well as the belief that differences in social organization in societies inevitably converge, especially in the direction of Western industrial societies, which may too easily be regarded as the more modern and advanced. Rather, functional alternatives in organizational behavior should be sought and studied. Cole (1979) demonstrates this approach in his comparison of American and Japanese industry.

Theodore L. Reller

See also Administration of Educational Institutions; Comparative Education.

REFERENCES

Altbach, P. G. *Comparative Higher Education Research Trends and Bibliography.* London: Mansell, 1979. (ERIC Document Reproduction Service No. ED 169 872)

Ashby, E. *The Structure of Higher Education: A World View.* New York: International Council for Educational Development, 1973. (ERIC Document Reproduction Service No. ED 083 891)

Ben-David, J. *Centers of Learning: Britain, France, Germany, United States.* New York: McGraw-Hill, 1977. (ERIC Document Reproduction Service No. ED 136 712)

Bereday, G. *Comparative Method in Education.* New York: Holt, Rinehart & Winston, 1964.

Burn, B.; Altbach, P.; Kerr, C.; & Perkins, J. *Higher Education in Nine Countries.* New York: McGraw-Hill, 1971. (ERIC Document Reproduction Service No. ED 090 897)

Carnegie Council on Policy Studies in Higher Education. *Three Thousand Futures: The Next Twenty Years for Higher Education.* San Francisco: Jossey-Bass, 1980. (ERIC Document Reproduction Service No. ED 183 076)

Clark, B. Academic power: Concepts, modes, and perspectives. In J. H. Van de Graaff, B. R. Clark, D. Furth, D. Goldschmidt, & D. F. Wheeler, *Academic Power: Patterns of Authority in Seven National Systems of Higher Education.* New York: Praeger, 1978. (ERIC Document Reprodcuction Service No. ED 171 201)

Cole, R. *Work, Mobility, and Participation. A Comparative Study of American and Japanese Industry.* Berkeley: University of California Press, 1979.

Committee on Higher Education. Higher education in other countries (Appendix 5). In *Higher Education: Report of the Committee.* London: Her Majesty's Stationery Office, 1963.

Corson, J. *The Governance of Colleges and Universities.* New York: McGraw-Hill, 1975.

Culbertson, J. Educational administration: Where we are and where we are going. In R. Farquhar & I. Housego, *Canadian and Comparative Educational Administration.* Vancouver:

University of British Columbia, Center for Continuing Education, 1980.

Eckstein, M., & Noah, H. *Metropolitanism and Education: Teachers and Schools in Amsterdam, London, Paris, and New York.* New York: Columbia University, Teachers College, 1973. (ERIC Document Reproduction Service No. ED 085 444)

Edwards, R.; Holmes, B.; & Van de Graaff, J. H. (Eds.). *Relevant Methods in Comparative Education.* Hamburg: UNESCO Institute for Education, 1973. (ERIC Document Reproduction Service No. ED 096 191)

Farquhar, R., & Housego, I. *Canadian and Comparative Educational Administration.* Vancouver: University of British Columbia, Center for Continuing Education, 1980.

Getzels, J. Alternative directions for research in educational administration. In R. Farquhar, & I. Housego, *Canadian and Comparative Educational Administration.* Vancouver: University of British Columbia, Center for Continuing Education, 1980. (ERIC Document Reproduction Service No. ED 194 994)

Glenny, L. (Ed.). *Funding Higher Education. A Six-nation Analysis.* New York: Praeger, 1979.

Goldschmidt, D. Systems of higher education. In J. H. Van de Graaff, B. R. Clark, D. Furth, D. Goldschmidt, & D. F. Wheeler, *Academic Power: Pattterns of Authority in Seven National Systems of Higher Education.* New York: Praeger, 1978. (ERIC Document Reproduction Service No. ED 171 201)

Husén, T. *The School in Question. A Comparative Study of the School and Its Future in Western Societies.* New York: Oxford University Press, 1979.

Kandel, I. *Comparative Education.* Boston: Houghton Mifflin, 1933.

Kandel, I. *Types of Administration.* Auckland, New Zealand: Whitcombe & Tombs, 1938.

Kazamias, A., & Massialas, B. *Tradition and Change in Education. A Comparative Study.* Englewood Cliffs, N.J. Prentice-Hall, 1965.

Lijphart, A. *Democracy in Plural Societies. A Comparative Exploration.* New Haven, Conn.: Yale University Press, 1977.

McKelvey, T. (Ed.). *Metropolitan School Organization* (2 vols.). Berkeley, Calif.: McCutchan, 1973. (ERIC Document Reproduction Service Nos. ED 089 394 and ED 089 395)

Reller, T. L., & Morphet, E. L. (Eds.). *Comparative Educational Administration.* Englewood Cliffs, N.J.: Prentice-Hall, 1962.

Robson, W., & Regan, D. (Eds.). *Great Cities of the World: Their Government, Politics, and Planning* (2 vols.). London: George Allen & Unwin, 1972.

Van de Graaff, J. H. *Can Department Structures Replace a Chair System?: Comparative Perspectives.* Unpublished manuscript, New Haven, Conn.: Yale University Institute for Social and Policy Studies, 1980. (ERIC Document Reproduction Service No. ED 189 916)

Van de Graaff, J. H.; Clark, B. R.; Furth, D.; Goldschmidt, D.; & Wheeler, D. F. *Academic Power: Patterns of Authority in Seven National Systems of Higher Education.* New York: Praeger, 1978. (ERIC Document Reproduction Service No. ED 171 201)

Walsh, A. *The Urban Challenge to Government. An International Comparison of Thirteen Cities.* New York: Praeger, 1969.

Warren, R. The interorganizational field as a focus for investigation. *Administrative Science Quarterly,* 1967, *12,* 396–419.

Weiler, H. The future of educational planning: Some skeptical notes. In R. Farquhar, & I. Housego, *Canadian and Comparative Educational Administration.* Vancouver: University of British Columbia, Center for Continuing Education, 1980.

World Yearbook of Education. *Education in Cities.* London: Evans Brothers, 1970. (ERIC Document Reproduction Service No. ED 059 322)

COMPARATIVE SCHOOL ACHIEVEMENT

Achievement has been a central topic of interest to comparative educators since Marc-Antoine de Jullien first proposed his comprehensive schema for studying foreign educational systems in 1817 (Fraser, 1964). Throughout the nineteenth century, as school systems were developing in the more industrialized nations of the world, observers traveled abroad to study those practices and policies that might explain differences in the achievements of students and the contributions of a nation's schools to the well-being of their respective societies. American and other educators described and commented upon schooling in other countries and on their presumed outcomes, limited severely by the data available and the lack of research sophistication of their times.

A century later, in the aftermath of two world wars and of the dissolution of great European-based empires, new nations as well as old again concerned themselves with the potential of their school systems to serve their interests: economic growth, political stability, social development, and educational advancement. Comparative study was stimulated by the twin desires to learn from foreign examples and to seek yardsticks against which to measure performance. With the growth in communications through national and international organizations, the accumulation of educational and social data, and the rapid advances in research concepts and techniques, the possibilities of cross-national study of educational achievement were considerably enhanced.

Substantial progress may be observed from the early statistical studies and impressionistic observations of the later nineteenth century to the more systematic empirical studies of the mid-twentieth. Studies of curricula, examinations, textbooks, teacher training, and instructional practices compared across several countries, began to appear with increasing frequency, as did efforts to assess pupil attainment in such areas as arithmetic and reading (Eckstein, 1977). Nevertheless, despite its centrality as a topic for comparative investigation, achievement was relatively neglected in contrast to other aspects of education. The reasons are clear: cross-national assessment of student school performance is fraught with problems of equivalence and comparability, complicated by differences in national objectives and practices, and confounded by verbal and conceptual ambiguities. Small wonder then that comparativists leaned heavily upon such system variables as retention rates and promotion figures from one level to the next. Enrollment or attendance figures are generally available, rates can be calculated from official statistics, and thus seemingly reliable and objective measures may be used. That such figures are themselves not altogether unambiguous is acknowledged, but for international comparison, they appear to be far less troublesome than curriculum content, student performance, and instructional methods.

The IEA Project.   The first concerted effort to compare achievement levels according to internationally accepted measures is represented by the massive research project of the International Association for the Evaluation of Educational Achievement: the IEA Project. It began in the late 1950's when researchers from a dozen countries convened under UNESCO auspices to consider the feasibility of conducting such research. The report on the pilot study (Foshay et al., 1962) concerned itself with many of the administrative and methodological problems involved in international collaboration on this scale, while the mathematics study (Husén, 1967) presented the results of the first completed survey of student achievement in twelve countries.

Subsequent phases of the project encompassed six additional school subjects: science (Comber & Keeves, 1973), literature (Purves, 1973), reading comprehension (Thorndike, 1973), English and French as foreign languages (Lewis & Massad, 1975; Carroll, 1975); and civic education (Farnen, Oppenheim, & Torney, 1975). Twenty-one nations participated, though not all were involved in each subject. In addition to the achievement data of samples of students at several school grade-levels, information was gathered on the students' home and school backgrounds through questionnaires administered to principals, teachers, and the students themselves in each country. The IEA Project was an ambitious attempt along the lines of the Coleman study in the United States and the Plowden report in Britain to perform simultaneous national replications. And the central purpose of all this activity was to answer the question "What factors best explain differences in student achievement?" (Postlethwaite, 1974; Härnqvist, 1975).

That differences in achievement existed was clearly evident. In each subject at each age and grade, achievement was compared at several levels: among students within nations, among schools within nations, and among nations. In mathematics, for example, Japanese students scored higher than those in all other nations at the same age/ grade levels. Although the differences were not great, younger students (primary level) from Sweden and Italy performed better in the reading comprehension tests, while lower secondary students from New Zealand and Italy did well. In the same subject, average national scores of older students differed considerably, closely associated with the extent to which nations retained students of the appropriate age-group through the final year of secondary schooling. In English as a foreign language, Swedish students performed better than those of the other nine nations participating. And in science, secondary school students from New Zealand and the Federal Republic of

Germany led those of other nations involved in the study.

It was inevitable that some educators would respond to the fact that students from their own nation performed higher or lower than students from other countries in a subject. However, the researchers properly insisted that national averages could in no way be regarded as the results of an international competition, for obvious reasons. Their quest was for the associated factors that might explain the differences observed.

The six volumes on achievement in the several subjects cited above contain a host of data and interpretations relating to their own areas, but three additional IEA publications review the project as a whole: a technical report on the methodology (Peaker, 1975), a summary discussion of the findings as a whole (Walker, 1976), and a review of the findings in relation to differences of school-system structure and organization and socioeconomic characteristics of the twenty-one nations involved (Passow et al., 1976). Looked at in its entirety, the project confirmed and extended much that was known or suspected about the factors affecting student achievement: home background, comprising essentially the educational and social status of parents, by far the most influential force; school characteristics of various kinds; and features of the national educational system. But the relative significance of individual factors and of groups of variables was found to vary considerably among different countries, age levels, and subjects of study, provoking new questions about why achievement levels vary.

A number of more specific points may be selected from the total project to illustrate its capacity to illuminate and to provoke new questions. Although home-background factors tended generally to be more important than school-related characteristics, this fact varied greatly by subject, by grade level, and by nation. In science and foreign languages, for example, school factors were generally of greater significance than they were in reading comprehension and civic knowledge. Although, as expected, nations differed in curriculum content and curriculum emphases in particular subjects, they also differed in their orientations toward the subject matter itself and the very nature of learning. The mathematics study had revealed, for instance, that students of the United States were more inclined to guess than those from Belgium; the literature survey showed that students' attitudes toward literature and their approaches to interpreting and evaluating it also differed according to nation or culture. Certain achievement differences (science, foreign languages) were linked with sex. The study as a whole confirmed the gap that separates the less developed countries of the world (Chile, India, Iran, and Thailand participated in several phases of the study) from the rest, in school resources and student performance as much as in economic development. Finally, among the several more obviously policy-related aspects of the study, it was evident that national achievement norms tended to be lower in those nations that maintained nonselective school systems and relatively open access to upper secondary education.

Although the IEA Project is a landmark in quantitative comparative research—rigorous in design, catholic in perspective, comprehensive in scope (Inkeles, 1977)—its very strengths may also account for some of its limitations. The decision to perform a cross-sectional study and use linear multiple regression as the primary analytic tool imposed certain limitations from the beginning. Inevitably, explanations for the phenomena observed could only be based upon correlations among variables, a far cry from causal associations (Bridge, Judd, & Moock, 1979). The variables themselves comprised groups of separate but presumably associated indicators for samples of specified student populations, expressed in average values. And the cross-sectional approach made it impossible to investigate the developmental aspects of education, except by tentative inference. Just as causation cannot be assumed from correlation, the cumulative effects of schooling cannot be adequately considered merely by comparing the achievements of three (or more) different age levels at one time. Average values may obscure suggestive or significant relationships, and the difficulties of actual or proxy variables remain intractable. However, these deficiencies are generic to this particular research mode and common to all similar social science research. The IEA Project, despite its limitations, goes a long way to realizing many of the objectives of comparative study of education as outlined by Jullien over a century and a half ago.

That such issues have been taken to heart is indicated by certain new approaches in IEA work currently under way: revised replication of the mathematics study, which will incorporate a longitudinal dimension; smaller-scale observational studies of classroom interactions, which will attempt to remedy the neglect of subtler, qualitative aspects of teaching-learning processes; and a movement from largely uniform international measures to tests that contain both an international core and sections tailored to the concerns and the curricula of individual participating nations.

Comparative Research Findings. The possibilities of the IEA six-subject study have not yet been fully exploited. The data bank with its mass of educational and related information is available for new and revised analyses by the scholars of the world. Since the publication of the original IEA volumes, a slow but steady stream of studies has used these data for various purposes, often in conjunction with the results of additional research, both in a single nation and in several countries.

Home and school influences. The IEA results confirmed what had already been concluded from similar national-survey research studies and a host of more limited ones: on the whole, home background matters more than school-related variables in accounting for differences in student school performance. With one exception, specific school characteristics did not clearly or consistently relate to variance in student cognitive achievement.

Some have used this broad generalization to argue that in the absence of political or economic reforms that would radically alter the nature of home and society, changes in educational policy and practice can have little effect. Yet the evidence suggests otherwise. Although most school factors examined in the IEA Project bore no direct, consistent relation to achievement, the indicators of "opportunity to learn," that is, time devoted to teaching and studying a particular portion of knowledge in a subject, were important cross-nationally. Furthermore, school factors in general were substantially more influential in certain subject areas rather than in others—in science and foreign languages, for instance, rather than in reading comprehension in the native language and in civic education. The relative influence of school compared with home factors tended to increase with the age of the student. And, finally, the amount of influence ascribed to school factors varied from nation to nation. The conclusion can only be that differences in school policies and practices do matter, but that much remains to be explained: when, where, how, and why?

Several writers have raised the question, "Why do the IEA studies and similar large-scale surveys, such as the Coleman report, shed no more light on the influence of home and school factors on student achievement?" One answer proposed (Marjoribanks, 1973) is that the two environments are rather broad concepts, crudely measured and aggregated, and therefore unlikely to account reliably for more than small proportions of variance. The author reanalyzed a number of small-scale studies from England, the United States, Canada, and Australia, focusing upon the "learning subenvironment," those psychosocial factors that appear most likely to affect a student's cognitive performance at school. These include such factors as the intellectuality and "achievement press" of parents and their ambitions, aspirations, and attitudes toward school achievement. Marjoribanks found these to be highly predictive of children's school achievement in their different national settings.

The argument is taken a step further in the analysis of data from one less developed nation (Uganda) compared with certain evidence from the IEA Project (Heyneman, 1976). Although home background appears more influential in the developed countries, the effects of schooling on cognitive achievement appear relatively greater in the case of less developed nations. One inference to be drawn from such work is that there may be a threshold effect at work: or certain levels of social and educational development, school factors are highly influential; at more advanced levels, home background becomes more significant. Furthermore, this effect may be true not only between nations but also between segments or strata of society within a given nation.

On this issue of relative influence, it can be concluded that, in all likelihood, home backgrounds differ from each other far more than schools do, at least for the measures used in large-survey research. Secondly, the very nature of the research design may obscure rather than highlight the associations among factors: the need to use large numbers of indicators; the decision to aggregate a number of measures for a particular variable. The very comprehensiveness of studies that seek to test many elements of a complex explanatory model at one time is also a deficiency. Fine distinctions, qualitative dimensions, and exceptional relationships—all potentially highly significant—may be lost in the manipulation of average values. It is left to researchers without the resources and scope of the IEA teams to reanalyze portions of data already collected and, in complementary and exploratory smaller-scale studies, to investigate portions of the conceptual model. In this way, they can direct attention to specific variables in both the home and school environments of students and their relation to one another under specific conditions.

Teachers and instruction. The data base and the research model of the IEA Project enhanced the possibilities of systematic comparative study of teacher characteristics and instructional methods. For example, the first global study of reading and writing (Gray, 1956), a UNESCO-sponsored project, laid the foundations for comparisons of educational conditions and standards of literacy in the world. Nearly two decades later, a collection of essays and studies (Downing, 1973) delved further into the subject, although still limited by the lack of a unified set of concepts and information. Examples of individual efforts in various subject areas may also be found in Halsall's thoughtful attempt to study attainment differences in French in Holland, Belgium, and England (Halsall, 1963); in Trace's comparison of curriculum and textbook content in the United States and the U.S.S.R. (Trace, 1961); and in Wiersma's study of academic achievement of prospective teachers (Wiersma, 1969). Yet even the evidence from IEA studies provided no clear answers. On the whole, teacher and instructional variables bore no general, consistent relationship with variance in student achievement that was statistically significant.

It was left to subsequent analyses of IEA data and to reviews of additional information to cast light on the subject. One study concluded (Avalos, 1980) that neither higher academic qualification nor longer preservice preparation of teachers were in themselves important in explaining differences in student achievement, although they might be in conjunction with other variables. The same author also found that differences in instructional method were not influential, although she found discovery methods more effective than expository teaching at higher levels of intellectual achievement. This study, of data relating to less developed nations, is in part substantiated by two additional works (Husén, 1978; Simmons & Alexander, 1980). Although neither found clear and consistent, significant relationships among teacher training, several other school-related variables, and achievement, Husén's analyses firmly rejected the null hypothesis that the sixteen teacher-related variables studied were unrelated to achievement. Four characteristics were rather more important than others: qualifications, experience, amount of education, and knowledge. In addition, two demographic characteristics were important under specified conditions: teacher's sex and teacher's age (older teachers may be more successful with older, that is, upper secondary students). Finally, positive teacher expectations, so far as they could be identified, tended to produce positive results.

Simmons and Alexander (1980) found that teacher certification and academic qualifications were not so important at primary and lower secondary as at upper secondary levels and in certain subject areas (notably science). However, in their search for evidence to influence educational-policy decisions in less developed nations, they found teacher experience did have a positive effect on academic achievement in the lower grades (although it was not so important at upper secondary levels). In general, they concluded that gross expenditures on teacher salaries and school facilities were not significant, but that teacher motivation (as indicated by time spent on preparation and by membership on curriculum-reform committees) was a positive factor in student achievement. Finally, Simmons and Alexander found that the amount of homework done, the physical conditions at home, and the amount of reading done were all important predictors of student achievement. The conclusions are that increasing the quality or quantity of most of the traditional inputs to schooling, such as teacher training or expenditures per student, is not likely to increase student achievement. However, affective skills taught by the schools may be more important than cognitive skills, especially for postschool benefits (higher earnings and satisfactions in work).

Finally, still with reference to practice in less developed nations, Heyneman (1978) reviewed the published evidence on the relationship between availability of textbooks and academic achievement. Studies covering twelve nations were reviewed, including the IEA Project, Heyneman's own investigations in Uganda, and a number of other works. The availability of books is a consistently good predictor of academic achievement, Heyneman concluded, although the reasons why the associations are stronger in some cases and weaker in others are not at all clear. He recommends that investment in reading materials is likely to improve cognitive achievement in less developed nations.

All of the studies reviewed in this section exemplify the potentialities and the limitations of quantitative analysis made possible by IEA and similar investigations. They raise questions about the conventional wisdom on which educators base their actions; they are suggestive about possible and conceivably unanticipated association among variables; and they indicate most clearly that smaller-scale, rigorous studies of particular sets of phenomena are necessary to complement the broader surveys.

Sex and achievement. Much remains to be discovered about the relationship between sex and school achievement. Although the issue of separation of the sexes in school is quiescent in many countries, it remains controversial in various places because of social and religious values and customs. However, comparative study reveals that even where schools have been integrated, achievement often depends on the sex of the student. The sex of the teacher is probably also an important factor.

The IEA studies extended the general awareness that, on the average, the sexes perform differently in given school subjects; what was known to be true in certain instances, was found to be true internationally. Boys do better than girls in civic education, mathematics, and science, with the exception that, in some countries, girls excel in biology. On the other hand, although the differences are sometimes slight, girls tend to do better in foreign languages, reading comprehension, and literature. Such findings add to what is known about sex differences in education globally: literacy skills as estimated by United Nations statistics, enrollment and attendance figures, curricular and vocational choices, and achievement in specified school subjects (Finn, Dulberg, & Reis, 1979).

It can be no coincidence that male teachers appear to be more successful with their students' science achievement too, while their female colleagues are better able to enhance their students' foreign-language performance (Husén, 1978). As one comprehensive review of the topic makes evident (Finn, Reis, & Dulberg, 1980), patterns of performance are inextricably bound up with behavior models suggested in schools by teachers and textbooks, by curriculum exposure, by academic supports, and by vocational expectations and opportunity—all of which are deeply rooted in society's ideas and practices.

Yet the evidence is not all in, and the psychological and sociological dynamics remain unclear. Why, for instance, does it appear that male teachers influence male students positively in the middle grades, but negatively at upper secondary levels (they also influence female achievement negatively at the upper secondary level) (Simmons & Alexander, 1980)? In a four-nation study of reading achievement (Johnson, 1973–1974), boys scored higher than girls in Nigeria and England, while the reverse was true of samples of primary pupils from Canada and the United States. And a selection of IEA data (Passow et al., 1976) suggests that in those more developed nations of the world, where primary-school teaching is perceived as a career for females, primary-school achievement in basic skills (mathematics, reading comprehension) tends to be lower; where primary-school teaching is seen as a career for either sex, such achievement is higher. Comparative study demonstrates that school-achievement differences between the sexes are not easily or quickly reduced, even as social practices develop, economic conditions change, and school practices vary.

National School Policies. The continuing debates over how particular school policies affect performance are unlikely to be stilled easily, for they are often rooted in fundamental differences of philosophy, political ideology, and social values. It should make a difference whether compulsory schooling begins earlier or later, how long it lasts, whether classes are smaller or larger, at what age students are moved from primary to secondary levels of schooling, and what mechanisms, if any, are used at important transfer points. The controversies over the effect of classroom-grouping policies or the merits of selective versus comprehensive schooling cannot be assessed with respect to student achievement alone, for they are also involved with political and social effects.

These and many similar issues have been studied both in one-nation case studies and in cross-national investigations. In the IEA Project especially, in addition to the several volumes devoted to the separate subjects of study, the National Case Study volume (Passow et al., 1976) discussed associations between such issues and student achievement. However, since the nations were not selected as a sample for particular research purposes (participation was on a voluntary basis) and the ranges they represented on such variables were limited (and unrepresentative), no clear associations were found between such factors as national average class size, forms of compulsory schooling, and achievement. However, a number of suggestive points emerged, indicating that further analyses and added data would be fruitful.

The question of the effect of selective versus comprehensive secondary schooling may demonstrate how comparative study may dispel some confusion. The IEA Project produced national achievement norms for each participating nation in different subjects for students at different levels. On the whole, achievement norms were demonstrably lower in those countries that retained larger proportions of their youth in the education system by means of nonselective transition from primary to secondary levels and by providing various forms of comprehensive secondary schooling. It is to be expected, therefore, that such countries would have a wider range of student ability in the samples tested at middle and upper secondary school levels, and that national averages would consequently be depressed in comparison with those countries restricting advancement through the school system. However, as IEA analyses demonstrate, if comparisons are made among the top 5 to 9 percent of achievers in each country, the differences among countries are sharply reduced. The best students tend to achieve at very similar levels in different countries, regardless of whether the school system is more selective or more comprehensive.

The issue of how increased access to more schooling may affect outcomes is but one of the current concerns in the United States as in other nations of the world. So too are the issues of how to provide for cultural, linguistic, and other "exceptional groups" whose achievement levels are demonstrably below national norms and whose participation in the mainstream of national life is limited. Bilingual-education programs and compensatory school schemes of various kinds have developed in many countries of the world in order to meet similar kinds of problems: transient foreign workers in Sweden and West Germany, the Francophone communities of Canada, Asian refugees in the Netherlands, Indian and Jamaican immigrants in Britain, the poor in rural or urban areas everywhere. Such efforts to use the school system to achieve particular social as well as educational objectives are increasingly being described and analysed in the comparative literature.

However, as these examples of policy questions indicate, student attainment in basic skills such as reading the native language or in standard school subjects is but one way of defining the outcomes of different school policies. School achievement may also be considered as the capacity of the school system to produce what the educators, citizens, and the leadership of a nation deem important. To evaluate the performance of an education system calls for some understanding of the goals, costs, demands, and needs of the nation for which it provides. Although societies may agree on certain broad social and personal objectives of education, the many varieties of practice, organization, and criteria for evaluation among the schools of the world indicate that, in fact, the ends, the means, and the processes connecting them may vary considerably. Thus, Coombs and Lüschen (1976) propose four criteria by which to assess system performance comparatively: effectiveness, efficiency, responsiveness, and fidelity. They acknowledge the existence of many output measures, some more usable than others, but note the problems involved that may explain why so little has yet been achieved in comparing the achievements of school systems relative to their particular respective priorities and objectives. They conclude with a number of hypotheses suggestive of policy-oriented research.

Valuable as the comparative research has been, its potential for informing specific policy has been severely limited. One cause for this fact may be that the researchers have not adequately translated their findings into forms that educational practitioners and policy makers can grasp. In this respect, comparativists may be at one with other researchers in education and the social sciences generally. A second cause, quite evident in the IEA Project, lies in the research strategy that resulted in conclusions about the relative importance of one factor compared with another over entire nations. Eckstein (1977) summarizes the argument:

Teachers, curriculum makers, and educational policy makers, however, usually wish to know something more specific. They are more interested in those variables over which they have some control than in those less amenable to their decisions. They need to know the effect upon achievement of varying a particular item under rather specific circumstances. They are less interested in influencing achievement on an average, national basis than in, say, rural as compared with urban settings, boys vis-à-vis girls, students in poor neighborhoods as distinct from wealthier communities. What provides the largest increments to achievement for low achievers? For average or high achievers? The answers to these and similar questions require analyses that partition the national samples (singly and across groups of nations) so as to investigate relationships among variables for specified groups of students, e.g., rural/urban, poor/wealthy, high achievers/low achievers. The potential of the I.E.A. studies to inform policy making in education was neglected because insufficient attention was given to policy questions and because authors did not take care to express their findings in appropriately concrete form. (pp. 354–355)

Conclusions. The scope of this article has been restricted in two important senses. First, the word "comparative" has been taken to mean cross-national, although this is by no means the only possible usage. Much educational research is "comparative" in the intranational sense and faces similar possibilities and obstacles. Second, the term "school achievement" has been taken to mean student cognitive performance, rather than other contributions of a school system to individual or social benefit. As a result of these limitations, a substantial body of literature on both the politics and the economics of education has been excluded (e.g., Blaug, 1978; Merritt & Coombs, 1977; Messialas, 1977). It should also be noted that the discussion is based on two significant assumptions. The explanatory model for school achievement presupposes that there are explicit causes of differences in student performance and that they may be discovered in the patterns of relationships among a number of environments: the home, the school, and the larger contexts of the whole culture or society. And, it is held that comparative school research, whether of achievement or of other aspects of schooling, contributes substantially to our understanding of the complex processes of education and thereby to informing policy.

By moving outside the boundaries of a single nation, comparative study enables the researcher to include variables that may not be available at home. For instance, some practices, such as beginning age and duration of compulsory schooling, are generally uniform within a nation, so that the effect of varying this policy cannot be studied without comparison. Similarly, it may be possible to increase the range of variability of a given factor by using cross-national data when a given nation exhibits only limited variations. In fact, certain important policy differences and outcomes can only be investigated through cross-national comparison. As Wolf (1977) effectively demonstrates in his discussion of student performance in the United States in the IEA Project, reference to the larger number and wider range of variables represented in other countries can be most illuminating.

A second value of comparative study is its capacity to extend generalizations, to expand the scope and validity of a given finding. The conclusion of a one-nation study in education may hold true for a particular school system, but of necessity omits consideration of important national variables. Comparative study broadens the applicability of the conclusion, or, if not, poses new questions about the educational processes under investigation.

This is in fact the third value of comparative studies in achievement: their heuristic potential. They increase the number and variety of phenomena for study; challenge

the conventional wisdom in education; and, most important of all, as Bloom (1976) suggests, enhance the theoretical models posited to explain achievement.

All questions concerning school achievement do not require cross-national treatment, although comparison at a lesser level is likely to be necessary. Nor can the conceptual and operational difficulties of cross-national research be avoided. But the history of comparative education over the past century provides ample evidence of progress in defining important educational questions, developing means for studying them, and revealing, with increasing degrees of specificity, the possibilities and limits of such investigations (Noah & Eckstein, 1969). The variety of educational practices and their outcomes in the many nations of the world may be regarded as a series of natural experiments created by different political, social, and economic circumstances. Comparative study investigates their meanings and seeks to relate them to persistent problems in understanding education.

Max A. Eckstein

See also Achievement Testing; Change Processes; Comparative Education; National Development and Education.

REFERENCES

Avalos, B. Teacher effectiveness: Research in the Third World—Highlights of a review. *Comparative Education*, 1980, *16*, 45–54.

Blaug, M. *Economics of Education: A Selected Annotated Bibliography* (3rd ed.). New York: Pergamon Press, 1978.

Bloom, B. *Human Characteristics and School Learning.* New York: McGraw-Hill, 1976.

Bridge, R. G.; Judd, M.; & Moock, P. *The Determinants of Educational Outcomes: The Impact of Families, Peers, Teachers, and Schools.* Cambridge, Mass.: Ballinger, 1979.

Carroll, J. B. *The Teaching of French as a Foreign Language in Eight Countries.* Vol. 5 of *International Studies in Evaluation.* New York: Wiley; Stockholm: Almqvist & Wiksell, 1975.

Comber, L. C., & Keeves, J. P. *Science Education in Nineteen Countries.* Vol. 1 of *International Studies in Evaluation.* New York: Wiley; Stockholm: Almqvist & Wiksell, 1973.

Coombs, F. S., & Lüschen, G. System performance and policy-making in West European education: Effectiveness, efficiency, responsiveness and fidelity. *International Review of Education,* 1976, *22*, 133–153.

Downing, J. *Comparative Reading: Cross-national Studies of Behavior and Processes in Reading and Writing.* New York: Macmillan, 1973.

Eckstein, M. A. Comparative study of educational achievement. *Comparative Education Review,* 1977, *21*, 345–357.

Farnen, R. F.; Oppenheim, A. N.; & Torney, J. V. *Civic Education in Ten Countries.* Vol. 6 of *International Studies in Evaluation.* New York: Wiley; Stockholm: Almqvist & Wiksell, 1975.

Finn, J. D.; Dulberg, L.; & Reis, J. Sex differences in educational attainment: A cross-national perspective. *Harvard Educational Review,* 1979, *49*, 477–503.

Finn, J. D.; Reis, J.; & Dulberg, L. Sex differences in educational attainment: The process. *Comparative Education Review,* 1980, *24*, S33–S52.

Foshay, A. W.; Thorndike, R. L.; Hotyat, F.; Pidegon, D. A.; & Walker, D. A. *Educational Achievements of Thirteen-year-olds in Twelve Countries*. Hamburg: UNESCO Institute for Education, 1962.

Fraser, S. *Jullien's Plan for Comparative Education, 1816–1817*. New York: Columbia University, Teachers College, 1964.

Gray, W. S. *The Teaching of Reading and Writing*. Paris: UNESCO, 1956.

Halsall, E. A comparative study of attainments in French. *International Review of Education*, 1963, *9*, 41–59.

Härnqvist, K. The international study of educational achievement. In F. N. Kerlinger (Ed.), *Review of Research in Education* (Vol. 3.). Itasca, Ill.: F. E. Peacock, 1975.

Heyneman, S. P. Influences on academic achievement: A comparison of results from Uganda and more industrialized countries. *Sociology of Education*, 1976, *49*, 200–211.

Heyneman, S. P. *Textbook and Achievement: What We Know* (World Bank Staff Working Paper No. 298). Washington, D.C.: World Bank, 1978. (ERIC Document Reproduction Service No. ED 179 044)

Husén, T. *International Study of Achievement in Mathematics: A Comparison of Twelve Countries* (2 vols.). New York: Wiley, 1967.

Husén, T. *Teacher Training and Student Achievement in Less-developed Countries* (World Bank Staff Working Paper No. 310). Washington, D.C.: World Bank, 1978.

Inkeles, A. The international evaluation of educational achievement. *Proceedings of the National Academy of Education*, 1977, *4*, 139–200.

Johnson, D. D. Sex differences in reading scores across cultures. *Reading Research Quarterly*, 1973–1974, *9*, 67–86.

Lewis, E. G., & Massad, C. *The Teaching of English as a Foreign Language in Ten Countries*. Vol. 4 of *International Studies in Evaluation*. New York: Wiley; Stockholm: Almqvist & Wiksell, 1975.

Marjoribanks, K. Psychosocial environments of learning: An international perspective. *Comparative Education*, 1973, *9*, 28–33.

Merritt, R. L., & Coombs, F. S. Politics and educational reform. *Comparative Education Review*, 1977, *21*, 247–273.

Messialas, B. G. Education and political development. *Comparative Education Review*, 1977, *21*, 274–295.

Noah, H. J., & Eckstein, M. A. *Toward a Science of Comparative Education*. New York: Macmillan, 1969.

Passow, A. H.; Noah, H. J.; Eckstein, M. A.; & Mallea, J. *The National Case Study: An Empirical Comparative Study of Twenty-one Educational Systems*. Vol. 7 of *International Studies in Evaluation*. New York: Wiley; Stockholm: Almqvist & Wiksell, 1976.

Peaker, G. F. *An Empirical Study of Education in Twenty-one Countries: A Technical Report*. Vol. 8 of *International Studies in Evaluation*. New York: Wiley; Stockholm: Almqvist & Wiksell, 1975.

Postlethwaite, N. Introduction, and target populations, sampling, instrument construction, and analysis procedures. *Comparative Education Review*, 1974, *18*, 157–179.

Psacharopoulos, G. *Returns to Education: An International Comparison*. San Francisco: Jossey-Bass, 1973.

Purves, A. C. *Literature Education in Ten Countries*. Vol. 2 of *International Studies in Evaluation*. New York: Wiley; Stockholm: Almqvist & Wiksell, 1973.

Simmons, J., & Alexander, L. Factors which promote school achievement in developing countries: A review of the research. In J. Simmons (Ed.), *The Education Dilemma: Policy Issues for Developing Countries in the 1980s*. Elmsford, N.Y.: Pergamon Press, 1980.

Thorndike, R. L. *Reading Comprehension Education in Fifteen Countries*. Vol. 3 of *International Studies in Evaluation*. New York: Wiley; Stockholm: Almqvist & Wiksell, 1973.

Trace, A. S. *What Ivan Knows that Johnny Doesn't*. New York: Random House, 1961.

Walker, D. A. *The IEA Six-subject Survey*. Vol. 9 of *International Studies in Evaluation*. New York: Wiley; Stockholm: Almqvist & Wiksell, 1976.

Wiersma, W. A cross-national comparison of the academic achievement of prospective secondary school teachers. *Comparative Education Review*, 1969, *13*, 209–212.

Wolf, R. M. *Achievement in America: National Report of the United States for the International Achievement Project*. New York: Columbia University, Teachers College, 1977.

COMPETENCY-BASED TEACHER EDUCATION

"Competency-based teacher education" appears to be a term new in the educational lexicon since the 1969 edition of the *Encyclopedia of Educational Research*. Even though "Preservice Programs" in that edition cites Goodlad as recommending that future research be directed toward defining expectations of teachers in terms of behavioral objectives, nowhere in that article or related articles is the term "competency-based teacher education" to be found. Other terms that have been applied to the concept include "performance-based," "field-based," "certification of teacher behavior," and "performance assessment."

The concept probably emerged from the accountability movement of the late 1960s and early 1970s, which assigned responsibility to the schools and their staffs for demonstrating that students had mastered agreed-upon learning objectives. To accomplish this, it was proposed that objectives be specified and evaluated in performance terms.

It follows logically that those institutions and professionals preparing persons to teach should ensure that licensees possess particular competencies before being permitted to practice the profession. It is notable that in the competency-based movement both for teacher licensure and for certifying elementary and secondary school students for promotion from grade to grade or for graduation, the major responsibility has been shifted to the students, who must demonstrate competence according to predefined criteria.

The classic definition of competency-based teacher education (CBTE) that guided the movement at its height is as follows: "In performance-based programs performance goals are specified, and agreed to, in rigorous detail in advance of instruction. The student must either be able to demonstrate his ability to promote desirable learning or exhibit behaviors known to promote it. . . . Emphasis is on demonstrated product or output" (Elam, 1971, p. 2).

No broad consensus on this definition has been reached over the ten years that the concept of CBTE has been part of the professional literature. Moreover, a definition of quite different emphasis has been put forth by one large segment of the teaching profession, the National Education Association: "Performance-based teacher education is a procedure for helping prospective teachers and in-service teachers acquire those knowledges, skills, and attitudes that research, empirical evidence, and expertise indicate contribute most to providing learning opportunities that are consistent with objectives of schools" (Kemble & McKenna, 1975, p. 6).

Research and Development. To paraphrase the second definition, it is important to answer the question "What knowledges, skills, and attitudes do research, empirical evidence, and expertise show that teachers should possess in order to provide maximum learning opportunities for students?" Some of the earliest efforts to answer this and related questions took place in the late 1960s through the model programs of the National Center for Educational Research and Development of the U.S. Office of Education (USOE). In 1967 the USOE issued a request for proposals (RFP) for model elementary teacher education programs. The RFP indicated that "what is clearly needed at the outset is a variety of sets of detailed educational specifications which can be used as guides in developing sound teacher education programs" (U.S. Office of Education, 1967). The models were required to incorporate behavioral objectives, systems analyses and expected and measurable teacher behaviors (Hamilton, 1973; Shearron, 1973).

Ten sets of specifications were eventually developed. Assumptions underlying all of these models were both summarized and described in detail in the late 1960s and early 1970s (Burdin & Lanzillotti, 1969). The models represented a difference from traditional programs (Shearron, 1973) in shifts (1) from an experience base to a performance base; (2) from a primary focus on knowledge and skill to a focus on output; (3) from a mainly data-free mode to a data-dependent mode; (4) from an essentially training function to research, development, and training; (5) from an essentially impersonal mode to a personalized and student-oriented mode; (6) from an essentially college-centered or university-centered program to a field-centered program; and (7) from an essentially narrow and closed decision-making base to one that is broad and essentially open. Following model development, eight institutions carried out feasibility studies including resources and costs, for their implementation (Shearron, 1973).

The models produced a variety of delineations of teaching competencies (*Florida Catalog of Teacher Competencies*, 1973; Johnson, 1972) as well as task-analysis processes for identifying competencies (Houston, 1972). They were also characterized by module building, and procedures were developed for creating modules (Houston, 1972).

Antecedents to competency-based teacher education

prior to the models projects have been attributed to various Greek, European, and American scholars; to developments in educational theory; to the rise of teacher education and teachers' colleges; and to adaptations from systems models for planning and evaluation in other enterprises (Hamilton, 1973; Saylor, 1976).

The models projects were to proceed through three phases: design, feasibility studies, and demonstration. But because of leadership changes and shortage of funds the demonstration stage was not implemented (Hamilton, 1973). USOE activities and funding in a variety of forms were sustained at a high level from 1967 through 1973, with expenditures for that period estimated at more than 12 million dollars (Hamilton, 1973). Among these activities were the support of conferences, consortia, training institutes, and state and institutional projects.

The major dissemination effort was through funding to the American Association of Colleges for Teacher Education (AACTE), which served as a clearinghouse. This activity was coordinated by the AACTE Committee on Performance-Based Teacher Education established in 1970.

A second major activity that might be considered a dissemination effort for adaptations of the CBTE concept, or at least some aspects of it, has been reflected in the hundred-plus Teacher Corps programs, some of which have proceeded through more than a dozen cycles since their inception in 1965. Emphasis in Teacher Corps has been on those aspects of performance-based teacher education (PBTE) dealing with training and "field-basedness" rather than with research and development.

From 1970 to 1977 the AACTE published twenty-two monographs on the subject, ranging from governance for CBTE to design alternatives. Most of the monographs were favorable to and promotional of CBTE and took a "why" or "how-to-do-it" approach to their topics. But the movement was not without its detractors. Included in the AACTE series were at least two monographs (Broudy, 1972; Kemble & McKenna, 1975) and a number of articles (e.g., Atkin, 1975; Nash, 1970) that raised questions about the movement or took exception to it. A study separate from the AACTE series, prepared for the Office of Planning, Budgeting, and Evaluation of the U.S. Office of Education, raised questions about the theoretical and research base, instruction and evaluation, premature legislation, costs, exportability, and other issues.

Two critiques typical of the exceptions taken to the movement pointed out that although the CBTE concept might be generally sound, development and dissemination activities were far exceeding research. The critics recommended that the major participants in the movement "return to the drawing board," design and implement a broad range of research studies to validate teaching performances most likely to produce student learning, and develop sound procedures to assess levels of performance required to successfully practice the profession (Kemble & McKenna, 1975; Maxim, 1974).

In 1974 the AACTE published recommendations on

future directions for PBTE (Committee on Performance-Based Teacher Education, 1974). It included a historical review of the movement and a description of characteristics of PBTE programs as applied to teacher education. The committee found that CBTE's major shortcomings were superficiality and fragmentation resulting from attempting too much with limited resources, adopting too eclectic an approach, and making too narrow an interpretation. Nevertheless, the committee concluded that its potentialities justified a large-scale effort and made the following recommendations: (1) that CBTE roles be more clearly conceptualized; (2) that standards for developing materials and procedures for disseminating them be worked out; (3) that the roles of students in the process be more clearly defined; (4) that assessment plans be more fully developed; (5) that collaborative decision-making be implemented and that management responsibilities be clearly delineated; (6) that costs and factors that influence costs be identified; (7) that there be no mandating, either state or local, of CBTE; (8) that accreditation standards be applied rigorously to CBTE experiments; and (9) that research designs be integral parts in the development of all CBTE programs.

In 1974 a series of journal articles (*Phi Delta Kappan*, 1974) presented arguments for and against CBTE. And in 1975 the AACTE published a report of a task force (Drummond et al., 1975) that dealt with CBTE as a process, indicating current criticisms and concerns about how the concept was being viewed and implemented. This report reiterated a number of the recommendations made in an earlier monograph (Committee on Performance-Based Teacher Education, 1974).

The CBTE literature to 1975 appears to have been more expository, descriptive, and advocacy-oriented than research-based, and thus reflects the findings of the AACTE committee itself. The movement has never lacked for literary efforts. The ERIC Center for Teacher Education reports more than two thousand entries on the subject.

Trends. In 1977 a member of the AACTE's committee attempted to assess PBTE efforts up to then from the viewpoint of the committee (Kay, 1977). Reviewing a survey of the states written by Roth (1977), Kay pointed out that thirty-six states had been involved in one aspect or another of CBTE by 1976. Kay cited another survey (National Center for Educational Statistics, 1977) reporting that approximately half the nation's teacher education programs had developed and adopted written statements of learning objectives and competencies. The Kay report concluded that many members of the education community had embraced the CBTE concept and that its growth was continuing.

Also in 1977 Elam reported that the government was getting out of the movement as the funding for the Education Professions Development Act came to an end (Elam, 1977). At this time a conference (Southeastern Competency-Based Teacher Education Symposium, 1977) was held on the future of the movement. At about the same time a 1973 survey was updated by Villeme (1977) showing that whereas twenty-two states had been planning PBTE programs in 1973 only eleven reported using them in 1977, five were planning to use them, and thirty-four states had no specific commitments. The survey concluded that teacher certification based on demonstrated competencies would probably not become institutionalized.

Another survey (Sandefur & Westbrook, 1978) concluded that CBTE programs had actually expanded between 1975 and 1977. Piper & Houston (1980) pointed out, however, that programs can incorporate varying amounts of competency-based elements, which may explain discrepant survey results. Coker (1979) and Smith and Nagel (1979) indicated that a variety of characteristics of CBTE are present in many traditional teacher education programs. These include stipulation of objectives, instruction and assessment related to objectives, and advancement based on demonstrated proficiency.

Evaluation. The majority of the reported evaluations of CBTE are representative of three areas of application: vocational education; education for the handicapped; and early childhood education. The reports are descriptive, rather than research-oriented. Few compare CBTE to conventional approaches to teacher education to determine which is superior for particular purposes. The studies have produced such widely disparate findings as the following seven. (1) Modules have immediate effect on competency acquisition, but the competencies are not maintained over time (Stolovich, 1976). (2) A competency-based program seemed to have been operating in a superior fashion to a subject-centered program based on six measures (Enos, 1975). (3) A field-oriented and competency-based approach was judged a viable alternative to the traditional university approach to industrial teacher education, but the phases employed did not fully address the issue of competency-based vocational education. It was concluded that additional research is needed in this area (*Competency-based Industrial Teacher Education*, 1977). (4) The unavailability and complexity of materials and a lack of data evaluation can be serious impediments to widespread use of CBTE (Gall, 1979). (5) There is a set of commonly agreed-on competencies important to the individualization of instruction in vocational education (Mills, 1977). (6) An evaluation model selected for a CBTE program did not provide sufficient guidance in program description and had to be enhanced with two others (Hinely, 1979). (7) Generic teaching competencies do exist and can be measured, but special education teachers require additional specific assessment items (Stulac, 1978).

One study that reviewed the literature on program evaluation for CBTE (Kay & Schoener, 1979) reiterates theory in program evaluation, teacher evaluation, teacher assessment, and descriptions of existing programs and pays less attention to evaluation of CBTE implementations per se.

Promising as the concept may seem, and with as much residue as is reported remaining from the movement of the 1960s and 1970s, CBTE still lacks rigorous research, development, and evaluation. With current declining enrollments in teacher education institutions and severe budget restrictions on teacher education, the promise for substantially reducing these deficits in the foreseeable future is not great.

Bernard McKenna

See also Competency Testing; Evaluation of Teachers; In-Service Teacher Education; Teacher Certification; Teacher Education Programs; Teacher Effectiveness.

REFERENCES

Atkin, J. M. Professional leadership and PBTE. In R. A. Smith (Ed.), *Regaining Educational Leadership: Critical Essays in PBTE/CBTE, Behavioral Objectives, and Accountability.* New York: Wiley, 1975.

Broudy, H. S. *A Critique of Performance-based Teacher Education.* Washington, D.C.: American Association of Colleges for Teacher Education, May 1972. (ERIC Document Reproduction Service No. ED 063 274)

Burdin, J. L., & Lanzillotti, K. *A Reader's Guide to the Comprehensive Models for Preparing Elementary Teachers.* Washington, D.C.: ERIC Clearinghouse on Teacher Education, 1969. (ERIC Document Reproduction Service No. ED 034 076)

Coker, H. An empirical test of teachers' concepts of teaching. *Professional Educator,* 1979, *21*(1), 34–35.

Committee on Performance-Based Teacher Education. *Achieving the Potential of Performance-based Teacher Education: Recommendations.* Washington, D.C.: American Association of Colleges for Teacher Education, February 1974. (ERIC Document Reproduction Service No. ED 087 748)

Competency-based Industrial Teacher Education Project, Phase III: Inservice Program (Final Report). Tampa: University of South Florida, 1977. (ERIC Document Reproduction Service No. ED 145 222)

Drummond, E.; Kennamer, L.; Lindsey, M.; Massanari, K.; & Shearron, G. *Performance-based Teacher Education* (Report of a Task Force for the Committee on Performance-Based Teacher Education of the AACTE). Washington, D.C.: American Association of Colleges for Teacher Education, August 1975.

Elam, S. *Performance-based Teacher Education: What Is the State of the Art?* Washington, D.C.: American Association of Colleges for Teacher Education, December 1971. (ERIC Document Reproduction Service No. ED 058 166)

Elam, S. *Clarification: What Is the State of the Art?* Paper presented at the Southeastern Competency-Based Teacher Education Symposium, Western Carolina University, Asheville, N.C., March 1977.

Enos, D. F. *A Cost-effectiveness Analysis of Competency-based and Non-competency-based Teacher Education at San Diego State University.* San Diego, Calif.: San Diego State University, 1975. (ERIC Document Reproduction Service No. ED 148 729)

Florida Catalog of Teacher Competencies (Florida Catalog of Teacher Competencies Project). Tallahassee: Florida State Department of Education, 1973.

Gall, M. D. Competency-based teacher education materials: How available? How usable? How effective? *Journal of Teacher Education,* May-June 1979, *30*(3).

Hamilton, P. *Competency-based Teacher Education* (Research Memorandum 2158-9). Menlo Park, Calif.: Stanford Research Institute, July 1973. (ERIC Document Reproduction Service No. ED 087 770)

Hinely, W. H. *Development of an Evaluation Model for Competency-based Instruction* (Final Report). Tallahassee: Florida State University, 1979. (ERIC Document Reproduction Service No. ED 176 086)

Houston, R. W. *Strategies and Resources for Developing a Competency-based Teacher Education Program.* Albany: New York State Education Department, Division of Teacher Education, and the Certification and Multi-State Consortium on PBTE, 1972.

Johnson, C. E. *Competencies for Teachers: A Handbook for Specifying and Organizing Teaching Performances.* Georgia Education Models. Athens: University of Georgia, 1972.

Kay, P. M. *PBTE: Where to from Here?* Washington, D.C.: American Association of Colleges for Teacher Education, October 1977. (ERIC Document Reproduction Service No. ED 143 664)

Kay, P. M., & Schoener, J. E. *Program Evaluation for Competency-based Teacher Education: A Brief Review of Literature and an Annotated Bibliography.* New York: City University, Center for Advanced Study in Education, 1979. (ERIC Document Reproduction Service No. ED 164 615)

Kemble, E., & McKenna, B. H. *PBTE: Viewpoints of Two Teacher Organizations.* Washington, D.C.: American Association of Colleges for Teacher Education, September 1975. (ERIC Document Reproduction Service No. ED 111 770)

Maxim, G. W. The role of research in competency-based teacher education. *Education,* January 1974, *55*(5).

Mills, J. D. *Development and Validation of a Competency-based Preservice/Inservice Learning System for Vocational Teachers* (Final Report). Tallahassee: Florida State Department of Education, Division of Vocational Education, June 1977. (ERIC Document Reproduction Service No. ED 186 770)

Nash, R. J. Commitment to competency: The new fetishism in teacher education. *Phi Delta Kappan,* December 1970, *51.*

National Center for Educational Statistics. *Condition of Teacher Education.* Washington, D.C.: U.S. Department of Health, Education, and Welfare, 1977. (ERIC Document Reproduction Service No. ED 143 644)

Phi Delta Kappan (Special issue on competency/performance-based teacher education), January 1974, *55*(5).

Piper, M. K., & Houston, R. W. The search for teacher competence: CBTE and MCT. *Journal of Teacher Education,* September-October 1980, *31*(5), 37.

Roth, R. A. *Performance-based Teacher Certification: A Survey of the States, 1976.* Lansing: Michigan State Department of Education, January 1977. (ERIC Document Reproduction Service No. ED 070 753)

Sandefur, W., & Westbrook, D. Involvement of AACTE institutions in CBTE: A follow-up study. *Phi Delta Kappan,* 1978, *59*(9), 663.

Saylor, J. G. *Antecedent Developments in the Movement to Performance-based Programs of Teacher Education: An Historical Survey of Concepts, Movements, and Practices Significant in the Development of Teacher Education.* Lincoln, Nebr.: L & S Center, November 1976. (ERIC Document Reproduction Service No. ED 133 302)

Shearron, G. F. *Some Contributions to Competency-based Teacher Education Made by the Elementary Models* (Paper prepared for the annual meeting of the Association of Teacher Education, Chicago, February 1973).

Smith, H. R., & Nagel, T. S. From traditional to competency-based teacher education—and never back. *Phi Delta Kappan*, November 1979, *61*(3), 195.

Stolovich, H. D. *Reaching the Handicapped through Their Teachers: The Development and Evaluation of Two Competency-based Training Modules; Parents as Partners in Teaching Handicapped Children* (Final Report). Bloomington: Indiana University, May 1976. (ERIC Document Reproduction Service No. ED 163 681)

Stulac, J. F. *Special Education Competencies for Teachers Project, Final Report, Year II: A Validation Study in Identification and Measurement*. Atlanta, Ga.: Metropolitan Cooperative Educational Service Agency, August 1978. (ERIC Document Reproduction Service No. ED 169 708)

U.S. Office of Education. *USOE Request for Proposals* (No. OE-68-4). Washington, D.C.: The Office, October 16, 1967. (Mimeo)

Villeme, M. B. The decline of competency-based teacher certification. *Phi Delta Kappan*, January 1977, *58*.

COMPETENCY TESTING

The term "competency testing" encompasses a diverse set of phenomena that includes testing programs in the public schools, higher education, teacher education, and testing for certification, licensure, and maintenance of certification. The focus of this article, however, is on minimum competency testing (MCT) for secondary school students. Minimum competency testing is defined as a program mandated by a state or local policy-making body with the following characteristics: (1) all or almost all students at designated grades are required to take paper-and-pencil tests designed to measure basic academic skills, life or survival skills, or functional literacy; (2) a passing score or standard for acceptable levels of student performance has been established; (3) test results may be used to certify students for grade promotion, graduation, or diploma award; to classify students for or place students in remedial or other special services; to allocate compensatory funds to districts; to evaluate or certify schools or school districts; or to evaluate teachers (Madaus, 1981). A summary of the perceived benefits and costs of MCT is given by Perkins (1979) and in an ERIC compilation ("Minimum Competency: General Issues," 1979; see also Glass, 1979).

Minimum competency testing is not the result of a movement by educators; it is therefore important to try to understand the background of MCT programs and the social context in which they are embedded. The first section of this article describes the context of MCT. Since part of the impetus for MCT programs arises from an expressed dissatisfaction with the schools, the evidence for national deficiencies related to the skills assessed in these programs is described in the second section. The responsiveness of political bodies is examined in the third section, which describes the status of legislative activity at the local, state, and national levels and the variations in MCT programs. The fourth section describes the instruments that

have been used. Measurement issues and related research are examined in the fifth section, for example, standard setting and validity. The sixth section describes the legal aspects of MCT, that is, the court cases to date and the major statutes upon which cases have been based. The final section examines needed research on particular topics in MCT: effects upon students, teachers, and the curriculum; testing of the physically handicapped and other special students; the effectiveness of remediation; and the evaluation of MCT programs.

Background of MCT. An analogy can be made between the figure and ground phenomena in perception and the minimum competency testing program and its sociopolitical context. To some viewers, MCT is the figure, and the program components (legislative requirements, funding, remedial efforts, dropout and retention data, and effects on schools) are the ground. For others, MCT programs themselves are the figure, but the ground encompasses a diverse set of economic, political, social, and educational phenomena into which MCT programs may recede and constitute part of the background for other trends. To the first group of viewers, MCT is embedded within the framework of accountability and efficiency that has led to an increasing use of standardized tests within schools. To the second group, MCT programs are only a symptom or part of the attempt of diverse groups to respond to larger social problems. Since both sets of viewers offer insights into the issues of MCT and directions for research, both are included in this discussion.

The testing context. Resnick (1980), Britell (1980), and Perrone (1979) locate the roots of testing in the schools in the nineteenth century. The Boston School Committee administered written examinations in a number of subjects in 1845, and Horace Mann described their objective as follows: "The method of examination tests in a most admirable manner the *competency* or *sufficiency* of the teaching which the pupils have received." (Britell, 1980, p. 28). In 1956, Chicago provided an example of written examinations used in high school admissions that were later used for promotion. The Regents Examinations in New York were established for elementary schools in 1865 and for high schools in 1878. Examinations intended for national use—the work of Joseph Rice—appeared in the 1890s (Resnick, 1980). By 1916, there were thirty-eight standardized scales and tests described in the *Elementary School Journal*. These tests were broadly based, could be used by school systems having a variety of materials and methods, and were the forerunners of the standardized tests in use today.

Two uses of tests have been mentioned. One is for promotion, high school selection, and certification. The New York State Regents Examinations certified the attainment of a standard or minimum of competence, as do present day tests of credit by examination such as the Tests of General Educational Development. These functions are most like the MCT programs. The second use of tests, involving nationally standardized tests, have functions such as monitoring teacher, student, and program performance; comparison of student, class, and grade level performance with those of other districts; and use of the tests in grouping students for instruction. By the end of the 1890–1930 period, "the regular administration of educational tests had become a common practice in almost all the larger American schools" (Resnick, 1980, p. 7). Most importantly, the central administration in the local school district provided the impetus for these testing programs. Thus, the testing programs in local school districts in this country may be likened to some extent to the use of examining boards in England, which served as administrative devices (Montgomery, 1965). And in this regard the English examining system has other elements in common with state-level MCT programs, which provide further centralization of testing and hence control over local school districts (Wise, 1977).

The growth of state educational funding is related to the growth of state power over testing (Resnick, 1980). In 1930 local funding accounted for about 80 percent of the school's resources; by 1980 this percentage had declined to about 45 percent, with accompanying increases in state funding to 45 percent and increases in federal financing from about 0.5 percent in 1930 to about 10 percent in the late 1970s. Although there are expectations at present that changes in fiscal policies may reduce federal expenditures, the balance between state and local funding is unlikely to be fundamentally altered in the direction of more local funding. These funding balances will maintain state-level efforts to set policy as well as administrative means of implementing policy. MCT programs in some form are likely to remain; the current directions of control are reflected in the characteristics of MCT programs described below.

The MCT programs have also appeared at a time when developments in measurement influenced the form of testing. Changes in the technology of measurement were emphasized in the 1960s and 1970s (Airasian, 1979). The definition of competencies "fit" the increased attention to objectives in instructional psychology (Glaser, 1963; Gagné & Rohwer, 1969) and their continuing emphasis in education (Tyler, 1934; Bloom, 1956; Mager, 1962). Glaser (1963) also reinforced a view of measurement that examined the relation between tests and instruction, suggesting the need for criterion-referenced tests that indicated what pupils could or could not do. This idea led, in turn, to establishing a standard of performance and to technical work on cutting scores that would distinguish between those who were "competent" or had attained mastery, or, for MCT, had attained minimum competence.

Within the education and testing context, the rapid adoption of MCT programs in the states can be partially traced to the pressure to provide equal opportunity: first, through federal legislation such as the Elementary and Secondary Education Act of 1965 (ESEA), Title I, and special programs under the Office of Economic Opportunity as well as efforts to assess the outcomes of education, such

as the National Assessment of Educational Progress (NAEP); and second, through legal efforts to equalize the allocation of resources to schools and to attain desegregation. All of these federal efforts either required evaluation of programs, encouraged research to determine their effects (as in desegregation), or were assessments of achievement (Haney & Madaus, 1979; Pedulla & Reidy, 1979; Resnick, 1980).

There was disillusionment with the results of these programs as they were evaluated and did not produce the expected equalization of outcomes (Cohen & Haney, 1980) or resulted in what Lerner (1980) calls the failure of the judicial initiative. There were also a series of studies that appeared to show no relation between school inputs and student outcomes as well as apparent evidence of a national decline in test scores. All contributed to the rapid legislative activity for MCT and an expression of the need for schools to "return to the basic skills" in the curriculum. Testing activities, already well established in schools and states (Holmen & Docter, 1972; Resnick, 1980), became the administrative device for requiring the attainment of student competency that seemingly was not achieved with the allocation of special resources.

The economic and social context. The broader background of MCT rests on changing economic and social forces in this country and our relationship to other countries. Within the United States the rapid growth of the economy in the 1950s and 1960s resulted in expanding social programs (although aimed at what Cohen and Haney (1980) suggest are minimum goals) in such areas as public housing, Social Security, and Medicare. Expectations that were primarily egalitarian in character were fostered. Schools and postsecondary institutions expanded to meet demands. De S. Price (1981) estimated that the student population in secondary education had grown exponentially at about 6 percent a year, moving from an elite to a democratized higher education, until about one-half the age group were going to college and no further growth was possible. During this period, schooling was viewed as contributing to income. However, changes in age and employment patterns in the adult population were occurring, such as a higher proportion of elderly, a movement of workers from industry to the service sector, and increasing rates of employment for women. These patterns and the war effort, a decline in the value of the dollar, energy costs, a diminishing industrial base, increased inflation, and other factors all provided a brake to these growing expectations and expenditures from the late 1960s on.

These factors also culminated in greater youth unemployment, especially for minorities. The effects of increases in the service sector may have further emphasized the need for strengthening human resources through education (Ginzberg & Vojta, 1981). The extent to which unemployment is due to lack of competencies, as perceived by some proponents of MCT, to problems in high schools (Resnick, 1980), or to more fundamental structural problems in the economy—changing social patterns and impacts of age-structure effects in the labor market on the economy—is an important question in need of exploration. Such research is likely to affect the further development and focus of MCT programs, as well as schooling, more broadly. A broader historical analysis of critics of the schools may add further insights into the relationship between rates of social change, conservatism, and pressures on the schools (e.g., Brodinsky, 1977).

There is also a need to test some of the assumptions regarding the origins of MCT through research. Greene (1980), for example, questions whether the public dissatisfaction with the schools has in fact been the main impetus for MCT as a means of achieving accountability. The shifting basis for school funding and resulting administrative use of tests suggest otherwise. Careful studies and analyses of the origins of state legislation and board policies would assist in untangling the possible "causes" of the legislation and mandates. They would provide an understanding of the likely permanence of MCT and the further expansion of testing as administrative efforts. The review by Resnick (1980) provides a starting point for such studies. Also needed are comparative studies of the use of examinations in other countries, drawing on work such as that of Montgomery (1965) to provide further contrasts with MCT developments and their effects on local governance of education, curriculum, and potential for increased placement of students into separate tracks.

Evidence of National Deficiencies. The evidence of national deficiencies with respect to the skills assessed in MCT programs is inconsistent in terms of the comparability of samples across studies and particularly with respect to the link between tests and school curricula. The latter is important because, until recently, much of the evidence for deficiencies in basic skills was based upon the results of nationally standardized achievement tests. These tests are norm-referenced, with items selected to provide differentiation among individuals, not their achievement in relation to a "standard" or attainment of proficiency in a defined curricula. The evidence, which does not show declines in some skills, is limited by the time span covered by the results (i.e., the National Assessment of Educational Progress, starting in 1969); but it has advantages as an approach to measurement since performance on individual items is examined. One of the major tests on which the claim for the decline in national achievement data is based, the Scholastic Aptitude Test (SAT), is not an achievement test in the usual sense, and is less linked to the school curriculum than are the nationally normed achievement tests. However, analyses of the reasons for declines in the SAT are useful to an understanding of the scope of influences on test scores and the difficulties in interpreting the evidence to date on national deficiencies.

Viewed from an international perspective, it is not clear that there is a national deficiency in all of the basic skills. Tyler (1981) has summarized the cross-national data of the International Association for the Evaluation of Educational Achievement (a consortium of sixteen nations that has comparative test results in six subjects). The mean scores for the top 5 percent of youth completing secondary education in all the industrialized nations tested were about the same. The average score of U.S. 14-year-olds in literacy (reading comprehension) was 27.3, third highest of the fifteen nations tested. At age 14, the majority of the age group is in school. In literature, the average score (combined for comprehension and interpretation) was 16.5, exceeded only by New Zealand (18.7) and Finland (17.2). For secondary school students, data must be viewed in terms of the different national retention rates: the United States retained the highest percent—78 percent, through the final year of secondary school, whereas other countries retained an estimated 13 percent (New Zealand) to 70 percent (Japan). The U.S. average comprehension score on the reading test was the lowest, apart from the three developing nations (Thorndike, 1973), although literature comprehension and interpretation was bettered by only four of the other nations. Results in mathematics placed the United States in a much less favorable light (Tyler, 1981). Performance in the application of computational skills to common quantitative problems was low for 14-year-olds, and the United States made the lowest average mathematics' score for high school seniors. Differences in school retention rates have some influence, but Japan has similar retention rates and high attainment in mathematics.

Within the United States, an examination of evidence of achievement test score decline using the SAT, Preliminary Scholastic Aptitude Test (PSAT), American College Testing Program (ACT), Minnesota Scholastic Aptitude Test (MSAT), Iowa Tests of Educational Development (ITED), Iowa Tests of Basic Skills (ITBS), Comprehensive Tests of Basic Skills (CTBS), and National Assessment of Educational Progress (NAEP) was reported by Harnischfeger and Wiley (1976). Copperman (1978) cites similar data, including data on the lowered readability levels of textbooks and the NAEP conclusions about literacy rates. All the tests examined, with the exception of the natural science scores for ACT, the PSAT scores, and some areas of the NAEP, show a decline in average scores for either national or state samples over a ten-year period beginning approximately in the mid-1960s. The SAT is reported to still be declining (College Entrance Examination Board, 1980), although the rate of decline for 1980 is less rapid than in the 1970s.

The NAEP reported no change in reading skills between 1971 and 1975 for 13-year-olds and in-school 17-year-olds, and a slight improvement between 1971 and 1975 for 9-year-olds. There was a slight improvement in literal comprehension and a slight decline in inferential comprehension for 13-year-olds and 17-year-olds (Farr & Olshavsky, 1980). Data from the 1979–1980 assessment of reading skills provided evidence of improvement in the basic reading skills taught in the lower grades but declines in the inferential comprehension and critical reading skills necessary to demonstrate an increasingly higher level of understanding (Fiske, 1981; Maeroff, 1981; Morgan, 1981). Lerner (1980) is critical of concepts of literacy used to construct NAEP test items and of the NAEP definition of illiteracy (*Functional Literacy: Basic Reading Performance*, 1976). However, Tyler provided a long-term view of increases in reading comprehension in the general population and questioned whether 100 percent attainment is a reasonable expectation (cited in Ryan, Johnston, & Newman, 1977).

Declines occurred for 9-year-olds, 13-year-olds, and 17-year-olds in science, and there was no major change in writing skills during the 1970s ("Third NAEP Survey," 1981). A decline was reported for all ages in mathematics achievement, with 17-year-olds in 1978 performing an average of 4 percentage points lower than 17-year-olds in 1973 (Neill, 1979). Results of the mathematics items by area are given in a series of analyses (e.g., Carpenter et al., 1980), and Fey and Sonnabend (in press) also review the trends in mathematics scores and related research. Welch (1980) reported an interesting study of the decline in science scores. Jones (1981) examines the declines in both mathematics and science.

The decline in SAT scores has received the most attention, with a report of the advisory panel (Wirtz, 1977) summarizing interpretations of the decline. The verbal portion of the SAT includes four areas—antonyms, analogies, sentence completion, and reading comprehension—but subscores are not available to examine decline by verbal area. The mathematical section requires background mathematics taught in grades 1–9, but items are intended to measure problem solving in arithmetic reasoning, elementary algebra, and geometry. Thus, there is little relation to the "basic skills" emphasized in MCT programs, as Farr and Olshavsky (1980) have argued in stating that MCT is not the appropriate solution to the SAT score decline. (See also Elligett & Tocco, 1980.)

The factors examined for their relationship to decline in SAT scores ranged from composition of the student groups taking the SAT, school courses of study (the curriculum), learning standards, staff and facilities, parents (as teachers), television, other social events, and student motivation (Wirtz, 1977; Harnischfeger & Wiley, 1977; Eckland, in press). Changes during the 1960s were attributed to a considerable degree to changes in the population of those taking the SAT; later changes were attributed to lower education standards in required curriculum courses, a rise in absenteeism, grade inflation, social promotion, reduced homework, and a marked drop in textbook level of difficulty. The panel recognized the broad constituency served by the schools, but did not suggest that students be uniformly held in grade until they reach a common standard, that they be suspended from school as a rigid penalty for absenteeism, that they be overloaded with homework, or that electives be removed from the curriculum (Eckland, forthcoming). The National Academy of Education (1978) listed four changes in school practice contributing to declines in writing and SAT scores: course

proliferation and less rigorous academic standards; confusion about appropriate methods of instruction; less direct teaching and learning time; and fewer opportunities for intensive academic study at the secondary level. The National Center for Education Statistics is initiating a study that will provide further evidence on national achievement trends: "High School and Beyond," a longitudinal study of the sophomore and senior classes of 1980, parallel to the national longitudinal study of the class of 1972 (Eckland, forthcoming).

Among the discussions of evidence for deficiencies in basic skills there is little analysis of the link between curricula and test items. Although mentioned by Harnischfeger and Wiley (1976), the point has received more analysis by Madaus and his colleagues (Madaus et al., 1979; Madaus, Airasian, & Kelleghan, 1980) in the context of studies of school effectiveness (see also Bridge, Judd, & Moock, 1979), and by Cooley and Leinhardt (1978, 1980) and Hanson, Schutz, and Bailey (1977) in evaluation studies. (A partial review of the methods and results of analyses of the match between curricula and tests is provided in Tittle, in press.) The evidence for a continuing decline in basic skills is not substantiated thoroughly by the evidence to date, and some NAEP data suggest that the problem is in the higher-level skills in curriculum areas (Fiske, 1981, Maeroff, 1981). Munday (1979) cites data that the sharp decline in the late 1960s has stopped, and the achievement of high school students is about at the level of the early 1960s. Copperman's interpretation of the data (1979) differs from that of Munday, and Eurich (1980) provided data showing that students at the University of Minnesota in 1928 performed better than a group of students in 1978 (same institution, same test, but again a changed college applicant pool). Unfortunately, since state MCT programs have not used any of the available NAEP items (National Assessment of Educational Progress, 1977a, 1977b), the type of information given by the NAEP cannot be examined for the large numbers in state testing programs.

Resnick (1980) cited estimates that functional illiteracy ranges from 15 million to 50 million individuals; yet, for those who graduate from high school the illiteracy rate is estimated at 1 percent. But the rate is quite different for those who drop out of high school. The dropout rate for high school begins with about 2.5 percent in grade 9 (school attendance is still mandated); but at grade 10 and grade 11, dropout rates increase to 9 percent and 10 percent; for grade 12, the dropout rate has remained steady since about the mid-1960s at 25 percent. MCT programs that focus only on 15-year-olds to 17-year-olds still in school cannot be expected to help reduce the number of functional illiterates in the population (Resnick, 1980) unless early identification of those in danger of failing MCT leads to successful remediation and school retention. Lerner (1980) has made a similar argument. Data on MCT programs in the states have not yet included cohort and time series analyses of the dropout patterns (examined for groups at, below, and advanced for age in grade, Price,

1969). The differing patterns of state program MCT requirements would permit examination of the effects of MCT programs on dropout rates.

Legislated and Policy-board Activities. Legislated activities related to MCT programs occur at the federal and state levels; at the state level, state legislatures and education policy boards have initiated mandates for MCT, and at the local level, school boards of education have required MCT. Federal-level activities have included the legislated transfer of the NAEP from the National Center for Education Statistics to the National Institute of Education (NIE). Further, the Elementary and Secondary Education Act Amendments of 1978 included provisions (Part B, Title IX, ESEA) for grants to implement education proficiency standards and achievement testing assistance (e.g., House Committee on Education and Labor, 1977). These activities would have supported state and local testing programs only, but no funds were appropriated in 1979/80 (Vlaanderen, 1980). There has not been, and is unlikely to be, any serious effort to have a national test that would have impact on local curricula. The negative reaction that such a proposal would bring is evident in the report of a federally sponsored National Conference on Achievement Testing and Basic Skills (National Institute of Education, 1979).

Other federal activities (not legislated) included a commission to the National Academy of Education to review achievement tests and provide policy recommendations, and support to the National Academy of Sciences for an analysis of testing theory and practice. Technical assistance and research and evaluation activities are being carried out by the NIE (Shoemaker, 1979, 1980).

The major sources for the current status of state and local initiatives in MCT are reports from the Education Commission of the States (Pipho, 1980b, 1980c) and a study of minimum competency testing programs commissioned by NIE (Gorth & Perkins, 1979a, 1979b, 1979c, 1979d). Mills (1980) provides another resource on state activities, as does an ERIC document, "Minimum Competency State Testing Programs" (1979). Ramsbotham (1980) has described MCT programs in twelve southern states, test results (if available), and has summarized policy issues. The reports by Pipho define MCT as any statewide call for MCT or standards or any call that would permit or give guidance to local school districts in establishing such programs. With this definition 38 states are included. Gorth and Perkins summarize data for 31 states and 20 (selected from 169 initially identified) local districts.

State-level education policy boards have been used by more states than legislation in initiating MCT (twenty-four vs. twenty), with six states using both. Activity on MCT peaked in 1977–1978; in 1979 only Arkansas, Texas, and New Jersey passed legislation, and the New York Board of Regents modified a 1977 decision. In 1980, MCT bills were in legislatures in Missouri, Nebraska, and Ohio. The earliest action was taken by the state of Michigan, with a state board of education resolution in 1969 for statewide assessment and in 1974 for minimum performance.

Among local districts, Denver has required tests for high school graduation since 1958 (implemented in 1960). Pipho states that MCT was more widely accepted in the western, southern, and eastern parts of the country, and primarily in states that had a history of strong central state control over education. Legislative activity is apparently moving to teacher competency testing (Pipho, 1980a, 1981). And one state, New Jersey, has used MCT results (and program review teams) to evaluate individual school districts, rating them as "approved" with recommendations and commendations, "interim approval," and "unapproved" (Burke, 1980). The states setting basic skills tests in postsecondary education are identified by Kraetsch (1980).

The categories used by Pipho (1980c) and Gorth and Perkins (1979d) identify some of the characteristics on which MCT programs differ. These include such aspects as grade levels included, use of the tests, skill areas to be assessed, source of competency definitions, responsibility for writing or selecting the test, responsibility for setting standards and their basis, provisions for special populations, parent or citizen involvement, reporting, and dissemination.

As of 1979, fourteen state and thirteen local MCT programs are fully implemented (Gorth & Perkins, 1979c). The goals most frequently cited for MCT programs are to identify students for remediation, to improve curricula, to increase accountability, and to certify basic skills prior to graduation. All programs test reading and mathematics skills using, in most cases, multiple-choice tests. Twenty-seven states include language arts and/or writing; most programs include elementary and high school students (either MCT at several grades or state-level assessment tests) and recognize special education and bilingual populations. Sources of tests vary: in-house, commercial, or tailored. Responsibility for setting standards varies also: state, local, or shared. All tests were locally administered. Most reported results to students, teachers, parents, administrators, and school boards. Few states or districts have conducted any evaluation of the MCT programs; (NIE is planning a study of the impact or consequences of the MCT programs). Gorth and Perkins (1979c) provide a wealth of detail on state programs, the result of site visits; but the data are not consistent across sites, and further research is needed to develop consistent information.

The most common mandates are at the state level, expressing a commitment to MCT, requiring all local education authorities (LEAs) to participate, and giving varying responsibility to the LEAs (twenty-seven states). Within states, the responsibilities for state and LEA differ. In Florida, the state assumed responsibility for major tasks, such as test development. In New Hampshire, the LEA is required to carry out tasks, but in both states the LEA must initiate MCT. Only two states have a different type of mandate—the optional LEA participation or district option program. Idaho has a program in which the State Department of Education (SDE) has invited LEAs to participate, and those that do are then subject to state requirements. In Illinois, technical assistance is given by the SDE to LEAs that voluntarily decide to adopt MCT. The third type of mandate is that of the state authorizing study of MCT to decide whether or not to implement it. Two states, Kansas and Maine, take this approach; testing has been initiated only on a temporary basis. It is primarily the public schools that are affected by MCT mandates. Connecticut and North Carolina originally included private schools in their mandates, but in North Carolina, due to legislative changes, private school participation is strictly voluntary.

One of the major issues for MCT programs has been the use of minimum competency tests for identifying or classifying students for remediation (with the potential for resegregation and tracking), grade promotion, and awarding high school diplomas. Mandatory remediation is specified by ten states, and optional remediation by fifteen (with often the cost to be borne by the LEA). Anderson (1977) reports that add-on costs of compensatory programs range from $28 million to $94 million per year. Two states (Arizona and Nevada) use MCT as part of the basis for grade promotion. Fourteen states do, or plan to, require MCT for high school graduation. Three states plan to give attendance certificates if students do not pass MCT. Two states will place special recognition on the diploma for competency achievement, but will not require MCT for the diploma (Idaho, New Mexico). Alternate routes to the diploma are allowed by Maryland and New York. In New York, the Regents examinations and acceptable scores on standardized college admissions examinations are alternatives.

Defining and setting standards are generally done by the state if the state has responsibility to develop the competency tests and by the LEAs if they have that responsibility. Only two programs set standards for a total test. Others set a standard for each competency or major subject area. Although the data are fragmentary in Gorth and Perkins (1979c), nine of the states report setting standards based upon field test or test administration data. Two states use the contrasting group method, one uses the Nedelsky method for some tests and the Angoff method for others, three define standards as part of their competency definition, and five determine standards by "administrative decision." (That other than a "standard" enters into settings of standards is evidenced by Sallander's descriptions (1980) of the decisions MCT poses for educators, including cutoff score costs in terms of the dollars districts have available for remedial programs.)

In all cases, tests are administered at the local level, and typically by teachers. In large-scale testing programs there will be irregularities, and in one LEA program, teachers were assisting students; as a result, classroom teachers no longer administer tests to their own students. A New Hampshire LEA has a specially trained team that administers tests. (Where funding or other major decisions rest on tests, scores may well be "corrupted"; see Feldmesser, 1975; Campbell, 1977; Cochran, 1978.) Scoring and

analysis of these programs are carried out by the states themselves in about half the programs, and by consulting agencies or publishers in the remainder. Reporting and dissemination data show that information that does not identify individual students or teachers is open to the public and often released to the media. Procedures are similar across programs, and most schools enter test results in the student's permanent record and inform parents. Reports also go to school administrators (twenty-four states), boards of education (twenty-three), teachers (thirteen), and the legislature (seven states).

Funding is provided by the state in twenty programs, with ten state programs supported primarily by local funds. The cost data given for the states in the Gorth and Perkins survey (1979c) are fragmentary. Apparently no state has developed full costs for an MCT program. Anderson (1977) has suggested the categories for which costs need to be developed:

1. Set-up costs of legislation and any recurring costs
2. Implementation costs, including costs to the regulatory agency in deciding how to implement the law and to determine what is required of others (in Oregon, for example, LEA costs were reported to range from $26,500 to $173,000); administrative, record-keeping, and reporting expenses to regulatees; enforcement costs to regulator (e.g., to see that remedial dollars are not put into general funds nor substituted for local efforts); test development costs; any avoidance costs from LEAs
3. Excess burden from compliance, as in court cases
4. Induced neglect of information, as schools restrict other activities
5. Foregone monitoring of other public policies

Airasian et al. (1979) also suggest cost categories.

The costs reported to date are in test development, test administration, add-on costs of compensatory programs, and bureaucracy (Anderson, 1977; Gorth & Perkins, 1979c). The development of full costs for different types of MCT programs remains to be done, and would, if it included estimates of foregone costs as suggested by Anderson, provide guidance to states and other policy makers in making future decisions about MCT programs. Cost estimates would be especially valuable if carried out for programs for which LEAs are responsible. Such cost analyses would be part of a full-scale evaluation of MCT programs.

Gorth and Perkins (1979a, 1979c) also report any efforts that states have made to evaluate MCT programs. Seven states have conducted some level of evaluation. For example, New Hampshire has reviewed materials and interviewed teachers and administrators. Two states have had outside reviews by groups affected by the programs; for example, the Florida MCT was the subject of a review sponsored by the National Education Association (Tyler, 1978), and the Michigan MCT program has been reviewed (House, Rivers, & Stufflebeam, 1974). California has used a survey questionnaire for a sample of districts and conducted personal interviews in LEAs. Questions concerned standards, the assessment process, costs, estimates for remediation, and attitudes toward different standards and the certificate of attendance. Kentucky planned a similar survey of LEAs. New Hampshire had an initial review of materials by a college evaluation team. North Carolina reports pass rates by school, sex, ethnic group, amount of parent education, handicapping condition, and has contracted several studies related to the MCT program, for example, on standard-setting procedures (Jaeger et al., 1980) and on pass rates for successive test administrations to the same group of students (Parramore, Serow, & Davies, 1980). A pilot study in Rhode Island (Gorth & Perkins, 1979a) examined the average score and range of scores registered by all students who had been judged "borderline" by their teachers in the skills specified. In addition, the commissioner proposed "that the standards not be set higher than the lowest scores attained by those involved in planning and implementing the program, including members of the State Standards Council and the Board of Regents" (Gorth & Perkins, 1979a, p. 604). Utah reported a compliance evaluation.

Two studies were conducted in Vermont and illustrate the type of research that needs to be done where LEAs are responsible for MCT. Vermont has an LEA program, with no state test. In the first study, consistency of judgments of mastery (competence) were made. SDE staff and LEA staff both assessed students using district materials. Agreement between the two groups ranged from 59 percent on reading competency to 85 percent on mathematics competency, with overall agreement (on eight competencies) at 69 percent. A comparability study between LEAs was also conducted. SDE staff rated local materials as to whether for each competency they were above, in agreement with, or below a level most closely associated with the wording of the competency and the material in the state manual provided for LEAs. The SDE found that "some had attached specific time requirements for the completion of the task while others had not. Some used group situations for all the competencies reviewed, while others used some individual assessment. Some schools used the same methods throughout the school, while others left the method up to individual teachers. Some had very specific guidelines for evaluation, while others left the standards to individual teachers" (Gorth & Perkins, 1979a, pp. 690–691).

With the exception of small-scale studies dealing with particular aspects of an MCT program, or reporting of statewide results on pass rates, little attention has been given to the evaluation of MCT programs. Some planning has started (e.g., Hartman, 1980), but little systematic work has taken place. Major attention has been given to instruments and standards as states work on the implementation phases of MCT programs.

Instrumentation. The assessment measures used in minimum competency programs can be the responsibility of the state education agency (SEA), the LEA, or can be shared by the two. As of 1979, fourteen states had complete responsibility, eight shared responsibility with the LEA, and in seven states the LEA had complete responsibility (Gorth & Perkins, 1979c). Regardless of where the responsibility for the assessment instrument rests, several approaches to developing a test are possible. These methods, and the number of states using them in 1979, are as follows: "in-house" or state agency development only (three states); consulting service or contracting agency only (four); commercial tests and/or tests tailored by a publisher only (five); in-house development and use of consulting service or contractor (six); in-house development and use of commercial test or test tailored by a publisher (two); use of consulting service or contract and use of commercial or tailored test (one); in-house development and consulting service or contractor and commercial or tailored test (three). According to Gorth and Perkins (1979c), no one commercial test is used more than others. Among the instruments used are the Senior High Assessment of Reading Performance (SHARP), the Test of Proficiency in Computational Skills (TOPICS) and the California Tests of Basic Skills (CTBS) published by CTB/McGraw Hill; the Gates-McGinitie Reading Tests, Survey F, published by Teachers College Press; the Beckman-Beal Mathematical Competency Tests for Enlightened Citizens and the SOBAR reading test published by Science Research Associates; tests published by Stanford Research Associates; the Adult Performance Level Test published by American College Testing; and the Iowa Tests of Basic Skills (ITBS) published by Houghton Mifflin. (See also an earlier report on basic skills assessment programs, Educational Testing Service, 1977.)

The N-ABELS instruments developed by the state of Nebraska are entirely performance-based. For example, students may be required to read aloud, to locate words in a dictionary, or to locate a topic and cross reference in a card catalog. By far the majority of instruments are multiple choice in response form, regardless of whether they are developed by the SDE, commercial publishers, or are tailored (adopted from) commercial tests. Open response forms are proposed for use in the assessment of writing in eleven states.

The tests developed or selected are primarily criterion-referenced, defining the skills and knowledges (competencies or domains) to be tested in detail. Minimum competency instruments are said to vary as to whether they measure functional literacy, basic skills related to school curricula, and/or basic skills related to "real life" settings, the so-called life skills.

The process of defining competencies or skills to be measured in minimum competency instruments has also taken several forms. This process is important to the MCT program not only from the standpoint of the validity of competencies and instruments but also from the political and potential legal views of the program. The major parts of the process are described in Perkins (1979a). The steps in the process of developing competencies, when carried out thoroughly, have much in common with the steps in developing test items: establishing a task force or advisory committee; developing a competency framework or skill emphasis, defining competency content domains; writing and selecting competencies; reviewing, refining, and validating competencies; and selecting the final set of competencies. As with the item writing process, no research exists on variants in the process or factors that may affect perceptions of various groups regarding the fairness of legitimacy of the competencies (outcomes) selected. This is an area in which measurement, the political process, and the educational process are intertwined, in which little or no research exists, and in which research should be useful, both politically and legally, as we begin to define what it means to "validate" competencies.

Competency validation. Validation of competencies may imply at least two approaches, depending on whether the source of competencies is in the school curricula or in the life skills area. In the area of the school curricula, validation of competencies (and, by implication, assessment tasks or items) may require the type of analysis reported for reading and mathematics tests and curricula as defined by school textbooks and accompanying student instructional materials. Armbruster, Steven, and Rosenshine (1977) and Jenkins and Pany (1976, 1978) reported the analysis of beginning reading series and test items. Freeman et al. (1980) and Kuhs et al. (1979) developed a taxonomy for classifying elementary school mathematics content and analyzed both textbooks and test items for grade 4. Anderson and Anderson (1981) analyzed the overlap of a functional literacy test (FLT) in mathematics and a ninth-grade textbook. They found a low page overlap (28 percent) with the fourteen goal areas of the FLT. Whereas these analyses indicate the overlap in textbooks and test items (and should be done for competencies and textbooks), they do not indicate whether the overlap also exists in the instructional process. Teachers may choose or emphasize different competencies in the instructional process (Freeman & Belli, 1981). This suggests the importance of obtaining observations, ratings, analysis of lesson plans, or another estimate of the match between competency and instruction as part of the competency validation process. In a court case involving the Florida MCT, the Court of Appeals remanded the case because the state had not made any effort to make certain whether the test covered material actually studied in the classroom of the state. If not, it would be unfair and violate the equal protection and due process clauses of the Constitution (*Debra P. v. Turlington,* 1981).

Cooley and Leinhardt (1978, 1980), Leinhardt (1980), and Leinhardt and Sewald (1980) have discussed the importance of assessing overlap in the evaluation setting—in effect, establishing part of the construct validity of both "treatment" and test. Construct validation is a more inclusive and appropriate concept, since "competence" is used as a psychological construct and inferences about performance go beyond the specified content domain (Linn, 1979). Cronbach (1980) has argued that content validation includes more than specifying a domain of tasks and sampling rigorously: "The 'defense' must be prepared to show that the domain is relevant and that weight is properly distributed over it" (p. 105). Research is needed concerning the methodology of this process and the agreement across different approaches. Research is also needed on perceptions of the fairness and validity of MCT held by the various groups concerned with the outcomes of MCT programs: students, parents, teachers, administrators, and employers.

If the minimum competency instrument or performance task is intended to assess life skills, the competency validation process would have another component. There would be a validation of the student's opportunity to learn the life skill in the school setting and there would be a validation of the occurrence of the skill, and presumably its critical nature, in settings outside the school. A number of approaches are possible, some of them based upon methods used to show the job-relatedness of knowledge, skills, and abilities in work settings. These range from the application of job analyses procedures (McCormick, 1976; Teryek, 1979) to ratings of the importance of competencies by job incumbents and supervisors (Rosenfeld & Thornton, 1974). Basic discussions of validity in both education settings (e.g., Cronbach, 1971) and in the employment setting (Guion, 1976) can help to expand the framework for validation of competencies in MCT programs and to guide research. The scope of such an undertaking should not be underestimated. "Generic" multiple-choice tests of verbal and mathematical skills have not held up well in court cases dealing with employment settings (*Luevano et al. v. Campbell,* 1981) and may face similar challenges in education. Fillbrandt and Merz (1977) have provided one example of an application to life skills of standard setting (determining a cutting score) by stratified sampling of entry-level jobholders in small and large businesses and government jobs, in the clerical, service, sales, and operatives occupational categories. King's review (1977) of the validity of the Florida Functional Literacy Test indicated the difficulty of establishing content validity, and Hills and King (1978) provide limited validity data.

To gain an overview of the test development process and the procedures for standard setting as part of the MCT programs as of 1979, two resources are helpful. Priestley (1979) provides a review of the test selection and development process, including developing test and item specifications, writing, review and editing of items; field testing; and establishing validity and reliability. Validity is discussed primarily in terms of content validation by a group of judges (content experts). This view of validity should be expanded to establish more clearly the relationships of the minimum competency test, school curriculum materials, and classroom instruction. And, where life skills or functional literacy are involved, construct validation should involve settings outside the school. Nassif (1979) discusses several standard-setting approaches as applied in minimum competency programs. The standard-setting approaches are used to identify a single score on minimum competency tests or performance tasks below which performance is unsatisfactory and above which performance is satisfactory. Among the issues to be considered are the use of single or multiple cutoff scores, whether student performance levels should enter the decision process, and whether students are correctly classified. The methods used in standard setting vary as to whether students are judged or test items are judged, but all make use of judgments.

Measurement Issues. The measurement issues in minimum competency programs include those central to all measurement efforts—validity, reliability, item bias and equating—and some specific to the use of tests to classify individuals into groups, that is, the classification of individuals as competent or not by the use of cutting scores (setting standards). Issues of validity have been mentioned earlier, in connection with the validation of competencies. Some of these ideas will be repeated here, because if the competencies are not subject to formal validation procedures, the full burden is shifted to the measurement instrument.

Validity. Shepard (1980) has reiterated the view that validity depends upon both the logic of the test development process and the validation process itself. The logic of the test development process includes the empirical evidence gathered at each step of the process. Initially, for MCT this includes selection of the domains to be assessed, the definition of the domain, and whether the items selected are adequately representative of the domain. Here the evidence may include judgments by groups; and the rationale for the use of the groups or individuals making judgments is important for the validation process.

Although judges are often used, rarely are the results of the judgments presented. For example, evidence is typically not available with respect to the degree of agreement among judges (see Rovinelli & Hambleton, 1976, for some data and questions to be asked about the development of a methodology for the use of judgments of content specialists). The documentation of the results of judgments of the domain, the domain definition, and the relation of items to domain statements should be reported along with other evidence of the appropriateness of tests, for example, reliability and data on cutoff scores (standards). For MCT the logic and documentation of the test development process is as important for local district-based test development as it is for state-level efforts. Research is needed to determine the extent to which local and state-level programs provide documentation on this aspect of the validation process and on a methodology for the judgment of content. Linn (1980) has emphasized the need for a theory of content.

Another perspective on validity emphasizes the importance of the relationship between MCT and what is taught in the schools as evidenced by curriculum materials and the instructional process. From this perspective, MCT programs are presumed to base their domains of content on the school curriculum; and analyses of the relationship or overlap between the school curriculum, instruction, and test content would constitute part of the evidence of validity. There is little evidence of such analyses in the MCT program descriptions to date. The importance of these analyses in areas such as reading and mathematics is found in research that has examined the overlap in content categories and format of test items and textbooks (e.g., Bianchini, 1977; Armbruster, Steven, & Rosenshine, 1977; Jenkins & Pany, 1976, 1978; Porter et al., 1978; Kuhs et al., 1979; and Freeman et al., 1980). Similarly, differences in the degree to which teachers rate student opportunity to learn individual test items is predictive of student gains in the early grades (Cooley & Leinhardt, 1980; Leinhardt, 1980; Leinhardt & Sewald, 1981. The advantage of the text analyses and indicators of instruction would be not only in their contribution to the accuracy of inferences from test scores but also in the information they provide to link instruction and assessment.

The usual emphasis on content validation in achievement measures is not sufficient for the validation of MCT. "Competency" is a construct, and further evidence of validity is required for the use of the MCT in making promotion and classification decisions. Shepard states this requirement succinctly: "The theoretical relationship of test performance to other performances must be confirmed by reality" (1980, p. 39). The use of competency tests for grade-to-grade promotion should include demonstrations that the students who are retained would benefit from additional instruction and could not have functioned in higher-level curricula. Similarly, MCT programs that claim to anticipate the requirements for success in adult life should examine the relationship between the MCT and adult performance in various life settings. Such an approach was proposed by Byrne (1980) for developing reading standards using degrees of reading power units, as is done already with school texts; the job analysis approaches used in employment settings may also be applicable (e.g., McCormick, 1976; Teryek, 1979). There are often group differences in performance on MCT, and the economic implications of diploma denial (Eckland, 1980) suggest that guidelines for Equal Employment Opportunities (EEOC) might well be taken as a standard for the demonstration of validity (*Uniform Guidelines on Employee Selection Procedures*, 1978).

Reliability. Reliability issues for MCT are based upon the distinction between reliability estimates appropriate for criterion-referenced measures and those developed by classical test theory. An issue with respect to reliability is the extent to which the degree of mastery or nonmastery is assessed or whether the focus is upon classification errors (Hambleton & Novick, 1973). Whereas minimum competency testing has not been concerned with estimates of domain scores, minimum competency tests that make competent/not competent classifications should examine the consistency of decisions at the cutting scores. Shepard (1980) has summarized the various approaches, including the observed proportion of agreement as an index of reliability, a coefficient adjusted for chance, estimates based upon single administrations, and generalizability theory. She recommends using a combination of approaches to summarize both decision consistency and magnitude of errors. Research is needed to develop what she labels an "ideal index," one that would reflect misclassification errors and weight the degree of error. Another area of research for MCT programs is the examination of decision-consistency data, magnitude of errors, their effects on numbers of students being denied diplomas or promotions, and the influence of these data upon judges' decisions about cutting scores.

Standard setting. The use of multiple-choice measures means that MCT programs assume a continuous underlying variable, and this variable is artificially dichotomized to classify students as competent or not competent. A variety of procedures have been proposed and used to set a cutting score, and a number of reviews are devoted to or contain sections on standard setting (e.g., Millman, 1973; Meskauska, 1976; Subkoviak & Baker, 1977; Glass, 1978; Hambleton et al., 1978; Jaeger, 1979; Hambleton & Eignor, 1980; Shepard, 1980; and Weiss & Davison, 1981). Hambleton and Powell (1981) have provided a useful list of questions which must be addressed in the standard-setting process. An important issue that underlies many of the arguments about the appropriateness of MCT use of multiple-choice tests is the use of an artificial dichotomy, the cutting score. Unreliability of measuring instruments will always result in misclassifications. There will also be little difference between individuals, even though correctly classified, who are close to either side of the cutting score. In this sense, there is no "true" standard to be discovered for MCT, only a continuum with an artificial dichotomy.

There are two general approaches to setting standards. (Detailed descriptions of the approaches are found in Zieky & Livingston, 1977; Popham, 1978; and Nassif, 1979, as well as the original articles.) One approach, applied most frequently, uses judgments of item content. Variants of the approach are found in the type of judgments the raters are asked to make. In the Nedelsky (1954) procedure for multiple-choice items, raters delete responses that students who are at the lowest levels (grades D or F) or are minimally competent should be able to reject as incorrect, and the minimum passing level for each item is computed as the chance score for the remaining items. These scores are summed across items for the minimum passing score for each judge, and then the scores from all judges are averaged. Angoff (1971) proposed that each judge estimate the probability for each item that a minimally competent individual will get it correct. Ebel (1972) asked judges to categorize items by both difficulty and relevance and then assign probabilities of passing items so categorized. The second approach to setting standards uses judg-

ments of students. In the "contrasting groups" method (Zieky & Livingston, 1977), judges (usually teachers) are asked to classify a sample of students as competent or not competent, relative to the content being assessed. Based upon group membership and actual test scores, a standard is derived using statistical maximum-likelihood ratio procedures to minimize the probability of misclassifying students into groups. Another method using judgments of students is the "borderline groups" method. Judges are asked to identify students whom they consider to be borderline masters in the area being assessed; the MCT is administered, and the median score is chosen as the cutoff. Livingston (1980) proposed a variation of this method using stochastic approximation techniques. Huynh (1976) described a method using an external criterion, and Garcia-Quintana and Mappus (1980) applied the method using a norm-referenced test as a criterion. (See Huynh and Saunders, 1980, for an examination of measurement error and passing scores.)

A small set of reported studies compared the results (cutting scores) obtained by using these different procedures. Anderson and Hecht (1976), Koffler (1980), Rock, Davis, and Werts (1980), Archambault, Behuniak, and Gable (1981), Baron et al. (1981), and Poggio, Glasnapp, and Eros (1981) all compared at least two methods of setting standards. All of the studies report both differences in cutting scores using either different procedures and (for most) different groups of judges using the same procedure. This is not surprising, since judges are asked to make different decisions in each procedure, and groups of judges also differ in their knowledge of students. Poggio, Glasnapp, and Eros (1981) reported the largest study, using over nine hundred teachers in a statewide sample in Kansas, and four methods—Nedelsky, Ebel, Angoff, and contrasting groups. In this study, the Ebel method produced the highest cutoff score, followed by the Angoff and Nedelsky procedures. The contrasting-groups procedure fell between the Nedelsky and Angoff cutoff scores. Data are reported showing the effects on students—increases in numbers failing—of these procedures in regard to the Kansas State Board of Education (1980). For example, in eleventh-grade mathematics, the Nedelsky method resulted in 92 percent passing, Angoff in 59 percent passing, and Ebel in 46 percent passing. The results of these studies forcefully reiterate the problem of defining a standard. The variations in "standards" mean that different numbers of individuals would have been classified as competent or not competent.

Jaeger et al. (1980) provided data on the distributions of recommended passing scores of groups of voters, high school teachers, high school principals, and counselors. The study used judgments on items, and provided judges with data concerning student performance to enable them to adjust their initial judgments in a modification of the judging-items approach. Judges differed substantially in their recommendations, again emphasizing the need carefully to study, document, and present the logic for choices made in test development and establishment of cutting scores.

Researchable questions can focus upon many issues in standard setting. For example, there is little study of the variables that may affect the ratings of judges in MCT settings. Huynh (1981) reported that judges' achievement in the area covered by the test does influence their recommended passing score (accounting for about 9 percent of the variation in passing scores). The methods by which judges attach weights to classification errors—that is, false-positive and false-negative errors—is not well-described or examined for different types of judges with regard to their resulting influence on pass rates and failures of individual students. Although judges have been asked to carry out the various procedures, emphasis has been placed on the results, with little attention given to judges' attitudes toward the task or their perceptions of its fairness for students. Other researchable questions could examine the variables that may lead to more homogeneity in judgments within an individual procedure, for example, defining the "expertise" of judges in particular categories and the identification of "poor" judges. Hambleton and Powell (1981) provide a list of other questions that should be examined. MCT has brought about renewed interest in the underlying concepts and results of standard-setting procedures.

Item bias. In a reanalysis of the Florida Functional Literacy Examination (FLE), Linn and Wise (1981) illustrated the effect for whites and blacks of small reductions in the number of correct answers required to pass the mathematics and communications sections of the 1977 FLE. When three items were removed that were judged or statistically identified as biased against blacks, differential effects on the pass rate were found. For example, if three fewer items were required on the communications test, an additional 189 white students and 400 black students would pass. This differential impact suggests the importance of using item-bias review methods, both judgmental (Tittle, in press) and statistical for MCT (Angoff, in press; Ironson, in press; Scheuneman, in press; and Schmeiser, in press).

Judgments of item bias in the representation of women and minorities, stereotyping and degree of familiarity of items to various subgroups are part of the process of test development in MCT. In domain specification, item writing, item review, item tryout, and selection of final items, there is a need to use judges, to provide judges with training and guidelines, and to document the outcomes of such judgments. These judgments are necessary and independent of the statistical or experimental procedures to examine item bias. Earlier research found material offensive to women and minorities, stereotyped portrayal of members of these groups, an overall lack of representation in standardized achievement tests (Tittle, McCarthy, Steckler, 1974), and some relationship of these variables to performance (Donlon, Ekstrom, & Lockheed, 1979). States and LEAs selecting or constructing tests require systematic review procedures. Other judgments regarding overlap of test items and texts and regarding opportunity to learn individual test items also need to be formalized, both

for validity and user perceptions of "bias" in inferences from test scores.

Statistical item-bias methodology is an active field of research and one in which a variety of procedures are being used to examine whether item-by-group interactions are found for individual test items. (The procedures are appropriate for situations in which no external or outside criterion is to be used in the validation or bias-detection process.) That is, do groups perform consistently, in the same relationship to each other, throughout the item series in tests or are there unexpected between-group differences? Linn and Wise (1981) used transformed item difficulties for comparison (Angoff, in press). Chi-square procedures (Scheuneman, 1979) provide an approximation to latent trait (item response theory) procedures, which assume that the test as a whole is less biased than the individual items (Ironson, in press). Item response theory develops procedures to describe "item characteristic curves" that mathematically describe the relationship between ability and the probability of getting an item correct. Three parameters are used to describe a cumulative logistic or normal ogive function: a difficulty parameter, the discrimination value, and a guessing parameter. Some research examines whether one, two, or all three parameters are necessary to "fit" the model and observed data. If an item is unbiased, it should have the same item characteristic curve in the groups of interest. Because, in theory, there is parameter invariance across samples of different abilities, item-response-theory procedures are the object of considerable research; the practical utility of the chi-square approaches, however, ensures their continued study. Ironson (in press) indicates that studies to date show that the methods are not interchangeable but that agreement between the chi-square and three-parameter item characteristic procedures appears to be highest. Unless sample sizes are large, however, chi-square procedures are preferred, although Linn and Harmisch (1981) have proposed an alternative procedure using the three-parameter model when one of the groups is small.

Test equating. The problems in equating minimum competency tests are similar to those for other tests, although of critical concern where MCT are used alone for decisions in promotion and graduation, and fairness dictates a constant "standard." Test-equating procedures are used in situations where multiple forms of tests are constructed and used from year to year, and some method of rendering the scores comparable is necessary. Lord (1977) and Angoff (1971) provide definitions that describe when test forms can be considered equated. Various designs—single group, random groups, and anchor tests—are used with either linear or curvilinear equating methods. There are also item response theory (IRT) equating methods, an active area of research in MCT programs as well. Cook (1981) provides a comprehensive description of conventional and IRT equating procedures, and cites research comparing the two approaches. IRT methods were found to be superior to conventional methods for equating SAT *V* and *M* forms. Bock (1979) compared IRT models for reporting school scores in the California assessment program and found that the two-parameter solutions provided the best fit. Among recent studies on the use of the Rasch (one-parameter IRT) model to establish equivalence of forms of items in minimum competency tests are those by Davis and Moriel (1980) and Golub-Smith (1980). The latter study reports finding differences between Rasch equating and linear equating in the development of conversion tables. Further studies comparing the various IRT and conventional approaches to equating are needed to establish the conditions under which the various methods function efficiently.

Legal Aspects of MCT. Minimum competency testing programs have resulted in consideration of a number of legal issues. These have focused primarily upon the use of MCT to deny a regular high school diploma. A number of writers have examined the basis for law suits and summarized the results of court decisions (e.g., McClung, 1977, 1978; Tractenberg, 1977, 1980; Tractenberg & Kahn, 1979; Carter, 1978, 1979; Pabian, 1979; Beckham, 1980; Commander, 1980; Mahon, 1980; Pinkney, 1980; Schreiber, 1980; Tuttle, 1980).

Tractenberg (1980) describes six categories of legal provisions that may be relevant to MCT: federal and state due process clauses; federal and state equal protection clauses; state education clauses; statutory provisions of state education laws that directly or indirectly relate to operation of MCT; state education authority regulatory policies and rules; and common law—legal principles that evolve through litigation. The majority of writers have stressed federal laws and regulations, including the due process and equal protection clause of the Fourteenth Amendment to the U.S. Constitution. Others (Beckham, 1980) have suggested that Titles VI and VII of the Civil Rights Act of 1964 and section 504 of the Rehabilitation Act of 1973 may also be relevant, as well as Public Law 94-142, which requires the development of Individualized Education Programs (IEPs) for each handicapped student.

By 1979 several court cases had directly involved MCT. In North Carolina, *Green* v. *Hunt* was filed by the Southern Christian Leadership Council on grounds that the law requiring MCT for high school graduation violated equal protection laws; but there was a summary judgment for the defendant (Tractenberg & Kahn, 1979) because the plaintiffs lacked standing to bring the challenge (Green was not yet subject to the eleventh-grade examination required for the diploma). One case (Virginia) was concerned with release of the graduation competency test to the public and another (Delaware) with the release of the test results.

The most widely noted case has been *Debra P.* v. *Turlington* (1979) in the state of Florida. The case provided a ruling in the situation where failure to pass the test was used to deny a high school diploma. In October 1978 a class action suit was filed in the Tampa Division of the U.S. District Court on behalf of three classes of plaintiffs:

(1) all present and future twelfth-graders in the Florida public schools who have failed and continue to fail the State Student Assessment Test, Part II (SSAT-II); (2) all present and future black students in the same schools who have failed and would continue to fail the SSAT-II; and (3) all present and future black twelfth-graders in Hillsborough County who have failed and who continue to fail the SSAT-II (Gorth & Perkins, 1979c). The plaintiff claimed that the test was racially biased, that neither adequate notice nor preparation time was given, and that the use of SSAT-II to classify and group students in need of remediation reinstituted segregation in the public schools. In July of 1979 the court found that the schedule for implementing the SSAT-II was a violation of the due process clause of the Fourteenth Amendment and that until the 1982/83 school year, the requirement to pass the SSAT-II in order to receive a diploma was a violation of the equal protection clause of the Fourteenth Amendment. The judge concluded that "the legitimate interests in the test program are substantial, but the timing of the program must be questioned to some extent because it sacrifices through the diploma sanction a large percentage of black twelfth-grade students in the rush to implement the legislative mandate" (Tractenberg & Kahn, 1979, pp. 38–39). The court did not find the test invalid nor racially or ethnically biased. The court also found that although black students were represented disproportionately in a remediation program, the purpose of the program was to assist and not resegregate; and therefore the use of the results for remediation was neither a constitutional nor a statutory violation. In 1981, however, the appeals court (*Debra P.* v. *Turlington*, 1981) remanded the case for further findings because the state had not made any effort to make certain whether the test covered material actually studied in the classrooms of the state. If the test does not, "it is unfair and violates the Equal Protection and Due Process clauses of the United States Constitution" (p. 6767). Several other cases in Florida challenged various aspects of MCT, for example, the authority to establish scoring criteria (Carter, 1979).

Wells v. *Bank* in the state of Georgia challenged a county school system on the use of a test as a high school graduation requirement. *Hernandez* v. *Board of Education of Lynwood Unified School District* in California is a different type of challenge. This suit is based on the alleged failure of the LEA to implement the California basic skills proficiency program in conformity with the governing state statute (in particular, failure to involve parents and students). In Illinois, handicapped students have brought suit *(Debra B.* v. *Illinois State Board of Education)*, claiming the Peoria School District has violated Public Law 94-142, section 504 of the 1973 Rehabilitation Act, and the Fourteenth Amendment due process clause in denying the diploma on the basis of a local competency test. A New York state judge ruled *(Northport–East Northport Union Free School District* v. *Ambach)* that handicapped students could keep their diplomas although they had failed the MCT. The decision cited inadequate notice of graduation requirements ("Illinois Handicapped Students Challenge Competency Test," 1981).

Whereas writers on legal issues and MCT have emphasized due process, procedural fairness, and equal protection (as have the courts), they have also given attention to issues of test validity. McClung (1978), for example, used the idea of fairness to argue that the school's curriculum and instruction should match in some way whatever is measured by a test (Tractenberg & Kahn, 1979). He suggested that curricular validity is a measure of how well test items represent objectives of the curriculum, and instructional validity measures whether or not the school district or state objectives were translated into topics actually taught in classrooms. The concept of instructional validity is not well suited to traditional interpretations of content validity. Both concepts, however, fit well with earlier discussions of a more unified view of validating the construct of competence, in school and, in "life" settings.

In the instance where minimum competency tests are used to deny the high school diploma, a diploma is required by an employer for employment, and an applicant is denied employment on this ground, Lynch (1979) has raised the question whether the school can be construed as an employment agency and hence subject to the *Uniform Guidelines on Employee Selection Procedures* (1978). (See Tittle, 1979, for a similar question in the context of tests used in vocational education.) The *Uniform Guidelines* are explicit in describing validation requirements for tests used in the selection process and in defining adverse impact. As Lynch accurately notes, minimum competency tests in use to date would not be able to meet these guidelines.

Issues of due process, procedural fairness, reasonableness of procedures, and discrimination (adverse impact) underlie the legal challenges to MCT. The relationship between court cases in employment testing and MCT have only been suggested and not closely examined to date for concepts of test validity and fairness in all the procedures leading up to testing and the use of test information. Particularly as court cases move to local school district MCT, documentation of procedures to justify claims of fairness and validity will come under close scrutiny (Mahon, 1980).

Special Topics and Policy Issues. The topics noted here warrant research since they also have policy implications. These topics include the effectiveness of remediation programs; the effects of MCT on students, the curriculum, and teachers; assessing students in special groups; the use of tests alone to deny promotion and certification; and the evaluation of MCT. Topics are identified for the reader, but are not elaborated.

Remediation. Parramore, Berow, and Davies (1980) reported only limited support for the effectiveness of remedial programs (comparing students with no remediation versus remediation) in improving MCT passing rates for a sample of about seventeen hundred North Carolina students. Archambault (1979) has reviewed the results of re-

medial programs more generally, and suggests that students failing MCT are comparable to the types of students served by ESEA Title I. There is related research on individualizing instruction, use of small groups, class size, use of pullout programs, planning and management variables, and the variable time-on-task. Changing the research focus for compensatory or remedial programs from elementary to junior and senior high school students in MCT may result in other variables becoming more prominent, for example, motivation (Harnisch, 1981), test-taking skills, and the social context of instruction. Research on the relation of these variables to the instructional process is needed, as well as research on the funding and resource allocation patterns between and within states and LEAs for remedial programs.

Effects on students. Remediation programs are only one facet of the possible effects of MCT on students. As mentioned earlier, research has not yet focused on the impact of MCT on dropout and retention data, student course-taking patterns, student self-perceptions, and employment, both immediately and long-term (see Eckland, 1980, for estimates of adverse impact on black students of diploma denial). Richman and Wooldridge (n.d.) and Shane (1981) report a small-scale study (using paper-and-pencil tests) of students at high and low risk on the North Carolina MCT. Self-esteem appeared negatively affected by MCT failure, scores on an alienation measure increased, and high-risk students who passed the MCT apparently had decreases in academic achievement motivation. Blau (1980) interviewed thirty-five students "not doing well in school" and reported that poor students saw the tests as an additional barrier to success and good students saw the tests as another "piece of nonsense" that wastes time during high school.

Also of concern is the development of due process procedures in schools. For instance, if a student is predicted to fail MCT (on the basis of an earlier test), placed in special courses, and the student (or the student's teacher) states that the classification is in error and choices are being taken away, what recourse is available? The use of tests alone to classify students may be subject to court challenge (as they have been in educable mentally retarded placements, e.g., *Diana* v. *State Board of Education; Larry P.* v. *Riles;* and *P.A.S.E.* v. *Hannon*). Zettel and Abeson (1978) have summarized the reasons why tests alone are not used for decisions affecting special education students—the right to nondiscriminatory testing and evaluation.

Assessing students in special groups. Two groups of students are of concern here—special education students and bilingual students. Public Law 94-142, the Education for All Handicapped Children Act of 1975, makes provision for a free appropriate public education in the least restrictive environment; it includes extensive due process procedures, prohibits discrimination on the basis of disability, and provides for individualized educational plans. Of particular concern in MCT is the fairness and legality of exemptions for handicapped students, the individual determination of the use of MCT, differential diploma standards, and differential assessment procedures (McClung & Pullin, 1978).

Gorth and Perkins (1979c) have summarized the provisions made by states for special education or learning disabled, multilingual or limited English-speaking, and migrant or transfer groups of students. Some fourteen states have provisions to exempt special education students; nine use tests with different formats or administration procedures; one permits differential standards; and two provide for case-by-case decisions. (See also Ewing, 1979; Rosewater, 1979; Galloway, Schipper, & Norman, 1979; McCarthy, 1980; Olsen, 1980; Safer, 1980; Smith & Jenkins, 1980; and, for an example, Nazzaro, 1979; Grise, 1980). Morrissey (1980) described the needs for "adaptive" testing for handicapped students, and Grise (1980) described one study that found increased student performance with audio tests and a large print edition. In the New Jersey state assessment program, modifications of Braille, large print, and a signed test version were used with fourth-grade, seventh-grade, tenth-grade, and twelfth-grade students. For reading, the modified versions were better at grade 7, grade 10, and grade 12, and there were no differences in mathematics test performance (Greenberg, 1980). In North Carolina, McKinney and Haskins reported misclassification of students, dropouts after failing MCT, the need for better guidelines at the local level, and generally lower pass rates for handicapped students. Little research has been reported on adaptations in MCT, and it is urgently needed where MCT is required for handicapped students.

Bilingual or limited English-speaking students are another group for whom MCT programs have adopted different approaches. Three state programs exempt students in this category, three use different administration procedures, and five provide for delay or testing under other programs (Gorth & Perkins, 1979c). There is apparently no research comparing alternate testing and procedures for these students as well as MCT validity, classification decisions, or the use of other tests with this group of students.

Effects on teachers and curriculum. Almost no research was located on the effects of MCT on teachers and the curriculum, although MCT is expected to influence the instructional process and goals. Ward (1980) had a low response rate to a survey of teachers belonging to the American Federation of Teachers (AFT). Teachers reported low involvement in selecting competencies or passing scores for MCT, held favorable or neutral views toward MCT (about 20 percent had negative opinions), and about one-third reported changes in instructional program or reduced attention to important curricular goals. These changes were not specified. Bardon & Robinette (1980) suggested some of the varied effects of MCT on teachers, but direct studies are not available. Similarly, little research is available regarding curricular effects of MCT, although several writers have suggested potential effects, for example, Broudy (1980) and Amarel (1980), who suggest a general move toward constriction of the school curriculum. Broudy also suggested that this development would involve a two-tier school system. As MCT is implemented in different patterns in state and local districts, research is needed in this area to inform future decisions about MCT.

Evaluation and policy studies. The above topics have special relevance for evaluation and policy studies. They are included in the list of questions proposed for an evaluation in one state (Hartman, 1980), and they include some of Baratz's list (1980) of policy issues in MCT. Added to these topics is the effect of the MCT program on community support for schools. Other areas to be considered for evaluation studies are the costs and management burdens of MCT programs. Of particular interest would be estimates of opportunities forgone in student programs for those at risk on MCT or for other groups of students. Some studies have followed the approach used by Coleman in the Equality of Educational Opportunity study, that is, to relate characteristics of students, schools, or teachers as predictors of student gain or scores on MCT. Poggio and Glasnapp (1980) found school building characteristics were not related to MCT, nor were pupil characteristics, generally, and concluded that there was little information to be gained from the use of status variables as in the EEO study. Revicki (1980) used path analysis and found that pupil-teacher ratio was the only organizational variable (of four) related to competency test results. These types of studies are unlikely to yield much more information without examining in greater detail the types of variables reported in Cooley and Leinhardt (1980), which are concerned with the curriculum and instructional practices.

New Jersey local and state competency standards were examined for their relationship to socioeconomic status (Tuckman & Nadler, 1979). Local standards were more stringent in some instances, and this was associated with wealthier school districts. Such findings have implications for policy and further examination of the relationship of resources, standards, and student "competency." Ogden (1979) examined data on one school district, and concluded that minimum competency standards and establishment of remedial courses were likely to raise scores of low achievers on district-wide tests.

These evaluation-related studies, and the others reported earlier, are fragmentary and likely to leave unanswered many of the questions of policy makers. One of the directions that evaluation and policy studies can take is the consideration of alternative approaches to the apparent issue of concern—the "competence" of high school graduates and, by association with the basic skills, the "literacy" of high school dropouts. Airasian, Madaus, and Pedulla (1978) tried to categorize three MCT program models on seven policy issues. Lerner (1980) has proposed to approach the problem from yet another alternative—the use of vouchers for private schools for those students whom the public schools are unable to reach. Other alternatives to the current MCT focus on individual assessment of competencies by SEAs and LEAs is the approach taken by the National Assessment of Educational Progress—developing information about the performance of groups of students with respect to individual sets of items (Bayless & Nix, 1979; Keppel, 1980). This approach might offer information that can be more directly related to school instructional practices, avoiding some measurement problems, posing a different type of standard-setting situation, and hence reducing legal challenges to assessment.

As research and experience with MCT accumulate, it will be possible to determine whether Wise's prediction (1977) is accurate: that MCT will not solve the problem of the minority of teachers who fail to teach and the minority of students who fail to learn. It is also clear from these research areas that there are many philosophical issues in education and schooling that are brought into sharp focus by the form and substance of MCT programs. Policy issues range from the very broad in scope (What are the roles of schools and their relationship to society?) to highly specific issues (What are the alternatives to MCT for "improving" education?). Research and evaluation can illuminate these issues for policy makers and all others concerned with education in the schools.

Carol Kehr Tittle

See also Achievement Testing; Competency-Based Teacher Education; Evaluation of Teachers; Licensing and Certification; Measurement in Education; Promotion Policy.

REFERENCES

Airasian, P. W. Educational measurement and technological bases underlying minimal competency testing. In P. W. Airasian, G. F. Madaus, & J. J. Pedulla (Eds.), *Minimal Competency Testing.* Englewood Cliffs, N.J.: Educational Technology Publications, 1979.

Airasian, P. W.; Madaus, G. F.; & Pedulla, J. J. *Policy Issues in Minimal Competency Testing and a Comparison of Implementation Models* (Report submitted to the Policy Subcommittee of the Massachusetts Advisory Committee on High School Graduation Requirements). Dedham, Mass.: Heuristics, Inc., April 1978. (ERIC Document Reproduction Service No. ED 174 650)

Airasian, P. W.; Madaus, G. F.; Pedulla, J. J.; & Newton, K. B. Costs in minimal competency testing programs. In P. W. Airasian, G. F. Madaus, & J. J. Pedulla (Eds.), *Minimal Competency Testing.* Englewood Cliffs, N.J.: Educational Technology Publications, 1979.

Amarel, M. Comments on H. Broudy's "Impact of minimum competency testing on the curriculum." In R. M. Jaeger & C. K. Tittle (Eds.), *Minimum Competency Achievement Testing.* Berkeley, Calif.: McCutchan, 1980.

Anderson, B. D. *The Costs of Legislated Minimal Competency Requirements* (Background paper prepared for the Minimal Competency Workshops sponsored by the Education Commission of the States and the National Institute of Education). Denver: Education Commission of the States, 1977. (ERIC Document Reproduction Service No. ED 157 947)

Anderson, B. J., & Hecht, J. T. A preliminary investigation of two procedures for setting examination standards. *Educational and Psychological Measurement,* 1976, *36,* 45–50.

Anderson, L. W., & Anderson, J. C. Functional literacy tests: A case of anticipatory validity? *Educational Evaluation and Policy Analysis,* 1981, *3*(2), 51–55.

Angoff, W. H. Scales, norms, and equivalent scores. In R. L. Thorndike (Ed.), *Educational Measurement.* Washington, D.C.: American Council on Education, 1971.

Angoff, W. H. Use of difficulty and discrimination indices for detecting item bias. In R. A. Berk (Ed.), *Handbook of Methods for Detecting Test Bias.* Baltimore: Johns Hopkins University Press, forthcoming.

Archambault, F. X., Jr. Remediation in minimum competency testing. *Education and Urban Society,* 1979, *12,* 31–46.

Archambault, F. X., Jr.; Behuniak, P.; & Gable, R. K. *A Comparison of the Angoff and Nedelsky Procedures for Setting Standards on Reading and Mathematics Proficiency Examinations.* Paper presented at the annual meeting of the National Council on Measurement in Education, Los Angeles, April 1981.

Arbruster, B. B.; Steven, R. O.; & Rosenshine, B. Analyzing content coverage and emphasis: A study of three curricula and two tests (Technical Report No. 26). Urbana-Champaign: University of Illinois, Center for the Study of Reading, 1977. (ERIC Document Reproduction Service No. ED 136 238)

Baratz, J. C. Policy implications of minimum competency testing. In R. M. Jaeger & C. K. Tittle (Eds.), *Minimum Competency Achievement Testing.* Berkeley, Calif.: McCutchan, 1980.

Bardon, J. I., & Robinette, C. L. Minimum competency testing of pupils: Psychological implications for teachers. In R. M. Jaeger & C. K. Tittle (Eds.), *Minimum Competency Achievement Testing.* Berkeley, Calif.: McCutchan, 1980.

Baron, J. B.; Rindone, D. A.; & Prowda, P. *Setting Statewide Proficiency Standards: A Multi-method Multi-fate Analysis.* Paper presented at the annual meeting of the National Council on Measurement in Education, Los Angeles, 1981.

Bayless, D. L., & Nix, C. W. *Competency Testing: Setting Educational Performance Standards for the Group.* Paper presented at the annual Conference on Large-Scale Assessment, Denver, June 1979. (ERIC Document Reproduction Service No. ED 186 452)

Beckham, J. *Legal Implications of Minimum Competency Testing* (Fastback 138). Bloomington, Ind.: Phi Delta Kappa Educational Foundation, 1980. (ERIC Document Reproduction Service No. ED 190 629)

Bianchini, J. C. Achievement tests and differential norms. In M. J. Wargo & D. R. Green (Eds.), *Achievement Testing of Disadvantaged and Minority Students for Educational Program Evaluation.* New York: CTB/McGraw-Hill, 1977.

Blau, T. H. Minimum competency testing: Psychological implications for students. In R. M. Jaeger & C. K. Tittle (Eds.), *Minimum Competency Achievement Testing.* Berkeley, Calif.: McCutchan, 1980.

Bloom, B. S. (Ed.). *Cognitive Domain.* Handbook I of *Taxonomy of Educational Objectives.* New York: McKay, 1956.

Bock, R. D. *A Feasibility Study of the One-, Two-, and Three-parameter Item-Response Models for the Analysis and Reporting of California Assessment Data.* Chicago: International Educational Services, 1979.

Bridge, R. G.; Judd, C. M.; & Moock, P. R. *The Determinants of Educational Outcomes.* Cambridge, Mass.: Ballinger, 1979.

Britell, J. K. Competence and excellence: The search for an egalitarian standard, the demand for a universal guarantee. In

R. M. Jaeger & C. K. Tittle (Eds.), *Minimum Competency Achievement Testing*. Berkeley, Calif.: McCutchan, 1980.

Brodinsky, B. Back to the basics: The movement and its meaning. *Phi Delta Kappan*, 1977, *58*, 522–527.

Broudy, H. S. Impact of minimum competency testing on the curriculum. In R. M. Jaeger & C. K. Tittle (Eds.), *Minimum Competency Achievement Testing*. Berkeley, Calif.: McCutchan, 1980.

Burke, F. G. Testing in New Jersey. *Educational Leadership*, 1980, *38*, 199–201.

Byrne, C. D. *Setting the State Reference Point for the Reading Test for New York State Elementary Schools*. Paper presented at the annual meeting of the American Educational Research Association, Boston, March 1980. (ERIC Document Reproduction Service No. ED 193 289)

Campbell, D. T. Keeping the data honest in the experimenting society. In H. W. Melton & D. J. H. Watson, *Interdisciplinary Dimensions of Accounting for Social Goals and Social Organizations*. Columbus, Ohio: Grid, 1977.

Carpenter, T. P.; Corbitt, M. K.; Kepner, H. S., Jr.; Lindquist, M. M.; & Reys, R. Results of the second NAEP mathematics assessment: Secondary school. *Mathematics Teacher*, 1980, *73*, 329–338.

Carter, D. G. *Proficiency Testing and the Law: An Old Problem with a New Twist*. Paper presented at the annual convention of the National Organization on Legal Problems in Education, 1978. (ERIC Document Reproduction Service No. ED 170 837)

Carter, D. G. The emerging legal issue of competency testing. *Education and Urban Society*, 1979, *12*, 5–18.

Cochran, N. Grandma Moses and the corruption of data. *Evaluation Quarterly*, 1978, *2*, 363–374.

Cohen, D. K., & Haney, W. Minimums, competency testing, and social policy. In R. M. Jaeger & C. K. Tittle (Eds.), *Minimum Competency Testing*. Berkeley, Calif.: McCutchan, 1980.

College Entrance Examination Board. *National College-Bound Seniors, 1980*. New York: CEEB, 1980.

Commander, M. G. Minimum competency testing: Education or discrimination? *University of Richmond Law Review*, 1980, *14*, 769–790.

Cook, L. L. The application of item-response theory to test equating. In M. L. Stocking, L. L. Cook, D. R. Eignor, J. D. Scheuneman, J. B. Sympson, & M. S. Wingersky, *Item-Response Theory: Concepts, Tools, and Applications*. Princeton, N.J.: Educational Testing Service, 1981.

Cooley, W. W., & Leinhardt, G. *Design and Educational Findings of the Instructional Dimensions Study*. Paper presented at the annual meeting of the American Educational Research Association, Toronto, March 1978.

Cooley, W. W., & Leinhardt, G. The instructional dimensions study. *Educational Evaluation and Policy Analysis*, 1980, *2*, 7–25.

Copperman, P. *The Literacy Hoax: The Decline of Reading, Writing, and Learning in Public Schools and What We Can Do about It*. New York: Morrow, 1978.

Copperman, P. The achievement decline of the 1970s. *Phi Delta Kappan*, 1979, *60*, 736–739.

Cronbach, L. J. Test validation. In R. L. Thorndike (Ed.), *Educational Measurement* (2nd ed.). Washington, D.C.: American Council on Education, 1971.

Cronbach, L. J. Validity on parole: How can we go straight? *New Directions for Testing and Measurement*, 1980, *5*, 99–108.

Davis, J. M., & Moriel, J., Jr. *Using the Rasch Model to Establish Equivalent Certification Tests*. Paper presented at the annual

meeting of the American Educational Research Association, Boston, April 1980. (ERIC Document Service Reproduction No. ED 191 865)

De S. Price, D. R & D and productivity. *Science*, 1981, *211*, 1116.

Debra P. v. *Turlington*, 78-892-Civ-T-C (1979).

Debra P. v. *Turlington*, U.S. Court of Appeals, Fifth Circuit, Unit B (No. 79-3074), May 4, 1981, 6762–6774.

Diana v. *State Board of Education*, Civil Action No. C-70 37 R.F.P. (N.D. Cal., Jan. 7, 1970 and June 18, 1973).

Donlon, T. F.; Ekstrom, R. B.; & Lockheed, M. E. The consequences of sex bias in the content of major achievement test batteries. *Measurement and Evaluation in Guidance*, 1979, *11*, 202–216.

Ebel, R. L. *Essentials of Educational Measurement*. Englewood Cliffs, N. J.: Prentice-Hall, 1972.

Eckland, B. K. Sociodemographic implications of minimum competency testing. In R. M. Jaeger & C. K. Tittle (Eds.), *Minimum Competency Achievement Testing*. Berkeley, Calif.: McCutchan, 1980.

Eckland, B. K. College entrance examination trends. In G. R. Austin & H. Garber (Eds.), *The Rise and Fall of National Test Scores*. New York: Academic Press, forthcoming.

Educational Testing Service. *Basic Skills Assessment Around the Nation: An ETS Information Report*. Princeton, N.J.: ETS, 1977. (ERIC Document Reproduction Service No. ED 152 796)

Elligett, J., & Tocco, T. S. Reading achievement in 1979 versus achievement in the fifties. *Phi Delta Kappan*, 1980, *61*, 698–699.

Eurich, A. E. Student readers: The fifty-year difference. *Change*, 1980, *12*(3), 13–15.

Ewing, N. J. Minimum competency testing and the handicapped: Major issues. *High School Journal*, 1979, *63*, 114–119.

Farr, R., & Olshavsky, J. E. Is minimum competency testing the appropriate solution to the SAT decline? *Phi Delta Kappan*, 1980, *61*, 528–530.

Feldmesser, R. A. *The Use of Test Scores as a Basis for Allocating Educational Resources: A Synthesis and Interpretation of Knowledge and Experience*. Princeton, N.J.: Educational Testing Service, 1975. (ERIC Document Testing Service, 1975. ED 121 839)

Fey, J. T., & Sonnabend, T. Trends in school mathematics performance. In G. R. Austin & H. Garber (Eds.), *The Rise and Fall of National Test Scores*. New York: Academic Press, forthcoming.

Fillbrandt, J. R., & Merz, W. R. The assessment of competency in reading and mathematics using community-based standards. *Educational Research Quarterly*, 1977, *2*, 3–11.

Fiske, E. B. Low reading comprehension found. *New York Times*, November 12, 1981, p. 13.

Freeman, D., & Belli, G. *The Impact of Differences in Textbook Use on the Match in Content Covered by Textbooks and Standardized Tests*. Paper presented at the annual meeting of the American Educational Research Association, Los Angeles, April 1981.

Freeman, D. J.; Kuhs, T.; Porter, A. C.; Knappen, L. B.; Floden, R. E.; Schmidt, W. H.; & Schwille, J. R. *The Fourth-grade Mathematics Curriculum as Inferred from Textbooks and Tests*. Paper presented at the annual meeting of the American Educational Research Association, Boston, April 1980.

Functional Literacy: Basic Reading Performance. An Assessment of In-school 17-year-olds in 1974. Denver: Education Commission of the States, National Assessment of Educational Progress, 1976. (ERIC Document Reproduction Service No. ED 112 389)

Gagné, R. M., & Rohwer, W. D., Jr. Instructional Psychology. *Annual Review of Psychology*, 1969, *20*, 381–418.

Galloway, J. R.; Schipper, W. V.; & Norman, M. E. *Competency Testing, Special Education, and the Awarding of Diplomas.* Washington, D.C.: National Association of State Directors of Special Education, 1979. (ERIC Document Reproduction Service No. ED 185 785)

Garcia-Quintana, R. A., & Mappus, M. L. Using norm-referenced data to set standards for a minimum competency program in the state of South Carolina: A feasibility study. *Educational Evaluation and Policy Analysis*, 1980, *2*, 47–52.

Ginzberg, E., & Vojta, G. J. The service sector of the U.S. economy. *Scientific American*, 1981, *244*(3), 48–55.

Glaser, R. Instructional technology and the measurement of learning outcomes. *American Psychologist*, 1963, *18*, 519–521.

Glass, G. V. Standards and criteria. *Journal of Educational Measurement*, 1978, *15*, 237–261.

Glass, G. V. Looking at minimal competence testing: Educator versus senator. *Education and Urban Society*, 1979, *12*, 47–55.

Golub-Smith, M. *The Application of Rasch Model Equating Techniques Applied to the Problem of Interpreting Longitudinal Performance on Minimum Competency Tests.* Paper presented at the annual meeting of the American Educational Research Association, Boston, April 1980. (ERIC Document Reproduction Service No. ED 187 749)

Gorth, W. P., & Perkins, M. R. (Eds.). *A Study of Minimum Competency Programs: Final Comprehensive Report* (Vols. 1 and 2). Amherst, Mass.: National Evaluation Systems, 1979. (a) (ERIC Document Reproduction Service No. ED 185 123)

Gorth, W. P., & Perkins, M. R. (Eds.). *A Study of Minimum Competency Testing Programs: Final Program Development Resource Document.* Amherst, Mass.: National Evaluation Systems, 1979. (b) (ERIC Document Reproduction Service No. ED 185 126)

Gorth, W. P., & Perkins, M. R. *A Study of Minimum Competency Testing Programs: Final Summary and Analysis Report.* Amherst, Mass.: National Evaluation Systems, 1979. (c) (ERIC Document Reproduction Service No. Ed 185 124)

Gorth, W. P., & Perkins, M. R. *A Study of Minimum Competency Testing Programs: Final Typology Report.* Amherst, Mass.: National Evaluation Systems, 1979. (d) (ERIC Document Reproduction Service No. ED 185 125)

Greenberg, L. *Test Development Procedures for Including Handicapped Students in New Jersey's State Assessment Program.* Trenton, N.J.: New Jersey State Department of Education, 1980. (ERIC Document Reproduction Service No. ED 187 767)

Greene, M. Response to "Competence and excellence: The search for an egalitarian standard, the demand for a universal guarantee," by Jenne K. Brittell. In R. M. Jaeger & C. K. Tittle (Eds.), *Minimum Competency Achievement Testing.* Berkeley, Calif.: McCutchan, 1980.

Grise, P. J. Florida's minimum competency testing program for handicapped students. *Exceptional Children*, 1980, *47*, 186–191.

Guion, R. M. Recruiting, selection, and job placement. In M. R. Dunnette (Ed.), *Handbook of Industrial and Organizational Psychology.* Chicago: Rand McNally, 1976.

Hambleton, R. K., & Eignor, D. R. Competency test development, validation, and standard setting. In R. M. Jaeger & C. K. Tittle (Eds.), *Minimum Competency Achievement Testing.* Berkeley, Calif.: McCutchan, 1980.

Hambleton, R. K., & Novick, M. R. Toward an integration of theory and method for criterion-referenced tests. *Journal of Educational Measurement*, 1973, *10*, 159–170.

Hambleton, R. K., & Powell, S. *Standards for Standard Setters.* Paper presented at the annual meeting of the American Educational Research Association, Los Angeles, April 1981.

Hambleton, R. K.; Swaminathan, H.; Algina, J.; & Coulson, D. B. Criterion-referenced testing and measurement: A review of technical issues and developments. *Review of Educational Research*, 1978, *48*, 1–47.

Haney, W., & Madaus, G. F. Making sense of the competency testing movement. In P. W. Airasian, G. F. Madaus, & J. J. Pedulla (Eds.), *Minimal Competency Testing.* Englewood Cliffs, N.J.: Educational Technology Publications, 1979.

Hanson, R. A.; Schutz, R. E.; & Bailey, J. D. *Program-fair Evaluation of Instructional Programs: Initial Results of the Kindergarten Reading Readiness Inquiry* (Technical Report No. 57). Los Alamitos, Calif.: SWRL Educational Research and Development, 1977.

Harnisch, D. L. *A Test of a Structural Model of Student Background and Motivational Variables.* Paper presented at the annual meeting of the American Educational Research Association, Los Angeles, April 1981.

Harnischfeger, A., & Wiley, D. E. *Achievement Test Score Decline: Do We Need to Worry?* St. Louis: CEMREL, 1976.

Harnischfeger, A., & Wiley, D. E. *The Decline of Achievement Test Scores: Evidence, Causes, and Consequences* (ERIC Clearinghouse TM Report 59). February 1977. (ERIC Document Reproduction Service No. ED 141 412)

Hartman, A. S. *Overview of a Policy Evaluation Design for Determining the Effectiveness of a State Minimum Competency Policy.* Paper presented at the annual meeting of the American Educational Research Association, Boston, 1980. (ERIC Document Reproduction Service No. ED 186 472)

Hills, J. R., & King, F. J. *Construct Validity of the Florida Functional Literacy Test.* Tallahassee: Florida State University, August 1978.

Holmen, M. G., & Docter, R. *Educational and Psychological Testing: A Study of the Industry and Its Practices.* New York: Russell Sage, 1972.

House Committee on Education and Labor. *Part II. A Bill to Provide Educational Proficiency Standards. Hearings before the Subcommittee on Elementary, Secondary, and Vocational Education of the Committee on Education and Labor, House of Representatives.* 95th Cong., 1st sess. on H.R. 6088 (September 12 and 15, 1977). Washington, D.C.: Congress of the U.S., 1977. (ERIC Document Reproduction Service No. ED 159 609)

House, E. R.; Rivers, W.; & Stufflebeam, D. L. An assessment of the Michigan accountability system. *Phi Delta Kappan*, 1974, *55*, 663–670.

Huynh, H. Statistical consideration of mastery scores. *Psychometrika*, 1976, *41*, 65–78.

Huynh, H. *Technical and Practical Considerations in Setting Standards.* Paper presented at the annual meeting of the American Educational Research Association, Los Angeles, April 1981.

Huynh, H., & Saunders, J. C. *Solutions for Some Technical Problems in Domain-referenced Mastery Testing: Final Report.* Columbia: University of South Carolina, 1980.

Illinois handicapped students challenge competency test. *Report on Education Research*, March 18, 1981, p. 5.

Ironson, G. H. Chi-square and latent trait theoretic approaches. In R. A. Berk (Ed.), *Handbook of Methods for Detecting Test Bias.* Baltimore: Johns Hopkins University Press, forthcoming.

Jaeger, R. M. Measurement consequences of selected standard setting models. In M. A. Bunda & J. R. Saunders (Eds.), *Practices and Problems in Competency-based Measurement.* Washington, D.C.: National Council on Measurement in Education, 1979.

Jaeger, R. M.; Cole, J.; Irwin, D. M.; & Pratto, D. J. *An Iterative Structured Judgment Process for Setting Passing Scores on Competency Tests, Applied to the North Carolina High School Competency Tests in Reading and Mathematics.* Greensboro: University of North Carolina, Center for Educational Research and Evaluation, 1980.

Jenkins, J. R., & Pany, D. *Curriculum Biases in Reading Achievement Tests* (Technical Report No. 16). Urbana: University of Illinois, Center for the Study of Reading, November 1976. (ERIC Document Reproduction Service No. ED 134 938)

Jenkins, J. R., & Pany, D. Curriculum biases in reading achievement tests. *Journal of Reading Behavior,* 1978, *10,* 345–357.

Jones, L. V. Achievement test scores in mathematics and science. *Science,* 1981, *213,* 412–416.

Kansas State Board of Education. *Kansas Competency-based Education Statewide Assessment Report: School Year 1979/80.* Topeka: The Board, 1980.

Keppel, F. Education in the eighties. *Harvard Educational Review,* 1980, *50,* 149–153.

King, F. J. *Studies of the Validity of the Florida Functional Literacy Test.* Tallahassee: Department of Education, September 1977.

Koffler, S. L. A comparison of approaches for setting proficiency standards. *Journal of Educational Measurement,* 1980, *17,* 167–178.

Kraetsch, G. A. What's new in literacy legislation. *Change,* 1980, *12*(3), 44–45.

Kuhs, T.; Schmidt, W.; Porter, A.; Floden, R.; Freeman, D.; & Schwille, J. *A Taxonomy for Classifying Elementary School Mathematics Content* (Research Series No. 4). East Lansing: Michigan State University, Institute for Research on Teaching, April 1979.

Larry P. v. *Riles.* Civil Action No. 6–71–2270 343 F. Supp. 1036 (N. D. Cal., 1972).

Leinhardt, G. Modeling and measuring educational treatment in evaluation. *Review of Educational Research,* 1980, *50,* 343–420.

Leinhardt, G., & Seewald, A. M. Overlap: What's tested, what's taught? *Journal of Educational Measurement,* 1981, *18,* 85–96.

Lerner, B. *Minimum Competence, Maximum Choice: Second Chance Legislation.* New York: Irvington, 1980.

Linn, R. L. Issues of validity in measurement for competency-based programs. In M. A. Bunda & J. R. Sanders (Eds.), *Practices and Problems in Competency-based Education.* Washington, D.C.: National Council on Measurement in Education, 1979.

Linn, R. L. Test design and analysis for measurement of educational achievement. *New Directions for Testing and Measurement,* 1980, *5,* 81–92.

Linn, R. L., & Harnisch, D. L. Interactions between item content and group membership on achievement test items. *Journal of Educational Measurement,* 1981, *18,* 109–118.

Linn, R. L., & Wise, S. L. *Summary of Analyses of the Florida Functional Literacy Examination.* Champaign: University of Illinois, 1981. (Mimeo)

Livingston, S. A. Choosing minimum passing scores by stochastic approximation techniques. *Educational and Psychological Measurement,* 1980, *40,* 859–872.

Lord, F. M. Practical applications of item-characteristic curve theory. *Journal of Educational Measurement,* 1977, *14,* 117–138.

Luevano et al. v. *Campbell,* 79–0271. U.S. District Court for the District of Columbia (Joint motion to amend the consent decree). (February 24, 1981.)

Lynch, P. Public policy and proficiency testing. *Education and Urban Society,* 1979, *12,* 65–80.

Madaus, G. F. Description of the clarification hearing. Chestnut Hill, Mass.: Boston College, Center for the Study of Testing, Evaluation, and Educational Policy, 1981. (Mimeo)

Madaus, G. F.; Airasian, P. W.; & Kellaghan, T. *School Effectiveness: A Reassessment of the Evidence.* New York: McGraw-Hill, 1980.

Madaus, G. F.; Kellaghan, T.; Rakow, E. A.; & King, D. J. The sensitivity of measures of school effectiveness. *Harvard Educational Review,* 1979, *49,* 207–230.

Maeroff, G. I. Educators' new worry: Lack of reading insight by pupils. *New York Times,* April 30, 1981, p. 8.

Mager, R. F. *Preparing Instructional Objectives.* Palo Alto, Calif.: Fearon, 1962.

Mahon, J. P. Competency-based education: What are the legal issues? *National Association of Secondary School Principals Bulletin,* 1980, *64,* 98–106.

McCarthy, M. M. Minimum competency testing and handicapped students. *Exceptional Children,* 1980, *47,* 166–173.

McClung, M. S. Competency testing: Potential for discrimination. *Clearinghouse Review,* September 1977, 439–448. (ERIC Document Reproduction Service No. ED 164 643)

McClung, M. S. Are competency testing programs fair? Legal? *Phi Delta Kappan,* 1978, *59,* 377–400.

McClung, M. S., & Pullin, D. Competency testing and handicapped students. *Clearinghouse Review,* March 1978, pp. 922–927. (ERIC Document Reproduction Service No. ED 164 644)

McCormick, E. J. Job and task analysis. In M. R. Dunnette (Ed.), *Handbook of Industrial and Organizational Psychology.* Chicago: Rand McNally, 1976.

McKinney, J. D., & Haskins, K. G. Performance of exceptional students on the North Carolina minimum competency test, 1978–1979. Final Report. Chapel Hill: University of North Carolina, 1980. ED 193 236

Meskauska, J. A. Evaluation models for criterion referenced testing: Views regarding mastery and standard setting. *Review of Educational Research,* 1976, *46,* 133–158.

Millman, J. Passing scores and test lengths for domain-referenced measures. *Review of Educational Research,* 1973, *43,* 205–216.

Mills, G. H. *State Minimum Competency Testing Programs: Resource Catalog* (Final report). Denver: Education Commission of the States, 1980. (ERIC Document Reproduction Service No. ED 190 657)

Minimum competency: general issues. *ERIC Highlights.* Princeton, N.J.: ERIC Clearinghouse on Tests and Measurements, 1979.

Minimum competency state testing programs. *ERIC Highlights.* Princeton, N.J.: ERIC Clearinghouse on Tests and Measurements, 1979.

Montgomery, R. J. *Examinations: An Account of Their Evolution as Administrative Devices in England.* Pittsburgh, Pa.: University of Pittsburgh Press, 1965.

Morgan, D. Study shows young blacks improved as readers. *Greensboro Daily News,* April 29, 1981, p. A2.

Morrissey, P. A. Adaptive testing: How and when should handicapped students be accommodated in competency testing programs? In R. Jaeger & C. K. Tittle (Eds.), *Minimum Competency Achievement Testing.* Berkeley, Calif.: McCutchan, 1980.

Munday, L. A. Changing test scores, especially since 1970. *Phi Delta Kappan,* 1979, *60,* 496–499.

Nassif, P. M. Setting standards. In W. P. Gorth & M. R. Perkins (Eds.), *A Study of Minimum Competency Testing Programs: Final Program Resource Document.* Amherst, Mass.: National Evaluation Systems, 1979. (ERIC Document Reproduction Service No. ED 185 126)

National Academy of Education, Committee on Testing and Basic Skills. *Improving Educational Achievement.* Washington, D.C.: NAE, 1978. (ERIC Document Reproduction Service No. ED 157 919)

National Assessment of Educational Progress. *Math Resource Items for Minimal Competency Testing: A Collection of Math Items for State and Local Education Agencies to Draw upon in Custom-building Their Own Minimal Competency Instruments.* Denver: Education Commission of the States, 1977. (a) (ERIC Document Reproduction Service No. ED 173 395)

National Assessment of Educational Progress. *Reading Resource Items for Minimal Competency Testing: A Collection of Reading Items for State and Local Education Agencies to Draw upon in Custom-building Their Own Minimal Competency Instruments.* Denver: Education Commission of the States, 1977. (b) (ERIC Document Reproduction Service No. ED 173 394)

National Institute of Education. *Achievement Testing and Basic Skills: Conference Proceedings.* Washington, D.C.: The Institute, 1979.

Nazzaro, J. N. Minimum competency testing programs and handicapped students: A conversation with J. Howard Hinesley. *Education and Training of the Mentally Retarded,* 1979, *14,* 282–285.

Nedelsky, L. Absolute grading standards for objective tests. *Educational and Psychological Measurement,* 1954, *14,* 3–19.

Neill, G. Washington report. *Phi Delta Kappan,* 1979, *61,* 157.

Ogden, J. *High School Graduation Requirements: Do They Result in Better Graduates?* Paper presented at the annual meeting of the American Educational Research Association, San Francisco, April 1979. ED 173 416

Olsen, K. R. Minimum competency testing and the IEP process. *Exceptional Children,* 1980, *47,* 176–183.

Pabian, J. M. Educational malpractice and minimum competency testing: Is there a legal remedy at last? *New England Law Review,* 1979, *15,* 101–127.

P.A.S.E. v. Hannon. U.S. District Court for the Northern District of Illinois, Eastern Division, No. 74C 3586. (July 17, 1980.)

Parramore, B. M.; Serow, R. C.; & Davies, J. J. *Effect of Mandated Competency Testing in North Carolina: The Class of 1980.* Paper presented at the annual meeting of the Evaluation Research Society, Washington, D.C., November 1980.

Pedulla, J. J., & Reidy, E. F., Jr. The rise of the minimal competency testing movement. In P. W. Airasian, G. F. Madaus, & J. J. Pedulla (Eds.), *Minimal Competency Testing.* Englewood Cliffs, N.J.: Educational Technology Publications, 1979.

Perkins, M. R. Defining competencies. In W. P. Gorth & M. R. Perkins (Eds.), *A Study of Minimum Competency Testing Programs: Final Program Resource Document.* Amherst, Mass.: National Evaluation Systems, 1979. (a) (ERIC Document Reproduction Service No. ED 185 126)

Perkins, M. R. To implement or not to implement MCT. In W. P. Gorth & M. R. Perkins (Eds.), *A Study of Minimum Competency Testing Programs: Final Program Resource Doc-*

ument. Amherst, Mass.: National Evaluation Systems, 1979. (b) (ERIC Document Reproduction Service No. ED 185 126)

Perrone, V. Competency testing: A social and historical perspective. *Educational Horizons,* 1979, *58,* 3–8.

Pinkney, H. B. Florida's minimum competency program: Two years later and the judge's decision. *Clearinghouse,* 1980, *53,* 318–322.

Pipho, C. News from the states. *NCME Measurement News,* 1980, *23*(3), 7–8. (a)

Pipho, C. *State Activity: Minimum Competency Testing,* Denver: Education Commission of the States, 1980. (b)

Pipho, C. *State Minimum Competency Testing Programs: Analysis of State Minimum Competency Testing Programs for the National Institute of Education—Final Report* (NIE-G-79-0033). Denver: Education Commission of the States, 1980. (c) (ERIC Document Reproduction Service No. ED 190 675)

Pipho, C. News from the states. *NCME Measurement News,* 1981, *24*(1), 2–3.

Poggio, J. P., & Glasnapp, D. R. *Report of Research Findings: The Kansas Competency Testing Program—1980.* Lawrence: University of Kansas, School of Education, December 1980. (Mimeo)

Poggio, J. P.; Glasnapp, D. R.; & Eros, D. S. *An Empirical Investigation of the Angoff, Ebel, and Nedelsky Standard Setting Methods.* Paper presented at the annual meeting of the American Educational Research Association, Los Angeles, April 1981.

Popham, W. J. *Setting Performance Standards.* Los Angeles: Instructional Objectives Exchange, 1978. (ERIC Document Reproduction Service No. ED 171 755)

Porter, A. C.; Schmidt, W. H.; Floden, R. E.; & Freeman, D. J. Practical significance in program evaluation. *American Educational Research Journal,* 1978, *15,* 529–539.

Price, D. O. *Changing Characteristics of the Negro Population.* Washington, D.C.: U.S. Bureau of the Census, 1969.

Priestley, M. Test selection and development. In W. P. Gorth & M. R. Perkins (Eds.), *A Study of Minimum Competency Testing Programs: Final Program Resource Document.* Amherst, Mass.: National Evaluation Systems, 1979. (ERIC Document Reproduction Service No. ED 185 126)

Ramsbotham, A. *The Status of Minimum Competency Programs in Twelve Southern States.* Jackson, Miss.: Southeastern Public Education Program, April 1980.

Resnick, D. P. Minimum competency testing historically considered. In D. C. Berliner (Ed.), *Review of Research in Education* (Vol. 8). Washington, D.C.: American Educational Research Association, 1980, pp. 3–29.

Revicki, D. A. School district organization and competency test performance. *Carolina Journal of Educational Research,* 1980, *1*(2), 13–29.

Richman, C. L., & Wooldridge, P. W. Competency test failure and its consequences. Winston-Salem, N.C.: Wake Forest University, Department of Psychology, n.d.

Rock, D. A., Davis, E. L., & Werts, C. *An Empirical Comparison of Judgmental Approaches to Standard Setting Procedures.* (RR-80-7) Princeton, N.J.: Educational Testing Service, 1980.

Rosenfeld, M., & Thornton, R. F. *The Development and Validation of a Public Selection Examination for the City of Philadelphia.* Princeton, N.J.: Educational Testing Service, Center for Occupational and Professional Assessment, 1974.

Rosewater, A. *Minimum Competency Testing Programs and Handicapped Children: Perspectives on Policy and Practice.* Washington, D.C.: Institute for Educational Leadership, 1979. (ERIC Document Reproduction Service No. ED 177 807)

Rovinelli, R. J., & Hambleton, R. K. *On the Use of Content Specialists in the Assessment of Criterion-referenced Test Item Validity.* Paper presented at the annual meeting of the American Educational Research Association, San Francisco, April 1976. (ERIC Document Reproduction Service No. ED 121 845)

Ryan, K.; Johnston, J.; & Newman, K. An interview with Ralph Tyler. *Phi Delta Kappan,* 1977, *58,* 544–547.

Safer, N. D. Implications of minimum competency standards and testing for handicapped students. *Exceptional Children,* 1980, *46,* 288–290.

Sallander, R. Competency tests: Decisions for educators. In R. M. Jaeger & C. K. Tittle (Eds.), *Minimum Competency Achievement Testing.* Berkeley, Calif.: McCutchan, 1980.

Scheuneman, J. A new method for assessing bias in test items. *Journal of Educational Measurement,* 1979, *16,* 143–152.

Scheuneman, J. D. A *posteriori* analysis of biased items. In R. A. Berk (Ed.), *Handbook of Methods for Detecting Test Bias.* Baltimore: Johns Hopkins University Press, forthcoming.

Schmeiser, C. B. Experimental designs for statistical item bias studies. In R. A. Berk (Ed.), *Handbook of Methods for Detecting Test Bias.* Baltimore: Johns Hopkins University Press, forthcoming.

Schreiber, S. High school exit tests and the Constitution: *Debra P.* v. *Turlington. Ohio State Law Journal,* 1980, *41,* 1113–1143.

Shane, S. Failing test a real blow. *Greensboro Daily News,* January 25, 1981, p. B1.

Shepard, L. Technical issues in minimum competency testing. In D. C. Berliner (Ed.), *Review of Research in Education* (Vol. 8). Washington, D.C.: American Educational Research Association, 1980, pp. 30–82.

Shoemaker, J. S. The federal approach to testing. *Educational Horizons,* 1979, *58,* 20–25.

Shoemaker, J. S. Minimum competency testing: The view from Capitol Hill. In R. M. Jaeger & C. K. Tittle (Eds.), *Minimum Competency Achievement Testing.* Berkeley, Calif.: McCutchan, 1980.

Smith, J. D., & Jenkins, D. S. Minimum competency testing and handicapped students. *Exceptional Children,* 1980, *46,* 440–443.

Subkoviak, M. J., & Baker, F. B. Test theory. In L. S. Shulman (Ed.), *Review of Research in Education* (Vol. 5). Itasca, Ill.: F. E. Peacock, 1977.

Teryek, C. J. An overview of job analysis: Methods, procedures, and uses in vocational education. In T. Abramson, C. K. Tittle, & L. Cohen (Eds.), *Handbook of Vocational Education Evaluation.* Beverly Hills, Calif.: Sage, 1979.

Third NAEP survey of student writing contains mix of good and bad news. *Phi Delta Kappan,* 1981, *62,* 464.

Thorndike, R. L. *Reading Comprehension Education in Fifteen Countries.* New York: Wiley, 1973.

Tittle, C. K. Test bias: Current methodology and implications for evaluation. In T. Abramson, C. K. Tittle, & L. Cohen (Eds.), *Handbook of Vocational Education Evaluation.* Beverly Hills, Calif.: Sage, 1979.

Tittle, C. K. Use of judgmental methods in item bias studies. In R. A. Berk (Ed.), *Handbook of Methods for Detecting Test Bias.* Baltimore: Johns Hopkins University Press, forthcoming.

Tittle, C. K.; McCarthy, K.; & Steckler, J. F. *Women and Educational Testing: A Selective Review of the Research Literature and Testing Practices.* Princeton, N.J.: Educational Testing Service, 1974.

Tractenberg, P. L. *The Legal Implications of Statewide Pupil Performance Standards* (Background paper prepared for the Minimal Competency Workshops sponsored by the Education Commission of the States and the National Institute of Education). Denver: Education Commission of the States, 1977. (ERIC Document Reproduction Service No. ED 156 725)

Tractenberg, P. L. Testing for minimum competency: A legal analysis. In R. M. Jaeger & C. K. Tittle (Eds.), *Minimum Competency Achievement Testing.* Berkeley, Calif.: McCutchan, 1980, pp. 85–107.

Tractenberg, P. L., & Kahn, L. *State Minimum Competency Testing Programs: Legal Implications of Minimum Competency Testing: Debra P. and Beyond* (Final report). Denver: Education Commission of the States, 1979. (ERIC Document Reproduction Service No. ED 190 658)

Tuckman, B. W., & Nadler, F. F. *Local Competency Standards versus State Standards and Their Relation to District Socioeconomic Status.* Paper presented at the annual meeting of the National Council on Measurement in Education, San Francisco, April 1979. (ERIC Document Reproduction Service No. ED 177 198)

Tuttle, S. G. Education and the law; Functional literacy program—A matter of timing. *Stetson Law Review,* 1980, *10,* 125–139.

Tyler, R. W. *Constructing Achievement Tests.* Columbus: Ohio State Press, 1934.

Tyler, R. W. *The Florida Accountability Program: An Evaluation of its Educational Soundness and Implementation.* Washington, D.C.: National Education Association, 1978.

Tyler, R. W. The U.S. vs. the world: A comparison of educational performance. *Phi Delta Kappan,* 1981, *62,* 307–310.

Uniform Guidelines on Employee Selection Procedures, 43 Federal regulations 38290, 1978. (*Federal Register,* August 25, 1978.)

Vlaanderen, R. B. *State Minimum Competency Testing Programs: Reviews and Resources—Federal Efforts in Minimum Competency Testing* (Final report). Denver: Education Commission of the States, 1980. (ERIC Document Reproduction Service No. ED 190 676)

Ward, J. G. *Teachers and Testing: A Survey of Knowledge and Attitudes* (Research report). New York: American Federation of Teachers, 1980.

Weiss, D. J., & Davison, M. L. Test theory and methods. *Annual Review of Psychology,* 1981, *32,* 629–658.

Welch, W. W. A possible explanation for declining test scores, or: Learning less science but enjoying it more. *School Science and Mathematics,* 1980, *80*(1), 22–28.

Wirtz, W. *On Further Examination: Report of the Advisory Panel on the Scholastic Aptitude Test Score Decline.* New York: College Entrance Examination Board, 1977.

Wise, A. E. *A Critique of "Minimal Competency Testing."* (Background paper prepared for the Minimal Competency Workshops sponsored by the Education Commission of the States and the National Institute of Education). Denver: Education Commission of the States, 1977. (ERIC Document Reproduction Service No. ED 156 724)

Zettel, J. J., & Abeson, A. The right to a free appropriate public education. In C. P. Hooker (Ed.), *The Courts and Education: Seventy-seventh Yearbook of the National Society for the Study of Education.* Chicago: University of Chicago Press, 1978.

Zieky, M. L., & Livingston, S. A. *Manual for Setting Standards on the Basic Skills Assessment Tests.* Princeton, N.J.: Educational Testing Service, 1977.

COMPREHENSIVE HIGH SCHOOL

See Junior High and Middle School Education; Secondary Education.

COMPULSORY EDUCATION

See Attendance Policy; History of Education; Legislation; State Influences on Education; Truants and Dropouts.

COMPUTER-ASSISTED INSTRUCTION

See Computer-Based Education.

COMPUTER-BASED EDUCATION

A definition and description of common computer-based education (CBE) techniques and the application of those techniques in instruction are presented. The techniques include computer-managed instruction; computer-based interactive instruction, sometimes referred to as tutorial or computer-assisted instruction (CAI), drill-and-practice; and computer-based instructional simulations. Then the historical development of CBE (including a brief history of computing and its impact on education) is presented followed by a review of hardware developments and instructional materials (courseware) considerations that have specific implications for education. The work of significant CBE centers in academia, the military, the private sector, and professional associations is reviewed and summarized followed by a summary of evaluative studies of the effectiveness of CBE in a variety of settings. Benefits of CBE for learners, faculty, and institutions are summarized; conclusions are drawn; and finally the implications of microcomputers for education are summarized.

Techniques and Applications. The term "computer-based education" (CBE) is used instead of "computer-assisted instruction" (CAI) to encompass a broader spectrum of computer applications than CAI. The latter has come to mean primarily tutorial instruction. CBE, as used here, includes computer-managed instruction, interactive instruction, instructional simulation, and inquiry.

Each of the instructional applications (management, interactive instruction, and simulation) employs the computer in a different role in instruction. Computer-managed instruction (CMI) in its least complex application is relatively simple, relying principally on the record-keeping and summarizing power of the computer to assess, diagnose, prescribe, and monitor each learner's progress. Interactive instruction (II), which subsumes the concepts of tutorial instruction and drill-and-practice, presents instructional material to the learner, accepts and judges responses from the learner, provides feedback, and alters the flow of subsequent instructional material based upon the learner's responses. Instructional simulation (IS) causes learners to apply, analyze, integrate, and synthesize their knowledge as they solve "real life" problems that have been stored in the computer. The continuum of these CBE techniques (CMI, II, and IS) parallels the increasing complexity of (1) the computer programming required for implementation of the techniques and (2) both instructional tasks and learning tasks as the learner moves through the three stages of learning (acquisition, transfer, and integration). The locus of control shifts from computer in CMI to learner in IS as the learner advances through the stages of learning.

Each succeeding instructional application requires (1) all learner knowledges, skills, and behaviors provided by the preceding application and (2) all curricular products produced for the preceding applications. Therefore, it is suggested that normal development of CBE courseware should proceed from computer-managed instruction to interactive instruction to instructional simulation (Hall, 1978).

Computer-managed instruction. Computer-managed instruction (CMI) employs the computer as a record-keeping device and does not provide any direct instruction to learners. Mitzel (1974) identified three levels of CMI. In level I, the instructor provides data to the computer in a batch-processing mode, frequently through optically scanned student-response sheets or instructor-generated evaluations of student performance. The computer sorts, tabulates, and provides printed, summary reports about student progress to the instructor. In level II, the computer is still used in a batch-processing mode to accumulate student-performance records and provide summaries. Additionally, level II provides instructional prescriptions to learner (and instructor) for remediating deficiencies identified in evaluation. Level III incorporates all features of level II but is characterized by a *real-time,* interactive interface between learner and computer and by a diagnostic-prescriptive strategy based on the learner's responses to material stored in the computer system. CMI in its most sophisticated levels provides the following instructional functions: (1) assesses the learner's present level of knowledge, (2) diagnoses weaknesses or gaps in the student's learning, (3) prescribes learning activities to remediate the identified weaknesses, and (4) continuously monitors progress of the learner.

Baker (1971) presented a state-of-the-art review of computer-based instructional management systems with focus on the underlying structures and features of the systems. Mitzel (1974) presented summaries of CMI projects in academia, industry, and the military services. Significant CMI applications since Mitzel's summary include the Individually Guided Education program (Belt, 1975; Belt & Spuck, 1974; Spuck et al., 1975); the college freshman biology program BIO/CMI (Burnard, 1978) designed to integrate books, computers, slide-tape lectures, laboratory experiences, and live teachers; preservice teacher education

(Countermine & Singh, 1977); dentistry (Fast, Stringfellow, & Cammett, 1980); introductory psychology (Kasschau & Halpern, 1979); military science (Rockway & Yasutake, 1974; Van Matre, 1978) and the Response System with Variable Prescriptions (RSVP), which augments instruction (sometimes presented via broadcast television) with computer-assembled, prescriptive paragraphs mailed to learners (Anandam, Eisel, & Kotler, 1980).

Computer-based interactive instruction. The term "interactive instruction" refers to two instructional strategies: tutorial instruction (frequently referred to as computer-assisted instruction) and drill-and-practice. Tutorial instruction (CAI) assumes that the learner is approaching the content to be learned for the first time. Therefore, new content is presented in an expository style, followed by (1) a question to which the learner will respond, (2) a computer analysis of the learner's response, (3) appropriate feedback, and (4) presentation of new material (or questions) to fit the demonstrated need of the learner. Drill-and-practice assumes that the learner has learned certain facts or concepts prior to using the computer program. Therefore, the program does not present new content, but rather, through a series of questions and responses (usually programmed to bring the learner to some predetermined level of performance) provides an opportunity for practicing what has already been learned. Separation of the two instructional strategies into two separate CBE techniques has caused instructional programs to be written according to the needs of the techniques rather than according to the needs of good instruction. Learning new material, for example, regardless of the nature of the learning task (facts, skills, comprehension, analysis, or synthesis) requires practice, a feature not often included in sufficient quantity in a tutorial program. Similarly, practicing of material already presented (drill-and-practice) frequently could be enhanced by re-presenting the material, an option precluded in a drill-and-practice paradigm.

Instructional functions of interactive instruction include the following: (1) display content to the learner, (2) provide opportunity for practice on the content, (3) provide feedback to the learner, (4) consolidate learning, and (5) enhance retention.

Early CBE programs were designed as either drill-and-practice or tutorial and were written in highly structured, hierarchical disciplines. Mathematics (Mitzel et al., 1967; Suppes, Jerman, & Brian, 1968; Suppes & Morningstar, 1972), reading (Atkinson & Hansen, 1966; Fletcher & Atkinson, 1972; Obertino, 1974), chemistry (Lower, 1973; Smith, 1970), physics (Bork, 1975), and electronics (Ford & Slough, 1970; Longo, 1969) were all popular topics for computer-based education. Although by today's standards, these pioneering efforts were limited by instructional strategy and by severe hardware constraints, they demonstrated clearly that the electronic computer provided potential and significant power for improving instruction.

Computer-based instructional simulation. Computer-based instructional simulation (CBIS) is one of the most powerful applications of computers to education (Greenblat, 1975; Rosenfeld, 1975; Tansey & Unwin, 1969). Instructional simulations cause the learner to analyze, integrate, synthesize, and apply basic knowledge to a complex problem-solving situation—learning activities frequently not included in formal education except in such life-and-death applications as medical diagnosis and military-command applications (Abrahamson, Wolf, & Denson, 1969; Feurzeig, 1968; Harless et al., 1973a, 1973b). CBISs provide realistic substitutes for natural experiences that might otherwise be impractical, time consuming, costly, or even dangerous.

CBISs establish (1) a model situation that imitates some aspect of reality and (2) a problem that utilizes the model. The model may be either a static situation, in which conditions do not change during the student interaction with the model, or a dynamic situation, in which conditions change as a result of the learner's actions and solutions (Farquhar, Hoffer, & Barnett, 1978), for example, the distillation equipment displayed by the computer may explode if heat is not controlled properly by the learner.

Crawford (1966) identified five dimensions of simulations: (1) scope or segment of the environment represented in the simulation, (2) duration of the experience provided by simulation, (3) degree of mediacy between the person and the raw environment, (4) degree of centrality of interpersonal relationships, and (5) degree of apparent cognitive involvement. CBISs provide opportunities for systematic application of problem-solving skills: collect, analyze, and interpret data; sequence priorities and decision making; manipulate a situation to alter it; monitor consequences of the decisions or actions; and respond to the altered situation (McGuire & Weyeman, 1974).

Instruction and evaluation can both be implemented through CBISs. Teaching applications should allow the learner to make repeated use of the simulation to explore the effect of alternative decisions without physical danger or risk and without risk of being evaluated during the exploration. The same simulation can be used for student evaluation by invoking a scoring routine to evaluate the learner's decisions, and the sequence of those decisions where sequence is critical. Student evaluation through use of CBISs ensures that all students will experience exactly the same problem and will be judged by exactly the same criteria, an almost impossible accomplishment in a clinical environment.

Disciplines in which CBISs have been developed and used successfully include medicine (Harless et al., 1973a, 1973b; Skakun, Taylor, & Wilson, 1978); chemistry (Smith, 1970; Gerhold & King, 1974); physics (Hughes, 1974); biology (Rubin, Geller, & Hanks, 1977); and reading (Boysen, Thomas, & Mortenson, 1979).

History of Computer-based Education. The first working computer was constructed in 1949. A commerical computer, UNIVAC, was produced the following year (Barnes, 1969). In 1950 there were about twelve computers in the United States, served by fewer than 1,000 programmers, analysts, and operators. By 1960 the number of installations had grown to 6,000 and the manufacture, service, and use of them employed between 500,000 and 1 million persons (Levien, 1972). The early computers were large, slow (by today's standards), expensive, and susceptible to frequent malfunction. Between 1950 and 1980 external dimensions decreased by more than 1,000-fold; speed of operation multiplied by more than 60,000; mean time before failure, then measured in hours, is now measured in years; and cost has plummeted: a computation costing $1 today would have cost $28,000 in 1950, and high-speed data storage costing $1 today would have cost $2,600 in 1950 (Resnikoff, 1981). These technical advances have not been fully felt yet in the field of education, nor perhaps in most fields.

The early computers operated in batch mode, that is, programs and data were loaded into the computer in a group, or "batch," usually via punched cards, and the output from the computer was delivered in a batch, usually via a printer, to the user. CBE demands an "interactive" mode in which the computer displays information to the learner, receives a response from the learner, evaluates the response, provides feedback to the learner regarding correctness of the response, and alters the flow of instructional events to provide instruction tailored to the individual needs of each learner. Gentile (1967) provided an evaluative review of first-generation CBE systems, and Zinn (1967a, 1967b) provided a review of early systems and projects. Large central computers developed for business applications provided the computing power, and teletypes or electric typewriters, modified to communicate with computing equipment, allowed the computer to interact with the learner (Atkinson & Wilson, 1968). Many early projects explored the potential of CBE using "off-the-shelf" equipment (Adams, 1969; Impellitteri, 1968; Mitzel, 1969; Mitzel, Brown, & Igo, 1968; Mitzel et al., 1967; Pagen & Arnold, 1970).

The earliest CBE applications occurred in the computer industry for employee training (O'Dea, 1971). Instructional modules, developed in complicated languages not readily understood by non-computer specialists, were presented to learners who responded with one-character or one-syllable responses. By 1960 the International Business Machine Corporation (IBM) developed the first CBE language, Coursewriter, designed to enable educators to develop instructional modules without the aid of a computer specialist (Suppes & Macken, 1978).

In 1959 engineers, physicists, psychologists, and educators at the University of Illinois under the leadership of Donald Bitzer began developing a system to automate individualized instruction. The system known as PLATO has evolved into a powerful CBE system (Lyman, 1978). In 1963 the Institute for the Mathematical Studies in the Social Sciences began research and development in CBE at Stanford University. Research, development, and implementation in CBE were initiated at Penn State University when the CAI Laboratory was established in 1964 under

the leadership of Harold E. Mitzel. Early in 1972 MITRE Corporation in cooperation with C. Victor Bunderson and Brigham Young University began developing and testing time-shared, interactive, computer-controlled information television (TICCIT) for instruction. More complete descriptions of these significant projects are included in a later section of this article.

Hardware. From the educator's viewpoint, the terminal was the most severe limitation of early CBE equipment (Wodtke, 1967). Teletypes print only in uppercase at fairly low speeds, and the electric typewriters, although printing at somewhat faster speeds and providing lowercase and uppercase, still imposed significant pedagogical limitations. The terminals would display for the learner anything that could be typed on a typewriter, but educators needed facilities to display anything that could be drawn on a chalkboard. Television screens (cathode-ray tubes, or CRTs) offered many of the features needed, but required that the image displayed on the screen be refreshed thirty times per second. The frequency of screen refreshing and the high volume of data required to refresh the screen required that the terminals be connected to the computer with coaxial cable, because telephone communication lines with sufficient speed and capacity were prohibitively expensive. Therefore, pedagogically desirable terminals had to be placed in close proximity (within 2,500 feet) to the computer or pedagogically limited terminals could be used through telephone communications.

A short-term solution to the problem was employed to provide in-service education to teachers and nurses (Hall, 1976; Mitzel, 1974). A mobile van was built that contained a complete minicomputer and sixteen student terminals. The solution was successful and met a need until advanced technology provided a midrange solution to the problem: the plasma-panel terminal invented at the University of Illinois (Arora et al., 1967; Bitzer & Slottow, 1968). The plasma panel incorporated 512 horizontal and 512 vertical electrical conductors in a gaseous chamber. A charge of electricity transmitted through a horizontal conductor and another charge transmitted through a vertical conductor would cause the plasma to glow at the point where the two conductors intersected. A series of instructions could turn on a pattern of dots to create an alphabetic character (or any other symbol) for display on the screen. An entire display could be created and displayed very quickly by the computer. And most important (from a cost standpoint), those dots of light would continue to glow until another signal was given to turn them off, thus eliminating the need for high-capacity, high-cost telephone lines. Although the plasma terminals could be used on standard telephone lines at remote distances from the main computer and appeared to be the wave of the future, they were more costly to produce than CRT terminals. Integrated circuits soon provided the needed refresh capability for CRTs so they also could be supported on standard telephone lines, and thus CRTs have come into standard use. Not only have integrated circuits been used in terminal devices but they have also revolutionized the field of CBE.

The first computing equipment was large, bulky, and required a specialized staff to operate and maintain it. These large, centralized systems became even larger and more powerful over the years and have commonly been referred to as "main frame" or "maxi" systems. Integrated circuits have allowed more and more computer power to be built in smaller and smaller physical enclosures. The progression has gone through three stages: (1) maxisystems, (2) minisystems, and (3) microcomputers. Only three characteristics seem to adequately discriminate among the three stages. A maxisystem will fill an entire room, will cost six or more digits (of dollars) to purchase, and will require an entire institution to agree to its acquisition. A minisystem will fill one corner of a room, will cost five digits to purchase, and will require that only one part of the institution (department, division, or school building group) agree to its acquisition. A microcomputer will sit on a desk, will cost four digits, and the decision to acquire the system can be made by one individual. The increased power of microcomputers, low cost, small space requirements, and ease of making a purchase decision have all contributed to the sudden availability of computers in schools.

Microcomputers have caused the user to learn considerably more about computers and to develop skills formerly left to specialists in the computer room. Although computers are somewhat frightening at first, once the knowledge and skills have been developed, the user can be creative in using the power of the system without excessive dependence on others.

One's relative evaluation of maxisystems, minisystems, and microcomputers for educational uses is heavily colored by past experience. A user of maxisystems will typically underestimate the power of microcomputers and view them as toys rather than as computer systems. A user of microcomputers who has had no experience with maxisystems will overestimate the capability of micros and view maxisystems as too expensive and cumbersome for practical applications in education. Both viewpoints contain some truth. The maxisystems do have greater power and capacity for storing large volumes of courseware and student-performance records, and the costs of system use (rental) and telephone communication are continuous. Student terminals available for maxisystems generally do not provide color or graphic displays for lessons. Microcomputers, on the other hand, are limited in amount of storage capacity, but there are only minimal continuing costs and microcomputers frequently provide color and graphic displays.

Users of maxis and micros are independently pursuing means of acquiring the benefits of both systems. Maxi users are attempting to interface their large systems with microcomputers so (1) courseware can be down-loaded onto microcomputers for independent student use and (2) student-performance records can be up-loaded to the maxisystem for storage and analysis. Micro users are pursuing methods of networking their units so they can communicate with other micro users and with maxicomputers.

Regardless of users' perceptions of maxicomputers and microcomputers, there are hardware and software similarities and differences. Although early uses of computers for education relied on terminals that printed information on paper, virtually all materials are being developed for video display terminals that appear as small television screens. Keyboards have been the standard means of interacting with programs, but other devices are becoming more common: touch-sensitive screens and light pens for responding directly to material displayed on the screen, joysticks and game paddles for moving materials to different locations on the screen, graphic tablets for drawing on the screen, and audio units for input and output. Random-access discs have been the standard storage medium on maxisystems and are becoming the standard on micros, replacing cassette tapes, which are less expensive but are slower than discs and provide only linear access to stored materials.

Courseware. Publishing and distributing courseware (the materials that provide instruction to the learners) is prerequisite for CBE to be widely used for education. Courseware development requires specialized knowledge, skill, experience, and time that are not readily available to everyone who might want to use CBE. Development and use patterns are likely to parallel those of other instructional materials: the major portions will be purchased but will be supplemented with locally produced courseware. Distributing courseware for maxisystems has been limited because of minor differences between systems which require that courseware be modified before it will execute properly. Control Data Corporation (CDC) has been successful, however, in maintaining intersystem compatibility among the installed PLATO systems and has become the publishing company for courseware on those systems, publishing several thousand clock hours of instructional materials in almost all academic disciplines and at almost all grade levels. The company has established criteria and review processes quite similar to those found in book publishing. In contrast, publishing courseware for microcomputers has become the domain of almost anyone who owns a micro and decides to produce and sell courseware, resulting in a plethora of "publishing" companies and widely varying qualitative standards for their products. (It has been said that one could randomly choose any three letters from the alphabet and have the acronym of an existing publishing company for microcomputer courseware.)

Early CBE courseware was documented in a series of catalogs (Hoye & Wang, 1973; Lekan, 1970; Wang, 1976). The 910 entries in 1970 and 1,837 entries covering 137 subject areas in 1976 reflect rapid growth. Kearsley (1976) summarized the 1976 index as follows: (1) the largest proportion of reported courseware was in mathematics, foreign language, and health professions; (2) TUTOR, APL, Coursewriter, BASIC, and FORTRAN were the most frequently used languages; (3) the IBM 360/370 computer was the most frequently used system; (4) drill-and-practice was the most frequently used single instructional strategy, although most courseware used a mixture of strategies; (5) a few major centers had large collections of courseware, whereas most centers had one to five lessons; and (6) most courseware provided one to five hours of instruction, although the average completion time was one hour or less. The plethora of microcomputers and the ease with which courseware can be written (ignoring quality) have made it difficult to assess the trends of courseware development except to say that a lot of small bits and pieces of courseware are available.

Computer-based Education Centers and Activities.
When computers were first used for instruction, a variety of funding programs were available in the federal government. This support enabled and encouraged sizable CBE centers to develop; many in higher education with research and development interests (e.g., Florida State University; University of Illinois; Massachusetts Institute of Technology; The Ohio State University, College of Medicine; The Pennsylvania State University; Stanford University; State University of New York at Stonybrook; and the University of Texas), some in public schools with primarily implementation interests (e.g., Chicago; Montgomery County, Maryland; and Pontiac, Michigan), and some in the private sector (e.g., TICCIT and World Institute for Computer-Assisted Teaching—WICAT) in addition to considerable resources and activity in military training commands. Other centers developed with internal institutional support or with private funds. Some of these centers continue to operate, and others are no longer in existence for a variety of reasons. Documentation of projects and programs from the centers is not systematic and in many cases not available through traditional retrieval systems, such as ERIC, thereby causing omissions in the summary of activities reported here. The following accounts are arranged alphabetically within four groups: (1) academic centers, (2) military applications, (3) the private sector, and (4) professional associations.

Academic centers. This heading includes CBE developmental activities that took place both in higher education institutions and in schools.

The Division of Educational Research Services under the direction of Steven Hunka at the University of Alberta has been active in CBE since 1968, when they installed an IBM 1500 Instructional System (Hunka, 1973). Their work can be characterized as demonstration, research, and production, that is, using CBE to provide instruction to regularly enrolled students at the university. CBE is often the major source of instruction rather than voluntary or experimental instruction assigned as back-up to regular teaching sessions. The following CBE courses characterize the work at Alberta: (1) major heart murmurs and electrocardiography (25 hours); (2) identification of mildly handicapped children (25 hours, developed at Penn State University); (3) beginning high school French (25 hours); (4)

basic electrical theory (45 hours); (5) descriptive statistics (70 hours); (6) programming of the CBE system (18 hours); and (7) simulated patient management problems (20 hours). Short courses, complete in themselves, but which do not replace the major source of instruction include optics laboratory, food sciences, microbiology, educational finance, nursing, anesthesiology, and pharmacology (Hunka, 1976).

The city of Chicago drill-and-practice CBE program began in 1971 with 105 cathode-ray tube (CRT) terminals and 7 hard copy printers equally divided among 7 Elementary and Secondary Education Act (ESEA) Title I schools. It was expanded to 54 elementary schools with similar equipment configurations and to 6 special education schools with smaller equipment configurations. Each CBE laboratory serves 150 or more students per day, and each student receives one CBE session per day in reading and one session per day in either language arts or mathematics. In addition to CBE's serving more than 100,000 students with more than 30 million student sessions during the first 10 years, more than 2,500 teachers have received in-service training in CBE concepts and curricula (Litman, 1981). An evaluation that compared students who used CBE with students who did not found that (1) students who used CBE made significantly better achievement scores in reading (and when those achievements were converted to grade-equivalent scores, they were judged to be important and desirable), (2) the achievements were accomplished by middle-grade students who had been considered hopelessly unsuccessful in special reading programs, and (3) the increased achievement of CBE participants was obtained at relatively low cost (Litman, 1977).

The University Committee on Computer Applications in Education initiated a program of seminars and demonstrations of PLATO in the fall of 1974 to explore the potential of CBE in the university and to evaluate the role that CBE might play in the future of the university community. The first terminal was installed in the spring of 1975, and courseware development projects were initiated in a wide variety of disciplines including agriculture, art, computer science, education, home economics, music, nursing, physical education, and sociology. Additional terminals were installed, more courseware was proposed and developed, and a full PLATO system was made operational in the spring of 1978 (Hofstetter, 1978).

The Delaware PLATO project, under the leadership of Fred Hofstetter, has become a leader in the use of CBE for teaching music. Auxiliary, electronic music boxes under computer control play musical passages for the student to transcribe on the musical scale presented on the computer screen. The University of Delaware has also provided leadership in forming discipline-based national consortia in music education, home economics education, and mathematics education, which furnish forums for professionals to exchange and share knowledge, materials, and methods nationwide.

Research was begun in 1960 in the Coordinated Science

Laboratory at the University of Illinois to explore automating individual instruction. A teaching system called PLATO (Programmed Logic for Automatic Teaching Operations) was invented and developed under the direction of Donald Bitzer (Bitzer, Braunfeld, & Lichtenberger, 1962). During the next 7 years the system grew from 1 terminal to 71 (20 of which were operable simultaneously), and 180 lessons were written to demonstrate the teaching flexibility of the system (Lyman, 1980).

In January 1967, the University of Illinois established the Computer-based Education Research Laboratory (CERL) and moved the PLATO project into the new laboratory. Work in the laboratory emphasized efficient use of the system, hardware development, and courseware development for a large-scale CBE system (Bitzer, 1969). From 1967 through 1972 approximately sixty hours per week were assigned to student use, while authors and system programmers worked late evening and early morning to develop new courseware and to experiment on and correct operating system problems. Disk storage replaced magnetic tape storage for lesson material, and the operating system for the TUTOR language (Avner & Tenczar, 1969) was improved to allow students and authors to work simultaneously on the system (Lyman, 1980).

Testing of the large-scale CBE system, PLATO IV, began with development of extended-core storage and arrival of many commercially manufactured plasma display panels during the summer of 1972. Extensive development of the TUTOR language for PLATO IV enabled authors to convert their PLATO III lessons to PLATO IV without rewriting the materials. In 1977 a microprocessor and a floppy disk system were designed to provide local mass storage at the terminal, making it possible to operate the PLATO terminal independent of the central computer system and still deliver courseware of the same quality (Lyman, 1980).

The present University of Illinois PLATO system supports approximately 1,100 terminals at about 200 locations and is connected to all other PLATO systems for intersystem communication. Although all systems operate independently, the intersystem and interterminal networks facilitate message exchange, forums, rapid information interchange, consultation for lesson writing, and other programming aid (Lyman, 1980). Use of the system has grown dramatically over the years. Student and author use averaged about 87,000 hours per month from 1974 through 1976 and over 135,000 hours per month during the year ending July 1980, for a total of 8 million hours of use since July 1, 1974. The amount of available courseware has also grown from 720 hours in the summer of 1970 to about 7,000 instructional hours in about 150 subject areas in 1980 (Lyman, 1980). Funding support for the development of the PLATO system has come from a wide variety of sources including the joint departments of the Army, Navy, and Air Force; U.S. Office of Education; Control Data Corporation; the National Science Foundation; the National Institute of Education; and the University of Illinois (Lyman, 1980).

CBE work at the Massachusetts Institute of Technology (MIT) has been done largely in the Artificial Intelligence Laboratory (Goldstein & Miller, 1976) and by the LOGO group in that laboratory. Their work has to a great extent reversed the roles of learner and computer and allows learner to instruct (or program) computer. Seymour Papert and his colleagues have created learning environments in which children communicate with computers in a natural and easy way (Papert, 1971; Abelson, Goodman, & Rudolph, 1973).

The Division of Computing Services for Medical Education and Research (DCS) of the Ohio State University (OSU) College of Medicine provides centralized development and support for (1) design, implementation, and maintenance of health-related CBE materials, both on campus and for a state and national CBE network; (2) research and development in CBE; and (3) system analysis, programming, and statistical support of medical-related research programs. The CBE program library of approximately 480 hours of courseware developed over the past 10 years represents one of the largest bodies of health-related CBE materials in the world. Students from the OSU College of Medicine and students and health practitioners from 50 other institutions in the United States logged over 26,000 hours of usage during the 1979/80 fiscal year.

The CBE courseware library includes a broad range of materials for medical students and practitioners as well as for patients. Major courseware includes PILOT, self-evaluation modules for students in the independent study program; PHYSEU, physiological self-evaluation units; and CASE simulations of the patient encounter. Although the work of the division in the past used a maxisystem and a nationwide communications network, the staff is investigating the potential role of microcomputers to meet their needs (Division of Computing Services, 1980).

Since the inception of the Computer Assisted Instruction Laboratory in 1964, research and development sponsored both by the Pennsylvania State University and by agencies outside the university have been the primary focus of effort there. Some thirty-four projects were completed which resulted in a considerable amount of curriculum aimed at, among others, health care professionals (Estes, 1977; Mitzel et al., 1968), teachers (Cartwright & Cartwright, 1973; Golub, 1975; Hall et al., 1970), public school classes (Mitzel et al., 1971), and adult vocational education audiences (Impellitteri, 1968).

The goal of the CAI Laboratory was improvement of instruction through computer application, and the focus was on three objectives: (1) courseware development, (2) systematic investigation to optimize the learning effect of CBE courseware, and (3) computer systems development and research. Several research projects had as their specific missions to develop courseware for use by designated audiences, whereas other projects saw courseware as by-products necessary to perform required research studies. Applied-research problems dealt largely with evaluation techniques and measurement tools, for example, summative evaluation of a self-contained CBE course for training regular classroom teachers to identify handicapping conditions among children in their classroom (CARE I) indicated that students completed the course in 33.3 percent less time and scored 24 percent higher on the final exam than did students in the traditional class (Cartwright & Cartwright, 1973). A continuing effort was made to identify variables that could best be managed by the computer in adapting instruction to individual differences. Development of an authoring language called TACL (Teaching And Coursewriting Language) greatly increased productivity of authors in developing new courseware (Countermine, 1973).

An IBM 1500 Instructional System, the first computer system designed and built specifically for instructional purposes, was installed at Penn State in December 1967, expanded, and used for ten years. The 1500 system used a televisionlike screen as a display device (with a light pen and keyboard for student responses) along with an optional image projector and audio playback equipment. Student terminals had to be located within 2,500 feet of the computer itself, a severe limitation for a geographically dispersed university. Three custom-designed, expandable, mobile vans each housing a complete computer system and sixteen student stations were built and used for transporting the CBE programs around the state and eventually around the nation (Mitzel, 1974), providing over 38,000 academic credits to 16,000 in-service teachers at 45 sites. The mobile vans and the IBM 1500 systems served well in their time, but have since been surpassed by microcomputer technology.

Work in CBE at the Institute for Mathematical Studies in the Social Sciences, Stanford University, began in 1963. During the first decade courseware in mathematics and reading was developed for elementary schools (Suppes, 1972), but during the late 1960s the focus shifted to university-level courses including first-year Russian (Suppes & Morningstar, 1969); old church Slavonic, linguistic history of the Russian language, logic, and music (Suppes, Smith, & Beard, 1977).

Although early work at Stanford focused on large-enrollment courses, the recent focus has been on small-enrollment, relatively esoteric courses as a matter of productivity (Suppes, 1975). The strategy has been to meet declining or fixed budgets and the concomitant pressure against specialized, small-enrollment courses by using CBE to provide effective instruction with little or no instructor intervention.

Work at Stanford has included paradigms for computer-generated courseware, audio input and output devices, computer-generated speech, natural language processing, and computer systems configurations for instructional purposes (Suppes, Smith, & Beard, 1975).

Military applications. CBE applications in the military services have often been on the cutting edge of developments. Three different services—Air Force, Army, and Navy—have provided research and development.

The Advanced Instructional System (AIS) is a develop- ment of the Air Force Human Resources Laboratory, Technical Training Division, and represents the major effort by the Air Force in CBE (Rockway & Yasutake, 1974). AIS will support individualized instruction in four courses: Inventory Management, Material Facilities, Weapons Mechanic, and Precision Measuring Equipment. AIS, a full-scale, instructional system designed to increase the cost-effectiveness of multimedia programs, represents a major effort to develop a computer-directed system for a large, centralized training facility and to optimally synthesize current technology into an integrated system for administering and managing individualized instruction on a large scale.

Although AIS is the major air force CBE activity, there are other projects as well. A twelve-week, adjunctive CBE course in special-vehicle maintenance was developed at Chanute Air Force Base as part of the experimental evaluation of PLATO IV (Navy Personnel, 1973). Twenty-nine learning objectives were presented on PLATO, and the remainder of the course was provided through hands-on instruction. The Air Force School of Health Care Services at Sheppard Air Force Base uses twenty PLATO IV terminals to present clinical simulations to trainees studying to become physician's assistants (Navy Personnel, 1973).

The army interest in use of computers for instruction is strong, with emphasis on immediately practical and specific aspects of training rather than on theoretical aspects. Rich and Van Pelt (1974) reported that fifteen of the thirty-four army training activities surveyed used computers to support training. Army CBE activities include the following: (1) the Signal Center and School, Fort Monmouth, Computerized Training System (CTS) is a project that developed and evaluated a 128-terminal system for use in Army training activities (Hinkle, 1974; Seidel et al., 1978); (2) Command and General Staff College, Fort Leavenworth, provides sufficient training about computer terminals and the BASIC programming language to student officers to enable them to use the computer as a tool; (3) at Engineer School, Fort Belvoir, CBE is used to provide drill-and-practice on teletypewriters; (4) Infantry School, Fort Benning, uses computer-based simulations to provide decision-making training; (5) Ordnance Center and School, Aberdeen Proving Ground, uses and evaluates PLATO IV as part of machinists' training (Navy Personnel, 1973); (6) Quartermaster School, Fort Lee, uses a variety of simulations to provide training in stock control and accounting to enlisted students; (7) Logistics Management Center, Fort Lee, uses computer-based simulations to extend the case method by actively involving the student in the case and by using time compression (Rich & Van Pelt, 1974); (8) Security Agency Training Center and School, Fort Devens, uses CBE to provide 260 hours of instruction in Morse code to each student; and (9) Academy of Health Science, Fort Sam Houston, used an IBM 1440 Coursewriter I system (probably the first hardware and software assembled for CBE by a commercial organization, and the installation at Fort Sam Houston was probably the last one in existence) until 1975 to provide tutorial instruction to students (Fletcher, 1975).

The navy emphasized research and development of a variety of CBE techniques rather than a single project such as the air force AIS or the army CTS projects. Much of the navy work was funded by the Navy Personnel Research and Development Center, San Diego, the Office of Naval Research (ONR), and the Department of Defense Advanced Research Projects Agency (ARPA) but has been conducted at a variety of military and nonmilitary sites. PLATO IV was evaluated at the Naval Training Center, San Diego, and at the Naval Air Station, North Island, using five training courses: (1) Multimeter Simulation and Training, (2) Recipe Conversion, (3) Low-cost Trainer Simulation (as a substitute for the more expensive airplane simulators), (4) Oscilloscope Training through Simulation, and (5) Computer-based Guidance of Oscilloscope Training (to provide computerized guidance of hands-on training) (Fletcher, 1975). The Shipboard Computer Training Project addressed the feasibility of using minicomputer systems aboard ships for instruction and training administration purposes (Fletcher, 1975; Flint & Graham, 1971; Navy Personnel, 1973). Starting in 1975, approximately 15–20 percent of the training given to air crews of the S-3A military plane at North Island Naval Air Station was presented by a TICCIT system. TICCIT was chosen on the basis of cost, system size, and availability of contractor personnel to assist in development of courseware (Fletcher, 1975).

The Advanced Computer-based Training Research project had four principal research areas: (1) computer-assisted instruction study-management system (CAISMS) conducted at the University of Illinois (R. Anderson et al., 1974; T. Anderson et al., 1974); (2) CAMELOT/GRAIL conducted at the San Diego State University to support CBE simulation research (Fletcher, 1975); (3) Automatic Question Generation and Response Evaluation to explore and develop techniques for automatically generating questions from text material (Fletcher, 1975); and (4) Lesson Translator, a terminal-based system for dispersed training, a software program that accepts lesson material, translates it into computer instructions, and displays it on shipboard computer consoles (Fletcher, 1975).

The navy computer-managed instruction system, a large, multisite program, not only yielded significant cost savings of over $10 million during fiscal year 1975 (Hansen et al., 1975) but also produced better end-of-course performance while maintaining more positive attitudes among students and lower attrition rates than did conventional instruction.

Early CBE work at the U.S. Naval Academy, Annapolis, was directed toward tutorial instruction in three programs: (1) CBE based on teletypewriters, (2) CBE based on the IBM 1500 system, and (3) a U.S. Office of Education project that supported the development of multimedia course presentations (Hoye & Wang, 1973). These efforts were terminated in 1972–1973 in favor of a more general approach

of providing computer skills as tools and literacy for a technological society.

Although much of the effort of the navy has been focused on strictly military needs and objectives, use of CBE in teaching basic skills has also been explored. Stolte and Smith (1980) found a basic-reading-skills program for recruits reading below the sixth-grade level to be cost-effective in light of escalating instructor-related costs. Wisher (1980) found that literacy instruction in phonics using a computer-driven voice synthesizer produced student performance comparable to student performance in the control group.

Private sector. The private sector includes both profit and not-for-profit organizations that have exhibited research and development activities in CBE.

Since 1962, when Control Data Corporation (CDC) started providing support to the University of Illinois for development of PLATO, the corporation has invested more than $750 million in the product (Hayes, 1981). The PLATO community has grown from a single system at the University of Illinois to a second system at CDC headquarters in Minneapolis in the spring of 1974, a third one at Florida State University in the fall of 1974 (Lyman, 1980), until the most recent report (Francis, 1981) of the following additional system sites: University of Delaware; University of Alberta; University of Quebec; London; Brussels, Belgium; Johannesburg, South Africa; Korean Advanced Institute of Science and Technology, South Korea; and four additional systems at CDC headquarters in Minneapolis. These systems use compatible operating software so courses can be exchanged among systems and be available to all users. Communications links also exist among systems so messages regarding courseware and courseware development can be exchanged quickly.

Although much of the courseware developed at the University of Illinois has been made available on the other systems, CDC has supported development of courseware in significant areas of social need: basic skills in mathematics, reading, and language and courseware to prepare non–high school graduates to take the General Educational Development (GED) test and earn a high school diploma equivalency certificate (Five years old, 1979; PLATO's popularity, 1979). The social usefulness of CBE was also demonstrated by the HOMEWORK program, which enables CDC employees who are disabled and on medical leave to return to productive work via a PLATO terminal in their home (Homework, 1980).

A new system, called Micro-PLATO, uses a terminal and flexible disk drives to deliver PLATO courseware independently of a central host computer and thus avoid the expense of telephone communications. Because Micro-PLATO uses the standard PLATO terminal (plus disk drives), students can use the same equipment for central-system instructional delivery as well (Micro-PLATO, 1980).

Four converging economic factors indicate rising demands for using PLATO for instruction: (1) costs of central computers and terminals are dropping; (2) performance of computer-based training to date is stimulating interest; (3) rising transportation costs and instructor salaries have dampened the appeal of centralized training centers; and (4) the number of PLATO lessons (courseware) is growing by more than 2,000 per year. Moreover, the increasing number of home computers is expected to provide access to PLATO courseware to many more people (Hayes, 1981).

The Minnesota Educational Computing Consortium (MECC) was formed in 1972–1973 to facilitate and coordinate use of computers in the elementary, secondary, and collegiate schools of Minnesota. MECC provides management information services, offers instructional services, and conducts special projects. During the 1979/80 school year 96 percent of Minnesota students had access to the MECC Timeshare System, one of the world's largest general purpose educational time-sharing systems. In addition to providing direct computing services, MECC also negotiates statewide contracts with hardware and software vendors to assure compatibility of equipment, simplify procurement, and gain significant cost reductions throughout the state. During the 1979/80 school year, over 1000 Apple II microcomputers were sold and installed in Minnesota, bringing the total of Apple IIs ordered through MECC to over 1,500. Additionally, MECC completed over 150 Apple II computer programs that are available to Minnesota users at no cost and to users outside Minnesota for a modest charge (Minnesota Educational Computing Consortium, 1980).

In 1971 the National Science Foundation awarded a contract to the MITRE Corporation, McLean, Virginia, to develop and demonstrate Time-shared, Interactive, Computer-controlled Information Television (TICCIT, pronounced "ticket"). Using inexpensive minicomputers, standard color television receivers, and typewriterlike keyboards, a TICCIT installation can serve as many as 128 students simultaneously (Rappaport & Olenbush, 1975). The project began with the combined efforts of engineers from MITRE and educators from the CAI Laboratory at the University of Texas and later the Institute for Computer Uses in Education at Brigham Young University (Alderman, 1978a). Unique goals of the TICCIT project that distinguish it from other CBE development efforts include (1) to make the system a market success (legal agreements now permit the Hazeltine Corporation to market the system), (2) to design TICCIT as a local facility with local control, (3) to use available hardware, (4) to provide learner control of instruction (Bunderson, 1973; Reigeluth, 1979), and (5) to provide "main-line" rather than supplementary instruction. The field test (Alderman, 1978a, 1978b) of mathematics and English courseware for community colleges is reported in the section on evaluation of CBE.

The World Institute for Computer Assisted Teaching (WICAT) is an independent, nonprofit institute formed to enable such new technologies as the microcomputer and videodisc to be instructionally usable at all levels of instruction and education (preschool, elementary, secondary, college, adult, and home populations, as well as government, industrial, and corporate training). The purposes of WICAT include the following: (1) to develop a permanent institute with sufficient capital to attract and hold experts from a broad range of disciplines who are committed to the use of technology in education; (2) to develop educational standards for the use of new technologies to ensure that users receive maximum benefit from the equipment while being protected from overzealous applications; (3) to develop exemplary courseware, particularly in such basic skill areas as English, mathematics, and reading; (4) to conduct research in learning and teaching through use of capabilities generated by the new technologies; (5) to influence hardware development and ensure that a broad range of educational capabilities is included; (6) to develop implementation strategies to ensure that technology enters the mainstream of education; and (7) to develop a private laboratory school where innovative teaching and learning techniques can be investigated. The WICAT organization includes (1) an instructional systems group that specializes in analysis, design, implementation, and evaluation of technology-based instructional systems; (2) a courseware development group that produces computer and videodisc materials; (3) a computer systems group that designs, programs, and tests the software needed for technology-based instructional systems; (4) an engineering design group that designs, fabricates, and tests hardware prototypes; and (5) a management group (Bunderson, 1981).

Two groups have evolved from the interest in CBE and provide opportunities for information exchange on CBE through professional meetings and publications: (1) the Special Interest Group on CAI (SIG/CAI) in the American Education Research Association (American Educational Research Association, 1981) and (2) the Association for the Development of Computer-based Instructional Systems (ADCIS) which publishes the *Journal of Computer Based Instruction* and proceedings of the annual conference (Association for the Development of Computer-Based Instructional Systems, 1981).

Evaluation of Computer-Based Education. Computer-based education, *per se*, cannot be evaluated any more than all textbooks, lectures, or films can be judged as effective or ineffective instructional materials or techniques by evaluating a single example (Jamison, Suppes, & Wells, 1974). An evaluation study can examine only a single instance where CBE has been implemented and cannot generalize to the technique itself. The following summary of early investigations of CBE shows that, in these instances, CBE was effective.

Studies reviewed by Edwards et al. (1975) and by Vinsonhaler and Bass (1972) were unanimous about the effectiveness of supplemental CBE at the elementary school level. Hartley (1977) also reported differences favoring CBE at the elementary school level of at least 0.5 standard deviation between students receiving CBE instruction and those who did not. Twelve CBE evaluative studies (Abramson et al., 1970; Atkinson, 1968; Cartwright, Cartwright, & Robine, 1972; Ford & Slough, 1970; Hall & Mitzel, 1974; Harless et al., 1969; Hurlock, 1971; Longo, 1969; Pagen & Arnold, 1970; Robinson & Lautenschlager, 1971; Scrivens, 1970; Suppes & Morningstar, 1969) reported on the performance of 11,877 students with 7,266 of them receiving instruction through computers and 4,611 of the students receiving conventional instruction. A wide variety of students (elementary through post–high school, military, and postbaccalaureate college students) and subject matter (elementary mathematics and reading, post–high school electronics maintenance and theory, college-level Russian, and teacher education) were included in the studies using drill-and-practice, tutorial, and remediation paradigms. CBE consistently produced more learning than conventional instruction; considerable savings in time were also shown when time was investigated. Although direct comparisons between studies were difficult because of the differing objectives, student characteristics, and content, there appeared to be an increase in learner performance related to CBE in every instance.

Kulik, Kulik, and Cohen (1980) conducted a meta-analysis of fifty-nine independent evaluations of CBE uses at the college level and reported findings related to student achievement, aptitude-achievement correlations, student attitudes, and instructional time, which are summarized as follows: (1) the computer has made a small but significant contribution to the effectiveness of college teaching, raising exam scores by about 0.25 standard deviations (a change that was as noticeable in high-aptitude and low-aptitude students as it was in average students); (2) CBE has had small but positive effects on attitudes of college students toward instruction and toward subject matter; (3) in a few cases CBE has had a strong, positive effect (Cartwright, Cartwright, & Robine, 1972; Grandey, 1970; Roll & Pasen, 1977); (4) CBE produced learning in about two-thirds of the time required by traditional instruction; and (5) accomplishments of CBE must be considered modest at the college level.

Educational Testing Service (ETS) has reported on the evaluation of major CBE implementation efforts of PLATO IV in a community college (Murphy & Appel, 1977), TICCIT in a community college (Alderman, 1978a, 1978b), and drill-and-practice materials in the Los Angeles Unified School District (Ragosta, 1981). The findings are complex in all cases, they often reflect evaluation of specific courseware rather than of CBE systems, and they are generally consistent with the meta-analysis reported by Kulik, Kulik, & Cohen, (1980).

Findings from CBE studies seem consistent with findings from studies of teaching effectiveness (Rosenshine & Furst, 1971) and studies on effectiveness of educational programs (Gordon, 1971). The studies all indicated that the following attributes should be included in the instructional environment: (1) frequent feedback to learners, (2) tutorial relationship, (3) individual pacing, (4) individual programming, (5) clarity of presentation, (6) motivational factors, (7) variability in classroom activities, (8) enthusiasm, (9) task-oriented or achievement-oriented instruction, and (10) opportunity for students to learn criterion material.

Many of these attributes can be provided by computer technology because computers allow us to store and present stimulus materials to learners, receive and evaluate student responses, present evaluative feedback, and alter the flow and sequence of instruction according to student performance (very much the same as live tutors do) but with the added advantages of recording and/or replicating the exact sequence of instruction for careful scrutiny and analysis. The computer's capability to capture instructional interactions for repeated use with students, analyze the interactions, and refine the data provides the "flexibility for successive incremental improvement" identified by Glaser (1972, p. 8).

Benefits of CBE for learners include (1) flexibly scheduled instruction at locations convenient to school, home, and/or work; (2) adaptive instruction that can include variations in speed with which courses are completed, instructional method (e.g., pretest, off-line instructional resources, on-line drill-and-practice, individualized instructional prescriptions, on-line interactive instruction, and instructional simulation), remedial choices and enrichment excursions, diagnosis of individual errors and assignment of remediation, immediate feedback; (3) private instruction, response, and feedback (which removes the social stigma of learning slowly or making errors); (4) assured progress in skill development; (5) reduced student time; (6) continuous report to the learner of progress and accomplishments; (7) specified performance criteria; (8) increased achievement; and (9) increased retention.

Benefits of CBE for the faculty include (1) released faculty time for teaching higher-level, specialized courses; (2) released faculty time for faculty-student interaction; (3) professional publications from the research and development effort; (4) additional class time for higher-level instruction by removing basic skill development from the classroom and assigning it to the computer system; (5) assured minimum student competency before class lectures and discussions, allowing classwork to move at a faster pace; (6) opportunity for creative development of innovative curriculum materials; (7) inclusion of objectives that are otherwise impossible (e.g., ear training in music, graphic display and solution of student problems in architecture, flexible presentation and manipulation of text and audio for language skill development); (8) professional recognition for curriculum design and development; (9) professional growth; and (10) increased enrollment in CBE courses that students perceive meet their needs (i.e., adaptive, responsive, goal-oriented, and efficient).

Benefits of CBE for the institution include (1) uniform, observable, high-quality instruction for students; (2) progressive improvement of instruction as student performance data are used for curriculum revision; (3) reduced course attrition and associated expense; (4) released faculty time for reassignment to higher-level courses (i.e., cost avoidance); (5) significant new student clientele served with existing faculty; (i.e., CBE is available on demand at remote sites); and (6) curriculum expansion by implementation of basic coursework via CBE with faculty reserved for specialized coursework.

Conclusions. High-quality CBE requires a systematic approach to the instructional development process that includes (1) analysis of curricular needs and existing courses; (2) instructional design to determine objectives, tests, entry knowledge, and scope and sequence of instructional events; (3) development and field-test validation of course materials; (4) course implementation; and (5) evaluation and revision. In addition to the quality of instruction for learners, the flexibility and adaptability of instruction via CBE are attractive to students. Instruction can be scheduled at any time and at any place where terminals (microcomputers) are located. The computer continuously monitors each student's progress and adapts the instruction to the learner, skipping portions where the learner has demonstrated competence and providing remedial instruction where the learner has demonstrated weakness. Research has consistently shown that CBE reduces learning time 40–50 percent with equal or increased retention when compared with traditional instruction.

The flexibility provided by CBE makes instruction possible to a wide variety of learners in a wide variety of environments: traditional school-age children in school and out; preschool-age children at home or in day care centers; and adults on the job, in social service centers, in health care centers, or at home. Potential students from other population groups include employed adults as part-time students, women reentering the work force, and practicing professionals in need of renewal education (e.g., current agribusiness concepts and techniques, update of tax laws, new products from the pharmaceutical industry, accounting fundamentals, refresher courses for licensing and certification, and city and regional planning for lay members of boards).

Of major concern to universities is the large number of entering freshmen who are poorly prepared to study and learn from traditionally taught college-level courses. These students have failed to learn effectively from traditional instructional methods in the past, and there is little reason to believe that one more exposure will make significant differences in their performance. The students themselves are discouraged and embarrassed at not progressing like their peers. CBE offers new techniques and a new environment with infinite patience and time so each student can learn privately without social failure, pressure, and stigma. CBE techniques have the instructional power and versatility to contribute to solution of these and other instructional problems.

Implications of microcomputers. The low cost and physical availability of microcomputers means that many individuals with many ideas will be working with micro-

computers in education. Being third-generation users (maxi-users and mini-users were the first and second-generation users), microcomputer users have the responsibility to study the work of the pioneers of the field and to apply their findings to their own work. Formal study of CBE is necessary as is formal study in other disciplines.

Physical mobility of microcomputers makes it possible to serve geographically remote learner populations without concern for access to large computer systems—a unique opportunity for serving new clientele with instructional programs as well as for gathering research data.

Congressional Hearings. In October 1977, the U.S. House of Representatives Committee on Science and Technology held hearings (U.S., Congress, House, 1978) to take testimony from informed observers in the field of CBE and found extensive agreement on the following: (1) the current performance of the nation's educational system leaves much to be desired; (2) judicious use of computer technology could make significant improvements in teacher effectiveness and student learning; (3) a microelectronic revolution is under way that will reduce the cost of computing and will probably make computers commonplace in homes and schools, thereby introducing new educational opportunities; and (4) the implications of computer technology are only vaguely understood and are not being studied or planned in a comprehensive manner. The Committee made specific recommendations to Congress for legislation to enable the nation to gain maximum advantage of computers for education. It is clear that informed observers believe strongly about the tremendous opportunities afforded by microelectronics for education. Although national economic factors may influence the speed at which computers become a significant factor in education, there is little doubt that they will become important to the broad scope of education in the United States.

Keith A. Hall

See also Games and Simulations; Individualized Systems of Instruction; Information Management and Computing; Media Use in Education; New Technologies in Education.

REFERENCES

Abelson, H.; Goodman, N.; & Rudolph, L. *Logo Manual* (LOGO MEMO 7). Cambridge, Mass.: Massachusetts Institute of Technology, LOGO Group, Artificial Intelligence Laboratory, August 1973.

Abrahamson, S.; Wolf, R. M.; & Denson, J. S. A computer-based patient simulator for training anestheseologists. *Educational Technology*, October 1969, *9*(10), 55–59.

Abramson, T.; Weiner, M.; Malkin, S.; & Howell, J. *Evaluation of the New York City Computer-assisted Instruction Project in Elementary Arithmetic* (Second year, 1969–1970, Title III Contract A-3968, Research Report 70-16) New York: City University of New York, Research and Evaluation Unit, Division of Teacher Education, October 1970.

Adams, E. N. Field evaluation of the German CAI lab. In R. C.

Atkinson & H. A. Wilson (Eds.), *Computer-assisted Instruction: A Book of Readings.* New York: Academic Press, 1969.

Alderman, D. L. *Evaluation of the TICCIT Computer-assisted Instructional System in the Community College* (Final report, Vol. 1). Princeton, N.J.: Educational Testing Service, September 1978. (a) (ERIC Document Reproduction Service No. ED 167 606)

Alderman, D. L. *Evaluation of the TICCIT Computer-assisted Instructional System in the Community College* (Final report, Vol. 2, Appendices). Princeton, N.J.: Educational Testing Service, September 1978. (b) (ERIC Document Reproduction Service No. ED 167 607).

American Educational Research Association. *Educational Researcher.* Washington, D.C.: The Association, *10*(5), 1981.

Anandam, K.; Eisel, E.; & Kotler, L. Effectiveness of a computer-based feedback system for writing. *Journal of Computer-based Instruction,* May 1980, *6*(4), 125–133.

Anderson, R. C.; Surber, J. R.; Biddle, W. B.; Zych, P. M.; & Lieberman, C. E. *Retention of Text Information as a Function of the Nature, Timing, and Number of Quizzes* (TR 74 28). San Diego, Calif.: Navy Personnel Research and Development Center, February 1974.

Anderson, T. H.; Anderson, R. C.; Dalgaard, B. R.; Wietecha, E. J.; Biddle, W. B.; Paden, D. W.; Smoch, H. R.; Alessi, S. M.; Surber, J. R.; & Klemt, L. L. A computer-based study management system. *Educational Psychologist,* 1974, *11,* 36–45.

Arora, B. M.; Bitzer, D. L.; Slottow, H. G.; & Willson, R. H. The plasma display panel: A new device for information display and storage. In *Proceedings of the Eighth National Symposium of the Society for Information Display,* San Francisco, May 1967.

Association for the Development of Computer-Based Instructional Systems. *Computer-based instruction: Frontiers of thought* (1981 conference proceedings). Bellingham, Wash.: The Association, 1981.

Atkinson, R. C. Computerized instruction and the learning process. *American Psychologist,* 1968, *23*(4), 225–239.

Atkinson, R. C., & Hansen, D. N. Computer-assisted instruction in initial reading: The Stanford project. *Reading Research Quarterly,* 1966, *2*(1), 5–25.

Atkinson, R. C., & Wilson, H. A. Computer-assisted instruction. *Science,* 1968, *162,* 73–77.

Avner, R. A., & Tenczar, P. *The TUTOR Manual* (Report X-4). Urbana: University of Illinois, Computer-based Education Research Laboratory, 1969.

Baker, F. B. Computer-based instructional management systems: A first look. *Review of Educational Research,* 1971, *41*(1), 51–70.

Barnes, B. J. Hardware, software, technique, and philosophy. *Drexel Library Quarterly,* April 1969, *5,* 63.

Belt, S. L. *Some Design Considerations to Meet the Requirements of Individually Prescribed Education.* Madison: Wisconsin University, Research and Development Center for Cognitive Learning, 1975. (ERIC Reproduction Service No. ED 107 219)

Belt, S. L., & Spuck, D. W. *Computer Applications in Individually Guided Education: A Computer-based System for Instructional Management, Needs, and Specifications* (Working Paper No. 125). Madison: Wisconsin University, Research and Development Center for Cognitive Learning, 1974. (ERIC Reproduction Service No. ED 094 692)

Bitzer, D. L. Economically viable large-scale computer-based system. In R. T. Heimer (Ed.), *Computer-assisted Instruction and the Teaching of Mathematics.* Washington, D.C.: National Council of Teachers of Mathematics, 1969.

Bitzer, D. L.; Braunfeld, P. G.; & Lichtenberger, W. W. PLATO II: A multiple-student, computer-controlled, automatic teaching device. In J. E. Coulson (Ed.), *Programmed Learning and Computer-based Instruction.* New York: Wiley, 1962.

Bitzer, D. L., & Slottow, H. G. *Principles and Applications of the Plasma Display Panel.* Paper presented at the Office of Aerospace Research Applications Conference, Office of Aerospace Research, Arlington, Va., March 1968.

Bork, A. *Current Status of the Physics Computer Development Project.* Irvine, Calif.: University of California at Irvine, Physics Computer Development Project, 1975. (ERIC Document Reproduction Service No. ED 107 201)

Boysen, V. A.; Thomas, R. A.; & Mortenson, W. P. Interactive computer simulations of reading skill weaknesses. *Journal of Computer-based Instruction,* 1979, *4*(3), 45–49.

Bunderson, C. V. *The TICCIT Project: Design Strategy for Educational Innovation* (ICUE Tech. Rep. No. 4). Provo, Utah: Brigham Young University, Institute for Computer Uses in Education, September 1973. (ERIC Document Reproduction Service No. ED 096 996)

Bunderson, C. V. Personal communication, February 10, 1981.

Burnard, R. K. Computer-managed instruction with individualized instruction in general biology. *Journal of Personalized Instruction,* 1978, *3*(3), 165–167.

Cartwright, G. P., & Cartwright, C. A. A computer-assisted instruction course in the early identification of handicapped children. *Journal of Teacher Education,* 1973, *24*(2), 128–134.

Cartwright, G. P.; Cartwright, C. A.; & Robine, G. C. CAI course in the early identification of handicapped children. *Exceptional Children,* 1972, *38*(6), 453–459.

Countermine, T. A. *The Development and Evaluation of a Teaching and Coursewriting Computer Language (TACL).* University Park: Pennsylvania State University, Computer Assisted Instruction Laboratory, June 1973. (ERIC Document Reproduction Service No. ED 089 794)

Countermine, T. A., & Singh, J. M. A computer-managed instruction support system for large group individualized instruction. *Journal of Computer-based Instruction,* 1977, *4*(1), 17–21.

Crawford, M. P. Dimensions of simulations. *American Psychologist,* 1966, *21*(8), 788–796.

Division of Computing Services for Medical Education and Research. *Annual Report: July 1979–June 1980.* Columbus: Ohio State University, College of Medicine, 1980.

Edwards, J.; Norton, S.; Taylor, S.; Weiss, M.; & Dusseldorp, R. How effective is CAI? A review of the research. *Educational Leadership,* 1975, *33,* 147–153.

Estes, C. A. *Mobile Education for Nurses in Remote Areas* (Final Report R77). University Park: Pennsylvania State University, Computer Assisted Instruction Laboratory, January 1977.

Farquhar, B. B.; Hoffer, E. P.; & Barnett, G. O. Patient simulations in clinical education. In E. C. Deland (Ed.), *Information Technology in Health Science Education.* New York: Plenum Press, 1978.

Fast, T. B.; Stringfellow, H. R.; & Cammett, S. M. Computer-based management of a clinical teaching program. *Journal of Dental Education,* May 1980, *44*(5), 264–267.

Feurzeig, W. *Educational Potentials of Computer Technology* (Report No. 1672). Cambridge, Mass.: Bolt, Beranek & Newman, September 1968.

Five years old and already a math whiz. *Contact for Control Data People,* May 1979, 2–3.

Fletcher, J. D. *Computer Applications in Education and Training: Status and Trends* (NPRDC TR 75 32). San Diego, Calif.: Navy Personnel Research and Development Center, April 1975.

Fletcher, J. D., & Atkinson, R. C. An evaluation of the Stanford CAI program in initial reading (grades K through 3). *Journal of Educational Psychology,* 1972, *63*(6), 597–602.

Flint, H. M., & Graham, T. S. *Computer Applications in Education and Training: Status and Trends* (Special Report ADO-43-03X). Washington, D.C.: Washington Navy Yard, Naval Personnel Research and Development Laboratory, August 1971.

Ford, J. D., Jr., & Slough, D. A. *Development and Evaluation of Computer-assisted Instruction for Navy Electronics Training: 1. Alternating Current Fundamentals* (Research Report SSR 70-32). San Diego, Calif.: Naval Personnel and Training Research Laboratory, May 1970.

Francis, L. SIG PUG. *ADCIS News,* May 1981, *14*(3), 2.

Gentile, J. R. The first generation of computer-assisted instructional systems: An evaluative review. *AV Communication Review,* 1967, *15*(1), 23–53.

Gerhold, G. A., & King, D. M. Computer-simulated qualitative analysis without flowsheets. *Journal of Computer-based Instruction,* 1974, *1*(2), 46–49.

Glaser, R. Individuals and learning: The new aptitudes. *Educational Researcher,* June 1972, *17*, 5–13.

Goldstein, I., & Miller, M. *AI-based Personal Learning Environments: Directions for Long-term Research.* Cambridge, Mass.: Massachusetts Institute of Technology, Artificial Intelligence Laboratory, LOGO Group, December 1976.

Golub, L. S. *A Computer-assisted Bilingual/Bicultural Teacher Education Program* (Report R66). University Park: Pennsylvania State University, Computer-assisted Instruction Laboratory, January 1975.

Gordon, E. W. *Utilizing Available Information from Compensatory Education and Surveys* (Final Report). Washington, D.C.: U.S. Office of Education, 1971. (ERIC Document Reproduction Service No. ED 055 664)

Grandey, R. C. An investigation of the use of computer-aided instruction in teaching students how to solve selected multistep general chemistry problems. (Doctoral dissertation, University of Illinois, 1970). *Dissertation Abstracts International,* 1971, *31*(12-A), 6430. (University Microfilms No. 71-14, 764)

Greenblat, C. S. Teaching with simulation games: A review of claims and evidence. In C. S. Greenblat & R. D. Duke (Eds.), *Gaming-Simulation: Rationale, Design, and Applications.* New York: Wiley, 1975.

Hall, K. A. *The Development and Utilization of Mobile CAI for the Education of Nurses in Remote Areas.* Paper presented at the annual meeting of the American Education Research Association, San Francisco, April 1976. (ERIC Document Reproduction Service No. ED 121 281)

Hall, K. A. Computer-based education: Research, theory, development. *Educational Communication and Technology Journal,* 1978, *26*(1), 79–93.

Hall, K. A., & Mitzel, H. E. A pilot program of high school computer-assisted instruction mathematics program. *Journal of Educational Technology Systems,* 1974, *2*(3), 157–174.

Hall, K. A.; Mitzel, H. E.; Suydam, M. N.; Riedesel, C. A.; & Trueblood, C. R. *Inservice Mathematics Education via Computer-assisted Instruction for Elementary School Teachers in Appalachia* (Final Report R-26). University Park: Pennsylvania State University, Computer Assisted Instruction Laboratory, January 1970. (ERIC Document Reproduction Service No. ED 042 334)

Hansen, D. N.; Ross, S. M.; Bowman, H. L.; & Thurmond, P.

Navy Computer-managed Instruction: Past, Present, and Future. Memphis, Tenn.: Memphis State University, Bureau of Educational Research and Services, July 1975. (ERIC Document Reproduction Service No. ED 114 051)

Harless, W. G.; Drennon, G. G.; Marxer, J. J.; Root, J. A.; Wilson, L. L.; & Miller, G. E. CASE: A natural language computer model. *Computers in Biology and Medicine,* 1973, *3*, 227–246. (a)

Harless, W. G.; Drennon, G. G.; Marxer, J. J.; Root, J. A.; Wilson, L. L.; & Miller, G. E. GENESYS: A generating system for the CASE natural language model. *Computers in Biology and Medicine,* 1973, *3*, 247–268. (b)

Harless, W. G.; Lucas, N. C.; Cutter, J. A.; Duncan, R. C.; White, J. M.; & Brandt, E. N. Computer-assisted instruction in continuing medical education. *Journal of Medical Education,* August 1969, *44*, 670–674.

Hartley, S. S. Meta-analysis of the effects of individually paced instruction in mathematics. (Doctoral dissertation, University of Colorado, 1977). *Dissertation Abstracts International,* 1978, *38*(7-A), 4003. (University Microfilms No. 77-29, 926)

Hayes, T. C. Plato's logic spreads. *New York Times, Education Supplement,* April 26, 1981, pp. 5, 26.

Hinkle, L. R. *PLATO IV: First-year Report, Computerized Training System, Project ABACUS.* Fort Monmouth, N.J.: Army Signal Center and School, April 1974. (ERIC Document Reproduction Service No. ED 095 926)

Hofstetter, F. T. *Third Summative Report of the Delaware PLATO Project.* Wilmington: University of Delaware, 1978.

Homework. *Contact for Control Data People,* March 1980, pp. 2–7.

Hoye, R. E., & Wang, A. C. *Index to Computer-based Learning.* Englewood Cliffs, N.J.: Educational Technology Publications, 1973.

Hughes, W. R. A study of the use of computer-simulated experiments in the physics classroom. *Journal of Computer-based Instruction,* 1974, *1*(1), 1–6.

Hunka, S. The computer-aided instruction activities of the division of educational research services at the University of Alberta. *International Journal of Man Machine Studies,* 1973, *5*, 329–336.

Hunka, S. *Eight Years of Computer-assisted Instruction: Now What?* Edmonton: University of Alberta, Division of Educational Research Services, Faculty of Education, February 1976.

Hurlock, R. E. *Development and Evaluation of a Computer-assisted Instruction Course for Navy Electronics Training: 2. Inductance* (Research Report SRR 71-22). San Diego, Calif.: Naval Personnel and Training Research Laboratory, March 1971.

Impellitteri, J. T. *The Development and Evaluation of a Pilot Computer-assisted Occupational Guidance Program* (Final report). University Park: Pennsylvania State University, Computer-assisted Instruction Laboratory, 1968. (ERIC Document Reproduction Service No. ED 029 095)

Jamison, D.; Suppes, P.; & Wells, S. Effectiveness of alternative instructional media. *Review of Educational Research,* 1974, *44*, 1–67.

Kasschau, R. A., & Halpern, M. S. *Computer-managed instruction: Individualizing Introductory Psychology for One Thousand Students.* Paper presented at the American Psychological Association Meeting, New York, 1979. (ERIC Document Reproduction Service No. ED 190 126)

Kearsley, G. P. Some "facts" about CAI: Trends 1970–1976. *Journal of Educational Data Processing,* 1976, *3*(2), 1–12.

Kulik, J. A.; Kulik, C. L. C.; & Cohen, P. A. Effectiveness of computer-based college teaching: A meta-analysis of findings. *Review of Educational Research*, 1980, *50*(4), 525–544.

Lekan, H. A. *Index to Computer-assisted Instruction* (2nd ed.). Boston: Sterling Institute, 1970.

Levien, R. E. *The Emerging Technology: Instructional Uses of the Computer in Higher Education.* New York: McGraw-Hill, 1972.

Litman, G. H. *Relation between Computer-assisted Instruction and Reading Achievement among Fourth-, Fifth-, and Sixth-grade Students.* Unpublished doctoral dissertation, Northern Illinois University, 1977.

Litman, G. H. Personal communication, February 18, 1981.

Longo, A. A. *The Implementation of Computer-assisted Instruction in U.S. Army Basic Electronics Training: Follow-up of a Feasibility Study* (Tech. Rep. 69-1). Fort Monmouth, N.J.: U.S. Continental Army Command Computer-assisted Instruction Project, September 1969.

Lower, S. K. *CHEMEX: Understanding and Solving Problems in Chemistry: A Computer-assisted Instruction Program for General Chemistry.* Burnaby, B. C.: Simon Fraser University, Department of Chemistry, 1973. (ERIC Document Reproduction Service No. ED 081 202)

Lyman, E. R. *PLATO Highlights* (5th ed.). Urbana: University of Illinois, Computer-based Education Research Laboratory, March 1978. (ERIC Document Reproduction Service No. ED 161 435)

Lyman, E. R. *PLATO Highlights* (6th ed.). Urbana: University of Illinois, Computer-based Education Research Laboratory, March 1980.

McGuire, C., & Weyeman, F. *Educational Strategies for the Health Professions.* Geneva: World Health Organization, 1974.

Micro-PLATO. *Contact for Control Data People*, December 1980, pp. 2–3.

Minnesota Educational Computing Consortium. *1979–1980 Annual Report.* St. Paul, Minn.: The Consortium, 1980.

Mitzel, H. E. *Experimentation with Computer-assisted Instruction in Technical Education* (Final Report). University Park: Pennsylvania State University, Computer-assisted Instruction Laboratory, December 1969. (ERIC Document Reproduction Service No. ED 059 618)

Mitzel, H. E. Mobile computer-assisted instruction for inservice teacher education. *Journal of Educational Technology Systems*, 1974, *2*(4), 305–313.

Mitzel, H. E.; Brown, B. R.; & Igo, R. *The Development and Evaluation of a Teleprocessed Computer-assisted Course in the Recognition of Malarial Parasites* (Final Report R-17). University Park: Pennsylvania State University, Computer-assisted Instruction Laboratory, 1968. (ERIC Document Reproduction Service No. ED 042 325 and NTIS No. AD 702 476)

Mitzel, H. E.; Hall, K. A.; Kriner, B. H.; Johnson, D. W.; & Wodtke, K. H. *The Development of Four College Courses by Computer Teleprocessing* (Final report). University Park: Pennsylvania State University, Computer-assisted Instruction Laboratory, June 1967. (ERIC Document Reproduction Service No. ED 016 377)

Mitzel, H. E.; Hall, K. A.; Suydam, M. N.; Jansson, L. C.; & Igo, R. V. *A Commonwealth Consortium to Develop, Implement, and Evaluate a Pilot Program of Computer-assisted Instruction for Urban High Schools.* University Park: Pennsylvania State University, Computer-assisted Instruction Laboratory, July 1971. (ERIC Document Reproduction Service No. ED 059 604)

Murphy, R. T., & Appel, L. R. *Evaluation of PLATO IV Computer-based Education System in the Community College* (Final report). Princeton, N.J.: Educational Testing Service, June 1977. (ERIC Document Reproduction Service No. ED 146 235)

Navy Personnel and Training Research Laboratory. *Computer Applications in Education and Training: Status and Trends* (Special Report ADO 43 03X). San Diego, Calif.: The Laboratory, April 1973.

Obertino, P. The PLATO reading project: An overview. *Educational Technology*, February 1974, *14*(2), 8–13.

O'Dea, E. P. Computer-assisted instruction teaches computer system at IBM. *Training in Business and Industry*, 1971, *8*(3), 33–35.

Pagen, J., & Arnold, R. *Summary of the Activities and Findings of the INDICOM Project* (ESEA Title III, OEG 67-04301-0). Pontiac, Mich.: Waterford Township Schools, October 1970.

Papert, S. *Teaching Children Thinking* (LOGO MEMO 2). Cambridge, Mass.: Massachusetts Institute of Technology, Artificial Intelligence Laboratory, LOGO Group, October 1971.

PLATO's popularity raises Walbrook's reading rates. *Contact for Control Data People*, August 1979, pp. 14–15.

Ragosta, M. *The ETS-LAUSD Computer-assisted Instruction Project: Does CAI Work?* Paper presented at the annual conference of the American Educational Research Association, Los Angeles, 1981.

Rappaport, W., & Olenbush, E. Tailor-made teaching through TICCIT. *Mitre Matrix*, 1975, *8*(4). (ERIC Document Reproduction Service No. ED 121 328)

Reigeluth, C. M. TICCIT to the future: Advances in instructional theory for CAI. *Journal of Computer-based Instruction*, 1979, *6*(2), 40–48.

Resnikoff, H. L. Implications of advances in information science and technology for institutions of higher learning. *Educom*, 1981, *16*(1), 2–10.

Rich, J. J., & Van Pelt, K. B. *Survey of Computer Applications in Army Training* (CTS TR 74 3). Fort Monmouth, N.J.: U.S. Army Communications Electronics School, Office of the Product Manager, Computerized Training System, August 1974.

Robinson, T. E., & Lautenschlager, E. Preliminary evaluation study: Measuring computer-assisted instruction effectiveness in algebra II. In A. Dunn & J. Wastler (Eds.), *Computer-assisted Instruction Project Report* (ESEA Title III). Montgomery County, Md.: Montgomery County Public Schools, June 1971.

Rockway, M. R., & Yasutake, J. Y. The evaluation of the Air Force advanced instructional system. *Journal of Educational Technology Systems*, 1974, *2*(3), 217–239.

Roll, J. H., & Pasen, R. M. Computer-managed instruction produces better learning in an introductory psychology course. *1977 Conference on Computers in the Undergraduate Curricula*, 1977, *8*, 229–237.

Rosenfeld, F. H. The educational effectiveness of simulation games: A synthesis of recent findings. In C. S. Greenblat & R. D. Duke (Eds.), *Gaming-Simulation: Rationale, Design, and Applications.* New York: Wiley, 1975.

Rosenshine, B., & Furst, J. Current and future research on teacher performance criteria. In B. W. Smith (Ed.), *Research on Teacher Education: A Symposium.* Englewood Cliffs, N.J.: Prentice-Hall, 1971.

Rubin, H.; Geller, J.; & Hanks, J. Computer simulations as a teaching tool in biology. *Journal of Computer-based Instruction*, 1977, *3*(3), 91–96.

Scrivens, R. W. *Evaluation Monograph No. 1* (INDICOM Project, ESEA Title III). Pontiac, Mich.: Waterford Township Schools, 1970.

Seidel, R. J.; Rosenblatt, R.; Wagner, H.; Schulz, R.; & Hunter, B. *Evaluation of a Prototype Computerized Training System (CTS) in Support of Self-pacing and Management of Instruction* (HumRRO FR ED 78 10). Alexandria, Va.: Human Resources Research Organization, August 1978.

Skakun, E. N.; Taylor, W. C.; & Wilson, D. R. Computerized patient management problems as part of the pediatrics certifying examination. *Journal of Computer-based Instruction*, 1978, *4*(4), 79–83.

Smith, S. G. The use of computers in the teaching of organic chemistry. *Journal of Chemical Education*, 1970, *47*, 608–611.

Spuck, D. W.; Hunter, S. N.; Owen, S. P.; & Belt, S. L. *Computer Management of Individualized Instruction*. Madison; Wisconsin University, Research and Development Center for Cognitive Learning, 1975. (ERIC Document Reproduction Service No. ED 112 869)

Stolte, J. B., & Smith, S. C. *A Computer-based Approach to Functional Literacy Training for Recruits: Performance-related Enabling Skills Training (PREST)*. Philadelphia; Research for Better Schools, Inc., April 1980. (ERIC Document Reproduction Service No. ED 185 505)

Suppes, P. Computer-assisted instruction at Stanford. In *Man and Computer* (Proceedings of International Conference, Bordeaux 1970). Basel: Karger, 1972.

Suppes, P. *Research on the Uses of Audio and Natural-language Processing in Computer-assisted Instruction* (Annual Tech. Rep., July 1974/1975). Stanford, Calif.: Stanford University, Institute for Mathematical Studies in the Social Sciences, 1975.

Suppes, P.; Jerman, M.; & Brian, D. *Computer-assisted Instruction: Stanford's 1965–1966 Arithmetic Program*. New York: Academic Press, 1968.

Suppes, P., & Macken, E. The historical path from research and development to operational use of CAI. *Educational Technology*, 1978, *18*(4), 9–12.

Suppes, P., & Morningstar, M. Computer-assisted instruction. *Science*, 1969, *166*, 343–350.

Suppes, P., & Morningstar, M. *Computer-assisted Instruction at Stanford, 1966–1968: Data, Models, and Evaluation of the Arithmetic Programs*. New York: Academic Press, 1972.

Suppes, P.; Smith, R.; & Beard, M. University-level computer-assisted instruction at Stanford: 1975. *Instructional Science*, 1977, *6*, 151–185.

Tansey, P. J., & Unwin, D. Computers and simulation. In P. J. Tansey & D. Unwin (Eds.), *Simulation and Gaming in Education*. London: Methuen, 1969.

U.S., Congress, House, Committee on Science and Technology. *Computers and the Learning Society*. 95th Cong., 2nd sess. Washington, D.C.: U.S. Government Printing Office, June 1978.

Van Matre, N. *The Many Uses of Evaluation in the Navy's CMI System*. Paper presented at the annual meeting of the Association for the Development of Computer Based Instructional Systems, Dallas, 1978. (ERIC Document Reproduction Service No. ED 165 709)

Vinsonhaler, J., & Bass, R. A summary of ten major studies of CAI drill and practice. *Educational Technology*, 1972, *12*, 29–32.

Wang, A. C. *Index to Computer-based Learning*. Milwaukee: University of Wisconsin, Instructional Media Laboratory, 1976.

Wisher, R. A. *Computer-assisted Literacy Instruction in Phonics*. San Diego, Calif.: Navy Personnel Research and Development Center, April 1980. (ERIC Document Reproduction Service No. ED 190 067)

Wodtke, K. H. Educational requirements for a student-subject matter interface. *Proceedings of AFIPS Spring Joint Computer Conference*, 1967, *30*, 403–411.

Zinn, K. L. Computer assistance for instruction: A review of systems and projects. In D. D. Bushnell & D. W. Allen (Eds.), *The Computer in American Education*. New York: Wiley, 1967. (a)

Zinn, K. L. Computer technology for teaching and research on instruction. *Review of Educational Research*, 1967, *37*(5), 618–634. (b)

COMPUTING

See Archives and Records Management; Computer-Based Education; Information Management and Computing.

CONCEPT FORMATION

See Cognition and Memory; Learning; Psychology.

CONSUMER ECONOMICS EDUCATION

Consumerism grew into a powerful social movement during the 1970s as Americans became increasingly aware of their role as participants in the economic marketplace. Concurrent with that movement, consumer education reappeared on the educational scene following a fifteen-year absence. By the end of the decade, consumer education existed in some form in nearly forty states.

History. Chandler (1974), Langrehr and Mason (1977), and Royer and Nolf (1980) have documented the history of consumer education, tracing its roots to the consumer movement. The initial consumer movement developed near the close of the nineteenth century. Responding to rapid industrialization, its original concerns ironically were less with products and more with labor conditions. The National Consumers' League (NCL), founded in 1891, organized boycotts of businesses whose workers were mistreated. Only after two decades of popular literature by muckrakers, who exposed problems of consumers, did the NCL and others begin to call for government regulation and to support issues relating to product safety. In 1929, Consumers Research, Inc. was formed, marking the initiation of product testing.

During the first two decades of the century, consumer education appeared in formal schooling only in isolated locales. Courses or units were offered first in "domestic science" and later in homemaking. The curriculum had a decidedly antibusiness orientation and developed skills in choice making, budgeting, and buymanship. Hazel Kyrk (1923) and Henry Harap (1927) pioneered national attention for the need to educate consumers formally. Both writers attempted to move consumer education away from domestic science and to align it with economics.

The first major impetus for implementing consumer education coincided with the great Depression. The decline of real income due to wage reductions and high unemployment forced consumers to maximize their reduced buying power. Advocates of the Life Adjustment Education Curriculum, growing out of the Progressive Education Movement, claimed that nearly 50 percent of students were not college-bound. Citing the irrelevance of economic theory, many educators urged that economics education be made more practical and consumer-oriented.

The first text on consumer education for secondary schools appeared in the 1930s, and high schools began to incorporate consumer topics into home economics, business, social studies, and mathematics courses. Special emphasis on consumer conservation also appeared in the science curriculum. A trend against advertising, reflective of the broader consumer movement, was evident in these curricula. By 1939, 25,000 secondary schools offered courses in consumer education, although two-thirds of the students were female. A curriculum study conducted in the 1940s (*Consumer Education in Your School,* 1947) revealed that nearly one-quarter of all secondary schools offered consumer education as a separate course. The study, sponsored jointly by the National Association of Secondary School Principals (NASSP) and the National Council for Better Business Bureaus, helped shift the curriculum away from its antibusiness emphasis and broadened it to include economic decision making, value analysis, health, and use of leisure time, as well as buymanship. By the close of the 1940s, however, defense concerns of World War II predominated, and consumer education waned. Although the first two editions of the *Encyclopedia of Educational Research* (1941, 1950) contained entries on "consumer education," the third and fourth editions (1960, 1969) did not. Those deletions paralleled the declining interest in consumerism in general.

Russia's successful space program prompted reaction against the Life Adjustment Curriculum during the early 1960s. Opponents charged that its courses were largely anti-intellectual. As consumer education continued to lose favor, economics education and other college preparatory courses regained prominence because they were viewed to be pure sciences. By 1965, a bulletin on economics education, published by the former supporter of consumer education NASSP, contained no references to consumer issues.

The current revival of consumer education began in the mid-1960s. A high dropout rate renewed interest in the student not bound for college. As calls for a relevant curriculum were heard, consumer education found renewed favor, and some high schools replaced economics courses with consumer education. The federal government expressed interest in educating consumers for the first time when President Kennedy established a Special Assistant to the President on Consumer Affairs in 1962. A year later, he delivered a special message to Congress on consumer interests.

Current Status. Consumer education seems presently to be influenced more by federal regulation than by local impetus. The Vocational Education Amendments of 1968 appropriated the first federal money for consumer education. By 1980, the Department of Education contained an Office of Consumers' Education that issued grants and contracts for research and implementation projects to private and public nonprofit agencies as well as to local, state, and higher-education institutions. Legislation required bilingual consumer education; federally funded efforts also focused on other special groups, such as physically handicapped, mentally retarded, and poverty-stricken consumers.

The form that consumer education takes among the states varies considerably. A survey by Alexander (1979) reported policies for the fifty states and the District of Columbia. Thirty-eight have policies that include topics of consumer education; two of those policies are stated in competency requirements while seven policies merely encourage it to be taught. Six of the states mandate that the state education agency develop guidelines, but do not require that consumer education be offered by local schools. Twenty-four states require students to receive instruction in consumer education at the elementary and/or secondary level. In most cases, instruction may be integrated into other courses, including economics education. Only Idaho and Oregon require a separate high school course. Thirteen states have no consumer-education policy beyond policies (or regulations) applying to vocational education.

Curriculum. *Consumer Education in Your School* (1947) analyzed the curriculum of early courses. More recently, the Consumers Union sponsored a Consumer Economics Materials Project (CEMP) to review programs from early childhood through the years of higher education. In early-childhood education, young children usually are objects of study (Consumer Economics Materials Project, 1973a). Consumer topics in the elementary grades appear incidentally in mathematics problems and more systematically in some social studies curricula. Conservation and energy issues usually appear in elementary science. There are no formal textbooks on consumer education for these grades (Consumer Economics Materials Project, 1972).

At the secondary level, consumer education may be offered as a separate course or be integrated into an existing course in home economics, business, or social studies. Herrmann (1979) analyzed fifteen high school textbooks in consumer education published over a forty-year period and found little uniformity in content. Only four topics—budgeting, savings and investment, life insurance, and housing—were common to all texts. The textbooks, as a group, inadequately discussed the effects of inflation, the consumer movement, product safety, the growing influence of corporate power, or such social changes as the effect of having two wage earners in a family.

Adult consumer education abounds in the news media and agencies in the community. Colleges and universities offer formal courses through departments of home economics and business. Some social studies educators incorporate consumer education into their methods courses. A small number of universities offers graduate programs in consumer education, although the degree is in home economics, not in consumer education *per se.*

Research on Consumer Awareness. Numerous status studies document the consumer awareness (or lack of it) among adolescents. One of the most comprehensive surveys was conducted in a special probe of 17-year-olds by the National Assessment of Educational Progress (1979). Consumer competence was tested by evaluating skills related to consumer behavior, economics, energy, consumer mathematics, personal finance, and consumer protection. Groups that significantly exceeded the national average included males, whites, and students from the Midwest and from suburban areas. Scoring significantly below the national average were females, blacks, and students from the Southeast and the West and from big cities.

Relatively little attention has been given to children's cognitive development of consumer concepts. Two studies (Fox, 1978; McKenzie, 1970) have sought to assess the emergence as well as the confusion of such economic concepts among young children and preadolescents. Not surprisingly, they found that very little awareness of concepts existed. Another pair of studies focused on the behavior of young consumers. McNeal (1964) investigated middle-class children's independent purchases when shopping with their parents. A major study by Ward (1971) documented the effects of television advertising on children and adolescents.

Because courses in consumer education are offered in some middle and high schools, considerable attention has been given to the effectiveness of the curricula there. Most studies have been unable to distinguish a significant difference in consumer competency between students who took a single course in consumer education and those who took no course (see Langrehr, 1979). Only two studies (Langrehr, 1979; Cogle, 1977) have found significant gains among students enrolled in consumer education.

Research that compares two or more consumer-education curricula through experimental design is scarce. Nappi (1972) found that inquiry-oriented instructional materials were significantly more effective than were traditional materials among high school students in business and home economics, but not in social studies. Another study compared formal, systematic instruction with a series of informal shopping simulations among preschool children. Systematic instruction was significantly more effective (Stampfl, Moschis, & Lawton, 1978).

Problems of Consumer Education. Five major problems confront consumer education. They are the lack of professional orientation and of uniform curriculum content and the need for well-prepared teachers, adequate research funding, and a unifying national network.

Professional orientation. Most research and writing in consumer education is conducted by professional educators whose primary orientation is either home economics education, business education, or social studies education. Only a small cadre of persons are primarily dedicated to consumer education. Consequently, consumer education is largely a secondary field of study, and its focus is therefore diluted. Each discipline treats consumer topics differently. Home economists tend to emphasize personal finance and product testing; business teachers focus on consumer behavior; and social studies educators stress economic principles.

Curriculum content. Definitions of "consumer education" by the major advocates in the field vary so much as to defy agreement. The issue of definition is reflected in curriculum content which ranges from practical personal finance to a theoretical economic orientation. Textbooks and courses abound with facts, but generally lack basic principles to guide future decision making. The curriculum responds largely to the popular but changing concerns expressed by the consumer movement; it is less responsive to real social change. It also lacks the educational, and philosophical foundations that undergird most disciplines (Herrmann, 1979).

Royer and Nolf (1980) have singled out problems relative to curriculum materials. They indicate that the immediate nature of consumer concerns makes it difficult to produce textbooks that are current for any length of time. Publications for the elementary level are nearly nonexistent; at the secondary level they are inadequate. Some are biased by the business, consumer-advocacy group, or governmental agency that produces them. As a group, these publications tend to oversimplify complex issues and to present a single point of view. Rarely do consumer-education texts include economic aspects of consumer problems. Moreover, the field lacks widely accepted criteria for assessing either materials or programs.

Teacher training. One national assessment found that prospective secondary school teachers in all academic disciplines did not possess high levels of consumer understanding (Garman, 1979). Fewer than 12 percent had taken a college-level consumer-education course, although those who did scored higher. No states certify teachers in consumer education; teacher education and certification programs rarely single out consumer-education courses as training requirements. Although federal appropriations have included monies to train home economics teachers in consumerism, generally little effort has been directed at improving teacher education in the field. Even one CEMP study felt that "the interested educator needed only study the literature in the field" to meet students' needs in consumer-education adequately (Consumer Economics Materials Project, 1973b, p. 10). Many teachers who acquire responsibility for consumer-education instruction have had no course in either consumer or economics education.

Research funding. Federal money, susceptible to the whims of changing politics, is not a stable source for financing consumer-education research. In 1978 and 1979, the Office of Consumers' Education distributed $3 million in grants and contracts. Only 10 percent of the nearly 700 applications were funded; 80 percent were awarded to agencies outside of higher education.

National network. Several national organizations fulfill disparate needs of consumer educators. At the postsecondary level is the American Council on Consumer Interests (ACCI), originally named the Council on Consumer Interests when formed in 1953. Its members are predominantly university professors. The council publishes the semiannual *Journal of Consumer Affairs,* which contains articles on a wide range of consumer topics. Although, ACCI disdains financial support from business, the Conference of Consumer Organizations (COCO), formed in 1973, actively solicits research funding from the private sector. A grant from the Office of Consumers' Education also supports operation of the Consumer Education Resource Network (CERN), which disseminates consumer-education information. Nevertheless, consumer education lacks a single national network to unite classroom teachers, university researchers, and consumer agencies in the community. None of the existing organizations, including the Office of Consumers' Education, effectively orchestrates research, publication, or project development in the way that the Joint Council on Economic Education functions in economic education.

In spite of its nearly fifty-year history, consumer education is a largely undeveloped field. It lacks a definitive body of knowledge and seems to be constantly searching for academic respectability. In view of the present emphasis from the federal level, whether or not that respectability is attained may depend on the political biases of each political administration.

Sharon Pray Muir

See also Economic Education; Health Education; Home Economics Education; Nutrition Education.

REFERENCES

Alexander, R. J. *State Consumer Education Policy Manual.* Denver: Education Commission of the States, 1979. (ERIC Document Reproduction Service No. 168 926).

Chandler, C. Consumer education: Past and present. *Social Studies,* 1974, *65,* 146–150.

Cogle, F. L. The effectiveness of teaching consumer education concepts as determined by test scores of secondary students in home economics (Doctoral dissertation, Florida State University, 1977). *Dissertation Abstracts International,* 1977, *38A,* 2613–2614. (University Microfilms No. 77–24, 750).

Consumer Economics Materials Project. *Elementary-level Consumer Education.* Mt. Vernon, N.Y.: Consumers Union, 1972.

Consumer Economics Materials Project. *Early Childhood Consumer Education.* Mt. Vernon, N.Y.: Consumers Union, 1973. (a)

Consumer Economics Materials Project. *Preparing the Consumer Educator.* Mt. Vernon, N.Y.: Consumers Union, 1973. (b)

Consumer Education in Your School. Washington, D.C.: National Education Association, 1947.

Fox, K. F. A. What children bring to school: The beginnings of economic education. *Social Education,* 1978, *42,* 478–481.

Garman, E. T. The cognitive consumer education knowledge of prospective teachers: A national assessment. *Journal of Consumer Affairs,* 1979, *13*:1, 54–63.

Harap, H. *Economic Life and the Curriculum.* New York: Macmillan, 1927.

Herrmann, R. O. *The Historical Development of the Content of High-School-Level Consumer Education: An Examination of Selected Texts, 1938–1978.* Washington, D.C.: Office of Consumers Education, 1979. (ERIC Document Reproduction Service No. ED 185 431).

Kyrk, H. *A Theory of Consumption.* Boston: Houghton Mifflin, 1923.

Langrehr, F. W. Consumer education: Does it change students' competencies and attitudes? *Journal of Consumer Affairs,* 1979, *13*:1, 41–53.

Langrehr, F. W., & Mason, J. B. The development and implementation of the concept of consumer education. *Journal of Consumer Affairs,* 1977, *11*:2, 63–79.

McKenzie, R. B. The economic literacy of elementary school pupils. *Elementary School Journal,* 1970, *71,* 26–35.

McNeal, J. V. *Children as Consumers.* Austin: University of Texas, Bureau of Business Research, 1964.

Nappi, A. T. *A Project to Create and Validate Curriculum Materials in Consumer Education for High School Students.* St. Cloud, Minn.: St. Cloud State College, 1972. (ERIC Document Reproduction Service No. ED 072 514)

National Assessment of Educational Progress. *Teenage Consumers: A Profile.* Denver: Education Commission of the States, 1979. (ERIC Document Reproduction Service No. ED 174 801)

Royer, L. G., & Nolf, N. E. *Education of the Consumer: A Review of Historical Developments.* Rosslyn, Va.: Consumer Education Resource Network, 1980.

Stampfl, R. W.; Moschis, G.; & Lawton, J. T. Consumer education and the preschool child. *Journal of Consumer Affairs,* 1978, *12*:1, 12–29.

Ward, S. *Effects of Television Advertising on Children and Adolescents.* Cambridge, Mass.: Marketing Science Institute, 1971.

CONTINUING EDUCATION

See Adult Education; Distance Education; Experiential Education; Independent Study; Nontraditional Higher Education Programs.

CORRECTIONAL EDUCATION

Correctional education is the part of the total correctional process of changing behaviors of offenders that employs purposefully contrived learning experiences to develop knowledge, skills, attitudes, and values. It seeks to bring about behavioral changes that will be implemented in positive self-concepts and socially acceptable and productive roles in the free society (Ryan, 1970).

Correctional education is only about fifty years old, although prisons came into existence in this country some two hundred years ago (Eckenrode, 1971). The genesis of correctional education can be traced to early attempts by chaplains to reform prisoners. Conducted at night or on Sundays, "correctional education was . . . the chaplain standing in the semi-dark corridor, before the cell door, with a dingy lantern hanging to the grated bars, and teaching to the wretched convict in the darkness beyond the grated door the rudiments of reading or numbers" (Lewis, 1922, p. 341). In 1870 the American Prison Association, later to become the American Correctional Association, was formed and proclaimed in its declaration of principles that the primary goal of prisons was not to punish but to reform by providing academic education and vocational training to prisoners (Henderson, 1910). Education and vocational training were to receive primary emphasis in prisons. Correctional education for adults has had a continuous, though sporadic and nonsystematic, growth since the early efforts of the chaplains and the establishment of the American Prison Association. Every federal facility has correctional education. Almost all state prisons have some educational programs. To a lesser degree, education is provided in jails and detention facilities (Bell et al., 1979).

Correctional education for youthful offenders was provided by private agencies until 1847, when the Lyman School opened in Massachusetts. The juvenile court system that developed at the end of the nineteenth century reinforced the idea that youthful offenders needed education and training. Most juvenile training schools had academic educational programs through the eighth grade by 1970. A few had high school programs, but because of the relatively short length of sentence, few juvenile offenders graduated from high school. The underlying philosophy of institutions for youthful offenders, contrary to the philosophy of adult corrections, has been that juveniles should be educated and treated rather than punished.

Types of Programs. Correctional education is located within correctional institutions and in the community. Programs are found in adult prisons and jails and in juvenile training schools and detention facilities. A 1974 census of state correctional facilities found that at least 65 percent of the institutions had individual counseling, remedial education, job placement, group counseling, vocational training, prevocational training, and/or college degree courses (National Criminal Justice Information and Statistics Service, 1975). The United States Bureau of Prisons has the most extensive education and training programs for inmates.

The four correctional education programs most common in institutions are (1) adult basic education (ABE), (2) high school diploma–General Education Development (GED) Certificate, (3) postsecondary education and training, and (4) vocational education and training.

Adult Basic Education (ABE) programs are remedial in nature, designed to bring inmates at least to a sixth-grade level in reading, writing, and computation. Most inmates enrolled in ABE classes are functionally illiterate.

The high school diploma and General Education Development (GED) Certificate programs are the counterparts of the three-year or four-year secondary education programs in the public schools. There are relatively few high school diploma programs in which students are required to take specified subjects and earn a given number of credit hours with passing grades to earn a diploma. Most institutions have GED programs in which students are prepared to take the GED test and qualify for a High School Equivalency Certificate.

Postsecondary education is provided through college courses, usually offered as a cooperative effort between the institution and nearby two-year and/or four-year colleges. Courses are offered on a contract basis by faculty from the colleges and are held within the prison walls. Postsecondary education also is provided through correspondence courses. Payment for tuition and books usually is the responsibility of the students. However, inmate students generally are eligible for the same financial aid as students enrolled on college campuses.

Vocational education and training programs seek to develop job-related skills and to prepare inmates for gainful employment. Vocational education includes prevocational, formal vocational/technical, apprenticeship, and on-the-job training.

In addition to the four most common correctional education programs, social education, counseling, and recreation are found in increasing numbers in institutions. Social education in correction is designed to prepare inmates for reintegration into society and to help them develop self-understanding and healthy, positive self-concepts. Counseling usually is part of the admission and orientation program. Academic teachers, vocational instructors, and full-time counselors assist adult offenders in areas of personal problems, educational planning, and career development. The use of full-time counselors is relatively recent. Recreational programs include physical education, crafts, art, and music. The aim is to develop physical fitness and to provide opportunities for inmates to release tensions in healthy, positive ways while they learn satisfying and constructive ways of using leisure time.

Correctional education in jails differs from that in prisons. A 1979 American Correctional Association survey of local jails found little general education, academic education, study release, furlough, or vocational training in jails. One study of correctional education in jails concluded that custody and security issues take priority over educational programming, with the result that education is undermined (Mennerick, 1974). The physical facilities of the jails generally do not lend themselves to educational programs.

One of the largest educational programs in an adult jail is in the Cook County Jail in Chicago. Programmed

Activities for Correctional Education (PACE) was founded in 1968 by a prison chaplain who had concluded that religious training by itself was not enough to prepare inmates for a successful return to society (Grindstaff, 1980). The program offered by PACE Institute emphasizes individualized instruction and development of realistic self-concepts.

Whereas correctional education in adult facilities by and large relies on voluntary enrollment, participation in educational programs generally is compulsory for youthful offenders. Correctional education—including academic education, vocational education, counseling, and recreation—is in every juvenile training institution in the nation. However, the range of education opportunities for youth in detention facilities is greatly limited compared with the offerings in the training institutions (Fritsch & McCoy, 1979). Because of this limitation, there are more youthful offenders enrolled in community correctional education than adults. Correctional education in the community is provided through public and private schools and alternative schools. Alternative programs to meet the needs of socially deviant, primarily youthful offenders are used to divert juveniles who are first offenders. Two alternative schools cited by the Law Enforcement Assistance Administration (1977) as exemplary are Project New Pride in Denver and Providence Education Center in St. Louis. The primary focus of correctional education for adults and juveniles is on development of basic literary skills, after which the emphasis is on vocational training to develop job-related skills.

Administration. The administration of correctional education has no single or predominant pattern. State and local agencies of corrections, juvenile justice, and education—with varying degrees of autonomy—administer correctional education. Inmates are not involved directly in the administration of correctional education. Inmate councils may provide advice and counsel to correctional education administrators, and inmates may be employed as teachers, tutors, or teaching aides.

The administration of correctional education for youthful offenders is as varied as that for adults. In small juvenile facilities, one teacher responsible for programming in all academic areas may report to the chief administrator of the institution (Fritsch & McCoy, 1979). In large reformatories or training schools, the teachers and counselors may report to a principal or supervisor, who in turn reports to the superintendent.

Correctional education in a relatively small number of states is administered through special school districts. This is done by legislation to establish a nongeographical school district consisting of all the educational programs offered by the state correctional agency. The Windham School District, Texas Department of Corrections, is an example of a nongeographical school district. This school district provides education and training for inmates of the entire Texas prison system and is subject to the certification requirements and regulations of the Texas Education Agency and the State Board of Education (Murray, 1980).

There are advantages and disadvantages to the school district administration of correctional education. Although few states use the school district administration, it is generally agreed that the establishment of correctional school districts has been advantageous in separate funding for education and training programs (McCollum, 1977). The correctional school district is able to obtain federal funds routinely allocated to local educational school systems. The Windham School District budget for 1979/80, for example, was approximately $6.5 million (Murray, 1980).

A disadvantage to using the school district administration comes from not having a clearly defined chain of command. Parity of responsibility and authority is generally lacking. The administrators, teachers, counselors, and support staff for the correctional-education programs are employed by state educational agencies and hence are not responsible to correctional agency or institutional administrators.

In some states correctional education is administered through contract with local or county school systems. Administration of correctional education by local or county school districts has the same disadvantage as administration by state educational agencies. Employees tend to hold allegiance to the educational agency. They are not always familiar with problems peculiar to a prison school (Center, 1978).

Characteristics of Students. There are 5,312 correctional institutions in the United States, housing about 400,000 inmates, including adult and juvenile offenders. The individuals making up the prison population of adult and youthful offenders are as diverse in age, experience, aptitude, interests, and personal characteristics as the general population from which they come.

A study by the Education Commission of the States (1976) concluded that from 20 to 50 percent of adults incarcerated in federal and state prisons can neither read nor write, up to 90 percent are school dropouts, and more than 50 percent of adults over 18 years old have less than an eighth-grade education. Most adult offenders have distorted values, poor self-concepts, learning disabilities (Ryan, 1973).

There were 45,090 juveniles confined in institutions in the United States on December 31, 1977 (National Criminal Justice Information and Statistics Service, 1979). This statistic includes only juveniles already adjudicated as delinquents and does not take into account those in jails, detention facilities, group homes, and adult facilities. Delinquent youths typically are low in educational achievement, particularly in the skill areas of mathematics and reading (Jerse & Fakouri, 1978). They expect failure and lack self-discipline and self-confidence. The learning disabilities that are most common for youthful offenders are emotional handicap, reading difficulty, cultural disadvantage, and behavioral or social problems (Education Commission of the States, 1976).

Effects. Studies have been made that suggest that participation in correctional education reduces recidivism and rearrest rates (Bennett & Chatman, 1979; Clendenan & Severson, 1979; Constantine & Whitney, 1975; Neil & Harvey, 1976; Price & Price, 1980; Shandera, 1980). There is no doubt that the acquisition of job-related skills and the improvement of educational achievement may contribute to successful reentry to society after incarceration. However, correctional education in and of itself probably cannot significantly reduce recidivism or rearrest. Many factors are involved in reintegration of the offender into society, and the quality of correctional education is just one of these. The comptroller general of the United States (1979) concluded, "Even the most highly educated and trained offender will have difficulty in finding employment if there are poor economic conditions in his community" (p. 9). Often the physical facilities and equipment used for education and training programs are outdated. The comptroller general (1979) concluded that the Bureau of Prisons and state correctional agencies have not done enough to improve employability of inmates in their care. Postrelease employment requires an understanding of the job market and good academic and vocational counseling, and both are reputed to be missing from correctional programs (Polcyn, 1977).

Both adult and youthful offenders enrolled in correctional education while incarcerated can and do raise their levels of educational achievement significantly. Factors contributing to increase in educational achievement levels of adult and youthful offenders are performance contracting, individualized instruction, and computer-assisted instruction (Eller, 1979; McAfee, 1980; System Development Corporation, 1977). Programmed Logic for Automatic Teaching (PLATO) has been one of the most effective computer-assisted instructional programs for use with offenders.

There is not much research to support the assumption that correctional education leads to changes in attitudes, improvement in self-concept, and increase in motivation. The difficulties associated with operationalizing and measuring components of the affective domain generally have plagued researchers trying to establish links between correctional education and affective changes of inmates. Added to this is the fact that most, if not all, inmates tend to give socially desirable responses and are very adept at doing so. In their national evaluation of correctional education programs, Bell et al. (1979) found little to help develop inmates' motivation. With few exceptions, correctional education has not been successful in bringing about affective changes. The introduction of social education has brought attention to this important area of behavioral change.

Future. The Commission of Accreditation for Corrections sponsored by the American Correctional Association, adopted standards for adult correctional institutions (1977b), adult community residential services (1977a), adult local detention facilities (1977c), adult parole authorities (1976), adult probation and parole field services (1977d), juvenile probation and aftercare services (1978b), juvenile community residential services (1978a), juvenile detention facilities (1979a), and juvenile training schools (1979b). These standards, generally expected to be the norms of the future of corrections and juvenile justice, mandate quality education and training. The future will see dramatic changes in correctional education, both in quantity and quality. There will be a greater involvement of the community and private industry in planning and delivering correctional education, a greatly increased use of technology, and a strengthening of administration.

Alternative education programs will be increased for youthful offenders. Both adult and youthful offenders will be enrolled in local educational systems. More attention will be given to liaison between correctional education and job placement. The adaptation of community programs to the needs of ex-offenders and offenders will be realized in the future; however, in the face of the current state of the economy, a future of diminishing resources, and the shifting of priorities away from support for corrections, it can be anticipated that progress will be slow for the next two decades.

Correctional education programs will be open-entry, open-exit. Individually prescribed instruction will be supplemented by group-process dynamics. Social education, career education, recreation, and counseling will be greatly increased and improved. On-campus college enrollments, work-study programs, and study-release programs will be utilized much more extensively. Curriculum development will rely on behavioral objectives, task analyses, job analyses, skill clusters, and competency-based modules.

In the delivery of correctional education in the institutions, cells will be equipped with computer keyboards and viewing screens. Inmates will have access to telephones enabling them to discuss issues and ask questions of instructors and other students. The use of satellite technology will change the delivery of academic education, counseling, and job placement. It also will affect staffing, curriculum development, and instructional materials. Satellite technology permits an aggregate of widely dispersed individuals to share and use a resource that they cannot afford as individuals. Satellite technology will also make it possible for correctional institutions to pool their limited resources to obtain services that are not possible otherwise. Corrections will become a powerful reconstructive force, contributing to the positive development of youth and adults who have transgressed the laws and been sentenced or adjudicated to adult or juvenile correctional systems.

T. A. Ryan

See also Adult Education; Behavioral Treatment Methods; Vocational Education.

REFERENCES

Bell, R.; Conard, E.; Laffey, T.; Lutz, J. G.; Miller, P. V.; Simon, C.; Stakelon, A. E.; & Wilson, N. J. *National Evaluation Program, Phase I Report: Correctional Education Programs for*

Inmates. Washington, D.C.: Law Enforcement Assistance Administration, 1979. (ERIC Document Reproduction Service No. ED 175 982)

Bennett, L. A., & Chatman, L. What works in adult corrections? New careers revisited. *Offender Rehabilitation,* 1979, *3,* 325–339.

Center, S. Priorities and political considerations affect education programs at prisons in large cities. *American Journal of Correction,* 1978, *40,* 32–33.

Clendenan, R. J., & Severson, R. J. Project Newgate: The first five years. *Crime and Delinquency,* 1979, *24,* 55–64.

Commission on Accreditation for Corrections. *Manual of Standards for Adult Parole Authorities.* Rockville, Md.: The Commission, 1976.

Commission on Accreditation for Corrections. *Manual of Standards for Adult Community Residential Services.* Rockville, Md.: The Commission, 1977. (a)

Commission on Accreditation for Corrections. *Manual of Standards for Adult Correctional Institutions.* Rockville, Md.: The Commission, 1977. (b)

Commission on Accreditation for Corrections. *Manual of Standards for Adult Local Detention Facilities.* Rockville, Md.: The Commission, 1977. (c)

Commission on Accreditation for Corrections. *Manual of Standards for Adult Probation and Parole Field Services.* Rockville, Md.: The Commission, 1977. (d)

Commission on Accreditation for Corrections. *Manual of Standards for Juvenile Community Residential Services.* Rockville, Md.: The Commission, 1978. (a)

Commission on Accreditation for Corrections. *Manual of Standards for Juvenile Probation and Aftercare Services.* Rockville, Md.: The Commission, 1978. (b)

Commission on Accreditation for Corrections. *Manual of Standards for Juvenile Detention Facilities and Services.* Rockville, Md.: The Commission, 1979. (a)

Commission on Accreditation for Corrections. *Manual for Standards for Juvenile Training Schools and Services.* Rockville, Md.: The Commission, 1979. (b)

Comptroller General of the United States. *Report to the Congress: Correctional Institutions Can Do More to Improve the Employability of Offenders.* Washington, D.C.: The Comptroller General, 1979.

Constantine, M., & Whitney, G. PACE (Programmed Activities for Correctional Education) Institute versus traditional education. *Journal of Correctional Education,* 1975, *27,* 10–13.

Eckenrode, C. J. Institutional and community resources. Honolulu: University of Hawaii, Education Research and Development Center, 1971. (Mimeo)

Education Commission of the States, Correctional Education Project. *Correctional Education: A Forgotten Human Service.* Denver: The Commission, 1976.

Eller, B. F. An analysis of the effect of tutorial contracting on the academic grades and truancy rates of delinquent and low-achieving students. *Offender Rehabilitation,* 1979, *3,* 229–243.

Fritsch, R. E., & McCoy, K. M. The role of special education in the juvenile detention center. *Journal of Correctional Education,* 1979, *30,* 8–10.

Grindstaff, G. Volunteers: An invaluable resource at Cook County Jail. *Corrections Today,* 1980, *42,* 86–87.

Henderson, C. R. *Prison Reform and Criminal Law.* New York: Russell Sage, 1910.

Jerse, F. W., & Fakouri, M. E. Juvenile delinquency and academic deficiency. *Contemporary Education,* 1978, *49,* 106–109.

Law Enforcement Assistance Administration. *Exemplary Projects.* Washington, D.C.: The Administration, 1977.

Lewis, O. F. *The Development of American Prisons and Prison Customs, 1776–1845.* Albany: Prison Association of New York, 1922.

McAfee, D. T. Individualized instruction for residents. *Journal of Correctional Education,* 1980, *31,* 17–19.

McCollum, S. G. What works! A look at effective correctional education and training experiences. *Federal Probation,* 1977, *41,* 32–35.

Mennerick, L. A. Constraining influence of the custody-security emphasis on a county jail school. *Kansas Journal of Sociology,* 1974, pp. 29–41.

Murray, L. National Advisory Council: Public hearings on the status of vocational education in correctional institutions. *Journal of Correctional Education,* 1980, *31,* 8–11.

National Criminal Justice Information and Statistics Service. *Census on State Correctional Facilities, 1974.* Washington, D.C.: The Service, 1975.

National Criminal Justice Information and Statistics Service. *Children in Custody: Advance Report on the 1977 Census of Public Juvenile Facilities.* Washington, D.C.: The Service, 1979.

Neil, T. C., & Harvey, J. W. School attendance and discipline. *Journal of Correctional Education,* 1976, *28,* 10–11.

Polcyn, K. A. Communication satellite technology. *Journal of Correctional Education,* 1977, *28,* 7–15.

Price, T., & Price, L. Correctional education: A humanistic and treatment approach. *Journal of Correctional Education,* 1980, *31,* 8–12.

Ryan, T. A. *Model of Adult Basic Education in Corrections.* Honolulu: University of Hawaii, 1970. (ERIC Document Reproduction Service No. ED 124 711)

Ryan, T. A. A model for correctional education. In Policy Institute, *School Behind Bars.* Syracuse, N.Y.: Syracuse University Research Corporation, 1973, pp. 153–244. (ERIC Document Reproduction Service No. ED 083 340)

Shandera, D. Satisfaction in correctional education: A teacher's perspective. *Journal of Correctional Education,* 1980, *31,* 18–20.

System Development Corporation. Studies and Evaluation Department. In *Compensatory Education and Confined Youth: A National Evaluation of Title I Programs in State Institutions for Neglected or Delinquent Youth* (Vol. 1). Santa Monica, Calif.: The Corporation, 1977.

U.S. National Institute of Law Enforcement and Criminal Justice. *An Exemplary Project: Project New Pride.* Washington, D.C.: U.S. Government Printing Office, 1977. (ERIC Document Reproduction Service No. ED 145 178)

CORRESPONDENCE INSTRUCTION

See Adult Education; Distance Education; Independent Study; Individualized Systems of Instruction; Nontraditional Higher Education Programs.

COUNSELING

Counseling has moved from an almost exclusively student-focused orientation held prior to the 1950s and 1960s to an orientation that now emphasizes the life span. Counselors now work with individuals ranging from preschool to retirement age. Counseling with these individuals deals with issues that include careers and their many ramifications, social development and interpersonal skills, cognitive-skill development, performance skills and their development, family and marital relations (including divorce mediation), development of personal potential, remediation including rehabilitation of the disabled, health and leisure, psychotherapy for the psychologically disturbed, stress management, and cross-cultural matters.

Not only has the focus of counseling broadened from the original student orientation, but counselors also now function as consultants. Consultation differs from counseling in that it does not itself deal with a primary population, but rather with prevention and treatment of problems through an intermediary. Counselors also develop and evaluate training programs, do group counseling and intervention through several types of group activity, conduct individual evaluation and program evaluation, engage in program development and implementation, and are involved in job and educational placement.

The settings in which counselors perform these various functions still include, of course, schools, such as colleges and universities, secondary schools, and elementary schools, but have been expanded to include community agencies of various sorts, such as community mental health agencies, hospitals and convalescent settings, retirement homes, and private-practice settings.

Another major shift in focus in the 1970s and 1980s is an increasingly expanding set of counseling techniques and methods. Within the individual-interview setting, counselors engage in such techniques as reflection-oriented counseling, insight-oriented counseling, and Gestalt-focused approaches. Counselors also use behavior modification procedures, biofeedback, and cognitive-skill-development techniques.

In sum, the counseling effort has become incredibly diversified and specialized over the past decade.

Counselors are expected to read a large number of regularly appearing serial publications to remain contemporary in their skills and concepts. Some recent books of major interest to counselors include Burks and Stefflre's *Theories of Counseling* (3rd edition) (1979), Carkhuff's *Helping and Human Relationships* (1969), Crites's *Vocational Psychology* (1969) and *Career Counseling* (1981), Holland's *Making Vocational Choices* (1973), Ivey and Authier's *Microcounseling* (2nd edition) (1978), Krumboltz and Thoreson's *Behavioral Counseling* (1969), Mahoney and Thoreson's *Self Control: Power to the People* (1974), Osipow's *Theories of Career Development* (2nd edition) (1973), Patterson's *Theory of Counseling and Psychotherapy* (2nd edition) (1973), Whiteley's *History of Counseling Psychology* (1980), and Whiteley and Fretz's *The Present and Future of Counseling Psychology* (1980).

The major issues that dominated the field of counseling during the 1970s reflect concern with the difference between counseling and psychotherapy. A continuum of activities can be proposed that is anchored at one end by psychotherapy and at the other end by guidance. Counseling is conceived to be in the middle of that continuum. "Guidance" has been defined as a series of services that include appraisal, counseling, placement, and follow-up (Shertzer & Stone, 1976). Guidance is seen as a continuous, sequential, educational process and is therefore not isomorphic to counseling.

Examining the other end of the continuum, such writers as Hansen, Stevic, and Warner (1977) described "psychotherapy" as a set of services for which the clientele is unspecified. In contrast, "counseling" often defines services in reference to the group served. Traditionally, psychotherapy is perceived as focusing more on serious disorders, personality change, and individual interventions, whereas counseling presumably deals more with normal developmental problems and normal ranges of behavior and has less discrepant personality-change and behavior-change goals.

It is generally concluded that there is considerable difficulty in differentiating among guidance, counseling, and psychotherapy. Substantial overlap in function, technique, and clientele blurs the differences implied by these three terms; however, most psychologists agree that some difference in emphasis occurs from one end of the continuum to the other.

Difficulties in definition include such issues as whether individual as well as group approaches should be considered counseling and whether programmatic services can also be considered counseling.

Related to this difficulty is the issue of specifying the criteria to use in identifying successful counseling outcomes. Highly specific objectives for counseling lend themselves well to criterion statements; for example, clients seeking assistance in dealing with circumscribed mood states, such as anxiety or depression, can be exposed to intervention, and change in complaints can be evaluated. Very few clients, however, actually present such clearly circumscribed complaints. Often these mood states themselves are symptoms of other difficulties that are addressed in counseling.

Questions also arise regarding the degree to which the counseling process itself should be regarded as part of the criterion. In other words, counselors often teach clients techniques for dealing better with their difficulties, which include problems with decision-making skills, stress management, ability to resolve conflicting values and motives, and ability to be more self-disclosing and to develop a greater sense of intimacy with others. For such problems as these, criteria are somewhat difficult to isolate and identify. Interview approaches to counseling about such problems can be prolonged, and the specific goal may shift several times over the course of an intervention.

Where behavioral procedures are used, goals generally tend to be highly specific. Clients with phobias can be treated and the phobic reaction measured. Clients claiming sleep disorders, speech anxieties, or test-taking-skill problems can all be assessed with respect to those target behaviors following counseling intervention, and assessment of the intervention can be clearly made.

It is more difficult to help clients with career decision problems evaluate the outcomes of counseling efforts. Career decisions continue through the life span. At one stage, an individual may need information, so the proper criterion might be information-seeking behavior and processing of the information obtained. At another time, a decision needs to be implemented, and the adequacy of that implementation must be part of the criterion. At still another time, satisfaction and adjustment in the work situation or the decision to change to a more satisfying situation may be the appropriate criterion. Since these events are not unrelated to each other even though they occur at different times of life, the problem of relating an earlier counseling intervention to a later outcome becomes very difficult to solve.

Establishing criteria for the outcome of counseling is a serious, difficult problem. Gelso (1979) pointed out many of the pitfalls that investigators in counseling psychology encounter. Criterion problems include determination of goals; the duration of counseling that is most appropriate for assessment; adequacy of measures used; the expected duration of changes themselves, that is, how long they should last; the relative value of subjective and objective criteria. The difficulties involved in assessing counseling outcomes contribute to the "softness" that the field has endured over its lifetime.

All these evaluation problems have caused considerable difficulty for the counseling profession in establishing its credibility and in dealing with increasing demands to be accountable for the services it provides. Nonetheless, attempts have been made and evidence is accumulating to suggest that program evaluation can be done effectively and that a variety of intervention attempts can be sharpened to increase their effectiveness.

Counselors. Counselors are employed in a full range of settings. Ordinarily they work in elementary and secondary school settings, universities, and colleges. In addition, services provided by counselors are found in such agencies as the U.S. Employment Service, vocational rehabilitation bureaus, the penal systems of the states and federal government, the Veterans Administration, community mental health agencies, private-practice and pastoral settings, religious institutions, industrial settings, and specialized career-counseling agencies (Shertzer & Stone, 1976).

Data published by the former U.S. Department of Health, Education and Welfare indicated that student-counselor ratios in public schools had gone from one counselor to 960 students in 1958 to one counselor for each 490 students during the 1967–1970 period. The 1967–1970 period was the low point in terms of counselor-student ratio, which returned to a somewhat higher ratio of one counselor for each 522 students in data presented in 1975 and 1976.

Somewhat obscuring the number of counselors em-ployed in private-practice settings is the fact that many counselors work in educational institutions as a full-time activity, but are employed on a part-time basis as consultants and private practitioners. These individuals provide substantial services to the public and private sectors, but they do not regard themselves as private practitioners and often are not included in employment survey data (Tanney, 1980).

Counseling. The heart of the counseling system consists of the actual interchanges that occur between clients and counselors in individual-counseling activities. Counseling usually consists of an initial phase, during which time a client is introduced to the counseling process and a problem statement is generated; a planning phase, during which some kind of assessment and goal-setting activity occurs; and an intervention phase aimed at resolving the problem identified.

Assessment. Under the best conditions, the particular techniques chosen for intervention reflect a decision based on the assessment. Some of the critical variables involved in the assessment phase of counseling involve judgments of counseling readiness, diagnosis of the client's situation, and aspects of the counseling relationship.

Counseling clients have varying degrees of difficulty in exploring sensitive life areas. Client readiness, or the degree of motivation to change behavior, affects counseling success, but counselors occasionally explain failures by attributing them to a client's inability to profit from interventions rather than to the quality of counseling itself.

Diagnostic activity has not always been emphasized in counseling, but with the proliferation of techniques, it has recently become important. Because a large variety of techniques are available (Osipow & Walsh, 1970), selection should be based on understanding of the client's problems and the relationship of the diagnosis to the demonstrated adequacy of interventions. Literature is accumulating which identifies techniques that are most effective with specific problems. Selection is usually easier to make for behavioral interventions, where such techniques as desensitization can be effectively used with highly circumscribed complaints. Selection of techniques is more difficult with pervasive, subjective complaints, such as anomie, which typically require somewhat more diffuse interventions of a psychodynamic or insight-oriented nature.

Intervention. The counseling relationship underlies almost any kind of intervention in an interview setting. Rogers (1961) and Carkhuff (1969) gave prominence to such features as congruence, empathy, unconditional positive regard, and attention to the cognitive-affective dimension. "Congruence" refers to ability of the counselor to present an integrated self to the client. "Empathy" refers to ability of the counselor to understand the frame of reference from which the client speaks. "Unconditional positive regard" refers to a nonjudgmental attitude regarding the client's behaviors, and "attention to the cognitive-affective dimension" allows the counselor to focus on the proportion of rational thought to emotion the client is experiencing.

Also related is concern with the effect of concreteness, that is, ability of the counselor to be specific in helping the client understand events that are involved in troublesome situations.

General interviewing techniques have not changed substantially over the years. They still include structuring, reflection, leading, reassurance, listening, interpretation, and information giving.

"Structuring" refers to the explicit and implicit communication given to clients to describe proper roles and the source of responsibility for various events that occur in interviews. Structure is communicated concerning length of the interviews, behavior of the counselor to the client who comes late, specificity of goals, and allocation of responsibility in interviews.

"Reflection" and "leading" refer to the degree to which the counselor tries to move the client along in thinking and understanding about the problems of concern. Reflection of client feeling in properly phrased statements can lead the client to increasing levels of self-understanding.

"Reassurance" allows the client to feel the counselor is supportive, is an ally, and will assist the client in difficult times. This technique can help the client while more durable interventions are implemented.

"Listening skills" refers to ability of the counselor to attend to the significant elements of events the client reports. Counselors must be good listeners, demonstrating skills in both attention and selection of important themes in client talk.

"Interpretation," derived from psychoanalytic approaches, involves explaining to the client the meaning behind emotional disclosures. Usually, what can be manipulated in interpretation is the degree to which the counselor is ahead of the client's own awareness. Normally, interpretation should not be too far ahead of the client's own level of understanding, lest it be rejected and thus ineffective.

Finally, "information giving" focuses on those cognitive events that clients must have in order to function under certain conditions. Typically, information giving is greatest in decision-oriented counseling, such as career counseling, but may also be used in other settings, such as the family and child-rearing situations.

Termination, the last active counseling phase, involves identification of the degree to which counseling goals have been achieved. Problems encountered in terminating can include dealing with dependency that the counseling relationship itself raised and adequately assessing the degree to which the client has realistically achieved the goals stated earlier. Sometimes termination is postponed because the client has moved to another level of functioning and may seek to identify new goals and continue with counseling. The issue that must be raised at this point is whether continuation represents an improvement or an attempt by both counselor and/or client to perpetuate the counseling relationship inappropriately.

A follow-up phase, after termination, is not always con-ducted, but it is highly desirable. One of the ways in which counselors can properly assess the adequacy of their interventions is by finding out what has occurred to the client after counseling concludes. Although it is often difficult to maintain the proper degree of contact with clients after counseling, and although clients sometimes do not wish to maintain follow-up efforts, good practice requires counselors to follow up at least a sample of their clients.

Theoretical Approaches. During the 1960s and 1970s, some old and well-established theoretical positions continued to exert influence in the field of counseling, along with several newer trends. Psychodynamic approaches continued to be influential, along with client-centered, humanistic, Gestalt, and existential approaches. Newer approaches in the area of behavioral cognitive approaches, social-influence processes, and social-learning approaches were also apparent.

Behavioral approach. The 1960s saw the rise and increasing sophistication of a variety of very specific behavioral interventions that have been used by both clinical and counseling psychologists. The initial impetus for this work was the learning and conditioning approaches popularized and developed by Wolpe and extended by numerous other writers, such as Lazarus, Allyon and Azrin, and many others.

At the present time, several major behavioral approaches seem to exist. One is the original and extensions of the original reciprocal-inhibition approach proposed by Wolpe and others. This approach involves, basically, the rationale that it is possible to eliminate an undesirable or ineffective emotional response by pairing it with a stimulus situation that arouses an incompatible competing response. Thus, anxiety cannot be experienced in combination with sexual arousal, and depression is driven out by action. Relaxation approaches tend to be used to eliminate negative emotional affective responses. The typical approach involves teaching the client specific techniques of relaxation that can then be applied in the presence of either real or vicarious anxiety-provoking stimuli. The course of treatment is rather specific and lends itself well to highly circumscribed difficulties, such as phobic responses or stimulus-specific problem behaviors.

Considerable work has been done in refining these approaches over the years, and these approaches form a rather definite tool in the counselor's kit of techniques.

Social influence. One of the most useful major summaries of counseling as a social-influence process was recently published by Corrigan et al. (1980). From this viewpoint counselor impact is related to counselor credibility, the interpersonal attractiveness of the counselor, and such counselor variables as expertness and trustworthiness. Corrigan et al. summarized research that focused on the question of counselor influence on their clients and counseling as a social-influence process.

The social-influence approach dates to the work of Frank (1961), who pointed out that "certain types of therapy rely primarily on the healer's ability to mobilize healing forces in the sufferer by psychological means." Strong (1968) applied social-influence notions to the counseling setting. Strong postulated that counselors can reduce the likelihood of being discredited by their clients by being perceived as expert, attractive, and trustworthy. Strong proposed that counseling proceeds in two stages: first, counselors enhance their perceived expertness, attractiveness, and trustworthiness; second, counselors use the resulting influence potential to change opinions and behavior of clients.

Since Strong's early paper, a substantial literature has accumulated studying social influence in counseling by manipulating the three principal variables of expertness, attractiveness, and trustworthiness (Corrigan et al., 1980). A great deal of this literature has been based on analogue investigations, which have the advantage of allowing better control than field studies in counseling and the disadvantage of being somewhat removed from the real-life factors that operate in counseling situations.

Counselors who endorse a social-influence model pay most attention to variables of expertness, as defined in terms of counselor attire, setting, gender, and race; also involved are counselor reputation variables, defined largely in terms of things people say about the experience of the counselor. Manipulation of behavior cues is also important to counselors who are concerned with social influence.

Attractiveness cues related to physical attributes and attractiveness, dress, setting, race, and sex are seen to be important counselor attributes.

Counselor characteristics must be fundamentally related to the influence they have on clients in order for this model to be useful. Most research has suggested that counselors can influence clients, but because the experimental situations on which conclusions have been based have generally been analogue rather than real counseling situations, some question remains as to the actual influence of counselors. One important implication of the social-influence model is if it is valid, training of counselors should very clearly proceed along the lines of the important cues that counselors should display in order to generate maximum influence on their clients.

Social learning. Social-learning approaches to counseling represent a fairly new application of theory. Stimulated by the work of Bandura (1969), a number of individuals have tried to develop a system that emphasizes the role of models and vicarious learning in counseling and psychotherapy. Krumboltz and Thoresen (1969) made significant applications in this area.

In a paper entitled "Behavioral Self-Control and Career Development" (Thoresen & Ewart, 1976), a social-learning model of career selection was proposed as one example of social-learning approaches in counseling. Social-learning theory applied to vocational selection focuses on genetic characteristics involved in choice, environmental conditions, learning histories, and task-approach skills. A major part of any social-learning approach of this type is its em-

phasis on self-management. Thoresen and Ewart, for example, developed ways people can be helped to learn to solve many of their problems or to prevent them from developing in the first place through application of social-learning approaches to self-management. Self-control was seen as a "learnable cognitive process" used to develop actions that significantly affect other factors influencing behavior. According to Thoresen and Ewart, major aspects of teaching people self-control skills include motivation development, self-observation, environmental planning, and altering of reinforcement schedules. It should be evident that the social-learning approaches to counseling overlap substantially with the general behavioral approaches to counseling and, in fact, represent a specific example, albeit somewhat more differentiated than most applications of behavior theory to counseling.

Psychoanalytic approach. Although few counselors identify themselves as purely psychoanalytic in orientation, they admit being influenced by psychoanalytic theory (Brenner, 1974). So pervasive is psychoanalytic thinking that many of its hypotheses have become incorporated into other systems of counseling. To identify these underpinnings, a brief review of psychoanalytic theory is appropriate.

Psychoanalytic theory is a body of hypotheses concerning human mental functioning and development. The theories of psychoanalysis have been derived from observational data and attempt to order and explain these data. Two fundamental principles of psychoanalytic theory are psychic determinism (causality) and the "proposition that consciousness is an exceptional rather than regular attribute" of daily living (Brenner, 1974).

Although these two hypotheses are the *sine qua non* of psychoanalytic theory, they also compose important underpinnings in other systems of psychological theory. "Psychic determinism" maintains that events do not occur by chance, but rather are determined by earlier events. Gestalt theory, humanistic theory, and certainly existential theory all require that individuals assume responsibility for their actions and not attempt to avoid consequences of behavior by calling their actions "accidents."

The existence of unconscious mental process is the second fundamental hypothesis of psychoanalytic theory. Although psychoanalytic thinkers may have been the first to propose to increase the ratio of conscious to unconscious behavior, all systems of counseling seek to have individuals become more in control of their lives. Ergo, counselors implicitly accept the concept that their clients may not be aware (or conscious) of the environmental stimuli, reinforcement schedule, aspirations, false hypotheses (the language selected will depend on the orientation), etc., that are promoting their behavior.

Psychoanalytic thinking is also concerned with normal mental functioning: selection of vocation (e.g., Bordin, Nachmann, & Segal, 1963; Medvene, 1969; and Roe, 1957), choice of a marital partner, literature, childhood myths and legends (Bettleheim, 1976), artistic creativity, and politics. In these areas particularly, its tenets may be useful to counselors and their clients.

One recent outgrowth of psychodynamic therapy has been efforts to provide an abbreviated treatment model of psychotherapy. The brief dynamic therapies now practiced have developed largely from efforts of psychoanalytically oriented therapists to isolate and apply analytic theories, insights, and practices in a shorter therapeutic process. Counselors often work in agencies that limit the number of sessions available to clients. Pursuing the efforts of Bellak and Small (1977), Mann (1973), Malan (1963, 1976), Sifenos (1972), and Davaloo (1978) would enable the counselor to apply psychoanalytic theory within a time-limited framework.

Client-centered counseling. Carl Rogers was the originator of this system of counseling/therapy, which has as its basis an optimistic view of the nature of human beings, one that sees humans as essentially rational, socialized, forward moving, and realistic. The basic philosophy required by practitioners of this approach is characterized by respect for individuals and for their rights to self-direction.

Early Rogerians emphasized that the counselor should manifest the conditions of empathy, congruence, warmth, understanding, and positive regard during counseling interviews. The client's perception that the counseling process includes these ingredients is crucial. It is upon the client's perception of the counseling process and of the counselor's attitude, personality, and techniques that therapeutic change depends.

Client-centered therapy, like existential, Gestalt, and humanistic therapy, emphasizes that clients must assume responsibility for themselves in the relationship and, by extrapolation, in life. This emphasis may lead to various feelings of annoyance, anger, (existential) aloneness, but in the Rogerian system, eventually to an acceptance of responsibility (Rogers, 1961).

Self-exploration is facilitated by the accepting attitude of the counselor. The client's inconsistencies, contradictions, and ambivalences are discovered along with previously denied feelings, perceptions, and attitudes. Experiences inconsistent with the self-concept are manifested in awareness. These alterations of awareness require a reorganization of the self.

The continuing acceptance of the counselor is very important during this reorganization and provides the atmosphere in which façades may be dropped and feelings heretofore denied may be experienced to their limit (Rogers, 1951).

This reorganization transcends problem solving. It is the experiencing of feelings leading to the being of one's self. It is the full awareness of *all* aspects of humanness that makes it possible for a client to become a complete and fully functioning human organism.

Rogerian theory, like psychoanalytic theory, is ubiquitous in most counseling interactions. The importance of respect for the potential growth of the client and the ne-

cessity to communicate acceptance and understanding were greatly facilitated by client-centered therapy.

Humanistic counseling. The 1950s saw the establishment of a new ideological approach within the academic psychology so long dominated by scientific, positivistic behaviorism and Freudian psychoanalysis. This "third force" was humanistic psychology, so called because it emphasized those attributes that make human beings human (e.g., love, wishes, creativity, self-awareness, choice, values, growth, humor, affection).

Early humanistic psychology and the counseling/therapy that grew from it had a decidedly more positive orientation to human existence than the "sickness" models of Freudian psychoanalysis and the behaviorists. "Peak experiences," self-realization, encounter, and development of potential are all aspects this system emphasizes. A rejection of determinism and an emphasis on choice and responsibility are of great importance to this frame of reference.

Gestalt counseling. Gestalt counseling/therapy has its origins in the theories of Gestalt psychology and, in particular, the work of Max Wertheimer (Emerson & Smith, 1974). Fritz Perls, considered one of the founders of Gestalt therapy, dedicated his first book (Perls, 1947) to Wertheimer, whom he considered the originator of Gestalt psychology.

Gestalt therapy shares with existential therapy a strong emphasis on assumption of personal responsibility for the fact and quality of one's own existence. It rejects what Perls saw as existentialism's reliance on religious or philosophical support. Instead, Gestalt therapy posits that the need for events to come to a closure is the strong motivator of human behavior. Gestalt therapy borrowed much from the academic perceptual psychology tradition of Koffka, Wertheimer, and Köhler and their works on (1) the relation of figure and background; (2) the importance of interpreting the coherence or split of a figure in terms of the total contex of the actual situation; (3) the definite structured whole that is not too conclusive, yet is not a mere atom; (4) the active organizing force of meaningful wholes and the natural tendency toward simplicity of form; (5) the tendency of unfinished situations to complete themselves (Perls, Hefferline, & Goodman, 1951, pp. 237–238).

Perls added to this system the perception of one's own needs, feelings, and bodily awarenesses. He postulated that the same Gestalt-forming process would occur in this sphere as in the perceptual realm. His approach extends academic Gestalt psychology by adding needs and body awareness to the Gestalt-forming process. Problems and difficulties suffered by clients are viewed as interruptions in the completion of significant experiences (Gestalts) in their lives which have caused them to become blocked in fulfilling their contemporary needs. Therapy consists of using the insights gleaned from Gestalt psychology to help unblock their need-fulfillment patterns.

Two other academicians, Lewin and Goldstein (1940), had a significant effect on the development of Gestalt therapy. Their work extended the theoretical position founded on perception into the area of personality.

One of Lewin's students, Zeigarnik, studied experimentally what Perls would eventually call one's "unfinished business." The "Zeigarnik effect" is a phenomenon found when comparing short-term memory for finished and unfinished tasks. Zeigarnik (1927) found, consistent with Lewin's tension-system hypothesis, that unfinished tasks are remembered better (because of the remaining tension) than are finished tasks.

Interestingly, if the subject is fearful of failure in the task being performed, a reversal of the Zeigarnik effect is found. Completed tasks are remembered better than those not completed.

Goldstein (1940) also had a significant effect on Perls's extension of Gestalt psychology into Gestalt therapy. Goldstein developed the concept of *self-actualization,* which he called the sovereign motive of the organism. Organisms complete "figures" (satisfy specific needs) as they attempt to actualize themselves.

Anxiety also received Goldstein's attention. He viewed it as the result of expectations of catastrophe and suggested that anxiety can cause a splitting of the personality because it can lead to detachment and isolation of organismic parts. From Lewin's students' studies on the impact of incomplete activities and from Goldstein's view of anxiety as rehearsing in the present for a future calamity came Perl's emphasis on staying in the present to complete Gestalts and to confront only that which the organism could affect.

Goldstein can be credited also with influencing Perls in his emphasis on language. Goldstein maintained that loss of categorical thinking (inability to abstract and classify) results in a limitation of orientation and of action. Perls absorbed this belief and demonstrated both in his writings and in transcripts of his therapy interactions a strong emphasis on using words precisely. He encouraged learning of the value of each word and concretization (by the therapist) of clients' choice of metaphor. He thought that avoidance of ego language (use of "it" or "you" rather than "I" when speaking of one's own experience) and avoidance of personal responsibility (Perls, 1947) are closely related.

Many of the techniques of Gestalt therapy (taking responsibility for one's behavior, "empty chair" technique, "I" statements, localizing of tension within the body) are used by counselors. These devices are effectively outlined by Passons (1975).

Existential counseling. Yalom (1980) defined existential counseling/psychotherapy as a dynamic approach to therapy (conflicting forces on a conscious and unconscious level are operating within an individual) that focuses on concerns that are rooted in the individual's existence. In other words, existential counseling deals with confronting (or avoiding) the ultimate "givens" of human existence.

According to Yalom, these major concerns include death, freedom, isolation, and meaninglessness. Death is by far the most obvious universal human concern. It is inevitable. Yet, how terrifying to encounter the awareness of death and the wish to continue to exist. Freedom includes assuming sole *responsibility* for the fact and quality of one's existence and assuming responsibility for the conscious and unconscious will (Farber, 1966). Existential isolation concerns that fundamental aloneness that all humans bear: each of us enters existence alone and must depart from it alone no matter how close one may become to another. The fourth concern, meaninglessness, is inextricably involved with the preceding three. Since existence is finite, since the world is individually constituted, since humans are inevitably isolated from each other, what is the point of living? How can meaning-seeking creatures endure an existence in a meaningless universe?

Yalom (1980) maintained that the concepts of existential thought are often incorporated by therapists/counselors who may not be aware of the concepts' origins, and he believed that most therapists, regardless of theoretical orientation, use existential insights in their therapy.

Special Populations.   Recent interest has developed in several specialized areas of adult counseling, in part because of the upward shift in age of our population. Increasing attention is now being paid to counseling with adults at all stages of life.

Schlossberg, Troll, and Leibowitz (1978) observed that a general bias toward youth in our culture (from which counselors are not immune) has distracted counselor attention from the problems of the adult population and, in particular, the older adult. These authors also describe several recurring adult problem patterns that may be useful as guides for developing counseling programs. One pattern is first transitions in life that are not well executed, such as not getting a suitable job after graduation from college, not being married by the time one is 30, not getting the job promotions that one's peers are getting, and not having children if that is a personal expectation. A second pattern is a slow rate of career advancement. A third life pattern includes stresses defined in terms of changes in status, such as those involved in death of a spouse, divorce, illness, loss of a job; finally, the last pattern has to do with taking stock, a behavior that tends to occur past midlife. The definition of what is midlife, however, is not clear.

Schlossberg, Troll, and Leibowitz (1978) also identified the contexts in which adult counseling efforts are properly conducted. One context is the family. Counseling helps adults deal with their roles as parents, spouses, children, as well as siblings. The second context has to do with work roles. Counseling provides assistance with such issues as vocational maturity, career change in midlife, and retirement. The questions raised concerning career disappointment are also pertinent in this context.

Schlossberg and Entine (1977) summarized many of the issues involved in counseling through the life span, including specific developmental stages through the adult span, developmental counseling with adults, problems of age bias, and special problems of women and men as they mature which have implications for counseling.

Sinick (1977) pointed out some of the counseling-related concerns older people present which have often been ignored, such as career-choice counseling, counseling for changing one's career, problems with self-confidence, altering attitudes, and dealing with the anticipation of dying and death. Doyle (1980) in particular suggested treatment strategies to be used in counseling individuals about death-related problems. Clearly an important focus for counseling older people is death and dying. Landerth and Berg (1980) also provided strong evidence for the pervasiveness of counseling needs for an aging population.

Counseling the disabled. A large literature exists describing counseling with disabled individuals. Rusalem and Malikin (1976) summarized many of the issues of the mid-1970s dealing with vocational aspects of rehabilitation counseling. Among the major issues pointed out by Rusalem and Malikin's volume are special vocational problems the handicapped experience, the public's attitude toward disability, how vocational rehabilitation clients see the counseling services they receive and how they use them, and the special counseling implications for dealing with socially disabled, emotionally disabled, and mentally retarded persons. Many of the suggestions involve environmental changes and development of support systems that would make adjustment of the disabled easier. Thus, counseling disabled populations focuses heavily on the person-environment interaction aspect of counseling.

Substance abuse is a special aspect of counseling for disability that emerged in the 1960s and 1970s. Valle (1979) presented a model for alcoholism counselors that builds primarily on the counseling approach proposed by Carkhuff; the approach relies heavily on helpers who offer a high level of empathy, positive regard, and concreteness to their clientele. Alcoholic and drug abuse clients, in general, do not present fundamental counseling problems different from those presented by other clients. They display the same tendency to resist change and ambivalence toward their problems. What is different about substance abuse clients is that often they fail to have the social support systems that other types of clients have and therefore provide a special challenge to counselors. In addition, the particular nature of their disorder may foster deterioration of other potential resources they have, which adds to the difficulty in rehabilitation.

Parent counseling. Two major areas of parent counseling are of special interest to counseling personnel. One has to do with counseling parents of exceptional children and the other with counseling parents of intellectually gifted children. Stewart (1978) pointed out that parents need to be counseled so that they fully understand the nature and diagnosis of a child's handicap and can learn to deal effectively with the child as a consequence of this knowledge. Parents need to learn to deal effectively with

their own feelings of responsibility for the child's condition. Ziv (1977) discussed analogous problems in counseling parents of intellectually gifted children, pointing out that, although most of the time we focus on the advantages of being intellectually gifted, a gifted child is often disadvantaged in a number of ways, for example, by lack of environmental supports, difficulty in interacting with peers, and dealing ineffectively with parental expectations.

Gender issues. A major new development of the 1960s and 1970s was an interest in counseling related to gender issues. Work in these two areas is well represented by two basic volumes in the Brooks/Cole series in counseling psychology. *Counseling Women* (Harmon et al., 1978) and *Counseling Men* (Skovholt, Schauble, & Davis, 1980) deal very thoroughly with most of the major counseling issues.

Issues especially involved in counseling women include sex stereotyping, difficulties in displaying assertive behavior, career counseling stereotypes, counseling concerning physical sex differences and physiological processes, counseling involving marital issues, and sexual-abuse counseling. One issue not clearly resolved is the circumstances under which same-gender or opposite-gender counselors are appropriate. Issues in counseling of men include male violence, problems in intimacy, competitiveness, and aggressiveness.

Along with counseling regarding gender issues are problems of counseling gay males and females. Relatively little has been written in this area, but a recent publication by Woodman and Lenna (1980) described a process they have used in working with gays operating at various stages of self-awareness. The focus of the Woodman and Lenna book is on self-enhancement and development of humanistic values, increasing the client's self-esteem.

Family counseling. Brammer and Shostrom (1977) suggested that couple counseling as a major function of the work of the counselor involved the following two generalizations: (1) reconciliation of the couple is not always a reasonable goal, and (2) a major goal of couple counseling is to reduce the effect of couples' disruptions on children and the family. Brammer and Shostrom also talked about premarital counseling in terms of dealing with misconceptions about love and partner choice, sex-role stereotypes, sexual behavior itself, and such sources of conflict as religion and money. Finally, in family counseling they talked about counseling with children, but this discussion was not very specific.

One new trend has been to help couples deal more effectively with problems related to separation and divorce. Divorce mediation counseling tries to treat divorce counseling as a negotiation rather than as a counseling process and tries to lead the clients through the separation process by attending to all phases, emotional, economic, and social (Haynes, 1981).

Group counseling. Group work has come far from the initial attempts of Boston internist Joseph Hershey Pratt, who worked with advanced tubercular patients in 1905.

Pratt appreciated the importance of psychological factors in the outcome of treatment. He arranged regular sessions with groups of patients in which the focus was their weight loss and gain and the general state of their lives. Group cohesiveness and support helped stave off the depression and isolation associated with their disease.

Although some attempts to use group methods followed Pratt's work, the first concentrated effort to utilize a group format was stimulated by World War II. Enormous numbers of psychologically damaged individuals overextended the resources available for individual counseling and therapy. Group methods became much more common as a result of this need. Gradually, through experience and experimentation, practitioners came to see the cohesion, support, and potential for identification available in groups as therapeutically invaluable for certain types of problems.

Group approaches have become increasingly popular over the past twenty years. This popularity is based on several factors. One is the inherently attractive economies of group approaches: several clients can be seen by one counselor in the same unit of time that one counselor can see a single client. Or, where cocounselors work together, a fairly large number of clients can be seen by two counselors in a single time unit. Second, groups are attractive because they lend themselves to programmatic approaches: schools can use groups to deal with developmental problems most individuals are likely to experience, for example. Third, groups themselves possess certain distinctive and positive psychological features that help clients. Some of these features are, first, a group can provide extensive emotional support to an individual otherwise alone; second, group members can learn from the behavior of other individuals in the group; third, the interpersonal dynamics occurring in a group, such as being accepted by others, learning to trust, seeing how anger occurs in groups, can be useful; fourth, group counseling can serve as a useful adjunct to individual counseling; fifth, group members can learn that other people have problems similar to as well as different from their own, and that they are not alone in their discomfort; and sixth, groups can provide feedback to individuals about their behavior which has an element of reality and immediacy.

Groups can be of several types, including experiential groups, skills-acquisition groups, therapy groups, and problem-focused groups (e.g., focused on career decisions, alcoholism, parenting). Up to now, the focus has been on groups as treatments for pathological emotional conditions. Many other types of group formats are in use today. Self-help groups, such as those for alcoholics and drug abusers, are quite common. Groups for individuals with chronic medical problems (ileostomies, colostomies) or for those enduring a life crisis (dying children, divorce) are quite common. Groups with a time-limited, problem-centered focus often resemble small classes in which certain skills are taught (e.g., assertion training, weight loss methods). Additionally, some group formats (T-groups, sensitivity-training groups) are used in industry and schools to in-

crease the sensitivity and communication skills of participants.

Among the issues that cause difficulty occasionally in group counseling are maintenance of confidentiality and privacy for group members, the composition of the group (homogeneous versus heterogeneous), and the skill and self-awareness of the group counselor.

In sum, group counseling approaches represent a major kind of setting and set of techniques used increasingly commonly in counseling.

Special Counseling Areas. During the late 1970s a number of other specialized counseling settings became evident. Health counseling is a newly emerging specialty that focuses on issues of self-care, such as dealing effectively with smoking behavior and eating disorders; it also has implications for self-medication and for counseling families of patients. Sports psychology has some counseling implications, and a number of counselors are involved in dealing with not only world-class but ordinary athletes in trying to help them develop their potential and use their sports activities effectively. Counseling is being done increasingly in business and industry, and many of the traditional techniques and a few new ones are being applied (e.g., Osipow, 1982, in press; Toomer, 1982, in press).

Increasingly, counseling occurs in settings where the principal symptom and complaint of the client is psychological stress. Much stress counseling occurs in business settings (Osipow, 1982, in press; Toomer, 1982, in press). Business and industry are becoming more sensitized to the problems stimulated by the work place that employees experience. Elsewhere referred to as part of the occupational mental health efforts of counselors (Osipow, 1979), most of the interventions dealing with stress use behavioral techniques and environmental manipulation.

Not yet well developed, but growing, are abortion counseling and genetic counseling.

Trends and Issues. A number of writers have discussed the kinds of major issues and trends that face counselors in the 1980s and 1990s. A list of these might include, based on Shertzer and Stone (1976), career education, privacy regarding records, prevention, increasingly specialized personnel such as paraprofessionals, the increase in group counseling, the increase in consultative roles for counselors, the increase in part-time private practice. Others, such as Pietrofesa et al. (1978), described trends in terms of varied settings for counselors, accountability issues, increasingly directive and assertive counseling procedures, increased use of computer technology, and also group counseling. In addition, such issues as licensing; role definitions between school psychologists, social workers, clinical psychologists, and counselors; counselor self-awareness, and use of paraprofessional services seem important. Other issues that can be raised have to do with counseling with the handicapped and the aged. The newly emerging health counseling area focuses primarily on self-care and counseling for substance abuse.

Many of these issues will not be fully addressed in the

next decade. We believe that among the most likely salient issues will be those dealing with primary prevention, increasing counseling and consultation by counselors, increased part-time practice, increased work with the aging population, and increasing attention to specific techniques and how they apply to particular client concerns.

Credentials. Of great interest and attention now are the problems associated with professional counselor credentials. Conflicts here arise between counselors who are psychologists and those counselors who are not psychologists. The associated issues of licensing, third-party fee payment, and availability of services on a private-practice basis are sources of contention. Controversy will probably continue as the decade unfolds because of the shrinking marketplace and the increasingly rigorous attention paid by insurers to credentials of service providers. It seems evident that the source of support for psychological and counseling services has shifted from institutional bases to individual responsibility paid for by insurance companies. If this trend continues and is expanded outside the clearly psychotherapeutic sphere, increasing controversy and conflict between various service providers over credentialing is likely.

Prevention. Preventive efforts in mental health are those activities designed to reduce incidence of disorders. Removing the cause of the disorders or strengthening individuals' capacities to cope with stress are two general types of preventive strategies.

For the past twenty years, efforts have been under way to conceptualize and implement primary prevention programs to reduce incidence of emotional disorders. The report of the Joint Commission on Mental Illness and Health (1961) alluded to the necessity for preventive intervention. Kessler and Albee (1975) discussed the field of primary prevention in the *Annual Review of Psychology.* The Vermont Conference on Primary Prevention has for five years brought together theorists and researchers in the field of prevention. A Task Panel on Primary Prevention was appointed by the President's Commission on Mental Health (1978, pp. 1822–1863). Its report contained many useful ideas.

Preventive programs have many inherent difficulties. In times of limited resources, the "already ailing" demand attention and remedial efforts. They do not typically seek intervention before they are in pain and certainly not following the onset of disorder. The mental health job market favors opportunities for traditional practice. Training and credentialing for such efforts are already in place.

Logic tells us that there will never be enough mental health providers to assist those who need services utilizing traditional intervention methods. The rationale to "stop having to fish bodies out of the water downstream by stopping whatever is pushing them in upstream" cannot fail to appeal. Record-keeping problems and impact-verification difficulties thwart preventive intervention on a large scale. Specific intervention at recognized high-stress points (e.g., preparation via film models for small children facing

surgery), however, is quite possible to arrange. Data from these types of endeavors (Granziano, Giovanni, & Garcia, 1979; Melamed & Siegal, 1975) verified that unfortunate mental health outcomes can often be prevented by care before the stressful episode occurs.

Other issues. According to the American Psychological Association's ethical code (1972), it is the responsibility of the practitioner to maintain adequate files and records on the individuals one sees. These records should be sufficient to inform interested and relevant professionals (e.g., physicians) regarding the psychological development of the client at the written request of the client. Third-party payers, additionally, have a right to be informed regarding the psychological assistance provided a client if they are involved in reimbursement procedures. Government agencies also *may* have a legitimate right to information regarding clients or former clients if they are engaged in security-relevant occupations or security-threatening activities.

It is in the last two areas that counselors appropriately have the most concern. Recent disclosure of unauthorized access to medical records sobers many mental health professionals. Uncertainty regarding the use of psychological information may cause many counselors to be as taciturn as possible in their record keeping.

Optimum mental health treatment requires that the client reveal the most intimate thoughts and feelings to the practitioner. Any violation of this confidentiality adversely affects ability to assist a client. This principle has been relied upon by the public and has been, in a number of states, an expression of public policy, since even with assurances of confidentiality, some clients are reluctant to speak openly.

Federal law protects the identities of alcohol and drug abuse clients. It recognizes that society's gain from encouraging these individuals to seek treatment (or at least not impeding their seeking treatment by making them fearful of disclosure) overrides the potential advantages (law enforcement issues) of information availability.

The traditional service-delivery areas for counselors have been schools, colleges, universities, mental health centers, and rehabilitation centers. Recently, additional counselor employment centers have emerged. The most prominent new demands for counselors are found among the physically handicapped, aged, and terminally ill.

Legal mandates (e.g., Section 504 of the Rehabilitation Act of 1973, pp. 94–142) have enabled the physically handicapped to claim a larger share of what heretofore was only the purview of the "normal" (that is, not physically handicapped). Employment opportunities, travel facilities, education and training institutions have all been opened to the physically handicapped.

Categorization systems vary, but a recent estimate fixed the number of Americans afflicted by some significant physical handicap at 36 million. Although counselors specially trained in rehabilitation can offer assistance, many clients require help in coping with a noninstitutional environment. School counselors, counseling psychologists in universities, employment counselors, etc., all have unique training to help these individuals.

Institutions experiencing an influx of physically handicapped persons could also use counseling services, particularly development of programs to assist the nonphysically handicapped with their reactions to physically handicapped individuals (Kleck, 1968, 1969; Kleck, Ono, & Hastorf, 1966).

A youth-conscious society, such as late-twentieth-century America, is beset with a curious anomaly. Medical advances and better nutrition are enabling more Americans to live longer than ever before. It is in affecting the *quality* of these extended lives that counselors play a role. Vocational theories need to include information useful to assist retirement-age individuals in finding satisfactory employment. Counselor expertise in facilitating normal development (aging, like dying, is statistically quite normal) could merge with expertise in career development to provide a useful service to the elderly.

Counselors also need to assist the elderly with the tremendous shifts with which this life may confront them. Alterations in physical appearance and physical capacity, and frequent loss of loved ones, and the shifts within their families are all major adjustments that could certainly benefit from counselors' interventions.

Terminally ill persons and their families also have need for counselors. Death is one of the few universal experiences. Viewing dying as a developmental process, in both physical and psychological terms, enables the counselor to provide valuable assistance (Kubler-Ross, 1975). Expansion of this counseling area is a developing trend. Familiarity with new perspectives on the needs of the bereaved (Goddard & Leviton, 1980) can further enrich the traditional services counselors supply to those affected most directly by death, and counselors can also assist staff in hospices, nursing homes, and extended-care units by offering consultation for the severe burnout these settings pose (LeGrand, 1980).

Samuel H. Osipow
M. Faith Tanney

See also Affective Education; Career Guidance; Drug Abuse Education; Mental Health; Psychological Services; Rehabilitation Services; Student Personnel Work.

REFERENCES

American Psychological Association. *Ethical Standards of Psychologists.* Washington, D.C.: The Association, 1972.

Bandura, H. *Principles of Behavior Modification.* New York: Holt, Rinehart & Winston, 1969.

Bellak, L., & Small, L. *Emergency Psychotherapy and Brief Psychotherapy.* New York: Grune & Stratton, 1977.

Bettelheim, B. *The Uses of Enchantment: The Meaning and Importance of Fairy Tales.* New York: Knopf, 1976.

Bordin, E. S.; Nachmann, B.; and Segal, S. J. An articulated framework for vocational development. *Journal of Counseling Psychology,* 1963, *10,* 107–116.

Brammer, L. M., & Shostrom, E. L. *Therapeutic Psychology* (3rd ed.) Englewood Cliffs, N.J.: Prentice-Hall, 1977.

Brenner, C. *An Elementary Textbook of Psychoanalysis.* New York: Doubleday Anchor Books, 1974.

Burks, H. M., Jr., & Stefflre, B. *Theories of Counseling* (3rd ed.). New York: McGraw-Hill, 1979.

Carkhuff, R. R. *Helping and Human Relationships* (Vols. 1 and 2). New York: Holt, Rinehart & Winston, 1969.

Corrigan, J. D.; Dell, D. M.; Lewis, K. N.; & Schmidt, L. D. Counseling as a social influence process: A review. *Journal of Counseling Psychology Monograph,* 1980, *27,* 395–441.

Crites, J. O. *Vocational Psychology.* New York: McGraw-Hill, 1969.

Crites, J. O. *Career Counseling.* New York: McGraw-Hill, 1981.

Davaloo, H. (Ed.). *Basic Principles and Techniques in Short-term Dynamics Psychotherapy.* New York: Spectrum, 1978.

Doyle, P. *Grief Counseling and Sudden Death.* Springfield, Ill.: Thomas, 1980.

Emerson, P., & Smith, E. W. Contributions of Gestalt psychology to Gestalt therapy. *Counseling Psychologist,* 1974, *4*(4), 8–12.

Farber, L. *The Ways of the Will.* New York: Basic Books, 1966.

Frank, J. D. *Persuasion and Healing.* Baltimore: Johns Hopkins University Press, 1961.

Gelso, C. J. Research in counseling: Methodological and professional issues. *Counseling Psychologist,* 1979, *8*(3), 7–35.

Goddard, H. L., & Leviton, D. Intimacy-sexuality needs of the bereaved: An exploratory study. *Death Education,* 1980, *3*(4), 347–358.

Goldstein, K. *Human Nature in the Light of Psychopathology.* Cambridge, Mass.: Harvard University Press, 1940.

Granziano, A. M. D.; Giovanni, I. S.; & Garcia, K. A. Behavioral treatment of children's fears: A review. *Psychological Bulletin,* 1979, *86,* 804–830.

Hansen, J. C.; Stevic, O. R.; & Warner, R. W., Jr. *Counseling: Theory in Process* (2nd ed.). Boston: Allyn & Bacon, 1977.

Harmon, L. W.; Birk, J. N.; Fitzgerald, L. E.; Tanney, M. F. (Eds.). *Counseling Women.* Monterey, Calif.: Brooks/Cole, 1978.

Haynes, J. M. *Divorce Mediation.* New York: Springer, 1981.

Holland, J. L. *Making Vocational Choices.* Englewood Cliffs, N.J.: Prentice-Hall, 1973.

Ivey, A., & Authier, J. *Microcounseling* (2nd ed.). Springfield, Ill.: Thomas, 1978.

Joint Commission on Mental Illness and Health. *Action for Mental Health.* New York: Basic Books, 1961.

Kessler, M., & Albee, G. W. Primary prevention. *Annual Review of Psychology,* 1975, *26,* 557–591.

Kleck, R. Physical stigma and nonverbal cues emitted in face-to-face interaction. *Human Relations,* 1968, *21,* 19–28.

Kleck, R. Physical stigma and task-oriented interactions. *Human Relations,* 1969, *22,* 53–60.

Kleck, R.; Ono, H.; & Hastorf, A. The effects of physical deviance on face-to-face interaction. *Human Relations,* 1966, *19,* 425–436.

Krumboltz, J. D., & Thoresen, C. E. *Behavioral Counseling.* New York: Holt, Rinehart & Winston, 1969.

Kubler-Ross, E. *Death: The Final Stage of Growth.* Englewood Cliffs, N.J.: Prentice-Hall, 1975.

Landerth, G. L., & Berg, R. C. *Counseling the Elderly,* Springfield, Ill.: Thomas, 1980.

LeGrand, L. E. Reducing burnout in the hospice and death education movement. *Death Education,* 1980, *4*(1), 61–75.

Mahoney, M., & Thoresen, E. *Self-control: Power to the People.* Monterey, Calif.: Brooks/Cole, 1974.

Malan, D. H. *A Study of Brief Psychotherapy.* London: Tavistock Publications, 1963.

Malan, D. H. *The Frontier of Brief Psychotherapy: An Example of the Convergence of Research and Clinical Practice.* New York: Plenum, 1976.

Mann, J. *Time-limited Psychotherapy.* Cambridge: Harvard University Press, 1973.

Medvene, A. M. Occupational choice of graduate students in psychology as function of early parent-child interactions. *Journal of Counseling Psychology,* 1969, *16,* 385–389.

Melamed, B. G., & Siegal, L. J. Reduction of anxiety in children facing hospitalization and surgery by use of filmed modeling. *Journal of Consulting and Clinical Psychology,* 1975, *43,* 511–521.

Osipow, S. H. *Theories of Career Development* (2nd ed.). Englewood Cliffs, N.J.: Prentice-Hall, 1973.

Osipow, S. H. Occupational mental health: A new role for counseling psychologists. *Counseling Psychologist,* 1979, *8*(1), 65–70.

Osipow, S. H. Counseling psychology in business and industry. *Counseling Psychologist,* 1982, *10,* in press.

Osipow, S. H., & Walsh, W. B. *Strategies in Counseling for Behavior Change.* Englewood Cliffs, N.J.: Prentice-Hall, 1970.

Passons, W. *Gestalt Approaches in Counseling.* New York: Holt, Rinehart & Winston, 1975.

Patterson, C. H. *Theories of Counseling and Psychotherapy* (2nd ed.). New York: Harper & Row, 1973.

Perls, F. *Ego, Hunger, and Aggression.* London: Allen & Unwin, 1947.

Perls, F.; Hefferline, R.; & Goodman, P. *Gestalt Therapy.* New York: Julian Press, 1951.

Pietrofesa, J.; Hoffman, A.; Splete, H. H.; & Pinto, D. V. *Counseling: Theory, Research, and Practice.* Chicago: Rand McNally, 1978.

President's Commission on Mental Health. *Report of the Task Panel on Primary Prevention* (Appendix, Vol. 4). Washington, D.C.: U.S. Government Printing Office, 1978, pp. 1822–1863. (Stock No. 00-000-00393-2)

Roe, A. Early determinants of vocational choice. *Journal of Counseling Psychology,* 1957, *4,* 212–217.

Rogers, C. R. *Client-centered Therapy.* Boston: Houghton Mifflin, 1951.

Rogers, C. R. *On Becoming a Person.* Boston: Houghton Mifflin, 1961.

Rusalem, H., & Malikin, D. (Eds.). *Contemporary Vocational Rehabilitation.* New York: New York University Press, 1976.

Schlossberg, N. K., & Entine, A. D. *Counseling Adults.* Monterey, Calif.: Brooks/Cole, 1977.

Schlossberg, N. K.; Troll, L. E.; & Leibowitz, Z. *Perspectives on Counseling Adults: Issues and Skills.* Monterey, Calif.: Brooks/Cole, 1978.

Shertzer, B., & Stone, S. C. *Fundamentals of Guidance* (3rd ed.). Boston: Houghton Mifflin, 1976.

Sifenos, P. E. *Short-term Psychotherapy and Emotional Crisis.* Cambridge, Mass.: Harvard University Press, 1972.

Sinick, B. *Counseling Older Persons.* New York: Human Sciences Press, 1977.

Skovholt, T. N.; Schauble, T. G.; & Davis, R. (Eds.). *Counseling Men.* Monterey, Calif.: Brooks/Cole, 1980.

Stewart, J. C. *Counseling Parents of Exceptional Children.* Columbus, Ohio: Merrill, 1978.

Strong, S. R. Counseling: An interpersonal influence process. *Journal of Counseling Psychology,* 1968, *15,* 215–224.

Tanney, F. *Counseling Psychologists in Private Practice.* Paper presented at the American Psychological Association Convention, Montreal, 1980.

Thoresen, C. E., & Ewart, C. K. Behavioral self-control and career development. *Counseling Psychologist.* 1976, *6*(3), 29–43.

Toomer, J. Counseling psychology in business and industry. *Counseling Psychologist,* 1982, *10,* in press.

Valle, S. K. *Alcoholism Counseling.* Springfield, Ill.: Thomas, 1979.

Whiteley, J. L. *The History of Counseling Psychology.* Monterey, Calif.: Brooks/Cole, 1980.

Whiteley, J. L., & Fretz, B. *The Present and Future of Counseling Psychology.* Monterey, Calif.: Brooks/Cole, 1980.

Woodman, N. J., & Lenna, H. R. *Counseling with Gay Men and Women.* San Francisco: Jossey-Bass, 1980.

Yalom, I. D. *The Theory and Practice of Group Psychotherapy.* New York: Basic Books, 1975.

Yalom, I. D. *Existential Psycholotherapy.* New York: Basic Books, 1980.

Zeigarnik, B. Über das Behalten von erledigten und unerledigten Handlungen. *Psychologische Forschung,* 1927, *9,* 1–85.

Ziv, A. *Counseling the Intellectually Gifted Child.* Toronto: University of Toronto, Faculty of Education, 1977.

COVARIANCE ANALYSIS

See Analysis of Variance and Covariance.

CREATIVITY

In the past three decades there has been an enormous amount of research and writing on the topic of creativity. Many approaches to the study of creativity have appeared, and creativity's relationship to hundreds of other variables has been examined. Space limitations permit consideration of only a few central issues and topics.

This entry begins by drawing a distinction between creativity as measured by tests and creativity as measured by real-life accomplishments. There follows a discussion of the advantages and disadvantages of various criteria that have been used to assess real-life creativity. The issues of field and level differences in real-life creativity are presented. Next, we turn our attention to the use of tests as measures of creativity. A few of the widely used divergent-thinking tests are described. The issue of their independence and discriminability from conventional IQ tests is reviewed, followed by a consideration of their relation to real-life creative accomplishments. Next to be considered are the findings of some studies assessing real-life creativity in two areas: science and art. There follows a section on training and education for creativity. The entry concludes with a discussion of theories about the nature of the creative process.

Two Approaches.   The outpouring of research and theorizing about creativity has left the topic fragmented. There is still no consensus about how to define or measure creativity. Colloquial usage of the term "creativity" is one source of the problem. Mention creativity and some people immediately think of monumental achievements, such as Einstein's theory of relativity or Michelangelo's Sistine Chapel. Other people deem any activities in music, literature, and the arts to be creative by definition. Still others see creativity in the clever and original ideas expressed by young schoolchildren. Perhaps because of the diversity of phenomena that have been called creative, researchers studying creativity have developed different definitions.

Within this diversity, two fundamentally different approaches to the study of creativity can be distinguished. The first defines creativity in terms of test performance. The divergent-thinking tests developed by Guilford (Guilford, 1967; Guilford & Hoepfner, 1971), Torrance (1966), and others to measure divergent-thinking abilities have often been used as measures of creativity. Divergent-thinking tests use problems that allow many possible solutions. One type of problem often found in these tests requires a subject to think of a large number of ideas in connection with a new and unusual situation. For example, what would happen if people no longer needed to sleep?

Researchers who use tests to measure creativity assume that the abilities being tested are essential to real-life creativity and that persons with high test scores have high potential for creative accomplishments. Such researchers have studied educational and situational variables affecting creativity test scores, as well as other variables of interest, including IQ scores, academic and nonacademic achievement, and personality traits. However, if test performance does not correspond closely to real-life creative achievement, then the many studies defining creativity in terms of test performance are misleading. This point is critical, since Wallach (1971) has persuasively argued that creativity test scores do not vary one-to-one with real-life creative attainments and can be influenced by factors that have nothing to do with real-life creativity. For example, a person will score higher on a brick-uses test if eagerness to please the tester leads to extra effort or persistence in generating alternative uses.

The second broad approach to the study of creativity avoids such problems by attempting to measure real-life creativity directly and then relating it to other variables, such as personality characteristics and child-rearing experiences. Real-life creativity is expressed in products, such as poems, symphonies, books, inventions, and scientific theories. Jackson and Messick (1967) have proposed that creative products are characterized by four features: novelty, value, transformation, and condensation. A creative product must be novel or unusual, but this feature is insufficient to make a product creative. The suggestion that automobile tires be made of cloth is probably novel, but it is not creative, because it would not work. Creative products must possess some value or appropriateness in addition to novelty. Jackson and Messick also think that highly creative products are characterized by properties of transformation and condensation. Transformed products force the viewer to see something from a new perspec-

tive. For example, Heisenberg's uncertainty principle changed the way philosophers and physicists viewed the certainty of empirically based knowledge. Products with high levels of condensation possess a concentration of meaning, so that someone repeatedly examining the product is likely to discover additional meanings.

Criteria. Needless to say, the criteria for creativity products are relative. Judgments of novelty, value, transformation, and condensation must be made with respect to some reference group in a given field at a given time. What is novel at one point in time may not be novel later on. The early paintings of the impressionists were highly creative in their time, but a painting using the same techniques today would not necessarily be regarded as creative.

Defining the criteria for creative products does not by itself solve the problem of how to measure real-life creativity directly. To assess the creativity of a group of persons in a field, one might use expert ratings of a sample of each person's products. This approach appears to have some potential. Ultimately, expert ratings might be reduced to even more objective dimensions. For example, in the area of creative writing, Malgady and Barcher (1977, 1979) showed that teachers' judgments of creativity were influenced by such quantifiable dimensions as productivity, novelty, figures of speech, and flexibility. But because of the practical difficulties in getting groups of experts to rate large numbers of products, product ratings have seldom been chosen to assess real-life creativity. Instead, persons have been rated or nominated, usually by experts or supervisors. It should be noted that ratings of persons are potentially subject to contamination by other variables, such as intelligence, productivity, and professional visibility.

Another criterion for creativity is available for use in scientific fields. The reference journal *Science Citation Index* provides data on the frequency with which a scientist's work is cited by other scientists. If scientists generally cite work that they consider to be original and valuable, citation counts should provide reasonably valid measures of scientific creativity. Citation counts have been used frequently by sociologists (e.g., Chubin, 1973; Cole & Cole, 1971; Reskin, 1977) but only on infrequent occasions by educational researchers (e.g., Segal, Busse, & Mansfield, 1980; Walberg, Rasher, & Mantel, 1977).

Field and Level Differences. In studies of real-life creativity it is important to specify the field being studied. One cannot assume that the correlates and antecedents of creativity are the same across fields. Creative engineers and creative poets may show few similarities. The majority of studies of real-life creativity among adult professionals have been done with persons in scientific and scientifically related fields. The scattered results from other fields do not yet permit much generalization.

In addition to possible field differences in creativity, there may be differences stemming from different levels of creativity. For example, the antecedents of scientific creativity in high school students may be different from the antecedents of scientific creativity among adult professional scientists. A distinction between creativity at the adult professional level and creativity at lower, "amateur" levels seems justified, because products judged creative at the adult professional level are novel and valuable in relation to other existing products at the time of their creation. On the other hand, products at the amateur level may be relatively creative, when, for example, compared with the products of other high school students, but rarely, if ever, do they represent significant contributions to a field.

Some evidence bearing on this distinction comes from a study (Segal, Busse, & Mansfield, 1980) of several hundred male biologists selected from listings in *American Men and Women of Science*. Data on their amateur-level scientific interests and activities from grade school through graduate school were gathered by means of a questionnaire. The scientists' achievement and creativity at the professional level were measured by journal publications and citations to published work. These adult criteria were found to be predictable from a number of items in the graduate school years: publications, presentations at professional meetings, and various awards. Only a few activities and accomplishments from the college years predicted professional-level creativity, and very few items from grade school or high school showed relationships to the adult creativity criteria. At least in this field, biology, there were fewer links between amateur-level and professional-level creativity than might have been expected.

Cognitive Tests. Researchers using the first approach outlined above have developed a variety of tests to assess creativity. Usually, these researchers have assumed that cognitive abilities are central to creativity and have therefore used cognitive tests. Most of the commonly used tests derive from the work of Guilford and his coworkers (Guilford, 1967; Guilford & Hoepfner, 1971). Guilford developed a "structure of intellect" model that suggested the importance of numerous mental abilities distinct from those measured by conventional intelligence tests.

Although some of the tests Guilford developed to measure these abilities have been used in basic psychological research, educational researchers have most often used other divergent-thinking tests that were derived at least in part from Guilford's work. Two of the widely used cognitive test batteries will be briefly described here. Torrance (1966) developed a battery of tests called the Torrance Tests of Creative Thinking. The battery consists of several verbal and figural subtests yielding verbal and figural scores on four dimensions: fluency, flexibility, originality, and elaboration. Sometimes these tests are summed across dimensions and/or across the verbal and figural domains to yield summary scores. Wallach and Kogan (1965) developed a test battery consisting of three verbal and two figural subtests. Each subtest is scored for ideational fluency and for uniqueness of responses, and overall scores on these dimensions are then calculated.

Other cognitive tests sometimes used as measures of creativity include a battery developed by Getzels and Jackson (1962), the Remote Associates Test, devised by Mednick (1962), and Thinking Creatively with Sounds and Words (Torrance, Khatena, & Cunnington, 1973).

Problems with creativity tests. A focal issue among creativity researchers is the question of whether creativity tests really measure creativity. The validity of commonly used divergent-thinking tests have been analyzed in detail elsewhere (e.g., Crockenberg, 1972; Mansfield & Busse, 1981; Thorndike, 1966; Wallach, 1970, 1971). A few of the central questions will be highlighted here.

First, do creativity tests measure anything apart from what is measured by intelligence tests? Thorndike (1966) and Wallach (1970) have argued that in order to demonstrate the existence of a unitary and separate domain of creative or divergent-thinking abilities, one must demonstrate that different measures of creativity or divergent thinking correlate among themselves more highly than they do with measures of general intelligence. If this criterion is not met, there is no justification in postulating a separate domain of creativity, apart from general intelligence. Wallach (1970), reviewing the relevant evidence for the Guilford and Torrance batteries, concluded that neither battery meets this criterion. Not all researchers agree that a creativity measure must be independent of measures of general intelligence. Crockenberg (1972), for example, argues that even if there are moderate correlations between creativity and intelligence measures, much of the variance in creativity cannot be explained by variance in intelligence.

A study by Houtz and Speedie (1978) sheds some light on this issue. Fifth-graders were administered a battery of problem-solving and divergent-thinking tests. Many factor analyses were conducted, with the consistent finding for three-factor solutions of an ideational-fluency factor, a problem-solving factor, and a school-achievement factor. The latter two factors, which are conceptually closer to what intelligence tests measure, showed separation from the ideational-fluency factor.

The relationship between intelligence and creativity tests may depend on the level of intelligence under consideration. Some researchers have suggested that there may be a threshold of intelligence above which creativity scores are not correlated with IQ scores. Crockenberg (1972), reviewing the relevant evidence on the Torrance Tests of Creative Thinking, concluded that the evidence favors this interpretation.

Wallach and Kogan (1965) initially proposed that in order to measure divergent-thinking abilities uncontaminated by intelligence, it is necessary to avoid standard test-taking conditions, under which performance is timed and an evaluative context is apparent. Instead, Wallach and Kogan proposed that their divergent-thinking tests be administered under untimed, gamelike conditions. A number of studies bearing on this issue were subsequently conducted. Reviewing the evidence, Wallach (1971) concluded that ideational fluency and intelligence were largely independent, under both the gamelike, untimed conditions and the standard, timed conditions. This conclusion was corroborated more recently in a carefully controlled study by Hattie (1980), who also pointed out the greater feasibility of the standard approach for classroom use.

An equally important issue concerns the criterion-related validity of creativity tests. To what extent do divergent-thinking tests relate to measures of real-life creativity? One line of evidence comes from studies investigating relationships between divergent-thinking test performance and teacher judgments of creativity (e.g., Thacker & Rosenbluh, 1972; Treffinger, Feldhusen, & Thomas, 1970; Yamamoto, 1963). In a review of studies using the Torrance tests, Wallach (1970) concluded that teachers cannot judge the creativity of students apart from their general intelligence. And since the Torrance tests also correlate positively with intelligence, any correlations between teacher judgments of creativity and creativity test performance can be explained by common associations of these variables with intelligence. Thus, studies of teacher judgments of creativity do not provide very good evidence about the criterion-related validity of divergent-thinking tests.

Better evidence comes from studies relating divergent-thinking test performance to real-life creative accomplishments. A few such studies have been conducted involving the Torrance tests (Torrance, 1969, 1972a, 1972b; Torrance, Tan, & Allman, 1970), but these studies have serious limitations, chief among them being an inability to determine whether the creative accomplishments were in fact really creative. Somewhat better evidence is available for the Wallach and Kogan (1965) tests. For example, Wallach and Wing (1969) administered four of the Wallach-Kogan tests to students who were about to enter the freshman class at Duke University. Ideational productivity on these tests was significantly related to self-reported nonacademic attainments in art, writing, science, and leadership but not in dramatics, music, or social service. Uniqueness scores from these tests showed the same significant results, except for nonacademic attainments in leadership. A number of conceptual and methodological problems in this study have been pointed out by Feldman (1970). Results similar to those of Wallach and Wing were obtained by Bartlett and Davis (1974) in a study of college undergraduates in a creativity course, and by Milgram and Milgram (1976) in a study of Israeli high school seniors. These results indicate that the Wallach and Kogan tests sometimes show relationships to real-life accomplishments, some of which may be considered creative. On the other hand, less encouraging results were obtained by Kogan and Pankove (1972, 1974) in a longitudinal study of students progressing from fifth to twelfth grade.

Both the Torrance battery and the Wallach and Kogan battery are designed for children and therefore have not been studied in relation to the real-life creativity of adult professionals. But other cognitive tests, including several developed by Guilford and his associates, have been related to real-life creativity, mostly in scientifically oriented fields. Reviewing this evidence, Mansfield and Busse (1981) concluded that most of the divergent-thinking tests have failed to show relationships with measures of real-life creativity in scientific fields. The same negative results generally held for a variety of other cognitive and perceptual tests. It is still an open question whether divergent-thinking tests would show relationships to real-life professional-level creativity in nonscientific fields.

Even if divergent-thinking tests showed consistent relationships with real-life creativity, there would remain some serious logical problems with the assumption that we can understand real-life creativity by studying people identified as creative on the basis of divergent-thinking test scores. Wallach (1971) pointed out that if divergent-thinking test scores varied one-to-one with creative accomplishments, there would be no problem with using the test scores as a proxy measure of real-life creativity. But no creativity test even comes close to approximating a one-to-one relationship with real-life creativity. Moreover, divergent-thinking test scores are affected by many variables that have nothing to do with creativity. For example, divergent-thinking test scores can be enhanced if a person is obsessive or persistent in generating alternate responses, or if a person wants to please an experimenter and therefore tries harder. For these reasons, as Wallach (1971) concludes, real-life creativity can only be understood by studying it directly.

There might be less controversy about creativity tests if they were called by some other name. Since creativity tests usually involve the fluent generation of ideas, students who score high on the tests are very likely to be students who spontaneously generate many unusual ideas in the classroom. If this behavior is of interest, educational researchers may wish to study ideationally fluent students, just as they may wish to study reflective students or field-independent students. But the term "creativity," when applied to high scorers on divergent-thinking tests, suggests unwarranted connections to real-life creative accomplishments. And if it is those accomplishments that we wish to understand, we must study them directly.

Studies of Real-life Creativity. Studies using the second approach to the study of creativity, in which the creativity measure is based on real-life accomplishments, offer the best hope of illuminating the correlates, antecedents, and processes associated with creativity. The most useful studies of this type measure creativity within a group of adult professionals in a field and relate their creativity to other variables of interest. Studies comparing professionals in one field with those in another field or with general population norms are less helpful, since there probably are differences between fields in the variables associated with real-life creativity. Much of the research on real-life creativity has been conducted in scientific fields and related areas such as mathematics. This evidence will be considered first, followed by a section on artistic creativity.

Scientific creativity. On the basis of the results from personality and vocational tests, as well as personal-history questionnaires, Mansfield and Busse (1981) summarized the personal characteristics that appear to be associated with scientific creativity. First, three characteristics are viewed as preconditions for attainment of the professional level in a scientific field. These include above-average intelligence as well as field-specific cognitive abilities, extensive training in a field, and at least a minimal level of emotional adjustment. Beyond these three factors, several personality characteristics seem to differentiate more creative scientists from their less creative peers: autonomy, personal flexibility, originality and novelty, need for professional recognition, commitment to work, and need for aesthetic sensitivity. It appears that high levels of real-life scientific creativity depend on the joint occurrence of several of these personal characteristics. To some extent, moderate levels on one characteristic might be compensated for by higher levels on another characteristic.

Some of these characteristics may be manifested at amateur levels during the years before scientists formally enter their profession. In one study of male high school physics students (Walberg, 1969), a creative group showed evidence supporting the hypothesized adult characteristics of commitment to work and need for originality and novelty. The creative group, who reported having achieved public recognition or awards for scientific projects, were more persistent in carrying things through and completed their work faster than a less creative comparison group. In addition, the creative group felt more creative, imaginative, and curious and more often believed that it is important to be creative.

Mansfield and Busse (1981) also reviewed the evidence relating real-life scientific creativity to family child-rearing antecedents. Most such studies used only males. Family variables related to creativity in males include upper-middle-class status, frequent moving, and being a first-born. The scientifically creative male is likely to have shared scientific interests and hobbies with his father and to have received some intellectual stimulation from his parents. However, relationships with his parents were unlikely to have been exceptionally warm or close. His parents, in their child-rearing practices, were likely to have encouraged autonomy and independence.

Artistic creativity. The most complete study of artistic creativity is the work of Getzels and Csikszentmihalyi (1976). Almost 200 college art students were given cognitive, perceptual, and personality tests, as well as a biographical questionnaire. In addition, all students were interviewed and were asked to do a still-life drawing, during which various observational data were collected. These art students differed from the general population in a variety of ways. For example, although the art students scored near the average for college students on two IQ tests, they scored much higher on various perceptual tests, as well as on a measure of aesthetic judgment. On a test of values, they scored very high on an aesthetic dimension and considerably lower on social and economic dimensions. The art students were socially reserved and aloof, serious and introspective, low in superego strength, subjective, unconventional, imaginative, radical and experimental, and resolute and autonomous in making their own decisions. Female art students tended to be more dominant than other females, while male art students were more sensitive and effeminate in their feelings than other males.

These characteristics differentiated the artists from persons in other fields but did not necessarily differentiate creative from less creative artists. Getzels and Csikszentmihalyi presented other evidence about variables associated with creativity among the artists sampled. Measures of artistic achievement in school were related to several personality variables in males, including aloofness, low ego strength, introspection, sensitivity, imaginativeness, self-sufficiency, and lack of conformity to social norms. In addition, successful males tended to place very low priority on economic values. Female success in art school showed no relationships to personality variables but was related to perceptual ability.

A second approach to real-life creativity comes from ratings of the still-life drawings that thirty-one male fine arts majors were asked to produce under standardized conditions. The researchers were especially interested in the process of finding an artistic problem and hypothesized that this process is at the core of artistic creativity. On the basis of observations of the students while they worked on the drawings and on interviews with the students afterward, the researchers developed a series of problem-finding measures. An overall problem-finding measure correlated substantially with artists' ratings of originality of the drawings. This relationship showed almost no change when ratings for overall value and for craftsmanship were partialed out of the originality ratings.

A third set of findings relevant to artistic creativity came from a follow-up study of the thirty-one male fine arts majors. Seven years after the original data were collected, the artistic success of these fine arts students was crudely rated. The more successful artists were more likely to have had mothers who were employed, to have been first-born as opposed to middle-born children, to have indicated a religious preference other than Protestant, and to have come from a well-to-do, educated, higher-status family. Studio grades in art were correlated with later artistic success, but grades in academic courses were negatively related. Only one personality variable, low concern for social approval, was related to later artistic success. Some measures of problem finding, derived from the still-life drawing, also showed significant correlations with later success.

Several additional studies provide evidence that is generally consistent with the results of Getzels and Csikszentmihalyi. Barron (1972) administered two personality inventories as well as numerous other psychometric tests to a group of student artists. Summarizing his results, Barron (p. 49) characterized the student artists as "independent and unconventional, vivid in gesture and expression, rather complex psychodynamically but with an emphasis upon openness, spontaneity, and whimsicality rather than neurotic complicatedness." Roe (1975) observed that a basic personality characteristic of male artists is passivity and almost feminine submissiveness, which she interpreted as being due to a high level of responsiveness to external stimuli. Cross, Cattell, and Butcher (1967) compared visual artists with crafts students and a nonartistic control group. On a standard personality inventory the artists differed significantly from the controls on twelve of the sixteen measures. The artists were more reserved, assertive, self-sufficient, suspicious, guilt-prone, and tense than the controls. The artists were higher in bohemian tendency but lower in emotional stability, self-integration, and superego strength than the controls. The crafts students tended to score between the artists and controls but for the most part did not differ significantly from the controls. None of these studies measured creativity among artists. Thus the obtained characteristics may or may not be related to creativity among artists.

An additional study sheds light on the creative process in art. Eindhoven and Vinacke (1952) studied the processes of artists and nonartists who were asked to paint a picture to illustrate a poem. The artists spent much more time in the early stages (planning and the initial sketch) than did the nonartists and much more time on the final sketch. Artists also tended to produce more new sketches than nonartists in the early stages. These results are consistent with Getzels and Csikszentmihalyi's (1976) emphasis on the importance of problem finding.

Training and Education.   With the burgeoning interest in creativity over the last three decades, one popular concern has been the training of creativity. The wide variety of techniques and programs that have been developed to enhance creativity are described by Stein (1974, 1975) and by Mansfield, Busse, and Krepelka (1978).

The key question is whether people can be trained to be creative. Unfortunately, some of the widely used techniques have been infrequently or inadequately evaluated. The evaluation studies that have been conducted are reviewed by Mansfield, Busse, and Krepelka (1978). Space permits only brief descriptions of three of the more frequently evaluated programs. The Productive Thinking Program (Covington et al., 1974) is a self-instructional program for fifth-graders and sixth-graders, consisting of fifteen booklets depicting detective stories in cartoon format. Instruction is provided in a variety of problem-solving skills, including both divergent and convergent thinking but with an emphasis on the latter. The Purdue Creative Thinking Program (Feldhusen, Speedie, & Treffinger, 1971), consisting of twenty-eight audio tapes with accompanying exercises, is aimed at fostering divergent-thinking abilities in children at about a fourth-grade level. Each audio tape consists of a three-minute to four-minute presentation with specific creative-thinking suggestions, followed by a ten-minute historical story featuring an American pioneer. Printed exercises provide practice in divergent-thinking skills. A third program, developed by Parnes (Parnes, 1967; Parnes, Noller, & Biondi, 1977) for college students, highlights the idea-generating group technique of brainstorming. While brainstorming, participants are encouraged to state all ideas that come to mind, however wild or impractical they may seem. No evaluation or criticism of ideas is permitted. In addition to brainstorming, the Parnes program employs a wide variety of other techniques.

In studies evaluating these programs, divergent-thinking or other cognitive tests are typically administered before and after training, and the effectiveness of training is assessed by gains on these tests. The three programs described above, as well as many others, have often produced gains on divergent-thinking tests. Superficially, it would appear that creativity can be trained. But this optimistic conclusion is undermined by conceptual and methodological problems in most studies. Chief among these problems is the assumption that creativity can be equated with divergent thinking, as measured by divergent-thinking tests. As was stated earlier, there is little evidence that any relationship, much less a strong one, exists between divergent-thinking tests and real-life creativity, either at the professional level or at the lower, "amateur" levels. Thus, even if training programs could enhance divergent-thinking abilities, there would be little reason to suppose that these gains would be reflected in increases in real-life creativity.

It is not even clear that gains on divergent-thinking tests following training indicate that divergent-thinking abilities have been enhanced. As Wallach (1971) points out, these gains may result from extraneous factors such as increased persistence in the generation of responses, "Hawthorne effects," or an implicit demand from the experimenter for improvement. Another possibility is that the training may simply communicate a better idea of the kinds of answers that are valued on the tests. Indeed, studies have shown that it is possible to facilitate divergent-thinking performance simply by altering the instructions under which the test is administered. For example, instructions to brainstorm have shown facilitating effects in a number of studies (Bouchard, 1969; Meadow, Parnes, & Reese, 1959; Parnes & Meadow, 1959; Turner & Rains, 1965). Instructions to provide original, clever, or creative responses have also been effective (e.g., Christensen, Guilford, & Wilson, 1957; Gilchrist & Taft, 1972; Ridley & Birney, 1967).

Although it is not clear whether creativity training programs actually improve divergent-thinking abilities, the more important question is whether the programs affect real-life creativity. This question is largely untested. Keating (1980) argued that education for creativity has emphasized divergent thinking to the exclusion of three other, equally important components of real-life creativity: content knowledge, critical analysis, and communication skills. Content knowledge refers to a deep and thorough familiarity with previous work in a field. Without such knowledge, Keating believes, it is virtually impossible to advance beyond the status quo in a field. Critical analysis, although sometimes seen as antithetical to creativity, enables the individual to select promising from less promising avenues of inquiry, so that the chances of a creative discovery are maximized. Finally, communication skills are essential if a creative idea or an artistic conception is to be realized in some creative product. One implication of Keating's position is that programs designed to foster real-life creativity should exist within the context of rigorous instruction in a specific content area.

A different avenue to an understanding of education for creativity is to find some creative adults and ask them about teachers who influenced their creative development. In a study by Chambers (1973), chemists and psychologists, identified as creative on the basis of expert nominations and evaluations of published work, completed questionnaires about teachers who had had a significant facilitating or inhibiting effect on their creative work. The facilitating teachers were usually well prepared for class and taught in an informal manner. They accepted disagreement from students and were likely to use it to stimulate discussion. Their students saw them as hard-driving, dynamic, and intellectually demanding, with a personal interest in teaching and a high level of commitment to their field. They gave extensive encouragement to students outside of class. Inhibiting teachers were more concerned with memorization of materials, and they discouraged independent study. They were unenthusiastic and rarely showed originality or creativity in the classroom. They had difficulty accepting disagreement from students. Surprisingly, direct reinforcement for students' creative behavior was not characteristic of either group of teachers. The teachers who had the greatest influence on these scientists' work were encountered in the graduate as opposed to the undergraduate years. The most influential aspect of the facilitating teachers' behavior was the encouragement they provided to students outside the classroom.

Theories. Many theories attempting to describe the creative process have been proposed. The major ones are reviewed by Busse and Mansfield (1980). Two general observations can be made about these theories. First, most of them offer psychological rather than physiological explanations of creativity. Little is yet known about the neurological processes or structures relating to creativity, although there has been a flurry of speculation about left-brain, right-brain issues (e.g., Andrews, 1980; Bogen & Bogen, 1976; Rubenzer, 1979; Torrance & Mourad, 1979). Second, many of the theories, because of their vaguely defined concepts, are not easily testable. But we will review several of the main theoretical perspectives.

Psychoanalytic theorists, such as Kris (1952) and Kubie (1958), emphasize the importance of preconscious processes. These processes are believed to occur when the ego, with its emphasis on logical, rational thought, temporarily loosens its control of the thinking processes, so that an unorganized, drive-oriented type of thinking can occur. It is at this preconscious level of thinking that facilitating associations between ideas related to the immediate problem and other, apparently unrelated but potentially useful ideas are most likely to occur. The ideas produced in this way can later be evaluated in a logical, rigorous way. To engage in preconscious thinking, one must allow oneself to daydream and fantasize.

Gestalt psychologists (e.g., Köhler, 1969; Wertheimer, 1959) use the terms "productive thinking" and "problem solving" to refer to what others might call creative thinking. Wertheimer describes productive thinking as a process of successive restructurings of a problem. The structural features of the problem itself set up stresses and tensions in the thinker. By following up these stresses and tensions, the thinker is led to a restructuring of the problem. Successive restructurings occur until a solution emerges. This model of problem solving seems more applicable to convergent problems, with only one or a few right answers, than to divergent problems, with many possible solutions.

Associationist theories involve the common assumption that creativity results from novel or unusual associations. Mednick (1962, p. 221), for example, defines the creative process as "the forming of associative elements into new combinations which either meet specified requirements or are in some way useful." The degree of creativity depends on the relative remoteness of the elements used to form the new combination. When asked to respond to a stimulus word, creative people are likely to give some remote or uncommon responses, whereas less creative people tend to give only common, stereotyped responses. Many other persons (e.g., Gruber, 1974; Hadamard, 1945; Haslerud, 1972; Koestler, 1964, 1978) have incorporated associationist principles into their theories.

A number of theories are composites in the sense that they combine principles from psychoanalytic, Gestalt, and associationist theories. Hadamard (1945), focusing on mathematical creativity, developed a theory with psychoanalytic as well as associationist ideas. Hadamard proposed a sequence of four steps in the creative process: preparation, incubation, illumination, and verification. The initial preparation period is conscious, systematic, and logical, but sets in motion some unconscious thinking processes that are essential to the incubation and illumination phases. The unconscious mind produces a vast number of associations, most of which are useless. Only the potentially fruitful ideas, selected by the unconscious mind for their beauty or elegance, are allowed to reach consciousness in the phase of illumination. The last step of the creative process, verification of the value of the idea and establishing its implications, is entirely conscious.

Some theories combine psychoanalytic and associative elements. For example, Koestler (1964, 1978) developed a "bisociation" theory of creativity. In bisociation, two independent matrices of ideas come into contact, but this occurs only subconsciously, through a regression to the preconscious thinking processes stressed by psychoanalytic theorists. Rothenberg (1979) has proposed a psychoanalytically based theory that highlights two thinking processes that, like bisociation, facilitate association of independent ideas. Janusian thinking involves actively thinking of two or more opposite or antithetical ideas simultaneously. Homospatial thinking involves imagining two or more discrete entities simultaneously occupying the same space. Both of these processes are conscious and goal-directed, in contrast to the preconscious processes emphasized by other psychoanalytic theorists.

Gruber's theory (1974) draws on the associationist and Gestalt positions, as well as on Piaget's theory of cognitive development. In Gruber's view, creative accomplishments are fueled by conscious, purposeful action, and unconscious processes are not critical. Rather, when people direct all their efforts toward some goal, the problems occupying their conscious thoughts will also spill over into imagery and dreams. Creative thought is preceded by a period of persevering search and inquiry. After such a period, idea discovery can occur. Creativity occurs when previously independent systems of ideas interact. Discovery results not from a single association but from a succession of small changes or restructurings.

Mansfield and Busse (1981) proposed a somewhat similar model of the creative process in scientific fields, involving five steps: (1) selection of a problem that is both important and potentially soluble, (2) extended effort to solve the problem, (3) setting constraints on the solution of the problem, (4) changing the constraints through a restructuring process, and (5) verification and elaboration of the results.

Several other theories merit brief mention. Schachtel (1959) explained creativity in terms of a perceptual openness, which allows an individual to approach an object repeatedly, from varied perspectives. Rogers (1959) emphasized the uniqueness of individuals as a source of creativity. Personal characteristics, such as openness to experience, an internal locus of evaluation, and the ability to toy with elements and concepts facilitate creativity. Feldman (1974) viewed creativity as a special case of the more general intellectual advance through Piaget's stages of logical reasoning.

Most theories of the creative process have had relatively little effect on what happens in schools and classrooms, although, as noted earlier, there have been attempts to train divergent-thinking abilities. Perhaps the task of the next decade will be to apply these theories to education, especially with reference to programs for the gifted.

Richard S. Mansfield
Thomas V. Busse

See also Aesthetic Education; Art Education; Dramatic Arts Education; Gifted Persons; Individual Differences; In-telligence; Music Education; Writing, Composition, and Rhetoric.

REFERENCES

Andrews, M. F. The consonance between right brain and affective, subconscious, and multi-sensory functions. *Journal of Creative Behavior*, 1980, *14*, 77–87.

Barron, F. *Artists in the Making*. New York: Seminar Press, 1972.

Bartlett, M. M., & Davis, G. A. Do the Wallach and Kogan tests predict real creative behavior? *Perceptual and Motor Skills*, 1974, *39*, 730.

Bogen, J. E., & Bogen, G. M. Creativity and the bisected brain. In A. Rothenberg & C. R. Hausman (Eds.), *The Creativity Question*. Durham, N.C.: Duke University Press, 1976.

Bouchard, T. J. Personality, problem-solving procedure, and performance in small groups. *Journal of Applied Psychology Monograph*, 1969, *53*(1, Part 2).

Busse, T. V., & Mansfield, R. S. Theories of the creative process: A review and a perspective. *Journal of Creative Behavior*, 1980, *14*, 91–103, 132.

Chambers, J. A. College teachers: Their effect on creativity of students. *Journal of Educational Psychology*, 1973, *65*, 326–334.

Christensen, P. R.; Guilford, J. P.; & Wilson, R. C. Relations of creative responses to working time and instructions. *Journal of Experimental Psychology*, 1957, *53*, 82–88.

Chubin, D. On the use of the *Science Citation Index* in sociology. *American Sociologist*, 1973, *8*, 187–191.

Cole, J., & Cole, S. Measuring the quality of sociological research: Problems in the use of the *Science Citation Index. American Sociologist*, 1971, *6*, 23–29.

Covington, M. V.; Crutchfield, R. S.; Davies, L.; & Olton, R. M. *The Productive Thinking Program: A Course in Learning to Think*. Columbus, Ohio: Merrill, 1974.

Crockenberg, S. B. Creativity tests: A boon or boondoggle for education? *Review of Educational Research*, 1972, *42*, 27–45.

Cross, P. G.; Cattell, R. B.; & Butcher, H. J. The personality pattern of creative artists. *British Journal of Educational Psychology*, 1967, *37*, 292–299.

Eindhoven, J. E., & Vinacke, W. E. Creative processes in painting. *Journal of General Psychology*, 1952, *47*, 139–164.

Feldhusen, J. F.; Speedie, S. M.; & Treffinger, D. J. The Purdue Creative Thinking Program: Research and evaluation. *National Society for Performance and Instruction Journal*, 1971, *10*(3), 5–9.

Feldman, D. H. Faulty construct-ion. *Contemporary Psychology*, 1970, *15*, 3–4.

Feldman, D. H. The developmental approach: Universal to unique. In S. Rosner & L. E. Abt (Eds.), *Essays in Creativity*. Croton-on-Hudson, N.Y.: North River Press, 1974.

Getzels, J. W., & Csikszentmihalyi, M. *The Creative Vision*. New York: Wiley, 1976.

Getzels, J. W., & Jackson, P. W. *Creativity and Intelligence*. New York: Wiley, 1962.

Gilchrist, M. B., & Taft, R. Originality on demand. *Psychological Reports*, 1972, *31*, 579–582.

Gruber, H. E. *Darwin on Man: A Psychological Study of Scientific Creativity* (Together with Darwin's early and unpublished notebooks transcribed and annotated by P. H. Barrett). New York: Dutton, 1974.

Guilford, J. P. *The Nature of Human Intelligence*. New York: McGraw-Hill, 1967.

Guilford, J. P., & Hoepfner, R. *The Analysis of Intelligence.* New York: McGraw-Hill, 1971.

Hadamard, J. *The Psychology of Invention in the Mathematical Field.* Princeton N.J.: Princeton University Press, 1945.

Haslerud, G. M. *Transfer, memory, and creativity.* Minneapolis: University of Minnesota Press, 1972.

Hattie, J. Should creativity tests be administered under test-like conditions? An empirical study of three alternative conditions. *Journal of Educational Psychology,* 1980, *72,* 87–98.

Houtz, J. C., & Speedie, S. M. Processes underlying divergent thinking and problem-solving. *Journal of Educational Psychology,* 1978, *70,* 848–854.

Jackson, P. W., & Messick, S. The person, the product, and the response: Conceptual problems in the assessment of creativity. In J. Kagan (Ed.), *Creativity and Learning.* Boston: Houghton Mifflin, 1967.

Keating, D. P. Four faces of creativity: The continuing plight of the intellectually underserved. *Gifted Child Quarterly,* 1980, *24,* 56–61.

Koestler, A. *The Act of Creation.* New York: Macmillan, 1964.

Koestler, A. *Janus: A Summing up.* New York: Random House, 1978.

Kogan, N., & Pankove, E. Creative ability over a five-year span. *Child Development,* 1972, *43,* 427–442.

Kogan, N., & Pankove, E. Long-term predictive validity of divergent-thinking tests: Some negative evidence. *Journal of Educational Psychology,* 1974, *66,* 802–810.

Köhler, W. *The Task of Gestalt Psychology.* Princeton, N.J.: Princeton University Press, 1969.

Kris, E. *Psychoanalytic Explorations in Art.* New York: International Universities Press, 1952.

Kubie, L. S. *Neurotic Distortion of the Creative Process.* New York: Noonday Press, 1958.

Malgady, R. G., & Barcher, P. R. Psychological scaling of essay creativity: Effects of productivity and novelty. *Journal of Educational Psychology,* 1977, *69,* 512–518.

Malgady, R. G., & Barcher, P. R. Some information-processing models of creative writing. *Journal of Educational Psychology,* 1979, *71,* 717–725.

Mansfield, R. S., & Busse, T. V. *The Psychology of Creativity and Discovery: Scientists and Their Work.* Chicago: Nelson-Hall, 1981.

Mansfield, R. S.; Busse, T. V.; & Krepelka, E. J. The effectiveness of creativity training. *Review of Educational Research,* 1978, *48,* 517–536.

Meadow, A.; Parnes, S. J.; & Reese, H. Influence of brainstorming instructions and problem sequence on a creative problem-solving test. *Journal of Applied Psychology,* 1959, *43,* 413–416.

Mednick, S. A. The associative basis of the creative process. *Psychological Review,* 1962, *69,* 220–232.

Milgram, R. M., & Milgram, N. A. Creative thinking and creative performance in Israeli students. *Journal of Educational Psychology,* 1976, *68,* 255–259.

Parnes, S. J. *Creative Behavior Guidebook.* New York: Scribner, 1967.

Parnes, S. J., & Meadow, A. Effects of "brainstorming" instructions on creative problem-solving by trained and untrained subjects. *Journal of Educational Psychology,* 1959, *50,* 171–176.

Parnes, S. J.; Noller, R. B.; & Biondi, A. M. *Guide to Creative Action: Revised Edition of Creative Behavior Guidebook.* New York: Scribner, 1977.

Reskin, B. F. Scientific productivity and the reward structure of science. *American Sociological Review,* 1977, *42,* 491–504.

Ridley, D. R., & Birney, R. C. Effects of training procedures on creativity test scores. *Journal of Educational Psychology,* 1967, *58,* 158–164.

Roe, A. Painters and painting. In I. A. Taylor & J. W. Getzels (Eds.), *Perspectives in Creativity.* Hawthorne, N.Y.: Aldine, 1975.

Rogers, C. R. Toward a theory of creativity. In H. H. Anderson (Ed.), *Creativity and Its Cultivation.* New York: Harper & Brothers, 1959.

Rothenberg, A. *The Emerging Goddess.* Chicago: University of Chicago Press, 1979.

Rubenzer, R. The role of the right hemisphere in learning and creativity: Implications for enhancing problem-solving ability. *Gifted Child Quarterly,* 1979, *23,* 78–100.

Schachtel, E. G. *Metamorphosis.* New York: Basic Books, 1959.

Segal, S. M.; Busse, T. V.; & Mansfield, R. S. The relationship of scientific creativity in the biological sciences to predoctoral accomplishments and experiences. *American Educational Research Journal,* 1980, *17,* 491–502.

Stein, M. I. *Individual Procedures.* Vol. 1 of *Stimulating Creativity.* New York: Academic Press, 1974.

Stein, M. I. *Group Procedures.* Vol. 2 of *Stimulating Creativity.* New York: Academic Press, 1975.

Thacker, B. T., & Rosenbluh, E. S. Creativity as a reflection of teacher-pupil relationships. *Psychology,* 1972, *9*(1), 23–26.

Thorndike, R. L. Some methodological issues in the study of creativity. In A. Anastasi (Ed.), *Testing Problems in Perspective.* Washington: American Council on Education, 1966.

Torrance, E. P. *Torrance Tests of Creative Thinking: Norms-technical Manual.* Princeton, N.J.: Personnel Press, 1966.

Torrance, E. P. Prediction of adult creative achievement among high school seniors. *Gifted Child Quarterly,* 1969, *13,* 223–229.

Torrance, E. P. Predictive validity of the *Torrance Tests of Creative Thinking. Journal of Creative Behavior,* 1972, *6,* 236–252. (a)

Torrance, E. P. Career patterns and peak creative achievements of creative high school students twelve years later. *Gifted Child Quarterly,* 1972, *16,* 75–88. (b)

Torrance, E. P.; Khatena, J.; & Cunnington, B. F. *Thinking Creatively with Sounds and Words.* Lexington, Mass.: Ginn and Co., 1973.

Torrance, E. P., & Mourad, S. Role of hemisphericity in performance on selected measures of creativity. *Gifted Child Quarterly,* 1979, *23,* 44–55.

Torrance, E. P.; Tan, C. A.; & Allman, T. Verbal originality and teacher behavior: A predictive validity study. *Journal of Teacher Education,* 1970, *21,* 335–341.

Treffinger, D. J.; Feldhusen, J. F.; & Thomas, S. B. Relationship between teachers' divergent thinking abilities and their ratings of pupils' creative thinking abilities. *Measurement and Evaluation in Guidance,* 1970, *3,* 169–176.

Turner, W. M., & Rains, J. D. Differential effects of "brainstorming" instructions upon high and low creative subjects. *Psychological Reports,* 1965, *17,* 753–754.

Walberg, H. J. A portrait of the artist and scientist as young men. *Exceptional Children,* 1969, *36,* 5–11.

Walberg, H. J.; Rasher, S. P.; & Mantel, H. Eminence and citations in educational psychology. *Educational Researcher,* 1977, *6*(3), 12–14.

Wallach, M. A. Creativity. In P. H. Mussen (Ed.), *Carmichael's Manual of Child Psychology* (Vol. 1, 3rd ed.). New York: Wiley, 1970.

Wallach, M. A. *The Intelligence/Creativity Distinction.* New York: General Learning Press, 1971.

Wallach, M. A., & Kogan, N. *Modes of Thinking in Young Children.* New York: Holt, Rinehart & Winston, 1965.

Wallach, M. A., & Wing, C. W., Jr. *The Talented Student: A Validation of the Creativity-Intelligence Distinction.* New York: Holt, Rinehart & Winston, 1969.

Wertheimer, M. *Productive Thinking* (Enlarged ed.). New York: Harper & Brothers, 1959.

Yamamoto, K. Relationships between creative thinking abilities of teachers and achievement and adjustment of pupils. *Journal of Experimental Education,* 1963, *32,* 3–25.

CREDIT BY EXAMINATION

See Competency Testing; Experiential Education.

CULTURE AND EDUCATION POLICY

The general purpose of this article is to examine the phenomenon of cultural differences with a view to drawing out the relevance and significance of cultural diversity and cultural pluralism. Such issues as group identity and ethnicity will be considered, along with desegregation and bilingual education.

Identifying Cultural Differences. Today, as perhaps never before, there is an expanded interest in cultural differences. This is true not only of the United States but of many other countries of the world as well. Cultural differences, as an item of political and moral debate, have asserted themselves forcefully in civil rights legislation and, consequently, in admission policies, desegregation mandates, and bilingual education programs. Hence, the demands related to cultural differences are among the most forceful and persistent for educational policy makers.

The initial question raised is "What is a cultural difference?" This question can be construed in different ways. It is sometimes a question of concept, sometimes a question of fact, and sometimes a straightforward question for political decision. In each of these forms, however, it is a different question altogether and requires a different kind of answer.

For example, the question may be taken as a special case of a somewhat larger question, "What is it that we *mean* by 'cultural difference'?" We answer this by recognizing that every cultural difference implies that there is an unlikeness of either a relative or absolute kind. The difference factor may be exhibited in terms of language, literature, ethical or religious beliefs, and so on. We refer to these as intrinsic cultural traits or patterns. Other differences manifest themselves in terms of dress, speech patterns, emotional expressions, manners, and so on. These we refer to as extrinsic cultural traits. The first category of traits is basic or fundamental to the difference, whereas

the second category offers nothing significant to the sense of group identity and cultural history of the individual. If any of these were to change over time, nothing fundamental would be changed.

What the concept cultural difference "expresses," "mediates," or "reports on" is a notion of the world as specifically inhabited by groups of people who exhibit extrinsic or intrinsic unlikenesses. Hence, what we mean by cultural difference is a question of concept, and it is not an empirical question.

On the other hand, it is generally agreed that individuals and groups exhibit differences depending on time and place. Such differences are, we recognize, historically conditioned. At certain times and in certain societies, for example, we might see remarkable dissimilarities between groups based on intrinsic cultural traits. Yet, at another time the groups might exhibit a remarkable variety with regard to extrinsic traits. Or the groups might exhibit a pervasive sameness of extrinsic or intrinsic traits or both. So if the question is meant to ask, "What is a cultural difference?" in terms of what, historically, have we considered cultural differences to be, then the answer to that question will be determined by appeal to the relevant historical facts and to some understanding of the history of groups and societies.

Finally, the question "What is a cultural difference?" can be construed as a request for certain specific information: "What is it that has been decided?" "What have we decided about cultural differences?" Obviously, not all cultural differences are significant or important in society in terms of formulating social relations or an agenda of politics. Thus in an important sense we can and do answer the question quite simply by saying that a cultural difference is whatever has been decided by an appropriate legal authority of the polity.

Each of these answers offers some utility in directing our attention to certain relevant aspects of the question. But each alone does not present to our understanding the problem that needs investigation, for what is needed is a formulation of the problem so that the inquiry will focus on the relations between its conceptual, empirical or factual, and practical elements. Thus to satisfy this methodological requirement our inquiry is organized around three controlling problems. The first is to state those conditions basic or necessary to the employment of the phrase "cultural difference." The second is to examine what we have historically considered cultural differences to be. And the third is to examine which cultural differences loom large in the United States today in terms of the practical issues of group identity and ethnicity.

The reader will recognize that the three controlling problems reflect the three aspects of the question "What is a cultural difference?" The first problem is essentially the conceptual one; the second is the historically factual one; and the third is the practical side of the problem.

Conditions of Cultural Difference. The initial point is that differences of some sort exist everywhere and are visible everywhere. Every society and every member of society is different in some respect. But, and this is crucial, this observation can be made only from a certain point of view. It can be made only by somebody who looks at, say, a number of people and because of some reason or other finds it important to observe that some members are different.

Although every society and individual is different in some respect, we should recognize that it is we who, for some reason, make certain criteria rather than others count in establishing differences. To turn the coin over, when we say that a group is homogeneous, we mean simply that the ways in which the members differ are unimportant or irrelevant to any of our practical concerns. We do not mean to suggest, however, that there are no differences. Thus when we say that a group is different, we are saying that from a particular vantage point, and for some *ad hoc* reason important enough to mark off a group or individual as different, we find some intrinsic or extrinsic trait relevant.

The second point is the recognition that the selected difference marking off a group must be viewed as fundamental enough to be capable of producing dispositions, values, and beliefs that contribute to significantly different outlooks on the world. In other words, the mark of unlikeness must be capable of *making* a difference, such as giving the group a sense of peoplehood. The difference must take hold in the minds and behavior of persons, not merely in the eye of the beholder, and the difference must have a concrete social reality, being exhibited in the social behavior of some of society's members.

The points in the foregoing analyses are (1) that any notion of cultural difference will involve selected differences and (2) that the difference must be regarded as basic to the group's sense of peoplehood. These understood, we turn to an examination of the historically factual aspects of cultural differences.

Traditionally, national origin and religious affiliation, along with race, have been the most prominent group affiliations in the United States. But race is obviously not a cultural difference but a physical difference. Thus the claim that race is a traditionally cultural difference bears special attention.

It is important at the outset to note that race, technically, refers to differential concentrations of gene frequencies responsible for traits that, as far as we know, are confined to physical manifestations such as hair form or skin color. Race as such has no intrinsic connection with cultural patterns and institutions. On the other hand, national origin and religious affiliation are both cultural phenomena, having their embodiment in cultural institutions: national states and formal religion.

However, race, national origin, and religious affiliation have had the distinct function in society of serving to create, over time, a sense of peoplehood for groups. The history of the United States is replete with peoplehood identification along these lines. Indeed, the concept of WASP

(white Anglo-Saxon Protestant) embodies this point quite succinctly. Moreover, the history of American immigration and socialization cannot be told apart from these elements. Gordon (1964) tells us that the American who answers the question "Who are you?" commonly answers from an ethnic (race, religion, or national origin) point of view: "I am of the White or Negro or Mongoloid Race, I am a Protestant, Catholic, or Jew, and I have German, or Italian, or Irish, or English or whatever, national background" (p. 26).

With regard to ethnicity, Gordon employs the term "ethnic group" to refer to any group "which is defined or set off by race, religion, or national origin, or some combination of these categories" (p. 27). Similarly, Glazer and Moynihan (1970) treat blacks "as an ethnic group in New York, parallel to other ethnic groups" (p. xiii).

Finally, in ordinary language use, race, national origin, and religious affiliation have been employed in interchangeable fashion in referring to group identity, particularly ethnic identity, each being used as a common referent of peoplehood, often interchangeably, and reinforced by each other in the language.

When race is thought of with these consequences in mind—consequences that are simplified but not exaggerated—it can be seen that the race has indeed served as a mark of cultural difference. Moreover Title II of the Civil Rights Act of 1964 (P.L. 88-352, sec. 201) says: "All persons shall be entitled to the full and equal enjoyment of the goods, services, facilities, privileges, advantages, and accommodations of any place of public accommodation, as defined in this section, without discrimination or segregation on the ground of race, color, religion, or national origin." Also, Title VI (sec. 601) of the same act tells us: "No person in the United States shall, on the ground of race, color or national origin, be excluded from participation in, be denied benefits of, or be subjected to discrimination under any program or activity receiving federal financial assistance." The burden of the discussion is this: cultural differences historically have been reduced to those of race, national origin, and religious affiliation. In recent years, emphasis on the religious element has been somewhat reduced, but use of the term "ethnic" has expanded. This is a curious development.

Raywid (1975) has pointed out that the phrase "ethnic group" was "previously restricted to national groups, often in religious combination (as, for example, Irish Catholic) but the term has recently come prominently to apply to Blacks as well" (p. 89). She contends further: "We've not given much attention to the considerable switch this represents in identifying *cultural* difference or ethnicity: from acquired or learned differences like nationality, to biological differences such as race. According to current usage, Blacks are an ethnic group, and at least some women have acquired that particular consciousness of kind entitling them to ethnic group status too. And this, of course, represents an even further extension of ethnicity, from a racial to a sexual basis" (pp. 89–90). We are witnessing here a shift from a rather narrow view of cultural differences to a broader, more encompassing one. In effect, we can expect cultural differences to play a growing and more important role in social relationships, particularly in the arena of educational policy making, and this expanded role may not be welcome or pleasant for everyone.

The complete analysis of "What is a cultural difference?" can never be made merely by listing its conceptual and historical aspects. In addition, there is such a thing as the practical side of the problem.

Societies range from those composed of one group (monistic) or two groups (dyadic) to those that have many groups (pluralistic) (Newman, 1973). Societies that are customarily described as culturally diverse are composed of numerous groups that, either by virtue of political coalitions or on the basis of their own critical size, are able to resist being lumped into an undifferentiated mass. American society represents a clear case of cultural diversity, with many recognized and accepted large groups vying with one another in a political system of countervailing powers.

In this important respect, there is a practical dimension of the problem of cultural differences, and this practical dimension emerges in the consideration of cultural diversity. Cultural diversity is not identical with cultural differences, for one further condition marks cultural diversity: it is accomplished by cultural transmission, having a sociopsychological base. We know that for cultural diversity to exist in society, cultural differences must, over time, be made incarnate in terms of establishing a sense of peoplehood—historical identity—and this requires both an ancestral and future-oriented identification with the group. The intrinsic traits that mark group identity must be transmitted from generation to generation if the group is to continue to maintain itself. It is doubtful if cultural diversity would long exist if groups did not jealously guard their intrinsic traits and patterns as well as limiting the members' social sphere of relations, particularly in childhood.

Cultural diversity, then, suggests something more than cultural differences. It suggests group differentiation measured in terms of the number of groups in society. Unfortunately, there has not yet been enough comparative study to specify the exact limits of what is meant by cultural diversity. That is, what of the relative sizes of groups? When does a relatively small group become a small subgroup of the mass? This question is difficult to answer. It remains an open question whether there are significant limits in terms of group numbers, beyond which the group is no longer considered as having a significant critical mass.

This problem, although important, need not sidetrack us. The United States does reveal itself as a highly differentiated society containing a large number of groups that compete through effectiveness in organization and achievement. The broadening effect of ethnicity, with increasing numbers of ethnic groups and groups wishing to be called ethnic, has its basis in the legitimation of ethnicity in a society reinforcing the tendency of interest groups to become ethnic groups. Group strength and solidarity are functions of the degree to which individual members share a common set of values, live by a common set of norms, and aspire to a common goal or set of goals. The greater the number of ethnic groups competing for the scarce resources of society, the greater the tendency will be for cohesiveness in each group.

Hence, practically speaking, group participation along ethnic lines has become more salient than class in vying for society's goods because it can combine an interest with an affective tie. That is, group interests can be mobilized and made very effective in the political arena along the lines of ethnicity. Illustrative of this are various minority, feminist, gay, elderly, and fundamentalist movements.

Cultural Diversity and Cultural Pluralism.   We have seen that cultural diversity suggests sizable but different groups coexisting in a common society. This view, it should be noted, makes no judgment about whether this state of affairs is desirable or undesirable, for the phrase "cultural diversity" simply records the fact mentioned above. Beyond this there is nothing else implied by the phrase.

Cultural pluralism is, however, not merely a descriptive phrase. It is much more controversial, expressing a social ideal or ideology. Disputes over the meaning of cultural pluralism still exist, long after Kallen first introduced it in 1915 (Kallen, 1924). The disputes are primarily creedal, or ideological, since in all its employments or senses cultural pluralism speaks to the ways in which a society ought to be organized and the manner in which the young should be socialized. (This last point is immensely important for educators.)

It is thus misleading in the extreme to refer to cultural diversity either as cultural pluralism or as an ideology. Both notions are false. To do so is to confuse fact and value. Cultural diversity describes a factual state of affairs; cultural pluralism refers to a desired state of affairs. Hence, the latter concept is more controversial and debatable than the former.

Perhaps this point will be made clearer by the following. For simplicity's sake, it is assumed that cultural diversity may be symbolized by *A, B, C, D*, with each letter standing for a cultural group, be it religious, racial, or of national origin. Hence, we account for the marking off of cultural groups (difference criterion), but we do not need to know what the differences are or the criteria justifying the "difference."

The second element to be considered is what the proper goal or outcome of cultural groups in society should be. In effect, this element is a judgment about how to achieve the "good society." It gives its stamp of approval to a particular goal, and that goal need not be, nor usually is it, an existing state of affairs.

Thus, briefly, cultural diversity serves as a necessary condition of any cultural ideology, but it is not sufficient. There also must exist a judgment regarding the best goal of society. Moreover, although the goals or hoped-for results of ideologies differ, each assumes that the young should be socialized according to the goal. (Pratte, 1979).

What this sketch so far offers is the deep sense of kinship between cultural diversity and cultural pluralism: the belief that the true value of a society can be realized only in situations that promote cultural groups living together in the polity but separated by "differences" in order to guarantee the freedom of racial or religious communality and traditions. The differences, at the same time, should not interfere with the carrying out of standard responsibilities in American civil life. In this ideology, it should be noted, cultural diversity is valued and celebrated, but both assimilation and amalgamation deny the worth of cultural diversity. On the other hand, as viewed by cultural pluralists, the polity must acknowledge the reality and desirability of cultural diversity as well as the prior claim of the group entity to its members' obedience and loyalty.

It is obvious that cultural pluralism conceives of cultural diversity as fundamental to the good society. In simple terms, the ethnic enclaves of America are not its weakness but its strength. Ethnic group membership is not to be viewed as a marginal existence removed from the larger society but rather as a positive form of social identity— peoplehood—a way of knowing who you are, what your roots are within the larger, often depersonalized, society.

It is often unnoticed by either cultural pluralists or their opponents that, ideologically, cultural pluralism is celebrated not because it actually achieves any single function in society but because it is said to promote, more effectively than any other ideology, a belief in freedom of association, implying the further belief that a society must afford room for many competing life-styles and that no one style is superior to others. Herein lies a powerful tenet of cultural pluralism: the celebration of cultural diversity and the notion that society benefits as a whole from cultural pluralism (Kallen, 1954).

Let us be specific. What are some of the value assumptions of cultural pluralism? Kallen (1956) put it this way: "The freer, the more civilized, is likely to be the personality which lives and moves and nourishes its being among the diverse communions" (p. 25). The assumption here is that respect for and receptivity to different others is enhanced by an identity nourished in prideful cultural group attachment.

This notion is emotionally appealing, and some would argue that it is the least controversial assumption in cultural pluralism. Yet is it? First, the claim that identity that is rooted in prideful cultural group attachment produces a sense of place and security is questionable, and it does not follow that a sense of place and security ensures respect for different others.

Let us look at the first claim. One of the most important aspects of living in a culturally diverse society is that minority group members are always, to some degree, caught between their own identities as members of the larger society and their identities as members of an ethnic group. Being Irish, Puerto Rican, Jewish, or black has different meanings depending upon the audience to which that role is being played. Thus group members must continually cope with multiple roles and realities, which may often conflict with one another, and with their "hyphenated" identity. This is a difficult and, for many, a frustrating business. Individuals may tire of the required role playing and, in extreme cases, question their very sense of identity. In psychological terms, the most distressing instance of this kind of situation is when we have the "marginal man." A fine literary example of this is found in Piri Thomas's autobiography *Down These Mean Streets* (1967). Thomas is faced with at least three role choices: white, black, and Puerto Rican identity. His account provides a vivid account of how he vacillates among these different worlds, finally coming to grips with the meaning of yet another identity, that of being a Puerto Rican of mixed parentage in a culturally diverse society.

So the claim that identity that is rooted in prideful cultural group attachment produces a sense of place and security is not well established. But what of the second claim that a sense of pride and security ensures respect for different others?

It can be legitimately argued that there is little or no evidence for this claim. It is an assumption badly in need of empirical verification, and at this point in time we have no such evidence. Further, however, we are considering an identity rooted in prideful cultural group attachment, not just a sense of pride and identity/security. While acknowledging that respect for the values and customs of other peoples is certainly more desirable than bigotry or ethnocentricism, we should not forget that an identity rooted in a group works against respect for individuality. That is what Patterson (1975) has called the "pluralist fallacy." "The greater the diversity and cohesiveness of groups in a society, the smaller the diversity and personal autonomy of individuals in that society" (pp. 10–11). The depressing conclusion is that ethnic cohesiveness implies increasing individual conformity, for group diversity is antithetical to individual diversity and autonomy. It is the strength and cohesiveness of the group that determines its success in society, and as the struggle between groups becomes more desperate, the tendency is toward viewing others as hostile groups rather than as other individuals worthy of our respect.

Desegregation and Bilingual Education. It is often said that desegregation and bilingual education are not compatible. Segregation is seen as a necessary evil of bilingual instruction, because it is generally agreed that a homogeneous group of a minimum of twenty students (critical mass criterion) is essential for the school to provide cost-effective bilingual services. Indeed, laws mandating bilingual instruction usually do not require compliance if fewer than twenty students in the district are limited English proficient (LEP). Obviously, if bilingual programs are contingent upon the strength of numbers, the more students that can be clustered, the more comprehensive the program that can be offered. Desegregation, then, is seen as disruptive to bilingual education, because it disperses the critical mass necessary to justify bilingual education. Conversely, bilingual education is seen as disruptive to desegregation because it produces segregation.

The assumed dichotomy between school desegregation and bilingual education is a divisive issue in the United States today, especially because on the one hand bilingual instruction is the only educational service that the Hispanic communities collectively have demanded from governments and on the other hand desegregation is supported by a large segment of blacks.

The following, although oversimplified, sets forth the problem. If a school district does not respond to the special needs of LEP, then a federal statutory violation has occurred; on the other hand, to ignore school segregation is a constitutional violation. In short, if bilingual education programs increase ethnic or national origin segregation, then the ability to meet desegregation mandates is jeopardized.

Desegregation. The landmark decision of the United States Supreme Court in the case *Brown* v. *Board of Education* (1954) was a significant decision promising a new era of racial justice. The Court ruled that segregated schools were "inherently unequal" and indicated that these schools must be desegregated "with all deliberate speed." Through desegregation policies, those who had suffered the denial of educational opportunity were to have access to equal schooling facilities and all that is entailed by that description.

On another tack, desegregation, in addition to providing every child an educational opportunity commensurate with his or her abilities, posits the proposition that affirmative federal and state action is the proper remedy for the serious inequalities in American society. The idea is advanced that an individual's right to educational opportunity is a desirable social policy. Moreover, the policy is assumed to make the community more equal overall.

What is important in the foregoing is that desegregation policies can go far toward advancing the conditions of equality of educational opportunity. For example, teachers can help students to believe it possible for them to gain schooling benefits by showing them there are advantages in so doing. School practice and programs should be structured to emphasize that school personnel are on the side of students, exhibiting this in countless ways by showing students esteem and approval. Finally, all students, but especially minorities, need to be assisted in exercising educational opportunity. Students must be given countless opportunities to choose to gain schooling benefits. In this regard, they cannot be given the same education as others but must be given educational equity: advantages commensurate with their status as a deprived racial minority.

Thus the enterprise of desegregation policy, although not primarily a device to increase student achievement, or indeed to accomplish any other educational goal, can have as goals increasing minority student achievement and making schools generally more effective for all students (Crain & Mahard, in press). If the enterprise reflects such

goals, then computer-assisted instruction, organized use of audiovisual materials, carefully screened and structured reading curricula, extensive use of extracurricular activities, new methods of classroom organization, and improvisational teaching methods can be utilized as elements of desegregation planning. This claim, which is a recommendation that the enterprise of desegregation policy be amended so as to allow for attention paid to improving students' achievement, deserves consideration.

In short, although desegregation itself guarantees neither academic success nor academic failure, it does provide educational challenges and opportunities. Desegregation planners can use a desegregation order as an opportunity to institute new programs and, subsequently, will probably find test scores improving, at least for minority groups—and nonminority students as well.

Bilingual education. Bilingual education, whereby students receive instruction in their native language while simultaneously learning English as a second language (ESL), is directly traceable to the federal Bilingual Education Act of 1968, which provided the first federal funds for bilingual education, and the Bilingual Education Act of 1974. The landmark case in bilingual education, however, was *Lau* v. *Nichols* (1974). It presented the issue of whether non–English-speaking students who constitute national-origin minority groups can receive an education free from unlawful discrimination when instructed in English, a language they do not understand. *Lau* was based on Title VI of the Civil Rights Act of 1964 (Public Law 88-352): "No person in the United States shall, on the ground of race, color or national origin, be excluded from participation in, be denied benefits of, or be subjected to discrimination under any program or activity receiving federal financial assistance."

What was in question was whether non–English-speaking students can receive an equal educational opportunity when instructed in a language they do not understand. In short, *Lau* states that equality of education goes beyond providing the same "access"—buildings, teachers, curriculum, and textbooks—to all students. The Court reasoned: "Under these state-imposed standards there is no equality of treatment merely by providing students with the same facilities, textbooks, teachers, and curriculum; for students who do not understand English are effectively foreclosed from any meaningful education" (p. 566).

In principle as well as before the law, we violate the individual's right to educational opportunity when we teach entirely in English those students who do not understand English. Let us be specific. Consider the case of a bright 9-year-old Chicano who does not understand English but is taught entirely in English. Can we say that he is a student? That is, can the youth carry out the necessary student functions basic to gaining schooling benefits? Of course not. The youth is attending school, but by no stretch of the imagination would we say that he is "studenting." To put it differently, he has no opportunity to partake of the educational programs of the school. In short, he is not experiencing equal educational opportunity. Further, he and other LEPs cannot avoid evoking active contempt from the dominant group, for the dominant group have succeeded in bettering their condition, some through sheer force of will, and they see no flaws in an educational system that is deaf to non–English-speaking youths.

It is now possible to see that at the heart of the desegregation/bilingual controversy is the matter of cultural diversity. There are deep-seated fears of creating segregated Hispanic, Chinese, and other national-origin communities in a predominantly English-speaking society.

Also it is now possible to see that it is dangerous not to recognize that desegregation and bilingual education are valuable strategies for achieving equality of educational opportunity. The reason is straightforward. Within the public political realm, policy makers must grasp that it is dangerous to pit blacks against Hispanics.

It is suggested that the nesting (Kerr, 1976) of bilingual education within a desegregation policy might ensure the success of desegregation. If bilingual education policy is made an integral part of a district's school program, then the logistics of "desegregating" bilingual instruction and eliciting the support of, say, the Hispanic or the Chinese community for the desegregation process might be readily achieved.

This established, we return to the alleged school desegregation/bilingual dichotomy. For those who think in terms of equality of educational opportunity, desegregation and bilingual education are mutually supportive strategies for achieving equality of educational opportunity. If educational policy is made from this basis—that desegregation and bilingual education are essential elements leading to the achievement of equality of educational opportunity for different groups of students—then we might maximize educational opportunity for all children.

Social Policy on Education. At the heart of cultural pluralism in the United States is the belief that through social policy schools can come to honor and implement cultural diversity while increasing equality of educational opportunity and improving the outcome of education.

It is not an overstatement to claim that the problem of cultural inequality remains a standing reproach to American morality and to our hope for the future. Although tremendous progress has been made in recent decades in stamping out racial discrimination, economically troubled times always reveal its lingering presence. The fight against racism, ethnic and religious prejudice, sexism, and other injustices must continue, along with a good measure of affirmative action.

We need to understand how thoroughly the United States has become a national society. In reality, America has become, in an economic and political sense, an extraordinarily compact or interconnected society. Witness, for example, the national significance of such issues as nuclear power, the location of the MX missile sites, oil and airline deregulation, and the uses of federal lands.

The past few decades have demonstrated that the problems of equity are not likely to be resolved at the local level. The public schools, as local institutions, are the captives of pluralistic politics, intentionally and unintentionally, discriminating against weaker and poorer classes. It is now recognized that a judgment regarding inequality requires a frame of reference larger than the local level, one reached from a comparison of resources, opportunities, and programs spanning school districts and states.

This broader view plus the "legalization of education"— the view that legal reasoning not only regulates the schools but is the proper model for changing them—has placed state and local boards of education, institutional boards of trustees, school administrators, and faculty on the losing side in a struggle for power over who will run our nation's schools.

Nathan Glazer (1975, pp. 104–123) has argued that the reach of the law is being extended not only by court decisions but by the response of the executive and legislative branches as well. In turn, however, the actions of courts, legislatures, and executive orders have a powerful effect upon the schools. The process, then, is reciprocal, mutually reinforcing, and in the end, circular. In short, litigation concerning schools, especially regarding cultural differences, has the effect of shifting policy making away from the local level to the state and federal levels.

A clear example of the federal government's involvement in policy making that modifies education is seen in *Brown* v. *Board of Education* (1954). As suggested previously, the Supreme Court advanced the view that blacks were being denied equal educational opportunity. The original objective of the decision was to remove barriers to equal educational opportunity. In short, desegregation was ordered as the cure for segregation.

Desegregation orders, however, raise the question "Does desegregation cure the problems of segregation?" Practically speaking, desegregation is not enough; "successful" desegregation is required, and it is not measured merely by a "proper balance" of whites and blacks in schools but by scores on tests of academic achievement as well. The requirement of "successful" desegregation makes equality of educational opportunity less of a concern that the outcomes of the educational process (achievement).

The transition from a concern for equality of educational opportunity to a concern for the outcomes of the educational process can be seen in a series of federal initiatives designed to improve educational achievement among poor students. In 1965 Congress enacted the Elementary and Secondary Education Act (Public Law 89-10). Title I of that act (sec. 101) called for financial assistance to school districts with "concentrations of children from low-income families" to meet "the special educational needs of educationally deprived children."

In 1966 the *Equality of Educational Opportunity Report* (the "Coleman report") defined the policy debate in education. The study by Coleman et al. had the effect of shifting policy attention from its traditional focus on comparison of inputs to a focus on output. Indeed, social policy attention has become fixated upon outcomes rather than upon inputs or processes.

In 1972 the federal government officially concluded that none of its previous efforts nor those of local and state educational authorities had yet had the deserved educational outcomes. Congress, in Public Law 92-318, sec. 405, declared that the policy of the United States is "to provide to every person an equal opportunity to receive an education of high quality." With this statement, Congress gave birth to the National Institute of Education (NIE), which was to search systematically and scientifically for the means to achieve the desired outcomes of education, among which was equal educational opportunity and a high equality of education.

In sum, the federal government has attempted to evolve a standard of adequacy of educational opportunity and achievement, and in this regard the government has enlisted the cooperation of local and state educational agencies. Thus many school districts and states have mandated that learning occur in schools (performance-based learning, competency learning, accountability, etc.), demanding that learning goals be specified in measurable outcomes.

Overall, then, social policy reform began with a concern for equal educational opportunity, but by the 1970s the ideal of equal educational opportunity was replaced by the concept of adequacy of educational achievement. Today, in many states, a strong tone of accountability permeates the educational process, and this reflects a shift from increasing equality to increasing productivity.

Richard Pratte

See also Bilingual Education; Equity Issues in Education; Ethnography; Multicultural and Minority Education; Sociology of Education.

REFERENCES

Brown v. *Board of Education*, 347 U.S. 483 (1954).

Coleman, J. S.; Campbell, E. Q.; Hobson, C. J.; McPartland, J.; Wood, A. M.; Weinfeld, F. D.; York, R. L. *Equality of Educational Opportunity*. Washington, D.C.: U.S. Government Printing Office, 1966. (ERIC Document Reproduction Service No. ED 012 275)

Crain, R. L., & Mahard, R. E. How a desegregation order can affect student achievement. *Civil Rights: Civil Liberties Law Review*, in press.

Glazer, N. Towards an imperial judiciary? *The Public Interest*, No. 4 (Fall 1975), pp. 104–123.

Glazer, N., & Moynihan, D. P. *Beyond the Melting Pot* (2nd ed.). Cambridge, Mass.: MIT Press, 1970.

Gordon, M. M. *Assimilation in American Life*. New York: Oxford University Press, 1964.

Kallen, H. M. *Culture and Democracy in the United States*. New York: Boni & Liveright, 1924.

Kallen, H. M. *Cultural Pluralism and the American Idea*. Philadelphia: University of Pennsylvania Press, 1956.

Kerr, D. H. *Educational Policy*. New York: McKay, 1976.

Lau v. *Nichols*, 414 U.S. 563 (1974).

Newman, W. M. *American Pluralism*. New York: Harper & Row, 1973.

Patterson, O. Ethnicity and the pluralist fallacy. *Change*, March 1975.

Pratte, R. *Pluralism in Education*. Springfield, Ill.: Thomas, 1979.

Raywid, M. A. "Pluralism as a basis for educational policy: Some second thoughts." In J. F. Weaver (Ed.), *Educational Policy*. Danville, Ill.: Interstate Printers, 1975.

Thomas P. *Down These Mean Streets*. New York: Knopf, 1967.

CURRICULUM AND INSTRUCTION IN HIGHER EDUCATION

Understanding the issues that complicate curriculum and instructional discussions and developments requires some grasp of the historical and philosophical backgrounds from which these issues arise. Hence this article starts with a brief review of these backgrounds, presents five contrasting philosophical views, and remarks on other factors that influence program development. The discussion considers the various concepts and definitions essential to an analysis of the present scene and those structures constituting the major components for development of curricular and instructional variations. Preoccupation with these structures too frequently usurps the time and effort that should be directed to the more fundamental problems of how and what students do and should learn. The result is a proliferation of content coverage in an excessive number of courses and a duplication of programs, both of which heighten costs and dilute, if they do not destroy, quality.

Historical and Philosophical Differences. The confused state of college curriculums and instruction arises from diverse origins and conflicting expectations (Dressel, 1976; Levine, 1978; Rudolph, 1977). The ultimate origins lie in ancient Greece, where education was initially expected to produce good citizens. Contrasting views of "good" existed in Sparta and Athens. Sparta demanded soldiers; Athens wanted a composite ideal for war and peace. Both regarded the educated individual as serving the needs of the state.

As Athenian influence expanded, the emphasis in education shifted to personal development and advancement. This trend, viewed by conservatives as disruptive, led Socrates and others to seek a unifying and integrative concept or principle. Socrates proposed the "examined life" and the view that education should release the universal values and truths embedded in every man. Plato sought an integration of all knowledge (temporal and spiritual) around the idea of the "good." Aristotle distinguished between intrinsic worth and utilitarian applications of knowledge. Although he sought to unite sensory and rational aspects of cognition, philosophy and science still tended to develop independently. Rome emphasized utilitarianism and hence deemphasized distinctions between actions and reason. Yet the seven liberal arts of the Romans (the *trivium* and the *quadrivium*), viewed by early Christian educators as essential for understanding Christianity, became the basis for the medieval education. The medieval university also included professional studies—specifically, medicine, law, and theology.

The Renaissance emphasized reason as a means of discovering unifying cognitive and affective truths contributing to the perfection of humanity. Since reality (nature) is, in a measure, random or accidental, it was regarded as a fit subject for man to study, and reason (the means to truth) required that education employing and developing reason be available to all. The perfect society should emerge from perfecting individual capacity. But as resources were exploited to attain an industrial society, reason was turned to improvement of technology. The natural sciences supplanted the humanities.

In the nineteenth century, democratic education was directed toward attaining nationalistic ideals and emphasized the natural and social sciences. German universities were already sponsoring research within a scientific framework of thought. Oxford and Cambridge, in contrast, were slow to sponsor research. The early American college, modeled upon the English college, offered a classical curriculum emphasizing languages (Latin, Greek, Hebrew) and religion as means of providing an educated ministry. However, the combined impact of demand for modern languages; professors with Ph.D.'s from the German universities; technical and professional training in engineering, agriculture, veterinary medicine, business administration, and other fields; attention to the natural sciences; inclusion of social sciences (economics, sociology, political science, history, psychology, and anthropology); and the addition of creative and performing arts and modern literature led to curriculum expansion, to new institutions (land grant colleges, technical institutes), and to a broadened conception of the baccalaureate. Alternative programs, options, and electives became inevitable (Rudolph, 1977).

Community colleges made postsecondary education more readily available on an intermittent or continuing basis. This development encouraged interinstitutional transfers, leading to difficulties in maintaining unique institutional conceptions of degree programs. The baccalaureate came to be equated with the accumulation of a specified number of credits (Gerhard, 1955).

A spate of philosophical terms—"rationalism," "realism," "idealism," "humanism," "neohumanism," "electicism," and "instrumentalism"—reflect these developments. However, these labels have remained unknown to faculty members engrossed in defining introductory departmental courses and programs for majors. Depth in the major or vocational specialty should require 30 to 60 percent or more of a baccalaureate degree program, but increased general education (breadth) has become recognized as a way of preserving remnants of liberal education (Dressel & Mayhew, 1954; Hook, Kurtz, & Todorovich,

1975). The several philosophical views implicit in these developments may be characterized as

1. *Theocentric*, making divine sovereignty and glory the central truth, with all other truth dependent upon or emergent from that ultimate source (Hong, 1955);
2. *Ideocentric*, emphasizing the worth of the accumulated knowledge in the disciplines (Phenix, 1964);
3. *Sociocentric*, making individual service to society (or the nation) the central purpose of education (Greene et al., 1943; Handlin & Handlin, 1970);
4. *Idiocentric*, assuming that a democratic society requires maximal individual development (Chickering, 1969; Perry, 1968); and
5. *Eccentric*, a view highlighting the individual instructor as a model for student emulation (Eble, 1971).

These five views result in assignment of quite different priorities to disciplinary content, physical education, foreign languages, communication and mathematical skills, common experiences (core), performing arts, and career development.

The curriculum emerges from complex interactions among many factors. The influences of students (individually and collectively), faculty (also individually and collectively), administrators, academic traditions, and educational philosophies are at once apparent. Pressures derived from social needs and expectations, professional societies, employers, donors, and politicians play a significant role. Laws, accrediting agencies, and governing boards impose both general and specific requirements—often costly, though of dubious merit. Cataclysmic events (*Sputnik*, war, inflation) have major impact. Whatever exists in the curriculum is an artifact of diverse circumstances seldom fully recognized, yet so operative that threat of major alteration generates unified resistance. The needs of the student and their implications for revising educational objectives and experiences are easily ignored in the resulting turmoil.

Basic Concepts and Definitions. "Course" is derived from the Latin verb *currere* ("to run"). "Curriculum," in its origins, referred to a running or a race course. The curriculum and its component courses provide a structure through which a student is guided by a process of instruction. Curriculum may refer to the composite array of learning experiences provided by an institution or department or to a fixed course of study (program) leading to a certificate or degree (Dressel, 1976).

As Table 1 shows, instruction that provides structure has many synonyms: (1) catechization, coaching, schooling, teaching, tutoring (Briggs, 1970; Davis, 1976; Bruner, 1966); (2) conditioning, inculcation, drilling, indoctrination, rehearsing, training (McKeachie, 1963); (3) pedagogy, didactics (literally "foot guiding" in its Greek origins); (4) eduction, education, guidance; (5) exemplifying, modeling. Groups 1 and 2 emphasize teacher activity, the second suggesting a routine process yielding rote learning. Group 3 suggests a systematic or scientific approach to instruc-

TABLE 1. *Taxonomy of instruction and associated learning activities*

Types of instruction	*Learning activities*
1. Catechization or tutoring	Assimilation or memorizing
2. Conditioning or inculcation	Practicing or studying
3. Pedagogy or didactics	Psychology of learning
4. Eduction or education	Discovery or self-directed learning
5. Modeling or exemplifying	Imitation and internalization

tion. Group 4, in contrast with instruction, suggests influencing learning by motivation and suggestion. Group 5 presents the teacher as a model or exemplar for the learner.

In Table 1, learning as a goal of instruction has numerous synonyms (Claxton & Ralston, 1978; Gagné, 1970): (1) assimilation, absorption, cramming, memorizing; (2) studying, practicing, drilling, mastering; (3) learning psychology; (4) self-directed learning, ascertaining, determining, discovering; (5) imitation and internalization. The bases for learning are motivation, direct sensory experiences, activities, and mastery of an abstract symbolic language. Instruction facilitates learning by planning, directing, modeling, and evaluating appropriate experiences.

The incentive for human learning arose out of problems such as understanding the physical and human environment and the desire to explain, predict, and control events. Observations of and experiences with this reality yielded experiential knowledge and led to generalizations and explanatory hypotheses (both natural and supernatural). Abstractions and their manipulation generated theories based upon assumptions, definitions, and principles and laws describing relationships and interactions. As knowledge was accumulated and organized, disciplines developed. A technology (skills, rules, processes) arose to mediate between theory and practice (both direct application and creative adaptation). Disciplines became structured entities with a substantive content possessing demonstrated effectiveness in dealing with problems out of which the discipline arose, as well as having potential for solving problems not yet recognized (Ford & Pugno, 1964).

Because of the factors involved, courses may deal with the original problems (the subject matter) giving rise to a discipline, with the discipline itself, with the technology for applying discipline to new problems, or with an interdisciplinary approach to problems (Mayville, 1978). Content and the detail and extent of coverage of that content become significant concerns (Kaysen, 1973).

Instruction and learning always take place in some context. That context includes social needs and problems (Robinson, 1973), current issues and events (Association of American Colleges, 1964), immediate and remote environments, student skill deficiencies, and existing expectations

(Grant & Hoeber, 1978) regarding education. The near environment (Astin, 1968) includes the campus and associated facilities, such as auditorium, chapel, classroom, gymnasium, laboratory, lecture hall, library, museum, residence hall, seminar room, stadium, and student union. Each environmental structure implies or provides a distinctive learning experience.

Administrative, organizational, and curricular structures also influence educational processes, objectives, and outcomes (Bloom, 1956). Most of the learning experiences provided are determined by the faculty rather than by the students (Givens, 1972). The teacher lectures, demonstrates, assigns, conducts recitations (where students recite the teacher's citations), and presides over seminars and field trips. Students discuss, play roles, work, study, and travel under faculty supervision (Blackburn et al., 1976; Dressel & Thompson, 1973). The distinctions among these experiences, whether in activities or in results, are uncertain, since instructor preferences control the performance.

Higher education programs vary in several other ways. Lower-division undergraduate education tends toward common requirements, breadth, and the acquisition of fundamentals for further study. Upper-division undergraduate and advanced education highlights depth (specialization or vocational preparation). Much is made of general education, viewed variously (usually in the first two years) as the breadth component of liberal education, a needed common experience for all college graduates, or a concentrated extract of the liberal arts for all vocational and professional students (Belknap & Kuhns, 1977; Bell, 1968; Forrest & Steele, 1977; Harvard Committee, 1945; University of Chicago, 1950).

Liberal education is variously interpreted as an experience with the liberal arts, a knowledge of the essence of the human heritage (usually Western), or a commitment to humane values (Conrad, 1978; Conrad & Wyer, 1980). Enthusiastic proponents possess a sublime faith in its virtues and assert that it is destroyed by a demand for immediate relevance or long-run applicability. This contention engenders an almost unbridgeable, though artificial, barrier between liberal education and technical, business, and professional education.

Basic Development and Review Concepts. Curriculum or program development, review, and evaluation are complex because of the many interacting factors involved. Curriculum and instruction are means to encourage student involvement and facilitate student learning within the structure provided (Dressel, 1980). Curriculum planning must always take into account learner characteristics, course content, and instructional process. Course content includes organization of ideas, materials, and experiences and is based upon complexity and interdependence of concepts, requisite skills, cumulative learner proficiency in single-task performance, and integration of related tasks. Procedures for motivating, recognizing, and rewarding learning accomplishments and procedures for evaluating the efficiency and effectiveness of curriculum and instruction are components of the instructional process.

Structures and Practices.   The most obvious aspects of structure are disciplinary content selection, courses, types and places of class meetings, and academic calendar. Once commitments are made on these matters, both students and faculty members find that their efforts are constricted and that deviations are difficult and always suspect.

A common type of structure is exemplified by majors, minors, concentrations, combined majors, double majors, distribution requirements, core programs, options, and electives. These concepts offer choices, but they also structure and delimit choices. Although the terminology reflects a recognition of limitations, it also restrains individualization by terms and rules that reflect composite faculty distrust of their ability and integrity to develop sound individual student programs. Traditional disciplinary departmental–college organization makes any alternative other than departmental majors and distribution requirements difficult to attain. New interdisciplinary program units tend to seek departmental status in budget and staff and become equally rigid and self-perpetuating.

Delivery systems (lectures, textbooks, computer-assisted instruction, individually programmed instruction) often become so important that they usurp time and energy better directed to maintaining a flexible array of learning experiences.

Evaluation systems mold and are molded by instructional and curricular patterns. Factual testing engenders memorization of facts and both reflects and reinforces instructor emphases and behavior. Comprehensive examinations imposed to encourage integration across disciplines, problem solving, and high standards generate both faculty and student complaints of excessive work and irrelevance unless the curriculum and instruction already attend to these goals.

Structures affect student progress, mastery of material, coverage of content, and student perseverance in programs. Lack of sequence in courses and extensive options or electives weaken any sense of progress or mastery. Availability of all courses every term encourages stopouts and dropouts, and study abroad, travel, community service, and work-study programs may further encourage discontinuities. Most curricular changes have unanticipated results requiring yet other changes.

Innovators tend to be highly vocal and enthusiastic because they emphasize intent. Students and faculty are much less so because they find experiences and prospects falling short of both intent and claims. The success of curricular and instructional innovations is best assessed after an interval of five to ten years by noting what innovations remain and by seeking appraisals of the effects on graduates.

Proliferation and duplication.   The concern in state systems of higher education in regard to program quality,

costs, and unnecessary duplication is becoming a significant factor in forcing review of programs and instructional practices (Bowen, 1977; Lenning, 1977). Program addition or expansion requires advance approval. Faculty loads, class size, instructional models, and materials are increasingly subject to review in reference to both cost and quality. In general, it is evident that high costs, whether associated with use of traditional faculty models or innovations, do not ensure quality. It is also evident that there is little agreement as to what constitutes quality.

The natural concern of state coordinating agencies with course and program proliferation and duplication highlights what well may be the most significant factor in generating doubts about the benefits of higher education. Thoughtful and responsible citizens reasonably expect that colleges and universities display social responsibility by providing an education that is relevant to, if not specifically focused upon, attainment of the intellectual abilities and value commitments necessary for a productive and satisfying personal life in a democratic society. Internal institutional forces push in the opposite direction. The specialization of faculty lends to a proliferation of departments and of courses in them. This proliferation, in turn, results in emphasis upon students acquiring (and shortly forgetting) detailed factual knowledge with little relation to other courses in the same discipline and none at all to the long-term objectives descriptive of an educated person. Although administrators and faculty members may strive to make a virtue of this "rich array," the truth is that the wisdom required for defining meaningful individual student programs is not present either in the faculty or the students.

Institutions (ably abetted by faculty members, administrators, boards, and various public groups) aspire to expand into additional programs, because nearby institutions with these programs attract students and public recognition presently denied to the institution without the programs. This acquisitiveness can be viewed as a responsiveness to public need and demand, but response to special interests (be they internal or external) in such a context can be as irresponsible as is failure to respond in other contexts of educational needs.

In recent years, many institutions have acceded to demands by students, faculty members, and external agencies and groups for courses and programs on such diverse topics as women in history, black literature, African cultures, environmental problems, values, and esoteric languages. The acknowledged past omission or imbalance in treatment of these topics hardly justifies the addition of the many courses and degree programs in areas in which the lack of organized substantive knowledge defies development of sound programs. Moreover, as such courses develop, they overlap or duplicate materials and ideas that are or should be covered in existing courses and programs. Both the students and the faculty involved in such special program proliferation ultimately suffer by having avoided the major stream of development of knowledge and intellectual skill that are relevant and adaptable to satisfying and useful careers in many fields.

Innovative programs that attempt to reorganize and repackage knowledge ultimately face the same difficulty and are forced back into a more traditional structure. The central weakness of American undergraduate education is not in the curriculum or the patterns of instruction. These only reflect the inability of specialized faculty members and hence of institutions to come to grips with the essential nature and characteristics of college education and the means of acquiring it. When educational ends are unclear and commitments to them uncertain, the processes of education as reflected in curricular and instructional patterns are inevitably dominated by faculty concerns rather than by fundamental individual and social needs.

Paul L. Dressel

See also Effects of College Experiences; Higher Education; History and Philosophy of Higher Education; Undergraduate Instruction.

REFERENCES

Association of American Colleges. *Non-Western Studies in the Liberal Arts College.* Washington, D.C.: American Council on Education, 1964.

Astin, A. W. *The College Environment.* Washington, D.C.: American Council on Education, 1968.

Belknap, R. E., & Kuhns, R. *Tradition and Innovation: General Education and the Reintegration of the University.* New York: Columbia University Press, 1977.

Bell, D. *The Reforming of General Education.* New York: Doubleday, Anchor Books, 1968.

Blackburn, R.; Armstrong, E.; Conrad, C.; Didham, J.; & McKine, T. *Changing Practices in Undergraduate Education.* Berkeley, Calif.: Carnegie Council on Policy Studies in Higher Education, 1976. (ERIC Document Reproduction Service No. ED 130 575)

Bloom, B. S. (Ed.). *Cognitive Domain.* Handbook 1 of *Taxonomy of Educational Objectives: The Classification of Educational Goals.* New York: Longmans, Green, McKay, 1956.

Bowen, H. R. *Investment in Learning: The Individual and Social Value of American Higher Education.* San Francisco: Jossey-Bass, 1977.

Briggs, L. J. *Handbook of Procedures for the Design of Instruction.* Pittsburgh, Pa.: American Institutes for Research, 1970. (ERIC Document Reproduction Service No. ED 043 230)

Bruner, J. S. *Toward a Theory of Instruction.* Cambridge, Mass.: Harvard University Press, Belknap Press, 1966.

Carnegie Foundation for the Advancement of Teaching. *Missions of the College Curriculum: A Contemporary Review with Suggestions.* San Francisco: Jossey-Bass, 1977.

Chickering, A. W. *Education and Identity.* San Francisco: Jossey-Bass, 1969.

Claxton, C. S., & Ralston, Y. *Learning Styles: Their Impact on Teaching and Administration* (AAHE-ERIC/Higher Education Research Report No. 10). Washington, D.C.: American Association for Higher Education, 1978. (ERIC Document Reproduction Service No. ED 167 065)

Conrad, C. F. *The Undergraduate Curriculum: A Guide to Innova-*

tion and Reform. Westview Special Studies in Higher Education. Boulder, Colo.: Westview Press, 1978.

Conrad, C. F., & Wyer, J. C. *Liberal Education in Transition.* AAHE-ERIC Monograph No. 3. Washington, D.C.: American Association for Higher Education, 1980.

Davis, J. R. *Teaching Strategies for the College Classroom.* Boulder, Colo.: Westview Press, 1976.

Dressel, P. L. *Handbook of Academic Evaluation.* San Francisco: Jossey-Bass, 1976.

Dressel, P. L. *Improving Degree Programs: A Guide to Curriculum Development, Administration, and Review.* San Francisco: Jossey-Bass, 1980.

Dressel, P. L., & Mayhew, L. B. *General Education: Explorations in Evaluation.* Washington, D.C.: American Council on Education, 1954.

Dressel, P. L., & Thompson, M. M. *Independent Study.* San Francisco: Jossey-Bass, 1973.

Eble, K. E. *The Craft of Teaching.* San Francisco: Jossey-Bass, 1971.

Ford, G. W., & Pugnok, L. (Eds.). *The Structure of Knowledge and the Curriculum.* Chicago: Rand McNally, 1964.

Forrest, A., & Steele, J. *College Outcome Measures Project: Assessment of General Education Knowledge and Skills.* Iowa City, Iowa: American College Testing Program, 1977.

Gagné, R. M. *The Conditions of Learning.* (2nd ed.). New York: Holt, Rinehart & Winston, 1970.

Gerhard, D. The emergence of the credit system in American education considered as a problem of social and intellectual history. *American Association of University Professors Bulletin,* 1955, *41,* 647–668.

Givens, P. R. *Student-designed Curricula* (Research Currents). Washington, D.C.: American Association for Higher Education, 1972. (ERIC Document Reproduction Service No. ED 061 917)

Grant, M. K., & Hoeber, D. R. *Basic Skills Programs: Are They Working?* (AAHE-ERIC/Higher Education Research Report No. 1). Washington, D.C.: American Association for Higher Education, 1978. (ERIC Document Reproduction Service No. ED 150 918)

Greene, T. M.; Fries, C. C.; Wriston, H. M.; Dighton, W. *Liberal Education Reexamined: Its Role in a Democracy.* New York: Harper & Brothers, 1943.

Handlin, O., & Handlin, M. F. *The American College and American Culture: Socialization as a Function of Higher Education.* New York: McGraw-Hill, 1970.

Harvard Committee. *General Education in a Free Society* (Report of the Harvard Committee). Cambridge, Mass.: Harvard University Press, 1945.

Hong, H. (Ed.). *Integration in the Christian Liberal Arts College.* Northfield, Minn.: St. Olaf College Press, 1955.

Hook, S.; Kurtz, P.; & Todorovich, M. (Eds.). *The Philosophy of the Curriculum: The Need for General Education.* Buffalo, N.Y.: Prometheus Books, 1975.

Kaysen, C. (Ed.). *Content and Context: Essays on College Education.* New York: McGraw-Hill, 1973.

Lenning, O. T. *The Outcomes Structure: An Overview and Procedures for Applying It in Postsecondary Education Institutions.* Boulder, Colo.: National Center for Higher Education Management Systems, 1977. (ERIC Document Reproduction Service No. ED 157 454)

Levine, A. *Handbook on Undergraduate Curriculum.* San Francisco: Jossey-Bass, 1978.

Mayville, W. V. *Interdisciplinarity: The Mutable Paradigm* (AAHE-ERIC/Higher Education Research Report No. 9).

Washington, D.C.: American Association for Higher Education, 1978. (ERIC Document Reproduction Service No. ED 167 043)

McKeachie, W. J. Research on teaching at the college and university level. In N. G. Gage (Ed.), *Handbook of Research on Teaching.* Chicago: Rand McNally, 1963.

Perry, W. G., Jr. *Forms of Intellectual and Ethical Development in the College Years: A Scheme.* New York: Holt, Rinehart & Winston, 1968.

Phenix, P. H. *Realms of Meaning: A Philosophy of the Curriculum for General Education.* New York: McGraw-Hill, 1964.

Robinson, L. H. *Women's Studies: Courses and Programs for Higher Education* (Research Report No. 1). Washington, D.C.: American Association for Higher Education, 1973. (ERIC Document Reproduction Service No. ED 074 997)

Rudolph, F. *Curriculum: A History of the American Undergraduate Course of Study since 1636.* San Francisco: Jossey-Bass, 1977.

University of Chicago, Members of the Faculty. *The Idea and Practice of General Education.* Chicago: University of Chicago Press, 1950.

CURRICULUM DEVELOPMENT AND ORGANIZATION

Pronounced changes in the structures controlling curriculum in the United States have taken place within the last two decades. The final responsibility for the curriculum in local public school districts still resides with the local boards of education and their staffs, but they exercise their powers related to curriculum policy making and development within structures of authority and governance that have noticeably shifted (Boyd, 1979). Local boards of education continue to act under authority delegated to them by state statutes and within policies, regulations, and guidelines established by state educational officials. Gradually, however, they have become subject to a great many additional mandates emanating from other sources of authority greatly affecting their decision-making responsibilities for curriculum and other educational matters.

Sources of Mandates. The changes experienced by boards of education are well documented by van Geel (1976) and include four new sources of mandates.

First, there are federal court actions based on interpretations of First Amendment rights, equal protection provisions, due process provisions, and other provisions of the U.S. Constitution and of a variety of federal statutes. Mandates have arisen for meeting the language needs of non–English speakers, secular but not antireligious instruction, political education based on the marketplace-of-ideas doctrine, programs at least minimally adequate for students with special needs, and social and cultural studies that treat race, sex, age, handicaps, and other differences non-stereotypically. Federal court decisions in these areas, although not often directing exactly what must be done, set the bounds of permissibility and establish principles that must not be violated. Local school authorities cannot ignore mandates of this type.

Second, there is federal legislation establishing regulatory and/or funding powers of the executive branch of the federal government in the area of curriculum. Here mandates become applicable throughout the United States only when schools or states accept financial assistance from the federal treasury for programs allowable under legislation of this kind. The method of controlling curriculum is to make receiving funds contingent upon meeting established criteria. Numerous categories of funding have been given legislative approval by Congress: disadvantaged children, the handicapped, students of limited English-speaking ability, science education, mathematics education, environmental education, ethnic studies, foreign languages, vocational education, desegregation planning, reading, career education, consumer education, gifted education, libraries, and experimental projects. Congress has also authorized curriculum development projects to design programs and materials for use in various subject areas. Both of these forms of congressional action clearly influence the scope and content of local programs.

Third, state courts interpret state constitutional provisions on education and resolve conflicts over legislative or executive authority at state and local levels. For instance, systems for financing public education have been successfully challenged in state courts in California, New Jersey, and New York, as being in violation of equal protection clauses. Actions by the legislatures in these states to remedy these situations have simultaneously altered the allocation of authority over local schools and their programs. Formerly, state authority to tax and to control and operate school programs was delegated to local school authorities in differing degrees; now these states finance larger portions of the local school budgets, allocate funds more equitably among districts, and demand stricter accountability for the use of state moneys. In effect, more of the control of educational programs has shifted to the central authority in the states. Other cases dealing with discretionary powers of boards and school officials in fulfilling statutory duties or in offering particular courses or programs have also come before state courts. Like decisions by federal courts on issues of planning and implementing educational programs, state court decisions set parameters and precedents for future program decision making by comparable authorities. State courts, in defending the right to a public education, have created additional mandates and obligated local authorities to act upon them as well as upon the directives of state legislatures and state educational authorities.

Fourth, professional employee unions or other bargaining agents can now obligate boards of education through their negotiated contracts on matters affecting curriculum, such as provisions on class size, duty hours for teachers and pupils, time and resources for curriculum development, and the ground rules for participating formally in curriculum policy making and development. Citizens, parents, and pupils are also asking for participation privileges with the intent of influencing curriculum from their particular perspectives. Working agreements indicating the extent and form of these privileges are increasingly being made between local school boards and these groups. Those among employee or outside groups who become dissatisfied with certain substantive curriculum decisions being made by official bodies, or who believe the existing formal contracts or working agreements are not being adhered to by these authorities, frequently place their concerns before the courts for resolution rather than rely solely upon direct influence with school officials. The threat of such cases exerts a powerful influence on local educational authorities to enter into amicable, but binding, contracts or working agreements that will satisfy the interests of these groups.

It is fair to conclude that the control of curriculum is now a shared responsibility, no longer to be thought of as being primarily vested in local district educational authorities acting as agents of state governments. At the same time, it must be admitted that these local agencies are the places where all mandates set forth by those now sharing in authority for curriculum come into final focus and determine the actual educational program to be received by children, young people, and older persons in their respective districts. Authority is diffused throughout three levels of government—local, state, and federal—and emanates, as has been indicated, from all three branches of government—legislative, executive, and judicial. Local school authorities are also subject, through political and social channels, to the views of nongovernmental groups, professional educators, and parents. Final curriculum policy-making authority and the exercise of attendant administrative tasks at the local level are, therefore, complex and very difficult. A large part of the range of choice in curriculum matters has been preempted by mandates outside the immediate control of local school boards and educators. The entire system of curriculum control has shifted and become increasingly centralized, bureaucratized, legalized, and diversified (van Geel, 1979).

In attempting to account for this change in structures of curriculum control, Schaffarzick (1979) and Boyd (1979) have identified two major national shifts in social and educational values that created a political climate favorable to centralized control of curriculum. The first shift was the mounting dissatisfaction with the quality of education during the middle and late 1950s, and the second was the demand for increased justice and equality of the middle 1960s. Congress responded to dissatisfaction with the quality of education with the authorization of a series of curriculum reform projects under the National Science Foundation in 1954, the Cooperative Research Program in 1956, and the National Defense Education Act in 1958. The form that this response took was a result of the pervasive influence of a national coalition of educational experts who favored the research-and-development approach used in business and industry; subject matter programs were created, tested, and disseminated, but were left unmandated. Congress responded to the second shift in public opinion—seeking increased justice and equality for educationally neglected segments of society—with a series of categorical grant-in-aid programs to encourage state and local program improvements for preschool children, the disadvantaged, the handicapped, vocational education, ethnic studies, and bilingual-bicultural education. The form that this response took was a result of the overriding influence of various coalitions of educational reformers who found the equal rights argument persuasive with Congress for gaining funds to enhance curricula for a particular group. Sykes (1979) and Boyd (1979) suggest that the public sought government action in both instances to correct a perceived imbalance among three conflicting values: representativeness, technical competence, and leadership. The indirect approach of Congress, as well as the direct approach taken by the federal and state judiciaries and state legislatures, was supported by a public eager for increased leadership in education. In the 1950s and 1960s, these approaches were supported by public desire for technical competence in what was taught, how it was taught, and the results of this teaching. In the 1960s and 1970s, these approaches were supported by desire for equality of educational opportunity and diverse representation in curriculum policy making.

Shared authority over public school curriculum, bringing with it an array of interlocking governance structures, has been judged a mixed blessing on several counts, both political and technical (Boyd, 1979; Sykes, 1979; Atkin, 1980; Atkin & House, 1981). On technical grounds, the difficulties inherent in the current shared-control structures are quite numerous. Short (1981a) has analyzed the characteristics and consequences of using this pattern of authority and governance and found it inadequate in many ways for the task of curriculum policy making. On the basis of six criteria for adequacy, derived from the work of scholars analyzing the strengths and weaknesses of this pattern, several changes in the present authority and governance structure are recommended. The criteria stipulated are that an adequate structure of curriculum control should (1) have jurisdiction over a domain of activity that is clearly curricular in intent and function; (2) have its legislative, executive, and judicial powers systematically and compatibly allocated to its various component levels and units; (3) rely upon a thorough and viable system of interactive communication to keep its decisions and actions grounded in reality and responsive to civic desires; (4) issue only those mandates capable of being carried out within available financial resources and other administrative parameters; (5) be able to assure compliance with its mandates through formal, effective accountability procedures; and (6) prescribe a minimum of specific uniform regulations governing the implementation of its mandates.

A number of adjustments in the structure of curriculum control are implied by the analyses reported: (1) the restoration of authority over curriculum to states and local school districts should be considered, but this may be politically unfeasible; (2) if shared authority and governance in curriculum are to continue, this pattern must be re-shaped and restructured to meet the six criteria of adequacy; (3) control of curriculum by each of the various levels and branches of government must be limited, by statutory or constitutional provisions, to those that together make up a system of control having no conflicting authority and powers among its units; (4) as a step toward such restructuring, litigation on challenges to the exercise of arbitrary authority and/or conflicting authority in curriculum among such units should be initiated; (5) an intergovernmental conference should be called to sort out the powers deemed appropriate for each unit at each level and to recommend a body of legislation or constitutional amendments that would embrace an adequate structure of curriculum control; and (6) further study of curriculum policy-making processes and problems in the context of shared governance should be undertaken (Boyd, 1979; Goodlad et al., 1979; Griffin, cited in Goodlad et al., 1979; Mosher, 1980). Failure to act on these needed changes will mean that both the public's wishes about curriculum and the school system's ability to fulfill such mandates will continue to be greatly hampered.

Whatever structure of authority and governance is established to control curriculum, there is a second major organizational issue in curriculum that must be confronted: the choice of curriculum development strategy. Experience with various strategies for translating curriculum policies into particular educational programs suggests that it is now possible not only to discern distinct forms of curriculum development but also to assess their relative merits. Formal studies of these features have begun to appear, and the policy implications of these analyses are becoming clearer (Short, 1981b).

Development Strategies. The fundamental requirements of the curriculum development task (Kliebard, 1979), are to *specify* and to *justify* what should be taught, to which persons, under what rules of teaching, and how these should be interrelated. Even who should make these decisions is an issue to be resolved. All these are value questions; they are subject to social and moral choice rather than to the application of technical criteria (Reid, 1978; Macdonald & Clark, 1973; Hayes, 1977). As circumstances vary and what is considered worthy educationally differs, so will the resultant curricula. The processes by which these curriculum development decisions can be made, however, while not uniform, are quite formal and technical in nature.

Several forms of curriculum development have been identified through study of curriculum development in action. These forms represent contrasting positions taken on certain key variables in the process. Strategies vary in terms of (1) where evidence is collected, consensus is established, and consequences are projected (the seat of curriculum development); (2) who the participants are and what qualifications they possess (the expertise required);

and (3) how much attention is paid to the realities of the intended use-setting for which curriculum is developed (the teacher's role in the process) (Robinsohn, 1969).

The seat of curriculum development may be user-based or externally based with respect to the locus of decision making (Connelly, 1972); or, as Walker (1979) describes this variable, curriculum development may be site-specific (local development under specific policy guidelines) or generic (in centers developing for many localities but without particular policy guidelines from any of them). User-based, site-specific curriculum development exists where development is organized and conducted at the direction of local educational authority and where the resulting curriculum is to be used within the authority's area of jurisdiction. In contrast, generic, externally based development is performed under the direction of some agency that does not have legal and administrative jurisdiction over a particular educational community and, therefore, cannot authorize for any particular setting the use of the curriculum it develops. Generic development serves a broader constituency and purpose than does user-based development. These two types of places where responsibility for curriculum development may be lodged understandably affect the other variables in the process: the expertise required and the attention given to the realities of the intended use-setting.

The expertise required for conducting curriculum development may be drawn from (1) subject matter scholars, (2) experts on the educational potential of students, (3) experts on the social and cultural milieus in which education takes place, (4) persons familiar with teachers and teaching practice, and (5) specialists with knowledge of the curriculum development process itself (Schwab, 1978). Curriculum development strategies vary in terms of the representation given each of these bodies of expertise in the decision-making process. The process may be constituted, and personnel may be assigned, in such a way as to give the decisive role to one or another of these bodies of expertise; it may, on the other hand, call for a balance of power among them insofar as categories of expertise and numbers of persons in each category are concerned. Great care in determining the kind and mix of expertise desired on the curriculum development team is essential, but it does not guarantee that the available expertise will be taken into account in making the substantive decisions. Of the many possible mixes of expertise that could be put in place in various curriculum development settings, three are singled out here and given somewhat arbitrary labels. First, there is the scholar-dominated pattern; second, the milieus expert-dominated pattern; and third, the balanced-coordinated pattern of participation.

Forms of curriculum development also vary in terms of how thoroughly the development process takes into account the realities of teaching and learning that exist in the actual settings for which the curriculum under development is intended. Such realities include a wide range of considerations: age, ability, interests of students; constraints of time, cost, and organizational factors; ability of teachers to adopt the perspectives and adapt to the scope of change required by the new program; and many others. The degree to which these realities are intentionally dealt with in various forms of curriculum development varies considerably. One conception of curriculum use may be labeled "implementation as directed"; a second, "limited adaptation"; and a third, "open adaptation." If a curriculum is meant to be used essentially in the manner prescribed by the developers, regardless of the specific realities of the use-setting, it is of the implementation as directed type. If developers expect the use-setting of the curriculum to require limited adaptation of the program as a result of certain realities in that setting that could not be foreseen by developers, it is of the second type. And if, at the extreme of wishing to allow the realities of use-settings virtually to control the use of the curriculum, in ways perhaps even at odds with many of the developers' intentions, then this is an instance of the open adaptation type. Roughly corresponding to the three categories identified here, these variations are sometimes expressed as (1) the teacher-proof curriculum approach, (2) teachers as active implementers, and (3) teachers as user-developers (Connelly & Ben-Peretz, 1980).

Many different strategies of curriculum development have been identified in terms of the position each takes on these key variables in the process: where development takes place, who participates in it, and what conception of the realities of the use-setting is adopted. To provide a basis for reporting the results of policy analyses among alternative strategies, three types of strategies will be characterized. These descriptions are derived from systematic examination of case studies of curriculum development of each type (Eisner, 1971; Weiss & Edwards, 1971; Schaffarzick & Hampson, 1975; Connelly, 1978; Stenhouse, 1980; Short, 1981b).

Most of the available analyses of curriculum development strategies focus on the strategy of the type "generic/scholar-dominated/implementation as directed." Associated with this type of strategy is a technology of development that involves a process of research, development, field testing, revision, dissemination, and implementation that produces a product at a "center" for use at the "periphery" (Hemphill, 1973; Baker, 1971; Nedler, 1972; Walker, 1979). The dominant role in decision making is held by subject matter experts, usually academics, with lesser influence by experts in learning, society, teaching, and curriculum. The projects funded by the U.S. federal government in the 1950s and early 1960s, as well as much of the centralized curriculum development conducted in other countries by national authorities, are of this type.

This strategy typically

1. provides updated, authoritative content within a subject area;
2. follows a process of trial use, feedback, and refinement,

until the curriculum is reasonably perfected, before it is released for general use;
3. supplies developed materials for far-flung school use through contractual arrangements with private publishers for production and marketing, thereby providing economy of scale;
4. leaves to others the task of assisting with adoption, implementation, and articulation into local programs;
5. operates within temporary organizations that cannot always obtain enough appropriate staff for necessary lengths of time, on leaves from other organizations, or by other means;
6. designs subject matter and learning processes for use in conventional organizational structure of schools (e.g., grade levels, classes, subjects) rather than what might require alternative patterns of schooling;
7. specifies subject matter and learning processes that, if fully understood by teachers and implemented as directed, would require a deliberate disregard for the integrity and ecology of each educational situation and of variations existing among such situations;
8. depends upon teachers' manuals and/or in-service training materials, developed as supplements to student materials, to carry the burden of preparing teachers to change their outlook toward the curriculum, their procedures for teaching, and the milieu into which the curriculum is to be implemented;
9. succeeds in generating, in the schools that adopt the curriculum produced, only selectively and/or partially implemented versions of the intended curriculum— a consequence of issuing substantive directives for implementation without possessing the authority to compel compliance or sanction modifications, and of lacking on-site personnel to assist in making local adjustments necessary for accommodating the curriculum;
10. embraces the experimental ideal of scientific research, but in practice disseminates an "effective" curriculum without having made comparisons among alternative options aimed at identical goals but based on different premises, components, or content;
11. faces administrative red tape and restrictions from the project funding agency, a fact that hampers the making of prudent adjustments in goals, staffing, development and/or assessment procedures, dissemination, and follow-up in use-settings;
12. addresses one subject area per project, leaving unaddressed the problem of designing, coordinating, and balancing a series of subjects into a total unified curriculum, and thereby fosters competition among projects for limited development funds;
13. functions only under circumstances where a particular doctrine of curriculum development, often one not sanctioned by experts having a comprehensive view of the technical aspects of curriculum, has achieved a degree of national political support (e.g., the disciplinary doctrine typical of the projects of the late 1950s

and early 1960s), and where authorizing agencies are in a position to mandate development embracing the doctrine (when support for such a doctrine collapses or fails to be achieved, the strategy is not utilized).

Considerable analysis has been done of another type of strategy, "generic/milieus expert-dominated/limited adaptation." This type of curriculum development strategy exists when an agency outside any operating school or school system generates a curriculum that may be adapted, within limitations imposed by the developers, for use in any number of different settings. The process of curriculum construction and planning in this type of strategy reflects the dominant perspective of experts in the social and cultural milieus within which education takes place, especially those experts knowledgeable about certain educationally neglected segments of society for whom curriculum policy makers have authorized special programs or innovations—the young child, the potential dropout, the handicapped, the non–English proficient, the academically deficient, and so on. The technology of development utilized in this type of strategy parallels that of the first type to some extent, with the intention to allow some curricular modifications by local users dictating the development of less rigid specifications and, inevitably, a less resolute search for the one best form of plan or materials (Taylor & Richards, 1979; Stenhouse, 1975; Farrar, Desanctis, & Cohen, 1980). Because of the willingness to allow local adaptations, more teacher feedback is sought regarding the most useful form that guidance on adaptation might take rather than feedback primarily on effects of trial testing or strict implementation.

This strategy typically

1. is employed to address a wide range of curricular innovations in addition to content revisions;
2. is oriented around a single perspective on the situation and needs of a particular type of client population (milieu experts who differ from this view tend to be at work elsewhere on alternative development efforts; compromise among milieu experts within a particular project is seldom required);
3. incorporates into program plans and materials a variety of content and activities generated by project-affiliated teacher-developers who find them suitable and successful in practice;
4. releases a program for use, not as a definitive product, but as a springboard for further directed development locally, and provides some continuing assistance in making appropriate adaptations;
5. recognizes the importance of in-service teacher training in implementing a curriculum change and develops both material and human resource networks to assist in this task;
6. operates within relatively temporary organizations, which are not always funded well enough, or do not always exist long enough, to provide all the technical assistance its program users require over time;

7. cannot fully control the adaptations made locally, with the frequent result that the program's structure and intent are appreciably altered in the direction of locally defined desires not consonant with initial commitments to the use of the generically developed program;
8. runs into difficult-to-resolve accountability, ethical, or policy problems when schools that accept funds for implementation from the generic program source use them to adapt the program beyond expected limits;
9. functions most successfully when divorced from the need for it to exercise regulatory or fiscal responsibility over the users of its programs and services.

"Site-specific/balanced-coordinated/open adaptation" is a third type of curriculum development strategy. Curriculum development of this type takes place in the actual educational setting where the development work is expected to be utilized, either within a local school system or a school building. This strategy specifies that teachers who expect to use the resultant curriculum will be actively involved in its planning in order to ensure that it will be readily adaptable to the known circumstances of the schools, classrooms, and students for which it is developed. Cooperative interaction among all the relevant experts is required in arriving at decisions. A specialist in curriculum development exercises leadership during these deliberations until, in each instance, decisions incorporate a coordinated and balanced view of these areas of expertise. Technologies prescribing procedures appropriate to this type of strategy are numerous (Skilbeck, cited in Walton & Welton, 1976; Schwab, 1978; Reid, 1978; Saylor, Alexander, & Lewis, 1981; Eible & Zavarella, 1979).

This strategy typically

1. recognizes the essential unity of goal setting and designing the operationalization of curriculum and assumes that the potential of a policy idea can be more readily accepted and translated into classroom practice if conceived and developed together in the immediate use-setting;
2. functions most effectively when the social climate among developers is open, cooperative, noncoercive, imbued with mutual trust, and predisposed to change;
3. utilizes a collegial decision-making process involving joint planning and active participation by all appropriate experts, including intended teacher-users (all participants are concerned with both strategic and tactical questions; the former are not assigned to a developer group, and the latter are not assigned to an implementer group);
4. has a strong leader who understands and projects the required development tasks, can lead but not drive the participants to completion of these tasks, and can marshal the necessary resources to sustain the entire process adequately;
5. operates within known parameters of policy, administrative constraints and incentives, community expec-

tations, and authority delegated to the site-specific development team;

6. is set in motion when forces outside the immediate use-setting (administrators, policy bodies, pressure groups) have identified and sanctioned a clear target for curriculum development or change;

7. develops a sense of ownership of the resultant program in developer-users, who may either create their own or model a generically developed one (not simply adopt or adapt one), but one embedded in local realities and controlled throughout by beliefs and concepts locally arrived at and accepted—a curriculum achieved rather than ascribed;

8. estimates the impact of the proposed curriculum changes upon all who will be affected by them, especially teachers who will be responsible for their fulfillment, and nurtures the recognized behavior and attitude changes that will have to accompany the substantive changes (self-education of teachers and others is abetted by providing thorough programs of preparation for change; internal readiness is more important than the curriculum plan; planning is considered an educational experience for the developer-users);

9. allows teachers the freedom to use the curriculum in keeping with their practical knowledge of students, the educational potential of materials, and the exigencies of instructional problems and situations; and

10. takes long periods of time to accomplish a given development effort (it is difficult to sustain the necessary level of involvement until completion; settlement of some tough issues and conflicts between national and local values may be deferred to parochial interests for lack of time for adequate resolution).

A particular curriculum development strategy is chosen and used because it is judged capable of getting a certain task accomplished, that of translating specific curriculum policies into a particular educational program. This is a more or less technical process within which substantive options are weighed and decided upon. The wisdom of employing one or another of the three types of strategies depends upon whether one form of resolution of the where, the who, and the use-setting issues comes closer to fulfilling practical, technical criteria than any other form. The best strategy will be one most capable of meeting four broad criteria: the criterion of practicality, the criterion of purposiveness, the criterion of realism, and the criterion of judiciousness (Reid, 1979; Short, 1981b). Specific criteria are listed below for each of these broad criteria. They are reported as derived from analyses of the use of various strategies and of their positive and negative consequences.

The most desirable strategy will be one that

1. can put its program specifications and related practical guidelines for action into sufficiently concrete form so that they can become integral to curricular frames of reference at the operational level, rather than become, perhaps in part, tacked-on appendages *(practicality);*

2. recognizes that what is to be done in every local circumstance cannot be determined by a single theoretical prescription nor a common rule *(practicality);*

3. gives the leading role of keeping the curriculum development process on task—and of facilitating the work of all participants in the process—to a trained specialist in curriculum development who is fully knowledgeable about what issues must be addressed and what technically useful forms decisions should take *(purposiveness);*

4. proceeds rationally and in an orderly fashion toward the achievement of its goal and tasks, not by a linear process of technological rationality that unfolds foreordained decisions and guidelines, but by a dynamic process of deliberate practical reasoning that admits various perspectives and seeks decisions that are in harmony with the expectations of all participants *(purposiveness);*

5. is directed toward a common purpose, with compatible procedures, and uses language that communicates effectively among participants and others *(purposiveness);*

6. grounds its work in a thorough and accurate understanding of the particular concrete circumstances of the school, classroom, or teaching/learning environments toward which the development effort is directed *(realism);*

7. recognizes the key role that the teacher plays in interpreting curriculum specifications and guidelines and in making practical judgments necessary for their realization in particular educational environments *(realism);*

8. recognizes the influence of the larger social and political context upon the use-setting for which its development work is intended and consequently develops curriculum specifications and guidelines that can feasibly be enacted within the possibilities and constraints of such a context *(realism);*

9. is itself adequately financed and is sanctioned by appropriate power relationships among funders and users *(realism);*

10. has its decisions as to what should constitute the curriculum, its rationale, and its guidelines for use, arrived at by an open, unbiased search for the educationally sound, the wise, the just, and the good, involving all relevant bodies of expertise *(judiciousness).*

Conclusions. Measured by the ten criteria of strategy desirability, each of the three strategies for curriculum development has some strengths and some weaknesses. On the whole the "site-specific/balanced-coordinated/ open adaptation strategy" has the fewest deficiencies and is recommended as the one that best fulfills these technical, practical criteria for an effective curriculum development strategy. Its deficiencies suggest that it requires outside resources upon which it can draw—networks of scholarly resources, materials developed elsewhere, expertise of all kinds, and sometimes additional financial resources. If generic development work is available, local educational developers should explore its usefulness for their own development purposes and specifications rather than become an agent for realizing external developers' curricula.

In light of the analysis presented in the first section of this article on shared authority and governance structures, the analysis of development strategies suggests a limited role for the federal and state governments in development efforts because of the many deficiencies of the first and second types of strategies. Some technical assistance and some development of sample program components may usefully be provided by projects or agencies outside local educational settings. These efforts might or might not be governmentally supported (National Institute of Education, 1976; Walker, 1979; Tyler, 1979; Sykes, 1979; Connelly & Elbaz, 1980; Datta, 1980; McIntosh & Housego, 1974). Control and development strategies are ultimately interdependent; the best form of the latter requires the most adequate structure of the former.

Edmund C. Short

See also Curriculum History; Curriculum Research; Qualitative Curriculum Evaluation.

REFERENCES

Atkin, J. M. The government in the classroom. *Daedalus*, 1980, *109*(3), 85–97.

Atkin, J. M., & House, E. R. The federal role in curriculum development, 1950–80. *Educational Evaluation and Policy Analysis*, 1981, *3*, 5–36.

Baker, E. L. Curriculum development projects. In L. C. Deighton (Ed.), *Encyclopedia of Education* (Vol. 2). New York: Macmillan, 1971.

Boyd, W. L. The changing politics of curriculum policy-making for American schools. In J. Schaffarzick & G. Sykes (Eds.), *Value Conflicts and Curriculum Issues: Lessons from Research and Experience*. Berkeley, Calif.: McCutchan, 1979. (Also appears in *Review of Educational Research*, 1978, *48*, 577–628. An abridged version appears in *Educational Researcher*, 1979, *8*(2), 12–18.)

Connelly, F. M. The functions of curriculum development. *Interchange*, 1972, *3*, 161–177.

Connelly, F. M. How shall we publish case studies of curriculum development? *Curriculum Inquiry*, 1978, *8*, 73–82.

Connelly, F. M., & Ben-Peretz, M. Teachers' roles in the using and doing of research and curriculum development. *Journal of Curriculum Studies*, 1980, *12*, 95–107.

Connelly, F. M., & Elbaz, F. Conceptual bases for curriculum thought: A teacher's perspective. In A. W. Foshay (Ed.), *Considered Action for Curriculum Improvement: 1980 Association for Supervision and Curriculum Development Yearbook*. Alexandria, Va.: ASCD, 1980.

Datta, L. Changing times: The study of federal programs supporting educational change and the case for local problem-solving. *Teachers College Record*, 1980, *82*, 101–116.

Eible, C. V., & Zavarella, J. A. Curriculum development: A model for action. *Bulletin of the National Association of Secondary School Principals*, 1979, *63*, 85–90.

Eisner, E. W. (Ed.). *Confronting Curriculum Reform*. Boston: Little, Brown, 1971.

Farrar, E.; Desanctis, J.; & Cohen, D. K. Views from below: Implementation in education. *Teachers College Record*, 1980, *82*, 77–100.

Goodlad, J. I., & Associates. *Curriculum Inquiry: The Study of Curriculum Practice*. New York: McGraw-Hill, 1979.

Hayes, H. E. Curriculum development as a moral enterprise. *Curriculum Inquiry*, 1977, *6*, 229–235.

Hemphill, J. K. Educational development. In J. K. Hemphill & F. S. Rosenau (Eds.), *Educational Development: A New Discipline for Self-renewal* (Far West Laboratory for Educational Research and Development). Eugene, Oreg.: Center for the Advanced Study of Educational Administration, 1973.

Kliebard, H. M. Systematic curriculum development, 1890–1959. In J. Schaffarzick & G. Sykes (Eds.), *Value Conflicts and Curriculum Issues: Lessons from Research and Experience*. Berkeley, Calif.: McCutchan, 1979.

Macdonald, J. B., & Clark, D. Critical value questions and the analyses of objectives and curricula. In R. M. W. Travers (Ed.), *Second Handbook of Research on Teaching*. Skokie, Ill.: Rand McNally, 1973.

McIntosh, G., & Housego, I. Policy issues in curriculum development. In J. Blaney, I. Housego, & G. McIntosh, *Program Development in Education*. Vancouver: University of British Columbia, Center for Continuing Education, 1974.

Mosher, E. K. Politics and pedagogy: A new mix. *Educational Leadership*, 1980, *38*, 110–111.

National Institute of Education Curriculum Task Force. *Current Issues, Problems, and Concerns in Curriculum Development*. Washington, D.C.: The Institute, 1976. (ERIC Document Reproduction Service No. ED 124 530)

Nedler, S. A development process approach to curriculum design. In R. K. Parker (Ed.), *The Preschool in Action: Exploring Early Childhood Programs*. Boston: Allyn & Bacon, 1972.

Reid, W. A. *Thinking about the Curriculum: The Nature and Treatment of Curriculum Problems*. Boston: Routledge & Kegan Paul, 1978.

Reid, W. A. Schools, teachers, and curriculum change: The moral dimension of theory-building. *Educational Theory*, 1979, *29*, 325–336.

Robinsohn, S. B. A conceptual structure of curriculum development. *Comparative Education*, 1969, *5*, 221–234.

Saylor, J. G.; Alexander, W. M.; & Lewis, A. J. *Curriculum Planning for Better Teaching and Learning* (3rd ed.). New York: Holt, Rinehart & Winston, 1981.

Schaffarzick, J. Federal curriculum reform: A crucible for value conflict. In J. Schaffarzick & G. Sykes (Eds.), *Value Conflicts and Curriculum Issues: Lessons from Research and Experience*. Berkeley, Calif.: McCutchan, 1979.

Schaffarzick, J., & Hampson, D. H. (Eds.). *Strategies for Curriculum Development*. Berkeley, Calif.: McCutchan, 1975.

Schwab, J. J. The practical: Translation into curriculum. In I. Westbury & N. J. Wilkof (Eds.), *Science, Curriculum, and Liberal Education: Selected Essays*. Chicago: University of Chicago Press, 1978.

Short, E. C. *Authority and Governance in Curriculum Development: A Policy Analysis in the United States Context*. Unpublished manuscript, 1981. (a)

Short, E. C. *The Forms and Use of Alternative Curriculum Development Strategies: Policy Implications.* Unpublished manuscript, 1981. (b)

Stenhouse, L. *An Introduction to Curriculum Research and Development.* London: Heinemann, 1975.

Stenhouse, L. (Ed.), *Curriculum Research and Development in Action.* London: Heinemann, 1980.

Sykes, G. Government intervention in the school curriculum: Floating like a bee, stinging like a butterfly? In J. Schaffarzick & G. Sykes (Eds.), *Value Conflicts and Curriculum Issues: Lessons from Research and Experience.* Berkeley, Calif.: McCutchan, 1979.

Taylor, P. H., & Richards, C. M. *An Introduction to Curriculum Studies.* New York: Humanities Press, 1979.

Tyler, R. W., Educational improvements best served by curriculum development. In J. Schaffarzick & G. Sykes (Eds.), *Value Conflict and Curriculum Issues: Lessons from Research and Experience.* Berkeley, Calif.: McCutchan, 1979.

van Geel, T. *Authority to Control the School Programs.* Lexington, Mass.: Heath, 1976. (A briefer treatment of this material appears in *School Review,* 1978, *86,* 594–631, which is reprinted, with changes, in J. Schaffarzick & G. Sykes (Eds.), *Value Conflicts and Curriculum Issues: Lessons from Research and Experience.* Berkeley, Calif.: McCutchan, 1979).

Walker, D. F. Approaches to curriculum development. In J. Schaffarzick & G. Sykes (Eds.), *Value Conflicts and Curriculum Issues: Lessons from Research and Experience.* Berkeley, Calif.: McCutchan, 1979.

Walton, J., & Welton, J. (Eds.), *Rational Curriculum Planning: Four Case Studies.* London: Ward Lock Educational, 1976.

Weiss, J., & Edwards, J. Data banks: Observations on a methodology for securing curriculum development process data. In F. M. Connelly (Ed.), *Elements of Curriculum Development* (Curriculum Theory Network Monograph Supplement), 1971, *7,* 35–42.

CURRICULUM HISTORY

It can be said that curriculum has a long past but a short history (Tanner & Tanner, 1980). Although the concept of curriculum is implicit in the earliest educational prescriptions and programs of all civilized societies, curriculum as a field of systematic inquiry emerged only during the early 1920s (Foshay, 1969, p. 275; Koopman, 1966, p. 2). Kliebard (1968) pointed to the year 1918 as the juncture when "curriculum emerged as a self-conscious field of study" (p. 71), citing such seminal works published that year as Franklin Bobbitt's *The Curriculum,* Alexander Inglis's *Principles of Secondary Education,* and the report of the Commission on the Reorganization of Secondary Education, *Cardinal Principles of Secondary Education.* Kliebard acknowledged the earlier contributions of Dewey and others, but he noted that they did not regard themselves as curriculum specialists, "nor was there a readily identifiable field of curriculum specialization at that time" (p. 70). Nevertheless, Dewey's *Democracy and Education* (1916) expounded a systematic rationale that

was to serve as an underpinning of experimentalist thought in the emerging curriculum field.

Although Herbert Spencer's remarkable essay "What Knowledge Is of Most Worth?" (1860) can be characterized as having a self-conscious focus on curriculum, and although it exerted a significant influence on curricularists well into the twentieth century, it was not until after World War I that a noticeable literature began to appear, eventually giving rise to curriculum as a field of university study. Cremin has noted that curriculum became a distinct field of study through the rapid growth of professional training for educators and the burgeoning literature on curriculum development during the progressive period spanning the early decades of the twentieth century (1971, pp. 207, 212).

Dewey's laboratory school, established at the University of Chicago in 1896, and Parker's practice-demonstration school, which opened at the University of Chicago in 1901, exerted a powerful influence on progressive educational thought and practice. The emphasis given to curriculum unification and synthesis in both schools, consonant with the emerging findings on child development, helped lay the groundwork over the ensuing decades for child study and curriculum development as fields of university scholarship.

A Modern School, by Flexner (1916), orchestrated the theory of curriculum synthesis with the growing recognition of the need to modernize the curriculum in the light of developments in science, industry, and aesthetics and the growing concern for democratic citizenship. Flexner's proposed curriculum gave rise to the Lincoln School at Teachers College, Columbia University, in 1917 through funds from the General Education Board of the Rockefeller Foundation. Flexner envisaged the laboratory school as a center for scientific curriculum research and development, an issue that was to plague the Lincoln School to the point of its demise thirty-one years after it opened.

Unlike most works on educational history, which give incidental attention to the curriculum, Brubacher's *A History of the Problems of Education* devoted two entire chapters to curriculum history. According to Brubacher, "the almost exclusive theory of the nature and organization of the curriculum from earliest times down to the end of the nineteenth century" was based upon the logical classification of knowledge into subject matter divisions under the premise that "objective reality had a logical structure which could be known and stated." Accordingly, "Such a view of subject matter naturally made a Procrustean bed of the curriculum. The curriculum was fixed in advance. As the child alone was pliable, he was made to conform to it" (Brubacher, 1966, pp. 287–288). Although this traditional view of subject matter had been challenged by scholars from the latter part of the eighteenth century through the nineteenth century, it was not until the twentieth century that emerging knowledge on the nature of the learner, coupled with the renascent development of democratic social theory, produced systematic approaches to curriculum reconstruction, implementation, and evaluation.

Sponsored Curriculum Study. From the late nineteenth century to contemporary times, various committees and commissions have been formed on a temporary basis with the charge of studying curriculum problems and practices and formulating recommendations. Before the turn of the century, the National Education Association sponsored the Committee of Ten on Secondary School Studies and the Committee of Fifteen on elementary education. The 1918 report of the NEA's Commission on the Reorganization of Secondary Education, *Cardinal Principles of Secondary Education*, is regarded as a landmark. According to Cremin, "most of the important and influential movements in the field since 1918 have simply been footnotes to the classic itself" (1955, p. 307). The report not only served as a kind of declaration of independence of the secondary school from college dominance over the curriculum, but also endorsed the comprehensive secondary school as a prototype institution of democracy, advocated the unification of studies as a means of fostering democracy in the face of increasingly specialized studies, and formulated a comprehensive range of curriculum functions designed to meet the needs of youth.

A quarter of a century later, the NEA's Educational Policies Commission extended the *Cardinal Principles* report with a comprehensive volume, *Education for ALL American Youth* (1944), illustrating how the needs of all youth might be met through the secondary schools of the post–World War II years. The curriculum proposals in the report were widely discussed and debated, particularly those pertaining to common learnings and the needs of youth, but the report itself, along with the commission (which had been established by the NEA in 1930 on a continuing basis), was to become a casualty of the cold war.

The NEA was not alone as a professional association concerned with curriculum development and policy. Curriculum study had begun to gain visibility in the early yearbooks of the National Herbart Society, established in 1892, and in the yearbooks of its successor organization, the National Society for the (Scientific) Study of Education, established in 1902. But it was not until 1932 that curricularists reached sufficient numbers to organize an association expressly focused on the curriculum. This association, the Society of Curriculum Study, came about largely through the leadership of Henry Harap, a professor of education at Western Reserve University. The Society of Curriculum Study was to merge with the NEA's Department of Supervision and Directors of Instruction, leading to the creation of the Association for Supervision and Curriculum Development (ASCD) in 1943. However, the need for a separate organization of university curricularists led to the emergence of an association known as Professors of Curriculum, which has conducted almost all its annual meetings just prior to those of the ASCD.

The demise of the NEA's Educational Policies Commission in 1968 left a void that was quickly filled by the private foundations and, more recently, by federally sponsored panels and commissions. In the wake of the cold war, James B. Conant was enlisted by the Carnegie Corporation in 1957 to study the American high school. During his Harvard presidency, Conant had appointed a University Committee on the Objectives of a General Education in a Free Society, which issued its report in 1945. Known as the "Harvard Report," *General Education in a Free Society* presented a rationale and framework for the curriculum in general education in the secondary school and college for the post–World War II years. Conant, who had chaired the Educational Policies Commission when it issued its revised edition of *Education for ALL American Youth* in 1952, shifted to a more conservative curriculum stance in his Carnegie study on the American high school, issued in 1959, wherein he gave considerable attention to the academically talented. Nevertheless, Conant's report *The American High School Today* (1959) supported vocational education in the context of the comprehensive high school and served to strengthen the nation's commitment to the comprehensive high school at a time when it was under severe attack by those who favored the adoption of a dual European-type structure of secondary schooling.

Bruner's report (1960) on a conference of scientists and other university scholars, sponsored by the National Academy of Sciences, provided the rationale for the discipline-centered curriculum reforms for the elementary and secondary schools over the ensuing decade. The subsequent reaction to the excesses of the pursuit of academic excellence, the college-student protest movement of the late 1960s, and the problem of youth unemployment and disaffection led the U.S. commissioner of education to promote a program of career education in the early 1970s extending throughout the elementary and secondary levels of schooling (Marland, 1971). Some educators viewed career education as reflecting a conservative political effort to acculturate the rising generation into the status quo of the working world (Bowers, 1977). The career education proposed bore a striking resemblance to the Prosser Resolution of a quarter of a century earlier (U.S. Office of Education, 1951).

A signal reaction to the discipline-centered curriculum reforms during the late 1960s and early 1970s was the demand for curriculum "relevance" by college and high school students. The excesses of the discipline movement led to Silberman's *Crisis in the Classroom* (1970), commissioned by the Carnegie Corporation. Silberman advocated the adoption of the open classroom at the elementary level and other "liberalizing" reforms from elementary through secondary schooling for purposes of "humanizing" the school. However, the "humanizing" reforms of the late 1960s and early 1970s lacked the systematic curriculum reconstruction required for a sustained movement. At the secondary and collegiate levels, elective options largely replaced general education.

The forces of knowledge specialism and the resultant decline of general education during the 1950s and 1960s led Bell (1966) to embark on a study funded by the Carnegie Corporation, *The Reforming of General Education.* Four years earlier, Thomas (1962) had published his historical study of general education in the American college for the Carnegie Corporation. Although Bell's historical and sociological analysis was centered on the curriculum of Columbia College, with comparisons with the curriculum experience in general education at Harvard and Chicago, his study and curriculum proposals for Columbia College were germane to the wider problem in higher education of meeting the need for a common learning in the face of specialism. However, in viewing the function of the high school curriculum as merely preparation for college, Bell ignored the persistent problem of general education for the heterogeneous secondary school population (p. 181). The ensuing student protest movement and the growing curriculum fragmentation through elective options in response to the student demand for "relevance" was to eclipse, with few exceptions, any concern for undergraduate curriculum reconstruction for yet another decade. A notable exception was the Report of the Commission on MIT Education (1970), a commission comprising faculty and students, stressing that the age of knowledge specialization had led to curriculum fragmentation and calling for curriculum integration through interdisciplinary social-problem–focused studies for general education. However, for the most part, the recommendations of the report went unheeded.

By the late 1970s the fragmentation of the undergraduate curriculum catalyzed a rediscovery of general education at many universities and the issue of a series of studies on the history and mission of the college curriculum, sponsored by the Carnegie Foundation for the Advancement of Teaching, calling for curriculum reconstruction to create coherence and balance at the undergraduate level (Carnegie Foundation, 1977; Levine, 1978; Rudolph, 1977). The *Report on the Core Curriculum* by the Harvard Faculty (1978), calling for the restoration of a core curriculum, attracted widespread attention in the general press as well as in academe. In sharp contrast to higher education, in which general education had been rediscovered during the late 1970s, the elementary and secondary schools were submerged by the wave of curriculum retrenchment through "back to basics."

The decade of the seventies also was marked by a succession of reports sponsored by the private foundations and the federal government criticizing the comprehensive high school and advocating various alternatives to secondary schooling for the less academically talented youth (Carnegie Council on Policy Studies in Higher Education, 1979; Panel on Youth of the President's Science Advisory Committee, 1974; National Commission on the Reform of Secondary Education, 1973; National Panel on High School and Adolescent Education, 1976). These reports were criticized for auguring the abandonment of the comprehensive high school and universal secondary schooling (Tanner, 1979).

In 1980 the Carnegie Foundation for the Advancement of Teaching appointed a National Panel on the High School to study the high school curriculum in relation to the college curriculum. The Report of the Commission on the Humanities (1980) of the Rockefeller Foundation criticized the curriculum retrenchment as embodied by the back-to-basics movement, advocated that the elementary and secondary schools develop a well-structured curriculum in the humanities and arts, and recommended the strengthening of the humanities in undergraduate education. In an essay for the Carnegie Foundation for the Advancement of Teaching, Boyer and Levine (1981) examined current problems and issues in general education in terms of its historical evolution and social context, and called for a partnership between school and college leaders in reconstructing the curriculum in general education.

The ebb and flow of curriculum reforms and counterreforms over several decades caused some curricularists to raise the question of whether curriculum studies had been over the same issues in earlier epochs and to accuse the curriculum field of succumbing to the malady of ahistoricism (Bellack, 1969, p. 282; Goodlad, 1966, p. 91; Kliebard, 1968, p. 69). This cyclical problem began to receive some attention during the late 1970s through papers and symposia presented at annual meetings of the American Educational Research Association. In 1977 a meeting of curricularists was held at Teachers College, Columbia University, to address this problem. The result was the establishment of the Society for the Study of Curriculum History, which subsequently has conducted its annual meetings concurrently with the American Educational Research Association.

Curriculum as a Field of University Study. Toward the end of the nineteenth century, some systematic study of curriculum and curriculum history at leading universities made an appearance through specific courses such as Evaluation of the Curriculum, taught by Dewey at the University of Chicago during the 1895/96 academic year (University of Chicago, *Annual Register,* 1895–1904). At Teachers College, Columbia University, from 1905 to 1914 Dewey taught the course Social Life and the School Curriculum (Teachers College, *Announcements,* 1905). Although departments of pedagogy or education had been created at leading American universities during the last two decades of the nineteenth century, it was not until 1938 that the Department of Curriculum and Teaching was established at Teachers College through the efforts of Dean William F. Russell and under the leadership of Hollis L. Caswell, who served as the department's first chairperson and who was later to become president of the college. Within a few years following the establishment of a curriculum department at Teachers College, similar departments were organized at leading universities throughout the United States.

Curriculum Journals. In *Curriculum Construction,* published in 1923, W. W. Charters included a bibliography of studies on curriculum with a statement explaining that, in the absence of a specialized curriculum journal or central curriculum agency, it was unlikely that his list was definitive and that some of the studies cited had been found "quite by accident" (Charters, 1923, p. 169). Franklin Bobbitt's *The Curriculum*, published in 1918, is generally recognized at the first comprehensive book on curriculum development. A host of books on curriculum development were to appear from the 1920s onward, but no journals specifically devoted to the curriculum field were to appear until a half century later.

The advent of the school survey during the second decade of the twentieth century, coupled with unprecedented activity in the statewide construction and revision of courses of study as a result of progressivist influences, gave rise to the Curriculum Bureau at Teachers College in 1926, conceived as a kind of clearinghouse on curriculum development. During the early 1930s the *Bulletin* of the Society of Curriculum Study, a mimeographed newsletter, carried articles on curriculum issues, items on curriculum projects, and lists of doctoral dissertations on curriculum.

Although various educational journals were publishing articles on curriculum development, theory, and research (including history) during the formative years of the curriculum field, there were no national journals specifically devoted to this emerging specialty. The journal of the Association for Supervision and Curriculum Development, *Educational Leadership*, helped fill the void over a period spanning a quarter of a century, along with the yearbooks of the association and yearbooks of the National Society for the Study of Education. However, *Educational Leadership* was an eclectic publication for an eclectic audience. And although the National Society for the Study of Education issued some landmark yearbooks on curriculum, most notably the 1927 two-volume yearbook edited by Harold Rugg, the society's yearbooks spanned a very wide range of educational themes for a highly diverse readership. Over a period extending from 1931 to 1969, the *Review of Educational Research* devoted no fewer than thirteen issues entirely to the curriculum theme.

Toward the end of the 1960s, journals specifically devoted to the curriculum field began to appear. In 1968 the Ontario Institute for Studies in Education (Canada) began publishing *Curriculum Theory Network*. This publication was retitled *Curriculum Inquiry* in 1976 and has gained a significant and growing circulation in the United States as well as Canada. The *Journal of Curriculum Studies* has been published in England since 1969 and is presently edited by a group from the United Kingdom, the United States, and Australia. In 1980 the *Journal of Curriculum Theorizing* began publication in this country and *Curriculum Perspectives* appeared in Australia.

Search for Consensus. Thomas Kuhn has pointed out that a field can be said to have reached maturity when its practitioners share a sense of community through a consensus of ideas and methods governing their work. The relative fullness of professional communication and consensus of judgment in mature fields of scholarship is exemplified through a paradigm or set of paradigms (Kuhn, 1970, p. 142). In a search for such consensus in the newly emerging curriculum field, Harold Rugg convinced the directors of the National Society for the Study of Education to appoint the Committee on Curriculum-Making in 1924, with the charge of preparing the twenty-sixth yearbook of the society.

The emerging curriculum field was being buffeted by conflict and disputation between the traditional subject-centered approaches, based upon adult demands, and child-centered approaches in curriculum making. As early as 1902, Dewey attacked both sects and argued that the reflectively formulated experience of the human race must be brought into harmony with the experience and development of the learner (1902, pp. 10–11). In this same work, Dewey identified three fundamental factors in the educative process, factors that must be treated as interdependent rather than in opposition. These factors are (1) the learner ("the immature, undeveloped being"), (2) society ("certain social aims, meanings, values incarnate with the matured experience of the adult"), and (3) organized, systematized, reflectively formulated subject matter (pp. 4, 11–12). To bring organized subject matter into harmony with the growth of the learner, Dewey contended, would require a reconstruction of subject matter.

Harold Rugg was deeply concerned with this problem. As chairman of the Committee on Curriculum-Making of the National Society for the Study of Education, Rugg convened a series of round tables to identify problems and issues in the curriculum field and to search for common ground. The two-volume yearbook of the society, issued in 1927 under Rugg's editorship, was a monumental work. Part 1 of the yearbook, *Curriculum-Making—Past and Present*, reviewed critically the history of curriculum development in the United States and described leading innovative curriculum practices in the schools and school systems of that day. Rugg's introductory statement to the yearbook traced the historical background leading to the widening separation of the school curriculum from child growth and from the dynamic content of American life (Rugg, 1927a, p. 3). In this volume, Rugg and Counts advocated more scientifically controlled studies of innovative practices, a problem that was to plague not only the progressivists but all movements for educational innovation and reform to this day. This volume also identified recommended procedures for curriculum construction.

Never before had such an analysis been undertaken, linking the history of the curriculum field with emergent problems, issues, and practices in a search for common ground. It was in part 2 of the yearbook, *The Foundations of Curriculum-Making* (Rugg, 1927b), that the ambitious and unprecedented search for consensus in the embryonic curriculum field was attempted. Part 2 of the yearbook contained fifty-eight numbered paragraphs in a "Composite Statement" of points of consensus. The first set of paragraphs addressed the needed resolution of the conflict between the nature and interests of the learner and the demands of adult life, and the selection and organization of subject matter—the identical fundamental factors explicated by Dewey a quarter of a century earlier (1902, p. 4). Here it was noted that although the "thoroughly systematized and classified knowledge developed through a long social evolution has many elements of proved worth and should not be lightly discarded," it must be reformulated in terms of "the needs of the learner, irrespective of the content and boundaries of existing subjects" (Rugg, 1927b, p. 22). The committee rejected the traditional conception of curriculum as "formal subject matter (facts, processes, principles), set-out-to-be learned without adequate relation to life," and viewed curriculum as a succession of learning experiences "giving the learner that development most helpful in meeting and controlling life situations" (Rugg, 1927b, p. 18).

Although many of the elements in the "Composite Statement" indicated compromise of position rather than resolution or consensus, the key elements of conflict had been clearly identified and focus had been given to the needed interdependence of the three fundamental factors or sources in curriculum development—namely, the learner, society, and codified knowledge. Bode (1931) observed that the welter of diverse and conflicting curricular aims stemmed from treating these three sources in conflict and that the key to resolution lay in an emphasis in curriculum construction based upon democratic social outlook through "reflective consideration of what constitutes a good life in the social order." These factors or sources were to be reformulated as a curriculum paradigm for the "Eight-Year Study," as it was called (Giles, McCutchen, & Zechiel, 1942), and later in Tyler's *Basic Principles of Curriculum and Instruction* (1949). Nevertheless, curriculum reforms over the ensuing decades were marked by setting these fundamental factors in opposition to one another, with resultant repetitive counterreforms and upheavals.

Toward Consensus and Synthesis. Kuhn (1970) points out that as a field approaches maturity, balances are struck through a movement toward greater consensus of key theoretical ideas and practical operations. Although disputations continue, there is a growing basis for shared values through consensual models or paradigms (pp. 142, 200, 204).

In guiding the program of curriculum development and evaluation for the Eight-Year Study (1933–1941), the staff developed a model based upon the following three fundamental approaches or sources: (1) the social-demands approach, (2) the adolescent-needs approach, and (3) the specialized subject matter approach (Giles, McCutchen, & Zechiel, pp. 22–48). The isomorphism between these approaches, Dewey's fundamental factors (1902), and the factors identified in *The Foundations of Curriculum-Making* (Rugg, 1927a; 1927b) is indeed striking. The curriculum report of the Eight-Year Study went on to describe how the program of curriculum development and evaluation

required attention to the following four fundamental questions: (1) identifying objectives, (2) selecting the means for attaining these objectives, (3) organizing these means, and (4) evaluating the outcomes. These fundamental questions were presented as interdependent elements: objectives, subject matter, methods and organization, and evaluation (Giles, McCutchen, & Zechiel, 1942, p. 2). In essence, these processes are consonant with Dewey's advocacy of systematic modes of inquiry (1929, pp. 8–10). Taba (1945) elaborated on these three sources of data in curriculum development: (1) studies of society, (2) studies of learners, and (3) studies of subject matter content (pp. 85–92); and she later reformulated the four fundamental questions cited above into a seven-step sequence for curriculum development (1962, p. 12). Nevertheless, it was Ralph W. Tyler (1949) who orchestrated these key factors, elements, and sources of data into a curriculum paradigm, in his *Basic Principles of Curriculum and Instruction*. Key elements in this work are strikingly similar to the model developed by Giles, McCutchen, and Zechiel (1942) in their curriculum volume on the Eight-Year Study. Tyler had conducted the evaluation of the college success of the students in the Eight-Year Study and was undoubtedly influenced by the curriculum model developed for the study, as well as by the work of Dewey, Rugg, and other experimentalists. In *Basic Principles of Curriculum and Instruction*, Tyler viewed systematic curriculum development as a process stemming from the following four fundamental questions: (1) What educational purposes should the school seek to attain? (2) What educational experiences can be provided that are likely to attain these purposes? (3) How can these educational experiences be effectively organized? (4) How can we determine whether these purposes are being attained? (p. 1). In essence, curriculum development had come to be seen as a problem-solving process. The evolution of the conception of curriculum development as a problem-solving process is presented in Table 1.

In answering the first question on educational objectives, Tyler identified the same three sources that had been formulated by Dewey almost half a century earlier (1902) and that had been reformulated by Bode (1931), Giles, McCutchen, and Zechiel (1942), Rugg (1927), and Taba (1945). These sources, as reformulated by Tyler, were (1) studies of the learners themselves, (2) studies of contemporary life outside the school, and (3) suggestions from subject specialists (pp. 5–33).

Although Tyler's *Basic Principles of Curriculum and Instruction* is conspicuous by the absence of documentation and a bibliography to reveal the heritage of the curriculum field and the genesis of Tyler's ideas stemming from that heritage, Tyler's work must be regarded as a signal contribution for having systematically orchestrated the key elements, sources, and determinants in the process of curriculum development. Some students of curriculum history have come to regard this work as "the Tyler rationale" and have described it as "Tyler's version of how a

TABLE 1. *Curriculum development as problem-solving process*

Dewey, 1916	*Giles, McCutchen, & Zechiel, 1947*	*Taba, 1945, 1962*	*Tyler, 1949*
Situation of significant experience	Identifying objectives	Diagnosis of needs	What educational purposes should be sought?
Identification of problem(s) deriving from situation	Selecting the means for attaining these objectives	Formulation of objectives	What educational experiences can be provided that are likely to attain these purposes?
Observations and information bearing on the problem(s)	Organizing these means	Selection of content	
Formulation of suggested solutions (hypotheses)	Evaluating the outcomes	Organization of content	How can these educational experiences be effectively organized?
Application and validation of suggested solutions		Selection of learning experiences	How can we determine whether these purposes are being attained?
		Organization of learning experiences	
		Evaluation	

curriculum should be developed—not *the* universal model of curriculum development" (Kliebard, 1970). Although the model or paradigm can be faulted on a number of grounds—such as its linear sequence, as presented by Tyler and Taba—it has also been presented as an interactive schema (Giles, McCutchen, & Zechiel, 1942; Tanner & Tanner, 1980, pp. 81–90). And although Tyler does not appear to give adequate recognition to Dewey's and Bode's admonitions that curriculum objectives and methodology stem from philosophy, Tyler's reconstruction of the model or paradigm remains largely intact to this day.

The historic origins of this curriculum model or paradigm reveal that it is not merely one theorist's version of how a curriculum should be developed. Virtually every major graduate textbook on curriculum development in current use gives significant attention to this model or paradigm, and although criticisms and modifications are offered, no model or paradigm has been formulated to take its place. A survey asking curriculum professors to rank the significant works that have influenced the curriculum field since 1906 found the highest rankings given to Dewey's *Democracy and Education* and Tyler's *Basic Principles of Curriculum and Instruction* (Shane, 1981).

In essence, the historical record reveals that curriculum development must be conceived and conducted as a problem-solving process stemming from the educative process (Dewey, 1929, pp. 33, 74, 77). Otherwise curriculum development will merely be a process of temporal conformation or reaction to shifting sociopolitical forces and fashions external to the educative process, warned Dewey (1929, pp. 14–15).

Reform and Counterreform. Dewey noted that when educational reforms are based upon mere rejection of or reaction against existing practice, there is a failure to recognize problems, let alone to solve problems (1938, pp. 9–10). Historically, the curriculum field has been buffeted by a succession of repetitive reforms and counterreforms. Reviewing the discipline-centered curriculum reforms of the 1950s and 1960s, Goodlad observed, "A substantial

number of the new crop of reformers have approached the persistent, recurring problems of curriculum development in the naive belief that no one had ever looked at them before" (1966, p. 91). In his review of the curriculum field, Kliebard noted, "As a field of study, we have been a peculiarly ahistorical lot" (1968, p. 69). Bellack, too, concluded, "This ahistorical stance seems to be characteristic not only of the current crop of curriculum reformers, most of whom are university professors of academic disciplines, but also of educationists who claim curriculum building as their field of professional specialization" (1969, p. 283).

In sharp disagreement, Hazlett contended that curricularists have been acutely historical-minded, though he noted that the field has suffered from cyclical movements (1979, pp. 129–130). Regardless of the position taken regarding the historic consciousness of the field, there is general agreement that curricularists concern themselves mainly with reacting to external pressures for reform and counterreform and that this concern has distracted them from addressing and solving substantive problems. Tyler recommended that historical studies of such curriculum-reform cycles and reactions be undertaken, along with historical studies of leadership in curriculum development, so that contemporary curricularists might be better able to anticipate and approach problems constructively (1978, pp. 5, 9–10).

It has been observed that throughout the twentieth century, reform movements have been sharply divided as to which source and influence for curriculum development should be dominant (Tanner & Tanner, 1980, p. 96). Should it be the body of organized scholarship (the specializations and divisions of codified knowledge)? Should it be the learner (the immature, developing being)? Or should it be the demands of society and adult life? These three sources and influences clearly correspond to the curriculum paradigm discussed earlier and appear to provide an essential clue to understanding and even anticipating curriculum-reform cycles.

The progressive spiral of curriculum improvement as

envisioned by Dewey (1929, p. 77) has often been subsumed by cycles in which one source is given priority at the expense of others, only to be followed by a reform effort in which another source is allowed to dominate. Each cycle appears to be marked by a reform so extreme that it is eventually succeeded by an excessive counterreform allegedly intended to undo the excesses of the preceding movement. By treating these sources and influences in their separateness and as antagonisms, rather than seeking to reconstruct them in an interactive and interdependent whole, contended Dewey, we are left with an insoluble problem, a problem of endless opposition and conflict that underlies all educational opinion (1902, pp. 4–5). The concerted study of these oppositional movements and the heritage of the curriculum field, including the emergent paradigms, might enable curricularists to anticipate the forces at work and attack the extant problems of the field constructively (Tyler, 1978, p. 5).

Emergent Focus. Since the 1960s a vast literature on curriculum history has emerged. The opening section of the 1969 issue on curriculum of the *Review of Educational Research* was titled "History of Curriculum Thought and Practice" (Bellack, 1969). Part 1 of the 1971 yearbook of the National Society of Education bore the title *The Curriculum—Retrospect and Prospect,* a volume designed to examine the heritage of the curriculum field in terms of present-day practice and future prospects (McClure, 1971). A 1975 issue of *Curriculum Theory Network* (now *Curriculum Inquiry*) contained an announcement by the editors that it was that journal's first issue of "a series that examines the roots of curriculum thinking" (Berk & Weiss, p. 234). The 1976 yearbook of the Association for Supervision and Curriculum Development was devoted entirely to tracing the evolution of curriculum thought since the American Revolution (Davis, 1976). The seventy-fifth anniversary issue of *The Elementary School Journal* featured reprinted articles by Francis W. Parker, William C. Bagley, Carleton W. Washburne, Franklin Bobbitt, Charles H. Judd, and others, including analyses of the contributions of some of these early writers in the curriculum field. In the opening article, Dunkel (1975) noted that "The reader is repeatedly struck by the perennial nature of many educational issues and problems" (p. 3).

It is generally assumed that the systematic study of the heritage of a field will enable contemporary practitioners to benefit from past experience. An example of such an endeavor is the volume *Value Conflicts and Curriculum Issues: Lessons from Research and Experience* (Schaffarzick & Sykes, 1979). This volume was derived in large part from papers commissioned for the National Institute of Education's (NIE) Curriculum Development Task Force. The function of the task force was to study the problems and issues of federal involvement in curriculum development at the elementary and secondary levels, with a particular focus on the rise and collapse of the curriculum-reform projects in the disciplines over a twenty-year period, beginning with the mid-1950s. The opening chapter

by Schaffarzick leaves the reader with the impression that the collapse of the federal curriculum-reform projects can be largely attributed to the forces of censorship, capped by a congressional attack on one of these projects in 1975. This is puzzling in view of the fact that the "new" mathematics, physics, chemistry, and most of the elementary and junior high science projects were not targets of censorship and were already in a state of decline by the late 1960s, when secondary school and college students were demanding curriculum "relevance." And although the new biology projects were attacked in some quarters by antievolutionists, the concept of evolution has undergirded the serious study of biology throughout the century. Indeed high school biology textbooks had been under attack from the time of the Scopes trial to the advent of the "new" biology.

Some of the chief problems leading to the collapse of the federally sponsored discipline-centered reforms were (1) the narrow emphasis on puristic and abstract knowledge to the neglect of knowledge applications and social problems; (2) the resultant curriculum imbalance when priority was given to the sciences and mathematics; (3) the curriculum fragmentation created by a host of separate discipline-centered projects competing for a place in the school curriculum, and the failure to develop the projects within a holistic and coherent curriculum framework; (4) the questionable validity of the "structure-of-a-discipline" doctrine as the singular ruling "principle" for curriculum development, and the concomitant neglect of cross-disciplinary and interdisciplinary studies; (5) the priority given to the academically talented while neglecting the disadvantaged; (6) the failure to provide for independent formative evaluation studies in developing the curriculum packages; (7) the failure to take adequate account of the nature and interests of the learner; (8) the narrow, nationalistic, cold war basis for these curriculum reforms to the neglect of the wider social interest; (9) the disproportionate and narrow emphasis given the curriculum by a single specialized federal agency, namely the National Science Foundation (which came to overshadow the U.S. Office of Education as an agency for funding curriculum development); (10) the general failure of the discipline-centered projects to live up to the often extravagant promises and claims made by the project proponents; and (11) the misguided effort to develop "teacher-proof" materials.

In essence, the guiding forces for the federal discipline-centered projects had failed to take adequate account of the fundamental factors in the curriculum paradigm: (1) the nature and interests of the learner, (2) pervading social problems, and (3) alternative approaches to knowledge organization and application.

Although criticisms and warnings had been raised in some quarters during the 1960s (Caswell, 1962; Tanner, 1966; Weinberg, 1967), they went largely unheeded as the discipline-centered reforms took on a bandwagon effect. Caswell's brief historical review of the curriculum field in a paper delivered in 1962 at a conference at Teachers College, Columbia University, raised serious questions about the validity of the structure-of-a-discipline notion, the failure to deal with alternative curriculum frameworks and interrelationships of knowledge, the tendency to let the knowledge specialist dominate while neglecting the school curriculum director, who must see the school curriculum as more than the sum of its parts, the neglect of the teacher in curriculum development, and the failure to bridge the gap between subject matter and the learner (Caswell, 1962, pp. 106–111). Caswell's paper is a remarkable example of how a study of curriculum history can provide the insight and foresight for anticipating and preventing problems.

Despite the apparently misplaced conclusions in *Value Conflicts and Curriculum Issues* (the historical analysis of the federally supported discipline-centered curriculum reforms), the very fact that such an unprecedented historical review was commissioned by a federal agency (NIE) attests to the growing awareness of the need to undertake historical study of the curriculum field as a means of learning lessons from the past. Of course, such lessons are never guaranteed, even by the best historical scholarship. But such study can provide a needed perspective on the difference between change and progress and can provide needed clues on the underlying causes of the shifting curriculum-reform cycles and counterreactions that only serve to confuse movement with progress.

Bochner's study of the history of knowledge (1969) supports the premise that the twentieth century marks an era of knowledge synthesis in which new knowledge is accommodated without major disruptions into the mature areas of scholarship. The twentieth-century "Age of Synthesis" is contrasted with the "Age of Eclosion"—the period of the half century around 1800—when new knowledge created explosive changes in the relatively immature fields of scholarship. Bochner's thesis clearly runs counter to the notion of an incessantly accelerating knowledge explosion, a notion that became a fundamental premise of the discipline-centered curriculum reforms of the 1950s and 1960s.

The need for curriculum synthesis permeated experimentalist theory from its very beginnings. The reawakened interest in general education and the interdependence of knowledge as we entered the last quarter of the twentieth century appears to be a legacy of experimentalist ideas that permeated the curriculum literature during the field's formative years.

Daniel Tanner

See also Curriculum and Instruction in Higher Education; Curriculum Research; History of Education.

REFERENCES

Bell, D. *The Reforming of General Education.* New York: Columbia University Press, 1966.

Bellack, A. A. History of curriculum thought and practice. *Review of Educational Research,* 1969, *39,* 283–292.

Berk, L., & Weiss, J. Editorial. *Curriculum Theory Network,* 1975, *4,* 233–234.

Bobbitt, F. *The Curriculum.* Boston: Houghton Mifflin, 1918.

Bochner, S. *Eclosion and Synthesis: Perspectives on the History of Knowledge.* New York: Benjamin, 1969.

Bode, B. H. Education at the crossroads. *Progressive Education,* 1931, *8,* 548.

Bowers, C. A. Emergent ideological characteristics of educational policy. *Teachers College Record,* 1977, *79,* 33–54.

Boyer, E. L., & Levine, A. *A Quest for Common Learning: The Aims of General Education.* Washington, D.C.: Carnegie Foundation for the Advancement of Teaching, 1981.

Brubacher, J. S. *A History of the Problems of Education* (2nd ed.). New York: McGraw-Hill, 1966.

Bruner, J. S. *The Process of Education.* Cambridge, Mass.: Harvard University Press, 1960.

Carnegie Council on Policy Studies in Higher Education. *Giving Youth a Better Chance.* San Francisco: Jossey-Bass, 1979.

Carnegie Foundation for the Advancement of Teaching. *Missions of the College Curriculum.* San Francisco: Jossey-Bass, 1977.

Caswell, H. L. Difficulties in defining the structure of the curriculum. In A. H. Passow (Ed.), *Curriculum Crossroads.* New York: Teachers College Press, 1962, pp. 103–111.

Charters, W. W. *Curriculum Construction.* New York: Macmillan, 1923.

Commission on the Reorganization of Secondary Education. *Cardinal Principles of Secondary Education* (U.S. Bureau of Education Bulletin No. 35). Washington, D.C.: U.S. Government Printing Office, 1918.

Committee on the Objectives of General Education in a Free Society. *General Education in a Free Society.* Cambridge, Mass.: Harvard University Press, 1945.

Conant, J. B. *The American High School Today.* New York: McGraw-Hill, 1959.

Cremin, L. A. The revolution in American secondary education, 1893–1918. *Teachers College Record,* 1955, *56,* 295–307.

Cremin, L. A. Curriculum-making in the United States. *Teachers College Record,* 1971, *73,* 207–220.

Davis, O. L. (Ed.). *Perspectives on Curriculum Development, 1776–1976.* Washington, D.C.: Association for Supervision and Curriculum Development, 1976. (ERIC Document Reproduction Service No. ED 119 341)

Dewey, J. *The Child and the Curriculum.* Chicago: University of Chicago Press, 1902.

Dewey, J. *Democracy and Education.* New York: Macmillan, 1916.

Dewey, J. *The Sources of a Science of Education.* New York: Liveright, 1929.

Dewey, J. *Experience and Education.* New York: Macmillan, 1938.

Dunkel, H. B. Voices from the past. *Elementary School Journal,* 1975, *75,* 3–7.

Educational Policies Commission. *Education for ALL American Youth.* Washington, D.C.: National Education Association, 1944. (Rev. ed., 1952).

Flexner, A. A modern school. *American Review of Reviews,* 1916, *53,* 465–474.

Foshay, A. W. Curriculum. In R. L. Ebel (Ed.), *Encyclopedia of Educational Research* (4th ed.). New York: Macmillan, 1969.

Giles, H. H.; McCutchen, S. P.; & Zechiel, A. N. *Exploring the Curriculum.* New York: Harper & Brothers, 1942.

Goodlad, J. I. *The Changing School Curriculum.* New York: Fund for the Advancement of Education, 1966.

Harvard Faculty of Arts and Sciences. *Report on the Core Curriculum.* Cambridge, Mass.: Harvard University, 1978.

Hazlett, J. S. Conceptions of curriculum history. *Curriculum Inquiry,* 1979, *9,* 129–131.

Inglis, A. *Principles of Secondary Education.* Boston: Houghton Mifflin, 1918.

Kliebard, H. M. The curriculum field in retrospect. In P. W. Witt (Ed.), *Technology and the Curriculum.* New York: Teachers College Press, 1968, pp. 69–84.

Kliebard, H. M. Reappraisal: The Tyler rationale. *School Review,* 1970, *50,* 270.

Koopman, G. R. *Curriculum Development.* New York: Center for Applied Research in Education, 1966.

Kuhn, T. S. *The Structure of Scientific Revolutions* (2nd ed.). Chicago: University of Chicago Press, 1970.

Levine, A. *Handbook on Undergraduate Curriculum.* San Francisco: Jossey-Bass, 1978.

Marland, S. P., Jr. *Career Education Now.* Paper presented at the meeting of the National Association of Secondary Principals, Houston, January 23, 1971. (ERIC Document Reproduction Service No. ED 048 480)

McClure, R. M. (Ed.). *The Curriculum—Retrospect and Prospect: Seventieth Yearbook of the National Society for the Study of Education* (Part 1). Chicago: University of Chicago Press, 1971.

National Commission on the Reform of Secondary Education. *The Reform of Secondary Education.* New York: McGraw-Hill, 1973.

National Panel on High School and Adolescent Education. *The Education of Adolescents.* (Health, Education, and Welfare Publication No. (OE) 76-0004). Washington, D.C.: U.S. Government Printing Office, 1976. (ERIC Document Reproduction Service No. ED 130 379)

Panel on Youth of the President's Science Advisory Committee. *Youth: Transition to Adulthood.* Chicago: University of Chicago Press, 1974.

Report of the Commission on MIT Education. *Creative Renewal in a Time of Crisis.* Cambridge, Mass.: Massachusetts Institute of Technology, 1970.

Report on the Commission on the Humanities. *The Humanities in American Life.* Berkeley, Calif.: University of California Press, 1980.

Rudolph, F. *Curriculum: A History of the American Undergraduate Course of Study since 1636.* San Francisco: Jossey-Bass, 1977.

Rugg, H. (Ed.). *Curriculum-making—Past and Present: Twenty-sixth Yearbook of the National Society for the Study of Education* (Part 1). Bloomington, Ill.: Public School Publishing Co., 1927. (a)

Rugg, H. (Ed.). *The Foundations of Curriculum-making: Twenty-sixth Yearbook of the National Society for the Study of Education* (Part 2). Bloomington, Ill.: Public School Publishing Co., 1927. (b)

Schaffarzick, J., & Sykes, G. (Eds.). *Value Conflicts and Curriculum Issues: Lessons from Research and Experience.* Berkeley, Calif.: McCutchan, 1979.

Shane, H. G. Significant writings that have influenced the curriculum: 1906–1981. *Phi Delta Kappan,* 1981, *62,* 311–314.

Silberman, C. E. *Crisis in the Classroom: The Remaking of American Education.* New York: Random House, 1970.

Spencer, H. What knowledge is of most worth? In *Education: Intellectual, Moral, and Physical.* New York: D. Appleton, 1860, chap. 1.

Taba, H. General techniques of curriculum planning. In R. W. Tyler (Ed.), *American Education in the Postwar Period: Forty-fourth Yearbook of the National Society for the Study of Education* (Part 1). Chicago: University of Chicago Press, 1945, Chapter 5.

Taba, H. *Curriculum Development: Theory and Practice.* New York: Harcourt, Brace & World, 1962.

Tanner, D. Curriculum theory: Knowledge and content. *Review of Educational Research,* 1966, *36,* 362–372.

Tanner, D. Splitting up the school system. *Phi Delta Kappan,* 1979, *61,* 92–97.

Tanner, D., & Tanner, L. N. *Curriculum Development: Theory into Practice* (2nd ed.). New York: Macmillan, 1980.

Teachers College, Columbia University. *Announcements,* 1905.

Thomas, R. *The Search for a Common Learning: General Education, 1800–1960.* New York: McGraw-Hill, 1962.

Tyler, R. W. *Basic Principles of Curriculum and Instruction.* Chicago: University of Chicago Press, 1949.

Tyler, R. W. The curriculum field. In D. Tanner (Ed.), *What the Curriculum Field Needs to Learn from Its History.* American Educational Research Association, Special Interest Group on the Creation and Utilization of Curriculum Knowledge, 1978, pp. 4–10.

University of Chicago. *Annual Register.* Chicago: University of Chicago, 1895–1904.

U.S. Office of Education. *Life Adjustment Education for Every Youth* (Bulletin No. 22). Washington, D.C.: U.S. Government Printing Office, 1951.

Weinberg, A. M. *Reflections on Big Science.* Cambridge, Mass.: MIT Press, 1967.

CURRICULUM RESEARCH

In order to incorporate as many of the definitions in use as possible, it is best to define "curriculum research" quite broadly. "Curriculum" derives from Latin roots that refer to the course of a chariot race; and ordinary educational discourse designates the common dictionary usage of "course of study." Although curricularists have long debated the meaning of the term, "curriculum" can be treated as the essence and/or subject matter of educational experiences. Indeed, the etymological metaphor can be extended to designate not only a race course but also a journey, expedition, or even pilgrimage.

Curriculum research goes hand in hand with curriculum scholarship. Because educational research derives its character from inquiry in the social and behavioral sciences, and because curriculum would seem to be a subdivision of education, it might seem to follow that curriculum research is dominated by social and behavioral methodologies. This expectation is only partially true. Curriculum research is more broadly conceived. Although it often includes social and behavioral methodologies, curriculum scholarship is more properly denoted by the terms "inquiry," "studies," "theory," and "perspectives" rather than "research." This is reflected in the titles and contents of the four principal scholarly curriculum journals today: *Curriculum Inquiry, The Journal of Curriculum Studies, The Journal of Curriculum Theorizing,* and *Curriculum Per-*

spectives. Educational Leadership, the journal of the Association for Supervision and Curriculum Development (ASCD), addresses scholars but primarily treats concerns of curriculum practitioners. Each of these journals provides a greater variety of research orientations than one finds in most journals that use the "educational research" label. The broad conception of curriculum research is sometimes empirical, but more often analytic, conceptual, critical, and/or normative.

Thus, curriculum research concerns inquiry about the course of educational experiences. It usually focuses on experiences of students in schools, and embraces the formulation, implementation, and outcomes of curricular policy. Stated another way, curriculum researchers seek to explicate, understand, and guide the context, purposes, planning, delivery, and acquisition of the subject matter of education in schools and related learning environments.

The remainder of this article discusses curriculum research relative to the following topics: (1) origins; (2) perennial categories; (3) contexts; and (4) emergent trends.

Origins. Philosophers, literary figures, and sociopolitical analysts have long been concerned about curricular matters, that is, the purpose, substance, implementation, and outcomes of education. These issues were, however, treated as part of much larger portrayals of society and the human condition. The early twentieth century, influenced by specialization in business and industry and the growth of universal schooling as a basis of democracy, saw the development of an embryonic area of specialized inquiry known as "curriculum." Curriculum scholars had roots not only in the teaching profession but in scholarly disciplines such as philosophy and psychology. By the 1920s, curriculum was a subarea of educational inquiry, and major writers charted the course of curriculum prescription and description, namely the development, design, and research of programs. The emergent literature was disparate in orientation, although three general tendencies emerged: the intellectual traditionalist, social behaviorist, and experientialist (Schubert, 1980a). Each trend in inquiry embodied certain assumptions about curriculum knowledge, and each persists today, although labels may differ according to time of origin and author.

Intellectual traditionalist. The dominant mode of curriculum thought prior to 1900 coupled a reverence for classics with faculty psychology. Sometimes referred to as the "mental disciplines approach," this trend of thought likened the mind to muscles that improved with exercise of such faculties as reason or imagination, achieved through study of subjects derived from the classical *trivium* (grammar, rhetoric, dialectic) and *quadrivium* (arithmetic, geometry, astronomy, music). It sponsored a subject-oriented curriculum, the application of which ranged from rote memorization of skills and information to study of perennial human themes and paradigms that frame scholarly disciplines. The intellectual traditionalist orientation strongly influenced both curriculum practice and research, which were inextricably connected. The

search for paradigmatic structures of disciplines and the study of perennial human questions were thought to be the proper goal of scholar, curriculum designer, teacher, and student. As Broudy (1979) argued, it is the search for goodness and wisdom that professors of education have relinquished and that they must rekindle if they are to have knowledge worth professing to those who design and implement educational programs for schools and other institutions.

Social behaviorist. Trends and methods in business, industry, and science from 1900 to 1925 combined precise explanation, technological efficiency, and social utility. The outcome, curriculum research that sought social efficiency through inquiry, was called "activity analysis" by Bobbitt (1918, 1924). By studying what people do in order to perform successfully in adult life, he translated adult activities into objectives for learning activities of students. Similarly, Charters (1923) built a theoretical framework around dominant social ideals that he viewed as goals, maintaining that they could be scientifically translated into precise objectives and learning activities. Bobbitt and Charters assumed that society is best perpetuated by creating learning activities that foster dominant ideals and behaviors. Although the "activity analysis" of early social behaviorists no longer prevails, its regard for science persists in the behavioral inquiry dominating educational research today. The tendency to specialize and systematize exists in many spheres of curriculum research, namely, in the areas of behavioral objectives, process-product studies, systems language and modeling, competency-based programs, learning packages, and input-output orientations.

Today's social behaviorists trace their origins to the experimental psychology of Wilhelm Wundt (Schubert & Posner, 1980). Their position is that research should provide basic or applied knowledge for the development and implementation of measurable results or products. Curricular products may be seen as "packages" that take the form of textbooks, instructional modules, or multimedia kits. Less formal, unpublished packages are exemplified by curriculum documents designed by committees within school districts to be engineered for teacher and student use. In either case, curriculum is seen as a good or service to be delivered through a network consisting of administrators, supervisors, teachers, environmental arrangements, instructional models, and students. In a sense students also, become products as they are subjected to the quality control of accountability measures. As recipients of carefully specified treatments, students are viewed as curricular results to be verified by researchers who analyze implementation and outcomes and assess the degree to which treatment accountably produces specified ends.

Experientialist. At the onset of the twentieth century, prominent Herbartians (followers of Johann Friedrich Herbart, 1776–1841; e.g., Charles DeGarmo, Frank and Charles McMurry) emphasized the notion of "apperceptive mass," or the growing repertoire of experiences. The task of curriculum research was to discover ways to prepare and present desirable knowledge so that students could systematically associate and apply it within their evolving apperceptive masses. This orientation marked the beginning of a science of method based on interest, and evolved through the work of John Dewey, who offered a view of science as problem solving that guides individual and social action. Dewey argued that problem solving must be taught by first considering problems actually experienced. It follows that curriculum research becomes a science of discovering how to induct the young to human knowledge by means of increasingly expanded study of their own experience. Whereas such research could involve large-scale studies that yield generalizations about the teaching-learning process, primary importance is placed on situationally unique interactions among teachers and students.

Early research orientations. Intellectual traditionalist, social behaviorist, and experientialist positions proliferated and merged as curriculum inquiry grew into a specialized field. An increased number of articles and books guided practitioners to develop curricula for universal schooling. New topics emerged, as did expanded treatments of old ones, fashioning a broader definition of curriculum that included curriculum at the several levels of schooling, descriptions of practice, ideal planning models, as well as analysis of curriculum foundations, purposes, materials, activities, assessment, organization, administration, and supervision. By 1930, more than one hundred curriculum books existed (Schubert, 1980a). The growing diversity prompted two major theoretical assessments of assumptions, those by Bode (1927) and the National Society for the Study of Education (1927). The interplay of theoretical and practical inquiry within the several orientations to curriculum thought provided a precedent for three quite different dimensions of curriculum research that have persisted since the mid-1930s.

One dimension of curriculum research involves broad and penetrating exploration of fundamental human questions about the meaning of life and how we should live together (Macdonald, 1977). Such inquiry taps not only the variety of social and behavioral methodologies, but the arts, sciences, and humanities as well. The Deweyan question of how to induct the young into the best that humanity can offer embraces the limits of human knowledge. Some hold that curriculum inquiry should not exchange philosophical criticism for simplistic clarity, nor should it replace what Greene (1978) calls "wide awakeness" with reified procedures. As Walker (1980) concludes, "A rich confusion is the right state for curriculum writing" (p. 81).

A second dimension of curriculum research strives for practicality in the service of immediate applicability, a trait that led to the use of curriculum research in the service of universal schooling. Yet, there exists little agreement on the nature of practicality as evidenced by the various purposes of this dimension of research. These include (1) the need to set forth general formulas that are known as curriculum principles; (2) the provision of sets of atomistic competencies, strategies, and behavioral objectives; and (3) the provision of perspectives enabling educators to imagine possibilities and project consequences to guide decision and action.

A third dimension of curriculum research has its roots in the tradition of empirical investigation. In the early twentieth century, E. L. Thorndike conducted investigations that discredited the position that traditional intellectual studies discipline the mind better than other subjects. These investigations prompted de-emphasis upon the study of classics in transfer of learning. The decline of traditional curricula was accompanied by the rise of progressive education in the late 1920s, and the time was ripe for a study that compared traditionalist and experientialist curricula. The Eight-Year Study (1932–1940) represents the most extensive curriculum experiment during the first half of the twentieth century (Aikin, 1942). Its purpose was to discover whether success in college depended upon traditional curricula at the high school level. A total of 1,475 students of varied backgrounds in thirty schools throughout the United States were schooled by means of nontraditional curricula during secondary school. Each student was matched with a traditionally schooled student and his or her progress was followed throughout college. The graduates of the thirty schools were found to perform better academically, nonacademically, and in areas of general problem solving. Moreover, those in the six most experimental schools did even better in these areas. These auspicious results, however, were overshadowed by World War II, which was followed by a period of educational traditionalism, mechanization, and authoritarianism.

Paradigm and Its Categories. How was it possible to convey the many varieties of curriculum knowledge to curriculum developers and practitioners in schools by means of one or two university courses? In what form should curriculum knowledge be generated and disseminated? The response to such questions was the creation of synoptic curriculum texts (Schubert, 1980a), first developed by Caswell and Campbell (1935), that summarized existing developments. Synoptic texts also prescribed recipes for curricular decision and action. They amalgamated experientialist, social behaviorist, and intellectual tendencies, and became preservers of curriculum research from 1940 to the present. Some of them (Gwynn, 1943; Smith, Stanley, & Shores, 1957; Taba, 1962; Saylor & Alexander, 1974; and Tanner & Tanner, 1980) provided new perspectives, categorization schemes, and summaries; but others were repetitious and diluted. In large part, however, synoptic texts defined the curriculum arena by socializing curricularists.

A concomitant synoptic event was the forging of a paradigm, or analytic scheme of topics, to guide curriculum research and development. Prior to the 1950s, curriculum researchers built their research around a host of topics. Most synoptic texts presented categorizations of curriculum knowledge that were rather cumbersome, amorphous, and idiosyncratic. A perspective was needed to give shape and cohesion to this diversity. Drawing upon the thought of Dewey, Charters, and his own work as evaluation director of the Eight-Year Study, Ralph W. Tyler produced *Basic Principles of Curriculum and Instruction* in 1949. This small book articulated a paradigm that identifies four major curriculum topics: "purposes," "learning experiences," "organization," and "evaluation." Reflecting trends in social behaviorist, intellectual traditionalist, and experientialist thought, Tyler's treatment has served as a rationale for curriculum deliberation and prescription for over thirty years. The four topics (and subtopics) of the paradigm serve as an outline for portraying major categories of curriculum research.

The Tylerian categories are clearly evident in most curriculum texts and research reports. They also shape major documents used by practitioners, such as accrediting instruments, curriculum guides, curriculum evaluation forms, and lesson plans. In addition to his topics of purposes, learning experiences, organization, and evaluation, Tyler's rationale emphasizes the need for a guiding philosophy to provide a cohesive meaning and direction for all four topics, an important consideration too often neglected in favor of mechanistic applications. Since researchers also often neglect to specify their research orientations, the following discussion analyzes research perspectives related to each of Tyler's major topics.

Purposes. The terms "aims," "intents," "ends," "goals," and "objectives," as well as "purposes" are widely used to identify one of the major curriculum topics of the paradigm. Some use these terms interchangably, whereas others arrange them in a hierarchy from general to specific, although ranking is rather idiosyncratic. Furthermore, curricular purpose is studied relative to both form and substance: how purposes should be formulated and what virtues or excellences they embody.

1. *Form.* Today's emphasis on behavioral objectives is an example of the formulation of purposes that evolved from early social behaviorist tendencies. It requires that those who formulate purposes use highly specific language, that results be stated as observable behaviors, and that results be measurable if possible. This view of formulation is closely related to industrial training models promoted for educational purposes since the mid-1960s. Arguments in favor of behavioral objectives rest on the manageability of their tangible form as compared with global statements of purpose. An elaboration used by formulators of behavioral objectives is provided by the taxonomies of Bloom (1956) and Krathwohl, Bloom, & Masia (1964), in which levels of cognitive and affective functioning are spelled out in detail. The logical and epistemological defensibility of these taxonomies is seriously questioned by Travers (1980). Criticisms of behavioral objectives and competency approaches have been made by noted researchers such as Atkin, Stake, Stenhouse, and Eisner (Hamilton et al., 1977), asserting that it is impossible, impractical, and inde-

fensible to reduce educational purpose to sets of atomistic prescriptions. These critics espouse a Deweyan view that distinguishes between training and education and that treats purposes as ends in view, emerging out of present activity, and not as remote, preordained ends (Kliebard, 1972). Those who acknowledge curriculum design as an act of intentionality (e.g., Johnson, 1977) prefer a more conceptually rigorous and less atomistic approach than behavioral objectives; thus, they treat objectives as "intended learning outcomes." Eisner (1979), however, argues for "expressive outcomes," which emerge from engagement in worthwhile activities in unanticipated ways.

2. *Substance.* The search for a philosophic rationale for the determination of qualities to be fostered in students is the subject of much inquiry. Tyler (1949) called for studies of learners, contemporary life, and scholarly disciplines. This emphasis on learner, society, and knowledge is reflected in Dewey (1902), the Eight-Year Study (Aikin, 1942), and Taba (1962), among others. Tyler advocates a balance of study in all three areas; however, by skewing the emphasis, tendencies toward experientialist, social behaviorist, or intellectual traditionalist positions emerge. Thus, it is important to interpret descriptions of, or prescriptions about, curricular purpose in light of these assumptions.

Content or learning experiences. The vast literature on subject matter demonstrates that curriculum content is primarily viewed as specific subject matter to be conveyed. Content is also often referred to as skills, knowledge, and attitudes or appreciations. This article considers research about the nature of content and the methods for its selection. Content is conceived differently by different authors. One conception steadfastly holds to content as subject matter derived from scholarly disciplines (King & Brownell, 1976). Another stems from early social behaviorists and equates content with activities; hence, many curricularists refer to the selection of "learning activities." Tyler (1949) is often associated with either position, but he defines "learning experiences" to indicate the interdependence of content and the learning process. Accordingly, the planning of content should be a gathering of evidence that enables curricularists to predict and create desirable changes in the experiential repertoire of students (1949). To this end, Parker and Rubin (1966) and Berman and Roderick (1977) provide Deweyan interpretations that conceive of process as the most defensible content. That content is thought to derive from numerous sources is illustrated by Smith, Stanley, and Shores (1957), who present the following sources of content selection: academic subjects, student needs, scholarly disciplines, social practices, universal institutions, social trends, and significant social problems. Today's conceptions of content stem from a combination of such sources. For example, open education bases content upon student interest, whereas the bandwagon of published materials reflects social trends. Post-*Sputnik* curriculum reform emerges out of a concern with scholarly disciplines. Similarly, the views of contemporary revisionists who assert that schools reflect dominant ideologies are expressions of interest in universal institutions. These are merely examples that illustrate the need for researchers to clarify the character and sources of content and to design curricula suitable to that content.

Organization. The vast amount of research on organization can be categorized in terms of: scope and sequence; instruction and methodology; and several environmental dimensions (human, physical, material, and psychosocial).

1. *Scope and Sequence.* The scope of curriculum organization involves the range of content or experiences to be covered. Questions about the proper balance of curricular offerings, required versus elective subjects, and depth versus breadth are matters of scope. Sequence deals with the proper ordering of content, that is, the matter of prerequisite knowledge. Research reveals several different criteria for determining sequence. Dewey (1916) raised the primary distinction between "psychological" and "logical" organization. Psychological organization takes student interests or current sources of meaning in student lives as bases for sequence, whereas logical organization proceeds according to the structures of academic disciplines. Proponents of progressive and open education exemplify the psychological approach, whereas those who guided curriculum reform projects in the late 1960s followed the logical approach to organization. Dewey argued that we must overcome dualistic interpretations, begin with the psychological, and help students move toward acquisition of the logical. According to Kohlberg and Mayer (1972), this position is strongly consonant with Piaget's notion of developmentally appropriate learning. Gagné (1967), however, considers the problem of sequence best treated hierarchically; that is, sequence should move consecutively from simple to complex capabilities. He relates instructional conditions to learning theories as a central feature of sequence. Posner and Strike (1976) elaborate a number of alternative positions on sequence at the same time that they are probing their epistemological assumptions. Whereas opinions about sequence are quite rational, research on curriculum practice reveals the power of the less rational sources such as social trends, ideology, political pressure, teacher preference, and the marketing strategies of publishers.

2. *Instruction and Methodology.* An ongoing debate persists about the relation of curriculum to instruction. Some researchers prefer to separate the two for analytic clarity, whereas others regard separation as superficial since curriculum and instruction are thoroughly intertwined in practice. Most agree, however, that if curriculum emphasizes ends to be acquired, then instruction is a principal means of acquisition. An account of research on numerous instructional strategies is beyond the scope of this article, but several sources provide helpful overviews: Broudy and Palmer (1965) provide historical perspective on method; Travers (1973) adds research overviews; Dunkin and Biddle (1974) summarize empirical studies of

teaching; and Joyce and Weil (1980) explicate models. Much recent attention has been given to the topics of "mastery learning," which asserts that students can achieve if given sufficient time, and "aptitude-treatment-interaction," in which achievement is examined as an outcome of learner predisposition and educative input. Such studies encourage Gage (1978) to argue that ample evidence exists for the scientific basis of instruction. Clearly, current research points up the interdependence of instruction and curriculum.

3. *Environment (Human).* The grouping of human beings is a major field of study that has long involved the issue of homogeneous versus heterogeneous grouping and the concomitant criteria for group selection. The organization of teachers in relation to students is considered. Are certain subjects or achievement levels best served by departmentalization, self-contained classrooms, or newer patterns such as team teaching, nongradedness, multiage grouping, minicourses? Clearly, departmentalization is dominant in secondary schools and self-contained classrooms in elementary schools. The relative benefits of large-group, small-group, and independent study cannot as yet be given generalized support or criticism; the same is true for contract learning and personalized systems of instruction.

4. *Environment (Physical).* Arrangement of the physical plant is treated at many levels. The recent emergence of middle schools (Lounsbury & Vars, 1978) exemplifies study of the impact of schoolwide grouping by age patterns. Grouping within school buildings raises issues about the comparative worth of openspace, modular, and pod arrangements, as well as more venerable curriculum issues such as subject, activity, and core curricula. Strengths and weaknesses of the latter are carefully discussed by Smith, Stanley, and Shores (1957). Although current terminology varies for both physical and human arrangements, the subject, core, and activity patterns readily prevail. Variations on each curriculum pattern utilize distinctive physical arrangements of furniture and equipment that markedly influence purposes, content, and evaluation.

5. *Environment (Materials).* The organization of published and locally made instructional materials is studied in its many dimensions. Just as Tyler's categories of purposes, experiences, organization, and evaluation are used in large-scale curriculum planning, they are also used as guides for the everyday curriculum research involved in teachers' unit and lesson planning. Tyler's topics give direction to both construction and use of published materials. The Educational Products Information Exchange (EPIE) argues for greater clarification of selection and use procedures (1979), especially in view of the fact that more than 85 percent of teaching time is involved with instructional materials. EPIE tries to enable educators to clarify their needs and select materials that are designed with internal consistency as to intent, content, methodology, and evaluation. Goodlad, Klein, and Associates (1970)

found that implementation of innovative curricular materials rarely remains consistent with intent; moreover, Walker and Schaffarzick (1974) provide evidence that the perceived value of innovative or traditional materials is greatly dependent upon the innovative or traditional character of evaluation instruments used.

6. *Environment (Psychosocial).* Since the psychosocial dimension of organization is quite intangible, it is difficult to study. It is concerned with the educational atmosphere and its conduciveness to learning. Organizational patterns clearly produce side effects or subliminal learning, for the classroom is not only the scene of covert effects of school life but also of a labyrinth of knowledge stemming from the curriculum outside of schools. Schubert (1981) argues that nonschool curricula of homes, peers, media, occupations, and avocations greatly influence students' responses to school learning and ought to be the subject of curriculum research. Posner (1980) focuses on student perspectives by drawing upon research from cognitive psychology and science education. Van Manen (1979) and Pinar and Grumet (1976) explore phenomenological and psychoanalytic sources to provide alternative perspectives on the experiential repertoires of students. Researchers of learning environments increasingly probe psychosocial factors quantitatively. Walberg and Moos (1980) assess organizational, suprapersonal, and social as well as physical aspects. Fraser (1980) incorporates student perceptions of learning environments in curriculum decision making and evaluation.

Evaluation. Evaluative considerations constitute the fourth topic in Tyler's paradigm. Early in this century, evaluation was nearly synonymous with testing and measurement. Between 1930 and 1960, writers of synoptic texts expanded evaluation to include a variety of evidence on student performance and program effectiveness. Tyler's influence on the latter was great. In 1963, Cronbach (1963) solidified an emerging direction for curriculum evaluation by advocating course improvement as its purpose. While issues in tests and measurements (such as criterion versus norm-referenced tests or teacher-made versus standardized tests) are clearly curriculum-related, attention primarily focuses upon Cronbach's efforts.

As evaluation efforts sought curriculum improvement, they acknowledged the import of process variables. Scriven (1967) distinguished between "formative" evaluation, focusing upon implementation processes, and "summative" evaluation, (focusing upon outcomes.) Stufflebeam (1969) described formative elements in terms of "context," "input," and "process," but his interpretation of "product" can be associated with the summative approach. Stake (1967) added complexity to the conception of evaluation by positing three major variables subject to both descriptive and judgmental portrayal: "antecedents," "transactions," and "outcomes." More recently, he has advocated a form of evaluation in which researchers strive to be responsive to evolving client needs rather than to their preordained goals (Stake, 1975). Moreover, Scriven (1972) has suggested a goal-free mode in which evaluators portray curricular conditions without being biased by the goals that clients say they seek.

Today, the emphasis on portrayal leads a growing number of evaluators to use qualitative methodologies to interpret results of greater situational richness than some feel can emerge from quantitative study. The argument is made that quantitative evaluation is useful for subjects that can be numerically represented; other means (ethnography, criticism, autobiography) are necessary to portray aspects of context not readily amenable to quantitative representation. The distinction blurs, however, when one realizes that all research ought to deal with qualities. The desire to portray the complexities of curricular situations has brought about comparative analyses of evaluation modes (e.g., House, 1978; Pagano & Dolan, 1980; Stufflebeam & Webster, 1980). Most noteworthy is the distinct possibility of merging the qualitative and quantitative, as is evident in the treatment of program evaluation by Cronbach et al. (1980). Scriven (1980) not only argues that evaluation should involve multiple perspectives, but also that it should exert ethical leadership through self-assessment in a search for solutions, explanations, and practical wisdom.

Despite these expanding perspectives, the dominant approach to curriculum evaluation remains a rather straightforward seeking of evidence for accountability. It involves careful specification and verification of treatment, and results are usually portrayed statistically. Detailed renditions of this dominant view are provided by Fitz-Gibbon and Morris (1978) and by Lewy (1977).

Curriculum Contexts. Recent curriculum research draws upon historical, philosophical, sociological, psychoanalytic, scientific, literary, and artistic sources to deal with the following categories of curriculum context: (1) theory, (2) change, (3) policy, and (4) hidden curricula.

Theory. The study of assumptions is necessary for defensible curriculum research. During the first half of the twentieth century, one can find many curricularists who advocated the search for assumptions, but too few who seriously contributed to the development of theory. The need for more adequate theory prompted Herrick and Tyler (1950) to organize a curriculum theory conference at the University of Chicago in 1947. The influence of this conference is evident in the work of many curriculum writers who share the conviction that assumptions must be seriously explored if curriculum research and development are to be defensibly pursued. The range of perspectives on curriculum theory is indexed by Schubert (1980a) and sampled by the following recent contributions: philosophical collections by Martin (1970), Levit (1971), and Jenkins, Pring, and Harris (1972); theoretical perspectives on purpose by Morris (1972); theory as conceptual analysis by Hirst (1975) and Johnson (1977); a scientific systems approach by Beauchamp (1981); historical reviews of curriculum theory and practice by Zais (1976) and Tanner and Tanner (1980); theories of practical policy by Reid (1978) and Westbury and Wilkof (1978); critical or humanistic treatments by Apple (1979) and Pinar (1975); and categorizations of theoretical conceptions by Eisner and Vallance (1974) and Schiro (1978).

The more general theory of educational philosophers often provides a seedbed for curriculum theory. The paramount influence of Dewey on curriculum thought is a case in point. Cited profusely in curriculum literature, he characterizes education as more inclusive than training or schooling. For Dewey, education is a continuous reconstruction of experience that adds meaning and direction to subsequent experience (Dewey, 1916). If curriculum pertains to the plan of this notion of education, what should be the nature and scope of curriculum research? Clearly, it would be included in Dewey's ideal for a science of education (1929), the sources of which are: "Any portions of ascertained knowledge that enter into the heart, head and hands of educators . . . and render the . . . educational function more . . . educational than it was before. But there is no way to discover what *is* more truly educational except by the continuation of the educational act itself" (pp. 76–77). Interestingly, Dewey's conception of educational science is used in diverse and contradictory ways: to justify a wholly statistical-empirical approach to research; as a basis for systems orientations; to promote behavioral objectives; to support incrementalist approaches to problem solving; and to theorize that meaningful knowledge derives from critical, phenomenological, and psychoanalytic study of human lives. The diverse interpretations of Dewey's conception illustrates the need for theoretical clarification; and the problem is compounded by the fact that curriculum theorists dispute the nature of curriculum theory itself. An increasing number of theorists assert that it is unproductive to separate curriculum research and theory. According to Macdonald (1977), the essential point for researchers to realize is that all research is value-laden, and that the value premises upon which knowledge is created must be explicated. Such clarification can guide the uses of curriculum knowledge.

Change. Throughout the history of curriculum writing, major sections of books and large numbers of articles are devoted to change. An often unwritten assumption is that the purpose of curriculum research is to bring about change. Until the late 1960s, emphasis was placed upon models of instituting change, and was largely derived from change models for disseminating new agricultural procedures. Hamilton et al. (1977) labeled this the "agriculture-botany model." Curricularists who assume that change is to be preplanned and instituted envision it not merely as the installation of new courses but as sociopolitical engineering that involves client systems of parents, students, teachers, school systems, communities, and other relevant groups. Today, this orientation persists under the rubric of "organization development."

Another orientation to research on curriculum change focuses on the study of actual changes. Goodlad, Klein, and Associates (1970) documented impoverished classroom implementation of federally funded curriculum reform projects in the post-*Sputnik* era. More recently, the case study approach that interprets change in specific settings has contributed illumination on change processes (Reid & Walker, 1975; Willis, 1978). Sarason (1971) analyzed the problem of change as a function of school culture, as did Reynolds and Skilbeck (1976). The question of the relation between social and curricular change is addressed by Marks and Nystrand (1981), invoking anew Counts's (1932) query: "Dare the school build a new social order?" Recent arguments (Apple, 1979; Giroux, 1980) hold that schools reflect the social order; thus, curriculum change is largely superficial since it perpetuates dominant social class values and existing hierarchies.

Policy. Prior to the 1970s, study of political aspects of education was reserved for those in educational foundations and administration. However, problems associated with curricular change coupled with findings by Coleman (1966) and others indicated that curriculum outcomes were dwarfed by comparison to contextual forces. It became widely acknowledged that curriculum was a function of complex political and economic factors, and researchers turned their attention to policy matters. Walker (1971) offered a "naturalistic model" of curriculum as an alternative to Tyler's rational model (Tyler, 1949). Based on observations of curriculum designers, Walker revealed that they move from a platform (personal and political orientations), through deliberation (interchange of power and ideas), to *design* (product offered to students). Kirst and Walker (1971) studied curriculum from a policy perspective that explicates the complex forces creating the subject matter of schooling. This complexity of bureaucratic pressures, according to Kliebard (1977), promotes guiding metaphors such as pertained to early social efficiency language to those of management and performance in the 1970s.

Studies of curriculum policy making have diminished credibility in the explanatory power of purely rational models. Networks of contextual influences upon curriculum are explicated by Dahllof (1971) and Lundgren (1972), who sought to understand curricular organizational patterns that contribute to achievement. They devised the concept of "frame factors" to define dimensions of context influencing achievement, and they suggest that some of these factors (location of schools, general ability of students, or scheduling policies) are beyond the command of teachers, whereas others (level of objectives, intraclass grouping, or time) are subject to teacher influence. The time variable is widely researched today. Productive work by Harnischfeger and Wiley (1976) emphasizes time in relation to pupil pursuits, but much research on time also focuses upon teachers. Studies by the International Association for the Evaluation of Educational Achievement (1973) support time of exposure to subject matter as a key variable in achievement.

Curricular policy is presently investigated on many

fronts. Boyd (1978) has shown that local control is effected best by superintendents whose values are in harmony with the community. Hosts of studies exist on the relation of curriculum to ethnicity, race, sex and the handicapped. Boyd (1979) sees promoters of equity for such groups as a new force of professional curriculum reformers. Schaffarzick and Sykes (1979) portray value conflicts as major issues at the federal level that influence curriculum development, decision making, and implementation. Van Geel (1976) treats the growing power of collective bargaining on educational programs, asking whether appropriate authority exists to deprive school boards of powers that they were created to exercise.

A multitude of policy implications was unleashed by Schwab's (1973) opinion that curriculum is, in fact, the interaction of classroom commonplaces: teachers, learners, subject matter, and milieu. This view raises the complex possibility, explored by Pressman and Wildavsky (1979), that policy is guiding disposition (created by the flow of events, decisions, and actions) and that implementation is its evolution.

Hidden curricula. The notion of unwritten, unintended, or even unconsciously implemented policy requires special attention. It raises questions about the existence and importance of covert consequences of intended curricula. Such consequences may be unintended or subtly intended. By the early 1970s, sociological and educational writing convincingly pointed to the existence of hidden learning experiences. Jackson's sensitive investigations of elementary school life (1968) illuminate profound learnings associated with socialization—for example, that students learn to function in a crowd, incur continuous evaluation, and live under conditions of power. Snyder (1970) has shown that the sense of self-worth of students and faculty is less influenced by intended curricula than by the hidden curriculum of strategies one must learn to achieve success and/or recognition in school systems. As Tanner and Tanner (1980) caution, it should not be assumed that all aspects of hidden curricula are negative; some are indeed beneficial. They also note that the concept is not without precedent; for example, Dewey (1938) writes of "collateral learning," which can have greater effect upon enduring attitudes than intended skills and information. In 1972, Broudy called for investigation of "life uses of schooling," which would surely be a combination of overt and covert curricular effects.

The need for knowledge about hidden curricula was acknowledged by Overly (1970). Recent research provides at least two general approaches to creating such knowledge. One focuses upon the ideological, sociological, and political, and the other taps literary and artistic origins. Relative to the first approach, Young (1971), Apple (1979), and Giroux (1980) argue that schools must understand that they selectively empower and deny access to goods, services, work, life-styles, sources of meaning, and forms of political participation. As Huebner (1970) observes, the political aspect of curriculum must be continuously ana-

lyzed as we ask, "What educative content can be made present to what educatees within what sociopolitical arrangement to govern and adjudicate the distribution of power between educator and student?"

Research orientations that strive to portray hidden curricula often use literary and artistic criticism which starts with the image of connoisseur. Broudy (1961) characterizes this role as follows: "Being a connoisseur makes one dissatisfied with anything less than the best, and being a connoisseur means having standards that tell one what the best is" (p. 208). Eisner (1979) develops a method of educational criticism based upon connoisseurship. According to Willis (1978), the use of criticism in curriculum research stems from Mann (1968–1969), who argues that curriculum has a profoundly aesthetic character that can be better understood through methods derived from literary criticism. Examples of studies that apply such criticism are provided by Fraser and Godfrey (1980), Fraser and Smith (1980), Eisner (1979), and Willis (1978). Although Willis (1978) uses the label "qualitative evaluation" and Hamilton et al. (1977) refer to "illumination," both build upon Eisner's earlier work. Essentially, the critic observes, evocatively describes, interprets, and assesses in curricular settings (Willis, 1979); the goal is to illuminate the context and implications of curriculum, both hidden and intended. Questions about the validity, reliability, and objectivity of this method are often raised. However, it is questionable, whether scientific assumptions are wholly appropriate to an essentially aesthetic methodology. Standards of public explication, referential adequacy, and structural corroboration (McCutcheon, 1979) as well as personal and educational significance (Willis, 1978) are offered instead. Would one, for example, deny a kind of generalizable significance to the work of Dickens, Monet, or Mozart on the grounds that their work does not meet the canons of science? Nevertheless, the question prevails: who is capable of illuminating curricular contexts and how does one become capable?

Emergent Research Trends. This article began with a consideration of three tendencies in curricular research—intellectual traditionalist, social behaviorist, and experientialist—and will conclude with a review of emergent trends in each of these areas.

The late 1970s brought a resurgence of interest in general education at American colleges and universities. Research in this area indicates that the ideals of liberal education, the crux of the intellectual traditionalist tradition, are indeed realized but not widely implemented (Martin, 1981). In addressing the goals of the educational professoriate, Broudy (1979) contends that while scholarship can be enlightened by current scientific research, it must be more broadly conceived as the steadfast pursuit of truth, beauty, and goodness. This pursuit requires immersion in the array of arts, sciences, and professional studies at our disposal.

Social behaviorist research continues its quest to articulate curricular ends and means by striving for consistency and precision of language and measurement in statements of purpose, content, and organization. A major policy goal involves analysis of relations between such statements, their formulation, implementation, and outcomes. Improved studies of the impact of student background, teacher characteristics, organizational factors, and pupil pursuits upon achievement and related outcomes is a major focus. Researchers debate the possibilities for, and relative merits of, studying aptitude-treatment-interactions, disputing the possibility of producing generalizable knowledge for complex, dynamic situations (Phillips, 1980). Implications of brain research (Chall & Mirsky, 1978) promise to offer innumerable curricular implications, as do Posner's curricular applications from the cognitive sciences (1978).

Divergent experientialist origins relate to policy research at many levels. Schwab (1970) advocates *practical* research that focuses upon decision and action in specific situations rather than publishable generalizations (Schubert, 1980b). Schwab argues that curriculum study is immobilized by *theoretic* research that considers overgeneralized problems and employs an inductive method of inquiry in its search for general laws. He suggests practical research that addresses problems in actual affairs and studies them by interaction for the purpose of situationally specific resolutions. Reid (1978) builds upon Schwab's ideas (1969, 1971) by defining the policy consultant as one who practically expands clients' conceptions of possible courses of action relative to their problems and one who enables them to project probable consequences of these actions. Similarly, Wildavsky (1979) sees the public policy analyst's role as an art and craft of speaking truth to power. This practical function, which necessitates qualitative awareness of contextual factors, may best proceed by diminishing emphasis on experiments (Shulman et al., 1980); however, it does not deny the efficacy of quantitative approaches such as decision theory that have power to attend to many variables simultaneously.

Helping decision makers expand their awareness of context invokes the idea that curricular experience is broader than schooling; to this end, Cremin (1976), Tyler (1977), Martin (1980), and Schubert (1981) call for an "ecological" study of curriculum. According to Schwab (1971), knowledge relevant to an ecology of variables must be derived eclectically and adapted to situational problems with considerable inventiveness.

Acceptance of Schwab's curricular "commonplaces" of learners, teachers, subject matter, and milieu (1973) necessitates curriculum research that is both situational and continuous. Such research moves beyond the purview of policy consultants and detached theoretic researchers to involve another level of policy researcher, namely, participants in educational situations. Action research (Corey, 1953) represents an earlier attempt to enable teachers to pursue such problem solving more effectively. Tried in America in the 1950s and 1960s, and more successfully in Europe and Great Britain, the approach is practically implemented by Stenhouse (1980), who sees curriculum research as a process by which consultant-researchers interact with teachers in their environments, encouraging cooperative reflection upon and study of specific situations; the end is to improve the art of teaching by merging teacher and researcher. In a related vein, "autobiographical research" (Berk, 1980; Grumet, 1980; and Pinar, 1980) is a method that enables teachers and students to study the ways in which curriculum is reconstructed within their own educational lives. Similarly, educational criticism is extended to enable teachers (McCutcheon, 1980) and students (Vallance, 1981) to actively engage in criticism of their own educative settings. This type of research points to the curricular ideals of publics who direct their own curriculum (Bremer, 1979); educators who probe sources of their pedagogic life (van Manen, 1980); students whose education is a form of curricular research (Schubert & Schubert, 1981); and a Deweyan (1916) democratic living.

A rich and varied heritage of curriculum research points to a future of productive perspectives and possibilities. It also signals the need for cautious awareness of unproductive disconnectedness. Apparent disconnectedness can, however, be worthwhile if dissimilar research illuminates different dimensions of the curriculum domain.

William H. Schubert

See also Curriculum and Instruction in Higher Education; Curriculum Development and Organization; Evaluation of Programs; Qualitative Curriculum Evaluation.

REFERENCES

Aikin, W. M. *The Story of the Eight-year Study.* New York: Harper & Brothers, 1942.

Apple, M. W. *Ideology and Curriculum.* London: Routledge & Kegan Paul, 1979.

Beauchamp, G. A. *Curriculum Theory.* Itasca, Ill.: F. E. Peacock, 1981.

Berk, L. Education in lives: Biographic narrative in the study of educational outcomes. *Journal of Curriculum Theorizing,* 1980, *2*(2), 88–154.

Berman, L. M., & Roderick, J. A. *Curriculum: Teaching the What, How, and Why of Living.* Columbus, Ohio: Merrill, 1977.

Bloom, B. S. (Ed.). *Cognitive Domain.* Handbook 1 of *Taxonomy of Educational Objectives.* New York: Longmans, Green, 1956.

Bobbitt, F. *The Curriculum.* Boston: Houghton Mifflin, 1918.

Bobbitt, F. *How to Make a Curriculum.* Boston: Houghton Mifflin, 1924.

Bode, B. H. *Modern Educational Theories.* New York: Macmillan, 1927.

Boyd, W. L. The changing politics of curriculum policy making for American schools. *Review of Educational Research,* 1978, *48*(4), 577–629.

Boyd, W. L. The politics of curriculum change and stability. *Educational Researcher,* 1979, *8*(2), 12–19.

Bremer, J. *Education and Community.* Sheparton, Australia: Waterwheel Press, 1979.

Broudy, H. S. *Building a Philosophy of Education.* Englewood Cliffs, N.J.: Prentice-Hall, 1961.

Broudy, H. S. *The Real World of the Public Schools.* New York: Harcourt Brace Jovanovich, Inc., 1972.

Broudy, H. S. *What Do Professors of Education Profess?* Society for Professors of Education De Garmo Lecture, Chicago, February 1979.

Broudy, H. S., & Palmer, J. R. *Exemplars of Teaching Method.* Chicago: Rand McNally, 1965.

Caswell, H. L., & Campbell, D. S. *Curriculum Development.* New York: American Book, 1935.

Chall, J. S., & Mirsky, A. F. (Eds.). *Education and the Brain.* Chicago: University of Chicago Press, 1978.

Charters, W. W. *Curriculum Construction.* New York: Macmillan, 1923.

Coleman, J. S. *Equality of Educational Opportunity.* Washington, D.C.: U.S. Government Printing Office, 1966. (ERIC Document Reproduction Service No. ED 012 275)

Corey, S. M. *Action Research to Improve School Practices.* New York: Teachers College Press, 1953.

Counts, G. S. *Dare the School Build a New Social Order?* New York: John Day, 1932.

Cremin, L. *Public Education.* New York: Basic Books, 1976.

Cronbach, L. J. Course improvement through evaluation. *Teachers College Record,* 1963, *64*(8), 672–683.

Cronbach, L. J.; Ambron, S. R.; Dornbusch, S. M.; Hess, R. D.; Hornik, R. C.; Phillips, D. C.; Walker, D. F.; & Weiner, S. S. *Toward Reform of Program Evaluation.* San Francisco: Jossey-Bass, 1980.

Dahllof, U. S. *Ability Grouping, Content Validity, and Curriculum Process Analysis.* New York: Teachers College Press, 1971.

Dewey, J. *The Child and the Curriculum.* Chicago: University of Chicago Press, 1902.

Dewey, J. *Democracy and Education.* New York: Macmillan, 1916.

Dewey, J. *The Sources of a Science of Education.* New York: Liveright, 1929.

Dewey, J. *Experience and Education.* New York: Macmillan, 1938.

Dunkin, M. J., & Biddle, B. J. *The Study of Teaching.* New York: Holt, Rinehart & Winston, 1974.

Educational Products Information Exhange Institute. *Selecting Instructional Materials* (Part 1, Module 3). Stony Brook, N.Y.: EPIE, 1979.

Eisner, E. W. *The Educational Imagination.* New York: Macmillan, 1979.

Eisner, E. W., & Vallance, E. (Eds.). *Conflicting Conceptions of Curriculum.* Berkeley, Calif.: McCutchan, 1974.

Fitz-Gibbon, C. T., & Morris, L. L. *Program Evaluation Kit* (8 vols.). Beverly Hills, Calif.: Sage, 1978.

Fraser, B. J. *Learning Environment in Curriculum Evaluation: A Review.* London: Pergamon, 1980.

Fraser, B. J., & Godfrey, J. *Evaluation of Multi-arts Project in New South Wales.* Canberra, N.S.W.: Curriculum Development Center, 1980.

Fraser, B. J., & Smith, D. L. *Evaluation of Development Dissemination Activities of High School Education Law Project.* Canberra, N.S.W.: Curriculum Development Center, 1980.

Gage, N. L. *The Scientific Basis of the Art of Teaching.* New York: Teachers College Press, 1978.

Gagné, R. M. *The Conditions of Learning.* New York: Holt, Rinehart & Winston, 1967.

Giroux, H. A. Beyond correspondence theory: Notes on the dynamics of educational reproduction and transformation. *Curriculum Inquiry,* 1980, *10*(3), 225–247.

Goodlad, J. I.; Klein, M. F.; & Associates. *Behind the Classroom Door.* Worthington, Ohio: Charles A. Jones, 1970.

Greene, M. *Landscapes of Learning.* New York: Teachers College Press, 1978.

Grumet, M. R. Autobiography and reconceptualization. *Journal of Curriculum Theorizing,* 1980, *2*(2), 155–158.

Gwynn, J. M. *Curriculum Principles and Social Trends.* New York: Macmillan, 1943.

Hamilton, D.; McDonald, B.; King, C.; Jenkins, D.; & Parlett, M. (Eds.). *Beyond the Numbers Game: A Reader in Educational Evaluation.* Berkeley, Calif.: McCutchan, 1977.

Harnischfeger, A., & Wiley, D. E. Teaching-learning processes in the elementary school: A synoptic view. *Curriculum Inquiry,* 1976, *6*(1), 5–43.

Herrick, V. E., & Tyler, R. W. (Eds.). *Toward Improved Curriculum Theory.* Chicago: University of Chicago Press, 1950.

Hirst, P. H. *Knowledge and the Curriculum.* London: Routledge & Kegan Paul, 1975.

House, E. R. Assumptions underlying evaluation models. *Educational Researcher,* 1978, *7*(3), 4–12.

Huebner, D. *The Thingness of Educative Content.* Paper presented at the Conference on the Reconceptualization of Curriculum Theory, Xavier University, Cincinnati, 1970.

International Association for the Evaluation of Educational Achievement. *International Studies in Evaluation* (6 vols.). New York: Wiley, 1973.

Jackson, P. W. *Life in Classrooms.* New York: Holt, Rinehart & Winston, 1968.

Jenkins, D.; Pring, R.; & Harris, A. *Curriculum Philosophy and Design.* Bletchley, England: Open University Press, 1972.

Johnson, M. *Intentionality in Education.* Albany, N.Y.: Center for Curriculum Research and Services, 1977.

Joyce, B., & Weil, M. *Models of Teaching.* Englewood Cliffs, N.J.: Prentice-Hall, 1980.

King, A. R., & Brownell, J. A. *The Curriculum and the Disciplines of Knowledge.* Huntington, N.Y.: Kreiger, 1976.

Kirst, M. W., & Walker, D. F. An analysis of curriculum policy making. *Review of Educational Research,* 1971, *41*(5), 479–509.

Kliebard, H. M. Exemplars of curriculum theory. In C. S. Lavatelli, W. J. Moore, & T. Kaltsounis, *Elementary School Curriculum.* New York: Holt, Rinehart & Winston, 1972, pp. 84–101.

Kliebard, H. M. Bureaucracy and curriculum theory. In A. Bellack & H. M. Kliebard (Eds.), *Curriculum and Evaluation.* Berkeley, Calif.: McCutchan, 1977, pp. 608–625.

Kohlberg, L., & Mayer, R. Development as the aim of education. *Harvard Educational Review,* 1972, *42*(4), 449–496.

Krathwohl, D. R.; Bloom, B. S.; & Masia, B. B. *Affective Domain.* Handbook 2 of *Taxonomy of Educational Objectives.* New York: McKay, 1964.

Levit, M. (Ed.). *Curriculum: Readings in the Philosophy of Education.* Urbana: University of Illinois Press, 1971.

Lewy, A. (Ed.). *Handbook of Curriculum Evaluation.* Paris: UNESCO, 1977.

Lounsbury, J. H., & Vars, G. F. *A Curriculum for the Middle School Years.* New York: Harper & Row, 1978.

Lundgren, U. P. *Frame Factors and the Teaching Process.* Stockholm: Almqvist & Wiksell, 1972.

Macdonald, J. B. Value bases and issues for curriculum. In A. Molnar & J. A. Zahorik (Eds.), *Curriculum Theory.* Washington,

D.C.: Association for Supervision and Curriculum Development, 1977, pp. 10–21.

Mann, J. S. Curriculum criticism. *Curriculum Theory Network,* Winter 1968–1969, *2,* 2–14.

Marks, W. L., & Nystrand, R. O. (Eds.). *Strategies for Educational Change.* New York: Macmillan, 1981.

Martin, J. H. Reconsidering the goals of high school education. *Educational Leadership,* January 1980, *37,* 278–282.

Martin, J. R. (Ed.). *Readings in the Philosophy of Education: A Study of the Curriculum.* Boston: Allyn & Bacon, 1970.

Martin, J. R. Needed: A paradigm for liberal education. In J. F. Soltis (Ed.), *Philosophy and Education.* Chicago: University of Chicago Press, 1981.

McCutcheon, G. Educational criticism: Methods and application. *Journal of Curriculum Theorizing,* 1979, *1*(2), 5–25.

McCutcheon, G. *Educational Criticism: Reflections and Reconsiderations.* Paper presented at the *Journal of Curriculum Theorizing* Conference, Airlie, Va., October 1980.

Morris, B. *Objectives and Perspectives in Education.* London: Routledge & Kegan Paul, 1972.

National Society for the Study of Education. *The Foundation of Curriculum-making.* Bloomington, Ill.: Public School Publishing Company, 1927.

Overly, N. V. (Ed.). *The Unstudied Curriculum: Its Impact on Children.* Washington, D.C.: Association for Supervision and Curriculum Development, 1970. (ERIC Document Reproduction Service No. ED 043 577)

Pagano, J., & Dolan, L. Foundations for a unified approach to evaluation research. *Curriculum Inquiry,* 1980, *10*(4), 367–381.

Parker, J. C., & Rubin, L. J. *Process as Content.* Chicago: Rand McNally, 1966.

Phillips, D. C. What do the researcher and the practitioner have to offer each other? *Educational Researcher,* 1980, *9*(11), 17–20, 24.

Pinar, W. F. (Ed.). *Curriculum Theorizing: The Reconceptualists.* Berkeley, Calif.: McCutchan, 1975.

Pinar, W. F. Life history and educational experience. *Journal of Curriculum Theorizing,* 1980, *2*(2), 159–212.

Pinar, W. F., & Grumet, M. *Toward a Poor Curriculum.* Dubuque, Iowa: Kendall/Hunt, 1976.

Posner, G. J. Tools for curriculum research and development: Potential contributions from cognitive sciences. *Curriculum Inquiry,* 1978, *8*(4), 311–340.

Posner, G. J. *New Developments in Curricular Research: It's the Thought That Counts.* Paper presented to the Northeastern Educational Research Association, Ellensville, N.Y., October 1980.

Posner, G. J., & Strike, K. A. A categorization scheme for principles of sequencing content. *Review of Educational Research,* 1976, *46*(4), 665–690.

Pressman, J. L., & Wildavsky, A. *Implementation.* Berkeley: University of California Press, 1979.

Reid, W. A. *Thinking about the Curriculum: The Nature and Treatment of Curriculum Problems.* London: Routledge & Kegan Paul, 1978.

Reid, W. A., & Walker, D. F. (Eds.). *Case Studies in Curriculum Change.* London: Routledge & Kegan Paul, 1975.

Reynolds, J., & Skilbeck, M. *Culture and the Classroom.* London: Open Books, 1976.

Sarason, S. B. *The Culture of the School and the Problem of Change.* Boston: Allyn & Bacon, 1971.

Saylor, J. G., & Alexander, W. *Planning Curriculum for Schools.* New York: Holt, Rinehart & Winston, 1974.

Schaffarzick, J., & Sykes, G. (Eds.). *Value Conflicts and Curriculum Issues.* Berkeley, Calif.: McCutchan, 1979.

Schiro, M. *Curriculum for Better Schools: The Great Ideological Debate.* Englewood Cliffs, N.J.: Educational Technology Publications, 1978.

Schubert, W. H. *Curriculum Books: The First Eighty Years.* Lanham, Md.: University Press of America, 1980. (a)

Schubert, W. H. Recalibrating educational research: Toward a focus on practice. *Educational Researcher,* 1980, *9*(1), 17–24, 31. (b)

Schubert, W. H. Knowledge about out-of-school curricula. *Educational Forum,* 1981, *45*(2), 155–198.

Schubert, W. H., & Posner, G. J. Origins of the curriculum field based on a study of mentor-student relationships. *Journal of Curriculum Theorizing,* 1980, *2*(2), 37–67.

Schubert, W. H., & Schubert, A. L. Toward curricula that are of, by, and for students. *Journal of Curriculum Theorizing,* 1981, *3*(1), in press.

Schwab, J. J. *The Practical: A Language for Curriculum.* Washington, D.C.: National Education Association, 1970. (ERIC Document Reproduction Service No. ED 038 332)

Schwab, J. J. The practical: Arts of eclectic. *School Review,* August 1971, *79,* 493–542.

Schwab, J. J. The practical 3: Translation into curriculum. *School Review,* August 1973, *81,* 501–522.

Scriven, M. The methodology of evaluation. In R. W. Tyler, R. M. Gagné, & M. Scriven, *Perspectives of Curriculum Evaluation.* Chicago: Rand McNally, 1967, 39/83.

Scriven, M. Pros and cons about goal-free evaluation. *Evaluation Comment,* 1972, *3*(4), 1–4.

Scriven, M. Self-referent research. *Educational Researcher,* 1980, *9*(6), 11–18, 30.

Shulman, L.; Phillips, D. C.; Thorensen, C. E.; & Walker, D. F. *The True Experiment.* Symposium presented at the annual meeting of the American Educational Research Association, Boston, April 1980.

Smith, B. O.; Stanley, W. O.; & Shores, J. H. *Fundamentals of Curriculum Development.* New York: Harcourt, Brace & World, 1957.

Snyder, G. R. *The Hidden Curriculum.* New York: Knopf, 1970.

Stake, R. E. The countenance of educational evaluation. *Teachers College Record,* 1967, *68*(7), 523–540.

Stake, R. E. (Ed.). *Evaluating the Arts in Education.* Columbus, Ohio: Merrill, 1975.

Stenhouse, L. Curriculum research and the art of teacher. *Curriculum,* 1980, *1*(1), 40–44.

Stufflebeam, D. L. Evaluation as enlightenment for decision making. In W. H. Beatty (Ed.), *Improving Educational Assessment.* Washington, D.C.: Association for Supervision and Curriculum Development, 1969, pp. 41–73.

Stufflebeam, D. L., & Webster, W. J. An analysis of alternative approaches to evaluation. *Educational Evaluation and Policy Analysis,* 1980, *2*(3), 5–20.

Taba, H. *Curriculum Development: Theory and Practice.* New York: Harcourt, Brace & World, 1962.

Tanner, D., & Tanner, L. N. *Curriculum Development: Theory into Practice.* New York: Macmillan, 1980.

Travers, R. W. M. Taxonomies of educational objectives and theories of classification. *Educational Evaluation and Policy Analysis,* 1980, *2*(2), 5–23.

Travers, R. W. M. (Ed.). *Second Handbook of Research on Teaching.* Chicago: Rand McNally, 1973.

Tyler, R. W. *Basic Principles of Curriculum and Instruction.* Chicago: University of Chicago Press, 1949.

Tyler, R. W. Desirable content for a curriculum syllabus today. In A. Molnar & J. A. Zahorik (Eds.), *Curriculum Theory*. Washington, D.C.: Association for Supervision and Curriculum Development, 1977.

Vallance, E. *Promising Directions in Curriculum Knowledge: Focus on Students*. Symposium presentation at the annual meeting of the American Educational Research Association, Los Angeles, April 1981.

Van Geel, T. *Authority to Control the School Program*. Lexington, Mass.: Lexington Books, 1976.

van Manen, M. The Utrecht school: A phenomenological experiment in educational theorizing. *Interchange*, 1979, *10*(1), 48–66.

van Manen, M. *Pedagogical Theorizing*. Paper presented at the annual meeting of the American Educational Research Association, Boston, April 1980.

Walberg, H. J., & Moos, R. H. Assessing educational environments. *New Directions for Testing and Measurement*, 1980, *7*, 63–76.

Walker, D. F. A naturalistic model for curriculum development. *School Review*, 1971, *80*(1), 51–69.

Walker, D. F. A barnstorming tour of writing on curriculum. In A. W. Foshay (Ed.), *Considered Action for Curriculum Improvement*. Washington, D.C.: Association for Supervision and Curriculum Development, 1980, pp. 71–81. (ERIC Document Reproduction Service No. ED 186 428)

Walker, D. F., & Schaffarzick, J. Comparing curriculum. *Review of Educational Research*, 1974, *44*(1), 83–111.

Westbury, I., & Wilkof, N. J. (Eds.). *Science, Curriculum, and Liberal Education: Selected Essays, Joseph J. Schwab*. Chicago: University of Chicago Press, 1978.

Wildavsky, A. *Speaking Truth to Power*. Boston: Little, Brown, 1979.

Willis, G. *Qualitative Evaluation: Concepts and Cases in Curriculum Criticism*. Berkeley, Calif.: McCutchan, 1978.

Willis, G. *A Reconceptualist Perspective on Curriculum Evaluation*. Paper presented at the *Journal of Curriculum Theorizing* Conference, Airlie, Va., October 1979.

Young, M. F. D. (Ed.). *Knowledge and Control*. New York: Macmillan, 1971.

Zais, R. S. *Curriculum: Principles and Foundations*. New York: Crowell, 1976.

D

DAY CARE

See Early Childhood Development; Early Childhood Education.

DEAF EDUCATION

See Hearing Impairment.

DEINSTITUTIONALIZATION OF THE HANDICAPPED

Few public policies in our society have so radically transformed services for handicapped people as that of deinstitutionalization. For the most part, this policy has led to new patterns of residential living and community participation for dependent populations. The people most affected by this policy are those who are generally regarded as mentally disabled, including individuals characterized as mentally retarded and mentally ill. Less dramatic changes are apparent in services for other groups—for example, children and youth with serious visual and auditory handicaps—as a consequence of the deliberate policy of deinstitutionalization. The term "dependent populations" is used to refer to handicapped individuals whose "motor, self-help, cognitive, or personal-social skills . . . deviate significantly from the skill levels of their same age, cultural, or ethnic group peers" (Prehm & McDonald, 1979, p. 502), and who therefore require help from society for their development and adjustment.

Various definitions have been advanced for the policy of "deinstitutionalization." Bradley (1978) simply defined it as the process of removing people from institutions and placing them in less restrictive residential settings. A somewhat more complex view was presented in a policy paper by the National Association of Superintendents of Public Residential Facilities for the Mentally Retarded (1974). It described deinstitutionalization as comprising three related processes: (1) preventing admission to (generally large) public residential facilities by developing alternative community methods of care and training; (2) returning to the community all residents of public facilities after preparing them in programs of rehabilitation and training to function in appropriate community settings; and (3) establishing and maintaining responsive residential environments that protect human and civil rights.

In another definition, "deinstitutionalization" was held to be (1) a process, (2) a philosophy, and (3) a fact (Bachrach, 1981). This formulation provides a convenient framework for the examination of deinstitutionalization. Further, this article examines the impact on handicapped people of the public policy of deinstitutionalization, particularly population changes in residential-care settings and schools, and the underlying legal determinations of deinstitutionalization. Both are considered in the context of the sweeping social changes that characterized the past twenty years and expanded the economic, political, and social opportunities for less advantaged citizens in general.

Philosophical Premises. In examining the nature and structure of educational and social services for dependent populations, the role of ideology (Wolfensberger, 1972) is often overlooked. Typically, services for handicapped people are discussed in terms of the number of people who must be served and the funds that are available for their support. Nevertheless, attitudes toward and beliefs about the nature of handicapping conditions have greatly influenced the public policies and private actions that affect and control decisions on the scope, characteristics, and quality of services that are provided (Bruininks, Warfield, & Stealey, in press; Heal, 1980).

The process of deinstitutionalization is based, ideally, on three philosophical concepts: (1) normalization, (2) least restrictive environment, and (3) the developmental model of programming. As defined by Nirje (1976), "normalization" means making available to handicapped people the patterns, conditions, and opportunities that characterize the everyday life of people in the mainstream of society. This definition has been elaborated by Wolfensberger (1980); in his view, society must use culturally normative means both to provide handicapped people with life conditions that are at least as good as those of average citizens, and to establish, enable, and support behaviors, appearances, experiences, and interpretations that facilitate normal patterns of living.

Related to normalization is the idea that, of all the possible services for any given individual, the one selected should be the "least restrictive alternative." The importance of the least restrictive doctrine in educational and human services is evident in the language of several recently passed federal laws such as Public Law 94-142—the Education for All Handicapped Children Act of 1975—Section 504 of the Rehabilitation Act of 1973, and the Developmentally Disabled Assistance and Bill of Rights Act.

Our third philosophical concept, the "developmental model of programming," assumes that all handicapped people, regardless of their degree of impairment, have the potential for growth, learning, and development (Roos, 1970). Further, developmental programming assumes that people change during their lifetimes; that individual development generally progresses in a sequential, orderly, and predictable manner; and that development can be modified by education and training.

The policy of deinstitutionalization in our society is based substantially upon these three premises. However, despite their widespread acceptance in law, regulation, and practice, a gap between theory and practice still exists in many residential and service programs for handicapped citizens (Flynn & Nitsch, 1980).

Factual Aspects. In the United States, the effects of deinstitutionalization as a public policy, mostly in mental health services and in services for retarded people, are reflected in the various statistics on residential services. For example, the size of institutionalized populations peaked near the end of the 1960s and since then has dropped by roughly one-third. Prior to World War II, public residential facilities represented the major source of formal programming for retarded people. During the postwar period, the number of retarded children in public school programs exceeded that of retarded children in public residential facilities. Yet even with this growth of public school services, the populations in public insititutions for the retarded and in mental hospitals increased steadily until about 1967 (Lakin, 1979). From that peak year until the present, a reduction of mo·e than 30 percent has occurred in the populations of public institutions for the mentally retarded (Lakin, 1979; Scheerenberger, 1978). The populations of state and county mental hospitals changed even more dramatically; approximately 67 per-

cent fewer people were still held in the hospitals at the end of the 1970s (Bassuk & Gerson, 1978). The reduced size of institutionalized populations resulted largely from an increase in the rate of releases; the death rate and the admission rate were relatively stable (Butterfield, 1976; Scheerenberger, 1978). Currently, nearly 90 percent of the people residing in institutions are severely and profoundly retarded and display a large number of other physical, sensory, and emotional disabilities (Hill & Bruininks, 1981). Nevertheless, public education programs must be provided for those of school age under the provisions of Public Law 94-142 and related legislation.

Most of the people who have been released from public institutions for the mentally retarded are mildly or moderately retarded. The majority have returned to their parents and close relatives, and the remainder have been placed in various alternative living arrangements. Increasingly, people who are released from public institutions are placed in smaller communal settings (Best-Sigford et al., 1981). Best-Sigford et al. (1981) also found that almost 32 percent were 21 years of age or younger.

Deinstitutionalization is also reflected in the rapid growth of small, private, community residential facilities. Information on community residential facilities and their residents throughout the United States was summarized by Bruininks, Hauber, and Kudla (1979). They surveyed 11,351 facilities, of which 5,038 met the definition established for a community residential facility. About 88 percent of the latter kind of facility supplied the requested information. The investigators found that more than one-half (2,410) had opened in the three years prior to the survey, and 88 percent served fewer than twenty residents per facility. (However, it should be noted that at the time of the survey, about 50 percent of the mentally retarded population lived in community facilities that served more than thirty residents.)

Although smaller community facilities served fewer people than institutions, it is important to note that they served at least 62,397 people in June 1977. Nearly 40 percent of these residents were under 21 years of age, and almost two-thirds were moderately or severely retarded. The previous placement of residents of community facilities is particularly noteworthy in the examination of the factual aspects of deinstitutionalization. Not surprisingly, the largest single category of previous placements was placement in public institutions, although many residents had been living with their natural families. Earlier studies by O'Connor (1976) and Baker, Seltzer, and Seltzer (1974) also reported this strong trend toward the development of smaller community living residences for retarded people.

It is assumed that when various community services are increased, more severely handicapped children and youth either will enter community residences or will stay at home rather than be placed in institutions. In addition to the estimated 3,700 school-age individuals entering community facilities from institutions each year, an estimated 2,900 school-age retarded people return to their natural families. Furthermore, among the specifically licensed foster homes for retarded people, 30 percent house school-age individuals. Clearly, the impact of deinstitutionalization on education is greater than would be expected simply by examining the release rates of institutions (Bruininks, Hauber, & Kudla, 1979; (Bruininks, Hill, & Thorsheim, 1980).

The dramatic changes in the philosophy and direction of residential services for retarded people are made explicit by the data reported in this article. Deinstitutionalization as a policy, however, has affected all kinds of handicapped children and youth. For example, the populations of state schools for children and youth with vision and hearing handicaps also have declined in recent years, and equally startling changes have occurred in services for children with behavior problems.

Statistical indicators of deinstitutionalization for other categories of handicapped people (the blind, the deaf, those with behavior problems) are not readily available and are probably somewhat misleading. Historically, institutions for retarded people provided long-term care, whereas residential schools for visually handicapped and hearing-impaired people served primarily educational purposes rather than providing long-term care (Bischoff, 1978). Notwithstanding this important distinction, enrollments in residential schools for children and youth with sensory handicaps have also declined.

Schildroth (1980) confirmed this downward trend with results from a national study of sixty-two public residential schools for hearing-impaired students. Between 1970 and 1978, the population in these schools declined 9.8 percent, wheras the school-age population declined 8.0 percent. The investigator found proportionately greater decline among the residential schools located in northeastern and north central states, but some population increase in southern states. There was a proportionately greater increase nationally in minority students and in the admission of students with additional handicaps to these residential schools. These findings were largely corroborated by Salem and Herward (1978), surveying residential school directors to assess the impact of Public Law 94-142 on residential schools for the deaf.

During the 1970s, enrollment changes in residential schools serving visually handicapped students were less clear, owing to the lack of representative survey information. The available statistics, however, show a 37 percent increase in day-school enrollments in local schools and a drop of 11 percent in residential-school enrollments for the period from 1972 to 1976 (Willis, 1979).

The facts show that the populations of state residential facilities for retarded people and state schools for visually handicapped and hearing-impaired students declined at significantly greater rates than the general school enrollment during the 1970s. Concurrent with these declines were the significant increases in the number of handicapped children and youth attending local schools and in the number of handicapped people of all ages living in generally less restrictive living arrangements.

Legal Foundations. Although much of the substantial change that has occurred in institutionalization is ideologically based, the chief catalysts of these changes were the enactment of landmark legislation affecting handicapped people and the intervention of federal courts in local practices and conditions.

The passage or amendment of three statutes during the 1970s strongly supported the right to treatment and education, the policy of equal opportunity through architectural accessibility, employment, income support, transportation, and housing, and the right to treatment in the least restrictive setting. Public Law 94-142 (the Education for All Handicapped Children Act of 1975) affirmed the right of handicapped children and youth to a free and appropriate education in the least restrictive setting. Earlier, Section 504 of the Rehabilitation Act, passed in 1973, was written in language similar to that of the Civil Rights Act; it prohibits discrimination against otherwise qualified handicapped individuals in employment, education, and accessibility to community environments and services. The third important law affecting handicapped people is the Developmentally Disabled Assistance and Bill of Rights Act of 1975. This act strongly asserts the right of handicapped people to treatment in the least restrictive setting and strongly supports the national policy of deinstitutionalization. These laws have had a substantial impact on the development and expansion of services for handicapped people.

Perhaps even greater changes have occurred in treatment practices from the 1960s onward as a consequence of actions by several federal courts. Mickenberg (1980) insightfully summarized the trends in litigation, observing that residents of state hospitals and training schools have a constitutional right not only to treatment but to treatment in the least restrictive alternative; this has forced states to spend substantial sums to upgrade public institutions and to develop community alternatives. Right to treatment litigation during the past twenty years was influenced strongly by decision of Judge Bazelon of the United States Court of Appeals for the District of Columbia Circuit. He ruled that the only permissible reason for civil commitment is treatment, that the length of hospitalization must be reasonably related to the need for treatment, and that treatment must be provided in the least restrictive setting (Mickenberg, 1980). These principles formed the legal basis for a large number of important cases affecting retarded residents of public institutions.

An equally significant case in this line of cases is *Haldeman* v. *Pennhurst State School and Hospital* in Pennsylvania. The federal district court, under Judge Broderick, ordered a number of actions: discontinuance of admissions, appointment by the court of a master to formulate a plan for community-living alternatives and related services, and provision by the state of suitable community-living alternatives for current residents and possible future candidates for admission to Pennhurst. Requirements of the Development Disabilities Act provided much of the basis for these orders. The Commonwealth of Pennsylvania and other parties appealed the decision, first in the Appeals Court and later in the Supreme Court. The Supreme Court, when it reviewed the decision, adopted a more conservative posture than Judge Broderick toward the Developmental Disabilities Act, ruling that the act is voluntary and that Congress did not intend to mandate a particular level of institutionalization or community-based services. The case involving the individual claims of the plaintiffs was remanded to the lower court for consideration or reconsideration.

It is perhaps too early to conclude that this particular decision limits the principles of right to treatment in the least restrictive alternative when individuals are deinstitutionalized. It is quite likely that the courts will not impose a particular service strategy on the states; rather, further judicial review may be needed to clarify the practices affecting particular individuals in specific settings (Mickenberg, 1980). The effect of the decisions of the 1970s, notwithstanding the imposition of limits on particular service models by courts, has been to focus on the unacceptable practices that restrict the development of handicapped people and on the precept that active treatment in the least restrictive environment is the expected standard for residential, educational, and other social service programs (Willer, Scheerenberger, & Intagliata, 1980).

Community Services. There is little doubt that the policies of deinstitutionalization and "mainstreaming" (assimilation with the nonhandicapped) have increased the number of agencies and individuals responsible for providing handicapped individuals with educational and other opportunities. A persistent and vexing problem is coordinating needed community services with residential programs. Freeman (1978), in order to delineate the problem of coordinating the services of schools and agencies, gave the results of a pilot program to assess the value of foster family care as an alternative approach to serving people in public institutions. The children who were moved from institutions into foster care settings registered gains in intelligence-test scores and improvements in emotional behavior. Particular mention was made by Freeman of the difficulties encountered by his agency in working with the public schools.

Providing services and living opportunities consistent with the philosophical premises of deinstitutionalization is a complex undertaking. It demands the coordination of networks made up of many agencies and individuals if it is to succeed as a matter of fact and policy (Bruininks et al., 1980; Sarason, 1971).

Public Education. To meet the needs of millions of handicapped children who were not receiving appropriate educational services, the Ninety-fourth Congress enacted Public Law 94-142. Details of the law and the history and problems of its implementation are discussed insightfully in a number of publications (e.g., Abeson & Zettel, 1977; Ballard & Zettel, 1978; Meyen, 1978). The provisions of Public Law 94-142 are far-reaching, particularly for children and youth who have experienced deinstitutionalization. Chief among the many requirements of the law is that handicapped children receive a free and appropriate education that affords, as much as possible, experiences with nonhandicapped students in the least restrictive setting. This process is often characterized as "mainstreaming." Both the policy of mainstreaming in education and that of deinstitutionalization share a philosophical and legal orientation toward providing handicapped people with opportunities for maximum development, social integration, and participation in the normal aspects of society. Fulfilling this commitment requires accurate information on the learning and adjustment needs of handicapped children and youth, careful planning, and the provision of many specialized services.

Common requirements derived from the policy of deinstitutionalization and the implementation of Public Law 94-142 present four important challenges to educational personnel. The first challenge is derived from the obligation of schools to identify and meet the educational needs of unserved and underserved handicapped children. Schools must collaborate with other service delivery systems, given that such children are often in residential programs that typically fall under the aegis of welfare and social service agencies. Unfortunately, poor coordination among agencies with common interests and compatible responsibilities seems to be endemic in the fields of human services and education (Bachrach, 1978; Bradley, 1978; Bruininks, Hauber, & Kudla, 1979; Gettings, 1977; Government Accounting Office, 1977).

A second and related challenge is to alter the attitudes of educational personnel toward the purpose of schooling and the involvement of appropriate individuals, such as parents and parent surrogates, in planning and monitoring educational experiences for handicapped students.

The third challenge to educators stems from deinstitutionalization. It is to provide comprehensive and effective service programs for the new school population. The philosophical foundation of deinstitutionalization is the commitment to provide, in a community setting, life experiences that are as close as possible to normal patterns of living. This commitment implies that handicapped people will have opportunities to learn and develop personal, social, vocational, and community-living skills to the maximum of their capabilities. Considering that many people in institutional settings have lived significant portions of their lives in rather isolated surroundings and that many are severely and multiply handicapped (Hill & Bruininks, 1981), the task of providing an appropriate range of services assumes challenging dimensions.

The fourth challenge is to develop interventions that will enhance the learning and adjustment of handicapped people and their social integration in schools and other settings. This aspect is perhaps the most important in serving handicapped people who are affected by the policy of deinstitutionalization.

Community Adjustment and Environmental Quality. With the placement of handicapped people in less restrictive settings, timely investigations have been conducted of postrelease individual adjustment, and the quality of community living environments. (For a synthesis and extensive discussion of research findings and issues related to the community adjustment of retarded people, see Bruininks et al., 1981; Carver & McCraig, 1974; Heal, Sigelman, & Switzky, 1978.) It appears that former residents of institutions who are living in community settings spend considerable time in passive in-house leisure activities, such as watching television (Birenbaum & Re, 1979; Hill & Bruininks, 1981), and are rather limited in active community integration. Several factors appear to be related to successful community adjustment and continued community placement, for example, lower degrees of maladaptive behavior (Hill & Bruininks, 1981; Schalock, Harper, & Genung, 1981; Sutter et al., 1980); ability factors, such as achievement, IQ, and community living skills (Hull & Thompson, 1980); family participation in the placement decision and service-planning process (Schalock, Harper, & Genung, 1981); and the quality of community support services (Heal, Sigelman, & Switzky, 1978).

Successful adjustment seems to be related to the quality of the person's living and community environment. Several studies have documented that placement in smaller community residences from larger institutions does not, *ipso facto*, ensure highly normalized living environments (Bjaanes & Butler, 1974; Bjaanes, Butler, & Kelly, 1981; Pratt, Luszcz, & Brown, 1980). The evidence, albeit limited, shows wide variations in the quality of community residential living environments. The limited evidence from a number of studies suggests, however, that smaller facilities possess higher normalization qualities and appear to produce positive increases in clients' adaptive behavior than large institutions (Balla, 1976; Eyman, Demaine, & Lei, 1979; Pratt, Luszcz, & Brown, 1980; Rotegaard, Bruininks, & Hill, 1981; Seltzer, 1981).

Ecological research on deinstitutionalization is a relatively promising and recent development. In a summary of such research and the relevant issues, Lakin, Bruininks, and Sigford (1981) argued for continued emphasis on studies of environmental qualities and their effects upon the development of handicapped people in various living environments.

Community Attitudes and Family Impact. There is little doubt that the effective assimilation of handicapped people into community settings depends in considerable measure upon community acceptance and family support. Among families whose children reside in state facilities for retarded people and are likely to be affected by the policy of deinstitutionalization, the general preference is for continued placement in state programs rather than

in smaller community residences (Brockmeier, 1974; Meyer, 1980). In one study, training sessions were held for parents; the investigator reported progress in the families' ability to develop management and training skills to cope with their children (Bates, 1977). The importance of including family members in the deinstitutionalization process is supported by the results of studies on community adjustment and on gaining essential community support (Bruininks et al., 1981).

A frequent impediment to deinstitutionalization is the concern of homeowners that local property values will fall if community residences are established in their neighborhoods. Apparently, this fear has little substance, although it has generated a large number of local-court zoning suits throughout the country. The Louisiana Center for Public Interest (1981) documented the results of three major studies that indicated there was no significant negative effect on property values or residential turnover rates following the location of a group home for retarded people in a neighborhood. Nonetheless, deinstitutionalization continues to be perceived by some people as a threat to local interests. It is an important problem in successfully assimilating handicapped people into schools, neighborhoods, and communities (Kastner & Reppucci, 1979).

The Future. The decade of the 1970s was a period of rapid change in living patterns and community assimilation for handicapped people. This trend, stemming from the policy of deinstitutionalization, affected primarily mentally disabled people, that is, mentally retarded and mentally ill citizens. Its effects on other groups of handicapped people seem to have been less dramatic but are still apparent, according to the various statistical indicators of the decline of public residential schools for visually handicapped and hearing-impaired children and youth.

The policy of deinstitutionalization is not without its critics or its implementation problems (Bischoff, 1978; Bradley, 1978; Bruininks, Hill, & Thorsheim, 1980; Throne, 1979). It has led to radical changes in the way we think about handicapped people as well as in practices; the changes in the latter are likely to continue and to evolve for many years while a balance among conflicting pressures is worked out. In surveys using the Delphi methodology, panels of experts who were asked to predict the future status of residential services for retarded citizens (Roos, 1978) and of state schools for students with sensory disabilities (Pace, 1977) consistently projected the continued existence of state-operated facilities for severely handicapped residents, a continued decline in populations, and increased application of the least-restrictive-environment principle as a basis for organizing educational, residential, and other human services. Ultimately, conflicting points of view regarding the merits of deinstitutionalization as public policy for handicapped citizens will be resolved on moral and ethical grounds. The policy and process of deinstitutionalization had a profound impact upon public education and society as a whole during the past two decades, and its influence is likely to be increasingly evident in the years ahead.

Robert H. Bruininks

See also Attitudes toward the Handicapped; Behavioral Treatment Methods; Equity Issues in Education; Handicapped Individuals; Rehabilitation Services; Special Education.

REFERENCES

Abeson, A., & Zettel, J. End of the quiet revolution: Education for All Handicapped Children Act of 1975. *Exceptional Children,* October 1977, pp. 115–128.

Bachrach, L. L. A conceptual approach to deinstitutionalization. *Hospital and Community Psychiatry,* 1978, *29,* 573–578.

Bachrach, L. L. A conceptual approach to deinstitutionalization of the mentally retarded: A perspective from the experience of the mentally ill. In R. Bruininks, C. Meyers, B. Sigford, & K. Lakin (Eds.), *Deinstitutionalization and Community Adjustment of Mentally Retarded People.* Washington, D.C.: American Association on Mental Deficiency, 1981.

Baker, B.; Seltzer, G.; & Seltzer, M. *As Close as Possible.* Cambridge, Mass.: Harvard University, Behavioral Education Project, 1974.

Balla, D. Relationship of institution size to quality of care: A review of the literature. *American Journal of Mental Deficiency,* 1976, *81,* 117–124.

Ballard, J., & Zettel, J. The managerial aspects of Public Law 94-142. *Exceptional Children,* March 1978, pp. 457–462.

Bassuk, E., & Gerson, S. Deinstitutionalization and mental health services. *Scientific American,* 1978, *238,* 246–253.

Bates, P. Community transition: A behavioral approach with the severely/profoundly retarded and their families. *American Association for the Education of the Severely-Profoundly Handicapped, Review,* 1977, *2*(4), 217–223.

Best-Sigford, B.; Bruininks, R.; Lakin, K.; Hill, B.; & Heal, L. *Resident Release Patterns in a National Sample of Public Residential Facilities.* Minneapolis: University of Minnesota, Department of Psychoeducational Studies, 1981.

Birenbaum, A., & Re, M. Resettling mentally retarded adults in the community: Almost four years later. *American Journal of Mental Deficiency,* 1979, 323–329.

Bischoff, R. Least restrictive educational program: The residential school. *Education of the Visually Handicapped,* 1978, *9,* 106–108.

Bjaanes, A., & Butler, E. Environmental variation in community care facilities for mentally retarded persons. *American Journal of Mental Deficiency,* 1974, *78,* 429–439.

Bjaanes, A.; Butler, E.; & Kelly, B. Placement type and client functional level as factors in provision of services aimed at increasing adjustment. In R. Bruininks, C. Meyers, B. Sigford, & K. Lakin (Eds.), *Deinstitutionalization and Community Adjustment of Mentally Retarded People.* Washington, D.C.: American Association on Mental Deficiency, 1981.

Bradley, V. *Deinstitutionalization of Developmentally Disabled Persons.* Baltimore: University Park Press, 1978.

Brockmeier, W. Attitudes and opinions of relatives of institutionalized mentally retarded individuals toward institutional and non-institutional care and training (Doctoral dissertation, University of Nebraska, 1974). *Dissertation Abstracts International,* 1974, *35,* 5163A.

Bruininks, R.; Hauber, F.; & Kudla, M. *National Survey of Community Residential Facilities: A Profile of Facilities and Residents in 1977.* Minneapolis: University of Minnesota, Department of Psychoeducational Studies, 1979.

Bruininks, R.; Hill, B.; & Thorsheim, M. *A Profile of Specially Licensed Foster Homes for Mentally Retarded People in 1977.* Minneapolis: University of Minnesota, Department of Psychoeducational Studies, 1980.

Bruininks, R.; Meyers, C.; Sigford, B.; & Lakin, K. (Eds.). *Deinstitutionalization and Community Adjustment of Mentally Retarded People.* Washington, D.C.: American Association on Mental Deficiency, 1981.

Bruininks, R.; Thurlow, M.; Thurman, S.; & Fiorelli, J. Deinstitutionalization and community services. In J. Wortis (Ed.), *Mental Retardation and Developmental Disabilities* (Vol. 11). New York: Brunner/Mazel, 1980.

Bruininks, R.; Warfield, G.; & Stealey, D. The mentally retarded. In E. Meyen (Ed.), *Exceptional Children and Youth: An Introduction.* Denver: Love, forthcoming.

Butterfield, E. Some basic changes in residential facilities. In R. Kugel & A. Shearer (Eds.), *Changing Patterns in Residential Services for the Mentally Retarded.* Washington, D.C.: U.S. Government Printing Office, 1976. (ERIC Document Reproduction Service No. ED 148 061)

Carver, R., & McCraig, E. Placement of the retarded in the community: Prognosis and outcome. In N. R. Ellis (Ed.), *International Review of Research in Mental Retardation* (Vol. 7). New York: Academic Press, 1974.

Eyman, R.; Demaine, E.; & Lei, T. Relationship between community environments and resident changes in adaptive behavior: A path model. *American Journal of Mental Deficiency,* 1979, *83,* 330–338.

Flynn, R., & Nitsch, K. *Normalization, Social Integration, and Community Services.* Baltimore: University Park Press, 1980.

Freeman, H. Foster home care for mentally retarded children: Can it work? *Child Welfare,* 1978, *57*(2), 113–121.

Gettings, R. Hidden impediments to deinstitutionalization. *State Government,* 1977, *50,* 214–219.

Government Accounting Office. *Returning the Mentally Disabled to the Community: Government Needs to Do More.* Washington, D.C.: U.S. Government Printing Office, 1977.

Heal, L. Ideological responses of society to its handicapped. In A. Novak & L. Heal (Eds.), *Integration of Developmentally Disabled Individuals into the Community.* Baltimore: Paul H. Brookes, 1980.

Heal, L.; Sigelman, C.; & Switzky, H. Research on community residential alternatives for the mentally retarded. In N. Ellis (Ed.), *International Review of Research on Mental Retardation* (Vol. 9). New York: Academic Press, 1978.

Hill, B., & Bruininks, R. *Family, Leisure, and Social Activities of Mentally Retarded People in Residential Facilities.* Minneapolis: University of Minnesota, Department of Psychoeducational Studies, 1981.

Hull, J., & Thompson, J. Predicting adaptive functioning of mentally retarded persons in community settings. *American Journal of Mental Deficiency,* 1980, *85,* 253–261

Kastner, L., & Reppucci, N. Assessing community attitudes toward mentally retarded persons. *American Journal of Mental Deficiency,* 1979, *84*(2), 137–144.

Lakin, K. *Demographic Studies of Residential Facilities for the Mentally Retarded: An Historical Review of Methodologies and Findings.* Minneapolis: University of Minnesota, Department of Psychoeducational Studies, 1979.

Lakin, K.; Bruininks, R.; & Sigford, B. Deinstitutionalization and community adjustment: A summary of research and issues. In R. Bruininks, C. Meyers, B. Sigford, & K. Lakin (Eds.), *Deinstitutionalization and Community Adjustment of Mentally Retarded People*. Washington, D.C.: American Association on Mental Deficiency, 1981.

Louisiana Center for Public Interest. Impact of group homes on property values and the surrounding neighborhoods. *LINKS (Living in New Kinds of Situations)*, 1981, *11*(2), 1–2.

Meyen, E. *Exceptional Children and Youth; An Introduction*. Denver: Love, 1978.

Meyer, R. Attitudes of parents of institutionalized mentally retarded individuals toward deinstitutionalization. *American Journal of Mental Deficiency*, 1980, *85*, 184–187.

Mickenberg, N. A decade of deinstitutionalization: Emerging legal theories and strategies. *Amicus*, 1980, *5*, 54–63.

National Association of Superintendents of Public Residential Facilities for the Mentally Retarded. *Contemporary Issues in Residential Programming*. Washington, D.C.: President's Committee on Mental Retardation, 1974.

Nirje, B. The normalization principle and its human management implications. In R. Kugel & A. Shearer (Eds.), *Changing Patterns in Residential Services for the Mentally Retarded*. Washington, D.C.: President's Committee on Mental Retardation, 1976.

O'Connor, G. *Home Is a Good Place: A National Perspective of Community Residential Facilities for Developmentally Disabled Persons*. Washington, D.C.: American Association on Mental Deficiency, 1976.

Pace, H. Future functions of residential schools for the blind (Doctoral dissertation, University of Arizona, 1977). *Dissertation Abstracts International*, 1977, *38*, 1332–1333.

Pratt, M.; Luszcz, M.; & Brown, M. Measuring dimensions of the quality of care in small community residences. *American Journal of Mental Deficiency*, 1980, *85*, 188–194.

Prehm, H., & McDonald, J. The yet to be served: A perspective. *Exceptional Children*, 1979, *45*, 502–507.

Roos, P. Evolutionary changes of the residential facility. In A. Baumeister & E. Butterfield (Eds.), *Residential Facilities for the Mentally Retarded*. Hawthorne, N.Y.: Aldine, 1970.

Roos, S. The future of residential services for the mentally retarded in the United States: A Delphi study. *Mental Retardation*, October 1978, pp. 355–356.

Rotegaard, L.; Bruininks, R.; & Hill, B. *Environmental Characteristics of Residential Facilities for Mentally Retarded People*. Minneapolis: University of Minnesota, Department of Psychoeducational Studies, 1981.

Salem, J., & Herward, P. Survey to determine the impact of Public Law 94-142 on residential schools for the deaf. *American Annals of the Deaf*, 1978, *123*, 524–527.

Sarason, S. *The Culture of the Schools and the Problems of Change*. Boston: Allyn & Bacon, 1971.

Schalock, R.; Harper, R.; & Genung, T. Community integration of mentally retarded adults: Community placement and program success. *American Journal of Mental Deficiency*, 1981, *85*, 478–488.

Scheerenberger, R. *Public Residential Institutions for the Mentally Retarded, 1977*. Madison; Central Wisconsin Center for the Developmentally Disabled, 1978.

Schildroth, A. Public residential schools for deaf students in the United States, 1970–1978. *American Annals of the Deaf*, 1980, *125*, 80–91

Seltzer, M. Known effects of environmental characteristics on resident performance. *LINKS (Living in New Kinds of Situations)*, 1981, *11*(2), 10–11.

Pennhurst State School and Hospital et al. v. *Haldeman et al.* (April 20, 1981).

Sutter, P.; Mayeda, T.; Call, T.; Yanagi, G.; & Yee, S. Comparisons of successful and unsuccessful community-placed mentally retarded persons. *American Journal of Mental Deficiency*, 1980, *85*, 262–267.

Throne, J. Deinstitutionalization: Too wide a swath. *Mental Retardation*, 1979, *17*(4), 171–175.

Willer, B.; Scheerenberger, R.; & Intagliata, J. Deinstitutionalization and mentally retarded persons. In A. Novak & L. Heal (Eds.), *Integration of Developmentally Disabled Individuals into the Community*. Baltimore: Paul H. Brookes, 1980.

Willis, D. Relationships between visual acuity, reading mode, and school systems for blind students. *Exceptional Children*, 1979, *46*, 186–191.

Wolfensberger, W. *The Principal of Normalization in Human Services*. Toronto: National Institute on Mental Retardation, 1972.

Wolfensberger, W. The definition of normalization. In R. Flynn & K. Nitsch (Eds.), *Normalization, Social Integration, and Community Services*. Baltimore: University Park Press, 1980.

DENTAL PROFESSIONS EDUCATION

The Baltimore College of Dental Surgery was founded in 1840 as the world's first dental college. Prior to this time, dentistry was taught by master craftsmen as a mechanical trade. In a review of the evolution of the dental school curriculum, Vann (1978) noted that the institutionalization of dental education elevated the profession from the "era of apprenticeship" to a healing art. In 1863 Harvard became the first university to open a school of dentistry. However, the proliferation of proprietary schools during the last quarter of the nineteenth century and early twentieth century slowed the change to university-based training. Proprietary schools seemed to be motivated more by profit than by the purpose of preparing capable dental practitioners.

In a report issued to the Carnegie Foundation, Flexner (1910) advocated that courses in basic science be included in medical education. This report was critical of medical proprietary schools and led to their eventual demise. Following medicine's lead, an extensive study of dentistry led to the closing of the last dental proprietary schools and paved the way for the complete integration of predoctoral dental education into the university community (Gies, 1926). The Gies study demonstrated the need for improved quality of instruction in the technical and clinical areas of the dental curriculum. It also indicated the need to incorporate biomedical sciences with clinical dentistry. These studies provided the foundation for the traditional dental school curriculum.

The primary objective of the traditional predoctoral program in dentistry has been to prepare students for general practice. Most schools have accomplished this goal by means of a four-year curriculum culminating in the D.D.S. or D.M.D. degree. The first two years have been devoted to basic sciences and mechanical techniques. The last two years have focused on clinical practice and the application of basic sciences. Upon completion of the program, most graduates have entered general practice, enlisted in the military or public health service, or engaged in advanced dental education, including graduate programs and postgraduate or residency programs. Graduate programs have led to a master's or doctoral degree, usually in one of the biomedical sciences, public health, or education. Postgraduate and residency programs have led to a certificate in general dentistry or one of the clinical dental specialties.

Current Issues. Allen (1980) reviewed a number of factors that have influenced the dental curriculum during the decade of the 1970s. One such factor has been the continued development of dentistry as a university-based program, as required by the Commission on Accreditation. Dental faculty have become more scholarly by engaging in more research, professional endeavors, and community service within the university setting. There has been an increase in the number of career-minded educators and an increase in the proportion of full-time faculty to part-time faculty. However, faculty involved in clinical disciplines have had difficulty pursuing the research needed to attain promotions and tenure while also meeting the demands of clinical teaching. Another factor has been the increased number of behavioral scientists and educational psychologists on dental faculties. These educationists have promulgated an interest in workshops, in-service programs, and faculty development. They have also promoted a more systematic approach to the design and evaluation of educational programs. However, it has been reported that less than 15 percent of dental educators had an education degree, and greater than 80 percent had no formal training in education. (Boozer et al., 1977).

Other factors have influenced the development of the dental curriculum. The increasing prominence of dental specialties has inflated curriculum content beyond the basic requirements of training general dentists. The increase in size and number of specialty and general-practice residency programs have at times diverted faculty effort and facility resources away from the predoctoral curriculum. The Task Force on Advanced Dental Education noted that between 1972 and 1979 the number of positions in general-practice residency programs increased by 70 percent (American Association of Dental Schools, 1980). The task force also reported that the number of active specialists had increased approximately 500 percent from 1955 to 1979 as compared to a 46 percent increase for all active dentists. The knowledge explosion has saturated dental curricula in terms of the quantity of material presented. New Subjects including genetics, immunopathology, inhalation analgesics, special patient care, behavioral sciences, molecular biology, and hospital dentistry have added

breadth to the dental curriculum. Students have been increasing their input to the curriculum through membership on school committees, representation in the American Dental Association, and participation in the American Association of Dental Schools. Finally, state and national dental boards have influenced the curriculum as schools gear the subject matter to facilitate students passing these examinations.

Funding. Dental education has been financed through three general sources of funding: educational revenues, service revenues, and research revenues. Educational revenues have been derived from student tuition, private funds allocated for general use or special projects, and government funding. Service revenues have included monies derived from direct patient care, continuing education programs, and other professional services. Research revenues have primarily been allocated by private foundations or governmental agencies for support of specific research projects or training programs.

The influence of the federal government has been pronounced during the past decade. Since 1966, federal capitation grants to schools have been intended to improve the quality of instruction and to expand student enrollment. The funds have also aided faculty recruitment and retention by increasing salaries and have also supported curriculum innovation. The ultimate goal was to meet the perceived shortage in health manpower by increasing the number of primary health care professionals in medicine, dentistry, and osteopathy. The Comprehensive Health Manpower Training Act of 1971 provided substantial capitation payments to those dental schools that increased class size and total enrollment. Additional financial rewards were offered to schools willing to convert from a four-year to a three-year program. It was felt that this conversion would reduce the financial burden of students, result in more dentists graduating each year, and utilize educational institutions more efficiently. In 1974 the Council on Dental Education surveyed curricula in American schools of dentistry. The survey completed in 1976 and published in 1977, found that eleven of fifty-nine schools operated a three-year program (American Dental Association, 1977). Formicola (1978) noted that although fourteen schools converted to three-year programs in the early 1970s, nine of these institutions returned to a four-year curriculum. The reinstatement of the program occurred because the compressed nature of the three-year time frame limited student experience and created schedule inflexibility.

To maintain eligibility for these federal funds, many schools have increased their student body beyond the capacity of their facility and/or faculty, causing crowded conditions and compromised faculty-student ratios. The Health Professionals Educational Assistance Act of 1976 attempted to stimulate the practice of dentistry in underserved areas by providing an additional option through which dental schools could receive funding. Many schools utilized this option by providing students with six weeks or more of remote-site training in ambulatory care settings or underserved areas.

Dental Manpower. In a review of the status of dental manpower in the United States, Littleton (1980) noted the following recent changes and trends. Approximately twice as many dentists (5,324) graduated in 1978 than in 1950. Twenty-one new dental schools have been constructed since 1950, raising the total to sixty. Nearly 40 percent of the dental school graduates in 1978 entered dental specialties, general practice residencies, or other advanced dental education programs. The productivity of the dental profession has increased dramatically during the last twenty-five years. However, the increased size and productivity of the dental work force, and the expanded use of preventive measures such as water fluoridation, have not as yet eradicated dental disease. As evidence, Littleton cited data estimating that in 1974, the average person aged 6 to 74 had 1.3 decayed teeth and 6.3 missing teeth. Moreover, one-half of the population from 18 to 74 years of age had periodontal disease. Yet, only 50 percent of the population made yearly regular visits to the dentist in 1977, an increase of only 3 percent from 1970. It was also noted that less care had been rendered to people with lower socioeconomic status. Further, the dentist-to-population ratio in 1979 was approximately 1 to 1,900, but 218 of 3,141 counties nationwide had zero dentists, and 558 counties had dentist-to-population ratios of approximately 1 to 5,000. Douglas and Cole (1979) indicated that in 1964 a shortage of dentists was projected for the 1970s. However, by 1973 the supply trend reversed itself in that the number of active dentists was growing faster than the U.S. population. This reversal was due to the increased number of dental school graduates and the decline in the fertility rate during the 1970s.

It has been estimated that the demand for dental care has increased because of an increased consumer awareness and changes in the financing of dental services, such as increased prepayment dental coverage (Rovin, 1979). It has been thought that the increase in numbers and productivity of the dental work force will keep pace with the demand for services; yet the maldistribution of services has produced localized conditions of shortage or oversupply. A survey of dental schools conducted by the Administrative Board of the Council for Deans of the American Association of Dental Schools demonstrated that relatively little has been done to induce students to practice in underserved areas (McDonald & Barton, 1980). It was noted that extramural programs familiarize students with remote-site settings, but it has not been demonstrated that these programs act as incentives to practice in these areas.

Dental Auxiliaries. One approach to solving the dental manpower crisis has been to increase the number of dentists. Another approach has been to increase the productivity of individual dentists by enlarging the supply of auxiliary personnel and encouraging the efficient utilization of these auxiliaries. Since the early 1960s, federal grants to dental schools (Dental Auxiliary Utilization Program)

have supported the efficient use of dental assistants. It has been demonstrated that dental assistants can more than double dentists' productivity by means of "four-handed" dentistry. Littleton (1980) noted that the decade of the 1970s demonstrated more than a 200 percent increase in the number of allied dental health programs and graduates. The number of active auxiliaries for each 100 active dentists has increased from 128 to 189 during the period from 1965 to 1977 (Littleton, 1980).

A third approach for increasing the productivity of dentists has been to delegate procedures to dental auxiliaries trained to perform "expanded functions." Most states have revised their dental-practice legislation to permit varying degrees of expanded functions by hygienists and dental assistants. Corry and Dannavale (1972) showed that dental assistants can be taught to perform acceptable levels of expanded functions in a relatively short amount of time. A study by Hammans, Jamison, and Wilson (1971) at the University of Alabama demonstrated that the services provided by dental assistants are indistinguishable from similar services provided by dentists. Another study at Harvard University found no differences in clinical performance between dental therapist trainees and junior dental students (Powell et al., 1974).

Federal grants to dental schools for TEAM (Training in Expanded Auxiliary Management) were initiated in the early 1970s. The purpose of this program was to provide training to dental students in the management of dental practice using multiple auxiliaries. It was hoped that TEAM graduates would delegate duties to auxiliaries better and manage the dental office more effectively.

Curriculum Innovations. The Kentucky Conference on Dental Curriculum provided one of the most important stimuli to curriculum change since the Gies report (Durocher, 1961). Many of the changes advocated by this conference in 1961 were implemented through the 1970s. These changes included (1) emphasis on human qualities during the student selection process; (2) the individualization of instruction; (3) early patient contact in the dental curriculum; (4) the establishment of electives, free time, and independent study for students; (5) the reduction in laboratory teaching time; (6) the use of audiovisual aids to improve teaching effectiveness; (7) the encouragement of interdisciplinary teaching; and (8) an emphasis on comprehensive oral health care. Allen (1973) summarized additional trends away from the traditional curriculum that included (1) an increase in hospital and community setting experiences; (2) increased implementation of the behavioral sciences; and (3) increased correlation between the biological, behavioral, and clinical sciences.

The Personalized Approach to Clinical Education (PACE) program instituted at the University of Kentucky College of Dentistry put into practice some of these new concepts (Bellanti et al., 1973). This innovative program permits individualization and flexibility within the clinical curriculum. Students individually progress through four levels of classification (preventive therapist, clinical therapist, assistant dentist, and associate dentist) on the basis of attained skill and knowledge rather than on the basis of completed academic years.

Following Kentucky's lead, other dental schools experimented with curricular innovations. Since 1968 the University of Pittsburgh School of Dental Medicine has stressed early clinical experience, interdisciplinary teaching, individualization, and a correlation of biological and clinical sciences (Wintner, 1972). The University of Florida College of Dentistry implemented a "flexible modular curriculum" in 1972. This program utilized self-instructional teaching packages that allowed students to progress at their own rate of learning. Allen and Collett (1978), reporting on the first six years of this program, noted that the modular approach (1) allowed self-pacing by students; (2) considered students' background and entry-level skills; (3) facilitated communication between faculty and students; (4) allowed the integration of clinical activities at various stages of the curriculum; and (5) encouraged sharing of instructional materials among other dental schools. Problems with the program arose from the difficulty of reorienting faculty and involving all disciplines in the design and implementation of the curriculum.

Goldhaber (1971) summarized a number of problems with the curriculum at Harvard School of Dental Medicine. He noted that the basic sciences presented during the first two years of dental school focused on details, not concepts. These courses frequently lacked relevance to oral biology and limited the time students could spend with other aspects of the dental curriculum. Second, he observed that the clinical years focused on technical skill development in restorative dentistry at the expense of preventive dentistry, diagnosis, and treatment planning. Third, since students were relatively isolated in the dental school clinic, they had minimal exposure to the management of patients with medical problems. Finally, Goldhaber noted that the traditional "lockstep curriculum" inhibited students from pursuing their individual academic interests. In response to these findings, Harvard introduced a medicine-and-surgery clerkship, an oral biology–pathophysiology course concurrent with basic sciences and clinical courses, a hospital dental externship, and a fourth year consisting only of elective course work.

Tryon (1971) studied the degree to which curricular innovations were implemented at various dental schools. He observed that innovations related directly to the clinical education of students, such as the use of the high-speed drill and utilization of dental assistants, were readily integrated into dental programs. Innovations not directly related to the technical aspects of students' training, such as "social" dentistry courses and programmed instruction, met with mixed success. It is not surprising, therefore, to note the varied emphasis placed on the development of programs in behavioral sciences, public health dentistry, and community dentistry among the nation's dental schools during the 1970s.

For example, in 1976 an American Dental Association survey reported that 92 percent of the nation's dental schools required instruction in the behavioral principles of dental practice (American Dental Association, 1977). The total number of clock hours ranged widely from 2 to 422 (mean = 61.4 hours; median = 53.5 hours). These figures indicated a significant increase in the courses devoted to the behavioral sciences since the early 1960s. Yet, less than 2 percent of the entire curriculum of the "average" dental school was set aside for required courses in communication and human behavior.

Instructional methods. Instructional methods utilized in teaching the various dental disciplines have included large-group lectures, small-group seminars, and one-to-one supervision. Lectures have been the most common form of instruction. They have been used for the dissemination of information in a structured and efficient manner, facilitating the presentation of material not available from other sources, One-to-one supervision has been used primarily in the preclinical technical courses and during clinical practice. Although many dental faculty have used lectures exclusively because of unfavorable student-faculty ratios or personal preference, others have expressed a growing dissatisfaction with the lecture technique. Small group seminars permit student participation and feedback. They have been used extensively during the past decade for teaching problem-solving skills, as in diagnosis and treatment-planning courses. Small-group discussions have also provided a mechanism for sensitizing the dental student to the psychological needs of their patients. Techniques such as role playing have been used to develop interpersonal skills and insights needed in dental practice (Gershen & Handelman, 1974).

Numerous studies researching the efficacy of self-instructional methods surfaced during the 1970s. These studies arose from the need to increase the efficiency and effectiveness of instruction in order to matriculate larger graduating classes. The studies compared the effectiveness of self-instructional programs to conventional techniques of instruction in terms of cognitive gains, time expended, and student preference.

Evidence of cognitive gains differed depending upon the level of the student, the nature of the material presented, and the manner of presentation. Some studies demonstrated higher scores for the self-instructional group (e.g., Emling & Gellen, 1975), but other studies found no differences between treatment groups (e.g., Wolf & Abou-Rass, 1976). A study relating time expended (Dilley et al., 1978) reported that students in self-instruction worked at a faster rate than students using traditional methods. Although self-instructional methods required less in-class time from faculty, the time needed for the development of self-instructional materials usually exceeded that of traditional techniques. Surveys of student preference indicated that students favored the self-pacing aspect of self-instructional materials but preferred additional faculty contact provided by supplemental lectures or live demonstrations.

One major concern stemming from the proliferation of self-instructional materials was development cost. Also, schools were duplicating efforts by developing programs of similar content in isolation. In response to this dilemma, project ACORDE (A Consortium on Restorative Dentistry Education) was developed and included twenty-six units that presented techniques in restorative dentistry (Dreier, 1974). Each teaching unit consisted of a syllabus for students, a course manual for instructors, methods for evaluating performance of students, and appropriate teaching aids. A 1979 survey indicated that approximately 40 percent of American dental schools had purchased part or all of the units (Kress, Silversin, & Kolenback, 1979). Users agreed that product quality was high and cost was relatively low. The major reservation of nonusers was their unwillingness to accept standardized procedures and packaged instruction.

Computer-assisted instruction (CAI) was used by some dental educators to augment self-paced curricula. CAI utilizes a computer that presents problems to students, records and evaluates their responses, and provides feedback. Brigham and Kamp (1974) reported that thirty-eight CAI programs existed in dentistry but that only 25 percent of the dental schools were utilizing them. Content areas for available CAI programs have included oral cancer detection, diagnosis of toothache, treatment planning, dental statistics, and dental management. The potential for CAI remains relatively untapped. It seems unlikely that this promising methodology will be fully developed for some time because of cutbacks in federal grants and special project support.

Media approaches. As dental educators attempted to expand the use of individualized instruction during the 1970s, an assortment of new facilities and educational equipment appeared. Independent learning centers, such as the facility established at the University of Maryland School of Dentistry, became commonplace (Lunin & Moreland, 1972). Within individual study carrels, students used sound-synchronized slide presentations, filmstrips, audiotapes, microscopic slides, manuals, study guides, and programmed texts. To facilitate the development of instructional products, dental schools created and expanded word-processing centers and media departments with support from artists, photographers, and television technicians.

The increased reliance on the use of video facilities had a profound effect on dental programs. Goldman (1973) noted that almost all dental schools have video monitors strategically placed in lecture halls, laboratories, and seminar rooms. Most schools also have access to studios used for videotape productions. Videotapes have primarily been used for demonstrations of clinical and laboratory techniques. Closed-circuit television has also been used as a media adjunct in teaching interpersonal skills within the behavioral sciences. As described by Wepman (1977), videotaped simulations of interactions in the dental office have stimulated classroom discussion. Other behavioral sci-

ence programs have used videotapes of actual interactions between dentist and patient (Linton, McCutcheon, & Stevenson, 1975; Jackson, 1978). At the University of California, Los Angeles School of Dentistry, a series of videocassettes was developed that provided students with insight into the thoughts and feelings of both dentist and patient formerly unattainable by traditional methods (Gershen et al., 1980).

Students. Student performance, selection, and characteristics are subjects of interest to dental educators.

Evaluation of performance. An important component of the educational program of a dental school has been the evaluation of student performance. Dental educators have debated the efficacy of traditional A–F grading versus pass/fail grading in measuring student performance. Graham (1975) reported that the percentage of U.S. dental schools using the pass/fail system increased from 45 percent in 1971 to 62 percent in 1974. Proponents of the pass/fail system indicated that this type of grading (1) eliminated the anxiety associated with the pressure to attain high grades; (2) reduced competition between students; (3) allowed students to pursue individual academic interests without fear of lowering their grade-point average; (4) reduced instructor-student debates over grades; and (5) improved student attitude towards study. Opponents of the pass/fail system indicated that the system (1) inhibited competition and thus reduced achievement motivation of students; (2) failed to discriminate among students; (3) reduced chances of students being accepted to advanced programs because class rank is not computed; and (4) did not allow for detection of marginal students by faculty with requisite information. Hall and Taft (1976) at the University of Iowa carried out one of the few empirical studies comparing pass/fail and traditional grading in dentistry. Results showed no differences between grading systems on three achievement tests.

A number of novel evaluation approaches have been introduced in dentistry. One approach, contract grading, has been used by some dental educators as a means of improving the affective environment in dental schools (Lewis & Killip, 1971; Zucker et al., 1978). The contract was a formal agreement negotiated between teacher and student enumerating objectives that had to be attained for a student to pass the course. Minimum competency scores, dates of completion, and criteria for adequate performance were established at the onset. Another criteria-related approach to evaluation has been applied in the clinical areas of instruction. Traditionally, the evaluation of performance in the clinic was based solely on the end product of treatment, that is, on the technical quality of the completed restoration. Greene (1972) identified five factors assessing clinical performance: (1) diagnosis, information gathering, and problem solving, (2) selection of treatment, (3) clinical technique, (4) rapport with patients, and (5) professional behavior. Criteria for effective and ineffective performance were delineated for each factor, and students were graded by more than one instructor for purposes of reliability. Denehy and Fuller (1974) described a peer evaluation system that familiarized students with the evaluation process and enabled students to compare individual performance with performance of peers.

Selection. Traditionally, the most important factors considered by admissions committees during the student selection process have been (1) overall grade-point average; (2) grade-point average in the sciences; (3) Dental Admission Test (DAT) scores; and (4) manual dexterity examinations. Other factors considered have included interviews, letters of recommendation, and statements made by applicants on application forms.

More recently, admission committees have directed their efforts toward selecting minority students (including women) and students who studied the social sciences, and toward developing valid criteria for student selection. In 1970, the Council on Dental Education changed the guidelines of prerequisites for admission to dental schools (American Dental Association, 1970). These guidelines encouraged predental students to pursue course work in the social sciences and humanities in addition to their preparation for the biological and physical sciences. Waldman (1978) believed that the goal of the dental admissions process was to select a variety of students in order to create a more diversified profession. He also felt that selection of students who were nonscience majors and with community service experience better prepared the dental profession for changes in the delivery of oral health-care. Administrators from a representative sample of twenty dental schools were interviewed about the recruitment and selection of students at their schools (Petterson & Kreit, 1972). The majority of admissions committees at these schools used predental grades as the primary factor in selecting students. However, interviewers cited problems in their ability to change admissions procedures, hindering their desire to select more socially aware students.

One concern of admissions committees has been the recent decline of dental school applicants. Graham and Kinsey (1979) summarized data regarding the number of applicants for the DAT program. From 1945 to 1963, the applicant pool remained constant at about 6,000 per testing cycle. By 1971 there was an increase to about 11,000 applicants, and the ratio of acceptances to total applicants was about 1 to 2. The applicant pool nearly doubled from 1971 to 1975, and the ratio of accepted students to total applicants declined to about 1 to 3. However, the applicant pool declined by one-third from 1975 to 1978. Graham and Kinsey also analyzed thirty variables from a data base provided by the American Association of Dental Schools Application Service during these three years of decline. They found (1) an east-to-west geographic decline in the applicant pool; (2) an increase in the number of dental hygienists and nurses applying; and (3) a decline in lower-middle-class applicants. The latter finding suggested that a dental education might not be as accessible to students from economically deprived backgrounds.

Kreit (1971) indicated that dental educators, in researching the relationship between admissions data and success in dental school, found that predental grade-point average was the most consistent predictor. However, a study by Thompson, Ahlawat, and Buie (1979) demonstrated that the DAT science average predicted overall success for the first and second years of the didactic curriculum. Boyd, Teteruck, and Thompson (1980) noted that a number of investigators found positive correlations between chalk carving and success in dental technique courses. The Perceptual Motor Ability Test (PMAT) replaced the chalk-carving test in 1968, and it has been shown that the predictive validity of both tests was similar (Graham, 1972).

Of the nongrade selection factors, applicant performance at the admission interview has been most widely used. Weinstein and Milgrom (1977) reported that use of the interview format at the University of Washington School of Dentistry (1) allowed applicants to demonstrate interpersonal skills; (2) permitted faculty to form a direct impression of the incoming class; (3) provided an opportunity for prospective students to clarify information submitted in their application file; and (4) facilitated public relations. Morse and Moebes (1973) concluded that admissions decisions were not influenced by interview variables such as appearance, expression, motivation, extracurricular experience, or acceptability as a dental colleague. However, a study at the University of Iowa's College of Dentistry demonstrated a relationship between data collected during structured, standardized interviews and desirable characteristics of dental students and practicing dentists (Killip, Fuller, & Kerber, 1979). Gough and Kirk (1970) attempted to predict academic performance from particular personality traits but met with little success.

Characteristics. Dental educators have attempted to assess characteristics of dental students by using a variety of standardized inventories. One group of studies has focused on personality descriptions of the typical dental student. Fusillo and Metz (1971) reviewed the personality research with mostly male dental students. They suggest that the "average" student tends to be pragmatic, conforming, and conservative, with little "humanitarian orientation." But for the most part, the dental student is very similar to the general population. Waldman (1978) summarized the "image of dental students" as conforming, persistent and aggressive, methodical, and rigid. Further, the dental professional is viewed as a highly skilled entrepreneur motivated by financial betterment and upward mobility.

In 1970 women comprised about 1 percent of the dentists in the United States, 20–40 percent of the dentists in the Scandinavian countries, and about 80 percent of the dentists in the Soviet Union (Campbell, 1970). Affirmative action programs encouraged the increased enrollment of women and other minorities in professional schools. Therefore, an increasing interest in assessing the characteristics of these students has occurred. Coombs (1976) noted that both sexes possess similar motivations and values and that they particularly value independence as a motivating factor in selecting dentistry as a career. Gershen and McCreary (1977) found that personality profiles of male and female dental students are markedly similar to each other. Also, male and female students are more similar to each other than men and women are similar in the general population. Research has yet to substantiate the theory that admitting more women to dental schools would result in a more socially conscious student body or profession.

Researchers have also focused on the impact of the dental school environment on personality characteristics, attitudes, and values as students progress to graduation. Silberman (1976) noted the similarity of values between freshmen and senior dental students. However, most studies demonstrated significant changes in student characteristics after four years in the dental school environment (Sherlock & Morris, 1972; Moody, Van Tassel, & Cash, 1974; Vinton, 1978). These changes include a departure from idealism, decreasing humanitarianism, increasing cynicism, and an increasing concern for self-interests and goals. These negative attitudes may have resulted from a reaction to the pressures of the dental school environment and tend to disappear after graduation.

Challenges for Dental Education. In the early 1970s, most dental administrators believed that capitation support would continue indefinitely. However, by the end of the decade it was clear that federal funding to dental schools was in jeopardy. Cutbacks in funding and concern over the termination of capitation grants alarmed those schools who relied heavily on federal support. The extent of federal funding in future years will more than likely depend upon the public's perception of the dental profession's ability to meet the oral health needs of the population. Decreased governmental support, increased costs, and inflation have forced schools to cut spending and rely more heavily on tuition, service revenues, and private donations.

This policy of fiscal moderation has existed in an era in which major changes have occurred in the delivery of dental health care. Dentistry has entered an age of consumerism wherein the demand for dental care, prepaid dental insurance, and quality control has increased. Changes in the financing of dental care have removed some monetary barriers for the patient but have led to the dental profession's consideration of new models of health-care delivery. Recent trends to establish health maintenance organizations (HMOs) and large group dental practices have been among these new models.

The dilemma for dental educators has been how to make dental education responsive to recent social changes in light of a decreasing pool of resources.

Jay A. Gershen

See also Licensing and Certification; Professions Education.

REFERENCES

Allen, D. L. Current trends and projections in dental education. *Journal of Dental Education*, 1973, *37*, 32–35.

Allen, D. L. Status of the predoctoral dental education program and its impact on graduate dental education. *Journal of Dental Education*, 1980, *44*, 592–599.

Allen, D. L., & Collett, W. K. A progress report on six years' experience with a flexible, modular curriculum. *Journal of Dental Education*, 1978, *42*, 290–295.

American Association of Dental Schools. *Advanced Dental Education: Recommendations for the Eighties, Issues in Dental Health Policy.* Battle Creek, Mich.: W. K. Kellogg Foundation, 1980.

American Dental Association, Council on Dental Education. *Requirements for an Accredited School of Dentistry.* Chicago: The Association, 1970.

American Dental Association, Council on Dental Education. *Dental Education in the United States, 1976.* Chicago: The Association, 1977.

Bellanti, N. D.; Wiggs, J. S.; Kenney, E. B.; Laswell, H. R.; Saxe, S. R.; Spohn, E. E.; & Cooper, T. M. Individualization of clinical dental curriculum. *Journal of Dental Education*, 1973, *37*, 33–36.

Boozer, C. H.; Gaines, W. G.; Copping, A. A.; & Rasmussen, R. H. Formal training in education for dental educators: A pilot program. *Journal of Dental Education*, 1977, *41*, 248–252.

Boyd, M. A.; Teteruck, W. R.; & Thompson, G. W. Interpretation and use of the dental admission and aptitude tests. *Journal of Dental Education*, 1980, *44*, 275–278.

Brigham, C. R., & Kamp, M. The current status of computer-assisted instruction in the health sciences. *Journal of Medical Education*, 1974, *49*, 278–279.

Campbell, J. E. Women dentists: An untapped resource. *Journal of the American College of Dentists*, 1970, *37*, 265–269.

Coombs, J. A. Factors associated with career choice among women dental students. *Journal of Dental Education*, 1976, *40*, 724–732.

Corry, R. D., & Dannavale, L. F. Expanded functions training for dental assistants in the Indian health service. *Journal of the American Dental Association*, 1972, *85*, 1343–1348.

Denehy, G. E., & Fuller, J. L. Student peer evaluation: An adjunct to preclinical laboratory evaluation. *Journal of Dental Education*, 1974, *38*, 200–203.

Dilley, G. J.; Machen, J. B.; Dilley, D. C. H.; & Howden, E. F. Acquisition of psychomotor skills in tooth preparation utilizing self-paced instruction. *Journal of Dental Education*, 1978, *42*, 476–480.

Douglas, C. W., & Cole, K. O. The supply of manpower in the United States. *Journal of Dental Education*, 1979, *43*, 287–302.

Dreier, D. L. Project ACORDE: A new laboratory curriculum. *Journal of the American Dental Association*, 1974, *88*, 1319–1321.

Durocher, R. T. *Kentucky Conference on Dental Curriculum.* Lexington: University of Kentucky, 1961.

Emling, R. C., & Gellin, M. E. An evaluation of programmed text, slide/tape, and lectures at six dental schools. *Journal of Dental Education*, 1975, *39*, 72–77.

Flexner, A. *Medical Education in the United States and Canada: A Report to the Carnegie Foundation for the Advancement of Teaching.* Washington, D.C.: Carnegie Foundation, 1910.

Formicola, A. J. Reflections on the three-year program. *Journal of Dental Education*, 1978, *42*, 572–575.

Fusillo, A. E., & Metz, A. S. Social science research on the dental student. In N. D. Richards & L. K. Cohen (Eds.), *Social Sciences and Dentistry: A Critical Bibliography*. The Hague: Sijthoff, 1971.

Gershen, J. A., & Handelman, S. L. Role-playing as an educational technique in dentistry. *Journal of Dental Education*, 1974, *38*, 451–455.

Gershen, J. A.; Marcus, M.; Strohlein, A.; & Pretzinger, M. An application of interpersonal process recall for teaching behavioral sciences in dentistry. *Journal of Dental Education*, 1980, *44*, 268–269.

Gershen, J. A., & McCreary, C. P. Comparing personality traits of male and female dental students: A study of two freshman classes. *Journal of Dental Education*, 1977, *41*, 618–622.

Gies, W. J. *Dental Education in the United States and Canada: A Report to the Carnegie Foundation for the Advancement of Teaching*. New York: Carnegie Foundation, 1926.

Goldhaber, P. The curriculum must change. *Journal of Dental Education*, 1971, *35*, 29–32, 45.

Goldman, M. Widened horizons for videotape in dental education. *Journal of Dental Education*, 1973, *37*, 43–45.

Gough, H. G., & Kirk, B. A. Achievement in dental school as related to personality and aptitude variables. *Measurement and Evaluation in Guidance*, 1970, *2*, 225–233.

Graham, J. W. Substitution of perceptual-motor ability test for chalk-carving in dental admission testing program. *Journal of Dental Education*, 1972, *36*, 9–14.

Graham, J. W. The pass/fail system in dental education. *Journal of Dental Education*, 1975, *39*, 71.

Graham, J. W., & Kinsey, R. B. Analysis of the decline in dental school applicants, 1975–1978. *Journal of Dental Education*, 1979, *43*, 107–114.

Greene, C. S. Comprehensive approach to evaluation of clinical performance. *Journal of Dental Education*, 1972, *36*, 23–26.

Hall, D. L., & Taft, T. B. Pass/fail versus A–F grading: A comparative study. *Journal of Dental Education*, 1976, *40*, 301–303.

Hammans, P. E.; Jamison, H. C.; & Wilson, L. L. Quality of service provided by dental therapists in an experimental program at the University of Alabama. *Journal of the American Dental Association*, 1971, *82*, 1060–1066.

Jackson, E. Convergent evidence for the effectiveness of interpersonal skill training for dental students. *Journal of Dental Education*, 1978, *42*, 517–523.

Killip, D. E.; Fuller, J. L.; & Kerber, P. E. The admission interview: The validity question. *Journal of Dental Education*, 1979, *43*, 547–551.

Kreit, L. H. The prediction of student success in dental schools. In N. D. Richards & L. K. Cohen, *Social Sciences and Dentistry: A Critical Bibliography*. The Hague: Sijthoff, 1971.

Kress, G. C.; Silversin, J. B.; & Kolenback, E. R. A study of the impact of project ACORDE on dental education in the United States. *Journal of Dental Education*, 1979, *43*, 204–209.

Lewis, L. A., & Killip, D. E. Contract grading: An alliance for learning. *Journal of Dental Education*, 1971, *35*, 616–620.

Linton, J. C.; McCutcheon, W. R.; & Stevenson, J. M. Teaching behavioral principles to dental students: A pilot course. *Journal of Dental Education*, 1975, *39*, 149–151.

Littleton, P. A. Dental manpower supply and requirements: The effect of national estimates on individual dental schools. *Journal of Dental Education*, 1980, *44*, 241–245.

Lunin, M., & Moreland, E. F. Independent learning center in a dental school. *Journal of Dental Education*, 1972, *36*, 20–23.

McDonald, R. E., & Barton, P. Activities by the schools to improve the distribution of dentists: An AADS report. *Journal of Dental Education*, 1980, *44*, 246–247.

Moody, P. M.; Van Tassel, C., & Cash, D. M. Cynicism, humanitarianism, and dental career development. *Journal of Dental Education*, 1974, *38*, 645–649.

Morse, P. K., & Moebes, J. D. Effect of interviews on admission decisions. *Journal of Dental Education*, 1973, *37*, 26–28.

Petterson, E. O., & Kreit, L. H. Recruitment and selection of students in dentistry. *Journal of Dental Education*, 1972, *36*, 31–36.

Powell, W. O.; Sinkford, J. C.; Henry, J. L.; & Chen, M. S. Comparison of clinical performance of dental therapist trainees and dental students. *Journal of Dental Education*, 1974, *38*, 268–272.

Rovin, S. The future of dental specialization: Policy issues. *Journal of Dental Education*, 1979, *43*, 537–543.

Sherlock, G. J., & Morris, R. T. *Becoming a Dentist*. Springfield, Ill.: Thomas, 1972.

Silberman, S. L. Comparison of personal values among freshman and senior dental students and dental faculty. *Journal of Dental Education*, 1976, *40*, 334–339.

Thompson, G. W.; Ahlawat, K.; & Buie, R. Evaluation of the dental aptitude test components as predictors of dental school performance. *Journal of the Canadian Dental Association*, 1979, *45*, 407–409.

Tryon, A. F. Diffusion of innovation in dental education I: An analysis of the system. *Journal of Dental Education*, 1971, *35*, 109–117.

Vann, W. F. Evolution of the dental school curriculum: Influences and determinants. *Journal of Dental Education*, 1978, *42*, 66–73.

Vinton, J. C. A four-year longitudinal study of the impact of learning structure on dental student lifestyle values. *Journal of Dental Education*, 1978, *42*, 251–256.

Waldman, H. B. Eliminating some unexpected effects of the dental student admission process. *Journal of Dental Education*, 1978, *42*, 513–516.

Weinstein, P., & Milgrom, P. The applicant's perception of the admissions interview. *Journal of Dental Education*, 1977, *41*, 149–152.

Wepman, B. J. Communications skills training for dental students. *Journal of Dental Education*, 1977, *41*, 633–634.

Wintner, A. J. University of Pittsburgh: Curriculum in motion. *Journal of Dental Education*, 1972, *36*, 30–36.

Wolf, S. A., & Abou-Rass, M. Development and evaluation of a self-instructional program in endodontic diagnosis and treatment planning. *Journal of Dental Education*, 1976, *40*, 366–367.

Zucker, S. B.; Odom, J. G.; Cheney, H. G.; & Fretwell, L. D. Contract grading in community dentistry. *Journal of Dental Education*, 1978, *42*, 668–670.

DESEGREGATION

See Black Education; Culture and Education Policy; Judicial Decisions; Multicultural and Minority Education; Transportation of Students; Urban Education.

DISCIPLINE

A major responsibility of formal education is to pass on, from generation to generation, the fiber and substance of a moral order—a conglomerate of democratic social values and social knowledge that enables people to live harmoniously in a group (Butler, 1980). In the past, these social, political, religious, and economic goals and accepted standards of conduct have tended to be regimented and homogeneous. The school's authority to deal with student behavior problems has been accepted with little question. The use of punishment or reward as the primary means of establishing order also has been accepted.

In today's society, the school system still relies on social mandate when using authority to transmit the bases of democratic order. Conflict has arisen when students question the teacher's views of this mandate or authority to transmit this message. Blind obedience to explicit and implicit rules and regulations has lessened (Butler, 1980). In the midst of this give-and-take, classroom teachers have become confused and frustrated as they search for disciplinary standards or guidelines that work (Kohut, 1978).

The modern controversy surrounding school discipline must be apparent to anyone who has lived through the 1960s and 1970s. The public has declared discipline to be the major problem in the public schools in ten of the eleven Gallup Polls between 1969 and 1980 (McDaniel, 1980). Evidence that teachers, administrators, parents, and even students have become deeply concerned about discipline appears in a number of national and international editorials written about the scope of the discipline problem in schools (Cronley, 1978; "Help! Teachers Can't Teach," *Time*, 1980). Newspapers and magazines headline topics concerning violence, increased student absenteeism, and adolescent alienation. More scholarly works, such as that by McPortland and McDill (1977) report recent increases in student absenteeism, drug abuse, classroom disruption, disrespect for authority, violence, and criminal behavior. The age at which these problems appear is also changing. Elementary schools are now experiencing many of the problems previously found only in junior and senior high schools ("City Schools in Crisis," *Newsweek*, 1977).

Definition. Attempts to gain consensus among educators on a definition of such a controversial word as "discipline" has been a frustrating task (Kohut, 1978). The *American Heritage Dictionary* (1978) defines "discipline" as "training that is expected to produce a specified character or pattern of behavior," "controlled behavior resulting from training," and "a systematic method to obtain obedience." This definition reflects the traditional view of discipline. Modern views suggest that discipline involves control from within as well as imposition from without. When viewed in this light, discipline implies the development by individuals of the necessary self-control to allow them to be effective and contributing members of society (Perkins, 1969; Webster, 1968).

There are educators who view discipline as synonymous with classroom management (Doyle, 1980; Weiner, 1972); they assert that a well-developed lesson plan is the best deterrent to a noisy and disruptive classroom. Although most teachers agree that learning is not restricted to a quiet and orderly environment, many supervisory personnel and laymen equate the effectiveness of teaching with the noise level and orderly appearance of an individual classroom. Thus, classroom management continues to be a major concern of teachers and other school officials.

Most educators agree that discipline is best obtained by involving teachers, students, and parents. An effective program of classroom management and discipline should stress student awareness and self-discipline, and be balanced with a system of rewards and punishments used to maintain an effective learning environment. Varied discipline solutions are suitable for different situations, and it is of paramount importance that the selected approach provide for positive rather than punitive or negative interactions between teacher and students (Kohut, 1978) and that it be supported by parents.

Approaches to Classroom Discipline. Under pressure of court decisions, legislative mandates, mass media exposure, and a climate of rapid social change, the contemporary teacher confronts students from diverse ethnic and cultural groups who frequently bring to the classroom their conflicting needs and divergent value systems. Fortunately, as discipline problems have intensified so have attempts to provide assistance. In the last decade numerous strategies for better classroom discipline have been developed. Many of these discipline aids are total packages and include special workshops, audiovisual training units, theory and research, documentation, and a variety of written materials.

Large-scale research studies are as yet rare in the area of classroom discipline and management. Kounin (1970) identified two major teacher characteristics, termed "withitness" and "overlapping," which were associated with successful classroom management. Although this research is more than a decade old, his attempt to study classrooms for the effects of various disciplinary actions and to identify the characteristics of effective and ineffective disciplinarians remains a landmark effort. Most other research in discipline has been either indirect or principally concerned with the support of a particular model or approach.

Most of the writing in the field has assumed an eclectic tone with a strong emphasis upon surveys of various approaches with a "whatever works" direction. A recent volume by Tanner (1978) reviews various approaches and proposes an "eclectic-developmental" approach loosely based on Piaget's developmental stages of moral reasoning. Three disciplinary stages are proposed, each of which includes specific responsibilities for both students and teachers. The three stages are: (1) the basic disciplinary stage, in which pupils listen, follow directions, and ask questions when they don't understand; teachers are to explain, encourage questions, and provide good role models; (2) the constructive stage, in which students work cooperatively, take the role of others, and understand concepts of justice; teachers are to explain rules and reasons for the organization pattern, provide opportunities to participate and work cooperatively, and relate concepts of justice to everyday life; (3) the generative stage, in which students can operate autonomously, responsibly, and make choices when rules do not apply; teachers are to encourage moral development, help to develop and implement plans of action for social problems, and create an autonomous, principled classroom operation.

Curwin and Mendler (1980) propose an eclectic and humanistic position termed the "three-dimensional approach." This approach focuses upon methods of setting up a classroom for the prevention of disciplinary problems; ideas for action if and when misbehavior does occur; and resolution plans for chronic problem situations. Jones and Jones (1981) similarly provide a thorough study of classroom discipline and management by examining (1) theoretical foundations for understanding student behavior, (2) key factors necessary for the prevention of disciplinary problems, and (3) a wide range of techniques and specific methods for effectively dealing with disciplinary problems when they do occur. The writers also provide ideas for working with parents and strategies for using resource personnel. First and Mizell (1980) have assembled a rich and varied compilation of approaches to improving student behavior. Many of them are described in the words of the educators, parents, and students who have devised them. This book is unique in that it considers alternatives that have been specifically devised for both elementary and secondary school levels. An extensive chart of disciplinary procedures along with relevant information is provided.

Current Common Strategies.   Perhaps the most effective way to review the current state of the art relative to classroom discipline is to summarize the various strategies developed in recent years (First & Mizell, 1980; Usher & Taylor, 1981). In most instances each strategy is supported by a particular set of theoretical assumptions and research findings. In some cases, however, the approach is an outgrowth of a larger and more general body of research and theory regarding human behavior and conduct.

1. *Self-concept.* The key proposition of Purkey (1978) and Canfield and Wells (1976), for example, is that an individual's concept of self is the most important determinant of behavior. School conduct and achievement are best improved by the student who, in the process of developing a more healthy and positive self-concept, is learning self-discipline. Growth in self-concept occurs in an accepting, warm, empathic, open, and nonjudgmental environment, which allows students the freedom to explore their thoughts and feelings in order to solve their own problems.

2. *Communication skills.* Ginott (1972) calls for a firm setting of limits on behavior but never on feelings. All feelings are to be accepted, no matter how destructive or outrageous. But limits are to be placed on actions that might result from such feelings. Ginott's approach suggests

the following steps: (1) reflecting the feelings of the "misbehaver" to demonstrate understanding; (2) setting limits on the behavior; (3) providing a symbolic outlet for feelings; and (4) acknowledging that the symbolic outlet is not as good as the "real" thing.

3. *Natural and logical consequences.* Driekurs, Grunwald, and Pepper (1971) and Dinkmeyer and Dinkmeyer (1976) have stated that misbehavior occurs because children have developed faulty beliefs about themselves. These faulty beliefs lead to personal goals that may result in misbehavior. The goals for misbehavior are attention-seeking, power, revenge, and display of inadequacy. Two major types of response in dealing with misbehavior are suggested by this approach: (1) to pinpoint the goal of the behavior and thereby understand how to help the behaver work through the faulty belief, and (2) to use natural or logical consequences for misbehavior.

4. *Values clarification.* Values clarification (Simon, Howe, & Kirschenbaum 1972) is a process designed to help youngsters answer some of their questions about values and build their own value systems. According to this view, discipline problems are caused by two factors: (1) students with unclear values who experience inner turmoil that may result in troublesome behavior, and (2) conflicting and colliding value positions held by the student, on the one hand, and the school, principal, or teacher, on the other. Values clarification strategies include games, structured communication activities, and questioning skills.

5. *Teacher effectiveness training.* The aim of this approach (Gordon 1974) is to replace "repressive and power-based methods" (punishment, blaming, shaming, or threatening) with a model of communication based upon: (1) active listening—responding in a reflective manner to the feelings and content of the behaver; (2) I-message—responding in a nonblaming, descriptive manner to misbehavior that creates a serious problem for the teacher; (3) problem ownership—understanding the differences between situations in which the learner has a problem and those in which the learner has no real problem but is behaving in a manner that is giving the teacher a problem; and (4) negotiation and problem solving—use of a collaborative, "no-lose" approach to resolve classroom conflict and establish classroom rules and policies.

6. *Transactional analysis.* Discipline problems are to be viewed, according to Ernst (1972), in terms of the communications transactions between people and may be either avoided or confronted through an understanding of the ways in which a teacher gets "hooked" into playing a game with a disruptive student. Communication is strengthened by an understanding of the ego states of both teacher and student at the moment. Transactional analysis principles suggest that teachers should learn to stay in the "adult ego state," particularly when they face students who have problems with authority. The "adult ego state" is the rational, thinking "computer-like" mental state that involves reflection upon information from both the "parent ego state" and the "child ego state"; it is thus more likely to be able to deal with the daily turmoil of most classrooms.

7. *Reality therapy.* This approach (Glasser 1965, 1969) claims that disruptive events occur in the classroom when students lack involvement with the school, when they feel like failures, and when they do not take responsibility for their own actions. The school should attempt to eliminate failure and to increase involvement, relevance, and thinking. Responsibility is learned through a strong, positive, emotional involvement with a responsible person. Teachers need to be positive and responsible persons who are trained to implement Glasser's ten disciplinary steps and to conduct classroom meetings that lead to improved student involvement.

8. *The LEAST approach to classroom discipline.* This method (Carkhuff & Griffin, 1978), provides teachers with five main tools to improve classroom discipline. LEAST is an acronym based upon the following steps for good discipline: *(L)* Leave it alone; many actions may simply be left alone. *(E)* End the action; Many times teachers can simply end the misbehavior without undue emotion. *(A)* Attend more fully; if a teacher must take further steps beyond merely ending the disruption at the moment, then it is time to get to the root of the problem. *(S)* Spell out directions; if the procedures listed thus far do not work, it is time to clearly tell the student what to do. *(T)* Track the student's progress by keeping a simple, written private record of disciplinary encounters.

9. *Project TEACH.* This program (Project TEACH, 1977) combines a variety of strategies, skills, and approaches in an exacting manner. The training includes skills development in both verbal and nonverbal communication, positive reinforcement and related behavior modification principles, changing the environment, natural and logical consequences, and assertiveness. It is a highly eclectic approach that attempts to combine some of the best ideas of many different approaches and philosophies.

10. *Assertive discipline.* The major emphasis in this plan (Canter, 1976) is, and should be, upon the teacher's full control of the classroom. Strong assertiveness skills must be developed by all teachers in order to preserve and establish order. Systematic behavior modification principles are implemented in each classroom, including use of the chalkboard for recording the names of disruptive students and the placement of an easily visible glass jar of marbles in the classroom for use in reinforcing positive behavior.

11. *Behavior modification.* According to Skinner (1968), misbehavior occurs because it is reinforced by the environment. As a remedy, the child's behavior is changed by changing the environment, and thereby reinforcing appropriate behavior instead of reinforcing inappropriate behavior. This shaping process occurs through rewarding successive approximations of the target behavior. Other measures suggested by behavior modification principles include reinforcement of behavior that is incompatible with a student's misbehavior; use of extinction procedures to remove reinforcement from an undesirable behavior; scheduling of reinforcement of desired behaviors for maximum effectiveness; and the use of praise as an important mode of reinforcement.

12. *Dare to discipline.* This strategy (Dobson, 1971) is based upon a strong authoritarian approach that gives the teacher "absolute locus of control." The teacher is expected to be businesslike, highly organized, and in firm control. This approach assumes that children will test limits on the first day of school and that the teacher needs to let them know at the start who is in charge.

13. *Rational emotive education.* The ideas of Knaus (1974) are based upon a cognitive-behavioral approach to personal growth. Emphasis is placed upon the directive role of thought in the guidance of behavior, and a specific set of rational and irrational assumptions are presented that guide individual thought. Accordingly, an irrational assumption implies that in order to enjoy life one must have certain and perfect control. A rational assumption implies that in order to enjoy life one must accept that life is largely governed by probability and chance. This approach assumes that students will exhibit better behavior if their irrational beliefs are changed into more rational beliefs. Similarly, discipline can be improved if teachers are able to change their irrational beliefs into more rational ones.

Conclusions. Discipline has been the most troublesome problem in public education during the past two decades. Many approaches and strategies have been made available for educators in order to combat the problem. These approaches are based upon research, philosophy, theory, or various combinations of these elements. Currently no overwhelming evidence indicates which approach is best suitable to specific educational settings.

Public school officials are confronted with a muddled picture as they search for effective policies and procedures to combat the discipline problems in their schools. On the one hand they are caught with a lack of resources for the implementation of new strategies, and, on the other hand, with a mounting pressure from taxpayers, parents, and education critics to arrive at quick solutions of the problem. They are left to struggle with ineffective strategies which are already in use with little or no time for thorough research or local adaptation efforts.

Confronted by public demands, student diversity, and either unclear or outmoded policies, teachers have been the most active proponents of the development of concrete remedies. From their perspective, little time exists for the development of careful research or for gradual change when confronting the crisis in discipline. Rather, circumstances call for crisis intervention and immediate help.

No easy solutions exist for the discipline problems in the nation's schools; in addition, there is a shortage of carefully designed major research efforts. Yet, the overall direction of future efforts seems to be a gradual shift toward a more restrictive and prescriptive discipline policy that emphasizes improved classroom communications. As Jones and Tanner (1981) point out, classroom discipline as an area of research and theoretical study has been a largely unclaimed legacy for scholars in education. Citing the modern tendency to regard discipline as a strictly managerial problem, they believe that solutions to the problem must incorporate both concepts of self-direction and social responsibility and that discipline must be viewed as an educational problem, not merely a managerial or administrative one. Research and theory linking disciplinary concerns to the broader purposes of education are much needed. Studies need to be done that examine such issues as class, racial, cultural, and ethnic factors; classroom environments; teacher behavior and strategies; school policy; and the relation of discipline to the fundamental goals of responsible citizenship in a free society.

John G. Taylor
Richard H. Usher

See also Behavior Problems; Behavioral Treatment Methods; Counseling; Psychological Services; Truants and Dropouts.

REFERENCES

American Heritage Dictionary. Boston: Houghton Mifflin, 1978, p. 375.

Butler, M. *Discipline and the Educational Process: Coping in the Classroom.* Washington, D.C.: ERIC Clearinghouse on Teacher Education, 1980. (ERIC Document Reproduction Service No. ED 170 293)

Canfield, J. D., & Wells, H. C. *One Hundred Ways to Enhance Self-concept in the Classroom.* Englewood Cliffs, N.J.: Prentice-Hall, 1976. (ERIC Document Reproduction Service No. ED 117 031)

Canter, L. *Assertive Discipline.* Los Angeles: Lee Canter & Associates, 1976.

Carkhuff, R. R., & Griffin, A. H. *The LEAST Approach to Classroom Discipline.* Washington, D.C.: National Educational Association, 1978. (ERIC Document Reproduction Service No. ED 166 143)

City schools in crisis. *Newsweek,* September 12, 1977, pp. 62–64, 67–70.

Cronley, C. Blackboard jungle update. *Trans World Airlines Ambassador,* September 1978, pp. 25–28, 62–64.

Curwin, R. L., & Mendler, A. N. *The Discipline Book: A Complete Guide to School and Classroom Management.* Reston, Va.: Reston, 1980, p. xiii.

Dinkmeyer, D., & Dinkmeyer, D., Jr. Logical consequences: A key to the reduction of disciplinary problems. *Phi Delta Kappan,* 1976, *57,* 664–666.

Dobson, J. *Dare to Discipline.* Wheaton, Ill.: Tyndale House, 1971.

Doyle, W. *Classroom Management.* West Lafayette, Ind.: Kappa Delta Pi, 1980. (ERIC Document Reproduction Service No. ED 198 075)

Driekurs, R.; Grunwald, B. B.; & Pepper, F. C. *Maintaining Sanity in the Classroom.* New York: Harper & Row, 1971.

Ernst, K. *Games Students Play and What to Do about Them.* Milbras, Calif.: Celestial Arts, 1972.

First, F. M., & Mizell, M. H. *Everybody's Business: A Book about School Discipline.* Columbia, S.C.: Southeastern Public Education Program, 1980.

Ginott, H. *Teacher and Child.* New York: Macmillan, 1972.

Glasser, W. *Reality Therapy.* New York: Harper & Row, 1965.

Glasser, W. *Schools without Failure.* New York: Harper & Row, 1969.

Gordon, T. *Teacher Effectiveness Training.* New York: Wyden, 1974.

Help! Teachers can't teach. *Time,* June 16, 1980, pp. 54–60, 63.

Jones, R. S., & Tanner, L. N. Classroom discipline: The unclaimed legacy. *Phi Delta Kappan,* March 1981, *62,* 494–497.

Jones, V. F., & Jones, L. S. *Responsible Classroom Discipline: Creating Positive Learning Environments and Solving Problems.* Boston: Allyn & Bacon, 1981.

Knaus, W. J. *Rational Emotive Education: A Manual for Elementary School Teachers.* New York: Institute for Rational Living, 1974.

Kohut, S. Defining discipline in the classroom. *Action in Teacher Education,* 1978, *1*(2), 11–15, 13.

Kounin, J. S. *Discipline and Group Management in Classrooms.* New York: Holt, Rinehart & Winston, 1970.

McDaniel, T. R. Exploring alternatives to punishment: The keys to effective discipline. *Phi Delta Kappan,* 1980, *61,* 455–458.

McPortland, J. M., & McDill, E. L. *Violence in Schools.* Lexington, Mass.: Lexington Books, 1977.

Perkins, H. V. *Human Development and Learning.* Belmont, Calif.: Wadsworth, 1969.

Project TEACH Westwood, N.J.: Performance Learning Systems, 1977. (ERIC Document Reproduction Service No. ED 167 527)

Purkey, W. W. *Inviting School Success: A Self-concept Approach to Teaching and Learning.* Belmont, Calif.: Wadsworth, 1978.

Simon, S. B.; Howe, L. W.; & Kirschenbaum, H. *Values Clarification.* New York: Hart, 1972. (ERIC Document Reproduction Service No. ED 069 585)

Skinner, B. F. *The Technology of Teaching.* New York: Appleton-Century-Crofts, 1968.

Tanner, L. N. *Classroom Discipline for Effective Teaching and Learning.* New York: Holt, Rinehart & Winston 1978. (ERIC Document Reproduction Service No. ED 150 750)

Usher, R., & Taylor, J. *A Baker's Dozen for Classroom Discipline.* Louisville: Kentucky Education Association, 1981.

Webster, S. W. *Discipline in the Classroom.* San Francisco: Chandler, Intext, 1968.

Weiner, D. H. *Classroom Management and Discipline.* Itasca, Ill.: F. E. Peacock, 1972.

DISTANCE EDUCATION

Electronic technology may effect the greatest instructional revolution in education in five centuries (Carnegie Commission on Higher Education, 1972.) With the shortage of faculty members in the 1960s, technology made learning more independent of instructors. Although that method of learning did not save time or money in all cases, it proved advantageous for other reasons: allowing students a more active role in learning, providing alternative modes of instruction for students who do not learn well in conventional classes, and giving students greater flexibility in schedules and locations of classes. Commitments were made in the past fifteen years to humanize education by increasing access for all kinds of citizens and by making instruction more responsive to individual needs. As Cross (1976) observes, the commitment went from education for all to education for each. Distance education programs have emerged throughout the world to serve new students in ways that are important to them.

The term "distance education" is used interchangeably with the terms "open learning" and "extended-degree program" because these terms all represent greater opportunities for learning through flexible adjustments in the time schedule and physical location of classes.

Methods of Delivery

In times of increasing concern about providing the most cost-effective educational programs, high priorities within the media selection process must be given to what costs least, is least complicated, is most accessible, and produces desired results. To understand this process, various methods of delivering instructional materials are examined.

Print. In many instances, the best medium may be the printed word. In addition to being very familiar to almost all learners, it is inexpensive and portable. Since it offers a fixed presentation format, students can look at any part of its message in any order for any length of time. Furthermore, print materials are easily distributed to learners by existing mail-delivery and package-delivery systems.

Correspondence study. Distance learners are provided with a set of sequential instructional and testing print materials for each course in which the student is enrolled. Correspondence study was first employed in the United States by the University of Chicago under the leadership of William Rainey Harper and by the University of Wisconsin's Extension Division under William H. Lighty at the beginning of the twentieth century. An excellent guide to primary sources on the historical and organizational development of correspondence schools (public, private, and military) can be found in Mathieson (1971). A comprehensive international overview of correspondence instruction is also available in MacKenzie and Christensen (1971).

Programmed instruction. The most sophisticated instructional design for print materials is "programmed instruction" (PI), which presents material in a definite sequence of steps leading to a specified educational objective. Students work at their own pace by actively writing or selecting answers to questions. Students receive immediate feedback about the correctness of their responses. Several variations of PI exist. In a "linear program," the sequence of steps is identical for all students. A "branching program" offers instruction for any of the several responses (correct and incorrect) that a student may select. "Combination programs" employ both linear and branching formats. Another type, a "mathetics pro-

gram," employs branching as well as task simulations (Ohio State University Center for Vocational Education, 1977).

Research studies show that there are no overall significant differences in achievement produced by programmed instruction, on the one hand, and traditional instruction, on the other (Jamison, Suppes, & Wells, 1974; Nash, Muczyk, & Vettori, 1971). Each method is effective in developing intellectual skills, factual knowledge, attitudes, and motor skills. Yet, low-ability and high-ability students were observed to benefit more by PI than average students. A major difference observed was the substantially diminished student learning-time needed (Nash, et al., 1971). The chief policy question, then, is whether the saving of time is worth the additional cost and faculty time.

Modularized instruction. The use of instructional modules permits students to work at differing rates by employing single-concept units of study to construct learning experiences of any needed magnitude and content coverage. Modules provide students with immediate feedback so that they can determine if mastery is achieved. Modules can employ different media to heighten the chances that a student masters a particular concept. Cross (1976) found that about three-quarters of all community colleges are using such modules.

Emphases upon the written word, self-pacing, and unit mastery are key features of the general instructional approach known as the "Keller Plan" or "personalized system of instruction" (PSI) (Robin, 1975). The other two key features of PSI, meeting with proctors for periodic testing and feedback and attending periodic lectures for motivation, pose more difficulty for distance learners, unless they are near a study center offering such activities.

Whereas PSI is thought to have an emphasis on written materials strong enough to pose potential problems for poor readers, the "audio-tutorial approach" schedules students into study carrels with a tape recorder, film and/or slide projector, and physical models in addition to written modules. Taped instructions guide students through each unit. Informal small-group and large-group meetings are also held once a week.

Although research evidence shows a small significant increase in the achievement of audio-tutorial students compared with those in classroom-only courses—with little negative effect on attrition and no diminution of student attitudes toward learning—PSI has demonstrated more impressive results. Compared to the achievement of lecture classes, the end-of-course achievement of PSI students was 10 percent higher, long-term retention after several months was 13 percent higher, and attitudes toward learning were more positive. However, a 4 percent higher dropout rate was also noted (Robin, 1976). Another disadvantage that must be taken into account is that it takes a faculty member about one-and-one-half times as much effort to prepare a PSI course as to prepare conventional instruction (Johnston, 1975).

Newspaper. The use of newspapers to present college-level course materials was begun in the United States, in 1973, by the University Extension of the University of California at San Diego. Since that time, more than 700 colleges and universities and almost 1,200 newspapers have participated. More than 40,000 students have earned credit in the first ten courses offered (Colburn, 1978).

The U.S. National Endowment for the Humanities has given sustained financial support for the development of these newspaper courses as well as special financing to community forums on course topics in conjunction with the American Association of Community and Junior Colleges (AACJC). A staff of eight people is responsible for overall development and production. The annual budget is about $600,000. The national office receives $7.50 per enrollee from schools with enrollments of ten or more students, plus royalties from book sales. The newspaper articles and illustrations are distributed free by United Press International. Participating colleges are required to hold at least two contact sessions per course. A book of background readings and a study guide for review are available from publishers for each course. In the fall of 1980, a television series produced by BBC and Time-Life Films are joined with a national newspaper course, "Connections: Technology and Change," the first such merger on a national scale (Gross, 1979). The Department of Extramural Studies of Makerere University College uses Uganda's weekly newspaper as a medium of distribution. It has the same faculty and staff as the campus. Its courses cover the same content (Erdos, 1970).

Kelly and Anadam (1979) observe two basic truths about distance learners: (1) some must learn at a distance or not at all; and (2) most succeed with the assistance of external motivators or not at all. Print-based correspondence units are supplemented by media instruction in part for that reason. A weekly broadcast of radio or television lessons serves to pace students through the course material. The completion rates of correspondence courses have dramatically improved with the addition of regular television broadcasts (Lipson, 1977).

Audio Media. Audio media also address the needs of distance learners.

The telephone. Stemming from a long-term commitment to statewide outreach programs, the University of Wisconsin has employed the telephone for instruction on a wide scale. The chief advantages of the telephone are low cost, interactive communication, and flexibility. It can handle telewriters, graphic input devices (electronic blackboards), and slow-scan televideo systems. The major organizational mechanisms have been the Educational Telephone Network (ETN) and the Statewide Extension Education Network (SEEN). Together, these networks serve over 30,000 engineers, teachers, physicians, nurses, librarians, lawyers, business people, and others (Parker, 1976).

The Educational Telephone Network has tied together 210 meeting places in 100 cities and towns. Each location has a loudspeaker and four microphones to permit group interaction. Instruction has been offered for fifty-five hours each week in thirty-four courses involving 50 faculty members and 600 students. Most classes last ninety minutes and involve 100 students at a time. The cost is fourteen cents per student for production and operation. Two important conditions of operation are dedicated telephone trunk lines and the use of good written materials.

Evaluation of the network courses has been quite positive, with 88 percent of the students saying they would take another course taught that way. University costs were much below those of other short-term courses or workshops.

One of the few case studies of the use of the telephone in Europe, at the University of Lund in Sweden, was provided by Flinck (1975), who describes the telephone as a motivational feedback device in an educational psychology course. Of particular interest is the discovery that, in 10 percent of the phone calls, more than half the content was personal counseling. Anandam and Fleckman (1978) also describe the telephone as a successful motivator of students in the United States.

Radio. The Open University, in England, has drawn some conclusions about the pedagogical value of radio. It can pace students through the instructional material of a course. In addition, it can provide feedback to students so that they have a sense of belonging. At the same time, corrections can be made in existing materials. Primary resource materials, such as performances, speeches, and discussions, can be brought directly to students. Radio can influence the public at large as well as students. Finally, radio can modify student attitudes by presenting material in a novel or dramatic way or from an unfamiliar viewpoint (MacKenzie, Postgate, & Scupham, 1975). A more recent trend in the provision of audio materials is to use cassettes until the student enrollment reaches over 500, at which time it becomes cost-effective to use broadcast radio.

Radio Sweden broadcasts more than 166 hours of instruction a year to over 12,000 participating schools. In Colombia, the success of Acción Cultural Popular (Action for Popular Culture)—an effort of the Catholic church with some government help—has stimulated the continuing development of rural radio for education throughout Latin America.

Subsidiary communications authority. In addition to FM radio's providing a high-quality, static-free signal, U.S. radio stations, with the permission of the Federal Communications Commission, may broadcast programs for a general audience while simultaneously using a subchannel to deliver a subsidiary communications authority (SCA) program to a limited audience. In order to receive the subchannel, a radio with a special decoder is needed; it costs about $55 and is less movable than regular receivers. Since SCA signals must be transmitted at lower power, the reception is possible for a limited area only. Because capital costs for station equipment range from $10,000 to $100,000, only about fifty noncommercial stations employ SCA (Carnegie Commission on the Future of Public Broadcasting, 1979).

SCA was first used in the United States in 1961 by the University of Wisconsin to transmit postgraduate medical programs over the state's FM radio network. SCA has enabled Ohio University to offer special programs to bus-riding high school students. Special-reading services for the visually impaired learner exist in about twenty-five U.S. cities, with Oklahoma City having an impressive volunteer-staffed effort.

Video Media. Distance learning makes widespread use of video media.

Television: broadcast and cable. Of the almost 3,000 U.S. colleges and universities participating in the Higher Education Utilization Survey conducted by the Corporation for Public Broadcasting, 94 percent responded (Dirr & Pedone, 1980). Of the responding institutions, 71 percent reported using television for instructional and/or non-instructional purposes during 1978/79. Twenty-five percent (735) of the colleges and universities reported offering 6,884 courses over television to half a million students. Although 44 percent of these courses were viewed on-campus, 14 percent were viewed off-campus. Of the two-year colleges, about 50 percent of course use was off-campus. Almost one-quarter of the institutions using television for instruction worked with public television stations, while only 9 percent worked with cable television systems and 7 percent cooperated with commercial television broadcasters. In addition, almost 30 percent of the colleges and universities using television for instruction were members of consortia offering or producing courses (Dirr & Pedone, 1980).

The U.S. Public Broadcasting System (PBS) has recently begun to utilize television-based courses produced by colleges and universities on its network service beamed to adult learners.

Corey (1980) describes Japan as the success story among nations using instructional television, with two networks broadcasting forty to forty-five courses each week to about 950,000 viewers. He also describes impressive adult literacy efforts by Danmarks Radio, the British Broadcasting Corporation, Germany's Follow Me program, and Swedish broadcasters. In conjunction with experimental use of television in India, France, and Senegal, UNESCO has established teleclubs for discussion of educational and community issues.

Some cost comparisons of television-based distance courses have been collected by Schramm (1977). In 1971, Japan spent $308 per year per student in its NHK television-radio-correspondence adult high school compared to $540 per student for conventional schools. The Bavarian Telekolleg averaged $143 per student per year in 1972 versus $540 per student in conventional schools.

Chu and Schramm (1967) reviewed a total of 421 comparisons of instructional television with traditional instruction and found that students at all grade levels learn as well in almost every subject area. They also found that students favor television for instruction at younger ages.

The use of cable television for educational and community purposes was spurned in the United States by rulings of the Federal Communications Commission. In 1972, major market cable systems were required to maintain at least one channel each, for public, educational, governmental, and leased access. In addition, in 1976, any system with 3,500 subscribers (regardless of market size) was required to provide four public-access channels, if the demand for use was there and sufficient unused channels remained. As a result, many community groups were formed to utilize such public-access channels. Bender (1979) describes such groups in six U.S. cities.

About 25 percent of all television homes in the United States have cable television. There were about 4,000 cable companies in the United States in 1980. Since systems in major markets are required to have at least twenty channels, there is considerable opportunity yet for educational programming. The use of fiber optics promises to provide more channels and clearer screen images.

One exciting development is talk-back cable television, which allows subscribers to push response buttons that are recorded in a computer at the cable system's control center. It allows viewers to take course tests at home or to ask faculty members any questions they wish. Use of this option has begun to occur on the QUBE cable systems of Houston, Texas and Columbus, Ohio. Administrators of the largest distance-education institution in Canada, the University of Waterloo, are making plans to use the new Canadian interactive television systems, Telidon and Vista. It will be possible to provide students with rapid feedback solutions, as well as simulations with color and graphics (Knapper & Wills, 1980).

Instructional television fixed service. Instructional Television Fixed Service (ITFS) is a low-power, all-directional transmission system with a direct reception area of about twenty miles. The coverage area can be extended by signal repeaters and linked systems. It is narrow casting in the truest sense (Graff, 1980). Each ITFS licensee is allowed up to four channels that can be used independently to serve different audiences simultaneously. The special receiving equipment costs about $2,000 per site.

There is a provision for two-way audio communication (using FM frequencies), which permits students and faculty to ask questions of one another. Three typical uses of ITFS by higher education institutions include (1) a closed-circuit network for an institution with multiple locations; (2) a feed to the cable company, then to homes; and (3) a linkage of the college or university to businesses, industry, or medical institutions (Curtis, 1980). Baldwin (1975) provides a very comprehensive description of how ITFS systems have been used by urban universities to provide continuing-education courses in engineering. More distant distribution has been done by point-to-point microwave transmission or videotapes brought to industrial and government locations by a commercial delivery service.

Videocassettes and videodiscs. Since television does not stop to answer questions or adjust to individual differences, substantial use of videocassettes has emerged. Because videocassettes are relatively inexpensive, easy to use, and generally compatible with many different players, they have been put into use by many companies (e.g., Xerox, Burrows, Coca-Cola, IBM, and the Ford Motor Company) for employee training and marketing (Norwood, 1976). The use of videocassettes by professional associations is also extensive and growing. For example, there are 60,000 attorneys in California using cassettes explaining new legal developments and prepared by a self-supporting unit of the state bar association.

In 1978, the Corporation for Public Broadcasting assigned the Nebraska Educational Telecommunications Network to investigate uses of videodisc technology in instructional and public television programs. Each videodisc looks like a photograph record. A thirty-minute side contains 54,000 image frames. The videodisc player is attached to the antenna terminals of a television set and the set's tuner is dialed to an unused channel. A low-power laser beam scans the microtracks of the disc and changes the recorded signals into a television picture.

Graff (1980) observed that it is far cheaper to produce videodiscs in mass quantities than to produce videotapes. Much less storage space is required for the discs. Furthermore the variable speed control and frame-by-frame access capabilities permit greater options for presentation of materials. However, in contrast to videotape recorders, the videodisc equipment cannot collect programs from the broadcast signal available at the home television set.

Satellites. There are three functionally different kinds of satellite television systems. First, a point-to-point system has a relatively low-power transmitter that broadcasts over a large area. Since its signals are very weak when they reach the ground, it requires an antenna about eighty-five feet in diameter and expensive ($3 million) amplification equipment. The second system, a distributing one, uses more transmitting power and concentrates on a limited geographic area. This development permits the antenna size to be cut in half and the receiving equipment to be much less costly ($400,000). The third system, a broadcast one, uses very large transmitting power to permit the use of an antenna only ten feet in diameter.

Polcyn (1979) provided a comprehensive history of the development of communications satellites for educational training in the United States. A case study of one particular effort is useful. The Appalachian Education Satellite Program was created in 1973 by the joint efforts of a regional planning commission and local public educators in eight states. In the first few years, about 1,200 teachers received graduate credit from thirteen institutions. Since the satellite system was shown to have costs of delivery comparable to campus-based courses, with equivalent cognitive and affective outcomes, the network was expanded to include sites in twenty-three states, with academic credit now available at fifty-two colleges (Gross, 1979). Cable systems are also subscribers.

Computers. The two major classifications of computer applications for distance learning are "computer-assisted instruction" (CAI) and "computer-managed instruction" (CMI). In situations falling under the first classification, the student is interacting with a computer directly. In CMI situations, the student does not have direct interplay with a computer.

One of the more noteworthy systems of CAI is PLATO (Programmed Logic for Automatic Teaching), which had its early development at the University of Illinois. Its greatest assets include (1) remarkable graphic capabilities; (2) access to the calculating speed and power of a large computer; (3) student terminals that respond to the location of a touching finger; with random access sound segments; and video images; and (4) terminals that can operate anywhere with a long-distance telephone connection. The last characteristic is true of only certain CAI systems. In practice, the costs of long-distance telephone connections can be quite high. The highly versatile PLATO terminal is also expensive. What is beginning to happen in the United States is the establishment of regional networks of hardware and software to reduce the cost of connecting with such resources.

Many writers claim that CAI can help tailor instruction to individual student needs (Cross, 1976; Kelly & Anandam, 1979). Toward this end, Cooley and Glaser (1969) saw these functions for CMI: (1) to present alternative goals that students select to determine their learning paths; (2) to conduct continuous monitoring and assessment to gather information, such as how much practice a student requires, how well information is retained, and what methods of study are selected and work well; (3) to utilize previous performance data to prescribe specific methods of study or scope of testing; and (4) to provide the instructor with group and individual statistics to help in the revision of course materials.

Distance education programs, particularly, with their communications between faculty and students, have great power to motivate students to become capable, independent learners. Feedback to students about their performances has the greatest impact if it is prompt, clear, and carefully written to be motivating. The introduction, in 1970, at the Hermods Correspondence School in Sweden, of a CMI system known as CADE (Computer-assisted Distance Education) to provide feedback of that kind was prompted by two important observations. First, although students rated the assignments to be submitted as the most stimulating part of a correspondence course, they viewed the tutor's corrections and comments as the least stimulating part of the course. Second, a majority of students preferred receiving a simple answer key rather than instructor's corrections and comments (Bååth & Månsson, 1977). Students displayed a very favorable attitude toward the new CMI system because it is believed they preferred (1) legible, computer-printed comments to handwritten ones; (2) the detailed comments that were given (300 words by the computer versus 20 to 50 by a faculty member; and (3) the fact that the computer never gets tired or angry as faculty members sometimes do.

Ehin (1973) provided an overview of computer-support systems for distance education programs, including places such as Quadriga-Funkkolleg (West Germany), Teleac (Holland), and Open University (England). A staff member of the Open University (Hooper, 1974) emphasized that without the computer, the mass teaching system would be virtually impossible. Other systems include CAMOL (Computer Assisted Management of Learning) at the University of Ulster (Northern Ireland); TIPS (Teaching Information Processing System), headquartered at Duke University in the United States, but used at about 1,000 institutions worldwide; and RSVP (Response System with Variable Prescriptions) at Miami-Dade Community College and about ten other institutions in North America.

In a meta-analysis of fifty-four studies comparing computer-based instruction (CBI) with conventional classes on examinations at the college level, Kulik, Kulik, and Cohen (1980) found fourteen statistically significant differences, thirteen of which favored the computerized application. In all eight of the studies that collected data on the amount of time spent in instruction, the computer produced a substantial savings of time (about 25 percent). In summary, it is on the basis of saving time and allowing individualization that the computer will be used.

Organization and Administration

Distance education courses are available from institutions that were created to provide only that type of instruction or as another service of an existing campus-based college or university. Within existing institutions, distance courses can be offered through either continuing-education or special organizational units. Staff of extended-degree programs that are designed to be self-supporting found that administering the program through the campus continuing-education division was both efficient and effective (Medsker et al., 1975). In addition, staff in several case-study institutions warned that creating a new academic unit reduces both the interest and pressure on existing academic programs to be responsive to new clientele, curricular innovations, and delivery strategies. Thus, the goal of maximizing program flexibility to experiment is balanced against the need for engendering faculty participation and overall credibility.

Cooperation with Other Institutions. Cooperative arrangements have emerged among educational institutions to share instructional resources and smooth the transfer of students from one college to another. For example, students can be simultaneously enrolled in a two-year college, North Island, and a four-year university, Athabasca, in western Canada. Many legally recognized groups and con-

sortia operate in the United States to share the costs of televised instruction. Beaty (1979) discusses several governance, administrative, financial, and instructional aspects of such consortia.

Finances. McCabe (1979) noted that there are three major categories of cost in television-centered courses: (1) development or acquisition of instructional materials, (2) development of a basic delivery system and organization, and (3) delivery of the instructional services. These categories are valid for all distance education systems. The first two categories are fixed costs that must be spread out over many students.

There are substantial difficulties in making international cost-benefit comparisons of different distance education systems. To start with, what may be an expense under one system is not an expense in another, for example, the charge for radio or television broadcast time. Second, there are different costs, related to labor charges and materials acquisition, for the same service in different countries. Third, there can be large differences observed between actual expenditures and estimated costs. Furthermore, efforts on behalf of on-campus and distance learning students frequently overlap. In the same manner, benefits to nonenrolled individuals, some of whom may be enticed to enroll later, are seldom determined.

Bates (1980) noted that one way to minimize the difficulties of comparing costs is to compare different media within the same system, while stating clearly what affects particular costs. The size of expenditures for certain media differs dramatically when a distance education program is compared to a campus-based one. For example, the British Open University has spent 22 percent of its budget on production of radio and television programs, with an equal amount going to hire faculty and counselors (Perry, 1977). Most campus-based colleges would spend the 44 percent or more on instructional faculty.

The source of funds for noncampus colleges is similar to that for campus colleges. Very little accommodation has been made to the different operating conditions, the predominately part-time student enrollment, and the small, widely separated learning centers (Lombardi, 1977). Although extended-degree programs commonly have tuition and fees greater than those for campus courses, students save money by not having to miss work in order to drive to and from the campus and attend classes (Medsker et al., 1975). Another reason for lower costs is the use of part-time faculty or regular faculty on an overload basis.

Although Jamison and Klees (1973) found many cost-effective, multimedia-based open-learning projects, Klees (1975) found it disturbing to see many such systems concentrate on higher-cost video technologies, often to the exclusion of lower-cost audio and print technologies. He noted that simpler television productions could be done for one-twentieth the cost, that a costly high-quality production may not be easily revisable, and that more courses could be developed if the cost of each were not so great.

Because of the physical separation of teacher behaviors from learner responses in distance education, the instruction must be more carefully planned and executed than in the classroom. Frequently, this planning necessitates the use of an instructional design team of specialists. Accordingly, the materials development process takes more time and is more costly than that needed for the classroom. The added cost and time mean that revisions occur less often.

Student Services. Support services are almost as important to extended-degree programs as the curriculum and the delivery systems used (Medsker et al., 1975). One crucial service is the evaluation of students' previous life learning for course credits. The publications of the Council for the Advancement of Experiential Learning describe various approaches.

Certain factors make recruitment and counseling very important: some students lack confidence in their abilities as students; some adults are cautious about a degree program that is unconventional, and some adults are unaccustomed to reading, writing, and study skills. Common agents of recruitment are existing students or staff, faculty or counselors at another institution, an employer or employment agency, a friend or family member, and pamphlets.

From an analysis of state and local surveys of adult learning needs, Cross (1978) observed that from 20 to 50 percent of nonstudents indicated that job or home responsibilities were the greatest barrier to their attendance at college. When this fact is coupled with the lack of child care and transportation cited by nonstudents as barriers to enrollment, recruitment counselors must alert the public to the solutions that distance education programs can offer to these personal problems.

An excellent overview of the literature that describes different ways (mail, audiocassettes, telephone, and face-to-face meetings) of providing counseling services to distance learners was prepared by Thornton and Mitchell (1978). Attention was given to practices in Australia, the United Kingdom, and the United States. Variations of the use of the telephone included (1) students calling anytime, (2) written requests for faculty to return calls at specific times, (3) connecting groups of students with loudspeaker telephones, (4) conference calls from up to eight student homes at once, and (5) dial access to recorded information tapes. Also discussed were three methods of giving face-to-face counseling: campus counseling centers, regional centers, and itinerant counselors.

Arbeiter et al. (1978) describe the advantages and disadvantages of using paraprofessionals to provide telephone counseling to individuals trying to evaluate postsecondary learning opportunities. The most valuable types of counseling are judged to be self-exploration, goal setting, and career decision making. The similarity of the demographic characteristics of the counselors to the socioeconomic status of the students boosted their credibility.

Miami Dade Community College uses its computer-managed instruction system (RSVP) to provide academic-alert and encouragement letters to students who need improvement in performance and/or attendance. The computer makes it possible to track the importance of student characteristics, such as faculty- or self-advised, native English language–speaking or other, status of reading skills, and status of mathematics skills.

Two major aspects of course registration differ among distance education programs. Although many of the extended-degree programs examined by Medsker et al. (1975) that had used continuous registration processes decided to abandon that approach, some institutions do so with substantial computer support. The other varying aspect is the use of a provisional registration to permit students to sample courses.

Faculty and Students

Harris (1975) completed a survey of 569 faculty (tutors) from seven representatively sized correspondence institutions in England. He discovered that 99 percent of the faculty worked part-time, with 55 percent handling only one course. Three-fourths of the tutors were men, and one-tenth were retired from full-time work elsewhere. Although only 15 percent of the tutors were under age 30, 28 percent did not have previous teaching experience (although they did have considerable professional experience). Wide variation was noted in how often individual faculty members communicated with students. Although one-quarter of the faculty had written comments to from 40 to 200 students in an average two-week period, one-third of the faculty had written to fewer than five students during this time.

The overwhelming majority of instructors in U.S. non-campus colleges teach on a part-time basis. Typically, they are teachers from other educational institutions, recent university graduates, or nonteaching professionals (Lombardi, 1977). When the distance education unit is affiliated with a campus college, full-time faculty members from the institution are used in most cases to teach (deliver) distance courses. The employment of regular faculty provides increased capability to get approval from other faculty and to match instruction to college objectives.

Faculty Rewards and Roles. There are some disadvantages to using regular faculty. They have heavy workloads when teaching the distance education course as an overload. This condition may diminish the completion of some responsibilities and leave little time for professional development. Furthermore, their participation in distance education efforts does not always get adequate attention in promotion decisions. The type of generalist skills required of many tutors may prevent them from keeping up-to-date in specialty fields, thus reducing their attractiveness to other institutions when seeking subsequent, more traditional positions.

Medsker et al. (1975) found a variety of regular load and overload compensation patterns in their twelve extended-degree case-study institutions. Although regular load payments require negotiations with regular academic units about the proportion of time that will be devoted to distance education activities, regular loads do not entangle faculty in heavy work-load situations as do overload assignments. Faculty find overload payments attractive, although they are concerned about the detrimental aspects of overload. The distance education unit usually pays faculty at a lower rate as overload than regular load.

Fundamentally, the faculty member who is responsible for providing students media-based courses serves as a mentor who assists students in their independent learning. Such assistance might include (1) answering questions that arise in students' minds as they use the standard instructional materials of the course, (2) directing students to appropriate additional resources, (3) giving emotional support to students who want to continue or leave a particular course, (4) orchestrating group and individual meetings with students when needed, and (5) evaluating student achievements in structured and unstructured ways.

Because mass media–based courses are structured with reduced or minimal class meetings, instructional materials for these courses must be designed to be as self-contained as possible. In addition to utilizing formats for the materials that compel the student to make active responses to the concepts presented, the writer of the materials must anticipate what are likely to be commonly asked questions. As much as the tempo of the instruction permits, the answers to these common questions will be included. An excellent detailed discussion of development faculty roles can be found in Field (1979).

Student Characteristics and Attrition. Students in college-level distance education courses are considerably older than their campus counterparts, with a mean between 30 and 35 years of age. A majority of these students have taken some previous college courses. In general, the more education people have, the more likely they are to seek additional learning opportunities, regardless of delivery system. Although many open-learning systems were designed to serve previously underrepresented students, this change has occurred slowly. For example, only 10 percent of the students registered with the British Open University in its first year, 1971, came from blue-collar homes; just ten years later, almost one-half the students are from such homes. Schramm (1977) has observed that distance education courses for the working people of Europe attract a disproportionate number of men, but that the ratio is in favor of women in the United States.

Much of the existing research indicates that students do not complete distance education courses as often as they do classroom-based courses. Several researchers have observed how correspondence retention rates of 25 percent have increased to about 65 percent with the addition of a television component to the same course (Chamberlin & Icenogle, 1975; Lipson, 1977). Many students indicate that television lessons serve as a pacing mechanism (Brown, 1975). The criticality of a steady rate of progress

to a student's completion of a course has been demonstrated by DeGoede and Hoksbergen (1978).

A recent trend of retention research is to try to measure the extent to which students indicate they have met their own differing goals, rather than the singular goal of obtaining a degree. A longitudinal study of more than 32,000 students at thirty-two California community colleges over six semesters ending in 1976, showed 60 percent of the students leaving before their goals were completed, but more than one-third of them later reenrolling (Knoell, 1976).

Research and Evaluation

MacKenzie, Postgate, and Scupham (1975) noted that research and evaluation have greater importance in open learning than they have had in conventional education because (1) innovative proposals require more documentation; (2) distance learning systems involve such costs of advanced production and distribution that they are not easily modified and must be used for a considerable number of years; (3) authors do not come in close contact with students using the materials, making it hard to know when revisions are needed; and (4) visibility to the public as well as to students within some delivery modes reinforces the need for careful planning and analysis.

One of the few centers doing extensive research on aspects of distance education is the German Institute for Distance Studies at the University of Tübingen in the Federal Republic of Germany. Its research focuses upon the economics, planning, and impact of various delivery systems. In addition, it evaluates individual courses, produces a radio college series, and sponsors self-study projects. It publishes in German two series of research papers and annual reports.

In analyzing more than thirty major state and national assessments of the needs and interests of adult learners in continuing education, Cross (1978) reported extensive replications of methodology and findings similar to the seminal work of Johnstone and Rivera (1965) and Carp, Peterson, and Roelfs (1974).

Gooler (1979) has proposed a number of criteria for determining the success of an open learning program. The access criterion indicates how many and what kinds of people are served. A second criterion judges the relevance of the program to the needs and expectations of the community. The quality of learner outcomes and program offerings, as well as their cost-effectiveness, are additional criteria. Influences upon institutional goals, policies, and practices are known as institutional impact. There may be consequences for other kinds of institutions and society in general. An example of this last criterion would be the generation of new knowledge. A variety of evaluation efforts have employed criteria similar to these.

One noteworthy, comprehensive approach to determining the costs and benefits of nontraditional and traditional programs of colleges and universities is PERC (Program Effectiveness and Related Costs) (Palola, Sunshine, & Lehmann, 1977). It was originally developed at Empire State College in New York State, but it has been used by a variety of institutions in the past few years.

McIntyre and Wales (1976) compared the effectiveness and costs of the noncampus Whatcom Community College in Washington State with three similarly sized campus-based colleges. They found that Whatcom (1) seemed to perform as well in most operational areas, (2) performed no better in assessing and meeting the needs of target groups, and (3) spent 10 percent less money per student and 6 percent less per course.

Kiesling (1979) did an estimated cost comparison of the University of Mid-America (UMA) and a sample of thirty-seven traditional colleges and universities in Indiana, projecting that UMA would be cost-competitive with higher enrollments. Unfortunately, almost all published cost comparisons are based on estimated costs. The fact that the distance institution studied by Kiesling never did obtain those greater enrollments is a significant commentary on the use of estimated costs.

Summary

This review of distance education on the international level has shown the magnitude, diversity, and impact of the phenomenon. Despite a recent trend toward multiple-media use, the major way to provide distance education is still printed materials. Distance education is successful at all educational levels in many content areas in economically diverse countries.

It is only under conditions of high enrollment that the use of technology in courses, especially broadcast media, becomes more cost-effective in comparison to classroom-based achievement by students. Furthermore, in many cases, broadcast radio or audiocassettes can be substituted for broadcast television, which is about five times more expensive.

Distance education will become even more important than it is now, because a higher value will be placed on time saved by students away from work and on budgets spared the cost of transportation fuels.

Charles E. Feasley

See also Adult Education; Computer-Based Education; Experiential Education; Independent Study; Media Use in Education; New Technologies in Education; Nontraditional Higher Education Programs.

REFERENCES

Anandam, K., & Fleckman, B. Telephone dialogue intervention in open learning instruction. *Journal of College Student Personnel*, 1978, *18*, 219–227.

Arbeiter, S.; Aslanian, C.; Schmerbeck, F. A.; & Brickell, H. *Telephone Counseling for Home-based Adults.* Princeton, N.J.: College Entrance Examination Board, 1978. (ERIC Document Reproduction Service No. ED 162 089)

Bååth, J. A., & Månsson, N. *CADE—A System for Computer-assisted Distance Education.* Malmo, Sweden: Hermods Skola, 1977.

Baldwin, L. N. Videotape applications in engineering education. In S. A. Harrison & L. M. Stolurow (Eds.), *Improving Instructional Productivity in Higher Education.* Englewood Cliffs, N.J.: Educational Technology Publications, 1975.

Bates, T. Educational technology and its cost with special reference to distance education. *Higher Education in Europe*, July–September 1980, *5*(3), 25–30.

Beaty, S. V. Forming college television consortia. In R. Yarrington (Ed.), *Using Mass Media for Learning.* Washington, D.C.: American Association of Community and Junior Colleges, 1979. (ERIC Document Reproduction Service No. ED 165 856)

Bender, E. T. *Cable TV: Guide to Public Access.* South Bend: Indiana University, 1979. (ERIC Document Reproduction Service No. ED 194 051)

Brown, L. A. *Learner Response to the Use of Television in UMA Courses.* Lincoln, Nebr.: University of Mid-America, 1975.

Carnegie Commission on Higher Education. *The Fourth Revolution: Instructional Technology in Higher Education.* New York: McGraw-Hill, 1972. (ERIC Document Reproduction Service No. ED 061 994)

Carnegie Commission on the Future of Public Broadcasting. *A Public Trust: The Report of the Carnegie Commission on the Future of Public Broadcasting.* New York: Bantam, 1979.

Carp, A.; Peterson, R. E.; & Roelfs, P. J. Adult learning interests and experiences. In K. P. Cross, J. Valley, & Associates (Eds.), *Planning Nontraditional Programs.* San Francisco: Jossey-Bass, 1974.

Chamberlin, M. N., & Icenogle, D. *Courses from Television: Potential for International Education.* Paper prepared for the Wingspread Conference on the Media and World Understanding, November 1975.

Chu, G. C., & Schramm, W. *Learning from Television: What the Research Says.* Stanford, Calif.: Stanford University, Institute for Communications Research, 1967. (ERIC Document Reproduction Service No. ED 014 900)

Colburn, G. A. Courses by newspaper. *Alternative Higher Education*, 1978, *3*(2), 128–129.

Cooley, W. W., & Glaser, R. *An Information and Management System for Individually Prescribed Instruction.* Pittsburgh: University of Pittsburgh, Learning Research-Development Center, 1969. (ERIC Document Reproduction Service No. ED 026 862)

Corey, G. H. Television experiences of other nations. In M. N. Chamberlin (Ed.), *Providing Continuing Education by Media and Technology.* San Francisco: Jossey-Bass, 1980.

Cross, K. P. *Accent on Learning.* San Francisco: Jossey-Bass, 1976.

Cross, K. P. *The Missing Link: Connecting Adult Learners to Learning Resources.* New York: College Entrance Examination Board, 1978. (ERIC Document Reproduction Service No. ED 163 177)

Curtis, J. A. Instructional television fixed service: A most valuable educational resource. In J. A. Curtis & J. M. Biedenbach (Eds.), *Educational Telecommunications Delivery Systems.* Washington, D.C.: American Society for Engineering Education, 1979. (ERIC Document Reproduction Service No. ED 187 341)

DeGoede, M. P., & Hoksbergen, R. A. Part-time education at tertiary level in the Netherlands. *Higher Education*, 1978, *7*, 443–455.

Dirr, P., & Pedone, R. *Higher Education Utilization Study.* Washington, D.C.: Corporation for Public Broadcasting, 1980.

Ehin, C. Suggested computer applications in correspondence education. *Educational Technology,* 1973, *13*(10), 60–63.

Erdos, R. The administration of correspondence education. In L. Edstrom, R. Erdos, & R. Prosser, *Mass Education.* New York: Africana Corporation, 1970

Field, H. H. Role of the faculty in mass media courses. In R. Yarrington (Ed.), *Using Mass Media for Learning.* Washington, D.C.: American Association for Community and Junior Colleges, 1979. (ERIC Document Reproduction Service No. ED 165 856)

Flinck, R. Two-way communication in distance education: An evaluation of various modes. In Erling Ljosa (Ed.), *The System of Distance Education.* Malmo, Sweden: Hermods Skola, 1975.

Gooler, D. D. Evaluating distance education programs. *Canadian Journal of University Continuing Education,* Summer 1979, *6*(1), 43–55.

Graff, S. M. Alternative delivery systems. In K. S. Munshi (Ed.), *Telecourse Reflections '80.* Washington, D.C.: Corporation for Public Broadcasting, 1980.

Gross, R. *Future Directions for Open Learning.* Washington, D.C.: National Institute of Education, 1979. (ERIC Document Reproduction Service No. ED 185 892)

Harris, W. J. The distance tutor in correspondence education. In E. Ljosa (Ed.), *The System of Distance Education.* Papers given to the tenth International Council for Correspondence Education International Conference at Brighton, England, May 1975. Malmo, Sweden: Hermods, 1975. (ERIC Document Reproduction Service No. ED 170 549)

Hooper, R. New media in the Open University: An international perspective. In J. Turnstall (Ed.), *The Open University Opens.* London: Routledge & Kegan Paul, 1974.

Jamison, D., & Klees, S. *The Cost of Instructional Radio and Television for Developing Countries.* Stanford, Calif.: Stanford University, Institute for Communication Research, 1973. (ERIC Document Reproduction Service No. ED 077 213)

Jamison, D.; Suppes, P.; & Wells, S. The effectiveness of alternative instructional media: A survey. *Review of Educational Research,* 1974, *44*(1), 1–67.

Johnston, J. M. (Ed.). *Behavioral Research and Technology in Higher Education.* Springfield, Ill.: Thomas, 1975.

Johnstone, J. W., & Rivera, R. J. *Volunteers for Learning.* Chicago: Aldine, 1965.

Kelly, J. T., & Anandam, K. Communicating with distant learners. In R. Yarrington (Ed.), *Using Mass Media for Learning.* Washington, D.C.: American Association for Community and Junior Colleges, 1979. (ERIC Document Reproduction Service No. ED 165 856)

Kiesling, H. Economic cost analysis in higher education: The University of Mid-America and traditional institutions compared. *Educational Communications and Technology Journal,* Spring 1979, *27,* 9–24.

Klees, S. J. Postsecondary open learning systems: Cost-effectiveness and benefit considerations. In C. E. Cavert (Ed.), *Designing Diversity '75.* Lincoln, Nebr.: University of Mid-America, 1975. (ERIC Document Reproduction Service No. ED 118 109)

Knapper, C., & Wills, B. L. Educational technology in Canada: Recent developments and future trends. *Higher Education in Europe,* July–August 1980, *5*(3), 10–14.

Knoell, D. *Through the Open Door: A Study of Patterns of Enrollment and Performance in California's Community Colleges.* Sacramento: California State Postsecondary Education Commission, 1976. (ERIC Reproduction Service No. ED 119 752)

Kulik, J. A.; Kulik, C. C.; & Cohen, P. A. Effectiveness of computer-based college teaching: A meta-analysis of findings. *Review of Educational Research,* 1980, *50*(4), 525–544.

Lipson, J. Technology and adult education: A report on the University of Mid-America experiment. *Technological Horizons in Education Journal,* September–October 1977, *4,* 36–38, 49, 50.

Lombardi, J. *Noncampus Colleges: New Governance Patterns for Outreach Programs.* Los Angeles: ERIC Clearinghouse for Junior Colleges, 1977. (ERIC Document Reproduction Service No. ED 136 880)

MacKenzie, N.; Postgate, R.: & Scupham, J. (Eds.). *Open Learning: Systems and Problems in Postsecondary Education.* Paris: UNESCO, 1975.

MacKenzie, O., & Christensen, E. L. (Eds.). *The Changing World of Correspondance Study.* State College: Pennsylvania State University Press, 1971.

Mathieson, D. E. *Correspondence Study: A Summary of the Research and Development Literature.* Syracuse, N.Y.: Syracuse University, 1971. (ERIC Document Reproduction Service No. Ed 047 163)

McCabe, R. H. The economics of television-centered courses. In R. Yarrington (Ed.), *Using Mass Media for Learning.* Washington, D.C.: American Association for Community and Junior Colleges, 1979. (ERIC Document Reproduction Service No. ED 165 856)

McIntyre, C., & Wales, C. A. *Evaluation of a Nontraditional College: Costs and Effectiveness.* Seattle: Washington Board for Community Colleges, 1976. (ERIC Document Reproduction Service No. ED 131 881)

Medsker, L.; Edelstein, S.; Kreplin, H.; Ruyle, J.; Shea, J. *Extending Opportunities for a College Degree: Practices, Problems and Potential.* Berkeley, Calif.: Center for Research and Development in Higher Education, 1975. (ERIC Document Reproduction Service No. ED 125 418)

Nash, A. N.; Muczyk, J. F.; & Vettori, F. L. The relative practical effectiveness of programmed instruction. *Personnel Psychology,* 1971, *24,* 397–418.

Norwood, F. W. Communication technology: Means for outreach. In C. E. Cavert (Ed.), *Conference Proceedings: Forum 76.* Lincoln, Nebr.: University of Mid-America, 1976.

Ohio State University Center for Vocational Education. *Employ Programmed Instruction* (Module C-28 of Professional Teacher Education Series). Athens, Ga.: American Association for Vocational Instructional Materials, 1977.

Palola, E. G.; Sunshine, M.; & Lehmann, T. *The Methodology of PERC (Program Effectiveness and Related Costs).* Saratoga Springs, N.Y.: Empire State College, 1977. (ERIC Document Reproduction Service No. ED 175 517)

Parker, L. A. *The Status of the Telephone in Education.* Madison: University of Wisconsin Extension, 1976.

Perry, W. *The Open University.* San Francisco: Jossey-Bass, 1977.

Polcyn, K. A. Communications satellites for education and training: Past, present and future. In J. A. Curtis & J. M. Biedenbach (Eds.), *Educational Telecommunications Delivery Systems.* Washington, D.C.: American Society for Engineering Education, 1979. (ERIC Document Reproduction Service No. ED 187 341)

Robin, A. L. Behavioral instruction in the college classroom. *Review of Educational Research,* 1976, *46*(3), 313–354.

Schramm, W. *Big Media, Little Media.* Beverly Hills, Calif.: Sage, 1977.

Thornton, R., & Mitchell, I. *Counseling the Distance Learner: A Survey of Trends and Literature.* Adelaide, South Australia: Adelaide University, 1978. (ERIC Document Reproduction Service No. ED 177 296)

DRAMATIC ARTS EDUCATION

Drama in schools generally divides into two major categories: formal theater and creative drama. This article distinguishes between these two types and then summarizes and comments on the scholarship about creative drama. This scholarship is grouped into foundational or theoretical writing and research reports. In particular, this article reports research about the effects of creative drama on the psychological growth, language and reading skills, and creativity of students. Some weaknesses in the available research are also identified.

Drama in education dates from the fifth-century B.C. in Athens. Heffner's exhaustive summary extends through the twentieth century, providing a helpful introduction to drama's place in education (Heffner, 1969). He focuses on formal theater, that is, scripted plays, rehearsed with a cast and staged with lighting and costumes. Elementary school children are occasionally involved in play production. Most high schools and colleges provide electives in drama appreciation or performance (Peluso, 1970). Much has been written about technical aspects of play production (Ommanney, 1972).

Creative Drama. Unlike formal theater, creative drama is a classroom-based, nonscripted participation experience in which children use their bodies and voices to interpret a story or to develop their own scenes (McCaslin, 1980). A discussion of theories of human development and education underlying this subject is presented by Geraldine Siks (1958), a founder of the movement. Leaders are developing exciting new approaches to informal drama extending beyond simple story creation (Wagner, 1976).

Attendance at creative drama conferences indicates continuing interest in it. Periodical articles and books extol the virtues of drama for children. Despite this interest, few children experience a planned sequence of drama sessions that move from simple to complex, from movement and pantomime through story dramatization to more involved improvisation and scene creation.

The availability of creative drama education is surveyed by Siks (1965), who determines that it was first established in the 1920s, when Winifred Ward (1930), a drama specialist, began experimenting with informal drama for all children. Before this program began, dramatics training was limited to formal theater for a talented few. Siks also reports on college courses offered, but no survey data on elementary programs are provided. She concludes that creative drama remains peripheral rather than a central subject of study.

Indeed, although many teachers are interested, few regularly use drama with children. Littig (1975) surveyed 346 classroom teachers; 75 percent reported they favored creative drama, although less than 25 percent actually used it. A subject that articulate spokespeople have been advocating for fifty years should certainly have a secure place in elementary curricula.

The available literature about dramatics training is enthusiastic, but diffuse with respect to theory. Most attention has been given to describing specific techniques that have worked in a particular situation, one that students and teachers enjoyed. Attempts to provide theoretical or developmental frameworks for these techniques are minimal. Empirical research to determine effects on children is also minimal. Burton (1973) found virtually no substantive research. Massey and Koziol (1978) summarized research that provides a "wobbly" foundation for further work. In our accountability-conscious era, advocates of a subject without these two justifications (a developed theory of drama education and research on positive effects on children) find it difficult to establish a place in a crowded curriculum. Those interested in drama have little ammunition with which to defend it (Stewig, 1974).

Siks (1965) attempted to assemble such ammunition by surveying the dramatic education literature for studies assessing program effects. Of the 1,100 bibliographical items, fewer than 5 percent represent structured research. The review shows that few studies demonstrate that children are different after drama. Two general weaknesses are apparent: (1) rationales for drama, theoretical or philosophic examinations of its nature, or descriptions of the structure of the discipline are missing, and (2) research reports fail to identify benefits accruing from drama.

Foundational or Theoretical Writing. Theoretical writing, including rationales for drama and descriptions of its structure, is limited and is often unrelated to the structured research being conducted. McGregor (1973) presented a well-developed rationale advocating drama education because it encourages cognitive growth in four areas: synpractic language, differentiation, categorization, and constructive alternativism. She describes these, giving examples, but no research data are provided. Research is needed to determine if growth does occur.

Stewig's justification for drama in the curriculum is based on the types of language growth that may occur, including vocabulary, paralanguage, kinesics, and spontaneous oral composition (Stewig, 1972). As in McGregor's article (1973), no data are reported to indicate whether language growth actually occurs.

Some authors have identified specific behavioral objectives for drama. Shaw's meticulously conceived taxonomy goes far beyond scattered descriptions of techniques and activities available previously (Shaw, 1970). Clearly a milestone in writing about creative drama, her approach should be widely applied. Koziol (1973) analyzed the intellectual processes required of students during drama sessions. Although devoted to the high school, the analysis is equally applicable at the elementary level. Such behavioral objectives lead to a consideration of how children's behavior varies at different grade levels, within different instructional contexts. Such descriptions are not widely available.

Research on Effects. Although research on dramatic education is not theoretically cohesive, effects have been investigated in at least five areas; developmental changes in dramatic presentation, personality (psychosocial) change, expressive language skill, oral reading, and problem solving.

Changes in dramatic performance. Lazier (1971) investigated eight aspects of drama by videotaping performance at various age levels and recording specific behaviors. Lazier found changes in behaviors as children grow older. Students' improvisations become less fragmented, more specific, and less free. However, generalizations must be drawn carefully until the study is replicated with larger, more diverse populations.

Ayllon and Snyder's study (1969) is similarly limited: 6-year-olds and 7-year-olds responded individually to verbal prompts. The more prompts they received, the more responses they gave. Then, groups watched the responses of models who had either high or low scores on the first experiment. When children responded to a high-score model, they did well; when they responded to a low-score model, they did less well. Unrealistic conditions limit the study's usefulness, as in most drama classes children do not work alone, and are not encouraged to watch what others do.

To validate an earlier test, Hogya (1974) administered it five years later to part of the same sample. Students' responses were videotaped and analyzed. Hogya concluded that the test discriminated between differing abilities in drama and served as a valid predictor of achievement.

Personality growth. Ward (1930), a founder of creative drama, justified its inclusion in curricula because it encouraged personality growth, yet few studies document this view. Those that are available have been summarized (Stewig, 1976). Only studies published since 1976 are described fully here.

Prokes (1971) found significant growth in self-concept among gifted junior high students after two semesters of drama. Wright (1972) reported significant increases in role-taking ability among 10-year-old and 11-year-old students. Elementary children had a more realistic picture of their own and desired personalities after participation in drama (Henry, 1967).

An interesting study (Noble, Egan, & McDowell, 1977) investigated drama's effect on the self-concept of twenty 7-year-olds from deprived urban areas. After only six hours, students were significantly better able to describe themselves verbally and nonverbally and were more aware of themselves.

More such studies are needed before stating with certainty that one justification for drama in the curriculum is the personality growth it fosters.

Language improvement. Several studies investigated drama's effect on speech problems. Woolf and Myers (1968) worked with first-graders and second-graders with auditory discrimination and articulation problems. The creative drama group showed significant improvement over the control group. McIntyre's preadolescent and adolescent speech-handicapped students showed significantly fewer consonant articulation errors after drama sessions (McIntyre, 1958). Attention has also been given to language growth in normal children. Blank's drama group, which met weekly for creative drama, showed significant improvement over the control group in vocabulary and voice quality (Blank, 1954).

Several researchers have assessed language growth. In Lewis's correlational research (1972), kindergartners who did well in unstructured dramatics also had superior syntactic maturity, fluency, and language organization. Neidermeyer (1972) matched an experimental group of seven kindergarten and seven first-grade classes with thirteen control-group classes. After twenty weeks of varied dramatics experiences, the experimental groups improved significantly in several areas. Schmidt (1974) found that role taking effected greater syntactic complexity in kindergarten-through-sixth-grade students. Saltz and Johnson (1974) used thematic-fantasy play with low-socioeconomic preschoolers. After four months, experimental students were significantly better at remembering stories, at seeing causal relations between pictures, and at making inferences. Total verbal output of the experimental students was significantly superior. Tucker (1971) examined drama's effect on kindergarten students' language, giving one group traditional readiness experiences and another drama sessions. Although there was no significant difference on word-meaning tests, the drama group scored significantly higher on listening skills.

Fourth-graders in an experimental group, after fifteen weeks of dramatics, more than doubled the verbal growth of the control group (Weisberg, 1972). Stewig and Young (1978) investigated the effects of twenty drama sessions on the language growth of middle-class fourth-graders, using pretests and posttests. Students increased output of total words, T-units, clauses, and number of different types of words. In a replication (Stewig & McKee, 1981), oral language again showed significant increases. Using similar measures, Dunn (1977) did not find significant oral growth in multiethnic second-grade and fifth-grade students. Her study suggests that creative drama worked better with Chicano than with black or white youngsters in improving oral language.

Growth in vocabulary, syntax, and accent was reported by Hendrickson and Gallegos (1972), who gathered language samples from Mexican-American students before and after thirty hours of creative drama. Posttreatment results in Pate's study (1977) showed no significant verbal growth by secondary school students studying introductory drama.

Reading improvement. Few studies of reading have focused on the effects of creative drama. Carlton and Moore (1966) studied the effect of an individualized reading approach incorporating creative drama on disadvantaged students in grades 1 through 4. After treatment, students in the experimental group attained significantly higher reading scores. In another study using disadvantaged subjects (Davis, 1968), fourth-graders and fifth-graders in a reading program incorporating creative drama scored significantly higher than control-group students.

A more recent study (Henderson & Shanker, 1978) investigated the reading comprehension of black, low-socioeconomic second-graders representing three different reading levels. Two of three groups received basal reading instruction with workbooks, while one group received basal reading instruction with drama. Then groups were reversed. Teacher-made comprehension tests following each lesson indicated gains significantly greater when students participated in the drama groups.

Drama's influence on reading is not well documented. Although several researchers found positive results, Amato, Emans, and Ziegler (1973), reporting a study of 298 students, found no significant effect on reading achievement. Vogel (1975) did not find creative drama made significant differences in reading scores of second-grade and third-grade learning-disabled children.

Creativity and problem solving.   After a series of creative drama sessions, kindergartners made significant gains on a creativity test (Hensel, 1973). Following drama experiences, Hartshorn and Brantley's second-graders and third-graders responded significantly better to problem-solving questions from two standardized intelligence tests (Hartshorn & Brantley, 1973). Karioth (1970) studied fourth-graders who experienced creative drama for seven weeks, but a confusing research design led to equivocal results. Allen (1968) provided creative drama experiences for fifth-grade remedial readers and reported significant growth in creativity following the sessions.

Ridel (1975) worked with older students, administering pretests and posttests of attitudes toward English and drama and verbal forms of a creativity test. On the latter, experimental students showed differences significant at the 0.01 level.

Two researchers found no differences following drama lessons. Pisaneschi (1977) studied first-grade through third-grade remedial readers ($N = 28$) and attributed lack of difference on a creativity test to short-term intervention. Youngers (1978), using one of the largest samples reported (eleven intact, fourth-grade classrooms), provided an extensive treatment spread over seven months. Despite these design strengths, posttreatment results on a creativity test showed no significant effects.

Research Problems.   Much creative drama research is flawed. Several problems are evident. First, sample size is a continuing problem. It is difficult to advocate drama in the curriculum on the basis of such studies as Hedahl's study (1980). Although six classes were involved, final data were reported for only ten students. Second, duration of treatment is a recurring problem. Because most studies are research for dissertations, treatment time is unfortunately brief. Bellman (1974) reported results after only

seven lessons. Surely significant changes cannot be expected so quickly. Third, design flaws are recurrent. Johnson (1978) compared the effectiveness of three treatments, but used varying numbers of sessions for each group, raising serious questions about the results. Fourth, test instruments continue to provide problems. Faires (1976) reports creative drama had no significant language impact in preschoolers, but the test used has been widely criticized. Lastly, data-gathering conditions raise questions about the validity of some research. Ayllon and Snyder's study conditions are so artificial that teachers would not choose to replicate them even if they could (Ayllon & Snyder, 1969).

Conclusions.   Many teachers are interested in drama. How many actually use dramatics with children is unclear. Teachers must justify drama to those who determine the curriculum, yet they get limited help from writers and researchers in doing this. Clear, incisive reasoning and sequentially developed behavioral objectives are only now beginning to be available. Empirical research is limited almost exclusively to short-term doctoral dissertations. Replications or long-term studies are virtually nonexistent. More needs to be done before we can respond with authority to the question "What do we really know about creative drama?"

John Stewig

See also Aesthetic Education; Creativity; Speech Communication.

REFERENCES

Allen, E. G. *An Investigation of Change in Reading Achievement, Self-concept, and Creativity of Disadvantaged Elementary School Children Experiencing Three Methods of Training.* Unpublished doctoral dissertation, University of Southern Mississippi, 1968.

Amato, A.; Emans, R.; & Ziegler, E. The effectiveness of creative dramatics and storytelling in a library setting. *Journal of Educational Research*, 1973, *67*, 161–162.

Ayllon, M., & Snyder, S. Behavioral objectives in creative dramatics. *Journal of Educational Research*, 1969, *62*, 355–359.

Bellman, W. M. The effects of creative dramatic activities on personality as shown in student self-concept (Doctoral dissertation, University of South Dakota, 1974). *Dissertation Abstracts International*, 1975, *35*, 5668A. (University Microfilms No. 75-5287)

Blank, W. E. The effectiveness of creative dramatics in developing voice, vocabulary, and personality. *Speech Monographs*, 1954, *11*, 190.

Burton, D. Research in the teaching of English: The troubled dream. *Research in the Teaching of English*, 1973, *7*, 160–189.

Carlton, L., & Moore, R. H. The effects of self-directive dramatization on reading achievement and self-concept of culturally disadvantaged children. *Reading Teacher*, 1966, *20*(2), 125–130.

Davis, S. S. The Pied Piper way to reading. *High Points*, Winter 1968, 8–10.

Dunn, J. A. The effect of creative dramatics on the oral language abilities and self-esteem of blacks, Chicanos, and Anglos in the second and fifth grades (Doctoral dissertation, University of Colorado, 1977). *Dissertation Abstracts International,* 1978, *38,* 3907A. (University Microfilms No. 77-29,908)

Faires, T. M. The effect of creative dramatics on language development and treatment progress in a psychotherapeutic nursery (Doctoral dissertation, University of Houston, 1976). *Dissertation Abstracts International,* 1976, *37,* 1958-1959A. (University Microfilms No. 76-23,368)

Hartshorn, E., & Brantley, J. Effects of dramatic play on classroom problem-solving ability. *Journal of Educational Research,* 1973, *66*(6), 243–246.

Hedahl, G. O. The effects of creative drama and filmmaking on self-concept (Doctoral dissertation, University of Minnesota, 1980). *Dissertation Abstracts International,* 1980, *41,* 851A. (University Microfilms No. 8019533)

Heffner, H. C. Dramatic arts education. In R. Ebel (Ed.), *Encyclopedia of Educational Research* (4th ed.). New York: Macmillan, 1969.

Henderson, L. C., & Shanker, J. L. The use of interpretive dramatics versus basal reader workbooks for developing comprehension skills. *Reading World,* 1978, *17,* 239–243.

Hendrickson, R., & Gallegos, F. *Using Creative Dramatics to Improve the English Language Skills of Mexican-American Students.* Rohnert Park: California State College–Sonoma, 1972. (ERIC Document Reproduction Service No. ED 077 023)

Henry, M. W. *Creative Experiences in Oral Language.* Champaign, Ill.: National Council of Teachers of English, 1967.

Hensel, N. H. The development, implementation, and evaluation of a creative dramatics program (Doctoral dissertation, University of Georgia, 1973). *Dissertation Abstracts International,* 1974, *34,* 4562A. (University Microfilms No. 74-4816)

Hogya, G. W. Predicting achievement in creative drama (Doctoral dissertation, Northwestern University, 1974). *Dissertation Abstracts International,* 1974, *35,* 3932A. (University Microfilms No. 74-28,646)

Johnson, X. S. The effect of three classroom intervention strategies on the moral development of preadolescents: Moral dilemma discussion, creative dramatics, and creative dramatics moral dilemma discussion (Doctoral dissertation, Northwestern University, 1978). *Dissertation Abstracts International,* 1979, *39,* 4597A. (University Microfilms No. 7903291)

Karioth, J. Creative drama as an aid in developing creative thinking abilities. *Speech Teacher,* 1970, *19*(4), 301–309.

Klock, M. E. An annotated bibliography of works in English pertaining to the teaching of creative dramatics (Doctoral dissertation, University of Denver, 1971). *Dissertation Abstracts International,* 1972, *32,* 4759A. (University Microfilms No. 72-5045)

Koziol, S. Dramatization and educational objectives. *English Journal,* 1973, *62,* 1167–1170.

Lazier, G. A systematic analysis of developmental differences in dramatic improvisational behavior. *Speech Monographs,* 1971, *38,* 156–165.

Lewis, P. H. The relationship of sociodramatic play to various cognitive abilities in kindergarten children (Doctoral dissertation, Ohio State University, 1972). *Dissertation Abstracts International,* 1973, *33,* 6179A. (University Microfilms No. 73-11,525)

Littig, E. *Drama as an Important Classroom Tool: Project Overview.* Green Bay: Northeast Wisconsin In-School Television Project, August 1975.

Massey, J., & Koziol, S., Jr. Research on creative dramatics. *English Journal,* 1978, *67*(2), 92–95.

McCaslin, N. *Creative Drama in the Classroom.* New York: Longman, 1980.

McGregor, M. Cognitive development through creative dramatics. *Speech Teacher,* 1973, *22*(3), 220–225.

McIntyre, B. The effect of creative activities on the articulation of children with speech disorders. *Speech Monographs,* 1958, *25*(1), 42–48.

Neidermeyer, F. The development of young children's drama and public speaking skills. *Elementary School Journal,* 1972, *73*(2), 95–100.

Noble, G.; Egan, P.; & McDowell, S. Changing the self-concepts of seven-year-old deprived urban children by creative drama or videofeedback. *Social Behavior and Personality,* 1977, *5*(1), 55–64.

Ommanney, K. A.; & Schanker, H. H. *The Stage and the School.* St. Louis, Mo.: McGraw-Hill, Webster Division, 1972.

Pate, T. L. An investigation of the effects of creative drama upon reading ability, verbal growth, vocabulary development, and self-concept of secondary school students (Doctoral dissertation, East Texas State University, 1977). *Dissertation Abstracts International,* 1978, *38,* 6506A. (University Microfilms No. 7805471)

Peluso, J. L. *A Survey of the Status of Theatre in United States High Schools.* Washington, D.C.: U.S. Department of Health, Education, and Welfare, 1970. (ERIC Document Reproduction Service No. ED 053 117)

Pisaneschi, P. Creative dramatics experience and its relation to the creativity and self-concept of elementary school children (Doctoral dissertation, Temple University, 1977). *Dissertation Abstracts International,* 1977, *37,* 7648A. (University Microfilms No. 77-13,583)

Prokes, D. Exploring the relationship between participation in creative dramatics and development of the imaginative capacities of gifted junior high school students (Doctoral dissertation, New York University, 1971). *Dissertation Abstracts International,* 1971, *32,* 2555-2556A. (University Microfilms No. 71-28,561)

Ridel, S. J. An investigation of the effects of creative dramatics on ninth-grade students (Doctoral dissertation, Florida State University, 1975). *Dissertation Abstracts International,* 1975, *36,* 3551A. (University Microfilms No. 75-26,811)

Saltz, E., & Johnson, J. Training for thematic-fantasy play in culturally disadvantaged children. *Journal of Educational Psychology,* 1974, *66,* 623–630.

Schmidt, E. Syntactic and semantic structures used by children in response to six modes of story presentation (Doctoral dissertation, University of Washington, 1974). *Dissertation Abstracts International,* 1975, *35,* 4879A. (University Microfilms No. 75-4046)

Shaw, A. A taxonomic study of the nature and behavioral objectives of creative dramatics. *Educational Theatre Journal,* 1970, *22,* 361–372.

Siks, G. B. *Creative Dramatics: An Art for Children.* New York: Harper & Brothers, 1958.

Siks, G. B. An appraisal of creative dramatics. *Educational Theatre Journal,* 1965, *17,* 328–334.

Stewig, J. W. Creative drama and language growth. *Elementary School Journal,* 1972, *72*(4), 176–188.

Stewig, J. W. Bandwagons are for riding: Accountability and drama. *Elementary School Journal,* 1974, *74*(4), 192–195.

Stewig, J. W. What do we really know about creative drama? *Proceedings of the Second Annual Conference on the Language Arts,* 1976, *2,* 1–12. Buffalo: State University of New York.

Stewig, J. W., & McKee, J. A. Drama and language growth: A

replication study. *Children's Theatre Review*, 1981, *24*(4), 1–14.

Stewig, J. W., & Young, L. An exploration of the relation between creative drama and language growth. *Children's Theatre Review*, 1978, *27*(2), 10–12.

Tucker, J. K. The use of creative dramatics as an aid in developing reading readiness with kindergarten children (Doctoral dissertation, University of Wisconsin, 1971). *Dissertation Abstracts International*, 1971, *32*, 3471-3472A. (University Microfilms No. 71-25,508)

Vogel, M. R. The effect of a program of creative dramatics on young children with specific learning disabilities (Doctoral dissertation, Fordham University, 1975). *Dissertation Abstracts International*, 1975, *36*, 1441A. (University Microfilms No. 75-18,878)

Wagner, B. J. *Dorothy Heathcote: Drama as a Learning Medium.* Washington, D.C.: National Education Association, 1976.

Ward, Winifred. *Creative Dramatics*. New York: Appleton-Century, 1930.

Weisberg, N. Creative drama spurs verbal development. *Nation's Schools*, September 1972, *90*, 51–52.

Woolf, G., & Myers, M. J. The effect of two ear-training procedures. *Exceptional Children*, May 1968, *31*, 659–665.

Wright, M. E. The effects of creative drama on person perception (Doctoral dissertation, University of Minnesota, 1972). *Dissertation Abstracts International*, 1972, *33*, 1876A. (University Microfilms No. 72-27, 823)

Youngers, J. S. An investigation of the effects of experiences in creative dramatics on creative and semantic development in children (Doctoral dissertation, University of Iowa, 1978). *Dissertation Abstracts International*, 1978, *39*, 117-118A. (University Microfilms No. 7810405)

DRIVER EDUCATION

Driver education, a subject taught by secondary schools, consists of classroom and in-car phases. Offered to students as they approach or reach driving age, the course prepares students to function safely and efficiently as highway users and to act responsibly and actively in supporting efforts to improve the highway transportation system.

Historical Background. The development of driver education began in the late 1920s. Albert W. Whitney, a mathematician and philosopher with the insurance industry, promulgated the idea that school systems have responsibility for driver and safety education. A 1928 doctoral dissertation by Herbert J. Slack at Columbia University placed emphasis on the classroom phase of driver education.

In 1934, a complete driver education course, taught by Amos Neyhart at State College High School, Pennsylvania, received nationwide attention. The status of driver education was further enhanced by the establishment, in 1938, of the Institute of Public Safety at Penn State College and the Center for Safety Education at New York University and by the publication, in 1940, of the eighteenth edition of the yearbook *Safety Education* by the American Association of School Administrators. Then, in 1943, the National Commission on Safety Education was organized as a service unit of the National Education Association, and, in 1949, the First National Conference on Driver Education was held for the purpose of developing policies and recommendations.

Along with the rapid increase in schools offering driver education during the late 1940s and early 1950s, many other developments occurred. Instructional aids were developed, legislation was passed, state associations were formed, short courses offered by the American Automobile Association and the insurance industry were supplanted by college and university credit courses, and evaluative research was conducted.

The 1950s and 1960s saw an increased concern with highway safety. In 1956, Michigan State University's Highway Traffic Safety Center was established, and Michigan enacted a law requiring youths under 18 years of age to complete an approved driver education course as a prerequisite to driver licensing. In 1957, the American Driver and Traffic Safety Education Association was organized. And in 1966, the Highway Safety Act was enacted by the Eighty-ninth Congress. This act required each state to establish a comprehensive highway-safety program, which would include the opportunity for youth reaching driving age to enroll in a driver education course. Responsibility for administration of the act was assigned to the National Highway Safety Bureau.

Human Variability and Driver Behavior. Research and education need to consider two types of human variability related to operating a motor vehicle. First is the variation of performance by the same individual, and second is the difference in performance among individuals.

Variations within individual performance. The driving performance of an individual operating a motor vehicle at a specific moment may be placed at any point on a continuum. Safe driving is on one end, and unsafe driving is on the other. Internal and external forces determine the exact point of the performance. In addition to the perceptual-motor skills of the driver, these forces include the psychophysical condition of the driver, the relationships between the driver and passengers, and the highway environment.

Variations from person to person. Drivers vary markedly in their information about the driving task, in their perceptual-motor skills, and in their judgment when applying information and skills to various conditions. The basic personality of an individual has a significant influence on how knowledge and skills are applied to cope with roadway, traffic, and environmental conditions. If certain individuals generally resent authority and restrictions, lack respect for the rights and property of others, and display over-aggressiveness in interacting with others, they will not only demonstrate these traits when driving, but may intensify them in the depersonalized nature of the traffic scene. Driving behavior is simply one manifestation of human beings' overall behavior. In short, individuals tend to drive as they live.

Although there is a small segment of the driving population than can be classified as "collision repeaters," most traffic collisions involve drivers whose records are relatively free of accidents and violations. This fact can be explained partly by "temporary emotional stress": a death in the family, a loss of job, a divorce or other unpleasant event can contribute to a person having repeated accidents during the stress period.

The role of chance also seems to be involved. One can commit errors in routine driving with a low probability that the error will have a negative consequence. Such errors are reinforced by satisfying the need to get where one is going despite the error. Errors in performance fail to produce a collision only because other ingredients are not present. This pattern tends to build up a false sense of immunity.

With appropriate research results identifying the psychological and sociological factors that produce variations in driver behavior, driver education can help students (1) understand the factors that shape driving behavior, (2) analyze personal strengths and limitations in regard to such factors, and (3) implement self-improvement processes. Driver education cannot change a student's style of life, but it can influence a student's style of driving.

Sponsored Research and Developmental Activities. Research in the area of driver education increased sharply following enactment of the Highway Safety Act of 1966 and establishment of the National Highway Traffic Safety Administration (NHTSA).

NHTSA research and development. In 1967, the NHTSA launched a long-term, systematic research and development program in driver education. Initially, four contracting organizations with identical contract specifications developed plans for evaluating driver-education programs. Following completion of the four studies, a fifth contract was let for the purposes of synthesizing the four initial reports and recommending specific plans for evaluating and improving driver education. The National Academy of Sciences was selected as the contracting agency for this study, and it arranged a subcontract with the Educational Testing Service in Princeton, New Jersey. The final report (Harmon et al., 1969) stressed the need for a detailed driving task analysis to serve as the basis for identifying desirable driving performance and providing guidelines for developing instructional objectives, course content, and measures of driving performance. Following the recommendation of the fifth study, the NHTSA charged the Human Resources Research Organization (HumRRO) with contractual responsibility for conducting a driving task analysis (McKnight & Adams, 1970). A later contract with HumRRO produced curriculum-related performance objectives based on the driving task analysis (McKnight & Hundt, 1971).

Numerous NHTSA-sponsored research and development projects followed during the next six years, culminating in the Safe Performance Curriculum (SPC) Demonstration Project (Weaver, 1977) in DeKalb County, Georgia. Beginning in 1977, the SPC has been evaluated in an operational setting to determine its crash-reduction potential compared to an abbreviated course and also to a group without driver education. A total of 18,000 students, who volunteered for driver education, were randomly assigned to one of the three groups. A complete project report is scheduled to be available during 1982.

Another major research project by the NHTSA was initiated in 1979 (Pabon et al., 1980). The report, which will serve as a guide for NHTSA research activities in the 1980s, stresses the need for more innovative, noninformational approaches to the driver behavior problem. Emphasis is placed on research in such areas as young-driver risk acceptance, perception of hazards, safety-belt usage, drinking and driving, and identification of desirable teacher characteristics. Whereas research activities during the 1970s dealt largely with curriculum development and evaluation, research in the 1980s seems to be directed at more specific problems of a psychological-sociological nature.

Recent Trends. One of the most discernible and challenging themes emerging from the literature in driver education is the need to identify teaching methods that influence the beliefs, attitudes, and motivations of young people about the driving task. Although information and perceptual-motor skills are essential prerequisites to safe and efficient driving, they are not sufficient in themselves. If a person can drive safely, it does not necessarily follow that he or she will drive safely. Willingness to drive safely depends on control of emotions and attitudes.

Effective teachers of driver education go beyond imparting essential driving information and developing operational skill. Through group discussion, role playing, use of selected audiovisual aids, and other special techniques, these teachers are attempting to influence attitudes of students toward misuse of speed, drinking and driving, and traffic laws and enforcement procedures. Greatly increased attention is being given to (1) alcohol and drugs as they affect driving performance, (2) driver education for special students, (3) emergency driving situations—sudden braking, evasive turning, recovery from skids, (4) energy conservation, (5) motorcycle and moped safety education, and (6) parent-school cooperative arrangements.

Research Problems. Research has not produced conclusive evidence regarding the effectiveness of driver education as a traffic accident countermeasure. The difficulty lies in planning and implementing a research design that controls the variables that have an influence on collision causation.

To obtain control (lacking driver education) and experimental (having driver education) groups, presents a difficult problem. Although the need to deprive people of a potentially advantageous experience in order to create a control group is not confined to driver education, it is certainly prominent in this subject. Furthermore, many states have laws requiring that all youth under 18 receive driver education.

Another area of difficulty is the identification of realistic and meaningful criteria for determining the effectiveness of driver education. Much of the past evaluative research on driver education has been based on the assumption that the ultimate criteria are collision and violation records established by course graduates. From a theoretical viewpoint, this conclusion may be acceptable. However, researchers soon discover many deficiencies in the use of driving records. Besides the incompleteness and inaccuracies of the records, another problem plagues researchers: collisions and convictions for traffic-law violations are infrequent events for most drivers. Therefore, any study using these criteria must use extremely large numbers of subjects and follow driving records for a number of years.

For these and other reasons, many designers of evaluative research have sought to identify realistic intermediate criteria for determining the effectiveness of driver education. Perhaps the best effort in this regard is the Driver Performance Measurement developed at Michigan State University (Vanosdall et al., 1977). Despite the quality of this effort, skeptics point out that the test only reveals what drivers can do, not what they necessarily will do. To answer this criticism, it has been proposed that a driving-performance scale be developed that is based on observation of drivers who are not aware of being observed. At present, the necessary expenditure of time and operational funds makes this approach impractical.

Driver Education and Public Policy. Motor vehicle crashes produce a serious social and economic problem in the United States. Each year, more than 50,000 fatalities, millions of injuries, and economic loss in the billions result from traffic collisions. Only cancer exceeds auto accidents in producing financial losses such as medical bills and lost earnings. To emphasize the problem further, two out of three young people who die in the 15–24 age group die as a result of a motor vehicle crash. These facts support the premise that the traffic problem is a *public* matter.

To control and reduce the carnage of motor vehicle crashes require the cooperative effort of many public and private forces. Engineers, law enforcement officers, educators, and emergency medical-care teams are all involved in efforts to improve highways, vehicles, and drivers. Moreover, these forces need to be coordinated and managed by an efficient administrative system, and supported by the general public.

Although driver education is only one of the program components that influence the functioning of the highway transportation system, it can play a major role. A well-conceived and well-implemented course cannot only develop safe and efficient driving skills and habits, but can also produce enlightened citizens who will exercise their

civic responsibility with respect to the highway transportation system. Enrolled in driver-education classes are young people who will make future decisions regarding public policy on driver education and other components of a comprehensive highway safety program. Therefore, it is important that they experience a course of quality.

The effectiveness of driver-education programs is still undetermined, and the program is not without its critics. However, the rationale underlying the need for continuance of driver-education programs was best expressed some years ago by Daniel Patrick Moynihan (1968), then Secretary of the Department of Health, Education and Welfare:

Although there is no conclusive proof as to the comparative effectiveness of various driver education techniques or, for that matter, the whole of present driver education practice, there is even less proof of the efficacy and value of any alternatives to present practices for communicating to the young person the rudiments of how to handle a car in modern traffic, and the associated social responsibilities. But operational driver education programs must continue. The problem is no different in principle than that for education in general. We have to continue with present systems even while recognized needed improvements are being studied. One would hardly advocate a moratorium on all schooling while looking for proof of better methods. (p. 286)

Richard W. Bishop

REFERENCES

Harmon, H. H.; Seibel, D. W.; Rosenfeld, M.; & Schimberg, B. *Evaluation of Driver Education and Training Programs* (Subcontract No. HRB-48-69-4 for National Academy of Sciences). Princeton, N.J.: Educational Testing Service, 1969.

McKnight, A. J., & Adams, B. B. *Task Descriptions* (HumRRO Technical Report 70-103). Vol. 1 of *Driver Education Task Analysis.* Alexandria, Va.: Human Resources Research Organization, November 1970.

McKnight, A. J., & Hundt, A. G. *Instructional Objectives* (HumRRO Technical Report 71-9). Vol. 3 of *Driver Education Task Analysis.* Alexandria, Va.: Human Resources Research Organization, 1970. (ERIC Document Reproduction Service No. ED 072 249)

Moynihan, D. P. *Report of the Secretary's Committee on Traffic Safety.* Washington, D.C.: U.S. Department of Health, Education, and Welfare, February 1968.

Pabon, Sims, Smith, and Associates, Inc. *Development and Review of Driver Training Research Plan: Evaluation of Preliminary Research Plan, Project Task V* (Under contract DOT-HS-8-02064 for National Highway Traffic Safety Administration). Washington, D.C.: NHTSA, April 1980.

Vanosdall, F. E.; Allen, T. M.; Pawlowski, J. J.; Rohrer, J. M.; Nolan, R. O.; Smith, D. L.; Rudisill, M.; Specht, P.; Hockmuth, M.; Spool, M.; & Diffley, G. *Michigan Road Test Evaluation Study: Final Report, Phase III—Evaluation Study.* East Lansing: Michigan State University, Department of Psychology, and Highway Traffic Safety Center, 1977.

Weaver, J. K. Safe performance curriculum demonstration project. *Journal of Traffic Safety Education*, 1977, *25*, 29–30.

DROPOUTS

See Attendance Policy; Promotion Policy; Truants and Dropouts.

DRUG ABUSE EDUCATION

At the time of the fourth edition of the *Encyclopedia of Educational Research* (Ebel, 1969), the United States was entering an era of social change that had significant implications for drug education. The issues that were critical then were refocused as a result of the public reaction to an increase in consumption of drugs by young people (Johnston, Bachman, & O'Malley, 1979). In response to expressions of concern in their communities, the schools initiated new programs without addressing and defining goals that are appropriate for drug education activities and evaluation procedures that should be initiated to assess goal attainment. The lack of clear and/or appropriate goals for drug education and the paucity of evaluation procedures need to be discussed at the beginning of this article in order to set the stage for interpreting government activity, school models, and the limited evaluation literature that has become available. Consequently, this article begins with a discussion of goal development for drug education and the status of evaluation efforts, then examines the evolution of government and school programs, and concludes with descriptions of the major modes of drug education that have a data base in the evaluation literature.

Goals.   One of the major problems in the field of drug education is the lack of clearly defined goals, particularly in terms of their effect on an intended audience. Lewis (1969) commented that "I was struck by the large number of schools that have added drug education programs to their curricula without any clear notion of what they want to accomplish and consequently without any means of evaluating programs" (p. 87). Similarly, Braucht et al. (1973) noted that in spite of the almost universal state requirements for schools to include alcohol and drug education in the curriculum, most published curricula failed to articulate goals. Dorn and Thompson (1976) did an extensive analysis of data generated from a comprehensive evaluation. They concluded that goals of instructions were necessary for evaluation.

The absence of specified short-term instructional goals is further complicated by the assumption on the part of the public and professionals alike that the ultimate outcome of drug abuse education should be to prevent students from using drugs. For example, DeLone (1972) suggested that many drug education programs were inferior because they may have resulted in an increase in drug use among exposed students. Swisher and Hoffman (1974) posited that information was an irrelevant variable in drug education because increasing information did not appear to alter attitudes or use patterns. Stuart's results (1974) of increased use following a program contributed to a position that information about substances should be eliminated from the curriculum. Schaps et al. (1978) reviewed only those studies of drug education that included some measure of substance use as an outcome. Others have argued that an increase in less dangerous drugs with a concomitant decrease in dangerous drugs would be a positive outcome (Blum, Blum, & Garfield, 1976). It may be acceptable for some community agencies and groups serving youth (e.g., the YMCA) to define an acceptable pattern of consumption of drugs, but the schools should consider more carefully the complexities of such a stance.

One difficulty with clarifying goals for drug education programs has been the lack of a consistent definition for the term "abuse." One major flaw in the current federal and state legislation is the absence of a definition of this term (Swisher, 1977; however, all drugs are classified in part as a function of their potential for abuse. The logic appears circular; that is, any use of an illicit substance is considered abuse, but a substance is classified as illicit if it is used outside the law.

Another complicating factor has been the inconsistent laboratory findings with regard to the effects of some substances. For example, at one time it was believed that LSD caused chromosomal damage but subsequent research yielded equivocal results. Similarly, marijuana is classified legally as having a high potential for abuse and low medical use; yet several states (e.g., New Jersey) have recently approved the medical prescription of marijuana for glaucoma and as part of the chemotherapy to relieve the suffering of cancer victims. Alcohol by any criteria (e.g., extent of use or negative consequences), is clearly the major substance problem among youth and adults. The fact that it is so obviously harmful is an incongruity that many youth find perplexing.

These shifting positions regarding effects of various substances as well as the inconsistent behavior of adults further complicate the development of goals for drug education. It is unlikely that any health educator under present conditions would be allowed to recommend responsible individual choice with respect to illicit drug use as an alternative to abstinence. Conversely, drug educators will be criticized if they attack alcohol or tobacco as highly dangerous substances because some adults will adamantly defend their "drug of choice." Finally, health educators may lose credibility with their audience if attempts are made to defend certain drug laws (e.g., marijuana) on the basis of potential harm. The drug educator is confronted by a very difficult set of circumstances in which to accomplish any objective. There is an obvious need to determine appropriate goals for drug education and to articulate clearly those goals for students and the public.

FIGURE 1. *Availability of evaluation reports by year*

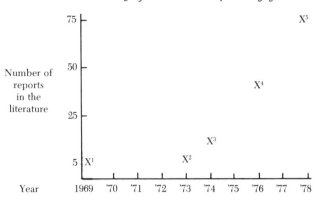

Sources of data: X[1] = Richards, 1969.
                   X[2] = Warner, 1973.
                   X[3] = Goodstadt, 1974.
                   X[4] = Berberian et al., 1976.
                   X[5] = Schaps et al., 1978.

Evaluation. Compared with other educational pursuits, drug education evaluation suffers from a lack of quality and quantity. Figure 1 charts the availability of reviews of drug education during the last twelve years by plotting the number of studies included in each review. The rate of productivity has increased; and if this rate were to continue, there could be a data base for future recommendations. However, the field at this point has had little data to direct its endeavors. The most comprehensive review by Schaps et al. (1978) revealed only seventy-five evaluation reports that were based upon studies of approximately 127 programs (several of the studies included more than one program). Of the seventy-five reports examined in this government-sponsored review, only twenty-three were in the professional literature, and another eleven were government reports. Forty-one of the studies were available only from the school or agency that conducted the original evaluation. Therefore, evaluators attempting to assess the state of the art through normal professional channels would have until recently been unable to find an adequate number of studies upon which to base their own work.

With regard to the quality of evaluations available from any source, Schaps et al. (1978) reported that only 31 percent of the reviewed studies included randomized control groups and another 9 percent had acceptable quasi-experimental designs. Sixty percent of the available literature would not qualify as acceptable by most standards of evaluation design.

In summary, health educators face a very tenuous situation. There is public and even professional pressure to do something to reduce drug consumption, but accomplishing such an objective requires surmounting numerous obstacles. This is particularly true for an educational setting in which it may be inappropriate to attempt to effect a behavioral outcome. Another major problem is the lack of research upon which to base the development of an educational plan. The remainder of this article examines the factors that have contributed to the present status of drug education; and it concludes with descriptions of the major approaches to drug education that are supported by data with respect to their efficacy.

Federal Policies and Programs. A critical incident for drug education in this country occurred in conjunction with the repeal of prohibition in 1933. At that time Harry Anslinger was responsible for implementation of the Eighteenth Amendment. Upon repeal of this amendment, Anslinger moved to the Bureau of Narcotics and Dangerous Drugs (BNDD) and continued to campaign against dependency on substances. His early writings revealed an antisubstance zeal that contributed to the growing public concern about the effects of drugs. According to Smith (1975), Anslinger argued that marijuana led users to commit violent, aggressive crimes, and that its users ultimately became insane. Although the validity of Anslinger's assertions regarding the effects of marijuana are questionable, one result of his campaign was an increased public concern for youth involvement with drugs. His approach also established the tenor of early drug education efforts, which mainly employed scare tactics.

In the late 1930s and early 1940s state departments of education following BNDD recommendations began to develop curriculum guidelines and regulations that required schools to include specific content about the "harmful" effects of substances, at least in health education classes. In the late 1960s drug use seemed to be becoming an even greater problem, and public concern this time resulted in the creation of the Special Action Office for Drug Abuse Prevention (SAODAP) as an advisory body to the president.

Except for BNDD efforts, the federal government was relatively uninvolved prior to 1970, but public concern for what appeared to be a growing problem (at least a growing awareness of an existing problem) resulted in two major developments. First, funds and direction were given to the U.S. Office of Education to develop an educational response to the problem. Second, the government created the National Institute on Drug Abuse and the National Institute on Alcohol Abuse and Alcoholism that also had responsibility for education and prevention activities. The offices with these responsibilities were recently disbanded, but the functions remain within the institutes.

For the most part, government agencies have judged programs to be successful to the extent that a program could demonstrate reduced use of drugs. For example, the grants program sponsored by the prevention branch of the National Institute on Drug Abuse clearly views reduced drug use as the primary indicator of success. Current evaluation grants are expected to include some measure of drug use as part of the study. Obviously, these government agencies have a clear mandate to influence drug use; however, some schools in their quest for funds have adopted the same objectives without careful deliberation.

The Office of Education's Alcohol and Drug Abuse Education Program (ADAEP) in 1970 initiated a national system of alcohol and drug education involving demonstration projects and teacher training activities (Pizza, 1980). These activities were a direct response to the Drug Abuse Education Act of 1970 and at the present time consist of four regional training centers that emphasize a community team approach to prevention and educational planning. In order to attend one of the center's programs, it is necessary to apply as a community team and to be prepared to engage in follow-up activities after the training center experience. The teams applying for training must demonstrate an awareness of the extent of the problem, have a representative membership, and some sense of direction. (The ADAEP system allows each team to develop its own objectives and correlated activities.) The future of the ADAEP system and its philosophy is presently in question, but it has made a major contribution by stimulating and supporting community and school-based program development.

The National Institute on Drug Abuse (1975) states that primary drug abuse prevention is a constructive process designed to promote personal and social growth of the individual toward full human potential; and thereby, inhibit or reduce physical, mental, emotional or social impairment which results in or from the abuse of chemical substances" (p. 16). In order to accomplish this basic goal, the prevention branch has identified four program service options.

1. *Information services* include media campaigns, clearinghouses, brochures, television documentaries, and other materials designed for dissemination to mass audiences.

2. *Alternative activities* encompass special projects or foster multiple activities as preferred by an individual. Specialized activities have included operating radio stations, restoring community buildings, or volunteering in special services.

3. *Intervention services* provide individual counseling for persons experiencing negative consequences from exposure to substances. These services are usually made available to clients who are considered to be high risk.

4. *Education services* are typically provided through schools, but are presently being expanded to include other settings and clients such as business and industry or the elderly. Education services are provided to groups and include information about substances (cognitive) as well as strategies for enhancing personal and/or social development (affective).

The preventions branch of the National Institute on Alcohol Abuse and Alcoholism (NIAAA) sponsored projects that were more systematically planned and included evaluation from the outset. Three types of projects were emphasized (not exclusively) by NIAAA, and these encompassed school curricula, college programs, and in-service education of teachers (Mong, 1980). The original projects were considered to be model demonstration projects and have subsequently entered a replication phase during which all replications are being individually evaluated; an approved project will conduct a comparative study. The three types of projects were

1. *School curriculum projects* that resulted in a comprehensive K–12 curriculum in King's County in the state of Washington. The curriculum included affective education techniques as well as sequential information regarding alcohol.

2. *In-service education programs* that were designed to help teachers of all subjects integrate alcohol education into their classrooms and to develop teaching types that facilitate affective development (e.g., better self-concepts among students).

3. *College programs* that were designed to intervene at an age and stage in which alcohol was a significant problem. The projects included an emphasis on facts about alcohol, personal understanding activities, and crises-intervention services.

Theoretical Perspectives. Another area that was an unintended victim of the crisis climate in which drug education programs were conceived concerned the theoretical foundation of curriculum development. Very little thought has been given to learning theory, personality theory, developmental theory, and other potentially useful considerations for guiding the development of drug education planning. Lettieri, Sayers, and Pearson (1980), along with the sponsorship of the National Institute on Drug Abuse, have attempted to compile the major theories that explain drug-using behavior. The four major sets of theories they described focused upon initiation of use, continuation of use, transition from use to abuse, cessation of use or abuse, and relapse into use or abuse. The theories can be grouped around intrapersonal, interpersonal, extrapersonal, and physiological dimensions. Although this study would serve as an excellent resource to guide future curriculum development, the vast majority of literature in the field of substance abuse education has not consistently been linked to a theoretical base. This article contains an *ex post facto* framing of the theoretical foundations of drug education, but it would not necessarily be accepted by practitioners and/or researchers in the field. Three major theoretical perspectives will be considered: the cognitive, affective, and behavioral.

Cognitive assumptions. One consistent finding in the sparse evaluation literature is that almost any form of drug education will significantly increase the information level of students. This literature has also consistently revealed that an increase in knowledge with respect to substances has not resulted in healthier attitudes toward personal use or changes in consumption patterns (Swisher & Hoffman, 1974). Consequently, health educators have begun to de-emphasize information about substances as part of the drug education curriculum. However, although such an action was well intended, from an educational perspective it is perhaps premature.

A base of factual information is crucial to making decisions regarding substance use for an individual. This position is not totally new (Ungerleider, 1968). For example, Besteman's committee (1977) advocated health information for families and schools as a foundation for prevention.

Several assumptions inherent in this point of view need to be made explicit. First, it is assumed that accurate facts are available and that those facts are conclusive. Glaser (1970), a psychiatrist with the Addictions Research Foundation, reviewed several sources of information about drugs and identified serious errors in the references critiqued. He concluded: "In this time of high drug consciousness, the importance of avoiding such errors in this field in relation to the general problem of closing the credibility gap between the generations must be stressed" (p. 607). One significant milestone in this field was an evaluation of drug education films (National Coordinating Council for Drug Education, 1973) funded by the Drug Abuse Council. This report revealed that one out of four films produced were scientifically inaccurate. As a direct result of these evaluations and other research, the American government declared a moratorium on funding the development of films and other materials (e.g., pamphlets) until 1980. It is important to recognize that accurate facts are difficult to obtain. Inaccurate statements must be avoided by health educators if they are to establish credibility with the information consumers.

Schaps et al. (1978) in a review of fifty-five outcome studies revealed that knowledge gains were the most likely outcome for any form of drug education program. Two-thirds of the programs that attempted knowledge gains were able to accomplish this objective. Stuart (1974) found that one particular program he evaluated resulted in higher levels of drug use among students exposed to the program in comparison to a control group of students who were not part of the program. The findings revealed a statistically significant increase in the use of alcohol, marijuana, and LSD, as well as an increase in the sale of marijuana. There is a need for research that examines types of information, levels of information, processes for dissemination (e.g., problem solving), and cognitive development with regard to formation of attitudes and, ultimately, decisions about use of substances. Most decision-making processes and behavior-change models include a cognitive component, and the schools could be considered negligent if they fail to provide a cognitive foundation for decision making. The school's responsibility for the cognitive domain should be (1) to obtain and disseminate objective information about drugs; (2) to monitor information sources in an effort to reduce existing inaccuracies; (3) to disseminate information that includes recognition of the complex interaction effects of multiple drug use; and (4) to develop curriculum materials that incorporate con-

ceptual levels, critical learning, and decision-making models.

Affective assumptions. The assumption that positively influencing the affective development of an individual will prevent excessive use of drugs is probably the most prevalent assumption underlying drug education efforts today. Most curricula appear to posit that enhancing some aspect of each individual's development (for example, self-concepts) will reduce the probability of use and/or negative consequences from use of substances at a later stage in development. The affective components frequently included in this broad assumption are (1) Intrapersonal developmental tasks and skills, such as self-understanding, self-acceptance, positive self-esteem, clarified values, moral reasoning, decision-making skills; and (2) Interpersonal development tasks and skills, such as effective listening, communication skills, leadership skills, resistance to peer pressure, acceptance of individual differences, group-participation skills, and assertiveness. Skills related to functioning in a complex society and participating in complex social institutions (extrapersonal) have not typically been included but could enhance any program in this domain.

Very few curricula have specifically identified a developmental theory and/or systematically developed a sequential curriculum based on affective theories. Vicary (1977) examined several developmental theories with the intent of evolving a rationale for the components and sequencing of affective education curricula. Her work related the three topics described above (intrapersonal, interpersonal, and extrapersonal) to the ideas of developmental theorists such as Peck and Havighurst (1960), Kohlberg (1975), and Piaget (1969).

Equally important in the field of affectively oriented drug education has been an emphasis upon the classroom climate in which the affective activities are implemented. The climate components have their origin in the facilitative conditions described by Rogers (1969), which include teachers demonstrating, understanding, and accepting students' expressions of feelings and ideas.

Somewhat more technique-oriented material designed to be implemented under facilitative conditions are the values clarification ideas fostered by Simon, Howe, and Kirshenbaum (1972) and Raths, Harmin, and Simon (1966). Spurred by the ideas and techniques in these materials, many teachers began applying this process to drug education units. Some evaluations of values clarification approaches to drug education have revealed significant results, including reduced levels of drug use among participants (e.g., Smith, 1973; Swisher & Piniuk, 1973).

Another major problem among drug abuse preventors has been the failure to recognize the audience's readiness to understand the material. Many of the prevention messages have not been designed in terms of the reasoning ability or emotional development of the potential recipient. For example, decision making appears to be too abstract a process for most children under the age of 10 to comprehend (Branca, D'Augelli, & Evans, 1975; Piaget,

TABLE 1. *Examples of matching needs with alternatives in Cohen's model*

Level of experience	Corresponding motives and needs (examples)	Possible alternatives (examples)
Physical	Desire for physical satisfaction; physical relaxation; relief from sickness; desire for more energy; maintenance of physical dependency.	Athletics; dance; exercise; hiking; diet; health training; carpentry or outdoor work.
Sensory	Desire to stimulate sight, sound, touch, taste; need for sensual-sexual stimulation; desire to magnify sensorium.	Sensory awareness training; sky diving; experiencing sensory beauty of nature.
Emotional	Relief from psychological pain; attempt to solve personal perplexities; relief from bad mood; escape from anxiety; desire for emotional insight; liberation of feeling, emotional relaxation.	Competent individual counseling; well-run group therapy, instruction in psychology of personal development.
Interpersonal	To gain peer acceptance; to break through interpersonal barriers; to "communicate," especially nonverbally; defiance of authority figures; cement two-person relationships; relaxation of interpersonal inhibition; solve interpersonal hangups.	Expertly managed sensitivity and encounter groups, well-run group therapy; instruction in social customs, confidence training; social-interpersonal counseling; emphasis on assisting others in distress via education.

1969). A growing body of knowledge has implications for how and when to present prevention messages on either the information or feeling level. Schaps et al. (1978) in a review did not find consistent experimental support for affectively based approaches to drug education. However, Skiffington and Brown (1979), in a large-scale analysis of Pennsylvania's Educational Quality Assessment data, reported that use of alcohol and marijuana could be differentiated as a function of high or low scores on affective dimensions such as self-esteem, understanding others, interest in school, social responsibility, and coping with change. Obviously, cause and effect cannot be determined from this analysis, but these data lend some support to the basic assumption of the affective approaches to drug education. Furthermore, Schaps (1981), in a very carefully controlled and designed study of combinations of affective-based approaches, has found some support for this type of curriculum approach. These results are described more fully with respect to multidimensional approaches.

Behavioral assumptions. A third cluster of theories that can illuminate drug education activities places a clear emphasis upon the non–drug-using behavior of the individual. The major assumption of such theories is that constructive alternative behaviors will preclude the opportunity as well as the motivation to participate in drug using. The most common rubric for this assumption is "alternatives," which is not to be confused with optional forms of punishment for apprehended drug users. Alternative behaviors can be designed to meet assumed needs (Cohen, 1973) or as reinforcements of successive approximations and actual alternative behaviors (Horan, 1973). Cohen's work (1973) has centered around the concept of matching alternative behaviors to the psychological needs of the individual. The assumption of this approach is that drug use is one expression of normal developmental needs. Table 1

presents two examples of Cohen's approach (1973). To implement Cohen's model, it is necessary to organize a large number of community groups and to recruit or recommend different programs to individuals (Cohen, 1973). One assumption of this approach is that individuals will gravitate to opportunities that meet their needs in a constructive manner. Unfortunately, the evaluation literature contains no references in which this model has been tested.

The second behavioral model was systematically developed around reinforcement principles applied in a small group context. This approach assumed that many individuals are currently participating in non–drug-using alternative behaviors and can be encouraged to maintain or increase these positive outlets. Furthermore, the process of discussing alternatives in a small group will result in vicarious reinforcement for those members who are less active. This approach has been implemented in health classes at the junior, and senior high school levels and at the college level (Swisher, Warner, & Herr, 1972; Swisher et al. 1973; Warner, Swisher, & Horan 1973). The results of this series of studies were that (1) knowledge gains were achieved at junior high, senior high, and the college level; (2) attitudes towards personal use became more conservative at the junior high level, did not change at the senior high level, and became more liberal at the college level; and (3) self-reported use of drugs did not change at any level. The inconsistent results appeared to be related to inconsistent implementation. The major difficulty with this approach to drug education was that it was not possible to adequately train and or supervise teachers or counselors to conduct the group process according to the basic principles involved.

Approaches to Implementation. The early strategies in schools included scare tactics, debates, and the use of recognized authorities (e.g., pharmacists). Contemporary

TABLE 2. *Summary of Blum, Blum, and Garfield's recommendations for extent of drug use and program responses*

Extent of drug use

	No drug use in community	Some drug use with complications	Drug problems associated with other problems in living	Normal drug use patterns	Extensive drug use
Recommended prevention activity	None	Crisis intervention	Teacher training in communication and mental health	Affective approaches (e.g., values clarification)	Change total school climate
Probable program impact	No stimulation to experiment	Fewer school problems Increase in referrals	Improvement in teaching Reduction in delinquency Increase in moral development	Increase in low-risk drugs Decrease in high-risk drugs	Empirical studies lacking

approaches have emphasized peer participation, media, curriculum development, and affective techniques. These approaches are not necessarily mutually exclusive nor are they very often seen in a pure form, but as approaches they represent major developments in drug education.

Scare tactics were seen most often in the first responses to the growing problem. Attempts were made to frighten the audience with syringes and other paraphernalia, as well as with demonstration of withdrawal symptoms and other phenomena. The intent was to demonstrate that drug abuse was high-risk behavior with dire consequences for the individual. This approach may have been effective with conservative audiences by reinforcing their fears (Richards, 1969). However, the more curious individuals probably could not associate their experiences with the problems portrayed and were usually unaffected by scare tactics.

An objective presentation of both sides of the issue in a debate format also had a great deal of appeal to an educational program that should also be concerned with academic freedom. However, as with many debates, the intent of the panelists was not to inform but rather to convince, and, consequently, the results of many debates depended upon style rather than a broad and objective review of information. The debate approach also served to highlight the fact that very little was understood about the effects of drugs on human beings. Recognized authorities were frequently included in the early drug-abuse prevention efforts. Very few teachers in schools felt comfortable with the pharmaceutical aspects of drug abuse and readily turned to external authorities such as physicians, pharmacists, and/or law enforcement agents. The recognized authority had the advantage of being a credible resource but the disadvantage of being a one-time inocula-

tion. The use of authorities also tended to lose some of the advantages of small groups and continuity in time.

Among other authorities frequently consulted were peers, and preferably, drug-experienced peers. It was assumed that a young person who could communicate effectively with other youth was a credible source of information and could model exemplary behavior. However, a series of controlled experimental evaluations have failed to support the efficacy of peers as drug abuse preventors (Swisher & Hoffman, 1974). Schaps et al. (1978) found programs led by peers to be the most effective means of providing drug education programs. However, this conclusion was based upon only 6 of the 127 programs reviewed.

Prescriptive. The prescriptive approach to drug education recommends program activities as a function of needs or current drug use patterns in a school. The program activities recommended are usually specific (e.g., health lectures in the seventh grade or meditation as an alternative), and there is usually a needs assessment required in order to prescribe appropriate program activities.

Blum, Blum, and Garfield's *Drug Education: Results and Recommendations* (1976) is a data-based example of the prescriptive program approach. Based on a three-year study of different types of drug education, these authorities developed a five-stage prescriptive approach that encompasses a variety of stages, activities, and probable outcomes. The stages range along a continuum of degree of drug use, whereas the parallel activities range from no response to complete revision of the school climate. Table 2 is a simplification of their recommendations. Of necessity, their recommendations have been greatly condensed, and the more detailed tables in their study should be consulted for better understanding of their conclusions (Blum, Blum, & Garfield, 1976).

Elsewhere Blum, Blum, and Garfield (1976) reported on trends in drug use patterns that would negate the realistic consideration of the option of "no activity." The trends included current use patterns changing from urban to rural, older to younger, and lower class to middle and upper class. If these trends are imminent, then a community cannot afford to choose no activity; or at a later point in time, they may be forced into poorly planned activities because of a sudden crisis. For most schools, the fifth option (change of total school climate) is also outside the realm of possibilities on a short-term basis and because of the extreme radical nature of its recommendations. Therefore, a school is left with three reasonably constructive responses to the problem of abuse prevention. Two of these options assume that drug abuse is related to developmental problems and that affective approaches combined with cognitive information will have beneficial results (responsible use and improved mental health).

One of Blum, Blum, and Garfield's conclusions (1976) was that information programs combined with personal and interpersonal growth opportunities were more likely to be successful. Apparently, it is important to examine one's values, decision-making skills, or susceptibility to peer pressure in the context of information about substances. Specifically, it might be possible to teach the steps in effective decision making; but unless those steps are applied to decisions one might confront with regard to substances, the decision-making skills will not transfer to the context of substance abuse. Regardless of personal and interpersonal skills or alternative activities, it is important to assist individuals with an examination of the implications of each affective component for their drug behavior.

One of the approaches (crisis intervention) is essentially reactionary in nature and is limited to only those individuals who demonstrate early signs of problems indicative of potential use. However, early identification is not an advanced science, and it is particularly questionable to trust it as a diagnostic tool on an individual level. Furthermore, if young people are classified as predrug abusers, they may be more likely to become drug abusers than if they were not so labeled.

A court in Montgomery County, Pennsylvania (United States District Court, 1975), was made aware of the potential hazards of this approach, and a program that called for the "early identification of high risk drug abusers" was not allowed. The program proposed to identify individuals judged to be very likely to use dangerous drugs (e.g., heroin) and to provide special services for them. The procedure used to identify the individuals was scientifically and conceptually sound (Streit, 1973), but the court felt that the plan for implementing the program was inappropriate and beyond the school's authority.

One disadvantage of prescriptive approaches is that they tend to be reactions to a problem rather than initiatives taken to prevent the occurrence of a problem. Ac-

cording to Blum, Blum, and Garfield's recommendations (1976), the extent of response is somewhat proportionate to the extent of the drug problem in a community. Another weakness in the prescriptive approach is that it tends to be more factual in nature. For example, the first two options presented by Blum, Blum, and Garfield (1976) are essentially recommendations for disseminating information, and the affective components do not appear until the later stages. An advantage to the prescriptive approach is that it allows a school to clearly define its position, state its goals, specify activities, and proceed. This is true for any of the five forms of action or any of the needs that could be targeted.

Multidimensional. The multidimensional approach is probably predominant in the drug education literature. This approach is the programmatic application of the assumption that improved affective development will preclude abuse of drugs. Accordingly, materials that foster positive self-concepts and improved interpersonal relationships are offered throughout all grade levels. In contrast to the prescriptive approaches, the multidimensional approaches do not require a needs assessment nor do they identify special populations at risk. Whereas the prescriptive approaches relate program recommendations to the extent of drug use in a school, the multidimensional strategy assumes that all students would benefit from enriched development and therefore provides for curricular activities at all grade levels.

The first compilation of multidimensional approaches occurred in the Pacific Institute for Research and Evaluation series entitled *Balancing Head and Heart* (Schaps, 1975–1976). The methods and materials recommended in this series included kits, "magic circle" activities, peer tutoring, role playing, values clarification, alternatives through service, peer counseling, family life education, and parent training. Those approaches were included if they had been successfully evaluated and if training were available for implementation.

Several states have adopted multidimensional approaches based upon the affective assumption. Ohio was one of the first to sponsor the development of curriculum guides known as *A World to Grow In*, which were developed in cooperation with the Ohio Department of Education and the Research Council of America (Meyers, 1975). North Carolina also developed a multidimensional approach known as Life Skills for Health (Frye & Rockness, 1974) and has implemented its curriculum guides through a teacher in-service training system. Pennsylvania, instead of developing a mental health or life skills curriculum, provides teachers with a library of affective materials and assists them through in-service workshops by integrating affective content based upon a multidimensional library into the regular classroom.

Two major studies, presently being completed, have carefully evaluated multidimensional approaches. The Life Skills for Mental Health program in Georgia, which created its own curriculum materials based upon a range of available materials, is being evaluated by Research for Better Schools (Dusewicz & Martin, 1981). Their preliminary results, presented at a special conference sponsored by the National Institute on Drug Abuse, indicated that the approach had reduced disciplinary incidents among younger children, increased teacher and pupil affective behaviors, but had not affected variables such as self-esteem and drug or alcohol use.

Schaps's evaluation (1981) of a multidimensional approach in the Napa Valley School District included an examination of each component in the approach as well as the effects of combinations of approaches that occurred over time. Schap's preliminary results indicated significant improvements in self-esteem and fewer disciplinary incidents among third-grade males exposed to the "magic circle" techniques. Fourth-grade, fifth-grade, and sixth-grade boys and girls were significantly higher in mathematics achievement, significantly less involved in disciplinary incidents, and the boys become more conservative in their attitudes toward alcohol as a result of being in classrooms where teachers had been given classroom management techniques. At the junior high school level in classrooms with increased affective emphasis, boys were absent less often and viewed their peers as more conservative with respect to drug use. Girls' self-esteem scores increased significantly. They saw their peers as more conservative regarding drug use and they reported less use of tobacco.

Both the Dusewicz and Martin (1981) and Schaps (1981) studies are the result of three years of program implementation and evaluation effort. Their full reports will be of importance to the field of drug education since they represent high-quality program implementation coupled with careful evaluation. Obviously, this discussion barely highlights the findings emerging from these two centers of evaluation.

One more extension of the multimodal approach that has some potential has been labeled "adaptive developmental" (Vicary, 1977). The two key elements in this approach include (1) integrating prevention messages (cognitive and affective) into regular subjects areas; and (2) adapting prevention messages (cognitive and affective) to the developmental age of the students. Instead of establishing new school courses, the adaptive developmental approach recommends training teachers to conduct their regular lessons in ways that also facilitate personal and social growth and provide for learning about socially responsible use of substances.

The concept of integrating prevention messages into existing activities of schools, communities, and families has its origins in the works of Brown (1974) and Kirschenbaum (1977). These authorities have been concerned with reasonable approaches to personal and social growth that recognize the realities and constraints of current cultural traditions.

An experimentally designed implementation of this model (Vicary, 1977) found significant changes among teachers who were trained and supervised in the process.

There were also significant improvements in self-esteem and interpersonal relations among students exposed to these teachers based upon one-year and two-year follow-up studies by French (1978) and Klein (1979). The affective integration model was one of the options for teacher implementation in the Life Skills for Mental Health program in Georgia.

A major weakness of a multidimensional approach is that each component is usually a separate activity requiring its own time slot in the school or agency schedule. For a short while, time may be found for several of these novel ideas, but ultimately the pressures of other more recent crises may push these programs aside. Furthermore, many of these modalities are never attempted because of a lack of available time in the school or agency's schedule. These modalities also tend to focus upon problem situations; consequently, rather than enhancing developmental skills, they teach people a variety of responses to encountered problems.

The greatest difficulty in a multimodality approach stems from lack of consistency in assumptions among component techniques. In fact, it is possible to engage in activities that are theoretically opposite. A conceptual rationale must be developed if a multimodality approach is chosen as the basis for a community, family, or school program.

Conclusions. Drug education, as it presently exists in the schools, is in its infancy in comparison to other areas of concern (e.g., reading readiness). There has been relatively little consideration given to appropriate goals for drug education, and there appears to be considerable disagreement regarding possible goals. Furthermore, basic learning and developmental theory has not been the basis for formulating curricular efforts, and the evaluation literature is sparse. It would appear that because of student motivation, students will learn about drugs regardless of the approach taken; but gains in knowledge do not necessarily relate to students' intended or actual use of substances. Two systematic approaches have appeared in the literature; one emphasizes program efforts in proportion to the drug problem (Blum, Blum, & Garfield, 1976) and the other provides for affective enrichment and information at all grade levels (Schaps, 1975–1976). As a function of their extensive data, these studies merit further attention. The problem of drug use and abuse appears to be growing, but it may be unrealistic to expect that the school could or should be the total solution.

John D. Swisher

See also Affective Education; Health Education; Mental Health; Psychological Services.

REFERENCES

Berberian, R.; Gross, C.; Lovejoy, J.; & Paparella, S. The effectiveness of drug education programs: A critical review. *Health Education Monographs,* 1976, *4,* 377–398.

Besteman, K. *Recommendations for Future Federal Activities in Drug Abuse Prevention: Report of the Subcommittee on Pre-*

vention. Washington, D.C.: U.S. Department of Health, Education, and Welfare, 1977.

Blum, R.; Blum, E.; & Garfield, E. Drug Education: Results and Recommendations. Lexington, Mass.: Heath, 1976.

Branca, M.; D'Augelli, J.; & Evans, K. Development of a Decision-making Skills Education Program: Study I (Final report to Governor's Council on Drug and Alcohol Abuse). University Park: Pennsylvania State University, January 1975.

Braucht, G.; Follingstad, D.; Brakarsh, D.; & Berry, K. Drug education: A review of goals, approaches, and effectiveness, and a paradigm for evaluation. Quarterly Journal of Studies on Alcohol, 1973, 1279–1292.

Brown, G. I. Human Teaching for Human Learning: An Introduction to Confluent Education. New York: Viking Press, 1971.

Cohen, A. Y. Alternatives to Drug Abuse: Steps toward Prevention. Washington, D.C.: National Clearinghouse for Drug Abuse Information, U.S. Government Printing Office, 1973.

deLone, R. H. The ups and downs of drug abuse education. Saturday Review of Education, November 11, 1972, pp. 27–32.

Dorn, N., & Thompson, A. Evaluation of drug education in the longer term is not an optional extra. Community Health, 1976, 7, 154–161.

Dusewicz, R., & Martin, M. Impacts of a Georgia Drug Abuse Prevention Program. Progress report presented to Prevention Evaluation Grant Management Review Meeting at the National Institute on Drug Abuse, Rockville, Md., March 1981. (ERIC Document Reproduction Service No. ED 195 890)

Ebel, R. (Ed.). Encyclopedia of Educational Research (4th ed). New York: Macmillan, 1969.

French, J. Second-year Evaluation of a Rural In-service Training Workshop in Affectively Integrated Developmental Education (Research report for the Pennsylvania Governor's Council on Drug and Alcohol Abuse). University Park: Pennsylvania State University, Addictions Prevention Laboratory, 1978.

Frye, R., & Rockness, P. Life Skills for Health: Focus on Mental Health. Raleigh: North Carolina Department of Public Instruction, 1974.

Glaser, F. Misinformation about drugs: A problem for drug abuse education. International Journal of the Addictions, 1970, 5, 595–609.

Goodstadt, M. S. Myths and methodology in drug education: A critical review of the research evidence. In M. S. Goodstadt (Ed.), Research on Methods and Programs of Drug Education. Toronto: Addiction Research Foundation, 1974.

Horan, J. Preventing drug abuse through behavior change technology. Journal of SPATE (Student Personnel in Teacher Education), 1973, 11, 145–152.

Johnston, L.; Bachman, J.; & O'Malley, P. Drugs and the Nation's High School Students: Five-year Trends. Washington, D.C.: U.S. Government Printing Office, 1979. (ERIC Document Reproduction Service No. ED 186 781)

Klein, M. Third-year Evaluation of a Rural Teacher In-service Training Workshop in Affectively Integrated Developmental Education (Research report for the Pennsylvania Governor's Council on Drug and Alcohol Abuse). University Park: Pennsylvania State University, Addictions Prevention Laboratory, 1979.

Kirschenbaum, H. Advanced Values Clarification. La Jolla, Calif.: University Associates, 1977.

Kohlberg, L. The cognitive-developmental approach to moral education. Phi Delta Kappan, 1975, 10, 670–677.

Lettieri, D.; Sayers, M.; & Pearson, H. Theories on Drug Abuse (National Institute on Drug Abuse Research Monograph No. 30). Washington, D.C.: U.S. Government Printing Office, 1980.

Lewis, D. G. Drug education. Bulletin, 1969, 53, 87–97.

Meyers, E. A World to Grow In. Cleveland: American Educational Research Council, 1975.

Mong, M. A Guide to Alcohol Education Curricula. Rockville, Md.: National Clearinghouse for Alcohol Abuse and Alcoholism, 1980.

National Coordinating Council for Drug Education. Drug Abuse Films. Washington, D.C.: National Coordinating Council for Drug Education and Information, 1973. (ERIC Document Reproduction Service No. ED 058 096)

National Institute for Drug Abuse. Toward a National Strategy for Primary Drug Abuse Prevention (Final Report, Delphi II). Rockville, Md.: National Institute for Drug Abuse, 1975.

Peck, R. F., & Havighurst, R. J. The Psychology of Character Development. New York: Wiley, 1960.

Piaget, J. The Mechanisms of Perception. New York: Basic Books, 1969.

Pizza, J. The School Team Approach (U.S. Department of Education, Alcohol and Drug Abuse Education Program). Washington, D.C.: U.S. Government Printing Office, 1980.

Raths, L.; Harmin, M.; & Simon, S. Values and Teaching. Columbus, Ohio: Merrill, 1966.

Richards, L. G. Government Programs and Psychological Principles in Drug Abuse Education. Paper presented at the Annual Convention of the American Psychological Association, Washington, D.C., September 1969. (ERIC Document Reproduction Service No. ED 033 428)

Rogers, C. Freedom to Learn. Columbus, Ohio: Merrill, 1969.

Schaps, E. Balancing Head and Heart: Sensible Ideas for the Prevention of Drug and Alcohol Abuse. Walnut Creek, Calif.: Pacific Institute for Research and Evaluation, 1975–1976.

Schaps, E.; DiBartolo, R.; Palley, C. S.; & Churgin, S. Primary Prevention Evaluation Research: A Review of 127 Program Evaluations. Walnut Creek, Calif.: Pyramid Project, 1978.

Schaps, E. Research Summary: NAPA Project. Progress report presented to the Prevention Evaluation Grant Management Review Meeting, National Institute on Drug Abuse, Rockville, Md., March 1981.

Simon, S.; Howe, L.; & Kirschenbaum, H. Values Clarification. New York: Hart, 1972.

Skiffington, E., & Brown, P. Personal, home and school factors related to eleventh graders' drug attitudes. Common Ground: Pennsylvania Prevention Forum, June 1979, 2–9.

Smith, B. Values clarification in drug education: A comparative study. Journal of Drug Education, 1973, 2, 369–376.

Smith, R. An historical perspective of drug use. In B. Corder, R. Smith, & J. Swisher (Eds.), Drug Abuse Prevention: Perspectives and Approaches for Educators. Dubuque, Iowa: Brown, 1975.

Streit, F. A Test Procedure to Identify Secondary School Children Who Have a Higher Probability of Drug Abuse. Unpublished doctoral dissertation, Rutgers University, 1973.

Stuart, R. B. Teaching facts about drugs: Pushing or preventing? Journal of Education Psychology, 1974, 6, 189–201.

Swisher, J. Drug use: Who is the victim? Law in American Society, 1977, 6, 21–26.

Swisher, J., & Hoffman, A. Information: The irrelevant variable in drug education. In B. Corder, R. Smith, & J. Swisher (Eds.), Drug Abuse Prevention: Strategies for Educators. Dubuque, Iowa: Brown, 1974.

Swisher, J., & Piniuk, A. An Evaluation of Keystone Central School

District's Drug Education Program. Harrisburg: Pennsylvania Governor's Justice Commission, Region 4, 1973.

Swisher, J.; Warner, R.; & Herr, E. An experimental comparison of four approaches to drug education. *Journal of Counseling Psychology,* 1972, *18,* 328–332.

Swisher, J.; Warner, R.; Spence, C.; & Upcraft, L. A comparison of four approaches to drug abuse prevention at the college level. *Journal of College Student Personnel,* 1973, *14,* 231–235.

Ungerleider, T. Drugs and educational process. *American Biology Teacher,* 1968, *30,* 627–632.

United States District Court, Eastern District of Pennsylvania, Montgomery County, Norristown. Civil Act #72–2057, *Michael Merriken et al.* v. *Wilmer B. Kressman et al.* Signed by Honorable John Morgan Davis, September 28, 1975.

Vicary, J. R. Toward an adaptive developmental education. In L. Rubin (Ed.), *Curriculum Handbook: The Disciplines, Current Movements, and Instructional Methodology.* Boston: Allyn & Bacon, 1977.

Warner, R. Research: An evolutionary perspective. In A. Abrams, E. Garfield, & J. Swisher, *Accountability in Drug Education.* Washington, D.C.: Drug Abuse Council, 1973. (ERIC Document Reproduction Service No. ED 075 918)

Warner, R.; Swisher, J.; & Horan, J. A behavioral approach to drug abuse prevention. *National Association of Secondary School Principals Bulletin,* 1973, *57,* 49–54.

EARLY CHILDHOOD DEVELOPMENT

The period of early childhood has been defined as the age range of 2 to 6 years, or the period known popularly as the preschool years. Other authors agree with this definition, with the exception that some consider the period to extend to age 8 or 9, when significant shifts in developmental influences and processes occur.

This article begins with an overview of the major concepts and theories of development relevant to the early childhood period. It is followed by a presentation of the important facts and generalizations about development of preschool children drawn from the research literature on physical and motor, cognitive and intellectual, language, social, and emotional domains of development. The article also includes a review of discursive and research literature concerning the relevance of theory and research for practice, especially theory-derived practices and programs in early childhood education. It concludes with a brief discussion of important issues and problems affecting children and families that must be addressed by policy makers during the remainder of this century.

Concepts and Theories

This article frequently comments upon the necessary interplay between developmental psychologists and educators, but, historically in the United States, the interaction between the two groups has been judged as minimal by some psychologists (Robinson & Hom, 1977; Spodek, 1977). The child study movement of the 1920s and 1930s certainly influenced nursery school practices (Lazerson, 1972; Sears, 1975). Teachers of preschool children functioned primarily as warm, nurturing adults, intent upon endowing the preschool with a home atmosphere and maternal environment for a few hours each day. Some authors have asserted that these teachers had no interest in the research findings of developmental psychology, whereas others have found that they showed considerable interest. The child study movement is partly responsible for greater interest in experimental scrutiny of children, but the interests of developmental psychologists and educators have often diverged.

Developmental Psychology and Education. Research in child development through the 1950s is characterized by a search for general developmental principles, mainly by applying work done with animals and adults to child populations (White, 1970; White & Siegel, 1976). However, in the late 1950s and early 1960s, the research literature reflects a new appreciation of the value of cooperative work between developmental psychologists and educators, with renewed interest in the complex, interactional nature of behavior and in the value of naturalistic observation (often in the preschool setting) as a research tool (Kilmer & Weinberg, 1974; McCall, 1977; Spodek, 1977; White & Fishbein, 1971). Recent interest in ecological approaches, the study of behavior in naturally occurring settings (Bronfenbrenner, 1974; Weisz, 1978), as well as large-scale research and interventions like Head Start, indicate intense interest on the part of both psychologists and educators in testing applications of research findings by means of intervention with children (Evans, 1975; Robinson & Hom, 1977; Sigel, 1972). These productive interactions between child development experts and early educators are no doubt the result of a variety of factors, some of them as yet undetermined. However, several reasons for the shift to greater cooperation between educators and psychologists are well documented. Accumulating evidence concerning the malleability of intelligence, recognition of the widening context of development (especially the sociocultural context of school and other child care settings), and increasing acceptance of the role of early intervention in later development have all contributed to recent positive interactions between child development and education (Bloom, 1964; Evans, 1975; Hunt, 1961; McCall, 1977; Zigler & Valentine, 1979).

Since the mid-1960s lines of inquiry in both fields have merged. Child development researchers understand that they provide the theoretical and knowledge base for child programs and services and are more interested in the practical applications of their work. Early childhood educators and policymakers now see more clearly the value of research and theory for programming and planning and recognize themselves as consumers of child development information and concepts.

Research Strategies: Commonalities and Variability. Fundamental research strategies used by developmental psychologists have influenced and will continue to influence the knowledge base as well as its application (Sigel & Brodzinsky, 1977). Child development research was, until recently, more nomothetic (concerned with general laws) than idiographic (concerned with individual cases). The nomothetic strategy de-emphasizes within-group variability, seeking generalizations about the behavior of large populations without special regard for discovering the determinants of individual behaviors. The idiographic approach, seeking to discover principles of individual development, is interested in exceptions rather than generic principles. Both approaches are necessary to research, since the identification of general principles of development allows prediction of group behavior, and the identification of intragroup variability extends understanding of the behavior of individuals (McCall, 1977; Sigel & Brodzinsky, 1977).

The age-level organization of most child development texts (Ambron, 1978; Biehler, 1981; Smart & Smart, 1977) indicates the dominance of the nomothetic approach prior to the 1960s. A substantial body of knowledge has accumulated about the significant behaviors considered typical of children at different ages in various developmental domains; this article includes a summary of significant research conclusions drawn from this literature.

Studying commonalities provides normative data about development, but careful review of these data indicates that much variability also exists in children's development. Normative information about child growth and development serves as a yardstick or standard to be used in judging "normal" behavior; whereas no single child is likely to be exactly average in all characteristics, most behavior, when measured according to norms, is considered to be within normal limits. Some differences in development considered too deviant from norms in either positive or negative directions are termed "exceptional" (Cartwright, Cartwright, & Ward, 1981).

Each human being has certain biological capacities, a genetic inheritance, prenatal experiences, and idiosyncratic life experiences. Obvious individual differences are present at birth, and, with each day of development, variability increases in both rate and type of behavior change. The study of individual differences provides for prediction and directs the course of intervention. Understanding variability in development is important in the search for the origins and meaning of uniqueness, but, more importantly,

understanding the determinants of individual and group differences is an effective strategy for extending understanding of the processes of development (Peters & Willis, 1977).

Developmental Processes. Development is change, and the period of early childhood is one of relatively rapid change compared to later stages in the life span (White, 1965). The general direction of development is from simple to complex and involves continuous differentiation and integration. Perhaps the most dramatic example of differentiation is reflected in the change from a single cell at conception to the complex set of organs and bodily systems present in the newborn. Change is generally gradual and occurs in relatively small increments, allowing the organism to adapt and remain in a state of balance. Influences are cumulative in the sense that every single small change influences and reorganizes the total organism. When change is too dramatic, the organism is out of equilibrium and vulnerable.

Some changes that occur are quantitative and occur continuously (for example, changes in height, weight, and size of vocabulary). Other changes are qualitative and produce a seeming discontinuity in development (for example, learning new problem-solving strategies or the concept of cardinal numbers); such changes do not occur incrementally, but rather in rushes or surges, and the result is generally construed as a sequence of qualitatively different stages of development (Bloom, 1964). Whatever kind of change is being studied, the change itself is usually explicable in terms of one or more change processes: biologically timed and regulated maturation, environmentally induced learning, externally induced organismic alterations, or some combination of the three (Peters & Willis, 1977). Examples of externally induced organismic alterations would include changes resulting from nutritional deprivation, drugs, accidents, diseases, and the like. Specific explanations vary somewhat with different theoretical perspectives.

Developmental Theories. The student of child development is faced with thousands of seemingly unrelated facts to consider, all subject to change at any time as a result of new research findings. Theories, the explanations for behavior change, also number in the hundreds. Clearly, some general conceptual framework is needed to organize and summarize theories and their related data; following is a review of the most important conceptions of human development along with related developmental theories.

World views. Three distinct frameworks for viewing the processes and products of human development are: the romantic (development as genetically predetermined and unfolding); mechanistic (development as a product of environment); and organismic (development occurring through reciprocal interaction between man and environment) (Harris, 1957; Kohlberg & Mayer, 1972; Lerner, 1976; Reese and Overton, 1970). These three viewpoints, often called "models" or "world views," represent different belief systems and assumptions about the nature of the world in general and the development of individual human beings in particular. They serve as constant reminders of the inescapable links between philosophy and science; the belief systems held by developmental psychologists determine the theories they espouse and delimit the content of research problems and research methodologies. The notion that there are predictable links between world views, theories of development, and optimal intervention practices is well established (Kohlberg & Mayer, 1972; Peters, 1977; Seaver & Cartwright, 1977; Sigel, 1972).

Presentation of facts and concepts about the various domains of development must be evaluated in terms of the implicit assumptions of the respective world views. For example, discussions of different conceptions of intelligence, such as the psychometric and cognitive-developmental, illustrate the pervasive nature of world views in the work of developmental psychologists. No single viewpoint is regarded universally as "correct," but each is thought of as providing a rich conceptual resource for theorists and practitioners.

Reese and Overton (1970) argued that world views are basically irreconcilable. In other words, they believe that different world views cannot be synthesized into a larger, more encompassing model that accounts for disparate beliefs about development. Others argue not so much for synthesis as for a greater understanding of the complementary nature of the models (Baldwin, 1967; Emmerich, 1977; Fowler, 1980; Kilmer & Weinberg, 1974; White & Siegel, 1976). Those who deal with intervention issues point out that theories often do not account adequately for all aspects of development and, as such, do not mirror reality. They see opportunities for shifting systematically among assumptions or combining assumptions in complementary ways (Emmerich, 1977; Forman & Kushner, 1977). In terms of early childhood programs, for example, cognitive tasks might be presented using a discovery or inquiry teaching approach (based on the organismic model), whereas group and individual discipline might be managed by means of a system of incentives and consequences (based on the mechanistic model).

General descriptions of each world view, along with related developmental theories and intervention methods are given in the following discussion. Excellent general resources for readers interested in greater depth are available (Baldwin, 1967; Crain, 1980; Harris, 1957; Langer, 1969; Lerner, 1976).

Romantic model and theories. One model of development is based on the notion that the identical factors that influence human biological development also function as determinants of psychological development. This view is based upon genetic predeterminism. As such, it assumes that humans are born with innate, predetermined patterns of behavior that are accompanied by internal regulatory mechanisms. If a human being is viewed as a biological product, then it follows that development is predetermined and maturation occurs as a function of time; for

example, new behaviors are expected with increasing age. Those who hold this view believe that individual potential will unfold in properly nurturant environments.

Among the important theories associated with this romantic, idealistic world view are the maturationist theory of Gesell (Yale University Clinic, 1940) and the psychoanalytic theory of Sigmund Freud (1949). Gesell and his colleagues believed that developmental change occurred as a result of the natural unfolding and maturing of physiological structures. The phrase "ages and stages" has become synonymous with maturationist theories that view ages as important benchmarks of increasing development, with each age characterized by certain personality patterns, language accomplishments, patterns of problem solving, and other skill achievements. Children are thought to move from one stage to another at their individual ages of readiness. Gesell emphasized a genetically programmed sequence of stages; and although he is generally well-known for his articulation of the norms of behavioral development, he also recognized the impact of individual differences (Caldwell & Richmond, 1967).

Freud proposed a structure of stages related to maturation, particularly movement of the child through predicted stages of psychosocial development (Baldwin, 1967). Freud believed that feelings and emotions have a biological basis and formulated his developmental sequence upon the resolution of internal conflicts at various stages.

Many current educational practices are based upon maturationist ideas (Seaver & Cartwright, 1977). For example, a typical assumption is that, given a supportive teacher and nurturant environment, the child will eventually perform expected, desired behaviors. Teachers are expected to become familiar with age-related behaviors and related age-appropriate experiences for children. They are encouraged to take advantage of sensitive periods for development and to have command of the concept of readiness. For example, maturationist teachers often stress social and emotional objectives for preschool children, along with a corresponding de-emphasis of cognitive objectives, since they believe children will not be ready for academic tasks until a later stage.

Organismic model and theories. The organismic model is based upon the notion of the individual as inherently active and seeking change. The individual is viewed as the organizing force in merging environment and heredity in an interactive process. In Langer's words (1969), "man develops to be what he makes himself by his own actions" (p. 7). The concept of self-organization as a critical component of development is embedded in the organismic model. Change is viewed as discontinuous and qualitative rather than the simple sum of the contributions of inheritance and environment. Development is thought to occur through reciprocal interaction between individual and environment. In this model, development occurs by means of active self-structuring on the part of the individuals, as they pass through a series of stages, each derived from and built upon preceding stages.

Theories derived from the organismic perspective use the concept of "stages" to refer to levels of organization representative of the individual's self-organization at various points in development. A stage refers to a level of internal organization that is qualitatively different from prior stages. The developmental theory that most closely adheres to the organismic model is Piaget's theory of cognitive development, often termed "cognitive-developmental" theory (Piaget, 1950; Piaget & Inhelder, 1969). Interested in explaining the growth of intelligence, Piaget postulated a set of biologically based processes known as the "stage-independent" component of his theory. These processes have been summarized as follows: "The fundamental cause of development is equilibration through self-regulatory activity on the part of the child. In attempting to assimilate new situations to old structures, the child experiences disequilibrium. Through further attempts at assimilation with accommodated structures, the child creates a new structure and arrives at a new level of equilibrium" (Rohwer, Ammon, & Cramer, 1974, p. 185).

Piaget also described a series of qualitative stages that he considered to be universal and occurring in invariant sequence. These stages make up the "stage-dependent" component of his theory (Honstead, 1968). Each stage is characterized by a particular level of mental operations, under the assumption that maturation, environment, social experience, and equilibration all contribute to development.

Curriculum planning and teaching practices derived from cognitive developmental theory are based upon two fundamental assumptions. On the one hand, the child is viewed as progressing through a sequential series of stages of mental development that must be taken into account in program planning. In addition, provisions must be made for active participation by the child in constructing and organizing experiences. Children and teachers are regarded as having complementary roles, each alternating between being passive and active, as the child is encouraged to stretch toward higher levels of development and to allow new levels of development to stabilize.

Mechanistic model and theories. The mechanistic, or empiricist, model ascribes to environment the major role in shaping development. The individual is regarded as basically passive, with activity prompted by environmental impingement. Age is considered an index against which to chart behavior change, and development is thought to occur through a series of antecedent-consequent functional relations. In this view, development is reduced to component elements and the linear accumulation of new skills. Inner states, while they are acknowledged as existing, are not involved in theory formulation since they are not overt, observable, countable, or directly measurable and, consequently, can only be inferred. Environment is understood to provide the structure for behavior, so that ultimately the individual becomes a product of the special stimulus situations and reinforcing elements of a particular individualized environment, in sharp contrast to the biological predeterminism of the maturationists.

Theories of development arising from the empiricist philosophical orientation are generally referred to as "behaviorist" theories, or sometimes as "learning" theories (more of a catch-all term). The basic building block of these theories is the stimulus-response (S-R) unit; the research emphasis is upon the operational definitions of both S and R components, and the main goal of theory building is discovery of functional relationships in the S-R unit. Theorists such as Skinner (1953), Bijou and Baer (1961), and Gagné (1970) take this fundamental approach to human behavior. For them, respondent and operant conditioning serve as basic explanations for the acquisition and modification of all behavior, whether it be positive and desirable or negative and undesirable. Complex learning is regarded as an extension of simple-order learning and is defined as chained sequences of the latter. Thus, the paradigm is additive.

Educators who espouse the behaviorist tradition follow a structured pedagogy and use teaching strategies that are based on empirically validated learning principles. Program planners are charged with deciding what the children are to learn since the theory itself is content-free. This contrasts with the maturationist view, in which the normal expectations for behavior at certain ages would dictate content. Adult initiative is usually paramount, and carefully sequenced and task-analyzed teaching materials as well as tightly structured teaching procedures are often used. The primary means for effecting change in the child is thought to be environmental manipulation or the arrangement of specified contingencies.

Developmental Characteristics of Young Children

Whatever theory is espoused, all developmental theorists acknowledge that no aspect of early childhood development proceeds independently of all others (Baltes, Reese, & Lipsitt, 1980; Baltes, Reese, & Nesselroade, 1977). Functional interrelations between aspects of development are important both for understanding the developmental process and for educating the child (DeVries, 1974). For example, the rate of a child's physical growth is important for intellectual development and emotional well-being, whereas the latter factors, in turn, influence how and when a child interacts with the environment during the development of motor skills (Tanner, 1970). In some cases, a substantial body of knowledge exists regarding how, and under what circumstances, different aspects of development interrelate; in others, it is less clear (Baltes, Cornelius, & Nesselroade, 1979). In either case, the known or potential interrelatedness should be kept in mind when different aspects of development are discussed.

Physical Development. Normative growth and development during the early childhood years may be described in several ways: in absolute terms, by comparing the growth rate during this period with growth rate during other periods, by determining the percentage of adult maturity attained, or by examining the qualitative developmental changes occurring during the period (Tanner, 1970).

From age 2 to age 6, children gain about four and one-half pounds (two kilograms) and add about three inches (seven centimeters) to their height each year. The average North American 5-year-old weighs about forty pounds (eighteen kilograms) and measures about forty-three inches (one hundred nine centimeters) (National Center for Health Statistics, 1976). There is quite a contrast between the proportion of adult weight and the proportion of adult height achieved during this period. Although the U.S. male achieves approximately 50 percent of his height during early childhood, he will not achieve 50 percent of his adult weight until about age 10 (Bloom, 1964). Because such a significant proportion of adult height is attained by the end of early childhood, height during this period is a fairly good predictor of adult height. By age 5 the correlation between preschool and adult height is .70 (Watson & Lowrey, 1962). Much of the weight gain is the result of muscular development and the increasing ossification of the skeletal structure. Approximately 75 percent of adult brain weight is developed by age 5 and 90 percent by age 6. This rapid growth reflects an increase in the size and complexity of brain cell size rather than in the increased number of cells.

Body proportion changes are quite noticeable in early childhood. The child's arms and legs grow more rapidly than the trunk; by age 6 the child's legs equal approximately half of total body length, whereas the head accounts for only one-fifth of total body length, proportions maintained through adulthood.

Since this is a period of very rapid growth and change, broad individual differences exist that are associated with sex, ethnic origin, and nutritional practices (Meredeth, 1978), and many body systems (for example, neural or skeletal) are particularly vulnerable to prolonged or serious illnesses or environmental deprivations (Bloom, 1964; Read, 1976).

Motor development. During early childhood, the child changes from a relatively helpless infant to an individual who has mastered most of the basic fine and gross motor skills. By age 3 the child is highly mobile; he or she can run and walk, stand on one foot, climb, and pedal some wheeled toys. At 4 to 5 years of age the average child is able to catch a bouncing ball and to hop, although he or she may still have difficulty with skipping. Fine motor or perceptual motor skills are somewhat harder for young children to master. These skills involve the coordination of motor skills with sensory information (visual, tactile, or auditory). For example, in building a block tower the child must learn to focus both eyes upon the same block and then must coordinate arm and hand movements with the visual focus. As the child adds the second, third, and fourth blocks to the tower, the coordination of visual and motor movements must become more precise. As with gross motor development, perceptual motor ability progresses from clumsy, inept attempts to smooth, precise movements. Perceptual motor ability plays an important role in the child's development of self-care skills, such as feeding and dressing, and enabling skills for academic work, such as using pencil, crayon, or paint brush.

Sensory and perceptual development. Sensory development in early childhood involves less physiological maturation or growth than it does advances in the child's understanding or cognition. The child's experiences and level of thinking and reasoning influence what is attended to and how it is interpreted. In early childhood the child is involved in coordinating sight, hearing, touch, smell, and taste. For example, the child learns to combine sight (a striped body, long tail, and slanted eyes) with touch (soft fur) and hearing ("meow") in order to determine that the animal in question is a cat. Young children need more sensory cues than adults and attend to certain distinctive features more than others (Gibson & Levin, 1975). During the early childhood period, children begin to employ increasingly sophisticated strategies of attention and exploration (Gibson & Levin, 1975; Zaporozhets & Elkonin, 1971).

Cognitive Development. Cognitive or intellectual development refers to changes in an individual's knowledge, understanding, and ability to reason about the world and the things in it. Research and theory about cognitive development blossomed in the 1960s and continue at a rapid pace. The aims have been to describe the particular cognitive processes occurring at different age levels and to identify specific etiological factors that determine development (Glick, 1975).

Two basic approaches to the study of cognition have had major impact on education: the cognitive-developmental approach of the Swiss scholar, Jean Piaget, and the psychometric approach of persons such as Alfred Binet, David Wechsler, and Robert Thorndike (Elkind, 1969). The Piagetian approach focuses upon intraindividual change—that is, how the same child's thinking changes as he or she develops—and on qualitative differences across stages of development. The psychometric view focuses upon interindividual differences—that is, how children of the same age differ from one another in their performance of intellectual measures—and upon the quantitative nature of intelligence (Elkind, 1969).

Cognitive-developmental theory. From the cognitive-developmental perspective the early childhood years are years of rapid and important changes. The child is moving from a form of thought Piaget has called "preoperational" to a form of thought called "concrete operational." It is believed that the young child's thought or construction of reality is different from that of the older child or adult, but that it has nonetheless, important cognitive capacity (Gelman, 1978).

The term "operation" in Piaget's work refers to flexible thinking; thus the expression, "preoperational thought" indicates a form of thinking that occurs prior to the development of flexible thinking (Piaget, 1950). It would be erroneous to say that all children's thinking in early childhood is inflexible. Rather, although variations exist, Piaget and others have found the thought characteristics of centeredness, egocentrism, and lack of reversibility to be common enough in early childhood to provide a useful basis for understanding and describing cognitive development during this period (Flavell, 1963; Flavell & Wohlwill, 1969; Piaget, 1952; Piaget & Inhelder, 1969; Pinard & Laurendeau, 1964). The term "centered" refers to the young child's difficulty in being aware of or taking into account more than one aspect of an object or event at a time. Preoperational children "center" upon one striking feature of an object such as its height and ignore other features such as width when reasoning about the object. This centeredness is related to the second characteristic of preoperational thought—egocentrism. "Egocentrism" refers to the child's inability to simultaneously consider both his or her own point of view and that of another. Young children assume that everyone sees and thinks and feels as they do. They lack awareness of their own cognitive strategies and thought processes. This awareness of one's own thinking has been called "metacognition" (Masters, 1981). Both centered and egocentric thinking indicate a lack of flexibility in the thinking process but not a lack of thinking per se (Gelman, 1978).

The third characteristic of the preoperational child's thinking is "lack of reversibility." In drawing conclusions from a series of events young children have difficulty reversing their thinking (thinking backwards); they focus only upon the final event in the series.

Centeredness, egocentrism, and lack of reversibility of thought decrease as children progress from early childhood to the school years. Children acquire the ability to classify, understand relations and sequences, and to follow logical rules that are shared by adults—particularly in concrete situations; that is, they become "concrete operational." However, it is not until later childhood that children can reason in hypothetical or abstract terms or handle questions involving metacognition (Piaget, 1950, 1952; Masters, 1981).

Psychometric theory.   The rapid changes in cognition that occur during the early childhood period create problems for the psychometric test builder. Since the psychometric approach is a comparative one—contrasting an individual's responses to others of a similar chronological age—normative tests are required. Descriptions of early childhood growth in intelligence are hampered by major scaling problems as well as by the changing nature of intelligence itself (Tuddenham, 1960); early measures of intelligence are unstable predictors of later intellectual ability (Lewis, 1976). Toward the end of the early childhood period some stability is found, but dangers are everpresent in interpretation. For example, when the average IQ of

groups of children are compared at age 6 and at age 18, the correlation is generally found to be about .80. However, when individual intellectual development, rather than group means, is studied, a somewhat different picture emerges. McCall, Appelbaum, and Hogarty (1973) found that normal middle-class children experienced average IQ changes of 28.5 points between $2\frac{1}{2}$ and 17 years of age and one child in seven displayed IQ shifts of more than 40 points.

There is evidence that in addition to these quantitative shifts in intelligence, some qualitative changes are also detectable by the psychometric approach. The psychometric approach describes qualitative changes in terms of changes in the relationships among measured intellectual abilities. Others have reported qualitative changes in verbal abilities as the child's use of language develops (Sigel & Hooper, 1968). The simple vocabulary factor of labeling, for example, present from 27 to 35 months of age, is replaced by the two factors of verbal imitation and verbal comprehension at 38 to 39 months. Conventional measures of mental ability continue to be used extensively for purposes of diagnosing developmental status, educational program planning, and program evaluation. By far the most frequently used measure of young children's intelligence is the Stanford-Binet Intelligence Scale. Other widely used measures are Goodenough's Draw-a-Man, the Wechsler Intelligence Scales, and the Peabody Picture Vocabulary Test (Evans, 1974). Scales based upon Piaget's cognitive developmental theory have also been developed (Goldschmid & Bentler, 1968; Laurendeau & Pinard, 1962). More specific cognitive measures that are not commercially available are described by Johnson and Bommarito (1971) and Johnson (1976).

Within both approaches to the study of cognition during the early childhood years the exact nature of the relationship between thought and language remains unsettled. However, there is general agreement that language acquisition is perhaps one of the most important developments during the early childhood years and that language and thought are intimately related (Hood & Bloom, 1979).

Language Development.   Language development in the young child is a truly remarkable phenomenon. What is impressive to researchers and parents alike is that children selectively learn the phonemes of their language, master the rules of combining phonemes into morphemes and words, induce basic rules for morpheme combination, and learn to apply transformational rules (semantic, syntactical, and phonological) to generate intelligent sentences all in a mere five or six years without formal education (McNeill, 1970; Menyuk, 1971). The rate of language acquisition is truly astounding. For example, the average 24-month-old has a vocabulary of about fifty words. During the next four years the child learns several new words each day, doubling his or her vocabulary every six months or less. The average 6-year-old knows between eight thousand and fourteen thousand words (Carey, 1977). The average 2-year-old can articulate correctly only about 32 percent of the phonemes he or she uses; by age 5 about 88 percent are correctly articulated; and by age 8 the speech of the child is for all intents and purposes that of the adult. Some of the usage of the young child does, however, tend to be idiosyncratic (deVilliers & deVilliers, 1978; Thompson & Chapman, 1977).

Grammar provides the rules for combining words and sounds into meaningful sentences. Chomsky (1965) proposed a theory that has three systems of rules: semantic rules for interpreting and conveying meaning in sentences (base structure); syntactical rules for interpreting and conveying sentence form, such as active versus passive (surface structure); and phonological rules for pairing sounds and meaning (speech) (DiVesta, 1974). The speaker originates a meaning to be communicated (base structure), applies transformational rules to generate a sentence (surface structure), and then transforms the sentence into a phonological system (speech). The listener reverses the process. By age 3 children demonstrate extensive grammatical knowledge. They can form plural nouns; past, present, and future tenses of verbs, and the objective, subjective, and possessive forms of pronouns (Brown, 1973). They have mastered the basics of all three sets of rules, although they tend to overgeneralize their usage (Gleason, 1967).

Language acquisition is at least partially attributable to the innate structure of the human mind and is related to biological and physiological development (Lenneberg, 1969; Slobin, 1973). It is also a function of experience (DiVesta, 1974). Imitation, feedback, and reinforcement have all been shown to contribute to the child's language development (Brown & Bellugi, 1964; Erwin-Tripp, 1973; McNeill, 1970). Experiential factors are particularly important in understanding how language develops within a larger psychological context (Danks & Glucksberg, 1980; deVilliers & deVilliers, 1978).

One of the most often used indicators of the development of vocabulary and grammar is the average number of morphemes in a sentence (MLU—mean length of utterance [Brown, 1958, 1973]). The MLU increases in size with both an increase in vocabulary and an increase in the sophistication and complexity of sentence structure, reflecting both more complex meaning and more versatile use of syntax. Other measures frequently used are the Peabody Picture Vocabulary Test and the Illinois Test of Psycholinguistic Abilities.

Social Development. Most societies view early childhood as the period of socialization, and social development has been a principal goal of most early childhood education programs. Socialization is the process by which children develop an awareness of and conformity to the roles and norms for behavior established by the culture. The product of socialization, in the ideal, is a socially competent adult. Social competence implies (1) normative patterning of social interactions and relationships and (2) effectiveness in reaching personal goals within or through social interactions.

The research literature has generally looked at social competence development as a product of predispositions, traits, or abilities as manifested in specific behaviors used by individuals across social situations (e.g., Anderson & Messick, 1974; Mischell, 1970). So, for example, physical appearance, cognitive abilities, motivation, and learning styles have been given prominent positions in theories of social competence development (Bronfenbrenner, 1979; Wohlwill, 1973), and sex and social class differences have been major organizing variables for research (Hess, 1970; Mischell, 1970). The dependent variables of such research have been behaviors such as attachment, dependency, and aggression (Feshback, 1970; Maccoby & Masters, 1970).

Dyadic relationships. More recently, social competence has been viewed as the quality and patterning of relationships at the dyadic level. That is, the construct has been viewed as a property of interactions between individuals rather than as qualities possessed by individuals themselves or as behaviors enacted by a single child (Gottman & Bakeman, 1979). Within this dyadic framework, socially competent relationships are seen as mutually satisfying, affectively positive, flexibly structured engagements that yield successful outcomes for the individuals involved (O'Malley, 1977). This conception has encouraged detailed study of children's peer relations and play.

During the early childhood years children begin to move outward from their home environment and begin to interact more with their peers. Children play with each other, and as they do so they learn from each other. Hartup (1970; 1979) has been one of the leading advocates of the view that child-child relations are distinctly different from adult-child relationships and singularly important for the development of social competence. He argues that the eqalitarianism, reciprocity, and frequency of peer interactions provide the quantity and quality of direct experience with many roles and models that is necessary for children to contribute to their own socialization (Hartup, 1979).

Play. The nature of the preschool child's play activity changes with age and experience. Parten (1932), for example, categorized children's play behavior into the following categories: (1) unoccupied, (2) solitary (independent play), (3) onlooker, (4) parallel play (playing alongside but not with another child), (5) associative (common activity with borrowing, lending, and taking turns), and (6) cooperative (different roles assumed by different children that supplement each other in the formation of a common goal). The latter categories more often apply to the play of older children, the former to the play activity of younger children.

Such changes in play behavior have been explained in terms of children's decreasing egocentrism and reflect a relationship between cognitive and social development. Piaget (1962) and Smilansky (1968) have defined a cognitive-developmental sequence for play. The sequence includes (1) functional play (simple repetitive muscle movements with or without objects); (2) constructive play (manipulation of objects to construct or create something; (3)

dramatic play (creation of imaginary situations in which the child acts out other roles or uses objects to represent other things); and (4) games with rules. These four types of play follow a developmental sequence, with functional play occurring most often in infancy and games with rules occurring only when the child reaches the stage of concrete operations. Rubin, Maioni, and Hornung (1976) studied the nature of children's play by combining both the Parten and Smilansky classifications. They report that younger preschool children engage in more solitary-functional and parallel-functional play and less parallel-constructive, parallel-dramatic, and group-dramatic play than older preschool children.

Although many unanswered questions remain concerning the nature of children's play and its relation to other aspects of children's development, there is general consensus in the current literature that play is central to children's development of symbolic representations of the world and to learning, in a safe environment, behaviors, including social behaviors, that are important for later adult functioning (Rubin, Fein, & Vandenberg, 1981).

Doll's Vineland Scale (1953) is one of the few standardized measures purporting to measure social competence (or social "adequacy") that has applicability to the early childhood years. Most measures reflect the unique definitions of the authors and use self-report, ratings by significant others, or observational procedures to assess the construct.

Emotional and Personality Development. Many personality characteristics or aspects of emotional well-being are believed to develop, or fail to develop, during early childhood. Examples include aggressiveness, achievement motivation, and conformity (Peters & Willis, 1978). Two aspects of this domain of development that seem particularly important and have received the attention of researchers and educators are "self-concept" and "locus of control."

Self-concept. During the early childhood years children are forming their self-concepts—a complex set of feelings, beliefs, and understandings about oneself (Peters & Raupp, 1980). A variety of definitions of "self-concept" exists, varying with the author's theoretical perspective. Most definitions include some notion of differentiation and value imposition. McDonald (1980), for example, suggests that during the early childhood period the child is developing (1) a body image—a sense of personal appearance and motor performance; (2) a social self—a sense of relationships; (3) a cognitive self—a sense of his or her ability to learn and solve problems; (4) an affecting self—a sense of his or her ability to control or affect change in the environment. As the child enters school, further differentiation with respect to school subjects, sports, or extracurricular activities occurs (Sears & Sherman, 1964). As the child places values upon each of these differentiated aspects of self, an overall sense of self-acceptance and self-respect emerges. This is generally called "self-esteem" (Sears & Sherman, 1964).

Children's ability to differentiate aspects of self and their assignment of value to these aspects are a function of their ability to "decenter" their cumulative experience, including social experience, and the feedback provided by others (Coopersmith, 1967). During the early childhood years children learn to differentiate themselves from others and to compare and contrast themselves and their performance with other children and with adult models. They develop an identity within a social context, becoming aware of themselves as members of a group (such as female or Hispanic), and they learn the social and cultural meaning of such group membership. Children also learn to differentiate their behavior in different settings (for example, home versus school), and with different people (grandmother versus teacher) (Samuels, 1977).

As this differentiation occurs, children begin to apply labels to themselves and to their behavior. At first their labels are just words, but by the end of the early childhood period they associate these evaluative components with the concept of who they are, what they are like, and what they should be (Hess & Croft, 1975). As such, the self-concept of the child plays a major role in determining his or her success in school and interactions with the world (Sears & Sherman, 1964).

Locus of control. During the early childhood period the child's world is expanding very rapidly. Each new experience contributes to the child's sense of efficacy or "personal agency" (Harter, 1978; White, 1959). What the child learns from these early experiences has major implications for later development. Whether individuals feel that they have the ability to control or affect change in their environment is an important determinant of their performance in a wide range of situations, including school. Children who feel they can make a difference and who attribute their successes to their own abilities and efforts are considered to have an internal locus of control. Such an attitude has been consistently related to cognitive development and problem-solving success (Gilmor, 1978; Strickland, 1977). Lefcourt (1976) suggests that people who perceive themselves as effective causative agents are more perceptive and ready to learn about the environment. They are more inquisitive and more curious. In contrast, those children who attribute outcomes to factors outside their control are prone to give up and to be passive (Abramson, Seligman, & Teasdale, 1978; Miller & Norman, 1979; Seligman, 1973, 1974, 1975). Such children are said to have an external locus of control.

Relevance of Child Development for Education

Well-accepted conceptual frameworks exist that can be used to organize the massive collection of research findings in child development, and these data have relevance for educators. Logic and persuasion are often used to discuss links between theories, facts, and educational practices. However, an important question remains: do teachers behave differently when they have at their disposal a solid foundation of theories, facts, and generalizations from child development research? This section will provide partial answers to the question.

Linking Theory and Practice. Several specialists in either child development or early childhood education have written cogently about the value of providing teachers with information about child development and an understanding of developmental theory. Biber and Franklin (1967) and Caldwell and Richmond (1967) presented important papers early in the development of Head Start in an attempt to persuade program developers of the value of developmental theory. Others analyzed program development and teacher training efforts that were part of the renewed interest in young children that coincided with Head Start (DeVries, 1974; Peters, 1977; Seaver & Cartwright, 1977; Sigel, 1972; Simmons, Whitfield, & Layton, 1980; Weikart, 1972). In addition to arguing the relevance of theory in formulating program practices, many of these authors used the Head Start model program experience to document that developmental theories had been used successfully for deriving program content and practices.

Although we advocate the relevance of developmental theories for curriculum design and educational practice, we recognize that logic and persuasion alone will not suffice to effect the link. Specific procedures for bridging theories and practices are needed. Ultimately, research and evaluation efforts, as well as children's experiences, benefit when systematic processes for deriving educational programs and practices from theories are carried out, since such procedures are the means of extending research results to applied settings.

Efforts to isolate salient components for program comparison provided preliminary information for those interested in proposing specific procedures for linking theories and practices. For example, Fein and Clarke-Stewart (1973) proposed several dimensions they had found helpful in determining important differences among early education programs. Four of the six dimensions were tied directly to key assumptions of developmental theories, and the remaining two were more procedural (concerning level of structure in the program and type of adult-child contacts). Theoretical dimensions included the conception of the nature of the child (the maturation-environment issue); judgments about goals for children (process-content issue); decisions about developmental aspects to be emphasized; and judgments about the value of intervening at various levels (for example, whether to change child, change family, or change both). Spodek (1977) suggested a different comparison approach that included some of the same elements but, in addition, added dimensions related to program effectiveness, practicality, and greater emphasis on procedural matters such as scheduling, grouping, and staffing.

These and other comparative approaches have been useful to authors interested in proposing processes for systematically linking developmental theories and program practices. Peters and Willis (1978) set forth three general

components of a translation model: product specification (to indicate desired results of interaction with child); process specification (to indicate what must be done to bring about desired changes); and modifiability index (to judge the likelihood of effective change). A somewhat more elaborate procedure has been described by Seaver and Cartwright (1977). They set up a conceptual hierarchy based upon the identification of the theoretical assumptions that dictate developmental expectations and change processes. In turn, related inferences about facilitating conditions and appropriate professional roles and behavior must be specified. These components, in turn, determine the selection of child activities, relevant content, and decisions about appropriate settings. The authors provide examples of conceptual hierarchies for each of the three major developmental world views.

Differential Effects of Early Education Programs. Perhaps the richest resource for information about children's educational experiences vis-à-vis different developmental theories is the Head Start and Follow-Through Planned Variation research literature. For example, our computer-based investigation of the topic turned up 337 citations. This body of research is important because it supports the notion that teachers can be taught to use different approaches (derived from different theories); that these approaches can often be documented as reliably implemented in classrooms; and that children perform differently depending upon the teaching approach and curriculum model in use.

Head Start and Follow Through programs. The entire Head Start effort for the past fifteen years was chronicled by Zigler and Valentine (1979) and is an excellent resource for those interested in the history and policy implications of Head Start. Rivlin and Timpane (1975) prepared a volume about the research and policy issues unique to the Planned Variation studies. Major research reports on Planned Variation should be consulted by readers interested in greater depth than space permits here (Bissell, 1971, 1972; Kennedy, 1977; Stallings, 1975; Stebbins et al., 1977). Excellent summaries of the Planned Variation research are also available (Hodges & Sheehan, 1978; Miller, 1979; Moore, 1977).

Two brief examples of major research projects designed to document differential model effects are presented, and many other examples are available. Miller and Dyer (1975) studied four model programs in an attempt to identify different program dimensions and differential effects upon children. Models included Montessori, traditional (maturationist approach), structured academic, and combination programs. Observations were conducted in classrooms to determine if models were being appropriately implemented. Results indicated that program differences were evident and, moreover, that they occurred along predicted lines related to their underlying developmental theories. In addition, the programs did have different effects on children, with respect to immediate impact as well as a four-year period. Generally, the more structured approach produced better immediate cognitive gains. Differential effects in both cognitive and noncognitive areas resulted from various combinations of approaches.

Stallings (1975) conducted an especially relevant observational study that proposed a major question about the relations of teaching practices to child outcomes. Seven Follow Through (primary grades) model programs were involved in the research, and observations indicated that important differences among models were evident in classrooms. In addition, it was concluded that structured classrooms in which teachers used systematic instruction contributed to higher scores on mathematics and reading achievement. Flexible classrooms that included more exploratory materials and options for child choices contributed to higher scores on a test of nonverbal reasoning and more willingness of children to work independently.

Day care services. Head Start and Follow Through are not the only programs involved in research on the relation of teacher approaches to child outcomes. In a recent nationwide study of day care services and policies in the United States, Ruopp and his associates (1979) reported that the most crucial variable in a child's day care experience was the care giver. Furthermore, in a detailed analysis of the characteristics of care givers that make a difference in child progress, the researchers reported that education or training in child-related fields such as developmental psychology and early childhood education was related to distinctive patterns of care giver behaviors and child behaviors, including higher gains in test scores for children. In centers where all care givers had such training, the children were found to have a significant advantage in the rate of intellectual growth over children in centers where only some care givers had training.

Policy Implications. The need for more well-prescribed national policies for children and families is a subject that is addressed frequently by researchers, educators, and other advocates for children (Haskins and Gallagher, 1980; Keniston, 1977; National Academy of Sciences, 1976; Roberts, 1980). We do not intend to present a thorough review of the literature on policy alternatives for children and families, but we do want to make two general points about policy alternatives in summary.

First, it is clear that research in early childhood development has advanced to the point where we can argue confidently (supported by facts and figures) about the value of early intervention in terms of immediate benefits to children as well as cost-effective long-range effects for all of us. Second, understanding the nature of developmental processes, especially their interrelatedness, should convince us to set aside our individual special interests, whether they be in fields such as child health and nutrition, early education, family aid programs, mental health, or others, and join together on behalf of the needs of children.

Carol A. Cartwright
Donald L. Peters

See also Early Childhood Education; Parent Education; Preschool Education for the Handicapped; Readiness.

REFERENCES

Abramson, L. Y.; Seligman, M. E. P.; & Teasdale, J. D. Learned helplessness in humans: Critique and reformulation. *Journal of Abnormal Psychology*, 1978, *81*, 49–74.

Ambron, S. R. *Child Development* (2nd ed.). New York: Holt, Rinehart & Winston, 1978.

Anderson, J., & Messick, S. Social competency in young children. *Developmental Psychology*, 1974, *10*, 282–293.

Baldwin, A. L. *Theories of Child Development*. New York: Wiley, 1967.

Baltes, P.; Cornelius, S.; & Nesselroade, J. Cohort effects in developmental psychology. In J. Nesselroade & P. Baltes (Eds.), *Longitudinal Research in the Study of Behavior and Development*. New York: Academic Press, 1979.

Baltes, P.; Reese, H.; & Lipsitt, L. Life-span developmental psychology. In M. Rosenzweig & L. Porter (Eds.), *Annual Review of Psychology* (Vol. 31). Palo Alto, Calif.: Annual Reviews, Inc., 1980.

Baltes, P.; Reese, H.; & Nesselroade, J. *Life-span Developmental Psychology: Introduction to Research Methods*. Monterey, Calif.: Brooks/Cole, 1977.

Biber, B., & Franklin, M. B. The relevance of developmental and psychodynamic concepts to the education of the preschool child. *Journal of the American Academy of Child Psychiatry*, 1967, *6*, 5–24.

Biehler, R. F. *Child Development: An Introduction* (2nd ed.). Boston: Houghton Mifflin, 1981.

Bijou, S. W., & Baer, D. M. *Child Development I: A Systematic and Empirical Theory*. New York: Appleton-Century-Crofts, 1961.

Bissell, J. S. *Implementation of Planned Variation in Head Start: Review and Summary of the Stanford Research Institute Interim Report—First Year of Evaluation* (Vol. 1). Washington, D.C.: Department of Health, Education, and Welfare Office of Child Development, U.S. Government Printing Office, 1971. (ERIC Document Reproduction Service No. ED 052 845)

Bissell, J. S. *Planned Variation in Head Start and Follow Through*. Washington, D.C.: Department of Health, Education, and Welfare, 1972. (ERIC Document Reproduction Service No. ED 069 355)

Bloom, B. *Stability and Change in Human Characteristics*. New York: Wiley, 1964.

Bronfenbrenner, U. Developmental research, public policy, and the ecology of childhood, *Child Development*, 1974, *45*, 1–5.

Bronfenbrenner, U. *The Ecology of Human Development*. Cambridge, Mass.: Harvard University Press, 1979.

Brown, R. *Words and Things*. New York: Free Press, 1958.

Brown, R. *A First Language: The Early Stages*. Cambridge, Mass.: Harvard University Press, 1973.

Brown, R., & Beluggi, U. Three processes in the child's acquisition of syntax. *Harvard Educational Review*, 1964, *34*, 131–153.

Caldwell, B., & Richmond, J. B. The impact of theories of child development. In H. W. Bernard & W. C. Huckins (Eds.), *Readings in Human Development*. Boston: Allyn & Bacon, 1967.

Carey, S. The child as word learner. In M. Halle, J. Bresman, & G. A. Miller (Eds.), *Linguistic Theory and Psychological Reality*. Cambridge, Mass.: MIT Press, 1977.

Cartwright, G. P.; Cartwright, C. A.; & Ward, M. E. *Educating Special Learners*. Belmont, Calif.: Wadsworth, 1981.

Chomsky, N. *Aspects of the Theory of Syntax*. Cambridge, Mass.: MIT Press, 1965.

Coopersmith, S. *Antecedents of Self-esteem*. San Francisco: Freeman, 1967.

Crain, W. C. *Theories of Development*. Englewood Cliffs, N.J.: Prentice-Hall, 1980.

Danks, J. H., & Glucksberg, S. Experimental psycholinguistics. In M. Rosenzweig & L. Porter (Eds.), *Annual Review of Psychology* (Vol. 31). Palo Alto, Calif.: Annual Reviews, Inc., 1980.

deVilliers, J., & deVilliers, P. *Language Acquisition*. Cambridge, Mass.: Harvard University Press, 1978.

DeVries, R. Theory in educational practice. In R. Colvin & E. Zaffiro (Eds.), *Preschool Education: A Handbook for the Training of Early Childhood Educators*. New York: Springer, 1974.

DiVesta, F. *Language, Learning, and Cognitive Processes*. Monterey, Calif.: Brooks/Cole, 1974.

Doll, E. *Measurement of Social Competence*. Circle Pines, Minn.: American Guidance Service, 1953.

Elkind, D. Piagetian and psychometric conceptions of intelligence. *Harvard Educational Review*, 1969, *39*(2), 319–337.

Emmerich, W. Evaluating alternative models of development: An illustrative study of preschool personal-social behaviors. *Child Development*, 1977, *48*, 1401–1410.

Erwin-Tripp, S. Imitation and structural change in children's language. In C. A. Ferguson & D. Slobin (Eds.), *Studies of Child Language Development*. New York: Holt, Rinehart & Winston, 1973.

Evans, E. Measurement practices in early childhood education. In R. Colvin & E. Zaffiro (Eds.), *Preschool Education: A Handbook for the Training of Early Childhood Educators*. New York: Springer, 1974.

Evans, E. *Contemporary Influences in Early Childhood Education* (2nd ed.). New York: Holt, Rinehart & Winston, 1975.

Fein, G., & Clarke-Stewart, A. *Day Care in Context*. New York: Wiley, 1973.

Feshback, S. Aggression. In P. Mussen (Ed.), *Carmichael's Manual of Child Psychology* (Vol. 2). New York: Wiley, 1970.

Flavell, J. *The Developmental Psychology of Jean Piaget*. New York: Van Nostrand, 1963.

Flavell, J., & Wohlwill, J. Formal and functional aspects of cognitive development. In D. Elkind & J. Flavell (Eds.), *Studies in Cognitive Development*. New York: Oxford University Press, 1969.

Forman, G., & Kushner, D. *The Child's Construction of Knowledge: Piaget for Teaching Children*. Monterey, Calif.: Brooks/Cole, 1977.

Fowler, W. Cognitive differentiation and developmental learning. In H. W. Reese & L. P. Lipsitt (Eds.), *Advances in Child Development and Behavior* (Vol. 15). New York: Academic Press, 1980.

Freud, S. *An Outline of Psychoanalysis*. New York: Norton, 1949.

Gagné, R. M. Contributions of learning to human development. In J. L. Frost & G. R. Hawkes (Eds.), *The Disadvantaged Child*. Boston: Houghton Mifflin, 1970.

Gelman, R. Cognitive development. In M. Rosenzweig & L. Porter (Eds.), *Annual Review of Psychology* (Vol. 29). Palo Alto, Calif.: Annual Reviews, Inc., 1978.

Gibson, E., & Levin, H. *The Psychology of Reading*. Cambridge, Mass.: MIT Press, 1975.

Gilmor, T. M. Locus of control as a mediator of adaptive behavior in children and adolescents. *Canadian Psychological Review*, 1978, *19*, 1–26.

Gleason, J. B. Do children imitate? *Proceedings of the International Conference on Oral Education of the Deaf*, 1967, *2*, 1441–1448.

Glick, J. Cognitive development in cross-cultural perspective. In F. Horowitz (Ed.), *Review of Child Developmental Research* (Vol. 4). Chicago: University of Chicago Press, 1975.

Goldschmid, M. L., & Bentler, P. The dimensions and measurement of conservation. *Child Development*, 1968, *39*, 787–792.

Gottman, J., & Bakeman, R. The sequential analysis of observational data. In M. Lamb, J. Suomi, & G. Stephenson (Eds.), *Social Interaction Analysis*. Madison: University of Wisconsin Press, 1979.

Harris, D. B. (Ed.) *The Concept of Development*. Minneapolis: University of Minnesota Press, 1957.

Harter, S. Effectance motivation reconsidered: Toward a developmental model. *Human Development*, 1978, *21*, 34–36.

Hartup, W. Peer interaction and social organization. In P. Mussen (Ed.), *Carmichael's Manual of Child Psychology* (Vol. 2). New York: Wiley, 1970.

Hartup, W. Peer relations and the growth of social competence. In M. Kent & J. Rolf (Eds.), *Primary Prevention of Psychopathology* (Vol. 3). Hanover, N.H.: University Press of New England, 1979.

Haskins, R., & Gallagher, J. J. (Eds.) *Care and Education of Young Children in America: Policy, Politics, and Social Science*. Norwood, N.J.: Ablex, 1980.

Hess, R. Social class and ethnic influences on socialization. In P. Mussen (Ed.), *Carmichael's Manual of Child Psychology* (Vol. 2). New York: Wiley, 1970.

Hess, R., & Croft, D. *Teachers of Young Children*. Boston: Houghton Mifflin, 1975.

Hodges, W. L., & Sheehan, R. Follow Through as ten years of experimentation. *Young Children*, 1978, *34*, 4–14.

Honstead, C. The developmental theory of Jean Piaget. In J. L. Frost (Ed.), *Early Childhood Education Rediscovered: Readings*. New York: Holt, Rinehart & Winston, 1968.

Hood, L., & Bloom, L. What, when, and how about why: A longitudinal study of early expressions of causality. *Monographs of the Society for Research in Child Development*, 1979, *44*(6, Serial No. 181).

Hunt, J. M. *Intelligence and Experience*. New York: Ronald Press, 1961.

Johnson, O. G. *Tests and Measurements in Child Development: Handbook 2*. San Francisco: Jossey-Bass, 1976.

Johnson, O. G., & Bommarito, J. *Tests and Measurements in Child Development: A Handbook*. San Francisco: Jossey-Bass, 1971.

Keniston, K. *All Our Children*. New York: Harcourt Brace Jovanovich, 1977.

Kennedy, M. M. The Follow Through program. *Curriculum Inquiry*, 1977, *7*, 183–208.

Kilmer, S., & Weinberg, R. The nature of young children and the state of early education: Reflections from the Minnesota Roundtable. *Young Children*, 1974, *30*, 60–67.

Kohlberg, L., & Mayer, R. Development as the aim of education. *Harvard Educational Review*, 1972, *42*, 449–496.

Langer, J. *Theories of Development*. New York: Holt, Rinehart & Winston, 1969.

Laurendeau, M., & Pinard, A. *Causal Thinking in the Child*. New York: International Universities Press, 1962.

Lazerson, M. The historical antecedents of early childhood education. In I. Gordon (Ed.), *Early Childhood Education: The Seventy-first Yearbook of the National Society for the Study of Education*. Chicago: University of Chicago Press, 1972.

Lefcourt, H. M. *Locus of Control: Current Trends in Theory and Research.* New York: Wiley, 1976.

Lenneberg, E. On explaining language. *Science,* 1969, *164,* 635–643.

Lerner, R. *Concepts and Theories of Human Development.* Reading, Mass.: Addison-Wesley, 1976.

Lewis, M. What do we mean when we say "infant intelligence scores"? In M. Lewis (Ed.), *Origins of Intelligence: Infancy and Early Childhood.* New York: Plenum, 1976.

Maccoby, E., & Masters, J. Attachment and dependency. In P. Mussen (Ed.), *Carmichael's Manual of Child Psychology* (Vol. 2). New York: Wiley, 1970.

Masters, J. C. Developmental psychology. In M. Rosenzweig & L. Porter (Eds.), *Annual Review of Psychology* (Vol. 32). Palo Alto, Calif.: Annual Reviews, Inc., 1981.

McCall, R. B. Challenges to a science of developmental psychology. *Child Development,* 1977, *48,* 333–344.

McCall, R.; Appelbaum, M.; & Hogarty, P. Developmental changes in mental performance. *Monographs of the Society for Research in Child Development,* 1973, *38*(3, Serial No. 150).

McDonald, K. Enhancing a child's positive self-concept. In T. Yawkey (Ed.), *The Self-concept of the Young Child.* Provo, Utah: Brigham Young University Press, 1980.

McNeill, D. The development of language. In P. Mussen (Ed.), *Carmichael's Manual of Child Psychology.* New York: Wiley, 1970.

Menyuk, P. *The Acquisition and Development of Language.* Englewood Cliffs, N.J.: Prentice-Hall, 1971.

Meredeth, H. Research between 1960 and 1970 on the standing height of young children in different parts of the world. In H. Reese & L. Lipsitt (Eds.), *Advances in Child Development and Behavior* (Vol. 12). New York: Academic Press, 1978.

Miller, I. W., & Norman, W. H. Learned helplessness in humans: A review and attribution-theory model. *Psychological Bulletin,* 1979, *86,* 93–118.

Miller, L. B. Development of curriculum models in Head Start. In E. Zigler & J. Valentine (Eds.), *Project Head Start: A Legacy of the War on Poverty.* New York: Free Press, 1979.

Miller, L. B., & Dyer, J. L. Four preschool programs: Their dimensions and effects. *Monographs of the Society for Research in Child Development,* 1975, *40*(Serial No. 162).

Mischell, W. Sex typing and socialization. In P. Mussen (Ed.), *Carmichael's Manual of Child Psychology* (Vol. 2). New York: Wiley, 1970.

Moore, S. G. The effects of Head Start programs with different curricula and teaching strategies. *Young Children,* 1977, *32,* 54–61.

National Academy of Sciences. *Toward a National Policy for Children and Families.* Washington, D.C.: The Academy, 1976. (ERIC Document Reproduction Service No. ED 142 272)

National Center for Health Statistics. NCHS growth charts, 1976. *Vital Statistics,* 1976, p. 253.

O'Malley, J. Research perspectives on social competence. *Merrill-Palmer Quarterly,* 1977, *23,* 29–44.

Parten, M. Social participation among preschool children. *Journal of Abnormal and Social Psychology,* 1932, *29,* 243–269.

Peters, D. L. Early childhood education: An overview and evaluation. In H. L. Hom & P. A. Robinson (Eds.), *Psychological Processes in Early Education.* New York: Academic Press, 1977.

Peters, D. L., & Raupp, C. Developing the self-concept in the exceptional child. In T. Yawkey (Ed.), *The Self-concept of the Young Child.* Provo, Utah: Brigham Young University Press, 1980.

Peters, D. L., & Willis, S. L. *Early Childhood.* Monterey, Calif.: Brooks/Cole, 1978.

Piaget, J. *The Psychology of Intelligence.* New York: Humanities Press, 1950.

Piaget, J. *The Origins of Intelligence in Children.* New York: International Universities Press, 1952.

Piaget, J. *Play, Dreams, and Imitation in Childhood.* New York: Norton, 1962.

Piaget, J., & Inhelder, B. *The Psychology of the Child.* New York: Basic Books, 1969.

Pinard, A., & Laurendeau, M. A scale of mental development based on the theory of Piaget. *Journal of Research in Science Teaching,* 1964, *2,* 253–260.

Read, M. *Malnutrition, Learning, and Behavior.* Washington, D.C.: National Institute of Child Health and Human Development, 1976. (ERIC Document Reproduction Service No. ED 133 395)

Reese, H. W., & Overton, W. F. Models of development and theories of development. In L. R. Goulet & P. B. Baltes (Eds.), *Life-span Development Psychology.* New York: Academic Press, 1970.

Rivlin, A., & Timpane, M. *Planned Variation in Education: Should We Give Up or Try Harder?* Washington, D.C.: Brookings Institution, 1975. (ERIC Document Reproduction Service No. ED 114 986)

Roberts, F. Child growth and development: A basic for policy. *Education and Urban Society,* 1980, *12,* 147–161.

Robinson, P. A., & Hom, H. L. Child psychology and early childhood education. In H. L. Hom & P. A. Robinson (Eds.), *Psychological Processes in Early Education.* New York: Academic Press, 1977.

Rohwer, W. D.; Ammon, P. R.; & Cramer, P. *Understanding Intellectual Development: Three Approaches to Theory and Practice.* Hinsdale, Ill.: Dryden Press, 1974.

Rubin, K.; Fein, G.; & Vandenberg, B. Play. In P. Mussen (Ed.), *Carmichael's Manual of Child Psychology* (4th ed.). New York: Wiley, 1981.

Rubin, K.; Maioni, T.; & Hornung, M. Free play behaviors in middle-and lower-class preschoolers: Parten and Piaget revisited. *Child Development,* 1976, *47,* 414–419.

Ruopp, R.; Travers, J.; Glantz, F.; & Coelen, C. *Children at the Center: Final Report of the National Day Care Study* (Vol. 1). Cambridge, Mass.: Abt Associates, 1979.

Samuels, S. *Enhancing Self-concept in Early Childhood.* New York: Human Sciences Press, 1977.

Sears, P., & Sherman, V. *In Pursuit of Self-esteem.* Belmont, Calif.: Wadsworth, 1964.

Sears, R. R. Your ancients revisited: A history of child development. In E. M. Hetherington (Ed.), *Review of Child Development Research* (Vol. 5). Chicago: University of Chicago Press, 1975.

Seaver, J. W., & Cartwright, C. A. A pluralistic foundation for training early childhood professionals. *Curriculum Inquiry,* 1977, *7,* 305–329.

Seligman, M. E. P. Fall into helplessness. *Psychology Today,* June 1973, pp. 43–48.

Seligman, M. E. P. Depression and learned helplessness. In R. J. Friedman & M. M. Katz (Eds.), *The Psychology of Depression: Contemporary Theory and Research.* New York: Wiley, 1974.

Seligman, M. E. P. *Helplessness: On Depression, Development, and Death.* San Francisco: Freeman, 1975.

Sigel, I. E. Developmental theory: Its place and relevance in early intervention programs. *Young Children,* 1972, *27,* 364–372.

Sigel, I. E., & Brodzinsky, D. M. Individual differences: A perspective for understanding intellectual development. In H. L. Hom & P. A. Robinson (Eds.), *Psychological Processes in Early Education.* New York: Academic Press, 1977.

Sigel, I. E., & Hooper, F. (Eds.). *Logical Thinking in Children: Research Based on Piaget's Theory.* New York: Holt, Rinehart & Winston, 1968.

Simmons, B. M.; Whitfield, E. L.; & Layton, J. R. The preparation of early childhood teachers: Philosophical and empirical foundations. In D. G. Range, J. R. Layton, & D. L. Roubinek (Eds.), *Aspects of Early Childhood Education: Theory to Research to Practice.* New York: Academic Press, 1980.

Skinner, B. F. *Science and Human Behavior.* New York: Macmillan, 1953.

Slobin, D. Cognitive prerequisites for the development of grammar. In C. A. Ferguson & D. Slobin (Eds.), *Studies of Child Language Development.* New York: Holt, Rinehart & Winston, 1973.

Smart, M. S., & Smart, R. C. *Children: Development and Relations* (3rd ed.). New York: Macmillan, 1977.

Smilansky, S. *The Effects of Sociodramatic Play on Disadvantaged Preschool Children.* New York: Wiley, 1968.

Spodek, B. Curriculum construction in early childhood education. In B. Spodek & H. J. Walberg (Eds.), *Early Childhood Education: Issues and Insights.* Berkeley, Calif.: McCutchan, 1977.

Stallings, J. Implementation and child effects of teaching practices in Follow Through classrooms. *Monographs of the Society for Research in Child Development,* 1975, *40*(Serial No. 163).

Stebbins, L. B.; St. Pierre, R. G.; Proper, E. C.; Anderson, R. B.; & Cerva, T. R., *Education as Experimentation: A Planned Variation Model* (Vol. 4-A). Cambridge, Mass.: Abt Associates, 1977.

Strickland, B. R. Internal-external control of reinforcement. In T. Blass (Ed.), *Personality Variables in Social Behavior.* New York: Wiley, 1977.

Tanner, J. M. Physical growth. In P. H. Mussen (Ed.), *Carmichael's Manual of Child Psychology.* New York: Wiley, 1970.

Thompson, J., & Chapman, R. Who is "Daddy" revisited: The status of two-year-olds over extended words in use and comprehension. *Journal of Child Language,* 1977, *4,* 359–375.

Tuddenham, R. Intelligence. In R. Ebel (Ed.), *Encyclopedia of Educational Research* (4th ed.). New York: Macmillan, 1960.

Watson, E., & Lowrey, G. *Growth and Development of Children* (4th ed.). Chicago: Yearbook of Medical Publishers, 1962.

Weikart, D. P. Relationship of curriculum, teaching, and learning in preschool education. In J. C. Stanley, *Preschool Programs for the Disadvantaged: Five Experimental Approaches to Early Childhood Education.* Baltimore: Johns Hopkins University Press, 1972.

Weisz, J. R. Transcontextual validity in developmental research. *Child Development,* 1978, *49,* 1–12.

White, R. W. Motivation reconsidered: The concept of competence. *Psychology Review,* 1959, *66,* 297–333.

White, S. H. Evidence for a hierarchical arrangement of learning processes. In L. Lipsitt & G. Spiker (Eds.), *Advances in Child Development and Behavior* (Vol. 2). New York: Academic Press, 1965.

White, S. H. The learning theory tradition and child psychology. In P. H. Mussen (Ed.), *Carmichael's Manual of Child Psychology* (3rd ed., Vol. 1). New York: Wiley, 1970.

White, S. H., & Fishbein, H. D. Children's learning. In N. Talbot, J. Kagan, & L. Eisenberg (Eds.), *Behavioral Science in Pediatrics.* Philadelphia: Saunders, 1971.

White, S. H., & Siegel, A. W. Cognitive development: The new inquiry. *Young Children,* 1976, *31,* 425–436.

Wohlwill, J. The concept of experience: S or R. *Human Development,* 1973, *16,* 90–107.

Yale University Clinic of Child Development. *The First Five Years of Life: A Guide to the Study of the Preschool Child.* New York: Harper & Brothers, 1940.

Zaporozhets, A., & Elkonin, D. (Eds.). *The Psychology of Preschool Children.* Cambridge, Mass.: MIT Press, 1971.

Zigler, E., & Valentine, J. (Eds.). *Project Head Start: A Legacy of the War on Poverty.* New York: Free Press, 1979.

EARLY CHILDHOOD EDUCATION

Early childhood educators view the young child within the contexts of the family and of society. Group programs are seen as tools to foster the child's total growth and development—physical, sensory-perceptual, cognitive-intellectual, linguistic, social, emotional, and academic. A common thread throughout the varying programs developed in the past fifteen years is a shift in emphasis from early childhood education as a means of encouraging socialization and emotional development of young children to a means of providing cognitive and academic education at a much earlier age.

Traditionally early childhood education has been viewed as one way to break the cycle of poverty and to raise the economic and educational levels of society. Never has this been more evident than in the early childhood programs developed since 1965. Preschool compensatory programs, Head Start, and publicly funded day care programs are direct results of this social emphasis. Research on child development has supported the notion that children can and do learn before the traditional school age of 6 years. Further, this research has suggested that environmental effects have an important effect on what young children learn as well as on how they learn. This research and its influence on group programs for young children (3 to 6 years) are reviewed in this article.

The variety of programs available for young children in the United States during the period from the mid-sixties to the early eighties will be described. Specific program variations to be reviewed include nursery school, kindergarten, preschool compensatory programs, Head Start, and day care. Group programs for infants and toddlers, programs for children with special needs, primary grade programs, and child development are discussed in other entries.

History. Previous articles in earlier editions of the *Encyclopedia of Educational Research* have provided overviews of the long-range history of early childhood education (Dowley, 1969; Fuller, 1960; Jensen, 1950). This historical review will focus on modern early childhood education in the United States as experienced since World War II. The social and political context that thrust early childhood education into public awareness in an unprecedented way during the 1960s and some of the major landmarks of this period will be identified.

Seminal thinkers. A useful starting point from which to gain an understanding of modern early childhood education as it is expressed in organized programs for children under 6 years of age is to note several major figures whose writings and works have directly influenced the form and function of current-day early childhood education programs. These persons include John Amos Comenius in the seventeenth century; Jean Jacques Rousseau in the eighteenth; Johann Pestalozzi in the eighteenth and nineteenth; Friedrich Froebel in the nineteenth; John Dewey, Maria Montessori, and G. Stanley Hall in the nineteenth and twentieth; and Edward L. Thorndike, Jean Piaget, and Arnold Gesell in the twentieth. This brief list omits a host of other philosophers, psychologists, child development specialists, and educators whose ideas have strongly influenced the development of modern early childhood education in its various forms, but these few do represent the major streams of thought and action. Braun and Edwards (1972), Frost and Kissinger (1976), Dowley (1969), and Osborne (1975) provide useful overviews of the history of early childhood education as it is related to these and other seminal thinkers. In addition, Ross (1976) and Weber (1969) focus on the development of kindergartens in the United States; Bremner et al. (1974) provide a documentary history, *Children and Youth in America;* deMause (1974) and Ariès (1962) give two accounts of the history of childhood; and Senn (1975) provides insights into the child development movement in the United States.

Social and political context. The history of early childhood education is intimately related to efforts to provide upward mobility in social status for children from poor families and to the desire to reform public schooling (Frost & Kissinger, 1976; Lazerson, 1972; Ross, 1976; Takanishi, 1977). There is still an expectation among many that preschool programs will influence the home and families, that their pedagogical techniques will influence changes in the primary schools, and that work with young children will break the cycle of poverty (Lazerson, 1972). Early childhood education has had to carry a host of high expectations ever since its beginning. For example, Comenius responded to the grimness of children's lives in his day by advocating "humor and lightness" in the children's lessons. Pestalozzi was an educational thinker and developer as well as a teacher who wanted to include poor children in the schools and liked to teach them. Montessori began her educational program specifically for children of the slums with the goal of helping them become independent citizens (Frost & Kissinger, 1976). The McMillan sisters in England and the Peabody sisters in Massachusetts opened kindergartens in urban areas to help eradicate poverty (Osborne, 1975; Ross, 1976). Modern early childhood education has developed from similar reform motiva-

tions, but with more sustained involvement at the federal level than ever before, with Head Start being the largest and longest-lasting federally funded program for children ever mounted (Klein, 1981).

During the Depression of the 1930s and also during World War II, the federal government sponsored child care programs for out-of-work families and for women working in the defense industries (Lanham Act). In 1946 the latter program was allowed to expire, with only one state, California, continuing the program. For the next twenty years the federal government was to provide little support for early childhood education or child care.

The years following World War II (mid-1940s to mid-1960s) were a period of accelerated social change. Women who had entered the work force during the war frequently kept their jobs or got others. More women joined the labor force. The shift from rural to urban centers of residence gained momentum. Extended families were separated. Minority groups began to press the struggle for their civil rights. Cold and hot wars kept both anxiety and industrial productivity high. Economic prosperity was available for many.

A normative-maturational view of child development prevailed in education and child rearing during this period. Neither preschool education nor day care was a high priority except where nursery schools were used to meet the socialization needs of young children of the middle socioeconomic level (SEL). By 1957 the schools were rapidly becoming the scene of the greatest social revolution of the century, as black citizens began to take advantage of the 1954–1955 Supreme Court decisions ruling that separate facilities were inherently unequal and that school boards should proceed with "all deliberate speed" toward racial integration.

Many influential persons believed that the educational system was not teaching children reading or producing enough young people interested and competent in science. The Russian launching of *Sputnik* in 1957 appeared to confirm what many had suspected: the U.S.S.R. was getting ahead of the United States in technological development. Near panic set in. The National Defense Education Act of 1957 focused on instructional improvement in math and science and on the use of guidance and counseling in order to increase both the quality and quantity of scientific personnel. Basic cognitive skills were to be emphasized in public education, and this emphasis later influenced early childhood programs.

The struggle of blacks in particular and of minorities in general to win their share of the economic well-being enjoyed by the other two-thirds of the population refocused attention during the mid-1950s on both the magnitude of poverty and on problems associated with it (Harrington, 1962). These problems included the problems of achievement in the schools noted by Davis (1948); Deutsch (1967); and Eels et al. (1951), in which it was documented that, as a group, low SEL children did not do well in schools. Low SEL is not isomorphic with race, but it is important to remember that minority groups, including blacks, had a greater proportion (but not absolute number) of persons who fell below poverty guidelines than did those in the majority.

During this same period, psychologists and educators in the United States were synthesizing knowledge concerning child development and learning and the variables contributing to the reduction of competence among infants and children—maternal deprivation, low income, poor nutrition, prematurity, and prejudice—to mention only a few. They were also being alerted to the provocative literature on child development created by Jean Piaget (Flavell, 1963; Hunt, 1961) and the growing technology emerging from the behaviorists (Skinner, 1968). The consequence was a reexamination of the maturationist school of thought (Bloom, 1964; Fowler, 1962; Hunt, 1961) and a modification in developmental theory. These changes led to a more predominant role for environmental influences in development and to an interactionist view of infants and children both influencing and being influenced by their human and physical environments.

It is within this postwar context of social awareness and revolution, with its accompanying violence, the irony of abject poverty within economic prosperity, international competition and fear, concern with intellectual development, rapid advances in communications technology, and the shift in thinking about child development that the major landmarks and features of modern early childhood education in the United States must be seen. These social, political, economic, and scientific trends were to lead once again to the use of early childhood education in the service of social and political ends and to the reentry of the federal government into the field. But in contrast to earlier periods, there has been greater vigor, variety, tension, and emphasis on the young child in modern early childhood education. Several landmarks are listed in Table 1 as a guide to the expansive nature of the past three decades, as compared with the slow growth of early childhood education in the three centuries preceding World War II.

Nursery Programs. Nursery school programs multiplied at a rapid rate during the 1970s. In spite of the development of Head Start and preschool compensatory programs for low SEL children, traditional middle SEL nursery schools continued to thrive and to be a significant part of the early childhood education scene in the United States.

Although there is great diversity among nursery schools, generally a nursery school program is a half-day program for $2\frac{1}{2}$-to-5-year-old children meeting from two to five days a week. Classes usually consist of groups of fifteen to twenty children with two or three adults per class. Most nursery schools still serve predominantly middle- and upper-SEL families (Lay & Dopyera, 1977). Sponsorship may be by churches, colleges, or private individuals or groups. Some privately owned nursery schools are run for profit; others are nonprofit. Cooperative nursery schools are parent-owned and managed. In most instances these parents are very involved with the cooperative program, serving as assistant teachers on a regular, rotating basis as well as serving on the board of directors, caring for the physical plant, hiring the teachers, and managing the fiscal affairs. Cooperative programs typically have a parent education component, with groups for discussion, speakers, and a parent library (Taylor, 1981).

Nursery schools are licensed in some states but not in others. Licensing usually guarantees a minimal amount of space per child, a minimal teacher-child ratio, and a minimal level of fire, safety, and health standards, but not teacher qualifications and proficiency or program quality. Although there are not generally accepted minimal professional requirements for nursery school teachers or directors in the United States, a survey of nursery schools across the country found that most nursery school directors had college degrees and that most teachers had some early childhood education training (Evans, 1975; Goodlad, Klein, & Novotney, 1973; Klein & Novotney, 1971). In many instances, nursery schools are staffed by trained, former teachers who currently prefer to have a part-time teaching position. Such positions are not usually available in the public schools, making nursery school teaching an attractive position in spite of the generally low salaries that most nursery schools offer.

Goals. The major purpose of nursery school programs seems to be the socialization of the young child. Program goals emphasize emotional development, development of the whole child, sensory-motor learning, and development of a positive self-concept (Klein & Novotney, 1971; Weber, 1973). Nursery school is seen as an extension of and supplement to the child's home. To this end over one-half of the nursery schools include the parents in some aspect of their programs (Butler, 1973; Klein & Novotney, 1971).

Play is seen as the medium of learning for children of nursery school age. Fantasy and sociodramatic play and creative art activities are central to the program, with play equipment and materials having a major influence on the activities. Traditional nursery schools are generally child-centered and rather permissive, with the teacher's intuitive grasp of child development providing the structure for the program. Within this permissive atmosphere, however, teachers demand compliance to routines, behavior control, and manners (Evans, 1975; Weikart, 1972b).

Parents' expectations for nursery school are generally consonant with the teachers' goals. Parents, nursery teachers, paraprofessionals, and early childhood education students were asked to rank nine values of nursery programs (Hildebrand, 1975). Individuality and socialization were ranked highest by 90 percent of all groups. Cognitive development was ranked higher by paraprofessionals than by any other group of respondents. In fact, 22 percent of the parents ranked cognitive development as the least desirable nursery goal.

Some specific nursery school objectives are to have the children develop sustained attention, the ability to stick to a task, positive interaction with peers and teachers, the

TABLE 1. *Selected landmarks in early childhood education*

	A. Before World War II[a]	
Year	*Item*	*Reference, author, or spokesperson*
1600	Children were economic assets.	
1628	Publication of *School of Infancy.*	John Amos Comenius
1619–1865	Children in slavery.	
1693	Publication of *Thoughts on Education.*	John Locke
1700–1850	Period of the Industrial Revolution and child labor.	
1762	Publication of *Emile,* start education at birth.	Jean Jacques Rousseau
1801	Publication of *How Gertrude Teaches Her Children;* base education on children's natural development.	Johann Pestalozzi
1815	Beginning of parent groups in the United States.	Maternal Associations
1826–1837	Beginning of kindergartens. Publication of *Education of Man.*	Friedrich Froebel
1840	*Parent's Magazine* begun.	
1856	First kindergarten in U.S. (German-language).	Margarethe Schurz in Wisconsin
1859	First English-speaking kindergarten in U.S.	Elizabeth Peabody in Massachusetts
1872	First kindergarten in public school.	William Harris & Susan Blow, St. Louis
1883	First scientific studies of children.	G. Stanley Hall
1896	University of Chicago Lab School begun.	John Dewey
1907	First "Children's House" opened in Rome as Montessori movement begins.	Maria Montessori
1921	Nursery school brought to U.S. from England.	Abigail Eliot
1923	Emphasis on maturationist view of development; fixed intelligence, predetermined development.	Arnold Gesell
1925	National Association for Nursery Education begun.	Patty Smith Hill
1928	Interest in study of cognitive development of young.	Jean Piaget
1930	Emphasis on the study of behavior in U.S. psychology.	John Watson
1930	Children no longer economic assets.	
1933	Beginning of WPA nurseries due to economic depression.	Franklin Roosevelt
1938	Child labor well regulated.	
1942	Beginning of wartime nurseries for working mothers.	Lanham Act
	B. World War II and after[b]	
1946	End of Lanham Act Nurseries.	
1946	Television begins rapid expansion; provides new eye on the world.	
1948	Publication of *Social Class Influences upon Learning.*	Allison Davis
1951	Publication of *Intelligence and Cultural Differences.*	Kenneth Eels, Allison Davis, Robert Havighurst, Virgil Herrick, & Ralph Tyler
1954/55	School desegregation decisions.	U.S. Supreme Court
1950's	Severe criticism of schools by influential persons.	Rudolf Flesch, Hyman Rickover, Arthur Bestor
1957	Public concern over education's shortcomings at peak as Russia launches *Sputnik.*	
1958	Federal general aid to education; federal intervention begins.	National Defense Education Act
1958	Preschool Compensatory Research Projects begin.	
1961	Concepts of fixed intelligence and predetermined development challenged in *Intelligence and Experience.*	J. McV. Hunt
1961	Rediscovery of Jean Piaget in the United States.	
1962	Publication of *The Culturally Deprived Child.*	Frank Reissman

TABLE 1. *Selected landmarks in early childhood education (cont.)*

	B. World War II and after[b]	
Year	Item	Reference, author, or spokesperson
1962	Poverty laid bare to U.S. public in *The Other America*.	Michael Harrington
1964	Importance of early learning reconfirmed in *Stability and Change in Human Characteristics*.	Benjamin Bloom
1964	Beginning of War on Poverty.	Economic Opportunity Act of 1964
1965	Head Start[c] begins; opens revolution in early childhood education.	
1966	Publication of *Adult Status of Children with Contrasting Life Experiences*.	Harold Skeels
1966	Full-year Head Start programs begin.[c]	
1967	Introduction of the British Infant School and open education to United States.	Joseph Featherstone
1967	Follow Through (on Head Start) and Parent-Child Centers begin.[c]	
1968/69	Beginning of instructional models used in Follow Through (1968) and Head Start (1969) Planned Variation.[c]	
1969	Children's Television Workshop begins work on preschool programming.	
1969	Publication of *The Impact of Head Start*.	V. Cicerelli
1969	Creation of Federal Office of Child Development.	Ed Zigler, first director
1971	Veto of Child and Family Services Act begins slowdown of the revolution.	
1972	Home Start and The Child Development Associate Program begin.[c]	
1973	Publication of *Federal Programs for Young Children: Review and Recommendations*.	Sheldon White et al.
1974	Beginning of Project Developmental Continuity.[c]	
1974	Publication of *Children and Television: Lessons from Sesame Street*.	Gerald Lesser
1974	Publication of *A Report on Longitudinal Evaluations of Preschool Programs* (Vol. II).	Urie Bronfenbrenner
1977	Publication of follow-up data from several Preschool Compensatory Research Projects gives new hope for young children through preschool education.	Irving Lazar et al. David Weikart et al.
1978	Publication of results of National Day Care studies.	Richard Ruopp et al.
1979	Basic Educational Skills Project[c] begins.	

[a] These landmarks are drawn from a number of sources, including Braun & Edwards, 1972; Bremner et al., 1974; Dowley, 1969; Frost & Kissinger, 1976; Hodges & Smith, 1978; Richmond, Stipek, & Zigler, 1979; Ross, 1976; Weber, 1969.
[b] Specific references to publications cited in Section B are listed in the references for this entry.
[c] These programs were all part of the Head Start family, and there were still other lesser known programs emanating from Head Start that are not involved in this chronology.

use of sentences in conversation, positive attitudes toward school, impulse control, social proficiency, a healthy personality, good manners, a sense of well-being, and feelings of accomplishment (Butler, 1973; Weikart, 1972b). General, all-round development of the child with emphasis on emotional and social development is sought.

Curriculum. Traditional nursery schools meet their social-emotional development goals by providing a child-centered program based upon play within a safe, adequately equipped physical environment. In a national survey of early childhood education programs, Klein and Novotney (1971) found agreement on nursery school activities and schedule. The most common nursery activities are blocks, outdoor play, storytelling, and informal math and science. Other common activities are cooking, dramatic play (including dolls and housekeeping), nature

walks, rhythms, and trips. Play with manipulative table toys is also common. The typical teaching environment in the nursery school is teacher-directed and whole-group oriented, with little individualization of activities. Positive reinforcement of behaviors is used for both classroom management and instruction.

A typical nursery school (half-day) schedule is as follows:

1. Unstructured free play (discovery time)
2. More-structured group time (circle time)
3. Snack
4. Unstructured outdoor play
5. Structured concluding activity

Discovery time activities include art, creative projects, sociodramatic play, blocks, cooking, informal science and math activities, and manipulative toys. Circle time activities include teaching specific concepts, oral language activities, and music and rhythms. Telling or reading stories is often used as the concluding activity.

The nursery school staff interacts with small groups of children during free play time, letting the materials structure the activities that the children choose. Children are actively involved with these concrete materials most of the time. Group time activities and stories are generally presented to the whole group by one teacher.

The most common curricular approach in traditional nursery schools is the unit-based curriculum, in which child-centered activities are developed around a central theme of interest to young children. Examples of such unit themes might be the zoo, holidays, foods, seasons, families, or pets. These units incorporate a variety of activities, including oral language, stories, music, art, trips, cooking, dramatic play, informal math and science, and creative projects. They are one way of providing the children with opportunities for social interaction, sensory-motor learning, and development of self-concepts. The nursery school curriculum is derived both from the children's interests and from the teachers' developmental assumptions about children. These assumptions about children are drawn heavily from the teachers' perceptions of the children's emotional needs. Generally, the programs are successful because the teachers create an environment for successful learning rather than because of the specific curriculum content (Weikart, 1972b).

Effects. An ecological study of the nursery school environment gives further information about the nursery curriculum and its effects upon children's development. One such study (Shapiro, 1975) of seventeen half-day nursery classrooms for 4-year-old children considered the issues of class size, adult-child ratio, and number of square feet of space per child. The environment of these classes was typical, with blocks, a doll corner, art, and manipulative table toys found in all of the classrooms. Library books, a water or sand table, woodworking, science, and music were found in most of them. No relationship was found between class size and social interaction among the children, but individualization of the program was affected by class size. The optimum adult-child ratio was found to be 1:8 within a class of fifteen children with two teachers. Increasing class size and adding more teachers to maintain the 1:8 ratio was not effective in maintaining optimum teacher-child contacts and individualization. Crowded classrooms had the highest percentage of noninvolvement (26 percent), and large classrooms (over 50 square feet per child) also had a high degree of noninvolved behavior. The optimum size classroom was found to be one that provides 30 to 50 square feet per child. Behaviors also varied with the activity center. The block area and the doll corner elicited the greatest amount of social interaction among children and the greatest amount of deviant behavior. These were also popular areas, with blocks or dolls being selected by the children 37 percent of the time and art 21 percent. Teacher-child interactions

were the greatest in art (35 percent) and much less (17 percent) in the block and doll areas. Teachers apparently deliberately allow spontaneous play in the dramatic play areas, leading to more social interaction and more deviancy.

The value of a heterogeneous environment in the nursery school was shown in an observational study of 3-, 4-, and 5-year-olds (Featherstone, 1974). Records of children's choices of activity areas revealed that some children sought out structured tasks with a stationary adult in places such as the project room or the cooking area. Other children consistently sought out child-structured areas without direct adult involvement; for example, the art table, blocks, or the rug area, which had manipulative toys. Both types of areas were necessary to meet the needs of all the children.

The environmental setting of the nursery school can also have an effect on the children's behavior within one activity area. The sociodramatic play of 4-year-olds was observed (Andalman, 1977) in three different nursery school settings—one unstructured, child-centered; one structured, child-centered; and one Montessori, academically oriented. Children were observed while playing school and playing doctor's office. The style of play was observed to differ systematically according to the setting. In the unstructured settings the children's play was role-oriented, highly imaginative, idiosyncratic, and unconstrained by external demands; in the structured settings the children's play was task-oriented, imitative, cooperative, goal-oriented, and anxious to please; and in the Montessori settings their play was prop-oriented, cooperative, creative on a reality-based level, and extremely verbal.

Effectiveness. Evaluation data for nursery schools are very limited. One reason may be the lack of a clear statement of mission. Without such a statement, it is difficult to determine an appropriate criterion measure for empirical testing of the nursery schools' influence. For the goals of emotional-social development, evaluation has usually been subjective (Evans, 1975; Goodlad, Klein, & Novotney, 1973).

Nursery school attendance for 4-year-olds has been related positively to children's extraversion and verbal competence as measured by the California Preschool Competency Test (Flint, 1979). A study of the long-term effects of nursery school attendance on the first-grade achievement of middle-SEL children (Morella, 1974) found that these children's reading, arithmetic, and perceptual-motor skills were no different from a comparable group of children who had not attended nursery school. A middle-SEL home environment was just as effective as nursery school in preparing children for first-grade academic work. This is not surprising, however, since nursery school goals are not academic. No assessment of social or emotional effects was made. Consideration of affective development would have been more in line with the nursery school's goals.

Nursery school attendance has been questioned especially in light of its current popularity (Moore, Moon, & Moore, 1972). Moore and Moore (1973) state that "there is much talk these days, stimulated partly by accident and partly by design, that a young child cannot normally be fulfilled and optimally developed unless he [she] goes to a good preschool" (p. 14). They review the maternal deprivation research and the research on early and late school entrants from the 1930s to early 1960s and conclude that nursery school attendance provides maternal freedom at the expense of the child and threatens the integrity of the home. They believe that early schooling separates the family, threatens the welfare of the child, and risks speeding the children's development prior to their neurophysiological and perceptual readiness for learning. Moore and Moore conclude that "for the highest and best cognitive, affective and physiological development, we should do all we can to develop a wholesome home and keep [the child] there" (p. 14). They suggest that schooling be delayed until the child is 7 or 8 years old.

Early childhood educators (Highberger & Teets, 1974) have commented on these proposals, noting the inappropriate equation of nursery school with maternal deprivation. They believe that nursery programs for 3- and 4-year-olds are not harmful because they keep the children in school for a shorter time than elementary school and provide more expressive language development. Further, the nursery staff know about child development and are able to provide meaningful environments in which the children can learn through play.

Summary. Nursery schools are usually half-day programs for middle-SEL 2½-to-5-year-old children. The program goals are to foster emotional development and to provide socialization experiences. The curriculum is based upon the teacher's concept of child development. Learning occurs through play, with creative activities and materials determining the environment rather than a structured curriculum. Sociodramatic play is a popular activity and increases both children's social interaction and their deviant behavior. Little evaluation information is available for nursery schools. What is available suggests that there is no evidence of either positive or negative long-term effects of nursery school attendance on later achievement and development.

Kindergarten Programs. A significant development in kindergarten programs in the United States during the 1970s has been the extension of public school kindergartens to all areas of the country—including the South, where previously only private kindergartens had been available. The majority of children, regardless of residence or family income, can now attend public school kindergarten.

Kindergarten is the early childhood program available to 5-year-olds the year before first grade. Some schools offer a half-day program, others a full-day program following the regular elementary schools' hours, with a hot lunch program. When the program is half-day, the kindergarten teacher usually teaches two classes, one in the morning and the other in the afternoon. Attendance at kindergarten is still voluntary in most states (Leeper, Skipper, & Witherspoon, 1979).

Kindergarten teachers within the public school system are certified under the same procedures as elementary and secondary teachers within the state. Some states require training in early childhood education (child development, nursery-kindergarten, or kindergarten-primary emphasis); others simply require elementary education with few additional courses dealing with kindergarten. Professional association standards for public schools apply to the kindergarten as well as to the primary-intermediate grades (Southern Association of Colleges and Schools, Commission on Elementary Schools, 1977). These early childhood program standards set minimal criteria for judging the kindergarten's philosophy and objectives, curriculum, administration, faculty, equipment and materials, and facilities. Private kindergartens, unless a part of an independent elementary school, usually do not adhere to teacher certification or professional accreditation standards for kindergarten.

Kindergarten classes vary in size from twenty to thirty children per class. There is an increasing trend toward the use of paraprofessional teacher aides, who work with the children, supervising and instructing them (Grangaard, 1977).

The kindergarten curriculum often is more flexible than the rest of the school's curriculum. Many administrators think of kindergarten as separate and different from "real" school. One result of this attitude is a lack of continuity and coordination of the kindergarten curriculum with the primary grade curriculum (Evans, 1975). Kindergartens offer varying degrees of emphasis on academic readiness but generally offer more print in the environment, more structured manipulative games, and more published materials than do nursery schools (Fromberg, 1977).

Goals. The traditional purpose of kindergarten was transition from home to school, giving the child an orientation to school and a readiness for formal learning (Leeper, Skipper, & Witherspoon, 1979). The proliferation of nursery schools, compensatory preschool programs, and Head Start programs makes this purpose obsolete except for those few children who have never attended a group program prior to kindergarten.

Some kindergartens have retained a traditional eclectic program, with socialization and overall development of the child as their main goals. In these programs, 40 to 50 percent of the children's time is spent on creative activities, music, and oral language, and the remaining time is spent on free play and self-care. The emphasis is on children as children rather than on children as future adults (Evans, 1975).

Traditional kindergarten objectives emphasized socialization or social adjustment, aesthetics, sensory-motor development, achievement motivation, positive attitudes toward school, health and security, individual personality development through group experiences, general readiness, and concrete learning based upon the child's experiences (Evans, 1975; Weber, 1973; Widmer, 1970).

In one study (Goulet, 1975) parents, kindergarten teachers, and first-grade teachers ranked goals for a kindergarten program. Parents selected social domain objectives (accepts authority, cooperates with others, accepts responsibility) as having the highest priorities in kindergarten; kindergarten teachers selected learning domain objectives (follows simple directions, uses memory skills, exhibits creative skills) as most important; and first-grade teachers selected self-concept domain objectives (accepts oneself, shows confidence in own ability, shows pride in oneself) as most desirable. All three groups ranked physical domain and sensory-perceptual domain objectives as having the lowest priorities. Emotional domain objectives were ranked second by first-grade teachers. Both language domain and academic domain objectives were ranked in the middle of the list by all groups; however, kindergarten teachers gave academic objectives a higher rank than did first-grade teachers or parents.

Traditional kindergarten goals have gradually become more academic. Kindergarten in the early 1980s can be more accurately described as the initial phase of the school's instructional program (Leeper, Skipper, & Witherspoon, 1979). More direct teaching and specific academic instruction is common. Many kindergartens use workbooks, readiness books, and instructional kits to accomplish their academic objectives. This shift in purpose seems to be a result, in part, of research from the 1960s indicating that children can and often do learn to read before first grade (Bryzeinski, 1964; Durkin, 1966; Teale, 1978). Sometimes this learning occurs at home within the natural language environment, and sometimes it occurs at school through planned kindergarten instruction.

Surveys of kindergarten teachers concerning instructional practices in prereading and beginning reading reflect this change in kindergarten goals. In a 1970 survey (LaConte), kindergarten teachers felt that some children were ready for reading in the kindergarten but that most were not. However, these teachers agreed that kindergarten reading was probably here to stay. They reported that they taught picture reading, sound-letter association, letter naming, word discrimination, and word reading spontaneously in their programs. Most kindergarten teachers said they used their classroom library and experience charts for this instruction. Alphabet charts were used in one-half of the classrooms, readiness books and tests in one-third, and preprimers in none. However, 70 percent said they used visual discrimination and visual-motor coordination ditto sheets.

A survey in 1974 (Scherwitzky) indicated that now 50 percent of the kindergarten teachers thought reading should be taught in the kindergarten, whereas 50 percent thought it should not be. Although most teachers stressed the need to consider individual differences among children in this matter, many taught reading in small groups, and 25 percent used a readiness workbook with the class as a whole group. A kindergarten reading program was seen as providing for those who are ready but possibly taking time from other important aspects of the kindergarten curriculum and placing pressure on the kindergarten children. Kindergarten teachers have indicated that they would like to make the choice to teach reading themselves; that is, they would like to retain control over the objectives for their program.

The greater emphasis on academic instruction in kindergarten is also reflected in a survey of the way kindergarten teachers spend their time (Berkeley, 1978). The largest percentage of time during the school day was devoted to procedural matters, cognitive activities ranked second, and social activities third.

Research supports the objective that children can be taught readiness skills in kindergarten and that such instruction improves their success in later reading programs. However, there is no general agreement as to the specific skill objectives that should be included in a kindergarten reading readiness program (Ollila, 1980). The advantage of an earlier start in reading instruction is lost unless later practices in the primary grades are altered accordingly (Durkin, 1974–1975).

Seven professional associations jointly published a statement of concerns and recommended practices for pre-first-grade reading (Joint Committee on Pre–First-Grade Reading Instruction, 1977). They stated that appropriate kindergarten reading instruction was an integrated language arts approach that included language experience, varied activities, concrete experiences and materials, and developmentally appropriate procedures.

Curriculum. The typical kindergarten program includes some choice of activities combined with more structured small group and whole class activities. A typical schedule would include

1. Free play, with a choice among centers of interest (blocks, dramatic play, art, manipulative games, books)
2. Work-play period (limited choices among activities presenting specific skills, often within a unit or theme) *or* planned academic instruction period (large or small group instruction in reading, language, and mathematics with workbooks and/or instructional kits)
3. Snack or lunch and rest
4. Group activities (music, oral language, storytelling, trips)
5. Outdoor play

The specific program objectives will determine whether a traditional work-play period is used for skill instruction or whether more structured academic periods are used (Ollila, 1980; Widmer, 1970).

Even within the greater academic emphasis now found in kindergartens, there is great variation in specific curricula. In most public and private, middle-SEL kindergarten classes, the curriculum is either an eclectic, teacher-planned, unit-based program or an academic readiness, school-planned, workbook-oriented program. In many federally funded, low-SEL kindergarten classes (e.g., Title I kindergartens), the curriculum follows one of the early childhood models developed for compensatory preschools, Head Start, or Project Follow Through (see Preschool Compensatory Programs section of this entry). In many cases the kindergartens have adapted these curricula, using their methods and materials during the planned academic instruction or work-play period. In some cases the curriculum model is selected to provide continuity with the child's prior experiences in Head Start or preschool, in other cases it is not. Similarly, continuity may or may not be provided with subsequent first-grade curricula (Evans, 1975).

Effects. Many research studies in the area of kindergarten curricula have investigated the effects of specific curricula or training programs on kindergarten children's learning and academic achievement in specific areas. Some show positive effects and others no effect. The following discussion presents examples of these research studies.

A sequential prereading program presenting materials and instruction in listening comprehension, auditory discrimination, visual discrimination, oral language, perceptual-motor skills, and sound-letter correspondence was successful in significantly improving kindergarten children's performance on the Murphy-Durrell Reading Readiness Test (Stanchfield, 1971a, 1971b).

Kindergarten instruction in mathematics skills such as rote counting, numeral recognition, addition, and subtraction produced significant achievement in both kindergarten and first grade (Runnels & Runnels, 1974). The method used for kindergarten mathematics instruction was also important. Children instructed in solving addition and subtraction story problems were more successful when they used concrete, manipulative materials than when they simply heard the story problems read to them (Lindvall & Ibarra, 1979).

Oral language fluency and listening skills have been improved through specific kindergarten activities. Storytelling significantly increased the quantity of different vocabulary words used by children in a Title I kindergarten (Delano, 1977). The use of the *Science: A Process Approach* curriculum significantly increased expressive fluency, expressive vocabulary, and sentence structure, as well as receptive listening skills (Huff & Languis, 1973).

The instructional method used to present the curriculum content to kindergarteners can also be important. Individual structured teaching (Blank, Koltuv, & Wood, 1972), encouraging symbolic play (Gillis, 1976), and involving the children's mothers in their education (Radin, 1969) have all been shown to be successful in increasing kindergarten children's performance on measures such as the Caldwell Preschool Inventory and the Metropolitan Readiness Tests as well as on intelligence measures.

A number of studies (Armbruster, 1973; Meier, 1973; Quarmley, 1974) have considered the addition of visual-motor coordination training to the kindergarten curriculum. Perceptual-motor and visual-motor coordination training activities are effective in significantly improving the children's performance on tests of visual-motor integration; however, there is no transfer to the children's academic readiness skills as measured by readiness or achievement tests.

The trend has been for kindergarten curricula to become more academic and more structured through the use of workbooks, readiness books, or specific instructional activities designed to improve readiness for and achievement in first grade.

Effectiveness. A number of school systems have experimented with variations on the half-day kindergarten schedule. One common variation is to have the children in each class attend school for a full day on alternate days. One evaluation study (Cleminshaw, 1978) found significant differences favoring the full-day alternate-day group in achievement, social behavior, and parental attitude but no difference in motivation of the kindergarteners. Another evaluation (Wenger, 1979) of low-SEL children found that children who had attended a half-day daily kindergarten scored significantly higher on the Metropolitan Readiness Tests at the beginning of first grade than did the children who attended full-day alternate-day kindergartens. Two further evaluations (Hatcher, 1979; Minnesota State Department of Education, 1973) of the half-day daily versus full-day/alternate-day kindergarten arrangement found no difference in the readiness or achievement levels of the children.

In a review of the literature on class size, length, and scheduling of the kindergarten day (Beckner et al., 1978), no conclusive evidence was found regarding either length or scheduling of the day, although it was noted that teachers preferred a full-day schedule. Smaller class size, however, was found to have a positive effect on cognitive, academic, social, and emotional development, as well as on teacher satisfaction and effectiveness.

Children who have attended kindergarten significantly outperform nonkindergarten children on academic readiness at the beginning of first grade (Pirkle, 1974; Williams, 1974); on report card ratings (Conway, 1968), school adaptation (Conway, 1968), language and social studies achievement (Chatburn, 1973; Lee, 1976), Piagetian cognitive development tasks (Russell, 1973), and measures of mental maturity in first grade (Conway, 1968); and in achievement in reading, spelling, and arithmetic in second grade (Conway, 1968). No significant effects were found for kindergarten children on personality measures (Williams, 1974) or achievement at the end of the third grade (Fitts, 1977; Lee, 1976). So kindergarten does have a positive effect on children's academic performance in the first and second grades, but that effect fades by the end of third grade.

Summary. Kindergarten has become more universal and more academic in purpose and goals. The kindergarten curriculum can be considered as the lower level of the elementary school, although continuity with the primary grades is still an issue of concern. More academic instruction is provided in kindergartens than formerly, often to whole groups with workbooks or structured tasks. No evidence exists to determine whether a full-day or half-day program is superior. Evaluation measures have shown that kindergarten attendance does have a positive effect on school achievement in the primary grades.

Preschool Compensatory Programs. The major focus of early childhood programs for more than two decades now has been compensatory education (Hellmuth, 1970). This focus grew out of the social ferment of the late 1950s and early 1960s as well as the rapid expansion of professional and scientific interest in children who did not succeed in school. Based on revised views about child development and learning, these programs changed both preschool curricula and the response of preschool faculties to children.

Data indicated that low-SEL children—whether from the slums of the big cities (Deutsch, 1963, 1964), the slums of the small rural towns of the South (Gray, 1962), the Appalachian Mountains (Sherman & Key, 1932), or the Southeastern region of the United States (Kennedy, Van de Riet, & White, 1963)—performed below their middle-SEL counterparts on both intelligence and readiness measures as they entered school. Further, as they progressed through school a cumulative deficit in academic achievement scores was apparent (Deutsch, 1964; Jensen, 1966). This cumulative deficit hypothesis was a basic part of the rationale for early compensatory education (Evans, 1975).

Gray (1962) suggested that low-income children might receive less, a more restricted range, or a different order of stimulation when compared with more affluent children. The ways in which low-income children were reinforced, however, might have even more negative influence on children's learning. Differences might occur in the absolute amount, the source, the kind, the direction, or the focus of reinforcement. These differences in stimulation and reinforcement might be related to differences in aptitudes for and attitudes toward achievement. Compensatory early childhood education was to make up for these presumed deficits among children. Even though this approach assumed something was wrong with the child, great efforts were made to change preschool practice, too.

Goals. Common practice in the nursery schools and kindergartens of the 1950s had been to focus on socialization and mental health aspects of child development with a secondary emphasis on intellectual or academic domains (Sears & Dowley, 1963). Nursery schools, in particular, but kindergartens, too, were more likely to serve middle-SEL children. Activities consisted of social play experiences among the children, and adults were not anxious to intrude upon the make-believe of children.

The shift in early childhood education from an emphasis on socialization and acculturation to a newer emphasis on the educability of intelligence, the malleability of the young, and cognitive development was reflected in the writings of Hunt (1961), Bloom (1964), and McCandless (1952) and in the experimental work of a number of social

scientists beginning in the 1950s and early 1960s. These studies included those of Kirk (1958), who studied the early education of mentally retarded children; Deutsch (1963, 1964), whose initial enrichment program in early childhood with nursery, kindergarten, and primary age children was carried out in several schools in the Harlem district of New York City; Weikart (Weikart, Bond, & McNeil, 1978; Weikart et al., 1970), who worked with five waves of 3-year-old children at home and at school in the Ypsilanti (Michigan) Perry Preschool Project; Gray and Klaus (1965, 1966, 1970; Klaus & Gray, 1968; Gray et al., 1965), who worked with groups of 3- and 4-year-old children in Murphreesboro, Tennessee, during the summer and sent visitors into their homes during the year; and Hodges, McCandless, and Spicker (1967), who worked with three waves of 5-year-old children in experimental and traditional kindergartens in and around Bloomington, Indiana. A number of other studies that can be classified as experimental preschool compensatory programs began at about the same time (early 1960s) or shortly thereafter. These early studies and reviews of them include Bereiter and Engelmann (1966); Bissell (1973); Blatt and Garfunkel (1969); Bronfenbrenner (1974); Di Lorenzo, Salter, and Brady (1969); Fouracre, Connor, and Goldberg (1962); Gordon (1967); Gordon and Guinagh (1974); Heber and Gardner (1975); Horowitz and Paden (1973); Karnes et al., (1969); Painter (1969); Palmer and Siegel (1977); Ryan (1974); Schaefer and Aaronson (1977); Skeels (1966); Sprigle, Van de Riet, and Van de Riet (1968); Stearns (1971); and White et al. (1973).

Curriculum. Most of the experimental preschool programs of this period emulated the traditional kindergarten or nursery school program. They varied in their structure; some were half-day, others full-day. The schedules provided for sharing, art, music, storytelling, rest periods, and for free play. Differences did occur, however, in the more favorable staff-child ratios, in the increased degree of parent education and involvement, in the use of a broader theoretical base, and in the addition of a more prominent thrust for cognitive-intellectual skills. The materials and methods for developing these cognitive skills were usually specified in detail.

The sheer quantity and vigor of the research and discussion cited above were the beginning of a revolution in early childhood education (Hodges & Smith, 1978, 1980) that quite rapidly yielded Head Start and its family of programs addressed to the needs of low-income children (see Head Start section, below). These studies also laid the foundations for the development of a variety of instructional models that were based on a range of different sets of guiding principles, were focused on a number of different goals, and used alternative ways to teach children (Bissell, 1973; Branche & Overly, 1971; Gordon, 1972; Weikart, 1972). Some programs derive their guiding principles from the interactionist cognitive theory of Piaget—for example, Weikart's Cognitively Oriented Curriculum (Weikart et al., 1971). Others use behavioral principles from operant conditioning—for instance, the Academic Preschool of Bereiter and Engelmann (1966). A third group maintains an allegiance to the normative-maturational principles that were predominant in the traditional nursery and preschool—such as the Developmental Interaction program of Bank Street College of Education (Biber, Shapiro, & Wicken, 1971). Each of these three specific examples of instructional models uses the preschool classroom or center as a major means of working with children, but the Cognitively Oriented Curriculum also adds home instruction. In that model, teachers visit the child and parent once a week in order to help parents become involved in the instruction of their children. A fourth type of model, based on communication and social-learning theories, uses television as an alternative system for reaching children. "Sesame Street," the preschool program developed through the Children's Television Workshop, is the prime example (Lesser, 1974).

The objectives of these four models differ, also. The Cognitively Oriented Curriculum places its emphasis on cognitive development, including productive language, grouping, ordering, space relations, and time relations. The Academic Preschool focuses on the academic skills of language, reading, and arithmetic. The developers' goal is to help low-income children catch up. The Bank Street model emphasizes helping children develop positive self-images and autonomy in learning. Specific goals and objectives evolve as children reveal their interests and skills. The objectives sought through "Sesame Street" are more similar both to the objectives of the Academic Preschool and to the Cognitively Oriented Curriculum than to those of Bank Street. These objectives include knowledge of letters, numbers, forms, perceptual discrimination, relational concepts, grouping, ordering, reasoning and problem solving, general information, and social interaction knowledge.

The teaching strategies derived from the theories that guide these models vary, too. For example, the Cognitively Oriented Curriculum includes children in planning, encourages them to act on the environment and to represent it in some way, involves them in many exploratory activities, and uses all activities in developing cognitive skills. The teachers have a framework that guides their activities with the children.

Teachers in the Academic Preschool follow a script when interacting with children during language, reading, and arithmetic lessons. These scripts are well-developed, sequential programs that require the teachers to engage small groups of children in rapid-fire verbal interaction and significant amounts of repetitive drill. Children receive immediate feedback, achieve high rates of correct responses, and are encouraged by the social reinforcement of the teacher.

Teaching in the Bank Street tradition is dramatically different from teaching in the Academic Preschool and significantly different from the Cognitively Oriented Curriculum. In the former, teachers have a script; in the latter, they have a framework; but in the Bank Street model

they have a child development orientation. Specific goals are not explicitly stated except as they emerge from the confluence of knowledge of the particular child with knowledge of child development. Children are provided choices from a wide range of possibilities. Classrooms are workshops that are richly endowed with materials such as blocks, clothing, sand, water tables, wood, tools, pets, books, and games. Interest centers are encouraged, as is spontaneous play. Motivation is assumed to be inherent in the activity of the child, and play is the major medium of learning for the preschooler.

The fourth model, "Sesame Street," provides still another view of learning and teaching. The producers of this series assume that children will learn from both form and content, from imitating the actors and action on the screen, by narrow focusing on the message being delivered, and from the cross-modal reinforcement inherent in words combined with pictures. The producers combine entertainment with instruction, trying to start with the familiar, using direct methods to teach basic intellectual skills and indirect methods to show social behavior, transporting the viewers to a variety of places that they would not normally see or hear, and avoiding preaching or talking down to the child viewers.

These four models are illustrative of the rich variety of instructional approaches that were developed as part of the preschool compensatory movement. In Table 2 a sample of programs is displayed according to theoretical orientation providing an overview of the range. There is, quite naturally, much overlap among the various approaches to early childhood programming, because no theory is currently capable of guiding the development of a complete model. In addition, the typical program in the field is more likely to be an eclectic one, especially when compared with the original models developed for experimental purposes.

The history of early childhood education, in contrast to public primary and secondary education, is notable for its concern with the role of parents and the family as educators. There are frequent examples of attempts to help parents become more adept at their roles as educators. A middle-SEL orientation in parent education was typical of the majority of efforts up to the 1950s and 1960s, when experimental early childhood education programs began to focus on the less well-to-do parent (Chilman, 1973).

It has already been noted that some of the preschool compensatory programs included a parent-involvement component, a parent-education component, or both. Other programs focused more directly on parent education. Many included a commitment to involve parents in policy-making councils. A number of these projects are reviewed by Chilman (1973) and Goodson and Hess (1975).

Effects. Evidence that some of these preschool compensatory intervention projects were succeeding in raising intelligence test and later achievement test scores of low-SEL children led to studies that compared different models (Di Lorenzo, Salter, & Brady, 1969; Hodges, McCandless,

TABLE 2. *Selected instructional models in modern early childhood education*[a]

A. *Developmental/maturationist theory models*		
Title and source	*Goals*	*Teaching style*
The Developmental Interaction Approach[b] Bank Street College of Education New York, N.Y.	Confidence. Creativity. Responsiveness. Productivity	Project-oriented. Classroom is workshop. Provides direct experience.
EDC Open Education Program[b] Education Development Center Newton, Mass.	Independence. Self-motivation. Social responsibility. Intellectual competence.	Teacher follows child's lead, responds, extends, and shows child ways to pursue his/her interest.
B. *Cognitive/interactionist theory models*		
Cognitively Oriented Curriculum[b] High/Scope Educational Research Foundation Ypsilanti, Mich.	Thinking skills. Self-discipline. Expression.	Teacher facilitates learning and creates proper environment.
The Montessori Curriculum Association Montessori Internationale Amsterdam, Holland	Learning how to learn. Autonomous functioning.	Teacher is resource and catalyst. Prepared environment.
C. *Behavioral/environmentalist theory models*		
Academic Preschool Direct Instruction[b] University of Oregon Eugene, Oreg.	Accelerated learning rate for academic skills.	Structured programmed lessons by teacher, using reinforcement principles.
Behavior Analysis Approach University of Kansas Lawrence, Kan.	Academic skills in language, number, reading concepts.	Token reinforcement system and programmed lessons for children.

[a] For descriptions of other instructional models see Rath, O'Neil, Gedney, & Osorio (1976).
[b] These models were used in both Head Start and Follow Through Planned Variation.

& Spicker, 1971; Karnes et al., 1969; Miller & Dyer, 1975; Smith, 1973; Soar & Soar, 1972; Stallings, 1975; Stanford Research Institute [SRI], 1971; Stebbins et. al., 1977; Weikart et. al., 1978; Weisberg, 1974). These comparisons suggested that different models did have different effects, depending upon the emphasis of the program within each model, but that no particular curriculum is consistently superior to the others. For example, programs that emphasized academic achievement and intelligence test score gain tended to be more likely to attain these goals. But in one well-controlled study (Weikart, Bond, & McNeil, 1978) three different curricula each resulted in substantial but similar intelligence test score gains. There were no significant differences among the curricula on that measure. Each model was well supervised, organized as part of a research project, and well publicized, which led Weikart to suggest that a variety of models can work and that the critical issue is to determine what the most important goals for young children are. Another outcome suggested by these studies is that because of individual variations, different children thrive better under different programs.

Research on the outcomes of "Sesame Street" was extensive and indicated that it was reaching about 80 percent of its possible and intended audience of 2-to-5-year olds in 1972; that these children were drawn from low-SEL as well as middle-SEL children; and that children learned from the series, as measured by an eight-test battery developed by the Educational Testing Service. Viewers showed greater gains than nonviewers, and children who watched the most gained the most on the test battery (Lesser, 1974).

Effectiveness. When the effects of the preschool intervention programs are summarized, a number of conclusions appear. First, children from poor families can perform well on a wide variety of tasks given them in compensatory preschool programs, as demonstrated in most well-organized projects.

Second, compensatory programs appear to result in immediate postintervention gains (on measures of broad intellectual functioning), which are greater for target children than for control children and greater than would be expected if they had not had the preschool experience. These broad gains appear to dissipate over time, however, so that scores for control and experimental children approximate both one another and their preintervention scores after a few years in elementary school (Hodges & Smith, 1978, 1980).

Third, and most important, long-term follow-up studies show that children who have experienced well-designed preschool compensatory education programs are more likely than their control counterparts to be in the approximate grade for their age and to use fewer special education services (Lazar et al., 1977; Schweinhart & Weikart, 1980; Weikart, Bond, & McNeil, 1978). In addition, a small number of these programs show long-term academic achievement differences in favor of the experimental children (Schweinhart & Weikart, 1980).

Fourth, a range of strategies has been used, including home visits, summer school, direct training, discovery learning, starting at various ages, using an extremely wide range of time in teaching contact with the child, focusing on specific skills, or working toward a more general set of objectives.

Fifth, a few other findings indicate that a majority of low-SEL parents are dedicated to helping their children and will use resources made available to them, such as home visits; low-SEL children lose more of their cognitive gains from preschool programs over a summer than do other children; direct training leads to direct and specific results when measured just at the end of the program; starting at earlier ages or using longer programs has not yet been shown to make major differences in outcome.

Summary. Preschool compensatory programs grew out of efforts to help low-SEL children reverse the cumulative achievement differences that occurred when their achievement was compared with that of middle-SEL children. A change toward greater emphasis on achievement and intellectual development was noted among the experimental preschool compensatory programs compared with traditional programs. A variety of specific models of early childhood education was developed, based on different views of child development, including the deliberate use of television as an intervention procedure. Parent education attained a renewed visibility as a means of addressing the problems of low-SEL children. The research has identified a variety of ways to adapt educational experiences to help young children improve their performance in school-related behaviors, but comparative assessment shows that these techniques have been only moderately successful.

Head Start. Head Start was a natural extension of the research projects in preschool compensatory intervention of the ten years preceding its initiation. If early childhood education has been used as a tool of social change and school improvement throughout its history, as has been suggested (Lazerson, 1972; Takanishi, 1977), then the creation and initiation of Head Start in 1964/65 can be considered as an escalation of that strategy on a grand scale. It appears, in retrospect, that early childhood education was a field whose time had come at last.

Head Start was the showpiece of the revolution that was taking place in early childhood education, but its originators did not necessarily embrace all the ideas that gave a new look to the field, such as (1) the emphasis on catching up on academic skills, best expressed in *Revolution in Learning* (Pines, 1966), (2) the radical behaviorism being applied to preschool children (Bereiter & Engelmann, 1966), or (3) the shift to environmental explanations for human development (Hunt, 1961). A developmental perspective persisted, and it was being rapidly modified by Piagetian theory (Flavell, 1963; Hunt, 1961).

Head Start began as a new approach to intervention in the cycle of poverty and as part of President Johnson's "war on poverty." The newness of the approach was in the commitments of its founders to have Head Start become more than just an education project. The 1967 Manual of Policies and Instructions (U.S. Office of Economic Opportunity, 1967) defined Project Head Start as a program for the economically disadvantaged preschool child based on the assumptions that "(1) a child can benefit most from a comprehensive interdisciplinary attack on his [her] problems at the local level, and (2) the child's entire family, as well as the community, must be involved in solving his [her] problems" (p. 1).

Five components are included in Head Start: (1) medical and dental services for children, (2) social services into the home and education of parents, (3) developmental services for children, (4) intensive use of volunteers, and (5) school readiness (Shriver, 1966). A major operating principle is that low-income persons are involved in the planning, establishing, and running of Head Start programs. Head Start is, thus, a broadly based, comprehensive community action program the most visible component of which is the child development center, where children congregate with teachers for a variety of preschool experiences. Child development centers are, however, only one of many ways of delivering services that have been developed through Head Start.

In fiscal year 1967 there were approximately 2.5 million 3-to-5-year-old children eligible for Head Start. The program served about 670,000 in full-year and summer programs combined, or about 26 percent of the need. In 1981 the program served approximately 378,000 children out of approximately 2 million who were eligible, or about 19 percent of the need. The reduction in number and proportion is largely due to the initiation of full-year programs and the phasing out of summer programs. Since 1965 the program has served about 7 million children, including close to 600,000 handicapped children (Klafehn, 1981).

A family of programs. Head Start was the base from which many innovations in early childhood education and other services for children and families have been launched. A number of these changes have come about because investigators, policy makers, and critics of the program have identified potential weaknesses or possibilities for enhancing the impact of early childhood services. Hodges and Sheehan (1978) and Richmond, Stipek, and Zigler (1979) have identified these potential weaknesses and the subsequent innovations.

First, some thought that the technology of preschool education may not have been robust enough to effect the growth in cognitive performance needed by poor children (Hunt, 1975). From this concern a number of the well-articulated instructional models that had grown out of the preschool compensatory programs (see above) were tested in both Follow Through Planned Variation (Haney, 1977) and Head Start Planned Variation (Smith, 1973; SRI, 1971; Weisberg, 1974).

Second, Head Start as a summer program alone may have provided too little time to have the desired effects. Data from a major study indicate an edge for full-year programs (Cicirelli, 1969), and as a result many summer programs were converted to year-round programs (Richmond, Stipek, & Zigler, 1979).

Third, Head Start may be discontinuous with the schools. Since children experienced cognitive gains immediately after well-run intervention research projects that were similar to, but not identical with, Head Start, and since these gains dissipated shortly after children entered school, it was clear that schools should become more adept at capitalizing on and maintaining the gains. Thus, a program was designed to "continue and build on the gains" accomplished in Head Start (Richmond, Stipek, & Zigler, 1979). This program, Follow Through, was established in 1967 and run by the U.S. Office of Education. Like its progenitor, Head Start, Follow Through is a comprehensive program aimed at children in kindergarten through the third grade (Haney, 1977; Hodges, 1978; Hodges et al., 1980).

Two other programs concerned with developmental and educational continuity between the preschool and primary years have evolved from the concerns illuminated by Head Start. The first, called Project Developmental Continuity, was begun in 1974 (Love, Granville, & Smith, 1978). It was designed to "assure greater continuity of services for Head Start children as they move from pre-

school to elementary school" (Richmond, Stipek, & Zigler, 1979, p. 145). The second was the Basic Educational Skills program (begun in 1979), intended to assure continuity of curricular, teaching, and parental activities with young children as they progress through the elementary grades.

Fourth, Head Start may have begun too late (Hunt, 1975). The response to this concern was the development of thirty-three Parent and Child Centers in 1967, serving children from birth to 3 years of age and their families. These centers sought to improve services for over 4,000 children as well as to help parents learn more about their children and the services available (Richmond, Stipek, & Zigler, 1979).

Fifth, Head Start may have been too narrow in its delivery system. In Head Start Child Development Centers, Follow Through, and Parent Child Centers, children had to leave home in order to receive services, and many child development specialists believed that center-based programs were not necessarily the best for children. They argued for a broader conception of the place where early childhood services could be delivered, and as a result the Home Start research and demonstration project was begun in 1972. This program provided health and educational services to more than 12,000 children in 280 full-year programs (Richmond, Stipek, & Zigler, 1979).

Sixth, Head Start may have been too narrow in that it served mainly children from poor families. In 1969, therefore, Congress made it possible for as many as 10 percent of the spaces in Head Start to be made available to children from families above the poverty line, and in 1972 Congress required that at least 10 percent of Head Start enrollees be handicapped children.

Seventh, Head Start may have been too narrow in another way. Its focus was largely centered on the child, but the health, education, and welfare of parents was later seen as important, too. A growing concern for parent education led not only to Home Start, which was mentioned above, but also to the Head Start Supplementary Training Program (begun in 1969), through which parents of children in Head Start could engage in higher education activities. The Education for Parenthood Program (begun in 1972) was designed "to help prepare teenagers for parenthood through working with young children in Head Start and other centers" (Richmond, Stipek, & Zigler, 1979, p. 145), and the Child and Family Resource Program (begun in 1973) allows Head Start centers to serve as a hub through which community services are made accessible.

Eighth, Head Start revealed the need for adults who can work well with young children. In 1972 the Child Development Associate (CDA) Program was begun to provide training for those who work in preschool child development, day care, or Head Start programs and to provide a credential for those who have demonstrated adequate performance in working with young children. This credential represents a first effort at developing a national certification of competence in the child care fields (Richmond, Stipek, & Zigler, 1979). At present, nineteen states and the District of Columbia have CDA as part of state licensing or certification, and 7,000 persons have obtained the credential, with another 8,000 in training (Klein, 1981).

Head Start has grown into a family of interrelated programs, some of which have come and gone (e.g., Home Start, Head Start Planned Variation) and some of which have remained as relatively permanent extensions of the basic concepts embodied in the original mandate (e.g., Parent Child Centers, Child Development Associate Program, Follow Through).

Goals. The purpose of Head Start has never been modest. It is to help break the "cycle of poverty" (U.S. Office of Economic Opportunity, 1967, p. 2). The broad goals of Head Start include improving children's health, emotional and social development, and ability to think, reason, and speak clearly; broadening children's experiences in order to "increase their ease of conversation and improve their understanding of the world" (p. 3); providing frequent chances to succeed and a climate of confidence; increasing children's interpersonal skills and strengthening the mutual understanding within families; developing responsible attitudes toward society and a sense of belonging in the community; providing opportunities for a variety of community groups to work with the poor in solving problems; reducing fear of authority figures; using other persons as models of manners, behavior, and speech; and improving confidence, self-respect, and dignity (U.S. Office of Economic Opportunity, 1967).

Curriculum. The Head Start Child Development Center is a place to play and learn for preschool age children (Stone & Janis, 1973). Each program must meet the Head Start Program Performance Standards (Office of Child Development, 1976), which have evolved during the development of the Head Start program. These standards include written and operational plans for education, medical and dental services, mental health services, nutrition services, social services, and parent involvement. Each year the program must undergo a self-assessment, and every three years a validation study of the program is conducted by a team of experts representing the six definitive services to be provided through the program.

The Head Start Child Development Centers more closely resemble the traditional nursery school than they do the experimental preschool compensatory education programs referred to above. Their general goal, like that of the experimental preschools, has been to help children cope with societal institutions, but like the traditional nursery schools, the centers have been organized with less-than-full-day schedules, forcing working mothers to make additional arrangements for their children in order to provide complete care. The staff usually consists of a teacher, aide, and parent volunteer for every classroom. The program is also similar to nursery schools, with an emphasis on learning through play, using concrete materials and centers of interest, and engaging in sociodramatic play and creative expression through art, music, and language.

Booklets describing the various components of Head Start are available in the Rainbow Series (e.g., Caldwell, 1968; Stone & Janis, 1973). Two of these booklets illustrate the educational philosophy of Head Start. Each local staff is encouraged to design its own curriculum as long as it meets the Performance Standards (Office of Child Development, 1976), which require (1) a supportive social and emotional climate; (2) provisions for intellectual skills development through problem solving, initiating activities, exploring, experimenting, and questioning; (3) balancing staff-directed and child-initiated activities; (4) promoting physical growth through space, materials, equipment, time, and appropriate guidance while children are engaged; (5) an individualized program; (6) a program that is relevant to and reflective of the population served; (7) a staff and resources reflective of the ethnic and racial nature of the population; (8) persons who speak the language of non–English-speaking children; (9) parent participation in curriculum development and as resources; (10) observation and evaluation of each child's growth and development; (11) a parent-involvement and parent-training program; (12) staff training and development; and (13) adequate and safe physical facilities. Head Start, across the nation, is a diverse set of programs held together by common guidelines and a general philosophy but not by a common curriculum model (Miller, 1979).

Effects. The literature concerning Head Start is large (Zigler & Valentine, 1979) and rich in the number of clues it provides for both program development and new research into the mysteries of child development, parent behavior, and teaching with young children.

The most agreed-upon findings concerning the educational effects of some of the Head Start programs are included in this section. The many positive effects of Head Start in community change will not be listed, although these changes have a salutary effect upon the education of children and the quality of life in a community (Kirschner Associates, 1970). Neither will the positive effects of parent participation in Head Start be explicated, even though it is assumed that these effects also have long-term educational benefits (Midco Educational Associates, 1972). A small but interesting set of findings emerge from a number of sources (Beller, 1973; Evans, 1975; Hunt, 1975; Mann, Harrell, & Hurt, 1976; and Stearns, 1971).

First, statistically reliable and substantial short-term gains (pre–Head Start to post–Head Start) have been shown in some research studies on task orientation, social adjustment, achievement orientation, and interpersonal relations among Head Start children based on comparisons of Head Start children's growth with the growth they were expected (predicted) to exhibit (Coulson, 1972; Datta, 1979; Dunteman, 1972).

Second, Head Start appears to increase school readiness scores when children are compared with what they would have been expected to achieve on these instruments without Head Start. These findings appear frequently on the Caldwell Preschool Inventory and on intelligence test performance but not consistently among all Head Start programs evaluated (Miller & Dyer, 1975; Smith, 1973; SRI, 1971; Weisburg, 1974). Pre–Head Start to post–Head Start gains in intelligence test scores gradually dissipate, however, as the children leave the preschool Head Start program and move through the kindergarten or elementary grades (Miller & Dyer, 1975).

Third, there do appear to be some differential immediate effects among different types of programs that were studied by Miller and Dyer (1975) and in the Head Start Planned Variation studies of 1969–1972 (Featherstone, 1973; Smith, 1973; SRI, 1971; Weisberg, 1974). One cluster of program characteristics appears to be helpful to children who score lower on intelligence tests and to older children. These characteristics include low pupil-teacher ratio and moderate to strong emphasis on academic achievement. A second cluster appears to benefit younger children with high pretest intelligence scores who live in urban areas. These characteristics include greater emphasis on independence, self-care, socialization, and dramatic play. In general, however, the data concerning preschools show few differences among curricula in effectiveness (Smith, 1973).

Effectiveness. Head Start has many goals and many programs. The effectiveness referred to in this report has centered mainly on the educational component represented in the mainstream of Head Start: the Child Development Center. Head Start should be judged in a much broader context than has been attempted here; but even taking the narrow view of these effects, one can conclude that Head Start is of social and educational benefit to children in the short-term. Longer-range benefits of Head Start programs are still unknown, even though the long-term effects of some of the experimental preschool compensatory programs have been shown (Lazar et al., 1977; Schweinhart & Weikart, 1980).

There are other provocative but less well-documented findings than those just presented. These include the effects on Head Start children who go into different types of Follow Through programs (Miller & Dyer, 1975; Weisberg & Haney, 1977), in which they appear to maintain some of their gain compared with Head Start children who do not go into a Follow Through program, and the tentative finding that Head Start graduates, like the graduates of several compensatory preschool experimental programs, are more likely to be in the usual grade for their age and less likely to be in special education (Datta, 1979). Given these encouraging signs, one can hope for continued research and confirmation of these promising leads.

Summary. Head Start began as a preschool intervention intended to help overcome poverty. It served as the base for the creation of a large number of innovative programs for children and families. Head Start has always worked toward multiple goals through its five service components: health, social, developmental, volunteer, and educational. The effects of Head Start on children, parents, and communities have been assessed in a variety of ways. The general conclusion is that Head Start exerts a positive influence in communities, is well supported by parents, and is modestly helpful in improving education-related skills among children.

Day Care Programs. Day care programs for young children began as a service to working parents, providing babysitting services for children too young to attend public schools. These programs have expanded rapidly during the 1970s, and many have added a child development and/or education program.

Day care is available for infants to 6-year-olds, eleven to twelve hours a day, five days a week, and for school-age children after school and during school vacations. Hot lunches, two snacks, and naps are provided. Some centers, especially those near hospitals, provide evening care, and others even provide twenty-four-hour, seven-day-a-week care. Most families use care located near their home, because centers located near or at places of work are very limited. Day care programs are either center-based, resembling nursery schools, with added facilities for meals, naps, and infants, or home-based, with care provided by a woman in her home for a small group of children. Almost all family day care providers in the United States are women.

Approximately 55 percent of day care in the United States is family, home-based care and only 2 percent of those homes are licensed (Day Care and Child Development Council of America, 1971). Family day care arrangements vary from informal arrangements made with a relative, friend, or neighbor to inhome care by a licensed family day care provider. Many family day care providers see themselves as babysitters only, not child development or educational specialists. They are often isolated from the professional child care community and may not take advantage of training or resources when these are made available to them (Peters, 1973; Rose, 1976; Wattenberg, 1977).

Some day care centers are private, proprietary centers serving primarily middle- and upper-income, often two-parent families. In some cases these centers are part of a local or national franchise. Other centers are nonprofit, either charitable (sponsored by a church or community agency) or publicly sponsored. Federal funds have been available for child care centers throughout the 1970s under a variety of social and poverty programs. In general, the nonprofit centers serve low-income families, many of which are also one-parent families. Those with public funding usually pay better salaries and provide more opportunities for professional growth of their staff members (Kayserling, 1972; Peters, 1973).

States license all center-based day care facilities, and most states have standards for home-based facilities also. Usually, the licensing standards cover the physical facilities; health, fire, nutrition, and safety requirements; adult-child ratio; administrative and business arrangements; and minimal qualifications for the staff, especially the director. Rarely do the standards cover the program, curriculum, materials, or education of the staff (Prescott & Jones, 1972).

Standards are intended to be minimum levels, but often they become maximum. Federally funded centers must also meet the Federal Interagency Day Care Requirements, which cover essentially the same areas as the state licensing requirements with the addition of social services and evaluation.

Day care center staff members exhibit a high rate of turnover, especially among male care givers. Low pay, low status, and limited opportunity for advancement are all given as reasons for this lack of stability (Anderson, 1980; Robinson, 1979). Directors often have only limited early childhood education (Day Care and Child Development Council of America, 1971). In a survey of thirty-six providers (Sheehan & Abbott, 1979), none had a college degree and 15 percent had less than a high school education. Only 51 percent had had any relevant training in early childhood education, and 51 percent were under thirty years of age.

An increasing need for child care has occurred because of the increase in the number of working women, the increase in the number of single-parent families, and the decrease in the number of extended families. It was estimated in 1975 that there were one million day care center spaces for 6 million children of working parents (Mondale, 1975; Schneider, 1971). Parents at the poverty level often need day care in order to enroll in job-training programs and to provide health, nutrition, and social services for their children. Parents of handicapped children also frequently need full-time care for their children (Hedrick & Fatland, 1971; Prescott & Jones, 1972).

Popular views disapproving of day care as a substitute for maternal home care have been common, especially among white, middle-SEL persons. Even many women using day care felt that "good" mothers stayed at home with their preschool children (Peters, 1973). These views were widely represented in popular magazines and child care books in the 1950s and 1960s (Etaugh, 1980). In the 1970s there was a shift from popular articles stating disapproval of day care except for mothers who "must" work to articles expressing positive views and even describing the benefits of the day care experience for young children. Child-rearing books have been slower in shifting toward more favorable views of nonmaternal care.

Goals. Day care centers vary in their primary goal. The most common goals are to provide custodial care, a child development program, or an educational program (Day Care and Child Development Council of America, 1971; Neubauer, 1974; Prescott & Jones, 1972). Custodial care is usually just babysitting, perhaps within a safe, healthy environment. Developmental programs are designed to meet social, emotional, and language development objectives and, in some cases, to provide social intervention (Peters, 1975). Educational day care programs are usually designed to foster academic and cognitive development and to provide cognitive intervention (Cahoon, 1975).

High-quality day care is described as providing a convenient, safe, stimulating environment for the child; working closely with the parents; having a professional staff; providing individualized child care; and being licensed (Maier, 1979); Prescott & Jones, 1972; Ristau et al., 1976). The development of cultural pluralism through the integration of children from varying socioeconomic and ethnic backgrounds has also been stated as a goal of day care centers (Grotberg, 1972; Langenbach & Neskora, 1977).

A survey of day care directors and child care experts indicated some differences in their goals for high-quality day care. The day care directors were more concerned with skills that allowed the child to function in the center, and the experts were more concerned with skills that allowed the child to learn in a group setting (Peters & Cohen, 1973).

Parents often do not know what to look for in day care and, therefore, frequently accept less than high-quality care for their child. Economic considerations, location, and availability also may determine their choice. In a survey of day care centers in Pennsylvania (Peters, 1973), it was noted that parents considered staff training and the educational aspects of a program when choosing a center for their children; however, most of the programs chosen supplied social experience clustered around people with frequent opportunities to interact with children from varying backgrounds rather than an educational program.

Curriculum. Developmental day care center programs usually focus on the child's play as a vehicle to explore the world, to develop cognitive structures, to learn how to learn, to develop a concept of self-worth, and to learn responsibility. These programs may resemble a nursery school with interest centers to foster symbolic, creative play (Langenbach & Neskora, 1977; Seefeldt, 1974). Educational day care center programs occasionally follow a planned curriculum, such as those developed for preschool compensatory programs and Head Start (Kirchner, 1973). (See the Preschool Compensatory Programs, above.)

The schedule for the day in a day care center depends on the degree of developmental and educational activities. The general schedule is as follows:

1. Free play
2. Snack or breakfast
3. Group time (varying degrees of structure and academic content)
4. Outdoor play
5. Storytelling, music
6. Lunch
7. Nap
8. Snack
9. Outdoor play
10. Storytelling
11. Free play

Television is frequently used as a choice during free play, especially when children's educational programs such as

"Sesame Street" and "Mr. Rogers' Neighborhood" are available. Storytelling is often a transitional activity used to settle the children down.

Observational studies of day care centers have described the materials and activities available and the behaviors and involvement of the providers and children. One such observational study (Sheehan & Abbott, 1979) included nine federally funded centers for 2-to-5-year-old, low-SEL children. Materials were generally available, in good repair, presented in an orderly manner, and varied. The provider behaviors noted were predominantly neutral in tone and were accompanied by relatively little physical affection. Activities were highly structured and usually initiated and directed by the providers, but there was a very low percentage of planned lessons observed. Providers used only limited language with the children, although they were usually engaged with the children. In spite of the fact that children exhibited a low level of involvement with activities, minimal negative involvement was observed. It was concluded that this survey described "custodial day care."

Observations of 4-year-olds in two day care centers, one serving middle-income and one low-income families, obtained similar results (Hough & Nurss, 1981). The centers had comprehensive, eclectic goals and provided some variety of materials. Most of the children were positively involved in activities within small or large groups. Routines were the only activities in which the children were engaged individually a majority of the time. Except during transitions, children exhibited a high level of involvement most of the time. Group size affected both involvement and behaviors, with whole-class organization eliciting minimal involvement. The teacher's role was influential in focusing children on the task at hand. Language was primarily receptive: listening to talk by other children or adults. Free play, outdoor play, and eating elicited expressive language more than directed activities, transitions, or routines. Listening to stories was a rare occurrence in these two day care centers.

The National Day Care Study investigated quality and cost of center-based day care for preschool children (3-, 4-, and 5-year-olds). The conclusions from this survey state that "smaller groups are consistently associated with better care, more socially active children, and higher gains on two developmental tests" (Ruopp et al., 1979, p. xxxvi). There was little difference in the quality of care associated with adult-child ratios of 1 : 5 and 1 : 10. Experience, formal education, degrees, and certification of the provider were not related to child gains, but caregivers with relevant training (in early childhood education and child development) provided care that yielded somewhat better developmental effects in the children. The recommendations of this study for high-quality, cost-effective care for young children were for groups of sixteen to twenty children with an adult-child ratio of 1 : 8–10. Relevant staff training, but not degree, certification, or experience requirements, were recommended.

Effects. Modifications of day care curriculum and instructional procedures have been shown to affect children's behavior and learning. Two methods of supervision were compared in one center serving low-SEL children (Lelaurin & Risley, 1972). During transition time from lunch to nap, the effects of "zone" supervision (one teacher assigned to an area) were compared with the effects of "man-to-man" supervision (one teacher assigned to a group of children). The "zone" supervision was more effective than "man-to-man" in preventing a decrease in child participation.

Observations were made to compare an options schedule, in which children had two or more activity choices, with a no-options schedule, in which the children did one activity at a time (Doke & Risley, 1972). Children's participation was equally high for the no-options schedule and for the options schedule under two conditions: when children were not forced to wait for others to finish (e.g., they were dismissed individually as they finished) and when there was an abundance of materials available for each required activity so children did not have to wait for materials.

The day care environment has been described as lacking in opportunities for children's expressive oral language, for hearing stories, and for developing concepts of print. The effects of this lack of an appropriate natural language and prereading environment may be seen in the limited prereading language skills of 4-year-olds in two day care centers (Nurss, Hough, & Goodson, 1981). The children were asked to describe a picture and to tell a story to a wordless picture book. They produced an average number of vocabulary words and average syntactic structure length for their age. However, they did not use any narrative conventions or display a sense of story. Their descriptions were only partially accurate, and they had very limited comprehension of the picture or the book. The limited language in the day care environment negatively affected their development of prereading skills. Similarly, significant differences in language fluency have been found favoring children attending day care less than six months when compared with children attending over twenty-four months (Eggleston, 1975).

Effectiveness. Many studies have compared home-reared children with children who have attended day care. Middle-SEL 3-to-4-year-olds were observed on several categories of social and nonsocial behaviors (Johnson, 1979). There were no differences between home and day care children on social tasks. However, day care children spent a larger amount of time cooperating with others than did home-reared children. Home children were rated significantly higher than day care children in conversation with others and in procuring service from others. In both settings the children spent more time on nonsocial than social tasks.

Contrary to many predictions, no differences have been found in day care and non–day care children's attachment to their mothers or in their dependency. Behavior of 3½-

year-olds in strange situations did not differ for day care and non–day care children (Moskowitz, Schwarz, & Corsini, 1977). A number of other studies found similar results, allowing the conclusion that bond formation of the child with the caregiver maintains the mother-child attachment (Anderson, 1980; Belsky & Steinberg, 1978). One exception to these findings occurred in a study of $2\frac{1}{2}$-to-$3\frac{1}{2}$-year-olds (Blehar, 1977). The day care children exhibited more disturbances in attachment than did home-reared children. No differences between day care and home children was found in dependency of 4- and 5-year-olds in situations with mothers, mothers and another adult, or mothers and another child (Cornelius & Denney, 1975). Day care children have been found to have higher levels of sociability and to exhibit more aggressive social behavior than their non–day care peers (Belsky & Steinberg, 1978).

Several studies have found positive intelligence test score gains for infants in high-quality day care centers (Belsky & Steinberg, 1978). One study, however, showed a reversal of that trend for children in center-based day care during preschool years (Fowler, 1978). The decreasing care giver–child ratio from infant to preschool day care classes and the high turnover of day care staff are given as possible explanations for these findings.

Day care has been shown to exhibit positive effects on families, children, staff, and community. Positive effects on families include increased family incomes, professional and personal growth of the mother, and increased marital satisfaction (Belsky & Steinberg, 1978; Winter & Peters, 1974). Positive effects on the child include increased self-esteem, expansion of the child's social interaction and roles, and increased cognitive development, especially for low-SEL children (Bronfenbrenner, 1979; Kirchner, 1973; Wexley, Guidubaldi, & Kehle, 1974; Winters & Peters, 1974). Positive effects on the day care staff include increased income and professional growth for public, center-based staff but not for proprietary or family-based day care staff. Positive effects on the community stem from the training of parents, especially low-income parents, as community leaders (Winter & Peters, 1974).

After completing an extensive, critical review of the literature on the effects of day care on children, Belsky and Steinberg (1978) conclude: "High quality, center-based day care (1) has neither salutary nor deleterious effects upon the intellectual development of the child, (2) is not disruptive of the child's emotional bond with his [her] mother, and (3) increases the degree to which the child interacts, both positively and negatively, with peers" (p. 929). Similarly, Etaugh (1980) concludes that "high quality nonmaternal care does not appear to have harmful effects on a preschool child's maternal attachment, intellectual development, social-emotional behavior, or physical health" (p. 313).

These conclusions are limited by the fact that they are based on short-term research on children in high-quality centers. Further study is needed to consider long-term

effects of day care, to consider the environmental and social context of behaviors in day care, and to consider both family-based day care and center-based care of the type available to the average family (Belsky & Steinberg, 1978; Bronfenbrenner, 1979).

Summary. Day care is very varied in type, quality, and availability. Different centers have different goals: custodial, developmental, or educational. Differences between children reared at home and those who have experienced day care can be summarized by stating that there are no differences in attachment and dependency but day care children exhibit greater aggression and home-reared children greater language skills. Many positive benefits accrue to the children and families when day care is used, including the positive attitudes of children of working mothers. High-quality, center-based care appears to have no harmful effects on young children.

Conclusions. Group programs for young children have greatly increased in quantity over the past fifteen years. Two general trends have been noted: (1) the shift in emphasis from social-emotional development and unstructured play to cognitive-academic development and more structured learning environments and (2) the increased number of compensatory programs available to children of low-income families, designed to provide both educational and social services.

The compensatory programs have been successful in increasing knowledge about how children learn and develop. Children who attended these programs have shown modest gains on various educational and social measures. Although none of these programs has eradicated poverty or changed the social order, there is a cautious optimism permeating the public, professional, and political communities, especially concerning the positive effects of Head Start.

Nursery schools continue to be popular among middle-SEL families, and kindergarten attendance is becoming nearly universal. Public attitudes toward day care are more positive, even though increased funding for such programs has not yet become a reality. There has been no clear technological breakthrough in early childhood education, but considering the complexity of the development of young children, there have been many positive steps in improving programs for them.

Several issues remain unresolved and will continue to dominate early childhood education research in coming years. These include: (1) long-term effects of group programs, especially day care, on children's later development and educational progress; (2) the continuity between the child's home and the early childhood programs and, more important, between early childhood programs and subsequent educational programs (elementary school); and (3) the advantages of specific curricula and methodology, especially the degree of structure and academic emphasis in early programs.

Joanne R. Nurss
Walter L. Hodges

See also Early Childhood Development; Parent Education; Preschool Education for the Handicapped; Readiness; Racism and Sexism in Children's Literature.

REFERENCES

Andalman, M. R. The effects of preschool environments on the sociodramatic play of young children (Doctoral dissertation, University of Chicago, 1977). *Dissertation Abstracts International,* 1977, *38,* 2657A–2658A. (Not available on University Microfilms)

Anderson, C. W. Attachment in daily separations: Reconceptualizing day care and maternal employment issues. *Child Development,* 1980, *51,* 242–245.

Ariès, P. *Centuries of Childhood: A Social History of Family Life.* New York: Knopf, 1962.

Armbruster, R. A. Perceptual motor, gross motor, and sensory motor skills training: The effect upon school readiness and self-concept development of kindergarten children (Doctoral dissertation, Wayne State University, 1972). *Dissertation Abstracts International,* 1973, *33,* 6644A. (University Microfilms No. 73-12,412)

Beckner, T. L.; Harner, J. H.; Kipps, B. M.; Kipps, D. M.; McCullough, M. S.; Trippe, S. L.; Williams, M. Z.; & Wilson, E. H. *A Study of the Relationship of Kindergarten Class Size, Length, and Scheduling of the Kindergarten Day and Teacher Self-concept to School Success.* Harrisburg, Va.: James Madison University, 1978. (ERIC Document Reproduction Service No. ED 165 891)

Beller, E. K. Research on organized programs of early education. In R. M. W. Travers (Ed.), *Second Handbook of Research on Teaching.* Chicago: Rand McNally, 1973.

Belsky, J., & Steinberg, L. D. The effects of day care: A critical review. *Child Development,* 1978, *49,* 929–949.

Bereiter, C., & Englemann, S. *Teaching Disadvantaged Children in the Preschool.* Englewood Cliffs, N.J.: Prentice-Hall, 1966.

Berkeley, M. V. Inside kindergarten: An observational study of kindergarten in three social settings (Doctoral dissertation, Johns Hopkins University, 1978). *Dissertation Abstracts International,* 1978, *39,* 1131A. (University Microfilms No. 78-11, 762)

Biber, B.; Shapiro, E.; & Wicken, D. *Promoting Cognitive Growth: A Developmental Interaction Point of View.* Washington, D.C.: National Association for the Education of Young Children, 1971.

Bissell, J. S. The cognitive effects of preschool programs for disadvantaged children. In J. Frost (Ed.), *Revisiting Early Childhood Education.* New York: Holt, Rinehart & Winston, 1973.

Blank, M.; Koltuv, M.; & Wood, M. Individual teaching for disadvantaged kindergarten children: A comparison of two methods. *Journal of Special Education,* 1972, *6,* 207–219.

Blatt, B., & Garfunkel, F. *Educability of Intelligence.* Washington, D.C.: Council for Exceptional Children, 1969.

Blehar, M. C. Mother-child interaction in day-care and home-reared children. In R. A. Webb (Ed.), *Social Development in Childhood: Day Care Programs and Research.* Baltimore: Johns Hopkins University Press, 1977.

Bloom, B. *Stability and Change in Human Characteristics.* New York: Wiley, 1964.

Branche, C. F., & Overly, N. V. Illustrative descriptions of two early childhood education programs. *Educational Leadership,* 1971, *28,* 821–826.

Braun, S. J., & Edwards, E. P. *History and Theory of Early Childhood Education.* Worthington, Ohio: Charles A. Jones, 1972.

Bremner, R. H.; Barnard, J.; Hareven, T. K.; & Mennel, R. M. (Eds.). *Children and Youth in America: A Documentary History* (Vol. III). Cambridge, Mass.: Harvard University Press, 1974.

Bronfenbrenner, U. *A Report on Longitudinal Evaluations of Preschool Programs* (Vol. II). (Publication No. OHD74-25). Washington, D.C.: Department of Health, Education, and Welfare, 1974.

Bronfenbrenner, U. *The Ecology of Human Development.* Cambridge, Mass.: Harvard University Press, 1979.

Bryzeinski, J. Beginning reading in Denver. *Reading Teacher,* 1964, *18,* 16–21.

Butler, A. L. Early childhood education: A perspective on basics. *Childhood Education,* 1973, *50,* 21–25.

Cahoon, O. W. Cognitive learning in group day care. *Child Care Quarterly,* 1975, *4,* 157–162.

Caldwell, B. M. *Daily Program II: A Manual for Teachers.* Washington, D.C.: Office of Economic Opportunity, 1968.

Chatburn, D. M. The influence of selected kindergarten programs on pupil achievement in language, social studies, and mathematics at the first-grade level (Doctoral dissertation, Utah State University, 1973). *Dissertation Abstracts International,* 1973, *33,* 6645A. (University Microfilms No. 73-13,291)

Chilman, C. S. Programs for disadvantaged parents: Some major trends and related research. In B. Caldwell & H. Ricciuti (Eds.), *Review of Child Development Research* (Vol. 3). New York: Russell Sage Foundation, 1973.

Cicirelli, V. G. *The Impact of Head Start: An Evaluation of the Effects of Head Start on Children's Cognitive and Affective Development* (Vols. 1–2). Washington, D.C.: National Bureau of Standards, Institute for Applied Technology, 1969.

Cleminshaw, H. K. Academic and social effects of all-day, alternate-day kindergarten versus half-day, everyday kindergarten in traditional and open-classroom settings (Doctoral dissertation, Kent State University, 1977). *Dissertation Abstracts International,* 1978, *38,* 7133A. (University Microfilms No. 78-08, 653)

Conway, C. B. *A Study of Public and Private Kindergarten and Non-kindergarten Children in the Primary Grades.* Vancouver: Educational Research Institute of British Columbia, 1968. (ERIC Document Reproduction Service No. ED 028 837)

Cornelius, S., & Denney, N. Dependency in day-care and home-care children. *Developmental Psychology,* 1975, *11,* 575–582.

Coulson, J. *Effects of Different Head Start Program Approaches on Children of Different Characteristics: Report on Analyses of Data from 1966–67 and 1967–68 National Evaluations* (Technical Memorandum TM-4862-001/00). Santa Monica, Calif.: Systems Development Corporation, 1972. (ERIC Document Reproduction Service No. ED 072 859)

Datta, L. Another spring and other hopes: Some findings from national evaluations of Project Head Start. In E. Zigler & J. Valentine (Eds.), *Project Head Start: A Legacy of the War on Poverty.* New York: Free Press, 1979.

Davis, A. *Social-class Influences upon Learning.* Cambridge, Mass.: Harvard University Press, 1948.

Day Care and Child Development Council of America, Inc. *Day-care Survey, 1970–71.* Rockville, Md.: Westinghouse Learning Corporation, 1971.

Delano, J. S. *Effects of Storytelling on Language Development.* Publication information not available, 1977. (ERIC Document Reproduction Service No. ED 168 674) deMause, L. *The History of Childhood*. New York: Psychohistory Press, 1974.

Deutsch, M. The disadvantaged child and the learning process: Some social, psychological, and developmental considerations. In A. H. Passow (Ed.), *Education in Depressed Areas*. New York: Columbia University, Teachers College, Bureau of Publications, 1963.

Deutsch, M. Facilitating development in the preschool child: Social and psychological perspectives. *Merrill-Palmer Quarterly*, 1964, *10*, 249–263.

Deutsch, M. *The Disadvantaged Child: Selected Papers of Martin Deutsch and Associates*. New York: Basic Books, 1967.

Di Lorenzo, L. T.; Salter, R.; & Brady, J. J. *Pre-kindergarten Programs for Educationally Disadvantaged Children*. Albany: New York State Education Department, Office of Research and Evaluation, 1969.

Doke, L. A., & Risley, T. R. The organization of day-care environments: Required versus optional activities. *Journal of Applied Behavior Analysis*, 1972, *5*, 405–420.

Dowley, E. M. Early childhood education. In R. L. Ebel (Ed.), *Encyclopedia of Educational Research* (4th ed.). New York: Macmillan, 1969.

Dunteman, G. *A Report on Two National Samples of Head Start Classes: Some Aspects of Child Development of Participants in Full-year 1967–1968 and 1968–1969 Programs*. Research Triangle Park, N.C.: Research Triangle Institute, 1972.

Durkin, D. *Children Who Read Early: Two Longitudinal Studies*. New York: Teachers College Press, 1966.

Durkin, D. A six-year study of children who learned to read in school at the age of four. *Reading Research Quarterly*, 1974–75, *10*, 9–61.

Eels, K.; Davis, A.; Havighurst, R.; Herrick, V.; & Tyler, R. *Intelligence and Cultural Differences*. Chicago: University of Chicago Press, 1951.

Eggleston, P. J. Language growth of day care children: Long-term enrollment effects on vocabulary, language comprehension, and language production (Doctoral dissertation, University of Illinois, 1975). *Dissertation Abstracts International*, 1975, *35*, 6935A. (University Microfilms No. 75-11,652)

Etaugh, C. Effects of nonmaternal care on children. *American Psychologist*, 1980, *35*, 309–319.

Evans, E. D. *Contemporary Influences in Early Childhood Education* (2nd ed.). New York: Holt, Rinehart & Winston, 1975.

Featherstone, H. *Cognitive Effects of Preschool Programs on Different Types of Children*. Cambridge, Mass.: Huron Institute, 1973. (ERIC Document Reproduction Service No. ED 082 823)

Featherstone, H. The use of settings in a heterogeneous preschool. *Young Children*, 1974, *29*, 147–154.

Fitts, R. T. The relationship of kindergarten attendance and later school achievement of children (Doctoral dissertation, University of Alabama, 1975). *Dissertation Abstracts International*, 1977, *37*, 7617A–7618A. (University Microfilms No. 77-12,259)

Flavell, J. *The Developmental Psychology of Jean Piaget*. New York: Van Nostrand Reinhold, 1963.

Flint, D. L. *Effects of Exposure to Pre-kindergarten on Five Social Competency Factors* (Technical Paper No. 8). Albany: New York State Education Department, 1979. (ERIC Document Reproduction Service No. ED 171 376)

Fouracre, M.; Connor, F.; & Goldberg, I. *The Effects of a Preschool Program upon Young Educable Mentally Retarded Children* (Vol. 2). New York: Teachers College Press, 1962.

Fowler, W. Cognitive learning in infancy and early childhood. *Psychological Bulletin*, 1962, *59*, 116–162.

Fowler, W. *Day Care and Its Effects on Early Development* (Research in Education Series No. 8). Toronto: Ontario Institute for Studies in Education, 1978.

Fromberg, D. P. *Early Childhood Education: A Perceptual Models Curriculum*. New York: Wiley, 1977.

Frost, J. L., & Kissinger, J. B. *The Young Child and the Educative Process*. New York: Holt, Rinehart & Winston, 1976.

Fuller, E. M. Early childhood education. In C. W. Harris (Ed.), *Encyclopedia of Educational Research* (3rd ed.). New York: Macmillan, 1960.

Gillis, M. F. Developing symbolic abilities of young children in play, drawing, and written language (Doctoral dissertation, Ohio State University, 1976). *Dissertation Abstracts International*, 1976, *37*, 2513A. (University Microfilms No. 76-24,599)

Goodlad, J. I.; Klein, M. F.; & Novotney, J. *Early Schooling in the United States*. New York: McGraw-Hill, 1973.

Goodson, B., & Hess, R. *Parents as Teachers of Young Children: An Evaluative Review of Some Contemporary Concepts and Programs*. Stanford, Calif.: Stanford University, School of Education, May 1975.

Gordon, I. *A Parent Education Approach to Provision of Early Stimulation for the Culturally Disadvantaged* (Final report to the Fund for the Advancement of Education, Ford Foundation). Gainesville: University of Florida, 1967.

Gordon, I. An instructional theory approach to the Analysis of selected early childhood programs. In I. Gordon (Ed.), *Early Childhood Education: Seventy-first yearbook of the National Society for the Study of Education* (Part II). Chicago: University of Chicago Press, 1972.

Gordon, I., & Guinagh, B. *A Home-learning-center Approach to Early Stimulation* (Final report to the National Institute of Mental Health). Gainesville: University of Florida, 1974.

Goulet, J. E. Curriculum priorities of teachers and parents in kindergarten classrooms. *Reading Improvement*, 1975, *12*, 163–167.

Grangaard, D. R. Perceptions of the functions of paraprofessionals in the kindergarten (Doctoral dissertation, Baylor University, 1976). *Dissertation Abstracts International*, 1977, *38*, 173A. (University Microfilms No. 77-14,543)

Gray, S. The performance of the culturally deprived child: Contributing variables. *Proceedings of the Seventh Annual Professional Institute, Section II, of the Division of School Psychologists of the American Psychological Association* (Today's Educational Programs for Culturally Deprived Children), 1962, pp. 30–36.

Gray, S., & Klaus, R. A. An experimental preschool program for culturally deprived children. *Child Development*, 1965, *36*, 887–898.

Gray, S., & Klaus, R. A. The early training project: An intervention study and how it grows. *Journal of School Psychology*, 1966, *4*, 15–20.

Gray, S., & Klaus, R. A. The early training project: A seventh-year report. *Child Development*, 1970, *41*, 909–924.

Gray, S.; Klaus, R. A.; Miller, J. O.; & Forrester, B. J. *The Early Training Project: A Handbook of Aims and Activities*. Nashville: George Peabody College for Teachers, 1965.

Grotberg, E. H. What does research teach us about day care: For children over three. *Children Today*, 1972, *1*, 13–17.

Haney, W. *A Technical History of the National Follow Through Evaluation* (Vol. V). Washington, D.C.: U.S. Office of Education, 1977.

Harrington, M. *The Other America*. New York: Macmillan, 1962.

Hatcher, B. A. A study of the cognitive, affective, and psychomotor development of children attending half-day and full-day state-supported kindergartens (Doctoral dissertation, North Texas State University, 1978). *Dissertation Abstracts International*, 1979, *39*, 6525A. (University Microfilms No. 79-11,074)

Heber, R., & Gardner, H. The Milwaukee Project: A study of the use of family intervention to prevent cultural-familial retardation. In B. Friedlander, F. M. Sterritt, & G. E. Kirk (Eds.), *Exceptional Infant: Assessment and Intervention* (Vol. 3). New York: Brunner/Mazel, 1975.

Hedrick, J. L., & Fatland, G. *Challenges in Day-care Expansion.* Minneapolis: Institute for Interdisciplinary Studies, 1971. (ERIC Document Reproduction Service No. ED 068 193)

Hellmuth, J. (Ed.). *Disadvantaged Child* (Vol. 3). New York: Brunner/Mazel, 1970.

Highberger, R., & Teets, S. Early schooling: Why not? A reply to Raymond Moore and Dennis Moore. *Young Children*, 1974, *29*, 66–77.

Hildebrand, V. Value orientations for nursery school programs. *Reading Improvement*, 1975, *12*, 168–173.

Hodges, W. The worth of the Follow Through experience. *Harvard Educational Review*, 1978, *42*, 186–192.

Hodges, W.; Branden, A.; Feldman, R.; Follins, J.; Love, J.; Sheehan, R.; Lumbley, J.; Osborn, J.; Rentfrow, R.; Houston, J.; & Lee, C. *Follow Through: Forces for Change in the Primary Schools.* Ypsilanti, Mich.: High/Scope Educational Research Foundation, 1980.

Hodges, W.; McCandless, B.; & Spicker, H. *The Development and Evaluation of a Diagnostically-based Curriculum for Preschool Psychosocially Deprived Children* (Final report to the U.S. Office of Education). Bloomington: Indiana University, School of Education, 1967.

Hodges, W.; McCandless, B.; & Spicker, H. *Diagnostic Teaching for Preschool Children.* Arlington, Va.: Council for Exceptional Children, 1971.

Hodges, W., & Sheehan, R. Follow Through as ten years of experimentation: What have we learned? *Young Children*, 1978, *34*, 4–14.

Hodges, W., & Smith, L. *Retrospect and Prospect in Early Childhood and Special Education.* Paper presented at the meeting of the American Psychological Association, Toronto, August 1978.

Hodges, W., & Smith, L. *Modern Early Childhood Education: A Review.* Manuscript submitted for publication. Atlanta: Georgia State University, 1980.

Horowitz, F., & Paden, L. The effectiveness of environmental intervention programs. In B. Caldwell & H. Ricciuti (Eds.), *Review of Child Development Research* (Vol. 3). New York: Russell Sage Foundation, 1973.

Hough, R. A., & Nurss, J. R. *The Ecology of Children in Day Care.* Paper presented at the meeting of the American Educational Research Association, Los Angeles, April 1981.

Huff, P., & Languis, M. The effects of the use of activities of *Science: A Process Approach* on the oral communication skills of disadvantaged kindergarten children. *Journal of Research in Science Teaching*, 1973, *10*, 165–173.

Hunt, J. *Intelligence and Experience.* New York: Ronald Press, 1961.

Hunt, J. Reflections on a decade of early education. *Journal of Abnormal Child Psychology*, 1975, *3*, 275–330.

Jensen, A. Cumulative deficit in compensatory education. *Journal of School Psychology*, 1966, *4*, 37–47.

Jensen, K. Preschool education. In W. S. Monroe (Ed.), *Encyclopedia of Educational Research* (2nd ed.). New York: Macmillan, 1950.

Johnson, R. L. Social behavior of three-year-old children in day care and home settings. *Child Study Journal*, 1979, *9*, 109–122.

Joint Committee on Pre–First-Grade Reading Instruction. *Reading and Pre–First Grade: A Joint Statement of Concerns about Present Practices in Pre–first-grade Reading Instruction and Recommendations for Improvement.* Newark, Del.: International Reading Association, 1977.

Karnes, M.; Hodgins, A.; Teska, J.; & Kirk, S. *Research and Development Program on Preschool Disadvantaged Children.* Washington, D.C.: Department of Health, Education, and Welfare, Office of Education, Bureau of Research, 1969.

Kennedy, W. A.; Van de Riet, V.; & White, J. C., Jr. A normative sample of intelligence and achievement of Negro elementary school children in the Southeastern United States. *Monographs of the Society for Research in Child Development*, 1963, *28*(6, Serial No. 90).

Keyserling, M. D. *Windows on Day Care.* New York: National Council of Jewish Women, 1972.

Kirchner, E. The sensitivity of selected measures of the day-care inventory to change-over time and to nursery school program differences. In D. L. Peters (Ed.), *A Summary of the Pennsylvania Day-care Study.* University Park: Pennsylvania State University, 1973.

Kirk, S. *Early Education of the Mentally Retarded: An Experimental Study.* Urbana: University of Illinois Press, 1958.

Kirschner Associates, Inc. *A National Survey of the Impacts of Head Start Centers on Community Institutions.* Washington, D.C.: Kirschner, 1970.

Klafehn, D. Personal communication, April 21, 1981.

Klaus, R. A., & Gray, S. W. The early training project for disadvantaged children: A report after five years. *Monographs of the Society for Research in Child Development*, 1968, *33*(4, Serial No. 120).

Klein, J. Personal communication, April 24, 1981.

Klein, M. F., & Novotney, J. American nursery schools—Help, hindrance, or enigma? *National Elementary Principal*, 1971, *51*, 85–89.

LaConte, C. Reading in the kindergarten: Fact or fantasy. *Elementary English*, 1970, *47*, 382–387.

Langenbach, M., & Neskora, T. W. *Day Care: Curriculum Considerations.* Columbus, Ohio: Merrill, 1977.

Lay, M. Z., & Dopyera, J. E. *Becoming a Teacher of Young Children.* Lexington, Mass.: Heath, 1977.

Lazar, I.; Hubbell, V. R.; Murray, H.; Rosche, M.; & Royce, J. *The Persistence of Preschool Effects: A Long-term Follow-up of Fourteen Infant and Preschool Experiments.* Ithaca, N.Y.: Cornell University, Consortium on Developmental Continuity, Education Commission of the States, 1977.

Lazerson, M. The historical antecedents of early childhood education. In I. J. Gordon (Ed.), *Early Childhood Education: Seventy-first Yearbook of the National Society for the Study of Education* (Part II). Chicago: University of Chicago Press, 1972.

Lee, B. A. *A Study of the Academic Achievement of Kindergarten and Non-kindergarten Children in a Rural School in Appalachia.* Johnson City: East Tennessee State University, 1976. (ERIC Document Reproduction Service No. ED 119 939)

Leeper, S. H.; Skipper, D. S.; & Witherspoon, R. L. *Good Schools for Young Children* (4th ed.). New York: Macmillan, 1979.

Lelaurin, K., & Risley, T. R. The organization of day-care environments: Zone versus man-to-man staff assignments. *Journal of Applied Behavior Analysis*, 1972, *5*, 225–232.

Lesser, G. *Children and Television: Lessons from Sesame Street.* New York: Random House, Vintage Books, 1974.

Lindvall, C. M., & Ibarra, C. G. *The Relationship of Mode of Presentation and of School/Community Differences to the Ability of Kindergarten Children to Comprehend Simple Story Problems.* Paper presented at the meeting of the American Educational Research Association, San Francisco, April 1979. (ERIC Document Reproduction Service No. ED 171 514)

Love, J.; Granville, A. C.; & Smith, A. G. *A Process Evaluation of Project Developmental Continuity: Final Report of the PDC Feasibility Study, 1974–1977.* Ypsilanti, Mich.: High/Scope Educational Research Foundation, 1978.

Maier, H. The core of care: Essential ingredients for the development of children at home and away from home. *Child Care Quarterly*, 1979, *8*, 161–173.

Mann, A. J.; Harrell, A.; & Hurt, M., Jr. *A Review of Head Start Research since 1969.* Washington, D.C.: George Washington University Social Research Group, 1976.

McCandless, B. R. Environment and intelligence. *American Journal of Mental Deficiency*, 1952, *56*, 674–691.

Meier, R. L. The effect of visual-motor training on readiness, intelligence of kindergarten children, and first-grade reading achievement (Doctoral dissertation, Indiana University, 1972). *Dissertation Abstracts International*, 1973, *33*, 5977A–5978A. (University Microfilms No. 73-06,988)

Midco Educational Associates. *Perspectives on Parent Participation in Project Head Start: An Analysis and Critique.* Washington, D.C.: Office of Child Development, 1972. (ERIC Document Reproduction Service No. ED 080 217)

Miller, L. B. Development of curriculum models in Head Start. In E. Zigler & J. Valentine (Eds.), *Project Head Start: A Legacy of the War on Poverty.* New York: Free Press, 1979.

Miller, L. B., & Dyer, J. L. Four preschool programs: Their dimensions and effects. *Monographs of the Society for Research in Child Development*, 1975, *40*(5–6, Serial No. 162).

Minnesota State Department of Education. *Kindergarten Evaluation Study: Full-day Alternate-day Programs.* St. Paul: The Department, 1973. (ERIC Document Reproduction Service No. ED 070 529)

Mondale, W. F. The need for children and family services. *Day Care and Early Education*, 1975, *3*, 14–15.

Moore, R. S.; Moon, R. D.; & Moore, D. R. The California report: Early schooling for all? *Phi Delta Kappan*, 1972, *53*, 615–621, 677.

Moore, R. S., & Moore, D. R. How early should they go to school? *Childhood Education*, 1973, *50*, 14–20.

Morella, J. R. Preschool education as a factor in first-grade performance of middle-class children (Doctoral dissertation, University of Oklahoma, 1973). *Dissertation Abstracts International*, 1974, *34*, 7590A. (University Microfilms No. 74-12,316)

Moskowitz, D. S.; Schwarz, J. C.; & Corsini, D. A. Initiating day care at three years of age: Effects of attachment. *Child Development*, 1977, *48*, 1271–1276.

Neubauer, P. B. Issues in early day care. *Psychosocial Process*, 1974, *3*, 1–6.

Nurss, J. R.; Hough, R. A.; & Goodson, M. S. Prereading/language development in two day-care centers. *Journal of Reading Behavior*, 1981, *13*, 23–31.

Office of Child Development. *Head Start Program Performance Standards Self-assessment/Validation Instrument.* Washington, D.C.: Department of Health, Education, and Welfare, 1976.

Ollila, L. O. Foundations: What have we learned about kindergarten reading programs? In L. O. Ollila (Ed.), *Handbook for Administrators and Teachers: Reading in the Kindergarten.* Newark, Del.: International Reading Association, 1980.

Osborne, D. K. *Early Childhood Education in Historical Perspective.* Athens, Ga.: Education Associates, 1975.

Painter, G. The effect of a structured tutorial program on the cognitive and language development of culturally disadvantaged infants. *Merrill-Palmer Quarterly*, 1969, *15*, 279–294.

Palmer, F. H., & Siegel, R. V. Minimal intervention at age two and three, and subsequent intellective changes. In M. Day & R. Parker (Eds.), *The Preschool in Action* (2nd ed.). Boston: Allyn & Bacon, 1977.

Peters, D. L. Day care: The problem, the process, the prospects. *Child Care Quarterly*, 1975, *4*, 135–139.

Peters, D. L. (Ed.). *A Summary of the Pennsylvania Day-care Study.* University Park: Pennsylvania State University, 1973.

Peters, D. L., & Cohen, A. Day-care centers and day-care homes. In D. L. Peters (Ed.), *A Summary of the Pennsylvania Day-care Study.* University Park: Pennsylvania State University, 1973.

Pines, M. *Revolution in Learning.* New York: Harper & Row, 1966.

Pirkle, G. O. A study of the effect of public school kindergarten experience upon readiness for first-grade learning experiences in a selected Texas public school system (Doctoral dissertation, Baylor University, 1973). *Dissertation Abstracts International*, 1974, *34*, 5490A–5491A. (University Microfilms No. 74-07,293)

Prescott, E., & Jones, E. *The "Politics" of Day Care* (Vol. 1). Washington, D.C.: National Association for the Education of Young Children, 1972.

Quarmley, L. L. The effect of perceptual motor training on reading readiness of kindergarten children (Doctoral dissertation, Lehigh University, 1973). *Dissertation Abstracts International*, 1974, *34*, 6983A–6984A. (University Microfilms No. 74-11,353)

Radin, N. The impact of a kindergarten home counseling program. *Exceptional Children*, 1969, *36*, 251–256.

Rath, S. W.; O'Neil, B. B.; Gedney, B. D.; & Osorio, J. *Follow Through: A Resource Guide to Sponsor Models and Materials.* Portland, Oreg.: Nero & Associates, 1976.

Richmond, J. B.; Stipek, D. J.; & Zigler, E. A decade of Head Start. In E. Zigler & J. Valentine (Eds.), *Project Head Start: A Legacy of the War on Poverty.* New York: Free Press, 1979.

Ristau, C. A.; Hamilton, V. J.; Gardner, A. M.; Hodges, W. L.; Bell, K.; Hammock, C. H.; Currier, C. E.; DeBovis, M.; Bell, P. B.; Baldwin, N. L.; Stephenson, D. P.; Hagler, R. A.; & Hodges, L. M. *West Virginia Paraprofessional Child-care Study.* Atlanta: Family Learning Centers, 1976.

Robinson, B. E. A two-year follow-up study of male and female caregivers. *Child Care Quarterly*, 1979, *8*, 279–294.

Rose, S. A. Independent family day-care mothers in the black community (Doctoral dissertation, Columbia University, Teachers College, 1976). *Dissertation Abstracts International*, 1976, *37*, 1834A (University Microfilms No. 76-21,035)

Ross, E. D. *The Kindergarten Crusade: The Establishment of Preschool Education in the United States.* Athens: Ohio University Press, 1976.

Runnels, P., & Runnels, L. K. A kindergarten mathematics program. *School Science and Mathematics*, 1974, *74*, 361–365.

Ruopp, R.; Travers, J.; Glantz, F.; & Coelen, C. *Final Report of* the *National Day Care Study* (Vol. 1). Cambridge, Mass.: Abt Associates, 1979.

Russell, W. L. Effect of preschool experience on performance of Piaget tasks in first grade (Doctoral dissertation, University of Tennessee, 1973). *Dissertation Abstracts International*, 1973, *34*, 3157A–3158A. (University Microfilms No. 73-27,744)

Ryan, S. *A Report on Longitudinal Evaluations of Preschool Programs* (Vol. I). Publication No. OHD 74-24. Washington, D.C.: Department of Health, Education, and Welfare, 1974.

Schaeffer, E., & Aaronson, M. Infant education research project: Implementation and implications of a home tutoring program. In M. Day & R. Parker (Eds.), *Preschool in Action* (2nd ed.). Boston: Allyn & Bacon, 1977.

Scherwitzky, M. Reading in the kindergarten: A survey in Virginia. *Young Children*, 1974, *29*, 161–169.

Schneider, H. *Public Opinion toward Day Care*. Minneapolis: Institute for Interdisciplinary Studies, 1971. (ERIC Document Reproduction Service No. ED 068 194)

Schweinhart, L. J., & Weikart, D. P. *Young Children Grow Up: The Effects of the Perry Preschool Program on Youths through Age 15*. Ypsilanti, Mich.: High/Scope Press, 1980.

Sears, P. S., & Dowley, E. M. Research on teaching in the nursery school. In N. L. Gage (Ed.), *Handbook of Research on Teaching*. Chicago: Rand McNally, 1963.

Seefeldt, C. *A Curriculum for Child-care Centers*. Columbus, Ohio: Merrill, 1974.

Senn, M. J. E. Insights on the child development movement in the United States. *Monographs of the Society for Research in Child Development*, 1975, *40*(3–4, Serial No. 161).

Shapiro, S. Preschool ecology: A study of three environmental variables. *Reading Improvement*, 1975, *12*, 236–241.

Sheehan, A. M., & Abbott, M. S. A descriptive study of day care characteristics. *Child Care Quarterly*, 1979, *8*, 206–219.

Sherman, M., & Key, C. B. The intelligence of isolated mountain children. *Child Development*, 1932, *3*, 279–280.

Shriver, S. Statement to Senate Subcommittee on Employment, Manpower, and Poverty of the Committee on Labor and Public Welfare. *Hearings on S. 3164*, Amendments to the Economic Opportunity Act of 1964, 89th Cong. 2nd sess., 1966, pp. 44–45.

Skeels, H. Adult status of children with contrasting early life experiences. *Monographs of the Society for Research in Child Development*, 1966, *31*(3, Serial No. 105).

Skinner, B. F. *The Technology of Teaching*. New York: Appleton-Century-Crofts, 1968.

Smith, M. *Some Short-term Effects of Project Head Start: A Report on the Second Year of Planned Variation*. Cambridge, Mass.: Huron Institute, 1973.

Soar, R. S., & Soar, R. M. An empirical analysis of selected Follow Through programs: An example of a process approach to evaluation. In I. Gordon (Ed.), *Early Childhood Education: Seventy-first Yearbook of the National Society for the Study of Education* (Part II). Chicago: University of Chicago Press, 1972.

Southern Association of Colleges and Schools, Commission on Elementary Schools. *Standards for Early Childhood Centers and Kindergartens*. Atlanta: The Association, 1977.

Sprigle, H.; Van de Riet, V.; & Van de Riet, H. *A Fresh Approach to Early Childhood Education and a Study of Its Effectiveness: Learning to Learn Program*. Gainesville: University of Florida, Department of Clinical Psychology, 1968. (ERIC Document Reproduction Service No. ED 019 117)

Stallings, J. Implementation and child effects of teaching practices in Follow Through classrooms. *Monographs of the Society*

for Research in Child Development, 1975, *40*(7–8, Serial No. 163).

Stanchfield, J. M. Development of pre-reading skills in an experimental kindergarten program. *Reading Teacher*, 1971, *24*, 669–670. (a)

Stanchfield, J. M. The development of pre-reading skills in an experimental kindergarten program. *Elementary School Journal*, 1971, *71*, 438–447. (b)

Stanford Research Institute. *Implementation of Planned Variation in Head Start: Preliminary Evaluations of Planned Variation in Head Start According to Follow Through Approaches (1969–1970)*. Washington, D.C.: Office of Child Development, 1971.

Stearns, M. S. *Report on Preschool Programs: The Effects of Preschool Programs on Disadvantaged Children and Their Families* (Publication No. 1792-003). Washington, D.C.: U.S. Government Printing Office, 1971.

Stebbins, L.; St. Pierre, R.; Proper, E.; Anderson, R.; & Cerva, T. *Education as Experimentation: A Planned Variation Model* (Vol. IVA). Cambridge, Mass.: Abt Associates, 1977.

Stone, J. G., & Janis, M. G. *Daily Program I for a Child Development Center: An Overview* (Publication No. OHD 73-1016). Washington, D.C.: U.S. Department of Health, Education and Welfare, 1973.

Takanishi, R. Federal involvement in early education (1933–1973): The need for historical perspectives. In L. G. Katz (Ed.), *Current Topics in Early Childhood Education* (Vol. 1). Norwood, N.J.: Ablex, 1977.

Taylor, K. W. *Parents and Children Learning Together* (3rd ed.) New York: Columbia University, Teachers College Press, 1981.

Teale, W. H. Positive environments for learning to read: What studies of early readers tell us. *Language Arts*, 1978, *55*, 922–932.

U.S. Office of Economic Opportunity. *Child Development Program: A Manual of Policies and Instructions*. Washington, D.C.: U.S. Office of Economic Opportunity, 1967.

Wattenberg, E. Characteristics of family day-care providers: Implications for training. *Child Welfare*, 1977, *56*, 211–229.

Weber, E. *The Kindergarten: Its Encounter with Educational Thought in America*. New York: Columbia University, Teachers College Press, 1969.

Weber, E. The function of early childhood education. *Young Children*, 1973, *28*, 265–274.

Weikart, D. Relationship of curriculum, teaching, and learning in preschool education. In J. C. Stanley (Ed.), *Preschool Programs for the Disadvantaged*. Baltimore: Johns Hopkins University Press, 1972. (a)

Weikart, D. A traditional nursery program revisited. In R. K. Parker (Ed.), *The Preschool in Action: Exploring Early Childhood Programs*. Boston: Allyn & Bacon, 1972. (b)

Weikart, D.; Bond, J.: & McNeil, J. *The Ypsilanti Perry Preschool Project: Preschool Years and Longitudinal Results through Fourth Grade*. Ypsilanti, Mich.: High/Scope Educational Research Foundation, 1978.

Weikart, D.; Deloria, D.; Lawser, S.; & Wiegerink, R. *Longitudinal Results of the Ypsilanti Perry Preschool Project*. Ypsilanti, Mich.: High/Scope Educational Research Foundation, 1970.

Weikart, D.; Epstein, A.; Schweinhart, L.; & Bond, J. *The Ypsilanti Preschool Curriculum Demonstration Project: Preschool Years and Longitudinal Results*. Ypsilanti, Mich.: High/Scope Educational Research Foundation, 1978.

Weikart, D.; Rogers, L.; Adcock, C.; & McClelland, D. *The Cognitively Oriented Curriculum: A Framework for Preschool Teach-*

ers. Washington, D.C.: National Association for the Education of Young Children, 1971.

Weisberg, H. *Short-term Cognitive Effects of Head Start Planned Variation: Third Year, 1971–72.* Cambridge, Mass.: Huron Institute, 1974.

Weisberg, H., & Haney, W. *Longitudinal Evaluation of Head Start Planned Variation and Follow Through.* Cambridge, Mass.: Huron Institute, 1977.

Wenger, E. B. The effects of time on the achievement of kindergarten pupils (Doctoral dissertation, Ohio State University, 1978). *Dissertation Abstracts International,* 1979, *39,* 4713A. (University Microfilms No. 79-02,243)

Wexley, J.; Guidubaldi, J.; & Kehle, T. An evaluation of Montessori and day-care programs for disadvantaged children. *Journal of Educational Research,* 1974, *68,* 95–99.

White, S.; Day, M.; Freeman, P.; Hartmann, S.; & Messenger, K. *Federal Programs for Young Children: Review and Recommendations* (Vol. III). Washington, D.C.: U.S. Printing Office, 1973.

Widmer, E. L. *The Critical Years: Early Childhood at the Crossroads.* Scranton, Pa.: International Textbook, 1970.

Williams, R. R. The influence of kindergarten experience on growth and development of pupils who have had kindergarten compared with pupils who have not had kindergarten experience (Doctoral dissertation, University of Georgia, 1973). *Dissertation Abstracts International,* 1974, *34,* 4976A. (University Microfilms No. 74-04,902)

Winter, M. L., & Peters, D. L. Day care is a human system. *Child Care Quarterly,* 1974, *3,* 166–176.

Zigler, E., & Valentine, J. *Project Head Start: A Legacy of the War on Poverty.* New York: Free Press, 1979.

ECONOMIC EDUCATION

It has been said that the American economy is the eighth wonder of the world and the economic ignorance of the American people is the ninth wonder (Garwood, 1964). Much of the blame for this ignorance has been placed upon the schools. Yet increasing attention is being given to the area of economic education at all levels of schooling. Educators have long acknowledged economic education to be an integral part of the school curriculum. In 1890, the American Economic Association established a Standing Committee on the Teaching of Political Economy, and a decade later, the National Education Association issued position papers favoring the teaching of economics as a separate discipline. The first conference convened specifically for the purpose of considering methods and problems of teaching economics was held at the University of Chicago in 1909. Economics gained general acceptance as a secondary school subject between 1900 and 1920, but it has never achieved the status of history, geography, or civics in the social studies curriculum, not even during the Great Depression era of the 1930s.

Perhaps the greatest impetus to economic education was the founding of the Joint Council on Economic Education in 1949. The council places major emphasis on training and development activities for classroom teachers. The council also publishes many teaching and resource materials for teachers. But its major contribution has been the establishment of local, state, and regional councils to implement the programs originated at the national level.

Since the publication of the fourth edition of the *Encyclopedia of Educational Research* in 1969, the volume of research literature in economics education has multiplied. It was not until the 1960s that journals began systematically to publish research in economic education. The *Journal of Economic Education* began continuous publication in 1969. Lewis and Orvis (1971), in an extensive review of the research literature, documented some 900 research projects of which 133 qualified as generic research studies. Since then, Dawson (1976, 1977) has reported on another 791 studies in the area of precollegiate economics education, and 700 studies at the college or adult level. A comprehensive review of postsecondary economics education research by Siegfried and Fels (1979) documented 179 more. This increase represents a dramatic turnabout in a period of just fifteen years. Also, during the mid-1970s, methodological strides in the sophistication of statistical techniques developed, especially under the leadership of Soper (1976) and Becker (1976), who confined most of their work to postsecondary studies, but whose "second-generation" research suggestions point the way for more elaborate studies and analyses at all levels of research.

The remainder of this essay will focus upon the major research findings, curriculum development efforts, instrument development, and trends in economic education since the fourth edition of the encyclopedia. Given space limitations, only the most significant developments will be reviewed.

Substantive Findings

The research of the past decade is founded upon the empirically tested belief that students at all levels of schooling can learn economics content (Darrin, 1958; Robinson, 1963; Spears, 1967; Dietz, 1963; Bach & Saunders, 1965; Dawson & Bernstein, 1967; Moyer & Paden, 1968; Bennett, 1968; and Dawson & Davison, 1973). Although a number of studies confirmed the feasibility of teaching economics to elementary-age students, the research is less conclusive in determining proper matches between students and curriculum content. Fox (1978) and Hansen (1980) suggest that better matches can be found if educators take into account experiences students have had with economics outside the school environment. In studies combining developmental theory with economic education, Burris (1976), Ward, Wackman, and Wartella (1977), Fox (1978), and Schug (1980) confirmed that the economic socialization of children passes through developmental stages paralleling Piaget's stages of cognitive thought, progressing from concrete to more abstract levels. But to date, no curriculum has been developed that is based upon these findings. It appears that a logical next step is to create curriculum materials that closely tie the experiences and developmental levels of children to appropriately placed content in economic education.

Problem Solving as an Instructional Technique. Although the link between children's experiences, developmental levels, and curricula has not been made, several studies have demonstrated the effectiveness of problem solving in learning economic content. Ellis and Glenn (1977) found that both real and contrived problem-solving approaches appear to be more effective than textbook/workbook methods. Furthermore, Kourilsky's work (1974) showed that students who participated in her "mini-society" program learned more economics than those in more traditional textbook programs, because they were required by the classroom structure to know economic content in order to succeed within the confines of the contrived classroom setting. Kourilsky's findings were supported by Cassuto (1980), who assessed the effectiveness of the mini-society approach in fifty-six classrooms in grades three through six.

Affective Learning in Economic Education. An entirely different thrust of research has been devoted to examining the affective realm of economics learning. This realm includes attitudes and attitudinal change relative to economics as a subject and opinions about economic issues. Dawson (1980) has documented some 180 studies in this area. MacDowell and Senn (1977) studied the relationship between cognitive and affective changes in more than 2,000 elementary-age students involved in an economics education program called the World of Work in Economic Education. They found that cognitive growth is positively influenced by attitudinal growth. In direct contrast to these findings, Walstad (1978) concluded that the attitudes of elementary-age students towards economics appeared to be positively and significantly influenced by achievement, but that achievement was not influenced by attitudes towards economics. The lack of research about student attitudes towards economics at the elementary level is in direct contrast to the substantial body of theory and research about the importance of early socialization and the development of attitudes. This is another area of study upon which researchers could concentrate in the coming decade.

Socioeconomic Status and Economic Learning. Regarding socioeconomic status and economic learning, studies by McKenzie (1969), Spears (1967), Davison and Kilgore (1971), Rader (1965), Sulkin and Friedman (1969), Dawson and Davison (1973), Hansen (1980), and Alexander (1969) confirmed that students whose parents have higher socioeconomic status learn more economics. The findings related to sex differences and economics learning are more mixed. Although studies by MacDowell, Senn, and Soper (1977), Jackstadt and Grootaert (1980), Nelson (1971), and Gentry (1969) concluded no major differences, Hansen (1980) and Bach and Saunders (1965) found that males perform better. The first two studies do show that sex-related factors do influence performance and this confirms

earlier studies at the postsecondary level. Finally, a number of studies have shown that students who score high on standardized tests, intelligence tests, or reading tests tend to learn more economics (Rader, 1965; Davison and Kilgore, 1971; Dawson and Davison, 1973; Hansen, 1980; Sulkin and Friedman, 1969; Wing, 1967; Lupher and Light, 1971; Hunt, 1968; and Soper, 1979).

Postsecondary Schools. Variables influencing college-student cognitive achievement are being specified and evaluated. Hansen, Kelley, and Weisbrod (1970) called attention to differential student achievement resulting not only from instructional technique but also from family background and social concerns. Weidenaar and Dodson (1972), in attempting to measure factors influencing student performance in two-year college economics courses, determined that instructor experience, student age and experience, and student major affect achievement. Swartz, Davisson, and Bonello (1980) and Bonello, Davisson, and Swartz (1975) more carefully specified a learning model that included high school rank, college entrance exam score, college grade-point average, and time devoted to the course as factors that influence student performance. Researchers need to combine student input variables, instructor variables, and instructional technique to identify factors influencing cognitive achievement more confidently.

Future Directions for Research. Despite the advances in knowledge based on research in economic education, most such research does not take advantage of research findings generated within the more expansive educational literature. Dalgaard and Dalgaard (1981) concluded, after reviewing articles published in the *Journal of Economic Education*, that economic education research tends to duplicate existing studies, to overlook major research findings within the general educational literature, and to utilize research techniques more consistent with the discipline of economics than education.

Instrument Development

Closely related to these research findings is the area of instrument development. A number of sophisticated, nationally normed evaluation instruments have been developed in economic education in the past fifteen years. The benchmark tool for measuring economic literacy was the Test of Economic Understanding (TEU), developed by the Joint Council on Economic Education in 1963. This fifty-item multiple-choice test served as the standard evaluation instrument in economic education for secondary school students for over a decade. In 1974, Schur et al. (1974) developed the Junior High School Test of Economics to extend the assessment of economic literacy to younger secondary students. Then in 1979, a group of nationally prominent economists were brought together by the Joint Council on Economic Education to update the TEU. What resulted was the Test of Economic Literacy (TEL). This instrument was normed nationally, using more than 8,000 high school students (Soper, 1979) and has also been translated into Spanish.

At the elementary school level, several instruments are also available. Rader (1965) developed three Elementary School Economics Tests for use with upper-elementary-age students as a part of his Elementary School Economics Program developed at the University of Chicago. At the primary level, Davison and Kilgore (1971) developed the Primary Test of Economic Understanding, which stands as the most definitive instrument for children in grades 1 through 3. Chizmar and Halinski (1980) completed development of the Basic Economics Test, which was nationally normed for upper-grade students and which is available in Spanish, as well, in an attempt to achieve cross-cultural analyses.

At the postsecondary level, the Test of Understanding in College Economics (TUCE), developed by the Joint Council on Economic Education in 1968, is by far the most widely used instrument. It has been used by researchers in more than seventy-one studies in the last twelve years.

Curriculum Materials Development. In July 1960, a National Task Force on Economic Education was appointed by the American Economic Association to set minimal levels of economic literacy and to establish objectives for high school economics curricula. In 1977, the Joint Council on Economic Education issued the first major updating of the National Task Force's efforts in the form of the *Master Curriculum Guide for the Nation's Schools, Part I, A Framework for Teaching Economics: Basic Concepts* (Hansen et al., 1977). The *Guide* outlines the major concepts that should be included in economics curricula at the precollege level and provides a wealth of strategies for teaching those concepts at the elementary and secondary levels. The *Guide* and the accompanying teaching-strategies booklets will stand as a benchmark in the area of curriculum development in economic education.

Trade-Offs: A Film-based Curriculum. Another curriculum development effort that has received widespread attention is *Trade-Offs*, a film-based curriculum series developed by the Agency for Instructional Television in cooperation with the Canadian Foundation for Economic Education and the Joint Council on Economic Education for 9-to-13-year-olds. The series has been found to be very successful in improving the economic literacy at those age levels. Some fifteen studies of *Trade-Offs* by eleven different researchers were reviewed by Shea (1981). The studies indicate that *Trade-Offs* significantly improved students' knowledge and attitudes about economics. Furthermore, the program also appeared to improve teachers' attitudes about the teaching of economics. The use of the program as an in-service tool in economics education has also proved effective. Studies by Walstad and McFarland (1980) and Cogan and Schug (1980) demonstrated that teachers who have been in-serviced via the program have had both their understanding of basic economic concepts and their attitudes towards economics improved.

Games and Simulations. Wentworth and Lewis (1973) reviewed the use of simulations and games in economics instruction and found mixed results. A number of studies have compared the effects of simulation games with more conventional methods. Wing (1966) found that two computer-based simulations designed for sixth-grade students were not significantly different in their effects on learning compared to more conventional methods. However, students in the simulation group learned the same material in significantly less time. The same finding was reported by Dooley (1969), although he did observe greater student participation and interest when the simulations were used. Fennessey et al. (1975) found that in their sample of more than 1,000 third- and fourth-grade students, there was no significant difference in the effectiveness of conventional versus simulation methods. Wilson and Schug (1979) describe eight studies at the secondary level in which games and simulations were used in the teaching of economics with the same mixed results. Cohen (1970) reported, however, that a game can be useful not only in teaching concepts to poorly motivated seventh-grade students, but that it can also improve motivation as measured by attendance and behavior in class. DeNike (1973) found that students who derive more knowledge from simulations tend to be those who speak and listen well; acquire meaning from sound; empathize; apparently are not greatly influenced by their peers, but usually do not exert their individuality; and can reason according to rules. In summary, it is safe to say that the effects of games and simulations on the ability to learn economics are inconclusive.

Televised and Programmed Instruction. Although research on simulations and games is sketchy at best, there are several studies that assess the effect of media-based curricula. Denton et al. (1974) found televised instruction and programmed instruction to be effective techniques for learning basic economic content. Walt Disney Productions' *The People on Market Street* has been shown to be effective in improving senior high school students' attitudes toward and knowledge of market economies (Educational Research Council of America, 1979). And considerable attention has been devoted to the use of technologies in college-level economic instruction. Initially, television was used to augment or replace traditional lectures. Paden and Moyer (1969) reported that student performance was not affected by use of television, but that attitudes were adversely influenced.

Computer-assisted instruction (CAI) has been the basis for considerable study since the early 1960s. Soper (1974) reviewed twenty-two research studies dealing with the use of computers in economics instruction. Kelley (1968, 1973) reported on a teaching-information processing system (TIPS), designed to improve instruction. Anderson et al. (1974, 1975) demonstrated that a computer-based system; Computer Assisted Instruction Study Management System (CAISMS), can manage student study, administer exams, and grade and record results without use of conventional classroom instruction. Paden, Dalgaard, and Barr

(1977) concluded that such a CAI system also leads to improved cognitive achievement, especially for slow learners, and more positive attitudes in the introductory college economics course. Davisson and Bonello (1976), on the other hand, reported no significant difference between the experimental and control groups in their CAI study. Additional research is needed, especially in the utility of computer-assisted instruction programs at the precollege level.

Teacher Training. The value of good materials is diminished unless teachers are carefully trained in using them. Foote, Bierman, and, Shelly (1967); Dawson and Davison (1973); Walstad and McFarland (1980); Cogan and Schug (1980); and Thornton and Vredeveld (1977) all conclude that the students of teachers who participate in in-service courses or workshops in economics show improvement in economic understanding and attitudes compared to students whose teachers have not been involved in in-service training. Studies have also been undertaken to assess the effectiveness of graduate-student instructors in economics. Articles by Oates and Quandt (1970) and by Saunders (1971) preceded an extensive graduate-student training program reported by Lewis and Orvis (1973). This integrated teacher-training program resulted in superior performance for students of the trained instructors and higher instructor ratings. A comprehensive training manual, at use in a number of universities, was published by Saunders, Welsh, and Hansen (1978).

Research findings at the postsecondary level are reported and analyzed in a comprehensive survey of the literature by Siegfried and Fels (1979). They concluded that a voluminous amount of research has been conducted at this level; that much of it is of high quality; that a variety of teaching strategies are desirable in meeting the differing needs of students; that computer-study-management programs, programmed learning, and self-paced instruction are efficient modes of learning; that graduate students are generally equally as good as regular faculty, although experience does result in better teaching; that graduate students who have received some training are better instructors than those who have not; and that a one-year course in economics has lasting effects in terms of greater economic competency.

The research reported in the preceding paragraphs is much improved both in quality and quantity since the fourth edition of the *Encyclopedia of Educational Research,* when a mere four paragraphs were devoted to the subject of economic education. Economic education is now a well-established field of study, which will likely develop even more rapidly in the decade of the 1980s.

John J. Cogan
Bruce R. Dalgaard

See also Consumer Economics Education; Social Sciences Education.

REFERENCES

Alexander, L. A. *Analysis of Economic Understanding of High School Seniors in Selected Schools in Alabama.* Unpublished doctoral dissertation, University of Alabama, 1969.

Anderson, T. H.; Anderson, R. C.; Dalgaard, B. R.; Wietecha, E. J.; Biddle, W. B.; Paden, D. W.; Smock, H. R.; Alessi, S. M.; Surber, J. R.; & Klemt, L. L. A computer-based study management system. *Education Psychologist,* 1974, *11,* 36–45.

Anderson, T. H.; Anderson, R. C.; Dalgaard, B. R.; Paden, D. W.; Biddle, W. B.; Surber, J. R.; & Alessi, S. M. An experimental evaluation of a computer-based study management system. *Educational Psychologist,* 1975, *11,* 184–190.

Bach, G. L., & Saunders, P. Economic education: Aspirations and achievements. *American Economic Review,* 1965, *55,* 329–356.

Becker, W. E., Jr. Programmed instruction in large-lecture courses: A technical comment. *Journal of Economic Education,* 1976, *8,* 38–40.

Bennett, R. G. *The Role of Economics at the High School Level.* Unpublished doctoral dissertation, St. Louis University, 1968.

Bonello, F. J.; Davisson, W. I.; & Swartz, T. R. Explaining cognitive achievement in economics: A test of alternative procedures. *Proceedings of the Illinois Economics Association,* 1975, pp. 90–98.

Burris, V. I. *The Child's Conception of Economic Relations: A Genetic Approach to the Sociology of Knowledge.* Unpublished doctoral dissertation, Princeton University, 1976.

Cassuto, A. E. The effectiveness of the elementary school mini-society program. *Journal of Economic Education,* 1980, *11,* 59–61.

Chizmar, J. F., & Halinski, R. S. *Basic Economics Test.* New York: Joint Council on Economic Education, 1980.

Cogan, J. J., & Schug, M. C. An inservice approach to improving the elementary teacher's economic knowledge and attitudes. *Principal, The Journal of the Minnesota Elementary Principals Association,* Fall 1980, pp. 36–37.

Cohen, K. C. *Effects of the "Consumer Game" on Learning and Attitudes of Selected Seventh-grade Students in a Target-area School.* Baltimore: Johns Hopkins University, Center for the Study of Social Organization of Schools, 1970. (ERIC Document Reproduction Service No. ED 038 733).

Dalgaard, K. A., & Dalgaard, B. R. *Educational Antecedents to Economic Education Research.* Unpublished manuscript, University of Minnesota, 1981.

Darrin, G. L. *Economics in the Elementary School Curriculum: A Study of the District of Columbia Laboratory Schools.* Unpublished doctoral dissertation, University of Maryland at College Park, 1958.

Davison, D., & Kilgore, J. *Primary Test of Economic Understanding.* Iowa City: University of Iowa, 1971.

Davisson, W. I., & Bonnello, F. J. *Computer-assisted Instruction in Economics Education: A Case Study.* Notre Dame, Ind.: University of Notre Dame Press, 1976.

Dawson, G. An overview of research in the teaching of college economics. *Journal of Economic Education,* 1976, *7,* 111–116.

Dawson, G. Research in economic education at the precollege level. In D. Wentworth, L. Hansen, & S. Hawke (Eds.), *Perspectives on Economic Education.* New York: Joint Council on Economic Education, 1977.

Dawson, G. *Research in Economic Education Report No. 2: Attitudes and Opinions on Economic Issues.* Old Westbury, N.Y.: Empire State College, Long Island Regional Learning Center, 1980.

Dawson, G., & Bernstein, I. *The Effectiveness of Economics Courses in High Schools and Colleges.* New York: New York University Center for Economic Education, 1967.

Dawson, G., & Davison, D. *The Impact of Economics Workshops for Elementary School Teachers on the Economic Understanding of Their Pupils.* New York: Joint Council on Economic Education, 1973. (ERIC Document Reproduction Service No. ED 090 093)

DeNike, L. *An Exploratory Study of Cognitive Style as a Predictor of Learning from Simulation Games.* Unpublished doctoral dissertation, Kent State University, 1973. (ERIC Document Reproduction Service No. ED 101 728)

Denton, W.; Holland, T. C.; Luker, W.; & Webster, W. *The Use of Educational Television as a Primary Delivery System for Economic Education.* Denton: North Texas State University, 1974.

Dietz, J. E. *Economic Understanding of Senior Students in Selected California High Schools.* Unpublished doctoral dissertation, University of California at Los Angeles, 1963.

Dooley, B. J. Research on the market game. In G. Dawson (Ed.), *Economic Education Experiences of Enterprising Teachers.* New York: Joint Council on Economic Education, 1969. (ERIC Document Reproduction Service No. ED 102 063)

Education Research Council of America. Market Street effective in teaching economics. *Market Street News.* Buena Vista, Calif.: Walt Disney, Inc., 1979.

Ellis, A. K., & Glenn, A. D. Effects of real and contrived problem-solving on economic learning. *Journal of Economic Education,* 1977, *8,* 108–114.

Fennessey, G. M.; Livingston, S. A.; Edwards, K. J.; & Nafziger, A. W. Simulation, gaming, and conventional instruction: An experimental comparison. *Simulation and Games,* 1975, *6,* 258–302.

Foote, E. W.; Bierman, M. L.; & Shelly, P. *The Teaching of Economics in the Primary Grades.* Montclair, N.J.: Montclair Public Schools, 1967.

Fox, K. What children bring to school: The beginnings of economic education. *Social Education,* 1978, *42,* 478–481.

Garwood, J. D. The need for economic education. *School and Society,* 1964, *92,* 289–291.

Gentry, A. D. *Economic Understanding of Non–college-bound Seniors in High Schools in Indiana.* Unpublished doctoral dissertation, University of Denver, 1969.

Hansen, R. *An Investigation to Determine if Early Economic Experiences Can Predict Third-grade Children's Economic Knowledge.* Unpublished doctoral dissertation, University of Minnesota, 1980.

Hansen, W. L.; Bach, G. L.; Calderwood, J. D.; & Saunders, P. *Master Curriculum Guide for the Nation's Schools—Part 1, A Framework for Teaching Economics: Basic Concepts.* New York: Joint Council on Economic Education, 1977. (ERIC Document Reproduction Service No. ED 148 648)

Hansen, W. L.; Kelley, A. C.: & Weisbrod, B. A. Economic efficiency and the distribution of benefits from college instruction. *American Economic Review,* 1970, *60,* 409–418.

Hunt, E. H. *An Experimental Study to Determine the Effectiveness of Teaching Economics at the Secondary School Level.* Unpublished doctoral dissertation, University of Maryland, 1968.

Jackstadt, S. L., & Grootaert, C. Gender, gender stereotyping and socioeconomic background as determinants of economic knowledge and learning. *Journal of Economic Education,* 1980, *12,* 34–40.

Kelly, A. C. An experiment with TIPS (Teaching Information Processing System): A computer-aided instructional system for undergraduate education. *American Economic Review,* 1968, *58,* 446–457.

Kelly, A. C. Individualizing instruction through the use of technology in higher education. *Journal of Economic Education,* 1973, *4,* 77–89.

Kourilsky, M. *Beyond Simulation. The Mini-society Approach to Instruction in Economics and Other Social Sciences.* Los Angeles: Educational Research Associates, Inc., 1974.

Lewis, D. R., & Orvis, C. C. *Research in Economic Education: A Review, Bibliography, and Abstracts.* New York: Joint Council on Economic Education, 1971.

Lewis, D. R., & Orvis, C. C. A training system for graduate student instructors of introductory economics at the University of Minnesota. *Journal of Economic Education,* 1973, *5,* 38–46.

Lupher, D., & Light, K. *Evaluation of "Adventure Economics" Telecasts.* Athens: Ohio University, 1971.

MacDowell, M. A., & Senn, P. R. *On the Problem of Measuring Affective Changes in Economic Education.* DeKalb: Northern Illinois University, 1977.

MacDowell, M. A.; Senn, P. R.; & Soper, J. C. Does sex really matter? *Journal of Economic Education,* 1977, *1,* 28–33.

McKenzie, R. B. *The Economic Literacy of Pupils in the Elementary Grades.* Radford, Va.: Radford College, 1969.

Moyer, E., & Paden, D. On the efficiency of the high school economics course. *American Economic Review,* 1968, *58,* 870–877.

Nelson, J. B. *An Evaluation of the ECON 12 Economic Education Project.* Unpublished doctoral dissertation, University of California at Berkeley, 1971.

Oates, W. E., & Quandt, R. E. The effectiveness of graduate students as teachers of principles of economics. *Journal of Economic Education,* 1970, *1,* 130–138.

Paden, D. W.; Dalgaard, B. R.; & Baar, M. D. A decade of computer-assisted instruction. *Journal of Economic Education,* 1977, *9,* 14–20.

Paden, D. W., & Moyer, E. M. The relative effectiveness of three methods of teaching principles of economics. *Journal of Economic Education,* 1969, *1,* 33–45.

Rader, W. D. *Results of the Evaluation Study on the Elementary School Economics Program.* Chicago: University of Chicago, Industrial Relations Center, 1965. (ERIC Document Reproduction Service No. ED 124 492)

Robinson, H. F. *Learning Economic Concepts in the Kindergarten.* Unpublished doctoral dissertation, Columbia University, 1963.

Saunders, P. More on the use of graduate student instructors in the introductory economics course. *Journal of Economic Education,* 1971, *3,* 36–40.

Saunders, P.; Welsh, A. L.; & Hansen, W. L. *Resource Manual for Teacher Training Programs in Economics.* New York: Joint Council on Economic Education, 1978. (ERIC Document Reproduction Service No. ED 173 258)

Schug, M. C. *The Development of Economic Reasoning in Children and Adolescents.* Unpublished doctoral dissertation, University of Minnesota, 1980.

Schur, L. M.; Donegan, R.; Tanck, M. L.; Zitlow, D.; & Weston, G. A. *Junior High School Test of Economics: Interpretive Manual and Rationale.* New York: Joint Council on Economic Education, 1974.

Shea, J. *The Impact of "Trade-Offs": What the Research Says* (Research Report No. 80). Bloomington, Ind.: Agency for Instructional Television, 1981.

Siegfried, J. J., & Fels, R. Research on teaching college economics: A survey. *Journal of Economic Literature*, 1979, *27*, 923–969.

Soper, J. C. Computer-assisted instruction in economics: A survey. *Journal of Economic Education*, 1974, *6*, 5–28.

Soper, J. C. Second-generation research in economic education: Problems of specification and interdependence. *Journal of Economic Education*, 1976, *8*, 40–48.

Soper, J. C. *Test of Economic Literacy: Discussion Guide and Rationale.* New York: Joint Council on Economic Education, 1979. (ERIC Document Reproduction Service No. ED 173 256)

Spears, S. *Concept Learning in Economics under Three Experimental Curricula.* Unpublished doctoral dissertation, University of California at Los Angeles, 1976.

Sulkin, H. A., & Friedman, C. (Eds.). *Research in Elementary School Economics: Occasional Paper No. 30.* Chicago: University of Chicago, Industrial Relations Center, 1969.

Swartz, T. R.; Davisson, W. I.; & Bonello, F. J. Why have we ignored the distribution of benefits from college instruction? *Journal of Economic Education*, 1980, *11*, 28–36.

Thornton, D. L., & Vredeveld, G. M. In-service education and its effect on secondary students: A new approach. *Journal of Economic Education*, 1977, *8*, 93–99.

Walstad, W. B. *Economic Problem-solving in Elementary Schools: Specification and Estimation of Alternative Learning Models to Measure In-service Program Impact.* Unpublished doctoral dissertation, University of Minnesota, 1978.

Walstad, W. B., & McFarland, M. "Trade-offs" and teacher in-service. *Social Education*, 1980, *44*, 410–411.

Ward, S.; Wackman, D.; & Wartella, E. *How Children Learn to Buy.* London: Sage, 1977.

Weidenaar, D. J., & Dodson, J. A. The effectiveness of economics instruction in two-year colleges. *Journal of Economic Education*, 1972, *4*, 5–12.

Wentworth, D. G., & Lewis, D. R. A review of research on instructional games and simulations in social studies education. *Social Education*, 1973, *37*, 432–439.

Wilson, C. R., & Schug, M. C. *A Guide to Games and Simulations for Teaching Economics* (3rd ed.). New York: Joint Council on Economic Education, 1979. (ERIC Document Reproduction Service No. ED 180 873)

Wing, R. L. Two computer-based economics games for sixth graders. *American Behavioral Scientist*, 1966, *10*, 31–33.